Contemporary
Literary Criticism

Guide to Gale Literary Criticism Series

For criticism on	Consult these Gale series
Authors now living or who died after December 31, 1959	*CONTEMPORARY LITERARY CRITICISM (CLC)*
Authors who died between 1900 and 1959	*TWENTIETH-CENTURY LITERARY CRITICISM (TCLC)*
Authors who died between 1800 and 1899	*NINETEENTH-CENTURY LITERATURE CRITICISM (NCLC)*
Authors who died between 1400 and 1799	*LITERATURE CRITICISM FROM 1400 TO 1800 (LC)* *SHAKESPEAREAN CRITICISM (SC)*
Authors who died before 1400	*CLASSICAL AND MEDIEVAL LITERATURE CRITICISM (CMLC)*
Black writers of the past two hundred years	*BLACK LITERATURE CRITICISM (BLC) AND BLACK LITERATURE CRITICISM SUPPLEMENT (BLCS)*
Authors of books for children and young adults	*CHILDREN'S LITERATURE REVIEW (CLR)*
Dramatists	*DRAMA CRITICISM (DC)*
Hispanic writers of the late nineteenth and twentieth centuries	*HISPANIC LITERATURE CRITICISM (HLC)*
Native North American writers and orators of the eighteenth, nineteenth, and twentieth centuries	*NATIVE NORTH AMERICAN LITERATURE (NNAL)*
Poets	*POETRY CRITICISM (PC)*
Short story writers	*SHORT STORY CRITICISM (SSC)*
Major authors from the Renaissance to the present	*WORLD LITERATURE CRITICISM, 1500 TO THE PRESENT (WLC)*
Major authors and works from the Bible to the present	*WORLD LITERATURE CRITICISM SUPPLEMENT (WLCS)*

ISSN 0091-3421

R

Volume 113

Contemporary Literary Criticism

Excerpts from Criticism of the Works
of Today's Novelists, Poets, Playwrights,
Short Story Writers, Scriptwriters, and
Other Creative Writers

**Jeffrey W. Hunter
Deborah A. Schmitt
Timothy J. White**
EDITORS

**Tim Akers
Pamela S. Dear
Catherine V. Donaldson
Daniel Jones
John D. Jorgenson
Jerry Moore
Polly Vedder
Thomas Wiloch
Kathleen Wilson**
ASSOCIATE EDITORS

GALE

DETROIT · LONDON

STAFF

Hunter, Deborah A. Schmitt, Timothy J. White, *Editors*

........., ..., Catherine V. Donaldson, Daniel Jones, John D. Jorgenson, Jerry Moore,
Polly Vedder, Thomas Wiloch, and Kathleen Wilson, *Associate Editors*

Tracy Arnold-Chapman, Jay Daniel, Linda Quigley,
Paul Serralheiro, Lynn Spampinato, *Contributing Editors*

Susan Trosky, *Permissions Manager*
Kimberly F. Smilay, *Permissions Specialist*
Steve Cusack, and Kelly Quin, *Permissions Associates*
Sandy Gore, *Permissions Assistant*

Victoria B. Cariappa, *Research Manager*
Julia C. Daniel, Tamara C. Nott, Michele P. Pica, Tracie A. Richardson,
Norma Sawaya, and Cheryl L. Warnock, *Research Associates*
Laura C. Bissey, Alfred A. Gardner I, and Sean R. Smith, *Research Assistants*

Mary Beth Trimper, *Production Director*
Deborah L. Milliken, *Production Assistant*

Barbara J. Yarrow, *Graphic Services Manager*
Sherrell Hobbs, *Macintosh Artist*
Randy Bassett, *Image Database Supervisor*
Robert Duncan and Mikal Ansari, *Scanner Operators*
Pamela Reed, *Imaging Coordinator*

Library of Congress Catalog Card Number 76-46132
ISBN 0-7876-2212-5
ISSN 0091-3421

Printed in the United States of America
10 9 8 7 6 5 4 3 2 1

Contents

Preface vii

Acknowledgments xi

Preface

A Comprehensive Information Source
on Contemporary Literature

Named "one of the twenty-five most distinguished reference titles published during the past twenty-five years" by *Reference Quarterly,* the *Contemporary Literary Criticism (CLC)* series provides readers with critical commentary and general information on more than 2,000 authors now living or who died after December 31, 1959. Previous to the publication of the first volume of *CLC* in 1973, there was no ongoing digest monitoring scholarly and popular sources of critical opinion and explication of modern literature. *CLC,* therefore, has fulfilled an essential need, particularly since the complexity and variety of contemporary literature makes the function of criticism especially important to today's reader.

Scope of the Series

CLC presents significant passages from published criticism of works by creative writers. Since many of the authors covered by *CLC* inspire continual critical commentary, writers are often represented in more than one volume. There is, of course, no duplication of reprinted criticism.

Authors are selected for inclusion for a variety of reasons, among them the publication or dramatic production of a critically acclaimed new work, the reception of a major literary award, revival of interest in past writings, or the adaptation of a literary work to film or television.

Attention is also given to several other groups of writers-authors of considerable public interest--about whose work criticism is often difficult to locate. These include mystery and science fiction writers, literary and social critics, foreign writers, and authors who represent particular ethnic groups within the United States.

Format of the Book

Each *CLC* volume contains about 500 individual excerpts taken from hundreds of book review periodicals, general magazines, scholarly journals, monographs, and books. Entries include critical evaluations spanning from the beginning of an author's career to the most current commentary. Interviews, feature articles, and other published writings that offer insight into the author's works are also presented. Students, teachers, librarians, and researchers will find that the generous excerpts and supplementary material in *CLC* provide them with vital information required to write a term paper, analyze a poem, or lead a book discussion group. In addition, complete bibliographical citations note the original source and all of the information necessary for a term paper footnote or bibliography.

Features

A *CLC* author entry consists of the following elements:

- The **Author Heading** cites the author's name in the form under which the author has most commonly published, followed by birth date, and death date when applicable. Uncertainty as to a birth or death date is indicated by a question mark.

- A **Portrait** of the author is included when available.

- A brief **Biographical and Critical Introduction** to the author and his or her work precedes the excerpted criticism. The first line of the introduction provides the author's full name, pseudonyms (if applicable), nationality, and a listing of genres in which the author has written. To provide users with easier access to information, the biographical and critical essay included in each author entry is divided into four categories: "Introduction," "Biographical Information," "Major Works," and "Critical Reception." The introductions to single-work entries--entries that focus on well known and frequently studied books, short stories, and poems--are similarly organized to quickly provide readers with information on the plot and major characters of the work being discussed, its major themes, and its critical reception. Previous volumes of *CLC* in which the author has been featured are also listed in the introduction.

- A list of **Principal Works** notes the most important writings by the author. When foreign-language works have been translated into English, the English-language version of the title follows in brackets.

- The **Excerpted Criticism** represents various kinds of critical writing, ranging in form from the brief review to the scholarly exegesis. Essays are selected by the editors to reflect the spectrum of opinion about a specific work or about an author's literary career in general. The excerpts are presented chronologically, adding a useful perspective to the entry. All titles by the author featured in the entry are printed in boldface type, which enables the reader to easily identify the works being discussed. Publication information (such as publisher names and book prices) and parenthetical numerical references (such as footnotes or page and line references to specific editions of a work) have been deleted at the editor's discretion to provide smoother reading of the text.

- Critical essays are prefaced by **Explanatory Notes** as an additional aid to readers. These notes may provide several types of valuable information, including: the reputation of the critic, the importance of the work of criticism, the commentator's approach to the author's work, the purpose of the criticism, and changes in critical trends regarding the author.

- A complete **Bibliographical Citation** designed to help the user find the original essay or book precedes each excerpt.

- Whenever possible, a recent, previously unpublished **Author Interview** accompanies each entry.

- A concise **Further Reading** section appears at the end of entries on authors for whom a significant amount of criticism exists in addition to the pieces reprinted in *CLC*. Each citation in this section is accompanied by a descriptive annotation describing the content of that article. Materials included in this section are grouped under various headings (e.g., Biography, Bibliography, Criticism, and Interviews) to aid users in their search for additional information. Cross-references to other useful sources published by Gale Research in which the author has appeared are also included: *Authors in the News, Black Writers, Children's Literature Review, Contemporary Authors, Dictionary of Literary Biography, DlSCovering Authors, Drama Criticism, Hispanic Literature Criticism, Hispanic Writers, Native North American Literature, Poetry Criticism, Something about the Author, Short Story Criticism, Contemporary Authors Autobiography Series,* and *Something about the Author Autobiography Series.*

Other Features

CLC also includes the following features:

- An **Acknowledgments** section lists the copyright holders who have granted permission to reprint material in this volume of *CLC*. It does not, however, list every book or periodical reprinted or consulted during the preparation of the volume.

- Each new volume of *CLC* includes a **Cumulative Topic Index,** which lists all literary topics treated in *CLC, NCLC, TCLC,* and *LC 1400-1800.*

- A **Cumulative Author Index** lists all the authors who have appeared in the various literary criticism series published by Gale Research, with cross-references to Gale's biographical and autobiographical series. A full listing of the series referenced there appears on the first page of the indexes of this volume. Readers will welcome this cumulated author index as a useful tool for locating an author within the various series. The index, which lists birth and death dates when available, will be particularly valuable for those authors who are identified with a certain period but whose death dates cause them to be placed in another, or for those authors whose careers span two periods. For example, Ernest Hemingway is found in *CLC,* yet F. Scott Fitzgerald, a writer often associated with him, is found in *Twentieth-Century Literary Criticism.*

- A **Cumulative Nationality Index** alphabetically lists all authors featured in *CLC* by nationality, followed by numbers corresponding to the volumes in which the authors appear.

- An alphabetical **Title Index** accompanies each volume of *CLC*. Listings are followed by the author's name and the corresponding page numbers where the titles are discussed. English translations of foreign titles and variations of titles are cross-referenced to the title under which a work was originally published. Titles of novels, novellas, dramas, films, record albums, and poetry, short story, and essay collections are printed in italics, while all individual poems, short stories, essays, and songs are printed in roman type within quotation marks; when published separately (e.g., T. S. Eliot's poem *The Waste Land),* the titles of long poems are printed in italics.

- In response to numerous suggestions from librarians, Gale has also produced a **Special Paperbound Edition** of the *CLC* title index. This annual cumulation, which alphabetically lists all titles reviewed in the series, is available to all customers and is typically published with every fifth volume of *CLC*. Additional copies of the index are available upon request. Librarians and patrons will welcome this separate index: it saves shelf space, is easy to use, and is recyclable upon receipt of the next edition.

Citing *Contemporary Literary Criticism*

When writing papers, students who quote directly from any volume in the Literary Criticism Series may use the following general forms to footnote reprinted criticism. The first example pertains to material drawn from periodicals, the second to material reprinted in books:

[1]Alfred Cismaru, "Making the Best of It," *The New Republic,* 207, No. 24, (December 7, 1992), 30, 32; excerpted and reprinted in *Contemporary Literary Criticism,* Vol. 85, ed. Christopher Giroux (Detroit: Gale Research, 1995), pp. 73-4.

[2]Yvor Winters, *The Post-Symbolist Methods* (Allen Swallow, 1967); excerpted and reprinted in *Contemporary Literary Criticism,* Vol. 85, ed. Christopher Giroux (Detroit: Gale Research, 1995), pp. 223-26.

Suggestions Are Welcome

The editors hope that readers will find *CLC* a useful reference tool and welcome comments about the work. Send comments and suggestions to: Editors, *Contemporary Literary Criticism,* Gale Research, 27500 Drake Rd., Farmington Hills, MI 48333-3535.

Acknowledgments

The editors wish to thank the copyright holders of the excerpted criticism included in this volume and the permissions managers of many book and magazine publishing companies for assisting us in securing reproduction rights. We are also grateful to the staffs of the Detroit Public Library, the Library of Congress, the University of Detroit Mercy Library, Wayne State University Purdy/Kresge Library Complex, and the University of Michigan Libraries for making their resources available to us. Following is a list of the copyright holders who have granted us permission to reproduce material in this volume of CLC. Every effort has been made to trace copyright, but if omissions have been made, please let us know.

COPYRIGHTED EXCERPTS IN *CLC*, VOLUME 113, WERE REPRODUCED FROM THE FOLLOWING PERIODICALS:

A Room of One's Own, v. 13, No. 1 & 2, for "A Slight Parodic Edge: 'Swann: A Mystery'" by Clara Thomas./ v. 13, July, 1989 for "Shield's 'Swann'" by Donna E. Smyth. Both reproduced by permission of the respective authors.—*The American Book Review*, v. 17, June-July, 1996. © 1996 by The American Book Review. Reproduced by permission.—*The Antigonish Review*, Summer-Autumn 1986 for "Mr. Prufrock's Big City Blues" by J. G. Keogh. Copyright© 1986 by the author. Reproduced by permission of the publisher and the author.—*Ball State University Forum*, v. VIII, Winter, 1967. © 1967 Ball State University. Reproduced by permission.—*Belles Lettres*, v. 9, Spring, 1994. Reproduced by permission.—*Books in Canada*, v. 11, November, 1982 for "Ordinary People" by Maria Horvath;v. 18, May, 1989 for "Telling it Slant" by Eleanor Wachtel; v. XXI, April, 1992 for "A Fine Romance" by Rita Donovan. All reproduced by permission of the respective authors.—*Canadian Forum*, v. LXXIV, January-February, 1996 for "Sadness and Light" by Christine Hamelin. Reproduced by permission of the author.—*Canadian Literature*, No. 130, Autumn, 1991 for "Impressions" by D. O. Spettigue. Reproduced by permission of the author.—*Chicago Tribune Books*, Section 14, July 10, 1994 for "A 'Gothic fantasia' from E. L. Doctorow" by Mark Shechner. © copyrighted 1994, Chicago Tribune Company. All rights reserved. Used by permission.—*The Christian Science Monitor*, for A review of 'Mrs. De Winter' by Merle Rubin. © 1994 by The Christian Science Publishing Society. All rights reserved. Reprinted by permission from the author./ April 20, 1994. © 1994 The Christian Science Publishing Society. All rights reserved. Reproduced by permission from The Christian Science Monitor.—*CLA Journal*, v. XXXVIII, September, 1994. Copyright © 1994 by The College Language Association. Used by permission of The College Language Association.—*Colby Quarterly*, v. XXVII, March, 1991; v. XXX, December, 1994. Both reprinted by permission of the publisher.—*Commonweal*, v. LXXXIX, October 25, 1968. Copyright © 1968 Commonweal Publishing Co., Inc. Reproduced by permission of Commonweal Foundation.—*Comparative Literature*, v. 43, Fall, 1991 for "Myth, Contingency, and Revolution in Carlos Fuentes's 'La región más Transparente" by Maarten Van Delden. Reproduced by permission of the author. A fuller exposition of this essay can also be found in *Carlos Fuentes, Mexico and Modernity*, by Maarten van Delden. Published by Vanderbilt University Press.—*Contemporary Literature*, v. 27, Fall, 1986. Reproduced by permission of the University of Wisconsin Press.—*Critique*, v. XXXIX, Fall, 1987; v. XXIV, Winter, 1993. Copyright © 1993, 1987 Helen Dwight Reid Educational Foundation. Both reproduced with permission of the Helen Dwight Reid Educational Foundation, published by Heldref Publications, 1319 18th Street, NW, Washington, DC 20036-1802.—*Éire-Ireland*, v. 28, Summer, 1993. Copyright © 1993 by the Irish American Cultural Institute. Reproduced by permission of the publisher.—*ELH*, v. 5, Fall, 1988. © 1988. Reproduced by permission of The Johns Hopkins University Press.—*English Journal*, v. 72, April, 1983 for "Recommended: Susan Hill" by Mary Jane Reed. Copyright © 1983 by the National Council of Teachers of English. Reproduced by permission of the publisher and the author.—*English Studies in Canada*, v. 7, Summer, 1981 for "Verbal Prisons: The Language of Albee's 'A Delicate Balance" by Patricia Fumerton./v. VI, Winter, 1980 for "'Prufrock: An Absurdist View of the Poem" by Shyamal Bagchee © Association of Canadian University Teachers of English 1980, 1981. Both reproduced by permission of the publisher and the respective authors.—*The Explicator*, v. 51, Fall, 1992. Copyright © 1992 Helen Dwight Reid Educational Foundation. Reproduced with permission of the Helen Dwight Reid Educational Foundation, published by Heldref Publications, 1319 18th Street, NW, Washington, DC 20036-1802.—*Extrapolation*, v. 26, Spring, 1985; v. 27, Spring, 1986. Copyright © 1985, 1986 by The Kent State University Press. Both reproduced by

Review of Books, v. VII, December, 1989 for "A World Made of Words" by Anita Clair Fellman./v. IX, April, 1992 for "A Passion for the Ordinary" by Jody Allen-Randolph./v. XI, May, 1994 for "Imagination's Invisible Ink" by Gail Pool./v. XIII, April, 1996 for "Smaller than Life" by Eunice Lipton. © 1989, 1992, 1994, 1996. All rights reserved. All Reproduced by permission of the respective authors.—*Theatre Journal*, v. 46, December, 1994. © 1994. Reproduced by permission of The Johns Hopkins University Press.—*Twentieth Century Literature*, v. 37, Winter, 1991. Copyright (c)1991, Hofstra University Press. Reproduced by permission.—*Washington Post-Book World*, June 23, 1996, © 1996, Washington Post Book World Service/Washington Post Writers Group. Reproduced by permission of the author.—*West Coast Review*, v 23, Winter, 1988 for "A Little Like Flying: An Interview with Carol Shields" by Harvey De Roo. Reproduced by permission of the publisher and the author.—*World Literature Today*, v. 59. Summer, 1985; v. 61, Winter, 1987; v. 69, Autumn, 1995; v. 69, Winter, 1995. Copyright © 1985, 1987, 1995 by the University of Oklahoma Press. All reproduced by permission.

COPYRIGHTED EXCERPTS IN *CLC*, VOLUME 113, WERE REPRODUCED FROM THE FOLLOWING BOOKS:

Barker, Clive. From "Stephen King: Surviving the Ride" in *Kingdom of Fear: The World of Stephen King*. Edited by Tim Underwood and Chuck Miller. New American Library, 1986. Copyright © 1986 by Tim Underwood and Chuck Miller. Reproduced by permission of the author.—Brustein, Robert. From *Dumbocracy in America: Studies in the Theatre of Guilt, 1987-1994*. Ivan R. Dee, 1994. Copyright © 1994 by Robert Brustein. All rights reserved. Reproduced by permission.—Burns, Gail E. and Melinda Kanner. From "The Perversion of The Female Principal in Stephen King's Fiction" in *Sexual Politics and Popular Culture*. Edited by Diane Raymond. Bowling Green State University Popular Press, 1990. Copyright © 1990 by Bowling Green State University Popular Press. Reproduced by permission.—Casebeer, Edwin F. From "The Art of Balance: Stephen King's Cannon" in *A Dark Night's Dreaming: Contemporary American Horror Fiction*. Edited by Tony Magistrale and Michael A. Morrison. University of South Carolina Press, 1996. © 1996 by the University of South Carolina. Reproduced by permission.—Casper, Leonard. From "'Tiny Alice': The Expense of Joy in the Persistence of Mystery" in *Edward Albee: An Interview and Essays*. Edited by Julian Wasserman with Joy Linsley and Jerome Kramer. The University of St. Thomas, 1983. Copyright © 1983 by The University of St. Thomas. All rights Reserved. Reproduced by permission of the editor.—Hofer, Ernest H. From "Enclosed Structures, Disclosed Lives: The Fictions of Susan Hill" in *Contemporary British Women Writers: Narrative Strategies*. Edited by Robert E. Hosmer, Jr. St. Martin's Press, 1993. Macmillan Press, Ltd. 1993. Copyright © 1993 by Robert E. Hosmer, Jr. All rights reserved. Reproduced by permission of Macmillan Press, Ltd. In North America by St. Martin's Press, Inc.—Jackson, Rosemary. From "Cold Enclosures: The Fiction of Susan Hill," in *Twentieth-Century Women Novelists*. Edited by Thomas F. Staley. Barnes & Noble Books, 1982. Macmillan, 1982. Copyright © Thomas F. Staley, 1982. All rights reserved. Reproduced by permission in North America by Rowman and Littlefield. In the United Kingdom by Macmillan, London and Basingstoke.—King, Kathryn R. From "Galesia, Jane Barker and a Coming to Authorship" in *Anxious Power: Reading, Writing and Ambivalence in Narrative by Women*. Edited by Carol J. Singley and Susan Elizabeth Sweeney. Copyright © 1993 State University of New York. All rights reserved. Reproduced by permission of the State University of New York Press.—Low, Donald A. From "Telling the Story: Susan Hill and Dorothy L. Sayers" in *British Radio Drama*. Edited by John Drakakis. Cambridge University Press, 1981. Copyright © 1981 Cambridge University Press. Reproduced with the permission of Cambridge University Press and the author.—Mahon, Ellen M. From "Eavan Boland's Journey with the Muse" in *Learning the Trade: Essays on W. B. Yeats and Contemporary Poetry*. Edited by Deborah Fleming. Locust Hill Press, 1993. Copyright (c)1993 by Deborah Fleming. All rights reserved. Reproduced by permission.—McDowell, Michael. From "The Unexpected and the Inevitable" in *Kingdom of Fear: The World of Stephen King*. Edited by Tim Underwood & Chuck Miller. New American Library, 1986. Copyright © 1986 by Michael McDowell. All rights reserved. Reproduced by permission.—Muir, Kenneth. From "Susan Hill's Fiction" in *The Uses of Fiction: Essays on the Modern Novel in Honour of Arnold Kettle*. Edited by Douglas Jefferson and Graham Martin. The Open University Press, 1982. Copyright © 1982 by The Open University Press. All rights reserved. Reproduced by permission of the Estate of Kenneth Muir.—Pearlman, Mickey. From "What's New at the Zoo?: Rereading Edward Albee's American Dream(s) and Nightmares" in *Feminist Rereadings of Modern American Drama*. Edited by June Schlueter. Associated University Press, 1989. Copyright © 1989 by Associated University Presses. All rights reserved. Reproduced by permission.—Schubert, Maria. From "Susan Hill Focusing on Outsiders and Losers" in *English Language and*

Edward Albee
1928-

(Full name Edward Franklin Albee III) American dramatist, poet, short story writer, and scriptwriter.

The following entry presents an overview of Albee's career through 1996. For further information on his life and works, see *CLC,* Volumes 1, 2, 3, 5, 9, 11, 13, 25, 53, and 86.

INTRODUCTION

An acclaimed and controversial playwright, Albee is best known for *Who's Afraid of Virginia Woolf?* (1962), his first full-length drama. Although initially characterized either as a realist or an absurdist, Albee combines elements from the American tradition of social criticism—established by such playwrights as Arthur Miller, Tennessee Williams, and Eugene O'Neill—with aspects of the Theater of the Absurd, as practiced by Samuel Beckett and Eugene Ionesco. While Albee's plays often portray alienated individuals who suffer as a result of unjust social, moral, and religious strictures, his works usually offer solutions to conflicts rather than conveying an absurdist sense of inescapable determinism. According to Allan Lewis, Albee "writes plays that grip an audience, that hold with their elusiveness, their obscurity, their meaning; and he has functioned in the true role of the playwright—to express the human condition dramatically and metaphorically." In a career spanning more than thirty years, Albee has received the Pulitzer Prize for Drama three times: for *A Delicate Balance* (1966), *Seascape* (1975), and *Three Tall Women* (1991).

Biographical Information

Albee is the adopted child of Reed and Frances Albee, heirs to the multi-million dollar fortune of American theater manager Edward Franklin Albee I. He began attending the theater and writing poetry at the age of six, wrote a three-act sex farce when he was twelve, and attempted two novels while a teenager. Many critics suggest that the tense family conflicts of Albee's dramas are derived from his childhood experiences. After attending several private and military schools and enrolling briefly at Trinity College in Connecticut, Albee achieved limited success as an author of poetry and fiction before turning to drama. Although he remained associated with off-Broadway theater until the production of *Who's Afraid of Virginia Woolf?,* he first garnered critical and popular acclaim for his one-act dramas, which prompted comparisons to the works of Williams and Ionesco. Albee has received three Pulitzer prizes, as well as several other prestigious awards, for his dramatic works.

Major Works

Albee's first one-act play, *The Zoo Story* (1959), is a satire set in New York City in which a young homosexual attempts to force conversation on a reticent conservative. After intimidating the man into defending himself with a knife, the homosexual purposely impales himself on its blade. His next one-act drama, *The Death of Bessie Smith* (1960), revolves around the demise of black blues singer Bessie Smith, who died after being refused treatment at a Southern hospital that catered exclusively to white patients. *The American Dream* (1961), another one-act play, focuses on a mother and father whose severe punishment of their adopted son resulted in his death many years before. Albee's most acclaimed drama, *Who's Afraid of Virginia Woolf?,* has generated popular and critical notoriety for its controversial depiction of marital strife. The play depicts the alternately destructive and conciliatory relationship between George and Martha, a middle-aged history professor and his wife, which is demonstrated during a late-night party in their living room with Nick, George's shallow colleague, and Honey, Nick's spouse.

As the evening proceeds, George and Martha alternately attack and patronize their guests before Martha, intent on wounding George, seduces Nick; George retaliates by announcing the death of their nonexistent son, whom they had created to sustain their relationship. The conclusion suggests that George and Martha may be able to reappraise their relationship based on the intimacy, which was both feared and sought all evening, that arises from their shared sorrow. In *A Delicate Balance,* a troubled middle-aged couple examine their relationship during a prolonged visit by two close friends. In *The Lady from Dubuque* (1980), Albee posited that reality is a subjective phenomenon open to multiple interpretations. This drama concerns a dying woman who vents her pain and hostility on her friends and husband prior to the arrival of an ambiguous, commanding woman who alternately evokes the images of archetypal mother and angel of death. *The Man Who Had Three Arms* (1983) centers on Himself, a man who acquired wealth and fame after growing a third arm that later disappeared. Addressing the audience from a lecture podium, Himself alternately pleads for sympathy and attacks his audience for his loss of prominence. Albee described his stylized drama *Finding the Sun* (1983) as "pointillist in manner." This play counterbalances characters, in one example contrasting a young man's forthcoming freedom with an old man's awareness of his impending death. In *Marriage Play* (1987), Albee returned to the themes of his earlier plays to portray the ambivalent relationship between a cynical woman and her detached husband. *Three Tall Women* (1991) begins with a meeting between an elderly woman in her nineties known as A, her middle-aged caretaker B, and a young lawyer named C who has come to help A settle her affairs. As the three women interact, each becomes aware of and impatient with the others' shortcomings. The first act ends as A suffers a stroke, and in subsequent scenes Albee departs from a strictly linear plot, having all three characters appear as various manifestations of A at different times during her life. The play concerns stereotypes and familial ties, and is considered largely autobiographical; the character A was based on Albee's mother and the relationship between parent and playwright mirrors that of A and her homosexual son. In *The Lorca Story: Scenes from a Life* (1995), Albee presents the story of Federico Garcia Lorca (1900-1936), a Spanish poet and playwright executed during the Fascist reign of General Francisco Franco.

Critical Reception

Beginning with reviews of his earliest works, Albee has garnered a wide variety of critical opinion, ranging from scathing to adoring; many commentators note Albee's inventiveness and insight into society and human nature while at the same time responding negatively to the tone or structure of his dramas. For example, although it was faulted by some as defeatist and nihilistic, *The American Dream* was also commended for its savage parody of traditional American values. Albee commented: "Is the play offensive? I certainly hope so; it was my intention to offend—as well as amuse and entertain." Similarly, even though some critics considered it morbid and self-indulgent, *Who's Afraid of Virginia Woolf?* was honored with two Antoinette Perry Awards and a New York Drama Critics Circle Award. Variously interpreted as a problem play in the tradition of August Strindberg, a campus parody, or a latent homosexual critique of conventional relationships, the drama has generated a wide array of critical analyses. *Who's Afraid of Virginia Woolf?* has more recently been assessed as a classic of American drama for its tight control of form and command of both colloquial and abstruse dialogue. While several of Albee's plays written since 1962 have failed commercially and elicited stinging reviews for their abstract classicism and dialogue, many scholars have commended Albee's commitment to theatrical experimentation and refusal to pander to commercial pressures. *A Delicate Balance,* while garnering approval for its synthesis of dramatic elements, was widely faulted for lacking action and cohesive ideas; when it was awarded the Pulitzer Prize, most regarded the decision as a belated attempt by the Pulitzer committee to honor Albee for *Who's Afraid of Virginia Woolf?* Although *The Lady from Dubuque* closed after only twelve performances, Gerald Clarke deemed it Albee's "best work since *Who's Afraid of Virginia Woolf?,*" and Otis Guernsey included it in *The Best Plays of 1979-1980. The Man Who Had Three Arms* also failed financially; although Albee denied any autobiographical intent, critics dismissed this play as a self-pitying portrayal of Albee, whose plays had been poorly received since the early 1960s. Critical reaction to *Three Tall Women,* for which Albee received a New York Drama Critics Circle Award as well as his third Pulitzer Prize, was generally positive. Although commentators have consistently identified C as the weakest character in the play, they have lauded A and B as well-defined portraits and praised Albee's focus on universal concerns. Many critics have additionally asserted that *Three Tall Women* is the most successful work Albee has written in years; they also note that due to its autobiographical content the play offers invaluable insights into Albee's life and career. John Lahr observed: "Far from being an act of revenge or special pleading, the play is a wary act of reconciliation, whose pathos and poetry are a testament to the bond, however attenuated, between child and parent. *Three Tall Women* bears witness to the son's sad wish to be loved, but with this liberating difference: the child is now finally in control of the parent's destiny, instead of the parent's being in control of the child's."

PRINCIPAL WORKS

The Zoo Story (drama) 1959

The Death of Bessie Smith (drama) 1960
Fam and Yam (drama) 1960
The Sandbox (drama) 1960
The American Dream (drama) 1961
Bartleby [adaptor; from the short story "Bartleby, the Scrivener: A Story of Wall-Street" by Herman Melville] (opera) 1961
Who's Afraid of Virginia Woolf? (drama) 1962
*The Ballad of the Sad Cafe [adaptor; from the novel by Carson McCullers] (drama) 1963
Tiny Alice (drama) 1964
A Delicate Balance (drama) 1966
Malcolm [adaptor; from the novel by James Purdy] (drama) 1966
Everything in the Garden [adaptor; from the play by Giles Cooper] (drama) 1967
Box (drama) 1968
Quotations from Chairman Mao Tse-Tung (drama) 1968
All Over (drama) 1971
Seascape (drama) 1975
Counting the Ways: A Vaudeville (drama) 1977
*Listening: A Chamber Play (drama) 1977
The Lady from Dubuque (drama) 1980
Lolita [adaptor; from the novel by Vladimir Nabokov] (drama) 1981
Finding the Sun (drama) 1983
The Man Who Had Three Arms (drama) 1983
Marriage Play (drama) 1987
Three Tall Women (drama) 1991
Fragments: A Sit Around (drama) 1993
The Lorca Story: Scenes from a Life (drama) 1995

*First produced as a radio play.

CRITICISM

Whitney Balliett (review date 4 February 1961)

SOURCE: "Three Cheers for Albee," in New Yorker, Vol. 36, No. 51, February 4, 1961, pp. 62, 64-66.

[In the following excerpt, Balliett offers a highly complimentary assessment of The American Dream and a negative appraisal of Bartleby.]

Classic tragedy is still kaput, and that rare and most admirable acrobat who, by managing the almost invisible tightrope between tragedy and comedy, produced the incalculably effective form known as tragicomedy no longer exists. He has been replaced by the horror-comic writer, who, like his progenitor, must have perfect equilibrium. If he slips, the results are either cruel or empty. Fortunately, it doesn't look as if Edward Albee, the thirty-two-year-old author of *The*

American Dream, a one-act play at the York Playhouse, will ever slip. His first and third plays, **The Zoo Story** and **The Sandbox,** which were successfully unveiled in New York early last year, are estimable demonstrations of his footwork, and this time around, Albee even flips over onto his hands, and without a single wobble. (His second play, **The Death of Bessie Smith,** inexplicably unproduced in this country, is quite different; it is an out-and-out horror story that all but dissolves in its own acidulous irony.) Indeed, **The American Dream** is a unique and often brilliant play. Its horrible aspects, which reach directly back to the butchery and perversion of the Greek theatre, are forbidding, for they have nothing to do with a stage business of moans and blood and bodies. Far worse, the play's horror is only reported or implied, and it is further pointed up by being juxtaposed with an unfailing and wholly original comic inventiveness that is by turns ridiculous, satiric, sardonic, and sensibly Surrealistic. No sooner has a Sophoclean dismemberment been mentioned than it is illumined by a comic sense that matches and often resembles the comic sense of Gertrude Stein, Lewis Carroll, and Jacques Tati. The play is not realistic, but neither is it purely illusory. It is, in the fashion of a comic nightmare, fantasy of the highest order.

> **Like most expert playwrights, who graciously underwrite in order to make room for their interpreters' artistic proclivities, Albee comes fully alive only when seen.**
> **—Whitney Balliett**

Like most expert playwrights, who graciously underwrite in order to make room for their interpreters' artistic proclivities, Albee comes fully alive only when seen. (The hot-and-heavy playwright usually regards actors and actresses as mere chimneys for his fire and smoke.) On paper, his work suggests a graceful but sketchy blueprint. *The American Dream* deals with a brief climactic period in the lives of five characters—Mommy, Daddy, Grandma (Mommy's ma), Mrs. Barker, and The Young Man. The setting is Mommy's and Daddy's plush apartment living room, which is succinctly suggested by William Ritman in a series of tall gray panels, Romanesque arches, heavy gilt-and-brocade furniture, and gilt picture frames, one of which is surmounted by two small crossed American flags—a touch that establishes the tone of the evening before a word is spoken. Since Albee doesn't have to worry about tragedy, Mommy is from the start a hideous caricature of a childless, waspish, well-to-do middle-aged American woman. Thin-lipped and snake-faced, she speaks in a voice that alternates between needles and syrup. She moves, her shoulders bent in witch fashion, in a series of sharp zigzags, and is smartly overdressed in a purple velvet suit, pounds of gold jewelry, and ugly harlequin glasses.

Daddy is mild, cowardly, conservatively dressed, and, since his digestive "tracts" have reportedly been replaced by "tubes," largely comatose. Albee sets his queer, singsong "Alice in Wonderland" dialogue, which reveals an impeccable ear, going at once. Mommy bullies Daddy into listening to a marvellously repetitious harangue about a hat and the subtle distinctions of color between beige and wheat. ("What did I say, Daddy? What did I just say?") The conversation veers with perfect aplomb to a broken toilet that no one seems able to get fixed. ("You can't get satisfaction any more," whines Daddy.) Then Grandma, who is short, spidery, blue-eyed, and eighty-six, and is dressed in black with a large pioneer-type shawl, appears and dumps at Daddy's feet an enormous bundle of boxes she has just wrapped. (The play is an endless series of surprises; in fact, it seems more improvised than written.) The boxes are fruitlessly discussed while Grandma, Mommy, and Daddy trade with glacial composure alternately hypocritical and vicious remarks about one another, including some indelibly libidinous remarks by Mommy about her sex life with Daddy. Mrs. Barker, the prototype of the American clubwoman, arrives, and is offered every comfort—a seat, a cigarette, a drink, the chance to cross her legs, and the suggestion that she remove her flowered silk dress, which she does, revealing a handsome black slip, in which she remains for most of the play. (No one seems to know Mrs. Barker or why she is there.) The rudeness and politeness, hypocrisy and truth, immediately envelop Mrs. Barker, who amiably joins in, and bit by bit the horrible vacuity of Mommy's and Daddy's life together is revealed. Grandma, who is unsentimental, plucky, shrewd, and funny, and who is Albee's sole but wholly adequate counter-balance to what goes on about her, is our chief informant. She tells with relish of how her daughter's head resembled a banana at birth, how she herself recently slipped secretly out of the apartment and entered a store-bought cake in a baking contest and won twenty-five thousand dollars, how Mommy and Daddy would like to shut her up in a home, and how the packages she has wrapped contain all the things Mommy and Daddy are always trying to take away from her, among them a blind Pekinese (a fine Albee touch) and her television set. In the meantime, Mommy has left the room with Mrs. Barker to show her where she can get a glass of water, and Daddy to search Grandma's room. Albee, though, is always a league or two ahead of us. Mommy cannot find the kitchen, and Grandma's room has disappeared. So it goes, through the revelation, ticked off like a shopping list, of how Mommy and Daddy, twenty years before, angrily dismembered an adopted child in an effort to remedy its illnesses and also to get their monetary "satisfaction." By this time, The Young Man, a vision of handsome, heartless muscularity (the American Dream), is on hand, and—well, the more one attempts to describe Albee the more elusive he becomes. Moreover, the play's resolution, which is critical, depends on considerable suspense. It is enough to say that Grandma gets full revenge on Mommy and Daddy through The Young Man, Mrs. Barker gets dressed again, and the play ends, leaving an irreparable and enormously comic hole in contemporary American middle-class life. . . .

A warning: This is a play for the resilient young and the wise old. All those paunchy, sluggish targets in between had best stay away.

Unfortunately, **The American Dream** is prefaced by **Bartleby,** an indigestible one-act opera skillfully adapted from the Melville story by James Hinton, Jr., and Albee, with music by William Flanagan. (**The Death of Bessie Smith** would have made a perfect twin.) **Bartleby** is a dead-end tale that deals with a mysterious and taciturn clerk of that name, who, when asked to do this or that by his employer, a New York lawyer, simply replies, "I prefer not to." The clerk even refuses to be fired, forcing the lawyer, a patient, kindly sort, to move his office. Left behind, the clerk is arrested as a vagrant and taken to the Tombs, where he dies of malnutrition. (In the opera, he expires in the lawyer's old office.) This is the sort of teasing, blank-faced symbolism that Melville revelled in, but its possibilities are pretty well buried by Flanagan's score, which is vaguely atonal and full of the difficult, craggy melodic content that Charles Ives invented.

Robert Brustein (review date 27 March 1961)

SOURCE: "Fragments from a Cultural Explosion," in *New Republic,* Vol. 144, No. 13, March 27, 1961, pp. 29-30.

[*In the following excerpt from a review of* The American Dream *and* The Death of Bessie Smith, *Brustein argues that Albee's talent as a playwright is underdeveloped and his plays lack depth, focus, and direction.*]

It is often taken as a sign of progress and maturity that our formerly Philistine fatherland has now begun to consume artistic objects with an appetite fully as ravenous as that once reserved for comic books. The phrase for this awesome phenomenon, I believe, is "cultural explosion"—but out of this explosion have come only scattered shell fragments which we vainly try to shore against our ruins. For despite increasing activity and interest, our culture is in a state of severe impoverishment. While everyone, including monkeys and IBM computers, is busy "creating," almost nobody is creating well, and the true appetite for works of art remains dreadfully undernourished by the native approximations. This fact is dimly, though indirectly, reflected in the various organs devoted to initiating cultural fashions. America's fascination with artists has always been much greater than its interest in art, but you can't have one without the other; and *Life, Esquire,* the women's magazines, and the newspapers are all revealing a measure of desperation in trying to unearth "exciting new personalities" to feed to an insatiable public. Years ago—and this may explain the comparative honesty of his early work—Tennessee Williams completed over fifteen plays before anyone took the slightest notice of him. Today, a Lorraine Hansberry and an Archibald MacLeish need produce only a single saleable commodity before their "dramatic genius" is proclaimed in every middle-brow publication in the land.

> **To be so easily gobbled up by the media would be a forbidding omen even in a playwright who has already proven his ability. But since Mr. Albee's talent is still in a rather immature stage of development, his premature fame may prove very damaging to his creative growth.**
> **—*Robert Brustein***

Edward Albee was first promoted into an "exciting new personality" on the basis of one short play (*The Zoo Story*), but now that he has added a couple more one-acters to the canon, the press is fairly bursting with enthusiastic epithets. In the last few weeks, he has been tin-typed by *Time,* interviewed by *Theatre Arts,* produced by *Omnibus,* and fluttered over by all the reviewers, with the result that we now know every detail of his life and his opinion on every conceivable theatrical subject. The irony of this situation is only surpassed by its essential sadness. To be so easily gobbled up by the media would be a forbidding omen even in a playwright who has already proven his ability. But since Mr. Albee's talent is still in a rather immature stage of development, his premature fame may prove very damaging to his creative growth.

The American Dream and *The Death of Bessie Smith* are further evidence that Albee's talent has not yet found its way out of chrysalis. Both plays are inferior to *The Zoo Story,* but all three embody the same vital defect: the absence of any compelling theme, commitment, or sense of life which might pull them into focus. Lacking this larger vision, Albee's plays—while beginning auspiciously, with a pyrotechnic display of arch, brittle irony—always collapse at the finish, either into whimpering melodrama (*Bessie Smith*) or into embarrassing self-exposure (*American Dream*). The consequence, reflected in both productions (which also end feebly after promising beginnings), is an abrupt switch in tone, and sometimes a sense of bewildering irrelevance—as in *Bessie Smith* where a Gothic report of the blues singer's death in an auto accident is forcibly superimposed on the main story of a malignant Southern nurse (out of Williams) and an idealistic interne who unaccountably pursues her.

The disunity of *The American Dream* is more damaging, since it mars a better work. The play begins as a scorching satire on upper middle class family life (aggressive Mommy and castrated Daddy tormenting sweet-crusty Grandma), in which the fatuities of daily conversation are brutally excoriated through the use of clichés, small talk, and illogical non-sequiturs. Albee, who has not yet developed his own style, borrows Ionesco's techniques here, and he manipulates them well in a somewhat febrile, bitchy manner. But while *The Bald Soprano* opened out onto all vacuous families, Albee closes in on one (probably his own); and with strong suggestions of personal bitterness, the play shifts into a story of adoption. This shift is signified by the entrance of the "Dream," a fully grown Adonis in regulation theater garb (blue jeans, tee shirt, cowboy boots) who proceeds to pour out toneless pathological confessions about his inability to feel, love, connect, be whole, etc. When Mommy, who has already dismembered his twin, adopts him, the curtain descends, while Grandma (now "dead") poignantly comments on the repetition from the wings. Thus, like *The Zoo Story,* this play begins as a whining letter to the chaplain, compromised by Albee's inability to objectify or transcend the wounded Self.

Harold Clurman (review date 27 October 1962)

SOURCE: A review of *Who's Afraid of Virginia Woolf?,* in *Nation,* Vol. 195, No. 13, October 27, 1962, pp. 273-74.

[*In the following excerpt, Clurman acknowledges Albee's technical skill, but faults his characterizations in* Who's Afraid of Virginia Woolf? *as one-dimensional.*]

Edward Albee's *Who's Afraid of Virginia Woolf?* . . . is packed with talent. . . . It may well prove the best of the season. Its significance extends beyond the moment. In its faults as well as in its merits it deserves our close attention.

It has four characters: two couples. There is hardly a plot, little so called "action," but it moves or rather whirls on its own special axis. At first it seems to be a play about marital relations; as it proceeds one realizes that it aims to encompass much more. The author wants to "tell all," to say everything.

The middle-aged wife, Martha, torments her somewhat younger husband because he has failed to live up to her expectations. Her father, whom she worships, is president of a small college. Her husband might have become the head of the history department and ultimately perhaps her father's heir. But husband George is a nonconformist. He has gone no further than associate professor, which makes him a flop. She demeans him in every possible way. George hits back, and the play is structured on this mutually sadistic basis. The first cause of their conflict is the man's "business" (or career) failure.

Because they are both attracted to what may be vibrant in each of them, theirs is a love-hate dance of death which they enact in typical American fashion by fun and games swamped in a sauce of strong drink. They bubble and fester with poisonous quips.

The first time we meet them they are about to entertain a new biology instructor who, at twenty-eight, has just been introduced to the academic rat race. The new instructor is a rather ordinary fellow with a forever effaced wife. We learn that he married her for her money and because of what turned out to be "hysterical pregnancy." The truth is she is afraid of bearing a child though she wants one. Her husband treats her with conventional regard (a sort of reflexive tenderness) while he contemplates widespread adultery for gratification and advancement in college circles. George scorns his young colleague for being "functional" in his behavior, his ambition, his attitudes.

So it goes: we are in the midst of inanity, jokes and insidious mayhem. Martha rationalizes her cruelty to George on the ground that he masochistically enjoys her beatings.

Everyone is fundamentally impotent, despite persistent "sexualizing." The younger wife is constantly throwing up through gutless fear. Her lightheadedness is a flight from reality. The older couple has invented a son because of an unaccountable sterility. They quarrel over the nature of the imaginary son because each of them pictures him as a foil against the other. There is also a hint that as a boy George at different times accidentally killed both his father and mother. Is this so? Illusion is real; "reality" may only be symbolic—either a wish or a specter of anxiety. It does not matter: these people, the author implies, represent our environment; indeed they may even represent Western civilization!

Albee is prodigiously shrewd and skillful. His dialogue is superbly virile and plaint: it also *sounds*. It is not "realistic" dialogue but a highly literate and full-bodied distillation of common American speech.
— *Harold Clurman*

The inferno is made very funny. The audience at any rate laughs long and loud—partly because the writing is sharp with surprise, partly because an element of recognition is involved: in laughter it hides from itself while obliquely acknowledging its resemblance to the couples on the stage.

When the play turns earnestly savage or pathetic the audience feels either shattered or embarrassed. Shattered because it can no longer evade the play's expression of the audience's afflictions, sins and guilts; embarrassed because there is something in the play—particularly toward the end—that is unbelievable, soft without cause. At its best, the play is comedy.

Albee is prodigiously shrewd and skillful. His dialogue is superbly virile and plaint: it also *sounds*. It is not "realistic" dialogue but a highly literate and full-bodied distillation of common American speech. Still better, Albee knows how to keep his audience almost continuously interested (despite the play's inordinate length). He can also ring changes on his theme, so that the play rarely seems static. Albee is a master craftsman.

Strangely enough, though there is no question of his sincerity, it is Albee's skill which at this point most troubles me. It is as if his already practiced hand had learned too soon to make an artful package of venom. For the overriding passion of the play is venomous. There is no reason why anger should not be dramatized. I do not object to Albee's being "morbid," for as the conspicuously healthy William James once said, "morbid-mindeness ranges over a wider scale of experience than healthy-mindedness." What I do object to in his play is that its disease has become something of a brilliant formula, as slick and automatic as a happy entertainment for the trade. The right to pessimism has to be earned within the artistic terms one sets up: the pessimism and rage of *Who's Afraid of Virginia Woolf?* are immature. Immaturity coupled with a commanding deftness is dangerous.

What justifies this criticism? The characters have no life (or texture) apart from the immediate virulence of their confined action or speech. George is intended to represent the humanist principle in the play. But what does he concretely want? What traits, aside from his cursing the life he leads, does he have? Almost none. Martha and George, we are told, love each other after all. How? That she can't bear being loved is a psychological aside in the play, but how is her love for anything, except for her "father fixation," and some sexual dependence on George, actually embodied? What interests—even petty—do they have or share? Vividly as each personage is drawn, they all nevertheless remain flat—caricatures rather than people. Each stroke of dazzling color is superimposed on another, but no further substance accumulates. We do not actually identify with anyone except editorially. Even the non-naturalistic figures of Beckett's plays have more extension and therefore more stature and meaning. The characters in Albee's *The Zoo Story* and *Bessie Smith* are more particularized.

If we see Albee, as I do, as an emerging artist, young in the sense of a seriously prolonged career, the play marks an auspicious beginning and, despite its success, not an end. In our depleted theatre it has real importance because Albee desperately wishes to cry out—manifest—his life. The end of his play—which seeks to introduce "hope" by suggesting that if his people should rid themselves of illusion (more exactly, falsity) they might achieve ripeness—is unconvincing in view of what has preceded it. Still, this ending is a gesture, one that indicates Albee's will to break through the agonizing narrowness of the play's compass.

Albee knows all he needs to know about play-making; he has still to learn something other than rejection and more than tearfulness. His play should be seen by everyone interested in our world at home, for as Albee's George says, "I can admire things I don't admire.". . .

A final note: though I believe the play to be a minor work within the prospect of Albee's further development, it must for some time occupy a major position in our scene. It will therefore be done many times in different productions in many places, including Europe. Though I do not know how it is to be effected, I feel that a less naturalistic production might be envisaged. *Who's Afraid of Virginia Woolf?* verges on a certain expressionism, and a production with a touch of that sort of poetry, something not so furiously insistent on the "honesty" of the materials, might give the play some of the qualities I feel it now lacks: it might alleviate the impression of, in the author's pithy phrase, "an ugly talent."

Robert Brustein (review date 3 November 1962)

SOURCE: "Albee and the Medusa Head," in *New Republic,* Vol. 147, No. 18, November 3, 1962, pp. 29-30.

[*In the following excerpt of a review of* Who's Afraid of Virginia Woolf?*, Brustein recognizes Albee's talent for compelling and clever dialogue and his inventiveness, but also notes what he perceives as the author's failure to create a cohesive drama.*]

Edward Albee's new work embodies both the failings and the virtues of his previous plays. But its positive achievements are substantial, and I am finally beginning to regard this playwright's future with real expectation. Albee's technical dexterity has always been breathtaking—for sheer theatrical skill, no American, not even Williams, can match him—but like Williams, he has been inclined to falsify his native gifts, distorting experience through self-defensive reflecting mirrors. In *Who's Afraid of Virginia Woolf,* Albee is still not looking the Gorgon smack in the eye. Still, he has conjured up its outline. And if he tends to focus more on writhing snakes than on the other features of this terrifying monster, then even these quick glances are more penetrating than I have come to expect; and they are always projected in steaming, raging, phantasmagoric the article images.

Virginia Woolf is an ambitious play, and it evokes the shades of the most ambitious dramatists. The central conflict—a Strindbergian battle royal between George, a contemplative History professor with an unsuccessful career, and Martha, his bitterly shrewish wife—proceeds through a series of confessions, revelations, and interior journeys which recall the circuitous windings of O'Neill's late plays. Glued together by mutual hatred and mutual recriminations, the couple can connect only through enmity, each exposing the other's failures, inadequacies, vices, and secret illusions in language of savagely ironic scorn. Though the climax of the work is built on such an exposure, however, Albee seems less interested in the real history of his characters than in the way they conceal and protect their reality: the conflict is also a kind of game, with strict rules, and what they reveal about each other may not be true. This comedy of concealment reminds one of Pirandello, and even more of Jean Genet. For George and Martha—each by turns the aggressor—shift their identities like reptiles shedding skins. And as the evening grows more alcoholic, and the atmosphere more distended and surrealistic, their "total war" becomes a form of ritual play acting, performed upon the shifting sands of truth.

> **Albee is a highly accomplished stage magician, but he fails to convince us there is nothing up his sleeve. His thematic content is incompatible with his theatrical content—hi-jinks and high seriousness fail to fuse.**
>
> **—Robert Brustein**

The "setting" for this play-within-a-play is a late night party; the "audience" is composed of a hollow young biology instructor, Nick, and his demure, simpering wife, Honey. A conventionally shallow couple, they are at first innocent bystanders embarrassed by the squabbling of their hosts, then full participants, as George sadistically exposes *their* guilty secrets. Nick's academic opportunism, Honey's surreptitious abortions. The waspish "fun and games" begin to take the form of ruthlessly aggressive charades. After "Humiliate the Host" and "Get the Guests" comes "Hump the Hostess" as Martha and Nick, in revenge against George, make a feeble attempt to cuckold him in the bedroom. The last episode, "Bringing Up Baby," constitutes George's revenge on Martha—not because she tried to betray him (her infidelities are apparently innumerable), but because she broke one of the rules of the game: she mentioned their "son" to strangers. Forcing Martha to recount the childhood history of this absent youth, George reads the requiem for the dead, climaxing this litany with the announcement that their son has been killed in an auto accident. But the child has never existed. He is merely the essential illusion of the childless Martha, a consoling fiction in her inconsolable reality. The play ends with Honey now determined to have a child, and Martha, submissive and frightened, being comforted by George.

Everyone seems to have boggled at this fictional child; and it is certain that the play collapses at its moment of climax. But the difficulty is not that the author introduces a spurious element into an otherwise truthful play. It is, rather, that he suddenly confronts us with a moment of truth after an evening of stage illusions. Albee's theatrical inventiveness rests mainly on incongruous juxtapositions: when George aims a shotgun at his braying wife, for example, it shoots not bullets but a Japanese parasol. These shock tactics are a sure-fire comic technique, but they have the effect of alienating the spectator from the action the very moment he begins to accept it. Thus, when George launches a blistering attack on the evils of modern science, Albee undercuts it with a ludicrous non-sequitur: "I will not give up Berlin." And when Martha speaks of her need to escape reality, he has her do so in a broad Irish brogue. George responds to Martha's infidelity by nonchalantly offering her flowers; he tells a harrowing story of matricide and patricide which is proved, first, to be autobiographical, and second, to be false; and when asked about the telegram announcing his son's death, he claims to have eaten it. Truth and illusion may be confused, as one character tells us, but after three and a half hours of prestidigitation, we become reluctant to accept one of these magical tricks as the real thing. In short, Albee is a highly accomplished stage magician, but he fails to convince us there is nothing up his sleeve. His thematic content is incompatible with his theatrical content—hi-jinks and high seriousness fail to fuse.

On the other hand, the author has a fine time showing off his sleight of hand, incidentally, I suspect, conjuring his action into the outlines of a classical myth (the evidence is jumbled, and I may be crazy, but I think I can detect elements of the story of Aphrodite, Ares, and Hephaestus, mixed with pieces from the story of Aphrodite and Adonis). . . .

In spite of all the excellence of play and production, however, I am left with my equivocal response. In his latest play, Edward Albee proves once again that he has wit, cunning, theatricality, toughness, formal control, poetry—in short, all the qualities of a major dramatist but one: that selfless commitment to a truthful vision of life which constitutes the universal basis of all serious art. Possibly out of fear of such commitments, Albee is still coquetting with his own talent, still resisting any real identification with his own material, so that he tends to confuse his themes, shift his attitudes, and subvert his characters. Yet, a genuine insight, merely

sketched in his earlier work is now beginning to find fuller expression: that in a time of deadened instinct, people will use any methods, including deadly hatred, in order to find their way to others. This, or something like it, may become the solid foundation of Albee's future writing; but whatever it is, I await what is to come with eagerness. For if Albee can confront the Medusa head without the aid of parlor tricks or mirrors, he may yet turn us all to stone.

Gerald Weales (review date 25 October 1968)

SOURCE: A review of *Box* and *Quotations from Chairman Mao Tse-Tung,* in *Commonweal,* Vol. LXXXIX, No. 4, October 25, 1968, pp. 120, 122.

[*In the following excerpt, Weales provides a favorable assessment of* Box *and* Quotations from Chairman Mao Tse-Tung.]

Edward Albee's new play and/or plays, **Box** and **Quotations from Chairman Mao Tse-Tung,** came into New York, burdened with a reputation that set up the worst kind of expectations. Reports from Buffalo, where the work had its premiere last spring at the Festival of the Arts, told of boredom and impatience. The creators' reaction to the critical response, both public (in the *New York Times Magazine,* Albee said of the non-speaking clergyman in **Mao,** "I suppose he's sort of a critic, except that he's sober") and private (the string of silly-ass telegrams that the author, director and producer sent to a Canadian critic) suggested infantile defense of a lost cause. The production of **Box** on educational television, divorced both from its companion play and the physical theater, was as empty as a visually flat box can be. The heart of the problem is that it is impossible to describe the new work without sounding as though one were inventing a parody of the most pretentious kind of avantgarde theater. The pre-judgment was in; the verdict, willful chi-chi. So I went to **Box-Mao** expecting nothing, or worse, and found myself fascinated by play and performance alike. What Albee is up to is not so much an examination of the contemporary situation as the rhetorical and artistic means of coping with it, an implicit critique of his own work that is harsher than that made by even his most vehement critics, and he is at once fragmenting and working with conventional theater responses.

Entering the theater, one is confronted with the frame of a gigantic box, filling the stage and, since the stage is an apron, reaching into the audience. A joke about the box stage? Obviously, but it becomes more than that. Before the house lights dim, a number of spots come on, fixing the frame so that it stands out, clean, functional, empty, once the house is dark. Then a voice begins—Ruth White on tape (since she was the motel-keeper's taped voice in *America Hurrah,* she is in danger of becoming one of the best actresses *not* in the theater). Given our listening habits, the aural-visual combination on which we usually depend for concentration, a disembodied voice in the theater should be impossible to follow, particularly when the monologue runs on and on, deliberately, unhurriedly, for a great many minutes (a reported 15, but I did not time the speech). I know that when I saw the play on television, my eyes and my mind wandered the room I was in and robbed the voice of meaning, turned it into White sound. Here, however, there was only the box and the voice and they seemed to belong to one another, so I listened. The monologue is at once an evocation of nostalgia and a lecture in aesthetics. The arts are gone, the voice says, and crafts have come if not to replace them, then to occupy the vacant space. Art that hurts by telling us of our losses is the final corruption in a corrupt world, but there is still room to move around in the box and the possibility of some kind of artistic order, always on its own terms.

> **What Albee is up to [in *Box* and *Quotations from Chairman Mao Tse-Tung*] is not so much an examination of the contemporary situation as the rhetorical and artistic means of coping with it, an implicit critique of his own work that is harsher than that made by even his most vehement critics, and he is at once fragmenting and working with conventional theater responses.**
>
> **—*Gerald Weales***

When the voice stills, *Mao* begins with the entrance of the man himself. He prowls the stage, the theater, the boxes, a little frightening in his mask, relentlessly quoting his Marxist platitudes. He shares the stage and the contrapuntal pattern with an old woman, played by Sudie Bond in the cartoon style she developed for Grandma in *The American Dream,* who does nothing but recite "Over the Hill to the Poorhouse," Will Carleton's marvelous exercise in 1930's poetic pop-schmaltz, and with a long-winded lady, as the program identifies her, who insistently tells the mute clergyman about the time she fell or jumped or was pushed off an ocean liner like the one on which they are riding at the moment. Once the three voices are established, they are joined by lines replayed from the opening tape, and the pattern is so organized that the lines are often direct comments on or oblique jokes about the speech that immediately precedes them. . . .

It is quickly clear that Mao's quotations, all jargonesque abstractions, and the old woman's poem, social criticism as a tear-jerker, are rhetorical devices to avoid the human situation with which they are presumably dealing, ways of not

seeing reality. The tricky thing about the play is Albee's use of the long-winded lady. As she tells the story of her fall, interrupted not so much by the other characters as her own verbal mannerisms—the familiar Albee hesitations, circumlocutions, searches for the precise word, new beginnings— she describes her own life, which, for all the admission of past affection, turns out to be as empty and meaningless as one has come to expect from an Albee heroine. She repeats her reaction to the official suggestion that she may have jumped, "I have nothing to die for.". . . Yet the story she tells—the dying husband, the defecting child—is the parallel of "Over the Hill to the Poorhouse" and, even while we are being touched, we know we are being had, that her rhetoric, that of heightened realism, is also an avoidance. Contemporary drama, Albee seems to be telling us, is at its best and its most corrupt when it treats of loss, as all of Albee's work does; craft, with a little box-room and its own sense of order, can at least recognize that fact. *Box-Mao* is a kind of confession, but, unlike so many confessions, one that is a pleasure to watch because it uses the tricks it admits.

M. Patricia Fumerton (essay date Summer 1981)

SOURCE: "Verbal Prisons: The Language of Albee's *A Delicate Balance,*" in *English Studies in Canada,* Vol. 7, No. 2, Summer, 1981, pp. 201-11.

[*In the following essay, Fumerton provides an analysis of Albee's use of language in* A Delicate Balance.]

A Delicate Balance forms part of Edward Albee's continuing exploration into the potentialities and limitations of language. Surprisingly, however, no one has yet provided a detailed analysis of the play's language. This work intends such a study. The characters of *A Delicate Balance* are conscious manipulators of their language: a frightened people who use language in an attempt to control or simply to survive fearful realities. They use the decorum of language to disguise anxieties, to balance between implications (as when Agnes habitually says "either . . . or" and "if . . . then"), and thus to evade truths and choices. At the same time, they sharpen their language of evasion into a precise instrument of persuasion—wielded by all, but most skillfully by the "fulcrum," Agnes. Yet in employing it to evade and coerce, the characters limit and distort their language, separating the "word" from its concrete and unconditional "meaning." Ironically—and tragically—they become trapped within the limits they themselves impose upon language.

The play opens with a conversation between Tobias and Agnes, a husband and wife who appear contented and very much in love. The mood is subdued, the characters are attentive, and the language, although formal, is cordial and pleasant. Agnes's opening speeches undulate like the rolling of hills, never descending into deep chasms nor climbing to mountainous peaks. She begins with an idea, glides into a parenthesis that becomes a digression (intermixed with questions to her husband), returns briefly to that idea—from which she again digresses—and finally completes this same thought three pages after it was originally introduced. Her sentences overlap, continually balancing and qualifying themselves:

> What I find most astonishing—aside from that belief of mine, which never ceases to surprise me by the very fact of its surprising lack of unpleasantness, the belief that I might very easily—as they say—lose my mind one day, not that I suspect I am about to, or am even . . . nearby. . . .

Placid and lamb-like, Agnes appears well-suited to her name. And the further association, through her name, with Saint Agnes, a virgin martyr of the third century, evokes no striking sense of incongruity.

[In *A Delicate Balance*] Agnes describes herself most aptly as the "fulcrum" of the family. A fulcrum is not only a support or point of support on which a lever turns in raising or moving something, but also a means of exerting influence or pressure. As the sole support of her family, Agnes must exert pressure to maintain its shape. She does so through language.
—*M. Patricia Fumerton*

As the play continues, however, it becomes apparent that Tobias and Agnes are not content and that even their love is to be questioned. Their language is a camouflaging tool that expertly conceals a depth of pain and fear. Rather than being an expression of love, the almost euphonious decorum permeating the play is a mark of heightened tension (as in the tea-pouring scene of Act III) or of extreme uneasiness (as in the exchange of names when Harry and Edna first arrive). Whenever uncomfortable or fearful, the characters turn to recognized formalities in order to distance what they fear and to conceal what they feel. Thus, when left alone in the living room in Act III, Harry and Tobias formally greet each other even though they have already been in this same room with the others for some time:

> HARRY: (*Watching them go; laughs ruefully*) Boy, look at 'em go. They got outa *here* quick enough. You'd think there was a . . . (*Trails off, sees* TOBIAS *is ill at ease; says, gently*) Morning, Tobias.

> TOBIAS: (*Grateful*) Morning, Harry.

Ironically, Agnes, the "saint," is the most expert manipulator of this language of disguise. Her *very* correct, *very* polite, and *very* balanced language is deceptively open and articulate—it conceals, in fact, rather than reveals. When Agnes distinguishes between an hysterical condition and an hysterical action (in response to Tobias's declaration that Julia is in hysterics), she is actually using articulation as a defense. Similarly, when Agnes responds with the expression "either . . . or"—an expression frequently mocked by Claire—she articulates the alternatives, but never makes a choice: "She [Julia] will be down or she will not. She will stop, or she will . . . go on." Agnes is as noncommittal as Tobias and the others. By repeatedly using this expression, as well as "if . . . then"—expressions balancing like teeter-totters—Agnes focuses upon the implications and thus evades rather than faces the truths (which demand that one not only recognize, but actively choose between alternatives). Claire sees this clearly:

> We live with our truths in the grassy bottom, and we examine alllll the interpretations of alllll the implications like we had a life for nothing else, for God's sake.

Claire's vision is indeed faithful to the meaning of her name:

> AGNES: (*An overly sweet smile*) Claire could tell us so much if she cared to, could you not, Claire. Claire, who watches from the sidelines, has seen so very much, has seen us all so clearly, have you not, Claire. You were not named for nothing.

Constantly striving to break the balance and expose truths, Claire threatens the equipoise Agnes so carefully maintains. Claire's sentences reach for peaks and descend into chasms. Stuffed with quick, short verbs, they build up and run head-long, rather than balance:

> Pretend you're very sick, Tobias, like you were with the stomach business, but pretend you feel your insides are all green, and stink, and mixed up, and your eyes hurt and you're half deaf and your brain keeps turning off, and you've got peripheral neuritis and you can hardly walk and you hate . . . and you notice—with a sort of detachment that amuses you, you think—that you're more like an animal every day . . . you snarl, and *grab* for things, and hide things and forget where you hid them like not-very-bright dogs, and you wash less, prefer to *be* washed, and once or twice you've actually soiled your bed and laid in it because you can't get up . . . pretend all that. No you don't like that, Tobias?

Like all potentially dangerous things, Claire must be controlled. With the mere mention of her name, before she even enters the room, Agnes's pleasantly rolling language becomes more forceful and oppressive. Her parenthetical comments (which had earlier acted digressively, dissipating her main idea) are now carefully laid one upon another in the building of her "mountain" of burdens. Note, in particular, the powerful accumulation of monosyllabic words in her first parenthesis:

> If I were to list the mountain of my burdens—if I had a thick pad and a month to spare—that bending my shoulders *most,* with the possible exception of Julia's trouble with marriage, would be your—it must be instinctive, I think, or *reflex,* that's more like it—your reflex defense of everything Claire. . . .

Agnes describes herself most aptly as the "fulcrum" of the family. A fulcrum is not only a support or point of support on which a lever turns in raising or moving something, but also a means of exerting influence or pressure. As the sole support of her family, Agnes must exert pressure to maintain its shape. She does so through language. Exemplary of this is Agnes's technique of ending a question with "was it not?" or "have I not?" thus adding assertive force to an interrogative sentence:

> AGNES: (*Quietly; sadly*) Well, it was your decision, was it not?
>
> TOBIAS: (*Ibid.*) Yes.
>
> AGNES: And I have made the best of it. Have lived with it. Have I not?

Harry and Edna are the only people Agnes cannot quite control. These two pose a far greater threat to Agnes than does Claire because they do not fall within Agnes's domain, the family circle. Indeed, the sudden arrival of Harry and Edna is seen as a hostile "invasion" (the verb "harry" means "to plunder"). Fearing for the safety of her stronghold, Agnes struggles to control these invaders—to grasp hold of them—by shifting her mode of address. Throughout the first half of the play, everyone, including Agnes, refers to them as "Harry and Edna." Midway, however, Agnes suddenly switches to "Edna and Harry" and she alone continues to address them in this way throughout the rest of the play:

> Would it seem . . . incomplete to you, my darling, were I to tell you Julia is upset that Har—Edna and Harry are here, that. . . .

But Harry and Edna remain ungovernable and, therefore, most threatening.

In all other cases, Agnes successfully exerts control through language. She is able to do so because language itself is presented as an authority. But it is only accepted as such if one has the "right" to speak authoritatively. Those who are not members of the family have no right at all—at least, not in the eyes of Julia and Agnes. Consequently, when Edna criticizes the way Agnes and Claire banter—"I wish you two would stop having at each other"—Agnes immediately questions her right to interfere: "Is that for you to say?"

In contrast with the above sequence is an exchange between two rightful members of the family, father and daughter:

> TOBIAS: (*Quiet anger and sorrow*) Your brother would not have grown up to be a fag.
>
> JULIA: (*Bitter smile*) Who is to say?
>
> TOBIAS: (*Hard look*) I!

Tobias, with verbal force, claims victory, and Julia silently accedes. However, the balance of power shifts at the beginning of Act III when, still dazed from his confrontation with Agnes, Tobias surrenders totally to what Julia says to him:

> JULIA: (*Setting the tray down*) There; now that's much better, isn't it?
>
> TOBIAS: (*In a fog*) Whatever you say, Julie.

In each of these dialogues one speaker emerges in control through the power of language alone. Of course, the right and ability to exercise this power rest foremost with Agnes. This is most evident when Agnes defines alcoholism:

> AGNES: (*Not looking at either of them*) If we change for the worse with drink, we are an alcoholic. It is as simple as that.
>
> CLAIRE: And who is to say!
>
> AGNES: I!

After an appeal to Tobias, which receives no response, Claire accepts the definition—she is what Agnes says she is: "Very well, then, Agnes, you win. I shall be an alcoholic." The very use of "if . . . then"—"If we change for the worse with drink, we are an alcoholic"—is authoritarian. This sentence structure leads one to focus upon the "then" clause while unquestioningly accepting or ignoring the "if" clause.

But because the family members have raised their language to an imperious position, even those who try to exert themselves through that language are actually controlled by it: captives of their own language, they think what they say rather than say what they think. Language is a ritual that has become separated from thought and, therefore, from real meaning. The characters are all extremely polite (they cordially address each other with "darling," "dear," "please," "thank you") but Tobias himself questions, as do we, whether this cordiality is only mechanical. Do they *really mean* "darling" and "thank you" or is this apparent sincerity, when actually analyzed, only conditional upon circumstances—like Agnes's "if ... then?":

> When we talk to each other ... what have we meant? Anything? When we touch, when we promise, and say ... yes, or please ... with our*selves*? ... have we meant, yes, but only if ... if there's any condition, Agnes! Then it's ... all been empty.

The emptiness of this ritual is most apparent when one compares the long exchange of personal names, upon the first appearance of Harry and Edna, with the similar yet confused voicing of names at the end of the same Act:

> AGNES: (*Reaches doorway; turns to* TOBIAS; *a question that has no answer*) Tobias?
>
> HARRY: (*Rises, begins to follow* EDNA, *rather automaton-like*) Edna?
>
> TOBIAS: (*Confused*) Harry?

Each individual calls out helplessly, expecting no answer to alleviate his or her isolation.

Like the rules of etiquette, the rules of grammar must always be observed in *A Delicate Balance.* Claire deliberately breaks one of these grammatical laws by saying "a alcoholic" rather than "an," but Agnes is quick to catch any irregularity in her speech: "I dropped upstairs—well, *that* doesn't make very much sense, does it? I *happened* upstairs ...." Here too, however, is an emptiness. The meaning which stands behind the order of language is missing:

> EDNA: Harry is helping Agnes and Tobias get our bags upstairs.
>
> JULIA: (*Slight schoolteacher tone*) Don't you mean Agnes and Tobias are helping Harry?
>
> EDNA: (*Tired*) If you like.

Individual words clank hollowly within this syntactical kettle-drum—as does the expression, "best friends," or Agnes's repeated use of "glad": "We're *glad* you're here; we're glad you came to surprise us!" The characters have command of their own language in the same way that Harry has mastered French:

HARRY: ... and I was reading my French; I've got it pretty good now—not the accent, but the ... the words.

They know the lexicon and syntax of their language, but have lost, or forgotten, its meaning.

Several attempts are made to define or to redefine words in *A Delicate Balance.* When Agnes defines Claire as an alcoholic, she does so to gain control over her by labelling her. Edna similarly tries to manipulate the others by defining "friendship," yet she is also actually attempting to understand the meaning—or what the others mean—by the word:

> EDNA: (*To* JULIA) You must ... what is the word? ... coexist, my dear. (*To the others*) Must she not? (*Silence; calm*) Must she not. This is what you have meant by friendship ... is it not?

But Edna's efforts are pathetically unsatisfactory. The language to which these people have reduced themselves is simply too limited for meaningful expression.

This is most evident when Harry and Edna try to explain their terror. Their language fails to provide an adequate description of this fear or of its cause: the characters can only repeat the adjectives, "frightened," "terrified," and "scared." The closest they come to identifying their fear is through a simile:

> HARRY: (*Quite innocent, almost childlike*) It was like being lost: very young again, with the dark, and lost.

Similarly, Julia, in her hysteria, is unable to express the full force of her pain and fear through language. In fact, the language actually disintegrates as she herself loses control: "Get them out of here, Daddy, getthemoutofheregetthemoutofheregetthemoutofheregetthemoutofhere ...."

In their struggle to express themselves, individuals often distinguish between synonymous words:

> AGNES: (*More curious than anything*) Do you really want me dead, Claire?
>
> CLAIRE: Wish, yes. Want? I don't know; probably, though I might regret it if I had it.

They will even differentiate between identical words—as in Act III when Harry tries to explain his relationship with Edna to Tobias: "We don't ... 'like.' Oh, sure we *like* ...." In this same Act, Tobias screams that he does not "want" Harry and Edna to stay and yet he begs them to stay.

This word, "want," takes on special significance in *A Delicate Balance.* It denotes both a lack and a need of something:

> EDNA: . . . if all at once we . . . NEED . . . we come where we are wanted, where we know we are expected, not only where we want. . . .

When Edna and Harry come to the house, Julia repeatedly asks, "What do they want?" In Act II, Julia's horror-filled declaration, "THEY WANT!", is followed a few lines later by the pathetic cry, "I *want!*" But like the other characters, Julia does not know specifically what she lacks and needs:

> JULIA: I *want!*
>
> CLAIRE: (*Sad smile*) What do you want, Julia?
>
> JULIA: I . . .
>
> HARRY: Jesus.
>
> JULIA: I WANT . . . WHAT IS MINE!
>
> AGNES: (*Seemingly dispassionate; after a pause*) Well, then, my dear, you will have to decide what that is, will you not.

"Want" lacks a definable object: it points to something beyond what each individual has, some unidentifiable thing that is missing from their lives:

> TOBIAS: (*Holding a glass out to* AGNES) Did you say you wanted?
>
> AGNES: (*Her eyes still on* CLAIRE) Yes, I did, thank you.
>
> HARRY: (*Subdued, almost apologetic*) Edna and I . . . there's . . . so much . . . over the dam, so many . . . disappointments, evasions, I guess, lies maybe . . . so much we remember we wanted, once . . . so little that we've . . . settled for . . . .

The word "want" exemplifies the casualties language suffers when warped into an instrument of disguise and control. Reduced to an evasive abstraction, "want" resonates with meaning yet is unable to communicate definite thoughts and feelings.

Dominated by this language, the characters themselves approach the undefinable and abstract. A distance separates them from the reader. Their talk is colloquial enough to be typically American, but elaborate enough to be found in a Restoration play like *The Way of the World.* Albee wishes

us to be at home with these people and yet to remove them to a more abstract sphere. They are familiar, yet strangers, human and yet less vital than, for instance, George and Martha in *Who's Afraid of Virginia Woolf?*:

> AGNES: Not even separation; that is taken care of, and in life: the gradual . . . demise of intensity, the private preoccupations, the substitutions. We become allegorical, my darling Tobias, as we grow older.

It is with the hope of arresting this process of substitution that Tobias reacts so violently against Agnes's evasively abstract use of language:

> TOBIAS: (*Frustration; anger*) I've not been . . . *wrestling* with some . . . abstract problem! These are *people!* Harry and Edna! These are our friends, God damn it!

Ironically, these "invaders," Harry and Edna, unwittingly open up a path to salvation through self-revelation. Lifting the veil that has shielded but blinded his eyes, Tobias comes to see himself and Agnes in the figures of Harry and Edna. Indeed, Edna speaks in the same manner as Agnes (she uses the royal plural, "we," the affirmative interrogative, "didn't we?" and the expression, "if . . . then"), and Harry's speech mimics the vague language of Tobias (such as his repetitive use of "sure"). In one attempt at defining "friendship," Edna offers a simile that most closely "hits home": "Friendship is something like a marriage, *is* it not, Tobias? For better and for worse?" Tobias comes to see that the meaning of his relationships with his family is mirrored in the meaning of his friendship with Harry and Edna. Although Claire may also see this, she refuses to act. It is only Tobias—the vague, taciturn, and evasive Tobias—who accepts the revelation and makes a final bid for salvation. With open eyes Tobias makes his choice: he decides to go against what he wants—self-protection—for something he wants more—a true and meaningful relationship. Struck with the fear that love could only be error—

> CLAIRE: What else but love?
>
> TOBIAS: Error?

—he struggles to define such words as "best friends" and "right" in order to give them meanings that are not only meaningful, but concrete and unconditional:

> YOU'VE GOT THE RIGHT!
>
> THE RIGHT!
>
> DO YOU KNOW THE WORD?

THE RIGHT!

(*Soft*)

You've put nearly forty years in it, baby; so have I, and if it's nothing, I don't give a damn, you've got the right to be here, you've earned it. . . .

Hoping to release himself and his family from their bonds, Tobias strives to reunite their divided language, to restore thought to language:

I came down here and I sat, all night—hours—and I did something rather rare for this family: I *thought* about something. . . .

But when Tobias calls out to Harry, "DON'T WE LOVE EACH OTHER?"—a pathetic repetition of Agnes's emphatic "do we not?"—he is begging for an affirmative response to what he fears is untrue.

Nevertheless, Tobias's "reaching out" is a saint-like gesture. As Agnes herself declares, "we quarantine, we ostracize— if we are not immune ourselves, or unless we are saints." The religious language in the play underscores this idea of sainthood. While such expressions as "for God's sake," "hell," and "Jesus" are commonplace expletives, they are selectively placed in *A Delicate Balance.* "For God's sake" is most conspicuous, occurring with unusual frequency throughout the play. Whenever upset, Tobias uses the adjective "goddamned." Here, in his hysterical speech to Harry, he pleads in the name of God:

I DON'T WANT YOU HERE!

YOU ASKED?!

NO! I DON'T

(*Loud*)

BUT *BY CHRIST* YOU'RE GOING TO STAY HERE!

. . . . .

. . . you've got the right to be here, you've earned it

(*Loud*)

AND *BY GOD* YOU'RE GOING TO TAKE IT!

. . . . .

I DON'T WANT YOU HERE!

I DON'T LOVE YOU!

BUT *BY GOD* . . . YOU STAY!! (my emphasis)

In fact, the name "Tobias" comes from the hebrew word "*töbhïyäh*" meaning "God is good." By extending hospitality to his neighbours (a connection with the Old Testament "Book of Tobias"), Tobias attempts to justify his name. But Tobias's offer is rejected and his name remains as split from his person as the language is split from meaning.

By the end of *A Delicate Balance,* language appears not as a medium for communication, but as a necessary protective device; it forms an impenetrable blockage, a thick layer of skin within which each individual may rest secure: isolated and lonely and—tragically—invulnerable.
—M. Patricia Fumerton

All of the characters in *A Delicate Balance* refuse to be saved—they dread upsetting the balance that so carefully hides and protects them from the naked truth. Each turns from salvation to the ritualistic language Agnes maintains. Indeed, the only religious expletives to be spoken after Tobias's scene with Harry—"good heavens" and "good Lord"—evoke a chilling sensation. For Agnes herself has become something of a substitute Lord. In fact, Agnes is a necessary factor in these people's lives: each individual—even Claire, the rebel—has fallen so low that the support Agnes offers, through language, has become both irresistible and indispensable.

The characters of *A Delicate Balance* momentarily waver between sanity and insanity, between revelation and self-deception. Drawn from their self-created—what Claire would call their "willfull"—illusions, they approach the truth, but quickly veer away from any openness, descending back into an even deeper mire of delusion. The language of the play follows a similar pattern: moving from a split between thought and language to a momentary union of words and meaning—the confrontation between Tobias and Agnes at the beginning of Act III, and Tobias' hysterical scene in the same Act—and outward again to a language even further divided from meaning and, therefore, to a language incapable of any real expression. By the end of *A Delicate Balance,* language appears not as a medium for communication, but as a necessary protective device; it forms an impenetrable blockage, a thick layer of skin within which each individual may rest secure: isolated and lonely and—tragically—invulnerable.

Katharine Worth (essay date 1981)

SOURCE: "Edward Albee: Playwright of Evolution," in *Essays on Contemporary American Drama,* edited by Hedwig Bock and Albert Wertheim, Max Hueber Verlag München, 1981, pp. 33-53.

[In the following essay, Worth examines Albee's treatment of evolution in his plays.]

Albee is a playwright whose great distinctiveness is peculiarly hard to name and define. He has been claimed for the Absurdists and linked with Ionesco on the strength of his early plays, *The Zoo Story* (1958) and *The American Dream* (1960); comparisons with Strindberg have been prompted by his relish for comic/ferocious sex battles, as in *Who's Afraid of Virginia Woolf?* (1961); and his use of polite social rituals to convey psychological malaise has called up thoughts of T. S. Eliot and Noel Coward. He has strong affinities with some of his American predecessors, notably with the O'Neill of *Dynamo* and *Welded,* and with Thornton Wilder, who has the same feeling for the poignant brevity of human life and the rapid passing of generations. In *The Long Christmas Dinner* Wilder represents this by an accelerated ageing process: as the members of the family join and leave the endless Christmas dinner, they put on wigs from time to time to indicate their movement from one generation to another. Albee's use of a wig in *Tiny Alice* (1964) to conceal the youth of Miss Alice and then as adornment on a phrenological head, as Julian dies, makes a similar suggestion of instability and mortal change. At the end of that same play the Butler goes round the room placing dust covers over the furniture, a prelude to Julian's death. We could hardly fail to think of *Endgame* at such a moment—and Albee, no less than other major modern playwrights, shows his awareness of Beckett in many subtle echoes of this kind.

To be aware of these affinities and resemblances is not of course to diminish Albee. On the contrary, whatever he takes he distils into a style which is entirely his own: no American playwright has a more distinctive voice. Its special quality comes partly from its ease in moving between an intellectual and an aggressively physical mode. Albee's characters usually belong to a well-to-do, educated middle class: typical is the Long Winded Lady in *Quotations from Chairman Mao Tse-Tung* (1968), described as 'very average and upper middle class. Nothing exotic, nothing strange'. We might question how 'average' she is in her reading tastes—Trollope and Henry James—but my point is that this cultivated, literate lady is the sort of person Albee favours. He is the most intellectual and literary of American playwrights. But he combines the cerebral with an extraordinary emphasis on the physical. His characters talk with often outrageous candour about their sexual and bodily activities: we are never allowed to forget that we live in an animal world. His plays

are full of animals, from the dogs, cats and parakeets of *The Zoo Story,* the 'little zoo', as Jerry mockingly describes them, to the talking lizards in *Seascape* (1975) who come on to land to join with a human couple in a symposium on the nature of human beings and animals. Like Jerry in *The Zoo Story* Albee seems inspired by the desire 'to find out more about the way people exist with animals, and the way animals exist with each other, and with people too'. He often uses people's relations with animals to measure their relation with each other and he can give a terrifying impression of the thin line dividing one world from the other, as when in *All Over* (1971) the Wife and Mistress relapse into animal fury, driving the newsmen out of the room, or in the same play, a woman who has had a mental collapse is said to have been sent 'spinning back into the animal brain'.

The seemingly comfortable position of his characters, their sophistication and self-consciousness, are useful to Albee, partly because he can quite naturally enrich the dialogue with the widely ranging cultural references and quotations his theme requires, partly because it allows him to 'disturb' his characters in interesting ways. Disturbance is above all Albee's theme, or as I am calling it 'evolution'. And it is that aspect of his drama I want to examine in this essay. He is an expert in contriving shocks and explosions to break up surfaces, façades, carapaces, and in so doing create new lines of direction. With increasingly fine instruments, as his art develops, he records what happens after these disturbances. Fine degrees of change, as well as spectacular ones, are recorded with the exactitude of a seismograph: it may be a collapse, as in *Listening* (1975) or a cataclysmic upheaval as in *Tiny Alice,* or a series of small adjustments resulting in the restoration of the status quo along with an almost imperceptible change as in *Who's Afraid of Virginia Woolf?* and *A Delicate Balance.* Albee himself sometimes talks so as to suggest his evolutionary interests. *The American Dream,* he said, was a 'stand against the fiction that everything in this slipping land of ours is peachy-keen'. The word 'slipping', so interestingly unexpected, surely suggests the sort of geophysical associations which underlie the intricate movements of Albee's dramatic action: earthquakes, tidal erosions, continents adrift.

When he was asked in 1968 what was the subject of his new play. Albee said he supposed it was about evolution. The play, *Seascape,* does indeed give an impression of the great stretch of human evolution, opening with the noise of jet planes screeching over the beach and ending, in one of Albee's most endearing and poignant scenes, with the creatures who have just come out of the sea contemplating their next movement:

> *NANCY:* You'll have to come back . . . sooner or later. You don't have any choice. Don't you know that? You'll have to come back up.

LESLIE: (*Sad smile*) Do we?

NANCY: Yes!

LESLIE: Do we have to?

NANCY: Yes!

LESLIE: Do we have to?

NANCY: (*Timid*) We could help you, please?

LESLIE: (*Anger and doubt*) How?

CHARLIE: (*Sad, shy*) Take you by the hand? You've got to do it—sooner or later.

NANCY: (*Shy*) We could help you. (*Leslie pauses; descends a step down the dune; crouches; stares at them*)

LESLIE: (*Straight*) All right. Begin.

There is a wonderful ring to this 'begin'. It has some of the heroic quality of the evolutionary drama of Shaw which is bound to come to mind when one contemplates Albee's absorbed interest in human development. Shaw's 'metabiological pentateuch', *Back to Methuselah*, begins in the Garden of Eden and ends with a scene showing how human beings have extended their life span indefinitely, and have become wise enough to win the approval of the Life Force: 'And because these infants that call themselves ancients are reaching out towards that [i.e. wisdom], I will have patience with them still: though I know well that when they attain it they shall become one with me and supersede me . . .'. This last play in the pentateuch is called 'As Far as though can Reach'. Albee's characters indulge a great deal in this kind of thinking, stretching their minds to contemplate the future of the race as well as their own. The conversation of Charlie and Nancy in *Seascape*—touching on everything from jet planes and world travel to sex, ageing, mortality and the meaning of things—is only one of many such dialogues where the characters' probing of themselves and each other opens up speculation on society and human life in general. Albee is often thought of as a pessimistic playwright, and certainly he depicts some pessimistic moods and situations, but there is a kind of Shavian optimism all the same in the spirited energy his characters bring to the contemplation of their own lives and to the puzzle of the world.

Albee's characters do not have much prospect of becoming supermen, like the Ancients of *Back to Methuselah*, but in their anything-but Arcadian world they do succeed in making readjustments which change their own lives and may, he sometimes seems to hint, be contributing, if almost imper-

ceptibly, to evolutionary change on a grander scale. Of course he is more interested in the dark undergrowth of his characters' psychology than Shaw; despite their wit and comic stylisations, his plays are often nearer to the tragic mood of O'Neill, the other American who shares with Albee and Shaw a preoccupation with the mysteries of evolution.

At its strongest, their urge to dramatise these mysteries drives them all into more or less fantastic modes which allow the non-human elements in the universe a vital role in the proceedings. Shaw has his talking snake in the Garden of Eden scene of *Back to Methuselah,* and in *Too True to be Good* the audience is addressed by a disgruntled microbe which, we are told, resembles a human being but in substance suggests 'a luminous jelly with a visible skeleton of short black rods'. O'Neill ends *The Hairy Ape* with a deathly encounter between man and ape in the zoo (anticipations here of *The Zoo Story*) and in *Dynamo* makes a destructive Mother Goddess out of electrical machinery. Similarly, Albee puts microcosm and macrocosm on stage in *Tiny Alice* and in *Seascape* brings out of the sea the creatures with unequivocal tails who identify themselves with such charming absurdity as Leslie and Sarah.

The function of Shaw's microbe is to draw attention to the wrong-headedness of human beings, the doctors, patients and fussy mothers who infect innocent microbes with measles and spoil their own lives by the unhealthy way they live them. Once the patient is set free from her genteel domestic prison by the anarchic Burglar her whole way of thinking changes totally, a change Shaw expresses through an instant physical change: in one scene a querulous girl wrapped up in blankets; in the next a beautiful animal, with hard, glistening muscles. The rebellious daughter eventually evolves to the point where she can accept her mother on terms which give them both an exhilarating new freedom. In the extraordinary last scene where one character after another is shown taking stock of his or her past life and making a choice for the future, the Elderly Lady announces her decision to change herself, move on to a different phase of evolution: 'The world is not a bit like what they said it was. I wasn't a bit like what they said I ought to be. I thought I had to pretend. And I needn't have pretended at all'.

This is very much the kind of activity Albee's characters are engaged in, a struggle to recognise what the world really is, what they really are and then to survive and evolve in the light of the knowledge they acquire or have thrust upon them. The aim is harder to realise in Albee's world than in Shaw's. Albee has in much higher degree a modern sense of the instability of the self, its lack of control over the deep movements of the psyche. There is certainly an abundance of strong-willed characters on his stage: we are always aware of the desperate will behind the 'fun and games' played out by Martha and George and the more deadly charades constructed by the unholy trio in *Tiny Alice*. But we are constantly aware too of the world beneath the will: the biological instincts, the subconscious, the many unknown forces that drive the human individual and the strange universe he finds himself in, along with all those animals. There is a much less strong illusion of mind controlling events than in the evolutionary comedy of Shaw or the evolutionary tragedy of O'Neill. The latter's battling characters often feel themselves driven in ways they cannot understand but they never really lose their heroic will: they retain a sense of purpose and meaning even when they are defeated, perhaps then most of all. Yet all three playwrights are linked by their fascination with the notion of tides sweeping men on to some unknown future and with their function as humans in a world which seems in a way better adjusted to animals, vegetables and inorganic elements. 'It was a great mistake, my being born a man', muses O'Neill's Edmund Tyrone in *Long Day's Journey into Night*, 'I would have been much more successful as a sea-gull or a fish'; while Shaw's Ancients in *Back to Methuselah* are steadily approaching the time when they will transmute themselves into a vortex of pure intelligence. One of the adolescents (newly born from an egg) puts the question, 'But if life is thought, can you live without a head?' 'Not now perhaps', replies the He-Ancient, 'But prehistoric men thought they could not live without tails. I can live without a tail. Why should I not live without a head?' The newly born then unwittingly helps to make the point by her innocent question, 'What is a tail?'; drawing from the Ancient a declaration of his evolutionary faith. The tail was a habit, no more, of which the human ancestors managed to cure themselves, and that is what must now happen with the whole body, the 'machinery of flesh and blood' which, he says, 'imprisons us on this petty planet and forbids us to range through the stars': men must free themselves from that tyranny and become the masters of matter, not its slaves.

Shaw plays with the evolutionary theme in witty argument, O'Neill uses it to fuel the tragic endeavours of his characters to rise above themselves and acquire heroic status. Albee incorporates it into the small change of life. The accidental, physical side of things looms much larger in his plays than in those of the other two: we hear more about the ordinary vicissitudes of the body, the 'machinery of flesh and blood'; in its various phases, health and illness, sexual excitement and frustration, need for procreation and disappointment in it, ageing and dying. Albee has really made himself the playwright of ageing: he studies with fascination the evolution of personality from one phase of life to another. He is interested in transitions and in the fineness of the line between different states of mind: between the vegetable and the animal, between real calm and the sinister quietness of malaise which is so often, in his plays, the stillness before the earthquake or the exhaustion following the after-shock when the troubled substance settles down again. He is acutely aware of the fragile equilibrium of the mind; no accident that one

of his plays is called *A Delicate Balance.* His characters have this awareness too: they fear madness or question whether they are hallucinated. Often they really are 'disturbed' in the common modern sense of being mentally unstable or ill, liable to break down altogether as a result of some clinical condition, like the suicidal girl in *Listening.*

They also, however, need to be disturbed. The games they play, the social strategies they devise, are a form of self-protection but also a means—perhaps unconscious—of galvanising themselves into the new situations which almost always seem of impasse. Like O'Neill's Dion Anthony in *The Great God Brown*, Albee is interested in the sort of doubt and disturbance which enters into the system, a germ which 'wriggles like a question mark of insecurity, in [the] blood, because it's part of the creative life . . .'.

In this drama of 'evolvings', death plays a major role. No playwright has paid more attention to the business of dying or to death as an ordinary part of life. In the early plays the deaths tend to be outrageous and symbolic; Grandma's playful exit with the Angel of Death in *The Sandbox* (1959), the ritual shooting of Julian in *Tiny Alice*. But in the later plays the focus is on more commonplace and quiet forms of dying, often protracted so that we are obliged to see this too as process, part of life's movement. 'Is he dead?' asks the Wife in *All Over,* as they sit and wait for the man to die (on stage but out of view). The Mistress refuses the expression, quoting the man himself on the inappropriateness of the verb to be to a state of non-being: 'one could be dying or have died . . . but could not . . . be . . . dead'. Language itself insists on death becoming an activity.

There are many different kinds of active death on Albee's stage. *All Over* shows us one kind. The dying man is in one way peculiarly helpless; until they brought him home from hospital he had been hooked up to a machine and was totally dependent on it for life. Looking at him, his wife conceived the strange fantasy that he had become part of the machine and that the machine had become organic, 'an octopus: the body of the beast, the tentacles electric controls, recorders, modulators, breath and heart and brain waves . . .'. For a moment it seemed to her that 'he was keeping it . . . functioning. Tubes and wires'. The image is painful and shocking but it keeps the man not only in life but powerfully so. And it is a true image, for by the power of his personality he has brought these characters together and holds them to him with the tentacles of feeling; memory, grief, hostility, desire. They are 'hooked up' to him, as one critic has said, as irresistibly as he to the machine.

Though his dying is so active and we can tell that he will continue to inhabit the minds on the stage, the man ceases to breathe at the close of *All Over.* Other kinds of death on Albee's stage are more metaphorical, deaths which contribute to the making of lives. As one of the characters says, 'Goodness, we all died when we were thirty once'. There is the little death of sexual consummation, the death of feelings, the deaths of the selves discarded in moving from one stage of life to the next. Albee shows us some bleak 'little deaths' but his characters pick themselves up and begin again; 'Well, we can exist with anything, or without. There's little that we need to have to go on . . . evolving'.

I want now to look at some of the methods Albee uses to show these 'evolvings', drawing on plays from different phases of his own evolution as a playwright.

Perhaps one of the most striking features of the early plays is Albee's youthful amazement at the difficulty of shaking people up, at their imperviousness to new thoughts or anything that might disturb their self-satisfaction. Along with this goes a profound feeling for the sense of loss and uncertainty which can be experienced in human relationships, especially the parent/child relationship. It is hard to avoid thinking of his own situation as an adopted child who has admitted to antagonistic feelings towards the natural parents who abandoned him at two weeks old. His achievement is to take up the personal distress into the dramatic structure of plays like *The American Dream* and use it to humanise the surrealist caricatures through which he satirises bourgeois complacency. What emerges in the end is a moment of good change, an 'evolving'. I want now to look at the working out of these changes in the first of his plays.

The satire in *The Sandbox* and *The American Dream*—the two plays in which Mommy, Daddy and Grandma figure— begins by being very funny, though with the touch of nightmare the theme of imperviousness requires. Mommy is the epitome of self-satisfaction. To poor browbeaten Daddy's choral comment 'That's the way things are today; you just can't get satisfaction; you just try', she replies with triumph, 'Well, I got satisfaction' and we can see she does. She dismisses anything likely to disturb her with the simple 'I won't think about it' and ruthlessly stamps on anyone who does not conform with her chosen way, as she has done, we are told in *The American Dream,* with the adopted child, 'the bumble of joy'. The horrific account of the dismemberment and castration of this child which is given by Grandma to the Young Man who appears out of the blue is the moment when the derisive glee aroused by the Ionesco-like stereotypes, Mommy, Daddy and Mrs. Barker, turns into something more human and more deeply disturbing. What Grandma describes, in her dry, laconic style, as a far-off fabulous event, is felt by the Young Man as a real nightmare, somehow associated with his lost twin, or perhaps, other self: without knowing how it happened, he has felt himself drained, emasculated and hollow. Grandma and the Young Man are victims of Mommy and this remains the Young Man's function: physically perfect but inwardly hollow he

is absorbed into the family as their American Dream. But Grandma has another role to play. She enlists his aid in her escape plan, and gathers together all her boxes, full of memories and dreams, and walks out on them, reappearing on the side of the stage, unseen by the dreadful family, to tell the audience:

> Well, I guess that just about wraps it up, I mean, for better or worse, this is a comedy, and I don't think we'd better go any further. No, definitely not. So, let's leave things as they are right now . . . while everybody's happy . . . while everybody's got what he wants . . . or everybody's got what he thinks he wants. Good night, dears.

What everybody thinks he wants is not perhaps what he would really want if he could be brought to understanding of himself, so Grandma implies. To be left with Mommy can be no happy ending for the Young Man, nor is there much prospect of happiness for Mommy with the 'clean-cut', midwest farm boy type, almost insultingly good-looking in a typically American way, as he detachedly describes himself. As for Grandma's exit, critics have been inclined to see this as a way of representing her death: reacting like the social worker, muddled Mrs. Barker, they feel incredulous about the possibility of a departure for a new life at her age: 'But old people don't go anywhere; they're either taken places, or put places.' Albee, however, corrects that view. Grandma dies, perhaps, but not in the usual sense: rather, he says, she moves 'out of the death within life situation that everybody else in the play was in'. She takes her boxes with her, loaded with the past—'eighty six years of living . . . some sounds . . . a few images'—but she has a lively sense of the future too, as her delighted reaction to the handsome young man suggests. 'Well, now, aren't you a breath of fresh air!', she says, and 'Yup . . . yup. You know, if I were about a hundred and fifty years younger I could go for you'. 'Yes, I imagine so', he spiritlessly replies, pointing up the sad difference between the young man who has become fixed in a deadly stereotype and the old lady who is still, despite all expectations, 'evolving'.

Evolution is a more painful matter in *The Zoo Story.* The complacent bourgeois here is not a monstrous caricature like Mommy, but a mild, well-mannered, believable man who attracts considerable sympathy for the plight he finds himself in: accosted while enjoying a quiet read, on a bench in Central Park on Sunday afternoon, by a youthful version of the Ancient Mariner looking for someone to listen to his story. The unwelcome apparition begins without preamble, 'MISTER, I'VE BEEN TO THE ZOO' and then proceeds to force on his reluctant auditor elaborate stories about squalid encounters with his landlady who pesters him with her 'foul parody of sexual desire' and with her dog, a 'black monster of a beast'.

Jerry is an alarming figure, sardonic and intense. When he says later in the play, as he drives Peter on, 'I'm crazy, you bastard,' we must wonder whether it is not in fact so. In the end he kills himself in a peculiarly whimsical way, forcing the unfortunate Peter to defend his place on the bench by thrusting a knife into his hand as a weapon, and then running on to it. Yet his is the perspective that triumphs. Though Jerry is clearly in a process of breakdown, it is equally clear that Peter is too undisturbed. He shares something with Mommy after all: despite, or because of, his interest in fiction as ordinary reader and as professional publisher, he finds it hard to face the harsh realities of life. His reaction to Peter's horrific tale of his landlady is to shrink away: 'It's so . . . unthinkable. I find it hard to believe that people such as that really are.' 'It's for reading about?' asks Jerry. He is mocking but Peter takes it seriously. 'Yes', he says.

He has to be jolted out of this inability to imagine the plight of others—'what other people need', in Jerry's phrase: Jerry's object from the start is to force him into a vital relationship. All this can be seen (and partly has to be) in psychological terms, simply as the effort of a lonely, suicidal outcast to find someone to really listen to him, and perhaps gain the impetus to finish himself off. But Albee takes pains to stress the biological and evolutionary aspects of the action. The two contrasting lives are expressed partly through their situation vis-à-vis animals. Peter is seemingly master of an orderly world where cats and two parakeets fit into a tidy scheme of things along with two daughters. The fact that he has no son and knows that he will have no more children is a flaw in the biological perfection which comes to the surface under the pressure of his encounter with Jerry. Jerry on the other hand seems unable to draw any line between the human and the animal world: dog and landlady equally rouse his loathing. We are made to think about what it is to be human by Jerry's emphasis on the hierarchy of evolution. The well-adjusted Peter is in Jerry's view no more than a vegetable: this is the insult he flings at him when goading him into defending his park bench (and by implication, of course, his way of life). The two men fight over territory like beasts—Jerry's dying scream 'must be the sound of an infuriated and fatally wounded animal'—and when Peter is at last enraged enough to fight he is paid the compliment. '. . . You're not really a vegetable: it's all right, you're an animal. You're an animal too'.

It is the highest term of praise the action allows, for both these characters are found imperfect in terms of the human culture they both in their different ways aspire to. Jerry is the more imaginative but he has found it impossible to establish a relationship with anyone, dog or human: hating and loving all end up as indifference. His efforts are admirable and pathetic: he is trying to climb the evolutionary ladder, one might say, when he confides in Peter, 'If you can't deal with people, you have to make a start somewhere. WITH

ANIMALS!' But he also has to be seen as an evolutionary failure, who falls out of the system. In his death he provokes Peter into a livelier awareness of 'others': this is presented as an achievement of a kind, which takes some of the depressing futility out of his life. Whether we can place much confidence on Peter's ability to advance as a human being is another question, but he has been given the chance: it is a moment of evolutionary choice.

The next two plays I want to consider form a 'pair' in the sense that the earlier two did, offering strikingly contrasting treatments of a similar theme. *Who's Afraid of Virginia Woolf?* operates within the naturalistic convention, though with a degree of stylisation which extends its possibilities. *Tiny Alice* on the other hand is a much more arcane piece which trumpets its symbolism from the start and indeed could hardly be interpreted on any but a symbolic level.

> **What is the purpose of all this play-acting? In each play [*Who's Afraid of Virginia Woolf?* and *Tiny Alice*] it is implied that a momentous psychic change is under way: something that has been gathering in the unconscious has reached a level of intensity that forces it out into the conscious, where it has to find theatrical form for expression, since it does not really belong in the world it has invaded. One part of the mind is acting another part, one might say.**
> **—*Katharine Worth***

Yet there is one striking affinity between the two plays. In each we must be struck by the remarkably elaborate nature of the preparations for the drastic change we feel preparing from the start: in one play it is a next step in the evolution of a relationship, in the other in an individual consciousness. In each play too there is a strong element of consciously histrionic performance. Martha and George act out their most intimate feelings in bold, exaggerated form for the startled benefit of their naive audience, the younger couple who seem to understand nothing of what is really going on until the very end. And in *Tiny Alice* the conspirators who change Julian's life flaunt their acting ability throughout, from Miss Alice's bravura impersonation of an old woman in her first meeting with Julian to the thoroughly professional 'blocking' of the death scene from a scenario the performers evidently know by heart and have played many times. As in a permanent ensemble company, they even take it in turns to play the lead: Butler and Lawyer have no names, only functions (though Butler claims to derive his function from his name) and they both give orders to and take them from Miss Alice, whose servant/lovers they are.

What is the purpose of all this play-acting? In each play it is implied that a momentous psychic change is under way: something that has been gathering in the unconscious has reached a level of intensity that forces it out into the conscious, where it has to find theatrical form for expression, since it does not really belong in the world it has invaded. One part of the mind is acting another part, one might say.

The differences of form between the two plays relate to the difference in the balance of conscious and unconscious elements. George and Martha have a pretty shrewd understanding of their own and the other's mental processes. This 'sensitive and intelligent couple', as Albee calls them, have lived together for so long that they can interpret pretty well every move in the games they play to exorcise their daemons. They share a language rich in private jokes, quotation and allusion, as they demonstrate at the start when they come home, rather drunk, and laughing, at two in the morning and go straight into one of their double acts. 'What a dump', says Martha, looking round, and, to George:

MARTHA: ... 'What a dump'! Huh? What's that from?

GEORGE: I haven't the faintest idea what ...

MARTHA: Dumbbell! It's from some goddamn Bette Davis picture ... some goddamn Warner Brothers epic ...

GEORGE: I can't remember all the pictures that ...

MARTHA: Nobody's asking you to remember every single goddamn Warner Brothers epic ... just one! One single little epic! Bette Davis gets peritonitis in the end ... She's got this big black fright wig she wears all through the picture and she gets peritonitis, and she's married to Joseph Cotten or something ...

GEORGE: ... Some*body* ...

MARTHA: Some*body* ... and she wants to go to Chicago all the time, 'cos she's in love with that actor with the scar ...

George comes up with the answer: '*Chicago*! It's called *Chicago*.' 'Good grief! Don't you know *anything*?' she taunts him, '*Chicago* was a 'thirties musical, starring little Miss Alice *Faye*. Don't you know *anything*?' But he wins the round, taking the opening she gives him to get in a customary tart reminder of their respective ages: *Chicago* was probably before his time. Every conversational movement, even the effort to remember an old film, affords them opportunities for the marital argument they both understand so well.

Albee points up their high degree of self-awareness by contrast with the young guests. Honey and Nick, who are at the opposite extreme, quite without self-knowledge and very much out in the cold altogether: the audience is presumably a few steps ahead of them in their struggles to catch the true drift of the caustic, funny and eliptical conversations between George and Martha.

In *Tiny Alice* the balance is the other way. The point here is that Julian does not understand himself. Among characters who are nothing but function, he alone has none: he is a lay brother, committed to the celibacy of a priest but without a priest's power. He is in a kind of limbo, not knowing which of his experiences are real, unlike George and Martha who know their imagined child is a fantasy (though that does not prevent them from thinking of him sometimes as real). Julian is much more confused: he is at the mercy of something he does not understand when he comes to the castle to be 'brought up' to Miss Alice. The first thing he does there, despite his conscious intention, is to confide in the Butler the traumatic tale of his six years' lapse of faith, when he had himself voluntarily committed to a mental institution. And the next is to confess to Miss Alice, at the moment of first meeting how, in that confused period, he had a sexual experience of great strangeness and intensity which he does not know whether to think of as dream, hallucination or reality. He lost his virginity, so it seemed, with a woman patient who imagined herself the immaculate Mother of God—but what she was bearing in her womb was a cancer. The dream, if such it was, is to be acted out in a new form with Miss Alice. It is as if he were meeting his own unconscious, in the romantically confused and sinister forms imposed by his imagination. The three who manage the machine (to borrow a phrase from Eliot's *The Cocktail Party,* a play with some obvious resemblances to *Tiny Alice*) make it clear enough that they in their turn are controlled from some other dimension. Miss Alice refers to herself as a 'surrogate' for the Miss Alice who resides in the model and the model itself is a perpetual reminder that the action is being conducted on more than one level. It stands there throughout, a man-sized replica of the castle, lighting up from time to time in its different rooms, following—or perhaps initiating—changes of location in the macrocosm. Albee had planned to have Julian bound to the model in the death scene; in the event he was made only to collapse against it, but the point is made, that in the end nothing but this would be left to him.

The process of effecting change is difficult, in one play because of the middle age of the characters, in the other because of immaturity. In *Who's Afraid of Virginia Woolf?* it seems at first as though there could be no breaking out of the fixed pattern of life George and Martha have established over many years: she is in her fifties, he is somewhat younger. Yet into their tired rituals—weariness is a feature of the proceedings—Albee artfully manages to insert growth points. Martha breaks the rules of the marital game by speaking to someone in the outside world of their fantasy son: she takes the young wife upstairs, confides in her, and then remains behind, disconcertingly, to change her clothes. George senses what this might mean. He dissuades the young couple from leaving, as they embarrassedly feel they should:

> Oh no, now . . . you mustn't. Martha is changing
> . . . and Martha is not changing for me. Martha
> hasn't changed for me in years. If Martha is chang-
> ing, it means we'll be here for . . . days.

It is the experience not of days but of years that is packed into the remaining small hours: George destroys the son who never was and perhaps in doing so frees himself from the obsessive dream or memory of a murderous relation between son and father which he tells of in the form of a story and seems to relate in some way to his own past. We cannot be sure of this, but there is a sense of relief as well as sadness in the ending. Perhaps Martha, despite all her bluster, knew at some deep level, as George does, that the change had to come. As he says, 'It was . . . time'. She receives the verdict with doubt and apprehension, but still, it is clear, with a readiness to move on with him to a new stage in their marriage: there has been an 'evolving' and it was necessary.

In *Tiny Alice* the difficulties are more obscure but are clearly to do with Julian's immaturity. At one point of his adventure, Julian muses about the possibility of avoiding experience:

> What may we avoid! Not birth! Growing up? Yes.
> Maturing? Oh, God! Growing old, and? . . . yes,
> growing old; but not the last; merely when.

In his proud demand for abstract perfection he shrinks from life, refuses procreation (except in dreams), resists the idea of God in man's image, although it is the idea on which his Church rests. 'Don't you teach your people anything?', sneers the Lawyer to the Cardinal. He has to unlearn his certainties, learn to know, as the Lawyer says, that 'We do not know. Anything'. He has to be 'brought up' to Miss Alice: the sexual/religious punning, like everything in the play, contradicts his idea that man can separate God from nature. In embracing Alice he accepts mortality (always implicit in the beauty of the flesh) and perhaps too the mystery he rejects: at the moment when they come together, she stretches out arms enclosed in very full sleeves so that the effect is of enfolding him 'in her great wings'.

Julian's is a martyrdom of a kind. The 'agents' leave, their work done, Alice telling him she is 'the illusion', the Lawyer counselling him to resign himself to the mysteries. Like the man in the story from which Albee said the play was de-

rived (he was imprisoned in a room inside another room), Julian is left to die by the model, unable to tell whether he is in microcosm or macrocosm. The model is a world without human figures in it and it is a horror. 'THERE IS NO ONE THERE', he calls in agony: the flesh and blood Alice is what he needs, after all. Some critics have taken this to be the moral of the piece; Julian, for them, is forcibly converted by secular evangelists who have proved to him sardonically that there is no world other than that experienced by the senses. That would be, however, to destroy the insistent ambiguity which is surely meant to convey something quite different, the necessity for symbols. As Miss Alice puts it, 'We must . . . represent, draw pictures, reduce or enlarge to . . . to what we can understand.'

And is there another dimension? In the play it is inescapable. Butler, Lawyer and Alice all assume it: the Lawyer is sarcastic about 'the mouse in the model' but he also promises Alice in the model, with 'no sarcasm', Albee says: 'You will have your Julian'. And Alice prays to the model to save the chapel when it seems in danger of burning down. 'Don't destroy!', she cries, and 'Let the resonance increase'. Though Julian cries in his agony 'THERE IS NO ONE THERE', yet as he dies we see on the empty stage lights descending the staircase of the model and 'the shadow of a great presence filling the room', while exaggerated heartbeats are heard. Audiences were inclined to rationalise these as Julian's own, but Albee has said that he expected people to think of this 'enormous' sound that engulfs Julian either as his hallucination or as the personification of an abstract force. There is no way of resolving the ambiguity. That is the painful truth Julian has to learn and the learning is an advance in maturity; he dies in the attitude of crucifixion—which in the religious imagery of the play must imply the possibility of resurrection. Though so cryptic and in many ways unpleasant and distasteful, the process has to be seen, I think, as evolution rather than catastrophic collapse.

The next play I want to consider, *A Delicate Balance,* draws into a new pattern threads from earlier plays. Again, as in *The Zoo Story,* animals are used to measure degrees of refinement in human consciousness. Tobias' story about the cat he grew to hate because it became indifferent to him tells us much about his self-mistrust: when Claire wants to convey the reality of her sordid experience as an alcoholic, she describes it as becoming more like an animal every day (to be an animal in this play is to go down in the evolutionary hierarchy). The structure resembles that of *Virginia Woolf*; a conversation among married couples (with complications in the form of a sister and daughter) goes on and on, with the aid of drink, through the hours of two nights, ending with breakfast, still intermixed with drinking, on the third day. As in *Virginia Woolf,* the talk is confessional in a thoroughgoing American style which makes one wonder how there could be anything left unrevealed, how indeed there could be any real movement or change. The play opens with Agnes confiding in Tobias her suspicion that she might one day go out of her mind and moves on to Tobias' confession to Claire that he had killed (or 'put down' as she softens it) the cat which grew to dislike him. Other more commonplace revelations come thick and fast; the whole idea of the confessional is indeed parodied in Claire's self-mocking account of how she rose to make a grand public confession at a meeting of Alcoholics Anonymous and turned it into bathos. 'I am Claire and I am a alcoholic', she said in her little girl's voice, then sat down.

These confessions are too easy, too familiar a feature of their daylight world. Albee wants to move in on the night, that limbo where thoughts are struggling out from the unconscious and the anxieties lie deeper, are kept closer. He brings this about by a brilliant invention, the arrival of Harry and Edna, the twin couple to Agnes and Tobias, their best friends, whose lives are 'the same'. These two have left their own home because they became frightened—of what they cannot say. They can only repeat: 'WE WERE FRIGHTENED ... AND THERE WAS NOTHING'. The scene of their arrival is comic in its lack of explanation and childlike suddenness, as when Edna says 'Can I go to bed now? Please?'. But they have brought into the house a disturbing sense of generalised anxiety relating to fears of darkness, nothingness and death. At the end of the play Edna articulates the unlocalised dread: 'It's sad to come to the end of it, isn't it, nearly the end, so much more of it gone by ... than left.' Under the pressure of this unease they all experience a revelation of their limits and breaking points. Agnes brings up from the abyss a misery she was not able to voice at the start, the memory of the time when her son died and Tobias refused her another child. She lay at night pleading, 'Please? Please, Tobias? No, you wouldn't even say it out: I don't want another child, another loss'.

Through it all runs a helpless longing to be safe and at home: the much married daughter hysterically claims her girlish room: Harry and Edna settle into it, like cuckoos in the nest. Yet changes occur, despite the characters' efforts to resist them: perhaps they occur because of that. Both married couples return perforce to the single room they had given up. Agnes expressing the shy hope that it may not be simply a temporary change: an elegiac tribute is paid to the sexuality that is leaving them. Various adjustments of feeling are made among the individuals in the group and finally Tobias, by enormous effort of will, looks at himself and forces himself to come out with an honest statement to the 'best friend' who has come to him for succour:

I DON'T WANT YOU HERE!

I DON'T LOVE YOU!

BUT BY GOD ... YOU STAY!

A deep obligation, running underneath all questions of personality, is faced and acknowledged under pressure of the night fears, the 'plague' that Harry and Edna have brought with them. Daylight returns, the intruders depart and Agnes is left contemplating what has happened—'They say we sleep to let the demons out'—and preparing to return to normal: 'Come now; we can begin the day'. Some critics have found this ending sentimental but there is no reason why it should have to be so taken: the tone is dry, matter-of-fact: the 'day' has its own problems, as we have seen. Beginning it again is all that can be done—yet the play makes us feel respect for the human resilience which allows for these routine adjustments.

In the plays that follow *A Delicate Balance* there is less room for radical changes of situation. The emphasis is on another kind of evolution, the development of finer understanding. Increasingly the characters watch and listen to each other with the sort of care and detachment described by Tobias when he tells Agnes of his reverie in the small hours: 'look at it all, reconstruct, with such ... detachment, see yourself ... look at it all ... play it out again, watch'. The style becomes increasingly delicate and oblique as Albee moves closer to the concept of 'static' drama most famously enunciated by Maeterlinck in his plea for recognition of the dramatic interest in an old man sitting in the lamplight. Maeterlinck is indeed referred to in *All Over,* where the Mistress tells us that he was once a topic of conversation for her lover, the man now dying. It is an appropriate reference for a play so Maeterlinckian in its situation—waiting for death—but in the other plays too Maeterlinck is brought to mind, especially by the musicality which becomes so marked a feature of the dramatic structure. In *Box* and *Quotations from Chairman Mao Tse-Tung* (1968) Albee makes a point of his concern with 'the application of musical forms to dramatic structure': he explains in his introduction that he has notated the dialogue on musical lines with an exceptionally precise use of punctuation, commas, semicolons and so on, with stage directions, with devices such as capitalising and italicising.

We have to listen exceptionally hard to follow this intricate dialogue, with its mesh of half-finished allusions, quotations, ambiguous sayings, ironies and fugue-like repetitions. It seems natural that in this phase of his art Albee should produce a play for radio called simply *Listening* (1975). Characters at this time tend to lose their names and be represented by function, like notes in music. The Wife amusingly calls attention to this phenomenon in *All Over* when she demands of Mistress, 'Me! Wife! Remember?'

Box and *Chairman Mao* are the first two plays constructed on Albee's new musical principle. They were written separately and can be so performed, Albee says, though surely he must be right in finding them more effective when 'enmeshed'.

The action of **Box** involves only a view of a box, or cube, and a Voice reflecting on it: the reflections widen out into a Jungian stream-of-consciousness which opens up beyond the personal life into 'the memory of what we have not known'. Throughout runs a theme of decline and loss—in art and craft (no one could make such a box now), in social responsibility (milk deliberately spilt when children are starving), and in understanding. Continually Voice returns to the sense of direction in art and the pain it can cause by contrast with loss of direction in life: 'When art hurts. That is what to remember'. Finally human artefacts and ideas give way to a vision of the sea, with birds skimming over it and only the sound of bell buoys in the fog to remind us of human presence.

When the second play begins, the outline of the box is still visible, creating the impression that the thoughts we now hear are taking place within the other consciousness: everything flows into and out of that empty space. The leading character in **Chairman Mao,** the Long-Winded Lady, is haunted by a memory she cannot assimilate, of falling into the sea from the deck of an ocean liner (such as she is now travelling on) after the death of her much-loved husband. The play ends with her repetition of the questions she was asked: 'that I may have done it on purpose? . . . thrown myself off?' Then, in one of Albee's delicate punctuation hints, she drops the question mark, turns 'tried to kill yourself' into a statement she has to deal with herself and arrives at the sad conclusion: 'Good heavens, no: I have nothing to die for'.

With her thoughts (they are supposedly voiced to a totally silent auditor, a Minister, who gives her no comfort) are interwoven the thoughts of two others. The Old Woman also tells a sad story of family loss, but in the more distant form of a poem, Will Carleton's ballad, 'Over the Hills to the Poor-House'. And in contrast to this limited personal view of history come the vast assertions of Chairman Mao proclaiming the class war and calling for revolution. The three lines of thought are separate but occasionally touch; the Old Woman nods approvingly from time to time when Mao refers to the hard life of the poor, but she also indicates silent sympathy with the unhappiness of the upper class lady. Mao's optimistic political simplifications are both reinforced and undermined by the experiences conveyed in the women's thoughts. His thoughts are crude and bracing, providing a strong upward thrust, a necessary counterpoint to the pessimism of Voice in **Box**. He does indeed at one point use an image of her kind. It is not a bad but a good thing, he says, that China's six hundred million people are 'poor and blank' because poverty stimulates the desire for change and 'on a

blank sheet of paper free from any marks, the freshest and most beautiful characters can be written'.

> **What may be the direction for human evolution? This is Albee's large theme. He makes it dramatically gripping through his mastery of form and his ability to interest us in the small changes and in the real lives of his people; even in the disembodied or fragmented shape which is all they have in [*Box*], they come through as vivid personalities.**
> —*Katharine Worth*

Of course there is irony in this: the image of the box perpetually filling up with inherited and fresh thoughts tells us that there is no such thing as a 'blank' human character. Still, even if it is an illusion, there is a need for the dream of 'beginning again'. Even the Long-Winded Lady feels it: whimsically she pictures herself 'falling up!' and reflects that 'One never returns from a voyage the same'. There is a suggestion of an 'evolving' here, and certainly there is an antidote to the emptiness portrayed by Voice in the complex texture of consciousness woven by the voices. When they die away, the light comes up again upon the empty box and we return to the Voice's elegy, to the contemplation of the painful beauty of a partita and the mystery of those memories we did not know we had. Voice reminds us that she could recognise the sound of bell buoys in the fog though she had never seen the sea: 'Landlocked, never been, and yet the sea sounds . . .'. It is with the miracle of the sea that the play ends and with the sense of mysterious direction: the birds are flying all in one direction, in 'a black net', only one 'moving beneath . . . in the opposite way'. What may be the direction for human evolution? This is Albee's large theme. He makes it dramatically gripping through his mastery of form and his ability to interest us in the small changes and in the real lives of his people; even in the disembodied or fragmented shape which is all they have in this play, they come through as vivid personalities.

As so often, we can see in these two plays the germ of the next one. The Long-Winded Lady sees one prospect of comfort: she might be able to forget the bitter detail of her husband's last illness: perhaps it is 'all over'. The phrase provides the title for the next play, **All Over** (1971), which explores the impact of a death about to happen on the five people closest to the dying man. We go in and out of their thoughts and memories in a pattern of engagement and disengagement which is something they have been painfully conscious of in their past lives. The Wife has been separated from her husband for thirty years and is alienated from the Daughter, seems indeed to be on better terms with the Mistress. The Mistress, though treated as a friend, is disengaged from them all and yet it is she who can best tell them about the phases in the dying man's withdrawal from life, the 'faint shift from total engagement'. The mood is one of 'languor' and exhaustion. The stories they tell to fill in the time of waiting tend to turn on various kinds of dying, including the sort of death which is to do with feeling: the Wife tells of a woman who died when she was twenty-six, 'died in the heart that is, or in whatever portion of the brain contains the spirit'.

Albee has commented that after a certain age arthritis of the mind sets in and 'change becomes impossible finally.' No sign of this with him: his later plays continue to show his own capacity to 'evolve'.
—*Katharine Worth*

A paradox develops. The little life the man has left is the source from which they draw: they are fired by him: and as they talk of him and more of their past life pours out, they become deeply and bitterly engaged with each other. There are moments of understanding and of violent hostility, till at last the Wife, looking into the landscape of the future, abandons her calm and acknowledges her need to 'feel something'. 'I'm waiting to' she says, and 'I have no idea what I'm storing up. You make a lot of adjustments over the years, if only to avoid being eaten away'. The cool politeness she has observed with the Mistress drops away, she accuses her: 'You've usurped'. And though she immediately apologizes, the frustration of thirty years at last erupts. 'I LOVE MY HUSBAND', she calls out in pain and in relief: we have an impression of parched land being flooded. Then it is, as we hear the doctor saying, 'All over'. But for the people waiting everything goes on: Albee has made us feel, through the unease of their conversational adjustments, something of the effort involved in that simple 'going on': it is an achievement.

Albee has commented that after a certain age arthritis of the mind sets in and 'change becomes impossible finally.' No sign of this with him: his later plays continue to show his own capacity to 'evolve'. In *Listening* and *Counting the Ways* (1976) he interestingly applied a vaudeville method—laconic, quick-firing cross talk and scenes punctuated by signs descending from the flies or a voice counting—to very different material, creating in one play a deeply sombre, in the other a genial, high-spirited mood. *Listening* was written for radio: it is about the need to listen and the difficulty of doing so. In the grounds of a one-time mansion, now a mental institution, by a dried up fountain, two of the staff, a Woman and a Man, meet to explore each other—and the Girl who is the Woman's charge—through strange, intense talk,

weighing words, testing nuances. The Girl has slipped half out of the human world; she reacts, we are told, like an animal, tensing and sensing her surroundings, then 'humanising' intermittently. 'You don't listen', she complains, 'Pay attention, rather, is what you don't do'. 'I listen', says the Woman, 'I can hear your pupils widen'. But she does not pay the attention the Girl needs; she and the Man abstract themselves, pursuing sexual memories they may or may not have shared, while the Girl takes her chance to find some broken glass and cut her wrists. Her last words are: 'Then . . . you don't listen'. She is an evolutionary failure, arousing pity and giving a dark colouring to the struggle—experienced in a bitter-sweet way by the other two—of listening to others in a fully human way.

In *Counting the Ways* also, a couple cross-question each other, listening hard for the implications in every reply. But this time the mood is happy, even though strains and small shocks occur. The play begins with her asking, 'Do you love me?' and ends with him answering that he does and then asking the question of her. In between, they count the ways—as in the poem from which the play takes its title, 'How do I love thee? Let me count the ways.' Whole phases of married life are traversed in a series of swift duologues: they count the petals of a rose, ask of each other en passant 'How many children do we have?', move into a new stage when she remarks of the roses that they should be in a vase on the table between their beds and there is a double-take before he realises the implications. 'When did that happen?' he asks, in comic anguish, and later, 'When did our lovely bed . . . split and become two?' 'Well, it happens sooner or later,' she says, and then, soothing him, 'May be we'll be lucky and it won't go any further'. He is left reeling from the impact of a new shock—'separate rooms'. But he picks himself up again. Despite the charming lightness of touch, the preoccupations are as serious as in *Listening:* all feelings are fragile and uncertain. When he asks 'Do you love me?' at the close, her 'I think I do' is a curtain line which leaves everything open: nothing can be done about the fragility of life.

The subsequent variation on the marriage theme, *Seascape,* opens with a similar marital cross-questioning act. Nancy and Charlie, lazing on the beach, are involved in one of Albee's typical stock-taking sequences—current state of feeling, hazy plans for the future now their children are grown up. It is the evolution of a marriage, treated in a gently, bantering naturalistic style. Then suddenly it widens out, through the alarming, only half-comic arrival of the animal couple, into a view of the whole of human evolution, seen entirely in terms of what these well-meaning intelligent but limited, groping individuals can make of it.

It is one of Albee's most touching moments when the animals achieve realisation of what it means to be human through learning of death, which must one day separate them from each other. 'I want to go back', wails Sarah, 'I don't want to stay here any more. I want to go back'. But there is no going back. The play ends with the creatures recognising this and preparing, with the aid of those of a little further on the way, to take the great evolutionary step: 'All right. Begin'.

It is a heroic assertion, unusual for our times, of faith in the capacity of human beings to learn from each other and evolve in good ways. And although nothing is more certain than that he will strike out in a different direction with other plays, this must all the same be a particularly appropriate point to conclude a discussion of Albee as the playwright of evolution.

Leonard Casper (essay date 1983)

SOURCE: "*Tiny Alice:* The Expense of Joy in the Persistence of Mystery," in *Edward Albee: An Interview and Essays,* edited by Julian N. Wasserman, The University of St. Thomas, 1983, pp. 83-92.

[*In the following essay, Casper explores the enigmatic quality of the structure, themes, characters, and language of* Tiny Alice, *and offers his own interpretations of the play.*]

When Edward Albee was asked by his publisher to provide a preface for *Tiny Alice* which would explain its peculiarities, he at first consented; then recanted, having decided that "the play is quite clear." Further, he declared that even more people shared his view than found his work obscure. Among the latter, however, were those daily reviewers who had the most immediate access to the Geilgud-Worth production in the Billy Rose Theater: Taubman of the *Times,* Kerr of the *Herald-Tribune,* Watts of the *Daily Post,* and Chapman of the *Daily News.* The bafflement of such otherwise friendly critics perhaps was epitomized best by contradictory reviews which appeared in *Time* early in 1965. The first, on January 8, referred to the play as a "tinny allegory," dependent more on mystification than mystery; more on echolalia than on eloquence; more on pretentious reprise of Nietzschean nihilism than on profound, fresh inquiry. Only one week later, the same source was at least willing, half-facetiously, to take part in the controversial deciphering of *Tiny Alice* by suggesting that meaning might lie dormant in such apparent clues as references to a "homosexual nightmare," Julian the Apostate, and cunning old Fury's decision in *Alice's Adventures in Wonderland* to try poor Mouse with intent to condemn him to death for lack of anything better to do that day.

Aside from agit-prop plays, whose ideological direction is extensively detailed, most plays submit to risks of misun-

derstanding involved in the indirection of their argument. But *Tiny Alice* has continued to be considered exceptionally difficult. Even critics who have tried to admire it have shown signs of testiness, undergoing trials originating at times in their own ingenuity. Harold Clurman, one of the earliest, was willing to say that he saw an allegory in which "the pure person in our world is betrayed by all parties," themselves corrupt. "Isolated and bereft of every hope, he must die—murdered." But the result, somehow, reminded him of a Faustian drama written by "a highly endowed college student." Later and more elaborately, Anne Paolucci described *Tiny Alice* as "the most impressive of Albee's paradoxical affirmations of negation." To be consistent with this conclusion, she was compelled to treat the play as an intricate allegory: the three agents of Alice, for example, compose a sinister "unholy trinity" concelebrating a parodic ritual of faith; the play is an extended enactment of the smaller scale sexual-spiritual abandon/abandonment experienced by Julian in the asylum. It is a confession of despair: the Invisible Presence is, in fact, an Immense Absence. Ruby Cohn's version of the play was similarly bleak, finding its central struggle in the wilful resistance of Julian's imagination to his pronounced desire for the real. A ceremony is contrived, to wed him to reality: "and even then he tries to rearrange it into familiar appearance." In the moment of death, Julian experiences "the prototypical existential confrontation"—complete isolation; but unable to bear it, invokes Christian allusions/illusions. Presumably, according to Cohn's version, reality = death = abstraction = Tiny Alice = self-negation. In her judgment, a man of true integrity should face this Absurdity with courage, not cower as Julian does, regressing to childhood. Michael Rutenberg's decoding of Albee's allegory perceived a diabolic force bartering a billion ordinary souls for one especially sensitive and worth corrupting, even as the visible conspirators form a chorus half-sympathetic with the victim. Although Rutenberg had to admit the ambiguity of the ending, however interpreted, Julian is lost—to Nothingness; or to an Evil Deity; or to a benevolent but all-devouring God. Positive projections of the ending have been rarer, perhaps because they have been considered too naive by the critical mind. And all have ignored the possibility that any definitive reading is too narrow for Albee.

But suppose *Tiny Alice* resists being treated as allegory because its meaning lies in the persistence, rather than the resolution, of mystery. Suppose risk, natural to reconnoitering the previously undiscovered or unexplored, is being offered as itself the supreme reality. Suppose *Tiny Alice* is a tribute to finite man's terrifying instinct for infinity. The play has at least two structural elements which provide a degree of stability to dimensions otherwise often in flux: the central presence of Julian and the strategic placement of visions at the climax of each of the three acts. As visions deriving from the virginal Julian, they are, of course, suspect. Two of them are even placed offstage and can therefore readily be dismissed as hallucinations in a disturbed mind. Albee offers no clear persuasion of his own but only suggests how best to submit to the play's passions and impressions: "Brother Julian is in the same position as the audience. He's the innocent. If you see things through his eyes, you won't have any trouble at all." Or, perhaps, just the trouble appropriate to flawed and still falling man—trouble not wholly distinguishable from the gift of choice to the half-informed.

Aside from agit-prop plays, whose ideological direction is extensively detailed, most plays submit to risks of misunderstanding involved in the indirection of their argument. But *Tiny Alice* has continued to be considered exceptionally difficult.
—*Leonard Casper*

When towards the end of Act I Julian reveals to Miss Alice his principal memory of all the six hermitic years spent sealed in an asylum, he cannot declare that it was not something wholly imagined. He had withdrawn so far from external realities that what he relates could have been pure fantasy rather than fabulous consummation. *Was* there an introverted woman who claimed to be the Virgin Mary? *Did* he ejaculate in ecstatic union with her? *Did* she become pregnant with the Son of God as a result? Julian's doctor advises him that some hallucinations are healthy and desirable: clearly *he* knows the difference between mystic insight and self-delusion. He informs Julian flatly that the woman died later of cancer of the womb. Julian, however, remains stricken with wonder.

The strangeness of this tale uncorroborated by onstage enactment, in addition to Julian's own indecisiveness about its nature, authorizes the greatest possible skepticism towards the play's final moments as a prelude to any Ultimate Vision. Are faith and sanity really one, as Julian declares? Or is his final submission, his passionate utterances of faith, a sign of a man now totally mad? Earlier, in Act III, Lawyer has been completely cynical about the consolations of self-delusion: Any man will "take what he gets for . . . what he wishes it to be. AH, it is what I have always wanted, he'll say, looking terror and betrayal right in the eye. Why not face the inevitable and call it what you have always wanted? How to come out on top, going under." According to the testimony of his own recollections, Julian has always associated sexual desire, death and union with God, in incongruous sublimation. Is that not how he sees the culmination of his life, with self-induced grace that eases the agony of the human condition? Is his vision not voided; any thought of his sanctification not sacrilegious? Are such inversions not to

be expected in Alice's Wonderland; such nihilism not inevitable in an Absurdist play?

But the sweet simplicity of that conclusion fails to account for the other vision at the end of Act II, which is unquestionably of the flesh, as naked to the eye as any revelation can be and, therefore, far from hallucinatory. It is precisely the very real presence of Miss Alice which makes possible serious consideration of *Tiny Alice* as an argument that things visible *may* be evidence of things invisible. The tableau in which Miss Alice offers herself as a transparency through which Alice can be seen might easily serve as illustration for Platonic Ideals or Christian Incarnation.

That so traditional a notion could be entertained by Albee should not be disquieting. From the beginning, his plays have complained about the decline of such "ancient verities" (to use Faulkner's words) as family cohesiveness, community life, and continuity in the history of evolving civilization. The Grandmother figure in the early one-act plays represents all of these ideals—as does George, on a more intellectual plane, in *Who's Afraid of Virginia Woolf?*. *Tiny Alice* provides dimensions that infinitely expand the dream/hope that there is more to life than our day-to-day living may signify. One begins to feel less ill at ease with *Tiny Alice* the moment one releases Albee from the box of Absurdism/defeatism where his techniques—the linkage of humor and horror, the seeming cross purposes and discontinuities—invited earlier critics to imprison him. For Albee such mannerisms are, simultaneously, metaphors for the dissipation of faith in meaningfulness and untraditional measures for reinvoking, resurrecting, reconstructing traditions at their best.

Albee does distinguish—again, like Faulkner—between dead convention and living tradition, between inflexible institutions and an order of growth congenial with diversity of direction and possibility. Daddy, in *The Sandbox* and *The American Dream,* is a figure of impotence, his human tracts having been replaced by tubes. Nick, in *Who's Afraid of Virginia Woolf?,* seems to epitomize health and youthful promise, but his proposed eugenics, a form of self-propagation, is indistinguishable from Daddy's living death. In *Tiny Alice,* the Church, represented by the most venal, most self-inflating aspect of the Cardinal, becomes one more Establishment mechanism for deadening human sensibilities.

Beyond its attempt to revitalize traditions of activated faith, *Tiny Alice* more subtly recognizes that the God-ache suffered by man is foremost an outcry to be born free but not abandoned. The play provides a continuous experience, rather than a philosophical discussion, of two profoundly permanent problems: how can man imagine the incommensurate (but we think we do), and how can man separate service from servitude (but we think we must)? Is there a discernible point beyond which the search for self in the other annihilates either that other or one's self? Can self-centeredness be transcended, yet selfhood be fulfilled? If we attempt to think of an unknowable unknown—such as God—do we delude ourselves more by conjuring anthropomorphic images or by approximating an abstraction of perfection? Do we earn an afterlife only by refusing to want one? Such are the dilemmas torturing the mind that aspires to be, become, belong and, especially, to define beyond desire.

Tiny Alice is replete with talk of serving. The Cardinal and Lawyer are, to a large extent, self-serving; so is Miss Alice, inasmuch as she finds a joy beyond pleasure in Julian's company; and even Butler often delights in comforting this unfortunate novice beyond the call of duty. Something of self is retained by all these four agents of causes/missions larger than themselves. Is this their flaw, or even in the worst of them is this some sign of grace, of a superior love that allows them a measure of freedom from complete depersonalization? Does omnipotence require impotence? In the last scenes, do not all these agents act out that love— though with varying degrees of reluctance—in their compassion for Julian? Or does their similarity lie in their failing to rise above self-pity mirrored in another's pain?

The question deepens when applied to Brother Julian himself. Early in the play he tells Butler that he committed himself to an asylum for six years because he was paralyzed by his inability to reconcile his own view of God, as creator and mover, with the popular view of God as a kind of miracle-worker on call. With Miss Alice he manages to be more open and confesses to having been impatient with God and excessively proud of his humility, as a lay brother in the pretended service of the Lord. Even now he wishes not to be forgotten for whatever services he renders; not to be unborn, in death. Miss Alice accuses him of still more ambition—negotiating martyrdom—and he admits that his unrelenting dream has been "To go bloodstained and worthy . . . upward." Immediately afterwards, she leads him from the ecstasy of that memory, to the sacrifice of himself, and to Alice through her own body.

Is this climatic moment of Act II the seduction of his soul or an advanced stage in its salvation? Julian wants his marriage to end in Miss Alice. It is required of him, however, that he not confuse symbol with substance, as the Cardinal regularly does. When Julian persists, despite Miss Alice's assurance that "I am the . . . illusion," he is executed by Lawyer. Julian feels forsaken by God as well as by those departing the scene. Finally, accepting his destiny, provided it is not eternal death, he prays in desperation: "Then Come and Show Thyself! Bride? God?" Lights move through the model/replica of the mansion; sounds approach, in rhythm with his heartbeat. Total darkness descends.

Has this entire drama been a hallucination in the mind of a

recluse become catatonic? Has Julian finally married himself? Or has his role merely served as insane filter, discoloring the reality of the others? Has this, after all, been a downfall into the void? Can one reconcile Albee's candid admission that "There are some things in the play that are not clear to me" with his assertion that if one positions himself in Julian's place, the play is as clear as need be/can be?

To argue that the direct vision of Miss Alice at the end of Act II may validate the reported visions that, respectively, climax the other acts still acknowledges ambiguities enough to satisfy many an alternate version of *Tiny Alice*'s meaning(s). Remembering Albee's bitter resentment of his abandonment two weeks after birth by his natural parents and his often unhappy childhood with his adoptive parents, one might be inclined to see as pure autobiographical projection this play about a She-God who gives life, only to demand its sacrificial return. Beyond the possibility that all this is personal complaint, problems that are more universal remain. Lawyer remarks in II, 2 that God is an abstraction which therefore can neither be understood nor worshipped; whereas Alice, "the mouse in the model," *can* be understood and worshipped, although it does not exist. What does existence mean, here? Does Alice have no permanent reality, no true substance, being only an exotic mask of God? Or is Alice a manifestation, a function of the Godhead, a further stage in man's adventuring towards divinity? Or is Lawyer, in his bitterness/limited knowledge, just distorting the truth? Are Lawyer, Butler and Miss Alice agents of a malignant surrogate God, and are all of them hyenas, scavengers of the dead vitals of men? Are they impure agents in prolonged process of purgation (Butler too still prefers Miss Alice to Alice) of a merciful and loving God or merely "angels of death," imperfect companions to those chosen for possible perfection? Is Alice, like the son in *Who's Afraid of Virginia Woolf?*, invented out of desperate human need to be part of, instead of apart from, some lasting meaning? Is Julian, secretly dedicated to his own destruction by denying that God may be gentle, courting death disguised as a demanding deity? Is his attraction to Miss Alice only a brief interlude in his inevitable marriage to darkness?

> **If one could appeal to the rest of Albee's work in this dilemma, the probability is that he would align himself with those who see *Tiny Alice* as a determined quest for spiritual coordinates, for opportunities to convert chance into choice and so to collaborate with life against one's own loneliness and that of others.**
> **—*Leonard Casper***

Or is this a parable of grace, one more fortunate fall? Does

Brother Julian lose his celibacy but gain proper priesthood? The name "Alice" derives from the Greek word for truth. Suppose Butler (the working class) once thought he possessed her; so, more recently, did Lawyer (law makers and stewards of justice). But what single system can speak for the whole Truth? The Church (Miss Alice as "missal"?) and, certainly, individual churchmen have their own insufficiencies; there are cobwebs in the chapel. Julian himself is no chaste Adam, as his childhood fantasies prove, and he falls again—not into the flesh, which has been sanctified by the Incarnation, but into a denial that flesh is symbol rather than substance. He becomes a proper man of God, not in retreat (the asylum) but in the world, in communion. Julian has equated faith and sanity, but at last he accepts the mystery, terror and all beyond reason and historic revelation and rituals that become routine. His uncertainty becomes his cause; he makes the desperate but not despairing mystic leap. Is it implied that we are all called to be Marys whose wombs bring God into his world and the delirious world to its destinate groom? All called but few chosen? And of those chosen, even fewer who reach supreme parturition? Or is such speculation itself not pretending to provide the sort of single-system answer which the general explication set out to refute?

If one could appeal to the rest of Albee's work in this dilemma, the probability is that he would align himself with those who see *Tiny Alice* as a determined quest for spiritual coordinates, for opportunities to convert chance into choice and so to collaborate with life against one's own loneliness and that of others. In his first four one-act plays, Albee implied that we try to compensate for our incompleteness by neglecting the needs of others, although, ironically, the only human strength lies in mutual aid among the weak. Albee at first wrote angrily because he resisted adding to the alienation and displacement and deprivation which some of his predecessors and peers considered *the* human condition. Those plays, like the violent act of Jerry in *The Zoo Story,* were cruel blows intended kindly. The same indignation and hope for reform, though presented with less grotesque humor, persist in *All Over,* one of whose attendants at a wake finally recognizes how they have wasted their lives, how corpselike *they* are: "All we've done is think about ourselves." In *The Lady from Dubuque,* when the dying woman receives little solace from her husband who is over concerned with himself, she has to turn to the kindness of strangers.

The surface of such plays to the contrary, Albee has been less death than dream-haunted: by the dream of a bond beyond bondage, a love that allows privacy but not loneliness. In *A Delicate Balance* a plague drives one family into the house of a friend, who then must decide if they have as much right to remain as his own daughter, who wants them out. Tobias the husband delays, reminded of his own terrors by

those of his friends, and when they finally leave, he knows that an opportunity to live generously and even expansively has been lost. The bonding of characters in *Who's Afraid of Virginia Woolf?* is more successful because not only is their reliance on one another renewed, but, in Nick and Honey's willingness to bear children, their passion for (re)generation is satisfied vicariously. The same sense of compatibility and continuity, the same ready submission to growth, flourishes in *Seascape* between different species in the same global enterprise.

Early and late, Albee's plays have sprung from a faith remote from both nihilism at one extreme and romanticism at the other. Like Eugene O'Neill before him, he knows the variety of dimensions in dreaming: they can be destructive or soporifically protective, as well as creative. The will-to-believe, therefore, has to be examined and re-examined scrupulously—man being a cunning, rationalizing animal—but that will-to-believe can be ignored or denounced only at the risk of sinking back into mindlessness.

Because of his constant attention to dreams, ultimately it is less important to argue that Albee leans toward the more positive interpretations of *Tiny Alice* than to recognize the implications of the play, itself, as exciting perplex. How it does *not* end is extremely significant. Each member of the audience is compelled to decide (those chronically passive, probably with reluctance) what the next moment after the death/descent of darkness will bring—if indeed there can even be a next moment. *Tiny Alice* is a dramatization of all that must remain tantalizingly beyond the mind's reach: all mysteries whose permanence we deny even as impressions of their persistence accumulate in our experience. The play solicits, proclaims, reveres man's active imagination, its thrust through symbols towards its outermost reaches, its visionary onsets.

In the end, *Tiny Alice*'s mystery is not only unresolved but not even well-defined. Yet, as irresistibly attractive as a black hole with all the blinding consequences of its super density, that mystery is retained. What is knowledge but a holding operation, a beachhead on the immense unknown? A plenitude of possibilities about the nature of the universe and man's miniscule/magisterial parts in it arise from doubt turned back on itself before achieving a dedicated nullity. Can we imagine man's lacking an imagination; can the mind unthink itself?

Tiny Alice is no facile confirmation of faith's efficacy. Even as it celebrates the mind's urgent outreach, the continuous Adamic demand to know the whole truth, it recognizes hazards: the smallness of man adventuring into vastness. The world is full of wonder. A variety of critical responses to his play not only is to be expected by Albee and tolerated; it is, in fact, invited and essential to this theme. Only when the questions end is there reason to worry about the human cause. No phrenological head can accurately map all the compartments of man's intelligence. As a realist of the irrational, Albee knows this—knows that serious literature, like life itself, is a trial embodiment of imagined purpose.

Julian N. Wasserman (essay date 1983)

SOURCE: "'The Pitfalls of Drama': The Idea of Language in the Plays of Edward Albee," in *Edward Albee: An Interview and Essays,* edited by Julian N. Wasserman, The University of St. Thomas, 1983, pp. 29-53.

[*In the following essay, Wasserman surveys the significance of Albee's treatment of language in his plays.*]

In response to an interviewer's question concerning the supposed lack of "realism" in his work, Edward Albee noted the implicit contradiction between the nature of drama as imitation, in the Aristotelian sense, and the expectation of realism on the part of a play's audience. The importance of this argument is that such a recognition goes far beyond the aesthetics of drama and touches upon the symbolic, that is imitative, nature of language—a problem that is frequently at the thematic heart of Albee's works. Indeed, the common thread that runs through many of his seemingly diverse plays is his characters' oft-stated concern with language and, in particular, the failures and limitations of the linguistic medium. For Albee, language is the medium or meeting ground which exists between the interior and exterior worlds of the speaker and the listener. As a playwright, he seems most interested in the function of language as a means of translating ideas into actions and in the role of language as mediator where a word, like a play, is an imitation which is a wholly independent sign, distinct and separate from that which it represents. As such, a word, like any piece of drama, is neither a pure idea of an action or event nor the event itself. In essence, the naming done by the semanticist and the storytelling practiced by the playwright are, for Albee, congruent if not identical actions.

The problematical nature of language is succinctly set forth in *Seascape* during an argument between Charlie and Nancy in the opening scene of the play. The practical onset of the debate is Charlie's use of the past rather than present perfect tense, and as so often happens in the works of Albee, the linguistic bartering over a particular term quickly evolves into a more general and abstract debate over the nature and function of language:

Nancy: Do you know what I'm *saying*?

Charlie: *You're throwing it up to me; you're telling me I've had a . . .*

Nancy: *No-no-no! I'm saying what you said, what you told me.* You told me, you said to me, "You've had a good life."

Charlie: (*Annoyed.*) Well, you have! You *have* had!

Nancy: (*She, too.*) Yes! Have *had*! What *about* that!

Charlie: What about it!

Nancy: *Am* not *having.* (*Waits for reaction; gets none*) Am not *having*? Am not *having* a good life?

Charlie: Well, of *course*!

Nancy: Then why say had? Why put it that way?

Charlie: It's a way of speaking!

Nancy: No! It's a way of thinking! *I* know the language and I know *you.* You're not careless with it, or didn't used to be. Why *not* go to those places in the desert and let our heads deflate, if it's all in the past? Why not just *do* that?

Charlie: It was a way of speaking.

Nancy: Dear God, we're *here.* We've served out time, Charlie and there's nothing telling us to do *that,* or any conditional; not any more. Well, there's the arthritis in my wrist, of course, and the eyes have known a better season, and there's always the cancer or a heart attack to think about if we're bored, but besides all these things . . . what is there?

Charlie: (*Somewhat triste.*) You're at it again.

Nancy: I am! Words are lies; they *can* be, and you *use* them, but I know what's in your gut. I *told* you, didn't I?

The problem, then, is that language, while it is the figurative medium through which Charlie is expressing the feelings in his "gut," is merely a symbol for those feelings and may, by nature, serve to obscure rather than to reveal them. As Nancy notes, her understanding of Charlie's meaning is intuitive rather than linguistic and is based first on her knowledge of Charlie and, second, on her understanding of the nature of language. Furthermore, an important part of the argument out of which these linguistic considerations arise is devoted to Charlie's and Nancy's discussion of their sexual fantasies, or as Nancy terms it, the problem of "when the real and the figurative come together." Remarkably, the discussion of these sexual imaginings which Nancy describes as "the sad fantasies, the substitutions, the thoughts we have" culminates in Nancy's discovery that Charlie's fantasy was to "pretend that I was me," thus again presenting the attempt to join the intangible product of the inner man with that which is experienced in the world of phenomena. Described in slightly different—though still in a combination of philosophical, linguistic and sexual terms—the same desire is expressed by The Man in *Listening:* "Odd, in retrospect: it's such a thing we all want—though we seldom admit it, and when we *do,* only part; we all wish to devour ourselves, enter ourselves, be the subject and the object all at once; we all love ourselves and wish we could." The goal is to make subject and object, idea and form, identical, and the pronouncement is immediately followed by a short interval of linguistic "bargaining" over The Man's use of the word "take."

For Albee, language is the medium or meeting ground which exists between the interior and exterior worlds of the speaker and the listener. As a playwright, he seems most interested in the function of language as a means of translating ideas into actions and in the role of language as mediator where a word, like a play, is an imitation which is a wholly independent sign, distinct and separate from that which it represents.
—Julian N. Wasserman

Furthermore, the conversation containing sexual fantasies which appears at the beginning of *Seascape* contains a likewise significant discussion in which Charlie and Nancy compare the difference between their memories of days past and their perceptions of their less pleasant present. Finally, the opening dialogue contains Nancy's suggestion that Charlie attempt to recapture those days, or make memory and fact one, by re-enacting his childhood act of holding stones and sinking to the bottom of the sea in order to escape, if only for a moment, the chaos of the world above. This, of course, all serves as a prelude to the face to face confrontation between the humans and their reptilian counterparts. As the dialogue between the beings from, in their own words, two different dimensions might suggest, the conjunction between the real and the ideal is clearly the central theme of the play.

As the lines from *Listening* suggest, the playwright's concern with the relationship between idea and actuality is certainly not limited to *Seascape.* The same nominalistic exploration is most elaborately set forth in the abstract in *Tiny Alice* with its butler named "Butler," a symbolic pre-

cursor of the joining of the real and the figurative in Charlie's sexual fantasies. The originally intended title of the earlier play, "Substitute Speaker," and its use of Alice as a substitute or proxy for the "Abstract" in the marriage to Julian further suggest a connection with the "substitutions" of which Nancy speaks in the discussion of fantasy. The same theme is no less forcefully, though a good deal less obliquely, presented in the battle over "Truth and Illusion" in *Who's Afraid of Virginia Woolf?* It is there that the illusionary is made real in the imaginary son and that the real is made illusion in George's "autobiographical" novel. Thus while Albee has enjoyed a reputation as an innovator whose constant experimentation has, to some, robbed his work of a clear and consistent stylistic voice, his plays have for the most part maintained a consistency of thematic concern. Significantly, most of those concerns will be seen to be the natural outgrowths or even elaborations of the material of his first play.

In *The Zoo Story,* the theme of the disparity between idea and experience is again presented in regard to sexual fantasy as is seen in Jerry's description of the pornographic playing cards: "What I wanted to get at is the value difference between pornographic playing cards when you're older. It's that when you're a kid you use the cards as a substitute for a real experience, and when you're older you use real experience as a substitute for the fantasy." What is important here is that, whether one begins with ideas and moves toward experience or whether one moves in the opposite direction, a disparity always remains. The recognition of that disparity is the essential content of Jerry's vision. Whether the process begins with either the idea or the object, one must inevitably be, in Nancy's terms, a "substitution" for the other and therefore different in actual identity. That is why the dialogue between Charlie, Nancy, and their reptilian counterparts must inevitably fail. No matter that they are joined by a verb; subject can never be co-incidental with objects, to borrow the terminology of The Man from *Listening,* no matter how much we may wish it. As with *Seascape,* the bulk of Albee's first play comes to be an elaboration of this vision whose content is the necessary failure of communication. To be sure, the action of *The Zoo Story* might be described as the process of translation of Jerry's death fantasy into action, just as the presence of the sea lizards in *Seascape* is the externalizing of objectification of the debate between Charlie and Nancy. It is important, however, to emphasize that the phenomenalization of Jerry's fantasy is brought about through language and that Peter is, significantly enough, a publisher by profession. Indeed, the process is overtly linguistic. It is the ongoing process of definition. The play reaches its climax over the argument as to whether or not Peter is a "vegetable." In the linguistic bargaining which takes place, Peter is called upon to take action in order to deny the validity of the name which has been applied to him. When in the final twist, Peter proves himself not to be a "vegetable" but rather an "animal," society, at large, is thereby defined as a "zoo," and it is this secret definition, a linguistic riddle of identity, that is the mystery which is at the heart of the play. The play as a whole might, then, well be taken as a type of extended definition. This idea of drama as linguistic process is likewise clearly seen in the playwright's **Counting the Ways,** which serves as little more than an extended definition of love. Remembering that Albee has throughout his career insisted that his writing begins with the creation of characters and then progresses to placing those characters in particular situations, the playwright's work, as has just been seen in **The Zoo Story,** may be seen as unfolding revelations of character and identity. Keeping in mind Elizabeth's pronouncement in **The Lady from Dubuque:** "In the outskirts of Dubuque . . . I learned—though I doubt I knew I was learning it—that all of the values were relative save one . . . "Who am I?" All the rest is semantics—liberty, dignity, possession," those exercises seem to be essentially semantic in nature.

While this preoccupation with the process of definition is not always as center stage as it is in **Counting the Ways,** it is without exception present in Albee's work. Whether in the more naturalistic dialogue of **Virginia Woolf** or in the seeming collection of non-sequiturs of **Listening,** a major topic of conversation—and admittedly there is a great deal more of talking than of action in Albee's plays—is language and, in particular semantics. In its most absurdist form, this preoccupation is present in the wonderfully comic tale of the confrontation between Mommy and Mrs. Barker over the color of their hats in **The American Dream,** a work which Albee has described as a play about failed communication. The same play also contains such semantic considerations as the difference between a "house" and an "apartment" or between an "enema bag" and an "enema bottle" as well as a wealth of word plays on such words as "badger" and "bumble/bundle." Each of Albee's plays has a host of similar verbal offerings. **Seascape,** because it deals so directly with the problem of language, again provides an excellent example of the relativity of definition through its comic debate between Charlie and Leslie, the male lizard, over the proper name for the front arm/leg. In a semantic exercise which is much in keeping with the debate over the color of Mommy's hat, Charlie begins,

> Charlie: When we meet we . . . take each other's hands, or whatever, and we . . . touch. . . .
>
> Nancy: . . . Let's greet each other properly, all right? (*Extends her hand again.*) I give you my hand, and you give me your . . . what *is* that? What is that called?
>
> Leslie: What?

> Nancy: (*Indicating Leslie's right arm.*) That there.
>
> Leslie: It's called a leg, of course.
>
> Nancy: Oh. Well, we call this an arm.
>
> Leslie: You have four arms, I see.
>
> Charlie: No; she has two arms. (*Tiny pause.*) And two legs.
>
> Sarah: (*Moves closer to examine Nancy with Leslie.*) And which are the legs?
>
> Nancy: These here. And these are the arms.
>
> Leslie: (*A little on his guard.*) Why do you differentiate?
>
> Nancy: Why do we differentiate, Charlie?
>
> Charlie: (*Quietly hysterical.*) Because they're the ones with the hands on the ends of them.
>
> Nancy: (*To Leslie.*) Yes.
>
> Sarah: (*As Leslie glances suspiciously at Charlie.*) Go on, Leslie; do what Nancy wants you to do. (*To Nancy.*) What is it called?
>
> Nancy: Shaking hands.
>
> Charlie: Or legs.

This verbal bartering continues until the inevitable result is achieved. The sea lizard, in a fashion highly reminiscent of Peter's anger at being called a "vegetable," takes umbrage at being termed a "fish." It would seem, then, that the major thrust of **Seascape** may be summed up in Leslie's annoyed response to Charlie's and Nancy's inability to define the human concepts of love and emotion: "We may, or we may not, but we'll never know unless you define your terms. Honestly, the imprecision! You're so thoughtless!" For his part, Charlie at a subsequent moment retorts in kind as he demands of Nancy, "What *standards* are you using? How would *you* know?" The point of these interchanges is that the existential situation of man is that he must, by the nature of his being, attempt to define his terms and standards, although he is also, by nature, incapable of doing so. Given the playwright's interest in Japanese *Noh* drama as well as Charlie's use of the Rinzai Zen Koan, "What is the sound of one hand clapping?", it would appear that Albee's concept of language is essentially Zen in nature. That is, language as a temporal creation is rooted in the phenomenal while the ideas which it attempts to convey find their source in the ontological. The result of this paradox is that definitions are futile attempts to cast the infinite in the garb of the finite and are of necessity doomed to failure. Such exercises ultimately obscure more than they reveal because of a mistaken notion of their completeness and an ill-placed faith in their ability to capture completely the essence of the subject being defined. Hence, all of the semantic debates, whether over the proper names of colors or anatomical features, are always unresolvable because, by presenting only partial or relative truths, language is a means by which one may, in the playwright's own words, go to "great lengths to avoid communication. . . . Talk in order not to have to listen."

In all of the naming contests which occur throughout his plays, what exists is for the most part a series of futile semantic debates in which each side insists on judging and defining according to its own perceptive standards.
—Julian N. Wasserman

In all of the naming contests which occur throughout his plays, what exists is for the most part a series of futile semantic debates in which each side insists on judging and defining according to its own perceptive standards. As George wryly tells Nick in *Virginia Woolf,* "Every definition has its boundaries, eh?" That definitions are thus implicitly faulty is seen in Oscar's use of the qualifier "as definitions go" in *The Lady from Dubuque.* To be sure, the implicit doubt of the validity of definitions is the key to the play as a whole. After all, the turning point of the play is the miraculous appearance of Elizabeth, the woman who claims to be Jo's mother. In its abruptness, the appearance of Oscar and Elizabeth is much like that of Leslie and Sarah, the sea lizards. Furthermore, as with the reptiles, their appearance seems to be an objectification of what has previously been presented only in the abstract, for the audience has already been given an indirect description of Jo's mother. The dramatic tension comes from the fact that Elizabeth, in the words of Lucinda, is simply "not what [she] imagined" and is completely unknown to Sam, Jo's husband. In other words, the objectification, as with the symbolic acts of both language and drama, conforms to neither the expected nor the known. The play, like so many others by Albee, ends with the audience left in doubt about the meaning of its title. If Elizabeth is aptly described by the title/name "The Lady from Dubuque," then she is, in fact, not Jo's mother since the latter lives in New Jersey. The situation is much like that of *Tiny Alice* where the audience must decide whether to apply the name of the play to the visible onstage character or the offstage abstraction. In each case, the title is a name and as such a definition which is part of each and applies fully to neither with

the result that the audience is left with the dilemma of how and when to apply the titular definition.

Albee's insistence on the relativity of words seems to rely heavily on the standard linguistic assertion that each speech act derives its meaning from three sources: the meaning of the word in the mind of the speaker, the meaning of the word in the mind of the listener, and, most importantly, the generally accepted meaning of the word in the speech community of which both speaker and listener are members. As has already been seen, Albee's plays can be viewed as his examinations of these complex relationships. The plays regularly take members from different speech communities, dimensions, worlds, or societies and present their attempts at forging or working out a new, common vocabulary. Even when speakers come from the same speech communities, they of necessity spend most of their time attempting to explain their private meanings. However, the lack of a common language can also be fostered in order to create an impassable gulf between characters. YAM in *FAM and YAM: An Imaginary Interview* reassures FAM in regard to a certain critic by saying, ". . . but after all, you and a man like that just don't talk the same language." Language is thus used both to include and exclude. YAM uses language to establish a communal bond between himself and FAM and at the same time to separate FAM from the community of critics.

Albee's insistence on the relativity of words seems to rely heavily on the standard linguistic assertion that each speech act derives its meaning from three sources: the meaning of the word in the mind of the speaker, the meaning of the word in the mind of the listener, and, most importantly, the generally accepted meaning of the word in the speech community of which both speaker and listener are members.
—Julian N. Wasserman

The same linguistic exclusion is readily apparent in *Virginia Woolf.* When asked if he and Martha have any children, George replies to Nick, "That's for me to know and you to find out." It is "finding out" or the solving of the riddle that is, within the play, the process of definition. It is only when Nick discovers that the child whom he assumed to be real is, in fact, the product of his hosts' imaginations that even a rudimentary understanding of the dialogue can begin. It is the final revelation that assumed fact is, in reality, fiction which gives all of the previous language its meaning. Before this final revelation, Martha has already berated Nick for his limited understanding:

You always deal in appearances? . . . you don't see
anything, do you?
You see everything but the goddamn mind; you see
all the little specks and crap, but you don't see what
goes on, do you?

Throughout the play, Nick deals only in the concrete while
George and Martha speak the language of abstraction. True
communication between Nick and his hosts is impossible,
so despite the fact that Nick tells George, "I'll play the charades like you've got 'em set up. . . . I'll play in your language. . . . I'll be what you say I am," Nick is doomed to
failure not merely because he is not as skillful as George at
word play but because he has no understanding of either the
vocabulary or the rules by which the linguistic game is
played, for as George makes clear at the end of the play, the
rules are definite and absolute, and there is a penalty to be
exacted for their violation.

Despite the fact that it is their immediate presence which acts
as the catalyst for the "fun and games" which are acted out
before them, Nick and Honey are, in essence, passive observers. When they enter the action at all, they serve solely
as the objects of manipulation, despite any illusions which
they may have to the contrary. For the most part, they are
mere sounding boards, a convenient direction in which to
aim speeches made about subjects in a *patois* which is both
unknown and unintelligible at the outset of the play. It is little
wonder, then, that there is no real communication between
the two couples in the course of the night's action. George
and Martha have, between themselves, all of the private,
mutually exclusive meanings which they assign to events in
their lives as well as a mutually agreed upon vocabulary and
an enforceable set of rules for its implementation. This is
the source of their togetherness, their comic unity. In contrast, there exists no such bond between either George or
Martha and either of their guests. When Nick attempts to
converse with George, it is as though the two were attempting to converse in two mutually exclusive tongues without
the aid of an interpreter. While George is aware of this fact,
Nick is not, and George refuses to explain or to translate.
In their linguistic exclusion from the conversations between
George and Martha, Nick and Honey are, themselves, models or metaphors for the members of the audience, objectified and placed on stage. Like Nick and Honey, the members
of the audience, although the "cause" or occasion of the
night's performance, are placed in the positions of passive
eavesdroppers to the verbal antics of their hosts. The process of the play is for the audience, as well as for the younger
couple on stage, the gradual understanding of those antics
and games and hence inclusion into the speech community
founded by George and Martha. The play, then, is a linguistic exercise, a teaching of language or at least a forging of a
common language founded on an initial act of exclusion and
followed by an initiation or movement toward inclusion. The

comic unity of the play, and Albee has from the outset stoutly
maintained that *Virginia Woolf* is a comedy, is its movement
from perceived disunity of George's and Martha's seeming
non-sequiturs and highly eccentric speech to a perception of
the unity or coherence of their speeches as we learn the semantic and lexical rules of their private tongue. This change
in perception takes place when the audience ceases to be excluded from and instead becomes a part of the speech community of George and Martha. And it is important to note
that this change is a change in the perception of the reality,
not in the reality itself. George was, despite appearances,
making "sense" all along. That is, the solving of the riddle,
the catharsis, the "finding out" as George puts it, is a linguistic and phenomenal rather than an ontological matter.
This is, in the last analysis, the same comic action that was
the essential structure of Albee's first play, where the solving of the riddle is the passive observer's ultimate recognition that Jerry's seeming nonsequiturs concerning "the zoo"
are not unintelligible ravings. Jerry's comments to Peter, like
those of George to Nick, make sense and are in fact seen as
truthful as soon as one understands the language in which
those "ravings" are cast.

Language, then, can serve as a bridge or medium between
speaker and listener but only when both parties are fully
aware of its rules and nature. When either half of the equation is missing, the result from the linguist's point of view
is not really true language. The point is made by Charlie who
in *Seascape* tells Nancy that "parrots don't talk; parrots imitate." Here the linguistic principle that thought must precede
the speech act is championed. The parrot does not talk because it does not think. It has no awareness of the fact that
its utterances comprise human words, and most important
of all, it has no understanding of their meanings, either public
or private. In this sense, the parrot is like Nick in *Virginia
Woolf* or Sam in *The Lady from Dubuque* who both find
themselves unwilling and even unconscious participants in
a repartee in which they know neither the rules nor the vocabulary. Albee's interest in the epistemological basis of
speech is most clearly seen in a brief interchange from *Listening:*

The Girl: You don't *listen.*

The Woman: (*As if the Man were not there.*) Well,
that may *be.*

The Girl: Pay attention, rather, is what you don't do.
Listen: oh, yes; carefully, to . . . oh, the sound an
idea makes . . .

The Woman: . . . a *thought.*

The Girl: No; an idea.

The Woman: As it does what?

The Girl: (*Thinks about that for a split second.*) Mmmmmm . . . as the chemical thing happens, and then the electric thing, and then the muscle; *that* progression. The response—that almost reflex thing, the movement, when an idea happens. (*A strange little smile.*) That is the way the brain works, is it not? The way it functions? Chemical, then electric, then muscle? (*The woman does an "et voila!" gesture.*)

The Man: (*Quiet awe.*) Where does it come from?

The Woman: What?

The Man: The . . . all that. Where does it come from?

The Woman: I haven't found out. It all begins right there: she says, "You don't listen." Every time, she says: "You don't listen."

The Man: To what!? You don't listen to what!?

The Woman: (*Sotto voce.*) I don't *know* what I don't listen to.

The Man: (*Accusatory.*) Yes, and do you care?

The Woman: (*So reasonable.*) I DON'T *know.*

The Man: (*Snorting.*) Of course not!

The Woman: (*Quite brusque.*) Defend the overdog once in a while, will you!? At least what you *think* it is. How do you know who's what!?

The Man: I don't!

The Woman: All right!

The Man: (Shrugs; throws it away.) Get behind that sentence, that's all you have to do. Find out what precedes.

The passage touches upon all the elements necessary for true linguistic communication as it follows the stages of the unconscious genesis of an idea to its establishment in the consciousness of the speaker to its final articulation and reception by a listener. As the title of the play suggests, the final stage is as important as the first. One must, to quote The Girl, not merely listen but also pay attention. A listener, then, is as important to language as a speaker; without a true listener who pays attention, language must out of necessity fail. As Albee has, himself, pointed out in several interviews, Mommy can tell Mrs. Barker, in *The American Dream* to take off her dress rather than her coat because no one in the room is paying any attention to what anyone else is saying. That is why the play is, according to its author, a play about the failure of communication. Significantly, the need for true communication is so great that its failure can result in madness. An important part of the "madness" of The Girl in *Listening* is her resentment over the fact that The Woman really doesn't "Listen." Similarly, Julian, in *Tiny Alice,* equates his own descent into madness with a loss of the ability to hear and comprehend language: "The periods of hallucination would be announced by a ringing in the ears, which produced, or was accompanied by, a loss of hearing. I would hear people's voices from a great distance and through the roaring of . . . surf. And my body would feel light, and not mine, and I would float, not glide."

If speaker and listener are essential to the linguistic process, then one must ask what is the nature of the operation which takes place between the two. To borrow a phrase from The Man in *Listening,* each attempts to "get behind" (that is, understand the generating idea) the sentence or public pronouncement between them. Without the kind of intuition which Nancy claims in regard to understanding what is in Charlie's "gut," one must of necessity rely on indirect means such as symbols or words which are by nature finite compromises for infinite complexities. An example of the kind of linguistic bartering that is necessary although futile is found in the description of the wrapped lunch in *The American Dream:*

Mommy: . . . And every day, when I went to school, Grandma used to wrap a box for me, and I used to take it with me to school; and when it was lunchtime, all the little boys and girls used to take out their boxes of lunch, and they weren't wrapped nicely at all, and they used to open them and eat their chicken legs and chocolate cakes; and I used to say, 'Oh, look at my lovely lunch box; it's so nicely wrapped it would break my heart to open it.' And so, I wouldn't open it.

Daddy: Because it was empty.

Mommy: Oh no. Grandma always filled it up, because she never ate the dinner she cooked the evening before; she gave me all her food for my lunch box the next day. After school, I'd take the box back to Grandma, and she'd open it and eat the chicken legs and chocolate cake that was inside. Grandma used to say, 'I love day-old cake.' That's where the expression day-old cake came from. Grandma always ate everything a day late. I used to eat all the other little boys' and girls' food at school, because they thought my lunch box was empty, and that's why I wouldn't open it. They thought I suffered from the sin of pride, and since that made them better than me, they were very generous.

The point here is that, while there is a seeming common understanding concerning the external appearance of the box, each person believed it to contain something different. In the same fashion, words which seem clear and apparent frequently have individual and sometimes antithetical, private meanings to the characters who use them within the context of the play. Thus, when Grandma in *The American Dream* presents the mysterious boxes around which everyone must negotiate, those boxes are in essence words, and, indeed, Grandma's most consistent complaint throughout the play concerns the way in which everyone speaks to the elderly. Words, then, are to Albee types of decorated boxes sometimes containing wonderful surprises as in the comic debates between Charlie and Leslie, or they can serve as virtual Pandora's boxes as they do in the cases of George and Martha. As FAM says in his interview with YAM, "Words; words . . . They're such a pleasure," and as George notes, "Martha's a devil with language: she really is."

As the case with George and Martha might suggest, the field of semantics is the arena in which the tug of war between reality and fantasy ultimately takes place. Nowhere is this made clearer than in *Tiny Alice.* In that play, many of Albee's concerns with the symbolic nature of language find their expression in the semantic debate over the curious relationship between the house in which Alice resides and the model which it contains. The house, it seems, was originally constructed in England and then disassembled and rebuilt in its present location. The house, therefore, is not by definition an "original" but is, rather, a "replica." Although built of the materials of the original, the replica can no more be the original than a word can be identical to the mental image which it signifies. The replica once again presents the playwright's preoccupation with the translation of ideas, persons, and objects. Translation, however, in these terms implies an absolute alteration of the item translated, for it implies a definite and distinct change from one location or state of being to another. In the midst of the replica stands a "model"—the proportionately correct although scaled down symbol which is derivative, though wholly separate from the original. It should, however, be noted that the model is subject to the vicissitudes which affect the replica and not *vice versa.* This is seen in the fact that while the fire is first noted in the chapel of the model it is, in fact, put out in the chapel of the replica. As in the case of the fire in the chapel, one learns about the house, the replica, by studying the model. If the model is to be exact, it must contain a model, which, in turn, must contain a model. The process must go on *ad infinitum.* The infinite nature of the series of reflec-

tive models required to establish the model as an exact duplicate of the replica presents an example of Xeno's paradox concerning the tortoise and the hare. Just as the hare can never in theory overtake the tortoise, so the model can never reach its goal of reduplicating either the replica or the original.

To understand the complex relationship which Albee is suggesting here, it is necessary to turn to a similar set of relationships in the later play, *Listening,* as The Girl describes the mysterious "blue cardboard":

> Yes. Most cardboard is grey . . . or brown, heavier. But blue cardboard is . . . unusual. That would be enough, but if you see blue cardboard, tile blue, love it, want . . . it, and have it . . . then it's special. But—don't interrupt me!—Well, if you want more value from it, from the experience, and take *grey* cardboard, mix your colors and paint it, carefully, blue, to the edges, smooth, then it's not *any* blue cardboard but very special: grey cardboard taken and made blue, self-made, self-made blue—better than grey, better than the other blue, because it's self-done. Very valuable, and even looking at it is a theft; touching it, even to take it to a window to see the smooth lovely color, all blue, is a theft. Even the knowledge of it is a theft . . . of sorts.

The blue is the Ideal. It is not only exclusive but practically unattainable. It is the "original" in that it is an intangible, unknowable form, in the Platonic sense. The grey is the common experience or phenomenon. What is of interest here in the artifice of the cardboard painted blue, for like a word or a play it stands mid-way between an action and the idea of that action, taking its identity from both but identical to neither. The artifice is just that; it is an artifice. It is a conscious creation. It is, however, as a result of the hands of the craftsman, no longer grey and yet not quite identical to the object, for it is neither purely an emanation, in the Neo-Platonic sense, nor is it uncreate or original.

However, if both the cardboard made blue as well as the model of the replica are merely finite, imperfect imitations, one must question the very act of resorting to such forms if they, like words, must inevitably fall short of what they attempt to portray or describe. While both the discussions of the model in *Tiny Alice* and the cardboard in *Listening* present the limitations of language as a mediating instrument between the abstract and the concrete, both simultaneously present the argument for the necessity of the linguistic medium, despite its imperfect status. In both cases, the model and the artifice are the only means by which the Abstraction and its relationship to the concrete may be observed and known. Ironically, the very imperfections of language may be said to be the source of its attraction for Albee since its failure to capture completely the Abstract, as it is termed in *Tiny Alice,* is what renders the Abstract comprehensible to the human intellect. Language, as the "glorious imperfect," allows the imperfect to know glory if not perfection.

As the meeting ground of the abstract and the concrete, language serves to help man understand the nature of each. Without that help, man is placed in the dilemma, so common in the plays of Albee, of not being able to distinguish between illusion and reality. This problem of illusion and reality is the exact source of Julian's dilemma in *Tiny Alice.* Such confusion is seen in Julian's remarkable description of an hallucinatory sexual encounter. Significantly, Miss Alice responds to Julian's account of his sexual/ecstatic experience with a fellow inmate by asking, "Is the memory of something having happened the same as it having happened?" Her question as to the actual relationship between the real and the imaginary remains the problem with which Julian must grapple throughout the rest of the play, and, in fact, it is central to incidents in the lives of the characters in several other plays as well, for the hallucinatory nature of sexual union is a recurring theme in the works of Albee. The theme is made manifest in *The Zoo Story* in Jerry's description of his relationship with his landlady:

> . . . and somewhere, somewhere in the back of that pea-sized brain of hers, an organ developed just enough to let her eat, drink, and emit, she has some foul parody of sexual desire. And I, Peter, am the object of her sweaty lust.

> But I have found a way to keep her off. When she talks to me, when she presses herself to my body and mumbles about her room and how I should come there, I merely say: but, Love; wasn't yesterday enough for you, and the day before? Then she puzzles, she makes slits of her tiny eyes, she sways a little, and then, Peter . . . and it is at this moment that I think I might be doing some good in that tormented house . . . a simple-minded smile begins to form on her unthinkable face, and she giggles and groans as she thinks about yesterday and the day before; as she believes and relives what never happened. . . .

For the landlady, one may indeed say that memory is the equivalent of event. Jerry's obvious distaste over the incident shows that he, like Julian, is as deeply affected by another's fantasy as if the actual events had taken place. The same problem arises in *Virginia Woolf* where it is not the sexual act that is fantasized but rather the product of that act, the imaginary son. In all of these cases, the best evidence points to the unreality of the events described, and yet in each case, the hallucination of the action produces the same effects as the actual event. Hallucination, then, provides a middle ground between idea and event for those who find the Ideal unattainable and the present unbearable. In *Virginia Woolf,* George makes a similar observation when he notes,

> It's very simple. . . . When people can't abide things as they are, when they can't abide the present, they do one of two things . . . either they . . . either they turn to a contemplation of the past, as I have done, or they set about to . . . alter the future.

Julian confirms the value of such mediation when he concludes his description of his hallucinatory encounter by noting,

> I was persuaded, eventually, that perhaps I was . . . over-concerned by hallucination; that some was inevitable, and a portion of that—even desirable.

In all three instances, Albee relies on the sexual metaphor for this commingling of illusion and reality, a metaphor commonly found in the writings of the mystics in their attempts to describe mystical union. Julian's confusion, here as well as throughout his life, is the direct result of his rejection of a middle ground, of the possible union of the Absolute and the relative which is achieved in both the made-over cardboard and the model of the replica. In the third act of the play, the other characters attempt to apprise him of this very folly:

> Lawyer: (*Sarcasm is gone; all is gone, save fact.*) Dear Julian; we all serve, do we not? Each of us his own priesthood; publicly, some, others . . . within only; but we all do—what's-his-name's special trumpet, or clear lonely bell. Predestination, fate, the will of God, accident. . . . All swirled up in it, no matter what the name. And being man, we have invented choice, and have, indeed, gone further, and have catalogued the underpinnings of choice. But we do not know. Anything. End prologue.

> Miss Alice: Tell him.

> Lawyer: No Matter. We are leaving you now, Julian; agents, every one of us—going. We are leaving you . . . to your accomplishment: your marriage, your wife, your . . . special priesthood.

> Julian: (*Apprehension and great suspicion.*) I . . . don't know what you're talking about.

> Lawyer: (*Unperturbed.*) What is so amazing is the . . . coming together . . . of disparates . . . left-

fielding, out of the most unlikely. Who would have thought, Julian? Who would have thought? You have brought us to the end of our service here. We go on; you stay.

Butler: May I begin to cover?

Miss Alice: Not Yet. (*Kindly*) Do you understand, Julian?

Julian: (*Barely in control.*) Of course not!

Miss Alice: Julian, I have tried to be . . . *her.* No; I have tried to be . . . what I thought she might, what might make you happy, what you might use, as a . . . what?

Butler: *Play* God; go on.

Miss Alice: We must . . . represent, draw pictures, reduce or enlarge to . . . to what we can understand.

Julian: (*Sad, mild.*) But I have fought against it . . . all my life. When they said, 'Bring the wonders down to me, closer; I cannot see them, touch; nor can I believe.' I have fought against it . . . all my life.

Butler: (*To Miss Alice; softly.*) You see? No good.

Miss Alice: (*Shrugs.*) I have done what I can do with it.

Julian: All my life. In and out of . . . confinement, fought against the symbol.

Miss Alice: Then you should be happy now.

Cardinal: Julian, it has been our desire always to serve; your sense of mission . . .

Lawyer: We are surrogates; our task is done now.

Miss Alice: Stay with her.

Julian: (*Horror behind it; disbelieving.*) Stay . . . with . . . her?

Miss Alice: Stay with her. Accept it.

Lawyer: (*At the model.*) Her rooms are lighted. It is warm, there is enough.

Miss Alice: Be content with it. Stay with her.

Julian: (*Refusing to accept what he is hearing.*) Miss Alice . . . I have married you.

Miss Alice: (*Kind, still.*) No, Julian; you have married *her* . . . through me.

Julian: (*Pointing to the model.*) There is nothing there! We are here! There is no one *there*!

Lawyer: *She* is there . . . we believe.

Julian: (*To Miss Alice.*) I have been with *you*!

Miss Alice: (*Not explaining; sort of dreamy.*) You have felt her warmth through me, touched her lips through my lips, held her hands, through mine, my breasts, hers, lain on her bed, through mine, wrapped yourself in her wings, your hands on the small of her back, your mouth on her hair, the voice in your ear, hers not mine, all hers; her. You are hers.

Cardinal: Accept.

Butler: Accept.

Lawyer: Accept.

This dialogue presents the beginning of Julian's awe-filled recognition of the price exacted by his rejection of symbols, for Alice herself admits that she is merely a symbol, an imperfect attempt to represent the abstract. Everyone is, as the lawyer notes, an "agent," a representative of a thing, rather than the thing itself. The wedding itself is a symbol of mediation or union. Julian as a *lay brother* is himself an apt symbol of the very kind of mediation which he has spent his life trying to reject. Yet Julian's rejection of such mediation has been his distinguishing characteristic throughout the play. The true extent of Julian's dualistic vision, as well as its dire consequences, is seen in his own account of the cause of his madness:

Julian: Oh . . . (*Pause.*) I . . . I lost my faith. (*Pause.*) In God.

Butler: Ah. (*Then a questioning look.*)

Julian: Is there more?

Butler: Is there more?

Julian: Well, nothing . . . of matter. I . . . declined. I . . . shriveled into myself; a glass dome . . . descended, and it seemed I was out of reach, unreachable, finally unreaching, in this ... paralysis, of sorts. I ... put myself in a mental home.

Butler: (*Curiously noncommittal.*) Ah.

Julian: I could not reconcile myself to the chasm between the nature of God and the use to which man put ... God.

Butler: Between your God and others', your view and theirs.

Julian: I said what I intended: (*Weighs the opposites in each hand.*) It is God the mover, not God the puppet; God the creator, not the God created by man.

Butler: (*Almost pitying.*) Six years in the loony bin of semantics?

Julian: (*Slightly flustered, heat.*) It is not semantics! Men create a false God in their own image, it is easier for them! ... It is not. ...

The passage is the key to Julian's thinking as it clearly shows that to Julian the difference between the First Cause and its emanations, between an object and the perception of that object, is both real and irreconcilable. Furthermore, the movement is essentially Neo-Platonic since the contrasting movement from experience to abstraction, namely man's creation of God, is rejected out of hand. Because the distinction is real, it is not in Julian's eyes "semantic," that is, without substance. Julian then is rejecting what he believes to be the relative in favor of the Absolute.

In order to understand more fully the exact nature of Julian's rejection of the label "semantic" to describe the difference between idea and emanation, it is necessary to consider a case in which he feels that the term is appropriate:

Butler: (*To Julian, pointing first to the model, then to the room.*) Do you mean the model ... or the replica?

Julian: I mean the ... I mean ... what we are in.

Butler: *Ah*-ha. And which is that?

Julian: That we are in?

Butler: Yes.

Lawyer: (*To Julian.*) You are clearly not a Jesuit. (*Turning.*) Butler, you've put him in a clumsy trap.

Butler: (*Shrugging.*) I'm only a servant.

Lawyer: (*To Julian, too sweetly.*) You needn't accept his alternative ... that since we are clearly not in a model we must be in a replica.

Butler: (*Vaguely annoyed.*) Why must he not accept that?

Miss Alice: Yes. Why not?

Lawyer: I said he did not *need* to accept the alternative. I did not say it was not valid.

Julian: (*Cheerfully.*) I will not accept it; the problem is only semantic.

To Julian the relationship between the model and the replica, as opposed to the relationship between God and the world, is semantic. The difference between idea and event is absolute; the differences between the various emanations of that idea are not. Language is, to Julian, part of the phenomenal. It is not, like the grey cardboard painted blue, a bridge from one realm to the other, for Julian would reject the artifice of the cardboard as an Aristotelian movement from the concrete to the abstract, since that is the movement which Julian wishes to avoid. Julian's reaction is to resolve the tension of that duality not by transcendence of the oppositions or by accepting their existence and arranging them hierarchically but rather through a complete dismissal of the phenomenal. Because Julian sees the use of symbols of a lessening of the Abstract, he rejects it out of hand. The Lawyer replies,

> I have learned ... Brother Julian ... never to confuse the representative of a ... thing with the thing itself.

In other words, the corruption of the Cardinal who is the subject of the dialogue in no way diminishes the God for which he stands. The manipulation of the symbol does not affect the idea which it represents. Again, that is why the fire, although first seen in the model, must be extinguished in the replica. The destruction of the chapel must be reflected in the model for its purpose is to reflect the replica as it is, not as it was. The fire, of course, has no effect on the original which exits only in memory and is no longer affected by events in the real world. Thus, Julian's fear that symbols constitute a lessening of the Abstract is proven to be groundless.

The lawyer, with the butler acting out the role of Julian, demonstrates the folly of the confusion under which Julian suffers:

Lawyer: But *shall* we tell him the whole thing? The Cardinal? What is happening?

Butler: How much can he take?

Lawyer: He is a man of God, however much he simplifies, however much he worships the symbol and not the substance.

Butler: Like everyone.

Lawyer: Like most.

Butler: Julian can't stand that; he told me so: men make God in their own image, he said. Those six years I told you about.

Lawyer: Yes. When he went into an asylum. YES.

Butler: It was—because he could not stand it, wasn't it? The use men put God to.

Lawyer: It's perfect; wonderful.

Butler: Could not reconcile.

Lawyer: No.

Butler: God as older brother, scout leader, couldn't take that.

Lawyer: And still not reconciled.

Butler: Has pardoned men, I think. Is walking on the edge of an abyss, but is balancing. Can be pushed . . . over, back to the asylums.

Lawyer: Or over . . . to the Truth. (*Addressing Julian, as if he were there; some thunder in the voice.*) God, Julian? Yes? God? *Whose* God? Have you pardoned men their blasphemy, Julian? Have you forgiven them?

Butler: (*Quiet echoing answers; being Julian.*) No, I have not, have not really; have *let* them, but cannot accept.

Lawyer: Have not forgiven. No Julian. Could you ever?

Butler: (*Ibid.*) It is their comfort, my agony.

Lawyer: Soft God? The servant? Gingerbread God with the raisin eyes?

Butler: (*Ibid.*) I cannot accept it.

Lawyer: Then don't accept it, Julian.

Butler: But there is *some* thing. There is a *true* God.

Lawyer: There is an abstraction, Julian, but it cannot be understood. You cannot worship it.

Butler: (*Ibid.*) There is more.

Lawyer: There is Alice, Julian. That can be understood. Only the mouse in the model. Just that.

Butler: (*Ibid.*) There must be more.

Lawyer: The mouse. Believe it. Don't personify this abstraction, Julian, limit it, demean it. Only the mouse, the toy. And that does not exist . . . but is all that can be worshipped. . . . Cut off from it, Julian, ease yourself, ease off. No trouble now; accept it.

Butler: (*Talking to Julian now.*) Accept it, Julian; ease off. Worship it . . .

Lawyer: Accept it.

This play within a play not only makes its point in and about the abstract but goes on to provide its corroboration in fact since the butler, named Butler in another convenient merging of idea and actuality, by acting the role of Julian has not affected Julian in any real sense. The problem, as the Lawyer sets it forth, is that the Abstract is, as Julian claims, unknowable and ineffable. Julian is correct to that extent, and yet like everyone else Julian has continued to pursue that unattainable knowledge. What sets Julian apart is his refusal to accept the necessary compromise or mediation which such a paradox demands. By refusing to accept mediation which others accept, Julian has only placed the Abstract farther beyond his reach. By rejecting symbols, Julian is abandoning all that may be known of the Absolute on the non-mystical, conscious level. Julian has ultimately deceived himself into believing that he has, in fact, completely rejected the mediation of language and symbol in his striving to experience the divine. Yet to speak and think of the Absolute as Julian does or, for that matter, even to resort to the term "Absolute" is indeed a denial of the recognition of its ineffability.

It is the recognition of this self-deception which comprises the bulk of Julian's final soliloquy. Deserted and dying at the play's conclusion, Julian realizes that in marrying Miss Alice he has, as the lawyer said, unknowingly accepted the symbol as a reality, for without the symbol "THE AB-STRACTION" is too terrible to behold. Julian's final words, as if in answer to the earlier pleas of both the lawyer and the butler are, "I accept thee, Alice, for thou art come to me. God, Alice . . . I accept thy will." The ultimate proclamation of Julian's folly, however, comes in Julian's realization that he is facing death. Julian has imagined Death, not dying. He knows life, the phenomenal, and has imagined Death, the ontological, but he has never given any thought to dying, the act of translation, the middle ground between the two.

Significantly, in the act of dying Julian assumes the attitude of the crucified Christ, another mediator between the Abstract and the concrete. Death is the ineffable state. Dying, however, may be known and described. In the last analysis, Julian is of a kind with Albee's many other characters such as Peter and Nick who are lost in the midst of verbal exchanges of which they had no understanding. However, while Julian's dilemma is ultimately linguistic in nature, he is not merely a man who cannot understand the language in which the oblique discussions of the mysterious Alice are couched. He is, until the final lines of the play, a man who will not understand because he rejects language and symbol as an unnecessary, even unacceptable compromise. He is not able to live comfortably in a world where all Truth and, therefore, meaning are in George's words, "relative." Yet, it is the very compromise which has been at the thematic and structural centers of Albee's work from its inception, and it is the basis for the playwright's initial reaction to the interviewers' question concerning the place of realism in theatre. As he has noted in several interviews, the ultimate task of the playwright is "to turn fact into truth," and this is the compromise of both the playwright and the linguist.

Edward Albee with Jeffrey Goldman (interview date 1989)

SOURCE: "An Interview with Edward Albee," in *Studies in American Drama, 1945-Present*, Vol. 6, No. 1, 1991, pp. 59-69.

[*In the following interview, conducted in 1989, Albee discusses his works, his artistic approach, critical reaction to his works, American theater, the arts, and contemporary social issues.*]

It was perhaps *the* most appropriate environment in which to interview Edward Albee: the rehearsal set for the Los Angeles production of *Who's Afraid of Virginia Woolf?* (1962). At center stage, a chipped wooden coffee table wobbled in front of faded green couch. Upstage right sat the play's ever-present bar, stocked with a variety of bourbon and whiskey bottles.

As the rehearsal broke up, and actors John Lithgow and Glenda Jackson exited the room, the Pulitzer Prize-winning American playwright took a seat on the tattered sofa.

Albee was preparing *Who's Afraid of Virginia Woolf?* for the opening leg of a tour that would take the play from the Doolittle Theatre in Hollywood to Houston to London and beyond. This was the second time Albee had directed *Virginia Woolf*—the first being the much-heralded 1976 Broadway production with Colleen Dewhurst and Ben Gazzara—and by the time the show left Southern California, it had garnered mixed reviews: an enthusiastic *Newsweek* announced, "the play hasn't lost its power to shock," while the lukewarm *Los Angles Times* complained that *Who's Afraid of Virginia Woolf?* "only stings us this time around, where once it stunned us."

But, then again, Albee has always had a precarious relationship with American theatre critics. Revered for such modern classics as *The Zoo Story* (1959), *The American Dream* (1961), *A Delicate Balance* (1966), *Seascape* (1975) and of course *Virginia Woolf*, he has also been vilified for writing *Malcolm* (his 1966 adaptation of James Purdy's novel), *The Lady from Dubuque* (1980) and *The Man Who Had Three Arms* (1982). The critical reaction to *The Man Who Had Three Arms* was highly representative. After a favorable response from the public in Miami, Chicago, and during its preview engagement on Broadway, the play opened to hostile reviews and closed soon thereafter. Subsequently, it went on to win a significant award and wide accolades at the Edinburgh festival in Scotland. Such is the life of a playwright who refuses to pull any punches with his potential critics.

The following interview took place on September 19, 1989. Albee was dressed in a simple black shirt, grey pants, and black Reeboks. He had salt and pepper hair, a greying moustache, and glasses, but his otherwise extraordinarily youthful appearance belied his true age—at the time 61 years old. The soft-spoken Albee offered intense, measured responses throughout the interview, although his infamous wry and subtle humor surfaced frequently. In the background, the stage hands broke down the set while a photographer snapped photos of the playwright, who is generally considered to be the finest American dramatist of the past three decades.

[*Goldman:*] *What are the primary ways the theatre has changed since the 1962 premier of* **Who's Afraid of Virginia Woolf?**

[Albee:] The theatre. Define what you mean by the theatre.

Okay, the American theatre.

The American theatre. What do you mean by that?

Well, how about Broadway?

There is more interesting theatre going on in the United States than you would ever know about if you only went to Broadway theatre. I mean, the best regional theatre, the experimental theatres, the university theatres, too—very, very interesting new work. I'm absolutely convinced that Broadway could vanish from the face of the earth and the American theatre as an art form would not be hurt at all.

And Broadway has become infinitely more difficult for valuable, useful, serious plays to get produced. When we first did *Who's Afraid of Virginia Woolf?,* we brought the play in and it cost $45,000 to get it open and ticket prices were $7—that was 1962. When we did a revival in '76 on Broadway, it cost $300,000 to open it, and ticket prices were up to $20. If we did it on Broadway this year, it would probably cost $800,000 or $900,000 to put it on and ticket prices would be up to $45. In the past, producers and theatre owners were more willing to take chances on tough, serious plays and bring them right onto Broadway. Now, almost always, a serious play has got to prove that it is both serious *and* commercial. Being serious is no longer enough.

Is this due to economic considerations?

Part of it has to do with the economics—the value of real estate, taxes, etc.—and part of it has to do with the fact that an audience that is paying $50 for a theatre ticket does not want to be hit over the head with ideas. They want *entertainment.*

Do you think that the influence of Hollywood has anything to do with this?

Maybe audiences want our theatre to be more like television and film. I'm convinced that our society wants less social and political engagement and more entertainment.

Is there a difference between European and American audiences?

This is a generalization, but European audiences tend to go to the theatre more regularly, are probably educated more in terms of serious theatre, and are more interested in theatre as an art form than as merely entertainment. But that's shifting—European audiences are probably getting just as lazy as some of our American audiences!

Why do you think critics often say that your work has a European feel to it?

Well, I'm not a regionalist like Tennessee Williams or Sam Shepard or David Mamet. I guess my plays seem to translate very nicely into other cultures. But they *are* set in America, and I'm *clearly* an American writer and my characters *are* American. But they're not regionalized, they're not that locale specific.

How have you changed as a playwright since the premier of **Virginia Woolf?**

Apparently, considering the fact that I run into so much trouble, I haven't changed enough.

Trouble with . . . ?

Oh, trouble with critics, management, audiences . . . I suspect that I haven't accommodated the way I am supposed to. I've always just written whatever's been inside my head, whatever came naturally.

Do you think that the initial popular support of **Who's Afraid of Virginia Woolf?** *made the critics suspicious and even hostile towards your work?*

I don't know what made those who became hostile hostile. Maybe they just disliked me, disliked the instant success, or maybe it was just dismay over things I was saying.

How do you deal with the reaction to, say, **The Man Who Had Three Arms,** *which was lambasted by the critics when it first appeared on Broadway in 1983, but which went on to win a prestigious award at the Edinburgh festival? Do you just laugh off the initial reaction?*

Oh, you have to in order to protect your sanity! If you know that the work you do is good and is unintentionally or intentionally misunderstood or shot down for reasons that have nothing to do with the quality of your work, then naturally there's nothing you can do except to just go about your business and assume that in a more rational time people will say, "Gee, I wonder why the critics behaved so irrationally about that play?"

Did this attitude take a long time to develop?

Not really. I've never been surprised by the reaction to plays of mine. I've been disappointed sometimes. Sometimes a play hasn't been allowed to reach the audience I thought it should. But if you know you've done your job properly you can't worry about it too much—you'd go crazy if you did.

What do you think about all of the talk about Los Angeles becoming the major cultural and theatrical center of the United States—and possibly the world—within the next decade or so?

When I see as many good plays coming from experimental theatre out here as I see in New York, I'll be more convinced. Though I must say I am more pleased with Los Angeles than I am with other large cities. But I still think that going to the theatre is somewhat of an unnatural occurrence out here. It is not like New York where going to the theatre is as natural as breathing.

Why is that?

I don't know! It's not a theatre town! It's a film and television town! And most actors I meet out here complain about the fact that they are really being pushed into film and television and do not have the opportunity to do live work on the stage.

Do you direct differently in Los Angeles than when you are staging a play in a theatre town?

No, I don't think so. You have to direct the play to know its intention. Trouble comes with too much accommodation. I would never cut a play of mine to make it more tolerable for an audience. You must make the assumption that an audience will come to the play and is interested in being in the theatre, interested in seeing the play, immersing themselves in it, and maybe even having a complex experience.

It's probably a little easier directing my work because I know a little more about what the playwright had in mind. I have to invent a little bit more if I'm directing somebody else's work.
                    —Edward Albee

You've directed work by such playwrights as Sam Shepard, Lanford Wilson, and David Mamet. Do you find directing your own work easier or more difficult than directing other playwrights' work?

It's probably a little easier directing my work because I know a little more about what the playwright had in mind. I have to invent a little bit more if I'm directing somebody else's work.

What do you think about the school of thought that says a playwright shouldn't direct his own play?

Well, I don't think anybody should direct a play unless they are a competent director. I've learned how to be a competent director. Lots of playwrights have directed their own work—besides Shakespeare and Moliere. In the 20th century, Brecht, Beckett, Gelber, Anouilh, Pinter, me. Lots of us direct our own work.

What do you consider to be your greatest play?

I don't know whether *any* of them are great.

How about your most satisfying?

I find this is to be true with every single one that I do. As I go on I find that the next one is always more interesting than the previous. You know, it would be an awful, terrible thing to think that you've done your best work. I like to think that maybe it's three plays down the line.

Who would you cite as your major influence outside of the theatre? For instance, I've read that you collect art.

I've been influenced by everybody, and I'd be a fool if I weren't. I don't think that anybody in the creative arts can be a well-rounded, well-informed person in the creative arts unless they're conversant in all the arts. A playwright who doesn't know painting and sculpture and classical music—especially classical music since composing music and writing for the theatre are so closely allied—and doesn't know what's going on in fiction and poetry is probably not an educated man and will put terrible limits on himself. All of the arts feed on each other, all of them influence each other, and it's very valuable and useful to know everything that you can.

Do you have a deep interest in classical music?

I wanted to be a composer when I was 13, but I didn't become one because I was incompetent. So I started studying music on the phonograph, and I would dare say that I've probably listened to—very conscientiously—more classical music than anybody who is not a composer.

You mentioned the similarity between the theatre and music, between dramatic structure and musical structure. Can you explain this to me?

Well, a string quartet is a performed piece that is heard and seen—so is a play. There are great similarities—structural similarities, psychological similarities. There are voices speaking, instruments speaking . . .

Does it primarily have to do with the language of the play?

No, it's in the psychology. A good piece of music has a structure which gives it a psychology, proper duration, whereas a bad piece of music doesn't end where it should—it goes on too long, ideas run out. The relationships are very complex and intertwined. A composer and a playwright use notation in very much the same way—rise, soft; fast, slow . . . it's a profound relationship.

Have you ever written a play with a particular piece of music in mind?

No, but I am aware sometimes when I'm writing a play that this section is a *passacaglia,* for example, or a theme and variation.

Can you describe the process you go through when writing a play? For instance, do you, as Pinter has said he does, begin with two characters in a room?

Doesn't everybody? Didn't Shakespeare, didn't . . .

Well, I don't know. Is that the germ? Or do you pick up ideas from something you read in the newspaper?

No, I've never—with the exception of *Bessie Smith*—never known where it came from. Everything starts coming into focus at the same time: the environment, and the characters, their relationship to each other—it just starts coming into focus.

Do you use an outline?

No. I will think about a play for quite a while before I start writing it down. The best way for me to lose interest in a play is to write it down.

You have said that the unconscious is the most efficient part of your mind. Why is that?

It must be since my conscious mind is very inefficient! I seem to come to lots of creative and dramatic conclusions which I inform myself of; so obviously I am moving from the unconscious to the conscious. I rely upon the unconscious mind for creativity just as most people do. And the conscious mind is a kind of translator.

For most good plays, the performance does not add anything to the play; it merely brings the play to its own life. You see, the better the actors you have, the closer the author's intention will be achieved. A great play is not *improved* by a performance, it is *proved* by a performance.
—*Edward Albee*

Do you believe that there is such a thing as the perfectly made play?

In which there is nothing missing and no excess?

Yes.

Oh, I've seen a few of them I think.

Care to name names?

A couple of Beckett's plays, one or two of Chekhov's . . . I see them now and again.

Do you still believe that, as you've once said, "a text is never dependent on performance and that no performance is as good as the performance the author saw when he wrote the play"?

I was talking about a good play. Now, a bad play . . . most performances are better than the play. For most good plays, the performance does not add anything to the play; it merely brings the play to its own life. You see, the better the actors you have, the closer the author's intention will be achieved. A great play is not *improved* by a performance, it is *proved* by a performance. The best actors in the world aren't going to make a Chekhov play any better than it is. Or a Beckett play. They're first rate! It's the responsibility of the actors to try to prove that they're as good as the play. In a lousy play, the actors have got to be compensated for the fact that the play is lousy.

Do you think there are many actors out there who would agree with you?

Yes. The professional and intelligent ones.

You once said that it was one of the responsibilities of playwrights to show people how they are and what their time is like in the hope that perhaps they'll change it. Do you still believe this?

Sure.

What other responsibilities does the playwright have?

Oh . . . to write as well as he can, to tell as much of the truth as he knows—as clearly and as honestly as he knows it. Not to lie, not to deal in half-truths. You see, all art is useful. There's no point if it's merely decorative. Art tells us who we are, how we live, our consciousness . . . The whole concept of metaphor is so important to the human animal, and that's what art does—deals in the metaphor. And so all good art is useful! And that's why the merely decorative, the merely escapist, is a big waste of everybody's time.

But you're not a great fan of social realism are you?

The only problem I have is that it limits its scope to accommodate the problems it addresses. I had a problem with a lot of the agitprop plays that were written in the 1930s—they just weren't very good plays. I have no objection to a first-rate play of social realism. But I don't think that you can justify writing a bad play just because it deals with social realism.

Do you see yourself as a social critic or as a writer interested more in metaphysical issues, interested in penetrating, as George in **Virginia Woolf** *says, "the bone and the marrow"?*

I don't see how you separate the two.

Really?

I mean, most of my plays do deal with people in the context of relationships, which is a microcosm and a macrocosm. If the play doesn't transcend what it is specifically about, it doesn't resonate and therefore isn't any good. It's got to be about not only how these couples live, but how we live as a society.

As a playwright, what do you think are the major issues confronting America today?

Too many people don't live their own lives, they pass through their lives half-asleep. I think that's a great waste of time. Most people do not wish life to be an adventure, they wish it to be a nice, slow descent. Most people are far more interested in comfort than they are in adventure, in escape rather than engagement.

What about on a purely social level?

How—how do, how do you separate these? A society is made up of people who run their society based upon their own needs, and how they wish to participate. If we have people who do not wish to be living in an adventuresome society, we end up with reactionary know-nothing dodos, which has been happening for quite a while in this country. You can't separate the two, they're desperately related!

What are your feelings on the current war on drugs in America? Are you interested in writing about this subject?

I'm less interested in addressing specific things than I am in addressing the kind of people we are that permit certain things to happen. Now, for example, there would be no drug problem in the United States if people did not want to take drugs. Right? So, really the way to address the drug problem is to create a society in which people do not want to take drugs. The people who take drugs are the people who are affluent and the people who are very poor. Right? People with money and people without money. That seems to be the division in our society, there being no middle ground anymore; people have money, people don't have money. People are enfranchised, people are disenfranchised in this society.

You have to make the people who have the money, who do drugs on a social level, want to participate so much in their lives that they don't want the escape of the drugs. Now, the people who are poor and desperate and are using drugs because reality is too hideous to tolerate—you've got to create a society in which they don't have to live in those conditions. If you accomplish both of those things there'd be absolutely no drug problem in this country.

The drug program the Bush Administration has put forward as I see it is spending infinitely too little money on alleviating the poverty in this country. You can take care of 9/10ths of the drug problem in this country by creating a society in which you don't have so many desperate, disenfranchised minority poor. The Bush Administration gives the impression that they are much more interested in solving the drug problems of the upper middle class white kids. And it strikes me as being ultimately, if not phoney, then certainly badly misdirected.

Let me ask you this since I think it ties in to what you've just said in a roundabout way. Your characters, versus those of a playwright like O'Neill or Williams, are always aware of the illusion they are creating around themselves. They admit that they invent an illusionary life. Do you think it is sometimes better to live life as a self-inflicted illusion rather than survive the day-by-day realities of it?

Well, obviously I prefer that people not have false illusions and that they participate completely in their own lives! The majority of my plays are about people who are deluded—consciously or unconsciously, in one way or another. And I want to say "Do it!" Shake 'em. "Stop it! Do it!"

Do you have any comments or predictions about the future of theatre and your role in it?

Oh, I don't know. I'm not a crystal ball gazer.

Mickey Pearlman (essay date 1989)

SOURCE: "What's New at the Zoo? Rereading Edward Albee's American Dream(s) and Nightmares," in *Feminist Rereadings of Modern American Drama*, edited by June Schlueter, Fairleigh Dickinson University Press, 1989, pp. 183-91.

[*In the following essay, Pearlman studies what she terms Albee's bitter, negative, and harsh treatment of women in* The Zoo Story, The American Dream, *and* The Sandbox.]

1

To reread Edward Albee's one-act play ***The Zoo Story***

(1958) is to reexperience the caustic, cryptic vision of an angry playwright thirty years after the play was performed (1959), in German, in Berlin.

The Zoo Story is a two-character dialogue of male strangers, both locked in rigidly defined "male" roles, with the resonately Christian names of Jerry (Jeremiah?) and Peter, whose chance encounter on a bench in Central Park provokes a clash of dichotomous visions of power, space, and society. Jerry is an antagonizing but isolated vagrant, whose life has been, in his opinion, short-circuited, if not exploded, by women. He lives in a West Side rooming house populated by "a colored queen" in a Japanese kimono, "who always keeps his door open . . . when he's plucking his eyebrows," a Puerto Rican family in "the two front rooms," a "lady . . . on the third floor [who] . . . cries all the time," and a landlady who is a "fat, ugly, mean, stupid, unwashed, misanthropic, cheap, drunken bag of garbage." He is a man out of society and out of control. Peter is Albee's archetypal insider, insulated but vacuous, who "wears tweeds, smokes a pipe, carries horn-rimmed glasses," and lives in the East Seventies with "one wife, two daughters, two cats and two parakeets," a fifties man who predates the culture clashes and role definitions of the sixties.

The women in this play appear only through the twisted memories of Jerry or the innocent reflections of Peter. All stereotypical characterizations of women, however, do appear, and, filtered largely through the mixed-up memories of Jerry, they emerge full force, tumbling into the hostile atmosphere of Albee's anti-female universe. That has been described as the product of a homosexual tirade, an American absurdist tableau, or a fragmented conversation about the inability of humans to communicate, locked as they are in racial, social, economic, and gender no-exit zones. As in Albee's later plays, these women are powerful and pathetic, damaging or deranged, vulgar and vicious, impinging on the spaces of men with damaging regularity.

The landlady [in *The Zoo Story*] is one of Albee's most unattractive women (she has plenty of competition for this dubious honor), and it is difficult to sympathize with her in a culture in which we are socialized to detest the licentious, out-of-control female. Actually, her out-of-control behavior is less damaging than Jerry's, but it is perceived as more detestable because it emanates from a woman.
—*Mickey Pearlman*

Jerry speaks first about his now dead "good old Mom" who "embarked on an adulterous turn of our southern states," the anti-earth mother as slut and alcoholic, whose "most constant companion . . . among others, among many others . . . was a Mr. Barleycorn." She is the prototypical Albee female—a symbol of betrayal, lust, and debasement—always the victimizer even when she seems helpless. The characterization is made more vicious and inexorable by its implied contrast to the usual explication of mother figure as dependable, sacrificing saint, a role usually created and then derogated by male writers. The strong implication is that she is responsible for Jerry's preoccupation with whores, the "pretty little ladies" whom he never sees "more than once" since he's "never been able to have sex with, or, how is it put? . . . make love to anybody more than once." And, he adds, "puberty was late . . . I was a h-o-m-o-s-e-x-u-a-l- . . . queer, queer, queer" for "eleven days . . . with the park superintendent's son." Mother love, in American fiction and drama frequently the source of emotionally crippled and childish or brutal heroes, is, in its absence, the genesis of a character similarly crippled who deserts his prostitutes as his mother deserted him. American literature is littered with the corpses of men who have been smothered by affection; here we are presented with the unmothered vision. "Good Old Mom" has a sister "who was given neither to sin nor the consolation of the bottle," who "did all things dourly: sleeping, eating, working, praying. She dropped dead on the stairs to her apartment . . . on the afternoon of my high school graduation. A terribly middle-European joke . . ." The untainted saint who never strays replaces the tainted sinner who always strays, but she also betrays Jerry by her emotional absence and inconvenient death. She is in attendance, but absent, and proves to be a disappointing mother figure who disappears in a dramatic and arbitrary moment, as did "Good Old Mom." The aunt is Albee's stereotypical version of the enervated, long-suffering woman as silent sufferer whose most lasting legacy is an unloved and empty male victim who feels betrayed, in different ways, by her sacrificial approach to reality. And Jerry is annoyed by her, and hostile to her memory, because her role as sacrificer and saint figure is part of his emotional powerlessness and his sense of social impotence. "Good Old Mom" and her sister are followed by the previously mentioned "lady living on the third floor, in the front." Her crying is "muffled, but . . . very determined. Very determined indeed," an unnamed Greek chorus of one, ostensibly helpless, because her response to life is unexplained weeping. She evokes in the reader neither pity nor pathos, nor is Jerry interested in finding out the source of her pain. In fact, her helplessness annoys him and reminds him of his own pain. But she serves as direct contrast to Jerry's central antagonist, the landlady (and her dog), "the gatekeeper[s]" of rooming house as Hell, whose trademark is vulgarity and who does not conveniently keep her pain behind closed doors. Jerry tells Peter that after "she's had her mid-afternoon pint of lemon-flavored gin she always stops me in the hall . . . presses her disgusting body up against me to keep me in a corner . . . The smell of her body and her breath . . . you can't imagine it." The landlady is a comic figure who lusts not only after Jerry but also after recognition, contact, and acceptance. In her daily, self-induced stupor, she cannot distinguish between reality and illusion. Jerry says that he has "found a way to keep her off. When . . . she presses herself to my body and mumbles about her room and how I should come there, I merely say: but, Love; wasn't yesterday enough for you, and the day before? . . . a simple-minded smile begins to form on her unthinkable face, and she giggles and groans as she thinks about yesterday and the day before; as she believes and relives what never happened. Then, she motions to that black monster of a dog she has, and she goes back to her room. And I am safe until our next meeting." The landlady is one of Albee's most unattractive women (she has plenty of competition for this dubious honor), and it is difficult to sympathize with her in a culture in which we are socialized to detest the licentious, out-of-control female. Actually, her out-of-control behavior is less damaging than Jerry's, but it is perceived as more detestable because it emanates from a woman.

[*The Zoo Story*] has often been said to be about alienation and the noncommunication that signifies the mechanized, urbanized, supposedly civilized western world. But in a feminist rereading, it is also an American absurdist work that, in its anger, displays all the usual stereotypical visions of women and enlarges the endless canon of plays, stories, and novels that agonize over the predicaments of men by further diminishing the emotional, sexual, and spiritual needs of women.
—*Mickey Pearlman*

When Jerry mixes rat poison into the hamburgers with which he tries secretly and unsuccessfully to neutralize the dog's power over him and to increase his power over the dog, the landlady turns from obnoxious aggressor to a "sniveling" antagonist who begs Jerry to "pray for the animal." The dog, which Jerry calls "malevolence with an erection," eventually recovers its former malicious state, having learned nothing about power. The landlady "recovered her thirst, in no way altered by the bowwow's deliverance." The dog returns to his previously vicious state, the landlady to her bottle, and Jerry to his nether-nether world where "neither kindness nor cruelty by themselves, independent of each other, creates any effect beyond themselves . . . the two combined . . . are the teaching emotion. And what is gained is loss."

The stereotypical woman as materialist and manipulator surfaces in Jerry's allusions to Peter's wife. She is unnamed, but in Jerry's eyes she is both powerful and incomplete. ". . . you're not going to have any more kids, are you?" says Jerry. "Is it your wife?" "That's none of your business!" Peter replies in fury, but adds: "Well, you're right. We'll have no more children." She is another woman who has failed, having produced two daughters but no sons. Peter points out that this is determined genetically, but he absorbs Jerry's accusatory point of view, although he knows that, scientifically, it is a ridiculous charge. They do have two cats. "But, that can't be your idea. No, sir. Your wife and daughters? (*Peter nods his head*)."

Peter's wife is in charge of one of the three demarcated spaces, or zoos, that Albee creates. She serves as zookeeper of the East Side apartment, a civilized institution of children, family, and jobs that marks the parameter of Peter's world. The landlady guards the gates of one rooming house-as-zoo that symbolizes the lonely, entrapping spaces of the societally displaced, most of whom are females or male homosexuals. The park becomes a symbolic microcosm of society as zoo, where dissimilarly caged animals, including the human variety, exist guardedly in an antagonistic state. All space delineations are limited and defined—the East Side apartment, the West Side rooming house, and the park bench over which the final, fatal fight occurs. The bench represents both safety and freedom to Peter; it is his space away from space. As he says, ". . . I see no reason why I should give up this bench. I sit on this bench almost every Sunday afternoon, in good weather. It's secluded here; there's never anyone sitting here, so I have it all to myself." For Jerry, the bench is initially an object of power and control ("Get off this bench, Peter; I want it"), a concrete symbol of his attempt to manipulate and dominate Peter and to become the chief zookeeper of the park as society. He sees the bench as part of his effort to make contact, to communicate, to be acknowledged at any cost. His efforts to jar Peter into acknowledging him and the encounters over the bench are replicated in his encounters with the dog. The setting changes—Jerry in the rooming house, the zoo, the park—but the common denominator of all three encounters is violence and encoded brutality. He is fierce and friendless, but there is something here that feminists who examine the silent loneliness of brutalized women will recognize—the desperate and pathetic need to be heard and to have that pain assuaged. How Jerry forces Peter to listen is part of what Emory Lewis called a "masochistic-sadistic interplay . . . [which reflects] a murky, homosexual milieu," with Jerry as the male partner and Peter playing the part of diffident, nonaggressive female, moving at Jerry's insistence into a smaller, more limited space (the end of the bench). Then he is trapped, defenseless, furious, and helpless. He says: ". . . I'm a responsible person, and I'm a GROWNUP. This is my bench, and you have no right to take it away from me." Similarly, the landlady's dog has been appropriating the space of the hallway, making Jerry into a defenseless, furious, and helpless victim.

The play ends as Jerry impales himself on his own knife that Peter is holding "with a firm arm, but far in front of him, not to attack, but to defend," and with Jerry's words: "Peter . . . Peter? . . . Peter . . . thank you. I came unto you (*He laughs, so faintly*) and you have comforted me. Dear Peter," and his final assurances to Peter that "you're not really a vegetable . . . you're an animal." These words have evocative New Testament and sexual overtones intertwined. The new designation was won apparently through Peter's inadvertent involvement with violence. What Jerry is saying is that Peter is no longer acting like a woman—at least an Albee woman—who deserts ship (bench), drops dead, silently weeps, or lives in a hermetic or fantasy world.

This play has often been said to be about alienation and the noncommunication that signifies the mechanized, urbanized, supposedly civilized western world. But in a feminist rereading, it is also an American absurdist work that, in its anger, displays all the usual stereotypical visions of women and enlarges the endless canon of plays, stories, and novels that agonize over the predicaments of men by further diminishing the emotional, sexual, and spiritual needs of women.

2

The American Dream, first performed in 1961, is a showcase for the four characters who also appear in *The Sandbox* (1960), a fourteen-minute sketch. Both plays are "an examination of the American Scene, an attack on the substitution of artificial for real values in our society, a condemnation of complacency, cruelty, emasculation and vacuity; it is a stand against the fiction that everything in this slipping land of ours is peachy-keen."

Twenty-eight years later, in 1989, American society is still not "peachy-keen," having endured, if not improved, through decades of Vietnam scar tissue, a generation of yuppies, and thirty years of ardent consumerism. America as marketplace has recently been elevated to an art form by eight years of a Washington glitzkrieg defined more by style than substance. Because it is American society in the fifties that Albee marks as "vapid, barren, and sterile . . . absurd and meaningless," *The American Dream* is both current and dated. For example, Albee would undoubtedly find plenty of material for act 2 in the hostile takeovers, Love Canals, AIDS epidemic, bridges falling down across America, insider trading scams, and drug-infested streets of the eighties to make the point again that noncommunication, artificiality, and false values are corruptive and destructive. But almost thirty years later, in a feminist rereading, it is doubtful that any audience will so blithely accept Mommy, Mrs. Barker, and Grandma, an odious triumvirate, as the matriarchal Murder, Inc. of the family and its natural legacy, society.

Mommy, who is emasculating, efficient ("I can get satisfac-

tion, but you can't") and cruel, is Albee's bad (American) dream, reducing Daddy, with snarls and sarcasm, to pathetic impotence. She is invested by Albee with tremendous power; Daddy is divested of energy and masculinity. Daddy is vague, respectful, and boring ("I am paying attention, Mommy"), like an over-disciplined child: rich but not powerful, an unlikely specimen in the U.S.A., where money and options are natural soulmates. He has been reduced by Mommy to the role of supplicant and cipher. As Mommy announces blatantly, "I have a right to live off of you because I married you, and because I used to let you get on top of me and bump your uglies; and I have a right to all your money when you die." "And aren't you lucky all I brought with me was Grandma. A lot of women I know would have brought their whole families to live off you. All I brought was Grandma." Daddy's role now is to put up with "it" and to shut up about it.

The problem with Mommy as female victimizer figure for the eighties is that few women in the audience want or expect to earn a gold Bloomingdale's charge card for thirty years of sexual service, and there are happily few, if any, men who would make this unspeakable, if unspoken, contract. In the eighties, Mommy's exaggerated power and manipulative skills would not be wasted on an unattractive wimp like Daddy but would most probably find their natural outlet on the playing fields of Wall Street, in board rooms of America, or in Silicon Valleys coast to coast. Woman as bloodsucking vampire figure is passé, although mothers, wives, and matriarchs are still suspect.

Mrs. Barker, a hermaphroditic screamer, "the chairman [sic] of your woman's club," is presented as an amoral pimpette who delivers "bumbles." (". . . I'm such a busy girl, with this committee and that committee, and the Responsible Citizens Activities I indulge in." The "bumbles," i.e., male babies, represent innocence and love and are delivered by her from the "Bye-Bye Adoption Service" to the Mommys and Daddys of America. Mrs. Barker is deeply committed, of course, like Mommy, to the unimportant non-issues—like the color of her hat. She is a veritable chargé d'affaires of the triviality and insensitivity of women à la Albee. ("What an unattractive apartment you have!", etc.) To quote Mommy, "She's a dreadful woman, you don't know her; she has dreadful taste, two dreadful children, a dreadful house, and an absolutely adorable husband who sits in a wheel chair all the time . . . She's just a dreadful woman, but she is chairman of our woman's club, so naturally I'm terribly fond of her."

Grandma, who is "feeble-headed" and "cries every time she goes to the johnny as it is," has spent the last twenty years of widowhood as an unpaid live-in servant to Mommy and Daddy. She is buried alive in *The Sandbox* and is immured in a sea of boxes in *The American Dream.* Grandma is a pitiful figure. ("Old people are very good at listening; old people don't like to talk; old people have colitis and laven-der perfume.") She is waiting for the arrival of the imagi-nary "van people" for a journey to an unnamed oblivion, the natural repository of the aged in Albee's U.S.A. They are expendable, dispensable, and disposable. As she says, "Old people aren't dry enough, I suppose. My sacks are empty, the fluid in my eyeballs is all caked on the inside edges, my spine is made of sugar candy, I breathe ice . . . old people are gnarled and sagged and twisted into the shape of a com-plaint." Her life, which consists of "some old letters, a couple of regrets . . . Pekinese . . . blind at that . . . the televi-sion . . . my Sunday teeth . . . eighty-six years of living . . . ," is packed in boxes in the smaller, confined spaces al-most always associated with women in American literature, and the spaces get smaller and more confining as her vic-timization nears completion.

The three women, therefore, epitomize the worst stereotypes of American females—Mommy is the evil, all-powerful emasculator; Mrs. Barker is the déclassé, intellectually va-cant instigator; and Grandma is the pathetic, ill-used, and nameless saint figure—Albee's offering of a treacherous trin-ity of female fates fatale.

The two men, of course, are victims, and more importantly they are innocents. ("You're the American Dream, that's what you are.") They are not party to the materialism and tawdriness that Albee is trying correctly to deride. Daddy's worst sin is that he has turned into an incompetent vegetable who "has tubes now, where he used to have tracts." This is hardly a surprising turn of events in an Albee Mommy-world dominated by an egregious stereotype, the Rambo of domes-ticity gone wrong. The Young Man, who represents what Albee believes America most adores—youth, beauty, and a modicum of brainpower—who will "do almost anything for money," recalls the sensory potential lost in the same way that a money-maddened, commercialized society devalues whatever cannot be arbitraged or sold short. The "bumble," we are told, had its eyes gouged metaphorically right out of its head; it cried its heart out, its eyes, heart, tongue, and hands were sacrificed, but "first, they cut off its you-know-what," and "it finally up and died." The Young Man is the twin of his castrated, blind, and adopted brother, the empty American ideal, the "bumble of joy" provided by Mrs. Barker. "I no longer," he says, "have the capacity to feel any-thing. I have no emotions. I have been drained, torn asun-der . . . disemboweled . . . I am incomplete . . . I can feel nothing . . . And it will always be thus."

The point is that there is no mattress beneath the American dream, and the sleeper is caught in an unending nightmare of vulgarity and crassness. For many theatergoers, that part of Albee's vision may still ring true. His implicit idea, how-ever, is that the malignancies ("I do wish I weren't sur-rounded by women . . .") that pervade the American

experience stem from the confused, craven, or contemptible influence of women. Women as enemies of the Dream is merely empty bombast, an outdated, outlandish vision of an angry young man of the sixties. In a feminist rereading, Mommy, Grandma, and Mrs. Barker seem to be only over-blown cartoon characters who predate what has been learned in the last twenty-eight years about the victimization of women and the pain of men. *The American Dream* is only a familiar, if painful, artifact of the historically long-lived vision of women as the progenitors and perpetuators of the end of Paradise and the decimators and destroyers of the potentially utopian ideal.

Marian Faux (review date December 1994)

SOURCE: A review of *Three Tall Women*, in *Theatre Jour-nal*, Vol. 46, No. 4, December, 1994, pp. 541-3.

[*In the following review, Faux provides a laudatory assess-ment of* Three Tall Women.]

Edward Albee's third Pulitzer prize-winning play *Three Tall Women* is a meditation on a woman's life and mortality clev-erly viewed from three different stages (no pun intended) of life: youth, middle age, and old age. In the first act, a woman known only as "A," played splendidly by English actress Myra Carter, who originated the role at Vienna's English Theatre in June 1991 (see *Theatre Journal*, 44: 251-52), is a stately and very rich powerhouse trying to come to terms with her diminished powers—physical, mental, and emo-tional.

As is usual in Albee plays, what is clear is also often con-tradictory. A's character being no exception, she was born to a lower-middle class family, to parents who may, or may not, have been overly strict, or overly permissive. In any event, they send her to live in New York City. Her mission: To marry rich. Because A has no fortune of her own, her choices are limited, and she ends up marrying a rich, short, one-eyed man whose wit and fortune are real enough but whose social cachet is obviously yet to be determined by her. By her own account, A does her job admirably, and she and her husband end up an American version of horsey country gentry.

A is attended by a crone named B, "crone" being the only word to describe Marian Seldes' first-act performance as A's solicitous (but perhaps malicious), mostly kind (but perhaps cruel) caretaker.

Also present when the play opens is a beautiful young law-yer—C—who has come to visit in order to lecture A on her financial affairs. (She's played by Jordan Baker.) With her beauty and youth, C is incapable of either sympathy or empathy, unable to imagine that she could ever turn into a peevish, impotent old woman. She's impatient at having to listen to the reminiscences of A, even though A was once a great beauty like herself.

Act 1 ends abruptly when A suffers a stroke in mid-sentence. In a wonderful kind of reversal of fates that can only happen in the theatre, in act 2 C does become A—at a slightly insipid and narcissistic twenty-six years of age. The only surprise from her is her determination to have a little fun before she settles down to a marriage that she openly acknowledges will be more about business than love. Carter's character becomes herself about twenty years earlier, still spritely and full of a kind of wisdom that had abandoned her in act 1. Most miraculously, B is transformed into A in sumptuous middle age, a woman truly in her prime. The women spar with one another to show what really happened, or should have happened, in their lives.

If a middle-aged A had the best perspective, an elderly A is the most contemplative, the most capable of parsing out what exactly it was that she accomplished—or failed to accomplish. She no longer cares about the luxurious surroundings she's spent her entire life struggling to obtain, and in fact is no longer sure the struggle was worth it: "It's all glitter," she observes. But her young self disagrees: "No, it's tangible proof we're valued."

This is a highly personal play. In countless interviews, Albee has said he wrote it as a kind of exorcism of his adoptive mother, who, he claims, never learned to like, let alone love him. If so, he appears to have come to terms with their relationship, including how she lived her life, and even manages to be quite generous toward her—and by extension, to other women like her. While making the point that this is a world where all women are kept in one way or another, he still manages to see what it took for her to survive. "They all hated me because I was strong," A recalls. "Strong and tall."

Albee is especially empathic to the middle-aged A. In our ageist society, where a woman's power is widely viewed as declining in direct proportion to her age (and diminishing beauty), he introduces a novel idea, namely, that age fifty can be as satisfying to a woman as to a man. Age fifty really was the best time, an elegantly mid-life Marian Seldes pronounces, the only time when "you're really happy," when you "get a 360-degree view" of your life.

James Noone has designed a set that is appropriately Park Avenue WASP—heavy draperies; a small French chair; a large, well-dressed bed; lush fabrics; and small pillows laden with fringe and braid. It all implies a sort of order than cannot be invaded by the outside world—although in this play, it is indeed order, of a most personal sort, that is crumbling

before our eyes. At various times, both C and B (the latter playing a middle-aged A) smooth the fringe on the same pillow. To the elderly A, though, the pillow no longer symbolizes anything. Order in her life now boils down to her daily struggle against the ravages of a weak bladder.

For a playwright who has built a career around challenging audiences with his minimalism and obscurantism, it's ironic that Albee's two most successful plays, *Who's Afraid of Virginia Woolf* and *Three Tall Women,* are his most accessible and also his most traditional, more so in their staging but also in their language and ideas. Can it be that his adoptive mother's death has freed him to confront his demons more directly than he has done in past plays? Like Tennessee Williams, the family—his family—has always been his great subject, but rarely has he managed to write about it with so little personal rancor.

Robert Brustein (essay date 1994)

SOURCE: "The Rehabilitation of Edward Albee," in *Dumbocracy in America: Studies in the Theatre of Guilt, 1987-1994,* Ivan R. Dee, 1994, pp. 204-9.

[*In the following excerpt, Brustein responds favorably to* Three Tall Women, *which he characterizes as "a mature piece of writing."*]

A number of years ago, while praising Edward Albee's much-reviled stage adaptation of *Lolita,* I commented on the startling reverses in the fortunes of this once lionized American dramatist: "The crunching noises the press pack makes while savaging his recent plays are in startling contrast to the slavering sounds they once made in licking his earlier ones. . . . If each man kills the thing he loves, then each critic kills the thing he hypes . . . brutalizing the very celebrity he has created."

I was generalizing not only from Albee's career but from that of Miller, Williams, and Inge, for although I had often depreciated works by these playwrights myself, it struck me as unseemly that mainstream reviewers were displaying such fickleness toward their favorite Broadway sons. This may sound territorial, but it's not. Readers expect highbrow critics to express dissent about an overinflated dramatic work, but it is an entirely different matter when those with the power to close a show become so savage and dismissive in their judgments. If it is a function of the weekly critic to try to correct taste, it is the function of the daily critic to guide theatregoers, not to trash careers or demolish reputations.

Fortunately, Albee's stubborn streak has kept him writing in the face of continual disappointment, a persistence he shares with a number of other artists battered by the New York press (Arthur Miller, David Rabe, Arthur Kopit, Christopher Durang, Philip Glass, and so on). I call this fortunate because Albee has a vein of genuine talent buried in the fool's gold, and, as I wrote then, there was always a hope, provided he was not discouraged from playwriting, that this would appear again in a world of some consequence. That work has now arrived in *Three Tall Women* (Vineyard Theatre), and I am happy to join his other former detractors in saluting Albee's accomplishment.

Three Tall Women is a mature piece of writing, clearly autobiographical, in which Albee seems to be coming to terms not only with a socialite foster parent he once satirized in past plays but with his own advancing age. Three women are discovered in a sumptuously appointed bedroom decorated with Louis Quatorze furniture, a rare carpet, and a parquet floor. They are called A, B, and C, which suggests a Beckett influence, though on the surface the play appears to be a drawing-room comedy in the style of A. R. Gurney. The oldest of the women is an imperious rich invalid (A) who appears hobbling on a cane, her left arm in a sling. She is attended by a middle-aged companion (B), an angular woman with a caustic tongue and a humped back, and a young politically correct lawyer (C) who has come to discuss A's business affairs.

[In *Three Tall Women*,] A is an entirely vicious old wretch, with a volatile tongue and a narrow mind, but it is a tribute to the writing and the acting that she gradually wins our affections.
—*Robert Brustein*

The first of the two acts examines some scratchy transactions among this symbiotic trio, consisting of A's recollections (clearly not in tranquility) and the shocked reactions of her companions. A has turned sour and abrupt in old age, and there are traces of Albee's celebrated talent for invective in her rage against life. Her spine has collapsed, she has broken her arm in a fall, and now the bone has disintegrated around the pins. Likely to wet herself when she rises from a chair ("A sort of greeting to the day—the cortex out of sync with the sphincter"), she is inordinately preoccupied with the aging process—"downhill from sixteen on for all of us." She even wants to indoctrinate children with the awareness that they're dying from the moment they're born, and anyone who thinks she's healthy, as C does, had better just wait.

In short, A is an entirely vicious old wretch, with a volatile tongue and a narrow mind, but it is a tribute to the writing and the acting that she gradually wins our affections. Although prejudiced against "kikes," "niggers," "wops," and

"fairies" (among them her own son), she is a model of vitality and directness when compared with the humor-impaired liberal democrat C, who protests A's intolerance. A remembers a past of supreme emptiness, of horse shows, dances, and loveless affairs, and particularly of the time her husband once advanced upon her with a bracelet dangling from his erect penis ("I can't do that," she said, "and his peepee got soft, and the bracelet fell into my lap"). That arid marriage, and the son who brings her chocolates but doesn't love her ("He loves his boys"), represent memories that can bring her to tears. They also bring A to a stroke at the end of the first act, as she freezes in mid-sentence describing her deepest family secrets.

Act II begins with A lying in bed under an oxygen mask. By this time B has been transformed from a sardonic hunchbacked factotum, slouching toward Bethlehem like Igor or Richard III, into a stately middle-aged matron in pearls, while C has become an elegant debutante in pink chiffon. Before long they are surprisingly joined by A, newly rejuvenated (the figure in the bed is a dummy), and the play shifts gears into a story of one woman at three different moments in time (A at ninety, B at fifty-two, and C at twenty-six). Just as B has shed her hump and C her primness, A has lost her feebleness. All three share the same history, the same child, the same sexual experiences, but A and B are united against C in their hatred of illusions. They warn C that her future will be one of deception and infidelity: "Men cheat a lot. We cheat less, but we cheat because we're lonely. Men cheat because they're men."

Beckett was the first dramatist to condense the past and present lives of a character into a single dramatic action, and *Krapp's Last Tape* is a play to which *Three Tall Women* owes a deep spiritual debt. . . . Beckett compressed youth and age through the device of a tape recorder; Albee uses doppelgangers; but both plays evoke the same kind of existential poignance.
—*Robert Brustein*

The prodigal child, now a young man carrying flowers, returns to sit by the bedside of his dying mother ("his dry lips on my dry cheeks"), silent and forlorn. None of the women will forgive him, nor will they forgive each other. A dislikes C, and C refuses to become A, while B bursts out bitterly against "parents, teachers, all of you, you lie, you never tell us things change." The inevitability of change is responsible for the obscenities of sickness, pain, old age, and death, but A, having accepted her fate, affirms that "the happiest moment is coming to the end of it." Taking a deep breath, she allows the action and her life to stop.

Beckett was the first dramatist to condense the past and present lives of a character into a single dramatic action, and *Krapp's Last Tape* is a play to which *Three Tall Women* owes a deep spiritual debt (it was also the companion piece to Albee's first New York production, *The Zoo Story*, in 1960). Beckett compressed youth and age through the device of a tape recorder; Albee uses doppelgangers; but both plays evoke the same kind of existential poignance. . . . Most of us have encountered horrible old women like A, fuming over their pain and helplessness. It is Albee's personal and professional triumph to have made such a woman fully human. His late career is beginning to resemble O'Neill's, another dramatist who wrote his greatest plays after having been rejected and abandoned by the culture. Happily, unlike O'Neill, he may not have to wait for death to rehabilitate him.

Jeane Luere (essay date Spring 1995)

SOURCE: "An Elegy for Thwarted Vision: Edward Albee's *The Lorca Story: Scenes from a Life*," in *Journal of Dramatic Theory and Criticism*, Vol. IX, No. 2, Spring, 1995, pp. 143-7.

[*In the following essay, Luere examines* The Lorca Story: Scenes from a Life, *in which, he asserts, Albee presents "an elegy for an artist's thwarted vision."*]

For over three decades, Edward Albee's controversial drama has kept him in the critical and public consciousness. With self-assurance, Albee has disregarded commercial pressure, experimented with dramatic form, and thrust innovative theater at his audiences. How natural, now, to find Albee evolving a play on artistic freedom. His present venture, *The Lorca Story: Scenes from a Life,* is more than a political or social tract; it is an elegy for an artist's thwarted vision.

The play's protagonist, Federico Garcia Lorca (c. 1900-1936), was the Spanish poet-playwright executed during the Fascist reign of General Francisco Franco. With two acts, ten scenes, and pageant-like structure, Albee takes us inside the soul of a casualty. Still in progress, the play dramatizes Albee's views on the thwarting of Lorca's literary vision by state and church throughout Franco's forty-year reign. Lorca had written his "unorthodox" poetry and plays when censorship momentarily lessened with the birth of the short-lived Second Republic (proclaimed in 1931). Without being an agit-prop piece, the drama is in part a polemic on the plight of artists in a culture that restricts and censors their work. Albee gives Lorca an appeal to us to feel the pain of curbed creativity: "Do you know what it's like to be me."

Like Albee's *Three Tall Women,* whose script was written

in 1991 but kept "in progress" until 1994, his *Lorca Play* will proceed to commercial venues when Albee deems it ready. The play was commissioned in 1992 by the Houston International Festival Committee for its "Centennial Celebration of Spain and the New World"; the project also entailed a trip to Spain for Albee's research on Lorca's life. Audiences applauded the Festival production for its freshness and relevance to our own culture's problems with censorship and diversity. The critics' reaction was mixed, some finding the play "timely and apt," "stirring and evocative," others hoping to view it again when Albee completes his "fleshing-out of characters and relationships."

Rather than belabor us with didactic monologues on repression, Albee uses parody to approach the parallels between Lorca's culture and our own. With Franco on stage in military uniform and the Cardinal in formal vestment, Albee's script quips, "Don't lose sight of *them* . . . it's people like that who run the world—people who define our faith, who give us our identity." Albee's lines alert us that "they" could be anywhere: "Sometimes they don't wear those uniforms; sometimes a suit and tie does them just fine; sometimes a suit and tie does them even better." Houston critics picked up on the parallels: one wrote that Franco's denunciation of Lorca's work "could have been lifted from a stump speech damning the N.E.A.'s funding of obscene and outside-the-mainstream art"; another critic echoed him, recalling "America's current art wars" in which writers had to "fend off attacks on their artistic content." Albee's action shows both Franco and the Catholic Cardinal harassing Lorca: Franco loathes his writing for its jabs at totalitarian rule, and the Cardinal threatens to excommunicate him for non-standard religious concepts.

Albee's play spans Lorca's life from childhood to sudden death. To stage the writer's hapless altercations with the church and state, a three-level set is used: the stage floor for the play's action, a mid-level with small platforms reached by stairs at either side of the stage, and, above continuing stairs, a catwalk extending across the stage. Albee places characters on levels appropriate to their relevance in the play's gruesome central conflict. General Franco and his Aide-de-Camp sit or stand on the top level Stage Left, and on the right, the Catholic Cardinal and his priest, where all sit in judgment on the thoughts, activities, and writings of the poet-playwright on the stage below. Our concentration shifts when spots go up or down on the catwalk or lower levels where Lorca, his family, and the play's ensemble actors mingle.

To give the audience a full acquaintance with his protagonist, Albee wants us "to see *all* of Lorca, not just the statue," to perceive him as "sad, funny, and even just plain silly," and to follow him from his youth to his death at thirty-six. For this purpose, Albee's script abandons Joseph Wood

Krutch's concept of "an identifiable and continuous self" for the role of Lorca. Albee had first envisioned three actors to depict the protagonist at different ages. Even before rehearsals, the playwright's careful objectivity led him to simplify the concept to two rather than three characters—Young Lorca and Lorca-as-adult—who often must appear on stage simultaneously. At times, they appear with their family, friends and figures from Spanish culture; in other scenes, while Young Lorca remains on stage, Adult Lorca must appear to cross the world, watch the Wall Street crash, dance with Cubans, then reappear abruptly in his home environment. The dialogue Albee has written for the two Lorcas reveals the love of the earth that lies in Lorca's poems and plays. Phrases like "the taste of blood and soil in my mouth," "a rip in the skin of the earth," show Lorca's immersion in nature, his blending of "poetic imagery with primitive passions"; many lines come from the pages of *Blood Wedding* (1933) and *Yerma* (1934), dramas considered "the finest Spanish works since the Golden Age."

To acquaint us with the culture that shaped Lorca as person and artist, Albee's scenes reach toward the land and people of Spain, "the country which birthed him . . . and the country which killed him." In action on the set's floor level, we see Young Lorca following the plow in Granada's countryside; we watch as Adult Lorca's spirited thoughts and antics upset distinguished friends and mentors like Salvador Dali and Manuel DeFalla; and we learn for ourselves that famous writers are human. Lorca meets and loses lovers, succeeds and fails with poems and plays. In the action, we also view comic and tragic scenes from Lorca's plays with actresses portraying Lola Membrives and Margarita Zirgu, famous Lorca thespians of the 1930s. Albee's dramatic choices disclose his protagonist's love of surrealism, symbolism, naturalism and his active involvement in theater and folklore.

To lift us over spans of time and space in the play's action, Albee has chosen an omniscient Narrator to stand at the set's mid-level platform and see all. With the heads of church and state high above the stage, he can get them out of our way by calling up, "You four go into limbo now," at which their space darkens until the playwright wants them back into action at an earlier (or later) chronological period. Then the Narrator will call, "You can come back now," and we move on undismayed through the years in which Franco and the Cardinal had inveighed against Lorca's artistic freedom, taken away his life, and for decades thereafter, hidden his literary legacy. At one point the Narrator may lean from his platform to point toward the boy on the first level, and reassure viewers that "The young Lorca stays with us of course . . . doesn't our young self always stay with us—lurk around the edges of our consciousness?" Albee's research in Spain confirmed the author's child-like nature; a Lorca letter reads, "In the depths of my being is a powerful desire to be a little child, very humble and very retiring."

Albee also uses his Narrator in droll scenes to mock the bogus ethics of the self-righteous clergy. When Act II begins, with Cardinal and Priest missing from their places near Franco and his Aide, the Narrator looks off, stage-right, and barks, "Would you two get out here, please?"; and his Aide suggests, "I think it's what they might have *been* doing." When the upbraided two slip in and begin to mount the stairs, we see the Cardinal "buttoning the front of *his* gown, followed by the Priest, pulling down the back of *his* gown," and we hear the Cardinal mutter, "All right! For heaven's sake." Although Albee tastefully keeps all other scenes between Cardinal and Priest (and between Lorca and his acknowledged intimates) tightly restrained rather than emotionally flamboyant, here he lets us smile very mildly at the hypocrisy of the church's ban on diversity.

To deride the states' brutal drive for conformity, Albee gives Franco and his Aide street-and-gutter-level language. When Franco offers asinine excuses for eliminating dissenters, Albee lets him brag coarsely that after he "saved the country from itself," there were "some people [who] just didn't make the cut, if you catch my drift . . . weren't worth talking about anymore. . . ." When the Narrator objects, "Oh, I see . . . so Lorca's name vanished, eh? . . . his poems taken out of print," Franco replies, "Yeah, like that. He wasn't worth the trouble . . . Who cares? Commie faggot!"

It was Lorca's theater work that deviated most pointedly from the state's main-line precepts. Albee's script sets up inescapable parallels, albeit unlabeled by Albee, with his own plight in the 1960s when a Pulitzer committee rejected ***Who's Afraid of Virginia Woolf?*** for supposedly offensive language and content. The criticism and publicity that Albee received at the time, though similarly unfair and damaging, proved less irrevocable, eventually, than the censorship Lorca faced for his unique dramas. In ***The Lorca Story***, Albee has an actor refer to a news report that charged Lorca with "perverting the peasants" through staged displays "of shameful promiscuity . . . of free love," and with "obedience to the dictates of Jewish Marxism, free love, and communism." Albee's Franco explicitly names the actors "atheists" and "homosexuals." Historically, Lorca had become active in the group to revive the "rancid and stagnant" Spanish theater from its "dead reproductions of the classics and escapist junk"; he preferred "theater for the *people*, about them." His insistence that theater "should immerse itself in the problems assailing humanity" resembles Albee's own drive for fresh and useful theater in the early 1960s. From start to finish, Albee's through-line for ***The Lorca Play*** is that Lorca's haunting, idealistic vision for theater was political poison for him in a Fascist country that subordinated the individual—creative artist or not—to the combined will of church and state.

To mock the inescapable outcome of church and state collusion, Albee gives amusing scenes with the Cardinal toadying to the overbearing egoism of Franco. Albee's dialogue lets Franco boast to the Cardinal, "My mother was a saint!", to which the Cardinal mumbles only, "She was?" But Franco quickly insists, "You don't think my mother was a saint?" The fawning Cardinal replies, "I do, I do . . . if you say she was a saint, she was a saint!" At another spot, Albee ridicules the church's subservience to the state by forcing Franco to overhear the Narrator's jest, "There's talk of making Isabella a Saint . . . shows you what a few good works can do!" (In Spain's early years, Isabella is said to have ordered her country's gypsies, Jews, and Arabs, "Convert or be killed!")

To end this requiem on the thwarting of Lorca's vision by political pressures, Albee chooses as his backdrop a full-sized canvas facsimile of Goya's "Executions of the Third of May." His choice broadens the relevance of Lorca's execution. Goya's canvas displays a group of Madrilenos facing a firing squad, with one young man flinging up his arms in opposition to the soldiers. Conceivably, the man could have cried out "This isn't fair!" By creating on stage a mirror of the Goya masterpiece, Albee dramatizes Spain's tragic loss: a lifetime of productivity from a literary giant. This finale confirms Albee's grasp of art and history, and heaps philosophical weight onto artists' protests against the narrowness of political and social repression—"This isn't fair."

William Hutchings (review date Autumn 1995)

SOURCE: A review of *Three Tall Women,* in *World Literature Today,* Vol. 69, No. 4, Autumn, 1995, pp. 799-80.

[In the following review, Hutchings examines Three Tall Women, *comparing it to works by Samuel Beckett.]*

Identified only as B and C, two of the three tall women of Edward Albee's Pulitzer Prize-winning drama are engaged in a deathwatch for the third, the ninety-two-year-old, bedridden, bitingly sarcastic A. B, according to Albee's production notes, "looks rather as A would have at 52," while C "looks rather as B would have at 26." In the first act the three are distinctly separate characters, generationally different but sometimes overcoming their mutual incomprehensions. The second act, however, perpetrates an intriguing, Pirandello-like change: the three generations represented on stage are no longer three separate people in the room at one time but *one* person at three separate ages in her life. As in the first act, though from an entirely different and newly subjective perspective, the women's interactions and mutual interrogations mingle past and present, youth and age, memory and desire.

> **With its relatively static dramatic form, its thanatopsic subject matter, and some of its specific imagery, *Three Tall Women* has strong affinities with a number of Samuel Beckett's shorter plays.**
> **—*William Hutchings***

Albee's three-page introduction provides particularly candid insights into his personal animus—in both senses of that word. The character of A is based on

> . . . my adoptive mother, whom I knew from infancy . . . until her death over sixty years later. . . . We had managed to make each other very unhappy over the years. . . . It is true I did not like her much, could not abide her prejudices, her loathings, her paranoias, but I did admire her pride, her sense of self. As she moved toward ninety, began failing both physically and mentally, I was touched by the survivor, the figure clinging to the wreckage only partly of her own making, refusing to go under.

Nevertheless, he insists, the play is neither a "revenge play" nor a search for "self-catharsis."

With its relatively static dramatic form, its thanatopsic subject matter, and some of its specific imagery, *Three Tall Women* has strong affinities with a number of Samuel Beckett's shorter plays. The second act's poignant juxtaposition of past and present selves resembles *Krapp's Last Tape,* though Albee depicts them as physical presences on stage rather than as a technologically evoked absence—and each can interrogate the others. The voices of Beckett's *That Time* are similarly identified as A, B, and C and are all the single character's own, coming from three distinct points in the darkness; the presence of the women for the deathwatch also suggests, in varying ways, *Footfalls, Rockaby,* and *Come and Go.* After much weeping (which Beckett's characters never do) and after talk of "going on" (that most familiar Beckettian refrain), A, dying, attains "the point where you *can* think about yourself in the third person without being crazy"—as in Beckett's *Not I.* In the final speech of Albee's play, A concludes that life's "happiest moment" is "coming to the end of it [her own existence]"—attaining (perhaps) the oblivion for which, futilely, many of Beckett's characters yearn.

With its realistic set of "a 'wealthy' bedroom" rather than the ominous darkness of the Beckettian void, with characters of a specific and privileged social class, *Three Tall Women* domesticates the dramatic territories that Beckett so relentlessly, evocatively, and innovatively explored. They have now been made accessible and—in every sense—plain.

James Campbell (review date 11 October 1996)

SOURCE: "The Habit and the Hatred," in *Times Literary Supplement*, No. 4880, October 11, 1996, p. 23.

[*In the following excerpt of a review of* Who's Afraid of Virginia Woolf?, *Campbell surveys the history of the play.*]

It is worth remembering, while enduring the three-and-a-half hour comic nightmare of *Who's Afraid of Virginia Woolf?*, that the play emerged from the Theatre of the Absurd. Albee's early one-acters, such as *Zoo Story* and *The American Dream* (in which a couple have gruesomely disposed of one of their sons in order to fit the picture of the American way of life), suggested a line of inheritance from Adamov and Ionesco. *Who's Afraid of Virginia Woolf?*, written in 1961 and first performed in the following year, was a departure: a well-made play, with a domestic setting, replete with wider references from the "world of ideas", particularly relating to science and civilization. In spite of its surface naturalism, however, the underlying spirit of this play draws on the farcical despair of Albee's dramatic mentors as much as his earlier work. It is the Theatre of the Absurd brought to your own fireside. In George and Martha's perfectly plausible living-room, where the young and innocent guests (innocent until now, that is) are introduced to the party games, Humiliate the Host, Get the Guests and Hump the Hostess, things get so mad and bad that the audience thinks they cannot get worse—whereupon they do.

> There can be few people who have left a production of *Who's Afraid of Virginia Woolf?* talking about its allusions to Spengler and Anatole France's novel *Penguin Island* (1908), a proto-*Brave New World* fantasy in which science would rule over human choice.
>
> —*James Campbell*

The ghost of childhood dominates *Who's Afraid of Virginia Woolf?* It is, of course, the play about bringing up the baby that doesn't exist—the "son" on whom Martha dotes and about whom she insists on boasting to the guests. The younger couple, Nick and Honey, have problems of their own, what with hysterical pregnancies and induced miscarriages. Yet each of the four principals is trapped in childhood, unable to grow up. The playwright has pursued variations on this theme ever since, from *The American Dream* (1960), where the child doesn't exist because it has been cut to pieces, to *Three Tall Women* (1991), a semi-autobiographical work with a dominant non-speaking part given to a young man who is seated by the bedside of his estranged, now dying, mother. Albee's latest, according to

the programme for this production, is actually called *The Play about the Baby.*

Who's Afraid . . . is also, less happily, the play about Western Civilization. The war between George and Martha rages side by side with another, between George, the professor of history, and the new-generation biology teacher Nick, whose personal and professional vigour greatly interest Martha. There can be few people who have left a production of *Who's Afraid of Virginia Woolf?* talking about its allusions to Spengler and Anatole France's novel *Penguin Island* (1908), a proto-*Brave New World* fantasy in which science would rule over human choice (for which read: Nick will rule over George). This perennially topical theme seems tired and affected in the play, as do further intended enlargements of the couples' discontents, signalled by the fact that George and Martha share Christian names with the first American President and his wife, and that the campus on which the men teach is called "New Carthage".

It is, rather, as a portrait of a marriage that *Who's Afraid* . . . has secured a place in the modern repertoire. . . .

It is unusual for a play's success to be measured against a cinematic version, but so it is with productions of *Who's Afraid of Virginia Woolf?*, which are inevitably compared to Mike Nichols's 1966 film, with its famed performances by Richard Burton and Elizabeth Taylor. Though it makes good viewing, the film relied on a truncated and altered script, with an added outdoors sequence, which fails to entrap the audience in the long night's journey into day of a good theatrical production.

FURTHER READING

Criticism

Campos, Carlos. "The Role of *Beyond the Forest* in *Who's Afraid of Virginia Woolf?*" *Literature/Film Quarterly* 22, No. 3 (1994): 170-3.
    Studies the significance of the film *Beyond the Forest* in terms of character, theme, and plot.

Herr, Denise Dick. "The Tophet at New Carthage: Setting in *Who's Afraid of Virginia Woolf?*" *English Language Notes* XXXIII, No. 1 (September 1995): 63-71.
    Discusses the degree to which the ancient city of Carthage and classical myths inform the setting of *Who's Afraid of Virginia Woolf?*

Kerjan, Liliane. "Pure and Simple: The Recent Plays of Edward Albee." In *New Essays on American Drama*, edited by Gilbert Debusscher and Henry I. Schvey, pp. 99-108. Atlanta, GA, and Amsterdam: Rodopi, 1989.

> Examines *The Lady from Dubuque, Listening,* and *Counting the Ways.*

Luere, Jeane. A review of *Sand. Theatre Journal* 46, No. 4 (December 1994): 543-44.

> A favorable assessment of *Sand.*

Roth, Philip. "The Play That Dare Not Speak Its Name." *New York Review of Books* 4, No. 2 (25 February 1965): 4.

> Highly negative assessment of *Tiny Alice.*

Sterling, Eric. "Albee's Satirization of Societal Sterility in America." *Studies in Contemporary Satire* 14 (1987): 30-9.

> Delineates Albee's negative portrayal of American society in *The Zoo Story* and *The American Dream.*

Additional coverage of Albee's life and career is contained in the following sources published by Gale: *Authors in the News,* **Vol. 1;** *Concise Dictionary of American Literary Biography,* **1941-1968;** *Contemporary Authors,* **Vols. 5-8R;** *Contemporary Authors Bibliographical Series,* **Vol. 3;** *Contemporary Authors New Revision Series,* **Vols. 8, and 54;** *DISCovering Authors; DISCovering Authors: British; DISCovering Authors: Canadian; DISCovering Authors Modules: Dramatists and Most-studied; Dictionary of Literary Biography,* **Vol. 7;** *Major Twentieth-Century Writers;* **and** *World Literature Criticism.*

Eavan Boland

1944-

(Full name Eavan Aisling Boland) Irish poet and critic.

The following entry presents an overview of Boland's career through 1997. For further information on her life and works, see *CLC,* Volumes 40 and 67.

INTRODUCTION

After struggling to find a place in the mainstream Irish literary canon, Boland has become a significant Irish poet. In a country with a strong patriarchal tradition, Boland has risen above classification as a minor "women's writer" to become an internationally studied poet. In her work she retains Irish mythology and lyricism while introducing feminist themes, uncommon in Irish literature.

Biographical Information

Boland was born in Dublin in 1944 to Irish diplomat Frederick H. Boland and painter Frances Kelly. She spent most of her childhood in London and New York while her father served Ireland beginning in 1950 as Irish Ambassador to the Court of St. James and then in 1956 as the President of the United Nations General Assembly. Boland found her time in London especially difficult due to the prevalent prejudice against the Irish. She would later write in both poetry and prose about the feeling of exile she felt during this period. When Boland returned to Dublin as a teenager, she continued to feel alienated from her culture because she did not speak Gaelic and was not raised in her own country. In 1959 Boland attended boarding school at the Holy Child Convent in Killiny, County Dublin. This time was very important to her development as an artist because she reconnected with her country and found the solitude at the school conducive to writing poetry. She published a pamphlet of poems called *23 Poems* in 1962 and began studies at Trinity College the same year; she received degrees in English and Latin in 1966. After graduation, she became a lecturer in the English Department at Trinity. Boland quickly became disenchanted with academic life, however, and left the university to pursue a career as a literary journalist and to write poetry. In 1967, she published a collection of poetry entitled *New Territory.* In 1969, Boland married novelist Kevin Casey and moved to Dundrum, a suburb of Dublin. Much of her subsequent work centers on her life as a wife and mother. Largely ignored but quietly building a reputation, Boland first stirred controversy with *In Her Own Image* (1980). The work brought Boland into debates over femi-

nism and the role of the woman poet in Ireland. Since then Boland has been an ardent voice for the equity of opportunity for female poets in the male-dominated literary climate of Ireland. More than just a vehicle for a cause, however, Boland's poetry has brought her international recognition as a literary figure.

Major Works

As Boland began writing poetry, she realized that her only models came from the patriarchal male-centered poetry of Irish literary tradition. Women were portrayed as decorative icons of Irish unity. Instead of abandoning national myths, however, Boland attempted to subvert traditional myths in her poetry and present an alternative look at women. Her style and themes developed slowly throughout her career. Her early poems were traditionally lyric and heavily influenced by William Butler Yeats. These early volumes were traditional in their focus and subject matter, but they touched upon issues that would later consume Boland's writing, including her examination of the role of women in Irish literature and society. Boland's style and themes underwent a drastic change with *In Her Own Image,* which addresses the difficult subjects of child abuse, wife abuse, anorexia, mastectomy, and victimization. The poems analyze female identity and challenge male-centered thinking by centralizing the experiences of the female body in short-lined stanzas which she refers to as "the anti-lyric." In *Night Feed* (1982), Boland again tackled the issue of female identity by looking at the domestic lives of women often overlooked in poetry and in Ireland's national myths. She used as her models the still-lives and domestic interiors of painters Jean-Baptiste Chardin and Jan Van Eyck. By turning to painting for her inspiration, Boland created a visual feel in the poems of this volume. The poems in *The Journey* (1983) expand the themes in *Night Feed* and continue to use the lives of women to redefine what it means to be Irish. The volume contains several poems which subvert the romanticized images of women found in Irish mythology. In this volume Boland also raises questions about the corruption and exclusion of art and the dangers of its use for ornamentation.

Critical Reception

Reviewers considered Boland a straightforward lyric poet with the publication of her first few volumes. Denis Donoghue stated, "When she published her first book of poems, *New Territory,* in 1967, it was hard to distinguish her voice from the common tone of English poetry at large: worldly, cryptic, Larkinesque." Many pointed out how much Boland's early poetry owed to Yeats, some criticizing Boland for imitation. Although Yeats was a strong influence on her poetry, critics noted her subversion of his themes. Most critics viewed Boland's *In Her Own Image* as a departure from the style and themes of *New Territory* and *The War Horse* (1980). Often reviews of this and subsequent works focused on Boland as a feminist, rather than as a poet. Many reviewers dismissed *In Her Own Image* as being too focused on feminine issues and some even found the themes offensive. The volume caused a stir and reviewers began characterizing Boland as a "women's writer." With *Outside History* (1990), Boland received critical acclaim in the United States which eventually brought her mainstream attention and praise in her own country. Critics disagree about whether Boland is more successful in her domestic or more politically oriented work. William Logan stated, "Poems of quiet desperation in the kitchen do not form an original aesthetic. . . . When Ms. Boland stops being the bard of fabric . . . she is truest to her own culture and most deeply coiled in its falseness." Other reviewers, however, found Boland's use of domestic scenes and topics a brave move for the poet, and preferred these poems to her more politically charged work. In recent years, reviewers have praised Boland for her unique presentation of women and political issues and her fusing of individual lives to public myths in her work. R. T. Smith asserted, "Reminding us that art is perhaps the most fruitful venue for the collaboration of public and private interests, [Boland] provides us with not only a map, but a compass as well, and perhaps a thirst for the journey."

PRINCIPAL WORKS

23 Poems (poetry) 1962
New Territory (poetry) 1967
W. B. Yeats and His World [with Michael MacLiammoir] (nonfiction) 1970
The War Horse (poetry) 1980
In Her Own Image (poetry) 1980
Introducing Eavan Boland (poetry) 1981
Night Feed (poetry) 1982
The Journey (poetry) 1983
A Kind of Scar: The Woman Poet in National Tradition (nonfiction) 1989
Selected Poems (poetry) 1990
Outside History: Selected Poems, 1980-90 (poetry) 1990
In a Time of Violence (poetry) 1994
Object Lessons: The Life of the Woman and the Poet in Our Time (nonfiction) 1995
An Origin Like Water: Collected Poems (1967-1987) (poetry) 1996

CRITICISM

Jody Allen-Randolph (essay date March 1991)

SOURCE: "Ecriture Feminine and the Authorship of Self in Eavan Boland's *In Her Own Image,*" in *Colby Quarterly,* Vol. XXVII, No. 1, March, 1991, pp. 48-59.

[*In the following essay, Allen-Randolph discusses the relationship among the poems in Boland's* In Her Own Image, *the female body, and the representation of women in patriarchal culture.*]

Alternately praised by the mainstream Irish literary establishment for her control, technical mastery, classicism, and lyric ear, and as frequently dismissed for her choice of subject matter, Eavan Boland has contributed significantly to the current debates concerning canon reformation and the nature of women's writing. Concurrent with attempts to marginalize Boland's poetry in Ireland is a steadily growing critical acclaim in the United States, where her poetry and essays have appeared regularly in *American Poetry Review, Partisan Review, Parnassus,* and, more recently, in *Contemporary Literature, Georgia Review, The New Yorker,* and *The Atlantic Monthly.* And although in the past year or two feminist critics have begun to accord Boland increasing attention, remarkably little has been said of her intricate explorations of the relationship between writing and gender, particularly notable in *Night Feed* and the more polemical 1980 volume *In Her Own Image.*

Written on the upswing of the French feminist movement linking sexuality to textuality in the late seventies, *In Her Own Image,* Boland's third major volume, was perceived by Irish, British, and North American critics alike as a major departure, eruption, and even mutation from the style and themes of her earlier volumes, *New Territory* and *The War Horse.* While recurrent images of imprisonment and claustrophobia in the earlier volumes can be seen retrospectively to hint at the thematic direction of the subsequent poems, *In Her Own Image* marks a period of experimental writing for Boland, a concentrated and focused experiment with what is now popularly referred to as *ecriture feminine,* writing located in and authorized by fundamental female experience: "writing the body." Ann Rosalind Jones's description of this principle, when applied specifically to *In Her Own Image,* provides an apt gloss to the volume's structure: "to the extent that the female body is seen as a direct source of female writing, a powerful alternative discourse seems possible: to write from the body is to recreate the world."

Positing the female body as the source and origin of the voice to be heard in all female texts, Helene Cixous sees an essential link between feminine writing and the female body.

By female texts she does not necessarily mean texts written exclusively by women, but texts which exhibit a particular kind of marked writing, "a decipherable libidinal femininity." In this context, femininity in writing can be read as a privileging of the voice where "writing and voice are woven together"; thus the speaking woman is entirely her voice: "She physically materializes what she is thinking; she signifies it with her body."

Cixous' theorization of feminine/female writing as a way of reestablishing a spontaneous relationship to the physical *jouissance* of the female body can be read as a utopian vision of female creativity in which change is both possible and desirable. In Cixous' poetic vision of writing, expressing the body's desire through language is an act of liberation. It is precisely this liberating function of ecriture feminine, I will argue, that Boland engages in *In Her Own Image.*

Alternately praised by the mainstream Irish literary establishment for her control, technical mastery, classicism, and lyric ear, and as frequently dismissed for her choice of subject matter, Eavan Boland has contributed significantly to the current debates concerning canon reformation and the nature of women's writing.
—*Jody Allen-Randolph*

Generally, a utopian vision takes off from a negative analysis of its own society in order to create images and ideas which have the power to inspire revolt against oppression and exploitation; this is arguably the net result, if not the point, of the first half of *In Her Own Image,* which probes such painful social problems as child abuse, wife abuse, and anorexia. The body, as Elizabeth Meese has noted, "is the site where the political and the aesthetic interpret the material." Boland makes this relationship explicit in the first five poems of the sequence with such stark titles as **"In Her Own Image," "In His Own Image," "Anorexic,"** and **"Mastectomy."** These opening poems make clear the connection between the female body and the body politic by staging an encounter between a generic Muse, erected by patriarchal culture as a kind of symbolic and ideal womanhood, and the suffering bodies of "real" women who are victimized by their acceptance of these patriarchal representations.

In the volume's opening poem, **"Tirade for the Mimic Muse,"** Boland interrogates masculinist representations of Woman by exposing and exploding the concept of a traditional female muse she ironically calls "Our Muse of Mimic Art," a title rich with parodic and religious associations. The

Mimic Muse, the "she" and "you" of the poem, is the female object of inspiration constructed by a masculinist discourse and within a masculine conception of aesthetic decorum. After an initial three-stanza outburst of incrimination ("I know you for the ruthless bitch you are: / Our criminal, our tricoteuse, our Muse—"), the speaker switches to a strategy of wily juxtaposition; the symbolic *Woman* is forced to confront the actual lives and suffering of ordinary *women,* women whose eyes are "lizarded" and "nipples whiskered" by an aging process to which the Mimic Muse is immune, both by the "deceits" of cosmetic application and by (male) definition.

In the opening stanzas Boland fashions the Mimic Muse from violent physical metaphors: she is a "slut," a "fat trout," poaching her face in "candle-stink." But halfway through the poem, her technique changes; she turns away from the distorting lens of metaphor to see the violence directly. Caught within the woman's poem, the Mimic Muse is forced to observe the exigencies of female experience whence she fled:

> The kitchen screw and the rack of labour,
> The wash thumbed and the dish cracked,
> The scream of beaten women,
> The crime of babies battered,
> The hubbub and the shriek of daily grief
> That seeks asylum behind suburb walls—
> A world you could have sheltered in your skirts—
> And well I know and how I see it now,
> The way you latched your belt and itched your hem
> And shook it off like dirt.

The following and final stanzas deepen Boland's condemnation of an aesthetic practice which segregates writing from the lived experience of (female) writers. Depending upon the Mimic Muse for direction, the lyric "I," here the female poet, recounts how she "mazed my way to womanhood / Through your halls of mirrors, making faces . . ." until, one day, surrounded by domestic debris, she has her epiphany:

> In a nappy stink, by a soaking wash
> Among stacked dishes
> Your glass cracked,
> Your luck ran out. Look. My words leap
> Among your pinks, your stench pots and sticks,
> They scatter shadow, swivel brushes, blushers.
> Make your face naked,
> Strip your mind naked,
> Drench your skin in a woman's tears.

In a final statement which is both a forecast of the poems to follow and an aesthetic credo, the speaker declares: "I will wake you from your sluttish sleep. / I will show you true reflections, terrors," implying that the reflections spawned by the Mimic Muse are false representations. Thus, as the poem ends, the patriarchal muse to which women writers have looked for definition and reflection is forced, by reversal, to look into "our mirrors. / Look in them and weep."

Immediately following **"Tirade for the Mimic Muse"** is a pair of poems which has as its central theme the ways that female identity gets distorted within patriarchal discourse. The first poem of the pair, **"In Her Own Image,"** explores the horrifying interiority, dangerous confusion, and retarded psychological development of a female speaker who has just strangled her own child. Strangely distanced in tone, subtle and extremely nuanced, the poem begins by contrasting the gold irises of the dead child's eyes with the speaker's wedding ring, an ironic framing of the speaker's estrangement from her primary relationships. In the next stanza, the eyes, like the ring, are distanced by "light years," which collapse in the third stanza into a confused series of negative definitions. Unable to describe herself in terms other than what-she-is-not, the speaker finds herself unable to extricate her sense of herself from her sense of her daughter. Having defined her daughter in terms of fragmentation (eyes, irises), she defines herself in terms of lack: "She is not myself / anymore, she is not / even in my sky / anymore and I am not myself." This fundamental confusion and alienation of identity at the core of the poem provides the psychological backdrop for what turns out to be a ritual of family violence; the death is revealed to be an act of self-hatred by a woman who has confused her own body with that of her female child. The speaker's roving identity, unfixed and unstable, confusing self and other, is in a state of retarded development. Not recognizing herself as a discrete subject, her boundaries are fluid, shifting. She perceives herself as a mess of uncoordinated movements and feelings rather than as a whole, constructed self.

Because the speaker cannot "see" herself, she is left without a positive sense of herself as a discrete body and an awareness of externality or otherness. As Lacan tells us, this lack of a sense of the other is extremely critical, for Lacan links the discovery of the other to our becoming social beings; without it we become overly attached to early, fluid fixations of identity, unable to adapt them as necessary to life's demands. In the speaker's confusion, the child becomes a former self, for whom she conducts an elegy as she buries her in the back garden at the poem's end. She wears "a family heirloom" of "amethyst thumbprints," "a sort of burial necklace" which hints at a sinister strangling of identity and loss of innocence through physical abuse, both in the speaker's actions and in her previous experiences of family. The only concession to identity is made in the final stanza where, after burying the former self/daughter in a garden safe from "surprises," the speaker tells us she "will bloom there, / second nature to me, / the one perfection among compromises." Thus the family ritual of violence upon female iden-

tity becomes, quite literally, the ground for a future, compromised identity.

Taking its cue from the foggy, brutalized identity of **"In Her Own Image,"** the companion poem, **"In His Own Image,"** begins with an incantatory echo of its precursor: "I was not myself, myself," and it too traces the connection between female identity and violence. Perhaps functioning as a palimpsest to the previous poem, as the source of the "family heirloom" of violence behind the violence of mother towards child, this poem explores the tragic consequences when women accept imposed masculinist systems of representation and expression. Searching for her identity among the "meagre proofs" of daily domestic debris (celery feathers, stacked cups, bacon flitch) and finding only fragments of her reflection (a cheek, a mouth) in the distorting mirrored surfaces of pot lids and tea kettles, the speaker experiences her identity as something fundamentally unstable:

> How could I go on
> With such meagre proofs of myself?
> I woke day after day.
> Day after day I was gone
> From the self I was last night.

This dilemma is resolved when the "he" of the poem comes home drunk and batters her into "a simple definition" by splitting her lip, blackening her eye, "knuckl[ing her] neck to its proper angle," and giving her a concussion "by whose lights I find / my self-possession, / where I grow complete."

> **Like ["In Her Own Image"], "In His Own Image" functions on the level of psychological realism by sketching a chillingly intimate view of domestic sexual violence.**
> **—*Jody Allen-Randolph***

"Coming to herself" means coming back to her body through the pain of the beating. She describes her domestic attacker as an artist; he is a "perfectionist" with "sculptor's hands" who summons form (her form, her image) from the "void" of her identity. The last line, "I am a new woman," vibrates with satire, inviting comparison between advertising images of the new woman stereotype and this woman's horrific reality. She is a new woman only in the sense that male violence has remade her into its image. Like the previous poem, **"In His Own Image"** functions on the level of psychological realism by sketching a chillingly intimate view of domestic sexual violence. However, in its use of the artist figure as the agent of the abuse, it also attempts a symbolic conjunction between the male victimizer and the patriarchal discourse which claims and defends authority over the powers of representation. Man, imitating the God of his Christian narrative of origin, is creating woman "in his own image." Man is the sculptor; he has the rights of definition and creation, and in her acceptance of his power woman is complicitous.

Boland continues her exploration of the relationship between female identity and victimization in the next poem, **"Anorexic,"** where she shifts her attention from child abuse and wife abuse to self-abuse. Using anorexia both as an illness and as a metaphor for culture, Boland probes the relationship between anorexia and myths of human origin which fashion women as virgins or whores. Building on the idea established by the previous poems, that alienation from the female body is a symptom of the violence directed toward female identity, **"Anorexic"** turns inward that alienation and its attendant violence. The speaker discusses her body as something separate from her; her body is an "it," a "bitch" with "fevers," a "witch" she is "burning." Alienation deepens into a sexualized self-hatred as the self-denial of food is transformed into a denial and rejection of female selfhood altogether: "Yes, I am torching / her curves and paps and wiles. / They scorch in my self-denials."

Anorexia is identified not only as a hatred of the female body but as a violent desire to annihilate it, "I am starved and curveless. / I am skin and bone. / She has learned her lesson." Subverting both female form and its biological origins in a maternal body, the speaker desires the shape of the phallic rib and "a sensuous enclosure" in a male body. Equating "foodless" with "sinless," spiritual purity with the atrophy and denial of a specifically female body, she yearns to decline herself back into the masculinist narrative of creation as Adam's rib: "I will slip / back into him again / as if I had never been away." Mythic narrative becomes blurred with physical reality as she speaks of accomplishing her return to the male body, where she will "grow angular and holy" in "only a few more days."

In the final two stanzas the anorexic structure of the poem, with its pared-down, three-line stanzas, fleshes out to a five-line description of the pre-anorexic female body. Here form imitates content as the penultimate stanza "falls" into the final stanza, in which female sexuality is described as a fall from (the) grace of the male body into the female body with its "python needs / heaving to hips and breasts." The speaker not only wishes to reverse this fall but to forget it, to erase from memory as from existence its catalogue of disembodied fragments: hips, breasts, lips, "and heat, and sweat and fat and greed."

On the level of representation, **"Anorexic"** shows how, within the masculine socio-cultural economy, accepted definitions, physical and spiritual, can impinge tragically upon women, shaping their ideas of themselves and their relation to their bodies. On the level of language and metaphor, the anorexic "fall" away from the female body, into a narrative of origin beginning and ending in the male body, becomes a model for the woman writing, representing herself within a masculinist discourse. The argument implicit in the poem, as in the poems preceding it, is the danger, undesirability, and even tragedy, of women, writers and otherwise, recognizing their "places" or finding their bearings within a masculinist system of definitions, representations, and narratives.

Exactly halfway through the volume, the focus shifts. The negative analysis of culture and victimization which fuels the first five poems gives way to an empowering, pleasure-based, even playful form of ecriture feminine. The next five poems, comprising the second half of the volume, champion a writing practice grounded in female experience, a practice which uses the female body as both vehicle and cipher, as both the site of female knowledge and writing and the interpreter of the knowledge unearthed. Thus *In Her Own Image* not only describes the feminine within a masculinist socio-cultural economy but also reinscribes it—simultaneously unwriting and underwriting the practice of representation.

While these poems—**"Solitary," "Menses," "Witching," "Exhibitionist,"** and **"Making Up"**—retain the insights of the previous poems, they suggest that a female-centered writing practice cannot emerge from the hollow shells of selfhood presented by the speakers of **"In Her Own Image," "In His Own Image," "Anorexic,"** and **"Mastectomy."** Instead of interacting with masculinist representations of female identity, as did the first half of the volume, these poems go about the task of reinscribing female identity from the experience of the female body and feminine pleasure.

According to Cixous, the discovery of desire necessarily precedes the discovery of a writing practice grounded in female pleasure and power. This process of discovering desire begins with the reappropriation of the body. Repossession of the body, in turn, encourages the speaker to seek selfhood and, later, to assert that selfhood through written language.

In *In Her Own Image* Boland recognizes a similar link between sexuality and textuality, but her insights function more on the level of content than of style. While Cixous envisions a new language based upon the rhythms of the body, Boland envisions a new aesthetic which reconceptualizes the body as a subject for poetry and as a mode of knowing. Thus in **"Solitary,"** a poem which explores and graphically documents female masturbation, desire functions not simply as the reality of the self but also as discovery of a mode of understanding, previously repressed. Desire is both the truth and the knowledge of the female self; it is not an abstraction, but an uncensored and embodied force to which the speaker abandons herself:

> no one's here,
> no one sees
> my hands
>
> fan and cup,
> my thumbs tinder.
> How it leaps
>
> from spark to blaze!
> I flush
> I darken.
>
> How my flesh summers.

Here the speaker desires not the body of her lover, but the pleasure of her own body, newly discovered, intimate and alien beyond all others, incomparably exciting.

By staging this masturbation scene at night, in "a chapel of unreason," the speaker suggests the female body as the source of a feminine spirituality, an empowering alternative to the encroaching male myth of origin in **"Anorexic."** The masturbating speaker is a "votary," "worshipping" in the "shrine" of female genitalia, her body a source of "sacred heat." In the fifth stanza, this alternative spirituality is juxtaposed to the prohibitions of the more orthodox spirituality of the Catholic Church, which teaches that masturbation is a mortal sin:

> You could die for this.
> The gods could make you blind.
> I defy them.
> I know,
> only I know
>
> these incendiary
> and frenzied ways.

The pleasure of the female speaker is a site of resistance and a territory of knowledge known only to herself ("only I know"), an observation echoed by Cixous in "The Laugh of the Medusa": "It is at the level of sexual pleasure in my opinion that the difference makes itself most clearly apparent in as far as woman's libidinal economy is neither identifiable by a man nor referable to the masculinist economy." Thus the orgasmic cry in the twelfth strophe which "blasphemes / night and dark" blasphemes masculinist discourse because it "makes word flesh," female flesh. An exuberant, sexualized creation has taken place, screaming "land from sea," giving form and flesh to female pleasure in its representation of a female sexual and spiritual identity based in the female body, "animal" and "satiate."

Boland's experiment in challenging male-centered thinking with a writing practice that foregrounds the experiences of the female body and its desire continues in the following poem, **"Menses,"** with an exploration of menstruation. However, as Luce Irigaray points out, women's discovery of their autoeroticism will not, by itself, enable them to transform the existing patriarchal discourse, nor will it arrive automatically: "for a woman to arrive at a point where she can enjoy her pleasure as a woman, a long detour by the analysis of the various systems which oppress her is certainly necessary." **"Menses,"** like **"Solitary,"** traverses territory absent from male discourse and transforms what has been defined by culture as a natural female handicap into a source of female empowerment.

In Ireland, as in most Western countries, periods are defined and controlled by exterior, cultural restraints. One hides one's sanitary napkins or tampons, and as French feminist materialist critic Christine Delphy has remarked, this "hiding appears to be the expression of the shame which in fact caused it." By exposing to public view in her poetry that which has been ignored and hidden as shameful by her culture, Boland revalues parts of female experience devalued within society. **"Menses"** is a refusal to devalue menstruation as a handicap, yet it denies none of menstruation's physical discomfort. The poem moves from a description of the physical sensation of menstruation: "I am sick of it, / filled with it, / dulled by it, / thick with it," to images of lunar entrapment and an analysis of menstruation as a force which binds the female speaker to a dioecious sexual practice. The speaker envies certain of her garden weeds which can reproduce independently:

> How I envy them:
> each filament,
> each anther bred
> from its own style,
> its stamen,
> is to itself a christening,
> is to itself a marriage bed.

Finally, she embraces menstruation precisely because of its relation to her sexual desire, as a part of what drives her to "moan / for him between the sheets" and "know / that [she] is bright and original / and that [her] light's [her] own." Again, female desire becomes both the truth and the knowledge of the self as the speaker discovers the potency and function of the female body and sets out to bring its value into the cultural discourse through the restructuring of a writing which flows from the experience of the body.

Having examined the first seven poems, one is tempted to critique Boland for subscribing to a narrow ultrarealist feminist aesthetic that considers "reality" and fidelity to lived experience as the highest goals of poetry, the truths of which must be rendered by literature. Indeed the statement of intent in the opening poem, "I will show you *true* reflections," would seem to substantiate this criticism of a reflectionism in the volume which has, so far, suggested that literary creation be measured against the female poet's perception of "real life" as experienced by the female body. However, in the next two poems, **"Witching"** and **"Exhibitionist,"** Boland anticipates this critique, playfully positing "the real" as something we construct, and a controversial construction at that.

> **What is most striking about Boland's change of technique and subject matter in** *In Her Own Image* **is not a deployment of anti-lyric, but rather her enlargement of the lyric mode to include aspects of experience from which it had previously remained detached. The site of this liberating new swelling of the lyric tradition is the experience of the female body, unsentimentalized, unprettified, and anti-lyrical.**
> —*Jody Allen-Randolph*

Both poems deal with writing as a mode of female transgression, informed by the poststructuralist insight that writing does not stand in a transparent relation to life or to reality. Re-invoking a category of female persecution by patriarchal culture, a category which had its roots in unresolved infantile fear of maternal omnipotence, Boland playfully and imaginatively "reverses the arson" by exploding the category in **"Witching."** The speaker is a writer figure, a witch who plays upon and delights within the male fear of an unrestrained, aberrant and devouring female sexuality. The writer/witch decides to "singe / a page / of history / for these my sisters / for those kin / they kindled" by making "a pyre" of her "haunch":

> and so
> the last thing
> they know
>
> will be
> the stench of my crotch.

The poem becomes a self-consuming artifact as the writer/witch claims "her turn" at fueling the fire and smelling "how well / a woman's / flesh / can burn." Thus the poem simultaneously and subversively re-invokes the image of the witch, laughs at and offends the sensibilities which created the category, and claims the power of representation both of the image and of its destruction. It is indeed "her turn."

"Exhibitionist" works along much the same lines, starting out with a gleeful presentation of writing as female exhibitionism, a double taboo in western society, and ending with a celebratory explosion of the category of exhibitionism out of the frame of realist representation into a powerful female imagination which is "unyielding," "frigid" (meaning in this context unresponsive to male lust), and "constellate." At the beginning of the poem, the writer awakens and "starts / working from the text" of the received "trash / and gimmickry / of sex." She is constructing, or rather salvaging, what she terms "her aesthetic" from the debris of received ideas about female sexuality, the "clothes / that bushelled me / asleep." She is liberating her aesthetic from those repressive packagings by writing the female body: "a hip first, / a breast, / a slow, shadow strip." She is "nippling the road" of tradition, "subvert[ing] sculpture, / the old mode," "dimpl[ing]" its "clay," "rump[ing]" its "stone." This process of writing the body is telescoped into the single phrase: "I flesh."

Having freed the female form and image, this powerful aesthetic then eclipses tradition, "blacks light," and becomes the night, "harvesting stars to its dark," and humbling phallic symbols and images of male power:

> Cast down
> Lucifers,
> spruce
> businessmen,
> their eyes cast down.

The poem ends by reversing conventional views of lust. Lust becomes a female desire to burn a dominating, self-created image of her own body into the discourse, to turn the tables of representation:

> Into the gutter
> of their lusts
> I burn
>
> the shine
> of my flesh.
> Let them know
>
> for a change
> the hate
> and discipline.
>
> the lusts
> that prison
> and the light that is
>
> unyielding
> frigid
> constellate.

Thus both poems, **"Witching"** and **"Exhibitionist,"** use writing and image making as modes of female transgression. Desire in these poems becomes a counterimpulse, and feminine writing, its expression, mischievously constructs counterimages which parody and explode received masculinist constructions.

The final poem of *In Her Own Image* makes more modest claims for a feminist aesthetic, exposing its predecessor, **"Exhibitionist,"** as a utopian ideal, an energizing myth rather than a model for how all women should write. The speaker in **"Making Up"** is once again a figure for the female artist. She wakes to her "naked," "pre-dawn" face, and "prinks" and "raddles" her blushers, eyeshadows, and lipsticks until her "face is made." Recognizing that all identities are constructions, the speaker's face tells the reader: "Take nothing, nothing / at its face value: / Legendary seas, / nakedness." The two stanzas which follow compact the ethos of the entire volume into a singsong, moral-of-the-story lyric. Like the speaker's make-up job, myths are "a trick," "made by men." But "the truth of this / wave-raiding / sea-heaving / made-up / tale" is also "made-up," and it is the writer's "own." She has managed, as Boland recently wrote of Sappho, "to harness the lyric tradition to her own private statement."

In an interview with Deborah Tall in 1987, Boland describes the sharp departure from her earlier style to the pared-down, short-lined stanzas of *In Her Own Image* as a determination "to write the anti-lyric"; "I was very conscious of the fact that the lyric as I had known it had been a constraint on me as a woman . . . but on the other hand these were degraded states." However, what is most striking about Boland's change of technique and subject matter in *In Her Own Image* is not a deployment of anti-lyric, but rather her enlargement of the lyric mode to include aspects of experience from which it had previously remained detached. The site of this liberating new swelling of the lyric tradition is the experience of the female body, unsentimentalized, unprettified, and anti-lyrical.

The female body in this volume functions as both subject which transgresses masculinist modes of representation and as an object which is de-scribed and re-inscribed. In this double role, it presents itself as a medium for connecting the contexts rent by relegation to the realm of "oppressor" or "oppressed." Boland's poetic practice turns specifically female experience into a powerful artifact that bears witness to the lived experience as well as the imaginative experience of woman. In many ways this is an act of recontextualization; using the limited materials at her disposal, the sticks and rouge pots, to color her own body and describe her own surroundings replicates an activity Boland implicitly ascribes to women in general: making up, the title of the volume's closing poem. In this way Boland recasts making up, both

the application of cosmetics and the narrative practice, as part of a heritage that she shares with a larger community of women, and one they can continue to participate in positively, taking responsibility for coloring in their own shades rather than those imposed by the patriarchal ideal.

By converting the action of making up into the poem **"Making Up,"** Boland makes clear the process by which physical female experience is converted into artifact. Because making up functions simultaneously as metaphor for a female decorative art, for self-creation, for literary creation, and for the oppression which created made-up images and myths inhospitable to women, it performs the recontextualizing so important to the volume as a whole. It accomplishes this both by constructing a female tradition out of the present self-liberating and utopian moment and by recuperating a past in that tradition which connects her with the silent artistry of other women. By subsuming the past in the present and vice versa, Boland is able, in the volume's final stanza, to point towards a future rather than remain in the angry exposition of the past and present which opened the volume; in a final symbolic act of repossession she declares:

> Mine are the rouge pots,
> the hot pinks,
> the fledged
> and edgy mix
> of light and water
> out of which
> I dawn.

It is the speaker's lyric "I" who gives these color tools their significance. As their repossessor and interpreter, she becomes the cipher that connects artistic endeavor to a specifically female heritage and experience.

In the same way, she makes the female body—its sensations and experiences—serve this ciphering function throughout the volume. By making the female body both the vehicle and the source of the discovery of a female knowledge repressed by masculinist discourse, as well as the interpreter of what is discovered, Boland casts her speaker(s) as an object lesson in both the reading and the authorship, the "making up" of self—the embodied connection between female experience and artistic expression. In this experimental role she attempts to create a context which will nourish the rituals of a previously nonexistent tradition of women's poetry in Ireland, one which posits an essential bond between female writing practice, female experience, and the female body.

"Making Up" is an affirmation that language need not remain as just an index and register of female grief over and estrangement from a patriarchal discourse which constructs feminine identity in its own image. The theme of the poem, and of the volume, is the necessity for the woman poet to re-image women and reshape tradition by feeling her way into words which dignify, reveal, and revalue female experience in all of its complexity. At the end of the final poem, when the speaker reclaims the truth, the tale, and the rouge pots as her own, we are in a place pregnant with possibility, a place where language and flesh have reached at least a provisional angle of repose. Each shines through the other for a brief lyric moment.

Eavan Boland with Nancy Means Wright and Dennis J. Hannan (interview date Spring 1991)

SOURCE: "Q. and A. with Eavan Boland," in *Irish Literary Supplement*, Vol. 10, No. 1, Spring, 1991, pp. 10-11.

[*In the following interview, Boland discusses the place of female poets in Irish literature.*]

[*Means Wright and Hannan:*] *A first-rate Irish woman poet would appear to receive less recognition in Ireland than even a third-rate male poet. Do you find this to be true?*

[Boland:] I was on a panel in Boston recently at a festival of Irish poetry, and exactly that point was with me. In the audience there were a number of male poets, but I knew of five or six wonderful Irish women poets that nobody in that audience would have heard of. And the breaking-through point for them is more at risk, I think, than for the male poet. My problem is, and certainly my ethical worry is that the woman poet doesn't even get considered: she's under so much pressure in this particular country.

Can you describe these pressures?

We like to think that in a country like Ireland that is historically pressured and has been defeated and has had minorities within it, that people get the permission equally to be poets. We like to think that, but they don't. There is not an equal societal commission here for people to explore their individuality in an expressive way—for a woman to cross the distance in writing poetry to becoming a poet. "If I called myself a poet," a young woman in one of my workshops told me, "people would think I didn't wash my windows." This was a piercingly acute remark on the fracture between the perception of womanhood in a small town in the southeast of Ireland and the perception of the poet. So the second part of the equation of not getting an equal societal permission is that I couldn't say that the people who have had permission—in other words, the bardic poets, who are male—that they have in every case generously held out their hand to these women, that they have equally encouraged them, given them a hearing. The proposals that happen under the surface to make a canon—that are subterranean and invisible—have been radically exclusive. The male writers in Ireland traditionally, in both prose and poetry, do have a kind of bardic stance; they do see themselves as inheriting a kind of bardic role. They have been disdainful of women writers with women's themes; they use a language I don't think you'd see in Canada or the United States. Only recently, for example, someone well involved with literary things in Ireland got up in a conference on "Women and Writing" to complain of the "pornography of childbirth and of menstruation in Irish women's writing."

> **"If I called myself a poet," a young woman in one of my workshops told me, "people would think I didn't wash my windows." This was a piercingly acute remark on the fracture between the perception of womanhood in a small town in the southeast of Ireland and the perception of the poet.**
> **—Eavan Boland**

This kind of discrimination has certainly existed in the United States.

Yes, but you have the huge diversity, that wonderful diversity of pressure and voices and liberalism. Ireland is a very small country, and its literary community is, over the past forty years, very staid in its perceptions. There isn't a lot of oxygen for the young woman poet—who is tremendously vulnerable to how she's perceived.

Rita Ann Higgins, for example, the young working class poet in Galway, or Moya Cannan or Eva Bourke, who can't find their books in the Dublin bookstores?

Yes, there's a huge amount of literary activity going in Galway. Jessie Lendennie [poet-editor of Salmon Press in Galway] was in my national workshop in 1984—a wonderful presence in it. I've known of those tentacles of energy for years, but it hasn't been easy to get any visibility for them. It's easier for me because I'm older, because I've always lived in a metropolitan area.

Is it easier for a women poet in academe, like yourself, to attain recognition?

I'm not in academe. I was a writer in residence last year at Trinity, and this year at University College Dublin, but I would think of myself as academically far from grace. Interestingly, the contemporary poetry course in Trinity this year carried not one woman poet! It's extraordinary to be taught outside in other countries and not anywhere in your own. This is the reason why when I'm in Boston I'm not inclined to be quiet or conciliatory about it: because these things have happened again and again and because they have been passively sanctioned. The male Irish poets have treated exclusion as invention, but there is absolutely no doubt that that exists. There is no give on this issue. It is a matter of fact.

Are there academics in Ireland who would promote the work of women? Women academics? The theme for the American Conference for Irish Studies conference this fall is "Women and Children First."

Yes, that's very interesting. If you look back at *Eire Ireland,* for example, there are almost no references to women's writing. The ACIS—yes, there are wonderful women there, but I think that ACIS itself has been conservative, the institution itself. The academic in Ireland has had remarkably little to do with the writing of poetry, but it has a great deal to do with the dissemination of it. The problem, I think, is a compound psycho-perception in this country that women are in many ways the caryatids of community. They hold on their shoulders the lives and the shelters—and it's not to say a great regard is not had for them—but as the unindividualized generic feminine presence.

In your American Poetry Review *essay,* **"Outside History"** [April 1990], *you rue the fact that male poets have made "the image of the woman the pretext of a romantic nationalism."*

Certainly: and the nation is an old woman and needs to be liberated. But she's passive; and if she stops being passive and old she becomes young and ornamental. Therefore, within our perception of women as being in the house, as being in the kitchen, holding things together, there's the perception of the male very often as the active and anarchic principle: and therefore nominated as male is the individual, the bardic, the dangerous, the expressive, partly because those were male, but partly because the transaction between the male and the female in literature is an active-passive one. But basically this community nominates women as the receptors of other people's creativity and not as the initiators of their own. Then we have the Church to support and give a sacro-quality to these perceptions. If you take a woman in a town which no doubt is strongly influenced by its Catholic past and its rural customs—where women were counseled patience and its silent virtues—a woman who suddenly says, "Now I'm going to express myself," that society is not going to give her the same permission as to a 23-year-old male with black curly hair. So she's already under a lesser set of permissions to explore her own gift, and a greater sense of inferences that that gift is dangerous to her tradition of womanhood. These are huge pressures!

I'm not a separatist. I think that separatism in a small country like Ireland would be another form of censorship. [But] in a funny way, being a separatist might have been advantageous to me.
—Eavan Boland

Enough to make feminists out of women poets?

I think it's important that women writers don't have to be feminists, don't have to be anything. They just have to have enough oxygen to write. I don't care what their political persuasions are.

You're not a separatist.

No, I'm not a separatist. I think that separatism in a small country like Ireland would be another form of censorship. In a funny way, being a separatist might have been advantageous to me. It would probably have made me a less suspect figure on the left of the women's movement here—who I think have had difficulties with me. They wouldn't see me as feminist enough, you see. It's the old story of the hare and the tortoise. They always see me as the tortoise. They don't understand that often you're just trying to get discriminatory funding out of the Arts Council so there are not six traveling fellowships for women under thirty, or artists under thirty, so that women with children can't take them up. But I think the maximum pressure should be kept up to bring these male resistances into the open.

About five years ago you would have found male writers saying, "Yes, there are women writers." But the inference would be: "These are women writers and not Irish writers—they don't belong to the great main discourse." One very eminent Irish poet said to me in New York: "I do accept that the energies of women writing are unctioned." Big deal! It's a very late in the day recognition! You can't be congratulating people on the recognition of human rights and the expression of it. So I think male writers might consider that I have an unconciliatory pose: and I think some of the left of the movement, as I said, too moderate. So it's an awkward position.

Your themes come out of women's experience. Won't the male poets and critics continue to object to that?

But it's the male poets who are separatist, you see; this is their separatism. They want to say, "There's a niche for this, a category for this. There's a cupboard for this—we can get rid of her: this is women's poetry." I certainly call myself a woman poet and I don't allow them to contaminate that particular category. But there is no way that they are not saying that ours are poems of human resonance and human import. I could certainly recommend to all women poets in this country that they argue on their own terms whether a poem is good or bad. We are not going to have an Irish poem to be a poem about a city or a bull or a heifer, but all the poems we write about—houses or children or suffering in the past—are women's poems. And that is where the argument is at the moment.

You won't get into a Virginia Woolfian dialogue on the aesthetics of the female sentence?

No, it's wonderful to talk about. But this argument may be in a cruder stage here. I think it may be at a more pressurized stage, and the ugly part is the intimidation for a woman to write a poem, get a book together, wonder where it's going to be published, how it will be received. In other words, the ugly part in every single minority in a writing culture is, "Where does the power lie? Who has the power?" I remember a women poet who said to me, "I can't publish with a woman's press. I have to publish with another one so that I have credibility." To me that was a heartbreaking sentence because it represented all the oppressions women are under in this country. A well disposed male poet said to me, "If Salmon publishes just women (which it doesn't), it will do them harm." I said, "Why will it do them harm? You have been publishing just men for years!" Tears come into these chaps' eyes because they think: Here's Eavan on a social occasion, saying these hard things to me. Here is one window that is shut off. I think you must be very careful and try to open the window and not break it. You come to a point, you know, where you feel like breaking all the windows. And I have really been getting near that point.

Can you talk about the critique in Ireland; where does it come from?

Everything I've been talking about is due to the fact or emanates from the fact that the critique in this country remains obdurately male and patriarchal. It's a complex matter where a critique in a country comes from. It comes in a very simple way from the contracting out to reviewers by the literary editors, and that's a complicated system. I no longer review any Irish writers. Five years ago I decided not to do that anymore; I wasn't going to waste time. Therefore you have a critique partly made by the reviews contracted by the literary editors. Then there are the critiques undoubtedly made in the universities; and there's a minimum interaction between the newspapers and the universities. Then there's the sort of hum in a literary writing community which is made up of short-hands and off-the-cuffs—that sort of hand-to-mouth critique, which I have a great respect for. Although a great deal of vital work by women has been done, the critique is really sitting on top of it. It's made up of the defense mechanisms of an older writing culture which is predominantly male, and it's made up of everything, I'm afraid, from sneers to pious statements of what makes excellence. The great cry is that all this terrible sewage that people like myself have released into the literary waters is diluting the excellence of our great literature. Though how you can get an excellent literature if it is exclusive, I don't know.

And the language used in this critique? Words like "miniature" and "painterly" and "she's not representative of her sex" as a kind of backhand approbation?

Yes, there are all these code words like "domestic," which imply a restrictive practice within the poem itself. A woman said to me of a male editor, "He said the best poems I wrote were the least female"—instead of looking at the thing the right way around, which is to look at the work of young women, and asking, "How are they putting together the Irish poem differently?" That is the real question. They are putting it together differently, and that means in itself to cast a light around what is being done in other ways and at other times. We need to look at all this as part of the legitimate energies that affect one another and country. But if you look at it that way, the critique is actually obstructing the perspective on that. So we are not able at the moment to consider in this country: how do young women put together that poem? What do they put into it and what do they leave out of it? We can't see that because the whole jargon surrounding it is very emotive. The most significant review to me was one in the *Irish Times* on my pamphlet, **"A Kind of Scar"**—the same essay that appeared later in the *APR* as **"Outside History."** The work was utterly dismissed. My editor said, "Should I do something about it?" I said, "Leave it." It's always to me a good thing when the murky undertoads come to the surface.

Is it difficult for these young women poets to be reviewed?

Yes, and therefore they get truly demoralized. The working conditions for young women poets are infinitely poorer than the conviviality and congratulations that surround their male counterparts. One of the important hidden agendas in this country is that poets emerge differently. The young male poets tend to emerge in their early twenties. They tend to be economically independent—even if they're restricted they don't have dependence. They're mobile; they can move to the centers of activity; they can move from the rural areas to the metropolitan areas. Although very often pressured, they have some flex on how they can move around. The traditional young Irish woman poet is in her thirties—at best in her late twenties. She may well at that point be economically dependent, be married, have small children. And above all be fixed in one place. She can't get to the local library easily, let alone get to Dublin. She doesn't have many of the available sustenances and none of the amenities. Yet I don't think either the critique or funding or the perception or the community support has followed her the way it has the young male writer.

The poet Rita Ann Higgins advises that women poets refuse inclusion in an anthology unless there is equal representation. Would you concur?

It's an interesting idea—one I'd be emotionally in sympathy with. But I would probably be cerebrally not in sympathy with token representation of any kind. I don't favor a woman being in an anthology just because she's a woman. I favor her being there because I know that many of the younger writers who are best in poetry are women. I think the right way is that women be the anthologists and the editors. I think it would be very interesting if Rita Ann would edit *Poetry Ireland*. And include men. And we could see what she saw of what is around her.

The periodical Krino *has just brought out an edition dedicated to women and writing. Is this a sign that the situation is changing?*

I think it's changing—but it's changing slowly. It's changing in ways that have to be closely looked at. I think that token representations in periodicals or conferences are not all the same as looking with a discriminatory eye at the body of literature in a country and saying, "If A is A, then B must be B. If there is a wonderful poem written in Galway in which the bus is put in and a woman on it, and she looks out the window—that has got to affect a poem written in Dublin five years before it or four years after it." I don't think we have recognition here, really. The names are known, but there is still tremendous controversy. There were no women in the communities in the '50s and '60s calling themselves poets.

People who say you can live in Ireland and not have an interest in the nation—they haven't lived in Ireland. They don't know how powerful these things are! The separatists want us to see the poetic past as patriarchal betrayal. I see that ideology as dangerous to the woman poet; I want to subvert the old forms.
—Eavan Boland

Your first book came out in 1967.

Yes, but you would find it hard to believe how persona non grata I was. I was regarded as a straight-up lyric poet with the first two books. There was no support of any kind from any male poet, and that was very difficult. I was growing uneasy about the way the thing was handled, from the minus of congratulations for women to the kind of bardic posturing of men at readings. The assumption was that all Irish poets drink, that they behave to women in a certain way. I am a poet who grew up in my generation hearing Sylvia Plath routinely slandered by male poets. I have to except from that some of the male English poets, whom I think were surprisingly graceful and atune to her work. But the Irish poets have continued to slander her.

Because they consider her too "confessional?"

Absolutely. And then, as I said, I became persona non grata. They were fairly happy to sit back and let me disappear. When I didn't completely disappear, I don't know that they knew I didn't disappear for a very long time. I do think you can pick up a number of books by Irish writers that make no reference to any woman writer in those years. *Irish Poetry After Joyce,* written by Dillon Johnston, came out in the middle of that decade. I think there are 500 pages in that book and two are on Irish women poets. The funny thing is that in my case it made the working conditions more definite; I found it liberating. It liberated me from the slightest interest in their views on these matters. It didn't stop me from liking some of the work they did, but it stopped me from having a huge regard for their views, because I thought they were thoroughly retrograde in many cases.

Adrienne Rich suggests the need for a woman poet to break with the male tradition and create her own personal myth—as she does in a poem like "Diving into the Wreck." Do you find this too separatist a view?

Well, of course, I love her work, and the last line in that poem is just prophetic: "A book of myths / in which / our names do not appear." But no, I'm not a separatist. I would be much more subversive by inclination. Ireland is a country with a strong history of subversion. I think the subversions in this literature have an interesting past. Joyce's *Portrait of the Artist* is simply a subversion of the Jesuitical program, that's what Joyce was out to do. He wanted to take the original repressive stance and subvert it to show that in another life, when you turned it backwards, it could be liberating. Yeats was more subversive of the British poet at the time than he appears. But by instinct I wouldn't wish to throw out capital labor or any of those things, and if I wished to I wouldn't find it possible because we are daily rooted in the past. People who say you can live in Ireland and not have an interest in the nation—they haven't lived in Ireland. They don't know how powerful these things are! The separatists want us to see the poetic past as patriarchal betrayal. I see that ideology as dangerous to the woman poet; I want to subvert the old forms. Where those elements of the Irish experience are repressive, I would rather subvert them than throw the baby out with the bathwater.

William Logan (review date 21 April 1991)

SOURCE: "Animal Instincts and Natural Powers," in *New York Times Book Review,* April 21, 1991, p. 22.

[*In the following excerpt, Logan asserts, "For all her virtuous, even virtuoso details . . . too many of Ms. Boland's poems lack definition; they fade into a reverie of revered objects."*]

Eavan Boland is domestic but not domesticated. Like other Irish poets, she has been formed by a national culture that has become national myth, however riven and violently marked that culture has been. **Outside History,** her third book to appear in America, slants against that culture in its devotion to women, whose lives have rarely figured in the national accounts. When she writes about Daphne, Daphne is trapped in a kitchen.

For Ms. Boland, the kitchen is a mortuary, but in poem after poem the kitchen and the garden remain scenes of her bloodless anger. When a poet is so self-divided, so drawn to the realms she despises, it should not be surprising if her poetry suffers division too, here between prose and the poetic. That division affects many poets, whose very inheritance may be division, but rarely does it do so as forcefully.
—William Logan

New mythologies are rarely less sentimental than the old, and Ms. Boland avoids few of the obvious risks. She is expert in the passionless household poem, its subject the incident reminiscent, its tone the retrospect melancholy, its diction the vernacular significant. She likes to start with a hard fact ("It is Easter in the suburb." "My mother kept a stockpot."), but she tends to drift off into the abstract language of "fluencies," "patterns," "complexities," "densities." Every object is a little too neatly or symbolically in order. When a mug breaks, a love affair is over.

For Ms. Boland, the kitchen is a mortuary, but in poem after poem the kitchen and the garden remain scenes of her bloodless anger. When a poet is so self-divided, so drawn to the realms she despises, it should not be surprising if her poetry suffers division too, here between prose and the poetic. That division affects many poets, whose very inheritance may be division, but rarely does it do so as forcefully. The featureless prose and aimless, airless philosophizing of Ms. Boland's work are transformed only by a love of pure detail, of the incandescence of the visual. A poem moony with memory is hardened into "the arc of the salmon after

sudden capture— / its glitter a larceny of daylight on slate." She has a gift for the graven phrase ("this rephrasing of the air") or the poetic tremor of a single word ("midges freighting the clear space between / the privet and the hedge"), though she uses it sparingly, as if too much of it might be a bad thing.

She seems to wish to be a poet of some mystic immanence, for whom the natural powers are landscape, garden, memory and children. She attempts to write by force of personality, which is difficult even when a poet has a striking personality. Whenever she nears the gravitational pull of the past, however, she becomes a darling of the sure particular:

> The German girls who came to us that winter and
> the winter after and who helped my mother fuel
> the iron stove and arranged our clothes in wet
> thicknesses on the wooden roll after tea was over,
>
> spoke no English, understood no French. . . .
>   To me, they were the sounds
> of evening only, of the cold of the Irish dark and
>
> continuous with all such recurrences: the drizzle in
> the lilac, the dusk always at the back door, like
> the tinkers I was threatened with, the cat inching
> closer to the fire with its screen of clothes, where
>
> I am standing in the stone-flagged kitchen; there are
> bleached rags, perhaps, and a pot of tea on the stove.
> And I see myself, four years of age and looking up,
> storing such music—guttural, hurt to the quick.

That is pure prose, but it has the eloquence of a remembered world. For all her virtuous, even virtuoso details (the best with the sharp sting of ammonia), too many of Ms. Boland's poems lack definition; they fade into a reverie of reversed objects. Poems of quiet desperation in the kitchen do not form an original aesthetic. Only when Ms. Boland's subjects impose design upon her do they have the bad manners of emotion:

> It was a school where all the children wore darned worsted,
> where they cried—or almost all—when the Reverend Mother
> announced at lunchtime that the King had died
>
> peacefully in his sleep: I dressed in wool as well,
> ate rationed food, played English games and learned

how wise the Magna Carta was, how hard the
Hanoverians

had tried, the measure and complexity of verse,
the hum and score of the whole orchestra.
At three o'clock I caught two buses home

where sometimes in the late afternoon
at a piano pushed into a corner of the playroom
my father would sit down and play the slow

lilts of Tom Moore while I stood there trying
not to weep at the cigarette smoke stinging up
from between his fingers and—as much as I could
think—

I thought this is my country, was, will be again,
this upward-straining song made to be
our safe inventory of pain. And I was wrong.

Here mere retrospection darkens past introspection. The poems of emigration, of the wear and tear between two cultures, make the dainty melancholies of her other poems seem crewel work. When Ms. Boland stops being the bard of fabric (in one stretch of 10 pages we find silk, lace, crepe de Chine, cotton, linen, damask, gabardine, synthetics, calico and dimity, some of them two or three times), she is truest to her own culture and most deeply coiled in its falseness.

David Baker (review date Summer 1991)

SOURCE: "Framed in Words," in *Kenyon Review,* Vol. XIII, No. 3, Summer, 1991, pp. 169-81.

[In the following excerpt, Baker discusses Boland's "double stance" toward traditional Irish poetry.]

Eavan Boland is only five years younger than Seamus Heaney, and she is the author of six previous books of poetry, but *Outside History 1980-1990* is her first collection to be widely distributed in this country. Ontario Review Press did publish its *Introduction to Eavan Boland* in 1981, and Carcanet distributed here, modestly, her 1987 *The Journey.* Still, while she clearly has not sprung overnight fully formed and brilliant, this collection may suggest so to an American audience. She is a splendid, graceful, demanding poet who has been evolving for some time, having published her first book, *New Territory,* in 1967.

I have been interested in showing how [Louis] MacNeice positioned himself outside the literal framework of Ireland and how Heaney situates himself at least partially outside, or apart from, the tradition of the Irish pastoral. Boland de-

rives much of her considerable power from a similar strategy, locating herself outside of history, as her title stipulates. More specifically, she pursues an important, feminist revision of the history-making so often praised or inherited by MacNeice and Heaney. Not so much outside of history as counter to it, or in the process of amending it through addition, Boland has developed in her poetry what Harold Bloom might call an agonistic relationship with the paternal, natural, and often silencing history of traditional Irish poetry.

> **While [Boland] clearly has not sprung overnight fully formed and brilliant, this collection [*Outside History 1980-1990*] may suggest so to an American audience. She is a splendid, graceful, demanding poet who has been evolving for some time, having published her first book, *New Territory,* in 1967.**
>
> **—*David Baker***

Recall, in reading the whole of Boland's **"Bright-Cut Irish Silver,"** the lineage specified in Heaney's "Digging":

I take it down
from time to time, to feel
the smooth path of silver meet the cicatrix of skill.

These scars, I tell myself, are learned.

This gift for wounding an artery of rock
was passed on from father to son, to the father
of the next son;

is an aptitude for injuring
earth while inferring it in curves and surfaces;

is this cold potency which has come,
by time and chance,

into my hands.

The scars earned in "Digging," by the passing down of male power and responsibility, are learned in Boland's poem—that is, gleaned as well as learned. In other words, what she inherits is a reminder or artifact of the male imagination dominant in the making of history and poetry. The male "gift" is a wounding one, a turning of the earth into scars, as well as a subtly misogynistic impulse to injure the female figure "inferred" onto the earth; recall, for instance, the fertile if impossible bog queen, and the violent act performed on her by the turfcutters and by history itself. Heaney's men loved the "cool hardness" in their hands as they performed their desires on the earth or on the page, but Boland finds such manipulation to be "cold," an oxymoronic potency at best—and in inheritance that she "takes down" only occasionally as a reminder of her own difference and obligation.

Eavan Boland is an attentive, powerful, encouraging poet. Part of her power derives from her ability to confront a past which might otherwise force her into complicity or silence. That dubious inheritance includes, in part, Louis MacNeice and Seamus Heaney. But there may be an equally remarkable kinship between her work and theirs: the consistent antagonism of modern Irish poets with their past.
—David Baker

The image of a cicatrix—a healed scar, specifically of a tree—provides Boland with a complex figure for the revising of poetic history. In **"Mise Eire,"** as she swears not to "go back to . . . my nation displaced / into old dactyls," she realizes again that her "roots are brutal." The brevity of her lineation suggests a clear-minded, resolute intent to confront

> the scalded memory,
> the songs
> that bandage up the history,
> the words
> that make a rhythm
> of the crime.

Here the speaker performs an act of sympathy and synthesis, imagining herself into the voice of a previously silenced persona:

> I am the woman
> in the gansy-coat
> on board the *Mary Belle*
> in the huddling cold,
>
> holding her half-dead baby to her.

Having identified and called into question the patriarchal character of history, Boland now seeks to replace that "criminal" paradigm with another model, maternal, uprooted, immigrant. It is most important that the female figure also possesses the skill of language—not the "old dactyls" of her antique nation, but rather

> a new language
> [which] is a kind of scar
> and heals after a while

> into a passable imitation
> of what went before.

Language frames or marks the location of the wound and, it provides as well the element which authorizes the wound to begin to heal.

To identify and name a problem is to make such a beginning. Boland's overall poetic involves an even more thorough transumption, and many of her strongest poems take up the challenge of containing the past while revising it into relevance. To amend the traditional estate of women in poetry, Boland locates her women in their more probable situations—not unreal nymphs or muses, but working, dignified, if domestically bound women. It's not that Boland wishes an exclusively domestic occupation for women, but that such an occupation (instead of membership in a male myth-wish) is their more likely accurate history. **"The Women"** presents a landscape and a vocation more like Dickinson's than Heaney's:

> This is the hour I love: the in-between
> neither here nor there hour of evening.
> The air is tea-colored in the garden.
> The briar rose is spilled crepe de Chine.
>
> This is the time I do my work best,
> going up the stairs in two minds,
> in two worlds, carrying cloth or glass,
> leaving something behind, bringing
> something with me I should have left behind.

The poet at work deals with a reluctantly inherited past and with the homely materials at hand, stitching them together. At the doubled crossroad—of night and day, and of the past and present—she witnesses in her lines a remarkable metamorphosis:

> in the words I choose, the lines I write,
> they rise like visions and appear to me:
>
> women of work, of leisure, of the night,
> in stove-colored silks, in lace, in nothing,
> with crewel needles, with books, with wide-open
> legs
>
> who fled the hot breath of the god pursuing,
> who ran from the split hoof and the thick lips
> and fell and grieved and healed into myth,
>
> into me in the evening at my desk. . . .

This is a "vision" of the history of women heretofore "outside" poetic history. So that "my sister will be wiser," as she writes in another poem, **"Daphne with Her Thighs in**

Bark," she exposes a past vulnerability toward the mythmaker, the "god pursuing":

> Look at me.
> I can be cooking,
> making coffee,
>
> scrubbing wood, perhaps,
> and back it comes:
> the crystalline, the otherwhere,
> the wood
>
> where I was
> when he began the chance.
> And how I ran from him!
>
> Pan-thighed,
> satyr-faced he was.

Boland repudiates the role of victim-shepherdess within the mythology of male history-making. Or, rather, she recognizes the role her gender has played in that mythology and refuses to frame herself there any longer. In **"The New Pastoral,"** Boland explores the possible hazards of cutting loose from such a pervasive system:

> I am a lost, last inhabitant—
> displaced person in a pastoral chaos.
>
> All day I listen to the loud distress, the switch
> and tick of new herds.

But her speaker reasserts that she's "no shepherdess," and turns instead toward the actual circumstances of women's lives. Even within the contemporary domestic scenery, Boland senses a possible, familiar (and familial) entrapment:

> am I
> at these altars,
> warm shrines—
> washing machines, dryers
>
> with their incense
> of men and infants—
> priestess
> or sacrifice?

The answer, here in **"Domestic Interior,"** depends on her ability to transform her circumstances past and present into art, into a schema of imagery appropriate to her own sense of self, and finally into an identity *she chooses* within and beyond the poetic tradition:

> The woman is as round

> as the new ring
> ambering her finger.
> The mirror weds her. . . .
>
> But there's a way of life
> that is its own witness:
> put the kettle on, shut the blind.
> Home is a sleeping child,
> an open mind
>
> and our effects,
> shrugged and settled
> in the sort of light
> jugs and kettles
> grow important by.

Boland seeks to describe a poetic location, and "effect"—that is, a property as well as a force—which includes an indicated past and a possibly ensnaring present. What prevents the continuation of oppression is the voice of the woman as she elects the substance of her own history and the manner of her own presentation. Even from within her daily surroundings, or perhaps especially within such, she finds an alternative to the unreal myth of her fathers:

> There is
> about it all
> a quiet search for attention,
> like the unexpected shine
> of a despised utensil.

Eavan Boland is an attentive, powerful, encouraging poet. Part of her power derives from her ability to confront a past which might otherwise force her into complicity or silence. That dubious inheritance includes, in part, Louis MacNeice and Seamus Heaney. But there may be an equally remarkable kinship between her work and theirs: the consistent antagonism of modern Irish poets with their past. Each of these poets very carefully and purposefully situates him or herself outside a large and traditional notion; most significantly, the stance of a chosen exclusion allows each poet to maneuver more freely *within* the conventions held in question. For MacNeice, exile provided him the freedom to retrieve his Irish birthright within the frame of his memory and art. Heaney questions the pastoral ideal to reinvigorate it, modernize it, even politicize it. Boland subverts the male ideal of history even while she instigates a parallel history—feminist and alternate—to witness the "unexpected shine" of otherwise mundane, mythologized, or suppressed lives. Due in part to their skeptical, doubled stances toward their respective subjects, these poets express a deep and intelligent love for something related to, but clearly not the same as, what they hold in doubt.

Jody Allen-Randolph (review date April 1992)

SOURCE: "A Passion for the Ordinary," in *Women's Review of Books,* Vol. IX, No. 7, April, 1992, pp. 19-20.

[*In the following review, Allen-Randolph calls the author's* Outside History *"a retrospective of Boland's most mature and best work."*]

Poetry in Ireland is still very much dominated by a male bardic tradition. Compared to their male contemporaries, women poets in Ireland get very little recognition and arouse tremendous controversy. Even as I write, the arts pages and opinion columns of Irish newspapers are crackling with a furious exchange of fire over the recently published *Field Day Anthology of Irish Writing,* the most comprehensive re-configuration of the Irish canon in this century. It seems the all-male editorial committee failed to notice the contribution Irish women have made to social change and contemporary writing in the last quarter century, and their omissions have become the focal point in the continuing debate over women's writing.

The controversy has created an atmosphere of intimidation which continues to help obstruct the emergence and recognition of women poets. When an arts administrator at a recent poetry conference complained of "the pornography of childbirth and menstruation in Irish women's writing," he went unchallenged. Critics and academics in Ireland still fail to take seriously even the most established women poets.

No one has done more to bring about a long-overdue reappraisal of this state of affairs than the poet Eavan Boland. In a series of essays and interviews over the past ten years she has borne passionate witness to the pressures placed on women writers in Ireland. More recently, she has written about how important it is for women poets who inherit a constraining national tradition to subvert that tradition.

Born in Dublin in 1944, the youngest child of an Irish diplomat, Boland spent most of her childhood in London and New York. Returning to Dublin as a teenager, she attended Trinity College and upon graduating was appointed lecturer in the English department. Deciding against an academic career, Boland worked for many years as a literary journalist. Her first collection of poems, *New Territory,* appeared in 1967. Since then she has produced six books, three of which (including the latest) were Poetry Book Society Choices.

Outside History is a retrospective of Boland's most mature and best work. It contains a generous selection of poems from her last two volumes, *Night Feed* and *The Journey,* and a large body of new work as well. (By reversing the order, however, putting the newest poems at the front of the book and the oldest at the back, it makes it hard for the

reader to follow the deepening patterns of meaning, resonance and reference over time.) Tucked away at the back of this book is a group of nine poems from *Night Feed* (now out of print), revised and rearranged into a sequence entitled **"Domestic Interior."** These are risky, short-lined poems, with a fresh, uncluttered, clean-edged presentation. Boland's acute observations of surfaces and textures in the ordinary world gives them their energy:

> This is my time:
> the twilight closing in,
> a hissing on the ring,
> stove noises, kettle steam
> and children's kisses. . . .
>
> the buttery curls,
> the light,
> the bran fur of the teddy bear.
> The fist like a nighttime daisy:
> damp and tight.
>
> **("Energies")**

Her descriptions of ordinary objects can resonate suddenly with a shimmer of enchantment. In a poem exploring the monotony of caring for a small family, for instance, we find this image of a doorstep milk bottle:

> Cold air
> clouds the rinsed,
> milky glass,
> blowing clear
>
> with a hint
> of winter constellations . . .
>
> **("Monotonies")**

The precedents for these poems are not in verse but in painting. Boland turned to the still lives and domestic interiors of Jean-Baptiste Chardin and Jan van Eyck for technical example. By conferring distinction upon the homely, Chardin and van Eyck revealed their objects as much as they described them, and Boland's technique of imbuing ordinary things with such fresh significance that they become a universe in themselves is learned from these painters. In the title poem of the sequence, a poem which takes van Eyck's *The Arnolfini Marriage* as its starting point, she explains:

> But there's way of life
> that is its own witness:
> put the kettle on, shut the blind.
> Home is a sleeping child,
> an open mind
>
> and our effects,
> shrugged and settled

in the sort of light
jugs and kettles
grow important by.

By taking as her subject the routine day that most women in Ireland live (caring for children, washing, cooking and sewing), Boland renews the dignity of demeaned labor and establishes a precedent for its inclusion in Irish poetry. By summoning up a tradition of artists like Chardin and van Eyck, she authenticates her own poetic stance. But by emphasizing her identification with the female subjects, rather than the male painters, she also subverts their tradition.

It is common for new landmarks in Irish literature to go unrecognized by its custodians. Yet when the dust kicked up by the current canon debate has settled, I expect we will see *Outside History* firmly ensconced. By then Eavan Boland's work will have made and found a context at the heart of her national literature, and in doing so, forced a more generous shape upon it.
—*Jody Allen-Randolph*

Her technique both in these poems and those of *The Journey* owes much to her fine understanding of light, tone, color and composition (Boland's mother, an early influence, is painter Frances Kelly). In **"Self-Portrait on a Summer Evening"** from *The Journey,* Boland examines a painting by Chardin:

> All summer long
> he has been slighting her
> in botched blues, tints,
> half-tones, rinsed neutrals.
>
> What you are watching
> is light unlearning itself,
> an infinite unfrocking of the prism.
>
> Before your eyes
> the ordinary life
> is being glazed over:
> pigments of the bibelot,
> the cabochon, the water-opal
> pearl to the intimate
> simple colors of
> her ankle-length summer skirt.

It is this talent—the skillful setting off of one light effect by another, the interplay of the smallest touches of color with touches of rhyme ("tints" with "rinsed," "blues" with "neutrals"), repeated as though at random, always discreet but always there—that gives us the sense of a delicate under-structure throughout Boland's work. At the end of this poem, the woman in the painting becomes the poet herself. As she crosses the yard, keeping one eye on the garden and the other on her children, she announces: "I am Chardin's woman / edged in reflected light, / hardened by / the need to be ordinary." It is this fidelity to ordinary human experience in the astute consciousness of the poet that makes these poems unpretentious, understated and exhilarating.

In the poems from *The Journey,* the ordinary experience of the present is layered with a rich sense of the past. The theme of storytelling as both the archive of female history and the memory of a nation is explored in **"The Oral Tradition."** The poet lingers in gentle reflection at the end of "a reading / or a workshop or whatever":

> only half-wondering
> what becomes of words,
> the brisk herbs of language,
> the fragrances we think we sing,
> if anything.

The leisurely pace of the slant rhyme ("words" with "herbs," "languages" with "fragrances") shifts into internal rhyme ("Wood hissed and split / in the open grate, / broke apart in sparks"), quickening the impact as the climax approaches. The poet overhears a story shared between two women, and is caught up in the drama as the great grandmother of the teller gives birth in an open field. The diction modulates from colloquial to poetic and the music rises as the poet imagines the moment when

> . . . she lay down
> in vetch and linen
> and lifted up her son
> to the archive
> they would shelter in:
>
> the oral song
> avid as superstition,
> layered like an amber in
> the wreck of language
> and the remnants of a nation.

It is this discovery of the past through recognizing the difficulty of turning it into the present that undergirds the *tour de force* of this book, the ambitious title sequence, **"Outside History."** The history of the title is at once Eavan Boland's personal history and the history of her nation. When she uses one as a metaphor for the other, as she does in **"The Achill Woman"** and **"What We Lost,"** she writes with an unforgettable mixture of courage and perception. In **"What We Lost,"** using a voice that has deepened in resonance and authority, Boland tells the story of a child (her mother) who is told a story which, "unheard" and "unshared," is forgotten:

> Believe it, what we lost is here in this room
> on this veiled evening. . . .
>
> The fields are dark already.
> The frail connections have been made and are broken.
> The dumb-show of legend has become language,
> is becoming silence and who will know that once
>
> words were possibilities and disappointments, . . .

The formal structure of the sequence is as fully accomplished as its themes. It has an ingenious clock-like configuration: twelve poems cycle through timescapes of changing light and changing seasons, suggesting both the twelve positions on a clock-face and the twelve months of the calendar. In a private interview, Boland described the sequence as a study in the breakdown of control: "It deals deliberately with the artificial construct of time and the seasons, and the ways in which these artifices of control ultimately break down." Myth for Boland is another form of control (earlier in the sequence she defines it as "the wound we leave in the time we have"). "The attachment of somebody like myself to myth," she explained, "is very much the flirtation and engagement with the idea of control, the way that we restrict meaning by controlling it. We restrict meaning and finally we restrict reality. We tamper with our own mortal nature, and therefore with love and therefore with time."

In the final poem of the sequence, which Boland describes as "an intense formalization of the breakdown of time," she rejects the controlling impulse of myth. The muscular cadences of the poem pull us along in their undertow:

> Out of myth into history I move to be
> part of that ordeal
> whose darkness is
>
> only now reaching me from those fields,
> those rivers, those roads clotted as
> firmaments with the dead.
>
> How slowly they die
> as we kneel beside them, whisper in their ear.
> And we are too late. We are always too late.
>
>   (**"Outside History"**)

The power and sweep of the sequence is a function of the silences into which it taps. The silences of women in these poems are all the more poignant because they are widened to include so many people, male and female, past and present: the conquered Gaels, the casualties of the potato famines, the immigrant Irish, and the victims of recent sectarian killings in the North.

It is common for new landmarks in Irish literature to go unrecognized by its custodians. Yet when the dust kicked up by the current canon debate has settled, I expect we will see *Outside History* firmly ensconced. By then Eavan Boland's work will have made and found a context at the heart of her national literature, and in doing so, forced a more generous shape upon it.

Deborah McWilliams Consalvo (essay date Summer 1993)

SOURCE: "In Common Usage: Eavan Boland's Poetic Voice," in *Eire-Ireland: A Journal of Irish Studies,* Vol. 28, Summer, 1993, pp. 100-15.

[*In the following essay, Consalvo argues that "Boland is a literary voice which cannot, and must not, be left to reside in the marginalia of the Irish literary canon."*]

Eavan Boland's literary achievement has established her as one of Ireland's foremost poetic voices. Born in 1945, Boland published *New Territory,* her first collection of poetry, in 1967. Her second collection, *The War Horse,* appeared in 1975. Since then, she has established herself as one of Ireland's leading literary figures with such works as *In Her Own Image, Night Feed,* and *The Journey and Other Poems.* Boland's most recent collection, *Outside History,* appeared in 1990. With the publication of her essay *A Kind of Scar,* she has become an outspoken critic of the traditional Irish patriarchy and a controversial figure within the Irish literary community. Yet, missing from any critical review of Boland's work has been an examination of her poetic contribution to the Irish literary canon—her *own* literary history. And so, the purposes of this essay are to consider the range of Boland's craft as a poet and to assess why her work not only has survived the critics' reviews but, indeed, has thrived.

My objective here is to argue that Boland is a literary voice which cannot, and must not, be left to reside in the marginalia of the Irish literary canon. As an established transnational voice, Boland helps bridge the gap between an Irish national voice and an international audience. However, within Ireland, her work is marginalized within the patriarchally determined Irish national canon. And, while Boland is identified as a leading female poet within Ireland today, her poetic voice directly challenges how the placement of woman writers is determined within that canonical tradition. What literary force or merit keeps Boland's poetic voice a powerful, growing force within the contemporary literary canon? There are, after all, many fine writers whose talents have not been able to mature in the political, competitive arena of the literary marketplace and whose works have not survived. So why does Boland's poetry seem actually to flourish?

In *Outside History*, Boland depicts a concept of national identity that, to a great extent, reflects a postmodern awareness of the national complexity of the Irish canon, of the literary expression of multivocality innate to literary Ireland. To Boland, the Irish people have a rich social and literary history, one which has both shaped and limited their ideals and identity as an independent, sovereign nation.
—*Deborah McWilliams Consalvo*

My own interest in Boland's work has spanned nearly a decade. Aside from some correspondence and occasional telephone conversations between Boland and myself, my first opportunity to pursue with her, in person *and* in depth, some of my ideas about poetic craftsmanship and style did not come until the summer of 1990 when I had the pleasure of visiting Boland near her home in Dublin. Boland then acknowledged her struggle to project an independent, female voice—both as a woman and as a writer living in Ireland, a country still scarred by a history of political turmoil and social discord. Boland contended that:

> Everything I am about to argue here could be taken as local and personal, rooted in one country and one poetic inheritance; and both of them mine. Yet, if the names were changed, if situations and places were transposed, the issues might well be revealed as less parochial. . . . Who the poet is, what she or he nominates as a proper theme for poetry, what self they discover and confirm through this subject matter—all of this involves an ethical choice.

After interviewing Boland, I began to understand that, for the handful of women writing in Ireland today, the conscious or unconscious decision to demand a place in Ireland's long tradition of male voices has been a costly one. Along with a few other Irish women writers, Boland has sought to shift attention within the literary debate. She wants women writers to be heard, to be allowed to be heard by publishers, readers, and critics. Boland argues for incorporation of women's voices into a literary tradition, to bring an end to their history of exclusion. She argues that women writers—because they *are* women—provide a different perception, a different literary imagination. Through images, motifs, and

themes of movement, place, and migration, Boland's poetry exemplifies an Irish struggle for independence; however, in Boland's case, the battle is fought in order to win a more authentic Irish canon.

Place and movement are spiritual concepts for Boland: both her expressive sense of place and her quest for a legitimate literary place illustrate her search for a renewed textual depiction—and definition—of national identity. She revisits the experiences she has inherited from Ireland's rich social and literary history as a single, independent nation, and she views them through her individual sensibilities. Thus, she uses poetry as a means of articulating a postmodern reformation of the Irish national experience and, by so doing, Boland is able to shape Ireland's national self-image into a more universal, global image—into a literary description of common humanity. In *Outside History,* Boland depicts a concept of national identity that, to a great extent, reflects a postmodern awareness of the national complexity of the Irish canon, of the literary expression of multivocality innate to literary Ireland. To Boland, the Irish people have a rich social and literary history, one which has both shaped and limited their ideals and identity as an independent, sovereign nation.

Through her poetry, Boland implores her reader to remember, recollect, and retrieve those individual experiences otherwise lost in the Irish canon. For her, it is through the individual memory that those events which shaped the history of civilization can be revised into a human history. Boland cautions that, if such individual narratives are not recalled and incorporated into the existing record of Irish social and cultural history, then the image of Ireland must remain a mythic image—the portrait of a flawed, heroic state. And, as Boland warns us, "myth is the wound we leave / in the time we have."

Boland's use of mythic constructs helps her to describe and depict her sense of place—sometimes social, sometimes personal, always historical. She believes "place" must involve the ideology of duality, claiming "there is the place which existed before you came to it, close in the secrets and complexities of history." If place involves myth, history, experience, and concealment, then what emerges through Boland's poetry is a literary representation of national identity that displays a more universal association: that is to say, an Irish canon correlative with other literary voices which form, as she proclaims, a more human text.

> . . . Although you live in a nation, it's a restricted category. You may have a powerful relation to the restriction, the restriction itself may be an emblem of other things that are much less restrictive. A nation can be a metaphor for a lot of powerful things. Above all, it's an archive. It's a file of suffering.

But in the end, it's the unidentified chapter that is more likely to be the one that people turn to.

Boland believes that it is the collective imaginative power of individuals, those who feel for the human suffering of others around them, that must reshape an understanding of national identity in Ireland. For if the very essence of human consciousness is deeply and historically embedded in the Irish longing for political unity, then the concept of national identity she addresses in her poetry is not a literary ideal *per se,* but, rather, an illustration of a postmodern polity, of the political force emerging through the voices of Irish women writers.

However, Boland values not only the content of the poetic text but also its source. For her, this poetic source lies deep within her own sense of self: "I found my voice where I found my vision, and I found my vision where I lived." Boland challenges what she perceives as a canonical history of patriarchal elitism in Ireland, and an exploration of the history of Irish poetry does, indeed, reveal an ideological superficiality that disproportionately projects a masculine perception and imagination. This male-dominated context not only provides a literary structure, it also establishes a literary authority to grant, or not, permission to those Irish women writers who wish to engage in the national discourse.

> **Boland's language, versification, and literary style reflect a complexity of poetic technique and skillfulness. But many critics have failed to address her compositional abilities, perhaps due to a preoccupation with *what* a writer says rather than *how* it is said.**
> **—*Deborah McWilliams Consalvo***

If Boland's principal objective in challenging the place of the woman writer in the Irish literary tradition is, as I would suggest, to transcend the cultural history of Ireland's patriarchy, then, in many ways, her only real source of power to do so must come directly from her own voice. And, if the source of Boland's poetic voice is, as I have mentioned, a force or power which emerges out of a particular individual experience—a singular moment in time—then the outgrowth of that personal experience becomes the experiential framework surrounding her literary expressions. That is to say, the origins of Boland's own poetic voice—the force or power of her poetry—emerge through the simple act of her reframing a particular moment in history, of her creating a timely reconsideration and reevaluation of an individual experience or event. As Boland comments,

all poetry commends to people that they hesitate in

that moment of time and look at the powers that are within rather than without. All poetry—all good poetry—commends a sort of interior moment.

The individual stories, narratives, and perceptions of her native Ireland provide Boland with the experiential source to stimulate her poetic imagination, and to craft a revised story of human history. She warns, however, that even this act of recollection is dangerous and that "memory is treacherous . . . [because] it confers meanings which are not apparent at the time." The poet recalls for and thus retells to her readership the temporary state, the unstable society, and the transitional factors that shape the tragedy of the Irish postmodern condition—an ideological atmosphere of political and national exile. And, it is in this atmosphere of exile that Boland's concept of "place" emerges and from which Boland's poetic voice receives inspiration. In this atmosphere Boland begins to develop her ideology of identity, which she defines as an individual's potential for self-improvement and self-realization.

Boland's language, versification, and literary style reflect a complexity of poetic technique and skillfulness. But many critics have failed to address her compositional abilities, perhaps due to a preoccupation with *what* a writer says rather than *how* it is said. If, however, a poet cannot effectively utilize language to articulate even a message, then that message is silenced or, at best, convoluted. In the case of Eavan Boland, her lines appear, initially, lightly lyrical; yet, a second or two after reading them, they reverberate with complex interpretations. In *New Territory,* for example, a twenty-two-year-old Boland writes about the world around her in the poem "**Mirages**":

> Reasonable men, however, hold aloof,
> Doubting the gesture, speech and anecdote
> Of those who touch the Grail and bring no proof—
> Failing to recognise that in their fast
> Ethereal way, mirages are
> This daylight world in summary and forecast.

Her verse constructs here a male-dominated narrative, a masculine discourse in which *she* wants a voice. In addition, Boland implies in these same lines that, because the feminine is absent, the conditions which the poem creates are, in actuality, nothing more than a mirage, a human myth.

In this same passage Boland uses images and events of Irish history to suggest that the woman writer complements a canonical representation of the human experience by projecting a different form of human consciousness. She thus challenges the external social and cultural forces which help to shape and condition the individual or private sense of self. Through this technique, Boland moves her reader away from a text which constructs an account of history to a text which reflects the construction of a mythic allegory—a record of Irish cultural history which is, essentially, no different than a Grail-like legend.

Boland's skillfulness as a poet is shown also by her diction, which is marked by her elaborate vocabulary and her frequent use of personification. In *The Journey,* for instance, Boland writes:

> The woman and the willow tree lean forward,
> forward.
> Something is near; something is about to happen
> . . . something more than Spring
> and less than history.

Here she works to redefine the position of the woman writer as one moving toward a revision of voice.

Boland believes that any type of long-lasting social and cultural change in women's roles must begin in the very place women reside—the domestic domain. Boland is not at all naive in this suggestion. She understands all too well that the domestic arena is not devoid of risk and warfare. However, she strongly believes that, as women gain ground through a continuous and conscious journey, they will acquire "new territory," new space in which to occupy, rebuild, and strengthen their self-perceptions and creative imaginations.

Through the voice of the poetic narrator in another poem, **"The Unlived Life,"** Boland considers the possibility of "another life" for women different from the domestic, from the home-based: "Suddenly I could see us / . . . wondering for a moment what it was / we were missing as we turned for home." But home *is* the narrator's domain, the place where the memory of her experiences resides. And so, along with her readers, the narrator leaves behind "the unlived life," the "texture of synthetics as compared / with the touch of strong cloth / and how they both washed." She turns to "formalize the terrors of routine / in the algebras of a marriage quilt / on alternate mornings when you knew / that all you owned was what you shared"—the communal experience of women sharing a renewed vision of the domestic ideal.

While Boland connects the inherent terrors of social, political, and economic isolation with the privacy of domestic life, she also uses the domestic framework's images of privacy and sensuality to describe the world around and external to her. The essential difference in Boland's reference to the domestic here, however, is that she never uses the domestic to *define* the complexity of a woman's individual self. Boland seems to think that a woman's struggle toward self-realization should begin at the domestic center—the place where women have historically resided and the origin, as well, of their independent experiences and communal existence. And

Boland suggests throughout many of *The Journey's* poems that within the domestic sphere there is a form of political power available to women which can be rechanneled to reshape the image of the Irish woman as something more than such a mythic motif as Ériu, Banba, Fodhla, Bridget, Maeve, and Cathleen ni Houlihan. As Boland defines from her own perspective the distinction between female as "subject" and the female as "voice," she argues:

> Yes, I'm a feminist. But not a feminist poet. I'm no more a feminist poet than if I [were] a Marxist and thus a Marxist poet. Those ideologies stop at the boundaries of poetry. You don't sit down and write as a Marxist poet and you don't sit down and write as a feminist poet.

Boland agrees that she has benefited from the women's movement in Ireland. She believes, in particular, that women writers simply do not experience the same permission, the same equalities, as do their male counterparts. She contends that throughout literary history, the canon has *remained* the product of a strongly male-oriented culture and that, for very "complex reasons of individuality and culture in [Ireland]," there are many good women writers who simply are not given a fair reading by the literary "elite." Boland goes even further to suggest that "the people who do have the permission to be a poet have [not] always generously held out their hand to those who do not have that permission." Despite what critics may say, Boland maintains that neither she nor her strategies are, by nature, confrontational:

> The poem is in the end the negotiator of [the] imaginative presence. I want that to be seen. I've no taste for these confrontational things. I'm not, by nature, a confrontationalist. I regret the confrontations that stem from within, men's writing and women's writing, in this country. And I absolutely blame it on the authoritative, radical, patriarchal structure in this country. I think that it has made dialogue difficult at this moment, but things are changing.

The changes Boland sees beginning to occur in Ireland today are emerging only after many, many years of social protest. And these alterations in the Irish social landscape are, like Boland's poetic diction, subtle and implied. Boland acknowledges the pain and fear attached to the process of change, to the maturation of oneself. In another of *The Journey's* poems, **"Growing Up,"** she recalls the innocence of girlhood, a time of fantasy, "of unschemed space / . . . indefinite and infinite with hope." But she observes that, as the natural process of maturation continues, those same young girls must learn to face the future with both courage and the ability to review the past before the "dreams blooding them with womanhood" became a part of the daily lives of those "full-skirted" and pregnant young women. Boland does not, however, suggest that the dreams of girlhood and the realities of womanhood should represent the only possible narrative of the female story. Instead, through her use of poetry, Boland articulates the multivocality of self-realization—the complexities of the female ascension into a new world.

Boland's poetry exhibits a lyrical quality, an emotional sense, and each poem is layered with allusions, annotations, and commentary. Part of the complexity of her poetry comes from its narrative quality which often explores "new possibilities for irony and paradox, new departures in style and tone." For instance, in her collection entitled *The War Horse,* the poetic persona speaks, in **"The Other Woman,"** about "a world [she] cannot share" and a place where "the married state" is not binding. Initially, these phrases appear to concern a simple indiscretion on the part of the male spouse, as told to us by the female spouse. However, a second reading of the poem reveals a different narrative: one about a novelist—suggestively, Boland's husband, the novelist Kevin Casey—whose personal time is filling up in "a world I can not share / . . . the pages of your novel / among the syntax and the sentences." The poem is brought to resolution both *in* and *through* the final two lines in the last stanza, where the persona comes to understand that her husband would forfeit his encounter with "the other woman" and "would exchange / Her speaking part for any of our silences."

In **"The Other Woman,"** the persona evidences a belief that both the family portrait and her domestic role as wife and mother will, in the end, remain intact. However, Boland ensures that the persona has been transformed by the poem's events and now becomes a more powerful voice. Boland constructs the final two lines of blank verse in iambic pentameter, the final line written in feminine meter. By that simple device of leaving an extra unaccented syllable at the end of the poem, Boland in effect disrupts the patriarchal canonical tradition of authority and, using language *and* versification together, emphasizes a reversal of both patriarchy and colonial ideology. It is, perhaps, Boland's use of this poetic device that is most exciting because of the subtle message it conveys against the currents of Irish conventionality and for the unique experiences and perceptions of women.

One last thing must be said about the schemes of versification in which Boland is most comfortable writing. Boland acknowledges that, in the context of a discussion of the techniques and principles of a poem's composition, critics cannot ignore that the creation of poetry involves some aspect of conversion—a transformation of thoughts, ideas, and feelings into the forms of metrical expression. In that conversion process, Boland contends that the perception and, thus, imagination of the female poet differs, in part, from that of the male poet:

> I want Irish women poets to be seen as poets who can put the poem together differently, because their imagination is differently scarred or is differently illuminated. The poem is in the end the negotiator of that imaginative presence.

Boland believes that it is the poem itself, not the poet, that must articulate a different way of reviewing our human histories, those stories and narratives which reflect aspects of human vulnerability and human complexity that, even now, remain "almost invisible to the naked eye."

Boland's technical skills and poetic craftsmanship help to restore the individual stories and unfamiliar voices unrecorded by social and literary history. Her poetry serves to reposition the significant forces that shape the literary landscape. She finds the familiar in language and discourse to be the most compelling:

> I might be the author of my poems; I was not the author of my past. However crude the diagram, the idea of a nation remained the rough graphic of an ordeal. In some subterranean way I felt myself to be part of that ordeal; its fragmentations extended into mine.

In this very way, Boland brings the myth out of history and into the familiar, moving her readers closer and closer to a common knowledge and a common idiom. In an important way, Boland's senses of versification and style are intrinsically linked: the form and the formation of her poems are interrelated, just as are the female imagination and the female voice.

What Boland wants to achieve as a poet, however, is not linked solely to the issue of female versus male voice or feminine versus masculine imagination. Rather, for her, the traditional form of poetry must itself be stretched and reshaped through the contributions of the female perception. In this, Boland acknowledges that the American poet Adrienne Rich has done much to advance the "place" of the female poet within the arena of contemporary literature. In bringing to the forefront of contemporary poetry the growing and "evolving consciousness of the modern woman . . . Rich commits herself to change in spite of the risks involved in having no preconceived idea of where she is going." Like Rich, Boland uses poetry as a means to explore the possibilities for overcoming the traditions of patriarchy through "rejecting patriarchal territoriality which defines women and children as possessions." Boland's lyrical style encourages, instead, individuality; she conveys a sense of the infiniteness of the exterior world in contrast to but not in conflict with the finite condition of the interior, domestic domain.

> **Boland uses allegory in many of her poems to construct a narrative form for her principle message, that of humanity's movement "out of myth into history." This textual shift provides a pattern throughout her work that depicts the threads of continuity and discontinuity throughout the Irish cultural fabric.**
> **—*Deborah McWilliams Consalvo***

Boland values a central ideal—literary discourse—and it is how that ideal is articulated that is the essential difference between Boland and many other women writers. Her language resounds in a type of lyrical concinnity, an elegance of literary style. As Boland has rebelled against traditional social patterns and cultural convention, so her poetic style articulates and encourages a sense of communal respect and a shared history. She suggests that

> If a poet does not tell the truth about time, her or his work will not survive it. Past or present, there is a dimension to time, human voices within it and human griefs ordained by it. Our present will become the past of other men and women. We depend on them to remember it with the complexity with which it was suffered. As others, once, depended on us.

For Boland, the internal force of self-reference is the filtering device for her concept of both individual *and* collective identity. She participates along with us, her readership, in reforming our own awareness and understanding of the complexity of our selves.

Boland uses allegory in many of her poems to construct a narrative form for her principle message, that of humanity's movement "out of myth into history." This textual shift provides a pattern throughout her work that depicts the threads of continuity and discontinuity throughout the Irish cultural fabric. Boland's poetry represents, thus, a sense of cultural awareness and progressive style, one which thematically focuses on the necessity of movement and relocation in the quest for a sense of self. Boland's poems each explore existing demarcations between historical events and human experience. Particularly relevant is how she employs mythical and historical elements as stylistic constructs. These two textual elements act as a type of containment, for they provide an enriching analytical framework inside of which Boland's poetic voices peacefully reside in, I would contend, unique cohabitation.

Added to the issues of place and position in Boland's work is the issue of perception. Boland compares and contrasts social conventions and individual perceptions, singularity and multiplicity, relativity and universality, cultural conditions and human contextures, and isolation and integration. She articulates the existence of the political force within the literary imagination. She contends that humankind is powerless if it does not expand beyond its current vision, perception, and imagination of either its past *or* its future. And, she observes that this expansion calls for the reforming and relocating of an individual sense of self. Boland speaks *through* the voice of a woman writer in Ireland, and *to* the place of the woman writer within Ireland's social history and traditional literary canon. But I believe that she speaks *first* to the issue of the common in humanity and *second* to the placement of individual voice. The female imagination reflects, in Boland's mind, a response that is fundamentally different from that perceivable by the male imagination. Examples of this difference can be found in particular throughout many of Boland's early poems. In the collection entitled *Night Feed,* for instance, she focuses on the domestic interior from the female perception.

Another aspect of Boland's poetic discourse involves the complex differences between self-identity and national identity. Throughout *Night Feed,* Boland explores aspects of procreation and motherhood, the mythic images of the domestic, and, finally, the particular atmosphere and sense of risk women experience in periods of transition and transformation. Her work illustrates how locality shapes the individual's concept and the manifestation of identity. In such poems as **"Night Feed"** and **"It's a Woman's World,"** Boland discusses the milestones and significance of the domestic experience. For example, Boland reminds women that a mother's milk is a life necessity, signifying the inherent power of mothering:

> The last suck.
> And now your eyes are open
> Birth-coloured and offended.
> Earth wakes.
> You go back to sleep.
> The feed is ended . . . we begin
> The long fall from grace.
> I tuck you in.

Although Boland is speaking both to her own daughter and to other mothers in **"Night Feed,"** she also is speaking to all women. And, it is with the final line of **"Night Feed"** that, I believe, Boland cautions the supporters and participants in the feminist movement. In that line, she recognizes that the domestic role for women may be somewhat a preordained condition, and yet she also recognizes that it is often a powerless role. Powerful or not, the notion of women's intrinsic role in mentoring other women through the generations in their own individual journey—"I tuck you in"—remains a strong, central message throughout her poetry.

Boland's poetry records the individual stories that collectively retell Irish experience as it relates to a universal, global humanity by skillfully interweaving domestic, private motifs with social, public themes. The images of the individual that emerge from her language reflect the individual stories, narratives, oral histories, and personal experiences that give voice to the history of Irish women. In an essay on the political force of poets, V. G. Kiernan claims: "Women—like the peoples of the Celtic fringe—represented a partially distinct race, indifferent to rules and conventions they have had no part in framing; and, being most of the time restricted to a narrow family circle, natural antinomians when outside it." Boland herself acknowledges that her poetic creativity is derived from a perception deeply rooted within a female imagination.

But what kind of pattern takes shape in her poetry to project the elements of territory, domain, abode, settlement, residence, exile, and so forth, which are such central themes in Boland's poetic discourse? Again, the American poet Adrienne Rich reminds her readers, including Boland, that we are "of woman born," that humankind is coupled with the maternal, domestic, feminine force. And, it is Boland who, in her collection *In Her Own Image,* reminds us that the feminine force is an agent of social and political re-birth. She writes: "She is not myself / anymore, she is not / even in my sky / anymore and I / am not myself."

In Her Own Image was received by the Irish literary establishment with more controversy than Boland had anticipated. In our 1990 Dublin interview, she admitted:

> At times I've run into very serious difficulties here [in Ireland]. In 1980, for instance, I published a book called *In Her Own Image* which got me into a certain amount of trouble, relatively speaking. Until then, I think, I was seen as a straightforward lyric poet. Then I began writing things which were perceived as feminist and sub-Plath, and so on. The result was that I was excluded, in some significant ways, from what was the so-called discourse at that time.

Boland observes that the "discourse" which then existed had essentially been governed by Ireland's male writers and was in great need of alteration. "There was a real element of distortion" in it, Boland said, because the editorial community found it nearly impossible to get beyond the controversy and to review *In Her Own Image* from a position of textual criticism. In Boland's view, it took many years of exposure to writers *outside* of the Irish literary community before her work could be critiqued in terms of its text rather than in terms of its argument.

Other poetic constructs are present in Boland's poetry. Ele-

ments of myth, history, origins, inheritance, past, recollection, and memory enrich her verse. Within the structure of Boland's poetry are motifs of myth, history, and migration, and from these emerge subthemes of immigration and emigration. In the case of *Outside History,* Boland's primary theme is migration, which she transforms into a type of emigration—the journey beyond the national landscape into an transnational or global sense of place. At times in her literary career, Boland has had to "turn [her] back on a lot of the motifs, arguments, and themes in poetry itself." She has resisted adopting cultural metaphors or incorporating those literary conventions traditionally used to describe the landscape and character of the Irish people and nation.

> I thought it vital that women poets such as myself should establish a discourse with the idea of a nation. I felt sure that the most effective way to do this was by subverting the previous terms of that discourse. Rather than accept the nation as it appeared in Irish poetry, with its queens and muses, I felt the time had come to re-work those images by exploring the emblematic relation between my own feminine experience and a national past.

Instead of representing a national discourse *per se,* Boland draws from a national history to illustrate human history. Her poetry reflects her literary sensitivity and technical imagination by depicting the narratives and stories of those individuals whose experiences and voices historically have been placed outside the literary mainstream of the national Irish canon.

In *Outside History,* Boland appears, at first glance, to present her poems in a loose structural arrangement comprised of three schematic divisions. But upon closer scrutiny, it becomes apparent that the trilogy accommodates a variety of elements that Boland considers significant to the Irish identity. The three schematic divisions consist of: "object lessons," those external forces which condition our perception and understanding of our environment; "outside history: a sequence," in which she writes "we are human history. We are not natural history"; and "distances," those memories we no longer choose to recall or revisit, but which are essential to a realization of our sense of identity, our selves. The theme of migration and the subthemes of immigration and emigration are joined through Boland's poetic voice in such a way as to suggest that one's concept of national identity is shaped by the images of locality and not defined by one's place of residence. Boland interlinks the concepts of identity—both individual and cultural—to forms of migration, involving issues of movement and place.

Irish women writers are engaged in a struggle for a sense of national voice—a literary place within the traditional Irish canon. They are attempting to negotiate, rather than to demand, idiomatic significance. Their intention is to reframe *and* expand the canonical domain, making it a place where the female imagination can find placidity. And, I believe that whatever literary place these women finally do secure is less significant than what they project by their collective idioms: the multivocality of Irish writers *and* of the Irish voice.

The literary debate that has occupied the last generation has been heavily centered on the concerns of gender. While those concerns still exist today, the current literary debate reflects a transformation of them. Political traditions and sectarian agendas are being replaced by cultural associations and the transformation of individual and national identities. The definition of what constructs national ideals is being expanded, and the sense of self-identity and origin is changing.

Boland not only is a poet addressing the Irish culture *per se,* but also an Irish voice in an international literary context. The social narratives and individual histories that contribute to the intensity of her work enhance, rather than limit, the global significance of Boland's poetry.
—*Deborah McWilliams Consalvo*

Consequently, what Eavan Boland faces, as the leading female poet in Ireland today, is an authorized national ignorance based in patriarchal myth, one which represents, in Richard Murphy's words, "what people believed took place, not always about what they did." Boland uses historical reference not to impose a rigid pattern upon the Irish landscape, but rather to bring forth a "sense of history [which] is essential to a poet . . . [and] of immense value in correcting those myths about the past, the errors of judgement that have biased people's minds," in order to expand the concept of national identity within the context of Irish literature.

Boland not only is a poet addressing the Irish culture *per se,* but also an Irish voice in an international literary context. The social narratives and individual histories that contribute to the intensity of her work enhance, rather than limit, the global significance of Boland's poetry. Her poems are filled with selected images, icons, and descriptions which reflect the universality of the isolated, individual perspective. Furthermore, while Boland acknowledges that there, indeed, may be images in her poetry that suggest a political symbolism, she claims that her poems are not consciously political. Instead, she maintains that they raise to a transnational level of consciousness the experiences of those who live inside a country still marred by political unrest. And, insofar as these individual voices narrate and influence Ireland's political landscape, Boland claims that those poetic voices are merely echoing a once-silenced historical tradition.

Through her poetry, Eavan Boland is able to create literary expressions that emerge out of perceptions, imaginations, and impressions of the individual experience. These voices describe a portrait of national identity which differs from the textual images found in traditional Irish literature. But along with that discourse on identity, there is embedded in Boland's poetry a political message as much as a political concern. She warns her audience, as well as other writers, not to

make [your] home in any comfort within a national tradition . . . however enlightened the climate, the dangers persist. So do the obligations. There is a recurring temptation for any nation, and for any writer who operates within its field of force, to make an ornament of the past; to turn the losses to victories and to restate humiliations as triumphs.

For Boland, there is "a human dimension to time, human voices within it and human griefs ordained by it." She uses language not as a medium to deny the truth about a particular historical event but, rather, to retell the truth about that time, about the complexity of the human suffering. And, out of these shared tragedies, Boland creates a sense of a collective voice that speaks of, and seeks to inform others about, a surviving human consciousness.

Ellen M. Mahon (essay date 1993)

SOURCE: "Eavan Boland's Journey with the Muse," in *Learning the Trade: Essays on W. B. Yeats and Contemporary Poetry,* edited by Deborah Fleming, Locust Hill Press, 1993, pp. 179-94.

[*In the following essay, Mahon analyzes Boland's* The Journey and Other Poems, *considering what the volume expresses about the poet's development as an artist.*]

A young Yeats in 1889 urged an aspiring poet to use Irish legend because it "helps originality. . . . Besides one should love best what is nearest and most interwoven with one's life." Yet thirty years later Yeats himself found *A Vision* necessary to give him "metaphors for poetry." Similarly Eavan Boland, born in Dublin in 1944, has searched long to find the right voice and subject. From her earliest volume, *New Territory,* to *Outside History,* she has published eight collections altogether, three of which incorporate poems from previous volumes. *Introducing Eavan Boland* reprints all the poems of *The War Horse* and *In Her Own Image* in order to bring this promising poet to a readership outside of Ireland. Juxtaposing the two early volumes points up her range, from Ireland's political unrest to feminist concerns. *Night Feed* shows Boland turning thematically to the "nearest and most interwoven with" *her* life in poems of domesticity and motherhood. It is five years later, however, in *The Journey and Other Poems,* that Boland comes to terms with her sources of inspiration. The two subsequent books, again collections or consolidations, contain actual revision as well as rearrangement of previous poems.

"As an Irish woman poet I have very little precedent," Eavan Boland explained in an interview shortly after the publication of *Journey:* "I didn't want to do without a discourse with my nation," but

> as a woman I didn't want to have a discourse with that national idea on the terms in which it was offered in Irish literature. So I had to rework some kind of relationship I could live with between my sense of being a woman poet and being a national poet—it was very slow and very hand-to-mouth.

Lacking a poet as precedent, Boland turned to a different kind of artist and dedicated *The Journey and Other Poems* to her mother. Certainly this dedication signifies her physical mother who was a painter, but there is a metaphoric suggestion as well. I believe that the "reworking" can be traced not only in the journey made in the title poem, where Sappho is guide and muse, but also by the entire volume full of relationships with women.

The title poem, **"The Journey,"** does not appear until the middle of the book where, with **"Envoi,"** it comprises the second section. Instead Boland begins with **"I Remember,"** an exploration of her "nine-year-old" consciousness in "the big drawing-room" of "bombed-out, post-war London" where she felt an "interloper" among her mother's "easel" and "portrait brushes" while "an eyebrow waited helplessly to be composed." From this meditation on her artist mother, the poet proceeds to consideration of her own art, one of language, in **"Mise Eire."** The title of this second poem evokes two· other sources of the author's life, Mother Ireland (Eire) and, in the near homonym "miserere," Mother Church. The "mise en scène," the given, of Eavan Boland's life is to be woman, Irish, and Catholic. It is here, as the poet asserts later, that her muse "must come . . . Let her come / to be among the donee, the given."

The thematic unity begun in the first two poems extends into the next three. Mother-painter and Mother Ireland produce the persona of **"Self-Portrait,"** the woman who herself finds a female heritage in **"The Oral Tradition."** In the fifth poem, **"Fever,"** the speaker seeks for her identity or heritage in her grandmother's story: "I re-construct the soaked-through midnights; / vigils; the histories I never learned / to predict the lyrics of." The process is one of considering some external event or historical fact and imaginatively reconceiving and interiorizing it. The result is that an ordinary moment or fact is illuminated with larger meaning.

"I won't go back to it—" Boland blurts out in the opening line, and stanza, of **"Mise Eire."** Then follow three full stanzas elaborating the refusal, qualifying the rejection. This second poem of *Journey* illustrates both the poet's method and her agenda. "It" is "my nation" but qualified as "displaced / into old dactyls" so that on one level it is epic poetry that is being renounced. The punctuation, making the second stanza a parenthetical expression, separates this rejection from the list which follows: "land of the Gulf Stream, / the small farm" begins stanza three nostalgically. As if examining a childhood memory from an adult perspective (or recalling Mother Ireland's shame as well as her glory), the speaker judges more harshly—"the scalded memory"—and returns to a consideration of language:

> the songs
> that bandage up the history
> the words
> that make a rhythm of the crime

only to climax in the fourth stanza, "where time is time past." The problem is identified and the refusal repeated: "No. I won't go back. / My roots are brutal."

The emphatic use of present tense accentuates rejection of the pastness of the past; "roots" convey the continuing sustenance of history in the present reality. In what appears to be a clear allusion to T. S. Eliot's "Tradition and the Individual Talent," Eavan Boland has confronted the discourse with her nation and taken her stand. A colon follows "brutal" in the text, and the fifth stanza, with personification reminiscent of Pearse, goes on to explain:

> I am the woman—
> a sloven's mix
> of silk at the wrists
> a sort of dove-strut
> in the precincts of the garrison—

who is paid for "delight" in "cambric" and "silks." In the interview cited above, Boland resolved the conflict between being a national poet and a woman poet "by feeling that my Irishness and my womanhood were metaphors for one another." The prostitute in **"Mise Eire,"** like the old "songs" and "words," is part of the historical past; she, and they, engender the present, and can be modified by it. Moreover, the spirit which enabled the prostitute to turn her historical situation to advantage is available to the poetess. "I am the woman" is repeated of the immigrant "in the gansy-coat . . . holding her half-dead baby to her / as the wind shifts," bringing the sound of a new language. Even as the poem, by its title, asks for mercy, it heralds a message from **"The Emigrant Irish"** in section three of *The Journey and Other Poems:* "it is time to / imagine how they stood there, what they stood with / that their possessions may become our power."

> **The poetic art of "Self-Portrait" deserves pause, for it shows Eavan Boland at work. It is definitely a poem of threes—indeed, the word "triptych" is used in it.**
> **—*Ellen M. Mahon***

Under the motif of a journey, the third poem suggests that the speaker takes the insights from poem two and applies them to the subject of poem one. On the level of poetic art, Boland combines the metaphors of womanhood and history with those of painting to draw her own **"Self-Portrait on a Summer Evening."** Choosing Jean-Baptiste Chardin (1699-1779) from history, the poet portrays him "painting a woman / in the last summer light." Unlike the artist-mother who would compose an eyebrow, thus metaphorically dealing with the hard realities of post-war London, this painter "has been slighting" his subject "in botched blues" and "rinsed neutrals"; following the line "All summer long," the word "slighting" echoes "sighting" as if the man were birdwatching. "Before your eyes" objects Boland, drawing the reader or a fellow observer into her confidence, "the ordinary life / is being glazed over." Twice more in the poem the line "before your eyes" is repeated as "her ankle-length summer skirt" becomes "my ankle-length / summer skirt," and the speaker realizes "I am Chardin's woman"

> edged in reflected light,
> hardened by
> the need to be ordinary.

The poetic art of **"Self-Portrait"** deserves pause, for it shows Eavan Boland at work. It is definitely a poem of threes—indeed, the word "triptych" is used in it. Dependent on three sources of metaphor, it is the third poem of a series; even in *Outside History* where the order of the poems is greatly rearranged it is placed third. There are three implied groups in the poem: the painter and his easel, the speaker who confides to a listener, and the children whom they are apparently minding. In measuring her position, there are three objects which locate the speaker—the garden, the house, and the whitebeam trees—and three things she keeps "an eye on": "the length of the grass, / the height of the hedge, / the distance of the children." The line "before your eyes" is repeated three times, and so, most interestingly, is "light."

The first stanza states that Chardin is painting "in the last summer light"; the last stanza depicts the speaker as "edged in reflected light." Perhaps the reflection refers to her relationship with the original portrait. Commenting on the neu-

tral tones employed by the painter, and indeed Chardin was famous for his "pastel portraits," the third stanza—in three trimeter lines!—reads:

> What you are watching
> is light unlearning itself,
> an infinite unfrocking of the prism.

Watching, unlearning, unfrocking: the three present participles connote an ongoing development, a journey, even as the root word "frock" relates both women to "light." This connection parallels the metonymous connection of "skirt," the term by which the two women are associated before the eyes of the watcher. That "light" is "unlearning" points to the symbolic meaning of light as intellectual insight or comprehension. The idealized woman under Chardin's brush, made neutral by restricting the prism's range of color, symbolizes the suburban wife and mother whose range of independence unlearns itself in the "reflected light" of her domestic relationships. Unlike the artifact "set upon a golden bough to sing / . . . Of what is past, or passing, or to come" (Yeats, "Sailing to Byzantium"), she is "hardened" by daily demands, "the need to be ordinary."

For purposes of the journey, the main thrust of **"The Oral Tradition"** is that the secrets of the trade can be passed down through a matriarchy. Putting on her coat—again one thinks of Yeats, in "I made my song a coat"—after a poetry reading, the speaker overhears two women speaking of a birth. They tell of a new mother who went out in her "skirt / of cross-woven linen" to "an open meadow . . . where she lay down / in vetch and linen / and lifted up her son." The appositive stanza which follows this delivery may refer either to the son or to the "shelter" mother and son together would find:

> the oral song
> avid as superstition
> layered like amber in
> the wreck of language
> and the remnants of a nation.

In the talk of the women—itself an oral passing on, in "a firelit room / in which the colour scheme / crouched well down" so that "the sole richness was / in the suggestion of a texture" like a "low flax gleam," the poet has a moment of insight. The fire images her illumination as a log "broke apart in sparks, / a windfall of light/ in the room's darkness."

Shrugging up her coat collar against the "winter's night," the speaker thinks of "distances / ahead," the "miles to go" of Robert Frost's snowy evening which for her are "iron miles / in trains." As her journey takes her home from the cultural evening, so the setting of the following poems shifts to the suburbs. The reconstruction of her grandmother's reality in

"Fever" parallels Boland's account in her essay **"The Woman, the Place, the Poet"** of her coming to terms with a suburban life. Searching out her roots, she discovers an ancestor, who became master of the Clonmel workhouse; ashamed of him, she "imagined a woman. A woman like myself, with two small children, who must have come to this place as I came to the suburb"; "more than likely she would have died" in the fever hospital—"Every few years typhus swept through the town."

Feeling solidarity with other mothers, Boland ponders in her essay the meaning of myth, and asks: "Is there something about the repeated action—about lifting a child, clearing a dish . . . which reveals a deeper meaning to existence and heals some of the worst abrasions of time?" Through the ritual of daily caring she came to see, as in the aesthetic of poetry and music,

> a sequence and repetition that allowed the deeper meanings to emerge: a sense of belonging, of nourishment, of a life revealed, and not restrained, by ritual and patterning.

Surely these are the sentiments evident in the sixth poem, **"The Unlived Life,"** where the speaker exchanges quilting patterns with a neighbor. Through wifely and motherly experience, the poet bonds with all the unsung women who have lived the daily ritual, who have known that the patterning of seasons like the patterning of quilts leads to contentment.

In *Woman and Nature,* the poet Susan Griffin comments on woman's relation to space "and the place which records her image. Space which she embroiders. Space which she covers in quilts. Space which she makes into lace." In Eavan Boland's *Journey* it is made clear that, within the limits of "jest so much caliker," "when it comes to cuttin' out / the quilt" one is "free to choose." Confronted with the passing opportunity represented in "the flange-wheeled, steam-driven, iron omen / of another life," the neighbor women do turn away "to choose . . . the unlived life, its symmetry / explored on a hoop with a crewel needle."

"Lace," the title and subject of the following poem, shows another kind of choice. "Bent over / the open notebook," the speaker begins,

> In the dusk
> I am still
> looking for it—
> the language that is
>
> lace:

and goes on to make a social comment. The "baroque obligation / at the wrist / of a prince / in a petty court," an insignificant adornment in his regard, "is still / what someone . . . in the dusk, / bent over / as the light was fading / lost their sight for."

How quickly "Adam's Curse" comes to mind, where Yeats puts forth the thesis that the finest things require the hardest work. The "stitching and unstitching" of a single line which "will take us hours maybe" is labor lost on "the noisy set / . . . The martyrs call the world." In the Yeats poem, both the sewing image and the concern with language are subordinated to the speaker's more immediate focus on love; however, in Boland's work, as we have seen, concern with language immediately evokes concern with cultural identity as well as attention to craftsmanship. Moreover, the needlework, while it connotes womanhood, is a sustained metaphor, part of a larger patterning. So we are not surprised to find **"The Bottle Garden"** treating lace as a pattern, this time the pattern that unifies life.

The speaker reflects on her bottle garden, decanted in an earlier time "into this globe which shows up how the fern shares / the invertebrate lace of the sea-horse." She then situates herself in time, "in my late thirties, past the middle way." Alluding not only to Dante, but to T. S. Eliot's use of *The Divine Comedy* in *Four Quartets,* she continues:

> I can say how did I get here?
> I hardly know the way back, still less forward.

Readers of the *Quartets* know that "the way forward is the way back," and Boland traces this way through repetition of the word "here."

Looking into the bottle-garden of her youth, the speaker names off the specimens she included: "well, here they are"—and then the transition, the imaginative leap to "here I am a gangling schoolgirl . . . reading the *Aeneid* as the room darkens / to the underworld of the Sixth book." The plants have bridged the watcher back to her schoolgirl self, the maker of the terrarium but also the student of the *Aeneid;* it is in Book VI that Aeneas has the future revealed to him by the sibyl of Cumae, and this discovery will bridge Boland's persona forward to **"The Journey"** with Sappho into the underworld. The "room darkens," as it did for the poet and for the lacemaker in the previous poem, and, outside, "the open weave of harbour lights" is a patterning like lace joining the moments of the speaker's life.

Other moments—more crewel needles, more dusk, more skirts—recur in the remaining poems of Part I, but Part II commences with **"The Journey"** and its opening line, "And then the dark fell." When one has walked awhile with this poet-mother to whom twilight means the calling in of children as well as the moment of myth and creativity, one sees that the dark would indeed fall in a child's illness severe enough to require "an antibiotic." The diction of "a poem to an antibiotic" brings a wince, as compared, Boland is quick to point out, "with the odes on / the flower of the raw sloe"; "Instead of sulpha we shall have hyssop dipped / in the wild blood of the unblemished lamb, / so every day the language gets less." The experience of redemption, symbolized by the paschal lamb, is what both the antibiotic and Sappho deliver.

The exhausted mother has been reading while keeping vigil; "the book beside me / lay open at the page Aphrodite / comforts Sappho in her love's duress." The allusion is to "A Prayer to Aphrodite," in which Sappho begs the goddess to come with comfort as she has before: "come to me now and free me / from fearful agony." In Boland's poem, the mother's fearful agony, like Sappho's, proceeds from love. In a state "not sleep, but nearly sleep," the tired persona announces, "she came and stood beside me":

> and I would have known her anywhere
> and I would have gone with her anywhere
> and she came wordlessly
> and without a word I went with her.

For Boland, Sappho has replaced the sibyl who guides Aeneas through the underworld, but like Virgil's seer, the mother of lyric poetry, whom Plato called the Tenth Muse, grants her initiate an underworld vision which illuminates her mission. Upon entering Hades, Aeneas first sees the souls of those who died as infants. "Cholera, typhus, croup, diphtheria," recounts Sappho, as the speaker makes out the shadows of "terrible pietas";

> ". . . these are women who went out like you
> when dusk became a dark sweet with leaves,
> recovering the day, stooping, picking up"

the toys that are "love's archaeology." Speechless with horror at their misery, the narrator wants to "at least be their witness," but Sappho replies: "what you have seen is beyond speech . . . not beyond love." Charging Boland's persona to "remember" as the two emerge again into the upper world, Sappho says:

> "there are not many of us; you are dear
> and stand beside me as my own daughter.
> I have brought you here so you will know forever
> the silences in which are our beginnings.

The narrator awakes—"nothing was changed; nothing was more clear . . . my children / slept the last dark out safely and I wept."

In a volume dedicated "For my Mother," in which Part I be-

gins with a poem about her physical mother, as she begins Part II, Eavan Boland effectively names Sappho, "Mother." I have tried to show the path by which the poet dramatizes coming to this recognition: her childhood memory of a female artist-model, her choice of lyric poetry over rejected dactyls, her imaginative entering into the mindset of other women or sharing the silent repetitions of daily ritual with them. That Sappho is the predominant inspiration for Boland's craft, seems substantiated by Lillian Feder's summation of the Greek exemplar's style:

> The conciseness of Sappho's style and her choice of exact details convey the quality of an intense personal experience. Though her artistry is exquisite, her poetry has a spontaneity and an immediacy which suggest that the poet is experiencing the emotional drama she both records and creates. Most of Sappho's poetry is written in short, simple sentences without subordination; exactness and simplicity of language, economy, and directness are her chief instruments for expressing intense and passionate feeling.

The partner piece to **"The Journey,"** once the speaker has returned from the underworld experience with Sappho, is **"Envoi."** The subject is the muse who "must come to me," the speaker insists, as we remember Sappho came, in the midst of everyday concerns. The poet needs confirmation of what **"The Journey"** has revealed, and Boland turns from classical allusions to the Bible and the Church's liturgy to structure **"Envoi."** "It is Easter," the poem opens, the liturgical season which celebrates Christ's passover and the redemption achieved by the "blood of the unblemished lamb" cited in **"The Journey."**

"It is Easter in the suburb": the prepositional phrase situates the speaker, as the stanza proceeds with other signs of Spring "in my neighbour's garden" and away towards the Dublin mountains. "In the suburb," therefore away from the center, may signify a positioning in time as well as a geographical positioning. Liturgically the Easter season lasts for forty days, during which time the Scriptural readings tell of appearances of the risen Jesus to his followers. Within the first few days after Easter Sunday, the gospel recounts the Emmaus story (*Luke* 24:13-35) where Jesus overtakes two disciples on the road and, unrecognized, enters into conversation with them. As they approach the village, the two urge him to remain with them, because the day is nearly over. Halfway through **"Envoi"** Boland says of her muse, "I need her to remain with me until / the day is over and the song is proven." In *Luke,* Jesus goes in with the disciples to dine, and in the breaking of the bread they recognize him, remembering suddenly the Last Supper and the institution of the Eucharist. The last stanza of **"Envoi"** recalls the Eucharistic transformation of bread and wine as Boland calls on her muse to "bless the ordinary" and "sanctify the common."

The purpose of Christ's appearances after Easter is to show his followers that he has truly conquered death and to confirm their faith in his teaching. Several stories tell of persons who visit the tomb where he was laid; he is not there, though other bright presences are, who reply that he has risen from the dead. Thus when Boland affirms "surely she comes to me," her muse does not show signs of age and decay— "no lizard skin . . . no podded womb"—but rather the "brightening" and promising "consequences of an April tomb." Like Mary Magdalen, who went alone to the tomb and learned Christ had risen, Boland can say:

> What I have done I have done alone.
> What I have seen is unverified.
> I have the truth and I need the faith.
> It is time I put my hand in her side.

The closing allusion is to the gospel of the first Sunday after Easter, the story of doubting Thomas (*John* 20:19-31). Because this apostle refused to believe the accounts of the others and the "verifications" of Peter and John, because he insisted on himself putting his hand into the wound made in Christ's side by the Centurion's spear, the risen Jesus appeared to Thomas and said: "Take your hand and put it into my side; be not faithless, but believing" (verse 27).

Christ's resurrection is a promise of transcendence, a life beyond the one we know. Eavan Boland asks no less for her poetry.
—*Ellen M. Mahon*

In **"Envoi"** Boland asks for a confirmation comparable to that given to Christ's disciples through the events following Easter. Critics have found in her conditional last stanza an insincere expression of self-doubt: if the muse does not come, "then here I am . . . the most miserable of women." In fact, the phrase echoes I *Corinthians* 15 for a fitting recapitulation of what the whole Easter mystery—and by extension, the descent with Sappho—has meant: "If in this life only," Paul writes, "we have hope in Christ, we are of all men most miserable" (verse 19, Douay translation). Christ's resurrection is a promise of transcendence, a life beyond the one we know. Eavan Boland asks no less for her poetry.

After the confirming experience with Sappho, Boland moves in Part III of *The Journey and Other Poems* to a new voice, a new sense of the speaker's self. The tone changes from one of tentative search to one of conviction, but all the poems in this section treat of displacement. The lovers of the first poem are on the move constantly, the emigrant Irish and the Irish child in an English classroom are out of their element, Canaletto of Venice fame is in the National Gallery of Ireland, and the Lyric Muse is bandaged up recovering from a facelift. Finally, the woeful mismatch between the Glass King and his wife mirrors the abyss between poetry of high romance and the ordinary world.

The poems of the last section seem concerned with working out Boland's assertion in **"Envoi"** that "My muse must be better than those of men / who made theirs in the image of their myth." Unlike the men's muse which is "made," the woman's muse seems to have an independent existence. Moreover the third person plural pronoun suggests that men collectively created both the myth and the muse, a creation challenged in **"Listen. This is the Noise of Myth":**

> Forgive me if I set the truth to rights.
> Bear with me if I put an end to this:
> She never turned to him; she never leaned
> under the sallow-willow over to him.
>
> They never made love; not there; not here;
> not anywhere; there was no winter journey;
> no aconite, no birdsong and no jasmine,
> no woodland and no river and no weir.

The noise of myth "makes / the same sound as shadow," the "Tricks of light" and "consolations of the craft" that "put / the old poultices on the old sores." No lasting cure is offered by the "old romances" because "when the story ends the song is over."

Rounding back on themes of **"Mise Eire,"** Eavan Boland rejects the "planets of a harsh nativity"—the possible allusion to "The Second Coming" could signify Yeats and male Irish poetry:

> They were never mine. This is mine:
> This sequence of evicted possibilities.
> Displaced facts. Tricks of light. Reflections.

"I didn't know what to hold, to keep," asserts the next poem, **"An Irish Childhood in England: 1951."** Here the speaker grapples again with myth and shadow under the guise of a child trying to fall asleep. Nor is the dilemma resolved by the last poem in which the speaker muses on the medieval world of **"The Glass King,"** the mad Charles VI of France. A familiar metaphor for poetry returns as the speaker muses, "under the stonesmith's hand / stone turns into lace. I need his hand now." The yoking of stone with lace expresses the poet's desire for a strong poetry, a poetic of truth, in contrast to romance's "unravelling" in **"The Noise of Myth."**

As the myth of men is rejected in the last section of *The

Journey and Other Poems, so is their muse. This is the muse of tricks and "reflections" castigated by Boland in her 1980 volume under the title **"Tirade for the Mimic Muse."** The tone of **"The Woman Takes Her Revenge on the Moon"** in *Journey* is very like the earlier **"Tirade";** with pots of make-up and false reflections of love the Mimic Muse eluded Time and Death, but the poet has found her out. Similarly the speaker of *Journey,* defying reflections, paints herself in sunrise crimson and goes out into the evening to outface the moon. Meanwhile the Lyric Muse lies "propped and swabbed," sutured and "shocked in cambric, / slacked in bandages." Visiting the patient, the speaker remarks: "You are the victim of a perfect crime"—lied to by Time which is personified as a cruel "he." Compassionately surveying the muse's "seams," "stitches," and "sutured youth," the poet articulates the healing relationship she wants with the muse—that of collaborator:

> We have been sisters
> in the crime.
> Let us be sisters
> in the physic:
>
> Listen.
> Bend your darned head.
> Turn your good ear.
> Share my music.

With the publication of *Outside History,* Eavan Boland repositioned the poems discussed here and moved beyond the vision represented by her 1987 volume. I believe that *The Journey and Other Poems* marks an important phase in her development as a poet. For the student of Boland's art, this volume demonstrates the way the contemporary poet followed her exemplar, Yeats, who "took a very powerful elite form," the lyric, "and subverted it thoroughly with a sense of private destiny."

Denis Donoghue (review date 26 May 1994)

SOURCE: "The Delirium of the Brave," in *New York Review of Books,* Vol. 41, No. 10, May 26, 1994, pp. 25-7.

[*In the following review, Donoghue analyzes several of Boland's poems and asserts, "Eavan Boland's best poems seem to me those in which she writes without apparent fuss or political flourish."*]

Like everything else in Ireland, poetry is contentious. There is always an occasion of outrage. Two or three years ago the choice of poems in *The Field Day Anthology of Irish Writing* made women poets feel yet again neglected, suppressed. Eavan Boland was their most vigorous speaker. With notable

success she made the dispute a public issue and set radio and TV programs astir. But she is not only a campaigner. Within the past few years and after a precocious start she has emerged as one of the best poets in Ireland. When she published her first book of poems, *New Territory,* in 1967, it was hard to distinguish her voice from the common tone of English poetry at large: worldly, cryptic, Larkinesque. It was the book of a young poet, premature in its certitude. She needed the reading and writing of several years to achieve the true voice of her feeling.

This is the achievement of *The War Horse, In Her Own Image,* and *Night Feed.* With *The Journey* and *Outside History* she took possession of her style. It was now clear that she could say with ease and grace whatever she wanted to say. Her new book, *In a Time of Violence,* does not mark a change of direction or a formal development: it is work of consolidation, culminating in **"Anna Liffey,"** a poem that brings together the preoccupations of several years. I should note, incidentally, that the time of violence referred to in the title is not in any direct sense the period since 1968 in Northern Ireland.

> **The choice of poems in *The Field Day Anthology of Irish Writing* made women poets feel yet again neglected, suppressed. Eavan Boland was their most vigorous speaker. With notable success she made the dispute a public issue and set radio and TV programs astir.**
>
> **—*Denis Donoghue***

Eavan Boland was born in Dublin in 1944, daughter of the artist Frances Kelly and the diplomat Frederick H. Boland. In 1951 she moved with her family to London, where her father served as Irish Ambassador to the Court of St. James. Several of her poems refer to the six years in London—"a city of fogs and strange consonants"—as an unhappy time. Later and more contentedly she spent a few years in New York where her father served as President of the UN General Assembly. She took a degree in English and Latin at Trinity College in Dublin, and started writing poetry. She lives in Dundrum, a middle-class suburb on the south side of Dublin. Many of her poems find themes in her domestic life as the wife of the novelist Kevin Casey and the mother of two daughters.

When Boland started writing poems, she soon decided that the major obstacle in her path was "the Irish poem." Not only was Irish poetry "predominantly male," which meant predominantly Yeats, but it presented images of women as "passive, decorative, raised to emblematic status." As in many other cultures, the spirit of the nation was regularly invoked as a woman—Dark Rosaleen, Cathleen ni Houlihan, Banba, Fodhla, the Sean Bhean Bhocht—beautiful in sorrow, triumphant at last in vision and prophecy. Boland resented that ideological formation and set about undermining it:

> I thought it vital that women poets such as myself should establish a discourse with the idea of a nation. I felt sure that the most effective way to do this was by subverting the previous terms of that discourse.

Besides, as she writes in *In Her Own Image,* "Myths / are made by men."

Boland does not advise women poets to practice a "separatist ideology." That, she believes, is a spurious device: it tempts women "to disregard the whole poetic past as patriarchal betrayal."
—*Denis Donoghue*

But Boland does not advise women poets to practice a "separatist ideology." That, she believes, is a spurious device: it tempts women "to disregard the whole poetic past as patriarchal betrayal." Boland has chosen instead to question "the Irish poem" by revising its myths, especially those which present women as archetypes, symbols of a fractured Ireland transformed into unity. She dislikes the way Samuel Ferguson, Thomas Davis, James Clarence Mangan, Yeats, Lady Gregory, and Padraig Pearse used those myths. "Forgive me if I set the truth to rights," Boland says in **"Listen. This is the Noise of Myth."**

Boland speaks of "the Irish poem," but there is no such limited thing. Irish poems are too diverse to be given such a category. Boland is familiar with modern Irish poetry written in English, but she has little or no direct knowledge of Gaelic poetry.
—*Denis Donoghue*

The issue is awkward. Since the early years of the seventeenth century, Ireland has been spiritually and emotionally divided. Most of the people in the northeast counties are Protestant and feel British, most of the people in the rest of the country are Catholic and feel Irish. (I have to present the matter briefly and approximately.) The Government of Ireland Act, 1920, gave that division a political and legal form, Partition. Eavan Boland evidently thinks it appalling that the myths which animate Irish poetry ignore the fact of difference and express a vision of unity as the true spiritual form of Ireland. I don't share her view. It seems to me that people who have lived in division are likely to sing of unity and to tell stories that aspire to it. I regard Partition as a disaster and the immediate cause not only of the Civil War but of the murders—by the Provisional IRA and the paramilitary Loyalists, the Freedom Fighters (UFF)—which persist to this day. The Downing Street Agreement, signed last December by John Major and the Irish prime minister, Albert Reynolds, guarantees that Partition will be maintained unless and until a majority of the people of Northern Ireland—not of Ireland as a whole—decide to end it. No article of the Agreement takes seriously the feelings of those who want to see Ireland united, the border removed. I am one of those. Perhaps I should also make it clear that I do not regard the achievement of Irish unity as justifying the spilling of blood.

Boland speaks of "the Irish poem," but there is no such limited thing. Irish poems are too diverse to be given such a category. Boland is familiar with modern Irish poetry written in English, but she has little or no direct knowledge of Gaelic poetry. She has satisfied herself that most of Irish poetry demeans women, but there is no evidence that she has reached this conclusion after a sustained reading of the *Tain, Buile Shuibhne,* the lore of the Hag of Beara, Eibhlin Dhubh ni Chonaill's *Lament for Art O'Leary,* and Brian Merriman's *The Midnight Court.* The women in those works are not the passive creatures Boland speaks of. Eibhlin Dhubh ni Chonaill is just as fiery as Eavan Boland. It is true that Yeats liked his women to be beautiful and quiet, but Maud Gonne, Constance Markiewicz, and Eva Gore-Booth chose otherwise; each went her own way. Yeats also wrote the Crazy Jane poems in which Jane is tough enough to please feminists, and the play *A Full Moon in March,* in which he set a queen dancing with a swineherd's severed head.

Boland has developed her complaint about men and their myths and images far beyond the brotherhood of Irish poets. She seems always ready to be incensed and to return to the scene of anger. She has two poems, twenty years apart, on Chardin's painting *Back from Market.* In the first, looking at Chardin's peasant woman, "her eyes mixed / Between love and market," Boland writes:

> I think of what great art removes:
> Hazard and death, the future and the past,
> This woman's secret history and her loves—

and she implies that Chardin gives the woman and her companions much diminished lives:

> He has fixed
> Her limbs in colour, and her heart in line . . .
> And even the dawn market, from whose bargaining
> She has just come back, where men and women

Congregate and go
Among the produce, learning to live from morning
To next day, linked
By a common impulse to survive, although
In surging light they are single and distinct
Like birds in the accumulating snow.

—**"From the Painting 'Back from
Market' by Chardin"**

"Although" is intrusive. Chardin's painting is domestic, but it does not withhold from the woman her single and distinct quality. Her presence exceeds her meaning. In the later poem, **"Self-Portrait on a Summer Evening,"** Boland writes of Chardin's peasant woman that

All summer long
he has been slighting her
in botched blues, tints,
half-tones, rinsed neutrals.

Slighting her? How?

Before your eyes
the ordinary life
is being glazed over.

If the viewer is still not convinced:

Can't you feel it?
Aren't you chilled by it?
The way the late afternoon
is reduced to detail—

I'm chilled by the poem, not by Chardin's picture. "Reduced" is impertinent, unless Boland claims to tell Chardin how he should choose his palette.

Perhaps she does. She tends to see herself in a dramatic and representative light, such that her censoriousness is to be understood as exemplary, her moods as universally significant. Her representative "suburban woman" has only to stand in a garden in Dundrum to feel the whole natural world ministering to her disposition as if the fate of nations hung upon it:

Late, quiet across her garden
sunlight shifts like a cat
burglar, thieving perspectives,
leaving her in the last light
alone, where, as shadows harden,
lengthen, silent she perceives
veteran dead-nettles, knapweed
crutched on walls, a summer's seed
of roses trenched in ramsons, and stares
at her life falling with her flowers,

like military tribute or the tears
of shell-shocked men, into arrears.

—**"Suburban Woman"**

One's life does not fall with one's flowers. It seems to me tactless to compare the movement of a secure life to the tears of shell-shocked men.

In **"Anna Liffey,"** Boland instructs the seabirds to mind her business in preference to their own:

I am sure
The body of an ageing woman
Is a memory
And to find a language for it
Is as hard
As weeping and requiring
These birds to cry out as if they could
Recognize their element
Remembered and diminished in
A single tear.

She evidently assumes that the natural world and the elements it contains have nothing better to do than to sustain her allegories.

Boland's common modes of poetry are lyrical and meditative. Her themes issue from her personal life or from other lives she draws into her own. She is especially tender toward "the unlived life," "evicted possibilities," "the lost, the voiceless, the silent," secret lives sequestered or suppressed in favor of an ostensibly higher cause, her own early restless self:

her mind so frail her body was its ghost.

I want to tell her she can rest,
she is embodied now.

—**"A False Spring"**

But if her tenderness takes the form of brooding on those lives, she rarely imagines them apart from her brooding. In recent poems she is concerned to rescue people from the myths in which they are allegedly imprisoned and to draw them into "history," a discourse she has not clearly established:

Out of myth into history I move to be
part of that ordeal
whose darkness is

only now reaching me from those fields
those rivers, those roads clotted as
firmaments with the dead.

—**"Outside History"**

Morally, the move does Boland credit. But the differences between myth, history, and fiction are left unclear, though her use of these words is peremptory. Each of them is a story. We are not saved from evil or untrue stories by coming out of myth into history. That, too, is a story, and it has death on its hands.

The crucial poem for an understanding of Eavan Boland's work is "The Achill Woman."

—Denis Donoghue

Boland writes of history as if it were true and solid beyond the telling. In **"It's a Woman's World"** she speaks for women, excluded from history:

> as far as history goes
> we were never
> on the scene of the crime.

Later:

> our windows
> moth our children
> to the flame
> of hearth not history.

> And still no page
> scores the low music
> of our outrage.

Sometimes the complaint against men becomes vindictive, and the low music nearly intolerable, as in **"Mastectomy,"** a poem unduly influenced I think by Sylvia Plath's rancor. **"Mastectomy"** denounces the surgeon who performs the operation: he does it, we are urged to believe, to satisfy the predatory character of men:

> So they have taken off
> what slaked them first,
> what they have hated since:

> blue-veined
> white-domed
> home

> of wonder
> and the wetness
> of their dreams.

But the crucial poem for an understanding of Eavan Boland's work is **"The Achill Woman."** In **"A Kind of Scar"** she describes how she came by it. One Easter when she was a young woman she had the loan of a friend's cottage in Achill and stayed there for a week. Mainly she spent the time reading for her courses in Trinity College and studying *The Court Poets of the Silver Age.* The cottage had no water, and every evening the caretaker, "an old woman who shared a cottage with her brother at the bottom of the field," carried up a bucket of water to the visitor. Boland and the old woman talked about the famine of the 1840s:

> but nothing now can change the
>   way I went
> indoors, chilled by the wind
> and made a fire
> and took down my book
>   and opened it and failed to
>   comprehend

> the harmonies of servitude
> the grace music gives to flattery
> and language borrows from
>   ambition—

> and how I fell asleep
> oblivious to

> the planets clouding over in the
>   skies,
> the slow decline of the spring
>   moon,
> the songs crying out their ironies.

In **"A Kind of Scar"** Boland complains that "the anguish and power of that woman's gesture on Achill, with its suggestive hinterland of pain, was not something I could predict or rely on in Irish poetry." But if it wasn't in Irish poetry then, it's still missing, because Boland's poem hasn't put it there. The poem expresses Boland's feelings, but it hasn't a word to say about the old woman's.

The poem I would like to read is one in which Boland would imagine how the old woman feels, carrying a bucket of water up the field every evening to the young woman from Dublin who has nothing to do but read Elizabethan poems. Could she not fetch the bucket for herself? Better still: I'd like to read a poem in which the old woman would express her own life and speak of the disharmonies of servitude and come into speech and history under her own auspices. Why should she be dependent upon Eavan Boland for her bounty?

In a Time of Violence has many of Boland's recurring themes: her sense of things diminished by the thought of them; unlived lives; terrains of suffering not indicated by maps:

> Where they died, there the road ended

and ends still and when I take down
the map of this island, it is never so
I can say here is
the masterful, the apt rendering of

the spherical as flat, nor
an ingenious design which persuades a curve
into a plane
but to tell myself again that

the line which says woodland and cries hunger
and gives out among sweet pine and cypress,
and finds no horizon
will not be there.
                    —**"That the Science of Cartography
                    Is Limited"**

In the new book, too, Boland writes of the Huguenot cemetery in Dublin, graves of the dispossessed; of Irish seamstresses in St. Louis in 1860, blinded by their craft; of lost arts; of things that happen out of sight and out of mind; and of how hard it is for a woman to become a figure in a poem. **"Anna Liffey"** has the problem of keeping Joyce's Anna Livia out of the poem or at a distance from it. A woman who identifies herself with the River Liffey is likely to have Joyce's woman taking over the show:

My great blue bedroom, the air so quiet, scarce a cloud. In peace and silence. I could have stayed up there for always only. It's something fails us. First we feel. Then we fall. And let her rain now if she likes. Gently or strongly as she likes. Anyway let her rain for my time is come. I done me best when I was let. Thinking always if I go all goes. A hundred cares, a tithe of troubles and is there one who understands me?

Boland's **"Anna Liffey"** can't rise or fall to that eloquence, and in the end it settles for a claim, the achievement of a voice, we might well have been left quietly to infer:

Consider rivers.
They are always en route to
Their own nothingness. From the first moment
They are going home. And so
When language cannot do it for us,
Cannot make us know love will not diminish us,
There are these phrases
Of the ocean
To console us,
Particular and unafraid of their completion.
In the end
Everything that burdened and distinguished me
Will be lost in this:
I was a voice.

My favorite poem in the new book is **"Lava Cameo,"** about a brooch carved on volcanic rock. Let's suppose there is such a brooch and that Boland associates it with her grandparents. But the detail must be improvised, and the moral of the made-up story is this:

there is a way of making free with
the past,
a pastiche of what is
real and what is
not, which can only be
justified if you think of it
not as sculpture but syntax:
a structure extrinsic to meaning
    which uncovers
the inner secret of it.

It strikes me that if Boland makes free with the past in this spirit, she should give Yeats the same concession; in which case the myths he recited have a right to be heard. They have a claim at least as good as Boland's to be a structure extrinsic to the meaning of Ireland which uncovers the inner secret of it.

Finally I should declare a preference. Eavan Boland's best poems seem to me those in which she writes without apparent fuss or political flourish. She gets on with it, writes the poem, and leaves the ideological significance of it to be divined. Her feeling is discovered through the words for it: "the line which says woodland and cries hunger." From the new book I quote **"The Pomegranate"**:

The only legend I have ever loved is
The story of a daughter lost in hell.
And found and rescued there.
Love and blackmail are the gist of it.
Ceres and Persephone the names.
And the best thing about the legend is
I can enter it anywhere. And have.
As a child in exile in
A city of fogs and strange consonants,
I read it first and at first I was
An exiled child in the crackling dusk of
The underworld, the stars blighted.
    Later
I walked out in a summer twilight
Searching for my daughter at bedtime.
When she came running I was ready
To make any bargain to keep her.
I carried her back past whitebeams.
And wasps and honey-scented buddleias.
But I was Ceres then and I knew
Winter was in store for every leaf
On every tree on that road.
Was inescapable for each one we passed.

And for me.
It is winter
And the stars are hidden.
I climb the stairs and stand where
   I can see
My child asleep beside her teen magazines,
Her can of Coke, her plate of uncut fruit.
The pomegranate! How did I forget it?
She could have come home and been safe
And ended the story and all
Our heartbroken searching but she reached
Out a hand and plucked a pomegranate.
She put out her hand and pulled down
The French sound for apple and
The noise of stone and the proof
That even in the place of death,
At the heart of legend, in the midst
Of rocks full of unshed tears
Ready to be diamonds by the time
The story was told, a child can be
Hungry. I could warn her. There is still a chance.
The rain is cold. The road is flint-coloured
The suburb has cars and cable television.
The veiled stars are above ground.
It is another world. But what else
Can a mother give her daughter but such
Beautiful rifts in time?
If I defer the grief I will diminish the gift
The legend will be hers as well as mine.
She will enter it. As I have.
She will wake up. She will hold
The papery, flushed skin in her hand.
And to her lips. I will say nothing.

My short list includes **"The Latin Lesson," "Fever," "The Women," "The Journey," "An Irish Childhood in England: 1951," "Domestic Interior," "Night Feed," "Suburban Woman: A Detail," "We Are Always Too Late,"** and **"Outside History."** From the new book I would add **"The Dolls Museum in Dublin," "Moths," "At the Glass Factory in Cavan Town," "Lava Cameo," "Love,"** and **"We Are the Only Animals Who Do This."** Each of these is a very good poem, if not quite the supreme poem Boland asks for in **"A Woman Painted on a Leaf"**:

   I want a poem
   I can grow old in. I want a poem I
     can die in.

But that is too much to ask. As my mother used to say, less will have to do.

Jan Garden Castro (review date 6 June 1994)

SOURCE: "Mad Ireland Hurts Her Too," in *Nation*, June 6, 1994, pp. 798-802.

[In the following review, Castro states that "the real beauty of reading the poems [in In a Time of Violence] *lies in discovering the difficulty in each and the delicacy with which Boland dismantles icons associated with Irish tradition and culture."]*

In a Time of Violence, Eavan Boland's seventh poetry book, held third place on the *Irish Times* best-seller list in mid-April, in the "non-fiction" paperback category. Although it was replaced a week later by Darina Allen's *Simply Delicious: Versatile Vegetables,* it is significant that a poetry collection should join other top-selling, socially conscious books in Ireland: Thomas Keneally's *Schindler's List,* Zlata Filipovic's diary and Roddy Doyle's Booker Prize-winning novel *Paddy Clarke Ha Ha Ha.* The serendipitous upsurge for poetry seemed tied to Boland's appearance on the leading TV late show and her headliner status in the A. T. Cross Cúirt Festival of Literature in Galway, which also featured Nobel Laureate Derek Walcott and American poets Denise Levertov and C. K. Williams.

Women poets in Ireland—or England or the United States—rarely achieve this level of commercial *and* critical success. For her part, Boland argues that in the past twenty years, Irish women have advanced from being anonymous mute witnesses in the belly of a male-created "mother" Ireland to being authors of literature. As she told interviewer Jody Allen-Randolph last year,

   the woman poet is an emblematic figure in poetry
   now in the same way that the Romantic and the
   Modernist poets once were. . . . [They] were emblematic not because they were awkward, or daring, or disruptive. But because the projects they set themselves—the way they approached poetry itself—internalized the stresses and truths of poetry at that moment in time. This is just what the woman poet does. This is her importance to the critique, outside the worth of any individual poems.

In a Time of Violence follows *Outside History,* a volume of selected poems, in its keen-edged deliberations about war, art and Irish, especially female, identities. To the first-time reader of Boland, this slim volume may appear easy to canvass. Even in the ominous title, the language is lilting, springy and not bookish. The poems, like gift boxes, tend to be filled with ironic yet delighting things—flowers, a party dress and a heather hillscape near the river Liffey inform images particularizing Irish famines, wars and legends. Even so, the real beauty of reading the poems lies in discovering the difficulty in each and the delicacy with which Boland dismantles icons associated with Irish tradition and culture.

Boland is literally freeing Irish poetry from its modernist moorings to oversimplified nationalist and Celtic myths, English meter and other conventions; her postmodern project permits the voices in the poem to debate among themselves, to encompass visual arts, history, philosophy and other disciplines and to navigate the Irish past and present without reducing or compromising truths she discovers.

Born in Dublin in 1944, Boland developed her distinctive voice in the course of a conservative upbringing in Dublin, London and New York City. She characterized her education good-humoredly for the *Dictionary of Irish Literature:* "I am convent-educated entirely.... I'm certain I lost my faith and kept my virginity there." During her father Frederick Boland's service as Irish ambassador to the Court of St. James's and to the United Nations, she faced encounters with anti-Irish teachers and childhood exile, which she recalls in such poems as **"An Irish Childhood in England: 1951," "In Exile"** (both in *Outside History*) and **"In Which the Ancient History I Learn Is Not My Own."** These poems let the victim reverse her fate. **"The Parcel"** re-examines the "dying arts" of Irish living, picturing her artist mother Frances Kelly using shears "the colour of the rained-on steps" and wrapping packages for destinations no longer traversed by "doomed steamships and outdated trains."

As a student and lecturer at Trinity College, Boland gradually realized she was not "one of the boys" and became disaffected from male perspectives in British and Irish literary legacies—the original oral tales as well as their incarnations by James Clarence Mangan and William Butler Yeats. At 22, in 1967, she published *New Territory,* her first book. Already she questioned Yeats's revival of legends to inspire pro-Irish warring factions; his story "Belief and Unbelief" suggests that beliefs, like leprechauns, may be "better than another's truth," and may sweetly feed wild bees. In her reply, **"Yeats in Civil War,"** Boland contrasts Yeats's voice, smelling honey "where honey could not be" (note the Platonic edge to the "bee" pun), with her own gentle questioning of his escapism "aboard a spiritship" in a land wasted by war. Boland's mixed identification with Yeats dates back to this period.

In *In a Time of Violence,* Boland continues to revise Yeats and others who valorize death and war. Her first section of poems reflects on historical moments including the increase in Huguenot settlements in Ireland after the French revoked the Edict of Nantes in 1685, the Protestant Peep-O-Day vigilante prosecutions of Catholics in the 1780s and the great potato famine of 1845-49. **"Writing in a Time of Violence"** is a memory of Boland's period at Trinity: The narrator cannot warn her youthful self, who is busy making "satin phrases" for a course in Rhetoric, that beautiful speech is dangerous and may contain and incite violent acts. In addition to targeting present bloodthirsty nationalist rivalries, this

is a veiled reference to Yeats's play *Cathleen ni Houlihan,* an adaptation of a Celtic myth featuring a man-eating enchantress; Maud Gonne's 1902 performance as the beautiful Irish revolutionary fueled men such as Sinn Fein founder Arthur Griffith to fight for Ireland. Using her own version of Virgil's voice, Boland censures the terrors hidden in language agendas that rally men to war. Instead, she describes a hill woman's memories of dire hardships.

> **Boland's present direction of including re-created artworks as visual metaphors hanging in defined settings in her poems is foreshadowed as far back as 1967, in "From the Painting 'Back From Market' by Chardin." Boland dismisses this as a student effort, yet it appears to me to grapple rigorously with the formal, spatial and linear complexities of words.**
> **—*Jan Garden Castro***

Boland also revises Yeats's views of females in her series on dolls and artifacts. Yeats's poems such as "The Dolls" (in which talking dolls criticize a crying baby as the dollmaker's wife apologizes for her child) and "Upon a Dying Lady" employ dolls as iconic references to a living child and a dying woman. Boland's **"The Dolls Museum in Dublin"** details the historical damage to the dolls in the Dublin museum as the narrator replaces them on the shelf as nonliving signs of "the hostages ignorance / takes from time and ornament from destiny."

Boland's present direction of including re-created artworks as visual metaphors hanging in defined settings in her poems is foreshadowed as far back as 1967, in **"From the Painting 'Back From Market' by Chardin."** Boland dismisses this as a student effort, yet it appears to me to grapple rigorously with the formal, spatial and linear complexities of words. The poem juxtaposes the narrator's speculations about the actual and dream life of Chardin's peasant woman with images of the woman as one among many:

> . . . I think of what great art removes:
> Hazard and death, the future and the past,
> This woman's secret history and her loves—
>
> And even the dawn market, from whose bargaining
> She has just come back, where men and women
> Congregate and go
> Among the produce, learning to live from morning
> To next day, linked
> By a common impulse to survive, although
> In surging light they are single and distinct,

Like birds in the accumulating snow.

The poem has formal and textual similarities to Auden's "Musée des Beaux Arts." Unlike his narrator, who observes the discrepancy in Bruegel's *Icarus* between the falling boy's disaster and the unruffled sailing ship, Boland's narrator considers the distances between truth, authorship and art. This poem is an early formulation of Boland's present practice of deposing some poet's notions and reinscribing values aligned with Virgil and Primo Levi.

It strikes me that many American poets of the generation matriculating in the sixties were exposed to totally different influences and expectations. My eclectic readings of E. E. Cummings, Robert Creeley, Pablo Neruda, Wole Soyinka, Elizabeth Bishop, A. R. Ammons, James Merrill, Adrienne Rich, Denise Levertov, Anthony Hecht and James Wright typify the age. We were going forward in history to hear Martin Luther King Jr.'s "I have a dream" speech at the foot of the Washington Monument and back to our disparate "roots." We protested the Vietnam War, acted up at poetry happenings. We were busy versifying the present. In search of individual identities, we set aside questions of our poetic inheritance from the above poets as well as from demonic types (Lowell, Bishop, Berryman, etc.) whose alcoholism, suicide or dysfunctional behaviors tended to be romanticized and even imitated. Many of those arguing for a public morality did not equally subscribe to a private morality, so it was an era of accumulating anxieties between men and women. "The canon" was a social club to which Emily Dickinson had not *yet* been admitted. Eliot, Joyce and Pound enthusiasts were careful *not* to associate their verse with my St. Louis hometowner and his cronies, while admirations for Gertrude Stein defied the fact that she was largely not on the syllabus.

Growing tensions regarding gender and genre added to the confusions of the Irish as well as the American seventies. In 1969, Boland married novelist Kevin Casey and moved to a Dublin suburb. Her volumes *The War Horse, In Her Own Image, Night Feed* and *The Journey* address Irish versions of the dilemma, which she now views as a cultural fiction:

> Ironically, in the Irish poem, the woman's image became a text of iconic nationalism. The sense of people addressing Ireland as a woman was a very interesting fiction and a deeply misleading one, because of course it excluded all the unglamorous, difficult, complicated lives led by silent people—women who were silenced by that metaphor. Therefore, what you were left with was an ingenious complex of silences that you had to dismantle.

One can see the poet setting about this project in *Outside*

History, which points to Boland's talent for creating fictions, paintings and philosophies in a poem. Her voice attains a satisfying resonance and depth in the course of addressing women's dilemmas and rethinking how and in what ways female consciousness could inform poetry. The five sections of poems, **"Object Lessons," "Outside History," "Distances," "The Journey"** and **"Domestic Interior,"** individually and cumulatively stitch, paint and interweave the viewpoints of varied individuals into the Irish picture. In **"Self-Portrait on a Summer Evening,"** Boland's narrator closes by saying:

> I am Chardin's woman
>
> edged in reflected light,
> hardened by
> the need to be ordinary.

Aileen McKeough's abstract, sun-colored tombstone on the cover of *In a Time of Violence* properly prefigures the roles of history, myths and memory in Boland's three sections of poems: **"Writing in a Time of Violence," "Legends"** and **"Anna Liffey."** The volume's primary distinguishing feature is an engaging narrative voice that acts as mediator between itself and other voices. The self-consciously interrupted narrative sequences facilitate Boland's destabilization of male hegemony over iconic references. This postmodern slant operates simultaneously on conceptual, factual and other planes, presenting sharply focused yet painterly images. The poet's beautiful-sounding lines employ irony and "metric shadows," her term for "a series of dissonances that are visibly connected to metric structure," as she replaces rhyme and traditional meter with reason and the rhythms of Irish syntax. (This contrasts with, say, Bishop's way of technically interpolating a strong meter and a strong vernacular.) The originality and the dynamic of these processes are illustrated in **"Lava Cameo"** and **"A Woman Painted on a Leaf,"** from the **"Legends"** section, which aligns personal stories and myths.

"Lava Cameo (A brooch carved on volcanic rock)" incises a tale based upon an oral fragment about Boland's grandmother meeting her sea captain husband at each port where his ship docked because she "feared the women." Both die young. Using the brooch as a controlling metaphor intended to be, Boland told one audience, "the inscribed face on the material of destruction," the poet invents a picture that speaks to and forges connections between the past and the present, as the narrator considers a core theme:

> there is a way of making free with the past,
> a pastiche of what is
> real and what is
> not, which can only be
> justified if you think of it

not as sculpture but syntax:

a structure extrinsic to meaning
which uncovers
the inner secret of it . . .

"A Woman Painted on a Leaf," the closing poem of *In a Time of Violence,* reaffirms the poet's intention to free or destroy stale and contrived images of women—to remove them from the imprisoning frame of disingenuous Irish and world mythology. (In fact, Boland has set up this *denouement* in **"Anna Liffey,"** by stating "The body is a source. Nothing more," and admitting that "In the end / Everything that burdened and / distinguished me / Will be lost in this: / I was a voice.") The twenty-eight-line poem appears simple, yet its complexities show, rather than merely describe, its injunction to destroy falsehood. First the narrator composes a scene:

I found it among curios and silver.
in the pureness of wintry light.

The narrator next decries the suffocating "suspension of life" seen in the face on the "veined surface":

This is not death. It is the terrible
suspension of life.

I want a poem
I can grow old in. I want a poem I can die in.

I want to take
this dried-out face,
as you take a starling from behind iron,
and return it to its element of air, of ending—

The narrator proceeds to free—or to project the freeing of—the artifact, until it is a leaf,

a crisp tinder underfoot. Cheekbones. Eyes. Will
be
a mouth crying out. Let me.

Let me die.

These last words are spoken by the artifact, in the sound of its own demise under someone's foot. This gives the image the last word but also puts words into the mouth of a leaf that is in the act of being destroyed by the narrator. In effect, this seems to leave suspended, in the place of the image on a leaf, the narrator's wish to face facts about aging and dying within the composed pictures in poems.

With apparent simplicity, Boland frames the large aesthetic and historic issues central to the poet's concerns. How can

a poem "age"? How can a poem convey life rather than a stale myth? In posing a philosophical and epistemological suggestion in the center of the poem, and in leaving it partially unanswered, Boland arrives at a meaningful ambiguity. Many qualities resonate beyond the poem's simple construction: the "I want" allusions to William Blake's *Songs of Innocence,* the lively assonance in "as you take a starling from behind iron," and the antithetical correlation between freeing a dead image and a live bird from false associations.

Boland combines impeccable craft, resilient metaphors and, above all, moral authority in order to witness human difficulties. Critics already align her ideas with those of Adrienne Rich and Margaret Atwood, and I'd add Toni Morrison, Nadine Gordimer and William Gass. Fictions and sustained metaphors enlarge her literal views of her Irish roots and culture. Boland's ethical perspective is as personal and universal as her focus on the dispossessed and war casualties and on roles within a family. Through her dedication to poetry, one might say Boland has "lost her virginity yet kept her faith" in a way few adults have done. As she squarely confronts the reader with everyday acts, you don't have to be Irish to understand that her messages point toward a future morality a long way off—one in which gender or other classifications do not diminish, essentialize or reduce, one in which our humanity toward one another is evenhanded.

Jody Allen-Randolph (essay date September-October 1994)

SOURCE: "Finding a Voice Where She Found a Vision," in *P. N. Review,* Vol. 21, No. 1, September-October, 1994, pp. 13-17.

[*In the following essay, Allen-Randolph traces Boland's career and defends her as a major poet.*]

It is hard to think of an Irish poet whose work has, over the last two decades, shown as much growth and courage as Eavan Boland's. Eight years ago the widespread establishment view in Ireland had branded her a technically gifted but minor poet. Today, with the recent publication by Carcanet of her latest volume of poetry *In a Time of Violence* and a selection of her prose essays on the way from Norton, she is increasingly officialized as the *feminine* laureate, or simply, and more accurately, as a major poet.

The quick shifts in recent years of Boland's status—from woman poet, to feminist poet, to leading woman poet, to major poet—reflect the stresses and turmoil in the Irish literary world as it struggles to come to terms with its own unwinding history of prejudice. Because Boland's trajectory as a poet is both emblematic and symptomatic of resistance and change in the critical environment of Irish poetry itself over the past twenty-five years, this may be the time to offer a cursory account of her achievement to date. And, at a few key points, to take a look at the equally interesting reception of that achievement in Ireland.

It is hard to think of an Irish poet whose work has, over the last two decades, shown as much growth and courage as Eavan Boland's.
—Jody Allen-Randolph

Boland became a poet in the early sixties as one of an extraordinarily gifted generation of Irish poets (Heaney, Mahon, Longley, Kennelly), among whom there was considerable contact, camaraderie, and debate. They were, in the sense that structure and form seemed second nature to them even as young practitioners, the last generation of nineteenth-century poets. The impressive first books of Boland's colleagues set them firmly on a course to inherit what was, until quite recently, an almost exclusively male establishment, and guaranteed their leadership of the literary field in the seventies and eighties. Boland's career and her reputation as a poet took a quite different course.

After what is customarily, and I think wrongly, viewed as 'a brilliant false start' with her first volume, Boland moved with each successive volume farther away from the old intersection between poetry and maleness which comprised the mainstream of Irish poetry. Consequently, her work lost status and grew less visible to that mainstream and status during the years between 1975 and 1987. Moreover, despite the consistency of her themes and obsessions, finding her voice as a poet came slowly over the course of her first three volumes. Looking back now, those early volumes chart a course, remarkable for its risk, experiment, and individual conscience.

Boland began as the exuberantly formal young poet of *New Territory,* an ambitious, dreamy, high-toned book, the most striking features of which were the young poet's lapidary genius for imagery, her command of a range of poetic forms, and a lyric voice so conventional that you would never know it belonged to a woman. Her chief influence was Yeats, and under his radiant shadow, she found her first subjects at the glamorous intersection between national myth and poetic legend. Central images of imprisonment—the metaphor which underwrites Boland's best work—dominate most of the poems. The volume's best poems ('**New Territory**', '**Athene's Song**', '**Back from the Market**', and '**The Winning of Etain**') are located in an anxiety about what must have seemed at the time an unbridgeable distance between being a poet and being a woman. Over the course of the next six volumes, this distance would become one of Boland's most abiding subjects, driving her to her deepest and richest themes, as she laboured to restore to poetry 'what great art removes: / Hazard and Death, the future and the past, / This woman's secret history and her loves. . . .'

By 1975 Boland's gifted colleagues were well on their way to being nominated as secondary superstars to the political situation in the North. Boland herself was making a less spectacular entrance into the realm of public poetry with her second volume, *The War Horse,* a searching, uneven attempt to articulate a relation between the escalating political violence, her vocation as a poet, and her identity as a woman. By reworking a vernacular voice across formal stanzas, Boland began to blend the formal elements of her craft with the familiar elements of her experience. Several first-rate poems—'**The War Horse**' for instance, and the beautiful elegy '**Child of Our Time**'—emerged from this effort. But the real break through poems, '**Suburban Woman**' and '**Ode to Suburbia**,' came at the end of the volume where Boland struggled to bring together unwieldy fragments of artistic, national and gendered identity. These were not good poems, yet their net effect was both important and disruptive. By constructing an encounter between two fractured elements of a single self—poet and woman—Boland mobilized gender into a sequence of debates with poetry, with violence, and with Irishness. At the end of the volume, poet and woman are 'defeated' by the unsuccessful effort, and 'survive, we two, housed / together in my compromise, my craft / who are of one another the first draft'.

The quick shifts in recent years of Boland's status—from woman poet, to feminist poet, to leading woman poet, to major poet— reflect the stresses and turmoil in the Irish literary world as it struggles to come to terms with its own unwinding history of prejudice.
—Jody Allen-Randolph

Over the course of her next two volumes, Boland would draft the lives and bodies of women into the very centre of the Irish poem, where she would deepen her exploration of the relation between gender, violence, and national identity. This new direction greatly perplexed her Irish male readership, who believed it was a movement off the chart of Irish poetry altogether. Written nearly simultaneously, then organized for publication as two sides—the lyric and the anti-lyric— of a single project, it was the first instalment of the two-volume effort, *In Her Own Image,* which so non-plussed Boland's Irish critics. One reviewer accused her of expressing in 'these curiously unpleasant and at times offensive poems', 'an extraordinary hatred of womanhood, an obsession with femininity regarded as an inferno of self-torture'. Another thought the poems were 'belligerently feminine' and dealt only 'with *strictly feminine* matters such as anorexia, mastectomy, and wife-battering' (italics mine). A third reviewer noted that while Boland 'had suffered a feminist vision,' there was nevertheless a 'triumphant affirmation of womanhood throughout the book'. Clearly Boland had hit a nerve, and the consequences she suffered in doing so threw the flaws and smallmindedness of the critical climate into bold relief.

The volume opens with a reproach to the Muse (**'Tirade for the Mimic Muse'**), a bitter attack on the national muse of Irish cultural unity: 'I know you for the ruthless bitch you are: / Our criminal, our tricoteuse, our Muse . . .' The vehicle of the poem is a dramatic encounter between muse and the woman poet who shows her the realities she has suppressed and the violences, public and private, she has colluded with. The volume then proceeds through a series of ten dramatic monologues whose subjects—anorexia, wife-beating, infanticide, masturbation, menstruation, mastectomy—are degraded states of experience and self-discovery. The point of this painful progress is to explore the interface between public-domain images of women, the uses to which those images have been put, and the privately suffered realities they edit. Or, as Boland once put it, to examine 'the weight of the feminine convention on the individual woman'.

> In my narrative of Boland's critical reception, I do not wish to imply that she was in any way excluded from Irish literary life. She wasn't. Indeed, as a staff reviewer for the *Irish Times,* and a radio presenter with her own poetry program on RTE each week, she had accesses and opportunities unimaginable to young poets in other countries.
> —*Jody Allen-Randolph*

With its angry, estranged tones, its pared-down stanzas, its fractured iambics, and its use of experience from women's lives as metaphors for human oppression, *In Her Own Image* was indeed a radical departure with a radical result: a very visible shift in Boland's readership and constituency. Her new constituency was comprised of the women whose lives, bodies and experiences she was carefully moving to the centre of her work, and it contained a growing, largely urban, feminist contingent. Yet, while the upsurge of feminism in the seventies and the Irish Women's Movement had helped to make women writers like Boland more visible, it did little to surmount the problem of ghettoization of those writers as women. Boland's establishment readership, dis-

missive of 'women's' themes in poetry, summarily dispatched the book as part of what they construed as a second-rate feminist trend, of sociological, not artistic impulse. So unquestioned was this orthodox view of poetry by women that an *Irish Times* reviewer wondered in print whether Boland would 'carry on down the thematically limiting road of the Sisters, or return to dance again on the general iambic table'.

In my narrative of Boland's critical reception, I do not wish to imply that she was in any way excluded from Irish literary life. She wasn't. Indeed, as a staff reviewer for the *Irish Times,* and a radio presenter with her own poetry program on RTE each week, she had accesses and opportunities unimaginable to young poets in other countries. What I am trying to establish here is some of the history, both within her poetry and outside of it, which might explain why her emergence and recognition as 'major' poet came relatively late in her publishing career, and by a seemingly more circuitous route than her generational colleagues.

Boland's fourth, and exceptionally brave, volume *Night Feed* was one of the most important volumes of Irish poetry produced by her generation, though it could not have been more unfashionable at the time, or more poorly welcomed. To the refined local ears of the elite establishment which continued to view 'women's' writing as a kind of provincial female backwater of domesticity and homelife, it must have seemed an astonishing choice. To her new feminist readership, the traditional female roles and values celebrated by the book seemed emphatically regressive. Not surprisingly then, the book was received on all sides with an embarrassed critical silence. One well-known male poet cited it, in a private conversation, as evidence that Boland's talent and ambition as a poet had gone seriously awry. There was, however, a huge, silent, powerless constituency for this volume: I can not count the number of times over the past decade that a woman in passing conversation has told me how much that book meant 'to those of us who were at home, raising our children and living that life'.

What was most anomalous about the silence which followed the release of *Night Feed* was that it was clearly Boland's breakthrough volume, in which she hit her stride as a poet, found her voice, and harnessed a poetic self to a powerful private vision. Thematically, the volume is centred in the series of domestic interiors it frames.

The precedents for these poems came not from verse but from painting. Boland turned to the still lives and domestic interiors of Jean Baptiste Chardin and Jan van Eyck, who, by recognizing the distinction in the homely, revealed their objects as much as they described them. Boland's technique of describing ordinary things with such fresh significance that they become a universe in themselves is learned from these painters. In **'Domestic Interior'**, a poem which takes van Eyck's *The Arnolfini Marriage* as its starting point, she explains:

> But there's a way of life
> that is its own witness:
> put the kettle on, shut the blind.
> Home is a sleeping child,
> an open mind
>
> and our effects,
> shrugged and settled
> in the sort of light
> jugs and kettles
> grow important by.

What gave this volume such rare lyric force was not just the happy combination of its fresh perspective, its thrillingly precise imagery, its clean-edged, uncluttered line, and speech rhythms, but the authoritative new voice it inscribed: ordinary, female and maternal. With the publication of *Night Feed,* a whole psychic terrain was written back into Irish poetry, one which restored its scope and complexity. Paradoxically, it was at this moment, when she was least visible to the literary mainstream, that Boland was in fact becoming the mainstream. Poems like **'Domestic Interior'** and **'Night Feed'** are written not, as her critics thought, from the outskirts of poetry, but from the lyric centre.

While the successes of *Night Feed* went largely unrecognized, they cleared the way for major leaps in Boland's technical development over her next two volumes, and unleashed a prodigious productivity both in poetry and in critical prose essays over the next twelve years.
—*Jody Allen-Randolph*

While the successes of *Night Feed* went largely unrecognized, they cleared the way for major leaps in Boland's technical development over her next two volumes, and unleashed a prodigious productivity both in poetry and in critical prose essays over the next twelve years. In *The Journey,* using a much longer, discordant, more flexible line, Boland brought together the combined achievement of her previous volumes—mixing lyric with anti-lyric, the dark with the celebratory sides of experience—within a single poem and project. *The Journey* made explicit the implicitly political project of *Night Feed:* making women's lives a source of redefinition for what is Irish. By taking the voice she'd found in *Night Feed,* and modulating it across different alignments of experience—maternal, national, literary—Boland began to write a formidable political poem.

More specifically, Boland was interested in disrupting the image of women and the family, essential to the iconography of nationalism, that had been a transcendent unity of identity enshrined in the Irish constitution, and inherited by Irish poetry, after the terrible disruptions of the famine. She accomplished this by several methods. In poems like **'Listen. This is the Noise of Myth'** and **'Mise Eire'**, she juxtaposed the romanticized fictions of female figures carried in traditional Irish myths, songs, and poems, with her own fictions of their 'bereavements of the definite'. In other poems, she juxtaposed inherited conventions with the vivid, everyday experiences and identities they excluded (see **'The Oral Tradition', 'The Glass King'**, and **'Tirade for the Lyric Muse'**). She combined these juxtapositions with expert modulations of voice and image. In **'Mise Eire'** ('I am Ireland') for instance, she invokes the latent idealized imagery of the Irish feminine emblem, Mother Ireland, only to destabilize it by flashing three voices across it in quick succession: the voice of the woman poet, a garrison prostitute, and an immigrant mother. By confronting the nation with its definitional others in poems like this, Boland began to reconfigure what counted as political.

Her efforts were not limited to the Irish poem however; many of the poems in *The Journey* raise ethical questions about the costs, corruptions, and exclusions of art, and the dangers of its ornamentalising tendencies. In poems like **'Self-Portrait on a Summer Evening'** and her impressive subversion of the dream-vision convention, **'The Journey'**, she chooses Chardin and Dante as starting points to show us what art has left out:

> Depend upon it, somewhere a poet is wasting
> his sweet uncluttered metres on the obvious
> emblem instead of the real thing.
> Instead of sulpha we shall have hyssop dipped
> in the wild blood of the unblemished lamb,
> so every day the language gets less
>
> for the task and we are less with the language.

The buzz of excitement about the political spirit and lyric maturity of *The Journey* was evident among communities of women poets and scholars and a growing ripple of acclaim was heard both in the universities and in some of the more progressive corners of literary establishment. The prejudicial cliché about second rate women's work soon evolved into a similarly-toned cliché about feminist politics in the mouths of the same influential arbiters who dismissed women poets for their politics as they admired male poets for theirs. From the loftiest heights of the establishment Boland's latest work could still be dismissed as 'feminist polemical verse', which 'suffers the constraints of intentionalism'. Again, what many critics failed to see was that Boland was not only writing some of the best Irish poetry of the day, but that what they saw as a feminist defilement of a great tradition was actually an essential contribution to it. What Boland was challenging, and the debate over her work was revealing, was an ethical fault-line in Irish poetry, and the small-minded views in the critical environment which supported it.

What many critics failed to see was that Boland was not only writing some of the best Irish poetry of the day, but that what they saw as a feminist defilement of a great tradition was actually an essential contribution to it. What Boland was challenging, and the debate over her work was revealing, was an ethical fault-line in Irish poetry, and the small-minded views in the critical environment which supported it.
—Jody Allen-Randolph

Returning to the territory of a public poetry she had not written since the seventies, Boland continued the work of untwining and redefining the feminine and the national in *Outside History*. After *The War Horse,* Boland had turned her attentions to the 'women's' worlds outside the acceptable borders of Irish poetry. Here, with a darkening lyric vision, an elegiac tone, and a high degree of technical finish, she turned those privately suffered and silent worlds into a powerful alternative history. By locating these worlds outside of history, as her title stipulates, Boland is calling attention to the unrecorded life which moves away from, or is edited out of, the official account of both literature and history.

The formal high-point of the volume is its ambitious title sequence which has an ingenious clock-like configuration: twelve poems cycle through timescapes of changing light and changing seasons, suggesting both the twelve positions on a clock-face and the twelve months of the calendar. Boland runs this nailed-down structure against the argument of the sequence: that time, like myth, is an artificial human construct—an attempt to restrict meaning by controlling it—which ultimately breaks down in the face of mortality. The history of the sequence's title is at once Eavan Boland's personal history and the history of her nation. When she uses one as a metaphor for the other, as she does in **'The Achill Woman'** and **'What We Lost'**, she writes with an unforgettable mixture of courage and perception. In **'What We Lost'**, using a voice which has deepened in resonance and authority, Boland tells the story of a child (her mother) who is told a story which, 'unheard' and 'unshared' is forgotten:

Believe it, what we lost is here in this room

on this veiled evening . . .

The fields are dark already.
The frail connections have been made and are
broken.
The dumb-show of legend has become language,
is becoming silence and who will know that once

words were possibilities and disappointments . . .

The power and sweep of the sequence is a function of the silences into which it taps. The silences of women in these poems are all the more poignant because they are widened to include so many people, past and present, North and South.

By self-consciously using the eye of the outsider in this book, Boland defies the distinctions of inside and outside. By relocating the significant experiences of Irishness in the voices of the traditionally marginalized, she challenges the notion of a central, orthodox Irishness through a perspective that is both subtle and daily, fully attentive to culture as it is constituted not necessarily in tradition but always in human interaction and suffering. Regardless of her subject, she locates history and politics in daily relationships of power, grief, alienation, identification and love.

In Ireland *Outside History* was received quietly and slowly at first, and then with growing enthusiasm, counterpointed by the immediate critical attention and acclaim it received in the United States, where critics were quick to notice the challenge it made to a narrow male appropriation of Irish writing and the Irish past. In the year immediately following the publication of *Outside History,* this challenge finally broke out in earnest in the form of a media debate over *The Field Day Anthology of Irish Writing*. By leaving women largely out of their 1980s redefinition of Ireland, the Field Day generation had exhibited a myopia symptomatic of a wider cultural one: they had failed to take account of the ways in which women were centrally concerned with the formation of national subjectivity and iconology. When the members of Field Day refused to debate the issue in Ireland (a subsequent Channel 4 debate with Tom Paulin representing Field Day only worsened matters), the Irish media supported the critique and the poets, Boland and Nuala Ni Dhomhnail, who launched it.

Two years have passed since the Field Day episode, and the enormous change in the critical environment is partially visible in the warm and immediate welcome of Boland's seventh and most recent volume *In a Time of Violence*. The sound of heavy hammering, of every element put perfectly into place, which was the trademark of *Outside History* is relaxed here into plainer speech, fewer technical props, and a warmer, looser tone reminiscent of *Night Feed*. Her primary mode is elegy, and her interest in the history of objects—a cameo, a hand-embroidered dress or doll, a glass-blown swan, a statue of a weeping woman—is elegiac: it deals with what is fixed, locked, lost, and loved. In **'The Parcel'**, written in free verse, Boland makes an argument about the mortality of art forms and their arbitrators. Here the art of parcel-preparing which the poet remembers from childhood, an art passed down from mother to daughter, has suddenly disappeared, and with it the life and circumstances which validated it. As art changes to meet the pressures of present realities, its arbitrators, here the blade sharpener, disappear overnight.

The volume is divided into three sections. The first is a pessimistic seven-poem sequence, **'Writing in a Time of Violence'** which builds incrementally an argument about the way powerful elements of expression, especially in times of violence, can repress or destroy elements of ethics. The danger of all writing, Boland suggests here, is that the furious forces engaged in the act get accessorized into ornament in the end. The sequence works by juxtaposition: each poem takes an expressive form or ornament—a map, a painting, a letter, a dress, a doll, a hand-carved cot, or a device of rhetoric—and sets it against the dark background of the violence of its age. Moreover, each expressive form or ornament survives as a witness to the elements of control and self-deception of its age, and gives the age a distorted meaning, devoid of the suffered lives which created them.

In the opening poem, **'That the Science of Cartography is Limited'**, Boland exposes the geography of human experience and suffering which remains outside the borders of the map-maker's art: 'the fragrance of balsam', 'the gloom of cypresses' and the abrupt end of a road, the only remaining sign of the terrible deaths of the 1847 famine. **'In a Bad Light'**, a poem about Irish seamstresses in St Louis during the American Civil War, pushes the argument further. All that survives of the 'coffin ships, and the salt of exile' are the dresses they sewed their deaths into for 'history's abandonment'. Abandoned by history, the suffered life is subsumed by the ornament of its labour. This, Boland tells us, 'is the nightmare'.

In the final poem of the sequence, **'Beautiful Speech'**, language itself is the dangerous ornament in a country 'already lost . . . in song and figure'. Here Boland employs the legend of St Patrick banishing the snakes from Ireland to show the dangerous underbelly of language and myth, where the very sweetness of the language and the old stories are seductions to collusion. With her beautifully handled time changes from past to present, and her implicit evocation of the Eve myth, Boland is addressing the temptations of language, ornament, and unexamined stances which confront young poets generally, and women poets specifically. But in her use of the pronoun 'we' and her choice of the word citi-

zen, implying as it does membership in collective identity ('we have lived / where language is concealed. Is perilous. / We will be—we have been—citizens of its hiding place') she widens the political sweep of the poem to include everyone who shares an Irish past or present. The poem expertly moves us through the local setting of the poet's youth 'where friends call out their farewells in / a city of whispers and interiors' and steps us squarely into the heartbreak of the national dilemma where:

> the dear vowels
> Irish Ireland Ours are
> absorbed into Autumn air,
> are out of earshot in the distances
> we are stepping into where we never
>
> imagine words such as *hate*
> and *territory* and the like—unbanished still
> as they always would be—wait
> and are waiting under
> beautiful speech to strike.

The second section of the volume, **'Legends'**, is a series of poems about children and growing older, lost stories and lost arts. The characters of legend here are not from some other world but are the husbands, daughters, and mothers of daily life. Their living presences, illuminated by the poet's love, are directly counterposed to the darker vision of ornamental objects in **'Writing in a Time of Violence'**, thus challenging the drama of power in the sequence with the drama of love in the following section. Here the poems take place in the realms 'between expectation and memory', and all involve myths of loss, 'the moment all nature fears and tends towards'.

In the last section of the volume, **'Anna Liffey'**, Boland picks up the argument about the ornamentalizing dangers of language again, and joins it to an argument about ageing. Stepping out of her house on a spring evening in **'Time and Violence'** the poet encounters a multiple aisling, a series of ornamentalized women, sexual captives within their frozen images—a shepherdess, Cassiopeia in the night sky and, in a pool beneath cherry trees, a mermaid with 'invented tresses'—who plead to be made human 'in cadences of change and mortal pain / and words we can grow old and die in.' But the radical heart of this new volume is the long title poem of this section, **'Anna Liffey'**.

'Anna Liffey' is Boland's usurpation of Joyce's riverized Molly Bloom, Anna Livia Plurabelle from *Finnegan's Wake*, and her version follows his fairly closely. Joyce's narrative begins with two young washerwomen at the source of the Liffey, having a conversation about their lives and the river. Anna Livia, the river personified, thinks back over her own life and remembers how she has been a cloud, a shower, a rivulet, a brook, before becoming a river. As the river progresses, Anna Livia becomes a woman. And as she flows downstream to the sea, she yields her place to her daughter who appears, as she did in youth, in the formation of rain. When the city is reached at dusk, the two washerwomen have grown old, turning into elements of the landscape in the form of a tree and a stone, and the river goes 'home slowly now by own way' until it is lost. But the narrative, imitating the circular geography of the Liffey, loops back around again to the beginning.

In Boland's version, like Joyce's, the river is made of language and memory. The poem is constructed as an open sequence of thirteen unnumbered sections which reflect the thirteen bridges the River Liffey crosses under on its passage from its source in County Wicklow to its destination in the Irish sea. Creating a kind of fragmented spatial argument about names, the body, identity, and language, the poem asks the central questions about consciousness, then extends them: What makes a self? Where is it located? What makes a place? A home? A nation?

Boland's poem follows the movement and theme of the Joycean narrative, the same succession of source, city, daughters and rain. However Boland omits Joyce's washerwomen and begins her narrative instead with the legend of how the river Liffey and the land around it got its name, from a woman who loved them. Against this myth, Boland counterpoints the growth of her own national consciousness: 'My country took hold of me. / My children were born.' 'The beautiful vowels sounding out home' are the names of her children, not her country; the love here is for the people, not the land. By thus conscientiously repositioning language and identity through the witness of the woman's life in poetry, Boland is creating a source for the redefinition of both poetry and national identity.

Technically speaking, **'Anna Liffey'** occurs at an important intersection of gender and genre: it is Boland's usurpation of the big, fragmented Modernist fusion poem proposed by Eliot. It employs a symbolist-cinematic technique which replicates the elements of perception by key repetitions of image and cadence—'a woman in the doorway of house. / a river in the city of her birth'. The images build to fuse into one intense central image at the end, in this case, the river. A series of fractured arguments are carried within the images, and they too fuse in the end into one intense argument about identity and mortality. The self, the woman in the doorway of her home, becomes the centrifugal force in the poem.

Here the high style of the great Modernist poem is subverted by using a non-high self. What we are watching is the poetically inadmissible self of the ageing woman, like the maternal woman in **Night Feed**, being made an admissible self in poetry. The static voice of the female figure is being

usurped, and made to age in the poem; it is being returned, like the tears, the rain, and the river, to a state of process. A revision of the poetic self occurs as the poem moves powerfully to align itself with the voices of the time. It does not foreground its alliance with the elite stance of the poet, but locates itself in the powerlessness of an ordinary figure: A woman standing in a doorway of a house, who changes and ages as she moves through her life, her motherhood and her sexual identity, and becomes a voice. It is the movement of this voice to the centre of lyric poetry, where it interrogates the huge constructs of literature and nation, which underwrites the radical accomplishment of the poem.

It would be difficult to over-estimate the influence and change Boland has brought both to perceptions of Irish poetry and to the practice of it over the last two decades. The life she has inscribed in poetry exists as a powerful challenge and corrective to tradition. The professional fraternities—literary and academic—who were so quick to assign her a marginal status must now accept that not only was she exploring a different register of experience, with a different audience, but that register and audience have become the mainstream. In Ireland, one week after its release, **In a Time of Violence** is at the top of the best-seller list for non-fiction. An indication, perhaps, that Boland's post-mortem prediction at the end of **'Anna Liffey'** is not so premature after all:

> In the end
> It will not matter
> That I was a woman. I am sure of it.
> The body is a source, nothing more . . .
> In the end
> everything that burdened and distinguished me
> will be lost in this:
> I was a voice.

Kerry E. Robertson (essay date December 1994)

SOURCE: "Anxiety, Influence, Tradition and Subversion in the Poetry of Eavan Boland," in *Colby Quarterly,* Vol. XXX, No. 4, December, 1994, pp. 264-78.

[*In the following essay, Robertson analyzes Boland's subversion of the male tradition in her poetry.*]

In his *Yeats,* Harold Bloom suggests that the greatest influence on a poet is his precursors and that the knowledge of this influence intimidates the ephebe, or fledgling, poet: "The ephebe cannot be Adam early in the morning. There have been too many Adams, and they have named everything." Because the precursors "have named everything," the ephebe experiences "a variety of melancholy or an anxiety-principle.

It concerns the poet's sense of his precursors, and of his own achievement in relation to theirs. Have they left him room enough, or has their priority cost him his art?" As Bloom developed these theories in *Anxiety of Influence,* the ephebe poet, in order to create the space he needs in which to write his poetry, consciously or unconsciously, but always deliberately, "misreads" his precursors. Every ephebe poet falls under the spell of those who have preceded him: "If he emerges from it, however crippled and blinded, he will be among the strong poets."

Unfortunately, as his theory is developed in *Yeats and Anxiety,* Bloom concerns himself almost exclusively with dead, white, male poets; he says nothing of either minority or female poets. Several critics have noted this gap in Bloom's theory and have attempted to fill it. These critics assert that while female writers do feel some anxiety about the influence of their precursors, it is not an anxiety as to whether the precursors have left them space enough in which to write. Their anxiety seems to arise from the fact that the male writers of the past do not address the issues in which the female writers are most interested or that they do not see shared concerns from the same perspective. The female writers feel they are breaking new ground, and they are anxious *because* they have no female precursors or at best these precursors are few and far between. The anxiety experienced by female writers could more accurately be characterized as one over a *lack* of influence.

When Virginia Woolf wrote *A Room of One's Own,* she was unable to locate any of those whom she called "Shakespeare's sisters," i.e., women writers of the Renaissance upon whom she could look as her precursors. She was forced to conclude that "no woman wrote a word of that extraordinary literature when every other man, it seemed, was capable of song or sonnet." In the years since 1929, we have discovered, much to our pleasure, that Woolf was mistaken. There were Renaissance women who were "capable of song or sonnet," women such as Elizabeth of York, Anne Boleyn, Mary Sidney Herbert, Anne Askew, Elizabeth Tanfield Cary, Aemilia Lanier, and Mary Sidney Wroth. In the seventeenth and eighteenth centuries, Margaret Cavendish, Aphra Behn, Katharine Phillips, Anne Finch, Anne Bradstreet, Anne Killigrew, and Fanny Burney followed their lead. These writers were succeeded in turn by the great female novelists of the nineteenth century: Jane Austen, Mary Shelley, Anne Bronte, Charlotte Bronte, Emily Bronte, Elizabeth Gaskill, and George Eliot.

Nonetheless, the canon of their work is still not extensive. The bulk of literature in English remains that of Bloom's dead, white, male poets. Therefore, female writers' anxiety is not confined solely to their lack of precursors; they also feel anxiety towards the very language in which they are forced to write. It has been, for most of recorded history, a weapon of the patriarchy which has been used over the centuries to silence women. Writing has been so closely associated with male power and authority that women who "attempted the pen," as Anne Finch described it, have felt it necessary to belittle their own accomplishments in order to escape condemnation as "unfeminine." The Renaissance women listed above struggled against charges of immodesty, even unchastity, when they dared to publish their works. In their discussion of nineteenth-century women writers, Sandra Gilbert and Susan Gubar explore the notion that the pen is a "metaphorical penis." According to their analysis, male poets have repeatedly expressed their capacity to write as "the begetting of one's thoughts on paper." The male writer is said to "father" his text in much the same way that God "fathered" the universe:

> The mimetic aesthetic that begins with Aristotle and descends through Sidney, Shakespeare, and Johnson implies that the poet, like a lesser God, has made or engendered an alternative, mirror-universe in which he actually seems to enclose or trap shadows of reality. Similarly, Coleridge's Romantic concept of the human "imagination or esemplastic power" is of a virile, generative force which echoes "the eternal act of creation in the infinite I AM," while Ruskin's phallic-sounding "Penetrative Imagination" is a "possession-taking faculty" and a "piercing . . . mind's tongue" that seizes, cuts down, and gets at the root of experience in order "to throw up what new shoots it will."

Because the act of composition is so fundamentally associated with the male gender, the female poet experiences an "anxiety of authorship," which is "an anxiety built from complex and often only barely conscious fears of that authority which seems to the female artist to be by definition inappropriate to her sex."

If language itself is overwhelmingly male, so also are the forms of poetry that that language has shaped: "Most Western literary genres are, after all, essentially male—devised by male authors to tell male stories about the world." When female poets come to write in these genres, there is a certain strangeness to their work:

> Many of the most distinguished late eighteenth-century and nineteenth-century English and American women writers do not seem to "fit" into any of those categories to which our literary historians have accustomed us. Indeed, to many critics and scholars, some of these literary women look like isolated eccentrics.

Gilbert and Gubar believe that the "eccentricity" and "isolation" common to these women's writing represent their attempts to create space for themselves amongst their male precursors. In Bloomian terms, the oddity in their writing is a result of their misreading of the male precursors. These female poets

> may have attempted to transcend their anxiety of authorship by *revising* male genres, using them to record their own dreams and their own stories in *disguise*. Such writers, therefore, both participated in and . . . "swerved" from the central sequences of male literary history, enacting a uniquely female process of revision and redefinition that necessarily caused them to seem "odd."

Virginia Woolf noted that the fiction and poetry which dealt with war were considered important, whereas those which concerned themselves with "the feelings of women in a drawing-room" were not: "A scene in a battlefield is more important than a scene in a shop—everywhere and much more subtly the difference of value persists." The situation remains much the same today. The labels "miniaturized," "domestic," and "interior" are frequently applied to women's writing, and these adjectives are then used to dismiss that writing. Even today, female poets must struggle to create a space for themselves in which they can write freely and feelingly of their worlds, only to discover all too often that that struggle is devalued in the still overwhelmingly male-dominated world of poetry.

For Irish female poets, especially those who, like Eavan Boland, Eilean Ni Chuilleanain, and Medbh McGuckian, write in English, this anxiety is compounded in two ways. First, not only are they forced to write in a language that is in many ways antagonistic to their gender, they also must write in one that is at odds with their national and cultural heritage. English is a transplanted language, one imposed on the Irish by those who colonized their country. Second, if the canon of English writers is weighted in favor of male writers, the canon of Irish writers in English is even more so. When contemporary female Irish poets look for their precursors, they find a dearth similar to the one Woolf experienced more than sixty years ago. A few Irish women—Maria Edgeworth, Emily Lawless, and Edith Somerville—were able to become novelists in the nineteenth century. There are only a few Anglo-Irish female poets; the vast majority of Irish female poets wrote in Gaelic, a language that is inaccessible to most of the poets writing today.

For these reasons, Irish women poets are trapped in a double bind: they are alienated from the tools of their trade both as women and as Irish people. These circumstances do create a certain "anxiety of influence," although not exactly the same as that described by Bloom.

Eavan Boland is one contemporary female Irish poet who has expressed her awareness of this double bind in both her poetry and her prose. She is extremely conscious that English, "the language in which we are speaking, is his before it is mine," is "his" in a dual sense: "his" as an *English man.* Unlike Adrienne Rich, who advocates a separatist movement for women poets, Boland believes that the Irish female poet can reclaim the English language and traditional poetic forms and make them her own through a subversion of them. She must do, as Emily Dickinson did: "Tell all the Truth but tell it slant."

In her essay on Elizabeth Bishop, **"An Un-Romantic American,"** Boland tries to explain why she, as an Irish female poet, has felt such a strong kinship with an American female poet of thirty years earlier. Her strong affiliation with Bishop's poetry is something of a puzzle to her because "the post-colonial aftermath made Irish poets often more interested in, and anxious about, British poetry than American." However, she feels part of the attraction towards Bishop's poetry lies in a shared sense of exile. Boland quotes Bishop as speaking of herself in interviews as "feeling 'like a guest'" in her own country. So does Boland: "It took me years—and a great many revisions of perspective—before I could connect my Irishness with my poetry and my womanhood." And so do most of those whom Boland calls "good Irish writers": Bishop "defines her country—as so many good Irish writers do—by her absence from it." There is a strong sense in Bishop of an "inability to belong" to her country, one that Boland sees paralleled in Irish literature: "Irish literature is primarily the record of a defeated people." Because "the Irish nation, more often than not, is occluded by humiliations and setbacks, its writers have had to invent, to improvise, to experiment." They are "aware that they [are] negotiating an experience of defeat into one of articulation and recovery." Boland recounts a story of an Irish folksinger of a hundred years ago which captures the misgivings she feels concerning the uneasy melding of Irish culture and English language. The folksinger was asked to sing an Irish tune, but to translate the words into English: "'I will do it,' she answered, 'but the tune and the words will be like a man and his wife quarreling.'" Something that, like a marriage, ought to be comforting and comfortable has instead become an occasion for argument.

Boland's **"Mise Eire"** offers a poetic discussion of these same feelings of misgiving and unease. The title of the poem is taken from the title of a popular Irish national anthem (comparable to "America the Beautiful" in the United States). It means, in English, "I am from Ireland." An English line immediately follows this Gaelic title: "I won't go back to it—." Using a title in Gaelic to head a poem written in English is the first of many suggestions that the relationship between the two languages and cultures is not an untroubled one. The title contains an assertion of place, of roots, of belonging, whereas the first line seeks to deny all these things.

The second stanza, an aside set off by dashes, reinforces denial by emphasizing the sense of displacement felt by the Irish:

> my nation displaced
> into old dactyls,
> oaths made
> by the animal tallows
> of the candle—[.]

The power and potency of a nation should find its expression in its people; Ireland, however, has been "displaced into old dactyls," into poetry and song. The dactyl is a verse foot composed of an accented syllable followed by two unaccented ones, as in the word "tenderly." In classical poetry it is associated with elegiac verse, but it is difficult to handle well in English because "its prolonged use tend[s] to override the normal word-accent and result[s] in a grotesque jigging."

The third stanza identifies the "it" of the first line, that to which the speaker refuses to return:

> land of the Gulf Stream,
> the small farm,
> the scalded memory,
> the songs
> that bandage up the history,
> the words
> that make a rhythm of the crime[.]

Ireland is indeed the "land of the Gulf Stream" in which "the small farm" is quite common, but it is more. It is also the "songs" and "words" of Irish poetry. This poetry tries to capture the glories of the past in the "dactyls" and perhaps even in the "oaths made / by the animal tallows / of the candle." This is the Ireland conjured by the male poets, but as Boland points out in her essay **"Outside History,"** "the Irish nation as an existing construct in Irish poetry was not available" to her. The "rhetoric of imagery" contained within it "alienated" her because its "fusion of the national and the feminine . . . seemed to simplify both." This simplification is referred to in her poem, in "the songs / that bandage up the history," songs that prettify it rather than tell the truth, and in "the words / that make a rhythm of the crime," words that disguise the anguish of Ireland's experiences in their "grotesque jigging."

The fourth stanza provides a transition from the present-day, mistaken visions of "time past" to a more realistic view of that same past:

> where time is time past.
> A palsy of regrets.
> No, I won't go back.
> My roots are brutal[.]

A "palsy" is a paralysis that can afflict any voluntary muscle, in the arms, legs, back, chest, throat or face, as the result of a nervous disorder. The loss of voluntary muscle control is often accompanied by involuntary spasms or tremors within the affected muscle. Therefore, the "palsy of regrets" that torments Ireland has paralyzed it. Its dactyls and oaths, songs and words, are merely involuntary spasms reflecting a wistful sense of what might have been or used to be. The speaker refuses to "go back" to this Ireland, because it is not her Ireland. Her Ireland is "brutal."

The brutality of the speaker's Ireland is captured in the two portraits of Irish women. The first is a prostitute, the second a mother. In these portraits, Boland consciously plays off two of the most ancient and common images of Ireland. In songs, stories, or poems, "Ireland almost always appears as a woman." On the one hand, this woman is a mother figure who is "both attractive and nurturing, requiring both defense and obedience." On the other, she is also a beautiful seductress yet eternal tease, who embraces one lover after another, but whose relations with them are never physically consummated. However, where other writers, almost exclusively male, use these archetypal images to represent Ireland itself, Boland insists that her women are not myths. They are real women who have first-hand knowledge of pain and loss.

The first such woman is a prostitute, one whose clientele is drawn from the soldiers of the British army of occupation:

> I am the woman—
> a sloven's mix
> of silk at the wrists,
> a sort of dove-strut
> in the precincts of the garrison—
>
> who practices
> the quick frictions,
> the rictus of delight
> and gets cambric for it,
> rice-colored silks.

A sloven is someone who is careless about his or her appearance, often dirty or untidy, yet this woman's slovenly state stands at odds with the silk lace that falls over her wrists. However, the oddness disappears when we learn that the silk, along with cambric, forms part of her fee, given in exchange for the "quick frictions" and "rictus of delight" of sexual intercourse. There seems to be little "delight" in this woman's couplings. "Rictus" is a striking pairing with "delight." Rictus specifically refers to the gaping of a baby bird's mouth as it waits for its parent to force food down its throat. From this more limited definition, the word has also come to mean any wide opening. It also carries a meaning more peculiarly applicable to human beings, that of a fixed, gaping grin. The "rictus of delight" experienced by this woman could refer to the opening of her vagina as her customers force their penises within her. It could also refer to the fixed, gaping grins that appear on their faces at the moment of orgasm. In either case, the "delight" is ironic, at least for her. There is no seduction here, no slow, tender, erotic build-up to mutual fulfillment. Instead, there are only "quick frictions," the discharging of a mere, physical need. The woman is but the necessary receptacle, to be discarded with "cambric" and "silk" when the need has been satisfied.

The second woman of the poem is a poor, immigrant mother, perhaps one of the thousands who fled the country to escape the famine wrought by the potato blights of the 1840s:

> I am the woman
> in the gansy-coat
> on board the *Mary Belle,*
> in the huddling cold,
>
> holding her half-dead baby to her
> as the wind shifts east
> and north over the dirty
> water of the wharf[.]

This poor mother wears only a "gansy-coat" to shield her from the cold. "Gansy" is another word for "jersey," a soft, elastic, knitted cloth of wool or cotton, indicating that her clothing is handmade. Perhaps she even made it herself. In any case, it offers little protection from "the huddling cold," a cold so fierce that it has rendered her baby "half-dead." This cold intensifies as the "wind shifts east / and north." East winds are usually considered ill-winds which bring disease and death in their wake; north winds reinforce the feelings of cold and death. Although the woman waits to disembark in her new home, which may be America, the winds that blow against her bring with them more than just the wet and salt of the ocean she has just traversed; because they are from the northeast, they might have originated in the land she has left behind.

The final two stanzas make overt the uneasy relationship that Boland perceives to exist between the English and Irish languages:

> mingling the immigrant
> guttural with the vowels
> of homesickness who neither
> knows nor cares that

> a new language
> is a kind of scar
> and heals after a while
>
> into a passable imitation
> of what went before.

The woman's "immigrant guttural" is her native Irish Gaelic. A "guttural" language is one that is composed of harsh, rasping sounds produced in the throat. Through the action of the bitter, northeast wind, her "immigrant guttural" is forcibly mixed with the "vowels of homesickness." The woman's homesickness is so profound that she cannot know, and even if she could she would not believe, that her pain will ease in time. Someday, this "new language" will become second nature to her, "a kind of scar" indicating that healing has occurred, presenting "a passable imitation / of what went before." Small wounds close without scarring; it is the deeper wounds that form scar tissue. Scar tissue is not the same as the original flesh. In many ways, it is more fragile. It lacks both elasticity and melanin: it cannot stretch as easily, and it does not tan. A scar is a visible reminder that the flesh has been damaged, that something which once existed exists no more.

> **If the Irish are indeed a "defeated people" as Boland maintains, then Gaelic is the sword they yielded to their conqueror to mark their surrender.**
> —*Kerry E. Robertson*

As **"Mise Eire"** demonstrates, Irish Gaelic is a dying tongue. Whether the instrument of that death is immigration or colonization or both, the hand which wields the instrument is English. This "new language" becomes "a kind of scar" on Boland's "displaced nation," but at least it may be hoped that the songs and poems in this language will not "bandage up the history" or "make a rhythm of the crime" perpetuated upon these two women and others like them. Perhaps this new language can tell their stories truly, in a way impossible for the old one. If the Irish are indeed a "defeated people" as Boland maintains, then Gaelic is the sword they yielded to their conqueror to mark their surrender.

In her essay, **"The Woman, the Place, the Poet,"** Boland voices the Joycean notion that "the language in which we are speaking in his before it is mine" in this manner:

> I learned quickly, by inference at school and reference at home, that the Irish were unwelcome in London. I absorbed enough of that information to regard everything—even the jittery gleam of the breastplates of the Horseguards as they rode through

the city—with a sort of churlish inattention. *All I knew, all I needed to know, was that none of this was mine.*

Boland could not love London, a city in which even "the iron and gutted stone of its postwar prospect . . . seemed to me merely hostile." This sense of hostility and alienation also found expression in her poem, **"An Irish Childhood in England: 1951."** In it she asserts that "all of England to an Irish child / was nothing more than what you'd lost and how." Her native Anglo-Irish dialect was ripped from her by the nuns in the English convent school she attended, women who "when [she] produced 'I amn't' in the classroom / turned and said—'you're not in Ireland now.'"

As an Irish female poet, Boland feels isolated, even alienated, from the language in which she must write, first because she is Irish, but also because she is female. To some extent, **"Mise Eire"** touches upon this isolation through its denial of the traditional depictions of Ireland as woman. As Boland explains:

> Images of nationhood in such poetry were often feminized and simplified. Cathleen ni Houlihan. Dark Rosaleen. The Poor Old Woman. These potent mixtures of national emblem and feminine stereotype stood between me and any immediate and easy engagement with the poetic tradition I inherited. It would take me years to realize that somewhere, behind these images, was the complex and important truth of Irishness and womanhood. (**"Un-Romantic"**)

The lives of the prostitute and immigrant in **"Mise Eire"** are part of this "complex and important truth of Irishness and womanhood." Boland's poem **"Envoi"** captures another aspect of it.

"Envoi" is a French noun meaning a "sending," a "parcel," or a "consignment." This poem, then, is Boland's "sending," her messenger into the world, or perhaps her message to her muse, since her relationship with her muse forms part of the basis of the poem. An envoi is also a specific French poetic form that originated during the period of the Provençal troubadours. The envoi was a short stanza used to end the poem. Originally, it served as a dedication to the poet's patron or some other important personage. Later, it came to function as a succinct summing-up of the poem itself. By giving her poem a non-English title, Boland again signals her unease with English as the poetic language of a defeated people.

The first stanza draws the reader into the world of the poem by introducing themes that will be developed more fully in the remainder of the poem:

> It is Easter in the suburb. Clematis
> shrubs the eaves and trellises with pastel.
> The evenings lengthen and before the rain
> the Dublin mountains become visible.

The poem is set in the suburbs in springtime. The suburbs are a place that carries special poetic importance for Boland. In **"The Woman, the Place, the Poet,"** she describes the impact that eighteen years of living in a suburb of Dublin had on her as a woman and a poet. Through it, she learned that the moments in one's life are not simply isolated incidents strung together to form one's life history. Rather, "they and we [are] part of a pattern—one that [is] being repeated throughout Ireland." These lives are "not lived . . . in any sort of static pageant; they thrive, wane, change, begin, and end here" in that suburb. In part, it is this pattern that Boland seeks to express in her poetry.

The word "Easter" is evocative as well. On one level, the holiday falls in the spring, when the wintery bleakness and cold of the land are erased by the returning warmth and light of the sun. Days become longer and there is a tremendous sense of rebirth, a pattern in which the seasons have waned, changed, thriven, begun and ended for countless centuries. This sense of reawakening and of variation within a pattern is reinforced by the clematis that "shrubs the eaves and trellises." Clematis is a perennial, vining plant from the buttercup family whose yellow flowers vary in size and form.

But Boland used the word "Easter," not "spring." This choice points the reader towards something more than the annual renewal of the earth. Easter is the moment upon which all of Christianity hinges, the day when an itinerant rabbi in Judea, one who was dismissed as just another crackpot with a Messiah complex, rose from the dead and altered the world forever. Again, we have variation within a pattern.

The second stanza presents an abrupt shift in direction from the first:

> My muse must be better than those of men
> who made theirs in the image of their myth.
> The work is half-finished and I have nothing
> but the crudest measures to complete it with.

The first two lines of this stanza address the same issue that was dealt with in **"Mise Eire,"** the idea that the male poet's muse is a female personification of Ireland. Boland describes the male impulse in this manner:

> The majority of Irish male poets depended on women as motifs in their poetry. They moved easily, deftly, as if by right among images of women in which I did not believe and of which I could not approve. The women in their poems were often pas-

sive, decorative, raised to emblematic status. This was especially true where the woman and the idea of the nation were mixed: where the nation became a woman and the woman took on a national posture. (**"Outside History"**)

Because Boland cannot believe in these images and cannot approve of them, she has found it necessary to shape her own images and myths, to vary them to suit her own experience. But the work she has begun is only "half-finished," and the tools with which "to complete it" are only "the crudest measures." Boland has a strong "need to locate [her]self in a powerful literary tradition," but she wishes to be "an agent of change," not merely "an element in [the] design," as occurs far too often with women in Irish poetry.

The third stanza swerves back to the suburb of the first stanza, to the ideas suggested by it:

> Under the street lamps the dustbins brighten.
> The winter-flowering jasmine casts a shadow
> outside my window in my neighbor's garden.
> These are the things that my muse must know.

Because of the light cast by the street lamps as they illuminate at dusk, even the trash cans take on a brightness. They too can participate in the general renewal of Easter. The "winter-flowering jasmine" she can see blooming in her "neighbor's garden" from her window provides a sense of community, of belonging, and of continuity. These are the things, what have traditionally been dismissed as "women's themes," her "muse must know." The last line of the stanza joins together the themes presented in the three preceding stanzas. The making of poetry must concern itself with the ordinary things of a woman's everyday world: the dustbins and the street lamps as much as with the clematis, jasmine, evening rain, and mountains. Traditional poetry, that of the men who made "theirs in the image of their myth," is "built on realities, like the elegy or the war poem, that have little to do with the daily life of women." A female poet must build her poetry by adapting these forms to her own realities.

The fourth stanza develops the role of the muse:

> She must come to me. Let her come
> to be among the donnée, the given.
> I need her to remain with me until
> the day is over and the song is proven.

She cannot go to the muse; the muse must come to her. This muse is not something that Boland can earn; her arrival is a gift, an unexpected present or "sending" (another dimension of the title, **"Envoi"**), that she needs to remain with her until the "song is proven," until she has captured, in poetry, what she sees around her.

The fifth stanza creates another kind of joining. It brings together, in the person of her muse, the male's "image of myth" and the religious images suggested in the first stanza:

> Surely she comes, surely she comes to me—
> no lizard skin, no paps, no podded womb
> about her but a brightening and
> the consequences of an April tomb.

The muse approaches Boland with confidence and assurance. There are no doubts, no misgivings. Nor is there any of the ugliness associated with the male poet's images of his muse: "no lizard skin, no paps, no podded womb." Boland's muse has nothing "about her but a brightening," the same illumination that touched the Dublin mountains and the dustbins, and "the consequences of an April tomb." The "consequences of an April tomb" are the resurrection of Christ, his return from seeming defeat and death, into a new, more glorious existence, one mirrored by the angels who appeared at that resurrection. Luke described the angel who guarded the tomb as wearing "dazzling apparel" whereas Matthew says of this angel that "his appearance was like lightning, and his garment was white as snow."

In both "Mise Eire" and "Envoi," Boland has a sense of what might be, if only the male muse and male tradition could be changed, varied, subverted. She does not wish to abandon either this muse or this tradition; hers are the same as the men's, only "better."
—Kerry E. Robertson

This resurrection points to Boland's own resurrection, one that is described in the next stanza:

> What I have done I have done alone.
> What I have seen is unverified.
> I have the truth and I need the faith.
> It is time I put my hand in her side.

The angels described in the gospels bore witness to the resurrection of Jesus, as did his apostles, the women who visited the tomb, and the men on the road to Emmaus. For Boland there are no such witnesses. What she has done, she has done alone; what she has seen has not been verified. She is the first, her own precursor. Where Elizabeth Bishop had Marianne Moore as a precursor, an example and guide, for Boland

> there are no parallels to this in anything [she] knew
> as a young poet, in or out of university. When [she]
> began writing, the Irish poetic tradition had been for

more than a hundred years almost exclusively male. . . . At times, and more and more as the years went on, [she] felt the absence of a female poetic precedent. (**"Un-Romantic"**)

What she came to acknowledge was that she was both a poet and a woman and that she could no longer separate the two, that she "regretted . . . the absence of an expressed poetic life which would have dignified and revealed" hers. Elsewhere Boland writes of this realization:

As an Irish woman poet I have very little precedent. There were none in the nineteenth century or early part of the twentieth century. You didn't have a thriving sense of the witness of the lived life of women poets, and what you did have was a very compelling and at times oppressive relationship between Irish poetry and the national tradition.

She knows, with her "half-finished work" and "crudest measures," that the time has come to tell all the truth. She has this truth within her; she simply needs the faith to put it into words. The time has come to "put [her] hand into [the muse's] side," even as Thomas had to place his hand into his master's side and his finger into the nail wounds before he could believe in that resurrection.

The final stanza captures the consequences of a failure of faith:

If she will not bless the ordinary,
if she will not sanctify the common,
then here I am and here I stay and then am I
the most miserable of women.

Boland's muse must come to her exactly where she is, in the suburbs among her dustbins and street lamps, among the "ordinary" and "common" things that make up her world. The muse must "bless" and "sanctify" her variations on the traditional themes. If she wills not to do so, then Boland remains trapped by the male images of that muse. If this is the case, then she is indeed "the most miserable of women," because she as a poet has some awareness that it need not be this way and some knowledge of what has been lost.

In both **"Mise Eire"** and **"Envoi,"** Boland has a sense of what might be, if only the male muse and male tradition could be changed, varied, subverted. She does not wish to abandon either this muse or this tradition; hers are the same as the men's, only "better." Her goal in her poetry is to resurrect the "devalued experiences" of women "by subverting the pre-existing structures" of traditional Anglo-Irish poetry "so that they have to include them." This is Boland's "swerve," her Bloomian clinamen. She works doggedly to escape the "postures" and "angers" that "glamourized resis-

tance, action" in order to tell the truth about "the wrath and grief of Irish history," to break free from the "exhausted fictions" that simplify, distort, and dehumanize both her nationhood and her womanhood. The truth she tells must be "slant." The current poetic structures do not allow her to tell it any other way, because, in a double sense, these structures, the language itself, was "his" before it was hers.

Gardner McFall (review date June-July 1996)

SOURCE: "Sappho's Daughter," in *American Book Review*, Vol. 17, No. 5, June-July, 1996, p. 14.

[*In the following review, McFall discusses what Boland's* An Origin Like Water: Collected Poems (1967-1987) *reveals about the poet.*]

Eavan Boland's work caught my attention almost ten years ago when a friend sent me three pages xeroxed from *The Journey and Other Poems,* published by Carcanet, a book which established her poetic maturity and stature. I instantly liked the selection: **"An Irish Childhood in England: 1951," "I Remember," "Fond Memory,"** and **"Canaletto in the National Gallery of Ireland,"** because of the truthful voice I heard, ardent and wise, committed to form, but not shackled by it.

Boland has been publishing poems for thirty years; in the last decade, she has emerged not only as a premier Irish poet and critic (her recent *Object Lessons: The Life of the Woman and the Poet in our Time* attests to that), but as a poet who transcends national boundaries. Since 1990, Norton has issued three volumes of her poems: *Outside History: Selected Poems 1980-1990, In a Time of Violence,* and her most recent, *An Origin Like Water,* which contains all the poems Boland wanted to preserve from the years 1967-1987, culled from *New Territory, The War Horse, In Her Own Image, Night Feed,* and *The Journey.*

The book is, roughly, an expanded version of Carcanet's *Selected Poems,* augmented with a preface by the poet, so that some of what has already been said about that volume still stands. There is the evidence of Plath in the poems from *In Her Own Image* and the charm of her poems dealing with the painters Chardin, Degas, and Ingres. The title of the last, however, has been astutely revised from **"Woman Posing"** to **"Pose,"** and **"On Renoir's** *The Grape-Pickers***"** has been omitted, perhaps because Boland found it wanting compared to others. Two additional poems, which appear in the *Night Feed* section of her *Selected Poems* and which are excised in the current volume, are **"A Ballad of Home"** and **"Before Spring"**; they are not missed, as their subjects are treated with greater complexity elsewhere.

> **Boland has been publishing poems for thirty years; in the last decade, she has emerged not only as a premier Irish poet and critic . . . , but as a poet who transcends national boundaries.**
> *—Gardner McFall*

That Boland still claims so much of her early work is lucky for readers who would trace her poetic development. In her preface, with its belated recognition of her enterprise, she asserts that her work has moved from that which "struggled for skill and avoided risk" to that which grew from a "forceful engagement between a life and a language," specifically a woman's life and language. Certainly, her starting point is common to all young poets, though the leap she makes would appear problematic given her gender, at odds with a male literary inheritance.

In the book's first poem **"Athene's Song,"** we glimpse the manifestation of Boland's dilemma in the figure of Athene, whose first utterance is "From my father's head I sprung" and whose "new music," created from her "pipe of bone," ultimately "like my mind / Remains unknown." Athene, like the female poet, is stuck, rendered mute by the pressures of history and expectation.

Driving this point home are Boland's programmatic iambic tetrameter line and the overshadowing influence of Yeats, whose "salmon-falls, the mackerel-crowded seas" from "Sailing to Byzantium" is recalled in her line "Fish sprung in the full river." Yet in the next poem, **"From the Painting *Back from Market* by Chardin,"** Boland augurs her later project and accomplishment, her account of "what great art removes: / Hazard and death. The Future and past. / A woman's secret history and her loves—."

Boland's selections from *New Territory* reveal a concentration on traditional form, which she later throws off, and numerous long-standing features of her work: her knowledge of myth, her attraction to literary and political history, her wit, her eye for the telling, ordinary detail, and her gift for extended metaphor. Her sensibility is keenly felt in her poem on Chardin and her imagination works impressively in poems like **"New Territory"** and **"Migration."** Yet Boland herself feels slightly absent, at a remove.

It is not until her second volume *War Horse* that her mission as witness to her experience as a woman and a poet takes off in poems that address violence and explore the bounds and bonds of marriage, family, and suburbia, "a devalued subject matter," as she has called it in *Object Lessons.* Poems from *In Her Own Image* and *Night Feed* deal with women's issues even more directly in form as well as

theme. With short, truncated lines, poems like **"Menses," "Mastectomy,"** and **"Anorexia"** examine women's sexuality. Boland dwells on the ordinary, domestic experience of women in the sequence **"Domestic Interiors"** and poems such as **"Degas's Laundress"** and **"Woman in Kitchen."** In **"It's a Woman's World,"** she coolly, ironically observes:

> Our way of life
> has hardly changed
> since a wheel first
> whetted a knife.
>
> Maybe flame
> burns more greedily,
> and wheels are steadier
> but we're the same
>
> who milestone
> our lives
> with oversights—
> living by the lights
>
> of the loaf left
> by the cash register,
> the washing powder
> paid for and wrapped,
>
> the wash left wet:
> like most historic peoples
> we are defined
> by what we forget,
>
> by what we never will be
> star-gazers,
> fire-eaters.
> It's our alibi
>
> for all time:
> as far as history goes
> we were never
> on the scene of the crime.

This poem, among others, illustrates Boland's particular, distinctive stance, developed over time. She stands within the parameters of traditional female experience and chronicles it in lyric (or, she would say, "anti-lyric") form, a form which historically has taken as one of its themes the woman as object. Speaking from this vantage point, she renders her project not only radical, but subversive, for she is able to draw back the blind, demythicize, and alter both the subject and subject matter of the genre.

Selections from *The Journey,* the final volume represented, epitomize this, especially the much praised title poem, which achieves that imperative articulated by Boland in an interview with Jody Allen-Randolph in the 1993 *Irish University Review*'s special issue on Boland: "The woman poet has to write her poem free of any resonance of the object she once was in it." To read **"The Journey"** is to see how clearly she has freed herself from that resonance, but only by the hard-won effort of her poems that have come before.

Bald, feminist statement is banished for an all-encompassing human and female poetic rendering of experience which stands inherited tradition on its head. Sappho (not Virgil) takes the poet on a journey to the underworld to discover and identify with a host of suffering women, whose children died before the advent of antibiotics. In this poem, Boland is claimed by Sappho as her "daughter" (as contrasted with the early figure of Athene, whose originator is Zeus) and is cautioned to remember what she's seen and "know forever / the silences in which are our beginnings, / in which we have an origin like water."

The poet's cathartic dream occurs in the intimacy of her bedroom, where she has been reading and is fueled by an incantation of repeated syntactical structures: "and I would have known her anywhere / and I would have gone with her anywhere. . . ." Idea and form are perfectly melded here, and we recognize that Boland has indeed found a language to embody her experience of being a woman as well as a poet with self-engendered authorial power.

Seven years ago, in *The London Review of Books*, Neil Corcoran observed about the Carcanet edition of Boland's *Selected Poems*: "[This] is one of those carefully pruned volumes in which a poet of quiet, meticulous, patient craft stands revealed as something more interesting and integrated than her individual books had led one to anticipate." His choice of words suggests a subversive activity. Whatever we call it, this new volume, enlarging on the old, reveals that while others weren't looking, Eavan Boland "made a new music" to reflect her mind as well as her life.

R. T. Smith (review date Summer 1996)

SOURCE: A review of *In a Time of Violence,* in *Southern Humanities Review,* Vol. 30, No. 3, Summer, 1996, pp. 304-7.

[*In the following review, Smith asserts that Boland's* In a Time of Violence *"counters any notion that poetry has retreated from the public forum or shies away from issues of great pitch and moment."*]

As an explorer of the terrible beauties Yeats witnessed and as a creator of language which radiates with both lyrical and intellectual beauty, Eavan Boland may be equal to any poet writing today. That she finds these beauties in the hard work

of rescuing her gender and Irish culture from repression, censorship, and self-imposed silence is both astonishing and inspiring. Her essays, introductions, and poems examine the "wrath and grief" that comprise Irish history as she lifts her voice to speak for a gender explored and exploited almost as if it were a "primitive" territory. Striking back, Boland's new volume, *In a Time of Violence,* employs subversive and disruptive rhetorical strategies to create a distressed beauty, witnessing to the fact that any time is a violent one for those who lack autonomy.

The seven poems of the title sequence revisit precincts in which Boland announced her citizenship as early as *New Territory,* but now she fuses landscape and temperament, exposing how the realities of both can be disguised in euphemism and inattention to detail. The introductory lyric, **"The Singers,"** asks if "the women who were singers in the west" ever found a moment when the song and the torturous weather were one, allowing them to record the joy with the danger because they had found "a voice where they had found a vision." In the poems that follow, Boland returns to a time of literal hunger when the Irish were starving under the gaze of their landlords. The initial poem, **"That the Science of Cartography is Limited,"** reveals a narrator who must quietly absorb the shock of discovery when her lover takes her to a forest where a famine road was built in 1847, a construction project whose workers died in harness and which maps do not yet record. Perhaps remembering Elizabeth Bishop's suggestion that "More delicate than the historians' are the map-makers' colors," Boland sets out to revise the maps of her country.

From this point of engaged imagination, the narrator recounts in **"The Death of Reason"** the bristling ironies of that "glorious Age" when the woman who allowed herself to be objectified in English portraiture—"Nameless composite. / Anonymous beauty-bait for the painter . . ."—was most likely oblivious to the conflagrations in embattled Ireland. The poem counterpoints "the dictates of reason and the blended sensibility / of tact and proportion" with the rage and violence across the Irish sea until "the eighteenth century ends here / as her hem scorches and the satin / decoration catches fire." Throughout this poem, the civilized forces strain to preserve decorum but cannot avoid the destruction born of blindness. The poem reveals Boland at her most poignantly skillful, interspersing fragments and abrupt short lines with elegant descriptions and quiet, often slant, rhyming. She also contrasts Irish geography—**"Antrim to the Boyne"**—with the artifice of painterly technique and ironizes the artist's discovery of "how difficult it is to make the skin / blush outside the skin," a discovery whose social and political implications are lost on the anonymous painter.

In the epistolary **"March 1, 1847. By the First Post,"** the poet renders the voice of one of the privileged ladies who writes of harebells, copper silk, opera, and picnics but is compelled to record the unpleasant sight of "*A woman lying / across the Kells Road with her baby*" and how the exposure to that suffering redirects the party on the return trip, while "*poor Mama was not herself all day.*" The poem is elegantly understated, revealing the author of the letter to be insulated and foolish, but not wholly denying her sympathy.

> **As an explorer of the terrible beauties Yeats witnessed and as a creator of language which radiates with both lyrical and intellectual beauty, Eavan Boland may be equal to any poet writing today. That she finds these beauties in the hard work of rescuing her gender and Irish culture from repression, censorship, and self-imposed silence is both astonishing and inspiring.**
> **—R. T. Smith**

In the sequence's final station, **"Writing in a Time of Violence,"** Boland takes the reader back to her college years, as in her well-known poem **"The Achill Woman."** The earlier poem presents a young woman's discovery of the dignity and endurance of the women of the extreme west of Ireland, while the narrator has set out only to learn the canonical "Court Poets of the Silver Age." In the new poem, studying rhetoric with all its "sweet euphony / and safe digression," she finds in the word *insinuate* a clue to language's perilous concealments and her own complicity as a rhetor. Finding the real thorns invisible at first to a girl working at her desk, the narrator begins to appreciate the danger "waiting under / beautiful speech. To strike."

Perhaps the most unforgettable and representative poem in the collection, **"A Sparrow Hawk in the Suburbs,"** demonstrates how Boland's diction and the weave of her imagination can lead to a language tortured until it reveals a life intensely and truly. In the suburban Dublin of this account, Boland's imagination and observation collaborate with great authority. The opening two stanzas reveal her economy and the sense of gathering significance in the quotidian activities:

> At that time of year there is a turn in the road
> where
> the hermit tones and meadow colours of
> two seasons heal into
> one another—
>
> when the wild ladder of a winter scarf is stored
> away in
> a drawer eased by candle-grease and lemon balm

is shaken out from
the linen press.

The air is expectant, the emphasis (through "heal" and "ease") is on mending. When the rain comes, it falls upon "The borrowed shears and the love-seat in the garden where / a sparrow hawk was seen through the opal- / white of apple trees / after Easter." In this climate of prescience and resurrection (reminding one of the Easter retreat in **"The Latin Lesson"** from *Outside History*), a visitation has occurred, something otherworldly and wild serving to focus attention through "the citrus drizzle of petals and clematis opening" and the shadows lengthening. Here her characteristic touch raises the poem to the muscular beauty of a Renaissance painting.

> **Boland's attention and rhythm make subordinate and strange structures perfectly clear.**
> **—R. T. Smith**

Boland's attention and rhythm make subordinate and strange structures perfectly clear. If the garden here is not lost, it is cold. If there are angelic wings, the narrator does not quite manage to see them, yet knows they belong to a raptor, whose threatening beak is mirrored by the shears on the love-seat. If it is a time ripe for revelation, what comes is at best a rumor, making darkness a sanctuary. The sense of exclusion heightens this poem about the near-miraculous, and the scraggly quatrains attempt to mute the assonances and intricate parallels, yet the visual precision and psychological intensity remind us how "wolves and dragons" sharpen our appreciation of sanctuaries.

If the final section of the book, **"Anna Liffey,"** is less successful, with its long title poem seeking an indelible emblem of the suffering and awareness of women, the book is not significantly damaged by the more naked search for "words we can grow old and die in." The quest for a preemptive personal elegy is perhaps doomed, but along the path Boland finds images that resist easy interpretation and formulation. One such is recorded in **"A Woman Painted on a Leaf,"** where the picture found "among curios and silver" reminds her that to separate a person from nature, to frame and preserve, is to divest, to remove him or her from the mortal cycle of what is begotten, born and dies. If she can return the painted leaf to earth, it will become "a crisp tinder underfoot," and the reader may infer the fires it will fuel to be those of transition, those pyres that shepherd us into the next realm.

In any time of violence, a guide as compassionate, informed, and accomplished as Eavan Boland is valuable, as her work counters any notion that poetry has retreated from the public forum or shies away from issues of great pitch and moment. Reminding us that art is perhaps the most fruitful venue for the collaboration of public and private interests, she provides us with not only a map, but a compass as well, and perhaps a thirst for the journey.

John Foy (review date 1997)

SOURCE: "Paroling Sweet Euphony," in *Parnassus,* Vol. 22, Nos. 1 and 2, 1997, pp. 223-46.

[*In the following review, Foy asserts that Boland's poems will stand "not on the politics that burdens and distinguishes them for now but on the hardihood of their afterlife as a lyrical voice."*]

Publicly, provocatively, and at length, Eavan Boland has ruminated on the issues that impel her poetry. These range from the Virgilian Latin, classical myths, and English poetry she learned in school to the "ordinary life" she stepped into as mother and wife in her beloved suburban Dublin. The burdens of this heritage come under her elegant scrutiny in the prose memoir *Object Lessons,* where we encounter the generous human perspectives that shape her work as well as the specifically Irish pressures—political and literary—that continue to inflect her voice. Behind and over all of these, however, looms a question as old as Plato. Though never fully sounded in the memoirs, it's a question that bears upon the poetry in *An Origin Like Water* as well as the earlier collections *In a Time of Violence* and *Outside History: Selected Poems 1980-1990.* It has to do with that ancient enmity between Truth and "sweet euphony." One of the pleasures of reading Boland is to eavesdrop on this quarrel mediated by a sensibility both political and lyrical—to watch her bicameral imagination play itself out in the very lines.

One wonders what Boland is up to with this suicidal gesture, posting Socrates' condemnation over the doorway into her poem. But it soon becomes clear. The seven-part sequence promotes truth ahead of beauty while inquiring into the physical and psychic violence that ravages those caught up in Irish history.
                                              —John Foy

The title sequence of *In a Time of Violence* opens with Plato's Socrates, the seminal indictor of poets. Given Boland's career-long, often brilliant, sometimes maddening arraignment of poetic norms, her invocation of this harsh judge sets up a density of meanings. As epigraph to the sequence, Boland excerpts the case against poets, from Book X of the *Republic:*

> As in a city where the evil are permitted to have authority and the good are put out of the way, so in the soul of man, as we maintain, the imitative poet implants an evil constitution, for he indulges the irrational nature which has no discernment of greater or less.

When Socrates damns the "imitative poets," he is, alas, damning all poets, who slink about in Plato's dialectics as poor simulators thrice removed from truth. In another passage from Book X (this one not cited by Boland), Socrates warns Glaucon of the mealy-mouths and their sweet, putatively ruinous influence:

> The poet with his words and phrases may be said to lay on the colors of the several arts, himself understanding their nature only enough to imitate them; and other people who are as ignorant as he is, and judge only from his words, imagine that if he speaks of cobbling, or of military tactics, or of anything else, in meter and harmony and rhythm, he speaks very well—such is the sweet influence which melody and rhythm by nature have. And I think that you must have observed again and again what a poor appearance the tales of poets make when stripped of the colors which music puts upon them, and recited in simple prose.

So Socrates sends the poet packing, who "awakens and nourishes and strengthens the feelings and impairs the reason." The real reprobates here turn out to be meter, harmony, and rhythm, all of which conspire to distort the simple truth. Always at the back of Boland's mind, this famous defamation fires her own doubts about the allurements of language.

One wonders what Boland is up to with this suicidal gesture, posting Socrates' condemnation over the doorway into her poem. But it soon becomes clear. The seven-part sequence promotes truth ahead of beauty while inquiring into the physical and psychic violence that ravages those caught up in Irish history. Among its virtues, the sequence both illuminates and enacts the long-standing quarrel by attending to the claims of historical fact while not wholly renouncing the linguistic surface. The lead poem of the sequence builds its conceit upon the image of the tragically futile "famine roads" in Ireland. These ghostly make-work roads were sponsored by the Relief Committees to provide starving Irish workers with employment during the worst of the famine. The poem demands quoting in full since it vividly displays Boland's contending impulses.

I **"That the Science of Cartography Is Limited"**

—and not simply by the fact that this shading of
forest cannot show the fragrance of balsam,
the gloom of cypresses,
is what I wish to prove.

When you and I were first in love we drove
to the borders of Connacht
and entered a wood there.

Look down you said: this was once a famine road.

I looked down at ivy and the scutch grass
rough-cast stone had
disappeared into as you told me
in the second winter of their ordeal, in

1847, when the crop had failed twice,
Relief Committees gave
the starving Irish such roads to build.

Where they died, there the road ended

and ends still and when I take down
the map of this island, it is never so
I can say here is
the masterful, the apt rendering of
the spherical as flat, nor
an ingenious design which persuades a curve
into a plane,
but to tell myself again that
the line which says woodland and cries hunger
and gives out among sweet pine and cypress,
and finds no horizon

will not be there.

Right away we witness the bicameral imagination in debate. A blunt, forensic assertion pushes the poem forward, obliging the title to run syntactically into the first stanza. While the stance is heavily rhetorical and the air a bit courtroomish (she's going to prove the truth of a proposition about the science of map-making), the insinuations of syntax (the abstract noun clause followed by the painterly particulars—the balsams and cypresses—in a long appositive with an iambic hint) whisper the intricate secrets of the lyrical.

Boland next lays down a line carrying the full genetic code of the Tradition: "When you and I were first in love we drove . . ." The line steps along in perfect iambic pentameter. But as if to show that what she considers imitative prosodic posturing cannot bear the moral import of her poem, Boland quickly jerks back to uneven, truth-telling lineation, closer to the simple prose prescribed by Socrates: "When you and

I were first in love we drove / to the borders of Connacht / and entered a wood there." The iambic pentameter's momentary poise and civility ("When you and I were first in love we drove . . .), along with its literary and political associations, are voted down by succeeding stanzas of varying lengths and unpredictable lineation.

This toying with sanctioned cadences is one of the means Boland has chosen repeatedly in her work to negotiate a new pact between Truth and prosodic tradition. She makes this point clear in ***Object Lessons:*** The old strains, representative of a male-dominated order of Irish poetry, are no longer up to the job of conveying truth, at least not the truths of her "hidden life" as suburban wife and mother and the heretofore silenced women in Irish poetry. The Tradition lets down its drawbridge automatically for no man, or woman. One must fight, and Boland has. Her way in as poet is to "subvert the old order" by advancing the ethical dimension over the formal and aesthetic. A part of the **"Cartography"** poem, fulfilling the ethical mandate, bears dangerously bald witness, in naked lines, to the obscure sufferings of famine victims in the mid 1800s:

Look down you said: this was once a famine road.

I looked down at ivy and the scutch grass
rough-cast stone had
disappeared into as you told me
in the second winter of their ordeal, in

1847, when the crop had failed twice,
Relief Committees gave
the starving Irish such roads to build.

The fact of the famine roads is a testimony to human suffering. But the fact alone does not constitute poetry—the lines themselves here are a little too bleached.

Luckily, the poem goes on to satisfy more fully its lyrical calling. Weaving through thirteen lines, the final sentence jaggedly generates itself out of plain statement ("Where they died, there the road ended") and into an emotionally charged, syntactically voluptuous reckoning:

Where they died, there the road ended

and ends still and when I take down
the map of this island, it is never so
I can say here is
the masterful, the apt rendering of
the spherical as flat, nor
an ingenious design which persuades a curve
into a plane,
but to tell myself again that

the line which says woodland and cries hunger
and gives out among sweet pine and cypress,
and finds no horizon

will not be there.

Here Boland voices a genuine indignation. Necessity's twisting power is conveyed in the long, periodic sentence whose syntax winds strenuously through the uneven cut of the stanzas. As if to compensate for the famine roads that peter out where the builders died, Boland's sentence drives ahead to its definite, incensed end. Read aloud, the last thirteen lines break convincingly, just about where the speaking voice might hesitate to isolate phrases and distribute weight. The line breaks are governed not by prosodic patterns but by the ebb and flow of an emotionally propelled argument. The quality of the phrasing and the involuted syntax (mirroring the complexities of emotion and conceit) together create the lyrical texture.

[Boland's] earliest work, well represented in *An Origin Like Water*, shows a precocious and enviable formal control.
—*John Foy*

The poem laments those things of deep human importance that never make it onto the official map—like the famine roads. These desperate, failed excursions work as metaphors for the women who, Boland argues, have not made it onto Ireland's literary map. And if we equate traditional stanzaic structures and iambic pentameter with the official *prosodic* map, as I believe Boland intends, then we see how, on the formal level, Boland has admirably extended the conceit: The subtext tells us that she is no longer interested in the official "apt renderings" and "ingenious designs" she mastered early on, in her Movement-influenced poems, which she refers to as "derivative, formalist, gesturing poems" marked by "the neat stanza, the well broken line." Her comments evince a mild disdain for the apprentice work, all those early raids on the Tradition that gave her form. Boland's exfoliating talents and dedication to the art have since enabled her to make those forms her own, to adapt and transcend them, and to move to the center of her poems whatever she has wished to.

Her earliest work, well represented in *An Origin Like Water,* shows a precocious and enviable formal control. "**The Poets,**" from *New Territory,* Boland's first book, was written before her 23rd birthday:

They, like all creatures, being made
For the shovel and worm,
Ransacked their perishable minds and found

Pattern and form
And with their own hands quarried from hard
words
A figure in which secret things confide.

They are abroad. Their spirits like a pride
Of lions circulate.

Are desperate. Just as the jeweled beast,
That lion constellate,
Whose scenery is Betelgeuse and Mars,
Hunts without respite among fixed stars.

And they prevail. To his undoing every day
The essential sun
Proceeds, but only to accommodate
A tenant moon
And he remains until the very break
Of morning; absentee landlord of the dark.

The only point a formalist could fault here is the Miltonic inversion endloading a Latinate adjective to give us "lion constellate." The slant rhymes work deftly at the ends of enjambed lines sustained by a compelling iambic pulse. The phrasing sparkles with power—the moon an "absentee landlord of the dark." Not men's power, and not women's power—just the linguistic firepower of a poet, albeit one Boland comes to question. Another of Boland's signature quirks is the syntactic fragment, which she often relies on, as in this case ("Are desperate."), to communicate a significant afterthought. Here she is again, doing the Movement, before age 23, in the last stanza of "**Belfast vs. Dublin**":

We have had time to talk and strongly
Disagree about the living out
Of life. There was no need to shout.
Rightly or else quite wrongly
We have run out of time, if not of talk.
Let us then cavalierly fork
Our ways since we, and all unknown,
Have called into question one another's own.

She knows her Auden and her Yeats. (In *Object Lessons,* Boland acknowledges her debts, paying particular tribute to Yeats.)

She demonstrates that fluent control and power again in her next book, *The War Horse.* In a poem dedicated to her husband, the novelist Kevin Casey, Boland weighs flesh and blood against imagination:

I know you have a world I cannot share
Where a woman waits for you, beautiful,
Young no doubt, protected in your care
From stiffening and wrinkling, not mortal

Not shy of her own mirror. How can I rival
Her when like another wife she waits
To come into the pages of your novel,
Obediently, as if to your bed on nights

She is invited nor, as in your other life
I do, reminds you daily of the defeat
Of time nor, as does your other wife,
Binds you to the married state?

She is the other woman. I must share
You with her time and time again,
Book after book. Yet I am aware,
Love, that I may have the better bargain:

I imagine she has grown strange
To you among the syntax and the sentences
By which you distance her. And would exchange
Her speaking part for any of our silences.

> ("*Dedication:* **The Other
> Woman and the Novelist**")

Nothing in these well-wrought stanzas chafes from undue strain or tweaking. The tender accusations come through softly, kept aloft on rhymes that evade a too-perfect equivalence, set up as they are at different syntactic junctures. Aside from being a masterly poem, this seems to me a fair assessment of a real woman's advantages over a fictive female. Life, the poem concedes, is different from art.

Many of Boland's poems, however, fume over the fact that a woman can be fixed, frozen, and distanced by sentences. This seems less a political posture than a kicking against the very nature of words and syntax. Boland is much enamored of both. I suspect that in the structurally looser **"Cartography,"** as in much of her later work, she is intent on delivering the formal control out of the hands of line and stanza (the traditional keepers) and into those of syntax alone—syntax "the controller," as Seamus Heaney has called it, "the compelling element that binds the constituent elements of sense into active unity." Boland expresses this beautifully in her own words:

> there is a way of making free with the past,
> a pastiche of what is
> real and what is
> not, which can only be
> justified if you think of it
>
> not as sculpture but syntax:
> a structure extrinsic to meaning which uncovers
> the inner secret of it . . .
>
> (from **"Lava Cameo,"** *In a Time of Violence*)

Of course, an impassioned syntax doesn't control and shape

in the same ways conventional line and stanza do. The "shape" that syntax alone imparts is a tonal one, an emotional and linguistic texture felt in the very way the phrase and clause are put together and broken; this, then, also unifies a poem and in the absence of conventional pattern defines what it is.

This force is felt in the syntactically complex lines that conclude **"Cartography."** Boland's breakaway tactics enable her to escape from the hothouse of formal expectation with her poems still unwilted. Some of the most engaging passages in *Object Lessons* describe her growing disillusionment with Anglo-Irish poetic form as an abstract entrapment:

> I had been born in a country where and at a time
> when the word *woman* and the word *poet* inhabited
> two separate kingdoms of experience and expression. I could not, it seemed, live in both. As the author of [formal, conventional] poems I was an equal
> partner in Irish poetry. As a woman—about to set
> out on the life which was the passive object of many
> of those poems—I had no voice. It had been silenced, ironically enough, by the very powers of
> language I aspired to and honored. By the elements
> of form I had worked hard to learn . . . However
> abstract it looked from outside, the paragraph of
> language and music was beginning to seem a crucial part of a whole, wider question of identity.

And then this insightful formulation, vital to anyone who claims to be a poet:

> But already I knew—from a few mysterious moments of writing—something about form. Already
> I sensed that real form—the sort that made time turn
> and wander when you read a poem—came from a
> powerful meeting between a hidden life and a hidden chance in language.

In Boland's best work, two hidden quantities meet and well up together: an avenging, subterranean moral imperative and an urge to sing. This confluence can't help setting in motion a strong, distinguishing current that cuts its own banks.

Boland's poems fare less well when, swayed by the admonitions of Socrates, they tilt towards documentary:

> This is St. Louis. Where the rivers meet.
> The Illinois. The Mississippi. The Missouri.
> The light is in its element in Autumn.
> Clear. With yellow Gingko leaves falling.
> There is always a nightmare. Even in such light.
>
> (from **"In a Bad Light,"** section 4 of the sequence
> **"Writing in a Time of Violence"**)

Even the few painterly details of light and Gingko leaves are not enough to energize this stanza. The speaker—it's Boland—stands in a museum in St. Louis inspecting a miniature display of nineteenth-century American riverboat culture:

> I stand in a room in the Museum.
> In one glass case a plastic figure
> represents a woman in a dress,
> with crepe sleeves and a satin apron.
> And feet laced neatly into suede.
>
> She stands in a replica of a cabin
> on a steamboat bound for New Orleans.
> The year is 1860. Nearly war.
> A notice says no comforts were spared. The silk
> is French. The seamstresses are Irish.

As if to demonstrate scorn for verbal discrimination, Boland here allows the preposition "in" to overcrowd the first three lines above. It has taken twenty lines, all quite ho-hum, to open on one fact: "The seamstresses are Irish." From then on, the poem rummages about in "human truths of survival and humiliation," to cite a keynote phrase from *Object Lessons.* The speaker imagines the exploited seamstresses working in gaslit backrooms, then suddenly switches to the communal "we": "We are bent over / / in a bad light. We are sewing a last / sight of shore. We are sewing coffin ships." The poem uses its final three stanzas to enlarge the diagram. As documentary and redress, this succeeds—it delivers information about injustice and sins of omission; as a poem, however, it founders with its cargo of uninflected fact. Chary of lyrical texture, the poem seems to prefer a threadbare line on moral grounds, recalling the epigraph from Plato.

Boland has her reasons for this approach, and she proclaims them clearly in *Object Lessons,* throwing gasoline on the embers of the old quarrel:

> All good poetry depends on an ethical relation between imagination and image. Images are not ornaments; they are truths . . . No poetic imagination can afford to regard an image as a temporary aesthetic maneuver. Once the image is distorted, the truth is demeaned. That was the heart of it all as far as I was concerned.

It's as if Boland felt any melody or rhythm, any linguistic sensuality, would risk distorting the image of the seamstresses. The assertion that "good" poetry has an ethical dimension is always ripe for debate. One could plausibly claim that the great poems of the Western Tradition have always served, in part, an extra-aesthetic end. *The Aeneid* glorifies the founding of the Roman state, *The Divine Comedy* underwrites the theology of Aquinas, *Paradise Lost* justifies the ways of Milton's God to man. But the unwitting paradox in Boland's rather fundamentalist legislation is this: If there is no *aesthetic maneuver,* no love in the language, the image and poem will perish, doomed to be short-lived victims of their own occasion.

"Maneuver," surfacing through French from the Latin, originally meant "work done by hand," implying close, craftsmanly work as humble, laudable, and upstanding as seamstressing; but Boland turns this linguistic broadsword in the sun to flash only its connotations of adroit trickery and deception, bringing us back to Socrates' misgivings about melody, harmony, and rhythm. Second, by deferring "aesthetic maneuvers" in Section 4 of **"Writing in a Time of Violence,"** Boland ensures that the poor seamstresses, propped up only as emblems, without nuance, will soon lapse back into oblivion. Of course, the poem's heart is in the right place. No one would begrudge the seamstresses our compassion as they labor in poor light to earn a paltry wage. But the language in which these women are depicted functions at minimal capacity, without the rich weave or visual vivacity that Boland can command.

A poem like **"The Achill Woman,"** written to fit a curriculum, ends up bereft of stereoscopic depth. Pumped up and pushed forward in the memoirs, this poem from *Outside History* recounts Boland's Easter-vacation trip as a college student to Achill, on Ireland's rugged Atlantic coast, where she met a simple working woman (perhaps a response to Yeats' "Fisherman"). The humble, work-hardened Achill woman, as the story goes, brought a bucket of water up to Boland's waterless cottage each evening, and they would chat. This woman came to stand in Boland's mind as a figure for all those women either wholly unrepresented in the Irish poetic tradition or reduced to silent, two-dimensional ornaments. Boland describes the condition this way in *Object Lessons:*

> The majority of Irish male poets depended on women as motifs in their poetry. They moved easily, deftly, as if by right among images of women in which I did not believe and of which I could not approve. The women in their poems were often passive, decorative, raised to emblematic status. This was especially true where the woman and the idea of the nation were mixed: where the nation became a woman and the woman took on a national posture.
>
> The trouble was these images did good service as ornaments. In fact, they had a wide acceptance as ornaments by readers of Irish poetry. Women in such poems were frequently referred to approvingly as mythic, emblematic. But to me these passive and simplified women seemed a corruption. Moreover,

the transaction they urged on the reader, to accept them as mere decoration, seemed to compound the corruption. For they were not decorations, they were not ornaments. However distorted these images, they had their roots in a suffered truth.

. . . It seemed to me a species of human insult that at the end of all, in certain Irish poems, they should become elements of style rather than aspects of truth.

Presented with this authoritative, just, and well-argued position, a reader comes to the poem itself with high expectations. Here is the beginning:

> She came up the hill carrying water.
> She wore a half-buttoned, wool cardigan,
> a tea-towel round her waist.
>
> She pushed the hair out of her eyes with
> her free hand and put the bucket down.
>
> The zinc-music of the handle on the rim
> tuned the evening. An Easter moon rose.
> In the next-door field a stream was
> a fluid sunset; and then, stars.
>
> I remember the cold rosiness of her hands.
> She bent down and blew on them like broth.
> And round her waist, on a white background,
> in coarse, woven letters, the words "glass cloth."
>
> And she was nearly finished for the day.

This is all we see of the actual Achill woman. The lines are somewhat inert; aside from the "zinc-music" and "fluid sunset," they tread along in the literal, weighed down by structural parity ("She came . . .", "She wore . . .", "She pushed . . .", "She bent . . .", etc.). The drama is nonexistent, at least until the end, when Boland goes back into the cottage with her copy of the English court poets of the Silver Age (she is preparing for a college exam) and fails "to comprehend / / the harmonies of servitude, / the grace music gives to flattery / and language borrows from ambition." Raleigh, one of those court poets (and sponsored by a queen), may have been a colonizer and tobacco advocate, but he, too, like the Achill Woman, knew a bit about truth and suffering. (Fifteen years in the Tower of London and death by execution should earn him some sympathy!) As for music and grace in language, need we damn them out of hand because of their historical association with the flattery and ambitions of Court life? One might just as well, then, abjure language altogether. **"The Achill Woman"** shows Boland moving closer to life for her inspiration, yet one would have hoped for more from the poem as poem. While its intentions are commendable, the argument is a bit too assured in the comfort of its affiliations.

At other points the poetry falls out of step with the ethical marching orders. An earlier and notorious poem entitled **"Mastectomy"** succeeds lyrically with its spare, haunting, oracular tercets, but all is spoiled at the end—if measured against Boland's benchmark—when the speaker blames male doctors for her loss:

> So they have taken off
> what slaked them first,
> what they have hated since:
>
> blue-veined
> white-domed
> home
>
> of wonder
> and the wetness
> of their dreams.
>
> I flatten
> to their looting,
> to the sleight
>
> of their plunder.
> I am a brute site.
> Theirs is the true booty.
>
> (from ***In Her Own Image,*** 1980)

Boland's moral authority doesn't live here. What, one wonders, has happened to the ethical dimension? Not only has the speaker failed to consider that the surgeon has saved her life (and holds a scarred human being more valuable than a cancer-ridden female sex object), but the speaker has also committed the sacrilege of reducing her *own* breasts to erotic objects upon which her sense of self depends.

The eponymous final section of **"Writing in a Time of Violence"** does greater justice to reality. In a complex gesture that refuses the stylish answer, Boland unloads bombs over *"sweet euphony" and* rhetoric in a poem both lyrical and rhetorical. She distinguishes *language* from *the Art of Rhetoric,* the former being the hero-in-hiding of genuine expression, the latter the blameworthy art of verbal trickery. It begins this way:

> In my last year in College
> I set out
> to write an essay on
> the Art of Rhetoric. I had yet to find
>
> the country already lost to me
> in song and figure as I scribbled down

names for sweet euphony
and safe digression.

And when I came to the word *insinuate*
I saw that language could writhe and creep
and the lore of snakes
which I had learned as a child not to fear—
because the Saint had sent them out of Ireland—
came nearer.

Chiasmus, Litotes, Periphrasis. Old
indices and agents of persuasion. How
I remember them . . .

When Stephen Dedalus, who also studied rhetoric and aesthetics, invokes the Father at the end of *Portrait of the Artist,* he does so with bittersweet fondness, knowing the necessity of artifice: "Old father, old artificer, stand me now and ever in good stead." But when Boland echoes that invocation, with "Old indices and agents of persuasion," it is as a looking back to a Fatherly art that has deceived her by painting over atrocities and agendas—an art behind which Boland no longer intends to hide.

Addressing both her current self and the increasingly wary college girl she was, Boland draws the line between language and the con-game of rhetoric: "we will live, we have lived / where language is concealed . . . / We will be—we have been—citizens / of its hiding place." But, Boland concludes, it is too late to ignore or deny the tenure of public, political, and literary rhetoric. She makes this point in a sentence that ventures out excitingly to the edge of syntactic control:

                    . . . But it is too late

  to shut the book of satin phrases,
  to refuse to enter
  an evening bitter with peat smoke,
  where newspaper sellers shout headlines
  and friends call out their farewells in
  a city of whispers
  and interiors where

  the dear vowels
  Irish Ireland ours are
  absorbed into Autumn air,
  are out of earshot in the distances
  we are stepping into where we never

  imagine words such as *hate*
  and *territory* and the like—unbanished still
  as they always would be—wait
  and are waiting under
  beautiful speech. To strike.

In one sense, this can be construed as a requiem for postlapsarian language, a medium whose sensuality is not to be trusted, where in every carefully wrought stone wall a snake waits to strike. Boland's specific premise is that, in a world as politicized as her Ireland, and for an Irish woman poet struggling to emerge in a predominantly male tradition, beautiful speech is not enough. Even satin phrases and sweet euphony—the whispers, the interiors, the dear vowels partake of the euphonious—are judged guilty by their association with public, political rhetoric, with "*hate* and *territory* and the like." Implying that the rhetorical *and* the dulcet both must be held for questioning in a time of violence, Boland honestly—and, for a poet, painfully—subpoenas the distinguishing powers of her art, coming full circle back to Socrates. She questions the poet's ways and means and implies the need for an ethical trellis up which the poetry must be trained. The adventure of reading Boland lies in watching her poetry, at its best, overwhelm the latticework.

"The Singers" is such a poem. It is dedicated to "M. R.," presumably Mary Robinson, the President of Ireland and one of Boland's most eminent admirers. (Robinson shares with Boland a characteristic mask, described by Declan Kiberd in his vast, new historical survey *Inventing Ireland* as that of a "classic Irish radical in deceptively conservative clothing.") **"The Singers"** goes forth with clear conscience, striding past Socrates with no second thought, and no homiletics. Yet it effortlessly fulfills both its duties, being in and out of its right mind:

  The women who were singers in the West
  lived on an unforgiving coast.
  I want to ask was there ever one
  moment when all of it relented,
  when rain and ocean and their own
  sense of home were revealed to them
  as one and the same?

                    After which
  every day was still shaped by weather,
  but every night their mouths filled with
  Atlantic storms and clouded-over stars
  and exhausted birds.

                    And only when the danger
  was plain in the music could you know
  their true measure of rejoicing in

  finding a voice where they found a vision.

If Socrates haunts these lines, it is not the forbidding censor of the *Republic* but the thinker of *Ion* looking enviously to the divine madness of *good* poets, who "compose their beautiful poems . . . because they are inspired and possessed," who are necessarily "not in their right minds" as they abandon themselves to the divine agents of music and meter.

Because Boland here allows herself this abandon, the unspecified women of the poem, and the poem itself, are rendered more memorable. The predicament of these "women who were singers in the West" is indeed "plain in the music." It's the difference between the prosaic chronicle, tethered to history and time, and the oracle, who speaks regardless of either. These lines, for instance, in the chronicle mode, merely allocate data:

> Two women
> were standing in shadow,
> one with her back turned.
> Their talk was a gesture,
> an outstretched hand.
>
> They talked to each other,
> and words like "summer,"
> "birth," "great-grandmother"
> kept pleading with me,
> urging me to follow.
>   (from **"The Oral Tradition,"** *Outside History*)

In contrast, the lines that open **"The Singers"** are alive with both oracular energy and sonic significance:

> The women who were singers in the West
> lived on an unforgiving coast.

These two lines do more than all ten quoted above. Working against the clear iambic suggestion set up by the first line, the harsher, foreshortened second suggests the rigors of the place: The abrupt, initial stress ("lived") and the final two consonantal stresses of "unforgiving coast" are rugged in their sound.

These women convey their measure of rejoicing in the vigor of the language; moreover, their rejoicing stems from finding a voice and vision that occur in the imaginative order, where each night "their mouths filled with / Atlantic storms and clouded-over stars / and exhausted birds." Human anguish presented in this oracular fashion—closer to the root of the lyric—will weather time better than sufferings merely chronicled. In fulfilling its double mandate, this poem abides by Aristotle's good horse sense from Book II of the *Nicomachean Ethics:* "The excellence of the horse makes a horse both good in itself and good at running and at carrying its rider and at awaiting the attack of the enemy."

The same may be said for the trend of Boland's more recent work, after 1987, as represented in Part I of *Outside History* and *In a Time of Violence.* In the former sits quietly, potently, one of Boland's most striking poems. **"What**

Love Intended" is a suburban elegy, though it requires no campaigning or pronouncements. The conviction of its own legitimacy runs deep in the music and cadences of the lines. It demands to be quoted in its entirety, as tribute to Boland at her best:

> I can imagine if
> I came back again,
>   looking through windows at
>
> broken mirrors, pictures,
> and, in the cracked upstairs,
>   the beds where it all began.
>
> The suburb in the rain
> this October morning
>   full of food and children
>
> and animals, will be—
> when I come back again—
>   gone to wrack and ruin.
>
> I will be its ghost,
> its revenant, discovering
>   again in one place
>
> the history of my pain,
> my ordeal, my grace,
>   unable to resist
>
> seeing what is past,
> judging what has ended
>   and whether, first to last,
>
> from then to now and even
> here, ruined, this
>   is what love intended—
>
> finding even the yellow
> jasmine in the dusk,
>   the smell of early dinners,
>
> the voices of our children,
> taking turns and quarreling,
>   burned on the distance,
>
> gone. And the small square
> where under cropped lime
>   and poplar, on bicycles
>
> and skates in the summer,
> they played until dark;
>   propitiating time.
>
> And even the two whitebeams

outside the house gone,
   with the next-door neighbor

   who used to say in April—
when one was slow to bloom—
   they were a man and woman.

This is masterful music. Boland does indeed make time "turn and wander" as she brings about that powerful, coveted "meeting between a hidden life and a hidden chance in language." The cadences are charged with elegiac love, not retributive ire. The diction is simple, but the words are carried in continuums of syntax that wind through the spare tercets with forceful elegance, sounding quiet off-rhymes at many of the turns to create a subtle, unprogrammed, but definite and sensuous echo. Boland conducts this score for one of her central themes: the ordinary, secret, uncelebrated life of a woman's suburban Dublin. The poem is all the more resonant for not getting bogged down in geographical particulars. At the end it gently but vastly opens out toward the mythic, its final line suggesting Ovid's faithful old couple, Baucis and Philemon, transformed together, by gods who loved them, into an oak and a linden tree in the Phrygian hills.

It's telling that [in "The Pomegranate"], as in many of her most intimate poems (as opposed to her stance pieces), Boland waives Socrates and paroles sweet euphony to go out and ravish the reader's willing ear.

—John Foy

Boland again mines the Tradition's classical legends in **"The Pomegranate,"** from *In a Time of Violence.* She appropriates the myth of Ceres and Persephone to explore the primal maternal love for a daughter and the ineluctable role reversal of child and parent. For the sake of space, I restrict myself to the first fourteen lines:

   The only legend I have ever loved is
   The story of a daughter lost in hell.
   And found and rescued there.
   Love and blackmail are the gist of it.
   Ceres and Persephone the names.
   And the best thing about the legend is
   I can enter it anywhere. And have.
   As a child in exile in
   A city of fogs and strange consonants,
   I read it first and at first I was
   An exiled child in the crackling dusk of
   The underworld, the stars blighted. Later
   I walked out in a summer twilight

   Searching for my daughter at bedtime.

The lines, stretched taut, defy the ear to ignore them. Their integrity dwells in several dimensions: an emotional necessity expressed so perfectly in a rhythm that the line is irrefutable and timeless ("The only legend I have ever loved is / The story of a daughter lost in hell"); an evocative mingling of image with abstract association ("A city of fogs and strange consonants"); and a deceptively relaxed, depressurized line enriched by the music of its vowels and mournful falling rhythms ("I walked out in a summer twilight / Searching for my daughter at bedtime.") It's telling that here, as in many of her most intimate poems (as opposed to her stance pieces), Boland waives Socrates and paroles sweet euphony to go out and ravish the reader's willing ear.

In another memorable poem, **"The Water Clock,"** Boland swan-dives into the purely lyrical:

   Thinking of ageing on a summer day
      of rain and more rain
   I took a book down from a shelf
      and stopped to read
   and found myself—
      how did it happen?—
      reflecting on
   the absurd creation of the water clock.

The first sentence, draped through eight lines, sparkles with classical clarity, poised at a sagacious distance from the world's wearisome political posturing. It maintains its imaginative elevation and complexity, working the image of the clepsydra, rather than collapsing into boilerplate rant. Boland continues to wonder about time's passing in **"Anna Liffey,"** which ruminates as much on the river through Dublin as on Boland's own history as woman, mother, and poet. With poignant wisdom and a degree of divulgence unseen in her poetry till now, Boland says outright:

   In the end
   It will not matter
   That I was a woman. I am sure of it.
   The body is a source. Nothing more.
   There is a time for it. There is a certainty
   About the way it seeks its own dissolution.

She goes even further toward revelation, lofted clear of contemporary orthodoxies:

   When language cannot do it for us,
   Cannot make us know love will not diminish us,
   There are these phrases
   of the ocean
   To console us.
   Particular and unafraid of their completion.

In the end
Everything that burdened and distinguished me
Will be lost in this:
I was a voice.

And the linguistic characteristics of that voice, its textures and persuasive melodies, will be its key to survival.

Boland knows that one need not smash the cello in favor of the horn: All resources are required to record *and* orchestrate the unrecorded life. If we judge from the textures of her newest poems, Boland is turning more fully now toward song.
—*John Foy*

While Boland still distrusts "the high-minded search for euphony," she nonetheless can sustain a superbly lyrical line, and it does not diminish her or us. It comes through clear as she praises the Liffey, "Spirit of water, / Spirit of place":

Its clarity as it flows,
In the company of runt flowers and herons,
Around a bend at Islandbridge
And under thirteen bridges to the sea.
Its patience at twilight—
Swans nesting by it,
Neon wincing into it.

Initiated in the consoling secrets of "these phrases of the ocean," the lines are more time-defying than a paragraph of deliberative oratory. These are the strains that set free the mermaid, the shepherdess, and Cassiopeia.

Boland knows that one need not smash the cello in favor of the horn: All resources are required to record *and* orchestrate the unrecorded life. If we judge from the textures of her newest poems, Boland is turning more fully now toward song. Even Socrates, in prison and preparing to die, gives in to a dream calling him to practice "the art." Boland, versed in the classics, is not unaware of this. Left behind as all writings are bound to be in time's democratic Circus Maximus, her poems will stand or fall—I suspect they will stand—not on the politics that burdens and distinguishes them for now but on the hardihood of their afterlife as a lyrical *voice*.

Brian Henry (essay date Winter 1997)

SOURCE: "The Woman as Icon, the Woman as Poet," in *Michigan Quarterly Review*, Vol. XXXVI, No. 1, Winter, 1997, pp. 188-202.

[In the following essay, Henry analyzes the connection between Boland's poetry collection, In a Time of Violence, *and her collection of essays,* An Origin Like Water, *and complains that the two works repeat too many themes and are too focused on Boland herself.]*

In what appears to be a bid to be considered *the* woman Irish poet, Eavan Boland has recently published two volumes of poetry—*In a Time of Violence* and *An Origin Like Water: Collected Poems 1967-1987*—and *Object Lessons,* a collection of essays subtitled "The Life of the Woman and the Poet in Our Time." The poems and essays reveal a powerful intellect at work, though her intelligence can at times seem like calculated shrewdness, especially when we examine the poetry and prose together. These three books allow us to trace Boland's progression as a poet and to evaluate her emergence as a significant literary figure, a spokeswoman for her generation. They are roles that she takes seriously and that, for her, are inextricably linked.

From the beginning, Boland's poetry is historically and politically aware as well as utterly humorless. Despite an evident ambition toward grandeur, her early poems emerge as stilted and pseudo-Yeatsian in rhythm and tenor. However, to loudly criticize Boland's early poetry would be redundant, for she herself dismisses these poems in the preface to *An Origin Like Water* because they "struggled for skill and avoided risk." She includes these early poems, "with their failures, their awkwardness, because although the connection [of her womanhood with her life as a poet] was often flawed and painful, [that connection] remains central." Although she criticizes these poems, she clearly does not expect us to follow suit. Her inclusion of a substantial number of poems that she considers failures compels us to consider them beside the later poems as stations on her journey toward a more capacious identity and vision. As with Adrienne Rich, one of Boland's obvious models in craft as well as ideology, the early work is exhibited as symptomatic of an undeveloped feminist sensibility in need of re-vision.

From the beginning, Boland's poetry is historically and politically aware as well as utterly humorless.
—*Brian Henry*

In Boland's first collection, *New Territory,* occasional dramatic monologues appear with more common third-person narratives, allowing the poet to remain outside the poems and to withhold feeling or emotion. We can see everywhere the work of a young poet struggling with form and slavishly imitating Yeats. In the first three quatrains of the sonnet **"Yeats in Civil War,"** one of the strongest poems in the collection, Boland forces several rhymes to achieve her line breaks; the slant rhyme of the final couplet, however, is a sign of formal rebellion, or at least innovation:

> In middle age you exchanged the sandals
> Of a pilgrim for a Norman keep
> In Galway. Civil war started. Vandals
> Sacked your country, made off with your sleep.
>
> Somehow you arranged your escape
> Aboard a spirit ship which every day
> Hoisted sail out of fire and rape.
> On that ship your mind was stowaway.
>
> The sun mounted on a wasted place
> But the wind at every door and turn
> Blew the smell of honey in your face
> Where there was none.
>   Whatever I may learn
>
> You are its sum, struggling to survive—
> A fantasy of honey your reprieve.

The "reprieve" is not only for the great poet, but also for the reader whose ear is jarred by the ostentatious rhymes.

In Boland's second collection, *The War Horse,* she becomes more historian than mythologist, and she eases up on her strict rhyme schemes. Unfortunately, most of the weaknesses of the poems in *New Territory*—especially the stiff cadences and the poet's distance from her subjects—are carried over to these poems. We see more dramatic monologues and the third-person narratives, but Boland's focus is more political now, in poems like **"The Famine Road," "A Soldier's Son,"** and **"The Hanging Judge,"** as well as two poems written "after" Mayakovsky. Her preoccupation with the suburbs, which strengthens with time, emerges in **"Ode to Suburbia,"** where the suburb is "an ugly sister" that "swelled so that when you tried / The silver slipper on your foot / It pinched your instep." Is the poet feeling hemmed in by her surroundings?

In the title poem, however, we see Boland for the first time entering and occupying her own poem. In its reliance on a first-person narrative and in its equating of the domestic world with the violent outside world, **"The War Horse"** foreshadows Boland's later poems. In the poem the passing of a horse is imbued with a sense of danger:

> This dry night, nothing unusual
> About the clip, clop, casual
>
> Iron of his shoes as he stamps death
> Like a mint on the innocent coinage of earth.

The slant rhymes and lack of regular meter give the poem a

more natural and more pleasing rhythm. When the horse passes by, the poem acquires a pentimento effect, as if Boland were rewriting Yeats's epitaph from "Under Ben Bulben":

> Cast a cold eye
> On life, on death.
> Horseman, pass by!

But here there is no horseman—no agent—only an unwitting and clumsy horse. After the horse disappears, the poet finds that "No great harm is done. / Only a leaf of our laurel hedge is torn / / Of distant interest like a maimed limb." Now the floral landscape, marred by this seemingly harmless horse, becomes a human landscape, with the rose bush "expendable, a mere / Line of defense against him, a volunteer," and the crocus "one of the screamless dead." Before she allows herself too much melodrama, Boland wisely remembers,

> But we, we are safe, our unformed fear
> Of fierce commitment gone; why should we care
>
> If a rose, a hedge, a crocus are uprooted
> Like corpses, remote, crushed, mutilated?

But the rose, hedge, and crocus are not corpses; and despite her inclination to make them so, Boland returns to the unwitting horse who "stumbles on like a rumor of war, huge / Threatening." The horse threatens neither the poet nor her suburban neighbors, but his passing through—the wreckage he leaves behind—reminds the poet of "A cause ruined before, a world betrayed." This hugely symbolic horse gallops improbably into Boland's milieu straight from the poetic tradition, as her historical analogies suggest—a masculine force of immense threat to the safe world of the suburban present.

Casting off her male influences, Boland delivers a cornucopia of psychological misfits in *In Her Own Image.* A cathartic collection of dramatic monologues, the book begins at a high pitch with **"Tirade for the Mimic Muse,"** a blast against everything poetically and politically oppressive. In its rhythm and tone, the poem reads like a re-tuned version of Plath's "Daddy." The poem steamrolls us with its Anglo-Saxon monosyllables, hard consonants, and loud internal rhymes:

> I've caught you out. You slut. You fat trout. . . .
> Anyone would think you were a whore—
> An aging out-of-work kind-hearted tart.
> I know you for the ruthless bitch you are:
> Our criminal, our tricoteuse, our Muse—
> Our Muse of Mimic Art.
>
>   . . .

How you fled
The kitchen screw and the rack of labor,
The wash thumbed and the dish cracked,
The scream of beaten women,
The crime of babies battered,
The hubbub and the shriek of daily grief
That seeks asylum behind suburb walls. . . .

After two books of mostly insipid poems, it is refreshing to encounter such voltage in Boland's language. But if we return to any stanza of Plath's "Daddy," we realize that **"Tirade"** is a weak imitation:

You stand at the blackboard, daddy,
In the picture I have of you,
A cleft in your chin instead of your foot
But no less a devil for that, no not
Any less the black man who

Bit my pretty red heart in two.

Boland's mimicking of Plath raises an important question: Does imitating a male poet (Yeats) produce bad poetry while imitating a female poet (Plath) produces good poetry? What kind of value system does that imply? Boland's acknowledgement of her debt to Yeats and her criticism of the resulting poems seem like a preemptive strike because she knows her readers will recognize the Yeatsian echoes in those poems. But she expects us to ignore that these poems mine Plath territory.

Boland's mimicking of Plath raises an important question: Does imitating a male poet (Yeats) produce bad poetry while imitating a female poet (Plath) produces good poetry? What kind of value system does that imply?
                    —*Brian Henry*

Although the other poems in *In Her Own Image* seldom attain the verbal power of **"Tirade for the Mimic Muse,"** they attempt to shock us with their content—domestic violence, breast cancer, anorexia, menstruation, masturbation. Because these subjects are common fodder for American poems, these poems carry the extra burden of convincing already skeptical readers. They seldom succeed. For example, the narrator in **"In His Own Image"** does not feel normal unless her husband beats her, ostensibly in order to recast her in his own image:

Now I see
that all I needed
was a hand

to mold my mouth
to scald my cheek. . . .

He splits my lip with his fist,
shadows my eye with a blow,
knuckles my neck to its proper angle.
What a perfectionist!
His are a sculptor's hands:
they summon
form from the void,
they bring
me to myself again.
I am a new woman.

Although the poem is a dramatic monologue, the narrator's total submission rings false to me. The cheap irony of the last line invites a programmatic feminist response: "Look how this poor woman has conspired in her own victimization! All her abuser has left her is a useless sarcasm." Readers of poetry are likely to resist this simplistic rhetorical stratagem.

In contrast, the dramatic monologue of **"Anorexia"** is faithful to the complexity of this disease: "Flesh is heretic. / My body is a witch. / I am burning it." Much of the poem recalls Plath's "Lady Lazarus," but Boland manages to fully explore the motives of the narrator who is destroying her body yet protecting her spirit:

I vomited
her hungers.
Now the bitch is burning.

I am starved and curveless.
I am skin and bone.
She has learned her lesson.

When Boland can transform her narrators from stock characters to fully realized women, the poems work as verbally taut performances. The too-close resemblances to Plath's staccato short-line speech acts, however, diminish these poems' long-term significance.

With *Night Feed,* Boland cools off a bit and enters her own territory rather than that of Yeats or Plath. The poems are carefully crafted and more subdued. In the opening poem, **"Degas's Laundresses,"** we hear Boland savoring the textures of language instead of the harshness of it:

You seam dreams in the folds
of wash from which freshes
the whiff and reach of fields
where it bleached and stiffened.
Your chat's sabbatical. . . .

But it is the domestic that dominates *Night Feed*—a domestic life that can be stultifying ("a room white and quiet as a mortuary") as well as exhilarating. In this white-washed suburbia—where **"It's a Woman's World"** is more than the title of a poem—Boland observes a seemingly static world that is actually full of flux. The possibility of transformation in such a setting is Boland's real concern here, whether physical (**"The Woman Turns Herself into a Fish," "Daphne with Her Thighs in Bark," "A Ballad of Beauty and Time"**) or cognitive (**"Woman in Kitchen," "It's a Woman's World," "Patchwork"**).

Transformation is paramount in the book's central poem, **"Domestic Interior,"** where the poet negotiates her world as a mother. Boland's treatment of this mother/daughter relationship can be touching, as in the section **"Night Feed"**:

> This is dawn.
> Believe me
> This is your season, little daughter.
> The moment daisies open,
> The hour mercurial rainwater
> Makes a mirror for sparrows.
> It's time we drowned our sorrows.
>
> I tiptoe in.
> I lift you up
> Wriggling. . . .

The scene is an ordinary one, but perhaps it seems more tender to us because of Boland's usually hardened stance. She is now looking beyond herself to another person who is completely reliant upon her ("we are one more and inseparable again").

Another transformation—the alternation between day and night—appears in **"Domestic Interior."** Boland treats this transformation deftly throughout the poem, where dawn becomes a prelapsarian world (after the feeding "we begin / The long fall from grace") and night is hardly innocent ("And in the dark / as we slept / the world / was made flesh"). What makes this poem succeed—in addition to its economy of language and tenderness of emotion—is how Boland inscribes an entire world into such a small, desultory space.

In *The Journey,* the final book represented in *An Origin Like Water,* Boland continues to explore the domestic life in an attempt to come to terms with "the terrors of routine." By now her poems focus almost exclusively on her life. But a new subject preoccupies her here: language. Whether she is searching for "the language that is / / lace: / / a baroque obligation" or asserting that "a new language / is a kind of scar / and heals after a while / into a passable imitation / of

what went before," Boland is intent upon the power of language—to oppress, to transform, to liberate.

In **"The Women,"** Boland explains her reasons for writing poetry:

> This is the hour I love: the in-between,
> neither here-nor-there hour of evening.
>
> . . .
>
> My time of sixth sense and second sight
> when in the words I choose, the lines I write,
> they rise like visions and appear to me:
>
> women of work, of leisure, of the night,
> in stove-colored silks, in lace, in nothing,
> with crewel needles, with books, with wide open
> legs
>
> who fled the hot breath of the god pursuing,
> who ran from the split hoof and the thick lips
> and fell and grieved and healed into myth,
>
> into me in the evening at my desk. . . .

Hence the women in her poems: Daphne, suburban women and country women, her daughter and mother and grandmother, women in paintings, the faceless women of history. These women were present in Boland's early poems, but by now their identities, or lack of identities, have acquired a sense of urgency for the poet. For her, no woman's life is too insignificant to enter a poem. Thus, when Sappho guides her to the Underworld in **"The Journey,"** she encounters women and children, victims of "[c]holera, typhus, croup, diphtheria," washerwomen, court ladies, laundresses; and she pleads, "'Let me be / let me at least be their witnesses.'" Sappho answers, "'What you have seen is beyond speech, / beyond song, only not beyond love'"; and, as they ascend, she tells Boland, "'I have brought you here so you will know forever / the silences in which are our beginnings, / in which we have an origin like water.'" Poetry, then, becomes a way to usurp those silences, to bring back from an immersion in the collective unconscious, like Dante from his journey, the language that can liberate an oppressed community.

This notion of empowerment through poetry energizes many of the poems in *The Journey.* By claiming "My muse must be better than those of men / who made theirs in the image of their myth," Boland rejects the conventional and depersonalizing perceptions that arise from myth. This is a theme that Boland also explores in her essays. Indeed, the strong connection between her poems and her essays makes a consideration of Boland's efforts in one genre contingent upon her efforts in the other.

> **Perhaps it is overly optimistic of me to expect Boland to reach out to her sister Irish writers, but her continual focus on "the woman poet" practically begs for such a communal gesture. . . . Boland's is the most familiar name to those of us interested in women's Irish poetry, and it seems that she wants to keep it that way.**
> **—Brian Henry**

The subtitle of *Object Lessons*—"The Life of the Woman and the Poet in Our Time"—makes a huge claim, leading one to anticipate a book devoted to a commentary on the woman poet's condition in Ireland today. But the book presents only essays on Boland's life and poetry: when Boland writes, her subject is always herself. While this can be an enjoyable and illuminating trait in poetry, in prose it comes across as egotistical. Part of the reason that Boland's recent publishing endeavors seem self-aggrandizing is her reticence about other women Irish poets—this despite all her talk about women progressing from being the objects of poems to being the authors of them. When she mentions other women Irish poets in these essays (she quotes Medbh McGuckian, Paula Meehan, and Eilean ni Chuilleanain), she does so only in passing. Her discussion of women Irish poets other than herself amounts to less than two pages of the 250.

Perhaps it is overly optimistic of me to expect Boland to reach out to her sister Irish writers, but her continual focus on "the woman poet" practically begs for such a communal gesture. When asked in a recent interview whom she considers to be successful writers of the political poem, Boland mentions only Seamus Heaney and Derek Mahon—male poets with firmly established reputations. In my mind, McGuckian's omission from that list is an egregious one, because of her ability to control her environment (Belfast) by means of linguistic innovations more original and remarkable than Boland's. Boland's is the most familiar name to those of us interested in women's Irish poetry, and it seems that she wants to keep it that way.

By holding herself up in *Object Lessons* as the model woman poet who struggled through Irish patriarchy and a male-dominated poetic tradition, she contributes to her relatively uncontested reputation. How unfortunate, then, that the book is so tedious. Although Boland has an elegant prose style, her essays rarely have true emotional power. And because she obsesses so much about herself, she often cannot connect with her readers, leaving us amazed at and increasingly intolerant of her infinite capacity for self-examination.

Boland divides her book of essays into two parts: "Objects"

and "Lessons." The essays in "Objects" explore the experiences that shaped her as a woman and as a poet and examine the relationships among gender, nationhood, and poetry. As an Irish citizen, she addresses the colonization and subjugation of Ireland by England; as a woman, she tries to find a place in her society and in the Irish poetic tradition. In these essays, Boland strives to articulate the impetus for and the consequences of her poetry because she will not allow her poems to speak for themselves. When read in tandem with her poetry, some of Boland's essays become redundant.

In her preface to *Object Lessons,* Boland explains (excuses?) the repetition in the essays as being akin to those in a poem, with "turnings and returnings." The way she describes her prose technique makes it seem attractive:

> Therefore, the reader will come on the same room more than once: the same tablecloth with red-checked squares; the identical table by an open window. An ordinary suburb, drenched in winter rain, will show itself once, twice, then disappear and come back. The Dublin hills will change color in the distance, and change once more. The same October day will happen, as it never can in real life, over and over again.

While this returning of details in the essays enriches them, the recycling of the same themes and issues as in her poetry is objectionable because it detracts from her poetry. The essay **"Lava Cameo,"** for example, is an expanded version of the poem of the same title in *In a Time of Violence.* The essay **"Outside History"** shares its title with Boland's volume of selected poems as well as a poetic sequence. The theme of the poem **"An Irish Childhood in England: 1951"** and most of its details reappear in the essay **"A Fragment of Exile."** At the risk of sounding puritanical, I believe that assigning the same title to an essay and to a poem diminishes the poem's importance, as if the poem could be written in prose with little difference. Ultimately, this book of essays negates the need for many of the poems in *In a Time of Violence* (or vice-versa).

Occasionally, an essay gives us the feeling that Boland has discovered something new about herself without writing a poem about it. In **"In Search of a Language,"** she explains the effect of her family moving to London when she was five years old. Not knowing the Irish language as a teenager (by now she had moved back to Ireland), she searched for both a mode of expression and an identity through that expression. With Irish closed to her and English oppressive to her, she found solace in Latin. Knowing Latin—the language that had "forged alliances and named stars"—gave her a sense of power and a path to clarity and safety. Because this feeling of possessing a language enabled her to write poetry, the language she discovers becomes her own.

In the "Lessons" section of *Object Lessons,* Boland becomes more political. She begins **"The Woman The Place The Poet"** with an eloquent consideration of the idea of place:

> There is a duality to place. There is the place which existed before you and will continue after you have gone. . . . there is the place that happened and the place that happens to you.

Boland has lived in Dundrum, a suburb of Dublin, for nearly half her life. Before moving to Dundrum (and she makes much of this forced displacement), she lived in London, New York, and Dublin itself. Her position as a suburban poet would merit little, if any, discussion if she did not feel compelled to rationalize it as a landscape for poetry. Perhaps she feels guilty, or uneasy, about her locale while other women Irish poets live in troubled areas such as Belfast. When Boland makes an argument for the "fragile and transitory nature of a suburb," or argues that lives in her suburb "thrived, waned, changed, began and ended here," she doesn't convince me. Don't lives thrive, wane, and change everywhere?

In **"Outside History,"** Boland gets to the heart of her project as a poet: her analysis of the idea of woman as object/subject/author in Irish poetry. She begins the essay with a formative event: an old woman—the caretaker of the cottage where Boland is vacationing—brings her water, and they talk about the famine. This encounter also comprises an earlier poem, **"The Achill Woman."** By beginning an essay on women with her own poetic experience, Boland makes herself a metaphor for all women: This is my experience, she says, this is our experience.

Boland then turns to the "virulence and necessity of the idea of a nation" and how male Irish poets blended the idea of the female with that of the nation. Mother Ireland, in their poems, becomes a woman raped and conquered by the English, violated while her poets/protectors can only watch and scribble in their notepads. Because these male poets created a poetic tradition and an idea of an Irish nation that excluded activist women, Boland as a young poet realized that "the Irish nation as an existing construct in Irish poetry was not available to [her]." The only way to enter that tradition was to repossess it. Thus, Boland, as well as other women (though, characteristically, none is mentioned in the essay), "moved from being the objects of Irish poems to being the authors of them." She perceptively exposes a tendency in Irish male poets to fetishize the female:

> The majority of Irish male poets depended on women as motifs in their poetry. . . . The women in their poems were often passive, decorative, raised to emblematic status.

The trouble was these images did good service as ornaments. . . . Women in such poems were frequently referred to approvingly as mythic, emblematic. But to me these passive and simplified women seemed a corruption. Moreover, the transaction they urged on the reader, to accept them as mere decoration, seemed to compound the corruption.

However convincing her argument might be, Boland's sweeping focus (she directs her attack at most male Irish poets, with "the later Yeats [being] a rare exception") inevitably leads to the author herself, forcing us to ask how Boland treats women in her poetry.

In fact, Boland can be as blinkered as her male predecessors in her treatment of the female, especially in her more recent poems. In **"The Death of Reason"** in *In a Time of Violence,* Boland contrasts the violence in Ireland with the "art of portrait-painting" in England. The woman sitting for a portrait emerges both as an anonymous female and as Brittania, the English version of Cathleen ni Houlihan:

> And she climbed the stairs. Nameless composite.
> Anonymous beauty-bait for the painter.
> . . . The easel waits for her
> and the age is ready to resemble her and
> the small breeze cannot touch that powdered hair.
> That elegance.

Boland strives to accomplish two tasks here: to reveal the objectification of women and to contrast the daily realities in Ireland and England. In the poem the violence in Ireland threatens the English: "The flames have crossed the sea. / They are at . . . the door. / At the canvas, / At her mouth." Because the woman represents the English and their enlightened ways, reason itself becomes engulfed in the spreading fire: "the eighteenth century ends here / as her hem scorches and the satin / decoration catches fire. She is burning down." Although Boland deftly uses the woman to represent several things (art, reason, England), she falls into the trap that she denounces in **"Outside History"**: she transforms the woman into an icon. The woman is faceless, a stock figure with no depth or humanity. On this central polemical point, then, Boland's credibility in her essay becomes questionable when we examine her treatment of the woman in **"The Death of Reason"** and elsewhere in *In a Time of Violence* (**"In a Bad Light," "Legends," "The Pomegranate"**).

In the very poem that emerged from Boland's encounter with the cottage caretaker, **"The Achill Woman"** (originally part of the **"Outside History"** sequence), she uses the woman as a token, as a way to give the poet a chance to arrive at the end of the poem. The title alone depersonalizes the woman; and because Boland ignores the class distinction between herself and the old woman, the woman becomes nothing more than an unrealized figure. She represents the peasantry and the Irish language while Boland, a privileged college student, speaks English, the language of the oppressor. By failing to remark on this distinction, Boland fails to do justice to the woman's story and the meeting between them. Perhaps Boland omitted this poem from *An Origin Like Water* because it represents exactly what she condemns in her male predecessors. In any case, the poem is an excellent example of Boland using the power of poetry to objectify other women while empowering herself.

Indeed, in both poetry and prose, Boland continually concerns herself with power: the power of language, the power of the woman, the power of the nation. However, the only woman in *In a Time of Violence* to acquire power is the poet herself; she never develops her female characters or narrators except when the central figure is the poet. When she comes to understand the power of language through rhetoric, Boland finds strength, for herself, in **"Writing in a Time of Violence."** She talks of the destructive power of language:

> we will live, we have lived
> where language is concealed. Is perilous.
>   . . . But it is too late
>
> . . . to refuse to enter
> . . . a city of whispers
> and interiors where
>
> the dear vowels
> *Irish Ireland ours* are
> absorbed into Autumn air,
> are out of earshot in the distances
> we are stepping into where we never
>
> imagine words such as *hate*
> and *territory* and the like—unbanished still
> as they always would be—wait
> and are waiting under
> beautiful speech. To strike.

Although she uncovers the terrors that lie under "beautiful speech," she serves merely as a distant witness, not as a participant. Rhetoric becomes a tool of persuasion, the people of Ireland the object of that tool. However, the poet lives far from this "city of whispers / and interiors" where language is concealed and veiled beneath glorious words. Her protests seem impotent even though she sees hateful language waiting to strike. By placing herself at the periphery of the poem, "at a desk in college," she fails to enter the realities of the poem.

Because most of the issues in *In a Time of Violence* also appear in *Object Lessons,* we must look to the language in the poems to notice the differences in her treatment of ideas in her poetry and prose. The language in most of these po-

ems vacillates between being purposefully flat and being perfectly crafted. The first three lines of **"The Parcel,"** for example, are prosaic, and the line breaks are weak: "There are dying arts and / one of them is / the way my mother used to make up a parcel." But the poem gathers momentum, and its ending is stunning:

> See it disappear. Say
> this is how it died
> out: among doomed steamships and outdated
> trains,
> the tracks for them disappearing before our eyes,
> next to station names we can't remember
> on a continent we no longer
> recognize. The sealing wax cracking.
> The twine unravelling. The destination illegible.

Many of these poems begin insipidly and end explosively. But the prosaic quality of much of the poetry again calls into question Boland's shifting between genres.

One poem in *In a Time of Violence* that avoids flat language, rehashed themes, and objectifying the female is **"Anna Liffey,"** the most ambitious and most human poem in the book. The "turnings and returnings" that Boland describes in her preface to *Object Lessons* occur here to great effect. Dublin's River Liffey courses through the poem: it is free, as it "rises in rush and ling heather and / Black peat and bracken and strengthens / To claim the city it narrated." But the poem's narrator is not so free: "If I could see myself / I would see / A woman in a doorway." The river frames the poem while the doorway (read: suburbia) frames (read: restricts) the woman. Because she displays both real emotion and technical adroitness here, this poem marks a significant departure from the other poems in this book and in *An Origin Like Water.* This emotion is restrained, yet we feel that Boland is barely holding it in:

> Make of a nation what you will
> Make of the past
> What you can—
>
> There is now
> A woman in a doorway
>
> It has taken me
> All my strength to do this.
>
> Becoming a figure in a poem.
>
> Usurping a name and a theme.

The locutions of Adrienne Rich are readily identifiable in such a passage. But influence need not be a problem. Boland is more human here than in any of her other poems. If she continues to explore these difficult areas in her poetry, her prediction at the end of **"Anna Liffey"**—"In the end / Everything that burdened and distinguished me / Will be lost in this: / I was a voice"—may prove true. But if she persists in self-aggrandizement in her poetry and prose and if she continues to ignore the valuable writing of the women around her, her work risks becoming overwhelmed by the weight of her ego.

FURTHER READING

Criticism

Henigan, Robert. "Contemporary Women Poets in Ireland." *Concerning Poetry* 18, Nos. 1 and 2 (1985): 103-15.
    Discusses the work of Boland and other Irish contemporary women poets and their presentation of the lives of women.

Kerrigan, John. "Belonging." *London Review of Books* 18, No. 14 (18 July 1996): 26.
    Reviews Boland's *Object Lessons* and *Collected Poems.*

O'Connell, Patty. "Eavan Boland: An Interview." *Poets & Writers Magazine* 22, No. 6 (November/December 1994): 36-45.
    Discusses Boland's growing U.S. audience and the difference between American and Irish poetry as Boland sees it.

Interview

Consalvo, Deborah McWilliams. "'Between Rhetoric and Reality': An Interview with Eavan Boland on the Place of the Woman Poet in the Irish Literary Canon." *Studies: An Irish Quarterly Review* 81 (Spring 1992): 89-100.
    Interview in which Boland discusses the relationship of her poetry to feminism, politics, and Irish literature.

Additional coverage of Boland's life and career is contained in the following sources published by Gale: *Contemporary Authors,* Vol. 143; *Dictionary of Literary Biography,* Vol. 40; and *DISCovering Authors Modules: Poets.*

E. L. Doctorow
1931-

(Full name Edgar Laurence Doctorow) American novelist, short story and novella writer, editor, essayist and dramatist.

The following entry provides an overview of Doctorow's career through 1995. For further information on his life and works, see *CLC,* Volumes 6, 11, 15, 18, 37, 44, and 65.

INTRODUCTION

Doctorow's work has been characterized as fabulist and described as allegorical romance. Although much of his fiction focuses on historical fact, Doctorow has stated his preference to "mingle the Marvelous" with the real, as can be seen in his most famous work, *Ragtime* (1975). Doctorow has explored several genres of fiction: western, science-fiction, historical, and science-detection mystery. In doing so he has produced works that, while provoking critical thought, have also had commercial success. Political issues are often raised in his work—as in *The Book of Daniel* (1971), a look at the communist scare of the 1950s in America. While he often represents the values of the political left, he has also been critical of the left. A post-modern novelist, deconstructing and refashioning myths of American culture, Doctorow has also been portrayed as a literary descendant of Nathaniel Hawthorn and Edgar Allan Poe: a teller of tales that both reflect the writer's time and heritage, and invite readers to see with the light of critical thought.

Biographical Information

Born January 6, 1931 in New York City, Doctorow was named after Edgar Allan Poe. He studied philosophy at Kenyon College, graduated with honors in 1952, and went on to perform graduate work at Columbia. From 1953 to 1955 Doctorow served in the U.S. Army Signal Corps. During his army service he married Helen Esther Setzer, a writer, with whom he has three children. Doctorow's professional work has included a position as script reader for Columbia Pictures in New York City. During his time as a script reader he completed *Welcome to Hard Times* (1960), his first novel, which was later turned into a film starring Lou Chaney and Henry Fonda. In his native New York City, Doctorow worked in publishing, serving as senior editor at New American Library from 1959 through 1964, and as editor-in-chief, vice-president and publisher at Dial Press from 1964 until 1969. *Big as Life* (1966) and *The Book of Daniel* were completed during this period. The rest of his writing, including

Ragtime, was completed while he held various academic positions. Doctorow was a visiting senior fellow at Princeton from 1980 through 1981 and has served as Glucksman Professor of English and American letters since 1982 at New York University in New York City.

Major Works

Doctorow's first novel, *Welcome to Hard Times,* was written as a reaction to bad film scripts for westerns that he read as part of his duties at Columbia Pictures in the late 1950s. An idea for a short story became the first chapter of this novel which presents a revision of the spirit of the old West. *Big as Life,* Doctorow's second novel, is the mythical story of two naked human giants who materialize in New York City. *Big as Life* was not a commercial success, though it did gain critical praise, as did *Welcome to Hard Times. The Book of Daniel* focuses on the case of Julius and Ethel Rosenberg, who were executed in 1953 for espionage, and the anti-Communist atmosphere of the 1950s. The novel explores the spirit of survival of those persecuted in the attack on left-wing supporters. Doctorow's biggest success, both critically and commercially, is *Ragtime,* an amalgam of fictional and historical figures, including J. P. Morgan, Harry Houdini, Henry Ford, and Emma Goldman. The novel was adapted for the cinema in 1981 by Dino De Laurentiis and Milos Forman, and starred James Cagney. The mixture of history and fiction presented in *Ragtime* is a device which has characterized much of Doctorow's work, and through which he has raised issues about the writing of fiction and the nature of history. A focus on language has marked the majority of Doctorow's works. Language plays a prominent role in his play *Drinks before Dinner* (1979), which Doctorow claims to have conceived first with sounds in mind, then words, then the names of the characters. As he explained in an interview, the inspiration came from the writings of Gertrude Stein and Mao Tse-tung, particularly their "rhythm of repetition" and "flexible language with possibilities of irony and paradox." *Loon Lake* (1980) and *Billy Bathgate* (1989), although different in narrative detail, both question and evaluate the myths of success and the self-made man of American history. *World's Fair* (1985) and *The Waterworks* (1994) each contain elements of reminiscence and recreation of the New York City of Doctorow's childhood. *The Waterworks,* ostensibly a science-fiction mystery, has also been seen as an allegory of the Reagan era. In his *Selected Essays 1977-1992* (1994), Doctorow covers a range of subjects that also appear in his fiction: for example, one essay deals with the effects of Reaganomics on American society, while another meditates on and describes 19th-century New York City.

Critical Reception

Many critics assert that Doctorow is the quintessential postmodern novelist whose work re-examines received ideas and reflects on its own nature and structure. However, "traditional fiction values" are not subverted, according to Stanley Kauffmann, who emphasizes Doctorow's storytelling skills. "Every sequence is handled by a dramatist, [and] is understood to its *conclusion,*" Kauffmann affirms. While telling tales, Doctorow also provokes critical thought: this is a strength repeatedly praised by reviewers. "Doctorow seeks a fiction," writes John G. Parks, "that is both politically relevant and aesthetically complex and interesting." Doctorow's mixing of historical reality and fiction is a feature generally admired by critics, who have asserted that the blend of fact and fiction provides fresh thought and breathes new life into mythical figures. Addressing this aspect of Doctorow's work, Michael Wutz praised Doctorow's "almost uncanny ability to reconstruct historical material and . . . spellbinding facility to tell a good tale." Commenting on *Welcome to Hard Times,* Stephen Cooper observed how Doctorow's portrayal of the early self-made men not as altruistic nation-builders but as "parasitic entrepreneurs" upset common perceptions of the mythical, and provoked readers to "struggle with our

relationship to our society with an open, flexible, critical mind." Doctorow's revisionism, however, is an area that gives rise to arguments about his political sympathies. Reviewing *The Book of Daniel,* Kauffmann pointed out that the "political radicalism" America inherited from late 19th-century immigrants, many of them east European Jews, is the source of Doctorow's critical thought and his power to stimulate the reader. However, many critics, like Carol Iannone and Joseph Epstein, object to Doctorow's slant on American history and culture. "[T]he ideological attitudes of the left . . . compromise everything he has written," wrote Iannone; and Epstein suggested that Doctorow's fiction verges on the anti-American. Most critics, however, support a more balanced view of the political elements that pervade Doctorow's fiction, agreeing that he does "target reactionary history," but at the same time "his postmodern method also questions the left-wing interpretations of history."

PRINCIPAL WORKS

Welcome to Hard Times (novel) 1960
Big as Life (novel) 1966
The Book of Daniel (novel) 1971
Ragtime (novel) 1975
Drinks before Dinner (drama) 1979
Loon Lake (novel) 1980
Lives of the Poets: Six Stories and a Novella (short fiction) 1984
World's Fair (novel) 1985
Billy Bathgate (novel) 1989
Selected Essays 1977-1992 (nonfiction) 1994
The Waterworks (novel) 1994

CRITICISM

Wirt Williams (review date 25 September 1960)

SOURCE: "Bad Man from Bodie," in *New York Times Book Review,* September 25, 1960, p. 51.

[*In the following review, Williams outlines the conflict and theme of* Welcome to Hard Times.]

"Once again, the legend of the Old West has been rescued for a serious literary purpose," say the publishers of this first novel by a philosophy major. Inevitably, they invoke *The Ox-Bow Incident*—a practice followed by many reviewers, who seldom fail to pronounce the work at hand the first serious fiction about the West since—well, almost always since *The Ox-Bow Incident* (e.g.: *The Authentic Death of Dendry*

Janes, Carrington, A Distant Trumpet, Warlock). It is time to acknowledge that the "serious Western" has established itself firmly on a sub-genre of fiction. ***Welcome to Hard Times*** is an exfoliation on a quite sturdy branch.

Thematically, E. L. Doctorow's short novel is concerned with one of the favorite problems of philosophers: the relationship of man and evil. Its structure is appropriately dramatic and simple. Into a small settlement in the Dakotas comes a Bad Man from Bodie. With easy and pleasurable cruelty, he destroys the town. It only takes a few brutalities, a couple of murders, and some simple arson.

Blue, self-appointed record keeper and honorific mayor, is too weak, too afraid—in a familiar tradition—to kill the Bad Man. Later, he sets about to rebuild the town. He also takes one of the brutalized bar girls, Molly, as common-law wife. The Bad Man comes back, of course. He has the inevitable confrontation with the Mayor, of course. But its inner meaning is a great distance from the business of "a man's gotta dew what a man's gotta dew."

It is time to acknowledge that the "serious Western" has established itself firmly on a sub-genre of fiction. *Welcome to Hard Times* is an exfoliation on a quite sturdy branch.
　　　　　—*Wirt Williams*

The book says that evil comes only when summoned. Blue tries to explain it to Molly: "You know something? Listen to me, you know why he came that time? We wanted him. Our tongues were just hanging out for him." And when the rebuilt Hard Times wants Evil again, the Bad Man returns. Blue finally kills him, perceiving that he has failed as badly in acting as he had failed earlier in not acting.

Perhaps the primary theme of the novel is that evil can only be resisted psychically: when the rational controls that order man's existence slacken, destruction comes. Conrad said it best in *Heart of Darkness,* but Mr. Doctorow has said it impressively. His book is taut and dramatic, exciting and successfully symbolic.

Gwendolyn Brooks (review date 10 July 1966)

SOURCE: "The Menace," in *New York Herald Tribune Book Week,* July 10, 1966, p. 17.

[*In the following review, Brooks provides a sketch of the plot, characters and ideas in* Big as Life.]

One day a gigantic, nude man and woman arrive in New York. They lean against the horizon. They are beautiful, burnished, odorous, and they have a powerful effect on the town, which proceeds to tumble over itself, to huddle, to pray. The town cries NO.

What can be done? Consultation, defense command, intellectual research, jetliner, helicopter, and practical philosophy are brought to bear. The President, the Cabinet, and the governors of New York, New Jersey, Connecticut, and Pennsylvania are interested, make suggestions.

Through the screen of hysteria we see most plainly Wallace Creighton, a professor of history at Columbia University, jazz bass king Red Bloom and Red Bloom's love, Sugarbush. These people inch their way through the violence, death, blanks, and quavers of their predicament and emerge, shredded, with new creeds. Thoughtful Creighton is at first convinced that the new people are unendurable, that they are overwhelmingly repulsive and subtly dangerous; for there is the possibility of mysterious and awful infection, and even though it is discovered that an hour of "normal" time is a month or two of giant time, there is the certainty that eventually the nameless ones will become aware of their small oppressors and will simply stamp them out. But after considerable mullings and veerings, Creighton decides that the invaders have become actually necessary, that they are stimulating the beginning of a "real history," that the net result may be "nice" for posterity, may improve the prospects of that little son Red and Sugarbush are expecting. To tamper with them might "touch some nerve, some key connection." Red, although still awed after a year of the mighty presences, decides that it will be all right if the big beauties remain. He can no longer imagine their non-existence. "I think if you take them away they'll still be there."

As for Sugarbush—her creed is comprised of Red, "love" with Red, housework, the coming baby, and making-the-best-of-things. In Essential Woman we meet the solving heart of things, the blood of this book. Making-the-best-of-things is E. L. Doctorow's recommendation. It is a good recommendation, so we water down our regret that his characters and style are servants to his message.

Stanley Kauffman (review date 5 June 1971)

SOURCE: "Wrestling Society for a Soul," in *New Republic,* June 5, 1971, pp. 25-7.

[*In the following review, Kauffman explains the intricacies of* The Book of Daniel, *revealing it as "a work of historic and psychic currents."*]

This is less a review than a celebration. [With *The Book of Daniel*,] E. L. Doctorow has written the political novel of our age, the best American work of its kind that I know since Lionel Trilling's *The Middle of the Journey.* Doctorow could hardly be less like Trilling in style or temper, but that's part of the point; it helps to make this novel the quintessence of the '60s, as Trilling, in 1947, fixed the political '30s.

The time of the book, the "present" time, is mostly 1967, between Memorial Day and Christmas. Daniel Lewin, twenty-seven, is a graduate student at Columbia, and this book is (and is not!) what he writes instead of a dissertation. He's the son of Communist parents, Bronx Jews, who were executed at Sing Sing in the early 1950s for conspiring to steal atomic secrets for Russia. He has a younger sister. The book is built on his attempts to find the truth about his parents, about himself in relation to them, and on his relations with his sister in her attempts to regain sanity.

> [With *The Book of Daniel*,] E. L. Doctorow has written the political novel of our age, the best American work of its kind that I know since Lionel Trilling's *The Middle of the Journey.*
> —*Stanley Kauffman*

The premise is only one of the potentially troublesome elements in the book that Doctorow converts into triumph. The Rosenberg parallel might have been a mere gimmick. (Trilling, triumphing likewise, based a major character on Whittaker Chambers.) There is no tricky plot. And most certainly it's not a forensic novel about whether the Rosenbergs were really innocent or really guilty. This is an artwork about the *idea* of the Rosenbergs and people like them, how they came into being in this country, why their trial was needed, what their legacy is, and the intertexture of that legacy with the social-political climate today. I haven't looked up the facts of the Rosenberg case; it would be offensive to the quality of this novel to check it against those facts. This is a work of historic and psychic currents.

The parents were named Isaacson. (Nothing has been chosen lightly in this book, including names. The first Isaac, we remember, was nearly sacrificed to his father's beliefs.) They were first-generation Americans, he a radio repairman with a tiny Bronx shop, she the daughter of a crazy old woman who wrote Bintel Briefs to a Yiddish newspaper, recounting persecution in Russia and fierce struggle on the lower East Side.

After the Isaacsons' execution, their two children, fourteen and nine, were adopted by a Boston law professor and wife named Lewin. The book begins with a trip that Daniel and

his young wife and baby make to Massachusetts, to join the Lewins in a visit to the mental hospital where his sister is confined. She was taken there after cutting her wrists in a Howard Johnson's ladies room nearby. The book ends—one of the three endings that are proposed—with the sister's funeral. In between we are pressed to a kaleidoscopic vision of the present and the intermingled past, of political history as it applies to the Isaacsons, of the fires of this century as they burn to and through the borders of all our lives.

A second triumph of Doctorow's is the form of the book. Daniel, the "author," often says that he hates the idea of sequence. The temporal urge of this book is toward simultaneity, not only of time planes but of different viewpoints. Not only are the present and various pasts closely interwoven but also various views of Daniel himself, who is seen in both the third and first persons—sometimes in successive sentences. As with many modern sensibilities, Doctorow has fractured seamless sequence because he felt, evidently, that the turbulence which bred and surrounds Daniel is always present with him, all of it, all the time. Doctorow's cascading form sweeps along with it occasional thematic variations, one of them a "True History of the Cold War" in the shape (says the author) of a raga.

> Every character in [*The Book of Daniel*], major or minor, is sharply visible, has a voice—even a peripheral character like the Isaacsons' Negro janitor, the black man whom these society-changing Communists, these Jews who have known persecution, are quite willing to relegate to a bare cot in the cellar; and who is symbolically waiting.
> —*Stanley Kauffman*

Another important part of the method, throughout the book, is the consciousness that the book is being written. For instance: "I suppose you think I can't do the electrocution, I know there is a you . . . I will show you that I can do the electrocution." And then Doctorow-Daniel does it, unforgettably. This now-familiar consciousness of art in the making of art, this attempt to fix the act of creation as part of the finished work, can be both disarming and enriching, as it is here. "Nothing up my sleeve" adds to the magic, for the modern consciousness that is suspicious of magic.

(In fact, I wish Doctorow had used this method in one "straight" section: the climactic meeting between Daniel and his parents' accuser, years after their death, in Disneyland at Christmas. The irony of the setting and season might have lost its slightly pat touch if Daniel had capitalized on the Disneyland aspects of the meeting.)

A third triumph is that this novel's untraditional form has not subverted traditional fiction values. Doctorow might have thrown all his creative energy into glittering sequences and like some contemporary writers, including some good ones—might have asked the fulfillment of the design to *be* the work. But he achieves other ends as well.

Character. Every character in this book, major or minor, is sharply visible, has a voice—even a peripheral character like the Isaacsons' Negro janitor, the black man whom these society-changing Communists, these Jews who have known persecution, are quite willing to relegate to a bare cot in the cellar; and who is symbolically waiting. Place. Every setting, every occasion has an essence, an odor: a dusty radio-shop window of the '40s, a Yippie pad in the East Village (where, fifty years before, Daniel's grandmother had struggled!), a Paul Robeson concert in the late '40s, a Washington Peace March in 1967. Drama. Every sequence is handled by a dramatist, is understood to its *conclusion*—just one example, the Dickensian episode in which the Isaacson children flee the children's shelter, while their parents are in jail awaiting trial.

And everything in this scintillating, yet deeply mined book feeds its theme. Here is an approximation of that theme. Political radicalism was brought to the US by late 19th-century immigrants, many of whom were East European Jews. Previous political impulses in this country had usually been comfortably meliorist, often theologically based. With increasing socio-economic pressures, partly caused by those very immigrants, the European ideologies that the immigrants brought with them became more and more germane. Therefore it's idle to speak of those ideologies as European concepts imposed on America: those immigrants, and their progeny, now are part of America, and the very changes caused by their interfusion have placed their ideologies among the American antecedents and options.

In its reaction against those ideologies, not an entirely deplorable reaction *in itself,* the US has gone through several spasms of purge, cruelly antithetical to our constitutional premises. One such spasm was the Red spy hunt, of the late '40s when this country needed victims to console itself for the fact that Russia was getting the bomb.

This novel faces up squarely and intelligently to the Jewishness of its subject. Jews had been persecuted, Jews are historically avid for social justice, Jews had less at stake in Anglo-Saxon-cum-Yankee traditions and rewards. Jews were in big cities mainly, cities were trouble spots, Jews were troublemakers. Doctorow refuses to blink any of this. On the contrary, by plunging his hands into the nettles, he plucks out the flower. By confronting the matter in fullest human resonance, he transforms parochialism into universals. His Jews become prototypical.

Out of all this background, partially in reaction against it, come many of today's revolutionaries. (No longer so markedly Jewish, by any means.) Their anti-intellectualism has its roots in impatience with the Bach-and-Shakespeare radicals of the past. Pop culture and pot culture are a reproof of all that Parnassian pipe-smoking culture that, in their view, merely mirrored the oppressive society at a different angle. Socially and psychically too, there have been both connection and change. Doctorow shows us how pervasively sexual the Isaacson marriage was. Daniel has inherited that sexuality, as he inherited radicalism, but has rejected his parents' "respectability," as he rejects formal ideology. A bizarre sex episode with his wife in a moving car is a declaration of continuity and independence.

And beneath the large theme that underlies the book is the even larger contemporary crisis in consciousness: the crisis of faith in rationalism, the faith so hard-won in the last few centuries; the resurgence of the Myth of Unreason because the Myth of Reason has not only failed so far to bring the promised grace but may have become a habit-forming narcotic. One need not subscribe to this belief, as for the most part I do not, to see its power in this novel. (Congruent belief is hardly necessary in art. I'm not a Catholic royalist, yet I think Evelyn Waugh's trilogy is the best fiction produced by World War II.)

> [*The*] *Book of Daniel* is beautiful and harrowing, rhapsodic and exact. Like all good artists . . . , Doctorow does not give answers but is not content only to pose questions.
> —*Stanley Kauffman*

"Existential" revolution, since 1967, has shown defects in dynamics, but Doctorow dramatizes the forces that produced it, along with the opposition to it—chiefly, the ingrained American hunger for innocence, a hunger that always gets vicious when frustrated. Fundamentally, the novel implies, the new revolution grew out of a break with a formal ideology that had its own innocence. Daniel's parents accepted the roles that society imposed on them in the prosecution; more, they accepted the roles that the Party imposed on them. (There is a masterly courtroom scene, imagined by Daniel, in which a mere exchange of glances reveals an intra-Party collusion.) The book chronicles a long break with acceptances, both conservative and radical. The end, the third and final ending, leaves the facts of the Isaacson case still mysterious for Daniel, but the forces that grew out of the radical past swerve until they reach the Columbia library-spring of 1968!-where he is writing.

E. L. Doctorow is forty, a former editor for book publishers, and the author of two previous novels that are not comparable with this work. His ***Book of Daniel*** is beautiful and harrowing, rhapsodic and exact. Like all good artists dealing with such subjects, Doctorow does not give answers but is not content only to pose questions. At one point Daniel says of his father: "He wrestled society for my soul." The line might be a motto for this fine book.

Joseph Catinella (review date 17 July 1971)

SOURCE: A review of *The Book of Daniel,* in *Saturday Review,* Vol. 54, No. 29, July 17, 1971, pp. 32, 61.

[*In the following review, Catinella comments on the devices and concerns of* The Book of Daniel.]

A dozen years after Paul and Rochelle Isaacson have been electrocuted for passing atomic secrets to the Russians, their son, Daniel, sits in the library at Columbia University, ostensibly working on his Ph.D. thesis. But he's actually jotting down notes about life in the Fifties and early Sixties, recalling how he and his sister, Susan, reacted to their parents' fate, wondering where the reckless course of late twentieth-century history is plunging America and the world.

To E. L. Doctorow politics is clearly a matter of life and death if men can be executed for their beliefs and actions. His third novel, more than a mere paraphrase of the Rosenberg Case, begins by evoking the cold-war tensions that, after Hiroshima, pitted Americans against each other, an era rife with political intrigues, witch hunts, blacklistings, and left- and right-wing propaganda which nurtured a national climate of fear.

By focusing on Daniel and his family, from the end of the Second World War to the peace march on the Pentagon in 1967, Mr. Doctorow creates a sharp, harrowing vision of people dedicated to ideologies that both heighten and betray their best impulses. Despite its questionable approach, ***The Book of Daniel*** is a plangent reading of recent history in which private and public events can clash and destroy human beings.

Before their arrest and indictment, the Isaacsons were familiar Old Left figures. They lived in a ramshackle house in the Bronx, attended square dances and Paul Robeson concerts, decried the country's cultural decadence, and raised Daniel on traditional Marxist dogma. As post-Depression Jews in an alien America, they believed that the eventual triumph of Communist ideals would vindicate "their poverty, their failure, their unhappiness. . . ."

Soon the tough, proud, slightly foolish Isaacsons—walking

about naked at home to prove their freedom from bourgeois restraints—are involved in a lurid espionage trial. Their chance of receiving justice is slim: the Korean War is in progress, conspiracy laws are being tightened, and all left-wing activities are under FBI surveillance. Fearing for its own survival, the Communist Party abandons the couple's defense. They're tried by newspapers, condemned by the testimony of Selig Mindish, a former friend, and sentenced to death.

> **Mr. Doctorow is that rare American novelist who is completely serious about politics, at ease with large abstractions, and capable of welding deeply human concerns with reverberant historical notes.**
> **—*Joseph Catinella***

Were they guilty? Unlike the biblical Daniel, favored by God with interpretive powers, their son has no gift for hindsight: "Of one thing we are sure. Everything is elusive. God is elusive. Revolutionary morality is elusive. Justice is elusive. Human character. Quarters for the cigarette machine." Privately debating his parents' guilt or innocence, Daniel vents frustrated rage on his wife and child. His New Left sister, after a suicide attempt, goes mad in a state asylum. Daniel hopes that Mindish may reveal some final truth about the case and flies to California to visit him, but Mindish is senile, frolicking in a toy automobile at Disneyland and unable to answer any questions.

These are desperate ironies, spiked with cruel wit, suggesting that behind all motives and actions lie dense ambiguities. Nevertheless, mediating between personal and national conflicts, Mr. Doctorow seeks some political truths. From the failures of communism, "the perfectionist dream of heaven on earth," have emerged today's New Left insurgents who, in another, more ruthless irony, dismiss the Isaacsons. "You want to know what was wrong with the old American Communists? They were into the system," a hyperthyroid radical declares. "You dig? Society is a put-on so we put on the put-on."

Mr. Doctorow is that rare American novelist who is completely serious about politics, at ease with large abstractions, and capable of welding deeply human concerns with reverberant historical notes. The form of the book, as anarchic as its material, encloses a "raga" on U.S. Soviet relationships, a running account of various methods of capital punishment, and even a discourse on the "political implications" of Disneyland.

The technical irony of the novel, however, is that although form mirrors substance, the Isaacsons' personal tragedy is often dwarfed by polemics, by Daniel's nervous shifts from first-to third-person narrative, by the skillful yet nevertheless modish intrusion of the author's voice, calling attention to the artifice behind all art: "I suppose you think I can't do the electrocution. I know there is a you. There has always been a you. YOU: I will show you that I can do the electrocution."

This is an art that frequently reveals its mechanics. But in certain reasonably pure dramatic passages—the FBI arrest, the young Isaacson children in a Bronx shelter, Daniel's Pentagon bust as he moves from neutrality to activism—the book asserts its power with a controlled urgency, which is the best tone Mr. Doctorow wields inasmuch as the final implication of the novel is apolitical.

On the eve of the Columbia University riots, Daniel shuts his "book"; the time for thinking and writing is over. Today's revolutionary must act, must confront injustice with all the vigorous self-possession he can command. But where is the New Left leading us? Will history unleash future terrors? God only knows. Or, in Daniel's rattled, secular universe, where "everything is elusive" and questions are seldom answered, perhaps God doesn't know.

Patrick Parrinder (review date 4 April 1985)

SOURCE: "Cover Stories," in *London Review of Books,* Vol.7, No. 6, April 4, 1985, pp. 15-16.

[*In the following excerpt, Parrinder discusses Doctorow's narration in the tales that make up* Lives of the Poets.]

'Here's something out of the quaint past, a man reading a book,' remarks E. L. Doctorow's narrator as he rides the New York subway. The other passengers in the subway are not readers but listeners, hooked to their earphones and tape-players, 'listening their way back from literacy'. And before literacy? 'The world worked in a different system of perception, voices were disembodied, tales were told.' If tale-telling is the sign of a primitive culture, we—this would seem to imply—have the novel; and the more self-consciously civilised among novelists have sometimes been anxious to disclaim the form's own origins. As E. M. Forster wearily put it, 'Yes—oh dear yes—the novel tells a story.' But storytelling will outlive the novel, and it is also elemental to the novel. It is not coincidental that each of the books under review ends with the lure of a further, untold story: a story which might or might not turn out to be the one we have just read.

In the closing paragraphs of *Out of the Blue* a CIA agent tells his 'truly horrific story' of the novel's central charac-

ter—a story, however, that the reader is not allowed to hear. *The Pork Butcher* finishes in exactly the same way. ('The story had begun. William's notebook was on his knee. For a moment he wished he could understand the man's language, but did it matter? . . .') And E. L. Doctorow's collection terminates at the point where the author-narrator surrenders his typewriter keys to another person, an immigrant child who, like himself, may conceivably grow up to be the 'writer in the family'. Other examples of this convention would be easy to find. Where earlier centuries preferred the modes of tragic or comic finality—'Go, bid the soldiers shoot' or 'And they all lived happily ever after'—we prefer the note of recurrence and renewed narrative promise. What satisfies us most is to be assured, not of the characters' eternal happiness, but of their continuing novel-worthiness: 'And that is another story.'

Where E. M. Forster was right, however, was in implying that the ostensible story the novel tells need only be a cover story. There is always an analogy between reading and detective work, and this is particularly clear in a book like *Lives of the Poets,* a series of 'six stories and a novella' potentially unified by the suggestion (made only in the dustjacket blurb) that the narrator of the novella is also the imagined writer of the stories. Is this, or isn't it, a meaningful hypothesis? The reader of these terse, stylish and varied pieces has a certain amount of sleuthing to do.

For an initial clue, we could take a passing reference to one of the principal figures of Doctorow's 1975 best-seller, *Ragtime:* Harry Houdini, the escape artist. In a story called '**The Leather Man**' the narrator, a policeman, is reminded of Houdini as he watches a girl doing weird gyrations in the midst of the crowd at a rock festival. Studying the film of her movements that he has shot, he sees 'someone in a straitjacket', 'the classic terror . . . of someone straitjacketed and trying to break free'. '**Lives of the Poets**', the novella which takes up nearly half of Doctorow's new book, is full of tales of men trying to escape from the institution of marriage. (Every middle-aged man his own Houdini?) Jonathan, the narrator of '**Lives of the Poets**', has gone to earth in a pied-à-terre in Greenwich Village, leaving his wife stranded in upstate New York. Jonathan's solitude is supposedly for writing in, though what he does, most of the time, is to mooch over his own and his fellow writers' marriages. His own domestic battles, he tells us, have 'reached the stage where we send in other marriages to do the fighting'.

These other marriages are the substance of the 'lives of the poets', a title that has little to do with Grub Street or Samuel Johnson. The favoured means of escape for Jonathan's colleagues consists in finding an even more constricting straitjacket, a solitary cell that women cannot enter. We hear of a writer burying himself in a sub-basement padlocked from the inside, and of another who is becoming a Buddhist monk.

The masculine hermitic ideal that is indulged (before being finally disclaimed) in this book suggests nothing so much as a male backlash against the demand for feminine *Lebensraum* which energises contemporary women's fiction.

If fear of women unites Doctorow's men, their solitude, once achieved, is shadowed by the contrary fear of abandonment and dereliction.
—*Patrick Parrinder*

Women come off badly in most of Doctorow's new stories. In **'The Writer in the Family',** the boy Jonathan is forced to aid a family conspiracy to hush up the death of his father. In another boyhood story, a Central European landowner's son catches his mother in flagrante delicto with the family tutor. Both stories end with the protagonist crudely and cruelly destroying the web of female deceit in which he feels he has been caught. In other stories, a schoolmistress new to her job is shown disastrously mishandling small-town life, and a schoolgirl is blown to pieces in an embassy bombing. The scrupulous impartiality of Doctorow's style refuses to interpret these events. What his impeccably self-contained stories have in common are notions of territorial rights, of a cherishing of (male) rituals, and the ever-present threat of female trespass. Neither sex can take much comfort from these sharp and dispassionate sketches.

If fear of women unites Doctorow's men, their solitude, once achieved, is shadowed by the contrary fear of abandonment and dereliction. As Jonathan puts it, 'dereliction is the state of mind given to middle-aged men alone, not to women. Middle-aged women alone turn feisty and keep busy and become admirable characters and achieve things.' The escape artist is most likely a sad and deprived individual; this may be true of all artists; and 'between the artist and simple dereliction there is a very thin line.'

In the end Jonathan seems to abandon his writing, and with it the state of the solitary artist. A sudden impulse turns him, instead, into an 'admirable character' who uses his apartment to shelter illegal immigrants. Here as in *Ragtime* his sympathy for the newly-landed immigrant plays a notable part in Doctorow's work. In *Lives of the Poets,* however, the socially-conscientious gesture does little to redeem our overall impression of Jonathan as a garrulous and unlovable first-person narrator. While two or three of the stories in this volume are timeless creations, the novella is not much more than a gossipy, up to-the-minute chronicle of New York life. There are reports of dinner-party conversations (Jonathan's attempt to live like a hermit does not extend to dining at home), scenes in the subway, political meetings and, for good measure, much reading of the junk mail that comes through

Jonathan's door. The result is distinctly ephemeral and, at the end, it was with relief that I found that Jonathan, as narrator and imagined writer, had served his turn. Not only have immigrants moved into his apartment but alien fingers (male fingers, needless to say) are entering his writing space and fumbling for his typewriter keyboard. 'Little kid here wants to type . . . hey who's writing this? . . . come on, kid, you can do three more lousy lines.' The rest is silence, or rather, the rest should be another (and conceivably much more memorable) story.

Richard D. Beards (review date Summer 1985)

SOURCE: A review of *Lives of the Poets,* in *World Literature Today,* Vol. 59, No. 3, Summer, 1985, pp. 427-8.

[*In the following review, Beards provides a brief survey of the stories collected in* Lives of the Poets.]

Subtitled "A Novella and Six Stories," E. L. Doctorow's collection of short works *Lives of the Poets* challenges the reader to create a heuristic writer whose imagination contains this conglomeration of fictions. The stories employ a variety of narrative stances and voices: first person, omniscient; journalist, police reporter, social psychologist.

The first story, **"The Writer in the Family"** (the title can be read to underscore the specialness of the writer or to suggest, emphasizing the last three words, the weight of the family on the imaginative soul), is comic, pathetic, and intriguingly reflexive at once. The deceased father's dream of a sea life has been destroyed by a demanding family, his immigrant-generated stabs at upward mobility, and perhaps by his own lack of will and determination. His son, the young writer who tells the story, while less a sharer of the immigrant ideology, is clearly up against family responsibilities and expectations as he pieces together the meaning of his father's failed life.

The novella (**"Lives of the Poets"**) that ends the collection gives us the writer at midlife, suburban family abandoned for a tiny space in the city where he can write, think, and act out his needs unhampered. Something about his intensely solipsistic life echoes the dreary popular accounts of midlife crisis so that the novella, far from pulling together the shorter works which precede it, vitiates their impact.

In addition to the pieces described above, *Lives of the Poets* includes a Winesburgish story about a sensitive single woman teaching grade school in a factory town and a clever parody of a government human-services investigative team in which derelicts are sought to be typed and catalogued. Titled **"The Leather Man,"** the story presents a number of variations on the derelict, including contemporary street people, Woodstock festival participants, a man arrested for voyeurism at his own house with his own wife, a failed astronaut. All are presumably, in their eccentricity, isolation, and private vision, versions of the artist-poet.

Marvin J. LaHood (review date Winter 1987)

SOURCE: A review of *World's Fair,* in *World Literature Today,* Vol. 61, No. 1, Winter, 1987, p. 101.

[*The following review provides a brief report of the contents and concerns of* World's Fair.]

Novels that are truly evocative of childhood are rare. It takes a special kind of talent to remember what the world looks and feels like through the sensibilities of a child. When it is done well, the remembrance resonates through the reader's own being in a way that is both pleasant and painful. *World's Fair* is one of the finest novels of this kind published in recent memory. It is a nostalgic and beautifully modulated look at New York City in the thirties through the eyes of a boy growing up there. Centered in the Bronx, it tells with poignancy the story of a Jewish family of four and their extended family, which includes scores of interesting grandparents, aunts, uncles, and cousins. The world of this family is seen not only though the boy's eyes, but in several chapters through those of his mother and older brother. This multiple view gives the world described a special sense of layered depth and breadth.

> **E. L. Doctorow's achievement [in *World's Fair*] is in both the remembering and the telling. The myriad details of life in the thirties are so brilliantly articulated that the reader is placed and kept in that time and in that place.**
> **—*Marvin J. LaHood***

E. L. Doctorow's achievement is in both the remembering and the telling. The myriad details of life in the thirties are so brilliantly articulated that the reader is placed and kept in that time and in that place. The boy's fears and hopes, triumphs and disasters are so effectively described that they are felt as one's own. The emotions are so true that the boy's life seems fact rather than fiction. The total effect is exactly that. There is little sense in the novel of the traditional elements of fiction: plot, character development, crisis, denouement. It seems more documentary than drama. This might be seen as a failing, yet Doctorow's novel of reminiscence works so well that it must be judged on its own obvious merits.

The final forty pages of the book are a detailed and wonderfully realized description of the nine-year-old boy's experiences of the 1939 New York World's Fair. In two visits, his feelings about the fair become a metaphor for his feelings about life. It is at once both glorious and mundane, glamorous and tawdry, stimulating and enervating. More than anything else, however, it symbolizes the boy's and the author's sense of wonder and hope in the world that stretches out in such infinite variety before them.

Michelle M. Tokarczyk (essay date Fall 1987)

SOURCE: "From the Lion's Den: Survivors in E. L. Doctorow's *The Book of Daniel*," in *Critique,* Vol. 29, No. 1, Fall, 1987, pp. 3-15.

[*In the following essay, Tokarczyk offers a psychological analysis of the characters in* The Book of Daniel.]

Upon its publication, ***The Book of Daniel*** was praised by reviewers for its stylistic excellence and imaginative treatment of a daring theme. Although the novel has received relatively little critical attention in subsequent years, it continues to be regarded as outstanding and insightful. In her article on ***The Book of Daniel,*** Barbara Estrin rightfully states the book is ". . . a description of the hysteria of McCarthyism as it surfaced during the trials of Ethel and Julius Rosenberg. Moreover, it shows the devastating effect of the mentality of the period on subsequent decades." Critics have likewise noted that the novel cannot be facilely categorized as a fictionalization of the Rosenberg case. Paul Levine, for one, contends that ***The Book of Daniel*** is about Daniel's personal legacy as a surviving Isaacson. Any perceptive reader will notice that the novel depicts the Isaacson children as seriously scarred by their parents' arrest and execution. What is not immediately obvious is that the children—Daniel and Susan Isaacson-Lewin and Linda Mindish—of the defendants in the fictional atom spy trial have psychological traits of survivors.

Psychologists broadly define survivors as those who ". . . have come into contact with death in some psychic or bodily fashion . . . and have remained alive." This definition can thus apply to people who emerge from things as diverse as personal accidents and natural catastrophes. But some literature (that on concentration camp victims in particular) suggests that survivors of political persecution or atrocities have unique problems. They know they are part of a group that has been targeted for destruction, but they have managed to escape while they saw many others perish. Like the Biblical Daniel, they have escaped from the lions' den.

Doctorow's ***The Book of Daniel*** portrays the scars of political persecution on its indirect victims, the children of those sentenced in a controversial trial. By doing so, it underscores the novel's theme that the anti-Communist hysteria of the 1950s was not, as many Americans would like to believe, a brief aberration washed away by the political progressivism of the 1960s.

While *The Book of Daniel* is not, as Doctorow himself has emphasized, a fictional account of the Rosenberg case, the actual case is obviously important to the novel. The political climate, disturbing features of the trial, and, most important, the left's view that post-World War II America was veering toward fascism, provide a convincing context from which survivors can emerge. For these reasons, it is useful to review some facts of the actual case and their adaptation in *The Book of Daniel.*

Upon its publication, *The Book of Daniel* was praised by reviewers for its stylistic excellence and imaginative treatment of a daring theme. Although the novel has received relatively little critical attention in subsequent years, it continues to be regarded as outstanding and insightful.
—*Michelle M. Tokarczyk*

Throughout the novel, there are many illusions to the postwar hysteria America was actually going through in the early 1950s. In one of his analyses, Daniel notes that after a war has ended, people are often still unable to give up the heightened patriotism and distrust of outsiders necessary for waging war. After World War II, Americans remained concerned about loyalty and increasingly intolerant of nonconformity. In March of 1947, President Truman issued an executive order calling for federal employers to take loyalty oaths. The government tried to enforce loyalty, or what might more accurately be called political conformity, in a number of ways. An estimated ten million people whose political allegiances were suspect were asked questions ranging from "Do you belong to an organization that is affiliated with the Communist Party?" to "Do you read the *New York Times?*"

America's post-war hysteria might not have persisted into the 1950s if anti-Communist feeling had not been aggravated by two events: the Russian explosion of an atom bomb and the Korean war. The fictional Rochelle Isaacson fears that she and her husband will pay for every setback in Korea; when the actual Rosenbergs were tried, headlines of their trial were beside news of American defeats in Korea. Judge Kaufman, who presided over the Rosenberg trial, probably was not alone in his belief that the couple had caused the Korean War.

Being Communists made the Rosenbergs targets of prejudice. So did being Jews. Many Americans harbored anti-Semitic feelings. In particular, there was a stereotype of Jews as Reds. The loyalties of Eastern European Jews with radical political ideologies were often questioned. An awareness of growing anti-Semitism possibly biased Judge Kaufman against the defendants. The issue of Jewishness was likely to rankle him. Like Doctorow's fictional Judge Hirsch, he could be described as an "assimilationist". His record was one of successful integration—at forty, he was the youngest judge. He had attended Fordham Law School and earned top grades in religion, thus gaining the nickname "Pope Kaufman." Distancing himself from his Jewish identity had helped his career. So he might have resented the unfavorable attention the Rosenbergs were drawing to Jews and been lax in protecting their rights.

Throughout the trial, the prosecution got away with many questionable tactics. Patriotism, not espionage, became the issue. In his opening remarks, the prosecution suggested Communists were likely traitors. The Rosenbergs, like the fictional Isaacsons, were cast as enemies of the American flag.

Such insinuations probably had a negative impact upon an already loaded jury. "Loaded" does not imply the jury was fixed to find the Rosenbergs guilty, but that it was not composed of peers who might be objective about the defendants. Rather, like the fictional Isaacson jury, it was devoid of Jews and political progressives. It consisted of a group of homogeneous, conventional Americans, including an examiner, an auditor, two bookkeepers, an accountant, and an estimator. Often those who choose such professions have authoritarian personalities, which are characterized by great respect for authority, little tolerance for nonconformity, and distrust of outsiders. A jury composed of people with such traits would be inclined to distrust the defendants and be uncritical of the government that represented the prosecution.

While many Americans did not recognize the injustices in the trial until years later, there were some substantial protests at the time. Distinguished scientists Albert Einstein and Harold Urey wrote to President Eisenhower, raising doubts about the validity of the prosecution's charges and asking the president to grant the Rosenbergs clemency.

This request was not granted. After numerous appeals failed and a stay of execution imposed by Justice Douglass was hastily removed, the Rosenbergs were executed. Throughout the world, many people were shocked. On the American Left, many feared this execution was only the beginning. They felt as Ethel Rosenberg had about herself and her husband: the couple were the first victims of American fascism.

In *We Are Your Sons,* the Rosenberg sons describe their anguish over their parents' arrest and execution. But the trauma did not make either of the boys anti-social or mentally unstable; both appear to be well adjusted. In a fictional work, portraying the offspring of political victims as well-adjusted people would suggest that the effects of the McCarthy Era outrages would be undone over time. By depicting the spy trial's children as people suffering from survivor syndromes, Doctorow suggests that injustice has lasting effects.

This theme is established early in the novel through the figure of the dead grandmother. As her "Bintel Brief" indicates, she has endured poverty, persecution, and the early death of loved ones: this is her legacy. That Daniel fantasizes she speaks to him, even smells her, indicates her suffering will have an enduring influence on him.

Daniel's parents' ordeal leaves a much stronger imprint. Even a quick analysis shows that the mature Daniel is not a normal, all-American man, even given the perspective of 1967, when it was trendy for students to act eccentrically against accepted values. He is intensely preoccupied with his parents' arrest, trial, and death; his relationship with his wife and child is often sadomasochistic; he is unable to commit himself professionally or politically. In essence, Daniel cannot recover from the trauma that took his parents from him and redefined his own identity. He is a survivor struggling to find his place in the society that killed his parents.

Daniel's problem of deciding how much of his survivor identity to maintain is complicated by the government's action to undermine his identity. Often oppressive governments eradicate opposition by killing subversives or, more subtly, by making them invisible. In *The Origins of Totalitarianism,* Hannah Arendt states that the ultimate deprivation of human rights occurs when one's voice becomes irrelevant because it is explained away as the result of something in one's background. Daniel's family background defines his political stance for the government. Despite his apolitical nature, the FBI routinely investigates him because he is an Isaacson. This identity in itself limits the political statements he can make: Burning his draft card is meaningless because the government would never draft such a potential subversive.

But the treatment he receives from his government is not nearly so difficult for Daniel as his own deeply rooted guilt. In his essay "Trauma and Regeneration," Bettleheim describes [in *Surviving and Other Essays* (1972)] the feelings of undeserved fortune among concentration camp survivors:

> Having to live for years under the immediate and continuous threat of being killed for no other reason than that one is a member of a group that is destined to be exterminated and knowing that one's close friends and relatives are indeed being killed—

this is sufficient to leave one for the rest of one's life struggling with the unsolvable riddle of "Why am I spared?" and also with completely irrational guilt about being spared.

As a child seeing his parents killed, Daniel undoubtedly felt that he too was in danger, and thus he has a survivor's feelings of having fortuitously escaped. Such feelings are hinted at in *The Book of Daniel* in Daniel's reference to the Negro spiritual which Robeson sang, "Didn't my Lord deliver Daniel . . . then why not every man?" What, Daniel, (as both child and adult) asks, makes him worthy of rescue, the chance to build a new life, when his family has suffered so. He can isolate nothing.

Feeling unworthy of rescue, Daniel is full of guilt that manifests itself in his negative self-image. Repeatedly he describes himself as a "criminal of perception" and "betrayer". Daniel does have horrible streaks of cruelty that are revealed when he burns his wife with a cigarette lighter and tosses his baby higher and higher, catching him lower and lower. However, Daniel thinks of himself as a bad person. His sadistic acts are consistent with his poor self-image.

Part of what contributes to this poor image is Daniel's experience of helplessly standing by while his parents were arrested and executed. In a novel that deals with power, it is significant that children are the most powerless, most vulnerable group, unable to act on behalf of themselves or their loved ones. Daniel's intense desire to aid his parents is first revealed in his attack on and death threats to the FBI men who arrest his father. During his first visit to the Death House, Daniel emphatically reiterates this desire: "I won't let them kill you . . . I'll kill them first." After leaving the prison, Daniel is haunted by his father's voice and the humiliation of having to leave his parents incarcerated.

A similar kind of guilt and failed sense of responsibility has been observed in Hiroshima survivors who have lost loved ones, particularly if the loved ones had helped to save the survivor's life (as Paul saved Daniel's life when a bus of radicals was attacked after a concert at Peekskill). Perhaps the greatest cause of guilt is the feeling that some unconsidered action might have saved lives. People cannot reasonably expect that they will think of all solutions, but emerging from a life-threatening situation is so extraordinary that it makes survivors have unreasonable expectations of themselves.

One of the most demanding burdens survival places upon a person is the sense of a survivor mission—the imperative to reveal what one has endured so others learn a crucial lesson. Susan feels compelled to get involved in radical politics, because she believes she has unique personal knowledge of government abuses. Her fury and hurt over Daniel's apparent rejection of his Isaacson mission are so great that she disowns him.

Although Daniel is not involved in radical politics, his fantasy of his dead grandmother's words to him shows that he also believes that he has a special duty: "I have recognized in you the strength and innocence that will reclaim us all from defeat. That will exonerate our having lived and justify our suffering". Along with his feeling that this burden is too great to bear must be one that the dead woman is wrong in her perceptions: the surviving Daniel is really a weak, evil person, unworthy of a special mission.

This sense of inadequacy is reinforced by others. Not realizing what a burden he places on his young son, Paul asks Daniel to help him with the defense. After Paul's arrest, Rochelle tells Daniel why his father was incarcerated, stopping herself only when the boy begins to cry. Even the pain of losing his parents might have been more bearable if it were not mixed with a relief that someone else died rather than himself. For many survivors, as for Daniel, this relief is a particularly painful component of survivor guilt. When Susan is hospitalized, Daniel at first feels he cannot go on without her, but then concludes: "I can live with anyone's death but my own". Daniel's survival is full of such discoveries about himself: that he is cunning, resilient, cruel. Although the knowledge of these traits makes him feel unworthy to carry on the family mission, it does not free him from his perceived bond to the Isaacsons.

The memory of their parents structures Daniel's and Susan's lives. Childhood days at the Lewins' are full of "ghosts" that manifest themselves in casual conversation, household rituals and, most important, in the parent-child relationship, all of which evoke painful recollections. The most powerful evidence of the pervasiveness of these memories is the structure of Daniel's account. Historical events, contemporary occurrences, and political theories are all juxtaposed with the narration of the Isaacson's arrests, trial, and death. Like a narrator in Eliot's *Waste Land,* Daniel has shored the fragments of his childhood memories and acquired knowledge against the ruin of his life. But the need to impose order by writing an account in itself suggests how obsessive Daniel's memories of his original parents are.

Clearly, Daniel feels a strong problematic pull to the deceased Isaacsons. Studies have shown that persistent identification with the dead is self-destructive for survivors; the living need to separate themselves from the dead (Lifton [*Death in Life: Survivors of Hiroshima* (1967)] p. 203). Daniel's need to do so is suggested in his account of his Death House conversation with his father: "'You're getting to look a lot like me,' he (Paul) said to his son". By referring to himself as "his son" rather than "me," Daniel attempts to distance himself from his father. As an adult, Daniel similarly questions the necessity of living in memorial to one's ancestors. Perhaps his desire to separate from his original family is best seen in his becoming a Lewin. This new identity enables him to live without people's constant suspicion and with the benefits of affluence. But in spite of the comforts his new life offers Daniel, he is not at ease with it. His discomfort is characteristic of survivor guilt defined by Lifton as "anger turned inward because the survivor cannot help but internalize the world in which he has been victimized". Such anger is apparent in Daniel's statement that his relationship to the society that killed his parents is constant and degrading. In an attempt to protest against this society and thus re-establish his Isaacson identity, Daniel participates in the "March on the Pentagon." After his beating and arrest, he sadly realizes, "It's a lot easier to be a revolutionary nowadays than it used to be". Nothing short of death can equal his parents' experience.

Susan's fate further attests to the impossibility of living as an Isaacson. Unable to aid revolutionary groups, she slashes her wrists rather than jeopardize her status as a progressive Isaacson. In part, her eventual death is the result of her refusal to compromise her radical beliefs.

Daniel's difficulty in choosing a middle ground between the Mindishes' total renunciation of their survivor identities and Susan's total embracing of hers is a typical survivor's dilemma.
—*Michelle M. Tokarczyk*

Complete rejection of one's past identity, however, is also dangerous. In blunting her memories, Linda Mindish blunts all her perceptions; thus, she does not immediately see Daniel as dangerous, but rather as pathetic. Shrewdly, Daniel observes: ". . . all she has accomplished is to fortify her fear. One sharp poke of the finger and the fortifications totter". Her father, Selig Mindish, is destroyed by his attempt to bury the past. Although his body survives in California affluence, his mind deteriorates into premature senility. His condition vividly illustrates that a survivor identity cannot be totally relinquished if one is to prevail mentally and emotionally.

Daniel's difficulty in choosing a middle ground between the Mindishes' total renunciation of their survivor identities and Susan's total embracing of hers is a typical survivor's dilemma. The healthiest alternative is what Bettleheim calls reintegration, which involves trying to pull something positive from a traumatic experience while at the same time accepting the extent of the traumatization. The process is complicated, however, for in order to derive something positive from a traumatic experience, the experience must be relived in one's mind. Memory is often not reliable in recalling emotionally charged events, and people are often reluctant to relate their traumas if they cannot recall them clearly. Hiroshima survivors, for example, often expressed hesitancy to relate their experiences because they were uncertain they could give authentic renderings.

Daniel likewise has special problems conveying the meaning of his parents' experience because he cannot verify their guilt or innocence. Since the truth is "irretrievable," he cannot know when he is lying, and often suspects that he is either doing so or exploiting his past. Linda Mindish and he, he believes, are "flawless, forged criminals of perception" who would use their sad lives to any end.

In a novel in which images of fire are so extensive, "forged" suggests one who has come through the flames and has not been destroyed but radically changed. The word also connotes a "forged" or false victim. In this sense, it suggests Daniel's pain cannot be trusted because he is so prone to fabrication. Going through the fire made Daniel a "criminal of perception." As Barbara Estrin explains in her essay: "Daniel and Linda understand the nature of the fires that burned them and their knowledge in turn renders them deadly. They become the objects of their perception, reciprocating the burden of evil without changing it. . . ." Essentially, Daniel and Linda Mindish are contaminated by their contact with evil. Daniel becomes a cruel child who spies on his aunt in the bathroom and a sadistic adult who torments his wife and child. Linda Mindish becomes a calculating person who goes to all lengths to divorce herself from her past, even if doing so is obviously detrimental to her father. Yet, if one does not understand the nature of evil, as Susan does not, one runs the risk of not developing the cunning necessary for survival.

Daniel bitterly recognizes that he had to become shrewd to continue to live in the society he views with contempt. His distrust of many social values is suggested in his pseudo-hippiedom, his failure to work on his dissertation, and his poor performance as a husband and father. He has become embittered, as is common for survivors (Lifton 256): Daniel is cynical about all ideologies and wary of the people who embrace them. Susan, in contrast, suffers because she blindly accepts the New Left's ideology. Her breakdown is partially triggered by the realization that young radicals view her parents with contempt and she is politically isolated.

The difficulty she and Daniel face in finding and maintaining ties is characteristic of survivors. Studies of Hiroshima survivors have found that the extensive physical and psychic damage of the bomb limited the possibility of cooperation among victims (Lifton 47). Bettleheim has pointed out that some of the concentration camp atrocities, such as leaving prisoners outside in freezing weather for long periods of time, gave many survivors increased confidence in their resilience as individuals, but destroyed any sense of group safety ("Individual," 66). The entire concentration camp experience undermined belief in group solidarity and safety through unity: People were not able to unite and resist.

The United States government was likewise successful in destroying the Left's sense of group safety. Numerous people were blacklisted or arrested, but there did not seem to be any cohesive resistance. Worse, the government persuaded many Communists to inform on and testify against fellow Party members.

In *The Book of Daniel,* Selig Mindish, although a government informer, is also arrested and imprisoned for atomic espionage. In a sense, the Mindishes and Isaacsons are co-victims. Upon meeting Linda, Daniel immediately feels a bond: "I recognize in you the same look I see in the mirror. It's like a community". Linda, in stating that she and Daniel had borne the brunt of the Isaacson trial, suggests that she feels a closeness to him. However, nothing can diminish the damning nature of Mindish's testimony in Daniel's mind. Linda, in turn, believes the Isaacsons were guilty and furthermore were contemptible people who exploited her father on many occasions. The thread of communion between Linda and Daniel cannot overcome familial hatred.

The resultant sense of isolation is particularly difficult for Daniel because, as someone who was tragically orphaned, he needs special caring. Yet often when Daniel does receive affection, he suspects that it is "counterfeit nurturance"—nurturance given out of guilt or obligation rather than genuine love (Lifton 193). Daniel is suspicious of the Lewins' motives for adopting him and contemptuous of their optimistic belief that they and the Isaacson children can be a normal family. Similarly, he suspects his wife Phyllis does many things (smokes marijuana, goes to bed on the first date) on principle. Thus he assumes she married him because he is from a notorious family. He is unable to accept her efforts to support him, as she tries to do when she offers to let Susan live with them and recuperate.

> **To a great extent, Daniel's inability to express emotion is caused by a survivor's characteristic fear of deep pain.**
> —*Michelle M. Tokarczyk*

Daniel is alienated from his wife by his belief that no one but Susan and, in a somewhat different way, the Mindishes have suffered as he. So Daniel feels survivor exclusiveness, a belief that "those who have survived, been through the experience, are radically different from those who have not" (Lifton 524). This sense perhaps discourages him from wanting to form relationships, for the gap between himself and others seems too great.

It is particularly difficult for outsiders to empathize with the survivor's plight if the survivor himself is emotionally deadened like Daniel. Often Daniel intellectualizes, offering theories about the causes of his parents' execution rather than agonizing over their deaths. He himself must constantly struggle to comprehend their pain, as he does when he stands in the men's room trying to imagine Susan slashing her wrists. His emotions, not imagination, fail; he cannot allow himself to experience Susan's pain. Likewise, he describes his parents' execution in great detail, but in an objective, unemotional account. The first sentence of this episode is: "First they led in my father"; the last is: "Later he (the executioner) said the first dose had not been enough to kill my mother Rochelle Isaacson".

To a great extent, Daniel's inability to express emotion is caused by a survivor's characteristic fear of deep pain. For example, many concentration camp survivors experienced what is termed psychic closing off. This emotional shutdown enabled them to get through their experiences: Most people could not feel the impact of mass executions or torture without breaking down. However, it was not easy for these survivors to re-activate their emotions. In particular, it was difficult for many to show affection, for they were deeply afraid of loving someone after having seen so many loved ones killed. Daniel has similar fears.

Sometimes his fear makes his behavior bizarre. On what had seemed to be a pleasant family outing, Daniel suddenly tosses his baby into the air, and catches him precariously close to the ground, while looking at the terrified "Isaacson face," which he cannot bear the thought of having to protect. As he is quick to abuse his child, he is quick to beat his wife or threaten Dr. Duberstein when the doctor proposes shock therapy for Susan (although Daniel's reaction is more understandable in the last case). His behavior in the car after visiting Susan is indicative of his propensity to rage when a simple whim is denied: He first terrifies, then tortures, the young wife who refuses to take off her pants at his request.

When Daniel is not actively enraged, he is brooding over memories. Part of his preoccupation is a repressed mourning that many Hiroshima and concentration camp victims also experienced. Under extreme conditions, many loved ones were lost, and there was not the time nor the proper circumstances for mourning. The Isaacson children too have scant opportunities for mourning. During the Death House visits, they feel obligated to relate stories of how well they are doing. When the execution day arrives, Daniel and Susan are not permitted at their parents' sides to say good-bye. These children could not vent their feelings through a nor-

mal mourning process, so they spend their lives trying to resolve repressed emotions.

Even though losing his parents was devastating, Daniel might have had a better foundation for rebuilding had he not also lost belief in the ideals that served as touchstones for his parents. His plight is similar to that of many concentration camp survivors:

> We see a picture characterized by the destruction of his (the concentration camp survivor's) world, the destruction of the basic landmarks in which the world of human beings in our civilization is based, i.e., basic trust in human worth, basic confidence, basic hope. Here, there is no trust, there is no confidence; everything has been shattered to pieces. (Epstein [*Children of the Holocaust* (1980)] 92)

As a young child, Daniel believed the Communist Party was the people's party, and when the government's oppression became clear, the people would rally behind the Party. With his parents' arrest, he learned that the Party acts in its own self-interest; his parents' names were quickly erased from the membership rolls.

Daniel copes with his resultant disillusionment by adopting a bitter, angry stance. For his sister Susan, however, such detachment is not possible; she needs to immerse herself in radical politics. Working for revolution is, for her, an attempt to reaffirm moral principles. A desire to re-establish moral principles is at the heart of many attempts at justice, such as the Nuremberg Trials, which did much more than sentence the guilty. They demonstrated something that is extremely important when society has been distorted by great violations of cherished values: Certain crimes cannot and will not be tolerated.

Susan wants to make a similar statement. Since it is impossible to retrieve her parents' lives, she tries to retrieve the ideals for which they stood and to testify that people will not again endure government oppression. Thus, she wants to establish the Isaacson Foundation for Revolution and to affiliate Daniel with this institution, thus indicating ". . . unanimity of family feeling, a proper assumption of their legacy by the Isaacson children". She is unsuccessful in her attempts to work with the New Left and can find no way to rectify the injustice that was done.

The Isaacson children's quest for justice is complicated by the absence of obvious heroes and villains in their parents' trial. Selig Mindish apparently did not lie on the witness stand; he is not a turncoat. If the Isaacsons were betrayed, they were betrayed by political progressives as well as the United States government. And the betrayal continues. When Susan says "They're still fucking us," she recognizes the

New Left is ready to exploit her just as the Old Left exploited the Isaacsons.

The New Left's scorn for her parents triggers Susan's breakdown—complete physical and psychic closing off in which she assumes the starfish position. Since the starfish retains one posture and shows no activity or emotion, Daniel correctly assumes there are not many forms of life below it. Susan in this state is similar to the "Musselmanner" in the concentration camps—those described as "walking corpses," seemingly unable to feel or act (Lifton 502). Like these victims, Susan senses her entire environment working against her. In a desperate attempt to protect herself, she eradicates her consciousness, stripping herself of all but the vital signs, and finally of these too.

Daniel does not withdraw psychotically or attempt to end his life, but he does discard many feelings (love, commitment to work) associated with a full life. As a survivor, Daniel feels he must minimize his life. His relatively easy adjustment to the affluence of the Lewin home makes him uncomfortable. Understandably, he is attracted to the deliberate poverty of Sternlicht's life, and perhaps for this reason lets Sternlicht insult him. At the anti-war rally, he seems to feel obligated to endure physical injury and incarceration. Although Daniel is not a true radical or a hippie, he cannot allow himself to enter the middle class. He owes a debt of suffering.

Neither can Daniel allow himself to fall into middle-class complacency. Being a survivor involves living with the knowledge that one has escaped death and may not again be so lucky (Lifton 481). It is necessary to live in preparation for renewed assault. The Isaacsons conveyed such wariness to their children even before their arrests: Repeatedly, Paul and Rochelle warned that the persecution of the working classes was "still going on." Years after his parents' death, Daniel is still not free to enjoy the relatively carefree life of the average citizen. His safety has been threatened, and he probably fears it will be threatened again.

As my numerous examples have shown, *The Book of Daniel* explores, with a psychological verisimilitude surpassing that in most other novels, the persistent conflicts of survivors. The especially acute characterization of Daniel as one with a survivor syndrome is an answer to the biblical depiction of the prophet Daniel who emerged unscathed from the lions' den. More important, it is a rebuttal to American optimism about the fleeting nature of political oppression in this country. According to *The Book of Daniel,* the McCarthy Era not only destroyed innocent people, but also left the victims' children with permanent psychological scars.

Two of the three children of the Isaacson Trial are unable to resolve their conflicts: Susan dies; Linda Mindish remains insulated from her past; and Daniel, through his investigation of his parents' case, is able to achieve reintegration and thus work through some personal problems. By the end of the novel, he has stopped abusing his wife and child and is even able to cry at his sister's funeral.

While minimal personal resolution might be possible, political resolution appears not to be. There seems to be no way for the American populace to learn the lessons of history. As *The Book of Daniel* ends, the students at Columbia are rebelling, intent on reforming American society. Yet without the voices of those who understand the nature of American oppression, revolutionary movements are likely to be ineffectual. And the last words of the novel tell us Daniel's survivor mission will go unfulfilled: ". . . Go thy way Daniel: for the words are closed up and sealed till the end of time".

John G. Parks (essay date Winter 1991)

SOURCE: "The Politics of Polyphony: The Fiction of E. L. Doctorow," in *Twentieth Century Literature,* Vol. 37, No. 4, Winter, 1991, pp. 454-63.

[*In the following essay, Parks applies recent critical theory to a study of the political and historical elements of Doctorow's fiction.*]

"The chief business of twentieth-century philosophy," R. G. Collingwood remarks in his *Autobiography,* "is to reckon with twentieth-century history." In the fifty years since Collingwood wrote those words that "reckoning" with history has become increasingly problematic, especially when considering the situation of the contemporary writer. Describing the writer's alienation from history in the modern period, as well as his loss of faith in the direction of history, Georg Lukàcs, in his work *The Historical Novel,* observes that history for the writer becomes either "a collection and reproduction of interesting facts about the past" or "a chaos to be ordered as one likes" (176,181). More recently, Philip Roth and David Lodge describe a similar division among recent writers, who have largely abandoned the social and political realm for the exploration of the self. As Lodge puts it: "Art can no longer compete with life on equal terms, showing the universal in the particular. The alternatives are either to cleave to the particular . . . or to abandon history altogether and construct pure fictions which reflect in an emotional or metaphysical way the discords of contemporary experience" (33). As Tony Tanner puts it, this "means that novelists have lost faith in the idea that the individual can ever realize himself in contemporary social territories" (297).

> **Doctorow sees himself as a novelist first and foremost, and rejects being labeled a "political novelist."**
> —*John G. Parks*

E. L. Doctorow is critical of the fiction of the private life, a fiction which abandons or neglects the social and political dimensions to feature, instead, what Doctorow calls the "entrepreneurial self." In developing his own poetics of engagement, Doctorow seeks a fiction that is both politically relevant and aesthetically complex and interesting. By blurring the distinctions between fact and fiction, Doctorow's fiction seeks to disclose and to challenge the hegemony of enshrined or institutionalized discursive practices. The narrative of fiction is thus the locus of battle, as it were, for freedom. It is the place, or rather, the process or event where the "regimes of power," as Michael Foucault says, may be challenged. The task of narrative is to disrupt or dismantle the prevailing "regimes of truth," including their repressive effects. Doctorow's ultimate political enterprise is to prevent the power of the regime from monopolizing the compositions of truth, from establishing a monological control over culture. A monologic culture is authoritarian and absolutistic and denies the existence and validity of the "other," of "difference." Culture is best seen as polyphonic, as a heteroglossic dialogue or conversation, to use terms from Mikhail Bakhtin and Kenneth Burke, which allows for the speaking and hearing of the many voices which constitute it. This, according to Bakhtin, is what prose can do best in an age of competing languages. In Doctorow, dialogue or polyphonic fiction is both disruptive or even subversive of regimes of power, and restorative of neglected or forgotten or unheard voices in the culture. It is this twin aim of disruption and restoration that characterizes Doctorow's own polyphonic fiction as it seeks to engage what he calls the "progression of metaphors" (Trenner, [Richard, ed. *Doctorow: Essays and Conversations* (1983)] 26) that constitute our civilization.

It is perhaps inevitable that a writer whose fiction is engaged in imaginative historical revisioning would be criticized for being a "political novelist," especially by those whose politics differ from Doctorow's. Carol Iannone, for example, writing in *Commentary,* criticizes Doctorow's fiction for having "the ideological attitudes of the Left, attitudes that pervade and, finally, compromise everything he has written" (53). Similarly, Joseph Epstein puts Doctorow's fiction in with writers he labels as "adversarial" and virtually anti-American. To Epstein, Doctorow's novel *The Book of Daniel* is rigged for political purposes. Agreeing with Epstein, Robert Alter, in an essay on "the American Political Novel" in the *New York Times Book Review,* argues that recent American political fiction falls into two categories—serious novels which see politics as farcical and which reflect the author's rage, and commercial novels which are basically conventional fictional documentaries, such as novels by Allen Drury. To Alter, *The Book of Daniel* fails to make "nice discriminations and complex judgments" because of its pervasive sense of oppression. But such facile criticism, as Susan Lorsch, among others, argues, misconstrues the central issues and strategies of a novel like *The Book of Daniel.*

Doctorow sees himself as a novelist first and foremost, and rejects being labeled a "political novelist." While his fiction shows his passion for justice, his passion is quite unprogrammatic. Indeed, he is suspicious of grand political schemes and knows that "no system, whether it's religious or anti-religious or economic or nationalistic, seems invulnerable to human venery and greed and insanity" (Trenner, 65). It is more useful to see Doctorow's fiction as illustrating what Foucault describes as a "battle among discourses through discourses" and of what Bakhtin calls "heteroglossia." As Geoffrey Harpham argues [in "E. L. Doctorow and the Technology of Narrative"(PMLA, 100 January 1985)] it is best to see Doctorow's fiction as developing "from a critique of the coercive power of the textual and ideological regime to a celebration of the powers of imaginative freedom"(82). While all of Doctorow's novels, in varying degrees, engage in the demythologizing of American history, the novels *The Book of Daniel, Ragtime,* and *Loon Lake* are arguably his most "political" books and thus clearly reveal his fictional project of disruption and restoration.

The Book of Daniel (1971) is many stories in one. It is a *Bildungsroman*—the story of Daniel Isaacson's struggle for manhood. It is a *Künstlerroman*—the story of a writer discovering his identity and his fundamental conflict with his society. It is the story of and by a survivor—a boy whose parents were executed for treason struggles for a narrative that will reconnect him to history. It is a revenge story—a son's obligation somehow to redeem his father's and mother's murder. And it is a story of a history graduate student searching for a topic for his dissertation. Daniel would avoid real history by writing it. But the radicalism of the late 1960s propels Daniel out of the stacks and into the streets, where Daniel must compose a book which avoids conceiving history as a series of repetitions and duplications or as an endless sequence of events. Because he inherits not a legacy of power but of powerlessness, Daniel, in responding to the historical summons of his time, must seize control of the narrative, and his resultant book is both a self-composition and an act of cultural hermeneutics. Daniel's narrative, his composition, as Harpham suggests, is an epistemology; it is how we know (85-86). For Daniel, telling leads to knowing. But knowing what? That reality is a function of power and the institutionalized discourses which constitute it. And that power must be challenged by a narrative which combines analysis and the ability to make truthful connections. Hence, Daniel's rather dissynchronous procedure—a calculated use of discontinuity. Like Hemingway's Jacob Barnes, Doctorow's Daniel must find a way to recompose history after a great wounding.

As Doctorow has said, his novel is not about the Rosenbergs but rather about the *idea* of the Rosenbergs. The novel is not a fictionalized attempt to prove the innocence of convicted conspirators—as Epstein would have it—but a polyphonic reopening of the case—a "re-hearing," or perhaps better, a "re-speaking," in the context of the New Left of the late 1960s, of the crucial issues connected with the trial of the Rosenbergs in the early 1950s. The ordeal that Daniel undergoes as a native son is America's as well, for the fate of both is interconnected. The genius of the narrative strategy is that it enables Doctorow to explore his themes in multiple contexts—the contexts of the New Left radicalism of the late 1960s, the Old Left radicalism of the 1930s, which faced attack during the virulent anti-communist hysteria of the Cold War of the 1950s, and the even larger context of biblical prophecy in the novel's allusion to the prophet Daniel and his struggle with exile and persecution. Thus, as children of executed parents, Daniel and his younger sister, Susan, must contend with a legacy of loss, of failure, of rejection. They must find some way of connecting the so-called "generation gap" between the two radicalisms, of ending their own exiles, and of rejoining American history.

Daniel sees that the story cannot be told in a straightforward, linear, chronological manner. Only a deconstructed narrative can destabilize the hegemony of official history enough to open up new possibilities for interpretation. Thus, Daniel's "book" is a virtual pastiche of genres—family stories, autobiography, essays, excerpts from newspapers and trial transcripts, letters, conflicting historical analysis, dissertation, biblical quotations—and abrupt shifts from first-to third-person points of view. The actual time of the novel covers less than a year, from Memorial Day in 1967 to the spring of 1968, when Columbia University is closed down by radical demonstrators and Daniel is forced to leave the library. Spatially, the novel moves from Massachusetts to New York to Washington D.C. to Disneyland on the west coast and back to New York.

Daniel's journey takes him from Susan's hospital room, after her attempted suicide in a Howard Johnson's toilet, to a confrontation with Artie Sternlicht, the New Left radical who wants to overthrow the country with images, and whose rejection of Susan's plan to memorialize her parents leads to her death (from a "failure of analysis"). It is significant, and not a little ironic, that Daniel's final interrogation occurs at Disneyland, which William Irwin Thompson calls "the edge of history," where history is essentially false and commodified. It is in Tomorrowland that Daniel at last confronts his

parents' betrayer. But Mindish's advanced senility prevents Daniel from hearing the truth about his parents. Daniel's quest ends in ambiguity and uncertainty, but not in futility, for the electric energy of his narrative has "resisted"—an electrical and political term—closing the circuit which leads to death. Avoiding the traps of deadly repetition and of meaningless sequence, Daniel composes a book implicating the reader in acts of participation and witness.

If *The Book of Daniel* is a tragedy of history, *Ragtime* (1975) is a comedy of history. While many people die in the book, it ends nevertheless in a marriage symbolizing some new and rich possibilities for America's future, after its innocence is lost. If the narrative of *The Book of Daniel* challenges the monologic power of the regime with its polyphonic quality, the narrative of *Ragtime* is a virtual carnival, an occasion for the reigning of the "jolly relativity" of all things. *Ragtime* is a text which resists organicism through the interplay of multiple voices, historical and fictive. The novel approaches what Roland Barthes calls a "plural text," a text that calls the reader not merely to consume the meaning but rather to produce it.

Like *The Book of Daniel, Ragtime* continues Doctorow's engagement with the problems of historical repetition and endless sequence, but this time during the first two decades of the twentieth century, the Progressive Era. As the little boy of the WASP family says: "It was evident to him that the world composed and recomposed itself constantly in an endless process of dissatisfaction" (135). The novel explores the changing compositions of history—replications and changes—and the possibilities of moral growth in history. One of the historical personages in the book, Henry Ford, who made history with his assembly-line techniques ("He had caused a machine to replicate itself endlessly," 155), is reputed to have declared that "history is more or less bunk," a view Doctorow's novel seeks to challenge with a prophetic vision of social justice.

In contrast to the intensity of the narrative of *The Book of Daniel,* the narrative of *Ragtime* is energetic, sprightly, and easy to read, giving rise to criticisms of the novel as shallow and superficial. But the book does not intend to be a dense study of character. Its pastiche quality intends to challenge conventional notions of plot. Its idiosyncratic blending of fact and fiction intends to challenge the privileged status of historical discourse. It is a text that illustrates Doctorow's ideas of history as spelled out in the *"False Documents"* essay: "There is no history except as it is composed. . . . That is why history has to be written and rewritten from one generation to another. The art of composition can never end" (Trenner, 24). The novel is not so much about the ragtime era as about how we view that era, and how we might compose and recompose it. For Fredric Jameson this narrative pastiche is evidence of the postmodern loss of the historical referent—a loss of connection between the writer's and reader's now and the past, and hence, a "crisis in historicity." The historical subject remains out of reach to us, problematizing interpretation. For this reason, Jameson [in "Postmodernism, Or the Cultural Logic of Late Capitalism." *New Left Review,* 146(July-August,1984)] sees Doctorow as "the epic poet of the disappearance of the American radical tradition"(68-71).

In any event, the ever-changing narrative surface of *Ragtime* is part of the "meaning" of a book concerned with changes. As the little boy learns from Grandfather's stories from Ovid: "the forms of life were volatile and . . . everything in the world could as easily be something else" (132-33). The book, we learn in the last pages of the novel, is the tale of the little boy grown up; it is his composition. In a real sense, moreover, the novel is a product of a warning read back into history after a terrible catastrophe—in this case World War I, the ending of American innocence and the real entry of America into the twentieth century. The little boy tells Houdini to "Warn the Duke" at the end of Chapter I, a warning which, of course, cannot be given and, hence, cannot be heeded. But as a composing artist, it is a gesture of freedom and historical consciousness that needs to be made. The boy's composition is a challenge to a view of history that forecloses the imagination and moral freedom.

> **What is at stake in [*Ragtime*] is a view of history that resists the temptations of myth, a view that accepts moral responsibility.**
> —*John G. Parks*

As a contemporary historical romance, the novel is a syncopation of a number of oppositions and tensions: degeneration and regeneration, static forms and volatile images, repetition and change, history and fantasy, self and other, rich and poor, white and black, WASP and immigrant, narcissism and self-divestment, journeys outward and journeys inward, departures and arrivals. These tensions are exhibited in the chance intermingling of three fictive families and various historical personages. As a result of their failed quests— Father's quest for new explorations, Coalhouse Walker's quest for racial justice, Tateh's quest for economic justice— only one of the fathers and one of the mothers survive the tumult of the era, and manage to direct their lives along the currents of American energy and generate a new history.

What is at stake in the novel is a view of history that resists the temptations of myth, a view that accepts moral responsibility. Most of the characters of the book are engaged in various forms of escape, like Houdini's relentless pursuit of the ultimate escape. J. P. Morgan and Henry Ford deny his-

torical responsibility through their belief in reincarnation. But such historical narcissism is doomed to failure. Obsessed with rebirth, Morgan, Ford, and Houdini see history almost wholly in terms of the self, an immature and infantile philosophy of history, one that is static and degenerate. But the Morgan-Ford-Houdini philosophy of escape endures, as the narrator says: "Today, nearly fifty years since his death, the audience for escapes is even larger"(8).

Reality, history, will not be pinned down. History refuses to succumb to the impositions of the human ego. Dreiser turns his chair all night "seeking the proper alignment" (30). Admiral Peary does not locate the exact spot of the North Pole: "On a watery planet the sliding sea refused to be fixed" (90). Only a novel like a motion picture can hope to catch the experience of history. Such is *Ragtime.*

Loon Lake (1980), published at the beginning of the Reagan era in national politics, is another contribution to that ongoing conversation in American culture on the moral and spiritual perils of success. Set in the 1930s, the novel is the story of the rise of a working-class boy to the pinnacle of wealth and power. As such, the work echoes earlier treatments of this theme—Dos Passos, Dreiser, Horatio Alger, and, of course, *The Great Gatsby.* The story of Joe of Paterson, like Gatsby's, is the story of how a son's choice of a father creates both an identity and a destiny. The novel is Joe's autobiographical grappling with that choice. In a tense moment of betrayal and accusation, Joe "finds his voice" and seizes control of his narrative in the action that also seals his fate.

Loon Lake, another polyphonic text to challenge the monologic powers of the regime, continues Doctorow's development of innovative narrative strategies. The novel is a demonstration of what Doctorow calls a "discontinuous narrative, with deferred resolutions, and . . . the throwing of multiple voices that turn out to be the work of one narrator" (Trenner, 39,41). Its shifts in scene, tense, and voice, along with interjections of poetry and computer biographies in the form of the résumé or curriculum vitae, give the effect of a cinematic montage, or what Harpham, among others, calls a "bricolage" (90). The overall effect of the narrative suggests destabilized genre forms, which reflect the hermeneutic predicament of the narrator.

In an early essay on the fiction of Henry James, T. S. Eliot comments that "the 'real hero' of James's novels is 'a collectivity'" (Miller, [in *Poets of Reality* (1974)] 137). This notion of the collective character is relevant to understanding the nature of the narrator/narration in *Loon Lake.* The ultimate master of Loon Lake, as well as the master of his text, is a master impersonator, a chameleon. He is the sum total of the voices he hears, denying and forsaking his own voice, if, indeed, he ever knew it. His text thus is a heteroglossic one, which reflects the multiple voices that shape, if not determine, human identity and constitute human selfhood. Joe's life is a paradox—while he appears shrewd and self-reliant, his survival and success stem from his ability to become somebody else. In an interview Doctorow commented on Joe: "*Loon Lake* suggests the act of self-composition on the part of Joe. It suggests that we all compose ourselves from other people in our experience. I think Joe's ability to jump around in voice and shift in time and be almost an impersonator as he writes these recollections of everyone else is a kind of ironic awareness of his inner failure to find out who he is." Hence, Doctorow's "collective hero" allows for a more socially and politically engaged fiction than a fiction focusing upon the psychologized ego written in the confessional mode so abundant in the 1970s and 1980s.

Loon Lake suggests a definition of culture as an encoded hero system. Such a system tells and shows us what to want and how to obtain it. In the novel the figure of F. W. Bennett is the hero of the system—he is what everybody wants; he embodies the dream. Hence, his power is much more than material; it is spiritual, for he, in effect, is the father-creator of our dreams, a godlike role. It is one of the main jobs of the hero to find out whose son he is and then to live out that heritage. All of America's sons are orphans, only winning or earning our fathers through a process of adoption. The father-hero is the self-made man, and the son creates himself in his image. To choose this as his life's trajectory is to strive for a kind of immortality, which is the promise of every hero system. But what are the costs of following such a code—for the individual as well as for the society? That is the major question *Loon Lake* raises for the reader.

> **Doctorow's novels, like Hawthorne's, are in the tradition of the historical romance which seeks to bring about social and moral changes.**
>   **—John G. Parks**

Loon Lake, stylistically and thematically, consists of a cluster of impersonations. Like its narrator it is always pretending to be something else, until the pretense becomes reality. Its mix of genres defamiliarizes the reader so that one shares in the sense of doubt and uncertainty regarding the narrator's sense of self. Showing his critical passage from youth to adult, Joe ends with a curriculum vitae, a summary of a life that was a replication of another. But the real tragedy is more than the personal spiritual failure of a man who betrayed his poetic heart to reach the pinnacle of the American system. Joe's failure, and hence his tragedy, is much greater. Like Robin, of Nathaniel Hawthorne's tale "My Kinsman, Major Molineux," Joe's life is an allegory of the repetitive failure of American history—at heart a failure of perception. Our choices at critical moments cut us off from our true history and lead us to duplicate false and empty options, ones not truly our own. At one point, when Joe is working in Bennett's factory, and the din of production echoes in his mind, Joe discovers "an interesting philosophical problem: I didn't know at any moment what I heard was what was happening or what had already happened" (164). For the reader the verdict of Joe's composition is that Joe's life is another version of "what had already happened."

Doctorow's novels, like Hawthorne's, are in the tradition of the historical romance which seeks to bring about social and moral changes. For Doctorow, as for such critics as Michel Foucault and Edward Said, discourse is worldly; power resides in discourse which is subject to change and has real world effects. Doctorow, as an artist, is committed to challenging the power of the regime with the power of freedom. The principle arena of that engagement is in discourse, in narrative, the range of discursive practices with their cluster of rules and codes which govern writing and thinking. The goal is to disclose and challenge the hegemony of enshrined or institutionalized discursive practices in order to make available new possibilities of thought and action. Doctorow's fiction shows a willingness to take risks, to counter the tendency of a culture to monopolize the compositions of truth with polyphonic and heteroglossic narratives.

Derek Wright (essay date 1993)

SOURCE: "*Ragtime* Revisited: History and Fiction in Doctorow's Novel," in *International Fiction Review,* Vol. 20, No. 1, 1993, pp. 14-16.

[*In the following essay, Wright considers Doctorow's narrative melding of historical fact and fiction in* Ragtime *and the themes that are developed in the novel.*]

Perhaps the crucial difference between E. L. Doctorow's *Ragtime* (1976) and other, more thoroughgoing fictional reinventions of history such as Barth's *Giles Goat-Boy* (1966) or Rushdie's *Shame* (1983) is that the latter use history to say something about fiction—they display the endlessly fertile capacity of the novelistic imagination to compensate for the stubborn limitations, or paucity, of facts—while Doctorow uses fiction to say something about history. Specifically, Doctorow calls into question the whole business of historicity and the origination of historical "fact" from possibly doubtful sources. Doctorow's metaphor for history in the novel is a "player piano" that plays its own tune, regardless of the style—classical, romantic, ragtime—which the pianist chooses to interpret it in. History, as the music of what happened, the events that actually took place, is not the same as history as it is received in the present from what historians have written down. Events are not scientifically mappable by "history" any more than, in Doctorow's novel, the North Pole is precisely locatable by the explorers of the Peary expedition or the correct alignment of the chair with the room by Theodore Dreiser. We put our flag or chair down anywhere: we make our own centers. As Doctorow, following Roland Barthes, has said in interview statements, there is no fiction or non-fiction, only narrative: the telling of a story.

Indeed, history, insofar as it is always narrowly partial and selective, is one of the least trustworthy and potentially one of the most fictional of narrative forms. As the opening pages of *Ragtime* demonstrate, whole racial groups have been written out of American history simply by not being mentioned, and the task of the novelist, as conceived by Doctorow, is to write them back in. The novelist's own pseudo-history parodies and then rewrites the falsely sentimental, nostalgic picture of the American past, as composed from the patriotic viewpoint of the dominant white middle-class culture which prevailed at the turn of the century. Not only are Doctorow's characters historically syncopated, fractionally offbeat on the historical chronometer like the base key which is marginally behind the melody in Scott Joplin's music (his Emma Goldman and Walker gang belong, in fact, to the 1960s), but his entire quasi-history is itself systematically unsynchronized or "in ragged time" with the school textbook, its facts always slightly askew from the received version. Against the known facts, Doctorow syncopates what he regards as "truthful fictions," which are poetically if not historically true: Freud and Jung mischievous shut up together in the Tunnel of Love on Coney Island and, on a more serious note, the Poverty Balls where guests dress in rags and the Stockyard Ball that is set in a mock-slaughterhouse. Concerning the latter two instances, which were certainly in the spirit of the times whether true or not, Doctorow's point is that in the early 1900s American reality was already becoming so incredible that it was most accurately located at the point where history fades into fiction, the factual into the fantastic.

Perhaps the crucial difference between E. L. Doctorow's *Ragtime* (1976) and other, more thoroughgoing fictional reinventions of history such as Barth's *Giles Goat-Boy* (1966) or Rushdie's *Shame* (1983) is that the latter use history to say something about fiction . . . while Doctorow uses fiction to say something about history.
                                            —*Derek Wright*

History, Doctorow subsequently implies, is so patently fic-

tional that there is no longer any felt need to preserve in separate categories fictional and historical plots and characters as, for example, Dos Passos had done in his trilogy *U.S.A.* (1937). Thus, all the canons of historical decorum are violated: personages from the newsreels and history books enter audaciously into the fictional life of the book either by performing fictional acts or meeting fictional characters.

And yet there are still a number of differences between the novel's fictional and historical material which assert themselves in its narrative form and serve to keep the two kinds of material in separate and clearly differentiated categories. Firstly, the historical vignettes of J. P. Morgan, Henry Ford, and Harry Houdini have a tendency to immobilize the narrative by the sheer mass of detailed information, to clutter it with blocks of fact, most notably in long accounts of the objects and properties the characters own. This draws attention obtrusively to the amount of undiluted factuality that has not been fictionalized, i.e., artistically shaped into dramatically interesting narrative material.

Secondly and more importantly, the abrupt shifts in locale in the historical material give the impression of history as a sprawling chaotic mass of unconnected facts. Doctorow's point, of course, is that history is plotless, playing its own heedless, incomprehensible music and plotted quite arbitrarily by the historian. But in practice this means that the novel acquires a sense of direction and causality, and indeed any coherence at all, only from the momentum of the fictional plots (of Tateh and Coalhouse Walker). Only then do we sense the presence of a causally related train of events and of mounting crisis, leading to a climax. The novel's underlying postulate, argues Barbara Foley, is that "whatever coherence emerges from the represented historical world is attributable to the writer's power as teller of his story, with the result that the process of historical reconstruction itself, rather than what is being represented, comes to the fore." What is implied by Doctorow's choice of form is a rather egotistical and paranoid view of history: that the only coherence history has is to be traced to the writer's superior talents as a storyteller.

Thirdly, there is the matter of characterization. We read of Tateh: "He began to create more and more intricate silhouettes, full-figured with backgrounds. . . . With his scissors he suggested not merely outlines but textures, moods, character, despair" (41). Tateh's brief silhouette-sketches illumine character in the light of background; they reveal personality in terms of the determining, victimizing forces acting upon it, and in this they act as a metaphor for the novelist's own flat, silhouettish, two-dimensional creations—in this case, the types of the Poor Jew and of the entrepreneurial Self-Made Man Tateh turns himself into once he has forsaken his victim-status. Doctorow's figures are essentially passive units impinged upon by social and economic forces, conductors of "the flow of American energy" which Tateh, like other American artists, learns to "point his life along" (102), and the novelist seems to be as much interested in this current of historical energy as in the characters it pulses through. The outcome is that the semifictional cast of *Ragtime* are at times presented as the puppet victims of history, jerked around in both comic and tragic ways by overwhelming forces, whether of repressed sexuality or institutionalized racism. Younger Brother by the rampant penis that "whips him about the floor" at the lesbian encounter of Evelyn Nesbitt and Emma Goldman (55), Coalhouse Walker by the firing squad that jerks his body about the street "in a sequence of attitudes as if it were trying to mop up its own blood"(222).

The aesthetic price paid by Doctorow's historical fiction is that the characters, real or invented, are like historical characters: they are thinly textured creations, seen from the outside, not as intricate, complex individuals. Thus we never know if Younger Brother, in joining the Walker gang, is motivated by a burning passion for justice or simply by thrills and excitement ("I can make bombs"), because we are not admitted to his psychological dilemmas and crises. If we are surprised at the end to find that Walker is really not a revolutionary but just wants his car back, it is because we too have seen him, externally, through the public responses of the media, cinema newsreels, and newspapers features.

It would therefore be fitting that Walker should end his life as a historical character. In fact he does not. His fate is not that of the historical nineteenth-century visionary Hans Kohlhaas, who saw himself as a millenial revolutionary and an avenging agent of the Archangel Michael come to form a new world government. It is, instead, that of the eponymous hero of Kleist's novella *Michael Kohlhaas* (1810) about the sixteenth century horse dealer Michael Kohlhaas (who here becomes "Coalhouse") and his pursuit of justice against the corrupt Junker Wenzel Von Tronka (here, Willie Conklin) over the wrecking of his horses (here, a car). Kleist's Kohlhaas simply wants his horses back but he has to murder, rob, and loot in order to get the injustice redressed and the price, as in Coalhouse Walker's case, is his own execution: the shining new horses are paraded past him as he climbs the scaffold. Society finally pays its debt to him, and he to it, for his crimes. Coalhouse Walker, though he appears to be perceived in historical terms, is really a derived fiction, and he ends as one, paralleling the fiction in which he has his origin. He ends as a character in somebody else's book.

Stephen Matterson (essay date Winter 1993)

SOURCE: "Why Not Say What Happened? E. L. Doc-

torow's *Lives of the Poets*," in *Critique,* Vol. 34, No. 2, Winter, 1993, pp. 113-25.

[*In the following essay, Matterson addresses the ideas about writing suggested by the stories in Doctorow's* Lives of the Poets.]

Lives of the Poets, E. L. Doctorow's seventh work, first published in 1984, occupies a unique space in his writings. Its most obvious difference from the other work is announced in its subtitle, *A Novella and Six Stories,* because, apart from the 1979 play, ***Drinks before Dinner,*** Doctorow's previous work had been in the novel form. A case could be made for considering ***Lives of the Poets*** almost an aberration within the Doctorow canon. Among its diverse themes and settings the collection becomes an exploration of the nature of writing itself and of the relation of writing to the life of its author. Doctorow had never before treated this issue so explicitly, though a debate about the reliability of fiction had often been implicitly present in his work. The style of the book is also markedly different from the other work. Doctorow appears willing to allow his self and voice to emerge more fully than they ever had before. ***Lives of the Poets*** could also be said to lack something of the ambitious breadth of Doctorow's novels. The multiple plotting and discontinuities that might be considered typical of Doctorow's writing are here apparently disregarded in favor of a series of self-contained stories. Doctorow's typically sustained focus on a particular time period is also absent. Whether writing of the 1870s, the turn of the century, the 1960s or the 1930s, Doctorow had maintained the focus on that time even while diffusing the action. In contrast, the short stories here range broadly in time and setting. However, in spite of the elements that would make ***Lives of the Poets*** an oddity among Doctorow's works, the book illuminates and adds much to our understanding of the novels. It may remain an aberration, but one that it was essential for Doctorow to write and that is in itself a major achievement.

For the reader to appreciate fully the unfolding of its meanings, ***Lives of the Poets*** must be read in sequence. It would be possible to detach particular stories and consider them complete in themselves, but Doctorow's achievement in the book is an overall one in which the stories are interdependent and contribute to a developing meaning. ***Lives of the Poets*** works in part through a series of correspondences that are established in the first story and are developed by the others.

These correspondences achieve two effects. First, they establish a series of connections, which, when taken together, make up the theme of the whole book. Second, the correspondences between this book and Doctorow's other writing indicate the seriousness and urgency of the themes and issues it raises. It addresses fundamental questions about the nature and function of the writer, questions that Doctorow is applying to himself and to his already published work. In some respects, chiefly through what it reveals about the writer and the need to write, *Lives of the Poets* could be said to alter our understanding of Doctorow's preceding novels. After reading this work we reconsider some aspects of *Welcome to Hard Times, The Book of Daniel, Ragtime,* and *Loon Lake. Lives of the Poets* is an outstanding example of the supposition that T. S. Eliot made in 1917 [in "Tradition and the Individual Talent"]: "The existing order is complete before the new work arrives; for order to persist after the supervention of novelty, the *whole* existing order must be, if ever so slightly, altered" (5). Indeed, it can be argued that one of the urges driving *Lives of the Poets* is Doctorow's need to re-examine some of the ideas that Eliot originated in that essay.

I

The situation established in the book's first story, **"The Writer in the Family,"** is important for appreciating this dual series of connections. The narrator, Jonathan, is in his early teens when his father dies, leaving a widow and two sons, Jonathan and his older brother Harold. The father's elderly mother, however, is still living, in a nursing home. Fearing that the shock of her son's death will be too much for the old lady, the narrator's wealthy Aunt Frances persuades Jonathan to write a letter purporting to come from his father, pretending that the family has moved to Arizona. Aunt Frances is delighted with the letter and prevails upon Jonathan to write more. Eventually the deceit disturbs the boy and to end the letters, he writes one that he knows Aunt Frances cannot show her mother.

> For the reader to appreciate fully the unfolding of its meanings, *Lives of the Poets* must be read in sequence. It would be possible to detach particular stories and consider them complete in themselves, but Doctorow's achievement in the book is an overall one in which the stories are interdependent and contribute to a developing meaning.
> —*Stephen Matterson*

Because of the dual system of correspondences in *Lives of the Poets,* **"The Writer in the Family"** is not a self-contained, straightforward story. It establishes within the book, a set of fundamental questions and observations about writing and the role of the writer. It is suggested that Jonathan has to give up the letters because they are dishonest. In anticipation of the novella "Lives of the Poets," young Jonathan is already haunted by Robert Lowell's question from the

poem "Epilogue," quoted in the novella: "Yet why not say what happened?" On one level, **"The Writer in the Family"** is about the boy's almost heroic stand, his refusal to use writing for deceit. Yet the story introduces other, potentially more important, areas. First, in spite of the deceit involved, Jonathan actually comes to a truthful image of his father by writing the letters through the fiction that he makes up. Thus, in the final letter, he invents the father's longing for the sea, and, in so doing, he uncovers two kinds of truth about his father, the factual and the psychological. His father actually was, as Jonathan later discovers, in the navy for a year. Psychologically, the father was restless and unsatisfied, a man for whom living in Arizona would have been a kind of death.

The second significant point about the fictive letters is that they come to have a function far beyond their ostensible one of deceiving the grandmother. Their immediate effect is somehow to keep the father's memory alive, to keep him real and living to the boy (he has a vivid dream that his father is still alive), and to Aunt Frances. The first brief letter has a profound effect on Aunt Frances:

> My aunt called some days later and told me it was when she read this letter aloud to the old lady that the full effect of Jack's death came over her. She had to excuse herself and went out in the parking lot to cry. "I wept so," she said. "I felt such terrible longing for him. You're so right, he loved to go places, he loved life, he loved everything."(5)

The talent of the young writer has given the father a truth, a reality, that keeps him alive for others. Jonathan never really grasps this fact, and Aunt Frances' motives are misunderstood. His brother, Harold, points out that the letters are unnecessary: "Grandma is almost totally blind, she's half deaf and crippled. Does the situation call for a literary composition? Does it need verisimilitude? Would the old lady know the difference if she was read the phone books?" (13). Both the brothers misunderstand Aunt Frances because they fail to realize how much the letters help in dealing with the loss of her brother.

For all of its darkly comic situation, **"The Writer in the Family"** concludes subtly with a complex and dual message: although fiction is deceit, made-up stories, it can reveal truths that facts alone cannot. Jonathan is as yet too young to grasp this fully; to him the letters are deceptions that he cannot continue. It is significant here to suggest the ways in which this dual approach to fictions pervades Doctorow's other works. **"The Writer in the Family"** forces the reader to recognize how much of Jonathan's situation has been repeated in the novels. This happens most obviously in *World's Fair,* which followed *Lives of the Poets;* there, Aunt Frances and the family all reappear at much greater length. There are particular changes; for instance, the brother Harold is renamed

Donald, and the family situation is amplified from **"The Writer in the Family."** Edgar in *World's Fair,* who wins a prize in an essay contest, resembles Jonathan in the earlier story. Though absent in **"The Writer in the Family,"** the father is a prominent figure in *World's Fair,* and his longing for the sea is further outlined, appropriately enough, by Aunt Frances herself (240-41).

In his first novel, *Welcome to Hard Times,* Doctorow had apparently avoided a reliance upon personal truth and fact. . . . However, in reconsidering even *Welcome to Hard Times* from the perspective made available by *Lives of the Poets,* the reader is likely to place more emphasis on the questions the central character, Blue, asks himself about writing and its effect.
—Stephen Matterson

There are also correspondences with the earlier novels. The reader recognizes much of the family situation from *The Book of Daniel.* Although the figure of Paul Isaacson is never explored as fully as the father in *World's Fair,* there are striking similarities between them. Like the father in *World's Fair,* Paul Isaacson has a shop; in *World's Fair* it is a record and radio shop, in *The Book of Daniel* a radio repair shop. The fathers also share a reciprocated devotion to their mothers and similar politics. The mother in *The Book of Daniel, World's Fair* and **"The Writer in the Family"** remains a constant and recognizable figure.

The similarities shared by these three works are especially striking because they suggest how far Doctorow has inserted himself and his own experience into *The Book of Daniel,* which often has been considered an exploration of an historical moment and an examination of the postwar period and of how the temper of the times could bring about the execution of the Rosenbergs. But, like **"The Writer in the Family,"** it also is concerned with the nature of writing and truth. On one level, this is obvious because Daniel self-consciously writes the novel in front of us as he sits in the library at Columbia. But, more covertly, Doctorow is considering the same questions that are raised explicitly in **"The Writer in the Family."** In repeating something of the childhood situation that existed in *The Book of Daniel,* he is already asking Lowell's question that will haunt him in *Lives of the Poets.*

In his first novel, *Welcome to Hard Times,* Doctorow had apparently avoided a reliance upon personal truth and fact. In part, the setting of *Welcome to Hard Times* in the 1870s, and in the West, which Doctorow had never visited, safeguarded him from the dangers of the overly autobiographi-

cal first novel. As he has said, "Somehow I was the kind of writer who had to put myself through prisms to find the right light—I had to filter myself from my imagination in order to write" (McCaffery [in "A Spirit of Transgression" (1982)] 34). However, in reconsidering even *Welcome to Hard Times* from the perspective made available by *Lives of the Poets,* the reader is likely to place more emphasis on the questions the central character, Blue, asks himself about writing and its effect. In the novel, Blue receives identity by his role as a historian; the role is analogous to his role as rebuilder of the town Hard Times. Yet he too doubts the validity of his writing as a means of interpreting and changing the world: "as if notations in a ledger can fix a life, as if some marks in a book can control things" (187).

When Doctorow said that he needed a prism through which to write, he was suggesting a strategy that is crucial to an understanding of *Lives of the Poets.* "The Writer in the Family" introduces a dilemma about the honesty of writing compared to the kind of truth that fiction offers. Taking Jonathan as the writer of the stories that follow, one sees how the dilemma is either avoided or further developed. The connections between **"The Writer in the Family"** and the subsequent stories are apparent even though they are not made explicit for the reader. In **"The Water Works"** a boy who is apparently shadowing an undertaker follows him one day as he collects a drowned corpse from the water works. The corpse, that of a child, is taken away, and the story ends with the boy observing the water workers drinking whisky; it represents one of their rituals for dealing with death: "There is such a cherishing of ritual too among firemen and gravediggers" (24). The boy and his family are curiously absent from this story. We do not learn his name or anything of his family situation. Strategically, the story represents one way of writing—distancing oneself from the theme. The self is extinguished, erased, in exactly the way that T. S. Eliot had described in "Tradition and the Individual Talent": "Poetry is not a turning loose of emotion, but an escape from emotion; it is not the expression of personality, but an escape from personality" (10) and "The progress of an artist is a continual self-sacrifice, a continual extinction of personality" (7). It is obvious that this erasing or distancing strategy is only apparently successful. Given the context of **"The Writer in the Family,"** **"The Water Works"** develops in different ways. It can be read as a deepening of the boy's fascination with death deriving from the death of the father in the other story. It also develops from one brief statement in **"The Writer in the Family"**; faced with his grief at the father's death, Jonathan is comforted by Harold who tells him:

> Look at this old black stone here. . . . The way it's carved. You can see the changing fashion in monuments—just like everything else. (9)

"The Water Works" is much more than an isolated epiphany, a Joycean moment of recognition and truth. It has a context that is provided by the previous story and by the overall questions about writing that *Lives of the Poets* considers. The story suggests the boy's unstated recognition that there are ritualistic ways of dealing with death. In seeing the water workers drinking the whisky, he immediately recognizes the ritual that is followed also by "gravediggers and firemen." The unspoken realization or implication is that the act of writing about the dead is in itself a ritualistic means of coping with grief and loss. But at that moment the boy gives no sign of recognizing this fact; and in effect, "The Water Works" is evidence of a split between the persona adopted for the telling of the story and the author of the tale. Mention of the rituals of firemen, is a glance toward *Ragtime;* one of its chief plots depends on how a ritualistic practical joke that the fireman play on their victim Coalhouse Walker turns into a shocking and extreme situation.

The division between author and narrator widens in the next story, "**Willi.**" Essentially, "**Willi**" is a boy's reminiscence of his mother's infidelity and what happens when he tells his father of the adultery. Like "**The Water Works,**" this story involves a moment of recognition and realization, not about death but about sexuality, jealousy, and, more personally, about the boy's learning that he is not exempt from feelings of sexual longing and arousal. "**The Water Works**" is in effect a fictionalization of Jonathan, using fiction to explore his feelings; this strategy is even more extreme in the case of "**Willi.**" Jonathan is erased from "**The Water Works,**" necessarily absent from it, and a further displacement takes place through the suggested displacement in time; the undertaker has a horsedrawn hearse. In "**Willi,**" there is displacement of time, place, and persona. The story is set in Galicia in 1910 and has a certain familiarity, even a predictability, with its props of aristocratic husband, younger wife, and adultery with the boy's tutor. On a more significant level, "**Willi**" is about displacement and comes to echo the displacement that made feeling into fiction. Galicia in 1910 is firmly invoked by the narrator (untypical of *Lives of the Poets* where most of the stories are not specific about time and place), as is the fact that the father is not at home there:

> He was a Jew who spoke no Yiddish and a farmer raised in the city. . . . We lived alone, isolated on our estate, neither Jew nor Christian, neither friend or petitioner of the Austro-Hungarians.(32)

Galicia itself occupied a precarious position in 1910, divided between Austria and Russia and agitating for autonomy. "**Willi**" has various effects. A satisfying and stimulating story in itself, but like a chameleon it takes on a variety of colors from the stories and contexts in which Doctorow has placed it. The narrator has created the persona of the boy and used the historical position of Galicia to find concrete analogies for his own puzzlement and alienation. The father, of course, reflects Jonathan's father; the Jew in a land of Gentiles, the would-be sailor living in the city. The implications of "**Willi**" are deepened further when, in "**Lives of the Poets,**" Doctorow uses the same phrases to describe the fighting of Jonathan's own parents (114-15). Whatever its theme, of adolescent longing, awareness, alienation, "**Willi**" is also concerned with how fiction starts in feeling and seeks concrete situations and symbols—objective correlatives—to explore and express that feeling. The feelings themselves may be explored more deeply through the very act of displacement, of locating them in a fresh context.

With this last recognition one starts to reach to the center of *Lives of the Poets.* Although the individual stories succeed on their own, the book as a whole takes for its theme the origin and purpose of fiction. The stories not only exist separately as units but also join together to form a much greater whole. Indeed, *Lives of the Poets* can be considered as a book that helps to unify Doctorow's own work up to that point. Like Jonathan in the book, Doctorow had transposed the self, seeking historical analogies and circumstances, recreating over and over the father, the mother, the family situation, the Jewishness. Even a brief tale such as "**Willi**" has implications for re-viewing Doctorow's other fiction because it makes explicit what had been implied in the recurring situation of father and mother seen from the child's perspective, the one offered in *The Book of Daniel, Ragtime,* and *Loon Lake.* Further, it suggests how the remote settings of *Welcome to Hard Times* and *Big as Life* can be considered self-consciously manipulative on Doctorow's part.

II

The first stories establish this questioning of the origins of fiction, in the second half of the book the stories go further and ask another, related question. In part, this is Lowell's question, "Yet why not say what happened?" It is another question too, which is not about the origins of fiction but about its usefulness and its responsibilities. That "**The Hunter,**" which follows "**Willi,**" raises these issues is not fully apparent until reading "**Lives of the Poets.**" The novella reveals that Jonathan had (and possibly is having) an affair with a woman who had taught in a grade school to pay for her university tuition. "**The Hunter**" represents Jonathan's imagining her situation; perhaps, though we cannot know this, deriving it from a story she had told him. Once this fact is revealed, "**The Hunter**" takes on various meanings. At first the story seems more remote from Jonathan than even "**Willi**" because the central consciousness is the young woman. But the story may also be read as Jonathan's self-examination because, being the story's maker, he has also entered into the life of another character, a young bus driver. Again, **"The Hunter"** explores aspects of alienation: the landscape is cold and bleak; the young woman is out of place in the town and is also deeply unhappy. In the story she apparently invites the bus driver's sexual attentions, but, then, in a moment of disgust, she spurns him. The act is one of both hope and despair; hope for love, yet despair at the predictability of the young man and at the restrictions in her life. She recognizes that an affair with the bus driver, rather than being a liberating force, will confirm her imprisonment in the small town and her self-restriction. In effect, she is the "hunter" of the title because, unlike the other characters, she seeks a life that is not predictable but imaginative and spontaneous.

Ostensibly **"The Hunter"** has a fairly standard theme, but **"Lives of the Poets"** suggests that it has other ones. On one level it is concerned with the writer's empathetic ability to enter and understand other lives, and perhaps it is also about the writer's need so to do. If we accept that the story is written by Jonathan, then it is also a story of self-examination because he has created the persona of the bus driver. Even the setting of **"The Hunter"** is glossed in **"Lives of the Poets"** as the town to which Jonathan and the woman go to be discreet in their love making (134-35). In this regard, the story could be read as a kind of disguise: guilt will not allow Jonathan to write frankly and honestly about the woman, but he needs to write about her, and thus the fictive displacement represented by **"The Hunter"** is born of guilt and the need to camouflage feelings. If this is the case, then the adult Jonathan is confronting the question of fiction in a much more complex way than could the child Jonathan. In **"The Writer in the Family,"** the dishonesty of the fictive letters forces him to stop writing them. But here Jonathan, is, as it were, using Eliot's "objective correlative" and the notion of the distanced, disguised self as a shield, a self-protective device, as if the insertion of one's self into a fictive self were one of the "deliberate disguises" that Eliot's "Hollow Men" sought. Jonathan has not yet reached the crisis brought on by the devastating simplicity of Lowell's question that is evident in the novella.

In the next two stories, **"The Foreign Legation"** and **"The Leather Man,"** Doctorow uses these by-now-established questions about fiction as a basis for exploring other themes, particularly variations on the theme of the writer's responsibility. Morgan, the chief (and, really, sole) character in **"The Foreign Legation,"** is not a creative writer but is used to represent aspects of the writer's apparent isolation and supposed self-reliance. Morgan's wife and children have left him (his story could have been suggested by those told in the novella about broken and failing marriages); alone in the house, he tends to brood. One day his habitual morning run takes him by the house of an unspecified foreign legation. At the end of the story Morgan is again jogging by the le-

gation one winter morning when a bomb goes off, and he is injured.

Like the other stories, **"The Foreign Legation"** establishes its meanings from different contexts. In part this story is about the impossibility of withdrawing from the world, either as an individual or as a nation. For instance, Morgan recognizes an analogy between his job as "assistant curator of pre-Columbian art at the Museum of the Under Americas in New York City" (57) and the international aspect of a diner he visits.

> The counterman handed him a large laminated menu and smiled a gold-toothed smile. Hey, compadre, he said.
>
> Morgan looked at the menu. He could have the chili, or the chicken soup, he could have pigs' feet or Irish lamb stew or lasagna or souvlaki. (61)

This recognition precedes the bombing, where the implication is that because we are all involved, no one can be entirely innocent or claim to have no interest in "foreign affairs." Doctorow makes the lack of insulation between the private and the political shockingly clear. Morgan's erotic fantasies about the girls in the convent school are brutally echoed when, after the bombing, he finds himself holding the severed leg of one of the girls. This theme alone makes the story a powerful one, but, once again, its placement in *Lives of the Poets* makes it resonate with other possibilities and analogies. It corresponds to **"The Leather Man"** and **"Lives of the Poets"** in that it is about the writer's responsibility in the world and his inability to withdraw from it. In several ways, Doctorow signals Morgan as surrogate writer. Like Jonathan in **"Lives of the Poets"** Morgan has, as it were, withdrawn temporarily into the self. If we read **"The Foreign Legation"** as a story explicitly written by Jonathan, we see again how he is exploring the self through displacement and how essential displacement is for such an exploration. Jonathan's voluntary withdrawal from his wife and family in **"Lives of the Poets"** is something he does not especially want to examine. In **"The Foreign Legation"** he avoids scrutinizing the act simply by making it an involuntary one. Morgan's wife and children have left him, allowing Jonathan to concentrate on the story's other themes. Further, Morgan's insight in the local diner is also Jonathan's, inserted into fiction:

> When I walk into the Bluebird Diner on lower Broadway the counterman gives me the gold-toothed grin. Hey, compadre, he says. He tosses me the laminated menu. . . . The plates slap through the slot, oh chili, soup of chicken, oh pigs' feet, oh lamb stew, lasagna (homemade), fried steak and souvlaki. (104)

Jonathan uses Morgan to exemplify the inability to be separate from the world, and this inability is part of his own self-examination as a writer, an examination that had started in **"The Writer in the Family"** and will reach a climax in **"Lives of the Poets."** However, the realization that the writer cannot be immune from politics and choice is also made by the authorities, as is evident in **"The Leather Man."** At first reading, this story, which directly precedes **"Lives of the Poets,"** makes little sense. Only on subsequent and careful readings does its point emerge.

"The Leather Man" has the not altogether convincing setting of a semi-formal meeting by a group, apparently the CIA. The meeting is concerned with whether vagrants and drop-outs can be considered politically or socially subversive and, if so, what subsequent course of action should be adopted toward them. Slater, who dominates the meeting, sees drop-outs and vagrants, characterized by a centenarian, the Leather Man, as necessarily subversive because they possess, and potentially provide, an alternative perspective on society.

What is the essential act of the Leather Man? He makes the world foreign. He distances it. He is estranged. Our perceptions are sharpest when we're estranged. We can see the shape of things. (74)

Because Slater accepts this as fact, his position is that the group should infiltrate and make contact with these individuals. One of the clues that this group is a CIA meeting is in Slater's reminiscence of having been part of the group that infiltrated the Woodstock festival (68-9). Once more, it is the writer, not just the drop-out who is the focus here. When Slater argues that the vagrant forces us to re-see the world, he is also detailing one of the effects that the writer achieves. Furthermore, Slater's final point concerning infiltration seems to be aimed deliberately at the writer rather than at the vagrant. The writer provides a perspective on society similar to that of the outsider, the Leather Man, and at first it appears that Slater wants to utilize the writer's perspective as a resource: "We've got thousands of people in this country whose vocation it is to let us know what our experience is. Are you telling me this is not a resource?" (76). The twist, however, is that rather than learning from the writer's perspective, Slater visualizes controlling the writer through infiltration. His group will seek to curb the writer's power by limiting the range or effectiveness of fiction as resource. The exact means of achieving control is not stated, but Doctorow is likely to have had in mind government patronage of the arts as a covert means of control. The *New York Times* of 11 January 1986 reported that Doctorow ob-

jected to then Secretary of State George Shultz's addressing the PEN conference (I, 23:2).

III

From the very opening of **"Lives of the Poets,"** it is obvious that the postures and stances that Jonathan has assumed in the other stories are now dropped and that the novella itself is exploratory, self-conscious. "My left thumb is stiff, not particularly swollen although the veins at the base are prominent and I can't move it backward or pick up something without pain" (81). As the novella develops, it is clear that the fictive personae Jonathan has used are not merely dropped but are being explained. He provides hints that lead to our detecting the sources of the preceding stories. In one regard, the novella is about a mid-life crisis, about turning fifty. Jonathan chronicles the anxieties and problems of his class and his age group. **"Lives of the Poets"** works successfully on this level alone, but it becomes immeasurably richer and finer because Doctorow is also examining the nature of writing and living. The questions that Jonathan faces—ones that he cannot even fully articulate—are about the nature of being a writer, about what the writer can hope to achieve, and about the responsibilities of fiction. In considering these issues, **"Lives of the Poets"** corresponds to the doubts that other writers have expressed in their work. These would include Shakespeare's "How with this rage shall beauty hold a plea,/ Whose action is no stronger than a flower?" (Sonnet 65); Auden's statement that "poetry makes nothing happen," ("In Memory of W. B. Yeats") and, as Jonathan himself indicates, Lowell's question, "Yet why not say what happened?"

> **From the very opening of "Lives of the Poets," it is obvious that the postures and stances that Jonathan has assumed in the other stories are now dropped and that the novella itself is exploratory, self-conscious.**
> **—*Stephen Matterson***

One way of considering **"Lives of the Poets"** is to see that Jonathan is asking such questions within a framework that provides their answers. The preceding six stories become variations of the possible answers about why one writes. Jonathan invents stories to make something real to him, to give comfort to himself and others, to deceive, to disguise the self, to explore his emotions and conflicts. Another answer to Lowell's question is that a kind of truth can emerge through fiction, though that truth is not necessarily factual. For example, Jonathan may learn something of himself through displacing his own situation, setting it in Galicia or making a fresh character for himself. Displacement represents another aspect of the Leather Man's significance: in making the world foreign for the reader, writers may also provide themselves with a fresh point of view. These are all sound reasons for writing. In **"Lives of the Poets"** Jonathan is at the end of his fictional resources, his Eliotean deliberate disguises. He drops his personae and in so doing, deftly (or, perhaps, to him, accidentally), reveals to us the sources of the preceding stories.

Doctorow's title for the novella and the book, *Lives of the Poets,* now reveals more of its significance. Perhaps more than any other art form, twentieth-century poetry has faced a crisis in the perceived relation between author and persona. For Eliot, at the start of modernism, the poet's progress, as outlined in "Tradition and the Individual Talent," was a "continual extinction of personality." When this process is made apparent in his poetry, however, it often appears as disguise, as in the "deliberate disguises," but it is there also in "Portrait of a Lady":

> And I must borrow every changing shape
> To find expression . . . dance, dance
> Like a dancing bear,
> Cry like a parrot, chatter like an ape.

The oblique revelation of the self through the dramatic monologue is a variation of this strategy of the impersonal. But Lowell's question strikes to the heart of this strategy, exposing it as somehow dishonest. Indeed, Lowell's question, "Yet why not say what happened?" comes from one of his last poems, published in his last book, *Day by Day* (1977). To reach the simplicity of the question in "Epilogue" Lowell himself had undergone the same process that Doctorow explores in *Lives of the Poets.* Starting off, as he often acknowledged, as a poet under the influence of Eliot and the New Critics, Lowell had espoused the impersonal in poetry. But his break with this aspect of modernism came with *Life Studies* in 1959. Strikingly, *Life Studies* itself follows something of the same pattern as *Lives of the Poets.* Lowell's book starts with monologues, as he invests his personality and feelings in figures such as Marie de 'Medici and a mad negro soldier. He continues through a prose reminiscence, which, like Doctorow's **"Lives of the Poets,"** provides essential clues to the other works in the book. After a section on four writers—Lowell's own "Lives of the Poets"—he comes to a series of poems that are, apparently, more nakedly about the self and the personal, undisguised by persona. Rather than being a continual extinction of personality, both *Life Studies* and *Lives of the Poets* represent a gradual emergence of the personality behind the fictions. An astute reader of **"Lives of the Poets"** makes a connection between Jonathan and Lowell because Jonathan attended Kenyon College (133-34), where Lowell and Randall Jarrell had followed their teacher John Crowe Ransom. Indeed, the ostensible gloss on the title *Lives of the Poets* derives in part from Jonathan's interest in poetry; it seems to have been the

title of a projected reminiscence about the poets he knew (123).

After he finished *Life Studies,* Lowell said that he was unsure whether the book was a "life-line" or a "death-rope" (277). Something of the same question is tackled in **"Lives of the Poets"** because Jonathan's new style of writing could represent either a dead end or a way out of his crisis. However, Doctorow complicates the question in several ways. The story ends with Jonathan's starting to become engaged in a political action, shielding Salvadorean refugees. This act can be seen as the logical consequence of one of the debates that has emerged in the second half of the book, about the impossibility of being self-reliant and disengaged from political realities. In theory, it could also mean the end of writing; hypothetically, Jonathan could find in political action an outlet for his temporarily suppressed creative energies. The choice between silence and action would be by no means new; it derives from Auden's "poetry makes nothing happen" and reflects, for example, the silence at the end of Saul Bellow's *Herzog* when Herzog is liberated from the compulsion to write his letters. The actual ending of *Lives of the Poets* is not so straightforward, however; it closes with the child refugee now assisting Jonathan at the typewriter:

> hey who's writing this? every good boy needs a toy
> boat, maybe we'll go to the bottom of the page get
> my daily quota done come on, kid, you can do three
> more lousy lines. (145)

The positive suggestion at the end is that political engagement, or, at least, a reawakening of the quality of compassion, can reinvest writing with the energy and power that are otherwise in danger of being lost. There is a neatness to this ending because man and boy now compose together, thus echoing and developing the situation in **"The Writer in the Family."** But rather than looking back to the first story, the novella ends by looking outward to a future that in other parts of the book seemed hopeless. Jonathan's action resolves nothing. It solves none of the dilemmas he had outlined, but it reveals a source of energy from outside the self. It is as though to be re-engaged as a writer Jonathan finds the advice of Yeats insufficient. Rather than returning to the "foul rag-and-bone shop of the heart" as Yeats advised in "The Circus Animals' Desertion," he must do the opposite and look outside the self.

In "Epilogue" Lowell's complaint about his "threadbare art" involved a doubt over whether he was a true artist. The artist, he suggests, transforms reality rather than reproduces it. Lowell's sense of failure derives primarily from a romantic view of the role of the poet, a view that stretched from Coleridge and Wordsworth to, in Lowell's time, Wallace Stevens. Rather than a romantic, Lowell designates himself a recorder, a photographer rather than an expressionist painter. Nevertheless, "Epilogue" ends with a note of triumph at this fact; art itself should be accurate, should exist in order to preserve because it involves the recognition that we are mortal and human:

> Yet why not say what happened?
> Pray for the grace of accuracy
> Vermeer gave to the sun's illumination
> stealing like a tide across a map
> to his girl solid with yearning.
> We are poor passing facts,
> warned by that to give
> each figure in the photograph
> his living name.

In some regards, *Lives of the Poets* closes with the same recognition, and, as for Lowell, "why not say what happened?" becomes not so much a question as a half-aggressive statement of post-romantic sensibility. For Jonathan, dropping fiction and saying "what happened" can be a refreshing, if temporary, triumph. Indeed, it is possible to see that **"The Hunter"** touches on this time. After her frustrated night with the bus driver, the teacher calls in the school photographer. To do so is most unusual because there is no special occasion, and the children are not dressed up for so unexpected a visit. They become uneasy and upset over the event and the teacher's vehement insistence. On one level, the teacher's gesture could be considered symptomatic of her overall frustrations. But the event becomes almost a trope for *Lives of the Poets.* Like the teacher, Jonathan finds authenticity in the snapshot rather than in the composed, formal portrait, in saying "what happened" as well as in the ways of disguising it.

Stephen Cooper (essay date May 1993)

SOURCE: "Cutting Both Ways: E. L. Doctorow's Critique of the Left," in *South Atlantic Review,* Vol. 58, No. 2, May, 1993, pp. 111-25.

[In the following essay, Cooper examines the political concerns of Doctorow's work.]

The experimental, "postmodern" elements in E. L. Doctorow's novels are remarked upon by virtually all his critics. In most of his major novels the narrative voice is self-conscious and calls attention to itself. In his first novel, *Welcome to Hard Times* (1960), the narrator Blue is writing his story in old ledgers and reflects on his penchant, even obsession, for record keeping and wonders if the truth of events can be captured in words. Daniel Isaacson, the narrator of *The Book of Daniel* (1971), begins his highly self-conscious story by commenting on his writing instrument (a felt-tip

marker), moves back and forth in time, frequently shifts from first- to third-person narrative, and interpolates numerous historical and analytical passages into his memoir. The narrative voice in *Ragtime* (1975) is flat and detached, a parody of the style used in documentaries or textbooks. This parody is given a twist when near the end of the novel we realize that one of the characters, the now grown Little Boy, is telling the story. In *Loon Lake* (1980) the reader confronts multiple narrative voices—first- and third-person, computer-generated text, poems, résumés, stream of consciousness—though in the end it turns out all has been composed by the central character, Joe of Paterson.

What makes Doctorow's postmodern narrative experiments noteworthy is that they occur in novels that deal with historical and political topics and characters. The way Doctorow "plays with" historical figures can be disconcerting to many readers who want certainty, who want to know what is "true" and what is invented. In his 1977 essay **"False Documents,"** Doctorow addresses this issue directly. He cites the historical origins of the novel and notes that writers such as Defoe and Cervantes presented their works as "histories," as "false documents." On the other hand, he argues that history is always "composed" and that it "has to be written and re-written from one generation to another" (24). Thus, history and fiction intermingle and always have. Both are ways of making sense out of the world, and as such, both are ideological to a greater extent than many writers would like to admit. As Barbara Foley [in "From *U.S.A.* to *Ragtime*" *American Literature* 50 (1978)] points out when she compares Doctorow to Dos Passos, "Doctorow treats with equal aplomb facts that are 'true' and those that are 'created,' thus calling into question our concept of factuality and, indeed, of history itself" (168). This position, that history is highly subjective, can be disquieting, as Foley notes:

> What I ultimately find disturbing about *Ragtime*—and about many other works of contemporary historical fiction, whether 'apocalyptic' or 'documentary'—is its underlying postulate that whatever coherence emerges from the represented historical world is attributable to the writer's power as teller of his story, with the result that the process of historical reconstruction itself, rather than what is being presented, comes to the fore. (175)

The main targets of Doctorow's destabilizing tactics are usually presumed to be traditional or conservative history and politics. In other words, as a writer associated with liberal or left-wing causes who knows well the history of radical dissent in the United States, Doctorow would target reactionary history to further his own political agenda. In fact, Doctorow does target such American shibboleths as free enterprise, individualism, self-reliance, and patriotism. But what makes Doctorow's fiction more than simply doctrinaire is that his postmodern method also questions the left-wing interpretations of history. Doctorow's liberal questioning of received opinion leads him to examine all such opinion, even the leftist view of history. For him, ossification wherever it is found represents a threat to human values. What I propose to examine is Doctorow's interrogation of the Left in five of his better known novels in an effort to see how his method pushes the reader toward a postmodern politics based on what Doctorow has called "a multiplicity of witness" ("Multiplicity" 184).

What makes Doctorow's postmodern narrative experiments noteworthy is that they occur in novels that deal with historical and political topics and characters. The way Doctorow "plays with" historical figures can be disconcerting to many readers who want certainty, who want to know what is "true" and what is invented.
—Stephen Cooper

The ways in which Doctorow's first novel, *Welcome to Hard Times,* challenges traditional myths about the American frontier are probably clearer than the ways it questions liberalism. The novel opens and closes with the Bad Man from Bodie destroying the small town of Hard Times in the Dakota Territory. After the town is destroyed the first time, the narrator of the novel and de facto mayor of Hard Times, Blue, works to rebuild and to attract people to the settlement. While the town has many of the character types from traditional westerns—from miners to saloon girls—Doctorow uses them to subvert the usual view of the frontier. Thus, the rugged individualists who are traditionally supposed to have tamed the frontier become greedy, parasitic entrepreneurs dependent on the miners in the hills who are in turn dependent on eastern business interests. Typical of these petty entrepreneurs is a Russian named Zar (a pre-Revolutionary figure, as his name indicates) who sets up a combination saloon and whorehouse. His sole aim is profit, and his capital is a large tent (formerly used for revivals), a quantity of liquor, and three prostitutes. The archetype of the successful pioneer becomes not the farmer, the cowboy, or the miner, but the entrepreneur, and the most profitable entrepreneur is the pimp.

A town based on these values is not a real community. When the mine closes and violence threatens, the town self-destructs. The critique of capitalist values is in the foreground. David S. Gross [in "Tales of Obscene Power," *Genre* 13 (1980)] has argued that Doctorow "makes his view the basis for a new de-mystified myth, a myth of sleazy self-inter-

est, fear, and macho violence" (136). In other words, Doctorow uses the mythic West to expose the myths of capitalism. Gross shows that because Hard Times is based on entrepreneurial capitalism, it is not a real community. The only thing holding people together in the town is a "cash nexus" that collapses in the face of violence or business failure (134). From this point of view, the novel can be seen as an allegory of the fragmenting, dehumanizing effects of capitalism, a kind of Marxist fable of greed and alienation.

It could be argued that in *Welcome to Hard Times* Doctorow does not despair of all social action, but only the kind of social action in which Blue engages, a boosterism firmly rooted in a capitalist framework. If we look at Doctorow's whole career, however, we will find that a skeptical attitude toward reform and progress is the rule rather than the exception.
—Stephen Cooper

But if the novel incisively looks at the self-destructiveness of a capitalist order, it does not provide any real alternative to that order. Indeed, I would argue that the book presents a profoundly pessimistic view of the possibilities for social change and that it differs greatly from the utopian vision of much classical leftist thought, which is based on the notion that positive change is possible, even inevitable. In *Welcome to Hard Times* violence and chaos seem an inescapable part of capitalism, but after the apocalypse there is no redemption, no brave new world. Paul Levine [in *E. L. Doctorow* (1985)] has noted that the vision of history presented in the novel is cyclical rather than progressive (29), and other critics have come to similar conclusions. The impossibility of escaping the deterministic cycles of history is explicitly stated by Blue near the end of his narration as he addresses a hypothetical urban reader:

> Do you think, mister, with all that settlement around you that you're freer than me to make your fate? Well I wish I knew yours. Your father's doing is in you, like his father's was in him, and we can never start new, we take on all the burden: the only thing that grows is trouble, the disasters get bigger, that's all.(187)

By denying the possibility of a new start, Blue also denies the promise of the New World and the West, which were settled in the belief that people could start anew. In addition, by putting this view in terms of an inheritance passed from father to son, he seems to suggest a sort of original sin, an innate something in man that progress and reform cannot overcome or erase. Blue has come to this conclusion from his own experience. After the first destruction of Hard Times, he devotes himself to rebuilding the town and making it a true community. When the Bad Man from Bodie returns, he stands up to him. The results of his social commitment are nil. The town is destroyed just the same. He could not get people to transcend their greed or overcome their selfishness and cowardice. The need for human reform and rebirth is clear in the novel, but the possibility of it occurring appears negligible.

It could be argued that in **Welcome to Hard Times** Doctorow does not despair of all social action, but only the kind of social action in which Blue engages, a boosterism firmly rooted in a capitalist framework. If we look at Doctorow's whole career, however, we will find that a skeptical attitude toward reform and progress is the rule rather than the exception. David Emblidge has argued that a cyclical, antiprogressive view of history runs through **Welcome to Hard Times, The Book of Daniel,** and **Ragtime, Loon Lake** and **Billy Bathgate** could easily be added to his list. In these later books radical and progressive causes are consistently thwarted, partly by capitalist oppression and partly by the human failings of the radicals themselves.

Although **The Book of Daniel** is based on the trial and execution of Julius and Ethel Rosenberg in the early 1950s, one of the Left's greatest causes célèbres, Doctorow has said he did not "write a documentary novel" but used "what happened to the Rosenbergs as *occasion* for the book" ("Spirit of Transgression" 46; italics in original). Certainly he uses the novel as an "occasion" to criticize the Cold War hysteria that kills Paul and Rochelle Isaacson, his fictional counterparts of the Rosenbergs. The Isaacsons may be Communists who are critical of the status quo and believe in the need for radical social change, but to think this lower-middle-class couple, leading a very ordinary life in most respects, is a mortal threat to US security is absurd. By having the novel's narrator, the Isaacson' son Daniel, writing during the late 1960s, Doctorow can also use the novel as an occasion to point out the continuing violence and paranoia of the US government. When Daniel participates in the October 1967 march on Washington, he is severely beaten by police, just as his parents were brutalized for their views. The novel also points out the narrowness and commercialization of American culture. In the 1940s when the Isaacsons take Daniel to see and hear Paul Robeson, their bus is viciously attacked by a mob yelling anti-Semitic and racial slurs. In the 1960s Daniel visits Disneyland and critiques the commercialization of history and literature it represents. In his father's generation the folk tradition Robeson celebrates is attacked, and in Daniel's generation it is debased and sentimentalized through commercialization. In neither era is it respected and seriously valued by mainstream American culture.

The Book of Daniel subjects the prevailing culture and

power structure to an incisive analysis, but it also questions and critiques the radical tradition. John Clayton [in "Radical Jewish Humanism: The Vision of E. L. Doctorow" (1983)] has called the novel "a work of brilliant cultural criticism, demolishing the American official myth of the Cold War, the sentimental counter-myth of heroic communist resistance, and even the myth of youth revolt of the sixties" (116). Although Doctorow undoubtedly has more sympathy with the radical tradition than Clayton's quotation seems to indicate, he is right in pointing out that Doctorow's analysis extends to those with whom he sympathizes.

Doctorow's use of the Isaacson' son Daniel as narrator is a brilliant device for capturing just the right blend of sympathy and criticism. As the son not just of the Isaacsons but of the radical tradition, Daniel has both the affection and the bitterness of a child of difficult parents. He is aware of the great flaws in his parents but retains a basic affection and respect for them. The fractured form of his narrative mirrors these divisions. He shifts back and forth from third to first person. Highly personal confessions about everything from his feelings toward his parents to sex with his wife are juxtaposed with impersonal analyses of post-World War II history and the radical mentality. As Daniel questions the meaning of his parents' radical activities and their fate, he utilizes academic analysis (he is a PhD candidate at Columbia), but the personal anguish he feels continually breaks through the objective facade. The result is a sympathetic but clear-eyed view of his parents and their politics.

Paul and Rochelle Isaacson emerge not as the heroic martyrs portrayed in leftist propaganda but as people from a particular time and place who adopt Communist ideology but are beset by the ordinary psychological, social, and economic concerns of the petite bourgeoisie and who are overwhelmed by events beyond their control. For Paul, Communist ideology provides the tools to analyze and understand the injustice he sees around him. The attraction is intellectual and idealistic, and Paul endlessly analyzes news events and the media that report events. As Daniel says of his father, "He was tendentious!" (47). For Rochelle, politics are not theoretical or abstract but personal and emotional. Daniel compares his mother's communism to his grandmother's Judaism—both represent "some purchase on the future against the terrible life of the present" (53). The coming of socialism is like the promise of heaven—a reward for those who suffer and keep the faith.

Although very different, Paul's idealism and Rochelle's emotionalism and cynicism are both out of touch with reality, are both extreme attitudes that leave them ill-prepared for their persecution by the government. As Levine has pointed out, their limitations and those of the Left contribute to their destruction:

Guilty of self-deception, both parents become accomplices in their own destruction. This illuminates one of Doctorow's themes: the compulsion of the American Left to implicate itself in its own martyrdom. . . . So we may say that the Isaacsons are co-conspirators along with the FBI and the Communist Party in their own immolation. (43)

Indeed, when the Isaacsons are arrested, the Communist party disclaims them and only later reclaims them when it sees their potential propaganda value as martyrs. Daniel's parents and their friends see themselves at the heart of a great movement in the vanguard of history, but Daniel comes to see them as marginalized figures whose significance in postwar America is grossly overestimated both by themselves and the US government.

Both the limits and the value of a radical viewpoint are present in very different ways in *Ragtime*. Whereas Doctorow uses Daniel's analysis and his flamboyant ironies and narrative tricks to present the radical view in *The Book of Daniel*, he utilizes a flat, pseudotextbook style filled with implicit ironies and contradictions in *Ragtime*.
—Stephen Cooper

When Daniel meets the New Left in the person of Artie Sternlicht, he encounters someone aware of the failures of the old Left but unaware of his own shortcomings. Artie's critique of the 1940s radicals centers on their participation in the system of American life and their reliance on the Soviet Union. Artie concludes, "The American Communist Party set the Left back fifty years. I think they worked for the FBI" (166). While Artie's analysis has some validity, he seems unaware of his own limitations. He has a general disregard for history—he has a mural on his wall entitled "EVERYTHING THAT CAME BEFORE IS ALL THE SAME" (151). Without some ability to understand the past and make distinctions, the New Left will have difficulty analyzing the present. Also, even though Artie Sternlicht may have contempt for the Isaacsons, like them he believes he is in the vanguard of a great movement. Granted, the antiwar movement of the 1960s enlisted more people and had more effect than the American communism of the 1940s, but Daniel knows from bitter experience the powers of the establishment. When Daniel is beaten and arrested during an antiwar march, his attitude is different from that of the other protesters—he sees their joy in being jailed as naive. Finally, Daniel recognizes the severe limits in the ideological temperament. When he leaves Artie Sternlicht's apartment, he says, "And I went home reacquainted with the merciless radi-

cal temperament" (170). Even though the radical's analysis of economic and social phenomena may be correct, the single-minded focus can miss important aspects of reality. As Sam B. Girgus [in "In His Own Voice: E. L. Doctorow's *The Book of Daniel*" (1988)] has said, "Whatever else Daniel's book achieves, it certainly promulgates an idea that love, liberation and oppression require a discussion that includes more than class warfare and historical materialism" (86).

Both the limits and the value of a radical viewpoint are present in very different ways in *Ragtime*. Whereas Doctorow uses Daniel's analysis and his flamboyant ironies and narrative tricks to present the radical view in *The Book of Daniel*, he utilizes a flat, pseudotextbook style filled with implicit ironies and contradictions in *Ragtime*. The racism and cultural tunnel vision of America at the beginning of the twentieth century is concisely captured in the opening description of the novel: "There were no Negroes. There were no immigrants" (4). Doctorow uses the humorist's method that often served Mark Twain so well: making outrageous or shocking statements in a matter-of-fact voice. Embedded in lists of social data on turn-of-the-century America are sentences such as, "Across America sex and death were barely distinguishable" (5), and "America was a great farting country" (94). Using the textbook language so often employed to create and perpetuate the myths of America, he destroys those myths, especially the myth of America as the melting pot where anyone with determination can succeed.

Doctorow applies this method with devastating effect to such historical figures as J. P. Morgan and Henry Ford. These great capitalists are shown to be greedy, egomaniacal men, but Doctorow's weapons are humor and irony rather than analysis and denunciation. He simply lets each man present his ideas on success and reincarnation—Morgan's based on extensive research, Ford's on a twenty-five-cent pamphlet—and the ironies are manifest. Their philosophies simply justify their own greed and sense of power. Doctorow deals in a similar manner with his purely "fictional" characters. The destruction of Coalhouse Walker's car by Willie Conklin and his eventual destruction by white society are presented matter-of-factly, and this very flatness of presentation highlights the horror of the racism in this society. The only ideological critiques are Emma Goldman's relatively simple statements, such as: "The oppressor is wealth, my friends. Wealth is the oppressor. Coalhouse Walker did not need Red Emma to learn that. He needed only to suffer" (322). Within *Ragtime*, the reader need only see the suffering to learn Emma Goldman's simple message.

Although Emma Goldman is presented favorably, the possibilities of radical action are clearly questioned. Coalhouse Walker is driven by injustice to take violent, seemingly revolutionary action. His followers feel they belong to an integrated community committed to social justice. During the course of events, "they were so transformed as to speak of themselves collectively as Coalhouse" and to believe they could "do something so terrible bad in this town, no one ever mess with a colored man for fear he belong to Coalhouse" (284-85). But while his followers are turning his cause into a crusade for social justice, Coalhouse sticks to his simple demand for personal justice—the restoration of his car by Willie Conklin. Coalhouse gets his car fixed, but the wider ambitions of his followers are thwarted. He makes a deal to save his followers, a deal they object to because it denies their revolutionary ambitions and focuses on Coalhouse's car. His followers escape to a life of underground, ineffective resistance, while Coalhouse stays to be gunned down by the police. Mother's Younger Brother plays the most exotic revolutionary role, becoming for a while a bomb maker for Emiliano Zapata in Mexico. However, Zapata's revolution fails and Mother's Younger Brother is killed. The triumph of the powers that be can be seen in the fact that the impetus for the resolution of Coalhouse's occupation of the Morgan Library comes from J. P. Morgan himself in a short telegram: "GIVE HIM HIS AUTOMOBILE AND HANG HIM" (331). Despite their appeal and the excitement they create, these revolutionaries stand little chance against capitalist power.

> **Although *Ragtime* provides an incisive, humorous critique of American society from a leftist perspective, it provides little hope of real progress or change.**
> —*Stephen Cooper*

Unlike Coalhouse Walker, Tateh, the Jewish immigrant in the novel, begins as a self-conscious social activist, but the system does not destroy Tateh, it co-opts him. As a Socialist working under horrible conditions in the textile mills of Lawrence, Massachusetts, Tateh is overjoyed when the workers go out on strike. He offers what help he can to the strike committee, but as time passes he becomes more concerned with the fate of his daughter, the only family he has. After police violence turns public opinion against the owner, the strikers win their demands, but Tateh feels alienated from industrial life and the working class by his experience in Lawrence. He realizes that the "victory" of the strikers is largely illusory: "The I.W.W. has won, he said. But what has it won? A few more pennies in wages. Will it now own the mills? No" (149). So Tateh turns his back on his Socialist past and points "his life along the lines of flow of American energy" (153), becoming an entrepreneur, then a movie director, thus realizing the "American dream" by selling it. What makes Doctorow's portrait of Tateh interesting is that even as he seemingly "sells out" his radical past, Tateh remains a likable figure. His motives, particularly his concern

for his daughter, are human and understandable. Doctorow has said, "As compassionate as we feel for Tateh and as much as we love him, here's a man who has betrayed his principles and sympathies and gotten ahead that way" ("Spirit of Transgression" 45). Through Tateh, Doctorow shows us the very real and understandable temptations for an intelligent, energetic man to compromise his principles in order to succeed within the system he supposedly opposes.

Although *Ragtime* provides an incisive, humorous critique of American society from a leftist perspective, it provides little hope of real progress or change. Arthur Saltzman notes, "Little has changed despite all that has occurred in *Ragtime;* the novel opens with Father making a living from patriotism, and the market still exists when the novel's frame is completed years later. Thus, as in every Doctorow novel, the dominant American mythology remains relatively intact" (99). The American mythology may mask many forms of iniquity and oppression, but it is a powerfully appealing myth. In *Ragtime* and in other works, Doctorow provides a clever critique of the myth without losing sight of its basic appeal and the problems that appeal causes for radical critics and reformers.

The appeal of the myth of the powerful self-made man is explored in depth in *Loon Lake.* F. W. Bennett, the original proprietor of the remote Adirondack estate called Loon Lake, has been described as an archetypical capitalist by Gross, as "an allegorical representative of that obscene power of money in capitalism, especially in its imperialist, monopoly stage" (141). Yet the narrator of the novel, Joe of Paterson, comes to identify with Bennett and eventually becomes his adopted son and replicates his life. In pointing out Joe's identification with Bennett, Jochen Barkhausen [in "Determining the True Colors of the Chameleon" (1988)] describes Bennett as a "personal incorporation of the American Dream, of absolute power and freedom and manic energy" (134). Gross's view of Bennett needs to be balanced by Barkhausen's if we are to understand why Joe is fascinated by Bennett. Wealth in America may be obscene power, but to someone like Joe—born poor, forced to live by his wits at a young age—money can become equated with freedom and energy. In some sense, Joe does what Tateh does in *Ragtime*—he points "his life along the lines of flow of American energy" and the current in those lines is money.

Joe is not alone in this novel when he turns his back on his working class origins. Levine has noted that Joe, Penfield, the poet who is the son of a coal miner, and Clara, Joe's mistress, all flee their backgrounds, and, "[i]n renouncing their respective familial legacies they all reject the ideal of class solidarity for the ideal of individual realization" (73). In the careers of these characters, and of the traitorous union officer Red James, Doctorow illustrates the difficulties of constructing a meaningful, broad-based opposition to American business interests. Not only must such a movement face entrenched, well-financed power, but there is always the temptation for talented, intelligent members of the working class to sell out. The reader can easily see why Joe would want to escape from Paterson or why Penfield would not want to become a coal miner. It is also no surprise that their notions of success—economic and literary—should be based to some extent on the powerful and privileged in their society. Thus, even the clearly articulated plight of their fellow men and women is not always enough to convince working people to subsume their individual desires in the interest of the common good.

All this is not to say that in *Loon Lake* Doctorow abandons his leftist ideals. In fact, the impersonal, predatory nature of capitalism is made clear whether the businessman is the industrialist Bennett or Sim Hearns, the proprietor of the carnival that Joe works for. What makes this indictment of capitalism and of Bennett interesting is that it is composed by Joe, who in many ways becomes Bennett. Barkhausen sees Joe's criticism of and ambivalence toward Bennett as a "displaced confrontation with himself" (135) and maintains that his story is an indictment of Bennett's life despite Joe's identification with Bennett (136-37). Barkhausen remarks, "No doubt, in reviewing his life Joe comes to the conclusion that the beginning of his career marked the death of the substance of his life" (135). Despite his tremendous financial and political success, Joe comes to realize that he has sacrificed some essential part of his self to achieve it. In his reckoning of his life, he sees that the freedom and power he had wanted are not identical with the freedom and power of wealth symbolized by F. W. Bennett. When Joe returns to Loon Lake after his cross-country flight with Clara, he finds Bennett a distraught, broken man after the death of his wife Lucinda. Bennett had tried and failed to isolate and protect himself with wealth. When writing his book years later, Joe has learned the same lesson after following in Bennett's footsteps—money may isolate, but it is not a real escape from the pains and limitations of life. While making Joe's career and his choices understandable, Doctorow, through his use of Joe as narrator and the ironies that entails, has shown the value of a leftist view and class solidarity through the career of someone who betrayed that solidarity. Ironically, that value is as much emotional and personal as it is social and political—the two strands cannot be separated.

Doctorow's most recent novel, *Billy Bathgate* (1989), has much in common with *Loon Lake.* Both novels tell the story of a poor working-class boy who escapes his past to achieve wealth and success. Like Joe of Paterson, Billy Bathgate has a powerful mentor and briefly runs off with his mentor's mistress. Both novels describe the attraction of money and power for a poor young man. The chief difference between the novels is that Joe's mentor is a "legitimate" businessman,

whereas Billy's mentor is the notorious gangster Dutch Schultz.

> In *Billy Bathgate,* as in *Welcome to Hard Times,* Doctorow uses a popular genre, in this case the gangster story, to project and critique the myths of American capitalism. In many ways this indirect, mythic approach is more devastating than the direct presentation of a rich businessman in *Loon Lake.*
>
> —Stephen Cooper

On the surface there may seem a great difference between the polished, sophisticated F. W. Bennett and the violent, uncouth Dutch Schultz, but Doctorow shows us that Schultz thinks of himself as just another businessman. Schultz tells Billy that "the crime business like any other needs the constant attention of the owner to keep it going" and that his business is "a very complex enterprise not only of supply and demand but of subtle executive details and diplomatic skills" (64-65). Even slitting a rival's throat in a barber's chair is described as "a planned business murder as concise and to the point as a Western Union telegram" (106). When Abbadabba Berman, Schultz's top aide, explains to Billy why cooperation and merger seem inevitable among the crime syndicates, he uses the example of railroad companies "cutting each other's throats" (144) before merging and forming monopolies for each section of the country. The gangsters simply make the metaphor literal.

In *Billy Bathgate,* as in *Welcome to Hard Times,* Doctorow uses a popular genre, in this case the gangster story, to project and critique the myths of American capitalism. In many ways this indirect, mythic approach is more devastating than the direct presentation of a rich businessman in *Loon Lake.* Doctorow shows us that the brutal world of the gangsters is not an aberration but the natural outgrowth of a social order based on wealth. Is there much difference between the F. W. Bennett who hires gangsters and industrial spies to protect his profits and to keep his work force in line and the Dutch Schultz who uses his violent outbursts to control his subordinates and to intimidate his rivals in order to keep the money flowing? Are the desires of Dutch and Billy for the luxury, respect, and style that money can buy different from those of most ambitious businessmen? When Billy Bathgate, through luck and pluck, acquires a rich benefactor and begins his rise in the world, he is reenacting a version of the Horatio Alger myth, albeit with many ironic twists. The irony is emphasized for the reader at the beginning because Billy's vision is unironic—he intends to rise in the organization through hard work and loyalty, as if he were a management trainee for GM rather than an errand boy for the mob.

Doctorow's use of the gangster genre and the Horatio Alger myth helps us see the attraction of the very institutions he criticizes. Billy's adolescent view of organized crime is glamorized by the myths and legends surrounding the crime bosses. The popularity of books and movies about gangsters shows the fascination of money and power, no matter how obtained, for ordinary people. For a boy of the streets such as Billy—poor, fatherless, yet ambitious—the pull of the mob is strong. Once again, Doctorow creates a tension between the political critique embedded in his novel and the understandable personal motives of a central character. He acknowledges the great attraction of power based on wealth while at the same time revealing the corrupting force of money.

Paradoxically, Doctorow's novels seem to assert simultaneously the value of political analysis and its limitations. The value of a radical viewpoint is that it can force us to see things in new ways, that it can shake us out of our complacencies. In this sense it is an appropriate subject or motif for fiction. Doctorow has said, "Fiction has no borders, everything is open. You have a limitless possibility of knowing the truth" ("Spirit of Transgression" 47). Doctorow uses a political perspective in his novels to point out the unpleasant truths we would rather ignore. In a sense his novels do what Emma Goldman does in *Ragtime*—they raise difficult questions for our society.

But because "everything is open," Doctorow does not stop his criticism and analysis at the borders of radical thought. Although sympathetic to the radicals' views, he does not exempt them from scrutiny. In particular, he seems to reject any special utopian claims for socialism or communism. In his novels there are no magical transformations. In fact, the prospects for social change are almost nil at the end of each of his novels. A sort of radical skepticism seems to be at the root of Doctorow's politics. He has said:

> But surely the sense we have to have now of twentieth-century political alternatives is the kind of exhaustion of them all. . . . But certainly everything else has been totally discredited: capitalism, communism, socialism. None of it seems to work. No system, whether it's religious or anti-religious or economic or materialistic, seems to be invulnerable to human venery and greed and insanity. So it seems to me that anyone who likes to think about these things seriously in an effort to find some mediation between individual psychology and large social movements has to be going in the right direction.
> (**"The Writer as Independent Witness"** 65)

The point of his fiction then becomes not the elucidation of a principle but the exploration of the always dynamic interaction of the individual and society, of the believer and reality. His interest is less in the symmetry of an ideological position than in how real people with human drives and limitations wrestle with social ideals, sometimes accommodating them and sometimes compromising them.

I have said that the possibility for social change seems slim in most of Doctorow's novels. This statement does not mean that his work is defeatist or cynical. The dynamic between individual characters and their social circumstances is often riveting and lively, and the possibilities for growth are never denied. Doctorow has pointed out that "the radical ideas of one generation make up the orthodoxy of subsequent generations" (**"Spirit of Transgression"** 44). Perhaps the real point of the novels is that we cannot lose our humanity if we continue to struggle with our relationship to our society with an open, flexible, critical mind.

Ann V. Miller (essay date Summer 1993)

SOURCE: "Through a Glass Clearly: Vision as Structure in E. L. Doctorow's 'Willi'," in *Studies in Short Fiction*, Vol. 30, No. 3, Summer, 1993, pp. 337-42.

[*In the following essay, Miller provides a detailed analysis of* "Willi," *from* Lives of the Poets, *pointing out its psychological complexities.*]

In his significant work on *Remembrance of Things Past*, Roger Shattuck argues that three principles of vision clarify the division of Proust's book and constitute its most fundamental structure. Borrowing his terms from film, Shattuck names these principles cinematographic, montage, and stereoscopic. The young see through only one lens: their first experience of reality, Shattuck asserts, "is cinematographic and linear, . . . conveying a sense of cause and effect. . . . Subsequently, this secure sense of predictability is disrupted when we encounter contradictions and alterations in Nature and, above all, in people" (57). A second phase, corresponding to the montage principle, is roughly one of disenchantment and "makes one aware of conflict and contrasts" (58). Finally the stereoscopic principle "allows our binocular (or multi-ocular) vision of mind to hold these contradictions in the steady perspective of recognition . . ." (51), in effect, to balance them so that the "mature" vision ultimately accommodates opposing views.

The first two modes of vision may be seen as operating in the fiction of initiation. Such a notion as prototype or model is entirely too restrictive for the range and scope of this genre but can perhaps be useful in exploring the journey, however tentative, from innocence to experience. E. L. Doctorow's **"Willi"** is particularly appropriate to examine this movement from one vision to another: specifically, that of the adolescent foray into montage.

Surely one of the most lyrical statements of the loss of innocence in contemporary fiction, Doctorow's **"Willi"** is central to his 1984 collection, *Lives of the Poets,* accurately dramatizing what Doctorow refers to in the title story as "a state of clarity, of coming into being" (125). Achingly meditative, the story is one of apocalyptic vision, set in Galicia just before World War I will bring to an end the Austro-Hungarian Empire. Formalist in treatment—at points a metafiction—the story strikes the familiar Oedipal note. The young protagonist, Willi, witnesses his mother's act of infidelity and subsequently both desires and betrays her, inexorably bringing about his family's doom. "I was the agency of [my father's] downfall. Ancestry and myth, culture, history, and time were ironically composed in the shape of his own boy" (33).

> **Surely one of the most lyrical statements of the loss of innocence in contemporary fiction, Doctorow's "Willi" is central to his 1984 collection, *Lives of the Poets,* accurately dramatizing what Doctorow refers to in the title story as "a state of clarity, of coming into being."**
> —*Ann V. Miller*

"Willi" is a fiction of memory, but memory that has been filtered, and that is still being filtered through a narrator—now child, now adult—presenting an impression of immediacy yet of subtly detached understanding. "We posit an empirical world, yet how can I be here at this desk in this room—and not be here? . . . memory is in the ontological sense another reality" (29). This fluid point of view fuses adult-observer and youth-participant into one narrative voice, making it possible for Doctorow to avoid both the limits of language and the limited perspective of youth and thus encompass all three visions.

Thirteen-year-old Willi has lived the most sheltered of existences: aside from his family and a tutor who lives on the premises, he is totally "alone, isolated on our estate . . ." (32). Doctorow focuses precisely on the absence of any contact with other children. In his rural isolation Willi "has no friends": he is "not allowed to play with the village children, or to go to their crude schools" (32). Nor is he "permitted to play with the children of the peasants" who work on his parents' estate. In such limiting circumstances, Willi has made a "trinity of Mother and Tutor and Father" (31).

Doctorow's use of the words "crude" and "peasant" clearly reflect both the prominence and the arrogance of the father, who is for Willi "the god-eye in the kingdom, the intelligence that brought order and gave everything its value" (32). The young son is "in awe" of and in effect worships this patriarchal figure, seeing him as a sort of mythical presence. "He lived in the universe of giant powers by understanding it and making it serve him . . ." (32). "A strong man, stocky and powerful" (32), Willi's father is fiercely independent, existing in "the pride of the self-constructed self" (33). "A Jew who spoke no Yiddish, and a farmer raised in the city" (32), his father denies "every classification society imposes," living "as an anomaly, tied to no past . . ." (33), "in the state of abiding satisfaction given to individuals who are more than a match for the life they have chosen for themselves" (31). In this essentially autonomous world, Willi places his father as its "owner and manager" (32), even as its creator. "Papa," the narrator as grown-up son says, "I see you now in the universe of your own making" (29).

The mother—many years younger than the father—is also for Willi the object of deep affection, fully as significant in his life as the father. His reference to her at one point as "my kind sweet considerate mother" (31) scarcely catches the intensity of his feelings. It is she to whom Willi turns in moments of trouble, wanting her "to hug me and to hold my head and kiss me on the lips as she liked to do, I wanted her to make those wordless sounds of comfort as she held me to her when I was hurt or unhappy . . ." (30). And, as with the father, there is a sort of reverence, as if she is for him a madonna at whom he gazes "in wonder and awe" (35).

Altogether secure in this adult world but lacking the companionship of his peers, Willi spends much of his time alone, wandering the fields. His youthful response to nature is characteristically romantic. He feels "rising around me the exhalations of the field, the moist sweetness of the grasses, . . . the golden hay meadow, the blue sky" (27), and sees himself as an intimate of this world that has "chosen" him, communicates with him, and indeed "was giving [him] possession of itself" (28).

Against this solid sense of security and this radiant natural backdrop, Willi is forced to see with blinding sight another, darker universe. The climactic epiphany takes place within the first two of the story's nine pages: thereafter all is denouement. And it is precisely this drawn-out ending, with its fluid chronology, that affords the temporal dimension necessary for Willi to become an initiate into the multi-ocular stage of vision, in which he accepts that it is possible for a person to both love and betray at the same moment.

The earlier visions are dramatized in a single five-page unbroken paragraph. The first, set "one spring day" in a sundrenched meadow, depicts one of those enchanted and enchanting moments in which the child does not exist apart from the world but is "mingled in some divine embrace" (27). In Joycean fashion, style and content here coalesce: the sweeping rhythms of the sentences perfectly conjoin Willi's ecstatic state of consciousness, a "trance" in which he remains "incredibly aware." Such states, the narrator tells us, "come naturally to children. I was resonant with the hum of the universe, I was made indistinguishable from the world in a great bonding of natural revelation. . . . and I rose and seemed to ride on the planes of the sun" (27-28).

The felt immediacy of the boy's mystical ecstasy, the shock of recognition that propels him into manhood—these first visions of experience are rendered episodically and constitute the body of the narrative. But the stereoscopic is given only in brief flashes of philosophical insight by the narrator-protagonist, who has come to accept that no action, no sentiment, no person is simple or consistent. "I know now," he says, that "each moment has its belief and what we call treachery is the belief of each moment, the wish for it to be as it seems to be. It is possible in joy to love the person you have betrayed, and to be refreshed in your love for him, it is entirely possible" (30).

As is characteristic of stories dealing with initiation, Willi faces his traumatic experience alone. And, in what William Peden [in "Recent Fiction" *Western Humanities Review* 39 (1985)] describes as "an appalling climax . . . out Kafka-ing Kafka" (268), the young protagonist is cast out of his edenic state into a holocaust that tears his world apart. Doctorow has Willi move "along the white barn wall . . . to the window, a simple square without glass" (28), meeting—in mid-sentence, with no stylistic shift—the epiphanic moment of shock. From sun and sky, he is cast down into the awful mystery of some bestial floor:

> I moved my face into the portal of the cool darkness, and no longer blinded by the sunlight, my eyes saw on the straw and in the dung my mother, denuded, in a pose of utmost degradation, a body, a reddened headless body, the head enshrouded in her clothing, everything turned inside out. . . . all order, truth, and reason, and this defiled mama played violently upon and being made to sing her defilement. . . . My heart in my chest banged in sickened measure of her cries. (28-29)

"I was given," the narrator says, "double vision, the kind that comes with a terrible blow" (31). This montage vision, with its violently opposed contradictions, is expressed in the boy's ambivalent summing up: "I felt it was my *triumph*, but I felt *monstrously betrayed*" [emphasis added] . . . I wanted to leap through the window and drive a pitchfork into his back, but I wanted him to be killing her, I wanted him to be killing her for me" (29).

Doctorow carefully dramatizes this "double vision," juxtaposing to the scene of degradation its contrast: a dining room where Papa sits admiring and admired, godlike at the head of his table. Here the light is focused sharply on the mother's face. "Mama is so attentive. The candle flame burns in her eyes." In her "long neck, very white, . . . a soft slow pulse beats . . . Her eyes are for her husband, she is smiling at you in your loving proprietorship, proud of you, pleased to be yours, and the mistress of this house and the mother of this boy" (30).

The defiled body, the saintly face. Willi sees through each glass, clearly, but he cannot focus these opposing visions into one person. Nor can he find in Ledig, his tutor and his mother's adulterous partner, any duality, "any sign of smugness or leering pride or cruelty. There was nothing coarse about him, nothing that could possibly give me offense" (31).

The ending of the five-page paragraph signals the end of his childhood: "this unholy trinity of deception . . . had excommunicated me from my life at the age of thirteen. This of course in the calendar of traditional Judaism is the year a boy enjoys his initiation into manhood" (31). The sordid vision of his mother, headless on the barn floor, prevails. He cannot purge from his mind "the image of her overthrown body, . . . her shoed feet in the air"—an image reenacted nightly in his dreams, with Willi himself as the violator.

E. L. Doctorow's small masterpiece ["Willi"] catches the precise moment in the young protagonist's life when he is most happy, and most vulnerable. The author holds the binoculars steady, bringing the contrasts into a focus so sharp and clear that Willi's vision is irrevocably altered to a world that will hereafter include both beauty and terror, both the "divine embrace" of the beginning and the expulsion of the end.

—Ann V. Miller

Moving from panoramic to scenic, the narrator-as-adult holds time still to describe the mother as the young Willi gazes at her. Focusing on the physical, Doctorow suggests in ambiguous phrasing the adolescent vision of the mother both as chaste and as object of sexual desire. "She was incredibly beautiful, with her dark hair parted in the center and tied behind her in a bun, and her small hands, and the lovely fullness of her chin . . . her neck, so lovely and slim . . . the high modestly dressed bosom . . ." (34-35).

For several days the boy watches his mother, feeling such shame and terror that he is "continuously ill" to the point of nausea and "terrible waves of fever" (33). Having pitched the story to such a level of intensity, Doctorow pushes toward a second epiphanic moment in two brief and brilliant sentences holding both panorama and scene: "I made her scream ecstatically every night in my dreams and awoke one dawn in my own sap" (33). Guilt-ridden, Willi blurts out to his father as he mates a pair of hunting dogs, "Papa, they should be named Mama and Ledig" (34). The son, in Saltzman's words, "completes the Freudian wish by destroying the father" (87).

The final scene of the story constitutes one further crushing "terrific blow." Willi's father, who has been for him the embodiment of commanding dignity and self possession—"the intelligence that brought order and gave everything its value" (32)—is suddenly wrenched into unleashed animal fury. In this deconstructive final section, Doctorow's masterful handling of time (worthy of Borges or Faulkner) affords glimpses of all three visions—a sort of dialectic of *past* and what would become *future,* dissolving into observations by a narrator in the *present.* Structurally, this fluid chronology is here largely accomplished with a single interpolated sentence: "I have heard such terrible sounds of blows upon a body in Berlin after the war, Freikorps hoodlums in the streets attacking whores they had dragged from the brothel and tearing the clothes from their bodies and beating them to the cobblestones" (35). It is a remarkable sentence, exactly placed. Temporally, it bisects the scene, bringing the violent streets of the future into the bedroom of the past. That one brief statement hurls time forward into World War II, beyond the final sentence, which alludes to the destruction wrought by World War I. Rhetorically, it reduces the mother to "whore," the father to "hoodlum." The verbal constructions—"attacking," "tearing," "beating"—dramatize with terrible immediacy the possibilities of rage in the most disciplined of men.

And from this stereoscopic point of view, the mature Willi is forced to see in his younger self these same contradictions of love and betrayal. Both shocked and excited by the screams of his mother, terrified but "undeniably aroused", the boy attempts to retreat, "shouting at my father to stop, to stop." Then the narrator, as if escaping into the present, shifts radically from lyric passion to flat prosaic statement in an independent coda of two brief sentences that mark the end of youth, of empire, of all but memory: "This was in Galicia in the year 1910. All of it was to be destroyed anyway, even without me." Yet, in Saltzman's words, the protagonist "keeps witness and takes responsibility" (87). In its almost unbearable dramatic intensity **"Willi"** exemplifies not only a boy's terrible thrust into manhood but his maturation into the artist-writer, who is "now a man older than my father when he died" (29).

At 13, Willi is like the speaker in Houseman's *Last Poems:*

"a stranger and afraid / In a world [he] never made" (Housman 79). E. L. Doctorow's small masterpiece catches the precise moment in the young protagonist's life when he is most happy, and most vulnerable. The author holds the binoculars steady, bringing the contrasts into a focus so sharp and clear that Willi's vision is irrevocably altered to a world that will hereafter include both beauty and terror, both the "divine embrace" of the beginning and the expulsion of the end.

Stephen Fender (review date 27 May 1994)

SOURCE: "The Novelist as Liar," in *Times Literary Supplement,* May 27, 1994, p. 20.

[*In the following review, Fender considers points raised in essays in* Poets and Presidents *and discusses the thematic and aesthetic aspects of* The Waterworks *in relation to Doctorow's previous fiction.*]

"The development of civilizations", writes E. L. Doctorow in the earliest of the essays in ***Poets and Presidents,*** "is essentially a progression of metaphors." At this level of abstraction, the narratives of history and fiction are indistinguishable. On a more specific level, they diverge. The difference is that novelists are "born liars", who are to be trusted precisely because they admit to lying. Their documents are false, whereas the historians' can be verified. "History is a kind of fiction in which we live and hope to survive, and fiction is a kind of speculative history . . . by which the available data for the composition are seen to be greater and more various in their sources than the historian supposes."

The trouble is that so many others seek to break into the novelist's domain. Advertising transforms factual products into fiction. Even the "weather reports are constructed on television with exact attention to conflict (high pressure areas clashing with lows), suspense (the climax of tomorrow's weather prediction coming after the commercial), and other basic elements of narrative". Does Doctorow feel threatened by these inroads? Not at all. "The novelist's opportunity to do his work today", he concludes, "is increased by the power of the regime to which he finds himself in opposition."

Not everyone approves of that oppositional stance. As another essay reminds us, Robert Alter has claimed that *Catch-22* and Doctorow's own ***The Book of Daniel*** "were flawed by a spirit adversarial to the Republic". This comes as a bit of a shock: one of the brightest American critics attacking two of the best American novels written since the Second World War. Do even clever and learned Americans have trouble with political novels?

Doctorow thinks they do. "If a novel is about a labor union organizer, for example, or a family on welfare, it is assumed to be political, that is, impure, as for example a novel about life in a prep school is not." Political novels are all right if they're written by foreigners—by Nadine Gordimer or Milan Kundera or Günter Grass—but not if they come from Americans on the domestic scene. "This is analogous to President Reagan's support of workers' movements as long as they are in Poland."

This "aesthetic piety" Doctorow traces to the American tendency, even among working people, to refuse to assign people to a class, and instead to define themselves "not by their work but what they own from their work". So the American novel values the individual predicament, almost irrespective of the historical forces that condition it. Hemingway's Robert Jordan dies alone, loyal not to a cause but to his own code of honour. "The most international of American writers was, morally speaking, an isolationist. War is the means by which one's cultivated individualism can be raised to the heroic. And, therefore, never send to ask for whom the bell tolls; it tolls so that I can be me."

As its title makes clear, *The Book of Daniel* (1971) elevates this contrast between official and hidden history to the urgency of an apocalypse.
—*Stephen Fender*

Trenchant and illuminating as they are on topics ranging from Dreiser and Jack London to popular songs and the American Constitution, these essays provide a key to the author's own work in a way that no other criticism by a contemporary novelist does. For the project of Doctorow's fiction has been to deconstruct crucial episodes in American political history and to rebuild them out of the hidden, or suppressed, or forgotten "false documents" of his own speculative imagination. *Welcome to Hard Times* (1961) is an anti-western, morally demoting the romantic outlaw to an impersonal, destructive force. In order to explore that restless era before the First World War, when conventional social and political categories were being undermined—and reality itself rendered problematic by the movies and the new "science" of publicity—the plot of *Ragtime* (1974) brings the narratives of fiction and history together, involving imaginary characters with actual figures like Emma Goldman, Harry Houdini and Evelyn Nesbit.

As its title makes clear, *The Book of Daniel* (1971) elevates this contrast between official and hidden history to the urgency of an apocalypse. Against the red scare following the Second World War, the institutionalization of the Cold War in the Truman Doctrine and the execution of the Rosenbergs,

the novel juxtaposes an alternative politics known only to an elect group of adepts. Daniel's father tells him "things I could never find in my American History, about Andrew Carnegies's Coal and Iron Police, and Jay Gould's outrages . . . about using imported Chinese labor like cattle to build the West, and of breeding Negroes and working them to death in the South".

If Doctorow's false documents were just false, they would stand no chance against the official facts they confront. It is their documentary nature—or the appearance of it—that makes them authentic. Early novels like *Don Quixote* or *Clarissa* often disclaimed their fictions, pretending merely to be transmitting editions of letters or long-lost manuscripts. Their authors' tactic was "to use other voices than their own . . . and present themselves not as authors but as literary executors". Doctorow doesn't revert to these expedients, but in his more recent novels, he distances the narrative voice from his own, to suit it to theme and period. *Ragtime* is written in short, clipped, impersonal sentences. Not until the penultimate page of the novel does the narrative abandon the "documentary" mask of the third person. By contrast, the indulgent first-person narrative of *Billy Bathgate* moves in long, sinuous sentences often filling whole paragraphs.

The Waterworks takes the experiment a stage further. The new novel is voiced in a first-person which uses the balanced periods and formal address of Victorian prose, while reaching out, like Walt Whitman, to shake a later generation by its lapels:

> You may think you are living in modern times, here and now, but that is the necessary illusion of every age. We did not conduct ourselves as if we were preparatory to your time. There was nothing quaint or colourful about us, I assure you. New York after the war was more creative, more deadly, more of a genius society than it is now. Our rotary presses put fifteen, twenty thousand newspapers on the street for a penny or two. Enormous steam engines powered the mills and factories. Gas lamps lit the streets at night. We were three-quarters of a century into the Industrial Revolution.

What sort of book is *The Waterworks*? It is a Poe-like novel of detection, but a story in which the mystery, as befits Doctorow's project, involves civic, as well as familial and individual issues. Martin Pemberton, who works as a freelance for the journalist narrator, thinks that his rich father has died, leaving him penniless after an argument over the sources of the old man's wealth: slave trading and the supply of shoddy goods to the Union Army. Then one day, Martin sees an uncanny thing. "At the intersection of Broadway and Prince Street . . . was a white city stage. . . . The passengers consisted solely of old men in black coats and top hats. Their heads nodded in unison as the vehicle stopped and started again in the impacted traffic." One of those old men Martin recognizes as his father. Delusion? Actuality? Read it and find out. The answer is perfectly rational—frighteningly so. The inventive details of this improbable but believable chain of events are what make the novel worth reading.

It may be too pat to characterize *The Waterworks* as Doctorow's allegory of the Reagan era. But that is what it is—just as *Catch-22,* though set in the Second World War, is Heller's comment on McCarthyism. In both worlds (that's why Doctorow's narrator has insisted on the modernity of post-Civil War New York), technology has institutionalized the efficient production and distribution of every civic good save one: information, charity, law enforcement, power and light, are organized; only wealth remains undistributed. Rich old men can rob their families and corrupt the system to corner the most advanced medical care in the world, while their fellow citizens—a phrase they would never use except in a political speech—die of hunger and common-place diseases. And the more monolithic the civic system becomes, the better its networks and connections, the more easily it can be corrupted.

The Waterworks, like all good novels of detection, resolves its mystery through the patient investigations of freelancers and renegades: reporters and policemen out of favour with their bosses. And that's what Doctorow is too. Though hardly out of favour with his public and hardly languishing for want of sales and literary prizes, he remains something of a renegade in his pursuit of the American historical imagination.

John Whitworth (review date 28 May 1994)

SOURCE: "A Wonderful Town, Even Then," in *Spectator,* Vol. 272, No. 8655, May 28, 1994, p. 33.

[In the following review, Whitworth informs the reader of the style and thematic concerns of The Waterworks.*]*

The Waterworks is a marvellous book, gathering such momentum that I read the last 120 pages in one go at four o'clock in the morning. Doctorow has given us a novel of the prelapsarian state, a late 19th-century novel. something out of Conrad and James, out of Stevenson and Wells and Conan Doyle. Of course it's a bit of a cheek, taking this American for our own, for this is a book about New York in the years after Lincoln's assassination. And perhaps Doctorow would prefer to make his bow to Theodore Dreiser (on whom he has written two fine essays); he quotes F. O. Mathiessen—Dreiser was "virtually the first major American writer whose family name was not English or Scotch-

Irish." And therefore, I take it, a direct literary ancestor of Doctorow himself.

The novel is a celebration of 19th-century New York in the grip of a Boss called William Marcy Tweed. Deep in British ignorance, I was unsure whether Tweed was fact or fiction, a historical fiction like the South American dictator of Conrad's *Nostromo.* But fat, bald, red-bearded, twinkling Tweed is fact. So much I gleaned from Doctorow's essay **"The Nineteenth New York."**

The waterworks is also fact, together with the white-painted stages of the omnibus company. Lincoln's funeral and all the careful documentation of New York in 1871. And the plot, "one man's search for the truth about his father's death" (the publisher's words), is fiction, beautiful fiction like a well-oiled piece of machinery, one of those Conradian plots before plot descended from the "literary" to detective stories and science fiction and P. G. Wodehouse, before people like me stopped reading those damned thick books with "literature" written all over them.

> **Of course the waterworks is a symbol.
> Why else give a novel such a boring title?**
> *—John Whitworth*

Conrad for the fictionalised history, James (or Conan Doyle) for the unravelling of crime. Stevenson/Wells. *Dr Jekyll and Mr Hyde* and *The Island of Dr Moreau* for the frisson of horror as the scientist steps into our century, announcing coolly that God is dead and stirring up what might be better left alone. Doctorow's scientist is Dr Sartorius, who goes in for a ghoulish form of tailoring.

I am reduced to this obliqueness because the book is so like a detective story in one respect, that if I revealed the machinations of the plot I would be as bad as those biro-wielding autodidacts, scribbling "The Butler done it" at the top of page one.

Of course the waterworks is a symbol. Why else give a novel such a boring title? Doctorow tells us in his essay that New York's waterworks system was put in place in the 1840s. He mentions a viaduct with 15 Roman arches, and keeps up the conceit of New York as an industrialised ancient Rome, a technological, godless marvel, the New City, the first modern city.

And it is to the Croton holding reservoir that New Yorkers go (for there is as yet no Central Park)—"They strolled along the parapet arm in arm and were soothed in their spirits." "This," says the narrator-newspaperman, "was the closest we could come to pastoral." But a lowering pastoral, for "the bouldered retaining walls were 25 feet thick and rose 44 feet in an inward-leaning slant. The design was Egyptian." Which is seemly, for the pyramids stand for a kind of godless immortality of the rich. If there is no transcendental reality then not-dying is the summit of all happiness.

Getting rich and living for ever!

> The war of secession made New York rich. When it was over there was nothing to stop progress—no classical ruins of idea, no superstitions to retard civil republican ardor. Not that much had to be destroyed or over-turned . . .

This is from the essay, and also, with minimal changes, from the novel. And the novel goes on:

> Nowhere else in the world was there such an acceleration of energies. A mansion would appear in a field. The next day it stood on a city street with horse and carriage riding by.

Why are there no long poems now—or not many you and I would want to read? Because the long poems are novels. This is one, written in a supple and subtle, multi-claused and pre-modernist prose, a voice which isn't quite (it is clear from other essays) Doctorow's distinguished professional one. He is Professor of American and English Letters at NY University. And a wonderful novelist.

Jonathan Franzen (review date 19 June 1994)

SOURCE: "Where Our Troubles Began," in *Los Angeles Times Book Review,* June 19, 1994, pp. 1, 8.

[*In the following review, Franzen discusses the setting, character and plot of* The Waterworks *and compares the book to* Ragtime, Billy Bathgate *and* The Book of Daniel.]

The imaginative universe of E. L. Doctorow is as unbounded in time as it is spatially restricted by his love and hatred of New York. He travels through history by means of inference, from old buildings. His characters are like genies conjured up by the mental stroking of New York City landmarks—the Morgan Library in *Ragtime,* Bathgate Avenue in *Billy Bathgate,* the fairgrounds in *World's Fair,* P.S. 70 in *The Book of Daniel.*

His new book, *The Waterworks,* seems to have been inspired by the reservoir and dam at Croton, just north of New York City. (I venture this guess in part because Croton appears in the book, and in part because I've been there myself. I've looked out on the imposing dam, the impounded water and I've had the thought: There's a novel here.)

Doctorow has found the novel not in any realistic history of the waterworks, but in their mythic being, their symbolic pairing of nature's immensity and civilization's presumption. What makes Doctorow our most exciting historical novelist, aside from sheer talent and audacity, is his perception that history can only be reconstructed, never re-experienced. However anxious a character named Eisenhower may be on the eve of D-day, it's hard for readers in 1994 to share in his suspense. Hindsight inevitably estranges us from historical figures, punctures the illusion of their free will, and so undermines the sense of identification on which realism depends. This is why Doctorow's best novels (*Ragtime, Billy Bathgate*) aspire less to be imitations of life than to be sophisticated toys for grownups.

> The imaginative universe of E. L. Doctorow is as unbounded in time as it is spatially restricted by his love and hatred of New York.
> —*Jonathan Franzen*

The setting of *The Waterworks* is New York City in 1871. The industrialized North has recently won the Civil War, and Boss Tweed and his ring are milking a metropolis financially engorged by victory. "Almost a million people called New York home, everyone securing his needs in a state of cheerful degeneracy. Nowhere else in the world was there such an acceleration of energies. A mansion would appear in a field. The next day it stood on a city street with horse and carriage riding by."

The narrator of the novel, whose voice is heard here, is a newspaper editor named McIlvaine, a man whose poetic gifts do interesting battle with his rationalism. In lieu of children, the unmarried McIlvaine has a "clutch" of free-lance writers, and one afternoon his favorite of them, an angry young man named Martin Pemberton, comes into the newspaper office with a bloodied face and torn shirt and says: "He's alive . . . my father, Augustus Pemberton. He is alive."

McIlvaine the rationalist knows that Augustus Pemberton, a vilely wealthy wartime profiteer and former slave trader, has been dead and buried for half a year. He shrugs off the son's words as "a poetic way of characterizing the wretched city that neither of us loved, but neither of us could leave." Soon enough, however, Martin vanishes from New York. The story he leaves behind with friends contains the first of the series of powerful images that together form the novel's mainspring.

In roaming lower Manhattan in a rainstorm, it seems, Martin has caught sight of a horse-drawn city omnibus occupied by six somber men in black coats and black top hats. "They are old men, or ill enough to look old, and eerily unmindful of the world." One of them, from the egg-like wen on the back of his neck, Martin identifies positively as his father.

Lest there be any doubt about the young man's sanity, we learn that the same thing has happened a second time, on 42nd Street during a snowstorm. Again a public conveyance, again the men in black. And again a glimpse of old Augustus, "who at the same moment turns an incurious gaze upon [Martin]. A moment later the entire equipage is swallowed up by the storm."

These twin sightings, with their Gothic atmospherics, set the novel's machinery in motion. To reveal more of the story would spoil the book's main pleasure, which consists of McIlvaine's investigation of Martin's disappearance, the alternate confounding and confirming of his rationalism. *The Waterworks* is a detective quest of exceptional single-mindedness.

Exceptional, and in some ways lamentable. Readers of this book will wait in vain for the irony and sensuality of *Ragtime,* the sumptuous prose and vivid characters of *Billy Bathgate,* the viscerality of *The Book of Daniel.* Despite the occasional anachronism (my Webster's has him using *intelligentsia* 35 years too early), the novel is notable for sounding genuinely old-fashioned. The author achieves a woodenness of character reminiscent of William Dean Howells, and the narration tends, like much of Wilkie Collins, to be both laborious and overheated.

> The *longueurs* and fascinations of *The Waterworks* are those of a toy whose colorful casings have been removed. We're given the austere spectacle of shiny gears and naked symbols; also the tedium of a toy that leaves little to the imagination; and finally the mystery that a thing so frankly contrived can still affect us. Uningratiating but visionary, the book invites us to peer back to the verge of modern industrial society—and shows us ourselves peering forward.
> —*Jonathan Franzen*

The pages are weighted with unnecessary recapitulations and heavy-handed underlings of abstract themes. There are several thousand sets of portentous ellipses, in passages like this: "I had staked out my claim to a story, in effect negotiating with the police for my rights in it . . . but, after all, how

phantom it was . . . no more than a hope for words on a page . . . insubstantial words . . . phantom names. . . ." Everywhere, you get the sense of an author who has despaired of showing and begun to tell.

And yet, and yet—what a kicker of an insanely dark secret Doctorow has planted at the center of his machine! Despite the novel's Gotheric rhetoric and rhythms and allegorical transparency, the ultimate shock to McIlvaine's ordering of the world comes not from any supernatural horror but from the vastness and modernity of the urban conspiracy that he unearths. Doctorow is pointing less to Transylvania than to Auschwitz when McIlvaine, near the novel's climax, speaks of feeling "not fear or dread . . . but a desolate bleakness." A few pages later he speaks again of being "haunted . . . not by ghosts, but by Science."

Apparently any universe both finite and unbounded, even an imaginative one, exhibits paradoxes of curvature. Following the history of modern New York back to its earliest limits, to a time when Central Park and the Brooklyn Bridge are works in progress, we find ourselves emerging into a world more late-20th-Century than any Doctorow has written about before. Evil old Augustus Pemberton, with his "loyalty not to any one business, but to the art of buying and selling them," could be Donald Trump or T. Boone Pickens. The twistedness of every father-son relationship in the book, the depiction of industry's orphaning of an entire generation, amounts to a refreshingly hardcore Marxist comment on the contemporary breakdown of the family. And the novel as a whole bears with uncanny directness on, of all things, our country's health-care crisis in 1994.

The *longueurs* and fascinations of *The Waterworks* are those of a toy whose colorful casings have been removed. We're given the austere spectacle of shiny gears and naked symbols; also the tedium of a toy that leaves little to the imagination; and finally the mystery that a thing so frankly contrived can still affect us. Uningratiating but visionary, the book invites us to peer back to the verge of modern industrial society—and shows us ourselves peering forward.

Simon Schama (review date 19 June 1994)

SOURCE: "New York, Gaslight Necropolis," in *New York Times Book Review,* June 19, 1994, p. 1.

[In the following review, Schama focuses on the historical aspects of The Waterworks.*]*

"The fact that Henry Armstrong was buried did not seem to him to prove that he was dead: he had always been a hard man to convince." Thus begins "One Summer Night," one of Ambrose Bierce's most wicked short stories: two pages long, a coffin-side view of an exhumation. An exhumation also plays an important part in E. L. Doctorow's startling and spellbinding new novel, *The Waterworks.* But what Mr. Doctorow has truly exhumed are the remains of the 19th-century genre of the science-detection mystery, originated by Poe and richly developed by Bierce and Wilkie Collins.

This is not to say that *The Waterworks* is mere Gotham Gothic. As Mr. Doctorow makes his narrator, a newspaper editor named McIlvaine, insist, this is no ghost story. For although he uses all the classic devices of the genre—a body that refuses to stay dead, an incredulous storyteller sucked into the Perilous Pursuit of Truth, an omniscient, laconic and socially awkward policeman—his book is actually designed to be a heavyweight novel of ideas, an allegory of vitality, mortality and the manipulation of nature. It is as though, descending at La Guardia Airport, he saw the welcome mat of the cemeteries in Queens, extending all the way to the horizon of towers, and wanted to have the populations of the dead and the living mingle in one vast literary commotion.

Almost all of Mr. Doctorow's novels have been, to some degree, documents of New York history, and one of his greatest strengths has been the richness of his descriptions of its cultural landscape, from turn-of-the-century New Rochelle and Manhattan in *Ragtime* to the Jewish Bronx of his 1930's childhood in *World's Fair.* But in *The Waterworks,* New York is no longer a setting for the action: it is the action, the principal character, the presiding genius and the trap of history.

Ostensibly, Mr. Doctorow lands the reader in Boss Tweed's city in 1871, at the precise moment the Tweed Ring is about to fall apart. New York is a gravy-stained, spit-flecked, bituminous, rough-necked, livid place that we fall into in his pages, and if this sounds familiar, it should. For although the odors are coal-sulfur and horse manure rather than pretzel scorch and subterranean steam, Mr. Doctorow's postbellum Gehenna is plainly held up as a mirror in which we are meant to see our own time and manners. And more than is usually the case with Mr. Doctorow, this is not a pretty picture.

Of the Ring, McIlvaine editorializes, "They were nothing if not absurd—ridiculous, simple-minded, stupid, self-aggrandizing. And murderous. All the qualities of men who prevail in our Republic." This New York of then and now and ever is a place imprisoned in thuggish corruption, where the police conspire with, rather than against, crime; a lair of vampire capitalism, a warren of alleys crawling with the urchin "street rats" who subsist on the refuse of the city's wants and needs, darting beneath the wheels of indifferent carriages, vending the news, loitering at the edge of scummy saloons.

> **The self-conscious choice of a broken style will not please those for whom the pleasure principle has always been a major reason to read Mr. Doctorow, whether dancing to the lilt of his deceptive jauntiness in *Ragtime* or enfolded in the lyric intensity of *The Book of Daniel.* But it is of a piece with his other courageous formal reinventions.**
> **—*Simon Schama***

Mr. Doctorow has caught this vision of a gaslight necropolis, where distinctions between the living and the dead are blurred by the presence of so many species of dead-and-alive souls, with forensic precision. His New York is also a residence of the mutilated. In one stunning episode, the artist Harry Wheelwright, possibly the most memorable of the characters in the novel, is seen painting the torso of a Civil War veteran, horribly deformed by the wounds of battle. Appropriately, then, Mr. Doctorow also gives his narrator, McIlvaine, a mutilated diction, broken by elisions and compressions of thought and utterance. This positions him to value the aggregating skills of the police officer, Donne, since "enlightenment comes . . . in bits and pieces of humdrum reality, each adding its mosaic bit of glitter to the eventual vision."

The self-conscious choice of a broken style will not please those for whom the pleasure principle has always been a major reason to read Mr. Doctorow, whether dancing to the lilt of his deceptive jauntiness in *Ragtime* or enfolded in the lyric intensity of *The Book of Daniel.* But it is of a piece with his other courageous formal reinventions. Just as he was able to concoct a kind of peculiarly furtive flatness for the voice of the title character of *Billy Bathgate,* he has produced an extraordinarily fretful, glance-over-the-shoulder writing style for McIlvaine, the purveyor of easy commonplaces.

The understated edginess of the writing serves the intensity of the story very well, as if it were overheard or glimpsed rather than seen dead on. One of McIlvaine's freelance culture reviewers, Martin Pemberton, habitually dressed in an ancient Union Army greatcoat and roiling in righteous misanthropic rage against the vulgar iniquities of the Gilded Age, announces to the editor that he has glimpsed his father, whom the world believes dead and buried, riding in a white municipal omnibus together with a company of spectral old men.

Bierce, among other writers, specialized in what he called "the parenticide club." And it turns out to be filial loathing rather than piety that drives Martin to discover the truth behind the apparition. His father, Augustus, had accumulated a fortune from running African slaves to Cuba in the very midst of the Civil War while also selling shoddy goods to the Union Army. Having gone to great pains to disinherit himself, the better to lead a life of virtuous chagrin, Martin is haunted by the thought that his father might have cheated the grave much as he cheated the Union. Pursuing the truth, he disappears, and McIlvaine goes after him.

The book limps a little in the opening stages of the search. Perhaps it is just because Mr. Doctorow is so successful at sketching New York and its Hudson Valley landscapes that his characters often seem swallowed up in its scenery. The two women in Martin Pemberton's life, for example, Emily Tisdale, who has loved him long to no effect, and his young stepmother, Sarah Pemberton, are seen only through the intermittently lecherous survey of McIlvaine's jaundiced eye, though as usual Mr. Doctorow is phenomenally good at erotic summaries. The wanly intelligent Emily arouses McIlvaine by the thought of penetrating all that woolen-skirted virtue. Sarah, on the other hand, is a peculiar combination of the motherly and the voluptuous: "The recessiveness of spirit that made her so lovely, even gallant, would appeal to any man who wanted endless reception, endless soft reception of whatever outrage he could conceive."

It is a part of the devilish cunning of this most intellectually designed of all of Mr. Doctorow's books that characters who superficially resemble their prototypes in 19th-century fiction, notably the policeman and the God-usurping scientist, refuse to be confined within their allotted conventions. Even the names Mr. Doctorow has chosen are themselves a kind of artful literary and philosophical riddle. The full name of the detective, for example, is Edmund Donne, equipped to unravel a mystery that is less paranormal than metaphysical, where the articulations between body and spirit are the crux of the matter. More mischievous still, the extraordinary figure at the heart of the story, who delivers a set speech of such terrible cogency that the reader has to fight not to be implicated in its logic, is called Dr. Sartorius. But his message is, in fact, the exact opposite of that which Thomas Carlyle puts into the mouth of Professor Teufelsdrockh in "Sartor Resartus." For where the metaphysical Teufelsdrockh argues that the tailored garment of our bodies is but a fabric for our divine spark, Mr. Doctorow's stitcher and weaver of bodies, Sartorius, who has won fame by the merciful speed of his battlefield amputations, insists that we are nothing but our biological matter. Perhaps Mr. Doctorow falters a little in a predictable passage where Sartorius's experiments are catalogued in such a way as to horrify a 19th-century reader, but provoke our own amused recognition of a medicine of interchangeable parts and an industry of cosmetic immortality.

The Waterworks is, however, much more than the sum of its own ingenuity. For all its rootedness in the social reality of New York, the story is carried along by a poetic flow of myth. Literature itself dissolves into this bath of memory when we realize that the site of the present public library on 42d Street and Fifth Avenue was once the great Croton Holding Reservoir. McIlvaine is haunted by the memory of having witnessed a child drown in the reservoir, the boy's toy boat drifting helplessly against the Egyptian Revival walls of the tank. And Mr. Doctorow knows that it was in Egypt that the original mythic connections between sacrifice and immortality, blood and water were first launched into the stream of our culture.

None of this formidable erudition gets in the way of the force and pace of the novel. Even former editors—like Mr. Doctorow—occasionally need editing, though. The image of "a great caesura of air, a gorge of sky that implied the Hudson" is so brilliantly judged the first time it appears that when it shows up again as "the peculiar implication of a river in the lighter sky between the bank and the far bluffs," the reader is made aware of the valves and pistons of Mr. Doctorow's formidable literary engine working up and down like the hydraulic monster at the heart of his story. For the most part, though, the reader is helplessly and gratefully caught in the current. For the waters that lave the narrative, from the sooty rains of the metropolis to the single bead of fluid Mr. Doctorow suspends on the tip of a priest's nose, all run to the great confluence, where the deepest issues of life and death are borne along on the swift, sure vessel of his poetic imagination.

Mark Shechner (review date 10 July 1994)

SOURCE: "A 'Gothic Fantasia' from E. L. Doctorow," in *Chicago Tribune Books,* July 10, 1994, p. 3.

[*In the following review of* The Waterworks, *Shechner takes account of the novel's strengths and failings.*]

The germ of *The Waterworks* is a four-page vignette of the same title that appeared in E. L. Doctorow's *Lives of the Poets* (1984). In that sketch the body of a drowned child is plucked from a reservoir, presumably the Croton in New York's Central Park, and whisked away in a horse-drawn carriage, while the silent narrator looks on.

I am fond of *Lives of the Poets,* the least celebrated of Doctorow's books, because it pretends to be nothing more than it is, a book of etudes for the left hand. Doctorow's troubles begin where the ambition swells and etudes get inflated into historical novels—mournful fanfares given a social/historical spin. That was the problem with *Ragtime;* so it is with *The Waterworks.*

Another of Doctorow's crabbed rhapsodies to New York City, *The Waterworks* is set in 1871. Its nominal plot is the search for a missing book reviewer, Martin Pemberton, among the streets of New York, webbed with intrigue and thuggery under the reign of William Marcy "Boss" Tweed.

Pemberton's editor, one McIlvaine, knows him only as the best of his free-lancers and "a moody distracted young fellow." Pemberton is also son of one of the city's robber barons, the late Augustus Pemberton, who ran slaves into Cuba as late as the 1860s and made a killing in the Civil War selling "boots that fell apart, blankets that dissolved in the rain" and such to the Army of the North. For that, his funeral catafalque was marched up Broadway, and the city was draped in black muslin.

When Martin disappears shortly after announcing that he has seen his father still alive, McIlvaine sets out on the trail, accompanied by a police captain, one of the few who is not in Boss Tweed's employ, Edmund Donne. This serves to get us into the city, a gaslit phantasmagoria of ambition and squalor.

Donne and McIlvaine go about like Watson and Holmes, rounding up the usual suspects. Martin's landlord complains of unpaid rent; his lady friend, Emily Tisdale, complains of unpaid attention; his mother complains of her husband's disappearing fortune. Harry Wheelwright, an impecunious artist, was last to see Martin alive; Dr. Thaddeus Mott, had diagnosed Augustus Pemberton with "irreversible anemia" and then lost track of him when a Dr. Sartorius was called in on the case.

Wheelwright's is the critical, if predictable, testimony. He and Martin Pemberton had dug up the casket of Martin's father and found the body within was that of a young boy. Fingers point toward Augustus Pemberton's bookkeeper; toward Sartorius, a renegade medicine man; toward an orphanage and to various and sundry thugs.

I am fond of *Lives of the Poets,* the least celebrated of Doctorow's books, because it pretends to be nothing more than it is, a book of etudes for the left hand.
                                    —*Mark Shechner*

The last third of the novel features a triple unraveling so dizzying that the reader may need Dramamine. All pretense of social realism collapses into a Gothic fantasia that grinds urban bossism into crypto medicine, zomboid tycoons and organs harvested from the dead. At this Doctorow hurls his most gorgeous prose, as if he were turning up the soundtrack to distract us from the gore and a plot in which anything goes.

Here, for example, is the discovery of Sartorius' "conservatory," "an indoor park, with gravel paths and planting and cast-iron benches . . . all set inside a vaulted roof of glass and steel. . . ."

"The effect . . . was of a Roman bath, had Rome been industrialized. The greenish light from the conservatory roof seemed to descend, it sifted down, it had motion, it seemed to pulse. Gradually I became aware that I was hearing music. First I felt it as a pulse in the air . . . but when I realized it was music, it broke over me, swelling and filling this vaulted place. . . . It was as if I had stepped into another universe, a Creation, like . . . an obverse Eden."

Boss Tweed's New York is material that any novelist-cum-urban historian might long to dirty his hands with. But since his one great novel, *The Book of Daniel,* Doctorow has adopted a clean hands strategy, side-stepping character development in favor of special effects. Thus McIlvaine, this book's central figure, is only a cipher, much like his predecessor in Doctorow's last novel, Billy Bathgate.

As for Boss Tweed himself, McIlvaine describes him as "a big ruddy son of a bitch, he ran about three hundred pounds. Bald and red-bearded, with a charming twinkle in his blue eyes. He bought the drinks and paid for the dinners. But in the odd moment when there was no hand to shake or toast to give, the eye went dead and you saw the soul of a savage."

Oh, for more of that, for there was the promise of this novel: that massive son of a bitch with the soul of a savage.

Andrew Delbanco (review date 18 July 1994)

SOURCE: "Necropolis News," in *New Republic,* Vol. 211, Nos. 3 & 4, July 18, 1994, pp. 44, 46-8.

[*In the following review, Delbanco presents an appreciation of the symbolic features of* The Waterworks *and comments briefly on the essay collection* Jack London, Hemingway, and the Constitution.]

Everybody's favorite stage set this year has been old New York. It first turned up in Martin Scorsese's movie of *The Age of Innocence,* which made viewers feel as if they were inside a meticulously accurate diorama of Edith Wharton's fashionable Manhattan in the 1870s. Then Caleb Carr enlarged the set for his murder mystery of the 1890s. *The Alienist,* to include the wharves and the dark alleys where

Wharton's grandees would never venture. Now E. L. Doctorow has returned to the immediate post-Civil War period for his own New York tale.

If the setting of *The Waterworks* is similar, Doctorow's way of representing it is entirely different. This is a writer who—ever since the first chapter of his first book, *Welcome to Hard Times* (1960), in which we meet a character known simply as "the Bad Man"—has been committed less to realism than to a kind of allegorical romance. Descended from the line of American fabulists that runs from Hawthorne to Malamud, Doctorow has always disavowed what Hawthorne (referring to the conventional fiction of his day) dismissed as "minute fidelity . . . to the probable and ordinary course of man's experience," in favor of a more imaginative "latitude . . . to mingle the Marvellous" with the real.

Late in *The Waterworks,* Doctorow sums up the dream effect he is after:

> There are moments of our life that are something like breaks or tears in moral consciousness, as caesuras break the chanted line, and the eye sees through the breach to a companion life, a life in all its aspects the same, running along parallel in time, but within a universe even more confounding than our own. It is this other disordered existence . . . that our ministers warn us against . . . that our dreams perceive.

To catch this "disordered existence" in fiction, the logic of the work must be more associative than sequential. Accordingly, the speech of the narrator is continually interrupted by ellipses that give his sentences a fractured quality and seem to represent a habitual pause—a hesitancy to deliver consecutive thoughts. "There is a difference," he remarks, "between living in some kind of day-to-day crawl through chaos, where there is no hierarchy to your thoughts, but a raucous equality of them, and knowing in advance the whole conclusive order . . . which makes narration . . . suspect." Yet, at the same time, a fiction that takes seriously this suspicion must commit itself to achieving something like the fluent exfoliation of images that one expects from poetry.

In the case of Doctorow's new novel, the images are those of a city closer to one of Red Groom's cartoonish ensembles than to any actual New York. Doctorow calls this city a "necropolis." Its "paving stones pound . . . with horse-droppings," while carrion birds swoop in between the carts and carriages, "picking out their meals" from the dung. Wooden remnants of the antebellum town are being literally burned away ("we had fire all the time, we burned as a matter of habit") and replaced by the city of iron and stone that survives today in patches of cast-iron buildings, mainly below Houston Street. This New York was already the "huge jagged city" that Henry James would describe at the turn of the century as ". . . looking at the sky in the manner of some colossal hair-comb turned upward and so deprived of half its teeth that the others, at their uneven intervals, count doubly as sharp spikes."

This is the gothic setting for a story that, briefly told, sounds outlandish. It begins with a tycoon named Augustus Pemberton, who grew rich during the War of Secession by abetting death itself—by "supplying the Army of the North with boots that fell apart, blankets that dissolved in rain, tents that tore at the grommets and uniform cloth that bled dye." Under sentence of death from pernicious anemia, he tells his family that he is going to an Adirondack spa to seek a cure. There he—apparently—dies. With due Episcopal ceremony, he is seemingly buried. But his estranged son, a free-lance journalist—one "of that postwar generation for whom the materials of the war were ironic objects of art or fashion," who "walk[s] down Broadway with his Union greatcoat open, flowing behind him like a cape"—thinks he sees his father alive.

> **No symbolic fiction can be fairly described by summarizing its plot (*Moby Dick,* in paraphrase, becomes a ridiculous story about a ship captain chasing the whale that ate his leg); and so it is difficult to convey the "sulphurous" atmosphere of Doctorow's book.**
> **—*Andrew Delbanco***

The startled young man, Martin Pemberton, is one of those whom Whitman had in mind when he wrote, in 1870, that "the aim of all the *littérateurs* is to find something to make fun of." A believer turned ironist, he produces caustic book reviews and half-fawning, half-mocking articles for the society page in which he enumerates the carats in the ladies' diamonds. Now, suddenly, he becomes the credulous object of scorn, surrounded by doubters. One stormy morning, while on his way up Broadway to deliver a review, he encounters a city omnibus carrying a group of pale old men who sit eerily still, oblivious to the lurches of the carriage and the bursts of lightning and the pedestrian shouts and traffic gongs. Peering in the carriage windows at its ghostly passengers, he sees that one of them has "the familiar hunch of his father's shoulders . . . and the wizened Augustan neck with its familiar wen, the smooth white egglike structure that from Martin's infancy had always alarmed him."

Most people dismiss Martin's report as fantasy or hoax, though a few take him seriously and even grope toward an explanatory idea of the Oedipal unconscious (everyone knows he loathed his father) to account for his delusion.

When Martin himself disappears, his soft-boiled editor, McIlvaine—whose "newsman's cilia [are] up and waving" at the smell of a good story—joins the chase to find out what, if anything, his young free-lance has really seen. After some further twists and turns the road of detection leads to a Mephistophelian character named Doctor Sartorius, who is a cross between one of Hawthorne's mad scientists and one of Poe's reclusive aesthetes. Ahead of Pasteur and Koch, he has intuited the germ basis of disease. He has transfused blood and is preparing to perform organ transplants. We discover him deep within the massive stone structure of the waterworks at a suburban reservoir, where, in a sort of futuristic bunker, he rests untried technologies on patients (including Augustus Pemberton) so rich and desperate that they are willing to try anything, pay anything, to forestall death. The medicines that Sartorius administers are derived from fluids extracted from children. "Shrunken, unnaturally darkened and sunk in on themselves, like vegetable husks," these old men have literally become vampires, feeding on the blood of the young.

No symbolic fiction can be fairly described by summarizing its plot (*Moby Dick,* in paraphrase, becomes a ridiculous story about a ship captain chasing the whale that ate his leg); and so it is difficult to convey the "sulphurous" atmosphere of Doctorow's book. The seed of his strange fable had been growing in his mind since he published a short story in *Lives of the Poets* in 1984, in which two men find a toy boat capsized in a reservoir, and discover the body of a drowned child in the adjacent waterworks. Now, in the novel that emerged from this image ten years later, the figure of the lost child is kaleidoscopically multiplied into clusters of "undersized beings on whose faces were etched the lines and shadows of serfdom." One of them turns up in what is supposed to be Augustus Pemberton's coffin (which Martin, in a half-parodic graveyard scene, digs up and pries open in the dark of night), laid out within on a "padded white silk couch," its "tiny leathered face with its eyes closed and lips pursed." These doomed children function in the novel as symbols of the age when, for the first time, American civilization began to produce more human refuse than it could dispose of or hide away:

> Vagrant children slept in the alleys. Ragpicking was a profession. . . . Out on the edges of town, along the North River or in Washington Heights or on the East River islands, behind stone walls and high hedges, were our institutions of charity, our orphanages, insane asylums, poorhouses, schools for the deaf and dumb and mission homes for magdalens. They made a sort of Ringstrasse for our venerable civilization.

As for those who stay within the ring, they scratch out a liv-

ing as messengers, peddlers, shopsweepers, hawkers, newsboys and involuntary whores:

> More than one brothel specialized in them. They often turned up in hospital wards and church hospices so stunned by the abuses to which they'd been subjected that they couldn't speak sensibly but could only cower in their rags and gaze upon the kindest nurses or ministrants of charity with abject fear.

In imagining this world of brutalized children, Doctorow wants to drive home—sometimes relentlessly—its affinity with our own age. A purposeful war has just ended ("I am a man," says McIlvaine, who narrates the story in the first-person voice, "who will never be able to think of anyone but Abe Lincoln as president"), and has given way to "a conspicuously self-satisfied class of new wealth and weak intellect . . . all aglitter in a setting of mass misery."

The men who have taken over this postwar America have, like the arbitrageurs of a century later, no "loyalty . . . to any one business, but to the art of buying and selling them." Pallid and glazed-eyed, the old men whose dying is retarded by Dr. Sartorius have a zombie inertness that seems the final stage in the natural course of their lives—lives that have been spent in a moral obtuseness that, when they were young, might have taken the form of insouciance or arrogance or blinding greed. The parasitism of their dying is not fundamentally different from how they lived: as blood-suckers indifferent to the human cost of their getting and spending. Augustus Pemberton, for example, is rumored to have been financially involved, even during the war, in the slave trade.

That Doctorow conceived this fantastic novel as a sort of moral prehistory of our own age becomes clear when one dips into the essays that he collected under the centerless title *Jack London, Hemingway and the Constitution,* while *The Waterworks* was taking form. In the introduction to this rather haphazard collection, he likens the impact of Reaganism on American society—deregulation, the politicization of the courts and the distribution of "the enormous costs of the cold war democratically among all classes of society except the wealthiest"—to "the effect . . . [of] a vampire's arterial suck." Another essay, a meditation on nineteenth-century New York written for *Architectural Digest* in 1992, contains blocks of descriptive writing that are reiterated, verbatim, in McIlvaine's voice.

Doctorow's implicit subject in these pieces seems to be the end of our "fifty-year nuclear alert" and its replacement by a restless waiting for some yet-to-be-defined menace that might revive a sense of common purpose. We live, he believes, in a "stillness between tides, neither going out nor coming in," bewildered to the point of paralysis about how to deal, for instance, with the thousands of people in our midst "sleeping in doorways, begging with Styrofoam cups." One suspects that he also had in mind for *The Waterworks* the increasingly evident possibility that—for those able to pay—medical technology may someday sustain almost indefinitely a grotesque simulacrum of life.

> **When, in the essays, Doctorow asks us to "pray for the dead and for the maligned and destitute," it feels as if we are being dunned for the annual charitable appeal. But when, in *The Waterworks,* he concentrates his pity and horror into images rather than arguments, the result is a persuasive portrait of an era akin to our own, when Americans found themselves living in cities of unprecedented scale, in which, for the first time, human beings had become indistinguishable from litter.**
> **—Andrew Delbanco**

Many of Doctorow's points border on cant. He is not an essayist. The most arresting piece in this collection is the least discursive. It is the one that was not commissioned—a brief rumination called **"Standards,"** about the "self-referential power" of songs. A charming imaginative frolic, it moves among associated topics that include the origins of lullabies in mothers' crooning, the mixture of irony and militancy in wartime songs like "Goober Peas," the "compensatory" function of ballads about lost love. But when, in the other essays, he turns away from the associative mode and becomes resolutely expository in the service of an argument, he tends to sound callow and even pontifical. Here is a piece written before the 1992 election out of disgust at George Bush and with high hopes for Bill Clinton:

> The true president would have the strength to widen the range of current political discourse, and would love and revere language as the best means we have to close on reality. That implies a sensibility attuned to the immense moral consequence of every human life. Perhaps even a sense of tragedy that would not let him sleep the night through.

Weakened by this mixture of outrage and sentimentality, the essays are more an expression of an offended sensibility than a serious effort at political analysis or understanding. They have a thin, sloganeering quality—and, finally, a columnist's transience. But when, in *The Waterworks,* the same sentiments are realized as images and put to use within the context of a story of loss and res-

cue, they work to greater effect. "I have dreamt sometimes." says McIlvaine.

> . . . that if it were possible to lift this littered, paved Manhattan from the earth . . . and all its torn and dripping pipes and conduits and tunnels and tracks and cables—all of it, like a scab from new skin underneath—how seedlings would sprout, and freshets bubble up, and brush and grasses would grow over the rolling hills. . . . A season or two of this and the mute, protesting culture buried for so many industrial years under the tenements and factories . . . would rise again . . . of the lean, religious Indians of the bounteous earth. . . . Such love I have for those savage polytheists of my mind . . . such envy for the inadequate stories they told each other, their taxonomies, cosmologies . . . their lovely dreams of the world they stood on and who was holding it up. . . .

In earlier works, like *Loon Lake* (1980) and *World's Fair* (1985), Doctorow indulged in this kind of reverie at the expense of narrative momentum. But in *The Waterworks,* he has pulled off the difficult literary trick of combining the grit and pith of a precisely located fiction with the reach of a moral exemplum independent of time and place. When, in the essays, Doctorow asks us to "pray for the dead and for the maligned and destitute," it feels as if we are being dunned for the annual charitable appeal. But when, in *The Waterworks,* he concentrates his pity and horror into images rather than arguments, the result is a persuasive portrait of an era akin to our own, when Americans found themselves living in cities of unprecedented scale, in which, for the first time, human beings had become indistinguishable from litter.

William Hutchings (review date Winter 1995)

SOURCE: A review of *The Waterworks,* in *World Literature Today,* Vol. 69, No. 1, Winter, 1995, pp. 138-39.

[*In the following brief review, Hutchings outlines the elements of* The Waterworks *and considers its literary predecessors.*]

Walking down Broadway in 1871, a young freelance journalist named Martin Pemberton notices a horse-drawn omnibus containing several old men dressed in black. Among them, he recognizes his dead and supposedly buried father—a businessman who was as notoriously corrupt as he was socially eminent; his fortune, based in part on slave-trading and war-profiteering, has been mysteriously unlocatable since his death. While pursuing his investigation into this strange event, Martin Pemberton disappears: perhaps kidnapped, perhaps murdered, but by whom and why?

From this scenario, E. L. Doctorow has constructed *The Waterworks,* an intriguing if implausible moral fable that is also a stylish whodunit and a masterfully detailed evocation of Boss Tweed's New York—and, implicitly, of specific literary precedents from nineteenth-century American literature. Doctorow's narrator, like the one in Melville's tale of "old" New York, "Bartleby the Scrivener," is a genial bachelor who defines himself through his work—though as an editor at one of the city's fifteen newspapers, he is more cynical and streetwise than Melville's bond lawyer. Doctorow's narrator McIlvane, like Melville's unnamed narrator, becomes increasingly involved in the life of his strange and ascetic employee—though it is his disconcerting *absence* from the office (in contrast to Bartleby's unremitting *presence*) that eventually dislodges the narrator from "the state of irresolution most of us live in with regard to our moral challenges." Eventually, at the city's reservoir (the waterworks of the title), he discovers secrets that are as dark and nefarious as those concealed at (and ultimately in) the murky tarn in Poe's "Fall of the House of Usher."

Notwithstanding such precursors from earlier American fiction, the foremost literary precedents for *The Waterworks* are the stories of Arthur Conan Doyle: McIlvane's investigation proceeds with Holmes-like logic and tenacity from a phenomenally startling initial incident (the supposedly dead man sighted among the living) and an ensuing ominous complication (the disappearance of the witness and estranged heir). Eventually he uncovers a bizarre and extravagant plot devised by the elusive archcriminal mastermind Dr. Sartorius, a Moriarty-like evil genius who profits inordinately from the hopes and fears of his elderly victims: extremely wealthy patients who trust his hubristic claim that human will and knowledge—specifically, his scientific expertise—can prevail even over mortality itself. McIlvane's position as a newspaperman affords him an intimate knowledge of the seamier aspects of life in his city, while the paper's "morgue" (clipping files) yields even more vital information than Holmes's library. The city-wide network of ever-observant newsboys constitutes a plausible American counterpart of the Baker Street Irregulars.

The world of New York in 1871 is often explicitly compared to and contrasted with a deliberately undefined "now" that is also referred to (wholly implausibly) as "your time" by Doctorow's elderly, retrospective narrator. Then-and-now analogies about such issues as medical technology and the prolongation of life, moral and political corruption, wealth and poverty, and neglected and exploited children can all easily be drawn, but the fundamental seriousness of such concerns is undercut repeatedly in *The Waterworks* by the

Doylean conventions of the detective story cum entertainment.

E. L. Doctorow with Michelle M. Tokarczyk (interview date Winter 1995)

SOURCE: "The City, *The Waterworks,* and Writing: An Interview with E. L. Doctorow," in *Kenyon Review,* Vol. 17, No. 1, Winter, 1995, pp. 32-7.

[*In the following interview, Doctorow discusses his views of* The Waterworks *and elaborates some ideas on writing fiction.*]

The author of nine novels—*Welcome to Hard Times, Big as Life, The Book of Daniel, Ragtime, Loon Lake, Lives of the Poets, World's Fair, Billy Bathgate,* and *The Waterworks,* as well as a play, *Drinks before Dinner,* and a collection of essays, *Hemingway, Poe and the Constitution*—E. L. Doctorow grew up in New York City and was educated at Kenyon College and Columbia University. A recipient of the PEN/Faulkner Award for fiction, the National Book Critics Circle Arts and Letters Award, and the National Book Award among others, Doctorow teaches creative writing at New York University.

[*Tokarczyk:*] *I've been intrigued by your choices to set so many of your novels—*The Book of Daniel, Lives of the Poets, World's Fair, Billy Bathgate *and now* The Waterworks—*in New York City. How do you think being a New Yorker who has lived in the City for most of your life has affected your writing, your outlook in general?*

[Doctorow:] It was a very fortunate thing for someone who was going to be a writer to grow up at the cutting edge of American culture. In those days the country was more regionally directed than it is today. What went on in New York wasn't as well distributed, so there was a tremendous advantage to living here. New York was a very rich experience for a child. As a teenager, I used to go almost weekly to the Museum of Modern Art. I'd look at the permanent collection, look at the new work, go downstairs to the theater and see a foreign film. As a boy I went matter of factly to plays, to concerts. And as I grew up, I was a beneficiary of the incredible energies of European émigrés in every field—all those great minds hounded out of Europe by Hitler. They brought enormous sophistication to literary criticism, philosophy, science, music. . . . I was very lucky to be a New Yorker.

And, I was also in touch with, what turned out to be, although I couldn't realize it at the time, the last vestiges of Jewish immigrant culture. Those vestiges were in my grandparents, and to a lesser extent in my parents, who were born here. But it was enough for me to pick up on that wonderful sort of beautiful trade-union spirit of the early twentieth century—the expectation that this was a country where you could work out some justice for yourself and everyone else in your situation if you worked at it. So I was lucky in that sense. I was nourished by that Jewish humanist, not terribly religious, spirituality. I imagine that's another part of the New York mind-set.

And then, of course, the place itself, the city as spectacular phenomenon. All writers find a place for themselves, a home for their imaginations, and I suppose the city is mine. It's the quintessential city—so much so that I've felt at home in every city I've been anywhere in the world.

How did you come to **The Waterworks?**

It began with the very short dream story in *Lives of the Poets,* "The Waterworks." I never fully got that story out of my mind. I kept thinking about it.

It is a puzzling and eerie story.

I would think about it, and go on to a novel, and come back to it. I understood eventually that image, the waterworks, meant I was in the industrial nineteenth century. Transporting water to the city, to any city, was a great engineering feat of that time. Then, of course, the reservoir described could have been the Croton holding reservoir at Forty-second Street and Fifth Avenue.

> **My studio looks south over Soho to lower Manhattan. One night a heavy fog came down and covered the World Trade Center, covered all the big glass, steel buildings of lower Manhattan, then the Woolworth Building of the 1920s. The entire twentieth century was erased until all I could see was the ground-level city. It was the most uncanny experience: I was looking at the city that Melville walked in. I was looking at the nineteenth century. So in this way, step by step, [*The Waterworks*] proposed itself to me.**
> **—E. L. Doctorow**

Oh, I didn't know there had been one there.

Where New York Public Library is now. The reservoir walls were over forty feet high, twenty-five feet thick, and inward slanted. The style was ancient Egyptian. You could walk from the street through these temple doors, go up a flight of

stairs, and come out on the embankment. People went up there to take the air, to stroll about. That was the New York version of pastoral, Central Park not having been built yet. Once I was into the book I realized how much of the nineteenth century city is still with us—not in just the obvious architecture—Central Park, the Brooklyn Bridge, the Sixty-seventh Street Armory, the row houses in the West Village, the Jefferson Market Courthouse and so on—but even the shape of the streets, the widths, and the names of them. My studio looks south over Soho to lower Manhattan. One night a heavy fog came down and covered the World Trade Center, covered all the big glass, steel buildings of lower Manhattan, then the Woolworth Building of the 1920s. The entire twentieth century was erased until all I could see was the ground-level city. It was the most uncanny experience: I was looking at the city that Melville walked in. I was looking at the nineteenth century. So in this way, step by step, the book proposed itself to me. In a sense the entire book is deduced from the story. For instance, the drowned boy who is carried off by the man in the black coat: I reflected on the uses of children in the nineteenth century. There were thirty to forty thousand vagrant children running around. Children who were unclaimed, who were totally on their own. People called them street rats. The city, my sense of the city of the time—New York in the post-Civil War—is what that story speaks to. And once I realized that, I was able to do the book.

Talking about the urchin children in nineteenth-century New York reminded me how much of your work is concerned with children. Particularly I thought about Billy Bathgate. *I am very curious about him. He is, like Daniel Isaacson in* **The Book of Daniel,** *such a ruthless child. I wonder how you see his corruption.*

Billy Bathgate is everything that you would want a boy to be; he's bright, he's loyal, he's enterprising, he's observant, a quick learner. He has feelings, he is connected to his feelings, he works things out. But all these virtues are in service to the underworld, which fascinated him.

When I first read **Billy Bathgate** *in the late 1980s I was reminded of crime's attraction—especially drug dealing—to many slum children. Criminal lives are incredibly dangerous but still alluring.*

Crime—along with sports and the arts—is the instant way up from the lower depths. They want the same things, those kids who sell drugs. They want what they see on television; they want the good life. They want a nice house, they want a car. A place in the world.

After **Billy Bathgate** *came out, you published an essay* **"A Gangsterdom of the Spirit"** *in the* Nation. *I wondered if* *there was some connection between that gangsterdom you write about in the essay and the crime in* **Billy Bathgate.**

I suppose there may be some connection. It's not the kind of thing you can afford to think about in the writing. But it is a fact that this book about crime came to me in the 1980s. That's all I can say. It's a strange thing. I have never had the sense of enormous, indiscriminate power that would allow me at a given time to write any number of books. I have never had that feeling about myself. I find myself in a book and my understanding is: This is my book. There is nothing else I can do right now. At any given time you can do only the book that you are given to do.

The Waterworks *is very interesting in the context of your other work. It seems that there are some recurring themes: Sartorius's quest for immortality reminds me of Ford and Morgan in* **Ragtime.** *McIlvaine's relentless search for the truth reminds me of Daniel's search for the truth about his parents' case.*

Comparisons to my other works don't occur to me because I don't think that way when I'm writing. If I did it'd probably worry me. The work has to dominate. That's where you live, in those specific sentences. But all writers have preoccupations, things they're attached to. So I suppose there must be recurring themes.

As I was thinking of the vagrant children Sartorius exploited, one of the things that came to mind was Stephen Dedalus's words in A Portrait of the Artist as a Young Man, *"Ireland is a sow that eats its farrow." Are you perhaps suggesting something similar about American society during this period?*

I think what Joyce meant is something different. He's writing about Irish culture and a provincial repressive Catholicism that permeates every aspect of life and discourages vitality in the people. *The Waterworks* is a different sort of story. I think it's more a novel about all modern industrial culture, its presumption of continuous modernity, and the extent to which modernity is an illusion.

There seems to be a connection between the various kinds of evil depicted in the novel—Tweed's corruption, Sartorius's experiments, and slavery.

Or among government, wealth, and science. But the discovery that came over me in writing the book was more the despair of being locked in history. I was very interested in the city's architecture, not only in the waterworks and the reservoir, but in the orphanage, and the grid layout of Manhattan. The narrator is quite sensitive to such things; in fact, at one point he talks of how architecture can inadvertently express the hideousness of a culture.

The main character, as a newspaper editor and reporter, reminds me of a writer as you've often depicted writers: that is, he searches out the truth. He's as relentless in his pursuit as Daniel in **The Book of Daniel.**

I suppose *The Waterworks* is like *The Book of Daniel* in that each describes a process of discovery. Something is unfolded.

I was struck by the book's oral quality, by the sense that McIlvaine was indeed telling his story. I believe that when you wrote **World's Fair** *you were striving for a sense of oral history. Were you doing so in* **The Waterworks?**

In *World's Fair* the oral history passages were set off from the main text. Here the narrator is meant to be talking all the way through. It's a spoken book. At one point I was thinking of indicating through another voice—in a prologue, afterword, or introduction—that McIlvaine in the last year of his life had dictated what he had to say to a stenographer. He says at one point, "You have your motorcars and telephones and electric lights." He's looking back thirty years or so, you see, motorcars and electric lights and telephones being the glories of the period after the turn of the century. I always imagined he was dictating, that the unnamed stenographer—me possibly—became the captive audience. But I decided I didn't have to frame it all up, as Conrad does when an unnamed narrator gives us the scene—everyone sitting on the afterdeck smoking cigars, the sun going down over the Thames, as Marlowe begins one of his marathon monologues.

I had thought of Hawthorne and Poe as possible influences here, particularly because Hawthorne wrote sinister stories like "Rappacini's Daughter" about scientific experiments.

Undeniably. *The Waterworks* is a tale.

> **Words have no physical existence. Books are events in the mind. You don't know as time passes if what was in your mind as you wrote is really what's on the page. I find my view of my books shifts as I continue to think about them, but certainly my relationship to the books that have been done is distant.**
> **—E. L. Doctorow**

Aside from the narrative tale-telling voice, what other features of the book were particularly important for you?

There are certain gifts that the book gave to me—for instance, the idea of the elusiveness of villainy. If you think about it, the old man Augustus Pemberton is never seen alive. His existence is reported secondhand from the newspapers or the fact that his son saw him. His factotum, Simmons, is found only after he's dead. As for Tweed, you never see more than a glimpse or two of him. He's a ruling ethos, a configuration of the clouds. As McIlvaine says, you can't really get your hands on these people. The only one who finally appears as a presence—in the end and after great delay—is Sartorius. His elusiveness, however, is not physical, it's intellectual. A man with his own standards, not society's.

In reflecting on **Lives of the Poets** *especially, I've been thinking about something you said in an interview with Christopher Morris, "All writers have doubts about the value of their work as compared with, for example, a well-made house."*

Words have no physical existence. Books are events in the mind. You don't know as time passes if what was in your mind as you wrote is really what's on the page. I find my view of my books shifts as I continue to think about them, but certainly my relationship to the books that have been done is distant. I think, "Well, all right, but with this new one I'm really going to do it." You always have the "this one."

I meant . . . that you can look at a house and walk around it and live in it; the windows are built so that the light comes in, the stairs are here, and you know where the closets are. Space is measured and defined. The house is solidly constructed, the floors are parqueted floors, and there's nice tile in the bathroom.

Right, it's very solid.

Several people can walk into the house and more or less agree that it's a useful, livable house, but I'm not sure that the house of fiction is ever something most people would agree on. I mean, there are obviously great works that we admire. But I don't think self-satisfaction is very useful or constructive for an author, even if I were capable of it to any great degree. Maybe to people who write one book and stop. If you did something perfectly, what would be the need to go on? But it all operates in the mind. Words are there . . . and not there. Books are, and are not. When you've finished with a book, nothing will ever match the experience you've had writing it.

Michael Wutz (review date Spring 1995)

SOURCE: A review of *The Waterworks*, in *Review of Contemporary Fiction*, Vol. 15, No. 1, Spring, 1995, pp. 177-78.

[*In the following review, Wutz outlines the elements of* The Waterworks *and considers its place in Doctorow's oeuvre.*]

An almost uncanny ability to reconstruct historical material and a spellbinding facility to tell a good tale—these are the qualities that have made E. L. Doctorow one of America's most distinguished literary practitioners and the qualities that are again evident in **The Waterworks,** a fascinating science-detection mystery centered in post-bellum New York City. Framed by the atmospherics of a city bulging out of its seams, the novel tells the story of young Martin Pemberton, a caustic free-lance literary critic, who claims to have seen his deceased father in a city omnibus. The ensuing search, told in the form of a memoir by a newspaper editor named McIlvaine, plunges Martin into the city's dark underbelly and eventually brings him face to face with the "mad" German scientist, Dr. Wrede Sartorius, the genius responsible for his father's ostensible resurrection and the mastermind behind an ominous operation. Housed in the underworldly catacombs of the city's waterworks on Forty-second Street, Sartorius has established a factory of immortality, a medical facility in which body fluid injections taken from children give old geezers illusory glimpses of rejuvenation and eternal life.

If this sounds like the reworking of the stuff that nineteenth-century fictions are made of, it is meant that way: the omnipresent oppressiveness of the city, as well as the delightful circumlocution of the narrative, are reminiscent of Dickens; the morbid subject matter and intuitive brilliance of the police officer solving the case suggest Poe's Gothic ratiocination; and the scientific rivalry between Sartorius and his colleagues, as well as the search for the elixir of life, recall Hawthorne's hybristic scientists. These are just a few of the literary voices echoing through the book. Indeed, in a novel about exhumed bodies, the self-conscious exhumation of literary models is only appropriate and part of its postmodern texture. Just as McIlvaine's narrative understands itself as a collage of archival materials, assembled from eyewitnesses and cross-referenced newspaper files, so Doctorow's *Waterworks* is an ingenious mosaic of the narrative raw material of his predecessors, framed by his own artistic vision.

> **An almost uncanny ability to reconstruct historical material and a spellbinding facility to tell a good tale—these are the qualities that have made E. L. Doctorow one of America's most distinguished literary practitioners.**
> —*Michael Wutz*

Readers of Doctorow will find much that is familiar and important here: McIlvaine's incessant concern with the slipperiness of language is at the heart of Doctorow's project as a language worker, beginning with *Welcome to Hard Times.* Similarly, McIlvaine's quest for meaning, especially as he attempts to adjudicate Sartorius's sanity, leads him into the quagmire of truth and justice, those Imponderables that define, in their elusiveness, the unmapped gray zones of the human mind, as they do in *The Book of Daniel, Ragtime,* and *Loon Lake.* But Doctorow also breaks new ground. Under the guise of a historical reconstruction, Doctorow may have written his most political novel yet; it certainly is a retrospective vision into the present. The financial regimes of Boss Tweed and Martin's father, Augustus, suggest the machinations of today's corporate capitalism, as do the squelched labor unrests in favor of an eight-hour workday. More importantly, in the allegorical figure of Sartorius, Doctorow evokes the controversies surrounding contemporary medical technology, the need for egalitarian health care reform, and our cultural fear of mortality. *The Waterworks* reminds us that the increasing cultural authority of science is a matter of precarious balance: it can lead to genuine human welfare and, at the same time, if left unquestioned, legitimize the inhumanly human cruelties of Auschwitz. In more than one sense, the novel is a "panoramic negative print" of our post-modern condition.

FURTHER READING

Criticism

Iannone, Carol. "E. L. Doctorow's 'Jewish' Radicalism." *Commentary* 81, No. 3 (March 1986): 53-6.

> Considers the impact of Doctorow's Jewish heritage on his work.

Jones, Malcolm Jr. "A Gothic Tale of Horror in Old New York." *Newsweek* (27 June 1994): 53.

> Provides a synopsis of the plot of *The Waterworks,* and considers the novel's borrowings from works in the horror/science fiction mystery genre.

Rovit, Earl. "The Miraculous Conjunction." *Sewanee Review* 104, No. 2 (Spring 1996): 325-29.

> Offers reflections on the essay genre and contains a brief review of Doctorow's *Selected Essays, 1977-1992.*

Additional coverage of Doctorow's life and career is contained in the following sources published by Gale: *Authors in the News,* **Vol. 2;** *Bestsellers 1989,* **Vol. 3;** *Concise Dictionary of American Literary Biography,* **1968-1988;** *Contemporary Authors,* **Vols. 45-48;** *Contemporary Authors New Revision Series,* **Vols. 2, 33, and 51;** *DISCovering Authors Modules: Novelists* **and** *Popular Fiction and Genre Authors; Dictionary of Literary Biography,* **Vols. 2, 28, and 173;** *Dictionary of Literary Biography Yearbook,* **1980; and** *Major Twentieth Century Writers.*

"The Love Song of J. Alfred Prufrock"

T. S. Eliot

(Full name Thomas Stearns Eliot; also wrote under the pseudonyms Charles Augustus Conybeare; Charles James Grimble, Reverend; Gus Krutzch; Muriel A. Schwartz; J. A. D. Spence; Helen B. Trundlett) American-born English poet, critic, essayist, dramatist, and editor.

The following entry presents criticism on Eliot's poem "The Love Song of J. Alfred Prufrock" (1915). For further information on Eliot's life and career, see *CLC,* Volumes 1, 2, 3, 6, 9, 10, 13, 15, 24, 34, 41, 55, and 57.

INTRODUCTION

"The Love Song of J. Alfred Prufrock" is considered one of Eliot's finest and most important works. With the help of Ezra Pound, the poem was accepted for publication in *Poetry* in 1915—four years, it is believed, after Eliot (1888-1965) completed it. Through this poem Eliot established himself as a modern voice in literature, creating profoundly innovative, erudite poetry which mixes classical references with industrial twentieth-century images. It is the first work among many which would earn him a place as one of the most important and revolutionary poets of the twentieth century.

Plot and Major Characters

"The Love Song of J. Alfred Prufrock" is a lyrical, dramatic monologue of a middle-class male persona who inhabits a physically and spiritually bleak environment. The title of the poem is misleading since it is neither a love poem nor a song in the classical sense. Approximately 130 lines long, it follows the ramblings of J. Alfred Prufrock, the would-be suitor of an unnamed and nebulously developed woman. While Eliot provides little description of Prufrock's person, he does reveal a great deal about Prufrock's personality and state of mind.

Major Themes

Prufrock is full of self-doubts, with a pessimistic outlook on his future, as well as the future of society and the world. This pessimistic view renders him unable to declare his love to the unnamed woman. He describes himself as "almost ridiculous," "almost . . . the Fool." Although aware of the possibility of personal fulfillment, Prufrock is afraid to act, unable to claim for himself a more meaningful existence. The poem also contains numerous biting images of the industrial landscape with its insidious "yellow fog," "narrow streets," "lonely men in shirt-sleeves," and "soot that falls from chimneys." "Prufrock" is also replete with classical references to such literary and historical figures as John the Baptist, Lazarus, and Hamlet and to the literary works of Hesiod, Andrew Marvell, Dante, and Jules Laforgue.

Critical Reception

"The Love Song of J. Alfred Prufrock" has sparked tremendous interest and dissension among literary scholars. It is considered by many to be one of the principal poems of this century, and is listed with *The Waste Land* (1922) and *Four Quartets* (1943) as Eliot's best work. Often analyzed by line, incident or reference, the poem continues to confound scholars. Eliot pioneered an innovative and often fragmentary style centered upon modernity and the use of startling metaphors; Louis Untermeyer calls it "sensitive to the pitch of concealment." Critics such as Robert M. Seiller, Elizabeth Drew, George Williamson, Cleanth Brooks and Robert Penn Warren all argue that Prufrock never articulates a question: he is too overwhelmed by modernity and the state of his existence to formulate it. J. Peter Dyson contends that Eliot utilizes a literary reference to Hamlet in which to indirectly frame Prufrock's question. In a separate but related inquiry, Bruce Hayman questions whether Prufrock is proposing marriage or making a sexual proposition to the woman in the poem. Critics agree that in the end Prufrock is too overwhelmed by the bleakness of his own life and his view of the urban landscape to take any action, so paralyzed is he with fear and uncertainty. Scholars have focused a great deal of energy on unraveling the meaning of the literary references with which Eliot peppers the poem. There is disagreement over the allusions to John the Baptist and Lazarus, and argument over which Hamlet reference he employs. Several scholars have marked Dostoevsky's influence on Eliot, although Eliot himself pointed out that *Crime and Punishment* was not available to him when he wrote this poem. Critics list among Eliot's influences Lord Alfred Tennyson, Henry James, Matthew Arnold, Charles Baudelaire, Edgar Allan Poe, and Laforgue.

PRINCIPAL WORKS

Prufrock, and Other Observations (poetry) 1917

Poems (poetry) 1919

*The Waste Land (poem) 1922

Fragment of a Prologue (play) 1926

Journey of the Magi (poetry) 1927

Fragment of the Agon (play) 1927

A Song for Simeon (poetry) 1928

Animula (poetry) 1929

Ash-Wednesday (poetry) 1930

Marina (poetry) 1930

Sweeny Agonistes: Fragments of an Aristophanic Melodrama (play) 1932

The Rock (play) 1934

Murder in the Cathedral (play) 1935

Collected Poems, 1909-1935 (poetry) 1936

The Family Reunion (play) 1939

†Old Possum's Book of Practical Cats (poetry) 1939

East Coker (poetry) 1940

The Dry Salvages (poetry) 1941

Four Quartets (poetry) 1943

The Cocktail Party (play) 1950

The Confidential Clerk (play) 1954

The Elder Statesman (play) 1959

Collected Poems, 1909-1962 (poetry) 1963

Growltiger's Last Stand and Other Poems (poetry) 1987

*First published in *Criterion,* October, 1922.

†Later adapted by Andrew Lloyd Webber as the Broadway musical *CATS.*

CRITICISM

George Fortenberry (essay date Winter 1967)

SOURCE: "Prufrock and the Fool Son," in *Ball State University Forum,* Vol. VIII, Winter, 1967, pp. 51-54.

[*In the following essay, Fortenberry explores the influence of Jules Laforgue on "Prufrock" and considers the role of the fool.*]

How much or how little the title of a poem means is, of course, left to the whim or decision of the poet. Upon occasion, however, a title will furnish the best clue to the meaning and significance of a poem. It is quite possible that the title, **"The Love Song of J. Alfred Prufrock,"** could furnish us with meaning we have not found before. This title has received very little attention considering the great attention which the poem itself has received. The following remarks focus upon the title of the poem, especially its use of the term "song."

In spite of the fact that **"The Love Song of J. Alfred Prufrock"** has fostered many articles, enough, in fact, to make it one of the best understood works in our language, the poem is not well read by—not well explained to—thousands of college freshmen each year who find it in the section of their readers devoted to the latest poetry to be anthologized. Often they are rather shocked to learn that the poem is vintage 1915, which, although a good year, seems long ago to a freshman. They are also shocked to learn that it has been in print longer than some Thomas Hardy and a great deal of Housman and Hopkins. **"The Love Song of J. Alfred Prufrock"** is no longer young. It is of such an age that coming to terms with it becomes very important.

Those who have long used the Brooks and Warren explanation of the Prufrock poem and are satisfied need go no further. It is a reasonable and sound explanation and one of the few attempts to deal with the whole poem by bringing some semblance of unity to it. Unfortunately for those who seek further than Brooks and Warren, most articles on the poem deal almost entirely with fragments, with single lines or single words, with Mermaids, rolled trousers, or gastric problems caused by peaches. This line-by-line approach is entirely natural because lines of the poem, especially those in the last section, seem to lack unity. Other essays are concerned with the sources of various lines in the poem. This approach is also a natural development which grew out of Eliot's own precedent of publishing notes on **"The Wasteland."** One of the best articles of this type, John C. Pope's "Prufrock and Raskalnikov," was provocative enough to merit a reply by Eliot in which he claimed the source for the Hamlet in **"The Love Song of J. Alfred Prufrock"** to be the work of Jules Laforgue, not Dostoyevsky's *Crime and Punishment,* as Pope had contended.

> It is quite possible that the title, "The Love Song of J. Alfred Prufrock," could furnish us with meaning we have not found before.
> —*George Fortenberry*

Explanation of **"The Love Song of J. Alfred Prufrock"** should begin with attention to the work of Jules Laforgue where Eliot has directed us. Not only that, but attention should be given to Laforgue's Hamlet, a character not too much like Shakespeare's Hamlet. Critics have known for a long time of Laforgue's influence. They have not, however, paid much attention to his Hamlet in trying to interpret the poem.

To return to the title, we observe that Eliot's poem is about a love song. As we read, however, we are soon aware that this is not the regular boy-girl love song but is an attempt to communicate a message of importance to the world, a message Prufrock wants to deliver but has great difficulty expressing. In spite of the difficulty, the love song is finally sung. It is sung by the Fool, and it is within the Fool Song that we may find the comment that Prufrock wants to make, one which Eliot himself continued to make in later poetry. The song of the Fool begins in much the same way that any ditty of a Fool in Shakespearian or other seventeenth-century drama might begin. But this resemblance does not mean that Eliot got his Fool from these sources, even though no smaller Fool than Falstaff admits, "I am old, I am old." (2 *Henry IV.* II. iv. 294) Much more likely it is that Eliot got his Fool, along with his Hamlet, from the work of Jules Laforgue, for both **"The Love Song of J. Alfred Prufrock"** and **"Portrait of a Lady"** are Laforguian poems. Eliot has indicated his indebtedness to Laforgue for his method. Tindall comments upon this method at length:

> The essays of Jules Laforgue tell almost as much about him as his verse. Inflated at first with transcendental yearning, he was deflated, he says, by Darwin. Hence the inflation and deflation of the poet's metaphors and the painful joy of punctured sentiments. But in Hartman's theory of the unconscious Laforgue found peace and a literary method. It was the job of the poet, he felt, to follow the vagaries of the life force beyond limits, categories, and reason. "The wind of the unconscious blows where it will," he exclaims. "Let it blow." Meanwhile the poet's face assumed the expression of the *fumiste* and man about town.

Laforgue's *fumiste* should interest us as a key to the mean-

ing of the Prufrock poem, for it is as *fumiste,* or Fool, that J. Alfred Prufrock makes his last attempt to communicate with the world. It is as Fool that Eliot has Prufrock show his own disenchantment with the modern world. In Eliot's poem Prufrock yearns to communicate with the world, and he makes at least two attempts before he gives up, resorting at last to the Fool Song. First, Prufrock is a man of society, one who is all-knowing and rather worn out with it all, or as Laforgue says in his criticism of Corbiere, who was adept at revealing only "mild waterfront sensuality," "He has known the Paris prostitute on his Paris holidays . . . and has known her also from the tropics to the pole." In spite of his all-knowing guise, Prufrock is not able to sing his love song to the world. He does not think the world would understand. The one he told his love song to would merely answer, "That is not what I meant at all./ That is not it, at all."

Prufrock does not come any nearer communicating with the world in the role of prophet than he did as a man of society. He is unable to sing his song as a prophet crying out a great truth to the world; even as one who has returned from the dead he would not be able to do it. By means of a quotation from Dante concerning Guido, and by using a reference to Lazarus, Eliot stresses the impossibility of communication and understanding between dead and living. In fact, the idea of communication with the dead is so strong in the poem that one is tempted to include Shakespeare's Hamlet here as one who has talked with the dead, sealing his own doom in the process. Prufrock, however, is not Prince Hamlet. The great void between dead and living holds a fascination for Eliot, a fascination well expressed in **"Little Gidding"** when he writes:

> And what the dead had no speech for, when living,
> They can tell you, being dead: the communication
> Of the dead is tongued with fire beyond the
> language of the living.

At this point it is important to return to Laforgue and also to remember that Prufrock says, "Almost at times, the Fool." It is at this moment that the Fool Song begins with the plaintive lines, "I grow old, I grow old." The next eleven lines have perhaps called forth more questions and more speculation than any other part of the poem. They are lines which have added great difficulty to interpretation chiefly because they are made up of an inane ditty, the type a stage Fool would sing. Eliot here is following the theory he borrowed from Jules Laforgue. It is well known that Laforgue was fond of fools and clowns, and the last six lines of his "Apotheosis" show his method of ending a poem. He gives us a picture of a man who has contemplated the stars in the process of trying to find his role in the universe.

> His family: a host of heavy blossoming globes, And
> on one, the earth, a yellow point, Paris, Where un-

der a swinging lamp, a poor fool sits. A weak phenomenon in the universal order, Knowing himself the mirror of a single day, He thinks of all this, then composes a sonnet.

Laforgue has his Fool compose a sonnet after he has made the discovery that he is of little importance in the universe. Prufrock becomes convinced that he is of little more importance than something crawling along the sea bottom. His Fool Song of twelve lines very effectively ends the poem.

There is a strong possibility that having failed to communicate with the world, Prufrock conveys his disillusionment as well as his love song and message through the song of the Fool.
—George Fortenberry

It is also interesting and perhaps significant that Eliot uses a Laforguian Hamlet. Laforgue had a very special feeling for Hamlet which led him to create his own modern version of the character. The translator of Laforgue's *Selected Writings*, William Jay Smith, observes that:

> Max Beerbohm once said that he thought that the scene with Yorick's skull would have been more effective if Shakespeare had given us an example of how the fool once entertained the royal table.

and himself adds: "This Laforgue has done; for he has written, as he expressed it, *à la* Yorick, combining hero and fool." What Laforgue actually did was create a Hamlet who was a brother of Yorick. His "Hamlet or The Consequences of Filial Piety" depicts them as having the same gypsy mother. Even a hasty look at this work of Laforgue will show that Eliot was saturated not only with Laforgue's method, but also with some of his words.

There is a strong possibility that having failed to communicate with the world, Prufrock conveys his disillusionment as well as his love song and message through the song of the Fool. Whether it is Darwinian disillusionment does not matter much for an interpretation of the Prufrock poem. Eliot's "Till human voices wake us and we drown." may be the equivalent of his lines in later poems:

> And any action
> Is a step to the block, to the fire, down the sea's throat.
>   or:
> We are born with the dead.
>   or:
> In my beginning is my end.

In any event, and entirely aside from Eliot's philosophy, both Yorick and Hamlet would, I believe, be happy to know that they have a delightful half-brother named Prufrock.

J. Peter Dyson (essay date 1978)

SOURCE: "Word Heard: Prufrock Asks His Question," in *Yeats Eliot Review,* Vol. 5, No. 2, 1978, pp. 33-5.

[*In the following essay, Dyson contradicts Robert M. Seiler's arguments, stating that Eliot does pose a question in "Prufrock."*]

An assumption seems to have grown up over the years that no precise meaning can be assigned to the "overwhelming question" in T. S. Eliot's **"The Love Song of J. Alfred Prufrock."** When Prufrock cries, "It is impossible to say just what I mean!" one is meant, apparently, to see the impossibility as referring, above all, to the formulation of the question. One can certainly agree with Balachandra Rajan, in his recent book, *The Overwhelming Question,* that **"Prufrock"** owes its effect as much to what is not in the poem as to what is, but Rajan's denial of the question's presence in the poem tends to diminish unnecessarily Eliot's accomplishment. Surely the "overwhelming question" *is* there in the poem, there in the way demanded by the methodology of the poem. One of the stranger aspects of the Prufrock "question" is the way in which critics, whether assuming the question to be present in the poem or not, have refrained from making clear what the question actually is and how it is present if, indeed, it is present.

One of the stranger aspects of the Prufrock "question" is the way in which critics, whether assuming the question to be present in the poem or not, have refrained from making clear what the question actually is and how it is present if, indeed, it is present.
—J. Peter Dyson

It seems for a moment as if Robert M. Seiler, in his interesting article, "Prufrock and Hamlet," is about to elucidate the matter once and for all since he recognizes that the imaginative link between the two characters rests on their respective capacities to approach the great question. However, Seiler quickly allies himself with such predecessors as Elizabeth Drew, George Williamson, Cleanth Brooks and Robert Penn Warren, who posit Prufrock's inability to identify the question. "The fundamental difference between [Hamlet and Prufrock]," writes Seiler, "is a psychological one: Hamlet formulates his 'question' while Prufrock can only hint that he has one in the back of his mind."

The difficulty stems, apparently, from Prufrock's nebulousness of mind—that mind which wanders about and slithers through the digressions of the poem like the enigmatic fog-cat which is its metaphor. Prufrock's intelligence lacks the all-encompassing grip of Hamlet's, the argument goes; it cannot come to terms with the complexities of modern life in the way that Hamlet's was able to get the measure of the (lesser?) complexities of the Renaissance. It is precisely because he senses life to be so overwhelming that he finds it impossible to ask any relevant question—let alone expect an answer; Prufrock cannot, therefore, objectify or universalize his plight. The poem is reduced to a digressive exploration of an emotional state; the logical exploration of the "human condition" represented in *Hamlet* is not possible in the twentieth century. By accepting Seiler's premises, one is forced to accede to his conclusion that "Prufrock's inability to formulate any of Hamlet's questions or answers, according to T. S. Eliot, prevents him from being able to say, 'I suffer'."

> **To think of Prufrock as merely incapable of formulating the question is to expect Eliot to depart from the poetic presuppositions of the poem, which are that everything Prufrock aspires to appears in the poem as echo, including the "overwhelming question." One need only read the relevant line of "Prufrock" with the proper stress for the question to leap into focus.**
> **—*J. Peter Dyson***

Seiler seems to be about to grasp the central truth concerning Prufrock's relationship to his question when he writes, "In his 'To be or not to be' soliloquy (III, 1, 56-88), for example, Hamlet confronts the abyss with his typical rigorous self-analysis, and confesses his procrastination." But, in restricting the meaning of *Hamlet* to Hamlet, Seiler is led to restrict the meaning of "**Prufrock**" to Prufrock. To limit the vision of the poem to the vision of the protagonist is to miss the central poetic device of the poem and the climactic working-out of the Hamlet-Prufrock link. The reason Prufrock has no "To be or not to be" is simplicity itself; he has none because he uses Hamlet's.

To think of Prufrock as merely incapable of formulating the question is to expect Eliot to depart from the poetic presuppositions of the poem, which are that everything Prufrock aspires to appears in the poem as echo, including the "overwhelming question." One need only read the relevant line

of "**Prufrock**" with the proper stress for the question to leap into focus. The line is, of course, the climactic line of the poem: "No! I am not Prince Hamlet, nor was meant to be." If one stresses it, "No! I am not Prince Hamlet, nor was *meant* to be," the meaning is, "No! I am not Prince Hamlet, nor was meant to be [Prince Hamlet]." If, however, one uses the obvious alternative stress, the meaning of the line becomes simply, "No! I am not Prince Hamlet, nor was meant to *be.*" The echo is immediate: "No! I am not Prince Hamlet, nor was meant to be or not to be, *that* is the question" [emphasis added].

Prufrock does, in effect, formulate his question, Hamlet's question—*the* question of the ages, Renaissance and twentieth-century—but he can do it only indirectly, by allusion. Characteristically, he poses it by answering it negatively and, by Eliot's brilliant manipulation of tenses, simultaneously in advance yet as part of the already vanished past. The questions within the poem modulate from the direct possibility of "Do I dare?" and "Shall I say?" through the dubious possibility of "How should I?" to the past impossibility of "Would it have been?" The allusive structure of the "**Prufrock**" climax means both that the reply to the question—"No?"—is given prior to the posing of the question and that the verb identifying Prufrock's reason for responding negatively—"am not meant"—assigns the initiative elsewhere. Hamlet's question, posing direct though opposite possibilities, is made, by Eliot's syntactical manipulation of the echo, to express the impotence of present impossibility. Prufrock's version of the Hamlet question then takes its place naturally in the sequence started by Prufrock's initial "do not ask 'What is it?'" as the technical and emotional climax of what Rajan has called "the outline of failure."

While it may be possible to argue about whether or nor Prufrock is conscious of the echo, it is not possible to wonder whether Eliot is. "**Prufrock**" remains a poem about the difficulties of realizing one's nebulous potentialities, but the framework retains a precision that serves to place Prufrock and his predicament not outside the formulations available to the English literary tradition, as critics such as Seiler would suggest, but emphatically within them.

Shyamal Bagchee (essay date Winter 1980)

SOURCE: "'Prufrock': An Absurdist View of the Poem," in *English Studies in Canada*, Vol. VI, No. 4, Winter, 1980, pp. 430-43.

[*In the following essay, Bagchee argues that "Prufrock" should be reinterpreted in terms of post-modern theories.*]

I

The aim of this article is to reclaim one of T. S. Eliot's most celebrated poems as a truly modern poem: as poetry that is as significant in our post-Modernist times as it was in 1915 when it was published at the beginning of the Modernist movement in Anglo-American literature. For much too long it has been admired and interpreted mainly from narrowly Modernist or Eliotic perspectives. Most existing readings of the **"Love Song of J. Alfred Prufrock"** ridicule the poem's main character for his timidity and self-deception. He is blamed for surrendering too easily to the petty vanities encouraged by a shallow and self-conscious society. The poem is admired mainly for its supposedly Modernist irony and its stylistic innovations. It seems to me that this "standard" approach fails to explain the poem's strange and powerful hold on the imagination of twentieth-century readers. There is an inexplicable gap between the critics' high-minded rejection of Prufrock and his world, and the incontrovertible appeal of the poem itself. The important concerns of the poem are those of the central character, yet critics have continually berated that character.

The view that Prufrock is a damned soul or a morally flawed character is popular also because it ties in well with the moral and religious concerns of Eliot's later writings. But this acceptance of the "integrity" of Eliot's *oeuvre,* though attractive in its neatness, tends to make us overlook significant differences between the poems. Today Eliot scholarship has advanced far enough for us to demand an analytical rather than a synthesized view. By making the right distinctions between the various kinds of creative impulses which inform the different poems we will better understand the poet.

> **Most existing readings of the "Love Song of J. Alfred Prufrock" ridicule the poem's main character for his timidity and self-deception. He is blamed for surrendering too easily to the petty vanities encouraged by a shallow and self-conscious society. The poem is admired mainly for its supposedly Modernist irony and its stylistic innovations. It seems to me that this "standard" approach fails to explain the poem's strange and powerful hold on the imagination of twentieth-century readers.**
> **—*Shyamal Bagchee***

In view of the continued appeal of **"Prufrock"** and *The Waste Land* at a time when Modernist poetic ideals have fallen in general disfavour, one may perhaps rightly conclude that in spite of certain superficial affinities with the deliberately iconoclastic and abrasive poetry of the early Modernist period, these poems never really belonged to that literary school or period. I think it can be profitable to examine Eliot's poetry from such post-Modernistic positions as the Existentialist and Absurdist. The poems indicate the inadequacy of reason and morality to make sense of our experience. **"Prufrock,"** in particular, depicts a rational, sensitive, and sensual individual's exasperatingly pointless encounter with reality. The poet seems unable to suggest a path that will lead to sense and will impose some meaning upon experience.

Given Eliot's natural inclinations (which were towards order, some system of belief whether literary or religious) it is difficult to believe that he would ever have accepted this absurdist stance as the final view of life. Therefore, it is not surprising that Eliot did not write about an absurdist view in his prose criticism. For him the *ideal* was always a system of order, but his poetry was not merely the versification of what he thought; it embodied his experience of reality. On the one hand, Eliot was far too sensitive to be able to ignore the pervasive and painful irrationality of the world around him; on the other hand, he was not one who could, like Yeats and Lawrence, fight that reality passionately and imaginatively. Eliot must be seen apart from other writers who underwent the modern experience. He did not have Joyce's fine sense of proportion about the absurd which gave *Ulysses* its moral-comedic vitality. Neither was he temperamentally equipped to persist indefinitely in a view of amoral-irrationality; therefore, he did not develop into a writer like Kafka. Eventually Eliot had to discover tradition and religion as his symbols for order, but in these early poems he was mainly free from religious predilections and was close to the world of the absurd. It cannot be said that he was ever quite convinced about the inevitability of the absurd world (though he was surely, for the time being, painfully aware of its inexorability); for this reason he never became a comedic-nihilist like Samuel Beckett.

II

"Prufrock" is more an inconclusive question (both for the protagonist and the poet) than it is a solution effected through social or moral satire. The poem does not invite us to force an absolute distinction between the poet and the protagonist; rather it invites us to regard Prufrock as a likely mask for the poet and for many of the poem's readers—the deliberately conflated "us" in the opening line.

What I would like to suggest is that Prufrock should be regarded as Eliot's Everyman. Of course, Everyman is never really *every* man and Eliot's is no exception. What makes Prufrock an Everyman is that in him acceptable notions of the self, of both the poet and the reader, find expression. Needless to say Everyman is not a heroic character; but this Everyman, being the Everyman of a particularly sensitive, learned, literary-minded, intelligent poet, is at least a special person. So is, in a way, the ideal reader of Eliot's poetry.

> **Prufrock should be regarded as Eliot's Everyman. Of course, Everyman is never really *every* man and Eliot's is no exception. What makes Prufrock an Everyman is that in him acceptable notions of the self, of both the poet and the reader, find expression.**
> —*Shyamal Bagchee*

Far from being a damned soul, or a social nincompoop, Prufrock is actually quite admirable, especially when we contrast him against his social milieu. Moreover, Prufrock proves himself capable of describing and interpreting astutely the moral pointlessness of the world in which he lives.

It has often been pointed out that the poem highlights lack of communication between individuals, and that Prufrock's main guilt is his refusal or inability to sing his "love song." However, throughout the poem it is Prufrock who worries most about the impossibility of such communication. Prufrock's most urgent wish is to convey his feelings. He is the most humane of Eliot's early protagonists and is flanked on one side by the silent and solipsistic Narcissus ("stifled and soothed by his own rhythm"), and on the other by the pathetic and gregarious lady of **"Portrait of a Lady."** Prufrock does not sing his "love song." But this is not because he wants to remain aloof from people who surround him. Rather, unlike the lady, he is acutely conscious of the insensitivity and callousness of his society and can see the futility of expressing his true feelings. Whatever else the unuttered "love song" may be, the bit of it that is actually verbalized by Prufrock is neither solipsistic nor lofty in any philosophical sense. In fact these are words that try to reach out to other people, words that are pregnant with great sympathy for fellow human beings:

> Shall I say, I have gone at dusk through narrow streets
> And watched the smoke that rises from the pipes
> Of lonely men in shirt-sleeves, leaning out of windows?

We should pay particular attention to these lines. Within the poem's fragmented narrative framework, they represent Prufrock's first tentative formulation of the song. For most readers these lines are overshadowed by the more transparently rhetorical hyperbole of Prufrock's rehearsing of his "speech" a few lines later:

> "I am Lazarus, come from the dead,

Come back to tell you all, I shall tell you all"—

That this is really a "speech," or the beginning of one, is indicated by the inverted commas used to emphasize its theatricality. This "speech" has no thematic substance at all; it gives no indication of what it is that is bothering Prufrock; it is merely a pose, deliberate histrionics.

By contrast, in the earlier quotation Prufrock attempts to bring to the attention of a gregarious but uncaring society the real sense of isolation, of loneliness, that exists under the surface. It is not necessary to assume that this loneliness affects only the protagonist who loves to luxuriate in imagined suffering and eventually becomes an enervated solipsist through sentimental overindulgence. What makes the poem relevant to our age is our recognition of both the validity of what Prufrock wants to say and of the fact that the women in the room will never really understand what he means. In fact what Prufrock wants to say in these lines is echoed by Eliot in **"Morning at the Window"** and **"Preludes,"** two of the most compassionate of his early poems. In **"Preludes IV"** an "I" voice, who is probably the poet himself, confesses:

> I am moved by fancies that are curled
> Around these images, and cling:
> The notion of some infinitely gentle
> Infinitely suffering thing.

Critics often point to these lines when they seek to defend Eliot from charges of indiscriminate irony and lack of human sympathy. I think Prufrock's lines belong with these. But Prufrock is not a poet, he is merely the poet's Everyman. The poet is in a special sense a hero, a creator; he can live through the images he creates. To Prufrock such life is not available. In spite of these differences between the "I" of **"Preludes"** and Prufrock, the similarity of the message strengthens my view that Prufrock is actually quite close to the poet, for even the poet admits that in the face of our unthinking, heartless reality his images are, perhaps, no more than "fancies" to which he "clings." This is the most that is available to sensitive individuals—to hope for a more tangible solution to one's anxiety is to deceive oneself.

Eliot does not depict Prufrock as a prophet or even a prophet *manqué.* Prufrock's prophetic voice in the Lazarus speech is really a joke, and Prufrock intends it to be seen as a joke. It is not correct to imagine that Prufrock unrealistically or obtusely thinks of himself as one who has come back from the dead. As a matter of fact, Prufrock knows himself quite well. When he pictures himself making the speech, he does not see himself as being tense or overly serious, rather as being amused at the incongruous image of "squeezing the universe into a ball." He thinks of himself as casually "biting off the matter *with a smile*" (italics mine). This is one of Prufrock's private jokes: private because he cannot share it with anyone who is around him. Only he can see it as a comic invention, and he alone is capable of imagining such an improbable scheme with which to provoke his stupid audience. It is worthwhile to remember that Prufrock is not seeking to ask *the* overwhelming question but merely "some" overwhelming question—any that would be suitably highfalutin, outrageous, and improbable. In the opening stanza of the poem we are told that the overwhelming question is to be asked *of* Prufrock, not *by* Prufrock.

> **Mainly, Prufrock wishes to tell his listeners that "No man is an island, entire to itself." But Prufrock is not a hero; he does not have a prophet's power to convince others, nor does he have the self-assurance needed to convince himself that he should at least try.**
>
> **—*Shyamal Bagchee***

Prufrock already knows that his humane appeal to his listener's conscience will inevitably fail: "I have seen the moments of my greatness flicker." He fully understands that he must not expect from either the woman or anyone else in his world sympathetic imagination and genuine concern. In fact, his lines about "lonely men in shirt-sleeves" are not obtuse enough to attract his listeners' attention or to interest them. His words may contain truth but they sound too simple, too low-key. What should he do instead? Use a special style, even if a false one? Speak in an artificial, theatrical rhetoric? Assume the tone and diction of a prophet? He is not convinced that doing any of these things would help him in any way: "Would it have been worth it after all?" he asks. The answer, obviously, is "no." Nevertheless, he tries to imagine what he would sound like if he did; he may even be able to startle his audience with this improbable form of speech. It is Prufrock himself, with his definite sense of irony, who tells how incongruous any show of human concern will be

> After the cups, the marmalade, the tea,
> Among the porcelain, among some talk of you and
> me.

In pointing out the irony Prufrock makes it quite clear that he has the ability to judge the true worth of the norms of social behaviour expected of him, the behaviour he regretfully conforms to. His sensitivity makes him vulnerable. He is an outsider and is treated as such by the women who discuss him as they would anyone similar to him—"some talk of you and me." The "you" here, as in the first line of the poem, includes the reader and the poet, both of whom are outsiders in that society.

Mainly, Prufrock wishes to tell his listeners that "No man is an island, entire to itself." But Prufrock is not a hero; he does not have a prophet's power to convince others, nor does he have the self-assurance needed to convince himself that he should at least try. Instead, he despairs and gives up. Numerous critics have dwelt upon Prufrock's "failure," his inability to "force the moment to its crisis." But this inability has been unjustly seen as moral failure, even more turpitude. Such a view of morality may be appropriate in the context of traditional ethical expectations, particularly to the conventional notion of a hero, but it is out of place in the amoral world of this poem. Ideally, Prufrock should have persisted in making his point; but to insist on such positive action from an unheroic character is to force a heroic concept on a world where notions of heroism have become inoperable. Prufrock is not a leader of men, but in not being one he does not automatically become insignificant to the reader. The disapproval of Prufrock's failure is quite simplistic and indicates our inability to enter imaginatively the existential and kinetic (rather than ideal and absolute) world of the poem.

> **The special feeling of the absurd in the poem arises from Prufrock's, and our, apprehension that although the world is amoral and illogical, we are not yet prepared to accept it as such. This makes for a peculiar dilemma: is one what one thinks one ought to be, or is one someone one has never been taught to recognize?**
>
> **—*Shyamal Bagchee***

The important question to ask is, "What could Prufrock have done being who he is?" To say that he should have been a different kind of person is to overlook the essential existential problem outlined in the poem. Prufrock comes at the head of the long list of non-heroes in recent literature. As a non-hero Prufrock is not better or worse than we are; therefore, we understand what he has to say while his listeners in the poem do not. This is one of the major indications of the poem's absurdity, its absurd world, and its absurd process of communication. Like many post-Modernist works of literature, **"Prufrock"** arranges its communicative pattern in a non-static, spatial way. What Prufrock fails to say to the lady in the poem, the very act of his failure makes most meaningful to the reader. I am not talking about dramatic irony, allegory, or any such referential rhetorical device that makes us understand a created literary piece—an object stable in time—from the outside of it. **"Prufrock"** is not to be understood merely by reference to stable intellectual and moral notions outside the poem. In fact **"Prufrock"** should not be approached referentially at all. Its dimension is that of space and it grows spatially into our, the readers', world. The creation of the relationship between the protagonist and the reader, in the "us" of the opening line, is vital to the poem's intended significance. It is not Prufrock's failure that we are shown in the poem; rather we are given an unmistakable sense of *deja vu*. The poem's world and its agony, despair, and uncertainty reach our world by extending a number of tentacles—various and complex patterns of images, emotional vibrations, and voices. Among these must be mentioned strange and compelling imagistic features like the "street" that follows like a "tedious argument," the fearful and mechanistic shadow of nerve patterns on the wall, and the silently scuttling crab that Prufrock wishes he was.

The special feeling of the absurd in the poem arises from Prufrock's, and our, apprehension that although the world is amoral and illogical, we are not yet prepared to accept it as such. This makes for a peculiar dilemma: is one what one thinks one ought to be, or is one someone one has never been taught to recognize? These critics who suggest that the "overwhelming question" is not really an "insidious" one but a profoundly moral one fail to understand the way in which the poem works. The questions about what Prufrock did, what he should have done, and what he should not to have done are quite out of place and deserve Sweeney's firm but impatient disapproval:

> What did he do! what did he do?
> That don't apply.

When Prufrock admits with much agony, "it is impossible to say just what I mean!"—lines that can be placed next to Sweeney's words, "Well here again that don't apply/But I've gotta use words when I talk to you" we should not assume that this is merely because Prufrock cannot articulate recondite ideas.

To understand the absurdist intentions of the poem we must consider the character of Prufrock in the context of the world in which he lives. We should not approach the poem from preconceived moral or satirical premises.
—*Shyamal Bagchee*

The tragedy of Prufrock, if the word tragedy is not inappropriate here, is that he, like most of the poem's readers, has been brought up on the idea of a hero ("Prince Hamlet") and therefore cannot now reconcile himself to the notion of a non-hero. In other words, Prufrock is quite unlike Murphy, the protagonist of Samuel Beckett's novel *Murphy*. Caught between two worlds, the reasonable and the moral, and the irrational and the amoral, Prufrock epitomizes one of the most central and most perplexing of modern dilemmas. And it is my view that the communication of this dilemma ac-

counts for the continued appeal of **"Prufrock."** In the poem and in its portrayal of the protagonist we recognize the "divorce between man and his life, the actor and his setting," which according to Albert Camus constitute the feeling of Absurdity.

To understand the absurdist intentions of the poem we must consider the character of Prufrock in the context of the world in which he lives. We should not approach the poem from preconceived moral or satirical premises. The poem is about a man who is neither so naive as to overlook the irrationality of the world around him, nor so pessimistic as to accept the failure of reason as final and absolute. This hesitation makes Prufrock a special person. Prufrock is not like the others in the poem who appear to be utterly ignorant of what it is that is happening to their world. Some degree of sympathetic and intellectual understanding of life is necessary before questions about reason and irrationality, meaning and absurdity become important to an individual. Such questions do not trouble obtuse minds. It is an indication of the special nature of Prufrock's character that these questions bother him; his predicament is of half knowing and half not knowing the issues involved. When one is not thus bothered one can afford to be dogmatic, smug, and self-assured as the woman in the poem is when she says so emphatically, "That is not it, *at all*" (italics mine). By contrast Prufrock hesitates, vacillates, and is diffident. He is not one of the "low"

> on whom assurance sits
> As a silk hat on a Bradford millionaire.
>   (*The Waste Land*)

It is instructive to contrast Prufrock with the house-agent's clerk in *The Waste Land*. Prufrock, middle-aged and neat of appearance, is an antithesis of the "young man carbuncular" even though both are shown visiting their ladies. Eliot's early poetry demonstrates the several levels at which individuals encounter reality. Among the various characters who populate the early poems Prufrock is alone in believing that no individual, however competent and intelligent he may be, can truly have his whole meaning by himself. Yet having a meaning, or at least believing that meaning is important, is one of major concerns. The young man in *The Waste Land* is not in the least bothered by the fact that his overtures to his mistress have no effect on her. His assurance and self-sufficiency are disgusting:

> The time is now propitious, as he guesses,
> The meal is ended, she is bored and tired,
> Endeavours to engage her in caresses
> Which still are unreproved, if undesired.
> Flushed and decided, he assaults at once. (Lines 235-39)

For Prufrock, polite and sceptical, time is never "propitious" in the world in which he has to live.

Although Prufrock never sings his "love song," neither does he reduce his love to an "assault." Prufrock is diffident not because he believes that his song is unworthy of being sung; his main fear is that it will be ridiculed and defiled by an uncaring world. In the world of the poem, the emotional, lyrical quality of his sensitive mind makes Prufrock an exceptional person, but it also makes him especially lonely. However, the inexorable fact about both love and song is that they need at least two people to give them meaning.

What can a person like Prufrock do? The poem's stark answer is "nothing." That is precisely what Prufrock does. One cannot, as the protagonist of *The Waste Land* foolishly imagines possible, set one's own lands in order. It is an intellectual self-deception to presume that there are "my lands" which can be separated from lands that belong to others, and it is equally self-deceiving to believe that one can, by oneself, set any land in order. The only things one can truly have by oneself are one's dilemma and anxiety. Eliot's personal, and it would appear inevitable answer to this dilemma in later life was the rejection of the world itself. But such a drastic metaphysical position is not maintained in the early poems, where the concerns of the absurd world are unmitigated by any ascetic desire for withdrawal into a spiritual world. In the world of the early poems such withdrawal can merely "confirm a prison." Many of Eliot's early protagonists are solipsistic and ego-bound: Narcissus, the young man in **"Portrait of a Lady,"** Gerontion, and several characters in *The Waste Land.* Only Prufrock, even in his faltering ways, desires to break open the prison of the complacent self. In a vague way he is similar to the woman in **"Portrait of a Lady"** who also believes in friendship: "Without these friendships—life, what *cauchemar*!" What makes this woman pathetic is that she foolishly declares her love to a world that cares little for such an emotion. She sings her love song and confirms the validity of Prufrock's fears. In spite of the strong erotic attraction of the woman in the shawl Prufrock does not sing his song to her; in doing what Prufrock does not do, the woman in **"Portrait"** acquires a lover who trifles with her affection.

What is, in effect, absurd about the world of Prufrock is that even the most apparently right gestures and efforts lead only to wrong solutions—or to no solutions at all. No easy reconciliation with this irrational world is possible for the person who expects reasonable and humane solutions. The unthinking woman whom Prufrock loves, or the cruel young man of **"Portrait of a Lady,"** are least bothered by this absurdity. But Prufrock and many of the poem's readers are not such people. Unlike the protagonist of Thom Gunn's poem "Innocence," Prufrock is *not*

ignorant of the past:

Culture of guilt and guilt's vague heritage,
Self-pity and the soul.

Rather, he is an heir to all these, especially "soul"; perhaps "self-pity" is a more human manifestation of soul's "vague heritage" than the arrogant, upstanding qualities our world loudly proclaims in public and expresses in clichés. In Gunn's ironic poem the "hero" has forged, out of such "finitude of virtues" (line 13) as "Courage, endurance, loyalty and skill" (line 10), a conscience that "No doubt can penetrate, no act can harm." Prufrock's soul is not composed of such innocent and sturdy ingredients. On the other hand, Prufrock's recent literary inheritors include many of Philip Larkin's sensitive but non-heroic protagonists. This comparison goes against the generally held view of the works of these two poets. For instance, C. B. Cox has recently written that "there is a compassion which sharply differentiates Larkin's democratic sympathies from T. S. Eliot's assumptions of superiority." The misunderstanding is due mainly to the Modernist readers' fastidious cultivation of a taste for ironic and abrasive literature. **"Prufrock"** has often been admired for wrong reasons—reasons which are, to some extent, based on pre-conceived assumptions about Modernist literature. Today we recognize the humanity of Joyce's *Ulysses,* although for a long time Joyce was regarded primarily as an iconoclastic writer. Such change of attitude towards Eliot's works is not yet evident. At least partly, **"Prufrock"** is a humane poem.

III

Our understanding of Prufrock's character has been influenced also by our notion of Eliot's poetic techniques. For example, critics often quote approvingly Eliot's statement, made several years after he wrote **"Prufrock,"** that a modern poet must become more and more "allusive, more indirect, in order to force, to dislocate if necessary, language into his meaning." But this is not the only way poetry can be written. Obliqueness in poetry, as the context of Eliot's statement makes quite clear, is the result of cultural contingency and is not in itself a special poetic virtue. Although the modern world has cultivated to a high degree its habit of not paying attention to simply expressed words, this is not necessarily because such words are inevitably inadequate. In a kind of two-tiered logic **"Prufrock"** seems to make this very point. The protagonist's words about lonely men in shirt-sleeves are quite direct and make no attempt to "dislocate" language. But they fail to satisfy the fastidious listener, who demands something rich, strange, and obviously different from normal speech; this expectation leads Prufrock to contemplate half mockingly his speech about Lazarus. In Pound's words, "The age demanded an image/Of its accelerated grimace." In **"Prufrock"**, a highly innovative poem, the complex, disjointed structure and indirect mode of expression are undercut by a deeper, persistent belief that it is the condition of the world itself that has banished from it both natural feelings and a natural kind of poetic expression. It is impossible to make sense in this world unless one joins hands with it. This is the contingency the poet faces and he adjusts his expression accordingly. The form of the poem is a living, spatial symbol of that reality.

> **Sisyphus is an appropriate symbol for Prufrock and we may, in viewing them together, see why Prufrock fails to ask his question although he tries repeatedly and almost achieves success.**
> —*Shyamal Bagchee*

I wish now to examine a specific aspect of the poem's spatial nature—the central method of its depiction and embodiment of the absurd. In **"Prufrock"** a number of inanimate, or at least non-human, objects acquire a living quality. The most important of these is the "street" of the opening paragraph. Both the descriptive words used to signify it, and the effect it supposedly has on the protagonist, give the street a sinister character. The street forms not merely a part of the landscape—the celebrated opening "scene" of the poem— it assumes an *active* role in the poem. The street is described as a "muttering retreat." This phrase stands in ambiguous syntactical relationship with the cheap hotels as well as the street. The street not only "mutters" but it also "follows" while at the same time that it, paradoxically, "leads." The street is not stationary, nor is it merely a long, curving line drawn in a painting; it chases the speaker from behind, while it is also ahead of him, beckoning him toward "an overwhelming question." Apparently, its intentions are far from benevolent; they are "insidious": lying in wait somewhere along the street, in ambush, is the question one cannot foresee or formulate, the question that one suspects exists, that one knows one will never be prepared for. The anxiety that propels the protagonist, who from time to time glances fearfully backwards over his shoulder (how else would he know that the street was following him?), makes him step cautiously (the insidious question lying in wait for him, ahead of him) but hastily (for he is also being pursued) into a future which seems to continue unendingly. . . . The point I am trying to make is that the "street" is not a symbol or a metaphor. Eliot's "multifoliate rose" is a symbol—a complex one, but still only a referential signpost. So are the "rock" and the "rose garden." But this sinister, slithering, and self-willed street is an active agent of the anxiety that haunts the protagonist. For the individual, who exist between birth and death—Eliot does not appear to be concerned with Christian salvation in this poem—the anxiety has no beginning which he can manipulate, nor can he know where its end lies. The street is a continually self-regenerating image. Unlike

the "rock" in *The Waste Land* it is not stable and finite. The "rock" is stable and solid, both semantically and in the range of its traditional symbolical meanings.

As the spatial vehicle of Prufrock's anxiety about not knowing what it is that he should do, the street extends into the reader's world and adds a concrete dimension to the poem. From the beginning Prufrock and the reader are walking, escaping, and following the same street. If the street is to be taken as a metaphor, then it must be seen as a deliberately misapplied one: it suggests a meaning—the journey, the path, the anxiety—and yet it remains itself—concrete, menacing, advancing. The word "street" suggests a range of possible meanings, then it proves all those meanings (what it *stands for*) highly inadequate and *becomes real itself.* In a way, it is a catachresis rather than a metaphor. In another sense, the "street" is what phenomenological critics call an essential "experiential pattern" which embodies an author's experiential world, or his *Lebenswelt.*

The street recedes backward into the remote distance, but it never actually ends; beyond every curve on the way it is still there. Ahead, it lies on and on; even when out of view it is unmistakably there. This creates a *mise en abîme* effect. It recedes but does not disappear; its validity is both continuous and continually revived. The street engulfs both Prufrock and the right reader. To cover it, to travel to its end, to reach some meaning, to hope to have the overwhelming question asked is to engage in the labour of Sisyphus, the most absurd and nerve-wracking of all endeavours. Sisyphus is an appropriate symbol for Prufrock and we may, in viewing them together, see why Prufrock fails to ask his question although he tries repeatedly and almost achieves success. Prufrock is doomed continually to try to sing his love song, to waver between a desire to sing his song and a desire to conform to the trivial wishes of the world, to hear "human voices" telling him to roll his trousers and forbidding him to eat peaches, and to expect to hear the "mermaids singing"—who sing "each to each" but never to him.

The street runs out of the page and into the reader's world; at the same time it runs through the poem from the half deserted streets, to the strand at the end of the poem where Prufrock contemplates walking in white flannel trousers. The street is always there, even when we are indoors, insidiously lying in wait for us just outside or watching us through the "window-panes." While Prufrock attempts to ask his question—which is not *the* "overwhelming question"—he is also mindful that the insidious, inexorable "overwhelming question" may be asked of him at any time. These two ironically juxtaposed "questions" make the protagonist's double-edged dilemma visible to the reader. In fact, when he first formulates *his* question he mentions *his* walks "at dusk through narrow streets" where he was expecting to have the overwhelming question" asked of him.

> **We misread Prufrock's thoughts when we say that he prefers to withdraw into a hard shell and *wants* to become a crab "scuttling across the floors of silent seas." He is merely saying that in the society in which he lives there is as little communication and reaching out towards others as there is between crabs. . . . A much-distressed Prufrock wonders why he too could not have been such a silent hardshelled crustacean; had he been one he would not have felt so out of tune with his world.**
> **—*Shyamal Bagchee***

Prufrock does not know the exact nature of the "overwhelming question." However, in his absurd and pointless life the encounter with this question is likely to be the only significant thing to happen to Prufrock. We may call it a "spot of time" or the point of the intersection between time and eternity although it is likely that the high experience suggested by the two phrases may be entirely out of place in the life of a non-hero. But that absurdity is in itself an indication of the overriding absurdist view presented in the poem. A more positive character, a hero, a saint, or a poet, may be able to create such special moments, or may know how to make his life an appropriate context for such moments. But Prufrock does not know anything about the nature of that special hour. He merely hopes that his life, too, will have such a moment and his worst fear is that it might come upon him when he is least prepared for it. Therefore, he is afraid of the street by the side of which the overwhelming question lies in wait to spring before him at any random moment. Unlike others in the poem, Prufrock cares very much for such a moment of illumination. So far his life has been far from remarkable and he knows that. He is not so cynical as to imagine that such moments are of no worth, nor is he so much enlightened as to have any prior notion of what it can mean. He is both afraid and hopeful. The important thing is that Prufrock can, even at his humdrum level of existence, contemplate the existence of an "overwhelming" question. His impatient "Oh, do not ask, 'What is it?'" is quite understandable. To ask for its definition is to limit its awesome dimensions, whereas Prufrock needs something that is infinite. In his finite world everything he knows is frustratingly insignificant. If the poem was meant to work within an idealistic framework—moralistic, aesthetic, or religious—the question would have been more definite and its significance more fathomable, although it still may not have been within the power of the individual to will it. In *Murder in the Cathedral* Becket does not, cannot, take the "decision" but can, as Prufrock cannot, with his "whole being give entire consent." But we cannot compare Becket with Prufrock for their worlds are seen from very different points of view. **"Prufrock"** is a more revealing picture of the reader's world than are the later works. This is not a world where empty pools in the rose garden suddenly get "filled with water out of sunlight" (**"Burnt Norton"**); it is a world where "eyes . . . fix you in a formulated phrase" not only because you are painfully conscious of what people think of you but also because the "eyes" themselves get metamorphosed, abstracted from the rest of the body and dominate the scene as in a surrealistic painting. It is a world where "hands" drop questions "on your plate," and "arms" acquire separate identities. Prufrock has not lost his senses; it is merely that he alone seems to be aware of the strange but real landscape. In a way he is no more insane than Salvador Dali. We misread Prufrock's thoughts when we say that he prefers to withdraw into a hard shell and *wants* to become a crab "scuttling across the floors of silent seas." He is merely saying that in the society in which he lives there is as little communication and reaching out towards others as there is between crabs. It is not he who is a crab or wants to be a crab, it is the woman—synedochically expressed as "Arms that are braceleted," therefore comparable to "a pair of ragged claws"—who behaves as a crab. A much-distressed Prufrock wonders why he too could not have been such a silent hardshelled crustacean; had he been one he would not have felt so out of tune with his world.

This poem is spoken by Prufrock, and much of what we know about the world around him is reported to us by him. It is not necessary to blame him for every action he reports. It is unfair to imagine that *only* Prufrock has measured out his life with coffee spoons. Of course he has done so, as have others, but only he seems to recognize that there should have been more to life. Similarly, Prufrock is bothered by the women's opinion of his appearance, but they themselves are not above such petty concerns. His reaction to the women's trivial behaviour is not exemplary, but it is real and not idealized. It is unlikely that even if Prufrock was made of worthier stuff, if he had been a real hero, he would have had a different reception from the women.

Again, when Prufrock says:

> I shall wear the bottoms of my trousers rolled.
> Shall I part my hair behind? Do I dare to eat a
> peach?
> I shall wear white flannel trousers, and walk upon
> the beach

we may not assume that he is expressing his most cherished desires. It is much more likely that he is merely hoping that by conforming to the standards expected by society he may be able to keep the backbiting women ("some talk of you and me") at bay. Like Kafka's K he, too, cannot understand what crime he has committed, and is unable to find an explanation for society's irrational displeasure with him. These lines show Prufrock's defeat at the hand of "human voices."

Yet it is not a final defeat, for end of the poem is a great lyrical outpouring, with Prufrock on the beach within earshot of the women *and the mermaids.* One imagines that Prufrock's vision of sea-girls will not allow him to be irredeemably drowned by "human voices."

In the religious phase of his career Eliot said "in our beginning is our end" and the "end is where we start from" (**"Little Gidding,"** v). By that time the road itself had become manageable, comprehensible, and even dispensable. But in **"Prufrock"** neither the beginning nor the end is known, and the road is not inconsequential. The path is not cyclical; it is lateral, infinite, and insidious. Most of Eliot's early poems show only arbitrary beginnings and arbitrary ends; the beginnings mock each other as the ends do themselves. The poems themselves become icons for the "insidious" and "cunning" streets and corridors, as well as for movements along them. The final existential anxiety that perplexes a Prufrock is a convincing representation of the Absurd—not knowing where the road started, not knowing if it leads to any place, and waiting in fear and hope for the "overwhelming" question, "Pressing lidless eyes and waiting for a knock upon the door."

J. G. Keogh (essay date Summer-Autumn 1986)

SOURCE: "Mr. Prufrock's Big City Blues," in *Antigonish Review*, Nos. 66-67, Summer-Autumn, 1986, pp. 75-9.

[In the essay below, Keogh compares Eliot's poem "Prufrock" with blues music.]

Marshall McLuhan was fond of saying that the love-song of Eliot's **"Prufrock"** is a blues song, and he related it to the interface between urban and agrarian life in the American South. In "Mr. Eliot and the St. Louis Blues," McLuhan wrote

> Further, the peculiar character of jazz derives from the South, perhaps because of the interplay between industrial and metropolitan life, on one hand, and agrarian life, on the other hand. People situated on the frontiers between metropolitan and agrarian culture are naturally inclined to interplay them. The sounds of the city can be poured through the spoken idiom in such areas.

I suppose the original nostalgia of the slave for his African homeland eventually mutated into the urban black's anguished longing for rural roots on the farm and the plantation. That same lonesome whistle blew, more wistfully, for the newly urbanized white at the turn of the century (when

"Prufrock" was written, at Harvard), no longer down on the farm, whether native emigrant or foreign.

While visiting his birthplace in Missouri in the 1950s, Eliot referred to the yellow fog in **"Prufrock"** as being "a St. Louis fog, now abated by the timely St. Louis smoke ordinance." The region of southern Illinois, just across the river from St. Louis, is quite notorious for the polluting qualities of its soft, high sulphur coal. **"The Love Song"** begins with an invitation to the reader to visit an urban inferno whose streets are full of sliding yellow smoke, a forbidding region whose smoggy river mist has anesthetized even the evening sky. Invisible only to the eye, gas-lamps only "mutter" (just as electric carbide lamps "sputter" in a later poem), and place the reader in an enchanted and acoustic space.

Eliot's poem is prefixed with an earlier revelation from below, Dante's fraudulent Count Guido in the *Inferno,* a spectre speaking from within a shaking flame. Prufrock's equivalent seems to be the magic lantern in the medical theatre, with its anatomy chart of the nervous system flung out in patterns on the screen. Controversial, polygraph. But Prufrock's depths are watery, not fiery; and when, sprawling and wriggling, he finds himself in the poison bottle or in a bit of hot water, he retreats into his shell. He can think only of a pair of ragged claws, scuttling for safety across the sea-floor.

Discussing the significance which Baudelaire held for him in **"What Dante Means to Me"** (*To Criticize the Critic*) Eliot quotes Baudelaire's description of the swarming city,

> Fourmillante Cité, cité pleine de rêves,

> Où le spectre en plein jour raccroche le passant

a city full of dreams, where ghosts in broad daylight clutch at the passer-by. Eliot's comment: "I knew what that meant, because I had lived it before I knew that I wanted to turn it into verse on my own account." And he continues,

> From him, as from Laforgue, I learned that the sort of material that I had, the sort of experience that an adolescent had had, in an industrial city in America, could be the material for poetry; and that the source of new poetry might be found in what had been regarded hitherto as the impossible, the sterile, the intractably unpoetic.

Watched by lonely men in shirt-sleeves, this is the sort of experience which Prufrock has had too ("young man," Eliot called him) but like Count Guido he recounts it as discarnate spectre.

What Dante could turn to poetic account in the *Inferno* and

Eliot in his **"Love Song,"** the wailing horns of jazz and the blues did for urban America—a good half-century before the Beatles learned to do it for the industrial midlands of England. In view of McLuhan's insights into these and other matters, it is in no way surprising that the composer of "Mood Indigo," Duke Ellington, should have held him in such high regard.

In **"The Music of Poetry"** (*On Poetry and Poets*), one of the essays of Eliot from which McLuhan quoted frequently, there appears the following intriguing passage about blues and the nonsense verse of Edward Lear.

> His non-sense is not vacuity of sense: it is a parody of sense, and that is the sense of it. *The Jumbles* is a poem of adventure, and of nostalgia for the romance of foreign voyage and exploration; the *Yongy-Bongy Bo* and *The Dong with a Luminous Nose* are poems of unrequited passion—'blues' in fact.

Eliot's **"Prufrock"** certainly reveals its affinity with the nonsense world of Carroll and Lear. Of equal interest is Eliot's statement in **"From Poe to Valéry"** (delivered in America) that the only poet in England or America whose style appears to have been formed by a study of Poe was—Edward Lear. He mentions this while discussing the exceptional feeling of Poe for "the incantatory element" in poetry. Eliot owned several of Lear's landscape paintings, but we can be sure that the incantatory rhythms and interior landscapes of Lear's poetry influenced him far more.

If Prufrock in his morning coat earlier in the poem, in his boiled shirt and tails, did not so much suggest the lobster (even to himself) we might even take him for Alice's white rabbit—no longer preoccupied with time and an approaching appointment, but lounging on the beach with a copy of the latest Playboy.

—J. G. Keogh

Incantation ("There will be time, there will be time") is noticeably present in **"Prufrock,"** and is largely responsible for the aura of self-hypnosis which hovers about the poem. And of course the blues, with their traditional repetition in the first two lines of any stanza, are the archetype of incantation. The closest thing we have to a blues lyric in the poem can be found in the three elaborately wrought stanzas beginning, "For I have known them all ready, known them all." They are, like many blues songs, sung by Prufrock to himself. They even include a reference to the Elizabethan mu-

sical term "a dying fall," a melancholy harmonic progression found in love songs of the period (the 'blacks' as it were).

It does not seem to have been noticed that the verses in the scene at the end of **"Prufrock"** share a music-hall rhythm with Lewis Carroll.

> Shall I part my hair behind? Do I dare to eat a peach?
> I shall wear white flannel trousers, and walk upon the beach.

Momentarily jarred from the depths of his dreamy sea-cave, and debating whether to sport about on the sunlit strand, Prufrock with his rag-time question seems to echo Carroll's "Lobster Quadrille" ("Will you join the dance?") and the rhythm of

> "Will you walk a little faster?" said whiting to the snail,
> "There's a porpoise close behind us, and he's treading on my tail."

If Prufrock in his morning coat earlier in the poem, in his boiled shirt and tails, did not so much suggest the lobster (even to himself) we might even take him for Alice's white rabbit—no longer preoccupied with time and an approaching appointment, but lounging on the beach with a copy of the latest Playboy.

We have lingered. But Count Guido assures us from the epigraph that "none ever did return alive from this depth." No survivor, and certainly no social butterfly, Prufrock is unable to skim the social surface, and remains sunk in the social whirl. Unlike Strephon, Prufrock never saw his goddess go. His mermaids ride, while he walks. They sing, while he talks. Their world has ever gone on wheels. And so they sing to each other, but he does not expect them to sing to him.

Surrounded and confounded by the variety of life, Prufrock is locked into one mood, as in the blues, or according to Eliot as in any of the successful poems of Edgar Allan Poe. Eliot explains the success of Poe's magical verse and richness of melody in the same essay

> It has the effect of an incantation which, because of its very crudity, stirs the feelings at a deep and almost primitive level.

This is the very technique employed by the creators of contemporary rock music, as they stir the global village, mixing memory and desire. Any too abrupt surfacing from such moody depths entails the risk of blood froth and of bends. As we emerge from the anesthetic the pain returns, along with more prosaic voices. A song lulled us to sleep, now human voices wake us. We are unable any longer to drown our sorrow in song, so now our sorrow drowns us. This is the music we must face once the ether has worn off, and the butterfly taken out of the chloroform bottle. After a night of singing the blues, the morning has come to consciousness. We are once again on display.

Robert McNamara (essay date Fall 1986)

SOURCE: "'Prufrock' and the Problem of Literary Narcissism," in *Contemporary Literature,* Vol. 27, No. 3, Fall, 1986, pp. 356-77.

[In the following essay, McNamara analyzes "Prufrock" in terms of realism and subjectivity.]

The central failure of modernist literature, according to Georg Lukács's vehement critique in "The Ideology of Modernism," is that it denies the historically situated character of human thought and action and in so doing denies the power of human actions to effect social change. Modernist literature, says Lukács, is rooted in a bourgeois ideology, at the center of which a self-made and self-contained individual confronts history, but history given a static, and as such fundamentally ahistorical, form. Like the bourgeois ideology in which it is rooted, modernist literature denies that history is a changing ensemble of human activities, and therefore subject to change by human action. Modernism rejects the tradition of realist literature in which the human individual is conceived of as an essentially social and historical being, both formed by and forming his or her environment. In modernism, that "concrete typicality" of the realist view is replaced by an "abstract particularity" that is grounded in a view of the human individual as essentially solitary and asocial, capable at best only of superficial contacts with others. Human action, particularly action aimed at effecting social change, is thereby rendered impotent.

Lukács asserts that Hegel's distinction between concrete and abstract potentiality is crucial to an adequate conception of the relation between human subjectivity and the objective world. Where concrete potentiality is concerned with the dialectical relationship between individual subjectivity and objective reality, abstract potentiality is wholly subjective, and much richer than actual life. Abstract potentiality is at once infinite and highly individual, and as such cannot determine actual development. In Lukács's view, modernism voids the distinction between concrete and abstract potentialities. It violates the crucial Hegelian distinction "by exalting man's subjectivity," and thereby, against its own intentions, impoverishing it. Modernism's view of the human individual as essentially solitary and asocial, and of self-development as

a fundamentally inward, subjective matter, violates the principle that it is in the interaction of character and environment, by decision and action, that concrete potentiality is singled out from the "bad infinity" of abstract potentiality. Modern subjectivism confuses abstract potentiality with the actual complexity of life, and as a consequence, personality, which can only be strong in relation to a strong reality, begins to disintegrate, to fragment. Subjectivity, says Lukács, succumbs to fascination and melancholy.

Along with this disintegration of personality, says Lukács, comes the modernist obsession with psychopathology. We may see the obsession either as an escape from the reality of life under capitalism or as a critique of daily life under capitalism, but neither escape nor critique, says Lukács, leads anywhere: because the psychological view grants primacy to origins and sources and posits no real goals, no ideals to be realized, it condemns action to impotence.

> **Certainly criticism has seen in "Prufrock" a weakened, severely fragmented personality, one paralyzed by possibility, with virtually no capacity for effective action, more often than it has seen a heroic liberation of desire. But there is another side of "Prufrock" . . . that offers a critique of the fantasies of coherent selfhood and the representational forms that support it, and that shows Prufrock's paralysis as the result, in large part, of his desire for a totalizing image of himself.**
> **—*Robert McNamara***

Much of the force of Lukács's critique, I find, derives from his use of Hegel's distinction between concrete and abstract potentialities to describe and critique the ethos of modernist literature. Lukács's description seems, on the level of character, both accurate and insightful, and it pointedly raises what I believe are crucial questions about the relation of notions and representations of self to the possibilities of social change.

But there are two claims in Lukács's argument that I think it important to resist. The first is that the realist mode provides the framework necessary for establishing characters as developing in dialectical relationships with their social environments and capable of effecting social change. The second is that modernist literature is unself-consciously the literature of abstract potentiality, of exalted subjectivity. The first I want to address only briefly, and primarily as an aid to formulating the second, which will be the main focus of this paper.

Leo Bersani has offered what seems to me a strong, and for my purposes, useful, case against realism. Bersani sees realism as a fundamentally conservative mode, one whose ideological interests are those of the bourgeois status quo. According to Bersani, the central assumption of the realist ideology is that the self is an intelligible structure. This is evident in the ways in which the movement toward significant form in realist literature serves the cause of coherently structured character: incidents reveal personality, beginnings and endings are purposeful, and desire, which for Bersani is by nature unbounded, is circumscribed by being forced to take form either as a ruling passion or as an abstract faculty. These strategies, as Bersani notes, serve social ends: the hero in realist works is defeated not only by his society but also by the psychology of realist form-the psychology of the "coherently structured and significantly expressive self". We see this as well in the two primary forms that heroism takes in realist literature: first, there is the hero who embodies disruptive desire, rejects social definitions of the appropriate limits of the self, and is consequently submitted to "ceremonies of expulsion" by which the anarchic impulses are socially contained; and second, there is the hero who smothers desire, either in unambiguous warning or as a strategy of retreat from the social order.

Desire cannot, Bersani argues, be fully and finally contained by the ordering strategies of descriptive narrative, and eventually fragments it into juxtaposed images. Under the pressure of desire, realist form shatters. But where Lukács sees a loss, a weakened sense of reality, a weakened personality and hence a diminished capacity for effective action, Bersani sees a potential for liberating desire from its traditional channels and hence an opening up of possibilities for social change.

Using Bersani's critique of realism to reformulate my second question with specific reference to **"Prufrock,"** we may ask: is the disjunctiveness of the poem primarily mimetic of the fragmentation of Prufrock's personality, or is it a critique of totalizing forms of desire? Certainly criticism has seen in **"Prufrock"** a weakened, severely fragmented personality, one paralyzed by possibility, with virtually no capacity for effective action, more often than it has seen a heroic liberation of desire. But there is another side of **"Prufrock,"** as I will attempt to show, that offers a critique of the fantasies of coherent selfhood and the representational forms that support it, and that shows Prufrock's paralysis as the result, in large part, of his desire for a totalizing image of himself. Eliot is aware of the problem Lukács identifies, but unlike Lukács, Eliot recognizes that the ideology of the unified, coherent self is part of the problem, not part of the solution.

The issues of selfhood involved in **"Prufrock"** gain clarity when we see the poem in literary context. I shall begin by briefly examining a number of examples of the dominant lyrical mode at the turn of the century, in order to characterize the fundamentally narcissistic ethos to which Eliot is responding in **"Prufrock."**

The dominant poetic mode at the turn of the century was a poetic of mood. It was grounded in the nineteenth-century culture of feeling and claimed as of primary value the recovery of moments of intense feeling as they provided for the momentary recovery of a unified self. The Aesthetes, continuing the anti-Victorian revolt of Swinburne and the Pre-Raphaelites, produced a poetry that moved toward Symbolism, but without the Symbolist emphasis on rendering a transcendental reality. Taking the conclusion to Pater's *The Renaissance* as providing their rationale, these poets produced a body of work characterized by sentimental emotion and poetic artifice. The poets of the Decadence, at the other pole of the poetic of mood, replaced the Aesthetes' sentimental emotion with eroticism and a libertine nostalgia. But for all these poets, poetry was a badge of sensitivity, and as such a sign of the poet's superiority, his greater capacity for life.

The poetic of mood has been succinctly characterized by Cairns Craig as the late nineteenth-century heir to the English associationist tradition, which he traces from Hume through Archibald Allison, James Mill, John Stuart Mill, and Pater. The poems in this mode are, characteristically, poems of reverie, particularly a reverie in which the poet's recovery of memory serves as a recovery of self-depths. They display the poet's acute sensitivity, and the poetic implies a hierarchy of people ranked according to their receptivity, their sensibility. Emotion supplies the poem's unity, and the poet's associations supply its diversity. The poetic values permanent over accidental associations, but, Craig argues, can provide no way of knowing one from the other. The associationist aesthetic is, he claims, essentially solipsistic, with no way of testing or grounding its claims, no way of insuring that the poet's associations are more than individual quirks.

Even the Symbolist influence on this poetic is filtered through the English associationist tradition. Symons, generally acknowledged as a primary force in bringing Symbolism into English literary culture, does so, according to Craig, by domesticating it with associationist principles that find their place in Hallam's defense of Tennyson. Nor does Anglo-American modernism, in Craig's view, break these associationist chains.

The poetic is as well closely tied to a number of features of the general culture. As late Victorian culture forbade the public expression of feeling, the poetic, like the culture of feeling in which it was grounded, served a compensatory function, elevating the forbidden to a position of value. (We may see here a logic that would seem to require a Decadence: as the value of expressed feeling depended, in this compensatory scheme, on its illicitness, poets would be driven further and further from social norms to find their materials.) Further, the poetic was tied to particular notions of personality and selfhood that were dominant in the late nineteenth century. Personality, in this view, was largely seen as the capacity to recover one's emotions, and as such was controlled retrospectively, following emotional expression, by self-consciousness, a view which encourages the longing, nostalgia, and regret that were prominent emotions in the poetry of mood. The self, imprisoned by its appearances in the world, can only be recovered in its wholeness, and then only momentarily, by the recovery of feeling. Such recovery involves an acute sensitivity to the details of appearances for their deeper, more intense, psychological meanings—as in, at one extreme, commodity fetishism. But in a world without a generally accepted code for reading such appearances, readings always give way to remystification.

It is out of this poetic of mood, but also against it, and most powerfully against its ethos, I want to argue, that Eliot builds the modernist poetic of **"Prufrock"** and *The Waste Land.* Laforgue, the poet most commonly identified as the poetic father of **"Prufrock,"** was of value to Eliot, as Kenner has observed, primarily because he had "discovered the potentialities of self-parody not in poetry at large but in the poetry of a circumscribed era, in a lyric mode closely allied with that of Dowson and Symons, one along among the possible derivations from Baudelaire." That lyric mode is very much in evidence in **"Prufrock"**: the poem "most clings to the memory whenever it exploits . . . the authorized sonorities of the best English verse" of the period; "the effects themselves, the diction, the sonorous texture and the interbreeding of nuances, came in 1908 or 1909 from sources so diffuse as to be virtually anonymous, the regnant sensibility of those years."

But Kenner's careful attention to such effects does not show the critique **"Prufrock"** offers of the ethos of this "regnant sensibility." In order to make this critique clear and to show that what Eliot has to offer in **"Prufrock"** is more than, and other than, a continuation of the associationist line, I want to look at a number of poems in the dominant mode in an attempt to characterize both the powers and limits of its ethos.

First Symons's "Pastel":

> The light of our cigarettes
> Went and came in the gloom:
> It was dark in the little room.
>
> Dark, and then, in the dark,
> Sudden, a flash, a glow,
> And a hand and a ring I know.

> And then, through the dark, a flush
> Ruddy and vague, the grace
> (A rose!) of her lyric face.

The poem, in reverie, recalls a moment of epiphany: out of the gloom and darkness, light and grace. The poem exemplifies the poetry of mood as Craig describes it: an attempt to recover, through memory, in reverie, an association of some significance. The speaker's claim seems to be that the intensity of the experience, or the intensity of the recollection, is what gives the moment value: this is what happened, this gradual unfolding out of the gloom and darkness of a vision I spontaneously saw as "a rose." This is possible, in part, as a result of the speaker's acute sensitivity, revealed in his attention to and response to fairly common objects.

But these implicit claims are foiled by the poem's very deliberate rhetoric. The studied melodramatics of "Dark, and then, in the dark, / Sudden, a flash, a glow," the deliberate introduction of religious overtones through "grace" and "A rose!" to an experience that seems otherwise not to warrant them, and the heavy reliance on adjectives for both mood and value make it clear that we are in the presence not of spontaneous reverie but of careful artifice that would like to deny itself as such. And must, if we are not to see the speaker's sensitivity as a bit of self-satisfying self-staging.

Further, we may note that the speaker's epiphany depends on a vagueness filled in by desire—an "hallucinated satisfaction in the absence of the source of satisfaction," an "appetite of the imagination" that is inseparable from fantasizing. "Pastel," although its claim seems to be of an intensity that was produced by an encounter between the speaker and his world, has nothing to offer but the intensity of desire, manifest in its rhetorical artifice and, most clearly, in its heavy reliance on adjectives (especially the "lyric" of the final line). The world of the poem is a blur, a vagueness. What desire produces is a sense of mystery but without any real content; we have a mood, but no sense of particular feelings in response to an object. This is because what the speaker desires, finally, is not so much the face as it is the moment of emergence itself, presented here as a total state.

The power of this desire and its tendency to blur the lines between psyche and world are even more apparent in another Symons poem, "White Heliotrope":

> The feverish room and that white bed,
> The tumbled skirts upon a chair,
> The novel flung half-open, where
> Hat, hair-pins, puffs, and paints, are spread;
>
> The mirror that has sucked your face
> Into its secret deep of deeps,

And there mysteriously keeps
Forgotten memories of grace;

And you, half dressed and half awake,
Your slant eyes strangely watching me,
And I, who watch you drowsily,
With eyes that, having slept not, ache;

This (need one dread? nay, dare one hope?)
Will rise, a ghost of memory, if
Ever again my handkerchief
Is scented with White Heliotrope.

Here the air of illicitness about the relationship is stronger than it was in "Pastel," and the dark and gloom of that poem has given way to jittery disorder, a kind of neurasthenic scene, which the poem attempts to draw into a unified and unifying state. Again, power and value are connected with spontaneity: here, the scent "White Heliotrope" has, or so the speaker desires, the power to raise "this"—the scene of the first three stanzas. The poem achieves a satisfying closure if we accept this desire as fact, which the poem encourages us to do: the emotional response to the memory as prospective—dread and hope—are relegated to a parenthesis, and "this" scene has, after all, already been raised before us. (Here again the claims of spontaneity are undermined by their own rhetoric, the rhetoric that has, through its deployment of the resources of tone and diction, invested them with importance.)

The second and third stanzas shed interesting light on the totalizing desire expressed in the fourth: the mirror, the woman, and the speaker inhabit a world in which relations are reduced to the production and consumption of images, a process at most half-conscious ("you, half dressed and half awake"; "I, who watch you drowsily"). Watching here is a kind of visual vampirism: the mirror has "sucked" the woman's "face / Into its secret deep of deeps," the repository of "memories of grace," and the woman watches the speaker "strangely," while his eyes, sleepless, "ache." What each wants from the other is life for himself or herself, and the structure of the stanza, gaze balanced against gaze, and the relation of the second and third stanzas, gazes balanced against the image-consuming mirror, suggest that life, or selfhood, is a matter of one's appearances, and the register of appearances is the gaze of the other. For the speaker, the recovery of something like a unified selfhood—such "grace" as is available—will be possible only retrospectively, and through the resources of memory. And memory, in this associationist poem, will require jogging, an externally supplied mnemonic to get it moving: selfhood will be recoverable at the scent of White Heliotrope.

But White Heliotrope is, we see as well, a scent whose powers as a mnemonic reduce the world to a figure of fantasy.

Finally, we feel, the details of this scene don't matter. We sense, but vaguely, the presence of contradictory feelings playing over the objects, but the feelings remain unexamined beneath the pressure of totalizing desire. The result is a mood that gains its power from the unanalyzed complex of rhetorically evoked feelings, and the recovery of self that White Heliotrope will enable will be a mood-dominated recovery of the self as its prior appearances, such appearances, such "grace" as the mirror holds.

Symons seems, at times, aware of the pitfalls of constructing a unified and coherent self, and in "Prologue" offers a critique of one such self:

My life is like a music-hall,
Where, in the impotence of rage,
Chained by enchantment to my stall,
I see myself upon the stage
Dance to amuse a music-hall.

'Tis I that smoke this cigarette,
Lounge here, and laugh for vacancy,
And watch the dancers turn; and yet
It is my very self I see
Across the cloudy cigarette.

My very self that turns and trips,
Painted, pathetically gay,
An empty song upon the lips
In make-believe of holiday:
I, I, this thing that turns and trips!

The light flares in the music-hall,
The light, the sound, that weary us;
Hour follows hour, I count them all,
Lagging, and loud, and riotous:
My life is like a music-hall.

A life played for the approval of others, says Symons's speaker, is empty, and loud, and dull. His critique at first sight seems to extend to the narcissistic "I" in general, the part projected as a unified and coherent self: "I, I, this thing that turns and trips!"

But the limits of the critique soon become clear. How is the speaker different from the "I" that "turns and trips"? If the "I" is, in its other-directed vain gaiety, an empty mask, is not the voice just one more self-satisfying staging of the self, albeit played to a classier audience? The speaking voice, full of an empty, decadent sense of its social inauthenticities, participates in the same narcissistic dynamic: the part projected as the whole, the self staged as unified and coherent. Vain weariness and self-contempt answer vain gaiety. Voice claims for itself an authenticity its performance belies. The speaker, motivated, we may feel, by a desire for an act that would allow for an expression of the self without residue, can offer no alternative to the life he critiques. He is, for all the vehemence of his attack, impotent.

The desire for an act that fully expresses the self, running as an unspoken desire through "Prologue," is an expression of what Harold Rosenberg has called "the Hamlet problem": the problem of living in a world in which actions no longer represent a person without remainder. The search for such an act can claim to be self-grounded only by denying its own rhetoricity: to admit rhetoricity is to admit that the self depends on a prior authorizing ground. The self seems inescapably, and uncomfortably, a social construction and the occasion of self-alienation. The attempt to deny their own rhetoricity leads these poems, in their quest for a totalizing act or state, to blur the lines between psyche and world, and at the same time to make claims that depend on these same lines being clearly drawn.

> **If we can, after years of hearing "Prufrock"'s first three lines as an indivisible gem, a touchstone of modernist poetry, pause long enough after the second line to hear the invitation to a journey, with its sense of expansive possibilities, we may recognize a strain of romantic pastoralism that would be right at home, say, in Wordsworth's "Stepping Westward."**
> **—*Robert McNamara***

What I offer is far from a survey of the dominant mode of the late nineteenth century. But the analyses are, I hope, adequate to reveal general tendencies, which we can readily recognize as well in Wilde's "Impression du Matin," or Dowson's "Non Sum Qualis Eram Bonae Sub Regno Cynarae," or even some of Yeats's early poems. And adequate to showing the use Eliot makes of the dominant mode in **"Prufrock."**

> Let us go then, you and I,
> When the evening is spread out against the sky.

If we can, after years of hearing **"Prufrock"**'s first three lines as an indivisible gem, a touchstone of modernist poetry, pause long enough after the second line to hear the invitation to a journey, with its sense of expansive possibilities, we may recognize a strain of romantic pastoralism that would be right at home, say, in Wordsworth's "Stepping Westward": given such an invitation, "who would stop, or fear to advance, / Though home or shelter he had none, / With such a sky to lead him on?". Admitting the third line, at this point, we may hear just how forcefully the tone set

by this gentle invitation, and the suggestion "of something without place or bound," is disrupted by it: "Let us go then, you and I,/ When the evening is spread out against the sky / Like a patient etherised upon a table." Possibility at once expands and contracts: the patient may dream anything, do nothing. And who, we must ask in another vein, has seen such a sky? Can we take this as a descriptive metaphor, or must we see it, as it seems to be, as a symptom of Prufrock's psyche? The juxtaposition of violently disjunctive images opens as a problem the tendency we have seen in the poetry of mood toward blurring the line between world and psyche. But Prufrock's unwavering voice seems unaware of the problem the juxtapositions have opened up. Prufrock does not, however, resume his pastoral tone; rather, he extends his invitation for a journey into a "quiet *fin-de-siècle* inferno" whose objective status is in doubt:

> Let us go, through certain half-deserted streets,
> The muttering retreats
> Of restless nights in one-night cheap hotels
> And sawdust restaurants with oyster-shells:
> Streets that follow like a tedious argument
> Of insidious intent
> To lead you to an overwhelming question . . .
> Oh, do not ask, "What is it?"
> Let us go and make our visit.

Prufrock's invitation is a composition of contraries: an image of both paralysis and violence disrupts a pastoral invitation; streets appear "tedious," but their motives are "insidious"; beneath an "etherised" sky, a nervous, aimless, undefined, and illicit energy runs on. Yet the contraries seem less intentional figures than inadvertent self-disclosures. Prufrock, in Kenner's phrase, is "a name plus a Voice", and the voice does not register the contraries as such. What we sense here is the play or tension that will produce the central drama of the poem: the tension of Prufrockian Voice, deploying the commanding rhetoric of the dominant mode, played against the authorial acts that reveal the contradictions the Voice would conceal.

Prufrock's refusal to stop to discuss the "overwhelming question" and his insistence on first-hand examination of the empirical data that lead toward it may be taken as a refusal of what Charles Altieri has characterized as Victorian discursiveness, the poetic deployment of reflective consciousness which too often became for the Victorians less a means to self-transcendence than "an endless hall of mirrors", a self-paralyzing of the mind focused on its own activities and processes, and cut off from action. But Prufrock's refusal may be no more than an expression of his awareness that he cannot give any meaning, even to the extent of deriving an overwhelming question, to his impressions. The impressions and images Prufrock presents, as Altieri has observed, "are not simply objects but rhetorical figures insisting on their own utter facticity while performing and deforming the traditional symbolic gestures of relating the world to the demands of the psyche." We cannot, as we have noted, tell with any certainty where the world begins and Prufrock's psyche ends. Once again, it is in the tension between these two readings that the novel life of this poem resides: the mood that the Voice evokes, asking, I think, our identification with its seemingly bold and adventuresome empiricism, is punctured by the authorial acts that partly deconstruct it, revealing, or suggesting, a fear and fragmentation at work behind the bravado. Here authoriality opens up, as problems, features of the lyric poetry of mood, and the poem gains its distinctive energies from this tension.

The poem, as we have seen, frustrates any expectations we may have had for clear distinctions between inner and outer worlds, and for a coherent speaking identity. In its foregrounding of authorial acts, it also distinguishes itself sharply from the traditional dramatic monologue. We may note another mark of this distinction in the authorial disruption of the linearity of Prufrock's discourse:

> In the room the women come and go
> Talking of Michelangelo.

We seem far from the slightly sordid lower-class haunts of the first stanza, but where is this room, who are these women? And what are Prufrock's feelings? Desire? Fear? Both? It's hard to say.

If we can't know the answers to these questions, what we can know, as Kenner has observed, is that "The closed and open o's, the assonances of *room, women,* and *come,* the pointed caesura before the polysyllabic burst of 'Michelangelo,' weave a context of grandeur within which our feeling about these trivial women determines itself." The tone surrounds these aimless, ethereal women, speaking of an intensely physical artist, with an aura of seemingly undeserved grandeur. We are in the realm of effects we observed in "Pastel," but with a difference: **"Prufrock"**'s foregrounding of the authorial act plays against the mood of grandeur the voice creates, drawing attention to the constructed nature of the voice and allowing us to glimpse behind the grandeur the inappropriate objects to which the mood has been attached.

Prufrock, unlike the speaker of "Pastel," is not to be taken as the source or voice of affectively grounded truth: he is, rather, a constructed voice, one capable of powerful evocations of mood, and as well the objects of an analysis that begins to sort out the particular objects and feelings that are blurred into these moments of totalizing mood:

> The yellow fog that rubs its back upon the
> window-panes,

The yellow smoke that rubs its muzzle on the window-panes
Licked its tongue into the corners of the evening,
Lingered upon the pools that stand in drains,
Let fall upon its back the soot that falls from chimneys,
Slipped by the terrace, made a sudden leap,
And seeing that it was a soft October night,
Curled once about the house, and fell asleep.

The catlike fog seems the perfect figure for the totalizing desire at work here and in the poetry of mood, surrounding and suffusing all the disparate details with its vague inclusiveness. Rhetoric here is at work in the service of fantasy, as it has been in the previous stanzas. Once again, however, authorial action both analyzes and deconstructs its totalizing thrust: the tone of gentle, domestic reverie jars with the often crude physicality of the cat, who appears covered in soot, lingering over waste-water. And at the center we notice a curious emptiness: what's in this house? The Victorian domestic ideal evoked by the Prufrockian voice is ruptured by authorial action, from without by the physicality the ideal denies or excludes, and from within by its own emptiness.

What we have been given, thus far in the poem, are three stanzas, each deploying different resources of the dominant mode in order to construct a voice, or voices plus a name, speaking first of its setting off on a quest, second of the object of its quest, and third of the goal or end of the quest. In each stanza, we have seen the same play of identification and authorial act, of mood and discriminated feelings, opening up for dramatic possibilities and for critique the unexplored problems of the dominant mode.

> **Authorial acts make clear the poem's judgment of the smallness of Prufrock's concerns: the references to Hesiod and *Ecclesiastes* expose as trivial the life Prufrock engages.**
> **—*Robert McNamara***

Having presented Prufrock defining his quest in the first three stanzas, the poem now gives us Prufrock, as though in response, backing off from it:

> And indeed there will be time
> For the yellow smoke that slides along the street,
> Rubbing its back upon the window-panes;
> There will be time, there will be time
> To prepare a face to meet the faces that you meet;
> There will be time to murder and create,
> And time for all the works and days of hands

That lift and drop a question on your plate;
Time for you and time for me,
And time yet for a hundred indecisions,
And for a hundred visions and revisions,
Before the taking of a toast and tea.

Backing into discursivity, the Prufrockian voice backs further into the realm of abstract potentiality. Here, where everything is possible, everything is leveled: this is the realm of a "modern doubt" in which all hierarchies have collapsed. The parataxis suggests that murder and creation are on a level with preparing a social mask, that such moral and practical advice as Hesiod offers a rural peasantry in *Works and Days* is on a level with a concern with dinner-party conversation. Authorial acts make clear the poem's judgment of the smallness of Prufrock's concerns: the references to Hesiod and *Ecclesiastes* expose as trivial the life Prufrock engages.

What authorial action plays against here is a vaguely Polonian public rhetoric, managed in a voice that is calm, measured, avuncular in tone, that offers its assurance and advice with the certainty that they are wise. And what authorial action reveals here, through juxtapositions, is the powerfully motivated nature of this would-be objective pose: the pose provides a defense against the kinds of clear, discriminating responses to, and valuations of, particular objects and actions, responses that would move from the vague moods of a world of abstract potentiality into a world of commitment to concrete particulars and to action.

The Polonian features of this pose are picked up more directly later in the poem in what is perhaps the poem's finest parody of late Victorian discursiveness and self-analysis:

No! I am not Prince Hamlet, nor was meant to be;
Am an attendant lord, one that will do
To swell a progress, start a scene or two,
Advise the prince; no doubt, an easy tool,
Deferential, glad to be of use,
Politic, cautious, and meticulous;
Full of high sentence, but a bit obtuse;
At times, indeed, almost ridiculous—
Almost, at times, the Fool.

The stanza, as John Jackson has observed, is distinctive in the assuredness of its tone, and the seemingly lucid external perspective on himself that Prufrock here achieves. Such, we might say, is the lure of reflective consciousness. But authorial action undermines this lucidity from the start: Prufrock begins this self-explanation by denying precisely what we have come to suspect about him, namely that he suffers from the Hamlet problem. There is, of course, some truth in his denial, even if it is only the truth of his defensiveness: unlike Hamlet, he will protect his own paralysis, maintain his incapacity to act. Reflective consciousness, as

the authoriality of the poem reminds us, is less the servant of Truth than of self-interest.

Assuredness of tone here is finally no more persuasive than lucidity. Fully identified with the Polonian public stance, the Prufrockian voice is made to choose for itself virtues befitting a late Victorian civilized bourgeois: it is "Deferential . . . Politic, cautious, and meticulous." The logic of this identification leads the voice first to an unintended description of its own rhetoric: it, too, is "Full of high sentence, but a bit obtuse," blind to the dimensions of its predicament—and finally to its logical conclusion—that it is "At times, indeed, almost ridiculous— / Almost, at times, the Fool." And never more so than at this moment, in which Prufrock is trapped in the rhetorical machinery of the self-enclosed public voice of late Victorian discursivity. The logic of identification is here carried to its comic limits, and such foolishness as it produces is the inevitable result of trying to create an assured, totalized, and coherent self in an available public voice.

We should note here too, regarding this passage that would pass as self-analysis, that such analysis as is successfully carried out in this poem is the result of authorial action. The voice of self-analysis, as we have seen it at work in the poem, produces only one more identification with an established, conventional, and hence falsifying pose, and repeatedly proves, despite its implicit claims to disinterest, to be fully self-interested. Authorial action takes place in a space not falsified by rhetorical masks and the demands of personality, and as such can make and sustain greater claims than can be sustained by such a voice.

In the Prufrockian voice, rhetorical powers are repeatedly deployed to invest the trivial with grandeur and to mask Prufrock's affective life. When the women return in lines 35-36 speaking of Michelangelo, and we see them set against Prufrock's concern, in the previous stanza, with social success, the women seem more threatening that they did in their first appearance. Juxtaposition reveals, or suggests, what Prufrock's tone does not: how Prufrock feels. The juxtaposition also allows us to see that these women are an objectification of Prufrock's desire for the satisfaction of his own unrecognized feeling of lack. These ideal or idealized women, we may come to sense, have the power to fill that lack, to affirm Prufrock's being, but they also, as such, have the power to deny him:

And indeed there will be time
To wonder, "Do I dare?" and, "Do I dare?"
Time to turn back and descend the stair,
With a bald spot in the middle of my hair—
(They will say: "How his hair is growing thin!")
My morning coat, my collar mounting firmly to
the chin,

My necktie rich and modest, but asserted by a
simple pin—
(They will say: "But how his arms and legs are
thin!")
Do I dare
Disturb the universe?
In a minute there is time
For decisions and revisions which a minute will
reverse.

Repeatedly the Prufrockian voice rhetorically invests parts
with an emotional charge more appropriate to wholes. To
"dare" is to risk all because rejection would leave Prufrock
hopelessly empty and would shatter his self-contained world
of limitless possibility. Daring might force Prufrock to confront an actual woman, not a figure of his own fantasy, invested with a grandeur and mystery no real woman could
support. The passage quoted above plays with this dynamic
of parts and wholes, constructed as it is out of vocal
attitudinizings that attempt to master the flickers of doubt
the passage registers, attempts that are repeatedly undermined by the triviality of the objects on which desire is made
to fall. Further, the passage neatly dramatizes within
Prufrock's voice a tension that we have seen to exist between
voice and authoriality: Prufrock fears being defined and falsified by the voices of others. In the language of a later passage, he fears "The eyes that fix you in a formulated phrase."
He fears, that is, what authoriality enables Eliot to avoid:
self-enclosure in the rhetoric of the dominant mode.

> **Prufrock, we come to feel, is trapped in
> and by the rhetorical stances in which he is
> constructed, partial stances invested with
> the desire for wholeness. As Kenner has
> observed with regard to "Prufrock"'s debt
> to the soliloquies of Elizabethan drama, the
> moods of the soliloquies "are affectingly
> self-contained, the speaker imprisoned by
> his own eloquence, committed to a partial
> view of life, beyond the reach of correction
> or communication, out of which arises the
> tragic partiality of his actions."**
> **—Robert McNamara**

Having seen the analytic force of the poem's juxtapositional
aesthetic at work within and between stanzas, we may now
note its force in structuring larger units of the poem. We may
see it in the juxtaposition of the stanzas governed by "I have
known them all" against stanzas governed by the repeated
"There will be time." One effect of this juxtaposition is to
make clear that, despite their obvious differences in meaning, the two claims share a motivation: to block the route to
action and to forestall Prufrock from having a life in the

present. This effect is compounded later in the poem when,
after Prufrock fails to imagine himself acting, a block of stanzas governed by the question, "would it have been worth it,
after all?" completes this larger structure and reveals the
poem to be structured around an absent center: the act of
lovemaking Prufrock seeks, an act that would make the poem
a love song.

Prufrock, we come to feel, is trapped in and by the rhetorical stances in which he is constructed, partial stances invested with the desire for wholeness. As Kenner has
observed with regard to **"Prufrock"**'s debt to the soliloquies
of Elizabethan drama, the moods of the soliloquies "are af-
fectingly self-contained, the speaker imprisoned by his own
eloquence, committed to a partial view of life, beyond the
reach of correction or communication, out of which arises
the tragic partiality of his actions." Authoriality in
"Prufrock" multiplies such partial views: Prufrock bravely
off on his quest, Prufrock in wonder at the grandeur of the
women "talking of Michelangelo," Prufrock claiming that all
is possible, claiming that he has known all possibilities and
that none are worth pursuing, and wondering whether or not
his contemplated action would have been worth the risk it
involved. Juxtaposing these disparate stances, authoriality
renders Prufrock not as a unified and coherent self, but rather
as a figure paralyzed by his narcissistic investments in each
of these partial positions.

Prufrock suffers from what Eliot describes in an early essay
as the Victorian "pathology of rhetoric." **"Prufrock"** treats
the disease in the only way Eliot acknowledged it could be
treated: "the only cure for Romanticism is to analyse it."
Rhetoric is pathological, in Eliot's view, when it becomes a
vehicle for evading feeling, for creating self-satisfying illusions, and for producing a sense of wonder or mystery that
is not supported by the facts. To cure the disease, Eliot calls
in that essay for a literary "intelligence, of which an important function is the discernment of exactly what, and how
much, we feel in any given situation." In **"Prufrock,"** such
discernment and analysis is not possible in any of the public, discursive voices given to Prufrock: here, what would
pass as objective analysis is bent to serve self-interest. The
emotional discernment achieved in the poem is the work of
authorial actions that enable us, if not to see clearly and unambiguously the particular feelings that Prufrock's mood-
producing rhetoric denies or obscures, at least—and this is
certainly a major contribution of the poem—to gain insight
into the problems of narcissism, rhetoric, and self-represen-
tation.

Action, in this poem, is the province of authoriality; Prufrock
cannot act, in part because in his grandiosity he cannot accept that a requisite of action is that he locate himself in a
middle: "And how should I begin?" he asks, wanting an en-

tirely self-determined and fully self-expressive act. Prufrock does try, however, to imagine himself taking action:

> And the afternoon, the evening, sleeps so peace-
> fully!
> Smoothed by long fingers,
> Asleep . . . tired . . . or it malingers,
> Stretched on the floor, here beside you and me.
> Should I, after tea and cakes and ices,
> Have the strength to force the moment to its crisis?
> But though I have wept and fasted, wept and
> prayed,
> Though I have seen my head (grown slightly bald)
> brought in upon a platter,
> I am no prophet—and here's no great matter;
> I have seen the moment of my greatness flicker,
> And I have seen the eternal Footman hold my coat,
> and snicker,
> And in short, I was afraid.

To imagine action, even the act of lovemaking, Prufrock must first imagine the afternoon or evening tamed or asleep: he must see his action as self-generated, and not as a response to a prior condition. He must then imagine himself as possessing the masculine strength, force, and crisis-orientation necessary to answer the highly civilized, and feminine, "tea and cakes and ices." Rhyme undermines Prufrock's melodramatic staging of the scene, a staging that, due to his inability to claim the strength he believes he needs, leads Prufrock to imagine himself not as agent but as patient, as the victim of women and servants: he has been treated by women as John the Baptist was by Salome, he has been victimized by a Fate that has refused him, despite his suffering and fasting, the role of prophet (a role that would allow him, as John Jackson has astutely observed, to name "l'être aimé comme parole fondatrice", and he has fallen from his (fantasized) greatness to the low point of being laughed at by his inferiors.

> **To say, simply, that Fate has refused Prufrock the role of prophet is to miss the distinctive thrust of the poem. Prufrock, a construct of available rhetorical stances, cannot be a prophet because prophecy is not one of these stances, is not possible in the poetic of mood.**
> **—*Robert McNamara***

But to say, simply, that Fate has refused Prufrock the role of prophet is to miss the distinctive thrust of the poem. Prufrock, a construct of available rhetorical stances, cannot be a prophet because prophecy is not one of these stances, is not possible in the poetic of mood. When later in the poem

Prufrock melodramatically imagines his own emotional assertion as prophecy, as a witness to eternal truth, by imaging his heretofore buried affect as "'Lazarus, come from the dead'", he fears being told that he has misread the scene, misunderstood what "one" has told him. The poetic of mood, and the Victorian cult of feeling, which was closely tied to the tendency in nineteenth-century liberal Protestantism to shift the ground of faith from doctrine to affect, cannot provide the certainty Prufrock desires. Desire may produce vague religious feelings, the sense of mystery without the facts that Eliot describes as the "pathology of rhetoric," but it cannot produce either the clear discrimination of objects and feelings that would enable action or the public framework that would authorize prophetic utterance. One is consigned, in the associationist poetic of mood, to patient status.

Prufrock fears not only misreading but both being misread and being fully read. He fears that having "bitten off the matter with a smile," having "squeezed the universe into a ball / To roll it toward some overwhelming question," he will be confronted by "one, settling a pillow by her head," saying to him "'That is not what I meant at all. / That is not it, at all'." He fears that what he says will be taken as a full expression of who he is: "It is impossible to say just what I mean!" But this is not to say that Prufrock desires to be fully seen: the following line, "But as if a magic lantern threw the nerves in patterns on a screen," suggests that Prufrock feels more expressed than self-expressing and is anxious about the prospect of inadvertently revealing himself, or rather, of being revealed by a "magic lantern" or an unconscious capable of expressing him beyond the control of his conscious mind. Wanting nothing less than the ability to fully articulate and control an image of himself, Prufrock is afraid of both himself and others.

But the "magic lantern" that reveals Prufrock's nerve patterns is not an unconscious but the authoriality of "**Prufrock.**" What authoriality reveals through Prufrock is the danger of the collapsing of psyche and world that is characteristic of the poetic of mood: the desire informing or producing this collapse, the desire for a totalizing state or act in which or of which one is fully in control, denies the agency of others and forecloses the possibility of action, since no act can be fully expressive of the self. The desire for authenticity and control produces self-enclosure.

Here, I think, we find the peculiar pathos of "**Prufrock,**" in the dramatization of the desire for such self-sufficient modes and the limitations of such modes as are available. Prufrock's desire exceeds what authoriality reveals to be the limited rhetorical solutions to his problem:

> I grow old . . . I grow old . . .
> I shall wear the bottoms of my trousers rolled.

Shall I part my hair behind? Do I dare to eat a
peach?
I shall wear white flannel trousers, and walk upon
the beach.

Prufrock will remain a spectator as well as a spectacle. He
may hear the mermaids singing, but they will not sing to him;
he may see them riding on the waves, and even linger with
sea-girls in the "chambers of the sea," but only "Till human
voices wake us, and we drown." The human voice exerts
claims of limited relations, of limited powers: to enter into
discourse with those voices would, for Prufrock, require that
he give up his melodramatic claims to specialness, the grandiosity of his self-staging, his repeated evasions of feeling
in self-serving and self-enclosed rhetoric. Further, it would
require that he confront a lover who is neither sea-girl, mermaid, nor ethereal aesthete, "Talking of Michelangelo": that
his lover be not the Woman of abstract potentiality but a concrete woman, with whom he can interact without fear of disturbing the universe.

For Prufrock, this would be a drowning, in a world of
middles, of contingencies—and others—beyond his control.

The absent center of **"Prufrock"** is an act of lovemaking.
Prufrock, as we have seen, cannot imagine himself making
love to a woman, nor can he make the poem the vehicle of
lovemaking that would make it truly a love song. Prufrock
is, as many critics have observed, a narcissist, and the symptoms are everywhere in the poem: Prufrock's sense of
specialness, his grandiose sense of election, coupled with a
powerful and debilitating sense of worthlessness (which
stands behind the Hamlet-like excesses of his responses and
his inability to act); his fear of rejection as a possible cause
of fragmentation, of loss of control; his hypercathexis of images, his sense of visibility as corrosive, and his fear of being defined by, of capitation by, the image of the
other—those "eyes that fix you in a formulated phrase."

These symptoms appear in, and as signs of, Prufrock's romantic posturing, closely tied to the poetics of mood, with
its characteristic desire for a totalizing state in which a unified and coherent selfhood can be recovered, by means of
association and memory, from its dispersal in its appearances, and its equally characteristic blurring of the edges of
psyche and world. Prufrock is the vehicle of Eliot's critique
of the mode. Eliot relocates the nineties vagueness we saw
typified in "Pastel," placing it not in the scene, where it can
support vaguely mystical feelings, but in the rhetoric of the
Prufrockian voice. Prufrock is, as Kenner has observed,
"strangely boundless", and he is so, we are made aware,
because authorial acts in the poem construct him so as to
foreground his collapsing of world and self in ways that
generate powerful moods but not discriminated objects
and feelings.

"Prufrock" is, clearly, a departure from the associationist
line. If we return to Craig's schema, discussed earlier, we
can see the ways in which **"Prufrock"** represents both a critique and a significant departure. In **"Prufrock,"** unity is
provided not by emotion but rather by the analysis of a condition—or, we might say, by the condition analyzed. Depth,
or what depth we find, is not a matter of singular and profound experience, but is, rather, triangulated by the structure of the poem from its series of lyric poses, each a
self-enclosed moment. And variety in **"Prufrock"** is not simply a matter of the speaker's associations, but is as well a
symptomatology, a presentation of the various forms that repressed desire takes. Variety, too, is a function of analysis:
the foregrounding of authoriality makes clear that what
Eliot's poetic values is analysis. Sensitivity, the highest value
in the poetic of mood, becomes in **"Prufrock"** the rough
equivalent to sentimentality, and what sentimentality indicates is a lack of self-awareness.

Eliot's critique is a powerful one, and its mode offers considerable resources for analysis. But it has, we should note,
serious limitations. The use of a persona limits the range of
problems that can be addressed. The poem can, and does,
deal powerfully with the difficulties of how we stand in relation to particular states of self. But the world of the poem
is limited to that of a single consciousness, and a very narrow consciousness, and cannot take up the significance of
what that consciousness excludes.

Perhaps a more serious limitation is that the analytical mode
of the poem seems incapable of addressing the problem of
actionable values. It can analyze romanticism, narcissism,
and bourgeois evasiveness, and can do so because
authoriality accepts its position in a middle—the middle of
literary conventions and modes—as a condition of action,
but what can it offer as an alternative? Only more analysis.
As such, it seems, it becomes one more form of paralysis,
repeating the problem of the Victorian discursivity it sought
to replace. It may be only one more version—perhaps the
most modern—of modern doubt.

Donald J. Childs (essay date Fall 1988)

SOURCE: "Knowledge and Experience in 'The Love Song
of J. Alfred Prufrock'", in *ELH*, Vol. 5, No. 3, Fall, 1988,
pp. 685-99.

[*In the following essay, Childs argues that in order to fully
comprehend "Prufrock" the poem must be considered in
light of Eliot's dissertation on F. H. Bradley.*]

But what a poem means is as much what it means
to others as what it means to the author; and indeed,

in the course of time a poet may become merely a reader in respect to his own works, forgetting his original meaning—or without forgetting, merely changing.

—T. S. Eliot, *The Use of Poetry and the Use of Criticism*

Although scholars and critics became aware of F. H. Bradley's influence upon T. S. Eliot at a relatively late point in the latter's career, the relationship between the two writers has now been extensively documented. The studies of Kristian Smidt and Hugh Kenner led to a number of books and articles on this subject in the early sixties. This research culminated, largely through the efforts of Anne C. Bolgan, in the publication in 1964 of *Knowledge and Experience in the Philosophy of F. H. Bradley*—in effect, Eliot's 1916 dissertation on **"Experience and the Objects of Knowledge in the Philosophy of F. H. Bradley,"** supplemented by his articles on Bradley and Leibnitz in *The Monist* (1916). Not surprisingly, the publication of Eliot's dissertation only increased enthusiasm for research into Bradley's influence upon his criticism and poetry. Indeed, so much has been published on the subject throughout the sixties, seventies, and eighties that a recent reviewer for the *Times Literary Supplement,* perhaps intimidated by the sheer amount of such research, attempted to dismiss most of it as unimportant. Reviewing yet another book on Bradley and Eliot, he suggested that "The pioneer work on Eliot's philosophy and its pervasive presence in his poetry was done by Hugh Kenner in *The Invisible Poet* and there is not a very great deal of importance to be added." He did allow, however, that the book he was reviewing had advanced the subject beyond Kenner in providing "a much stronger sense than we had before of how profoundly imbued with philosophy is Eliot's imagination, both as critic and poet." This, in fact, has been the general achievement of the research that the reviewer so easily dismissed; one can no longer hope to comprehend Eliot's imaginative achievements without also comprehending Bradley's pervasive influence upon them.

> **"The Love Song of J. Alfred Prufrock" is a poem closely linked to Eliot's work on Bradley. It is a poem that influences Eliot's understanding of Bradley, and it is also a poem that Eliot comes to see in a Bradleyan light. In fact, the poem offers a reading of the dissertation and the dissertation a reading of the poem.**
> **—*Donald J. Childs***

In the end, then, scholars and critics have been trying to prove what Eliot announced in the very beginning:

Few will ever take the pains to study the consummate art of Bradley's style, the finest philosophic style in our language, in which acute intellect and passionate feeling preserve a classic balance: only those who will surrender patient years to the understanding of his meaning. But upon these few, both living and unborn, his writings perform that mysterious and complete operation which transmutes not one department of thought only, but the whole intellectual and emotional tone of their being.

Those who have taken Eliot's implied advice here and studied Bradley (and studied him with Eliot in mind) have concluded that virtually everything Eliot wrote after encountering Bradley's philosophy is colored by it. The metaphor here is Kenner's: "it is precisely as a stain, imparting color to all else that passes through, that Bradley is most discernible in Eliot's poetic sensibility." Eliot's first important poem, however, **"The Love Song of J. Alfred Prufrock,"** would seem to be uncolored by Bradley's thought, for the poem was completed between 1910 and 1911, and Eliot apparently did not begin his study of Bradley until 1913. As Kenner observes, "there is no evidence that Eliot paid [Bradley] any attention until after he had written 'Prufrock' and 'Portrait of a Lady.' (He did not buy his own copy of *Appearance and Reality* until mid-1913)." In fact, Eliot may have been reading Bradley before 1913, but it is not likely that he was reading him before he composed **"Prufrock."** Granting all this, however, I would nonetheless like to argue that **"The Love Song of J. Alfred Prufrock"** is a poem closely linked to Eliot's work on Bradley. It is a poem that influences Eliot's understanding of Bradley, and it is also a poem that Eliot comes to see in a Bradleyan light. In fact, the poem offers a reading of the dissertation and the dissertation a reading of the poem.

That **"The Love Song of J. Alfred Prufrock"** was on Eliot's mind in 1915 and 1916, as he was completing his dissertation, seems certain. He sent the finished dissertation to Harvard in January or February of 1916. In January of 1915, in a letter to Harriet Monroe attempting to persuade her to publish **"Prufrock,"** Ezra Pound explained that Eliot would not agree to the deletion of the "Hamlet" verse paragraph. Pound had been campaigning, and would continue to campaign for the next six months, to have Harriet Monroe publish the poem (which she did in June of 1915). As the letter of January 1915 suggests, Pound probably kept Eliot informed of his progress with Monroe while the campaign was under way. In August, Pound sent Monroe another batch of Eliot's poems. Finally, in June of 1916, Eliot himself wrote to Monroe, explaining that he thought **"Prufrock"** better than his other poems written between 1909 and 1911. By this point, furthermore, it would seem that Eliot was suffering from a period of poetic sterility so severe that he felt he might never again produce anything as good as **"Prufrock."**

He wrote to his brother in September of 1916, in fact, to say that **"The Love Song of J. Alfred Prufrock"** might prove to be his "swansong."

> Let us go then, you and I,
> When the evening is spread out against the sky
> Like a patient etherised upon a table.

Critics have made these opening lines to **"The Love Song of J. Alfred Prufrock"** the cornerstone of their readings of the poem. The central preoccupation has been with the notorious distinction between "you and I." According to George Williamson, the reference of the pronoun "you" is not at all clear: "The 'I' is the speaker, but who is the 'you' addressed? The title would suggest a lady, but the epigraph suggests a scene out of the world, on a submerged level." Grover Smith, however, explains the reference of the pronoun "you" and suggests that the distinction between "you and I" is the framework for the Prufrockian dialectic: "By a distinction between 'I' and 'you,' [Prufrock] differentiates between his thinking, sensitive character and his outward self. . . . He is addressing, as if looking into a mirror, his whole public personality. His motive seems to be to repudiate the inert self, which cannot act, and to assert his will." In her Jungian interpretation of the poem, Joyce Meeks Jones reaches a similar conclusion: Prufrock, she argues, is an extrovert "who is unable to resolve the conflict between the demands of his own individuality, and those of his persona, or social mask. In consequence, he struggles helplessly in an eternal hell of self-estrangement and moral indecision." Carol T. Christ finds that Prufrock's "fictions insulate and preserve him in a solipsistic dream world, a chamber of the sea." **"Prufrock,"** she writes, "begins with a definite address and invitation . . . but . . . so deliberately avoids defining its events and audience that we question whether the poem records any interchange with a world external to the speaker's consciousness." Hugh Kenner looks to the epigraph for a clue as to the function of "you and I"; he sees in the poem a liaison between Dante's journey through hell, led by Virgil, and Prufrock's journey through the city streets led by "you"—"a liaison between [Prufrock's] situation and Dante's which is all the smoother for the reflective, lingering rhythm of the opening phrase." Joseph Chair develops a similar line: "you and I" are part of "an internal monologue which is not meant to be heard," just as Guido de Montefeltro's words are not to be taken back to the land of the living. "Obviously it is not only the evening which is etherized upon a table but also the speaker, who is in a kind of inferno-like situation."

For F. O. Matthiessen, however, the question is academic. That is, the first three lines of **"Prufrock"** are too academic; they are "too studied." The conceits in the lines in question have the look of "coming into existence not because the poet's mind has actually felt keenly an unexpected similarity between unlikes but as though he too consciously set out to shock the reader." The problem for Matthiessen lies not so much in the distinction between "you and I" as in the comparison between the evening spread out against the sky and the patient etherized upon a table: "Even though the reader can perceive wherein the comparison holds, he may still have the sensation that it is too intellectually manipulated, not sufficiently felt."

I would agree with Matthiessen that the opening metaphors are to some extent "intellectually manipulated." I would perhaps disagree with his charge that they are "not sufficiently felt." As Eliot himself pointed out in his dissertation, "There is no greater mistake than to think that feeling and thought are exclusive—that those beings which think most and best are not also those capable of the most feeling." I would obviously agree with all of these scholars and critics that the "you and I," the "evening spread out against the sky," and the "patient etherised upon a table" are essential elements in any interpretation of **"The Love Song of J. Alfred Prufrock."** But what concerns me here are the implications of the distinction between "you and I" for the poem and the dissertation as readings of each other.

That Eliot actually recalled the first three lines of the poem in the very act of writing the dissertation is suggested by his use of the image that begins **"The Love Song of J. Alfred Prufrock"**—the image of a patient spread out upon a table. The physician-patient metaphor, in which the subject or observer is the physician and the object or thing observed the patient, is one of Eliot's favorites. The Prufrockian patient appears in the dissertation:

> Our only way of showing that we are attending to an object is to show that it and ourself are independent entities, and to do this we must have names. So that the point at which behaviour changes into mental life is essentially indefinite; it is a question of interpretation whether . . . expression which is repeated at the approach of the same object . . . is behaviour or language. In either case, I insist, it is continuous with the object; in the first case because we have no object (except from the point of view of the observer, which must not be confused with that of the patient under examination), and in the second case because it is language that gives us objects rather than mere 'passions'.

The relation between subject as physician or "observer" and object as patient is central to understanding both the dissertation and the poem. In this passage, Eliot argues that subject and object are continuous except from the point of view of an observer (another subject that is a truly subjective self) who is able to regard the original subject as an object (an objective self)—in other words, as a "patient under examination." The consciousness that is the speaking voice in **"Prufrock"** is apparently just such an observer, articulating the discontinuity between "you and I." In the dissertation's terms, the Prufrockian observer is not the self as object or patient (the "I" observed), but the truly subjective self that is able to distinguish between object and objective self (that is, between "you and I"). That which is "spread out" and "etherised upon a table," in short, is not just the evening, but also the self as object. Prufrock, as object, is the patient. And yet it is his absolutely subjective self that is the observer or physician. Just as there is no patient without physician, so in the poem there is no "you" without "I," and so in the dissertation there is no language or object without observer. The metaphysical and epistemological implications of the Prufrockian metaphor, it seems, unfold in the dissertation.

Eliot develops the same medical metaphor in his early essay **"The Function of Criticism"** (1923): "Comparison and analysis need only the cadavers on the table," he writes, "but interpretation is always producing parts of the body from its pockets, and fixing them in place." Eliot's concern here is the same as that expressed in the epistemological context of his dissertation: he finds that interpretation introduces an epistemologically necessary second point of view, but he also finds that such a point of view inevitably produces only a relative truth—a truth relative to the point of view introduced, the point of view of the critic or reader. By the terms of Eliot's metaphor, then, the critic or reader is inevitably a coroner (dealing with dead fact or dead language, not with life or language as lived and living), but the critic or reader *as interpreter* is worse, for he or she is a dishonest coroner who supplies the body of fact or the body of the text with its missing parts from the pockets of his or her interpretation. As elaborated in 1923, therefore, the medical metaphor is still part of the original quest in **"Prufrock"** and the dissertation to discover an objective point of view on the relation between the self and its object—its objects being determined, according to the dissertation, by language. In the poem, the dissertation, and the essay, the body on the table is a linguistic object. The poet (Prufrock), the philosopher (Eliot), and the critic (Anonymous) are all physicians, and in each case the fate of the patient is in doubt. In 1923, then, Prufrock's overwhelming question remains unanswered: "What is the nature of the relation between subject and object?"

The same medical metaphor appears in *Four Quartets:*

> The wounded surgeon plies the steel
> That questions the distempered part;
> Beneath the bleeding hands we feel
> The sharp compassion of the healer's art
> Resolving the enigma of the fever chart.

In the Christian context of Eliot's writing in the 1940s, of course, the physician has become Christ. For Eliot at this time, poetry, philosophy, and criticism (or the act of reading in general) begin and end in a Christian point of view. But the patient remains the individual human self, the self as objectified in language (whether the language of *Four Quartets* or the language of the Christian liturgy). And just as in **"Prufrock,"** the dissertation, and **"The Function of Criticism,"** so in *Four Quartets* the relation between physician and patient is all important. Upon it—that is, upon the relation between self and other selves, subject and object, language and observer (or poem and reader)—depends the very nature of reality. As always, furthermore, the Eliotic inquiry into the nature of this relation produces not answers, but questions: questions about the nature of the relation between distempered part and wounded surgeon, between cadaver and coroner, between patient and physician, between language and observer—in short, questions about the relationship between "you and I". I would suggest, then, that the metaphor in **"Prufrock"** that introduces this fundamental metaphorical, metaphysical, and epistemological relation gathers much of its subsequent significance from the implications for the relation between subject and object suggested in Eliot's dissertation on Bradley.

The Prufrockian echo of the word "patient" in *Knowledge and Experience* is admittedly not very loud, but the echo of the Prufrockian words "spread out" and "table" is: "We can never . . . wholly explain the practical world from a theoretical point of view," Eliot suggests, "because this world is what it is by reason of the practical point of view and the world which we try to explain is a world spread out upon a table—simply *there*!" Similarly, in his conclusion, he reminds his reader that "Theoretically, that which we know is merely spread out before us for pure contemplation, and the subject, the I, or the self, is no more consciously present than is the inter-cellular action."

What were the first three lines of **"The Love Song of J. Alfred Prufrock"** bringing back to mind? I suggest that by recalling them in 1915 Eliot was reevaluating the philosophy embodied in the poem. In these lines, that is, we find the philosophical attitude to the relationship between "you and I" that Eliot held in 1910 and 1911, an attitude that seems to have been informed by Bergsonism. Over thirty years after writing the poem, Eliot told an inquirer that he was a Bergsonian when he composed **"The Love Song of J. Alfred Prufrock."** Piers Gray, exploring the Bergsonian dimensions of the poem, notes that in the opening lines "the world, at least in so far as the evening may be synecdochic of it, is in a state of deep unconsciousness." In the Bergsonian universe, he points out, such a state holds the greatest potential for real life, for it is not bound by the practical, goal-oriented consciousness. According to Bergson, consciousness restricts its use of memory to those memories which bear on the present goal: "the a recollection should reappear in consciousness, it is necessary that it should descend from the heights of pure memory down to the precise point where *action* is taking place." "It is form the present." Bergson continues, "that comes the appeal to which memory responds, and it is from the sensori-motor elements of present action that a memory borrows the warmth which gives it life." Only in an unconscious state, then, can pure memory—in which resides the total of one's past—reappear. "To be etherized," Gray therefore concludes, "is to be potentially open to the totality of one's past life." The first three lines of the poem, therefore, suggest the etherized abdication of goal-oriented consciousness, an abdication that allows the uncontrolled descent from "pure memory" of the particular memories and images that haunt Prufrock throughout the poem and thwart action at every turn. As J.S. Brooker observes, "Prufrock, not the evening, is etherized upon a table. Like everything else in the poem, the tired, sleepy evening is an aspect of Prufrock's mind."

But the first three lines of the poem are even more closely related to Eliot's study of Bergson than this brief analysis of certain Bergsonian concepts might suggest. One finds the metaphor of the world "spread out" in space in *Time and Free Will,* Bergson's first book and the book Eliot quoted most frequently when writing on Bergson. "Our conception of number," Bergson complains, "ends in spreading out in space everything which can be directly counted." The problem with western philosophy, he suggests, is that we have imported the quantifiable aspects of that which is external and material into our notions of what is properly unquantifiable, that which is internal and immaterial: the unextended is thought of as though it were extended; in other words, it is spread out in space. In the end, the externality of material objects, he explains, "spreads into the depths of consciousness." Consciousness, according to Bergson, is not a multiplicity of states, but a pure, undifferentiated duration; in fact, a plurality of conscious states is not observable, he argues, unless consciousness is "spread out" in space.

Eliot picked up the same metaphor when as a graduate student in philosophy at Harvard he wrote about Bergson: "Berkeleyan space, I believe, as adapted by Bergson becomes, on the one hand, extension; and Bergson's space is the Berkeleyan *pure* space; for Berkeley non-existent; for Bergson the homogeneous medium spread out by our understanding as a substratum for extrinsic relations." The image is as pervasive in Eliot's understanding of Bergson as it is in Bergson's writing: "The 'travail utilaire' of the 'esprit,'" Eliot writes, "consists in a kind of *refraction of pure duration across space.*" There can be no doubt, then, that the opening lines of **"The Love Song of J. Alfred Prufrock"** establish a Bergsonian context for the relation between "you and I," sky and evening, patient and physician, and objected and subject. And of course the relation is false, the distinc-

tion artificial. In Bergson's world, reality is a timeless, distinctionless, pure duration. The falseness of Prufrock's world, therefore, stems in part from the falseness of the categorical distinctions (between "you and I") by which his consciousness proceeds.

> **In noting in his dissertation that the epistemologist's world is "a world spread out upon a table—simply *there*" Eliot distinguishes between the epistemologically theoretical and practical points of view. Reality, he suggests, is "an approximate construction, a construction essentially practical in its nature."**
> **—Donald J. Childs**

What, then, did Eliot see in **"Prufrock"** four or five years after completing it? How did he himself read the opening lines of the poem in 1915 and 1916? What light does the dissertation throw upon Eliot's later interpretation of the distinction between "you and I"? In short, what was Bradley's influence upon Eliot's reading of **"The Love Song of J. Alfred Prufrock"**?

In noting in his dissertation that the epistemologist's world is "a world spread out upon a table—simply *there*" Eliot distinguishes between the epistemologically theoretical and practical points of view. Reality, he suggests, is "an approximate construction, a construction essentially practical in its nature." In other words, reality is a function of preconscious self-interest. The attempt to step beyond this point of view; that is, the attempt at objectivity, merely results in confusion, for one must then comprehend the internal from the point of view of the external. In the end, "We forget that what has grown up from a purely practical attitude cannot be explained by a purely theoretical [attitude]." In short, "this world is what it is by reason of the practical point of view," whereas the world one tries to explain by epistemological theory is placed before the mind as "a world spread out upon a table—simply *there.*" The epistemologist, in other words, is inevitably a dishonest coroner, producing parts of the body from his or her pockets and fixing them in place to suit his or her culturally and historically relative interpretation.

In rereading **"Prufrock"** during the writing of his dissertation, therefore, Eliot discovered that Prufrock's dilemma is the epistemologist's dilemma: how does one reconcile practice and theory, action and contemplation? On the one hand, Prufrock responds, or wishes to respond, to the exhortation to action ("Let us go then"), while, on the other, he contemplates—contemplates himself, that is, as though he were spread out upon an examination table. The disjunction is between the world as it exists according to Prufrock's practical point of view and the world as it exists beyond his immediate, practical interest—the world of theory, "spread out upon a table—simply *there.*" The disjunction, in other words, is between the practical point of view interested in women "Talking of Michelangelo" and "Arms that are braceleted and white and bare / (But in the lamplight, downed with light brown hair!)", and the theoretical or absolute point of view of "Lazarus, come from the dead, / Come back to tell you all"—presumably to tell of the absolute beyond the practical world.

Eliot also seems to have noted, while writing his dissertation, that the desire to contemplate the world spread out upon a table produces in both Bradley's and Prufrock's worlds a distinction between "you and I." In theory, Eliot notes (using the Prufrockian metaphor), "that which we know is merely spread out before us for pure contemplation, and the subject, the I, or the self, is no more consciously present than is the inter-cellular action." In practice, however, this pre-occupation with a theoretical world spread out upon a table requires a relation between the world, as object, and the self, as object—"a relation which is theoretical and not merely actual, in the sense that the self as a term capable of relation with other terms is a construction." That is, the self that does not immediately live or feel its experience is an object; the self as object (the "patient under examination") is related to experience as object within the whole that is the self as subject. But "this self which is objectified and related is continuous and felt to be continuous with the self which is subject and not an element in that which is known."

Two selves, therefore, are necessary to any attempt to know the world that is simply there, spread out upon a table. And yet one must know more than one's objective and subjective selves before one can determine the nature of that world; one must also know other selves. On the one hand, granted, the self "seems to depend upon a world which in turn depends upon it." This is the substance of the quotation from Bradley's *Appearance and Reality* that Eliot includes in the infamous notes to **The Waste Land:** "My external sensations are no less private to my self than are my thoughts or my feelings. In either case my experience falls within my own circle, a circle closed on the outside; and, with all its elements alike, every sphere is opaque to the others which surround it. . . . In brief, regarded as an existence which appears in a soul, the whole world for each is peculiar and private to that soul." On the other hand, however, Eliot affirms that "the self depends as well upon other selves; it is not given as a direct experience, but is an interpretation of experience by interaction with other selves." We thus "come to interpret our own experience as the attention to a world of objects, as we feel obscurely an identity between the experiences of other centres [or selves] and our own" (143). It is this felt identity, Eliot suggests, "which gradually shapes itself into the external world."

It is presumably the defective relation of selves in **"Prufrock,"** the defective relation between "you and I," that brought the poem to mind as Eliot wrote his dissertation. Prufrock's first distinction, between "you and I," is necessary and inevitable, according to both Bradley and Eliot. Ultimately, however, Prufrock's self, both "you and I," must interact with other selves—this is the "overwhelming question"—in order to begin to forge the identity of experience that will "gradually shape itself into the external world." In adapting the Prufrockian metaphor to the Bradleyan context of his dissertation, Eliot seems to realize that both the Prufrockian and Bradleyan universes depend upon the relation of selves within them. Ironically, then, Prufrock's "overwhelming question" is just as important as he thinks it is. The nature of the universe actually does depend on whether or not he disturbs it.

In *The Matrix of Modernism,* Sanford Schwartz suggests a similar approach to the poem. He finds that the self-conscious personae of Eliot's early poems "constantly agonize over their encounters with other persons." He explains the significance of the personae's confrontations with others in terms derived from Eliot's dissertation: "They are suspended between their external apprehension of others, whom they know directly through observable behaviour alone, and their internal apprehension of others as active centers of consciousness. These personae also experience a subject/object split within themselves. They are at once detached observers and conventional agents, spectators of their own participation in the social world." **"Prufrock,"** Schwartz suggests, follows this pattern very closely. He warns, however, that "We should avoid the misconception that Eliot first formulated the 'half-object' [the Prufrockian object observed from both an internal and an external point of view] and then dramatized it in his poetry." "Long before he wrote his dissertation," Schwartz notes, "Eliot had composed **'Prufrock,'** **'Portrait of a Lady,'** and several other poems that exhibit the [dissertation's] internal-external point of view of the half-object."

> **In the end . . . Eliot provides by means of his dissertation on Bradley a thoroughly modern map for reading "Prufrock." The resurrection of the Prufrockian metaphor of a patient spread out upon a table points the way to the passages in *Knowledge and Experience* most directly relevant to this reading.**
> **—*Donald J. Childs***

But as Schwartz himself implies, that **"The Love Song of J. Alfred Prufrock"** preceded *Knowledge and Experience* does not mean that there is no connection between the poem and the dissertation. In fact Eliot's recourse in his dissertation to certain Prufrockian metaphors suggests that he himself was aware of the connection. If in the usual chronology of cause and effect it would seem that Bradley did not influence the composition of **"Prufrock,"** the poem certainly influenced Eliot's articulation of his philosophical point of view in *Knowledge and Experience.* The Prufrockian metaphors repeated in the dissertation signal not just a coincidence of phrasing but also a coincidence of thought and feeling. The Bergsonian exploration in 1910 and 1911 of the way the subject distinguishes itself from the object (and so creates reality) by means of contaminated categories of time and space is taken up again in 1915 and 1916 in order to sort out the overwhelming question once more, this time from a Bradleyan point of view. Eliot began **"Prufrock"** from the Bergsonian presupposition that the relationship between sky and evening, object and subject, and "you and I" is false if that which is nonspatial is defined in terms of that which is spatial. The conclusion Eliot reached was that the Prufrockian self was indeed a false self, a self estranged from itself by its displacement in a fractured social space. When he came to Bradley several years later, Eliot recognized a point of view compatible with that in **"Prufrock,"** for Bradley's philosophic exploration of the relation between self and other selves articulated dialectically what Prufrock had articulated dramatically—that is, that self depends upon other selves, subject upon object, and "I" upon "you." According to Bradley, "man is a social being; he is real only because he is social, and can realize himself only because it is as social that he realizes himself. The mere individual is a delusion of theory; and the attempt to realize it in practice is the starvation and mutilation of human nature, with total sterility or the production of monstrosities." Prufrock, Eliot discovered in 1915 and 1916, is a monster accounted for by Bradley.

In the end, then, Eliot provides by means of his dissertation on Bradley a thoroughly modern map for reading **"Prufrock."** The resurrection of the Prufrockian metaphor of a patient spread out upon a table points the way to the passages in *Knowledge and Experience* most directly relevant to this reading. After five years, a poem born presumably of an almost inarticulable experience of self-estrangement became for Eliot an allegory of the epistemological dependence of reality upon a construction of self and selves—an allegory, that is, of the conclusions he was reaching in his dissertation. Insofar, then, as Eliot's work on Bradley in his dissertation seems to have prompted him to reread or reinterpret the poem from a Bradleyan point of view, Bradley does indeed seem to have influenced **"The Love Song of J. Alfred Prufrock."** In effect, Eliot has taken his own advice and reinterpreted the lived experience he captured in "Prufrock" in the way he suggested, in his dissertation, that all such necessarily "partial and fragmentary truths" should be reinterpreted: "the finest tact after all can give us only

interpretation [of lived truths], and every interpretation, along perhaps with some utterly contradictory interpretation, has to be taken up and reinterpreted by every thinking mind and by every civilization." *Knowledge and Experience,* I suggest, is in part a reinterpretation or rereading of "Prufrock." In the course of time, Eliot has "become merely a reader in respect to his own works, forgetting his original meaning—or without forgetting, merely changing." At the same time, **"Prufrock"** suggests a reading for the dissertation; indeed, it writes part of the dissertation insofar as its metaphors surface at important moments in the epistemological inquiry. If we attend carefully to the reinterpretation of the "world spread out upon a table" in Eliot's dissertation, in other words, we will perhaps find Eliot's final draft of the poem. At the very least, we will find that there is something of *Knowledge and Experience* in **"The Love Song of J. Alfred Prufrock."**

David Ayers (essay date October 1988)

SOURCE: "Two Bald Men: Eliot and Dostoevsky," in *Forum for Modern Language Studies,* Vol. XXIV, No. 4, October, 1988, pp. 282-300.

[*In the essay below, Ayers considers whether Dostoevsky's novel* The Double *influenced Eliot's writing of "Prufrock."*]

Students of the influence that one author has had on the work of another have at all times had reason to be careful, not to give too much importance to the superficial resemblance, the odd verbal parallel, while seeking deeper structural affinities—without, that is, making one or two centuries of highbrow literary effort appear to have repeatedly produced the same thing.

In the case of Eliot, possibly the most influence-prone writer of an age, the scholar must be doubly careful. At all points Eliot seems to have anticipated the influence-hunter's search and to have laid false trails—I say "seems" because, once possessed of the notion of Eliot's duplicitousness, it becomes impossible not to take it into consideration at every stage—what started life as a phantom becomes an everyday reality.

Examining the influence of Dostoevsky on Eliot might seem a potentially fraught task.
                                    —David Ayers

The notorious **"Notes on the Wasteland"**—hard to take seriously, hard to ignore—are perhaps a prime example of this. Many of Eliot's essays, while purporting to be objective criticism seem, under scrutiny, to be oblique meditations about the influence that an author might have had on Eliot's own work. The 1918 Lecture, **"From Poe to Valery",** finds in the work of Poe "nothing but slipshod writing, puerile thinking unsupported by wide reading or profound scholarship, haphazard experiments in various kinds of writing . . ." Yet Eliot admits that he shall "never be sure" what influence Poe's work has had on him. The essay then proceeds effectively to mitigate the effect of this influence by refracting Poe through Baudelaire, Mallarmé and Valéry—far more elegant peers than the stylistically crude and obsessive Poe.

Examining the influence of Dostoevsky on Eliot might seem a potentially fraught task. The first attempt to do so was an article by John C. Pope, "Prufrock and Raskolnikov," which appeared in *American Literature* in 1945. Pope gives weight to some very slight verbal parallels between Eliot's poem and Garnett's translation of *Crime and Punishment,* and additionally points out parallels of symbolic language—fog, streets, stairs (fairly ubiquitous phenomena, on any account) and references to Hamlet and Lazarus.

A study of the possible influence of Dostoevsky's early novel *The Double* on "Prufrock" and later works of Eliot seems . . . to have a profound obstacle in its path—Eliot does not admit to having read the book.

—David Ayers

While Pope's intuition was undoubtedly correct, he had made one fatal mistake, which Eliot himself pointed out in a personal letter. **"The Love Song of J. Alfred Prufrock"** had been completed in the summer of 1911, several years before any English translation of *Crime and Punishment* had appeared. This made nonsense of Pope's verbal parallels, as Pope himself acknowledged. However Pope did draw from Eliot the valuable information that he *had* been reading Dostoevsky in French translation, under the influence of his French tutor, Alain Fournier, while writing **"Prufrock",** although Eliot carefully disperses the question of influence on the poem by pointing out that parts of the poem, including the reference to Hamlet, were written *before* he had encountered Dostoevsky. Further, in addition to *Crime and Punishment,* he claims to have read *The Idiot* and *The Brothers Karamazov.*

A study of the possible influence of Dostoevsky's early novel *The Double* on **"Prufrock"** and later works of Eliot seems then to have a profound obstacle in its path—Eliot does not admit to having read the book. This at first seems disabling, but in fact it is liberating. It is possible that Eliot was misleading Pope while at the same time seeming to help the influence-hunters—just as the **"Notes on the Wasteland"**

seem to do. The French edition of *The Double,* had already in the Winter of 1910 run to several editions, and would have been easily available to Eliot. Even discounting this possibility, *The Double* dating from before Dostoevsky's exile, had an acknowledged effect on the work of his later period, and indeed he was working on a revised version of *The Double* some twenty years after its first publication—working at the same time on *Crime and Punishment.* So the question of influence might then be a question of refracted influence. Just as Poe was received by Eliot refracted through the French symbolistes, perhaps he received *The Double* (a tale with gothic elements possibly drawn from Poe, and immature in style) refracted through Dostoevsky's later and allegedly greater works. Yet there remains the tantalizing possibility, that Eliot's silence about *The Double,* like his distancing himself from Poe, is the product of a guilty affinity.

The hero of *The Double,* Titular Councillor Golyadkin, Yakov Petrovich to his friends, is a balding civil servant who is every bit as belated, indecisive, evasive and impotent as J. Alfred Prufrock himself. The narrative of the tale, which playfully blends the comic and the Gothic, brings Golyadkin into collision with his exact double, who comes to work in his office, impresses himself on his superiors in a way that Golyadkin has never done, and finally drives Golyadkin to madness. The story of Golyadkin finds its ancestry in Gogol's *The Nose,* Pushkin's *The Bronze Horesman,* and Cervantes' *Don Quixote,* but in its narrative method it is profoundly modern, blending the comic monologue of Dickens—a style itself sometimes named as the precursor of the stream-of-consciousness method in English—with a prediction of Jamesian point-of-view narration. The result is that rather than witness the decline of Golyadkin into madness the reader is inextricably involved in that decline. Much of what occurs is presented in Golyadkin's own words. Even when this is not so, the narrative voice increasingly adopts Golyadkin's own phrases and expressions, and as the persecution inflicted on him by his double grows, there is no relief for the reader who would seek to distinguish the projections of Golyadkin's own fevered mind from a sober and objective understanding of events. Indeed, the status of the reader with respect to the reality of the narrative mimics Golyadkin's own relationship to his double—each is shown a reality which, however implausible, becomes the only possible reference point.

The Double opens with Titular Councillor Yakov Petrovich Golyadkin awakening from a long sleep, and finding himself unable to decide "whether what is happening around him is real and actual, or only the continuation of his disordered dreams". This blurring of the distinction between reality and fantasy, subjective and objective, is in its various forms the archetypal romantic legacy for both Dostoevsky and Eliot alike, refracted through Baudelaire, transported to

Dostoevsky's Dickensian St Petersburg or Eliot's Dickensian London, and rendered ineluctable. Although Golyadkin quickly shakes himself awake to the grimy reality of St Peterburg, out of the "far-distant realm" of his dream, he will find the confusion recurring in his waking life, as he is forced to pinch himself to test his own wakefulness, considers pinching others also (but dare not), and is cruelly pinched on the nose and cheek by the taunting double.

For the moment, however, Golyadkin's possession of self and reality seems not to be threatened. He begins the morning by taking possession of his own image in the mirror. Considering what is about to happen, it is a greatly ironical moment, and one which enacts in microcosm the troubled heart of the Golyadkinesque dilemma:

> Although the sleepy, short-sighted, rather bald figure reflected in the glass was of such an insignificant character that nobody at all would have found it at the least remarkable at first glance, its owner was evidently quite satisfied with all he saw there. 'It would be a fine thing if something was wrong with me today, if a pimple had suddenly appeared out of the blue, for example, or something else disastrous had happened; however, for the moment, it's all right; for the moment everything is going well.'

In the heart of the metropolis the individual is utterly anonymous, the civil servant like any other good Russian citizen must dedicate his life to the service of his country, and entrust his fate to the authorities as to the father. The self then can only be recognised as an individual in its own eyes, it can only possess itself as an image, a mirror-image perhaps, or an imagined one, but always one mediated by that of which it is an image. The self and the self-image can never coincide, just as the individual in the parental state must go always unacknowledged, and the result is an interminable anxiety which can only increase the more the incomplete and never self-sufficient self tries to cross the gap. This, roughly expressed, seems to be the Dostoevskian formula not only for Golyadkin—whose name is derived from goli = "naked"—but for mass urban man in general. The nakedness of Golyadkin is in his very typicality, a typicality arrived at by stripping urban man to a core of anxiety, stripping his language down to a mixture of state-inspired platitudes and romance-inspired desires. Indeed the self-satisfaction of Golyadkin contemplating himself in the mirror is presented in terms of a platitudinous satisfaction with reality which Golyadkin continually reproduces throughout the novel as his situation deteriorates with increasing speed.

Golyadkin's possession of self and reality alike appear, even at this early stage of the narrative, to be tenuous. On waking, Golyadkin had looked around his room at his furniture and clothes which "all looked familiarly back at him". After looking in the mirror he takes out a bundle of notes in a wallet, which also seems "to look back at Mr Golyadkin in a friendly and approving fashion". This is the pathetic fallacy—the objects in question look approvingly back at Golyadkin only as a projection of his own self-satisfaction. Yet a reality seen in this way can equally become a menace. What if the pact with reality is broken by reality itself, approval for Golyadkin withdrawn, and a pimple erupts or some worse disaster takes place? As if to underline this threat, Golyadkin's samovar is found "raging and hissing fiercely, almost beside itself with anger and threatening to boil over any minute, gabbling away in its strange gibberish, lisping and babbling to Mr Golyadkin." Yet perhaps this too is a projection of Golyadkin—during the course of the narrative he too frequently threatens to boil over with anger, is almost metaphorically beside himself, and is finally literally beside himself. Golyadkin's consciousness attempts equally to contain a potentially explosive reality and a potentially explosive self. When the attempt at containment fails, Golyadkin's grasp on reality and on his self-image depart together, the self-image conspiring with a malevolent reality to expose the thoroughly dispossessed Golyadkin to his own naked anxieties.

These first pages then present a microcosmic view of the whole tale, although it is not at first apparent how out of hand Golyadkin's affairs already are, let alone how far astray they are going to go. Indeed most of the action of the story has taken place already, and the narrative deals only with the final dissolution. The first incongruities emerge when Golyadkin looks for his servant, Petrushka. Golyadkin is only a minor civil servant in a dingy fourth floor apartment, yet his aspirations to social position, arising from his sheer lack of position, lead him to keep a manservant who must sleep behind a partition, and who accords Golyadkin no respect whatsoever, despite frequent admonitions that he should do so. This morning Golyadkin finds Petrushka joking with other servants, he surmises about himself, and dressed in a ridiculously ill-fitting livery for the purpose of a coach-journey which he is to undertake with his master. For someone of Golyadkin's status, a journey with a liveried coachman is inappropriate. One purpose of the journey is a shopping expedition at the fashionable Arcades of the Nevsky Prospect. It is a ghost expedition: Golyadkin orders many items, some destined for a lady, promises a deposit, and leaves without giving his address: in short, an almost maniacal social masquerade born of Golyadkin's deep-seated wish to be someone. Yet at the same time, an incident on the journey from his own home shows exactly the opposite impulse. First, Golyadkin sees two younger colleagues from his own department. They are surprised to see him dressed up and in a carriage, clearly beyond his station, and call out to him. He hides in the corner of the carriage but consoles himself with aggressive thoughts:

"I know them, they're nothing but schoolboys still
in need of flogging . . . I'd have something to say
to the lot of them, only . . ."

Golyadkin's self-communion of consolation rests on knowing the others already, feeling able to look down on and contain them in a fantasy of domination, and on the security that
he *would* have something to say, even though he hasn't said
it, if only . . . his remarks trail off in suspension points.

The suspension of "only . . ." serves to isolate the most common rhetorical device of Golyadkin's almost constant pat-
ter of self-justification. It is not suspended because
Golyadkin is lost for argument—indeed later passages show
that his rhetoric of the conditional provides him with an un-
limited fund of argument—but that a second encounter provides a sharp intrusion into his interior monologue. He
encounters his immediate superior in the Department,
Andrey Phillipovich, in a carriage traveling in the opposite direction. He is in anguish trying to decide whether
or not to greet the other, or to take refuge in self-effacement:

> ". . . shall I pretend its not me but somebody else
> strikingly like me, and look as if nothing's the mat-
> ter?" . . . "I . . . it's all right," he whispered, hardly
> able to speak, "it's quite all right; this is not me at
> all, Andrey Phillipovich, it's not me at all, not me,
> and that's all about it."

Once his boss has passed, Golyadkin is consumed by anger
at his own pusillanimity, and directs "a terrible challenging
stare at the opposite corner of the carriage, a stare calculated to reduce all his enemies to dust".

This is a fascinating incident, and a crucial one. The urge
to self-effacement is born ultimately from the guilt of
Golyadkin's desires, both for social status and for the respectable lady whom, it later emerges, he would like to
marry. Thus the rhetoric of satisfaction and summary finality—"it's all right . . . that's all about it"—is an anxious attempt to contain the anxiety of an incomplete desire, one that
is embarrassed by its own incompletion in the face of the
seemingly self-sufficient other. Golyadkin's guilty reaction
to his own embarrassment—a reaction he repeats several
times during the course of the narration, always belatedly—
projects enmity on to a reality which is merely uncompliant
to his fantasy, and expresses a desire to exterminate that reality and replace it with fantasy. Indeed, Golyadkin's interior monologue throughout the narrative claims a knowledge,
and very often a foreknowledge, of events, particularly of
the thoughts and words of others, which it does not and cannot possess. In an effort to contain the other, the self attempts
to substitute itself for the other—but only belatedly. In the
face of an otherness which appears increasingly hostile to

the desire of the self, the self steps sideways evasively—"this
is not me at all".

Golyadkin is caught in an anxious oscillation between the
wish to manifest his individuality—in whatever this may consist—and wish to conceal it—often expressed as the wish
to hide in a mousehole, or as assertions about the normality
and acceptability of his own actions or situation. This oscillation becomes a general indecisiveness on his part which
almost entirely paralyses his will. This begins to become
clear during the encounter with Andrey Phillipovich, and assumes its extreme form during Golyadkin's next encounter—
with his new Doctor, Christian Ivanovich Rutenspitz. The
visit to Rutenspitz is an impromptu one, impulsively decided
upon after the encounter with Andrey Phillipovich and seemingly arising from that. On the way there, Golyadkin is tortured by doubts about the correctness and acceptability of
his action, in that language of self-questioning which becomes the most persistent index of his character:

> "Will it be all right though? . . . will it be all right?
> Is it a proper thing to do? Will this be the right time?
> However, does it really matter?" he continued as he
> mounted the stairs, breathing hard and trying to con-
> trol the beating of his heart, which always seemed
> to beat hard on other people's stairs; "does it mat-
> ter? I've come about my own business, after all, and
> there's nothing reprehensible in that . . . it would be
> stupid to try and keep anything from him. So I'll
> just make it appear that it's nothing special, I just
> happened to be driving past . . ."

It will be seen from this extended quotation that Golyadkin's
habitual discourse with himself, the precursor of the staircase torment of Raskolnikov, is like a perpetual attempt to
judge himself from an alternative viewpoint. He always wonders "what people might think", and substitutes his own
voice for the voice of the imagined others. Yet while the later
Dostoyevskian hero is troubled by issues that seem much
weightier, Golyadkin's doubts are about almost nothing at
all. That "almost nothing" is Golyadkin's own lack, that
incompletion which is the anxious heart of urban man. This
anxiety reproduces itself in an endless rhetoric of doubt. Indeed, it is about his state of anxiety that Golyadkin wishes
to see his doctor. But the will to self-revelation is countered
by the will to self-obliteration—to be no-one in particular,
self-sufficient, seen by others to be merely going about his
own business, as Golyadkin construes the self-sufficiency of
others. What results is the paralysis of the will by choice,
and this is dramatically enacted by Golyadkin at the door
of his doctor's house:

> Coming to a halt, our hero hastily tried to give his
> countenance a suitably detached but not unamiable
> air, and prepared to give a tug at the bell-pull. Hav-

ing taken hold of the bell-pull, he hastily decided, just in time, that it might be better to wait until the next day, and that meanwhile there was no great urgency. But suddenly hearing footsteps on the stairs, Mr. Golyadkin immediately changed his mind again and, while still retaining a look of the most unshakeable decision, at once rang Christian Ivanovich's bell.

The self is both subject and object—its own object and the object of the other, menacingly present here in the footsteps of the doctor's footman, ready to answer the door.

It is Golyadkin's constant claim that he is not duplicitous, that he makes himself plain, that he does not beat about the bush, that he does not wear a mask like others and, in short, that his objective image and his subjectivity are entirely coincident. It is a claim which is manifestly untrue—the incident at the door of Christian Ivanovich portrays a dramatic rupture between the oscillating anxiety of the self and the mask of "unshakeable decision" which Golyadkin presents. More than this, when Golyadkin goes to his superiors to explain himself, first about his designs on Carolina Ivanovich, daughter of the wealthy Olsufi Ivanovich, and later about the outrageous activities of his double, his rhetoric of self-revelation serves to so far defer and delay the actual moment of self-revelation that he is dismissed with impatience before any revelation has been made.

To complete this picture of Golyadkin before the appearance of his double—and it is a picture which accounts for most of his activities after the double appears—it need only be added that Golyadkin's linguistic attempt to contain the other and bend it toward his self-completion and self-sufficiency in the eyes of others is bound to fail, and continued frustration develops into a paranoia which sees enmity everywhere. Indeed, Golyadkin's rhetorics of self-questioning and of self-revelation are accompanied by an equally prolific and self-sustaining rhetoric of enmity. Not satisfied with one enemy, the allegation of enmity slips from one to another, frustrated of a final object, as Golyadkin is frustrated of his final revelation, another endless rhetoric of incompletion.

This is the prelude to the appearance of the double. The final precipitation is an abortive sexual encounter at a ball thrown by Olsufi Ivanovich, whose daughter has been wooed by a younger colleague of Golyadkin's, and in whose person therefore the whole of Golyadkin's anxiety of incompletion is embodied. Golyadkin is definitively not invited to the ball, and after a first abortive attempt at entry he is politely ejected. Instead of going home, he goes around to a rear entrance, and stands for three hours "in the cold among every kind of trash and lumber" assuring himself that his presence there means nothing, he could go in if he wanted to, it is not that he dare not, just that he does not choose to

at the moment, and so on. Having finally decided to go in and stepped up to the door, he retreats again into hiding. Having decided that he will go home, not only because he would like a warm cup of tea but also because his prolonged absence might upset his man-servant, Golyadkin states summarily "I'll go home, and that's all about it!" and steps straight inside the house. He proceeds to embarrass himself in the eyes of all present, and resorts to that device of self-detachment which enabled him to pretend not to be himself, this time to pretend to be merely a casual onlooker, and not a part of any scandal. Golyadkin's indecision and self-detachment, as well as his self-revelation when he tearfully tries to explain his presence in the sincerest manner, all reach their logical limit and, cast out on the streets of St Petersburg on a stormy night, Golyadkin first encounters his double, and follows him back to his own flat.

It should be apparent at this stage that while the doubling alluded to by the title of this novel is the eventual reduplication of Golyadkin himself, it might stand equally for a variety of reduplications at various levels which occur before the appearance of the double and which continue to manifest themselves after his arrival. From the first page where the fantasy of sleep and the reality of the waking world are confused, where everyday objects reflect back Golyadkin's gaze, and where a mirror offers him a specious moment of specular self-possession, doubling and duplicity become rampant. Doubling *and* duplicity, because every reduplication is seen to involve a treacherous loss. On his shopping expedition, Golyadkin takes his wad of high denomination notes to a money-changer. He comes away with a much thicker wallet—full of low-domination notes, having of course paid a commission on the exchange. Although he has lost by the transaction, it gives him the greatest satisfaction—the satisfaction, presumably, not only of appearing wealthier than he actually is, but also of a self-confirming exchange, the will to image the self and its true value being the same as the wish to image the true value of money in its bulk. It is a small moment, but one which neatly encapsulates the doubling process at work.

Perhaps this structural description of *The Double* has begun to hint too at aspects of Eliot's work—particularly **"The Love Song of J. Alfred Prufrock"**.

Prufrock in his balding and insignificant appearance certainly resembles Golyadkin far more than any other Dostoevskyian protagonist, least of all Raskolnikov, but it is parallels of structure rather than detail that most strongly suggest some kind of affinity.

The dramatic form of Prufrock, while it is drawn from a variety of traditions from the Elizabethan drama to Browning, serves, like the structure of *The Double,* to limit the perspective to that of the protagonist himself, a protagonist known therefore only by his language, his voice. What we learn about Prufrock's situation we know only from him, and his words seem often more symptomatic of his own malaise than indicative of any external reality—Prufrock imaging himself in his own discourse in that potentially endless exercise of attempted self-confirmation which constitutes the structural principle of Golyadkin's discourse. The opening words of **"Prufrock"**, "Let us go then, you and I", while they speciously suggest a link with one English translation of Golyadkin's address to the double, "Let's go somewhere now, you and I", are, more importantly, a key to the structural affinities and differences which link the two works.

If the words are read as Prufrock's own, which they need not be if it is not assumed that the poem is a dramatic monologue, then they might equally be addressed to his author, his reader, or to himself. If to himself, they suggest the gesture of self appropriation in the mirror which opens *The Double.* To whomever they might be addressed, they suggest that tone of attempted familiarity which characterizes one aspect of Golyadkin's relationship to others and especially to his double, an attempt to equate others with himself and to fix others, or the other, inside his own discourse. But no comfortable reading of these words is possible, as they are positioned with such wilful obscurity. They might be taken equally as the words of the author (or of a narrator) as of Prufrock himself, addressed possibly to the reader or to the protagonist. Suggesting all of these relationships without favouring any, the words come to stand generally for a language which seeks to appropriate the other to complete and satisfy the self, and in which the other, conversely, acquires a power to menace the self with what it has once taken to be its own image. Reader, author, Prufrock, and anyone else for that matter, are trapped in relationships of guilty complicity, drawn on and paralysed by specular images amongst the tawdry rubble of the godless city streets. Something like this is evidently how Eliot would have things, following quite a different brief from Dostoevsky in *The Double,* where author and reader alike are, despite superficial narrative complicity, placed at an aloof distance from Golyadkin's encroaching madness. Here, despite the humour at Prufrock's expense, there is a significant degree of endorsement of the Prufrockian position, not least by Eliot himself who, in a later interview, identified Prufrock as in part himself.

Prufrock the frustrated prophet might not at first seem to have much in common with the socially unsituated Golyadkin, but on examination the similarities proliferate. In fact, Golyadkin fancies himself something of a prophet. Whenever he finds himself overtaken by some completely unpredictable circumstance, he offers himself the reassurance, manifestly untrue, that he has already foreseen it all. For instance, when the engagement with the double is already well developed, Golyadkin arrives home in a spirit of self-torment, and finds an unexpected letter, one which is possibly an illusion but which seems tangible enough. It is from a friend at the office, in connection with the scandal of the double, and comes in reply to an earlier letter of Golyadkin's which the latter had foreseen that his manservant had not delivered. Golyadkin contains his surprise on finding the letter: "'However, I foresaw all this,' thought our hero, 'and now I foresee everything I shall find in the letter.'" Having read the letter, Golyadkin is dazed and uncomprehending, but continues to reassure himself that he has forseen it all while still puzzling the meaning of the words. Despite Golyadkin's puzzlement with the letter, in fact, there is no evidence that the letter is indeed real and not another projection. The language of the letter resembles closely Golyadkin's own self-dialogue and evasively accuses him of his most guilty action. Further, in the morning he looks again at the letter, and its meaning has changed in an unspecified way, somehow. Finally, looking in his pocket for the letter at a later stage, Golyadkin finds that it has disappeared, only to be replaced by a letter from the desired Carolina Ivanovna, rejecting her fiancé and inviting Golyadkin to elope; a letter which leads to his final destruction. The implication is that Golyadkin's self-proclaimed foresight is an attempt to contain a reality inimical to the self's desires, and perhaps a process of redefining that reality at first with subtlety and finally by outright alteration of the image of the world in the consciousness. On this analysis, the prime weapon of the self in its struggle with the other is its ability to substitute its own voice for the voice of others—a prophetic ability which Prufrock certainly shares, anticipating remarks about his hair and musculature, and anticipating also the scene of miscomprehension when his auditor remarks: "That is not it at all. That is not what I meant at all." At this point it is the voice of the other which rejects the appropriative strategy of the self and marks the self's inability to substitute its voice for the other.

Golyadkin too fears misprision, and is indeed always met by it in his attempted confidences, except for that single scene of the novel in which he finds himself contented, the night at home with the double, when the double, who comes to be known as Golyadkin Junior, unburdens himself to Golyadkin Senior, adopting the confidential and occasionally tearful manner of the latter. In the discourse of others, self-illusions have no purchase, and the romantic self is threatened with annihilation. It is the eyes of others which hold this power to annihilate the romantic self. For Prufrock there is the foreknowledge of "The eyes that fix you in a formulated phrase" which pin him to the wall like an insect, and for Golyadkin, also compared to an insect in his moments of supreme abasement, there is the "annihilating stare" of Andrey Phillipovich for instance, and the recurrent fear of betrayal and loss of self possession in the conspiratorial words of others, words which he cannot hear. This fear is finally realized in the Judas-kiss of the double, and it is the person of the double who is finally construed as the enemy, a term which has to shift considerably in Golyadkin's discourse—he is at first sure that the double is the device of other unspecified enemies. But Golyadkin's social insecurity leads him to construe every social inferior as a betrayer, particularly as they never respond to his patronising manner, and Petrushka in particular will never show his master any respect. It is Petrushka who at the very opening of the novel is chatting and laughing with some other servants: Golyadkin fears that he has seen "sold for nothing", a fear which compresses anxiety about annihilation in the discourse of others with anxiety about his own exchange value, and reveals perhaps a desire to be exchanged, like the desire to be made fully manifest, if only for the right price.

The possibility of the transcendent state is not dismissed in "Prufrock". It remains as an inaccessible possibility and recurs subsequently in much of Eliot's central work. *The Double* too deals with the death-in-life state, but does not offer it a refuge.
—David Ayers

For Prufrock too there is betrayal, and humiliation before social inferiors. Here the footman is given a capital and made 'eternal', not only because in his manners he might seem that much more assured than Prufrock, but also because he is the archetypal other which fixes the self under its stare, and representative too of that absolute of revelation to which the prophet Prufrock aspires. Betrayal is writ large in **"Prufrock."** While Golyadkin is implicitly compared to Christ, Prufrock explicitly compares himself to John the Baptist, imagining his head "brought in upon a platter"—perhaps a tidier analogy than that of *The Double,* evoking the sexual factor, present in both works, as the motive of betrayal. Further, it serves to put Prufrock in his self-romanticization at one remove from Christ himself. John the Baptist merely foresees the coming of the one who shall be revealed as the Son of God, but the power of revelation is not his. In **"Prufrock"** as in *The Double,* revelation is deferred or, as here, displaced, projected on to another. Revelation is the product in Eliot of a mystical timeless state, imagined as in many religions as a return to life from death, or a suspended state of death-in-life. Prufrock imagines himself saying "I am Lazarus, come from the dead, / Come back to tell you all. / I shall tell you all." Again, like Christ returning from the dead, but unlike Christ not possessed of any revelatory or prophetic power. Indeed, the Biblical Lazarus, anticlimactically, never says anything about having been dead. The possibility of Prufrock as prophet is all but obliterated by this deadening analogy, and in any case his wish to "have squeezed the universe into a ball" with its allusion to Marvell denotes a thorough confusion of the prophetic and the sexual

urge to completion in a (Platonic and otherwise) ball. (For Golyadkin the wish to complete and summarize takes the form of a regret that he cannot cut off his finger as a means to settle the whole matter—a comically small sacrifice which nevertheless suggests castration and the mid-life impotence which the balding Golyadkin and Prufrock share—a diminutive version of Caligula's wish that the Roman Senate had only one throat which he could cut.)

Yet the possibility of the transcendent state is not dismissed in **"Prufrock"**. It remains as an inaccessible possibility and recurs subsequently in much of Eliot's central work. *The Double* too deals with the death-in-life state, but does not offer it a refuge. Dostoevsky himself suffered from epilepsy, and Golyadkin is made to suffer bouts of epilepsy or perhaps madness in situations of acute stress. He is described as "more dead than alive" and in reply to questions from his doctor about his current abode he miscomprehendingly replies: "I was living, Christian Ivanovich, I was living even formerly. I must have been, mustn't I?" At the height of one of his attacks Golyadkin is "dumb and motionless, seeing nothing, hearing nothing, feeling nothing". When less overwhelmed, he becomes tremendously distracted, his thoughts and conversation digress fantastically, and his mind becomes fixed on isolated images, much like the "sordid images" which brokenly fixate Eliotic protagonists. Golyadkin's death-in-life moments resemble nothing more than that moment in **"The Burial of the Dead"** in the presence of the "hyacinth girl".

'You gave me Hyacinths first a year ago;
'They called me the hyacinth girl.'
Yet when we came back, late, from the hyacinth garden,
Your arms full, and your hair wet, I could not
Speak, and my eyes failed, I was neither
Living nor dead, and I knew nothing,
Looking into the heart of light, the silence.

This is a complicated moment which begins from that basic Romantic premise which makes the woman that object which completes the man and offers him transcendence—just as the ultimate object of Golyadkin and Prufrock was sexual. Here, however, the scene is passed, the girl has no subjective recollection of it, and seems therefore an inadequate object of the man's rapture, while what the man recalls might equally be a fit of madness as of rapture, while the "heart of light" borrows the ineluctability of the "heart of darkness" to further veil the moment of transcendence.

There is a crucial difference between Eliot and Dostoevsky on the point of romantic transcendence. For Eliot, while directing his full satirical tones against a weak romantic notion of transcendence in "Prufrock", there still seems to be always an escape clause. The possibility of transcendence is never disallowed—it is instead always deferred, delayed or otherwise displaced, remaining "a perpetual possibility / Only in a world of speculation." We know that Eliot in his early period at least was very close to the philosophy of T. E. Hulme, and belief in the desirability at least of the concept of an Absolute, even if it were to be an entirely inaccessible one. Politically this idea manifested itself perhaps in Eliot's royalism, the concept of a state where the monarchy in mystical fashion secured social meaning, much like the framework satirized in *The Double* in which Golyadkin looks on the state and the highest officials of the state as a father who should secure his individuality by preventing what he calls "substitution"—meaning the substitution of the double for himself—in a chaos of social and semantic slippage. While Eliot harbours mysticism, Dostoevsky blows it away. While **"Prufrock"** defers the moment of transcendence, doubts it, but leaves it possible, *The Double* displays a rhetoric of self-revelation in a transcendent moment which is given the chance to play its last card. As *The Double* progresses, it becomes increasingly desireable for Golyadkin to make plain his case to some higher power, and in a late scene, having entered yet another social gathering uninvited, the chance at last arrives for him to explain to a supremo of the Civil Service known only as "His Excellency". "Well, what do you want?" asks His Excellency: "As I say, it's like this: I look on him as a father; I stand aloof in the whole affair—and protect me from my enemy! There you are!" Golyadkin's reply ends with an exclamatory flourish which shows that he does indeed consider that he has made all plain. His Excellency of course is baffled, having heard nothing of Golyadkin's minor scandal, and in the face of incomprehension, Golyadkin breaks down and is taken away. When Golyadkin thinks he is revealing himself in a transcendent moment, all he reveals is that nexus of anxieties that has produced his discourse and actions throughout: his urge to completion and security, thought to be offered by the father: the repudiation of the self in the wish to stand outside it, elsewhere a wish to disappear or be annihilated: the fear for the safety of an incomplete self which, meeting only a hostile world which refuses it completion, projects enmity everywhere. It is a final testing of Golyadkin's rhetoric to which the subtler and more thoroughly scrutinized rhetoric of Prufrock is never subjected.

When Eliot selected a quotation from Conrad's "Heart of Darkness" as the original epigraph for *The Wasteland* he was challenged by Pound that it could not bear the weight which its position put on it. Contemporaries considered the work light, an evaluation which Pound seems to have shared, although Eliot, who took from it the epigraph to "The Hollow Men", seemingly did not. It is an interesting disparity, because "Heart of Darkness" probably more than any modern work, relies on a rhetoric of ineffability which culminates in Kurtz's final words—"The horror! the horror!" For the early Romantic the transcendent moment might have

been a union with God, but for Kurtz it produces a reduplicated vision of terror. At least this is what we are told by Marlow—for this is a displaced moment of vision. "Did he live his life again in every detail of desire, temptation, and surrender during that supreme moment of complete knowledge?" It is an unanswered question, even though it strongly suggests its own answer. For Marlow himself, although he seems to have lived through Kurtz's "last extremity", the summary is impossible—"I was within a hair's-breadth of the last opportunity for pronouncement, and I found with humiliation that probably I would have nothing to say. Through a host of rhetorical devices, "Heart of Darkness" suggests complete revelation and summation in a transcendent moment which is however always on the other side of a ghostly line. For all its seriousness, the rhetoric of "Heart of Darkness", which places the word "horror" at its abysmal centre, has a buried affinity with the literature of gothic horror, which must always employ a rhetoric of ineffability to maintain its power to horrify—it must in short refuse completion.

And in the manner of the horror fictionist—perhaps in that of his contemporary H. P. Lovecraft, whose language of ineffability owed much to Poe—Eliot deploys a rhetoric of displaced transcendence which has its roots in the first doubts of a Romanticism herded from the countryside and penned in the city, of which Coleridge is perhaps the earliest spokesman. Dostoevsky too deploys the Gothic—although never after *The Double* in the same unmitigated form—yet the notion of ineffability is demolished, the product of urban displacement and not its absolute though inaccessible meaning. It is a fundamental difference and one which makes the gap between *The Double* and **"The Love Song of J. Alfred Prufrock"** as wide as it could be. So finally, what is their subterranean connection?

> O keep the Dog far hence, that's friend to men,
> Or with his nails he'll dig it up again!

Grover Smith (essay date 1988)

SOURCE: "'Prufrock' as Key to Eliot's Poetry," in *Approaches to Teaching Eliot's Poetry and Plays,* The Modern Language Association of America, 1988, pp. 88-93.

[*In the following essay, Smith discusses how teaching students the underlying structure of "Prufrock" introduces them to the broader concepts of Eliot's later works.*]

A strategy to identify the essence of Eliot beyond, as well as within, a single poem needs the right poem. To make **"The Love Song of J. Alfred Prufrock"** this poem, whether one is proposing to teach Eliot comprehensively or selectively, offers several advantages. **"Prufrock"** is familiar and is outstanding in interest and attractiveness; it comes near the beginning of the canon; it links in theme and technique with various other poems by Eliot; and, most useful, it anticipates certain equally familiar critical principles (two especially) that he was to declare. Those principles, though they only took shape ten years further on, in his most active period of critical theory, apply to **"Prufrock"** and other poems of the 1909-11 period because it was in these, as a practical exercise, that he discovered their necessity. In **"Tradition and the Individual Talent"** (1919) he set forth a kind of theory of mutual adaptation between the poet and the cultural past; in **"The Metaphysical Poets"** (1921) he pointed to certain distinguished cases of poetic excellence achieved through unity of thought and feeling. (These papers, reprinted in Eliot's **Selected Essays,** are extremely interesting to read and are of value to the teacher. The best introductory summary of Eliot's critical theories is still René Wellek's 1956 essay in the *Sewanee Review.*) Tradition in the poetry of Eliot represents the impact of the past on the thought-feeling unity of the achieved work of art—the old renewing itself in the fresh and original. The two principles thus combine into one. Each entails for critics a kind of pons asinorum; for tradition to Eliot meant adapting the past, not copying it, and the unity of thought and feeling meant a poetic formulation, not a discharge of personal philosophy and passion—though indeed these might be sources for poetic transformation. The principles work in **"Prufrock"** by giving technical significance to what happens there, and they can help a teacher open up the poem for students. They also provide standards and a vocabulary for treating **"Prufrock"** as a touchstone—not quite in Arnold's sense—for Eliot's subsequent development. With them, the teacher of **"Prufrock"** can introduce Eliot as poet and theorist together and prepare students for dealing with poems, similarly grounded, that lie ahead. And since in teaching Eliot one teaches tradition or nothing, in a more Arnoldian sense **"Prufrock"** may become a touchstone for the work of other poets, even for the genuineness of a poem.

The teaching of poetry calls for a certain restraint. Interpretation is next to falsification: therefore it has no value (unless sometimes comic value) for its own sake. Yet we must confess that we are all tainted with it. The only expiation is to devote ourselves as far as possible to letting the poem reveal its true nature as we read and teach it—its own point of view, not ours. Pedagogically one is probably unwise to begin with theory in teaching a poem, for theory demands from the student prior knowledge of the object. If one sets out by establishing that **"Prufrock"** is a monologue, or more privately a spoken reverie, and one gets the class to recognize through the grammar and syntax that the persona's "visit" on that foggy late afternoon takes place in time, not space, in his projective imagination, then the remaining essentials should prove easy to explore. Why Prufrock revolves in his mind, assisted by his memories, a program of action

that should lead to an amorous declaration but cannot even commence can be answered only by reference to his character. Partly he gains definition through his rhetoric of vacillation and diffidence, which the members of the class who have read the poem aloud to themselves, at home, will know is confirmed by the ruefulness of his tone. An unhurried reading of selected strophes in class, however, may be used to question the proposition that he only suffers, that mere ennui and frustration are his only portion. Partly he emerges through a rhetorical effect quite other than rueful, namely, his invocation of a personal mythology of power, according to which he transitorily takes to himself, soon after the middle of the poem, exaggerative guises such as "ragged claws," a great saint's severed head "upon a platter," the mana of the resurrected Lazarus, and the grave perplexities of Hamlet, and at last locates himself in the chambers of "sea-girls." The ambivalence of these images of power—images that he both dodges and embraces, illustrates the transformations of thought and feeling, their interpenetration. One scenario for the teaching of **"Prufrock"** will therefore involve an analysis of the persona's rhetorical division into a comically pathetic self and a boastfully poetic one, two selves that coexist. And Eliot's 1921 theory of a fusion of thought and feeling can, perhaps uniquely, provide the right clue to what is going on. Theory enters the scene precisely on time, its presence required and its message respectfully attended.

A strategy to identify the essence of Eliot beyond, as well as within, a single poem needs the right poem. To make "The Love Song of J. Alfred Prufrock" this poem, whether one is proposing to teach Eliot comprehensively or selectively, offers several advantages.

—Grover Smith

As likely as not, that scenario will fail to work in the classroom because the rhetorical effect fails to be noted before some different question intervenes. Unless one is simply lecturing, a student may short-circuit the line of development by asking, for example, what the Italian poetry, the epigraph, at the beginning of **"Prufrock"** is *for.* This is a fair question and provides a useful topic, which will guide one to the character of the persona by a different way, but hardly through the unity of thought and feeling. Either the epigraph, from Dante's *Inferno* 27, or the references to John the Baptist, Lazarus, and Hamlet can prompt a general explanation of the role played in Eliot by tradition. More urgently, a student may pose a question, based on outside reading or a detective instinct, that challenges Eliot as unoriginal, plagiaristic, or inaccessibly highbrow. To concede the reasonableness of these charges is good tactics; one need only show afterward that, once laid open to inspection, tradition is as accessible as anything else and that the originality of Eliot's recourse to it, for source material or whatever, lies beyond cavil. Meanwhile, as most of our students have no familiarity with Dante, Shakespeare, or the Bible, access should benefit them. It can make no difference whether, at any early stage, one introduces the principle of the enduring tradition or that of the unity of thought and feeling; indeed one may need to discuss them together, as accident or opportunity may suggest. Some teachers may be uneasy with this amount of improvisation and may wish to control the sequence of topics more strictly. On occasion I might agree; but among possible experiments the least promising appears to be that of teaching the theoretical principles as a separate unit while actually teaching a poem. One says enough about them in naming, explaining, and applying them. In a course where they can compose a unit apart from the poetry, poetry by Eliot might be instanced to explain them.

Most students will admit to some confusion over the "I-you" question: to whom really is Prufrock talking?
—Grover Smith

With **"Prufrock"** I prefer any scenario that deals with the man's character first and leaves until later the consideration of style in relation to the past and to literary models or sources. The epigraph from Dante suggests itself as a source of Prufrock's character as well as of his situation. (In Eliot the sources always furnish some essential fiber of significance.) Most students will admit to some confusion over the "I-you" question: to whom really is Prufrock talking? One may cut the Gordian knot by replying that he is talking to himself; but his reasons are not altogether simple. They seem to be involved with the answer to another question: what is Prufrock representing himself as? It may be expedient in teaching to note, with the help of a translation, the possible parallel between Prufrock and Guido. In *Inferno* 27, Guido speaks the lines of the epigraph to the poet Dante, who has "dropped in" and who, in a kind of treachery, reports (in the very poem they occur in) the secrets that Guido says can never leak out, from those depths, to the world of the living. An indicated corollary of the Dantean parallel is that Prufrock's treacherous confidant ("you") is (as it were) the poet Eliot. Like Guido, moreover, Prufrock is hoist with his own petard: not knowing that he is a character in a poem, he blabs. It is Eliot, not he, who doubles Prufrock with Guido and who offers himself ("you") as a double of the Dante with whom Guido converses; but since Eliot does not play a further role in the monologue, Prufrock has only himself to talk to, "after all." My account—an interpretation, the reader is warned—postulates a joke in the manner of Laforgue, played on Prufrock by his author; Eliot would again double him-self with Dante in *The Waste Land* and in **"Little Gidding"**. Prufrock's ambivalent assimilation to Guido, Hamlet, and others specializes Eliot's practice, in poems at every period of the canon, of fabricating poetry by means of transformed source materials bearing traditional weight. The models for Prufrock's character besides Guido illustrate the composite impact of tradition. Since some of them, furthermore, also derive historically from Hamlet, they show multiple linkage at work in the composite. (On this chain effect or "genealogy" of sources, see Smith, *The Waste Land.*)

A main source for Prufrock was Henry James's story "Crapy Cornelia," which I have briefly discussed elsewhere (*T. S. Eliot's Poetry and Plays*; the parallel was pointed out to me, in conversation almost forty years ago, by my then-colleague Richard Earl Amacher). In the middle-class would-be suitor White-Mason of "Crapy Cornelia," Eliot found a character that he endowed with certain pretensions to cultivation or dignity, as merited by Strether in *The Ambassadors* and over-reached by the dithering Marcher in "The Beast in the Jungle." Besides manifesting a Jamesian mold, Prufrock seems to regard himself in a Jamesian light. Unlike other sentimental bachelors, from Charles Lamb's to Ik Marvel's, he introspects to break his way out, not wholly unsuccessfully. For at least he achieves a rhetoric of mythic grandeur, though of absurd components. The "mythical method" greeted by Eliot in writing of Joyce a dozen years later was already invented in **"Prufrock."** The important issue for this method, and for all Eliot's manipulations of received material, of tradition, consists in the changes made in the specific sources. The teacher of **"Prufrock"** may wish to press this point. It becomes ever more cardinal in the teaching of the Sweeney poems, of **"Gerontion,"** of *The Waste Land,* and later work of Eliot. Prufrock is the first of Eliot's complex synthetics, his psychological lineaments along with his milieu being derived variously; and he seems too, as brought out, to feel that he is an artificial person, made by his tailor. He talks furthermore as if playing the part of a Henry James character, such is his mode of self-description. If so, he has obviously become entrapped in the role, so much so that he displays hardly any claim to natural as opposed to literary existence. Prufrock's artificiality results from literary artificiality and can with difficulty be separated from it. His effort to escape his role by finding his opposite does not deliver him from his antiheroic condition. An early text of the poem bore the title "Prufrock among the Women," perhaps in allusion to the least glorious stratagem of Achilles. The rhetoric with which Prufrock rehabilitates his vitality carries the general implication of heroic failure, death rather than triumph. Another model for him was the Hamlet of Jules Laforgue's *Moralités légendaires,* a very different personage from Shakespeare's, an alter ego of Yorick the fool and the living counterpart therefore of Death. Laforgue's Hamlet, in defiance of a really tender conscience, parades himself as antihero, antilover, and antinomian of a type that believes "anything is permitted" and hails the Unconscious as his liberator from the categorical imperative; in despair he plunges into cruelty. His nihilism resembles that of the unregenerate Raskolnikov in Dostoevsky's *Crime and Punishment*, another prototype of the solitary rebel for Eliot. (See John C. Pope's essays on Prufrock and Raskolnikov in *American Literature*.) Prufrock draws his urbanity from James, his bitterness and irony from Laforgue, his intensity from Dostoevsky; but the mixture is both unequal and innovative. Like the concoctions of mock epic, it leaves its originals undiminished but not quite the same—enhanced ever so slightly by feedback. Such is the possible reverse effect of Eliot's principle of tradition. In teaching, one can accordingly make **"Prufrock"** a touchstone for theory.

The unity of thought and feeling as a characterizing device brings singleness out of doubleness without blurring either. Prufrock is what he thinks in the course of the poem, but very little of his thought appears except as objective imagery, flashes of feeling. Before writing **"The Metaphysical Poets,"** which speaks of "a direct sensuous apprehension of thought" and "a re-creation [hyphen mine] of thought into feeling," Eliot had ventured to term it "impossible . . . to draw any line between thinking and feeling" (**"Prose and Verse"**). Of course the two faculties work together: the thought apprehended by feeling is not eliminated by it. That no line can be drawn between them, moreover, does not imply that they are the same. Their difference becomes glaring when they do *not* work together, when in poetry they fail to combine or there is too much of either of them. Because "Prufrock" is a persona poem, the known interaction occurs at Prufrock's point of view, between his thinking and his feeling, and not in the poet's sphere of being. And it occurs constantly, but not in a constant form; one needs to keep students alert to the subtleties of the shift into feeling as the thought is phrased with overtones of irony, indifference, distaste, or desperation. Thus in the lines about the women and Michelangelo, used first as a focus for the proposed departure and later as a definition of the limits imposed by an arrival, the thought is stretched into more than one shape of feeling, dependent on connotations of the confined, the superficial, the pompous, the transient, the magnificent, the incongruous, which diversely collide. That it is not merely a thought is the main point. Up to the "lonely men" and "ragged claws" passages, Prufrock keeps reiterating his superiority to circumstances and then producing an imagery of his humiliation; but in the latter part of the poem the boasts take fanciful forms with imagery and are followed by more matter-of-fact observations. It is as if his mind were gradually convulsed with spasms of suffering and then were intermittently rallied with a mythology of self-esteem, only to succumb each time to more rational despair. The thought and feeling interact both in the reflective and in the fanciful utterances but are always shifting in intensity.

It is more important to get students to hear **"Prufrock"** than it is to get them to "follow" it. The teacher who does not manage to convey those apposite rhymes, those lovely cadences into the presentation of it misses a fine pedagogic exercise. But I do not know how to systematize that undertaking except by reading the poem aloud. Alas—because the unity of thought and feeling inheres in the delivery of the lines. It is possible, once again, to illustrate Eliot's recycling of tradition by citing from **"Prufrock"** a couplet that renews the past by transforming it, the couplet

> Arms that are braceleted and white and bare
> [But in the lamplight, downed with light brown hair!]

The contrast of coldness and warmth, artificiality and animal intimacy, sums up so much of the thematic essence of **"Prufrock"** that nothing more is called for. Yet behind these lines lurks a world of more solemn implication. If one can hear in them the line they primarily echo from John Donne's poem "The Relique,"

> A bracelet of bright haire about the bone,

and remember the significance of this emblem of passion and devotion (found also in "The Funerall"), the concentration of feeling in the couplet undergoes a heightening almost, even, to a sensation of physical pain, as intense as Donne's grim consciousness of love triumphant over charnel mortality. I do not say that Mr. Prufrock can hear this echo—though why not?—for he creates it, varying "bracelet" and chiming "white and bare" with "bright haire" and then near rhyming "downed" with "bone" and finally repeating the near rhyme and definitely rhyming, himself, with "light brown hair." And what is more he borrows from "The Funerall," which has "That subtile wreath of haire, which crowns my arme," a rhyme to prove his near rhyme a true one and adopts the essential word "arms" that denotes the objects of his attention and absorption and frustration. Perhaps it was Mr. Eliot that did and felt all this. He would often in the future raise voices from the grave (as one's students are pleased to discover), though none more comically sad and musical than Prufrock's own. In them nevertheless something from Prufrock would be blended, having in some manner joined a tradition perpetually to be enriched by his thought and feeling.

James Ledbetter (essay date Fall 1992)

SOURCE: "Eliot's 'The Love Song of J. Alfred Prufrock'", in *Explicator*, Vol. 51, No. 1, Fall, 1992, pp. 41-5.

[*In the following essay, Ledbetter asserts that a more accu-*

rate interpretation of "Prufrock" may be garnered by re-thinking the roles of Lazarus, John the Baptist, and Guido da Montefeltro.]

The editors of anthologies containing T. S. Eliot's **"The Love Song of J. Alfred Prufrock"** invariably footnote the reference to Lazarus as John 11:1-44; rarely is the reference footnoted as Luke 16:19-31. Also, the reference to John the Baptist is invariably footnoted as Matthew 14:3-11; never have I seen the reference footnoted as an allusion to Oscar Wilde's *Salome.* The sources that one cites can profoundly affect interpretations of the poem. I believe that a correct reading of Eliot's **"Prufrock"** requires that one cite Wilde, in addition to Matthew, and Luke, in addition to John, as the sources for the John the Baptist and Lazarus being referenced. Furthermore, the citation of these sources can help explain Eliot's allusion to Dante's Guido da Montefeltro.

By a correct reading of **"Prufrock,"** I mean a reading consistent with the central theme of the poet's belief made mute because the poet lives in a culture of unbelief—that is, the "silence" of the poetic vision in modernity. Prufrock renounces his inherited, romantic role as "poet as prophet" and renounces poetry's role as a successor to religion. The future of poetry may have once been immense, but that future no longer exists for Prufrock, who is faced not only with the certainty of the rejection of his poetic vision but also with a situation in which there are no grounds for rhetoric: "That is not what I meant at all. / That is not it, at all." Fear of rejection leads Prufrock to the ultimate silencing of the prophet and hero within himself, to being "a pair of ragged claws." He cannot share his poetic vision of life: to do so would threaten the very existence of that life. Paradoxically, not to share his light, his "words among mankind," threatens the loss of the wellsprings of his creative force.

I believe that a correct reading of Eliot's "Prufrock" requires that one cite Wilde, in addition to Matthew, and Luke, in addition to John, as the sources for the John the Baptist and Lazarus being referenced. Furthermore, the citation of these sources can help explain Eliot's allusion to Dante's Guido da Montefeltro.
—James Ledbetter

Prufrock elaborates the extent of his renunciation of the romantic notion of "poet as prophet": Prufrock is no prophet—neither a John the Baptist, nor a Lazarus, nor is he even a hero.

But though I have wept and fasted, wept and
prayed,

Though I have seen my head (grown slightly bald)
brought in upon a platter,
I am no prophet—and here's no great matter . . .

The reference is not only to Matthew 14:3-11, but also to Oscar Wilde's *Salome,* the play upon which Richard Strauss based his opera *Salome.* In the biblical account, no motivation is ascribed to Salome for wanting John the Baptist killed. In the versions by Wilde and Strauss, however, Salome is passionately in love with the imprisoned John the Baptist, who, because he will not let the temptations of the flesh corrupt his pure love of God, rejects her advances. Wilde's Salome, determined that if she cannot have John no one will have John, asks Herod for the Baptist's head on a platter. John the Baptist spurned Salome's affections while he lived; now that he is dead, Salome lavishes her kisses upon the cold lips of the bloody corpse-head.

Prufrock, too, has had his moments of temptation: he has "known the arms already, known them all— / Arms that are braceleted and white and bare / (But in the lamplight, downed with light brown hair!)." And these very sources of temptation, these "arms that lie along a table, or wrap about a shawl", eventually emasculate Prufrock by rejection: "Would it have been worth while / If one, settling a pillow or throwing off a shawl, / And turning toward the window, should say: / 'That is not it at all, / That is not what I meant, at all'." Prufrock has seen his "head . . . brought in upon a platter." Like John the Baptist, Prufrock has fallen prey to the seduction of an impious age. But, unlike John, Prufrock declaims: "I am no prophet—and here's no great matter."

John the Baptist lived in an age of belief: he felt a privileged claim to transcendent knowledge that assured the victory, even in death, of his holy prophecy over the vicissitudes of worldly evil. Prufrock knows that he is subject to the same temptations of the flesh, knows that he ultimately will succumb to the same death at the hands of evil; but Prufrock, if he makes claim to privileged, poetic knowledge, feels no imperative to share that knowledge with a society rooted in unbelief. The martyrdom of prophecy is untenable in a modernity in which "God is dead."

And would it have been worth it, after all,
. . . .
Would it have been worth while,
To have bitten off the matter with a smile,
To have squeezed the universe into a ball
To roll it towards some overwhelming question,
To say: "I am Lazarus, come from the dead,
Come back to tell you all, I shall tell you all"—
If one, settling a pillow by her head,
    Should say: "That is not what I meant at all.
    That is not it, at all."

Prufrock's answer is a clear "No!" If he is not a prophet like John the Baptist, much less is he a Lazarusian savior.

In John 11: 1-44, Lazarus of Bethany is ill and dying, and Jesus promises Lazarus's sisters, Mary and Martha, that he will come and heal him. But Jesus tarries, and Lazarus dies. By the time Jesus and his disciples arrive, Lazarus has been dead four days. Martha laments that Jesus took so long, and Jesus replies, "I am the resurrection, and the life: he that believeth in me, though he were dead, yet shall he live." Martha misunderstands Jesus, thinking he is referring to the Judgment Day, and then Mary comes out and says, "Lord, if thou hadst been here, my brother had not died." Jesus " . . . groaned in the spirit, and was troubled. . . . Jesus wept." Despite Martha's protestations that by now Lazarus must stink, Jesus orders the stone of the tomb rolled away and raises Lazarus from the dead. The chief priests of the Pharisees, hearing of the resurrection of Lazarus, resolve that "Jesus should die. . . ."

This account of the resurrection of Lazarus is what Matthew Arnold, in *Literature and Dogma* and *God and the Bible,* calls *aberglaube,* or "after belief," superstitious accretions to the essentially ethical religious message of the historic Jesus: according to Jesus' own reaction, his weeping, the need to resurrect Lazarus to inculcate belief should have been redundant and is therefore pitiable. This account of Lazarus is irrelevant to **"The Love Song of J. Alfred Prufrock,"** except possibly as a foil to Luke's Lazarus; its very "aberglauberish" dramatics are antithetical to the central theme of a recalcitrant Prufrock. Furthermore, John's Lazarus never speaks, nor is he ever really expected to say anything. The account serves to demonstrate man's incorrigible obduracy to truth and to set up Jesus' Crucifixion and Resurrection as Christ, which would be irrelevant not only to the theme of **"Prufrock"** but, according to Arnold, irrelevant to the essentially moral message of Jesus as well.

The parable of Lazarus found in Luke, on the other hand, is relevant both to Jesus' moral teachings and to the theme of **"Prufrock."** In Luke 16:19-31, Lazarus is a beggar, "full of sores," who beseeches a rich man that he be allowed to eat "the crumbs which fell from the rich man's table." The rich man sends Lazarus away and sets his dogs on him. Lazarus dies and goes to the comfort of the bosom of Abraham; the rich man dies and is tormented in hell's flames. Seeing Lazarus in comfort, the rich man begs Abraham to allow Lazarus to bring him water, Abraham, however, reminds the rich man that in life he received "good things" and Lazarus received "evil things," and that it is fitting that Lazarus now be "comforted" and he, the rich man, "tormented." Seeing that there is no help for himself, the rich man entreats Abraham to send Lazarus back to life to warn his five brothers so that they will not end up in hell also.

29. Abraham saith unto him [the rich man], They have Moses and the prophets; let them [your brothers] hear them.
30. And he [the rich man] said, Nay, father Abraham: but if one [Lazarus] went unto them from the dead, they will repent.
31. And he [Abraham] said unto him, If they hear not Moses and the prophets, neither will they be persuaded, though one rose from the dead.

Prufrock knows that it would be futile to declaim, "'I am Lazarus, come from the dead, / Come back to tell you all, I shall tell you all'—." His audience—like the rich man's five brothers (and probably like the audience of Christ's parable)—would be deaf to the claims of any privileged knowledge of transcendent authority. Lazarus, had Abraham returned him from the dead, would have been wasting his breath—his exhalation and his spirit, and Prufrock feels that he, too, would be wasting his breath declaiming to a modern audience that which modernity not only will not accept but will not even allow a forum for refutation: "Neither will they be persuaded, though one rose from the dead."

Prufrock's renunciation of any role as "poet as prophet," either martyred or resurrected, climaxes in a resounding "No! I am not Prince Hamlet, nor was meant to be. . . ." Not only is Prufrock not a prophet sent to save the human race, he is not even a hero, destined to purge the state of its ills. Something may be rotten in the state of Denmark, but her redemption rests with someone other than Prufrock. With this renunciation comes the capitulation of that which is most dear to Prufrock: with his renunciation of prophecy and heroism, Prufrock fears the loss of his poetic vision.

Prufrock does affirm the source of his poetic inspirations: "I have heard the mermaids singing, each to each." The mermaids are the source of access to privileged, transcendent belief—to transmogrifying belief. However, Prufrock continues, "I do not think that they will sing to me." The hermeneutic circle—from transcendent inspiration, to poet, to audience, back to worship of that divine source of inspiration—cannot be broken without devastating consequences. However, Prufrock believes that he has no audience, and the consequences of his alienation will ultimately be, he fears, poetic sterility—the loss of the very source of his creative life.

The loss of Prufrock's poetic inspiration might explain Eliot's cryptic epigraph. The epigraph is taken from Dante's *Inferno* where the false counselor Guido da Montefeltro, enveloped in hell's flame, explains to Dante that he will speak freely only because he has heard that no one ever escapes from hell: "If I thought that my reply would be to one who would ever return to the world, this flame would stay without further movement. But since none has ever returned alive from this depth, if what I hear is true, I answer you without fear of infamy." Guido has no fear of answering all of Dante's questions—of letting his flame shine forth. Prufrock, on the other hand, lives with his light entombed in the dark hell of his own fear of rejection: he cannot share his "love song." He says, in effect, A prophet is never honored in his own time; therefore, this prophet shall remain silent. He says, in effect, Lazarus wasn't sent back from the dead—because you already have your prophets. So what need have you of me? The labyrinth of his own "love song" is the hell that Prufrock is certain no one of us will escape. His silence is assured.

Bruce Hayman (essay date September 1994)

SOURCE: "How Old Is Prufrock? Does He Want to Get Married?", in *CLA Journal*, Vol. XXXVIII, No. 1, September, 1994, pp. 59-68.

[*In the following essay, Hayman argues that two distinctly different interpretations of "Prufrock" develop depending upon how the reader interprets the character's age and intent.*]

Before I try to answer the two questions which entitle this essay, I would like to pose a third question and try to answer it: what difference does it make? What difference does it make whether Prufrock is young or middle-aged, or whether he wants to get married or not? For a number of reasons, I think that it makes a significant difference.

First, it is a question of reading T. S. Eliot's **"The Love Song of J. Alfred Prufrock."** *What* do we know about J. Alfred Prufrock, and *how* do we know that?

> **What difference does it make whether Prufrock is young or middle-aged, or whether he wants to get married or not? For a number of reasons, I think that it makes a significant difference.**
> **—Bruce Hayman**

Second, depending upon how we answer these two questions, we have very different poems. A poem in which a young Prufrock desires to sexually proposition the poem's unnamed female is very different from a poem in which a middle-aged Prufrock desires to propose marriage. The difference between a proposition and a proposal is significant because there are two different sets of sensibilities involved. Such a difference tells us a good deal about what Prufrock thinks about the unnamed female and how he considers himself. Of course, there are not just two possible answers to these questions. It could be that a young Prufrock is proposing marriage or that a middle-aged Prufrock desires to make a sexual proposition. Still, the questions and their attendant sensibilities need to be differentiated.

Third, if Prufrock is a young man, then the poem takes on a much more autobiographical meaning. Eliot, after all, was a young man when he wrote the poem—about twenty-two or twenty-three in 1910-11. If Prufrock is middle-aged, we would likewise need to ask why a young Eliot was attracted to creating a middle-aged narrator.

Fourth, if Prufrock is a young man, then the structural and thematic similarities between Prufrock and the young narrator of **"Portrait of a Lady"** become striking—so striking, in fact, that it would be valid to argue that the Prufrock character narrates both poems. If Prufrock is middle-aged, the similarity between the narrators is different and less obvious.

Fifth, there is one final, intriguing possibility. If Prufrock is a young man who is interested in a one-night sexual fling with a woman whom he cares little about, then that situation is very similar to the mechanical, sexual encounter between the "young man carbuncular" and the "typist" in the middle section (**"The Fire Sermon"**) of *The Waste Land.* The notes to *The Waste Land* tell us that "What Tiresias *sees,* in fact, is the substance of the poem." If Eliot was exploring the sensibilities of arbitrary sexual encounters in **"The Love Song of J. Alfred Prufrock,"** does that mean that he "had the experience but missed the meaning"—a meaning he realized a decade later in *The Waste Land* (194)? There is a possibility of a strong thematic connection here. On the other hand, if Prufrock is middle-aged and proposing marriage, such a thematic connection probably does not exist.

With this rationale in mind, we can turn to the original two questions, and I would like to examine first the question of whether Prufrock is contemplating marriage in this poem, because that is the easier question to deal with. Two critics, Elisabeth Schneider and Balachandra Rajan, have suggested that the "overwhelming question" is a marriage proposal, and while they have not enumerated their reasons, we can look to the poem itself for evidence.

What evidence is there that Prufrock wants to marry the poem's female? First, the title may offer two clues. A "Love Song" is usually sung to someone whom you know well and with whom you are in love. "Love" is more closely associated with marriage than with one-night sexual encounters. Also, the name "J. Alfred Prufrock" is about as asexual as one can find. One can more easily imagine someone named J. Alfred Prufrock being married than prowling the town as a sexual stud. The formality of the name suggests a more formal relationship like marriage. Second, Prufrock does not present himself as a sexual creature—far from it. His self-depiction is of a person who is prim, proper, fastidious—and fully clothed: "My morning coat, my collar mounting firmly to the chin, / My necktie rich and modest, but asserted by a simple pin." He also describes himself as thin and balding—altogether not a particularly seductive package. Third, Prufrock seems to come from an upper-middle class or upper-class environment, where marriage would be more the norm for love songs. He is well educated and articulate, and he seems to refer to drawing rooms where women discuss Michelangelo or from which music emerges. There are also a lot of proper, upper-middle class *things* in the poem: plates, toast, tea, marmalade, coffee spoons, cakes, ices, novels, dooryards, shawls, and terraces. All of these proper things suggest a proper environment where one has proper relationships. These are not the accouterments of seduction: there is not a lot of alcohol, loud music, or bawdy songs and conversation. Fourth, Prufrock is far more intellectual than physical. There are references in the poem to Dante, Michelangelo, Lazarus, John the Baptist, Hamlet, and Hesiod. Prufrock is a very bookish sort who seems more intent on writing a term paper than on seducing anyone. Fifth, Prufrock apparently feels that the question which he wants to ask the female is "over-whelming," that some sort of crisis is involved which may ruin the rest of his life. A proposition for a one-night encounter would not be so momentous, but an unreciprocated marriage proposal might be. Sixth, there is not much standard reference in the poem to the joys of sex. He does mention "one-night cheap hotels" obliquely, but there is no reference to beds, sheets, bodies, euphoria, or any other stock sexual symbol. Finally, we can compare Prufrock to Apeneck Sweeny, another Eliot character, who was very physical and sexual, and who rapes an epileptic and then calmly shaves. Such a comparison leaves Prufrock looking pale, prim, overdressed, intellectual, and therefore more probably singing a "love song" about marriage than about sex.

On the other hand, what evidence is there in the poem that Prufrock desires to make a sexual proposition rather than a marriage proposal? First, if Prufrock were trying to make a marriage proposal, he would know the female fairly well—well enough that her presence would figure in his imagination. But Prufrock seems to know very little about this woman. *She does not even have a name.* Second, there is no evidence in the poem that they have ever spent any time together, except for the fact that she allows him to be alone with her while she lounges on pillows on the floor. Had they spent any time together, those encounters would figure in his thinking, and he would have some indication that she might be receptive to his proposal. His rationale would be: because she smiled or laughed this day, or because we spent so many days or evenings together, or because we did this or that,

this marriage proposal is at least plausible. But this is a couple with no past, which suggests that he does not have marriage on his mind. Third, he depicts her as lounging on the floor beside him among assorted pillows. This depiction suggests a more relaxed, informal, and sexual environment. It is, at least, more seductive than is necessary for a proper marriage proposal. Fourth, what Prufrock does tell us about her is almost exclusively physical. He concentrates on her body and says nothing about her mind or personality. He is aware of her arms, her bracelets, and her shawl. He does not even seem aware of her face—a standard poetic source for observations about complexion, eyes, lips, and hair. Prufrock's mind is telescoped toward the woman from the neck down. Fifth, while it is true that Prufrock is fastidious and proper, he is also sensually aroused in this poem. There is, for example, a long sensual depiction of the cat-like fog at the beginning of the poem: "The yellow smoke . . . rubs its muzzle on the window panes, / [and licks] "its tongue into the corners of the evening." He is also aware that her perfume is affecting his thoughts ("Is it perfume from a dress / That makes me so digress?"). And he does focus on her arms, which are "braceleted and white and bare / (But in the lamplight, downed with light brown hair!)." The focus on her arms may seem odd until we remember that a woman in 1910-11 would be more fully clothed than a woman today, and her arms would have been the only exposed part of her body. The focus on the arms has a strangely endearing combination of propriety and sexuality—as though Eliot wanted to write a poem about sexuality but was afraid his mother might read it. Sixth, it is true that Prufrock is prim, proper, overdressed, well educated, intelligent, articulate, and at least upper-middle class. He also has a funny name. But none of those qualities means that he is necessarily not interested in sex; certainly those qualities never held back Bertrand Russell. Prufrock may be, to use an overused twentieth-century word, "repressed," and he is certainly extremely introverted. But sexual repression was much more the norm at the beginning of this century, and in any event, repression does not negate the validity of sexual desire—in fact, repression indicates a desire is there to be repressed. Finally, if Prufrock desires a one-night sexual encounter and feels that the woman may decline, why is he getting so upset? Surely there must be many more women in the world whom he could quickly come to know as well as he knows this woman. But Prufrock sees this woman as a test case, a kind of conscious Rubicon. If he cannot force himself to make a sexual proposition to this unnamed, generic female commodity, he feels doomed to an asexual life of virginity—a devastating prospect if it is undesired. To him, she is, in a sense, all women. In other words, he is thinking: "I cannot succeed with this woman; therefore, I will never succeed with any woman, and my life will always be a lonely, asexual hell." That is the prospect which makes this encounter so crucial to him and which makes it appear, along with the other evidence, that Prufrock's question is a sexual proposition.

There are thus valid reasons for arguing that Prufrock's aborted question is either a marriage proposal or a sexual proposition. In my judgment, that question is a sexual proposition, and the most persuasive argument for that interpretation is the fact that Prufrock seems to know so little about the woman or even care about her. She has no name, no distinguishable face, no personality, and no past history. I do not think that it is persuasive to assume that Prufrock would propose marriage to such a nonentity.

The second and more complex question is whether Prufrock is a middle-aged man or a young man. By "middle-aged" I mean around forty or older; by "young" I mean in his early twenties. There is some disagreement among Eliot's critics about the age of Prufrock, but the consensus is that he is middle-aged. For example, John Crowe Ransom notes that "Prufrock is of middling age"; A. G. George agrees: "Prufrock is a middle-aged man"; Lyndall Gordon calls Prufrock "the timid, aging lover"; George Williamson refers to Prufrock's "unromantic middle-age"; and Grover Smith finds a possible source for Prufrock in a character from Henry James's "Crapy Cornelia" named "White-mason, a middle-aged bachelor of nostalgic temperament." Elisabeth Schneider disagrees, in part, saying that Prufrock is "a young man who has never been really young," and Stephen Spender calls Prufrock "a man of uncertain age." Late in his life, Eliot himself ambiguously split the difference by saying that Prufrock was partly a forty-year-old man and partly himself.

What evidence is there, then, in the poem to indicate that Prufrock is middle-aged? First, Prufrock refers to himself as aging: "I grow old . . . I grow old . . . / I shall wear the bottoms of my trousers rolled." He also sees himself wasting away, growing slightly decrepit: "(They will say: 'But how his arms and legs are thin!')." A young man in his early twenties would normally not make such statements or be thinking about growing old. Second, Prufrock describes himself with middle-aged characteristics. Twice he refers to going bald. "And indeed there will be time / . . . to turn back and descend the stair, / With a bald spot in the middle of my hair—/ (They will say: 'How his hair is growing thin!')." Later, he says: "I have seen my head (grown slightly bald) brought in upon a platter." Worrying about balding is a normal preoccupation of middle-aged men, but not of young men. Third, Prufrock places repeatedly heavy emphasis on his considerable knowledge ("For I have known them all already, known them all"), which could probably only have been acquired during a more substantial life span. Also, his allusions to Hamlet, Hesiod, Lazarus, John the Baptist, and so on suggest a substantial education which would have required some substantial time span. Fourth, for me the best argument for his being middle-aged is a passage in the middle of the poem where he shifts into the present perfect tense and seems to indicate his past life:

But though I have wept and fasted, wept and prayed,
Though I have seen my head (grown slightly bald) brought in upon a platter,
I am no prophet—and here's no great matter;
I have seen the moment of my greatness flicker,
And I have seen the eternal Footman hold my coat, and snicker,
And in short, I was afraid.

The reference to his past is mainly metaphorical, rather than practical, but it does suggest substantial elapsed time. It also suggests that he is already going bald and feels strongly the passage of time flowing through him. Finally, at the end of the poem, Prufrock sees himself as Polonius, a middle-aged character in *Hamlet:* "Am an attendant lord, one that will do / To swell a progress, start a scene or two." All of these repeated references to aging, balding, education, and middle-aged characters, combined with his use of the present perfect tenses, suggest that Prufrock is a middle-aged man.

What evidence is there, then, for Prufrock being a young man? First, there is a freshness and an innocence in his worrying about this woman, as though he were confronting the situation for the first time. The poem is loaded with questions: "Do I dare disturb the universe?" "And how should I presume?" "And how should I begin?" "Is it perfume from a dress / That makes me so digress?" "Should I, after tea and cakes and ices, / Have the strength to force the moment to its crisis?" This flurry of questions suggests the bewilderment of youth over a new situation—everything is new and puzzling. Second, Prufrock is a character largely without a past. A forty-year-old man would have encountered other women previously, and those experiences would give him some clues about this situation. But Prufrock seems never to have encountered a woman before. He is totally inexperienced. He has no past to draw from to help him say the right words or make the right gestures. He is a social tabula rasa. Third, Eliot explains in *Four Quartets* how past consciousness merges with the present and the future. But Prufrock's mind is focused primarily on the present and the future. In a mind as active and lively as his, the past would certainly keep appearing in his confused mental state; but there is no past consciousness here swirling into the present. Fourth, it is true that Prufrock refers to himself as middle-aged or elderly, but he usually does so in the future tense (italics mine): "(They *will* say: 'How his hair is growing thin!')"; "I *shall* wear the bottoms of my trousers rolled." Further, the heavy emphasis on the extraordinary amount of time which he has available to him is more indicative of youth than of middle age: "And indeed there will be time / . . . There will be time . . . There will be time." A middle-aged Prufrock would probably at least mention the time that has already been spent. Fifth, but why should a young man keep referring to himself as middle-aged or elderly? The answer is in the structure of the poem's argument. Prufrock is trying to understand, with all of his conscious knowledge and abilities, why he cannot sexually proposition a woman. Because he has looked at his problem theoretically and because he is intensely frustrated, he finds it easy to wallow in a kind of self-pity: I cannot succeed with this woman because of my particular structure of consciousness; therefore, I will never succeed with any woman, and my life will always be hell—from now until I am middle-aged or elderly. Life is over for me. But, of course, this sense of fatalism is really immature—much like the distraught teenager who feels that her life is ruined because her parents will not let her go to a party. Frustration, especially in the young, often multiplies monstrously of its own accord and causes one to rush to wild, negative, and illogical conclusions. Sixth, Prufrock's claims concerning his broad knowledge ("I have known them all already") would seem more characteristic of middle age if we believe those claims. But, in fact, his claims to knowledge are wildly exaggerated, and these exaggerations are more characteristic of precocious youth than of middle age. Youth is often overly impressed with what it knows "already" (a word Prufrock repeatedly uses), while maturity more often appreciates its limitations. Prufrock's heady claims are immature bravado. Finally, Prufrock suffers from a case of debilitating self-consciousness. But nearly every youth suffers to some degree from such self-consciousness, and nearly everyone gets over it and learns to deal with it be the time he is middle-aged. **"The Love Song of J. Alfred Prufrock"** captures that youthful moment when life is being consciously born and is terrifyingly puzzling. Young Prufrock reminds us that "April is," indeed, "the cruelest month."

Those, then, are the major arguments for seeing Prufrock as either middle-aged or young. In my judgment, the evidence in the poem supports a youthful Prufrock. The major arguments which persuade me are that Prufrock has no past, that he is innocently and bewilderingly inexperienced, and that he immaturely leaps to the fatalistic conclusion that he will grow old unloved. I cannot see a middle-aged Prufrock having these characteristics. As I have indicated already, I believe that the questions of whether Prufrock is young or middle-aged and whether he wants to make a proposal or a proposition are important ones. Despite the wonderful complexity of Eliot's poems and ideas, and despite the wealth of entrenched criticism on those poems, we should never stop asking two basic questions: *what* do we know about Eliot's poems, and *how* do we know that?

FURTHER READING

Criticism

Bentley, Joseph. "Actions and the Absence of Speech in 'The Love Song of J. Alfred Prufrock.'" *Yeats Eliot Review* 9, No. 4 (Summer-Fall 1988): 145-48.
> Argues that what Prufrock is really afraid of is modern society and its language patterns, and thus is not the pathetic character portrayed in other criticism.

Blythe, Hal, and Charlie Sweet. "Eliot's 'The Love Song of J. Alfred Prufrock'." *Explicator* 52, No. 3 (Spring 1994): 170.
> Discusses the importance of shellfish to the imagery in "Prufrock."

Campo, Carlos. "Identifying the 'Lazarus' in Eliot's *The Love Song of J. Alfred Prufrock*." *English Language Notes* XXXII, No. 1 (September 1994): 66-9.
> Claims that the Lazarus referred to in the poem is from Luke's account and the more famous story in John.

Colum, Padraic. "Studies in the Sophisticated." *New Republic* 25, No. 314 (8 December 1920): 52, 54.
> Discusses the modernistic aspects of Eliot's poetry.

cummings, e. e. "T. S. Eliot." *Dial* XLVIII (June 1920): 781-84.
> Praises Eliot's technique in *Poems*.

Everdell, William R. "Monologues of the Mad: Paris Cabaret and Modernist Narrative from Twain to Eliot." *Studies in American Fiction* 20, No. 2 (Autumn 1992): 177-96.
> Considers the evolution of American literature as influenced by Mark Twain, culminating with Eliot's "The Love Song of J. Alfred Prufrock."

Fleissner, Robert F. "The Germanic Insect Image in *Prufrock*." *Germanic Notes* 20, No. 1 (1989): 2-3.
> Discusses insect imagery in "The Love Song of J. Alfred Prufrock."

————. "Eliot's *The Love Song of J. Alfred Prufrock*." *Explicator* 50, No. 2 (Winter 1992): 104-05.
> Suggests a reinterpretation of the poem's opening lines, arguing they are not as tentative and hesitant as critics perceive.

————. "Eliot's *The Love Song of J. Alfred Prufrock*." *Explicator* 48, No. 3 (Spring 1990): 208-10.
> Analyzes the influence of American popular music on Eliot's poem.

Helmling, Steven. "The Humor of Eliot: From 'Prufrock' to *The Waste Land*." *Yeats Eliot Review* 9, No. 4 (Summer-Fall 1988): 153-56.
> Considers the evolution of humor in Eliot's poetry from "The Love Song of J. Alfred Prufrock" to *The Waste Land.*

Krogstad, Christopher, and James D. Alexander. "Eliot's 'The Love Song of J. Alfred Prufrock'." *Explicator* 53, No. 1 (Fall 1997): 53-4.

Considers the influence of Omar Khayyam's *The Rubaiyat* on "Prufrock."

Monteiro, George. "T. S. Eliot and Stephen Foster." *Explicator* 45, No. 3 (Spring 1987): 44-5.

Compares "The Love Song of J. Alfred Prufrock" with Stephen Foster's "Jeanie with the Light Brown Hair."

Sherfick, Kathleen A. "Eliot's 'The Love Song of J. Alfred Prufrock'." *Explicator* 46, No. 1 (Fall 1987): 43.

Comments on Biblical references in "The Love Song of J. Alfred Prufrock."

"Not Here, O Appolo." *Times Literary Supplement,* No. 908 (12 June 1919): 322.

Claims that Eliot's attempt at sophistication and novelty in *Poems* leads him to say nothing in his poetry.

Untermeyer, Louis. "Irony de Luxe." *Freeman* I, No. 16 (30 June 1920): 381-82.

Praises "The Love Song of J. Alfred Prufrock" but finds the rest of *Poems* lacking.

Weinstock, Donald J. "Tennysonian Echoes in 'The Love Song of J. Alfred Prufrock'." *English Language Notes* VII, No. 3 (March 1970): 213-14.

Notes similarities between Prufrock and Tennyson's characters but concludes that Prufrock is doomed to paralysis while Tennyson's protagonists take action.

Additional coverage of Eliot's life and career is contained in the following sources published by Gale: *Concise Dictionary of American Literary Biography 1929-1941; Contemporary Authors,* **Vols. 5-8R, and 25-28R;** *Contemporary Authors New Revision Series,* **Vol. 41;** *Dictionary of Literary Biography,* **Vols. 7, 10, 45, and 63;** *Dictionary of Literary Biography Yearbook, 1988; DISCovering Authors; Major 20th-Century Writers; Poetry Criticism,* **Vol. 5; and** *World Literature Criticism,* **Vol. 2.**

Carlos Fuentes

1928-

Mexican novelist, dramatist, short story writer, scriptwriter, essayist, and critic.

The following entry presents an overview of Fuentes's career through 1996. For further information on his life and works, see *CLC,* Volumes 3, 8, 10, 13, 22, 41, and 60.

INTRODUCTION

Fuentes's overriding literary concern is to establish a viable Mexican identity, both as an autonomous entity and in relation to the outside world. In his work, Fuentes often intertwines myth, legend, and history to examine his country's roots and discover the essence of modern Mexican society. Fuentes once commented: "Our political life is fragmented, our history shot through with failure, but our cultural tradition is rich, and I think the time is coming when we will have to look at our faces, our own past." This tradition incorporates elements of Aztec culture, the Christian faith imparted by the Spanish conquistadors, and the unrealized hopes of the Mexican Revolution. Fuentes uses the past thematically and symbolically to comment on contemporary concerns and to project his own vision of Mexico's future.

Biographical Information

Born in Panama City, Fuentes is the son of a Mexican career diplomat. As a child, he lived at several diplomatic posts in Latin America and spent much of the 1930s in Washington, D.C. He attended high school in Mexico City and later entered the National University of Mexico. While studying law there, he published several short stories and critical essays in journals. After graduating from law school, Fuentes traveled to Geneva, Switzerland to study international law and in 1950 began a long career in foreign affairs that culminated in his serving as Mexico's ambassador to France from 1975 to 1977. Fuentes wrote throughout his diplomatic career, and in the late 1950s and early 1960s he gained international attention as an important contributor to the "boom" in Latin American literature. Along with such authors as Gabriel García Márquez and Julio Cortazar, Fuentes published works that received international acclaim and spurred the reassessment of the position Latin American authors held in contemporary literature. Fuentes has also served as a lecturer and visiting professor at several universities, and has received numerous honorary degrees and literary awards. He has married twice; he has a daughter with his first wife, Rita Macedo, and a son and a daughter with his second wife, Sylvia Lemus.

Major Works

Fuentes's work, like that of several writers associated with the "boom," is technically experimental, featuring disjointed chronology, varying narrative perspectives, and rapid cuts between scenes, through which he creates a surreal atmosphere. For example, in his first novel, *La región más transparente* (1958; *Where the Air Is Clear*), Fuentes uses a series of montage-like sequences to investigate the vast range of personal histories and lifestyles in Mexico City. This work, which provoked controversy due to its candid portrayal of social inequity and its socialist overtones, expresses Fuentes's perception of how the Mexican Revolution failed to realize its ideals. The frustration of the revolution, a recurring theme in his writing, forms the basis for one of his most respected novels, *La muerte de Artemio Cruz* (1962; *The Death of Artemio Cruz*). The title character of this work is a millionaire who earned his fortune through unscrupulous, ruthless means. Using flashbacks, the novel shifts back and forth from depicting Cruz on his deathbed to his participation in the Revolution and his eventual rise in business.

Through this device, Fuentes contrasts the exalted aims that fostered the Revolution with present-day corruption. *The Death of Artemio Cruz* is generally considered a complex work that demands the reader's active participation. In *Aura* (1962), Fuentes displays less concern with social criticism and makes greater use of bizarre images and the fantastic. The plot of this novella involves a man whose lover mysteriously begins to resemble her aged aunt. Fuentes employs a disordered narrative in *Cambio de piel* (1968; *A Change of Skin*) to present a group of people who relive significant moments from their past as they travel together through Mexico. Fuentes's concern with the role of the past in determining the present is further demonstrated in *Terra Nostra* (1975), one of his most ambitious and successful works. In *Terra Nostra* Fuentes extends the idea of history as a circular force by incorporating scenes from the future into the text. In *La cabeza de hidra* (1978; *The Hydra Head*), Fuentes explores the genre of the spy novel. Set in Mexico City, this work revolves around the oil industry and includes speculations on the future of Mexico as an oil-rich nation. *Una familia lejana* (1982; *Distant Relations*) involves a Mexican archaeologist and his son who meet relatives in France. In this novel, an old man relates a tale to a man named Carlos Fuentes, who in turn relates the tale to the reader. Through the inclusion of ghosts and mysterious characters, Fuentes also introduces fantastic events into otherwise realistic settings, a technique prevalent in Latin American literature that is often termed "magic realism." In the novel *El gringo viejo* (1985; *The Old Gringo*), which examines Mexican-American relations, Fuentes creates an imaginative scenario of the fate that befell American journalist Ambrose Bierce after he disappeared in Mexico in 1913. *Cristóbal nonato* (1987; *Christopher Unborn*), a verbally extravagant novel, continues Fuentes's interest in Mexican history. This work is narrated by Christopher Palomar, an omniscient fetus conceived by his parents in hopes of winning a contest to commemorate the quincentenary of Christopher Columbus's arrival in the Americas. The novel's nine chapters symbolize Christopher's gestation and allude to Columbus's voyage, which is presented as a symbol of hope for Mexico's rediscovery and rebirth. Narrating from his mother's womb, Christopher uses wordplay, literary allusions, and grotesque humor, combining family history with caustic observations of the economic and environmental crises afflicting contemporary Mexico. *Christopher Unborn* satirizes Mexico's government as inept and its citizenry as complacent, warning that the country's collapse is imminent without change. Fuentes returned to the historical novel with *La campana* (1990; *The Campaign*). Set in early nineteenth-century Latin America, this work chronicles the adventures of Baltazar Bustos, the naive, idealistic son of a wealthy Argentinean rancher, who becomes embroiled in the revolutionary fervor then sweeping the region. The novel *Diana: The Goddess Who Hunts Alone* (1995) revolves around the love affair of a Mexican novelist and an American film ac-

tress. In addition to his novels, Fuentes has written several plays, including *Orquideas a la luz de la luna* (1982; *Orchids in the Moonlight*), and has published the short story collections *Los dias enmascarados* (1954), *Cantar de ciegos* (1964), and *Chac Mool y otros cuentos* (1973). Many of his short stories appear in English translation in *Burnt Water* (1980; *Agua quemada*). Fuentes is also respected for his essays, the topics of which range from social and political criticism to discussions of Mexican art. In his essay collection *A New Time for Mexico* (1996), Fuentes, according to Walter Russell Mead, "[Combines] impressionistic accounts of the Mexican national soul with remarkably lucid summaries of Mexican history, snippets of literary autobiography, policy prescriptions and personal journals." In this manner, Fuentes provides a detailed account of the political, economic, social, and cultural crisis faced by Mexicans following the 1994-1995 failure of the policies of former Mexican president Carlos Salinas de Gotari to bring about the positive changes promised.

Critical Reception

Fuentes's works have generated much controversy and widely varying critical opinions; some critics have impugned Fuentes for the sexually explicit nature of some of his work, particularly *A Change of Skin*, and for disjointed, obscure narratives, while other critics have praised him for daring to present topics such as sexuality in a frank, direct manner, and have applauded his narratives as technically masterful and artistically brilliant. Saul Maloff concluded that the success of *Where the Air Is Clear* as a novel is due to Fuentes's "ability to manage firmly and sensitively—always as an artist, never as an ideologist—the kind of packed and turbulent social scene that is so often the undoing of the 'political' novelist." Many critics have echoed these sentiments in discussions of Fuentes's other works; these commentators point to the author's exceptional capacity for presenting simultaneously the atmosphere and physical details of the setting and events and the thoughts of the characters in such a way that all elements of the narrative are illuminated for the reader. In reviewing *The Old Gringo*, Michiko Kakutani commented: "[Fuentes] has succeeded in welding history and fiction, the personal and the collective, into a dazzling novel that possesses the weight and resonance of myth." In assessing Fuentes's career, Earl Shorris concluded that he "has been the palimpsest of Mexican history and culture separated into its discrete layers: Indian, Spanish, French, revolutionary, aristocratic, leftist, centrist, expatriate. In this analyzed presentation of the person, this soul shown after the centrifuge, Mr. Fuentes demonstrates the complexity of the Mexican character and the artistic difficulties peculiar to the novelist born in the Navel of the Universe, which is where the Aztecs placed Mexico."

PRINCIPAL WORKS

Los dias enmascarados (short stories) 1954

La región más transparente [*Where the Air Is Clear*] (novel) 1958

Las buenas consciencias [*The Good Conscience*] (novel) 1960

La muerte de Artemio Cruz [*The Death of Artemio Cruz*] (novel) 1962

Aura (novella) 1962

The Argument of Latin America: Words for North Americans (nonfiction) 1963

Cantar de ciegos (short stories and novellas) 1964

Paris: La revolucion de mayo (nonfiction) 1968

Cambio de piel [*A Change of Skin*] (novel) 1968

Cumpleaños [*Birthday*] (novella) 1969

Dos cuentos mexicanos (short stories) 1969

La nueva novela hispanoamericana (nonfiction) 1969

Casa con dos puertas (nonfiction) 1970

Todos los gatos son pardos (drama) 1970

El tuerto es rey (drama) 1970

Poemas de amor: Cuentos del alma (short stories) 1971

Tiempo mexicano (nonfiction) 1971

Zona sagrada [*Holy Place*] (novella) 1972

Chac Mool y otros cuentos (short stories) 1973

Terra nostra (novel) 1975

Cervantes; o, La critica de la lectura [*Don Quixote; or, The Critique of Reading*] (nonfiction) 1976

La cabeza de hidra [*The Hydra Head*] (novel) 1978

Burnt Water [*Agua quemada*] (short stories) 1980

Orquideas a la luz de la luna [*Orchids in the Moonlight*] (drama) 1982

Una familia lejana [*Distant Relations*] (novel) 1982

On Human Rights: A Speech (speech) 1984

El gringo viejo [*The Old Gringo*] (novel) 1985

Latin America: At War with the Past (nonfiction) 1985

Cristóbal nonato [*Christopher Unborn*] (novel) 1987

Myself with Others: Selected Essays (essays) 1988

Constancia y otras novelas para virgenes [*Constancia and Other Stories for Virgins*] (short stories) 1990

La campana [*The Campaign*] (novel) 1990

The Buried Mirror: Reflections on Spain in the New World (essays) 1992

The Orange Tree (novellas) 1994

Diana: The Goddess Who Hunts Alone (novel) 1995

A New Time for Mexico (essays) 1996

*These works were published in *Holy Place and Birthday: Two Novellas*, 1996.

CRITICISM

David Gallagher (review date 4 February 1968)

SOURCE: "Stifled Tiger," in *New York Times Book Review*, February 4, 1968, pp. 5, 40-1.

[*In the following review, Gallagher offers a primarily positive assessment of* A Change of Skin.]

In an interview Carlos Fuentes once said that the Latin-American novel was now firmly out of its epic, Manichean stage. Before World War II, the problems depicted by Latin-American novelists looked relatively straightforward. Primitive men confronted primitive nature; oppressors and oppressed were easy to classify; the struggle between good and evil was a clear one. The postwar generation has delved deeper into the life of the continent, investigating Latin-American history with a greater regard for its complexity.

Fuentes, naturally, concentrated on the complexities of Mexican history. He has been particularly energetic in his denunciation of what seems to him the inauthenticity of Mexico's "institutional" revolution. One oligarchy was exchanged for another; the process could not be reduced to obvious villains and obvious saints; and facades were established—of middle-class prosperity, decency, democracy, "good conscience." In *Where the Air Is Clear* (1958) and *The Good Conscience* (1959), Fuentes skillfully explored the insecurity, the poverty and the violence lurking behind those respectable facades. In *The Death of Artemio Cruz* he told the story of one of the new men—from his early fight for his ideals to his eventual corruption by the opportunity to exploit the revolution for personal gain—with dispassionate honesty, without condemnation.

> At its simplest level, this complicated novel [*A Change of Skin*] explores the attempts of a married couple approaching middle age to grip on to something of the initial vitality of their love.
> —*David Gallagher*

For Fuentes, Mexico is a tiger that has been artificially tamed. He appears to wish that the energies of the enchained animal be authentically unleashed. *A Change of Skin* is his most ambitious—if not his best—novel to date, because his notion of the stifled tiger is extended in it beyond Mexico to the whole of mankind.

At its simplest level, this complicated novel explores the attempts of a married couple approaching middle age to grip on to something of the initial vitality of their love. The man, Javier, is a failed Mexican writer, always ready to blame his Jewish-American wife for blocking his creative spirit with too many concrete emotional demands. Fuentes comes out with many perceptive remarks concerning Javier's and Elizabeth's problems, though one often wishes that he took this couple and they took themselves less seriously. There is a great deal of portentousness in their stylized reminiscences, their insistent exchange of lapidary phrases and dubious maxims, sometimes as bad as this: "The distance that separates us has not only more value but also more meaning than the closeness that joins us."

But *A Change of Skin* is a great deal more than just a love story. And to complicate matters, we are presented with another pair, Franz and Isabel, who accompany Javier and Elizabeth on a journey from Mexico City to Cholula. The fictional status of Franz and Isabel is more dubious than that of the first couple, Franz and Isabel being perhaps just phantom alternative versions of Javier and Elizabeth, although Elizabeth, being a generation older, could equally represent Isabel's potential future.

Just in case there is any doubt that all four characters are in fact wholly apocryphal, there is also a narrator who intervenes in their lives, yet at the same time flamboyantly exhibits his omniscience. He underlines the fact that the entire action of the novel is an apocryphal game conducted in his own mind, which is, of course, a figment of Fuentes's.

There is a great deal of mischievous skill in the manner in which much of the story is told—in the form of a second-person dialogue between the narrator and the characters. For the narrator takes the liberty not only of reminding his characters of events in their past life—which we, as readers, usefully get to know about simultaneously—but also occasionally hints playfully and conceitedly at their future: "Tonight one of you will die, Elizabeth. But don't worry about it. I won't and God won't."

Fuentes strains to reveal the apocryphal quality not only of his characters' love life, but also of their environment. History itself comes under the scrutiny of his hectic suspicion of reality. And when Franz's background as the resident architect of Theresienstadt is recalled, we are asked to contemplate the elusiveness even of life in the concentration camp. Moreover, since Javier and Franz are potential versions of one and the same being, we are asked to meditate on the fact that if Franz, being a "Sudeten German," was involved in the murder of women and children, so would Javier have been, if only he had been a Sudeten German. (Javier is after all himself capable of the murder of an innocent child by abortion.)

Descriptions of the concentration camp are interspersed with

evocations of Mexico's own fascist (Aztec) past, or with extracts describing violence and hysteria in the European Middle Ages and Renaissance. History in short, repeats itself, nothing changes, and all men have an equal capacity for evil, which they make manifest in so many different fictions.

The description of life in Theresienstadt reads like a tourist propaganda pamphlet. Whenever Fuentes describes a cathedral or a palace, whether in Prague or Cholula, he sounds as if he had taken his material straight out of dubiously sophisticated guide-books. When Elizabeth describes her childhood in the United States or Franz his youth in Prague, the scenes evoked come straight out of the movies. Reminiscence and history, then, are fictions, the events they recall having been edged into fiction not only by the nature of language itself, but also by environmental pressures controlled by mass media: the documentary or the tourist pamphlet turns concentration camps into fictions; the movies turn a childhood into a fiction.

The trouble is that Fuentes does not give the impression that he is always content to remain so impassively on the surface of his "pop" novel. He is not always content to accept the distance between all the events he describes and a more "real" world. I felt that there was at any rate one phenomenon in the novel which was posturing as "real": that is, that vital tiger lurking under the skin not only of Mexico but also of Franz's "German" and perhaps of all mankind.

Fuentes serves us up a great deal of dubious, hipster-existentialist, sub-Mailerish philosophy in *A Change of Skin,*— harmless enough in its praise of "the hipster, the son of man who lives on gut, must gamble everything, for only by doing so can he fuse opposites," but potentially objectionable when applied to the "Nazi experiment." It is all very well to (rather ludicrously) hail the Beatles for "setting us free from all the false and murderous dualisms" of our civilization. But is not Fuentes's anti-Manichean zeal being carried just a little too far when the Nazis are congratulated for enacting "that true freedom to accept all, not only what man is but what he may be," or having "the will to continue to the end, to the edge, to the precipice"?

Of course, all these passages that sound like undergraduate variations on Nietzsche may be just so many more fictions. Poor Fuentes's novel was, after all, recently banned in Spain for being "Communistic, pro-Jewish and anti-German." Yet I got the uncomfortable feeling that, beneath all his illusive facades, Fuentes was clinging to some sort of hipster life-force which apparently the Nazis (or the Beatles) had been most competent to enact.

At any rate, politically objectionable or not, Fuentes has written a challenging and interesting, if occasionally silly and pretentious, book, and he has been well served by his translator, Sam Hileman.

Carlos Fuentes with John P. Dwyer (interview date Fall 1974)

SOURCE: "Conversation with a Blue Novelist," in *Review,* No. 12, Fall, 1974, pp. 54-8.

[*In the following interview, Fuentes discusses his approach to writing, Latin American writers and literature, and his place in Latin American literature.*]

[*Dwyer:*] *On what project are you working now?*

[Fuentes:] It's an enormous novel, over seven hundred pages. I guess one might call it a Medusa of a thousand heads. I hope to be finishing it within a month.

Would you dare to telescope all those pages into a brief outline?

Look, I'll try. I guess that everyone, at least once, has asked himself what he would do if he had his life to live over. Well, what I do in this book is bring the question to the level of an entire civilization, the civilization of Spain and Latin America. What the novel essentially asks is what Spain and Spanish America would do if they had an opportunity to relive their history. I then narrate what would happen under those circumstances of having the freedom to repeat this history, of choosing to repeat the history of our civilization, of its gestation, of the encounter between European and Indian civilizations: in short, of the formation of what is Latin American culture. What would happen? Unfortunately, if history could repeat itself exactly as it occurred, it would be much easier because there would not be the tragic margin of choice. But since the margin of choice does exist, history does not repeat itself exactly as it was. Nevertheless, its essence is the same. Its tragedies are once again the same, as well as its errors. And in its freedom to err once again lies the true sense of tragedy of choice.

Even though your outline is relatively uncomplicated, I am sure that you will present the story in a narrative maze.

It has to be that way because once I, as the novel's author, decide to allow myself the luxury of offering these cultures a second chance, I can only accomplish my goal by erasing chronology, by wiping out conventional concepts of time and space, so as to recreate all to my own tastes, concentrating the whole into a Goyesque canvas, as it were. Basically, the novel is like an Escorial under construction, where at the same time and in the same place exist such interesting char-

acters as: Juana la Loca [Jane the Mad]; Felipe II; Carlos II, el Hechizado [The Bewitched]; Felipe el Hermoso [Phillip the Fair]; all the dwarfs, buffoons, albinos, doctors, lawyers, Jews, Arabs . . . the whole crew. . . .

You mention a recreation of the past. . . .

Yes, but this novel happens in the future.

I don't reread my works. Aguilar in Mexico is now publishing my "complete works" but I refuse to correct anything. They'll stay exactly as they first appeared. I think that rewriting one's works is a form of self-paralysis. Looking back turns an author into a pillar of salt.
—*Carlos Fuentes*

Of course, another chance to create itself again. Have you ever thought of rewriting any of your works, or giving them as it were, an opportunity to be recreated by their author?

No, never, I don't even reread my works. Aguilar in Mexico is now publishing my "complete works" but I refuse to correct anything. They'll stay exactly as they first appeared. I think that rewriting one's works is a form of self-paralysis. Looking back turns an author into a pillar of salt.

But doesn't seeing your works published as "complete," at this stage of your career, cause any mixed emotions?

No, not at all. Volumes will still be added. It really is nothing more than another edition, a new one with photos, a criticism section, and a prologue written by Fernando Benitez. One could hardly call it my "complete works" because I am now forty-four and I hope to continue writing for at least another quarter century.

How do you feel when you now see yourself mentioned by younger Mexican writers as having influenced them?

Like an ol' gran'daddy!

Of all that you have written, your plays have probably received the least critical attention. One especially, seems rather difficult to stage: **Todos los gatos son pardos,** *where at the end of the play dead vultures rain down upon the stage from high above the set.*

Actually, that play has yet to be staged. Barrault is planning to present it in France next year and Glauber Rocha, the Brazilian director, is going to make a movie of it. Barrault is going to use the Theatre of the Gare d'Orsay where Orson

Welles filmed *The Trial* by Kafka. He has converted the theatre into a type of amphitheatre or circus, and will present the play with all the things he needs. I really hope that it will rain those vultures from a high scaffolding. Rocha, of course, with all of his cinematographic means will be able to do just about what he pleases. It is a difficult play to perform. On the other hand, *El tuerto es rey* is much easier because there's only a set and two characters, and it has already been presented with a fair amount of success, especially in French.

Do you still write movie scripts?

Yes, from time to time. To help finance my novels I write movie scripts, but my attitude in regard to them is that of Woody Allen: "take the money and run." I'm not a good writer for the cinema because mine is a verbal world, not a visual one. I love the movies and learn a lot from them. But since I'm really a spectator at heart, when I write for the movies, I don't work out well. My methods are too literary. My projection is totally verbal and the cinema calls for just the opposite.

You once called Cortázar the Bolívar of language for the Latin American novel. In many ways, you too might be considered a Bolívar of. . . .

Oh, no. If anything, the most you could call me is a Benito Juárez.

A Juárez, then, in reference to eroticism in Mexican literature.

Oh, God. That is simply not true. Please no. What about all the poetry of Octavio Paz which is fundamentally erotic? You see, if we accepted your point, we would be forgetting about all those poems and poetic passages in *Sunstone,* which after all is extraordinarily erotic because Paz himself is a very erotic author. I might be best classified as a "pornographic writer," at times, anyway . . . an author of blue novels, or at least of blue passages, let us say.

Several sections of **A Change of Skin** *bear out your point.*

Agreed, but I really believe that eroticism in Mexican letters is due more to Paz's poetry and Luis Buñuel's films. Even if all Mexicans don't realize what Buñuel is doing, one has to acknowledge the eroticism of films like *El, Los olvidados,* or *Robinson Crusoe.*

In your statement on Neruda you mentioned the importance of poetry to all Latin American novelists but, in many ways, it's a subject of much less critical attention than the contemporary novel.

Those who ignore the importance of poetry do a great injustice. Historically, and to the present day, the novel has always been vitally linked with poetry in Latin America. One cannot understand our novel without reference to our poetry. The novel, after all, is a fairly recent phenomenon in Latin America, while poetry has represented an uninterrupted tradition dating back to colonial times. We have always had good poets. In fact, the most important Mexican—and perhaps even Latin American—poet was an eighteenth-century nun, Sor Juana. And so you see, the appearance of Latin America's novel is preceded, influenced and determined by a vast background of poetry with figures like Leopoldo Lugones. Rubén Darío. Vicente Huidobro. César Vallejo and Pablo Neruda. This has always been the case. Frankly, I would be unable to write novels if I didn't read poetry.

In your essays, you often speak of a tendency in the contemporary novel to move toward a poetic expression.

That's true. The traditional European novel, as far as I am concerned, has died. Take the English novel. If any country had had a continuity in its novelists, it's England. But this occurred in a tradition that was alive but now has ceased to be so. Today, any British novelist who tries to continue speaking about psychological relations, or about social or class relations, would probably write a rather poor novel. He would only be repeating the great discoveries of the past. I don't believe that anyone can still write the novel that Dickens did, or for that matter, even Flaubert. Bourgeois realism is dead. And this fact leaves the novelist in a difficult situation. Many of his techniques, and a good part of his story material, have been taken away by the mass media. The melodrama, mystery stories, these are all now the object of television serials, daily radio programs and films. They have all ended up as movie plots. Today Balzac wouldn't write *The Human Comedy.* He'd make a film. No, a series of films about the social and psychological life of France. This all leaves the novelist stripped of his story. As a result, he must ask himself what can his novel say and how can it say it. It's a difficult challenge. We are now faced with the problem of deciding what actually belongs to the novel. We then find ourselves left with the essential basis and fact of literature, which is poetry. Poetry, and its very name implies it, because of its all-relating and comprehensive nature simply is literature. The novel is divesting itself of many trappings that the mass media now employ. It's a task that must be done if we are to find the very basis of literature and its definition, which is poetry. This is all very evident in Joyce, in Herman Broch and Malcolm Lowry. And I believe that it is one of the definitions of the contemporary novel in Latin America, which in no way can be judged to be a naturalist or realist novel. Ours is a novel that attempts to create, to construct verbal universes, its own and, in a certain way, sufficient unto itself.

Your remarks on the destruction of "bourgeois realism" are very evident in **A Change of Skin.** *There your characters constantly remind the reader that he's participating in a novel. The traditional framework of realism is constantly being questioned.*

That's right. I believe that there's a constant reflection on the genre, a criticism of creation within the created work, that destroys any illusion, either naturalist or realist, that the reader might have. And for that reason, the reader is disturbed, disturbed because he formerly could rely on the novelist's assuring him that what he was reading was real, that the novel was reality, and that the characters actually existed—that in fact the novel was true. The soap opera tells us these things, flaunting its reality to the viewer, assuring him of its truth, while the authentic novelist of today is saying to his readers that what they believe is reality is not so. He's saying that there's something more than that reality. The novelist is then attacking the reader's conformity, his acceptance of what is presented, and forces him to participate as a co-creator of the novel. The author imposes upon his reader a responsibility identical to his own. As I said in my remarks about Neruda, the poem creates the author, and it also creates its reader. I believe that this is a must for today's new novel, and Latin American novelists realize it.

> **The essential struggle of the Latin American novelist is with his language and culture. We are very conscious of having inherited a language that died at the end of the eighteenth century, one that had fossilized, academized and refused to deal with the themes of eroticism, rebellion and criticism. We find ourselves at battle with a language practically dead. We are attempting to revive it, to shatter it and to put it back together again, to infuse it with a new substance.**
> **—Carlos Fuentes**

How, then, do you react to criticism of their novel as being realist or naturalist, an idea expressed very recently by a reviewer of several Latin American novels available in English translation?

Even if we include the best translations available, I doubt that the Latin American novel could have the resonance and importance in countries where it is translated as it does at home or in Spain. The essential struggle of the Latin American novelist is with his language and culture. We are very conscious of having inherited a language that died at the end of the eighteenth century, one that had fossilized, academized and refused to deal with the themes of eroticism, rebellion and criticism. We find ourselves at battle with a language practically dead. We are attempting to revive it, to shatter it and to put it back together again, to infuse it with a new substance. This is an essential aspect of the work by Cortázar, Vargas Llosa, Octavio Paz and Lezama Lima. And it is a phenomenon difficult to transfer to another language in translation. I believe that ours is a situation akin to that of Pushkin, who is apparently an untranslatable poet. According to my friends who read Russian, no translation accurately reflects Pushkin's greatness. I think that we have run into similar problems, at least in some cases. Since we are writing a literature of foundation, one that deals with the problems of a stagnant culture, of a dead culture and its language, the essential part of the phenomenon is produced from within that culture and from within that language. Its nature is not easily transferred to another language. On the other hand, I find it rather extraordinary that acceptable translations have been made, and actually some very good ones that now reach a growing public in the United States, in Europe and in Japan. I think we are fortunate that it has happened, a gift of the gods, if you will, that these novels are published, and that they attract a readership and a critical reception. The fact is that there is now, without doubt, a presence of Latin American literature in places today where none existed twenty years ago. But the main battle, the essential repercussion, will always have to be within our own cultural and linguistic sphere. I don't doubt that in the least.

You probably are familiar with José Donoso's Historia personal del "boom" (Personal History of the "Boom"). *How do you react to his characterizing a party at your home in 1965 as being the symbolic initiation of what later became known as the "Boom" in the Latin American novel?*

Your question calls for a comment on the comments by Donoso. Just let me say that the book is a bit uncommon in Latin America where people are usually more solemn and everything is taken on a very abstract and somewhat stuffy level. Donoso's book belongs more to the Anglo-Saxon tradition of personal recollections, of confidences, of memories brought back to life. I really liked the book. On one side. Pepe is a Henry James who coexists in a very mysterious way with his nocturnal and monstrous side, with that of the vulture in search of carrion. I think that he is half Dracula and half Elsa Maxwell. All this elegantly adds up to a type of Henry James.

What are your feelings now on the "Boom?"

I don't believe that there ever was such a "Boom"—it was really an invention of the publishers and bookstore owners. Actually the whole process of a literature comes before, dating from much further back in time. No one can really say when it started, much less at that party Pepe Donoso mentions in his book. We have had a long history of literature in Spanish. If instead of a "Boom" we wanted to discuss an authentic movement of renovation, then we would have to talk about Borges, about Neruda and Huidobro. And Macedonio Fernández. And then Onetti, a great novelist who began writing much before we did. And Alejo Carpentier, as well.

But you would agree that there was something to the "Boom" . . .

Oh yes, most certainly. There was, and still is, a fraternity among certain writers. Some of the members of the "Boom" are close friends. I believe that for the first time we have a generation of writers in Latin America who are friends, who respect each other, and who don't stick knives in each other's back. I guess you could say that about Cortázar, Vargas Llosa, García Márquez and myself. We are all very good friends. Among ourselves there is a feeling of group unity, a fraternity. There's no question about that.

The "Boom" has also inspired a look back to what came before it, a rereading of preceding works. Wouldn't you agree?

Yes, exactly. That is one point I'd like to emphasize, because some people have criticized us by claiming that we have a society of mutual admiration among ourselves, that we are each other's most conscientious promoters. But that isn't the case. In fact, if you look at the personal opinions and critical works of all the novelists I just mentioned. I believe that in nearly every instance what we've done is to say and to recognize that there is a literature and a tradition behind us: that we did not appear from nowhere, but rather that precisely writers like Vargas Llosa. Cortázar and I have given great credit to and underlined the importance of people like Onetti, who had been little read and recognized. We have recalled the existence of and insisted a great deal on the importance of the founding influence of the poetry of Pablo Neruda, of Huidobro and Paz. We always mention the existence of writers like Felisberto Hernández. Roberto Arlt and Macedonio Fernández. So you see, this is not a closed group but rather one that is attempting to understand the process and to point out the value of an entire literary tradition. What we are trying to say is that it all didn't begin with *La ciudad y los perros* [*The Time of the Hero*] or **La región más transparente** [**Where the Air is Clear**], or *Rayuela* [*Hopscotch*], but rather that there was a whole process of gestation that must be considered.

George Gordon Wing (essay date Summer 1988)

SOURCE: "A Gallery of Women in Carlos Fuentes's *Cantar de ciegos,*" in *Review of Contemporary Fiction,* Vol. 8, No. 2, Summer, 1988, pp. 217-24.

[In the following essay, Wing examines Fuentes's treatment of female characters in Cantar de ciegos.*]*

It was José Donoso who first drew my attention to what are central features of the six short stories and the novella that Carlos Fuentes published in 1964 as **Cantar de ciegos (Song of the Blind)**. Donoso finds in them a common theme—"the withdrawal of human beings from basic feelings." Fuentes's characters no longer recognize themselves in traditional concepts such as "love," "hate," "justice," etc. They find these abstractions useless precisely because they exist prior to and independently of concrete experience which might make them meaningful. Consequently, neither a fixed order, nor a rational organization of society, nor a transcendent purpose are possible for Fuentes's characters, who are adrift in a world of instants and tropisms. Donoso says that the hero of **Cantar de ciegos,** without any firm convictions, tries to enjoy life without committing himself—his positive values are embodied in the words "cool," "étranger," "outsider." He is a person capable of seeing clearly everything that takes place around him without being moved by it emotionally.

With the exception of one story, all of Fuentes's characters are immersed in a mass-consumer society. As Fuentes has said in an essay, the Mexican is now the contemporary of all men, but only to be confronted with all of the problems inherent in mass society. After describing at length its contradictions, Fuentes makes an observation that seems paradoxical: "We participate apocryphally in modernity." It is from this apparent paradox that Fuentes's realism derives a peculiar flavor. In speaking of realistic plays, especially modern ones, Arthur Miller has suggested that all of their great themes might be boiled down to a single sentence: "How may a man make of the outside world a home?" In the prose fiction of **Cantar de ciegos,** it is indeed the underlying theme as well as the major problem confronting all of the characters, a problem exacerbated by the essential split between modernity and tradition, a split internalized and reflected in their behavior. Above all, it generates a subtheme common to all of the works of **Cantar de ciegos**—*plus ça change, plus c'est la même chose.* The realization of this theme is due to Fuentes's talent for depicting so graphically the visible configurations of contemporary life, the manners and morals of an apparently nontraditional society. Just as important is Fuentes's gift for expressing the split between the surface and what is relatively unchanging in Mexico. Fuentes accomplishes this in a variety of ways—structure, psycho social analysis, dialogue, etc.—but what Joseph Sommers has said of Fuentes's methods of characterization in **Where the Air Is Clear** applies equally as well to **Cantar de ciegos.** He subordinates, says Sommers, psychological analysis to "experience, traits and thoughts which are susceptible to broader reference in the world outside the character." In short, "his interest lies more with representative qualities than with psychological idiosyncrasies."

Isabel Valles, the protagonist of the novella, *A la víbora de la mar* (*To the Snake of the Sea*), might well serve as a touchstone for measuring Fuentes's other female characters. Isabel, who has inherited money, is now the owner of a boutique in the fashionable Pink Zone. A fortyish spinster and virgin, her life extends no farther than the store where "she sells beautiful things to beautiful people" and her apartment where she lives with a maiden aunt. Apart from the movies, church, and lunch (alone) at Sanborns, she has no social life She lives in a world of repression, rigidity, and dullness—one of alienation and willed "claustrophilia." On the one hand, she is presented as a typical product of consumer society, and on the other, as one of its pathetic victims. Although her external life is patterned by this society, her super-ego survives from a much more traditional and puritanical way of life. In short, she is immersed in consumer society but somehow she is not really of it.

Persuaded by her aunt to take a vacation after fifteen years of continuous work, Isabel opts for a cruise on a British liner from Acapulco to Miami. It is apparent that she is extremely apprehensive and has a revulsion toward close contacts either emotional or physical. Courted by an American confidence man, however, Isabel gradually overcomes her fears and regrets. By playing on her snobbery and lack of self-confidence, he tricks her into a false marriage, after which he induces her to give him the money she has brought with her, an outrageously large sum for such a short cruise. He then has his homosexual lover court her to make her feel guilty, unworthy, and inferior. Finally, he allows her to discover the two of them in bed, a fact he knows will destroy her. In all probability, she commits suicide by drowning. One might say that in large part her tragic flaw was to have believed in the reality of the concept "love" in the abstract without ever having experienced it.

At first glance, it might seem that Elena, the young wife of the story **"The Two Elenas,"** has nothing in common with Isabel. Elena seems to be the prototype of the completely "liberated" woman of the sixties who delights in flaunting behavioral patterns and ideas that run counter to those of her mother's generation. Nevertheless, she too avoids close involvements, but the outward patterns of behavior and ideas she uses to maintain distance are much more typical of advanced consumer societies than those of Isabel. Christopher Lasch has argued convincingly that the great malady afflicting the United States (and by extension other contemporary post-industrial societies, including Mexico) is narcissism. What needs to be stressed is that in these societies, paradoxically, the narcissist becomes socially and sexually promiscuous in order to *avoid* all close involvements. Elena is doubtlessly a narcissist of the type described by Lasch, but she is also, to go back to Fuentes's phrase, living modernity apocryphally. To begin with, for all of her apparent "emancipation," Elena is unable to transgress a traditional moral code that is at odds with most of her behavior. She is completely faithful to her husband, and the fact that it is impossible for her to be sexually promiscuous is very significant, since the aesthetic effect of the story depends largely upon the different sexual attitudes of the three principal characters.

To Elena, reality tends to be merely "role playing," "the presentation of self in everyday life" (the title of Erving Goffman's book [New York: Doubleday, 1959]), although her "self" is little more than a series of predictable responses to random stimuli from the world around her. Her husband, the narrator, says that what he loves most about her is her "naturalness," but the reader soon realizes that his statement is deliberately ironic. The fact is that for Elena, "the only reality is the identity she can construct out of materials furnished by advertising and mass culture, themes of popular film and fiction, and fragments torn from a vast range of cultural tradition, all of them equally contemporaneous to her mind." In fact, the only sustained dramatic conflict (more apparent than real) in this story springs from Elena's faddish obsession with *completing herself* (*complementarse*) by acquiring a permanent lover, a notion that occurred to her only after seeing Truffaut's *Jules et Jim*. She tells her husband that he will have to buy her a sailor suit like that worn by Jeanne Moreau in the film, only to declare a few moments later to a mutual acquaintance that she remains faithful to her husband because unfaithfulness has now become the norm. In short, the super-ego that dictates her most profound behavior belongs to another era.

> **It is in "A Pure Soul" . . . that Fuentes gives us his most memorable portrait of a contemporary, intelligent, and apparently liberated young woman.**
> —*George Gordon Wing*

Fuentes sets up a deliberate contrast between mother and daughter, providing the reader with a catalogue of their respective activities. The mother, married to a boorish *nouveau riche,* dutifully follows the routine common to upper middle-class housewives: trivial, conformist, and snobbish. But the daughter, too, adheres to a routine that is only superficially more flexible: painting and French lessons, meeting with some Black Muslims, going to jazz, cine clubs, etc. It is obvious, however, that for all of her so-called "liberation," she too is trivial, conformist, and snobbish. Attracted to all the latest fads, she is flighty and shallow; she belongs to what Alfred Rosenberg has called in another context, "a herd of independent minds." It is the husband, "cool" and conde-scending, who after an amusingly subtle seduction scene, enjoys the sexual favors of his mother-in-law—he is the one who *completes* himself.

It is in **"A Pure Soul,"** however, that Fuentes gives us his most memorable portrait of a contemporary, intelligent, and apparently liberated young woman whose "inability to make of the outside world a home" results not only in her own withdrawal from life but also in her willful destruction of her brother and his mistress, although she protests her inno-cence. Claudia, the narrator, evokes an idyllic childhood and adolescence with her brother in which an incipient incestual relationship becomes obvious. After graduating from the university, however, her brother goes to Geneva to escape from what he considers the confinements of Mexican soci-ety, although the reader realizes that he is at the same time fleeing the incest taboo. When he writes to Claudia of his numerous transient love affairs, she is ecstatic, for it is as if she were enjoying them vicariously, especially since she knows they are ephemeral; they do not threaten his love for her. When he takes a permanent mistress, however, Claudia manages by subtle (but not really innocent or pure) means to entrap him, for to let him go would devastate her. The subtle maneuvers she uses are quite sufficient to keep him from really loving anyone else. It is almost certain, more-over, that by lying to his mistress about an incestuous rela-tionship with her brother that was never consummated, she is responsible both for the mistress's suicide and, unwittingly, that of her brother. Winner takes nothing in this hair-raising story.

Critics have said of **"The Doll Queen"** that it differs radi-cally from the other stories. Nevertheless, it has as its main theme, as do so many others, the search for identity in a past that is pure nostalgia. The narrator seeks out a little girl with whom he had passed many pleasant hours in a park years before. Unfortunately, he succeeds in his persistent attempts to find her. Now grotesquely deformed, she is forbidden by her parents to leave the house or to have friends. In fact, her parents have constructed an elaborately adorned coffin in which they have placed a doll that resembles her as she was as a child. One might say that the parents, imbued with the values of consumer society, prefer her dead rather than ugly. To use Veblen's phrase, there is "conspicuous consumption" in social relations that are independent of economies as such. Even more significant is the fact that the child, now a woman, cynically accepts her horrible fate. The lack of love and compassion of her parents seems to her merely an ex-tension of a normal condition of the society in which she lives.

In **"The Old Morality,"** the only story not set in Mexico City, three sisters from Morelia, pharisaic and self righteous women dressed in black, come to "rescue" their nephew from his grandfather, who lives with a young mistress on his ranch. The grandfather, an atheist and old fashioned liberal, gives his fourteen year old grandson no opportunity for formal schooling and also, according to the aunts, provides him with the worst kind of immoral and sinful examples. The boy's life is spontaneous and natural, though, compared to that of his aunts, who live in a narrow ultra-Catholic atmosphere of repression. Taken to Morelia to be brought up by his maiden aunt, a spinster in her mid-thirties, the boy, Alberto, is bored, although he remains "cool" and intelligently an-ticipates every wish and command of his aunt, while feel-ing no real affection for her. Naturally, he is obliged to take religious instruction, but during his first confession he is so innocent that he has to invent sins he has merely intuited as such from films he has seen. His aunt is extremely angry with him for having tried to fool the priest, since she would have preferred him to have described the sexual relations between his grandfather and the mistress so that she could enjoy them vicariously. When she prods him, he replies naïvely that, yes, they always sleep together. He even quotes his grandfather, without having understood him, that "a man who sleeps alone dries up. And a woman too." This reply merely arouses fur-ther the repressed prurience of the aunt and serves to release the bottled-up emotions that gradually surface as hysterical behavior with sexual overtones. When, inevitably, she se-duces the boy, although he never fully understands the subtleties of her sexual behavior, he finds it all so enjoyable that he cannot bring himself to ask his grandfather to take him back to the ranch. Although one sees the aunt through the eyes of the boy, who enjoys her sexually without really loving her, it is impossible not to suspect that Fuentes ad-mires her more than he does the urban middle-class women of the other stories. It is as if, paradoxically, her incest rep-resents not only a gesture of despair but also a thrust toward natural behavior for which most other channels are closed in the stifling atmosphere of traditional society.

The protagonist of **"Fortuna lo que ha querido"** (**"What Destiny Wanted"**) is a man incapable of genuinely human relations with anyone, an artist who lacks both imagination and feeling, who is not above plagiarism or spouting absurd theoretical clichés. He would like to believe his life and his art are hermetically sealed off from each other. In the last analysis, however, they are two sides of the same coin. It just happens, for example, that his mistresses, or rather the women he uses and debases, are almost without exception wives of his critics and friends. They all serve as masochis-tic foils for his misogynous and sadistic behavior. Their amo-rality springs in large part from their snobbishness, a hero worship of which he is unworthy. Perhaps it is also bore-dom that is responsible for their abjection and self-debase-ment, their willingness to be abused and insulted by him for his own selfish pleasures. Love and compassion, as in so many of these stories, are virtues of neither the women nor the men. When, at the end of the story, the artist does meet a North American woman who might present a challenge to his lack of humanity, might disturb his withdrawal from basic feelings, he rejects her. In summary, we might see this artist not only as a symbol of male indifference and condescension, but also as a symbol of a kind of symbiotic relationship between this type of macho and the women who, in most of the stories of *Cantar de ciegos,* accept this relationship as normal.

There is only one point I should like to make concerning **"El costo de la vida" ("The Cost of Life"),** the most Hemingwayesque story of this volume. The protagonist is a lower middle-class school teacher who spends a day teaching, lunching with a group of old friends, attending a meeting of his fellow teachers who vote to strike, getting a job moonlighting as a taxi driver, and picking up a girl all with his working wife sick at home in bed. The protagonist seems to feel no strong emotions about anything, not even about the proposed strike, a strike that ironically leads to his death. One of the points most relevant to my study hinges on the fact that the protagonist has married a woman of a social class somewhat higher than his own. Although they are in dire economic straits, they refuse to live in an extended family with relatives. In short, they have opted for the nuclear family, largely because of his wife. In this respect, then, they too are very much immersed in contemporary society.

> **Certainly no other Spanish American novelist has given us a more complete picture than has Fuentes of what Lionel Trilling . . . has called "manners": "a culture's hum of buzz and implication . . . the whole evanescent context in which its explicit statements are made . . . that part of a culture which is made up of half uttered or unuttered expressions of value."**
> **—George Gordon Wing**

In his first novel, *Where the Air Is Clear* (1958), Fuentes gives a vast panoramic vision of Mexico of the 1950s, a society whose roots he traces back to a partial failure of the Revolution of 1910. In a sense, Fuentes took as his subject the history of a period during which Mexico was being transformed from an essentially rural society into one dominated by urban capitalism. Although Fuentes has drawn his characters from the highest and the lowest social classes, it is the new middle-class that occupies center stage. Fuentes's own opinion of this new class is most nearly expressed by the courtesan Natasha:

> The new rich who don't know what to do with their money, and that's all they have the way a crab has a shell, but they don't have the circumstances, how

should one say . . . of the development which in Europe gives the bourgeoisie a certain class. Of course the bourgeoisie in Europe *is* a class; it is Colbert and the Rothschilds, but it is also Descartes and Montaigne and they produce a Nerval or a Baudelaire who reject them."

Certainly no other Spanish American novelist has given us a more complete picture than has Fuentes of what Lionel Trilling [in *The Liberal Imagination,* Doubleday, 1953] has called "manners": "a culture's hum of buzz and implication . . . the whole evanescent context in which its explicit statements are made . . . that part of a culture which is made up of half uttered or unuttered expressions of value." It follows, then, that "they are hinted at by small actions, sometimes by the arts of dress or decoration, sometimes by tone, gesture, emphasis, or rhythm, sometimes by the words that are used with special frequency or a special meaning."

Even a cursory glance at Fuentes's portrayal of the new middle class reveals its snobbery, its inordinate love of money, and its undeserved self assurance. One of the central characters of *Where the Air Is Clear,* Federico Robles, has made good use of his revolutionary experience to amass a fortune and accumulate power. He has married a ruthless social climber with whom he lives in a loveless union, and their lives, in [Herbert Marshall] McLuhan's words [in "John Dos Passos: Technique vs. Sensibility," *Dos Passos: A Collection of Critical Essays,* edited by Andrew Hook, Prentice Hall, 1974], are dramas of "pathos of those made incapable of love by their too successful adjustment to a loveless system."

In *The Death of Artemio Cruz* (1962), the central character does have what might be called an early "idealized" love affair, but as Keith Botsford has commented [in "My Friend Fuentes," *Commentary,* Vol. 39, No. 2, February, 1965, p. 65]:

> As a man, Artemio has not made much contact with other human beings. This novel is so much his book not only because he relates the story, but because he is alone in the profoundest sense; he is not merely the only protagonist, he is also alone within himself. For Artemio is the portrait of the Mexican *macho*—the he-man and narcissist, deflowerer of womanhood, tamer of bulls, wild horses, and all that. Today that macho is an utter fake. Money is the only object of his desire; politics and power its sublimation. For those without a hope of either money or power, there is still the image of the *macho.* Like all soi-disant Latin virility, it is a blend of impotent talk, childish rage, pasted on moustaches, and an atrocious ignorance about women. The modern *macho* is more concerned with his deodorants and brilliantine than with sex.

In his major novels of the fifties and sixties, as well as in *Cantar de ciegos,* Fuentes has indeed portrayed a variety of macho types. In the novels, however, Fuentes has also created some extremely sentimentalized heroines who represent for the macho the epitome of natural wisdom and innocence. In *Cantar de ciegos,* on the other hand, Fuentes does not depict any idealized women. Rather, he shows his male and female characters, incapable of mutual love or shared equality, as people who more often than not are locked into grotesque symbiotic relationships. In his major novels of this period, Fuentes's main theme is the partial failure or betrayal of the Revolution of 1910, a theme expressed explicitly in long discursive passages. In *Cantar de ciegos* the theme is implied in the bleak portrait of post-Revolutionary Mexico. Fuentes's criticism of the abuse of power, principally the exploitation of women, his presentation of problems of personal authenticity and identity represent ethical judgments with far-reaching implications. Mexico, Fuentes is both suggesting and warning, has reached a stage in its history where the Mexican might welcome, or look upon with indifference, an increasing abuse of power at the broader levels of the economy or politics, for this abuse would be but a "natural" extension of his private life.

Joseph Chrzanowski (essay date Winter 1989)

SOURCE: "Patricide and the Double in Carlos Fuentes's *Gringo viejo,*" in *International Fiction Review,* Vol. 16, No. 1, Winter, 1989, pp. 11-16.

[*In the following essay, Chrzanowski analyzes Fuentes's use of the "double" or "doppelgänger" literary device as well as the theme of patricide in* El gringo viejo, *and asserts that the author's employment of both "has imbued his novel with remarkable structural coherence and has touched upon human issues which transcend history, geography, and culture."*]

In reading Carlos Fuentes's *Gringo viejo,* (1985; *The Old Gringo*) one is struck by the masterful way in which he has conjoined fictionalized biography, dramatic action, and ideological concerns. It also becomes evident that it is a novel in which character psychology has a dominant thematic and structural role. Central to the psychological component are father-child conflict and the concomitant motif of patricide. This study examines Fuentes's use of literary doubling in his treatment of these themes and in his portrayal of the novel's three principal characters.

The "gringo viejo," of course, is a fictionalized Ambrose Bierce—the controversial American journalist and short-story writer of the late nineteenth and early twentieth centuries. In 1913, at the age of seventy-one, the historical

Bierce set out for revolutionary Mexico, aware of the likelihood of dying there. Although he did maintain some written correspondence with a friend in the United States, it was not long before Bierce disappeared without a trace. In *Gringo viejo,* Fuentes presents an imaginary account of the writer's experience in Mexico.

> **In reading Carlos Fuentes's *Gringo viejo,* (1985; *The Old Gringo*) one is struck by the masterful way in which he has conjoined fictionalized biography, dramatic action, and ideological concerns. It also becomes evident that it is a novel in which character psychology has a dominant thematic and structural role.**
> **—*Joseph Chrzanowski***

A second main character is Harriet Winslow, a young American who meets the "gringo viejo" in Mexico and whose recollections of him form the novel's organizational frame. In contrast to the disillusioned and cynical old man, she is portrayed as naive and idealistic. Contracted to tutor the grandchildren of a wealthy landowner, Harriet is present at his estate when it is over-run by a group of revolutionaries who have allowed the "gringo viejo" to join them.

The third major character is Tomás Arroyo, the leader of a band of insurgents and the illegitimate son of the owner of the estate where Harriet is employed. Also an idealist, Arroyo embodies the spirit of protest that has motivated the revolutionaries to rebel against a system and a history of oppression and injustice.

Readers familiar with Ambrose Bierce's life and works will recognize the biographical accuracy and inaccuracy of various situations, statements, and persons presented in the novel. They will also readily perceive Fuentes's allusions to some of Bierce's short stories. The most important of these references are to "A Horseman in the Sky," a story whose title is evoked in the following descriptive passage. "At this early hour the mountains seem to await the horsemen in every ravine, as if they were in truth horsemen of the sky."

Set in the United States Civil War, "A Horseman in the Sky" begins with a description of a young Federal soldier who has fallen asleep while on guard duty. A flashback provides information about him. The only son of a wealthy Virginia couple, the boy had unexpectedly decided to join a Union regiment that was passing through his hometown. Acquiescing to his son's betrayal of the State of Virginia, the father stoically advises him: "Well, go, sir, and whatever may occur do what you conceive to be your duty."[*The Complete Short Stories of Ambrose Bierce, compiled by Ernest Jerome*

Hopkins, Doubleday, 1970]. The reader is then returned to the war scene to witness the young man awakening to the sight of a horseman on a distant ridge that borders a cliff. A grey uniform indicates that he is a Confederate scout who has discovered the presence of the Union force. For several moments, the young man anguishes over whether to kill his enemy. Recalling his father's parting counsel, he finally takes aim at the rebel's horse and fires. The scene immediately shifts to a Federal officer who observes "a man on horseback riding down into the valley through the air" [*The Complete Short Stories of Ambrose Bierce*]—obviously the Confederate soldier upon whom the sentry has fired. Another shift in scene occurs as a Federal sergeant approaches the young guard and asks if he discharged his weapon. The boy acknowledges that he shot at a horse and observed it fall off the cliff. Responding to the sergeant's inquiry as to whether anyone was on the horse, the young guard hesitatingly states: "Yes . . . my father" [*The Complete Short Stories of Ambrose Bierce*].

A common treatment of decomposition or fragmentation in literature involves the creation of several characters, all of whom represent a single concept or attitude. This technique has been referred to as "doubling by multiplication." Borrowing the motifs of parental conflict and patricide from "A Horseman in the Sky," Fuentes employs doubling by multiplication to link his ostensibly dissimilar characters and to introduce the presence of psychological conflict in the novel. In doing so, he alters and simultaneously commingles historical fact and the fictional antecedent of Bierce's story. The "gringo viejo," who, like Bierce himself, had been a Union soldier, is described as experiencing a dream in which his father served in the Confederate army. Without elucidating the nature of the father-son conflict, Fuentes introduces the patricidal motif by attributing the following thought to the "gringo viejo": "He wanted what he had dreamed of the revolutionary drama of son against father."

Juxtaposed with this dream is a dramatic battle scene in which the "gringo viejo" single-handedly attacks a group of Mexican Federal soldiers. Reinforcing the dream's psychological symbolism, the narrator clarifies that the American's inordinate act of bravery was in reality the externalization of unconscious rage directed at his father's memory: "it was toward this horseman, flashing his anger from the mountaintop, the gringo rode, not toward them, their machine gun lost now." The thematic and structural importance of the "gringo viejo"'s dream and its patricidal implication is apparent in Fuentes's allusion to it on five other occasions in the novel. The conflictual nature of the paternal relationship is also underscored by the following description of the "gringo viejo"'s father: "a hell-fire Calvinist who also loved Byron, and who one day feared his son would try to kill him as he slept."

Harriet Winslow's father, like the "gringo viejo"'s, was a military man. Because of him, she too bears the burden of psychological scarring. The narrator singles out two circumstances that have had lasting impact on her: (1) her discovery of her father's licentiousness and infidelity with a black servant and; (2) his abandonment of his wife and daughter in order to live in Cuba with another woman. Recurring references to her father attest to Harriet's psychological struggle in dealing with her loss of him on both the ideal and real levels. Paralleling the characterization of the "gringo viejo," her latent patricidal inclination is also expressed symbolically. When Harriet and her mother are overwhelmed by the economic necessity occasioned by the father's disappearance, they declare him dead in order to obtain a government pension. Harriet's lexical choice in referring to the incident has obvious psychological significance in the context of the patricidal theme: "We killed him, my mother and I, in order to live."

Arroyo's father, while not in the military, was also an authoritarian figure by virtue of the absolute power emanating from his socioeconomic standing Like Harriet's father, he was licentious. In fact, Arroyo is a produce of his abuse of power and position to sexually exploit a family servant. Arroyo's hatred for his father stems from that circumstance, as well as from the latter's refusal to recognize him legally. Even as a child, he would have readily killed his father if given the opportunity: "I spied him as he was drinking and fornicating, not knowing his son was watching him, waiting for the moment to kill him." The intensity of his hatred only increased over the years, as evidenced in his virulent declaration to Harriet toward the end of the novel.

As these references indicate, the patricidal motif is developed in *Gringo viejo* in a concrete, insistent manner. A further examination of textual evidence points to the presence of a psychological paradigm that is less obvious, yet fully consistent with the motif as employed by Fuentes in his portrayal of all three characters. In his recent study, *The Son-Father Relationship from Infancy to Manhood: An Intergenerational Inquiry*, Peter Blos underscores the Freudian notion that usurpation of the father's position can be interpreted as an unconscious attempt to "annihilate" him. Interestingly, Blos uses the term "patricide" figuratively to describe such usurpation. Reflecting this phenomenon, there is a moment or circumstance in *Gringo viejo* in which each protagonist duplicates some important trait of his or her father and, moreover, is identified with him at that moment. (Consistent with the basic premise of psychological criticism that textual evidence can point to unconscious as well as conscious motivation in characterization, none of the protagonists in *Gringo viejo* perceives the psychological significance of these details.) In the "gringo viejo"'s case, it is repeating his father's trip to Mexico more than fifty years earlier and distinguishing himself as a brave soldier: "The gringo thought how ironic it was that he the son was travelling the same road his father had followed in 1847." For Harriet, it is her rejection of her cultural and religious values through surrender to her most primitive sexual desires with Arroyo. In doing so, she consciously identifies with her father: "Don't you know that with Arroyo I could be like my father, free and sensual." In Arroyo's case, it is returning to the Miranda ranch and acting with the same arrogance and violence as did his father. The parallel between the two is underscored by Harriet's admonition of Arroyo: "you provoked yourself to prove to yourself who you are. Your name isn't Arroyo, like your mother's; your name is Miranda, after your father." If it is true, as Jean-Michel Rabaté asserts, that "a father is not a 'problem' but a nexus of unresolved enigmas, all founded on the mysterious efficacy of a Name," then Arroyo's choice of surname and Harriet's comment have particular significance in the patricidal context. Similarly, it should be remembered that the "gringo viejo" does not reveal his family name to anyone except Harriet while in Mexico. These details substantiate that, even on the unconscious level, the patricidal wish is central to Fuentes's depiction of all three characters.

As the plot of *Gringo viejo* unfolds, the paternal issue has profound effect on the manner in which the three protagonists relate and respond to one another and to events. In this regard, the "gringo viejo"'s role as father figure for Harriet and Arroyo merits special discussion. Their disposition toward relating to him as such is consistent with their figurative orphanhood: "General Tomás Arroyo, who, like her, had no father, both were dead or unaware, or what is the same as dead, both unaware of their children, Harriet and Tomas." The "gringo viejo"'s role as surrogate father is compatible with his advanced age, position of respect among the revolutionaries, and the paternal affection and behavior he demonstrates toward both characters on several occasions.

As a father figure, the "gringo viejo" facilitates Arroyo's and Harriet's resolution of the psychological conflict they experience as a consequence of their individual relationships with their fathers. It is well to clarify, however, that neither father has any active contact with his offspring in the historical present recreated in the novel, and that Harriet's and Arroyo's fatherlessness, as is often the case in literature, "is not so much the absence of relationship as a relationship to an absence."

In relating to the "gringo viejo" as a substitute father, Harriet and Arroyo each embody one pole of a basic endopsychic conflict: the love-hate relationship of child to father. Consequently, Fuentes has drawn his characters by also utilizing the literary device of doubling by division: "the splitting up of a recognizable, unified psychological entity into separate, complementary, distinguishable parts represented by seemingly autonomous characters."

Arroyo, of course, represents the negative pole of the paradigm. The principal issues in his psychic struggle are lack of identity stemming from his father's refusal to acknowledge him, the hatred it engenders and the need to express that hatred and to avenge his father's treatment of him. (On a conscious level, the latter need is one factor which explains Arroyo's participation in the Revolution.) These issues play a decisive role in the culminating action of the novel: Arroyo's murder of the "gringo viejo." As the plot unfolds, a number of references are made to papers which Arroyo is safeguarding on behalf of his corevolutionaries. The papers date from the colonial period and constitute a legal claim to the land that Arroyo's family had appropriated. They also represent a de facto affirmation of personal and social identity: 'The papers are the only proof we have that these lands are ours. They are the testament of our ancestors. Without the papers, we're like orphans."

The "gringo viejo"'s eventual burning of the papers therefore acquires profound psychological significance. On the one hand, the papers are symbolic of Arroyo's identity and claim to legitimacy within the social system. On the other, the man who destroys them is, at this point in the novel, a substitute for his father. Consequently, the childhood trauma of the son being reduced to a nonperson is symbolically recreated and relived on an unconscious level. The destruction of the papers provokes the hatred underlying Arroyo's previously mentioned patricidal wish and is externalized and expressed through his murder of the "gringo viejo". The psychological dynamics of the act mirror the drama of the Revolution itself: the socially and economically disenfranchised striking out against the fatherland that has denied them their patrimony and identity. Hence, with consummate artistry, Fuentes intertwines the personal drama of his characters with the historical drama of the Revolution.

> *Gringo viejo* **is a multifaceted novel that deftly combines dramatic action, historical verisimilitude, and ideological statement. It is also a work of profound psychological dimension and implication.**
> —*Joseph Chrzanowski*

Harriet's relationship with the "gringo viejo" as a hypostatic father is developed more fully in the novel, and in a way which suggests her awareness of it. The exclusively positive nature of the relationship corroborates Fuentes's presentation of her and Arroyo as a "composite character." Having been deprived of a father from the age of sixteen, Harriet finds in the "gringo viejo" a person with whom she can openly share her innermost thoughts and feelings; an object of tenderness, concern, and love; and, ultimately, a literal replacement for her absent father. Her awareness of what the "gringo viejo" signifies for her is first alluded to in a conversation in which he states: "I thought a lot about you last night. You were very real in my thoughts. I think I even dreamed about you. I felt as close to you as a . . . ." Before he completes the thought, Harriet interrupts by asking: "As a father?" In a subsequent exchange, she explicitly and dramatically communicates to him that he indeed represents a father to her: "Don't you know . . . that in you I have a father? Don't you know that?" Similarly, when Harriet senses Arroyo's determination to kill the "gringo viejo," she begs him not to the kill "the only father either of them had known."

It is Arroyo's murder of the "gringo viejo," however, that provides Harriet a lasting solution for her psychological conflict. Having returned to the United States after his death, Harriet publicly states that she had gone to Mexico in order to visit her father, and that she had witnessed *his* assassination at the hands of Arroyo: "She says she saw him shoot her daddy dead." Some time later, when his body is disinterred, she identifies it as her father's and has it buried in the family plot next to her deceased mother. Her words to the lifeless body of the "gringo viejo" confirm the presence of unconscious as well as conscious psychological motivation in the novel: "An empty grave is waiting for you in a military cemetery, Papa." The abandoned child has fulfilled her need to have and love a father.

In sum, *Gringo viejo* is a multifaceted novel that deftly combines dramatic action, historical verisimilitude, and ideological statement. It is also a work of profound psychological dimension and implication. In utilizing the literary device of the double and developing the patricidal motif which he borrowed from Ambrose Bierce, Carlos Fuentes has imbued his novel with remarkable structural coherence and has touched upon human issues which transcend history, geography, and culture.

Denis Donoghue (review date 8 April 1990)

SOURCE: "Safe in the Hands of the Uncanny," in *New York Times Book Review,* April 8, 1990, p. 15.

[*In the following review of* Constancia and Other Stories for Virgins, *Donoghue notes Fuentes's ability to present bizarre, extraordinary elements in his fiction in a manner that is "at once objective and arbitrary."*]

The long short story is a form of fiction Carlos Fuentes cherishes, and here we have five new instances of the genre: **"Constancia," "La Desdichada," "The Prisoner of Las Lomas," "Viva Mi Fama"** and **"Reasonable People."** Each of them is bizarre, a tale lingered over by the teller to the point at which, if he were to stay with it a moment longer, he would have to explain everything, and ruin it. Nothing is explained. We may interpret each story as we choose, but we cannot call on the teller to endorse our choice.

Mr. Fuentes has shown himself willing to write a straightforward novel. In **The Old Gringo** (1985) nothing affronts one's ordinary sense of time and place. We are allowed to find the story plausible, the characters credible, the style responsive to high emotions: love, hate, vengeance and the gringo's determination to die in Mexico. But Mr. Fuentes writes such a book as if with one hand. His major fictions are projects of the bizarre and the uncanny. He is not content for long to gratify one's sense of the usual, or one's prejudice in its favor. I would not like to be asked to say what precisely happens in **Aura** (1962).

In Mr. Fuentes's fiction, a sense of the uncanny is always enforced by a presentation at once objective and arbitrary. Phenomena are never used to embody or illustrate any official pattern of meaning, least of all the supposed relation between a cause and a consequence. In **"Reasonable People,"** the final story in this collection, one of the Velez brothers steps onto a patio and sees nine women and a child: "In one hand, each holds an umbrella, in the other, they carry various objects, shielding them from the rain. The first a basket and the second a shepherd's staff. The third a bag full of teeth and the fourth a tray holding bread that's been sliced in two. The fifth wears bells on her fingers and the sixth has a chameleon clasped in her fist. The seventh holds a guitar and the eighth a sprig of flowers. Only the ninth woman does not hold an object—instead, she holds the hand of the drenched child with his eyes closed."

It is vain to ask: why nine? Or: who are these women and why do they spend an hour walking in circles in the rain? Mr. Fuentes's authority is absolute. He is peremptory in leaving his readers to their own devices, trusting them not to be dolts. He compels them to recognize that it is possible to maintain a relation to fictive things, other than that of belief. One's interest is not limited to the true or the probable.

In **"La Desdichada"** a model for Mr. Fuentes's peremptoriness is the poem by Gerard de Nerval to which the title refers. In the story, two students in Mexico City steal a wooden mannequin from a shop window and start endowing her with life. They call her La Desdichada, "the outcast." One of them muses: "La Desdichada does not smile; her wooden face is an enigma. But that is only because I am disposed to see it that way, I admit. I see what I want to see and I want to see it because I am reading and translating a poem by Gerard de Nerval in which grief and joy are like fugitive statues, words whose perfection is in the immobility of the statue and the awareness that such paralysis is ultimately also its imperfection: its undoing."

In the poem, the famous second line, "Le Prince d'Aquitaine a la tour abolie"—the Prince of Aquitaine of the ruined tower—is authoritative in the degree to which it silences our question: it is imperturbable, immobile. There is no further explication of it that will help; no interrogation embarrasses the line. Even to speak of its imperfection, its undoing, as Mr. Fuentes's student does, leaves it uncompromised. So, too, the story; it is what it is, it does not ask to be loved upon any extraneous consideration.

To clear a space for the uncanny, Mr. Fuentes dislodges the privilege we normally concede to anything that has occurred. As amateur historians we italicize what has happened and think it superior to all the events that didn't come into being. But Mr. Fuentes's readers are impelled to give up that favoritism, and to care just as much for what has not taken place as for what has. *Terra Nostra* (1975) has Philip II of Spain marrying Elizabeth of England, America being discovered a hundred years later than the standard histories say, and sundry characters being fetched from other novels to play further parts in this one.

Near the end of that Utopian fiction, one of the characters introduces another to his great Theater of Memory: "Look; see upon the combined canvases of my theater the passage of the most absolute of memories: the memory of what could have been but was not; see it in its greatest and least important detail, in gestures not fulfilled, in words not spoken, in choices sacrificed, in decisions postponed, see Cicero's patient silence as he hears of Catiline's foolish plot, see how Calpurnia convinces Caesar not to attend the Senate on the Ides of March, see the defeat of the Greek army in Salamis, see the birth of the baby girl in a stable in Bethlehem in Palestine during the reign of Augustus." And the same character tells King Philip: "Every identity is nurtured from all other identities . . . Nothing disappears completely, everything is transformed; what we believe to be dead has but changed place. What is, is thought."

It follows, though not as night the day, that in his stories Mr. Fuentes introduces a narrative wobble instead of the stability expected. In **"Reasonable People"** he entrusts the story not to the brother who takes part in it but to the other brother, who deduces what happened from appearances that are not necessarily reliable. In **"Viva Mi Fama,"** he confounds chronology, making Goya and John Dillinger contemporaries. In *Zona Sagrada* (1967) he had put the reader in the hands of a lunatic.

These procedures are normally accounted for by describing Fuentes as a post-modernist. This is not a term in chronology or literary history. It usually indicates that the writer regards every experience as belated, already formed when we come to it, that spontaneity or "firstness" is an illusion. The writer therefore exploits a relation, likely to be ironic or otherwise subversive, to an established cultural formation or an earlier genre; the historical novel, the epic, science fiction. Claims to immediacy or resemblance to experience are voided by a proliferation of allusions. But these procedures are not enough to distinguish post-modernism from modernism. Line 430 of one of the supreme poems of modernism, "The Waste Land," reads: "Le Prince d'Aquitaine a la tour abolie." "The Waste Land," like Pound's "Cantos" and Joyce's "Ulysses," is a tissue of allusions, a confession of belatedness.

So we have to add a further consideration, which we owe to the philosopher Jean-Francois Lyotard. In the major works of modernism, however belated, the writer still hopes to tell a story, a comprehensive narrative of life as such, a myth not necessarily floating free of history but unintimidated by the eventfulness of the past. Myths are meanings and values in narrative form. A post-modernist writer, by contrast, doesn't believe that one story is more comprehensive, more telling, than another. Such a writer is promiscuous in the presence of stories; none of them is credited with explanatory power. The third woman carrying a bag of teeth might just as well be the tenth woman carrying a basket of flowers so far as explanatory ambition is in question. Alternative history is just as valid as the official version, anachronism is not a disability, the second chance is no worse than the first, among the moods the pluperfect subjunctive is just as good as the past perfect.

It is possible to feel irritated by such assumptions in post-modernist writing, or by any device that makes the words on the page seem willfully arbitrary or weightless. Long before the post-modern condition was felt or named, Henry James was exasperated by Anthony Trollope's habit of "reminding the reader that the story he was telling was only, after all, a make-believe." Mr. Fuentes doesn't let the reader off as lightly as that. Indeed, he persuades the reader to care for the characters, to worry about them, and only then to find that the worry has to do the best it can in the increasing density of bewilderment and the uncanny. In **"Constancia"** we care for Dr. Hull, an aging surgeon, man of letters, bibliophile, Constancia's husband, and wish he could be allowed to remain pretty much as we first see him in Savannah, heavy in the reality he takes for granted. But he gets displaced from that solid presence.

James said of his ghostly or supernatural stories that he wanted the mutations and strange encounters to loom through some other history, "the indispensable history of somebody's normal relation to something." In Mr. Fuentes's new stories, there is no guarantee that anyone's normal relation to anything will survive the uncanny to which it is exposed. In **"La Desdichada,"** by the time one of the students comes to "kill" the wooden mannequin "because she refused to love me," he has moved beyond any of his normal relations to anything. Besides, in giving that reason for killing her, he says in the same breath that the reason is not true.

Maarten Van Delden (essay date Fall 1991)

SOURCE: "Myth, Contingency, and Revolution in Carlos Fuentes's *La región más transparente*," in *Comparative Literature,* Vol. 43, No. 4, Fall, 1991, pp. 326-45.

[*In the following essay, Van Delden explores Fuentes's treatment of the "nature of the self and its relations to history and the community" in* La región más transparente, *and also examines some of the author's other works.*]

La región más transparente (1958), Carlos Fuentes's first novel, oscillates between two different perspectives on the nature of the self and its relations to history and the community. On the one hand, the novel outlines a view of the self that derives primarily from existentialist ideas found in the works of André Gide, Jean-Paul Sartre, and Albert Camus. In this view, the self is discontinuous, contingent, wholly unaffected by any kind of socio-cultural conditioning permanently separated from a stable and enduring core of meaning—and it is precisely for this reason that it possesses an absolute freedom to mold itself into constantly new shapes. On the other hand, the novel proposes a vision in which the self loses all its vestiges of autonomy; the individual merges entirely with the communal past, specifically with Mexico's Aztec heritage. This past is viewed as the origin and ground of an unalterable, culturally determined identity to which the self is inextricably attached. I will proceed to examine the conflict between these two views on a number of textual levels, after which I will conclude by arguing that the rather remarkable final section of the novel constitutes an attempt to resolve this conflict through the aesthetic embodiment of a concept of revolution. Fuentes expresses his vision of revolution by means of an inventive appropriation of the modernist technique of "spatial form." I will also show how the concept of revolution evolves in Fuentes's more recent work.

Toward the end of *La región más transparente,* Manuel Zamacona, the novel's intellectual spokesman, is senselessly murdered by a man he has never seen before. Afterwards, the killer coolly states that he did not like the way Zamacona had looked at him. The incident is reminiscent of the *acte gratuit* motif as it appears in the works of Gide, Sartre and Camus. Fuentes himself suggested a link with the existentialist tradition in a 1966 interview with Emir Rodríguez Monegal. In speaking of how the social and cultural realities of Mexico had somehow managed to anticipate certain artistic and philosophical currents in Europe and the United States. Fuentes made the following observation:

Hay un existencialismo *avant la lettre,* y muy obvio, México es un país del instance. El mañana es totalmente improbable, peligroso: te pueden matar en una cantina, a la vuelta de una esquina, miraste feo, porque comiste un taco. Vives el hoy porque el mañana es improbable (**"Diàlogo"**)

Fuentes's comment can be read as a gloss on the scene of Zamacona's death, which stands, then, as an illustration of the existentialist quality of Mexican life.

However, the existentialist act in *La región* is presented in a manner radically different from similar incidents in the works of Fuentes's French precursors. Lafcadio Wluiki's gratuitous murder of a complete stranger—whom he pushes out of a moving train—in Gide's *Les caves du Vatican* (1914) and Meursault's unmotivated killing of an Arab in Camus's *L'étranger* (1942) are by no means identical actions, but what they have in common is that in each case the perpetrator is at the center of the narrative. The events are related from Lafeadio's and Meursault's points of view. In Fuentes, on the other hand, the perspective is completely inverted: the victim is the protagonist and the killer remains a shadowy, indistinct figure on the margins of the narrative.

The symmetry of this inversion is reinforced by a number of other details connected with Lafeadio's *acte gratuit* in *Les caves du Vatican.* Even before he thrusts his victim out of the train, Lafeadio has been planning to leave Europe for what he calls "un nouveau monde," the islands of Java and Borneo. And as he begins to speculate on the possibility of committing this unusual crime, he reminds himself that, in any case, the next day he will be "en route pour les iles," and so will never be found out. In this way, the two projects, the gratuitous murder and the voyage to a faraway place, become linked together. Both are strategies for asserting one's freedom, for rejecting the old, oppressive ways of Europe. "Que tout ce qui peut être soit! C'est comme ça que je m'explique la Création. . . ." Lafeadio exclaims at one point, and throughout the novel he remains intent on demonstrating his love for what he calls "ce qui pourrait être . . . ." The desire to transgress all limits, to expand the realm of the possible, is expressed both in geographical terms, in the plan to flee to the East Indies, and in ethical terms, in the unmotivated murder of a stranger. Both projects are ways of affirming that one is bound by nothing. Or, as Camus put it in *L'homme révolté* (1951): "La théorie de l'acte gratuit couronne la revendication de la liberté absolue."

In *La región,* Natasha, an aging singer from St. Petersburg, alerts us to a difference between Mexico and Europe that speaks directly to this question of freedom and the transgression of limits:

Poi le menos a nosotros nos queda siemptre eso: la

posibilidad de s'enfuir, de busear el là-bas. El
Dorado fuera de nuestro continente. ¿Pero ustedes?
Ustedes no, mon vieux, ustedes no tienen su là-bas,
va estain en él, ya están en él, ya están en su limite.
Y en él tienen que escoger, vero?

In Gide, the idea of the limit depends on a more fundamental conceptual division of the world into a center (Europe) and a periphery (the non-European parts of the globe). From the perspective of the center, the existence of the periphery guarantees the possibility of freedom and escape. From the periphery itself, however, things look very different. If one's existence is perceived as already being at the limit, then the possibility of further displacement is eliminated. The result is the undoing of the very concept of the limit, and the collapse of the chain of analogies whereby a writer such as Guide links the notion of the limit to the ideas of the escape to a new world, the *acte gratuit,* and freedom. This emerges very clearly in the case of Zamacona's death. Fuentes does not use the incident to demonstrate the absolute nature of individual freedom. Instead, with the focus now on the victim, the scene evokes the old Latin American theme of a violent and hostile environment from which there is no escape. And even if we were to extract from this episode a different kind of existentialist motif—such as the notion of the absurd—such elements would exist in a state of tension with the larger narrative pattern into which the episode is absorbed. For Zamacona is only one of many of the novel's characters who suffer a violent death on Independence Day, and this juxtaposition of death and celebration is clearly designed to recall the ancient Aztec belief that human sacrifices are necessary to ensure the continuity of life. The series of deaths at the end of the novel hints at the persistence of these mythical patterns beneath the surface of modern Mexico and at the fragility of the individual in the face of such forces.

This reading of Zamacona's death is at odds with the interpretation Fuentes himself offers in the interview with Rodríguez Monegal, where he proposes that we regard it as evidence of the instantaneousness of Mexican life, and not, as I have just suggested, of the continued power of ancient cosmogonies beneath the country's veneer of modernity. In fact, Fuentes never wholly eliminates either of these two possible readings. Two details in the scene of Zamacona's death indicate how Fuentes tries to hold together these alternative interpretations. First, when Zamacona gets out from his car and approaches the cantina, he recites a line from Nerval to himself: "et c'est toujours la seule—ou c'est le seul moment . . . ." Nerval's idea that each moment in time is unique anticipates the existentialist conception of time, in which every instant is a new creation, disconnected from past and future. This notion of temporality is a focal point of Sartre's well-known analysis of Camus's *L'étranger.* Sartre describes Meursault as a man for whom "Seul le présent compte, le

concret" (*Situations, I*). He links this vision of time to Camus's absurdist world-view in which God is dead and death is everything: "La présence de la mort au about de notre route a dissipé notre avenir en fumée, notre vie est 'sans lendemain.' C'est une succession de présents." Fuentes's use of the quotation from Nerval seems designed to allude to such ideas about time, and thus to prepare us for the sudden, inexplicable flare-up of violence that leaves Zamacona dead.

But if this leads to a view of Zamacona's death as an absurd, meaningless event, another feature of this episode suggests a quite different point of view; the emphasis on the eyes and on the act of seeing. Zamacona's killer, as I observed earlier, justifies his deed by saying that he did not like the way Zamacona had looked at him. Furthermore, the only mention of the murderer's appearance is of his eyes:

> Uno de los hombres le dio la cara a Manuel
> Zamacona: desprendido como un uompo de la barra
> de madera, con los ojos redondos y sumergidos de
> canica, disparo su pistola dos, tres, cinco veces
> sobre el cuer po de Zamacona.

The killer's submerged and marble-like eyes link him to the realm of the invisible, subsisting beneath the surface existence of Fuentes's Mexico. Invisibility is generally associated in *La región* with Mexico's origins in its pre-Hispanic past, a connection captured most vividly in the figure of Hortensia Chacón, the blind woman who leads the powerful self-made banker Federico Robles back to his indigenous roots. Hortensia represents the beneficent side of the dark world beneath the country's semblance of progress and modernity. The killer, on the other hand, represents the violent, menacing side of this world: figuratively blind where Hortensia is literally so, this anonymous figure wishes to punish Zamacona for the look in his eyes, that is, for his location within the visible world of modern Mexico. Wanting to blind him as much as to kill him, he demonstrates the enduring power of Mexico's past.

There can be little doubt that the manner of Zamacona's death reveals the persistence of an atavistic violence lurking beneath the country's surface life. The question that remains unanswered, however, is whether this violence remains integrated with ancient cosmological rhythms, or whether it has lost its connection with ritual and has been expelled into a world of existential absurdity. This ambiguity is sustained in the development of the novel's plot after Zamacona's death.

It is difficult to ignore the connection between Ixca Cienfuegos's search, at his mother's behest, for a sacrificial victim with which to propitiate the gods, and the series of deaths that occur toward the end of the novel. But we can never be entirely sure that the sacrifices really are sacrifices, nor that they are responsible for a renewal of the life-cycle. Ixca's mother, Teódula Moctezuma, for her part, does not question the significance of these events. After Norma Larragoiti dies in the fire that burns down her house, Teódula tells Ixca that she believes the sacrifice has now been fulfilled, and that the normal course of life will be resumed. At the same moment, as if to confirm Teódula's vision of life's rebirth, the sun begins to rise.

Fuentes leaves his readers suspended between a world ruled by profound mythological rhythms, and an alternative, modern world of drift and contingency. He never fully decides which of these two pictures is finally truer of the reality of Mexico.
—*Maarten Van Delden*

Fuentes does not always represent this idea of cyclical return with such solemnity. While Part Two of the novel concludes with the destruction or downfall of many of the central characters, Part Three resumes three years later with the description of a young couple falling in love. But both Jaime Ceballos and Betina Régules have such stale and conventional natures that we inevitably sense an element of the parodic in this vision of life's regeneration. The effect is reinforced when the scene shifts again to a party hosted by Bobó Gutiérrez, whom we observe greeting his guests with the exact same words he had used approximately three years earlier, near the beginning of the novel: "¡Caros! Entren a aprehender las eternas verdades." Bobó's eternal truths are clearly a mockery. We recognize here not return and renewal, but paralysis and decay.

Fuentes leaves his readers suspended between a world ruled by profound mythological rhythms, and an alternative, modern world of drift and contingency. He never fully decides which of these two pictures is finally truer of the reality of Mexico. This same conflict shapes the meditation on identity and authenticity that receives novelistic form through the contrasting careers of Ixca Cienfuegos and Rodrigo Pola. Although two other characters, Federico, Robles and Manuel Zamacona, are also central to the development of this theme, I shall focus on Ixca and Rodrigo, since their confrontation after Bobó's last party effectively brings the plot of the novel to a close, thus suggesting the importance of these two figure to Fuentes's articulation of the problem of subjectivity.

Rodrigo Pola is an emblematic modern personality—a type toward the definition of which the existentialists made a significant contribution. Rodrigo's connection with this tradition of the modern self is clear from the first words he

speaks. Into a discussion about the social function of art, he interjects the following observation" "No todos tenemos que ser el cochino hombre de la calle o, por oposición, *un homme révolté.* . . ." While Rodrigo appears to reject the opposition he posits here, these words in fact encapsulate the defining axis of his personality, a conflict between conformity and rebellion. The allusion to Camus is clearly meant to recall the existentialist emphasis on subjectivity, on the need for individuals to create their own values without references to a realm of *a priori* truths or to society's received notions. Initially, Rodrigo's actions are guided by a similar search for authentic self-definition.

As he grows up, Rodrigo—who wants to be a writer—has to struggle against the oppressive demands of his mother, Rosenda, who, having lost her husband during the Mexican Revolution, cannot bear the thought of her son also escaping from her grip. The conflict between Rodrigo and his mother revolves around the question of who creates the self and thus has power over it. Rosenda wishes the moment in which she gave birth to her son to be prolonged forever. She wants always to be the mother, the child owing its existence to her alone. Rodrigo speaks with horror of "ese desco de beberme entero, de apresarme entre sus piernas y estar siempre, hasta la consumación de nuestras tres vidas, dándome a luz sin descanso, en un larguísimo parto de noches y días y años. . . ." To this idea of the enduring power derived from the act of giving birth to a child, Rodrigo opposes a notion of figurative birth in which the self engenders itself: "me senti . . . hijo, más que de mis padres, de mi propia, breve, sí, pero para mi única, incanjeable experiencia . . . ." In this, he appears to be heeding the existentialist exhortation to free oneself from all forms of external conditioning.

It is worth recalling, however, that there were different phases within the tradition of French existentialism. While the earlier work of Sartre and Camus tended to emphasize the absolute nature of individual freedom and favored the themes of anxiety, absurdity, and superfluousness, their latest work sought to establish a more affirmative view of existentialist philosophy. In *L'existentialisme est un humanisme* (1946), for example, Sartre sought to demonstrate that existentialism provides a philosophical basis for an attitude of engagement with the world and commitment to one's fellow human beings. Camus's *L'homme révolté* interprets the act of rebellion against an intolerable situation not as an individualistic gesture, but as a sign of the fundamental truth of human solidarity. Rebellion, according to Camus, is always potentially an act of self-sacrifice, and so implies the existence of values that transcend the individual. Camus himself regarded the shift in his work from a concern with the absurd to a concern with rebellion as the sign of a new focus on the group instead of the individual: "Dans l'expérience absurde, la souffrance est individuelle. A partir du mouvement de révolte, elle a conscience d'être collective, elle est l'aventure de tous" *(L'homme révolté).*

Rodrigo, by opposing "l'homme révolté" to man in the mass ("el cochino hombre de la calle"), evokes the more strictly individualistic side of existentialist thought. But in the course of the novel, Rodrigo's efforts to assert his own uniqueness become increasingly fruitless. This failure implies a critique of the early version of existentialism, with its one-sided emphasis on self-creation and self-renewal as the path to authentic selfhood, and its neglect of the social dimension of human life. Rodrigo's pursuit of a total freedom from all external constraints leads first to feelings of alienation and inauthenticity, and eventually to a complete turnaround, an unconditional surrender to society's norms of success.

In one episode, we see Rodrigo making faces at himself in the mirror, rapidly shifting expressions, "hasta sentir que su rostro y el reflejado eran dos, distintos, y tan alejados entre sí como la luna verdadera que nadie conoce y su reflejo quebrado en un estanque." This scene recalls a similar moment in *La nausée* where Roquentin studies his reflection in a mirror and is struck by the incomprehensible, alien appearance of his own face. Fuentes's adaptation of this motif suggests a similar perspective on the impossibility of discovering a stable, continuous identity, and the consequent susceptibility of the self to being constantly remolded into new shapes. For a moment, Rodrigo seems to recoil from his performance; he feels an urge to sit down and write, to leave what he calls "una sola constancia verdadera." Ironically enough, the text he produces articulates a theory of the self as a mask, a form of play. Everything becomes arbitrary and gratuitous. The self is cast loose from any serious attachment, even from that most fundamental attachment, the body itself. Thus, Rodrigo is at one point led to assert that it is a matter of indifference whether one's face is, in actual fact, ugly or beautiful; the act of self-creation can apply even to one's physical appearance. The material world, even in its most primary manifestation, is fully subject to the individual will: "El problems consiste en saber cómo se imagina uno su propia cara. Que la cara sea, en realidad, espantosa o bella, no importa. Todo es imaginarse la propia cara interesante, fuerte, definida, o bien imaginarla ridicula, tonta y fea."

Fuentes's use of the pathetic fallacy encourages a view of the realms of the human and the non-human as deeply interrelated.
—Maarten Van Delden

If the theory of the mask is initially designed to free the self from all forms of predetermination, then Rodrigo's radical

application of this principle appears to produce the opposite result. Rodrigo himself eventually recognizes that the histrionic self-display into which he has fallen effectively obliterates the possibility of achieving genuine freedom; he admits that he has become a captive of his own game: "Se vuclve uno esclavo de su propio juego, el movimiento supera y condena a la persona que lo inició, y entonces sólo importa el movimiento; uno es llevado y traido por él, más que agente, elemento."

A few pages later, the description of a thunderstorm dramatizes the extent of Rodrigo's estrangement from the world:

> La tormenta lo envolvía en una peteusión líquida, implacable. Arriba, el espacio se canjeaba a sí mismo estrueudos, luz sombría: todos los mitos y símbolos fundados en la aparición de la naturaleza se concentraban en el cielo potente, ensambladon de un poderío oculto. Resonaba el firmamento con una tristeza ajena a cualquier circunstancia: no gratuita, sino suficiente.

Fuentes's conception of the natural world, as it emerges from this passage, has important implications for his view of the status of the perceiving subject. The storm's concentrated, implacable power, its relation to the deep, continuous rhythms of nature, and its aura of timelessness are at the farthest possible remove from the inconsequentiality and arbitrainess that define Rodrigo's relations to himself and to the world. The implications of this contrast for Fuentes's larger view of the self can perhaps be sensed most clearly through a comparison with certain passages in Sartre's *La nausée* that deal with the same issues.

Fuentes's use of the pathetic fallacy encourages a view of the realms of the human and the non-human as deeply interrelated. The reference to the sky's occult powers may appear to lift the natural world to a position that transcends the human, but it also implies that nature is pregnant with meanings that are of great consequence to human life. The use of the verb "envolver" defines the exact nature of the relationship: it is impossible to think of human beings as separate from the universe in which they live. Roquentin, in *La nausée,* recognizes this human inclination to search for connections between ourselves and the physical world, to treat it, for example, as a text waiting for its meaning to be unveiled. At one point he describes a priest walking along the seaside as he reads from his breviary: "Par instants il lève la tête et regarde la mer d'un air approbateur: la mer aussi est un bréviaire, elle parle de Dieu." But Roquentin furiously rejects this attempt at humanization: "La *vraie* mer est froide et noire, pleine de bêtes; elle rampe sous cette mince pellicule verte qui est faite pour tromper les gens." In *La nausée* the world of objects and natural processes does not envelop the human world in a transcendent, protective manner; instead, it is conceived as a realm of brute, unredeemable fact from which a lucid consciousness will recoil in horror.

If Rodrigo is a failed existentialist, part of the explanation may lie in the way Fuentes has stacked the deck against him. In a world where natural phenomena exude such a compelling and inscrutable sense of purpose and power, the individual can hardly presume to play God with his own existence. Fuentes has created a character with existentialist features, but has placed him in a setting entirely different from the kind that would have been envisioned by the existentialists themselves. As a result, the existentialist project is effectively invalidated.

Ixca Cienfuegos represents, on the level of character, the same mythical forces which Fuentes evokes through his description of the thunderstorm. Ixca, whose first name derives from the Nahuatl word for bake, or cook, and whose last name alludes to the original time in Aztec mythology when fires lit up the universe, is a shadowy yet central presence in the novel. One character compares him to God because of his seeming omnipresence. Ixca's search for a sacrificial victim is part of an attempt to reintegrate Mexican society into a sacred, cosmic order, and thus to overcome the kind of self-division and self-estrangement suffered by a typical product of the modern world such as Rodrigo. The contrast between the two men emerges clearly in the description of an early evening walk they take along the Pasco de la Reforma:

> Rodrigo miraba como el polvo se acumulaba en los zapatos amarillos. Se sentía consciente de todos sus movimientos nerviosos. Y Cienfuegos como si no caminara, como si lo feura empujando la leve brisa de verano, como si no tuviera esas piernas, esas manos que tanto estorbalan a Rodrigo.

While Rodrigo is severely afflicted with the modern disease of self-consciousness, Ixca is entirely at case, in possession of an unfissured consciousness that exists in harmony with the natural world. Ixca does not search for an increasingly intense awareness of his own separateness from others. He is deeply at odds with the idea of a unique, individual personality waiting to be liberated from external oppression. Fuentes shows him in an intense, sometimes conflictive relationship with his mother, in which he submits to her wishes instead of rebelling, as Rodrigo does. Ixca advocates self-forgetfulness rather than self-regard: "Olvidarse de sí, clave de las felicidades, que es olvidarse de los demás; no liberarse a sí: sojuzgar a los demàs." His vision ultimately evolves out of his belief in the absolute nature of the nation's origins, and the priority of these origins over the claims of contemporary individuals. Mexico, he claims, "es algo fijado para siempie, incapaz de evolución. Una roca inconmovible

que todo to tolera. Todos los limos pueden crecer sobre esa roca, pero la roca en si no cambia, es la misma, para siempre." At one point, Ixca urges Rodrigo to choose between the two Mexicos, the ancient and the modern: "Acá scrás anónimo, hermano de todos en la soledad. Allá tendrás tu nombre, y en la muchedumbre nadie te tocará, no tocarás a nadie." The possession of a name becomes an emblem of the barren, atomistic individualism that rules over the contemporary world. In the mythical world Ixca believes in, the individual is absorbed into a larger order of fraternal belonging.

Neither Rodrigo nor Ixca offers a satisfying solution to the problem of authenticity. Rodrigo's inner restlessness seems so gratuitous and self-indulgent that it comes as no surprise to see him eventually give up his rebellion against the world. If each new mask is the result of an arbitrary choice, then why not choose the mask that will bring success and prosperity? By the end of the novel, Rodrigo has become a successful writer of screenplays for the movie industry, a back who has cynically mastered a simple formula for success.

The plot of *La región* offers no clear resolution to the problems of authenticity and national identity which the novel articulates. Fuentes rejects the existentialist project of liberating the self from the past, of investing life with value simply through the agency of free individual choice, but he also rejects the attempt to provoke a return to the cultural origins of Mexico. Both these approaches to the problems of subjectivity and community are shown to be fruitless, even self-cancelling.
—*Maarten Van Delden*

But if Rodrigo's cult of individuality ultimately proves fruitless and self-defeating. Ixca's violent attack on the notion of a personal life does not seem much more appealing. His behavior becomes increasingly menaging, at times literally poisonous. We may note, for sample, the terror he inspires in little Jorgito Morales when he meets him outside the Cathedral and offers to buy him some candy. In order to escape from Ixca's grip, Jorgito bites his hand, drawing blood. But the next time we see him, over a hundred pages later, the boy is dead. Since it is never clear that the regeneration Ixca is after actually takes place, we are left simply with the image of a man who goes around causing havoc in the lives of others. If Rodrigo's emptiness is that of a life lived without reference to the transcendent, then Ixca displays the perhaps more sinister emptiness of someone who has voided himself of all human emotions: "en realidad Ixca se sustentaba sobre un imenso vacío, un vacio en el que ni la piedad, ni el clamor, ni siquiera el odio de los demás era admitido."

The final confrontation between Ixca and Rodrigo, three years after the main events of the novel, brings the plot to a close, and seems designed to show that while their respective destinies are diametrically opposed, they are equally stunted and unfulfilled. While Rodrigo scales the heights of social success, Ixca disappears from Mexico City altogether, living in obscurity with Rosa Morales, the cleaning lady, and her remaining children. On the surface, Rodrigo has been transformed into a new person, yet he is haunted by the post: "¿Crees que porque estoy aquí ya no estoy allá? . . . ¿Crees que una nueva vida destruye a la antigua, la cancela?" Ixca, on the other hand, while having apparently reconciled himself to the demands of the mythical past, now finds himself abandoned in the present, divided from the very past he thought he was embracing. He describes his condition in the same plaintive tones as Rodrigo: "¿Crees que recuerdo mi propia cara? Mi vida comienza todos los días . . . y nunca tengo el recuerdo de lo que pasó antes. . . ."

Wendy Faris has drawn attention to Fuente's fondness for the rhetorical figure of the chiasmus, which he employs not only at the level of individual sentences but also at the level of plot-structures. The paths followed by Rodrigo and Ixca trace a chiastic design. If at the beginning of the novel Rodrigo represents the present-oriented pole, and Ixca the past-oriented, then the final confrontation between the two men constitutes a complete reversal of this relationship. By the end of the novel, Rodrigo can no longer escape the past, while Ixca lives his life as though it were starting anew at every instant.

The result of this chiastic pattern is to lead the novel into an impasse. The plot of *La región* offers no clear resolution to the problems of authenticity and national identity which the novel articulates. Fuentes rejects the existentialist project of liberating the self from the past, of investing life with value simply through the agency of free individual choice, but he also rejects the attempt to provoke a return to the cultural origins of Mexico. Both these approaches to the problems of subjectivity and community are shown to be fruitless, even self-cancelling.

The novel, however, does not end with the conversation between Rodrigo and Ixca. After the two friends separate, the text undergoes a series of unusual transformations. Ixca gradually sheds his corporeality, and little by little absorbs the different facets of the surrounding city, until eventually he and the city become a single entity. In a subsequent transformation, Ixca becomes the characters of the novel itself, so that finally Ixca, the city, and the book become metaphors for one another, in an operation that may be understood as

an attempt to life the novel onto a plane distinct from ordinary narrativity. In a final transition, Ixca disappears into his own voice, but the voice that speaks in the novel's concluding chapter is one no longer tied to a particular space on time; it is a voice that aims to give a total and instantaneous vision of Mexico, as well as of the novel Fuentes has written about it. This final chapter, entitled "La región más transparente delaire," suggests an attempt to recapitulate and condense the novel; it is a mélange of densely metaphorical descriptions of the Mexican people, scenes from Mexican history, and echoes of the main narrative of the novel itself.

The guiding conception behind this remarkable novelistic flight is the attempt to escape from linear time, to propose and embody an alternative vision of temporality in which, as Fuentes writers, "todo vive al mismo tiempo." Among writers of the present century. Fuentes clearly does not stand alone in his fasination with the break with linear time. For Octavio Paz, for example, the idea of a zone of pure time, beyond chronology, provides the very basis for his definition of poetry: "El poema es mediación: por gracia suya, el tiempo original, padre de los tiempos, encarna en un instante. La succession se convierte en presente puro, manantial que se alimenta a sí mismo y trasmuta al hombre" (*El arco y la lira*). In the area of the novel, one of the most influential codifications of the modernist aesthetic is Joseph Frank's 1945 essay "Spatial Form in Modern Literature"; it centers precisely on this attempt to create forms that are not dependent on linear, chronological methods of organization. Frank's essay, particularly his discussion of the basic features of spatial form, and the type of content it conveys, clarifies Fuentes's relationship to modernist writing. It also contributes to an understanding of the function of the novel's final chapter, in which the techniques of spatial form are most emphatically deploved and appear to constitute an effort to escape from the impasse with which the actual plot of the novel concludes.

According to Frank, in the works of poets such as Eliot and Pound, and novelists such as Joyce, Proust, and Djuna Barnes, the normal temporal unfolding of the text is repeatedly interrupted, with the result that the unity of these works is no longer located in a continuous narrative progression, but in the reflexive references and cross-references relating different points in the text to one another. The reader, in reconstructing these patterns, must ignore the aspects of temporal flow and external reference that are fundamental to more conventional works of literature. The reconstructed patterns must be perceived simultaneously, as a configuration in space. Frank goes on to argue that the most important consequence of the deployment of spatial form in literature is the erasure of a sense of historical depth. Different moments in time become locked together in a timeless unity that evokes the world of myth rather than history.

Clearly, numerous objections could be made to the concept of spatial form, in particular to the term itself, which may seem inappropriately metaphorical. My interest here, however, is not in the accuracy of the term itself, but in the narrative techniques the term was designed to describe, and in the revolt against linear, progressive time implied by the use of these techniques.

Fuentes's attempt, in *La región,* to disrupt the straightforward temporal flow of the novel is not restricted to the final chapter. To the extent that the novel as a whole constitutes an attempt—along the lines of James Joyce's *Ulysses* (1922) and John Dos Passos's *Manhattan Transfer* (1925)—to recreate the life of a city within its pages, the rejection of a sequential organization of the text appears entirely fitting. What Frank would call the "spatializing" technique of the juxtaposition of unrelated textual fragments corresponds to the essentially spatial entity being represented. A typical instance of this technique occurs near the beginning of Fuentes's novel, where the narrator, in a decidedly small-scale imitation of the "Wandering Rocks" chapter of *Ulysses,* traces the simultaneous activities in different parts of the city of various characters on the morning after one of Bobó's parties. The revolt against linear time is also apparent in those moments in the text when past and present are conflated within the mind of an individual character. This device is used most strikingly in the case of Federico Robles, who, as a firm believer in economic progress and a builder of post-Revolutionary Mexico, represents the attachment to the singularity of chronological time in one of its most powerful forms. Although he rejects the past, Robles nevertheless, at Ixca's urging, undertakes the perilous journey inward, and is eventually led to an almost Proustian apprehension of pure time freed from the habitual constraints of consecutiveness. In one scene, while making love to Hortensia, Robles bites the woman's hair, an act that suddenly evokes an image from the day he fought at the battle of Celaya during the Mexican Revolution, and bit the reins of his horse as he rode into the fray. The menaging of past and present is underscored by the paratactia arrangement of the following two sentences: "I Jano ensangientado de Gelaya. Guerpo húmedo y abierto de Hortensia." Robles's vision is particularly significant since it seems to be at least partly responsible for his decision to abandon his public role as a powerful financier in the nation's capital and return to his obscure roots in the country. His decision constitutes an explicit rejection of the rigorously linear time of economic progress.

The important question is whether, as Frank would argue, the disruption of a continuous temporal progression within a narrative necessarily implies a return to the timeless world of myth. It seems doubtful, if only because it is not altogether clear why we should be looked into a binary opposition between history conceived purely in a linean fashion, on the one hand, and myth as the eternal repetition of the same, on the other. The question, then, is what purpose does Fuentes's use of these techniques serve? In answering, I want to focus in particular on the relationship between the main body of the narrative and the poetic finale with which it concludes. One of the most remarkable features of *La región* is that while most of the devices Frank enumerates in his article on spatial form are in evidence throughout the novel, they are most spectacularly exploited at the end, in a manner without real equivalent in the texts Frank discusses. This does not mean, however, that the reader is now truly transported into the realm of myth. I would suggest, instead, that the final section of the novel ought to be read as an attempt to lift the text onto a completely different level, in the hope of offering a resolution to the ambiguities with which the plot concludes. Since these ambiguities center on the opposition between the mythical and the existential views of life, it seems unlikely that such a resolution would take the form of a more determined affirmation of the mythical, a move that would simply eliminate one of the poles of the opposition.

We can begin measuring Fuentes's distance from the mythical approach by looking at the principal features of Frank's definition of myth. Frank quotes Mircea Eliade, who identifies myth as a realm of "external repetition," where time becomes "cosmic, cyclical and infinite" (*The Widening Gyre*). Frank discovers a similar emphasis on repetition and uniformity in the works of modernists such as Joyce, Eliot, and Pound, whose techniques of juxtaposition and allusion he believes underline the fundamental sameness of the human condition through the ages. Octavio Paz, in his discussion of the poetic technique of *simultaneísmo* (which we may regard as another term for spatial form), reaches a similar conclusion: he argues that Pound and Eliot developed their experimental poetic in order to "reconquistar la tradición de la Divina Comedia, es decir, la tradición de Occidente" (*Las hijos del limo*). Both projects, the return to myth and the recapture of tradition, are driven by a search for cultural coherence and identity.

Fuentes has frequently discussed the notion that different temporal planes may have a simultaneous existence, but he has a very different understanding of the implications of this fact. When he discusses "la simultancidad de los tiempos mexicanos" (**"Kierkegaard en la Zona Rosa"**) which he opposes to the linearity of European time, he does not mean that the juxtaposition of these different temporal levels would reveal an underlying continuity between the various phases of Mexican history. Nor is this the effect he pursues at the end of *La región.* The torrent of images, names, and historical episodes he unleashes here evokes a tumultuous, unrestrained multiplicity. In the same essay Fuentes writes that Mexican time "se divertee con nosotros, se revierte contra nosotros, se invierte en nosotros, se subvierte desde nosotros, se convierte en nombre nuestro." These verbs describe not continuity and coherence, but an unceasing process of metamorphosis. He argues that the simultaneous existence in Mexico of all historical levels results from a decision of the land and its people to maintain alive all of time, for the simple reason that "ningún tiempo se ha cumplido aún." Fuentes's Mexican past, in other words, is profoundly different from the past to which the Anglo-American modernists wished to return. It offers not the fullness of an established tradition, but a variety of unfinished projects. Fuentes attacks the proponents of modernization in Mexico, with their cult of the present and of progress, for having suppressed this feature of Mexican time. To return to the cultural and historical multiplicity of Mexico constitutes an act of liberation, a rebellion against the enslaving prejudices of modernity. Fuentes believes that such a rebellion in fact took place during the Mexican Revolution:

> Sólo la Revolución—y por eso, a pesar de todo, merece una R mayúscula—hizo presente todos los pasados de México. Lo hizo instantáeamente, como si supiera que no sobraria tiempo para esta fiesta de encarnaciones. (**"Kierkegaard"**)

This view of the Mexican Revolution is explicitly expressed in *La región* by Manuel Zamacona, who declares at one point that "La Revolutión nos descubre la totalidad de la historia de México," a statement that exactly replicates statements Fuentes has made elsewhere in his own name. It is an idea that can be traced on Octavio Paz, who in *El laberinto de la soledad* described the Mexican Revolution as "un movimiento tendiente a reconquistar nuestro pasado, asimilarlo y hacerlo vivo en el presente." My argument is that at the end of *La región,* Fuentes tries to reproduce on the aesthetic level this revolutionary resuscitation of Mexico's many-sided past. He creates a textual model of ferment, upheaval, and open endedness. This vision of the simultaneous coexistence of all times overturns the linear approach to time represented by Rodrigo Pola, and by the new Mexican bourgeoisie's deification of progress. But the constant process of change and dispersal implied by this vision of time as "fiesta" also subverts the obsession with the unity and singularity of origins expressed in the figure of Ixca Cienfuegos. Fuentes's alternative is his concept of revolutionary time, a vision of simultaneity that promises freedom and possibility, but does not dispense with a strong sense of the shaping powers of the past. This paradoxical fusion of freedom and necessity, of futurity and pastness, is made possible by an ambiguity in the word "revolution" itself, which generally refers to a clean break with the past, a drastic change in the social order, but, in an older version of the word, which Fuentes clearly wants his readers to recall, indicates a process of cyclical return. In the imaginative space Fuentes creates at the end of *La región* these two meanings are held together in an ultimately utopian gesture.

A utopian vision of revolution has been a consistent element in Fuentes's work. In the 1980s. Fuentes has continued to discuss revolutions, in Mexico and elsewhere, in the same terms he used in the 1950s. In his 1983 Harvard commencement speech, for example, he declared that the Mexican Revolution had brought to light "the totality of our history and the possibility of a culture" (*Myself with Others*). He went on to connect the Mexican experience with that of other countries now passing through revolutionary phases:

> Paz himself, Diego Rivera and Carlos Chácez, Mariano Azuela and José Clemente Orozen, Juan Rulfo and Rufino Tamavo: we all work and exist because of the revolutionary experience of our country. How can we stand by as this experience is denied, through ignorance and arrogance, to other people, our brothers, in Central America and the Caribbean?

In *Gringo viejo* (1985), Fuentes once again explores his ideas about the Mexican Revolution. At one point in the novel, the soldiers in the rebel army of Pancho Villa occupy the mansion of a wealthy family that had filed the country. When the soldiers enter the ballroom, with its huge mirrors, they are astonished at the sight of their own reflections; for the first time in their lives they are seeing their own bodies in their entirety. In this way, the Revolution has finally allowed these men and women to discover who they really are. A similar notion is articulated in the broad opposition the narrative constructs between Mexico before and Mexico during the Revolution. Before the Revolution the country was merely an aggregate of static, isolated communities. The Revolution sets the country in motion: the people leave their villages and towns and finally begin to discover the common purpose that binds the nation together as a whole. The Revolution, in this view, constitutes an explosive moment of self-recognition in the nation's history.

> **A final element in Fuentes's revised view of the nature of revolution consists of his rethinking the relationship between the erotic and the political.**
> **—*Maarten Van Delden***

Fuentes's most recent novel, *Cristóbal nonato* (1987), however, reveals a distinct shift in perspective: revolutions, both past and present, are now seen in a far less sanguine light. The spirit of the Mexican Revolution is recreated in a mocking, though affectionate, manner in the figure of General Rigoberto Palomar, who owes his high military rank to a somewhat unusual feat: at the age of eighteen he was elevated in one stroke from trumpeter to general for having recovered the arm General Alvaro Obregón lost during the battle of Celaya. In the novel's present, at the age of ninety-one, General Palomar is the last survivor of the Revolution, in which he maintains an irrational faith premised on two contradictory assumptions: "1) la Revolutión no había terminado y 2) la Revolutión había triunfado y cumplido todas sus promesas." This discrediting of the concept of revolution takes on a less light-hearted form when it comes to a depiction of the revolutionary spirit of the late twentieth century. The embodiment of this spirit is Matamoros Moreno, whose leadership of the revolutionary forces of Mexico is both absurd, in that it grows out of the resentments of a frustrated writer, and somewhat sinister, in that his name, the "Ayatollah," links him to a reactionary religious fanaticism. In this way, the belief in the possible emergence of a new, more benign, order is severely attenuated.

A final element in Fuentes's revised view of the nature of revolution consists of his rethinking the relationship between the erotic and the political. Wendy Faris has observed that in much of Fuentes's work "love and revolution are allied, the physical upheaval and implied freedom of eroticism often serving as analogues for social liberation, both moving us toward some kind of utopia" ["Desire and Power, Love and Revolution: Carlos Fuentes and Milan Kundera," *Review of Contemporary Fiction*, Vol. 8, No. 2, 1988]. In *Cristóbal nonato,* however, the personal and the political are no longer so easily reconciled: the relationship between these two dimensions of existence turns out to be fraught with difficulties. When young Angel Palomar abandons his wife in the middle of her pregnancy in order to pursue an infatuation with the vain and superficial daughter of one of Mexico's richest men, he managers to convince himself that he is doing it in order to keep alive his iconoclastic and rebellions spirit. He is, in other words, chasing Penny López for the right ideological reasons. But Angel is not entirely convinced by his own attempt at self-justification, he continues to be perplexed by "la contradicción entre sus ideas y su práctica" and he is finally unable to find the correct adjustment between his sex life and his politics: "Su sexualidad renaciente, era progresista o reaccionaria? Su actividad política, debía conducirlo a la monogamíao al harén?" The only possible conclusion is that these two realms are in some sense incommensurable: "ante un buen acostón se estrellan todas has ideologís." In this way, revolution, deprived of a clear basis in personal experience, becomes a far more complex, baffling and even improbable event. Whether *Cristóbal nonato* signals a major shift in Fuentes's work it is too early to say. What is clear, however, is that it is precisely Fuentes's persistent engagement with the question of the interrelations between the private and the public, between the individual self and its historical circumstances, that constitutes his most powerful claim on our interest.

Roberto Gonzalez Echevarria (review date 6 October 1991)

SOURCE: "Passion's Progress," in *New York Times Book Review,* October 6, 1991, p. 3.

[*In the following review, Echevarria provides a highly laudatory assessment of* The Campaign, *declaring it not only "Fuentes's best novel so far," but "also one of the best Latin American novels of the last 20 years."*]

Latin America's novelists have been obsessively drawn to their continent's history because it is a grand narrative, with a beginning portentous enough to satisfy yearnings for a sacred origin, yet historical in the sense of being human and secular. The conquistadors themselves, as well as the first historians of the New World, believed that the discovery of America by Columbus was the most significant event since the Crucifixion. It may very well have been the discovery, in fact, that created the modern feeling of being *in* history.

For this reason, Alejo Carpentier, Gabriel Garcia Marquez, Homero Aridjis and Carlos Fuentes, among others, have all written novels that begin at or near that beginning. Of late, however, perhaps saturated by the consecration of that moment, or by its repeated and predictable debunking in this quincentenary year, Latin American novelists have turned to another dramatic historical divide: the wars of independence from Spain in the early 19th century. These conflicts provide a wealth of epic characters and actions, and the founding of new nations a rich, polemical beginning that still has clear repercussions. Thus we have had the novelist and poet Augusto Roa Bastos' *I the Supreme,* about the 19th-century Paraguayan dictator "Doctor" Jose Gaspar Rodriguez Francia; *The General in His Labyrinth* by Mr. Garcia Marquez, which narrates Simon Bolivar's final days; the Mexican writer Fernando del Paso's *Noticias del Imperio,* about the French imperial adventure in Mexico, and now *The Campaign* by Carlos Fuentes.

It is, in my view, Mr. Fuentes's best novel so far, the one where he has found, after much experimentation, a genuine voice. *The Campaign* is also one of the best Latin American novels of the last 20 years, possibly destined to become a classic.

It focuses on the decade of the independence struggle from 1810 to 1820, spanning the continent from Argentina to Mexico, with stops in Peru, Chile and Venezuela. It offers a vast social, intellectual and political panorama of the wars, as seen through the lives of three young men in Argentina who are imbued with the ideas of Voltaire, Diderot and Rousseau. Like the political movement in which the three young men are involved, they represent the transition from the Enlightenment to Romanticism. This is particularly the case of the protagonist, Baltasar Bustos, a follower of Rousseau who believes in the efficacy of passion in bringing about a restoration of nature's balance in all realms. Though a bookish man, like his two companions Baltasar makes himself into a man of action in a Quixotic quest to make reality and his readings coincide. *The Campaign* is in good measure about the impossibility of applying European theories to the American continent, a dilemma constantly faced by Latin American rulers, from Spanish viceroys to Marxist *caudillos.*

Carlos Fuentes has been one of the most deliberate and Protean writers of the century. He has been not only a prolific novelist, but also a short-story writer, an essayist, a critic, a playwright, a lecturer, a journalist—everything but a poet. As a novelist he has nearly exhausted the possibilities available in the modern tradition.
—*Roberto Gonzalez Echevarria*

Mr. Fuentes exploits skillfully the dramatic and even comical results of this faulty fit. In contrast to other Latin American historical novels, which can be ponderous and complicated, *The Campaign* is a very entertaining book, with a finely wrought plot and memorable characters and scenes—all elegantly contrived, unobtrusive self-referential structure.

Carlos Fuentes has been one of the most deliberate and Protean writers of the century. He has been not only a prolific novelist, but also a short-story writer, an essayist, a critic, a playwright, a lecturer, a journalist—everything but a poet. As a novelist he has nearly exhausted the possibilities available in the modern tradition. He has been Joycean in *Christopher Unborn,* Jamesian in *Aura,* Faulknerian in *The Death of Artemio Cruz,* baroque in *Terra Nostra,* realistic in *The Good Conscience,* mythical in *Where the Air Is Clear* and camp in *Cumpleanos.* As a critic and essayist Mr. Fuentes has reflected, too predictably at times, the shifting ideologies of the last 40 years; he has discovered at one point or another existentialism, psychoanalysis, Marxism and poststructuralism, and it is clear that the Russian theoretician Mikhail Bakhtin is his latest find.

Mr. Fuentes's literary works often betray symptoms of this consuming anguish to be *au courant*—a very common affliction of us Latin Americans. This is not to say that the earlier novels are not of high quality, nor to imply that they lack a Fuentes signature. The core of Mr. Fuentes's fictional world is a primal story involving the interplay of birth, fate, love and guilt, all cast in quasi-religious terms. This story

is genuine in its pathos, aligning him with a powerful Hispanic tradition reaching back to Fernando de Rojas, Cervantes and Calderon in the Spanish golden age. This fable of origins could be either the source or the reflection of Mr. Fuentes's relationship with models and mentors, which inevitably include, early in his career, Octavio Paz.

While it is very much another version of the Fuentes trademark story, *The Campaign* is so freely narrated, so unburdened by its author's latest readings and so audacious in its approach to quite grandiose themes that it reads like the work of a truly renewed, even reborn, Carlos Fuentes. One could possibly attribute the novel's spontaneity to its theme, to the youthfulness inherent in the story of a young man inspired by Rousseau and driven by an ideal erotic passion to struggle for political justice.

Baltasar's pilgrimage through war-torn Latin America, from the peaks of the Andes to the frivolous salons of Santiago de Chile, where he is a spy for the revolutionaries, is told in confessional-style letters to his friend Manuel Varela, a printer and publisher in Buenos Aires who is the novel's narrator. The elusive object of Baltasar's lust is Ofelia Salamanca, the wife of the Marquis de Cabra, the presiding judge for the Viceroyalty of the Rio de la Plata. He ogles her magnificent alabaster body through a window as she dresses, unaware of the voyeur, who will be fatally smitten by her beauty and as a result become the protagonist of significant political acts. Baltasar kidnaps her child and puts in its place a black baby during the momentous night of May 24, 1810. Before the substitution is discovered, however, the black baby is burned in a fire accidentally started by Baltasar, and its charred body is taken for that of Ofelia's child. Meanwhile, the white baby is lost by Baltasar's accomplices in the confusion of the blaze and the tumultuous events following the installation of a junta—without the viceroy—the next morning.

The return of Ofelia's child is not the only treat the narrator has in store for us at the end of his Fielding-like romance, but I will not give away the plot. Suffice it to say that the final disclosures are akin to those in Agatha Christie's thriller *The Murder of Roger Ackroyd,* and that they loop together neatly mysteries about the paternity of Ofelia's child and the genealogy of the text itself. I am sure that the fake foundling will play a significant role in two more novels which, Mr. Fuentes has announced, will make up, with *The Campaign,* a trilogy about Latin American independence.

Ofelia's child is reborn, as it were, the night before the May Revolution of 1810 in Buenos Aires, an event that robs him of the privileges he acquired by his first birth. It is as if this white baby represented the new freedom sought by the revolutionaries: unburdened by the past, a fresh new world in which to build a new polity. In this, as well as in the story of Baltasar's strained relations with his father, the owner of a large estate in the Argentine *pampa,* as well as in many other details, Mr. Fuentes seems to be flirting with allegory. The characters and their actions, in other words, come to embody abstract notions such as freedom, authority, the Spanish past. This tendency seems to be a paradoxical habit of political romances of this kind; while revolutionary in theme and intention, they assume the most conventional and even reactionary of literary forms, which depend heavily on received knowledge and the tritest of symbols. Mr. Fuentes has avoided the solemnity inherent in allegory and its implicit submission to authority by the very ironic, novelistic form that the transmission of the text feigns: letters that we never read completely (the narrator sometimes quotes from them), but that are recast by the narrator so that their significant implications in the story are not revealed until the end. The thriller style that brings about closure can only be taken with a grain of salt.

> Reading *The Campaign* creates the illusion of returning to that heady moment (the time of the Congress of Vienna in Europe, the Congreso de Angostura in Latin America) when, in the turbulent wake of the Napoleonic wars, modern nations were created. The contrast between political projects and subsequent history is, needless to say, ironic.
> —*Roberto Gonzalez Echevarria*

The freshness of *The Campaign* could also be due to the fact that it covers the struggle for independence in Latin America and the initial moments of republican life, when, despite disagreements among the young revolutionaries, there is hope that their efforts will bring about not only freedom, but equality. The desire for political renewal and the expectation of a perfect society is one of the undying topics of American literature—North and South. One of the central themes of *The Campaign* is the premonition of an American utopia. This is highlighted in one of the most remarkable scenes of the novel, when Baltasar, led into caves in the Andes, has a vision of El Dorado, in this case a marvelous Inca city that is resplendent with purity and wealth. (He also catches a tantalizing glimpse of Ofelia's inviting body in a dreamlike sequence that blends erotic and political desires.)

The end of the novel does not bring about a loss of this hope. This is in sharp contrast with *The General in His Labyrinth* by Mr. Garcia Marquez. Mr. Fuentes playfully underscores the difference when he has the printer write: "While I waited for authors of our own to emerge, I already had before me a life of the Liberator Simon Bolivar, a manuscript stained

with rain and tied with tricolor ribbons, which the author, who called himself Aureliano Garcia, had sent to me, as best he could, from Barranquilla. It was a sad chronicle, however . . . I preferred to go on publishing Voltaire and Rousseau (*La Nouvelle Heloise* was the greatest literary success in the entire history of South America) and leave for another time the melancholy prophecy of a Bolivar as sick and defeated as his dream of American unity and civil liberty in our nations."

But *The Campaign* contains enough prophecies of its own about battles to come among the divisive groups that brought about independence, and about the fragmentation of Latin America after the Spanish departure. In this the novel is very topical, for it seems to allude to the struggles fostered by present-day nationalism and the resultant splintering of large political units.

Reading *The Campaign* creates the illusion of returning to that heady moment (the time of the Congress of Vienna in Europe, the Congreso de Angostura in Latin America) when, in the turbulent wake of the Napoleonic wars, modern nations were created. The contrast between political projects and subsequent history is, needless to say, ironic. But the young men in the novel, particularly Baltasar, are caught up in the enthusiasm of beginnings. They argue vehemently about how to achieve equality as if their intellectual jousting could really realize their utopias. For Latin Americans, particularly in the current time of ideological breakdown and forced pragmatism, their fervor cannot be but exhilarating, and even the cause of a bit of nostalgia. More generally, *The Campaign* seems to evoke promises and projects of the Enlightenment at a time when they appear most bankrupt and unattainable. Perhaps this is a call for a new beginning. Despite a labored and at times inexact translation, *The Campaign* is a pleasure to read—for its plot, the richness of its historical setting and the political issues it raises. I had never before finished a Fuentes book wishing for more, but after reading *The Campaign* I look forward eagerly to the next volumes of the trilogy.

Nicolas Shumway (review date 26 April 1992)

SOURCE: "In the Embrace of Spain," in *New York Times Book Review,* April 26, 1992, p. 9.

[*In the following review, Shumway offers a mixed assessment of* The Buried Mirror.]

In 1856, Argentina's first great historian, Bartolome Mitre, published a collection of short biographies titled *Gallery of Argentine Celebrities.* In the foreword he wrote: "Argentine history has been rich in noteworthy men. . . . The glory of those men is the Argentine people's richest heritage; rescuing their lives and qualities from obscurity is to gather and use that heritage, for our honor and our improvement." Mitre's affirmation of Argentina's greatness came at a time of serious crisis. Two opposing governments claimed to rule the country, and the threat of lasting fragmentation loomed at every juncture. Yet Mitre denied even the possibility of permanent failure. Whatever the problems of the moment, his book held that Argentina was a spiritual unit with a glorious past that can instruct an equally glorious future. Mitre, of course, was not the only historian of his century with such attitudes. In the 19th century, history was often written to undergird newly formed nations needing a sense of cultural and spiritual unity to justify their existence.

The Buried Mirror by the Mexican novelist Carlos Fuentes is a recent installment in this historiographical tradition. Mr. Fuentes confesses the gravity of today's political and economic crisis in Latin America, yet, like Mitre, he discounts such difficulties as a thing of the moment and claims a magnificent future to be had by unearthing the buried mirror of cultural identity that will reveal to Latin Americans their forgotten, spiritually authentic history. This book, he tells us, is "dedicated to a search for the cultural continuity that can inform and transcend the economic and political disunity and fragmentation of the Hispanic world."

The result of such concerns is an unusual book, both compelling and disturbing. As history it is anachronistic and occasionally unreliable, as narrative and commentary it is forceful and beautifully written. Two major items, however, separate Mr. Fuentes from historians like Mitre. First is the scope of his book. Mr. Fuentes seeks to retell *all* of Spain's and Latin America's cultural history, a daunting task by any standard. Second is his intended audience. Ostensibly he, like Mitre, addresses other Latin Americans. Yet when he uses images in which Gibraltar reminds "us" of insurance companies and Numantia—where the ancient Iberians resisted for decades the Roman conquest of Spain—becomes "a sort of Vietnam for Rome," he clearly hopes English-speaking Americans are listening. Indeed, since his book is meant to complement, albeit not duplicate, a television series co-produced by the Discovery Channel and the BBC and also called *The Buried Mirror,* it sometimes seems that North Americans are his principal concern.

The range of the book is both its principal defect and its chief virtue. Beginning with the prehistoric cave paintings at Altamira in Spain and ending with contemporary street art in East Los Angeles, Mr. Fuentes seeks to cover all of Spanish and Spanish-American history, with frequent digressions on a particular artist, political figure, novel or painting. Given the size of such a project, it is no surprise that *The Buried Mirror* covers too much to do all of it well. Yet what Mr. Fuentes does manage to distill in so few pages is truly

astounding. With his considerable gifts as a narrator, he captures much of the sweep and drama of Hispanic history and culture without bogging down in details. Although he devotes only a few paragraphs each to important figures like Alphonse the Wise, Miguel de Cervantes and Benito Juarez, what he loses in detail he often captures in essence.

In a year when bashing Columbus and the Spanish conquest is becoming a popular parlor game among the politically correct and minimally informed, Mr. Fuentes calls attention to the complexity of Hispanic culture and history. He frankly describes the cruelty of men like Francisco Pizarro, but he also portrays vividly the heroism of figures like the early missionary priests and historians Bartolome de las Casas and Toribio de Benavente (always called Motolinia, a name the Indians gave him), who battled tirelessly to protect America's native populations.

> **Perhaps the biggest problem in *The Buried Mirror* is its basic premise: that the Hispanic world forms a coherent unit reducible to a single cultural continuity.**
> —*Nicolas Shumway*

Unfortunately, not all of Mr. Fuentes's narrative is equally felicitous. His need to generalize and encapsulate inevitably distorts. For example, he makes a great deal about bullfights and gypsies as symbols of all Hispanic culture. In fact, these are the hoary cliches that play better in 19th-century French operas than in modern Latin America. Even more puzzling is his repeated insistence that Hispanic countries should seek inspiration for their political institutions in their own past and cease imitating English and French models. While this point strikes a nice emotional chord, he never explains which English and French models are inappropriate or why, nor does he specify which elements of the Hispanic past should be reproduced to solve today's problems.

But perhaps the biggest problem in *The Buried Mirror* is its basic premise: that the Hispanic world forms a coherent unit reducible to a single cultural continuity. A parallel study of the English-speaking world would assume that England, Canada, Australia, New Zealand, Jamaica, Ireland, South Africa, India and the United States form a single cultural unit because England "embraces us all" (as Mr. Fuentes says of Spain). Virtually any generalization about England and England's former colonies would surely be greeted with at least a "Yes, but. . . ." Similar doubts rise from Mr. Fuentes's insistence on continuity throughout all places and periods of the Hispanic world. Hispanic countries differ tremendously from one another, so much so that even using a term like "Latin America" can signal an intellectual laziness that refuses to recognize their complexity and variety. It would surely be ironic if **The Buried Mirror,** rather than bringing greater awareness to North Americans, merely contributed to our lamentable penchant for seeing everything south of the Rio Grande as a single entity.

For these reasons I read much of Mr. Fuentes's book with a "Yes, but . . ." I am grateful for his attempting such a large task, impressed by his phenomenal narrative gifts and happy to own the book, both for what Mr. Fuentes says and for the extravagant reproductions of Hispanic artworks generously included. But the book leaves me feeling like a tourist who sees 12 countries in seven days. The places visited are beautiful and fascinating, but on my next visit, I want to take more time in fewer places. I will see less but know more.

Maarten Van Delden (essay date July-December 1993)

SOURCE: "Carlos Fuentes' *Agua Quemada:* The Nation as Unimaginable Community," in *Latin American Literary Review,* Vol. XXI, No. 42, July-December, 1993, pp. 57-69.

[*In the following essay, Van Delden surveys Fuentes's handling of the identity of Mexico as a nation in his works, particularly in* Agua Quemada.]

George Orwell claimed that politics gave him the sense of purpose he needed to write good prose. What politics was for George Orwell, Mexico has been for Carlos Fuentes, with the difference that for Fuentes it is not so much good writing as writing *tout court* that appears to have been enabled by the possession of a literary polestar. Consider the fact that an autobiographical essay Fuentes first published in *Granta* as **"The Discovery of Mexico"** became **"How I Started To Write"** when it was later included in *Myself with Others,* a collection of Fuentes's essays. One can hardly imagine more vivid proof of the conflation, in Fuentes's conception of his own career, of two processes: the encounter with Mexico, where he did not go to live permanently until age sixteen, and the emergence of a literary vocation.

But while the idea of the nation has sustained Fuentes's literary imagination, he has not always returned the favor by sustaining the idea of the nation. Fuentes has regularly put forward a heroic vision of the Mexican nation as a unified, self-knowing whole, but he has been equally, if not to say more, inclined towards a view of Mexico as a violently conflicted, divided entity. A brief example from **La muerte de Artemio Cruz** (1962)—perhaps the most obviously "nationalist" text in Fuentes's corpus—will give a sense of how Fuentes swings between the celebratory and the deconstructive in his rendering of the Mexican nation. Eric Hobsbawm has noted how the "travelogue or geography les-

son" is a common technique for inculcating a sense of the nation as "a coherent whole, deserving love and patriotic devotion." The school is obviously the preferred medium for the transmission of such lessons, but they are also to be found in literary texts. Near the end of **Artemio Cruz** there is a long, evocative section about Artemio's relationship to his country that includes a kind of tour of the nation's territory. At first, the sheer variety of the Mexican landscape is still reconciled within a nation of unity-in-diversity (a common strategy in definitions of national identity):

> son mil países con un solo nombre . . . Traerás los desiertos rojos, las estepas de tuna y maguey, el mundo del nopal, el cinturón de lava y cráteres helados, las murallas de cúpulas doradas y troneras de piedra, las ciudades de cal y canto, las ciudades de tezontle, los pueblos de adobe, las aldeas de carrizo . . . los huesos delgados de Michoacán, la carne chaparra de Tlaxcala, los ojos claros de Sinaloa, los dientes blancos de Chiapas, los huipiles, las peinetas jarochas, las trenzas mixtecas, los cinturones tzotziles, los rebozos de Santa María, la marquetería poblana, el vidrio jaliscience, el jade oxaquefio . . . las traes amarradas al cuello . . . se le han metido al vientre . . .

It is above all the experience of the Mexican Revolution, conceived as an *encuentro amoroso,* the expression of an *extraño amor comùn,* that ensures that the multiple realities of Mexico can be reconciled within a higher unity. But a few pages later, the speaker imagines a profound and unbridgeable fault-line running right through the heart of the nation. "Habrá aquí una frontera, the voice declares, "una frontera que nadie derrotará." It is a frontier that separates a Mexico that is "seco, inmutable, triste," that belongs to the "claustro de piedra y polvo encerrado en el altiplano," a Mexico linked to the Aztec past, from the Mexico of "la media luna veracruzana," a Mexico tied to another history, a different world, the sensuous, voluptuous world of the Antilles, and, beyond, of the Mediterranean.

These kinds of discursive and descriptive passages in a work of fiction are one way of representing the large and somewhat nebulous entity that is a nation. But the novelistic representation of the nation may be lodged less in such isolated passages than in certain structural features of the text. Benedict Anderson identifies a structure of simultaneity in the novel that has allowed it to become one of the fundamental forms of imagining the nation. He evokes a standard novelistic plot in which a series of disparate events are described as occurring simultaneously, perhaps in order to interlock at some later point, perhaps in order to diverge. Anderson then wonders why the two characters in his imaginary plot who never meet, who "can even be described as passing each other on the street, without ever becoming acquainted," are nevertheless connected to each other. He offers two answers. On the one hand, he sees a modern notion of a uniform and measurable clock-time as providing a frame when within which to enclose a wide variety of events. On the other hand, he speaks of the embedding of these events in certain "sociological entities of . . . firm and stable reality." Anderson undercuts his own argument about the privileged relationship between the novel and the nation by offering entities (Wessex, Lübeck, Los Angeles) as example of such societies that are not nations. Even so, his suggestion that the nation offers a point of reference that ensures the unity of certain works of fiction provides a useful framework for an analysis of Carlos Fuentes' *Agua quemada* (1981).

Even though Anderson's discussion is concerned with the novel, his remarks can help us read *Agua quemada* because the four stories that make up this collection are all carefully interlinked, and so can be seen as constituting a single universe that is not so different from what we typically encounter in a novel. An examination of the nature of these links will give us an initial sense of Fuentes' conception of the community he is representing. It will also provide us with an insight into some flaws in Anderson's interpretation of his own model.

Each of the four stories in *Agua quemada* deals with a different set of characters, but each story intersects briefly with one or more of the other stories. Doña Manuela in "**Estos fueron los palacios**" was once a servant in the home of General Vicente Vergara, the main character in "**El día de las madres.**" The General continues to pay Manuela's rent in a building owned by Federico Silva, the protagonist of "**Las mañanitas.**" The Aparicios in "**El hijo de Andrés Aparicio**" also used to live in one of Silva's buildings. Moreover, Bernabé Aparacio's grandfather was an aide-de-camp to General Vergara during the Revolution, and two of his uncles now work at a gas-station owned by the General's son Agustín.

> **The links between the different stories in *Agua quemada* serve to turn a collection of disparate narratives into a general survey of an entire community. But the glancing nature of these connections creates a paradox: the connections, precisely because they are so tenuous, become an image of disconnectedness.**
> **—*Maarten Van Delden***

Fuentes's picture of a single spatio-temporal continuum within which a series of life-stories cross each other's paths would appear to offer a fitting illustration of Benedict Anderson's idea about how a novel imagines a national community. Yet the existence of a common frame doesn't necessarily mean that what transpires within that frame constitutes a *genuine* community. Anderson appears insensitive to the uses of irony, and so does not see that a particular literary technique can be used to question as much as to imagine a community.

The links between the different stories in *Agua quemada* serve to turn a collection of disparate narratives into a general survey of an entire community. But the glancing nature of these connections creates a paradox: the connections, precisely because they are so tenuous, become an image of disconnectedness. This fragmentation of the social body is an all the more bitter reality since it is so often the result of deliberate refusals on the part of individual characters to preserve and respect the bonds that tie them to their fellow citizens. General Vergara fires Manuela after the death of his wife because she triggers too many memories in him. He discontinues the invitations to the Aparicios for breakfast on the anniversary of the Revolution, perhaps for the same reason. Federico Silva knows absolutely nothing about the people who live in this buildings, which he has never even visited. Later we learn that he raises the rent *sin piedad* on the Aparicio family when the rent freeze is lifted, forcing them to move to a different part of the city. It seems, then, that whenever two stories in the collection are linked to each other it is in order to depict an act of severance, to describe an erosion of the sense of community. This sense of erosion is also conveyed through the way in which space is mapped in the stories. *Agua quemada* attempts to cover different points on the map of Mexico City, as well as to trace the interrelations between these points. We move from the exclusive Pedregal neighborhood where the Vergaras live to the old colonial center with its semi-abandoned palaces, then to Federico Silva's house sandwiched between the Zona Rosa and the Colonia Roma, and finally out to a nameless squatters' community on the outskirts of the city. But the inclusive gesture only serves to uncover a general loss of cohesion in the urban fabric. Two motions stand out: on the one hand, the city, as it spreads, becomes shapeless, loses solidity, as we see in the description of the nameless district were Bernabé Aparicio grows up, "un lugar pasajero, como las chozas de cartón y lámina corrugada"; on the other hand, the city erects barricades against itself, as in the description of the attempt at *castidad urbana* in the fortress-like Pedregal neighborhood.

The description of the city as chaste evokes the image of the community as a body. Octavio Paz remarks in *Corriente alterna* that "la nación es proyección del individuo," a link that provides another basis for the imaginative representation of the nation. *La muerte de Artemio Cruz* offers an excellent example of this technique: the vicissitudes of the protagonist's life are emblems of different stages in the modern history of Mexico. The hero's psychological disintegration (captured in the tripartite structure of the novel) and his physical dismemberment (most vividly depicted in the concluding image of the surgeon's scalpel slicing open Artemio's stomach for the final, unsuccessful operation) point to the disintegration and mutilation of the nation as a whole. In **Agua quemada** the image of mutilation crops up again: Federico Silva's throat is slit in the course of a robbery in his house, an incident foreshadowed in Silva's own detailed and gloating description earlier in the story of the workings of a guillotine. Silva, we are told, resembles "el perdido perfume de la antigua laguna de México"; he belongs, on other words, to a vanished Mexico. Like the victims of the guillotine in France, he is an anachronism. The fact that the woman who participates in the fatal robbery in Silva's house is named Pocajonta gives a further, paradoxical twist to Silva's role: he belongs to an older Mexico, but he is also an intruder, an outsider, a colonialist in his own country. And in this story, of course, the native princess will not reach out to save the doomed foreigner.

The depiction of Silva as both a native and a foreigner, both insider and outsider, reveals the instability of the notion of national identity. But the most effective vehicle Fuentes chooses in order to demonstrate this instability is not the individual, but the family. One of the strands that ties together the different stories in **Agua quemada** is the motif of the missing relative. In **"El día de las madres"** the mothers themselves are dead. In **"Estos fueron los palacios"** Manuela's daughter Lupe Lupita has run away from home. In **"Las mañanitas"** the protagonist Federico Silva is a convinced bachelor who is led to think at the end of his life about the son he never had. In the final story of the collection **"El hijo de Andrés Aparicio"** it is precisely the father named in the title who never appears. The case of **"El día de las madres"** is particularly interesting, however, because here the theme of loss is given an especially bitter twist: the absence of the mothers turns out to be not a symptom of familial disintegration, but rather the *sine qua non* of domestic harmony. The men of the Vergara family can only continue to live together thanks to the violence they perpetrate on women. They bond over the bodies of the women. To the extent that the history of the Vergara family is meant to recapitulate the history of twentieth-century Mexico, the story reveals that national unity is entirely a function of violence and repression. The mourning of a loss masks the fact that the loss energizes the survivors.

On a more or less explicit level, **"El día de las madres"** offers two answers to the question of what it is that brings all Mexicans together into a single, unified community. Near the beginning of the story we see General Vicente Vergara thinking nostalgically "en los años de la revolución y en las batallas que forjaron at México moderno." Here it is a shared, and, significantly enough, violent, past that has cre-

ated the nation. Later in the story, the General's grandson Plutarco, who is also the narrator of **"El día de las madres,"** in the course of querying his grandfather about his somewhat contradictory stance with regard to the Church, says: "usted también dice que la Virgen nos une a los mexicanos." This time it is a shared symbol—and the fact that it is a feminine symbol is what needs to be underlined—that acts as the guarantor of the nation's unity. But what the story shows is how both these techniques for making the nation are fraught with terrible contradictions. The violent past makes the present but also cripples it, while the idealization of womanhood is merely the gentler way of excluding actual women from the national community.

The relationship to the past and the relationship to the feminine are the focus of the story's opening lines:

> Todas las mañanas el abuelo mezcla con fuerza su taza de café instantánco. Empuña la cuchara como en otros tiempos la difunta abuelita doña Clotilde el molinete o como él mismo, el general Vicente Vergara, empuñó la cabeza de la silla de montar que cuelga de una pared de su recámara.

In just two sentences, Fuentes gives us a complex structure of comparisons and contrasts that prepares the way for the story's subsequent trajectory. The present brings forth the past; a simple domestic task evokes the period, violent days of the Revolution. But the resemblance between now and then, between the grandfather and the military hero, immediately collapses under the weight of a merciless irony. The similarity between the two actions, the grasping of the spoon and the grasping of the pommel of the saddle, is promptly stripped away to reveal an unbridgeable gulf separating the past from the present. The passage offers no more than an illusion of continuity. The unobtrusive shift from one name to another, the Grandfather of the first sentence becoming the General of the second, cannot conceal the fact that these two figures have very little in common, for only in the slightly hallucinatory world of an old man overcome with nostalgia can preparing coffee and fighting a military battle entertain a genuine resemblance with each other. Having established the link between past and present, the narrative proceeds subtly to draw attention to the distance that has been travelled between them through the detail of the saddle. Hanging on the General's bedroom wall, it has acquired a merely ornamental value in a thoroughly domestic setting.

Towards the end of the opening paragraph, the General himself, even while he has been busy recapturing the past in a cup of coffee, acknowledges that times are no longer the same. He remembers a time when "los hombres cran hombres," taking pleasure in getting drunk and going to war. The present, then, is characterized by the decline of machismo, a decline that affects the General himself, for the other link established in the opening lines of **"El día de las madres,"** besides the one that connects Vicente Vergara's present self to his past self, is the one that connects him to his deceased wife, and, therefore, to the realm of the feminine. In the act of preparing himself a cup of coffee, Vicente Vergara takes the place of his wife, and so becomes a domesticated, feminized figure. But as was the case with the crossing over between past and present, the exchange between masculine and feminine qualities proves to be illusory. The story's opening image of the feminized grandfather gives way in the course of the narrative to the portrait of a man (a community of men, really) fundamentally cut off from womanhood.

The relationship between past and present is embodied in the relationship between General Vergara and his grandson Plutarco. Near the beginning of the story Plutarco speaks of the "angustia de ratón arrinconado" he feels every time he sees General Vergara "recorrer sin propósito las salas y vestíbulos y pasillos." But Plutarco feels this way less out of pity for the aimlessness of his grandfather's existence than because the old man constantly reminds him of the futility of his own life. Immediately after the above passage, Plutarco runs out of the house, as if to escape from his grandfather's oppressive presence. He hops into his Thunderbird (an obvious symbol of Americanization, and hence of the distance between Plutarco and the General) and heads for the ring road around the city, where he will finally feel free and at ease: "podía dar la vuelta, una, dos, cien veces, cuantas veces quisiera, a lo largo de miles de kilómetros, con la sensación de no movement, de estar siempre en el lugar de partida y al mismo tiempo en el lugar de arribo." But the structure of Pluarco's action is ambiguous: on the one hand, he flees from his grandfather, on the other hand, he ends up imitating him. After all, the aimlessness of Plutarco's highway drive simply replicates the purposelessness he had sensed in his grandfather's wanderings through his house.

> **The rivalry between the General and Plutarco points to the presence of an Oedipal paradigm in "El día de las madres."**
> —*Maarten Van Delden*

It is this ambivalence that offers the key to the relationship between Plutarco and General Vicente Vergara. To the extent that the General, having fought in the battles that had forged modern Mexico, is a national hero, and as such a kind of embodiment of the nation, the complexities of his relationship with his grandson are symptomatic of the impasse that has struck the nationalist project. This impasse is captured most vividly in the following conversation between grandfather and grandson:

—Lo quiero mucho, abuelo.

—Está bien, chamaco. Lo mismo digo.

—Oiga, yo no quiero empezar la vida con la mesa puesta, como usted dice.

—Ni modo. Todo está a mi nombre. Tu papás nomás administra. Cuando me muera, todo te lo dejo a ti.

—No lo quiero, abuelo, abuelo, quisiera empezar de nuevo, como empezóusted . . . .

—Ya no son los mismos tiempos, ¿qué ibas a hacer? Sonreí apenas:—Me hubiera gustado castrar a alguien, como usted . . .

It is worth examining this passage in some detail so as to unravel the structure of the relationship between Plutarco and his grandfather. The first two lines of the dialogue set up a dynamic of repetition and imitation: the grandfather's feelings for his grandson are the same as the grandson's feelings for his grandfather. Their emotions mirror each other. But Plutarco's desire to be like the General runs into insurmountable difficulties. Plutarco's wants to imitate his grandfather, but his grandfather prides himself precisely on never having imitated anybody. If Plutarco wants to begin anew, to create himself, like his grandfather, he must begin by freeing himself of his dependence on the old man. In other words, if Plutarco wants truly to imitate the General, he will have to reject him. The impossibility of reconciling these two imperatives causes Plutarco's paralysis. And it is the nature of time itself that is responsible for this situation, as the General acknowledges with serene simplicity when he says "Ya no son los mismos tiempos." In a sense, what he means is that times are never the same. One of the ways in which time becomes concrete is through the succession of the generations, and it is the fact of generation that places the children at a permanent disadvantage in the struggle for originality. Plutarco says that he would have liked to castrate somebody, as his grandfather did, but we are given to understand that in effect his grandfather, simply by virtue of his priority in time, has already castrated *him*.

The rivalry between the General and Plutarco points to the presence of an Oedipal paradigm in **"El día de las madres."** The pattern is confirmed when we learn that Plutarco's first experience of sexual arousal occurred at age thirteen when a friend showed him a picture of a girl in a bathing-suit. The girl turns out to be Plutarco's mother, who died when Plutarco was five. Both the incest wish and the wish to take the place of the father-figure express what Freud calls the child's "wish to be the *father of himself*." That this particular reading of the sources of the Ocdipus complex is most pertinent to Fuentes' story is clear from the fact that what is at stake in the struggle between Plutarco and his grandfather is, as I have tried to show, the desire of the younger man to be self-created. We have seen, however, that Plutarco's desire to engender himself is paradoxically intertwined with his desire to imitate his grandfather. The doubleness of this structure can be elucidated with the help of René Girard's reading of the Oedipus complex in *Violence and the Sacred.*

Girard looks at Freud's writings on the Ocdipus complex through the prism of his theory of triangular desire. Girard argues that desire is never the spontaneous movement of a subject towards an object. Instead, desire is always borrowed desire. The subject, according to Girard, does not "choose the objects of his own desire" (*Deceit*). Desire is instilled in the subject by a model or mediator, a third person to whom the subject attributes a desire for a certain object. The subject will begin to desire this same object only because of the "illusory value" (*Deceit*) conferred upon the object by the rival's desire. The subject's desire, in other words, is mimetic rather than autonomous. In *Violence and the Sacred,* Girard argues that the mimetic structure of desire can give us a better understanding of the Oedipus complex. Picking up on Freud's notion that the male child seeks identification with his father, Girard concludes that this must mean that the son will "desire what the father desires" (*Violence*). Principal among these objects of desire, of course, will be the child's mother.

In the scene in **"El día de las madres"** where Plutarco contemplates, in a state of sexual excitation, the photograph of his mother, there is no sense that Plutarco's desire is modelled on his father's desire. However, there is another passage where the structure of rivalry to which Girard grants so much importance is vividly present. Plutarco deplores the impoverished quality of his sex life, and compares it to his father's: "yo no pasaba de irme de putas los sábados, solo, sin cuates. Quería ligarme a una señora de a deveras, madura, como la amante de mi papá, no a niñas bien que conocía en fiestas de otros riquillos como nosotros." It is clear that Plutarco wants a mature woman only because of his father's prior desire for such a woman.

The more important father-figure in **"El día de las madres,"** however, is the General. Girard points out that the child's relationship of his father results in a "mimetic double bind" (*Violence*). On the one hand, when the son conceives a desire for the mother he "is simply responding in all candor to a command issued by the culture in which he lives and by the model himself" (*Violence*), that is, the command to imitate his father. On the other hand, when the two desires, the father's and the son's, converge on the same object, the

stage is set for a terrible conflict. This results in an injunction that contradicts the first one; now the command is *not* to imitate. This notion of the double bind is clearly applicable to the relationship between Plutarco and his grandfather. Here, too, the two commands, to imitate and not to imitate, are spoken simultaneously. Conversely, the two desires, to be like his grandfather, and not to be like his grandfather, surge up side by side in Plutarco. What remains to be seen is how the women in **"El día de las madres"** are drawn into this scenario. The story reaches its climax in the nighttime scene in which the General and Plutarco visit various nightspots in the city and end up in a brothel. In the midst of the drunken revelry, the General cannot stop talking about his military exploits. The entire scene becomes a mock replay of the battles of the Revolution. The General calls the mariachis he has hired for the night his troops, and when he gets into a fight in a nightclub he orders the piano's guts ripped out "como a los caballos de Celaya." But the General must finally face the unheroic nature of the present when he fails in bed with the prostitute Judith. When Plutarco takes over from his grandfather and has sex with Judith, we can see this as an act of revenge both on Judith (who is blamed for the General's grandson) and on the General (for having tried to figuratively castrate his grandson). The General watches sadly "como si mirara la vida renacer y ya no fuera la suya." Plutarco takes the place of his grandfather, and takes possession of his own life. In the next few pages of the story, Plutarco's suddenly more mature and reflective voice takes center stage. The General falls asleep as Plutarco drives him home; when they arrive Plutarco must carry his grandfather into the house, "como a un niño." The order of the generations has been reversed. But if Plutarco feels sad in spite of what he feels is a victory over his grandfather, it is because the double bind described by Girard continues to haunt him. The son's appropriation of the father's desire entails the destruction of the latter, but this immediately leads to the cessation of the son's desire which cannot exist without the father's mediation. Plutarco wants to take the place of his grandfather, but he cannot do so without destroying his grandfather and thus nullifying his own project of imitation.

The women in this model are turned into a medium for the expression of inter-male rivalry. This is true for Judith, but even truer for Evangelina, Plutarco's mother. Plutarco's father and grandfather conspire to murder Evangelina. What did she do to deserve this? In essence, her sin was that she was not her mother-in-law. Clotilde, the General's wife, was war booty. Evangelina, by contrast, chose her husband. She actively desired him, where Clotilde passively accepted her fate. But as Becky Boling points out, Evangelina's challenge to "the patriarchy's exclusive right to power or desire" makes her a "pariah" for General Vergara. Her death reaffirms the patriarch's authority and restores the bond between the men of the Vergara family. René Girard speaks in *Violence and the Sacred* of a society's need to find a scapegoat onto whom to deflect intra-communal violence. The sacrificial process allows a community to establish the sense of unanimity it needs to sustain itself as a harmonious entity. This process is reflected in **"El día de las madres."**

The victimization of the women allows the men to fortify their sense of connectedness. But Girard believes that the sacrificial process is at the origin of human culture, that it is a way of finding a socially acceptable outlet for humanity's violent instincts. In Fuentes's story, on the other hand, there is nothing acceptable about the violence of the Vergara men. Instead of a community, Fuentes depicts a parody of a community. In this way, he questions the entire nationalist project in Mexico.

Perry Anderson has argued [in "Nation-States and National Identity," *London Review of Books,* May 9, 1991, pp. 3, 5-7] that the repudiation of the notion of national character in Europe in the early part of this century was a side-effect of the assault on the notion of individual character. Both literary Modernism with its "wide-spread rejection of any stable ego" and psychoanalysis with its weakening of "traditional assumptions of individual character as moral unity" contributed to this development. It is striking, in light of Perry Anderson's observations, to note the enduring link that exists in Mexico between psychoanalysis and the discourse on national character. Samuel Ramos based his analysis of the Mexican character in *Pérfil del hombre y la cultura en México* (1934) on Alfred Adler's notion of the inferiority complex. Octavio Paz rejected Ramos's interpretation in *El laberinto de la soledad* (1950), arguing that "más vasta y profunda que el sentimiento de inferioridad, yace la soledad." But Paz continued to rely on a psychoanalytic model for his reading of the national character, for in the key chapter of *El laberinto,* "Los hijos de la Malinche," where he finds the sources for the present-day Mexican's identify in the period of the Conquest, Paz offers what is essentially a rewriting of Freud's parricide-incest theme to fit Mexican history: "lo característico del mexicana reside . . . en la violenta, sarcística humillación de la Madre y en la no menos violenta afirmación del Padre."

The reliance on psychoanalysis implies that there is a pathological element in the national character. [In *América Latina en busca de una identidad: modelos del ensayo ideológico hispanoamericano 1890-1960,* Monte Avilar, 1969] Martin Stabb has drawn attention to the frequency with which the essayistic tradition in Latin America projects the image of the intellectual as a doctor whose task it is to cure the nation of its illnesses. There is a specifically psychoanalytic version of this motif in which the intellectual appears in the guise of the mental therapist. Again, Paz offers a good illustration of this motif: in *Posdata* (1970) he calls explicitly for "la crífica de México y de su historia—una crítica que se asemeja a la terapéutica de los psicoanalistas" (134). It is a call Paz answers in the very text in which he makes it, for the aim of *Posdata* is to trace Mexico's current pathologies—which have erupted most dramatically in the 1968 Tlatelolco massacre—to the nation's Aztec past, in a hermeneutic maneuver that is parallel in structure to psychoanalysis. In excavating the nation's history Paz performs the same operation as the therapist who brings to light the patient's unconscious. In Paz's model of the Mexican character, the Aztec period comes to occupy the same position as the unconscious in the psychoanalytic model. And his concept of criticism is analogous to the idea of the talking cure in psychoanalysis. In bringing the past to light, Paz hopes to dispel its noxious effects on the present. The only difficulty, perhaps, in making the translation between psychoanalysis and Paz's concept of the critic's task is the question of where the locate Paz himself, for Paz is both the doctor prescribing a cure, and, as the intellectual who engages in acts of criticism, the patient who does the talking.

Roger Bartra [in *La jaula de la melancolía: Identidad y metamorfosis del mexicano,* Grijalbo, 1987] describes Mexico as a "paraíso para las expediciones psicoanalíticas." But he believes these expeditions serve a very specific purpose: if the act of defining the nation in Mexico has generally meant trashing the nation, the point of the exercise according to Bartra has been to facilitate the ruling the nation. The producers of the discourse on the Mexican national character describe the masses only in order to dominate them all the more effectively. In an argument that is clearly indebted to Michel Foucault, Bartra claims that the essayistic tradition in Mexico identifies a "*sujeto* de la historia nacional" in order to make it easier to keep the Mexican "*sujetado* a una forma peculiar de dominación" (emphasis mine). The uncovering of specifically Mexican character traits serves to justify the existence of an authoritarian political system that is presumed to *fit* the peculiarities of the Mexican character.

To some extent, Fuentes follows in the footsteps of Ramos and Paz. **"El día de las madres"** is a good example of what Bartra calls a psychoanalytic expedition into Mexican society. But what conclusions should we draw from this? Does Fuentes denigrate the Mexican character so as to exalt himself? Does he fix the Mexican national identify in order to make it easier to subject the Mexican people to a project of political control? In the first place I would like to use Perry Anderson to refute Bartra: the psychoanalytic approach, as Anderson points out, destabilizes rather than stabilizes the notion of national character. The national character becomes both changeable, and in need of change. "El día de las madres" offers an even more radical vision: the entire nationalist myth is presented as a pathological fiction. My second point is that *Agua quemada* should not be viewed in isolation. It has to be set in the context of Fuentes' entire *ocuvre.* And as I pointed out earlier, there is a celebratory as a well as a deconstructive vision of Mexico in Fuentes' work. In *The Buried Mirror,* the text that accompanied the TV documentary Fuentes made to mark the quincentenary of Columbus's voyage to the New World, Fuentes describes the Mexican Revolution as an eroticized act of national self-recognition:

> A country in which the geographical barriers of mountains, deserts, ravines, and sheer distances had separated one group of people from another now came together, as the tremendous cavalcades of Villa's men and women from the north rushed to meet Zapata's men and women from the south. In their revolutionary embrace, Mexicans finally learned how other Mexicans talked, sang, ate, and drank, dreamed and made love, cried and fought.

This kind of celebration of the nation's cultural distinctiveness breaks out of the confines of the model sketched by Bartra. Bartra sees only *desprecio* in Mexicanist discourse. Fuentes mixes denigration with boosterism. To account for these contradictions we must see that Fuentes is the inheritor of two separate traditions. On the one hand, he has nourished himself on the skeptical, subversive tradition of modern literature. On the other hand, he has absorbed the traditional Latin American intellectual's sense of responsibility towards the community. The collision of these two paradigms is responsible for the curiously fractured quality of much of Fuentes's work. And it is this quality that helps us see that Mexicanist discourse need not be as monolithic as it appears in Bartra's account. The same writer can imagine a community, and unimagine it as well.

Merle Rubin (review date 20 April 1994)

SOURCE: "Fuentes's New/Old World Mirror," in *Christian Science Monitor,* April 20, 1994, p. 17.

[*In the following review, Rubin offers synopses of the novellas collected in* The Orange Tree.]

In the midst of his long literary career, Carlos Fuentes, Mexico's most famous living writer, also served as his country's ambassador to France from 1975 to 1977. The author of *Terra Nostra, Distant Relations, The Death of Artemio Cruz,* and much more, Fuentes has pondered the urgent questions of social justice and the underlying complexities of the interrelationships among different cultures.

The Orange Tree, his latest work, consists of five novellas, artfully arranged to serve as distant mirrors of one another. Each has its own distinct historical setting. Each involves a

moment when two cultures meet, clash, or embrace. Beginning with *The Two Shores,* Fuentes examines the convergence of the Old World and the New—here, seen through the eyes of Jeronimo de Aguilar, translator to the conquistador Hernan Cortes. Aguilar speaks from the sublime perspective of the far side of the grave. He has witnessed the horrors of conquest, the murder and enslavement of the Indians; he has also witnessed the violent and ignominious fates that overtook many of the conquistadores. Aguilar's own role as translator has involved treachery, but his aim of rousing the Indians to repel their invaders has backfired. Now, beyond death, he dreams of an Indian conquest of Spain, in which ecologically minded Aztecs and Mayans turn the tables on the Spanish Inquisition, construct an interfaith temple "inscribed with the word of Christ, Mohammed, Abraham, and Quetzalcoatl," revoke the expulsion of the Moors and Jews, and inaugurate a blending of cultures where Mayan songs mingle with calls of muezzins and lays of Provencal troubadours.

Sons of the Conquistador, the second novella, is narrated by two of Cortes's sons. Martin 2 is the child of an Indian mother, Martin 1 of a Spanish mother. The Indian son upbraids his Spanish brother for failing to liberate the beautiful land of Mexico from the iron hand of Spanish rule. The Spanish son declines a struggle that would cost him his luxurious lifestyle. The impasse leads to despair.

The third novella, *The Two Numantias,* is set in the 2nd century BC. For more than a century, Rome and Carthage have been at war, and the backward, formerly isolated peninsula of Spain has become one of the main battlegrounds. Even after defeating Carthage, the Romans are still "bogged down" in Spain, fighting guerrillas and refusing to withdraw out of stubborn pride. It falls to Scipio Aemilianus, adoptive grandson of the general who defeated Hannibal, to quell the Spanish rebellion by crushing the defiant city of Numantia.

In Roman eyes, the Spaniards are a savage lot, who need to be led, like it or not, toward Roman civilization. In the eyes of the Greek humanist and historian Polybius, Scipio's friend and mentor, it's the Romans who are in need of Greek civilization. Young Scipio is a divided man, eager to embrace the spiritual legacy of Greek culture but determined to carry on the Roman tradition of military conquest. He dreams of founding a great school, but his fame comes from his merciless destruction of a city.

In some ways, the most interesting of the five novellas, *The Two Numantias,* concludes with a voice admonishing the hero to listen beyond the clamor of fame to the celestial music of the spheres. Individual renown is nothing, it declares, the individual's ability to feel, think, create, remember, use language, and exercise self control are what link him to his creator.

It's a long way from Numantia to Acapulco in the 1990s, the setting of the fourth novella, *Apollo and the Whores,* but once again, themes reverberate. Vince Valera, a handsome "black Irishman" (quite possibly a descendent of the Celtiberians defeated in Numantia) is a Hollywood film star vacationing in the resort town. He invites several local girls on his chartered boat, where they take part in an orgy that inadvertently finishes him off.

Viewing them—and continuing to narrate his own story—from the perspective of death, Valera is able to see them as individuals and to meditate on the contrast between two worlds: his own overprotected life of individual fame and glory, and the Mexican world of suffering, undifferentiated, and unprotected humanity. The final novella, *The Two Americas* (which is also the name of the boat chartered by Valera in the previous story), imagines a Columbus who decides not to reveal the secret of a New World to those who would despoil it. This Columbus is a Sephardic Jew, whose family was forced to flee Spain. He has also witnessed the cruelties of the slave trade. In the New World, he finds a living example of the fabled Golden Age, an unfallen Eden he is determined to preserve.

The Indians, luckily, believe him to be the legendary white-bearded god sent to check up on how well they have fulfilled their task of caring for the earth. But Columbus cannot save "paradise" forever: At the story's close, a Japanese conglomerate is planning to turn the place into a tourist resort—a parody of paradise.

The many visible and hidden leitmotifs—parallels, contrasts, foreshadings, and aftereffects—that interlink these five novellas would furnish enough material for several scholarly monographs: Mirrors, masks, and the notion of a double all play a recurrent role. There are meditations on the role of language, which, unlike military power, grows by absorbing, not destroying, alien influences.

All five novellas address the contrast between the round, fertile "earth," enduring and bounteous, and the human-imposed "world" that threatens to despoil it. And each novella contains an orange tree, a kind of tree of life brought from the Orient to Arabia to Rome to Spain, flourishing still more brightly transplanted in the New World.

Amid chronicles of inhumanity and exploitation, the orange tree symbolizes the promise of the earth's renewal, the hope for a more respectful relationship between mankind and nature, and the omnipresent possibility of cultural intersections that will result in fruitful cross-pollination instead of crass destruction.

Michael Kerrigan (review date 10 June 1994)

SOURCE: "In Realms of Gold," in *Times Literary Supplement,* No. 4758, June 10, 1994, p. 23.

[*In the following review, Kerrigan offers a favorable assessment of* The Orange Tree.]

Carlos Fuentes established his international reputation over three decades ago, with *The Death of Artemio Cruz* (1962). That novel goes in search of the identity of a protagonist who is modern down to his Volvo, and Mexican down to the parasites in his gut, but the quest ends up taking in a past of conquest and revolution, and looks far beyond Cruz's native Veracruz to the shores of the Mediterranean. Like the stars Cruz sees overhead—"only the ghost of the light that began its journey countless years ago, countless centuries"—the past informs the present. Its churches the reconsecrated shrines of Indian deities and its public buildings based on Spanish models, modern-day Mexico is unthinkable without this past.

Not that history is necessarily glorious or even dignified, nor can it be relied on for comfort or support. The grotesque story of Queen Joanna of Spain stands as both example and fable: allowed sole possession of her philandering husband only by his death, she roamed the land with his cadaver, wandering dementedly from monastery to monastery, shunning convents in her terror that even in death he might prove unfaithful. Faced with the prospect of lugging such an uncomfortable history about with them, many in Latin America and Spain have sought to deny the past. Fuentes, however, has always urged them to acknowledge and embrace it, to carry the corpse, however unappealing. The imaginative task he has pursued in an extensive and inclusive corpus of fictional work has been the exploration of what he sees as a distinctive Hispanic condition. Rummaging through the historical archives of Spain and Spanish America, leafing' through its literature, poring over old masters, Fuentes has sought to re-animate history and reveal the Hispanic world to itself. It is a paradoxical world in which time plays tricks, in whose present the past everywhere comes blazing through. It is a world whose America contains its Europe and its Europe America. Its articulation has required innovative, often difficult forms-most controversially the fathomless epic of allusion Fuentes invented in *Terra Nostra* (1975), for some critics a glorious El Dorado of Hispanic culture and life, for others a vast Escorial of barren academicism.

A novel in five novellas, *The Orange Tree* is a more manageable work altogether, and it provides the English-speaking reader with an excellent introduction to these realms of gold. Stout Cortés stands at the centre of the first story, a savage personification of the European will to conquest. There is more to him than rapacity and lust, however, and less force to his will than he himself could have imagined. These are important themes in a book which finds in history a cycle of conquest and resistance which changes conqueror as much as conquered. The orange tree provides a recurrent emblem for this process. Its name derived from the Arabic *narandj,* the orange was native to the East. Its delicious, fragrant fruit, round and red as the sun or a gold coin, was brought back as booty by Syria's Roman invaders. When they set out to conquer the wild Celtiberians, the orange went with them. In the fullness of time, conquered became conquistadors, and the tree completed its westward journey. It ran wild in America, and its fruit acquired a different, more bitter taste. Taking five years to reach fruition, it could symbolize patient endurance; sleeping and gaining strength in winter, it drew life from death.

The first narrator in **The Orange Tree** speaks from his tomb, having just died of plague, but that is logical enough, once you accept the cyclical view of time at work. Death is where all the ladders start; for the Aztecs, it was the only guarantee of continuing life, the darkness that executes the sun and clears the way for a new dawn; for Fuentes, it is the path to understanding and the obvious place to begin. It is, none the less, strange to read a story which moves from experience into innocence. Cortés's interpreter, Jerónimo de Aguilar, is a wilfully unreliable narrator, telling his tale backwards, a caprice which cannot, however, make up for the authorial power he has lost. For a brief moment the only man capable of representing one world to another, he has fancied himself holding history in his hands and shaping events. Mistranslating Cortés's self-serving blandishments as the dire threats they concealed, Jerónimo offered Moctezuma the chance to avert catastrophe, to see the true nature of the brigand he was welcoming as a god. But the Aztec refused to see; his ancient fatalism was unready to comprehend a man like Cortés, a European who never doubted his freedom to fashion his own destiny.

Yet was Moctezuma really so mistaken? asks Fuentes. Did Cortés really make history, or did history make him? A strikingly unreflecting man in this tale, Cortés acquires an appreciable psychological and moral dimension only in the second, in which his two sons tell his story after his death. "Is reality only the sum total of physical events?", the Roman general Scipio wonders, in **The Two Numantias,** the third story here: "Are mental events only and always consequences of those material acts? Do we fool ourselves by thinking that it's the other way round . . . ?" The Cortés who emerges in his sons' accounts is an unexpectedly tragic figure, his relationship with the land he conquered intimate, compelling and finally self-destructive. Mexico changed him, though that change is plainly registered only in his children. Both named Martín, one is legitimate and white, with all the sense, pride and entitlement that entails, and the other illegitimate, born to Cortés's Indian mistress and hence the first

mestizo. Together they are the first modern Mexicans, and the first to revolt as Mexicans against Spanish rule.

Hard as they have striven to overturn his work, the Martíns represent part of their father's story, what he was and what he accomplished. Rather than asking what posterity has done for us, we have to see, implies Fuentes, that it is only in time and in other people that we are created at all. The notion of sacrifice is crucial to Fuentes as it was to the Aztecs, though it can take many different forms. There are the innumerable roads not taken: "What would have happened if what did happen didn't?" asks Jerómino, "What would have happened if what did not happen did?" There are the thousands who must live in poverty so that Artemio Cruz can have his wealth and power, their anonymity the price of his ego; there are the men who, in **Terra Nostra,** spend their lives building a royal mausoleum. And there are the warriors of Numantia who kill themselves so that their women and children can eat their flesh. We are part of a cycle of death and rebirth, Fuentes suggests; the idea that we exist as individuals is a problematical one.

The discovery of the New World shattered Spain's sense of itself, overturning all assumptions, and complicating everything with the revelation that things could be quite otherwise. To a nation which had laboured long and hard to establish a single, "Spanish" culture, purified of every trace of Moor and Jew, which offered sacrifices in the shape of heretics to the honour of One Holy, Catholic and Apostolic Church, the discovery of a second world came as a profound shock, especially when this world was so full of strange peoples, plants, animals and other "things not mentioned in the Bible". However unsettling that shock, the Spaniards hurled themselves into the task of possessing this world as if their lives depended on it; as if, indeed, something vital to life had been lost with the denial of multiplicity at home, something which now had to be sought abroad. This common project would do more than anything else to unite the rival kingdoms of Iberia into a single Spain.

In our own time—time measured out to the minute by a digital watch—an Irish actor, Vicente Valera, the protagonist in **The Orange Tree**'s fourth tale, dies during a visit to Acapulco. As he looks at the whores he has gathered around him, he feels, for the first time, how artificial and provisional is the person he has been:

> In all of their eyes, I saw a time which disregarded my individuality. Above all, I saw those Mexican children and felt afraid of escaping from my own more or less protected individuality, constructed with a certain care and lots of patience so I could face a helpless humanity in which circumstances neither respect nor distinguish anyone.

I realized what had happened. In death, I had become a Mexican.

Once more, however, the American dimension offers the European gain as well as loss. Poor and powerless as he may be, buffeted as he is by a violent, uncomfortable history which affords him no individual recognition, the Mexican has a share in a collective immortality. As Jerónimo puts it, "the greatness of power fell; the small lives of the people survived". The challenge and the opportunity *The Orange Tree* presents its reader are those of escaping from "a more or less protected individuality" into a wider existence of multiple possibility and a cyclical history which holds past and present in simultaneity and in ceaseless renewal. It is difficult to maintain negative capability faced with so many alternative possibilities; the temptation is always to reach for synthesis; reading such a history it is hard to resist trying to square the circle. But the rewards are immense: each of its five short novellas reflecting and refracting the last, *The Orange Tree* contrives to project—if only in image in hints and suggestions—the story of a world. The most important stories, the novel implies, are the interminable annals of the poor. What strikes the reader first in Fuentes's work may be his erudition and intellectual rigour, but what remains in the mind is his sympathy, his concern to commemorate the countless lives sacrificed in pain and obscurity so that we might live.

Kenneth E. Hall (essay date Spring 1995)

SOURCE: "*The Old Gringo* and the Elegiac Western," in *University of Dayton Review*, Vol. 23, No. 2, Spring, 1995, pp. 137-47.

[*In the following essay, Hall examines Fuentes's handling of the female perspective in* The Old Gringo *and illustrates parallels between the novel and "elegiac Western" films "which are characterized by a quality of lament for the passing of the hero, and by extension, of the heroic age of the American West."*]

The opening of *The Old Gringo* (1985), by Carlos Fuentes, sets in place the chief organizing principle of the novel, the narrated memories of Harriet Winslow, an unmarried schoolteacher from Washington, D.C., who, the reader discovers, once came to Mexico to instruct the children of the rich *hacendado* Miranda family and there became embroiled in the Revolution. Her contacts with the *uillista* general Tomas Arroyo and the Old Gringo polarize her experiences between an apparent infatuation with Arroyo and an attempt to substitute the Gringo for her lost father. In her memories of the incidents which led her to place the body of the Old Gringo in her father's empty tomb in Arlington, an elegiac tone—

one of mourning for lost experience as well as a questioning of the value of that experience—is clearly discernible. Like the heroine of a classic Western film such as *The Virginian* (1929), Harriet, as the "Eastern schoolmarm" character type, confronts the heroic Westerner, in this case "doubled" into the figures of the Old Gringo and Arroyo, and in the process re-examines her own preconceptions about civilization. She becomes conscious of her marginalization from the society around her, as an intellectual woman who questions her past and present. One concern of the discussion here will be the importance of the female perspective in the elegiac Western narrative: rather than a mere foil or pretext for the hero's actions, the female character serves a critical function in clarifying the degree and nature of the hero's loss of relevance in present-day society. The heroic figures themselves, the Old Gringo and Arroyo, can lay strong claim to kinship to the heroes (and villains) of Western film and fiction. Equally larger-than-life and ironically viewed, the Old Gringo has the superhuman marksmanship and courage of classic Western heroes such as the Ethan Edwards of John Wayne or the Shane of Alan Ladd. But he carries about him a cynicism and world-weariness which, though mirroring his real-life source in Ambrose Bierce, yet recall the elegiac musings of the aging gunfighters J. B. Books of *The Shootist*, Steven Judd of *Ride the High Country*, and Pike Bishop of *The Wild Bunch*.

The term "elegiac Westerns" has been applied by popular culture and film critics such as Michael Marsden and John Cawelti to Western films which are characterized by a quality of lament for the passing of the hero, and by extension, of the heroic age of the American West. These Westerns share the central element of a frequently poetic treatment, anywhere on a scale from ironic to tragic, of the myths and heroes of the Old West as cultural icons whose time has passed, usually with some indication of the influence of technology on their passing. They share the quality of nostalgia found in the literary Western as typified by Zane Grey and Owen Wister. The motif of the gunfighter cognizant that "his days are over," as the titular hero of *Shane* is told, is frequent, as is the tendency for many of the heroes of these films to be aging. The element of the now vulnerable hero, an erstwhile near-superman with a six-shooter, may be tragic, as in *Ride the High Country* or *The Man Who Shot Liberty Valance,* or it may be savagely, even morbidly ironic, as in *The Wild Bunch.* But in all cases, the once invincible hero of dime-novel Westerns has become a complex representation of a member of an age which has passed and whose violent solution to once simple situations has now become either outmoded, as in *The Man Who Shot Liberty Valance,* or merely criminal, as in *The Wild Bunch:* Pike and Bishop could at an earlier stage of their development (or decline) have been Stephen Judd and his friend Gil.

Much as the aging, sick, and outdated hero of *The Shootist*

(1976), played with understated sensitivity and power by John Wayne, wishes to die with self-respect, so too does the Old Gringo wish to die in a moment and manner chosen by him. Both characters shun their reputations. The Old Gringo avoids mentioning his name or revealing significant autobiographical data, such as his association with William Randolph Hearst, to anyone but Harriet. Similarly, Books, the aging shootist, is reluctant, at least at first, for the truth about his identity to get around the small town to which he has come, as he does not wish to give fame-hungry guns a chance to prove themselves. He even forces a Ned Buntline-like newspaperman to leave his boarding house at gunpoint after hearing his publicity scheme.

Important to *The Shootist* is the discrepancy between the myths or legends which have formed around Books and in general around the figure of the gunfighter, as opposed to the historical reality of such figures as well as, in this case, the personal biographical facts about J. B. Books. In *The Old Gringo,* a similar conflict between historical fact, legend, and falsification of history is established, since the character of the Gringo is based on the historical figure Ambrose Bierce: their "biographies." as Joaquin Roy has shown, tend to intersect in several ways, the chief of which is their journey to Mexico with the intention of dying or disappearing.

The picture given of Books and of the Gringo is well-removed from "history." The Fuentes narrative, filtered through the recollections of Winslow, presents a picture of the Gringo, who only slowly comes to be revealed as Ambrose Bierce; his anonymity is maintained during the earlier part of the novel. until he begins to reveal himself to Harriet. The Gringo character, presented in legendary proportions (as in the battle scenes or the early incident of heroic "proof," in which the Gringo demonstrates his marksmanship), is in part derived from legends about Bierce, especially the tale about his disappearance in Mexico. As Joe Nickell has suggested in his "Biography: The Disappearance of Ambrose Bierce" [*Literary Investigation: Texts, Sources, and "Factual" Substructs of Literature and Interpretation,* UMI Press, 1987] this tale may have been fabricated by Bierce to cover his withdrawal from society, perhaps to live in Colorado until his expected death, probably from suicide. In any case, the Gringo, or Bierce, becomes as much a part of Winslow's perspectivist recollections as does the portrait of the Mexican Revolution which emerges from such mythmaking works as *Vámonas con Pancho Villa!* [*Let's Go with Pancho Villa!*] (1949), by Rafael Luis Muñoz.

Similarly, J. B. Books is placed into parallel in an interesting manner with the filmic image, that is, the mythic or fictionalized image, of John Wayne. The film opens with clips from some of Wayne's earlier movies, all showing him in heroic or dynamic sequences. Here the effect is not, as Marsden and Nachbar have stated [in "The Modern Popular Western: Radio, Television, Film and Print," in *A Literary History of The American West,* Texas Christian University Press, 1987], to "suggest [ ] that Books and Wayne are identical," but rather on the one hand (1) to show the character of Books as derived from a corpus of myth; (2) to imply that the public image of Books as heroic may be as much of a fiction as was the image of Wayne as a frontier hero; and (3) to emphasize the elegiac core of the film, since the clips lead us to remember the past deeds of Books.

The Shootist in effect critiques the gunfighter persona, since Books, though indeed a man of singular prowess and integrity, does not himself romanticize his actions. Nor does he retreat into mysterious statements about his past as does Shane or Jules Gaspard (Yul Brynner), the gunfighter of *Invitation to a Gunfighter* (1964). To the contrary, Books (whose name indicates his fictive nature) is quite hard-nosed about the reasons for his actions; he says clearly that he only tried to defend his interests: "'I won't be wronged, I won't be insulted, and I won't be laid a hand on. I don't do these things to other people, and I require the same from them.'" He also pointedly debunks the legendary Bat Masterson, with whom he is, nevertheless, implicitly associated in the Western myth: "'But then, Bat Masterson always was full'a— sheep-dip.'"

As does Books, the Gringo remains marginalized, largely by choice. Despite his attempts to kindle an impossible romance with Harriet—who sees him as a surrogate father—he remains an observer, almost voyeuristically watching Harriet's affair with Arroyo. The gunfighter of the Shane-Books type, which is traceable to the wandering archetype of Wild Bill Hickok and earlier of Davy Crockett and Leatherstocking [see Rita Parks, *The Western Hero in Film and Television: Mass Media Mythology,* UMI Research Press, 1982] is typically either unaccepted into society or incapable of relating to it, whether because of its civilized values or, as in the case of the mulatto Jules Gaspard, because of some deep resentment from a childhood perceived as socially unjust. The Gringo is rather like Gaspard in his chosen marginalization; his cynicism seems defensive, since he really suffers greatly—as did the historical Bierce—from the loss of his family. The "outsider" status of the Gringo, like that of the Western hero, is both adopted by and imposed upon him; like Ethan Edwards in *The Searchers* (John Ford, 1956), the Gringo helps to heal the wounds of family loss (Harriet "finds" a father to put in her father's empty tomb. Martin rediscovers himself and his cousin Debbie with the help of Edwards) but cannot share in it. Edwards leaves the community, in a famous shot in which the door of the adoptive family of Martin frames his exiting figure, made vulnerable by Wayne's clutching his elbows as if chilled or crippled. The Gringo is the sacrificial catalyst of Harriet's resolution of her fixational conflict about her own father.

The sense of loss and marginalization felt by the Old Gringo is mirrored in Harriet Winslow, who has never, at least until the unfolding of the narrative here, become reconciled with her father's abandonment of her and her rather domineering mother and has in fact collaborated or acquiesced in fictionalizing the desertion into a heroic death for her father at San Juan Hill. Harriet, like the Gringo, and like Ned Buntline or any other popularizer of the Western hero, is engaged in "mythmaking," that is, lying and the falsification of history.

Or perhaps, one might say, in rationalization, since Harriet would rather eschew mention of her fixated concentration on her father, an undeserving object of such attention. The Electra motif here is similar to the less clearly expressed, but nonetheless central complex dramatized in *True Grit,* novel and film (1969), in which Mattie Ross (Kim Darby), a stubborn adolescent girl, enlists an aging marshal. Rooster Cogburn (John Wayne), to help her bring to justice the murderer of her father. She is inordinately determined to punish the killer, driving Rooster and a Texas Ranger who accompanies them sometimes to exasperation. One of the more interesting aspects of *True Grit,* clearer in the Charles Portis novel than in the more emotionally diffuse Henry Hathaway film, is the gradual transference of Mattie's affection from her father—who soon drops into the background of the narrative, becoming only a motivating plot element—to Rooster, whose "cussedness," at first repellent to the arch Mattie, gradually becomes endearing to her. Harriet Winslow, on the other hand, does not see the Old Gringo as repellent so much as she recoils from his cynicism; nevertheless, as does Mattie with Cogburn, she becomes fascinated with the Gringo and literally supplants her father with him. An interesting sidelight on *The Old Gringo* and *True Grit* is their narrative technique, as both are told in flashback (on much differing levels of sophistication, however) by their female protagonists.

The female perspective is often quite important to the elegiac Western. Just as Mattie criticizes and ironizes the action around her (especially in the novel), so Marian (Jean Arthur) in *Shane* provides a reasonable perspective on the rivalry between ranchers and homesteaders. It is she who perceives the truth about Shane's vulnerability and about his incapability of fitting into present-day society and who points up the absurdity of the hard-driving male solutions to range problems. Similarly, in *High Noon* (Fred Zinnemann, 1952) Amy (Grace Kelly) acts as a balance to her husband's sense of perhaps misplaced duty by questioning the morality of violence as a solution. Such female characters are not merely stereotypical "voices of civilization" who try to restrain male depredations: more than this, they serve as surrogates for a critical perspective on the essential absurdity of the hero myth. Thus, Laurie (Vera Miles), in *The Searchers,* generally treats Edwards and Pauley in a rather indulgent man-

ner, as if they were irresponsible adolescents who refuse to let the past alone and who thus jeopardize their present.

> *The Old Gringo* and *The Wild Bunch* are . . . quite parallel in several respects, not the least of which is their setting in the Revolutionary period of Mexico. Both the novel by Fuentes and the film by Peckinpah employ imagery to convey the cruelty of the Revolutionary process and the out-of-place quality of heroism in such an environment.
> —*Kenneth E. Hall*

The presence of the past is of course at the center of the elegiac Western. Much as Mattie recalls an earlier part of her life in which she knew a heroic figure, the boy in *Shane,* Joey Starrett (Brandon DeWilde), remembers not only the heroic Shane but the passing of the heroic age with the coming of civilization: and Hallie Stoddard (Vera Miles) in *The Man Who Shot Liberty Valance* remembers, through the symbol of the cactus rose, both the heroism of the dead Tom Doniphon (John Wayne) and the falseness of the legend built around her husband Ranse (James Stewart), now a United States Senator. So too *The Wild Bunch* shows characters who remember a complex past, one which is shown not to be heroic but rather filled with compromises, betrayals, and errors (as in Pike Bishop's desertion of Deke Thornton). Similarly, the Old Gringo regrets his errors as a father and his work as a journalist and author—this is shown more explicitly in the Puenzo film, when he theatrically drops his collected works on the floor during a speech in Washington—but does retain positive memories of his military service as a mapmaker in the U.S. Civil War. Part of his motivation for going to Mexico is to create for himself an inverse heroic image, that is, to serve on the side of a rebellion instead of against it, as he had when fighting for the Union.

The Old Gringo and *The Wild Bunch* are in fact quite parallel in several respects, not the least of which is their setting in the Revolutionary period of Mexico. Both the novel by Fuentes and the film by Peckinpah employ imagery to convey the cruelty of the Revolutionary process and the out-of-place quality of heroism in such an environment. A noteworthy example is the scene in the novel in which the Federal colonel is executed by Arroyo while the wild pigs snuffle at corpses from the recent battle; similarly, Peckinpah shows vultures—in close-up—ready for the battle which will close the film with the deaths of the Bunch. The physical quality of the desert is clearly conveyed in both media, in Fuentes' case with a cinematic technique which places elements of the general desert experience on a parallel level by means of sequential shots:

> Sand mounts the mesquite. The horizon shimmers and rises before the eyes. Implacable shadows of clouds clothe the earth in dotted veils. Earth smells fill the air. A rainbow spills into a mirror of itself. Thickets of snakeweed blaze in clustered yellow blooms. Everything is blasted by an alkaline wind.

The novel is in such instances not far from a filmscript: is the previous passage a description of terrain or setting, or is it an indication for a prospective director for the desired *mise-en-scène*? For his part, Peckinpah uses a highly effective "flatness of perspective" to convey a similar unromanticized feel [Paul Seydor, *Peckinpah: The Western Films*, University of Illinois Press, 1980].

Both *The Wild Bunch* and **The Old Gringo** feature heroes who also provoke their own deaths, as if admitting the truth of the proposition that their age is past. Pike Bishop, in *The Wild Bunch*, leads his remaining men to a warrior's death in an attempt to redeem himself for his past desertions of comrades: the other members follow him not from nihilism but from loyalty and shared heroic values. The death of the Gringo is similarly a statement of values, though a negative one; by burning the papers proving Arroyo's title to the Miranda land, he tries to demonstrate the worthlessness of his own career as a writer and also to allow Arroyo to free himself from his own past by parricide. The Gringo, like Pike, dies shot in the back by a "son"—in the case of Pike, a boy who was the protegé of Mapache, the Huerta-like Federal general. Incidentally. Books, in *The Shootist*, also dies, shot in the back by a bartender whose motives are murky at best but who may have wanted the "glory" of killing a legend.

The importance attached to the death of the gunfighter or hero in the Westerns considered here causes their treatment to shade into ritual. The somber and haunting presence of Doniphon's plain coffin, the deromanticized but tragic "funeral" scene in *The Wild Bunch* (with the dead heroes borne off on the bounty hunters' horses [Seydor]); the pains taken by Mattie Ross in the novel *True Grit* to bury Rooster: and the maturely accepting attitude of Gillom (Ron Howard) in *The Shootist* toward the death of Books all exemplify the importance of such funerary set-pieces to the elegiac Western form.

One of the more striking parallels, in this respect, between **The Old Gringo** and the elegiac Western is the strangely ironic funeral procession of Jules Gaspard at the end of *Invitation to a Gunfighter*. Both the Gringo and Gaspard are voluntary outcasts from their own societies, maintaining cynical poses to hide their vulnerability and hurt idealism;

both have "gone West" in search of "freedom of choice" (Mexico serves in **The Old Gringo** as the new frontier, replacing the closing West); and both die as a result of their own provocative actions. Both also gain the affection and admiration of previously antagonistic constituencies— Winslow and the townspeople—and both are given ironically celebratory funerals. Gaspard is borne in heroic fashion on a makeshift bier carried by the now-grateful townspeople; the Gringo becomes the surrogate father for Harriet when he is buried in her own father's empty tomb. The Puenzo film accentuates the elegiac nature of the Gringo's reburial by showing his disinterment in Mexico in a misty light, placing him seemingly into an epic or tragic realm.

One should not make the error of seeing the elegiac elements in **The Old Gringo** as positively nostalgic (as, perhaps, one could see *Ride the High Country*); if nostalgia is an element here, its core of loss is emphasized. Or it is shown as nostalgia without basis, as in the fond stories propagated by Harriet about her father. As *The Man Who Shot Liberty Valance* reveals the lie behind the fame of Ranse Stoddard and calls into question as well the myth of the Western hero (who, as Robert Ray has noted [in *A Certain Tendency of the Hollywood Cinema, 1930-1980*, Princeton University Press, 1985], is shown to be the other side of the outlaw coin), so too **The Old Gringo** questions and criticizes the revolutionary past of Mexico—Frutos Garcia dies a comfortable, scarcely heroic death in his house in Mexico City in 1964—while still not sparing the Porfiriato. Arroyo's fantasy about the Indians' land title is deflated by the criticisms of the Gringo concerning the lack of worth of the written word and by the inability of Arroyo to read, and is finally exploded by the Gringo's burning of the papers. The legalistic appeal by Arroyo is shown to be just as fruitless, one might suggest, as has been the sad appeal to treaties by the wronged original inhabitants of North America. The heroic myths about the U.S. Civil War are questioned by references to the ironic stories of Bierce about that war, in which its "glory" is deflated. Thus, **The Old Gringo** demonstrates its affinity less to autumnal elegies like *Ride the High Country* or to pastoral hymns like *Shane* than to more corrosive and demystificatory critiques such as *The Wild Bunch Little Big Man* (1970), and, occupying a middle ground. *The Man Who Shot Liberty Valance*. Like Pike Bishop in *The Wild Bunch*, the Old Gringo wishes to emend his compromised past with heroic action—however futile—and as do Pike, Tom Doniphon, and J. B. Books, he dies an outsider, only finding an ironic re-integration into the community after his death."

Paul Theroux (review date 22 October 1995)

SOURCE: "An Affair She Seems Not to Have Remembered," in *New York Times Book Review,* October 22, 1995, p. 12.

[In the following review, Theroux responds negatively to Diana: The Goddess Who Hunts Alone.*]*

Sexual postures can look so funny and vulnerable that the very notion of the distinguished author of this inch-from-the-truth novel, Carlos Fuentes—the Mexican Ambassador to France from 1975 to 1977, winner of the Biblioteca Breve Prize, the Romulo Gallegos Prize and the Miguel de Cervantes Prize—engaged in buccal coition with an American actress in a hotel in Mexico City is irresistible to the point where it is almost possible to overlook the book's excesses and delusions. That ***Diana: The Goddess Who Hunts Alone*** also seems a seedy form of self-parody is one of the crueler wounds the author inflicts on himself, but this is a risk you run when you embark on autobiographical fiction. Another issue is the question of tone: are you boasting or complaining? Yet another is pomposity: "I began to be haunted by the idea that Diana was a work of art that had to be destroyed to be possessed." (Trust a philanderer to have a fancy prose style.) Last, there is the confessional mode, which, except in enormously talented hands, creates such embarrassment that the lesser writer is often on firmer ground telling blatant lies.

There do not seem to be any whoppers here, which is a pity. I wish this book had been more perverse. I quite like the idea of a faux roman a clef that is a key to nothing except greater enigma, that tells nothing, that conscientiously and artfully misleads the reader—an elaborate fiction that college kids might call post-modernist, yet that is probably a throwback to an earlier, yarn-spinning time. In such a novel the author would falsely disclose a ridiculous job, a successful disappearance, a shameful crime, then brazenly acknowledge a double life, and perhaps the seduction of an aristocrat, a confrontation with the supernatural. By moving freely from one life to another in a baffling fashion, the author would totally blur the line that separates reality and imagination, allowing the fiction to occupy some middle ground of post-modernist mendacity between *Tropic of Cancer* and *The Larry Sanders Show.*

But ***Diana*** is a tell-all roman a clef. Not a lot to tell, actually: the affair in question lasted less than two months. Much is obvious. Surely that panting figure on top is none other than Carlos Fuentes, and the diminutive person supine beneath him ("Diana Soren") is Jean Seberg; the photograph of last month's lover on the bedside table is unambiguously Clint Eastwood. From internal evidence—dates, places and so on—even the most casual filmographer gathers that we are on the set of a terrible 1970 movie called *Macho Callahan,* starring Seberg, Lee J. Cobb, David Janssen and David Carradine. All the characters in the novel are given unconvincing names, including Seberg's estranged husband, the novelist Romain Gary ("Ivan Gravet"), and another of her lovers, the Mexican revolutionary who called himself El Gato ("Carlos Ortiz" here).

The humiliating aspect for Mr. Fuentes is that Seberg's history seems to have ignored him. Not a mention anywhere in the authorized biographies. He was not alluded to in a lengthy and sympathetic piece about Seberg by Mel Gussow that ran in *The New York Times Magazine* a year after her death in 1979. Mr. Gussow wrote that during the filming of *Macho Callahan,* "she rekindled her romance with Gary while having an affair with a Mexican revolutionary." It is as though with ***Diana*** Mr. Fuentes is trying to make himself a footnote to history, since, in the thundering herd of Seberg's lovers, he was lost in the shuffle.

Some months before the Mexican episode, Seberg was in Clint Eastwood's trailer on the set of *Paint Your Wagon,* and a bit later it was a Black Panther, Raymond Hewitt, and later still, another marriage, more dalliances and a destructive affair with one Hakim Jamal. This last person, a borderline psychopath and murderer, resurfaced as a co-conspirator with "Michael X" in Trinidad, a hideous episode described by V. S. Naipaul in an extended investigative report. Yes, this is far from a tryst in the (perhaps) Pancho Villa Suite in the Mexico City Hilton, but it was part of Seberg's world of racial paranoia, sexual manipulation and political confusion in, to use the painter Francis Bacon's phrase, her gilded gutter-life. Added to this is the admission by the F.B.I. that in the 1970's it had planted news stories that were intended to damage the beleaguered actress because of the various radical causes she had advocated.

Mr. Fuentes sheds no light on any of this wickedness in his novel about a recently divorced Mexican novelist, a self-proclaimed Don Juan, who believes he has effectively seduced an American actress. After a few weeks of sexual bliss a cloud appears, about the size of a photograph of Clint Eastwood. Then the novelist overhears nighttime telephone conversations between his lover and a person in America who is black and very fierce. The novelist withdraws to consult his friends, among them the distinguished director Luis Bunuel. On his return to the actress, the novelist discovers she has taken another lover, a Mexican. No wiggle room here: Don Juan beats a retreat. End of novel.

So what are we left with? The affair is so brief that it is like coitus interruptus. It is lacking in substance, it is mainly hyperbolic and devoid of any insight, a credulous infatuation with a rather pathetic young woman of the sort other women describe by saying "She's sad, plus she's got real low self-esteem." Soren/Seberg is distracted, needy and manipulative. She is lovely. She knows a few sexual tricks and she is deft with the needle. "You have no imagination," she cries to the novelist, and, as if this is not lacerating enough, later she says, "You're like an American liberal." Finally she accuses him of giving her no sexual pleasure.

Curiously, this proud Mexican does not in the least feel castrated by these remarks; he displays a more emotional reaction when he loses at Scrabble. He embarks on a number of excursions regarding the subject of Mexican machismo: "Women are great at the art of making us feel guilty" and "We Mexicans descend from the Aztecs but also from the Mediterranean" and then blah-blah-blah "Phoenicians . . . Greeks . . . Jews . . . Arabs . . . medieval Spain." Here and elsewhere I scribbled in the margin, "Tell that to the Zapatistas!"

> **One of the odd lessons of this book by a novelist of world-class stature is the way it demonstrates the artlessness and banality of machismo.**
> —*Paul Theroux*

This is advertised as a book about a great passion, but really the passion is not sexual; it is political and cultural. The novel was a hit in Mexico, and you can easily see why. First the author establishes his literary credentials; "literature" is his license to chase women. "I try to justify sex with literature and literature with sex" and "Literature is my real lover" and "If I wasn't being unfaithful to literature, I wasn't being unfaithful to myself." This word "literature" is interesting; if he called it "writing," would his sexual license expire?

In a fluent translation by Alfred Mac Adam, the novel contains extensive rants against the United States, barking with the sounds of old Albania. Here is a sample of the observations directed at Mexico's neighbor to the north, "a country that lost its soul in the 12 Reagan-Bush years of spurious illusions, brain-killing banalities and sanctioned avarice." The "sacrosanct streets" of our suburbs are "profaned by crime," with "fast-food customers machine-gunned with hamburgers still in their mouths." We hold parades for the "grand liars in the Iran-contra conspiracy." "Hollywood has been the U.S. Sodom that waves revolutionary flags to disguise its vices." There's more: "North Americans detest what they're doing because all of them, without exception, would like to do something else so as to be something more" (that "without exception" made me laugh out loud). The words "Americans," "North Americans" and "Yankees" give way, under stress perhaps, to the rather offensive and intentionally insulting word "gringo" (interesting—in Spanish it also means "gibberish"): "one of the most repulsive institutions in the world, the gringo cocktail party," and "I'd never taught in a gringo university," and yattering on about "the inevi-

table theme of the loss of innocence, which so obsesses the gringos." This man was a diplomat?

It seems he has totally identified himself with poor paranoid Seberg/Soren, weak and tricky, compulsively allowing herself to be seduced and then rejecting the men—using her connections, describing herself inaccurately as an exile, blaming America for all her ills. But Seberg/Soren really was persecuted and used—as much by her lovers as by the F.B.I. No wonder she rejected her lovers and husbands and fled from the F.B.I. by killing herself and leaving a bitter suicide note.

One of the odd lessons of this book by a novelist of world-class stature is the way it demonstrates the artlessness and banality of machismo. The character of Diana Soren has a weak ego and so she takes revenge on men, because they represent the authority of the United States. The novelist-narrator sees Americans as "without exception" problematical and lacking in substance, and so he rants. He is Mexico. You are a gringo. She is your victim. It makes for an entirely humorless and strangely sclerotic novel.

Walter Russell Mead (review date 23 June 1996)

SOURCE: "In the Shadow of a Colossus," in *Washington Post Book World*, June 23, 1996, p. 5.

[*In the following review, Mead provides a generally positive appraisal of* A New Time for Mexico.]

"We turn on the television sets of the Mexican mind," writes Carlos Fuentes in *A New Time for Mexico,* "and every night we hear the same evening news. Top of the news: THE SPANISH HAVE CONQUERED MEXICO. Second item: THE GRINGOS STOLE HALF OUR TERRITORY. After that, murders, arson, kidnappings and, five-legged cows."

The murders and five-legged cows have been coming thicker than usual since the policies of former Mexican president Carlos Salinas de Gotari collapsed ignominiously in 1994-95. Salinas had promised through the magic of NAFTA [North American Free Trade Agreement] to turn Mexico into a First World country. Instead, as Fuentes makes clear, the Mexican scene remains a kind of Jurassic Park inhabited by political dinosaurs and, increasingly, by a new species Fuentes calls "drugosaurs"—figures who combine the corruption and impunity long associated with Mexico's terminally corrupt ruling party with the money and brutality associated with the drug trade.

The American establishment has fallen silent on the subjects of Mexico and Salinas. Nobody wants to admit that for the last six years the United States utterly misread its closest, most populous neighbor. The only people in the United States who want to talk about either Mexico or NAFTA today are people like Ross Perot and Pat Buchanan. The result is more than depressing. At the moment, the United States seems more likely to build a wall along the common border than to undertake any serious initiative to help Mexico grow.

For Mexico, of course, the collapse was more than an embarrassment; it was one of the most humiliating fiascos in a painful national history. Once again it seemed that Mexico was doomed to fail while the United States went forward from strength to strength. Mexico's economy and political regime alike seemed unreformable and unworkable.

This is the background for Carlos Fuentes's new book, and in it we can see a passionate and committed Mexican intellectual struggling with his country's unhappy present and uncertain future. Combining impressionistic accounts of the Mexican national soul with remarkably lucid summaries of Mexican history, snippets of literary autobiography, policy prescriptions and personal journals, *A New Time for Mexico* is a challenging book, but the North American reader will find few more helpful introductions to the Mexican national crisis.

For Fuentes and for much of Mexican elite opinion, Mexico confronts the Colossus of the North alone. It is not just that many Mexican intellectuals dismiss such "backward" countries as Guatemala and Honduras in much the same way many United States intellectuals dismiss Mexico. It is that for Fuentes—and for his countrymen—even countries like Brazil, Chile and Argentina do not loom very large in the hemispheric political and economic environment.
—*Walter Russell Mead*

Unfortunately, the policy-wonk bits of the book are not very successful. Fuentes has a list, but he doesn't have a plan. Mexico must become more democratic. It must open itself to market forces while preserving, and even extending, a network of social benefits to protect and educate its poor. NAFTA must be reformed; the United States and Canada ought to be more generous to Mexico; Europe and the newly prosperous states of East Asia ought to be more involved. Mexican political parties must become more honest; they must agree on a fair and transparent system for future elections; fraud must be rooted out of politics.

Well, yes, of course. But how?

Fuentes is more impressive when he dissects the flawed psychology behind Mexico's repeated one-sided dashes for modernization in both the 19th and 20th centuries. For Salinas, like Porfirio Diaz a century ago, progress meant the Europeanization or, most recently, the Yankification of Mexico. The psychological and emotional landscape of the Mexican countryside had to be exchanged for the values and perceptions of the Manchester School one hundred years ago, and those of the Harvard Business School today.

Mexico, says Fuentes, needs another kind of modernization: one built on the celebration and affirmation of its national character and civilization. Rather than the autocratic, top-down reforms of a Salinas, Mexico needs decentralization and democratization.

This again seems indisputably true—and exquisitely difficult to do. And it involves a revolution in Mexican thinking beyond anything Fuentes contemplates in this book.

For Fuentes and for much of Mexican elite opinion, Mexico confronts the Colossus of the North alone. It is not just that many Mexican intellectuals dismiss such "backward" countries as Guatemala and Honduras in much the same way many United States intellectuals dismiss Mexico. It is that for Fuentes—and for his countrymen—even countries like Brazil, Chile and Argentina do not loom very large in the hemispheric political and economic environment.

In the early 1980s, Mexico refused to make common cause with fellow-debtor nations like Argentina and Brazil. Later in the 1980s it moved ahead with NAFTA, rejoicing that the other Latin American nations were excluded from this new, special relationship with the United States. By insisting on handling its relations with the United States on a bilateral basis, Mexico magnifies its weakness and its isolation. By imagining itself as isolated—so far from God, so close to the United States in Porfirio Diaz's famous phrase—Mexico achieves a kind of glamour and dignity, but also dooms itself to endless impotence and futility.

Many things will have to happen before Mexico's political system and its economy can fulfill the hopes of Mexico's people; one of those changes will have to involve a rediscovery and a celebration of Mexico's connections with its neighbors to the south. Until then, look for more murders and five-legged cows. Mexico is in the midst of a profound, possibly a violent restructuring. We must all hope that it will be sane, patriotic and thoughtful humanists like Carlos Fuentes, rather than drugosaurs and dinosaurs, who shape Mexico's new order. And the United States can never forget that, should Mexico's problems dramatically worsen, no wall can be high enough, no river deep enough, to keep those problems out of our lives.

Peter Canby (review date 11 August 1996)

SOURCE: "Betrayed by the Revolution," in *New York Times Book Review,* August 11, 1996, p. 14.

[*In the following review, Canby provides a mixed assessment of* A New Time for Mexico.]

Carlos Fuentes is many things: a diplomat and self-described "transopolitan" who wears Savile Row suits and didn't live in Mexico until he was 16; a "leftist" who was banned from entry into the United States under the McCarran-Walter Act during the 1960's but who, inside Mexico, is regularly derided for his gringo mentality; an accomplished novelist who is perennially nominated for the Nobel Prize; and, finally, an interpreter of Mexico to the United States and of the United States to Mexico. *A New Time for Mexico,* Mr. Fuentes's latest collection of essays, reveals the author in interpreter mode, and even though it contains several chapters that leave the impression of having been included only to pad out a thin manuscript, it is, at its heart, an insightful and often brilliant reflection on Mexican governance and the daunting problems the nation faces today.

Mr. Fuentes argues that Mexico's strength lies in its racial and cultural diversity, but adds that this diversity was suppressed until the 1910 Revolution. During the Revolution, the Government not only distributed land to Mexico's poor and eliminated the institutions of caste, but also allowed the country to acknowledge, for the first time, the complexity of its Indian, black and Spanish heritage.

Still, Mr. Fuentes continues, a centralizing, authoritarian legacy bequeathed by both the Aztecs and the Spanish existed in opposition to the liberating effects of the Revolution. This legacy was magnified over the centuries by a tradition of governing according to the tenets of scholasticism—a school of thought associated with Thomas Aquinas—which postulates the idea that the common good is greater and more important than the rights of individuals. Although this autocratic philosophy was part of the world rejected by the Revolution, Mr. Fuentes contends that between 1920 and 1940, when the Revolution consolidated itself into the present ruling party—the Partido Revolucionario Institucional, or PRI—it essentially adapted Mexico's Thomist traditions for its own ends.

The postrevolutionary Government was, according to Mr. Fuentes, a regime that managed to be at once authoritarian and progressive. Presidents were granted autocratic powers, but only for six-year terms, and the Government itself became a kind of Thomist hierarchy through which people fulfilled themselves.

This system worked well as long as the Government lived up to its implicit pact with the Mexican people to guarantee peace, stability and a broad-based prosperity. But after the presidency of Lazaro Cardenas (1934-40), and more particularly after the Mexican Government's massacre of students in Tlatelolco Square during the Olympic year of 1968, the ruling party became, in Mr. Fuentes's opinion, increasingly self-serving. A series of incompetent, greedy and corrupt presidents led Mexico to its current financial straits.

At the present time, however, Mr. Fuentes is concerned about what he sees as a greater problem. During the hundred years or so after independence from Spain and before the Revolution, Mexico, he argues, went through a period when its leadership developed an "extralogical" obsession with French, British and American forms of government. Particularly during the dictatorship of Porfirio Diaz, this outlook enabled the Mexican Government to dismiss its Thomist sense of obligation to its citizenry and allowed the ruling clique to enrich itself at the expense of the general population. Mr. Fuentes sees this dynamic echoed in Mexico's present leadership, many of whom, he notes, are graduates of Ivy League and Eastern colleges who have "centered their lives on the New York Stock Exchange." He is not particularly fond of the new President, Ernesto Zedillo, whose "lean and hungry look" he associates with the "trenchant consistency of the Anglo-American conservatives." The previous President, Carlos Salinas de Gortari, does not fare much better. While Mr. Fuentes concedes that Mr. Salinas tamed inflation and managed the debt, he alludes to Mr. Salinas's economic policies as "archaic, savage capitalism, concentrating wealth in a minority and waiting for the impossible miracle of trickle-down."

Although Mr. Fuentes approves of the North American Free Trade Agreement [NAFTA] in theory, because he feels it is important for Mexico to open up to the world, he disapproves of the specifics, which he says are rooted in the "gospel preached . . . by Reagan and Thatcher." Nafta, Mr. Fuentes declares, is collapsing the Mexican economy without creating the conditions for new investment, and he fears that United States loans to Mexico will be used as a means of compromising Mexico's sovereignty.

Mr. Fuentes's solutions run to the social democratic. He speaks of the need for an open government, for checks and balances, for redesigning loans so that foreign money has to stay in Mexico and can be invested productively. It's hard to fault Mr. Fuentes for any of these eminently sensible ideas, but it's also hard to take them too seriously. Mr. Fuentes is like a good dinner guest. He is articulate, charming, erudite and clever, but his proposed solution to everything seems to be to convene men of good will. The question is, can this approach address the depth of Mexico's problems today?

Mr. Fuentes hints darkly that Luis Donaldo Colosio, the assassinated PRI presidential candidate (with whom the author reveals himself to have been quite close), was killed by what he calls the dinosaur wing of the PRI because he was outspokenly intent on reforming a Government whose interests extended to wide-scale drug trafficking and money laundering. Yet nowhere, beyond a "Jurassic Park" joke or two, does Mr. Fuentes address the critical issue of the effects of the drug trade on Mexican politics.

Mr. Fuentes includes, in this collection, the diaries he kept during the traumatic years of 1994 and 1995. Toward the middle of 1994, he mentions an invitation he received from the guerrilla leader Subcommander Marcos to take part in Mr. Marcos's "National Democratic Convention." It is briefly amusing to hear Mr. Marcos and Mr. Fuentes trading oracular pronouncements as if they were on an episode of *Star Trek*. But after a while you want Mr. Fuentes to get on with it, to go to the convention and tell us what it's like. He never does.

Sidney Weintraub (review date 18 August 1996)

SOURCE: "Fuentes: Mexico's Smoldering Volcano," in *Los Angeles Times Book Review*, August 18, 1996, p. 4.

[*Below, Weintraub offers a predominantly negative review of* A New Time for Mexico.]

The focus of this collection of essays [*A New Time for Mexico*] is largely on events during the last two full calendar years—the breakdown of Mexico's economic fabric in 1994 and the calamitous depression that followed in 1995. The discussion is personal and idiosyncratic—how Carlos Fuentes views what happened and what are his Ten Commandments for the future.

Fuentes is a person of considerable distinction, and his writings therefore merit the attention of those who seek to understand the Mexican scene. His thoughts are often inspiring, such as the emphasis on democracy, liberty and justice in his Decalogue, but they are also often quite base, such as his crude anti-Americanism. His prose is full of flowery banalities: "To see Mexico from the air is to look upon the face of creation. Our everyday, earthbound vision takes flight and is transformed into a vision of the elements. Mexico is a creation of water and fire, of wind and earthquake, of the moon and the sun." These are the opening sentences of the volume. But he also creates powerful word pictures: "While

U.S. progress has produced garbage, Mexico's backwardness has produced monuments." His aspirations are commendable. But his political-economic analysis is often downright naive. (Mexico's reserves were not slashed by a wave of imports, as he states, but by capital flight stemming from a lack of confidence in the management of the country.)

> **Fuentes is a person of considerable distinction, and his writings therefore merit the attention of those who seek to understand the Mexican scene. His thoughts are often inspiring, such as the emphasis on democracy, liberty and justice in his Decalogue, but they are also often quite base, such as his crude anti-Americanism.**
>
> **—*Sidney Weintraub***

The essays tell us much about Fuentes, particularly about his noble hopes for his country, but they provide little that is new to informed Mexicans or observers of the Mexican scene. By all means, read this slim volume if you wish to understand what motivates Fuentes but don't also expect to learn much about the reasons for the economic horrors that beset Mexicans during the last few years.

Mexico has been on a downward slide for the last 25 years. Luis Echeverria, when he acceded to the presidency in 1970, shifted policy with the objective of narrowing Mexico's abysmal divide between the rich and the poor, but his populist effort to spend the country into greater equality led only to mountainous inflation and further deterioration in income distribution. His successor, Jose Lopez Portillo, despite huge inflows of oil revenue, left the country with a Popocatépell of debt that impoverished the country for the rest of the 1980s. (Fuentes describes Popo as a dead volcano, which it apparently is not.) Between them, the next two presidents, Miguel de la Madrid and Carlos Salinas de Gortari, did bring Mexico into the world economy, but the end result was what happened in 1994 and 1995. Every economic catastrophe has its antecedents, but these are largely absent in Fuentes' description.

Fuentes' hero among Mexican presidents of the modern era is Lazaro Cárdenas, on two grounds: his land reform accomplishments and his standing up to the United States in the nationalization of foreign oil facilities in 1938. Most Mexicans would share this sentiment. Cárdenas did nothing to stimulate democratic opening in Mexico, as Fuentes admits. His main villain among modern Mexican leaders is Gustavo Diaz Ordaz, who was president during the infamous 1968 student massacre. Fuentes invokes Diaz Ordaz's name again and again in connection with this event, but he ignores the fact that the minister directly responsible for the police action was Echeverria. It is almost as though he cannot find it in himself to attack a populist, whereas he has no difficulty in repeatedly berating the more conservative Diaz Ordaz.

For reasons that are not fully articulated, Fuentes admires Carlos Salinas, who shifted the direction of Mexican economic policy. However, he is critical of Salinas on two scores, first for neglecting political opening even as he opened the Mexico economy, and, second, for not carrying out a devaluation of the peso before he left office in order that his successor could consolidate his own absolute power. By contrast, Fuentes has harsh words for Ernesto Zedillo, the current president, for his "brutal" break with Salinas and his lack of political expertise, which "permits . . . many democratic slogans to be perverted." Fuentes is, of course, accurate that Zedillo is a political novice, but Zedillo has demonstrated that he is more committed to the rule of law than Salinas ever was and that his preference is to end the absolutist system that has typified Mexican presidential politics for the last 70 years.

It is almost as though Fuentes resents Zedillo for succeeding to the presidency after the first candidate chosen by Salinas, Luis Donaldo Colosio, was assassinated. Fuentes is explicit that he would have preferred either Manuel Camacho, the former mayor of Mexico City who rebelled openly when Colosio was chosen, or Jesus Silva Herzog, a former finance minister and now ambassador to the United States, a person Salinas would never have selected as the candidate.

Fuentes has spent much time in the United States, but his resentments run deep and his comments are hard to take. U.S. malaise, which he assumes now exists, is accompanied by the need for a foreign enemy, and the enemy, he implies, "lies waiting at the very doorstep . . . with a common border stretching over 2,000 kilometers." He draws an obscene analogy between the Holocaust and the anti-Mexican attitude of California politicians when he says that "xenophobia and racism lead to the pogrom and the concentration camp." He states several times that the purpose of the $20-billion U.S. loan in 1995 after Mexico's financial collapse was to repay U.S. banks and investors and that the foreign credits do nothing "to set Mexico on its feet and back on the road to greater production." Nothing is said about the long-term price Mexicans would have had to pay had the country defaulted its sovereign debt—which really was the only other immediate option when the loan was granted.

The phrase that most rankles is that "anti-Americanism is not enough" to save both Mexico and its culture. Necessary, but not enough? His main point is that Mexico must do more for itself, which is a sentiment with which few would quar-

rel, but this comes after repeated trashing of U.S. motives and actions.

Fuentes is a most unreliable source on U.S. habits of thought and behavior. Is he a good source for understanding Mexican thought and behavior? In part, yes. We know how costly the continued authoritarianism has been for Mexico, and Fuentes is a major voice for democratic opening. Fuentes is highly critical of the closed nature of decision-making in Mexico, a practice that surely contributed to the debacle of late 1994. Mexico's justice system is typically scorned by the population, and Fuentes is a powerful advocate for reform. He regularly reminds Mexicans of the deep poverty and social injustice that exist in the country, and respected voices like his are needed to bring about reform.

But, while he plays a valuable role in calling attention to these political, social, legal and economic deficiencies in Mexico, it is not clear that he understands the processes needed for correction. Mexico saves too little, and his panacea is to change the pension system. Don't borrow even if the alternative is default on sovereign debt, and damn the consequences. Entering into NAFTA was a useful step according to Fuentes, but it is not clear why he believes this, because he asserts that it serves "above all, national interests of the United States."

There is much to admire in what Fuentes writes and does. But there is also much that leaves the respectful reader nonplused.

FURTHER READING

Bibliography

Dunn, Sandra L. "Carlos Fuentes: A Bibliography." *The Review of Contemporary Fiction* VIII (Summer 1988): 150-52.

    Brief primary bibliography of Fuentes's works through 1988.

Criticism

Bradfield, Scott. Review of *Diana: The Goddess Who Hunts Alone*. *Times Literary Supplement*, No. 4826 (29 September 1995): 27.

    Negative assessment of *Diana: The Goddess Who Hunts Alone*.

Faris, Wendy B. "Desire and Power, Love and Revolution: Carlos Fuentes and Milan Kundera." *Review of Contemporary Fiction* 8, No. 2 (Summer 1988): 273-84.

    Compares the works of Fuentes and Milan Kundera,

both of whom, Faris posits, are interested in the relationship between erotic power and revolution and political power and revolution.

Gyurko, Lanin A. "Women in Mexican Society: Fuentes' Portrayal of Oppression." *Revista Hispanica Moderna* XXXVIII, No. 4 (1974-1975): 206-29.
> Examines the dehumanization of female characters in Fuentes's works.

Ibsen, Kristine. *Author, Text and Reader in the Novels of Carols Fuentes.* New York: Peter Lang, 1993, 182 p.
> Book-length critical overview of Fuentes's novels; includes bibliography.

Mead, Robert G., Jr. "Carlos Fuentes, Mexico's Angry Novelist." *Books Abroad* 38, No. 4 (Autumn 1964): 380-82.
> Surveys Fuentes's novels through 1964.

Payne, Judith. "Laura's Artemio: Failed Sexual Politics in *La muerte de Artemio Cruz.*" *Hispanofila,* No. 112 (September, 1994): 65-76.
> Studies the relationship between Laura and the title character in *La muerte de Artemio Cruz,* and considers how it alters Artemio's "image . . . in relation to women."

Thomas, Rosanne Daryl. "Affairs of Love and Death." *Chicago Tribune* (17 December 1995): 3.
> Laudatory assessment of *Diana: The Goddess Who Hunts Alone.*

Williams, Raymond Leslie. *The Writings of Carlos Fuentes.* Austin: University of Texas Press, 1996, 177 p.
> Book-length work that is divided into three sections, the first of which is a biography of Fuentes from 1928 to 1993; the last two sections deal primarily with connections between the works of other authors and *Terra Nostra,* and the relationships between *Terra Nostra* and Fuentes's other works. Includes bibliography.

Additional coverage of Fuentes's life and career is contained in the following sources published by Gale: *Authors and Artists for Young Adults,* **Vol. 4;** *Authors in the News,* **Vol. 2;** *Contemporary Authors,* **Vols. 69-72;** *Contemporary Authors New Revision Series,* **Vols. 10, and 32;** *Dictionary of Literary Biography,* **Vol. 113;** *DISCovering Authors; DISCovering Authors: British; DISCovering Authors: Canadian; DISCovering Authors Modules: Most-studied, Multicultural,* **and** *Novelists; Hispanic Literature Criticism; Hispanic Writers; Major 20th-Century Writers; Short Story Criticism,* **Vol. 24; and** *World Literature Criticism.*

Susan Hill

1942-

(Full name Susan Elizabeth Hill) English novelist, short story writer, dramatist, essayist, and children's writer.

The following entry presents an overview of Hill's career through 1996. For further information on her life and works, see *CLC,* Volume 4.

INTRODUCTION

Hill is largely known for a body of critically acclaimed works published over six years during the late 1960s and early 1970s, when she wrote six novels, two collections of short stories, and several radio plays. Comprised of brief narratives that rely on simple plots, Hill's award-winning fiction of that period avoids exploiting the human anguish—grief, loneliness, and fear—which they intensely realize. Her novels and short stories feature vivid landscapes charged with meaning and concentrate on both the conscious and subconscious workings of the human psyche. Critics have praised Hill's formal, precise use of language and her narrative technique, finding her reticent psychological analysis and restraint from sentimentality and explicit sexual reference remarkable by contemporary literary standards. Hill surprised critics in 1975 by publicly announcing that she had written her last novel, but she reversed herself almost a decade later and has returned to writing fiction occasionally. Kenneth Muir likened Hill's narrative gift and the gloomy atmosphere of her novels to Charles Dickens's, remarking that "she shares his appreciation of the odd and eccentric, a compassion for the aged, the lonely, and the persecuted, and his obsession with violence."

Biographical Information

Born February 5, 1942 in Scarborough, Yorkshire, England, a faded resort town similar to the settings of some of her novels, Hill attended grammar school in Coventry, publishing her first novel, *The Enclosure* (1961), her last year there. The next autumn she entered King's College at the University of London, taking a B.A. degree with honors in 1963, the same year her second novel, *Do Me a Favour,* appeared. Upon graduation, Hill worked as a literary critic for five years for *Coventry Evening Telegraph* and as a reviewer for various periodicals. Between 1968 and 1974 Hill wrote what she has termed her "serious books": the novels *Gentleman and Ladies* (1968); *A Change for the Better* (1969); *I'm the King of the Castle* (1970), which won the 1971 Somerset Maugham Award; *Strange Meeting* (1971); *The Bird of*

Night (1972), which won the 1972 Whitbread Literary Award for fiction; and *In the Springtime of the Year* (1974), as well as the short story collections *The Albatross* (1971), which won the 1972 John Llewelyn Rhys Memorial Prize, and *A Bit of Singing and Dancing* (1973). Meanwhile, Hill also wrote many radio plays, which she collected in the volume *The Cold Country and Other Plays for Radio* (1975). After marrying Stanley W. Wells, a Shakespearean scholar, on Shakespeare's birthday (April 23) in 1975, Hill stopped writing fiction and instead concentrated on composing radio plays and her monthly column—"The World of Books"—for *The Daily Telegraph* newspaper. The publication of the novel *The Woman in Black* in 1983, however, signaled Hill's return to fiction writing. Since then she has published other fiction—the novella *Lanterns across the Snow* (1987), the novels *Air and Angels* (1991) and *Mrs. de Winter* (1993), and the story anthology *Listening to the Orchestra* (1996)—in addition to many children's stories and books about literature, historical literary places, and English rural life.

Major Works

"A summary of [Hill's] plots would read like headlines from one of the more lurid Sunday newspapers," Muir observed. Hill's novels tend to focus on social misfits and outsiders situated in isolated yet highly atmospheric places and characterized largely through her use of language and dialogue. Referred to by Hill as her apprentice work, her first two novels are distinguished by their focus on male-female relationships: *The Enclosure* traces the dissolution of a marriage, and *Do Me a Favour,* though peopled with a large cast of characters, mainly records the vicissitudes of a relationship between a young woman writer and her journalist lover. *Gentleman and Ladies* recounts the bittersweet lives and sometimes cruel machinations of a group of elderly women in a small, rural village, one of whom is courted by—and eventually marries—a fifty-four-year-old bachelor who still lives at home with his domineering mother. *A Change for the Better,* set in "a world of private hotels, paid companions, and a genteel concern with keeping up appearances," as Catherine Wells Cole put it, relates a woman's futile struggle for freedom from her controlling mother, whose presence is minded even in death. *I'm the King of the Castle* portrays a bitter battle of wills between two eleven-year-old boys: one is the son of a newly hired, live-in housekeeper and the other the son of a recently widowed man, both of whom are forced to share the same place. *Strange Meeting,* notable for its convincing male perspective, relates the effects of a vital but doomed friendship on a reserved, introspective officer and his easygoing, generous comrade when they are thrown together in the trenches of Flanders during World War I. *The Bird of Night,* written in the form of a eighty-year-old scholar's memoirs, ruminates on half of a twenty-year friendship between the old man and a brilliant but insane poet, Francis Croft, speculating about the line between genius and madness. Reminiscent of a pastoral elegy, *In the Springtime of the Year* spans a year in the countryside and follows the gradations of grief endured by a young widow, whose husband accidentally died when a tree crushed him, and who comes to accept her loss. *The Woman in Black,* written in an elegant though past idiom and often compared to Victorian ghost novels, relates the story of a supernatural, sinister haunting, again narrated by a masculine voice. *Mrs. de Winter* purports to be a sequel to Daphne du Maurier's popularly acclaimed novel *Rebecca* (1938). Hill's short story collections form thematic refrains to her novels, favoring atmosphere over plot and examining the conditions of detachment, loneliness, and fear. For instance, *The Albatross,* a novella-length story set in a bleak fishing town, deals with a mentally challenged man seeking escape from his invalid mother, whom he eventually wheels into the ocean after burning their cottage; and "The Custodian" describes the devotion of an old man for the care of an apparently abandoned boy, whose father suddenly returns one day, leaving the man bereft of his sole reason for living. Notable among her substantial body of radio plays are *Lizard in the Grass* (1971), which recounts the experiences of an orphaned, highly imaginative schoolgirl who doesn't fit in with the others at a distinctly unfriendly convent; *The Cold Country* (1972), which concerns four hopelessly snowbound Antarctic explorers, only one of whom presumably survives; and *Consider the Lilies* (1973), in which a young girl slowly wastes to death while communing with a middle-aged botanist, coping with both his Blakean tendencies and overly ambitious assistant.

Critical Reception

The critical reception of Hill's writings has cooled somewhat since her prodigious literary debut, but signs of academic interest in her work, especially her early novels and stories, have emerged. Generally acknowledged as an accomplished stylist, Hill's lucid narrative technique and usually indeterminate yet powerfully described sense of place have received particular notice, as has her convincing display of a distinctly male perspective in some of her fiction. Hill's simple but effective narrative structures have fascinated scholars, who frequently have noted precision in the way she distances the story from readers: "By so structuring that tight enclosure . . . Susan Hill's persona come to life," Ernest H. Hofer explained, adding that "faithful adherence to structure . . . becomes a dynamic of exposure. We SEE." Commenting on Hill's reticence about sex, Maria Schubert observed that "the absence of explicit sexual reference . . . expresses a preference for an oblique mode of communication, almost innovative after years of the demonstrative breaking of sexual taboos, once doubtless a great merit in literature." Although some critics have suggested that Hill's fictions do not advocate a feminist perspective, others have shown that "the real issues behind her work are related to problems of female survival," as Rosemary Jackson stated: "It is no accident that Susan Hill's work has been so well received by a liberal literary tradition, for it ends by silencing its own timorous interrogation of some of the fatal and crippling effects of a patriarchal, 'male' culture and retreats into a familiar 'female' enclosure of defeatism." Mary Jane Reed summarized Hill's achievement: "Hill's style is clear and the structure of her work is simple. Her novels are a paradox, easy to read yet profound in exploring our complex behaviour and the universal problems we encounter—death, war, seclusion, even madness."

PRINCIPAL WORKS

The Enclosure (novel) 1961
Do Me a Favour (novel) 1963
*Gentleman and Ladies (novel) 1968
A Change for the Better (novel) 1969
I'm the King of the Castle (novel) 1970

The Albatross (short stories) 1971; also published as *The Albatross and Other Stories,* 1975

Strange Meeting (novel) 1971

The Bird of Night (novel) 1972

The Custodian (short stories) 1972

A Bit of Singing and Dancing and Other Stories (short stories) 1973

In the Springtime of the Year (novel) 1974

†*The Cold Country and Other Plays for Radio* (drama) 1975

The Magic Apple-Tree: A Country Year (essays) 1982

The Woman in Black: A Ghost Story (novel) 1983

One Night at a Time (for children) 1984; also published as *Go Away, Bad Dreams!,* 1985

Through the Kitchen Window (essays) 1984

Mother's Magic (for children) 1986

Through the Garden Gate (essays) 1986

Lanterns across the Snow (novella) 1987

The Lighting of the Lamps (essays) 1987

Shakespeare Country (prose) 1987

Can It Be True? A Christmas Story (for children) 1988

Family (autobiography) 1988

The Spirit of the Cotswolds (prose) 1988

Suzie's Shoes (for children) 1989

The Glass Angels (for children) 1990

I Won't Go There Again (for children) 1990

Septimus Honeydew (for children) 1990

Stories from Codling Village (for children) 1990

Air and Angels (novel) 1991

Beware, Beware (for children) 1993

King of Kings (for children) 1993

Mrs. de Winter (novel) 1993

The Christmas Collection (for children) 1994

Listening to the Orchestra (short stories) 1996

Reflections from a Garden [with Rory Stuart] (essays) 1996

*This work was adapted as the radio play *Miss Lavender Is Dead* (1970).

†This work includes *The Cold Country* (1972) *The End of Summer* (1971), *Consider the Lilies* (1973), *Strip Jack Naked* (1974), and *Lizard in the Grass* (1971).

CRITICISM

Times Literary Supplement **(review date 15 September 1972)**

SOURCE: "Poet's Pains," in *Times Literary Supplement,* No. 3680, September 15, 1972, p. 1041.

[*In the following review, the critic highlights the theme of insanity in* The Bird of Night.]

There have been clues here and there in her previous books that Susan Hill was, like many of the rest of us today, troubled and fascinated by the apparently arbitrary way in which human beings are dismissed as "mad", by the possibility that the so-called insane are saner than the world cares to admit. But even considering the wide range she has so far covered, it would have been a rare guess that hit on the subject of Miss Hill's new and strange novel. *The Bird of Night* is in the form of an old scholar's ruminative memoir, a last tribute to the only relationship that has in eighty years really counted, his painful, patient, generous love for the mad poet Francis Croft. We are to accept that Francis, a survivor of the Somme, has now been recognized as a genius, as the major English poet of the 1930s; young men plague his crippled, solitary friend with their tape-recorders and impertinent questions, begging for "papers", letters, anecdotes. But Harvey, now a recluse on a windswept Suffolk estuary, is still obstinately loyal—there are no papers, he will say nothing about the great man, he will only record, haphazardly, some incidents of the friendship he embarked on, little knowing how it would devastate his life.

At no point does Miss Hill refer, even obliquely, to any sexual expression of the love between Francis and Harvey. At no point does any woman appear in the story, and the two men—one already something of a literary lion, the other a meticulous academic—are scarcely ever shown except in each other's company. When, at one of his earlier mental crises, Francis is committed to hospital in Battersea, his dour Scots father visits, deeply embarrassed by the "odd" ménage and by the disgrace which, in his eyes, Francis's manic behaviour has brought on the family. There is a publisher, a doctor, a silent peasant family in Venice (for whom Francis insists on buying lavishly unsuitable presents)—otherwise, the memoir consists entirely of the old man's efforts to tell the truth about the poet and his madness.

> **Miss Hill has established in a remarkably short time that she writes with very considerable control and power, using the minimum of stylistic elaboration yet suggesting a strongly poetic instinct for precise images.**
> **—*Times Literary Supplement***

Miss Hill has tried hard, without too obviously avoiding the odd few lines "quoted" from Francis's work, not to give us too much evidence on which we might so easily disbelieve that genius was displayed. She relies on occasional references to public recognition of Francis as a great poet, on extracts from Francis's diary describing the pain of a poem's gestation, and on an assumption that the reader will spot how a midnight walk in a wood in deep snow became the "well-known" poem about the owl. It is a large assumption and a daring one for any novelist, and one is uneasily conscious throughout this book that Francis is under half-conscious scrutiny—would a genius babble so emptily about the delights of London society, about Harvey being his big brother, about being on the train to Venice? Is his petulant childish behaviour—a Hamlet telling Horatio he does not understand what life is about—intended to show us the genius or the madman? Francis is, indeed, very much a Hamlet figure, portrayed as lonely, manic-depressive, increasingly paranoid, given to sudden whimsical escapades. In his worst periods, when Harvey is nearly murdered or driven insane himself by incessant piano-thumping and alarming truculence, the poet is forgotten and the relationship between a man and his friend, the long despairing days and womblike existence endured for love, dominates the book. Here Miss Hill is very good indeed, suggesting the nightmare with amazing restraint, allowing us to see just how loyalty is capable of suffering, without a trace of self-pity appearing in the old man's account.

Of her own talent there can now be no doubt—Miss Hill has established in a remarkably short time that she writes with very considerable control and power, using the minimum of stylistic elaboration yet suggesting a strongly poetic instinct for precise images; she has also now shown that she is ready to tackle possibly the most risky and unlikely material open to a woman novelist—a depiction of genius, insanity, a tale of two men who loved each other many decades ago, a tale with no sex, no politics, no topicality. Even if we are not wholly convinced of the poet's greatness, this remains a brave and moving novel about madness, and the speculation it raises about the value we put on unbalanced lives is not to be lightly forgotten.

Alexander Theroux (review date 27 April 1973)

SOURCE: "A Tale of Madness," in *National Review,* Vol. XXV, No. 17, April 27, 1973, p. 479.

[*In the review below, Theroux details the character of Francis Croft of* The Bird of Night, *observing Hill's "uncanny insight" about insanity.*]

The "greatest poet of his age," as envisioned by Susan Hill in her novel *The Bird of Night,* is an owlish, manic-depressive Scot named Francis Croft, *aet.* 33, who courts death imprisoned in the land of catatonia, an insanitarium of self where his nerve ends, *always* exposed, show themselves each to be more sensitive than a rice-weevil's feeler. This isn't really a novel. It's a nervous breakdown. It's a confession. Croft as a real character is totally unrealized, but, rather, thesis-wise, he's shot to us right away in an indescribable shrill-

ness and stays that way: a casebook barmy whose eccentric and perverse behavior stands as the single sine qua non of a genius in him we see nowhere else, certainly not in the snippets, of which we're treated to samples, of his masterpiece, *Janus.* We just see Croft suffer, screech.

In a kind of reverse of James's "The Aspern Papers," Croft is protected from the world—which, true to type, of course, rudely seeks to burgle his letters, his diary, his soul—by a "guardian angel" figure, 34-year-old Harvey Lawson, scholar and Egyptologist, who has more patience than St. Monica and who, inexplicably (but I'll accept love), assumes the role of wet nurse to the mad, suicidal poet, chronicling their mutual voyage to the end of night, which goes from Dorset, to Venice, to California, to a final bird sanctuary, as it were, called Schloss Vogel in Germany. Everywhere is death, of which the owl—perhaps I should have mentioned this sooner?—is an augur.

[*The Bird of Night*] isn't really a novel. It's a nervous breakdown. It's a confession.
—*Alexander Theroux*

Actually, Lawson, we find, chronicles only ten of the twenty years they spend together, casually mentioning four pages from the end of his memoir (about 10 per cent of which is, literally, Croft's own diary) that he has omitted ten years from the tale and that, hohum, life went on that way pretty much the same—attempted murders, projected suicides, chronic remorse, aborted strangulations, and all of this, one assumes, without surcease of Croft's recorded hates and fears which include bats, landladies, photographs, "thundering" poems, bells, doctors, sun, night, and decaying Venetian houses. Croft, naturally, kills himself—with some pruning shears Lawson forgot to tuck away; no one expected otherwise. I guessed it, frankly, long before latecomer Lawson told us how Croft started looking up the word "hemlock" in his botany, and treasuring Marco-aurelian proverbs on death, and identifying with unattractive Gilly-white owls. How did I guess? Well, since the sun in England is not a constant, I guess I just banked on the inevitability of landladies. In any case, Lawson paternalistically burns Croft's every letter, every paper, and the poetic marriage ends with the memory of Lawson, a Shelley to Adonais, mourning: "I weep not for Francis but for myself, for the loss of him."

Susan Hill has both a keen poetic talent, native, I think, but undisciplined, and an uncanny insight into the deranged mind; much of her writing is original and beautiful and tender. Irksome is her tendency to constantly speak in metaphors, a self-indulgence that, because it prevents a forward movement in the novel, perhaps forces her to nip off ten years from the life of owl-haunted Croft which *can't* have been irrelevant. Over this novel, I'm afraid, I still opt for *The Diary of Nijinsky.*

Times Literary Supplement (review date 25 January 1974)

SOURCE: "Weathering the Calm," in *Times Literary Supplement,* No. 3751, January 25, 1974, p. 69.

[*Below, the critic considers the representation of grief in* In the Springtime of the Year *and its effect on the novel.*]

Some novels conjure up discreet, well lit interiors, where you notice people's accents, or opinions, or possessions. Others seem to happen in a moody, unpredictable out of doors, where what you attend to—though it sounds paradoxical—is the inner life, the spiritual "weather". Susan Hill's fiction is very clearly of this second kind. She invests her real energy in emotional events everything that is merely circumstantial or descriptive is tacitly excluded; there is no gossip, no clutter, no social masquerade. Places matter a lot, especially landscapes, but never names or dates. Although each of her books has had its own distinctive atmosphere, almost its own colour (the iron-grey of Flanders trenches in *Strange Meeting,* the purple-and-black of the poet's private hell in *The Bird of Night*)—they all focus on the same kind of lonely, dislocated experience. The characters are always somehow unaccommodated, outside ordinary intercourse; there is always the pathos of an excited, complex sensibility that has to stay closed-off and inarticulate. It is significant that Miss Hill seems most at home when she writes about old people and children: the gulf between what they can feel and what they can do or say is deepest, and she identifies with them because of that.

> **Miss Hill has said that [with *In the Springtime of the Year*] she has come closer to autobiography than in any of her other novels, and perhaps one might have guessed that from the frankness of the search for comfort.**
> **—*Times Literary Supplement***

In the Springtime of the Year would seem to offer an even more urgent occasion for empathy. It is about a young woman, Ruth, whose husband has died suddenly in an aimless, accidental way, and it follows the fluctuations of her grief from the first trance of anguish, through chafing, irritable heaviness, to—in the end—a glimmering, precarious acceptance. The whole, year-long process takes place in a countryside that seems at first oppressively quiet and empty.

Only gradually do its rhythms begin to assert themselves and make human sense, so that Ruth comes back to life with the return of spring, and dares to believe that her husband is living too. There are some vividly horrible moments—as when she tries to eat, and the food tastes rank, decaying—but what comes over most strongly is not, as you might expect, the specificity of the thing, the sense of getting inside someone's skin. Instead, it is the ritual, almost anonymous, aspect of grief that dominates the writing, a pattern of despair and consolation that is as intensely conventional as a pastoral elegy. *In the Springtime of the Year* is a fable about resurrection, and its characters are not really particular people at all.

Miss Hill has said that here she has come closer to autobiography than in any of her other novels, and perhaps one might have guessed that from the frankness of the search for comfort. Usually she works to make her people as painfully individual as possible, but here that's taken almost for granted, and the local suffering dissolves into all the deaths that have gone before, and all the births that will come after. And although the book retains her habitual air of dignity, the ritual slackens the writing:

> She thought, dying is like being born, and now I am doing both, with Ben. For she wanted to share everything with him, could not accept that, in death, he had to be alone. She said, I should have been with him when the tree fell, there when he died. I failed him, I left him by himself.

There isn't the feeling of control and tension you remember from her other books—possibly because the subject is just too close. Such speculation, though, has little point. In Miss Hill's lonely territory, the difficulties of keeping stock responses at bay are immense. Timelessness so easily slips into vacuum, and reverence into indulgence because there are no restraints except the ones that are self-imposed. This novel falters, perhaps not much, but enough to make the difference.

Irina Sofinskaya (essay date 1976)

SOURCE: "Susan Hill: A Soviet Critic's View," in *Soviet Literature,* No. 11, 1976, pp. 166-69.

[*In the following essay, Sofinskaya identifies the hallmarks of Hill's fiction, especially her short stories, indicating the significance of psychology, place, and death for her narrative art.*]

The Soviet reader first became acquainted with Susan Hill's work at the beginning of the year, when three of her short stories were translated into Russian and published in the magazine *Inostrannaya Literatura* ("Foreign Literature"). A collection of her stories to be published in English in Moscow is also in preparation. Articles about Susan Hill and the first reviews of her books had, in fact, already appeared in *Inostrannaya Literatura* several years before her stories were published. Like their English colleagues, Soviet critics consider her work to be one of the notable examples of English prose today. For instance, the well-known Soviet authority on English literature, Professor Valentina Ivasheva, who discovered Susan Hill for the Soviet reading public, has written: "This young and exceptionally gifted writer is one of the most noteworthy figures in English prose writing of the seventies."

Susan Hill's choice of the problems raised, her sensitive use of words, and her close attentiveness to man's inner world have won her recognition and popularity. It may seem surprising that in our age of great economic and social transformations she should write books in which the external signs of the times are almost totally absent. A car or a television set in her novels can strike the reader as something of an incongruity. Soaring prices, the scientific and technological revolution, pollution of the environment, the uneven development of economics, the woman's liberation movement, sex, violence, the growth of crime, and youth in revolt—in a word, everything characteristic of the West today, seem to remain outside Susan Hill's sphere of vision. What, then, is the secret of her success? Principally that she has opposed the transitory values of the contemporary "consumer society" with the world of nature and the inner life of man. Her short stories mostly centre on the eternal problems of life and death, love, fear, expectations and collapsing hopes. The action often takes place against a background of deserted holiday resorts by the sea in winter, fishing villages and isolated hamlets. Susan Hill does not idealise the simple life and does not call for a retreat from reality: she simply reminds the reader that nature, the sea, animals and birds will always be of true value to man.

Susan Hill has managed to see beauty where she feels it is no longer noticed: in the ordinary human feelings of sympathy, pity, attachment and compassion. With gentle lyricism, sometimes even with sentimentality, she describes the experiences of people who have nothing remarkable about them at all. There is something about her characters that suggests the "little man" of the Russian literary classics, the tradition associated with Gogol, Dostoevsky and Chekhov. Susan Hill has fully succeeded in doing what André Maurois asked for in his famous speech, "The writer's role in contemporary society": "The artist," he said, "must make sense of this senseless world. . . . Our duty is to help the reader to see Man in each man." The basis and main appeal of Susan Hill's work is that it makes us see the capacity for the deepest feelings behind the apparent shallowness and deformity.

> **Like their English colleagues, Soviet critics consider [Hill's] work to be one of the notable examples of English prose today.**
> **—Irina Sofinskaya**

Although she is primarily a novelist, one feels that her best work is in the short stories published in two collections, *The Albatross and Other Stories* (1971) and *A Bit of Singing and Dancing* (1973). As for her novels, they contain much that is alien to Soviet readers. For example, in *I'm the King of the Castle,* the author shows the triumph of sophisticated cruelty, all the more horrible for being practised by an 11-year-old boy. This novel, reminiscent of the Gothic horror novels, evokes associations with William Golding's *Lord of the Flies.* But whereas Golding's novel, a philosophical parable written under the direct influence of the Second World War, is meant to sound a warning to mankind of the dangers inherent in violence and fanaticism, Susan Hill's novel is just a thorough and skilful analysis of man's allegedly inborn evil instincts. In this article we mainly base our observations on her short stories, leaving the analysis of her novels for some other occasion. In her short stories, she smashes traditional notions about the supposed English passion for orderliness, reticence, an unswerving adherence to the rules of good tone, and a love of solitude. There is nothing of the traditional English "home" in her stories: Dickens' principles of family morality are a thing of the distant past. In her stories, we come across lonely and neglected children who have everything except a family (**"The Elephant-Man"**), a married couple painstakingly concealing their indifference to one another under a mask of concern and solicitude (**"The Peacock"**), a brother who hates his sister (**"Somerville"**) and, to crown all this, a son who has murdered his own mother (**"The Albatross"**).

There is an attractive psychological subtlety about her stories. They could be described as studies in psychology: the author is not interested in the events as such: what matters is their impact on the inner world of man. The elements of composition in her stories are therefore frequently geared to changes in a character's mental state and not to external action (**"The Custodian," "Missy"**). In concentrating on the exploration of the human psyche, Susan Hill portrays not only the conscious life of her characters, but the working of their subconscious minds. In this sense, her stories vividly exemplify the special features of the contemporary approach to psychological analysis.

The means of artistic expression are directly tied up with the "psychological" content of the stories. Thus, an important part in their imagery is played by symbolic detail which cannot always be reduced to a simple and unequivocal interpretation. At the same time, symbolic detail is successfully employed as an aid to the creation of a visual image that conveys accurately and almost tangibly the emotional experience of the character.

[*I'm the King of the Castle*], reminiscent of the Gothic horror novels, evokes associations with William Golding's *Lord of the Flies*. But whereas Golding's novel, a philosophical parable written under the direct influence of the Second World War, is meant to sound a warning to mankind of the dangers inherent in violence and fanaticism, Susan Hill's novel is just a thorough and skilful analysis of man's allegedly inborn evil instincts.
—*Irina Sofinskaya*

Landscapes are charged with meaning in Susan Hill's stories. Described with great verbal economy, but full of imagery and colour, they are directly tied up with the characters' moods. In **"The Albatross,"** for example, there is a clearly discernible parallel between the harsh inconstancy of the sea and the behaviour of Duncan Pike, the principal character, now quiet and fearful, now subject to fits of inexplicable fury. Thanks to her use of the precise simile or the right adjective, the economically worded descriptive passages evoke complex pictures in the reader's mind. Susan Hill always notices what is most characteristic of a landscape, and she often conveys a state of nature, and also the mood of her character, in only a single sentence.

There is a sad ending to **"Halloran's Child,"** the main theme of which is the tragic attachment of a deaf-and-dumb old man, Nate Twomey, to a little girl doomed from birth. Nate has become used to the child's presence in his workshop and to her stories which he has learned to understand by lip-reading. And the girl likes watching him at his work, breathing the fragrance of sawdust and wood shavings. Although Twomey sees that Halloran's daughter is getting worse each day, her foredoomed end seems remote and unreal to him. The theme of death, as interpreted by Susan Hill in her own original way, is heard in the story from the very beginning. The same theme permeates the close: but the girl's death brings the central character not only pain and suffering, but spiritual catharsis and even illumination.

This treatment of death is typical of Susan Hill. She is concerned with the mysteries of existence which man is so eager to fathom.

But it is not only the motif of understanding and enlightenment through suffering that comes with death that gives most of Susan Hill's stories a sad ending. The world she creates is one of unfulfilled hopes, of missed opportunities and of suffering. And so death, to her, seems the most natural resolution of the conflict and, in terms of plot, the simplest way out of the predicament. Many of her characters suffer from incurable illness; hence the motif of the transitoriness, the frailty and imperfection of all that exists.

What, then, can take a man out of the wretched round of day-to-day existence? Creativeness, the power of the spirit, replies Susan Hill. This is the subject of her novel *The Bird of Night* (1972), which tells of a young and talented poet who suffers from a serious mental ailment.

The novel consists, for the most part, of reminiscences about the poet by his close friend Harvey Lawson. They run as a free thought-stream, not following any chronological sequence, sometimes becoming confused and breaking off. The action of the novel is developed with equal freedom, consisting of vivid, complex, but profoundly interrelated inner fragments.

The technique of the vivid fragmentary miniatures is not only the basis for the novel's composition but is also the foundation for the creation of the images. Susan Hill does not tell us everything about her characters: on the contrary, she outlines only what is most typical and significant. Her aim is, without explaining anything, almost without drawing conclusions and making deductions, to convey the inner state of the character's mind through behaviour. This behaviour often seems strange at first, and even illogical; but it is always possible to find an explanation, to ascertain the underlying cause. This is what is most important in Susan Hill's works, and, although it is almost never clearly defined, this cause dominates the narrative and is palpable in everything that she describes. It is also typical that for all the restraint inherent in her style, she nevertheless "pushes" the reader very discreetly towards the right solution, the true interpretation of the inner conflicts. This is where we become aware of her skill in the use of such devices as telling detail, repetition, specific rhythm and sentence structure. The ending of her story **"The Red and Green Beads"** is touching and disturbing thanks to a detail brought out in the title. Marcel Piguet, sick and ugly from birth, brings to the grave of the only person who does not find him revolting the coloured glass beads which he has never parted with until this moment. Frequently, in order to stress something or evoke an essential analogy, Susan Hill elaborates on a secondary theme, while the main message in any of her works remains deep below the surface; it seldom emerges and, before it can declare itself, withdraws into the depths once more.

The result of this method of writing is an extreme succinctness which, so far from schematising the action, gives the narrative a special expressiveness and special imagery.

Susan Hill is very skilfull at the realistic creation of character. But she shows her protagonists in a grim and hopeless duel with life, or she artificially wrests them out of their habitual environment and puts them in conditions not typical of our times. Her characters, however much they may differ—shopkeepers, the owners of seedy hotels, wretched old men, mad poets—cannot understand the world around them and find their place in it. They often feel hopelessness of their attempts in advance, and this makes them suffer a great deal.

Much in Susan Hill's books suggests that she is engaged in a quest, that she is trying to find the answers to questions that have so far seemed insoluble to her. The Soviet reader awaits her next books with interest.

Donald A. Low (essay date 1981)

SOURCE: "Telling the Story: Susan Hill and Dorothy L. Sayers," in *British Radio Drama,* edited by John Drakakis, Cambridge University Press, 1981, pp. 111-38.

[*In the essay below, Low discusses the connection between Hill's fiction and her radio dramas, emphasizing the role of dialogue and the spoken word in her narrative style in both genres.*]

> When we go to Heaven, all I ask is that we shall be given some interesting job & allowed to get on with it. No management; no box-office; no dramatic critics; & an audience of cheerful angels who don't mind laughing. (Dorothy L. Sayers to Val Gielgud, 13 January 1942)

Radio is as rich a story-telling medium as any in the twentieth century. Given its appeal to the ear through speech—and also by means of music, silence, and sound—this is easy to understand. The novel and short story developed largely as forms for the printed word, and silent reading is a sophisticated activity with its own conventions and assumptions. But turn to young children anywhere: the first way in which most of us come across stories is by hearing them read aloud. 'Acting out' or drama is the next stage. What is more, all story-writing carries some echo and implication of human speech, most obviously in the form of dialogue. It follows that radio offers to the skilled writer a medium in which stories and drama belong naturally, and the chance to recover an old dimension while finding a new. The writer's passport into radio drama is a trained ear for dialogue.

There is a wry and truthful BBC boast that radio drama in Britain has launched on their careers a number of writers who have gone on to realise their dreams by working subsequently for the theatre, playwrights of the calibre of Harold Pinter and Tom Stoppard. But a quite different group of successful radio dramatists consists of writers who, before supplying scripts for radio, had already made their mark in the novel. Radio drama provides an additional outlet and resource for these writers, who do not necessarily ever aim for the kind of mastery of visual presentation which the stage requires. Some of the best of all British radio plays have been created by storytellers of long professional experience, novelists who possess narrative energy and a subtle auditory imagination.

The truth of this is borne out by the radio work of two novelists of different generations and different types, Susan Hill and Dorothy L. Sayers. Born in 1942, Susan Hill grew up an avid radio listener, familiar with *Under Milk Wood* and *The Dark Tower.* She published several novels before beginning to write for radio, but when she did, it was to find that 'I slipped into the medium as into an old glove, which seemed to have moulded itself long ago to the shape of my own hand, and I am still surprised that I did not make use of it much earlier.' In *The Cold Country and Other Plays for Radio* (1975), she reveals the sharp psychological intelligence of a novelist of the seventies adept in exploring the inner fears and loneliness, as well as the hopes, of her characters. Her special flair is for hinting at comedy and even beauty amidst insecurity and mounting anguish. No Beckett, she is nevertheless an 'endgame' writer, or what Denis Donoghue has called a 'connoisseur of chaos'; thus her work belongs to a mainstream twentieth-century tradition. The formula which she adopts to express this vision in her radio plays is essentially a simple one. Something which begins by being low-key and apparently trivial gradually gathers pace, is felt to be thoroughly ominous, and moves towards a desperate and painful ending. This sound-drama technique can be compared with her approach in fiction: in both media she makes use of a popular narrative type, the tale of doom or story with a horrifying crisis, and invests it with depth and unexpected meaning. As she has noted, the radio dramatist 'may do anything—except *bore*'. Susan Hill's radio Gothic spine-chillers are never boring.

Elwyn Evans has described the spare style of modern radio writing as 'essentially conversation, tightened, sharpened, made (often in the most literal sense) killingly funny; the phrases, the interruptions, the pauses all chosen and subtly counterpointed to make contact with the listener on a disconcerting variety of levels'. The context shows that he has in mind especially Stan Barstow and Giles Cooper in making this comment, but it might equally serve as a description of *The Cold Country.* In this play, four explorers are snowed up somewhere near the South Pole with no hope of getting away and nobody at hand to rescue them. Not even the radio is working any more, although it takes a long time for Jo, the most naive and trusting member of the group, to accept this. As the days pass, they all get on each other's nerves, and the resulting dissolution is grim: a hopeless walk undertaken by Jo out of guilt and ending in his death; a murder; a second, truly guilty exit into the icebound waste; and aimless guitar-playing by the sole survivor in the tent, merging into the Lyke-Wake Dirge. Susan Hill explains in her Introduction to the printed version of the play that ever since the news of man's conquest of Everest in 1953 she has been fascinated by 'cold white desolate worlds'. *The Cold Country* is anti-heroic, a study of defeat, and perhaps significantly of man's defeat—in her other plays, where there are female characters as well as male, the emphasis seems not quite so stark. The adroitness with which she handles phrases, interruptions, and pauses to communicate the tensions and faltering interaction of Ossie, Chip, Barney, and Jo is extremely sensitive. Chip, for instance, who is to end by killing his friend Barney in a moment of hysteria, begins by telling bright jokes in the teeth of adversity. Ingeniously, Susan Hill disturbs her listeners with words made familiar by Brian Cant's television programme for children, *Playaway:*

> CHIP. That's right, troops, keep up the old morale.
> JO. It's Ossie. Making all sorts of snap judgements. We don't get on, he says, we're driving one another mad. Well I think we're doing all right. As well as anyone else would do under the circumstances. I think . . .
> BARNEY. Oh, spare us the sermon.
> OSSIE. O.K., O.K., forget it, I only said . . .
> CHIP [*interrupting quickly*]. I say, I say, I say, my aunt's gone to the West Indies.
> OSSIE. Jamaica?
> CHIP. No, she went of her own accord. [*Pause*] Well come on! . . . All right, try again. I say, I say, I say, my aunt's gone to the *East* Indies.
> OSSIE. Jakarta?
> CHIP. No, she went by plane.
> JO. Oh, for God's sake!
> CHIP. Barney, why do cows wear cow-bells?
> BARNEY. I don't know, Chip, why do cows wear cow-bells?
> CHIP. Because their horns won't work. Da-da-dee-da-da-DA! [*Silence*] Oh, I give up, I do really.
> JO. Good.
> CHIP. What's on your mind anyway, Jo?
> JO. Oh, nothing, nothing. How to make you lot get off your backsides. Whether we're going to let ourselves live or die. Because it's up to us, you know. What we're doing here, what it's all about. What went wrong.

The trouble with Chip is that he does not wear motley consistently enough—in *King Lear* neither the Fool nor Edgar says, 'Oh, I give up, I do really.' But Susan Hill pays some kind of tribute to Chip for trying. Only Ossie lasts longer, it

may be because he has the superior consolation of art. He wears the rest down by playing 'Roses of Picardy' on the mouth-organ, then moves on to the guitar. Even as a time-killer, Susan Hill appears to imply, music-making has value, keeping alive the imagination and the will to live in harsh places.

Ossie has said with vindictiveness, 'When I get home, I'll write a book like they've never read before, I'll tell them how it really is.' Presumably at the end he somehow survives, and so gains the chance to write about his experiences; *The Cold Country* deliberately runs counter to what is held to be the false glamour of *Scott of the Antarctic.* Elsewhere, Susan Hill develops the theme of the solitary and apparently antisocial individual's imagination as the only way through hell, the single positive force worth holding on to in a welter of destructiveness all around. The radio play is particularly well suited to express such a theme. Words about solitude which are listened to in solitude communicate strongly the idea of human separateness.

Lizard in the Grass (1971) presents the extraordinary experiences of an intensely imaginative adolescent girl, an orphan, caught by unhappy chance in an uncongenial convent school where she rubs up both staff and pupils the wrong way. There are overtones of Joyce's *Portrait of the Artist as a Young Man* here in the way phrases of the institution are loaded with hostile feeling. It is hard to say which is worse, the taunts of Jane's classmates, or the inflexible lovelessness of Sister Patrick, but both are brought home to us in jingling words:

> CLARE. [*Sharp whisper, very close*]. Jane Pace . . .
> JANE. [*startled*]. What? What is it?
> CLARE. What have you done?
>   [*Other girls in the taunting chorus*]
> Now what have you done?
> You've been sent for.
> You're to see Sister Superior.
> Jane Pace.
> You got an order mark.
> Three.
> In one week.
> You're for it.
> Again.
> What have you done? What have you done? Jane Pace, in disgrace, Jane Pace, in disgrace, Jane, Jane, Jane . . .
>   [*A desk bangs suddenly. Scurrying. Silence. Scraping of chairs.*]
> SISTER PATRICK. Good morning, Four A.
> CLASS [*sing-song unison*]. Good morning, Sister Patrick.
>   [*Pause. Then Sister imitates sarcastically*]
> SISTER P. Good-*mor*-ning-*Sister-Pat*-rick.

[*A murmur*]
Listen to you. Listen! What do you sound like?
Stand up straight.
Stand up as girls should stand first thing each morning. Bright, Alert,
Attentive. Jane Pace . . .
JANE. I didn't . . .

Sister Patrick treats poor dreamy Jane as a deviant needing to be straightened out, and very nearly succeeds in breaking her spirit. However, the girl receives a crumb of affection from an eccentric old nun, Imelda, who is barely tolerated by the rest of the community, and Jane's love of unorthodox reading sees her through, after a fashion, so that she ends up holding conversations with the ghost of John Skelton, spirited out of a bone which she finds on the beach. He, it turns out, was treated somewhat shabbily in his lifetime, and he is glad to have the chance to share his troubles with Jane. His words 'come to me' form a distinctly sinister refrain towards the close. Susan Hill brings off the difficult feat of controlling her invention, so that the play does not topple over either into 'lonely-hearts' sentimentality or into that other trap for radio dramatists, 'twangling instruments' metaphysics. Unlike, say, Bruce Stewart's *The Tor Sands Experience* (BBC *Hi-Fi Theatre,* 1979), in which ingenious but finally tedious stereophonic effects failed to lift a weak philosophical idea, *Lizard in the Grass* develops a fantasy in words powerful enough to be believed in. 'There should be no time', says Sister Patrick, 'for a head full of peculiar imaginings. "This is the weather the cuckoo likes." That is what I have set her to learn.' But Jane's head is her own, and she chooses to learn much less comfortable verses, with the result that she is accused of harbouring simultaneously immodest and morbid thoughts 'about skeletons and wombs'. Susan Hill weaves in cleverly selected quotations at will, using them to distinguish her introspective heroine from everyone else in the play:

> MEGAN. Clare Boothright, just you get on, you stop talking to Jane Pace, it's forbidden, it's not allowed.
> CLARE. Well I can't shut my case
> [*A sudden screech of laughter goes up somewhere else.*]
> I can't take anything out, I need everything.
> JANE [*very quietly*].
> 'That when ye think all danger for to pass,
> Ware of the lizard lieth lurking in the grass.'
> CLARE. What?
> MEGAN [*calls*]. It's twenty past. Just gone twenty past.

Such words from the past are at once teasing and poetic in their suggestiveness, adding notably to the linguistic texture of the play.

What impresses most is that the different elements of *Consider the Lilies* blend together to operate successfully on the 'disconcerting variety of levels' noted by Elwyn Evans as characteristic of recent radio writing at its best.
—*Donald A. Low*

Susan Hill is able to capture in *Lizard in the Grass* the apparently random effect of different trains of thoughts cutting into each other because she has learned as a novelist to listen to people talking and to highlight moments of spoken interplay. This is common ground between fiction and the radio play, but there was much to learn about creating drama for the airwaves, and she gives full credit for vital encouragement to Guy Vaesen, the BBC producer of all but one of her plays, and also to Geoffrey Burgon, who wrote music for three of them. In the 1973 stereo play *Consider the Lilies,* Guy Vaesen's role as constructive critic was especially important, and the dramatist states that 'it ought to bear his name, as co-author'. *Consider the Lilies* breaks new ground in combining Susan Hill's characteristic honesty about suffering—in the course of the action a young girl dies of a wasting illness—with visionary optimism. A main source of inspiration this time is Blake. The central figure, a middle-aged botanist called Bowman, has intense moments of apprehension of heaven on earth very much in the manner of the revolutionary poet-artist; then he and Susannah, the girl who dies, commune with each other partly in allusive fashion.

> SUSANNAH. My nurse gets bored. 'All those trees', she says. 'All those trees.' I suppose it's tiring for her, pushing me everywhere. She likes a 'nice sit-down'. I look at the trees.
> BOWMAN. 'The tree which moves some to tears of joy is, in the eyes of others, only a green thing which stands in the way.'
> SUSANNAH. But I'm lucky. I haven't any troubles. They don't know when I'll die . . . I'd like to wait until the winter. Everything else will die then. But people look after me. I have every day to look at things. Everyone else has to work and worry. I learned something, too. I read a lot of books. I can always read.
> BOWMAN. What did you learn?
> SUSANNAH. 'The stars reflect the visions of holiness and the trees are uttering prophecies and speaking instructive words to the sons of men.'
> BOWMAN. That's the truth. That's what I see. Oh, Susannah, don't die. You mustn't die.
> SUSANNAH. I shall. I don't seem to belong here now. It's a nuisance. I feel like a shot bird. Heavy.

BOWMAN. We've reached the edge of the lake.
SUSANNAH. 'Every night and every morn
    Some to misery are born.
    Every morn and every night
    Some are born to sweet delight.'

There is a danger that such exchanges may seem flat, failing to move the listener in the manner that the writer intends; Susan Hill's sensibility is really very different from Blake's. To counter-point the visionary theme, she develops a comic sub-plot, in which Lesage, Bowman's statistically minded second-in-command, schemes with his garrulous mother about how to pension off the admirer of lilies so that he can get his job. This layer of the play works very well indeed, so characterful is the dialogue:

> LESAGE. Plants, flowers, the whole botanical gardens, the whole organisation . . . I could talk to him about my plans for a research programme in carnivorous plants. I could . . . I don't know. I can't seem to find a way through. We never meet. He lives in another world.
> MRS. L. It's not right, you're young, you're ambitious. You always liked plants, even from a little boy. You made a beautiful garden in a kitchen saucer when you were only three, the afternoon before those four houses in Albany Street got a direct hit, and not so much as a warning, not a peep were we given out of that siren, crash-bang, while I was peeling the potatoes, I thought the world was coming to an end.
> LESAGE. I still have dreams about that. The noise.
> MRS. L. You were too young to remember. And there you'd been, making that lovely garden, all neat it was, all orderly, little paths marked out in rows of pebbles, bits of twigs and so on, just like a proper laid-out public park.

What impresses most is that the different elements of *Consider the Lilies* blend together to operate successfully on the 'disconcerting variety of levels' noted by Elwyn Evans as characteristic of recent radio writing at its best. Bowman is no less a man of truth for being seen through the eyes of Lesage as culpably vague and absent-minded—their collision is genuinely funny, part of the price of Blakean change. And Susannah loses none of her vulnerability or dignity because of the ironies which attend Bowman's progress: 'you must tell your visions', she tells him. Affirmation and playful satire both have a place in the drama, just as they do, quite differently, in *The Marriage of Heaven and Hell.* Moreover, the work is genuinely stereophonic, as there is music and a chorus of plants, 'a male and a female chorus, set on either speaker . . . they are separate at the beginning, and join together towards the end, when the music becomes reminiscent of the music which will later "blossom out" into

the visionary theme'. Few radio plays to date have exploited the full resources of the medium with such assurance and tact.

What are the proper boundaries of the radio dramatist's role? Should he or she stay away from rehearsal, or is a place to be specially reserved in the studio? Susan Hill is clear about a lesson of experience gained during rehearsal of *Consider the Lilies:*

> I had never gone into the studio during the recording of any of my plays; I felt that the presence of the author (even when sitting mute in the background of the control room) would inhibit producer and cast. But I was persuaded to go down for the production of *Consider the Lilies,* only to find that, especially in the final scenes, the actors were having great problems with the interpretation of their parts, because of faulty writing. After long talks with Tony Britton, Helen Worth and, again Guy Vaesen, several scenes were rearranged, cut, or rewritten entirely in the margins of scripts, during lunch and coffee breaks. I still adhere to my rule that the author must not interfere in any way with the work of producer, actors or technicians, but I shall not be absent from studio during any future recordings, if only because a radio playwright's education is a continuous one, and a day spent listening and observing, in silence, can teach one more than weeks in the study with a script-in-progress.

This is an admirably frank and well-defined position. Only an outsider ignorant of production schedules would want to see writers continuously present among broadcasting staff, interfering in their work; yet the dogmatism which would exclude the radio dramatist from the studio is equally short-sighted. Much depends, clearly, on the quality of the relationship between writer and producer. Where there is trust, a constructive studio partnership involving writer, actors, and producer is possible.

Rosemary Jackson (essay date 1982)

SOURCE: "Cold Enclosures: The Fiction of Susan Hill," in *Twentieth-Century Women Novelists,* edited by Thomas F. Staley, Barnes & Noble Books, 1982, pp. 81-103.

[In the following essay, Jackson approaches Hill's fiction in terms of a tension between detachment from and desire for life, identifying the idea of coldness as its "imaginative centre" and relating its principal themes and motifs to feminist concerns.]

Susan Hill's fictional output has been substantial and has been well received by the English literary establishment. Between 1961 and 1976, she published nine novels, two short story anthologies, one collection of radio plays, and received recognition with the Somerset Maugham Award in 1971, the Whitbread Literary Award in 1972, and the Rhys Memorial Prize in 1972. Her success enabled her to be financially independent as a writer from 1963 onwards. Unlike many of her contemporaries, Susan Hill does not seem to be primarily concerned with the subject, or the subjection, of women. A female consciousness rarely forms the centre of her tales, and questions of women's social position appear merely as vague shadows hovering on the edges of her writing. Yet, in spite of this subordination of women, a close reading of Hill's work seems to vindicate a feminist approach. For her victims, her peculiar cast of artists, idiots, children, lonely and dying men and women, are all romantic figures who have given up the struggle to live in an adult, 'masculine' world. They are enclosed within their fears of engagement with a difficult, demanding actuality. They withdraw into passive, dependent situations, feeling that they do not know how to 'live'. Hill seems to pose their problems in metaphysical terms—as to whether life is worth living at all—but behind these there are considerable economic and emotional factors which have determined their senses of 'failure'. As her fiction develops, a resolution slowly emerges, but it is achieved at a considerable price, and it shows that the real issues behind her work are related to problems of female survival.

> **Unlike many of her contemporaries, Susan Hill does not seem to be primarily concerned with the subject, or the subjection, of women. A female consciousness rarely forms the centre of her tales, and questions of women's social position appear merely as vague shadows hovering on the edges of her writing. Yet, in spite of this subordination of women, a close reading of Hill's work seems to vindicate a feminist approach.**
> **—Rosemary Jackson**

I shall consider Hill's writing as a whole, and take it more or less chronologically, as it deals with these issues of detachment and desire for life. As a body of writing, it shows considerable unity: from *The Enclosure* (1961) to *The Land of Lost Content* (1976), the same preoccupations appear in it. Plots, themes, and motifs, recur with a striking similarity in different texts, as they move toward a resolution of a basic desire to enter life. Perhaps the most powerful of Hill's images, and the most central, is the one which is found in her work time after time, of a cold, frozen country, of ice, snow, still water, frost, winter. A tension between apprehending ice/winter/sterility and longing for warmth/summer/fertility is constant in her fiction. It is graphically expressed in two identical dream images, found in the openings of *Strange Meeting* (1971) and *The Bird of Night* (1972). These haunting images, primarily oneiric scenes which are not readily translated from visual into verbal discourse, can be regarded as the imaginative centre of Hill's fiction. The first tells of John Hilliard's (his name coincides with Hill's) wartime dream:

> at first, he dreamed only of horses, standing beside a hawthorn hedge in winter. The dark twigs were laced over with frost. There were four or five horses, and the breath came out of their nostrils and rose to hang and freeze, whitening on the air. He heard the soft thud of hoof on hard earth and the metal bits champing. Their muzzles were like the soft backs of moles.
>
> . . . For a while, half-sleeping again, he still heard the gentle tossing of the horses's heads, saw their breath smoking, saw ice meshed with cracks across a puddle.
>
> Outside in the darkness, a hundred yards away, the soil became paler and drier, became sand, and the path led down to the beach.

The second tells of Harvey Lawson's similar memory:

> How often I must have dreamed, every night of my long life perhaps, and forgotten all of them except this one.
>
> I was dreaming of winter. I stood in a lane beside a hawthorn hedge and the frost had laced the twigs over with delicate, brittle strands of ice, powdery snow lay balanced between. There was a puddle of water at my feet, iced over and transparent except in the centre, where it had been cracked by a single stone and the ice was meshed out in fine lines from a hollow core. Beside me stood two horses, and the breath came steaming out of their nostrils and froze at once upon the air, they tossed their heads and their eyes shone, I could hear the harness chinking. I had a hand on the neck of one horse, the muscle was thick and strongly fleshed, and the coat faintly sticky to my touch. The hawthorn hedge glittered. (p. 17.)

For both these dreamers, ice and snow represent their emotional isolation, whilst heat and breath indicate their desire that this coldness be counteracted by something more vital and physical. Frequently, coldness is associated with artistic control, with the act of writing, or with a quest for beauty/purity. Hill's novels and stories recount a gradual thawing of that ice landscape, in a slow renunciation of aesthetic withdrawal.

The title of Susan Hill's first novel, *The Enclosure,* indicates its concern with imprisonment and detachment. Its heroine, Virginia, uses novel writing to control experience. It gives her a sense of superiority over others, of (in-)difference. But her hyper-sensitivity is exposed as egotism. She regards others as less troubled, less perceiving than herself. Her son Philip turns Catholic, and Virginia 'wondered how anyone could be so obviously content and undisturbed', 'she was amazed again at the complacency with which he regarded life'. Her husband, Guy Stirling, she holds as less sensitive than she is, 'He bluffed himself, as always, into believing that everything was really quite normal'. The narrator permits no ambiguity in our response to this woman writer: she is a monster of egotism, and all her suffering constitutes a necessary penance for her selfishness. She is described as an 'emotional adolescent', insensitive to Guy's depths of feeling. 'Man, to her, was animal. She could never believe that Guy could experience a woman's subtlety of emotion . . . did not realise that almost physical pain her coldness gave him'. She is locked in an 'innate selfishness, which she projected so often on to other people and saw in them', being 'a woman whose understanding of men scarcely penetrated the surface, in spite of the influence of passionate love'. Moral judgements of Virginia, for not giving to others, are plentiful. It is 'her own fault' that her life sinks into 'futility and hollowness', and 'Any observer might have remarked, with justice, that it served her right . . . Virginia never tried to realise the fact that she was unhappy was basically her fault . . . she would not recognise her own selfishness'.

Virginia's eventual success as a writer, with a room of her own, is presented not only as a rather Pyrrhic victory, but as an absolute failure in human terms. She has been unable to respond to Guy's patient devotion, and unable to be a 'real' woman—her pregnancy is 'unreal' to her, and her child, a daughter, is stillborn. Virginia ends in the same enclosure in which she began, with a curious sense of hollowness, of wanting something more. 'She seemed to be living in an enclosure which she hated with an agonising intensity, but out of which she would not let herself escape.' 'The enclosure was still intact.' Unlike similar metaphors of imprisonment in Anais Nin's *Under a Glass Bell* (1944), Sylvia Plath's *The Bell Jar* (1963), or Anna Kavan's *Ice* (1967), Susan Hill's image in *The Enclosure* does not relate detachment from experience to specifically female anxieties. It allows for neither understanding nor pity. She does not consider the ideological implications of her explicit and implicit judgements about Virginia. She presents the issue as being beyond gender. In fact, her condemnation of a woman for giving priority to her work barely disguises a deep unease, verging on guilt, about her own position as a writer. Female freedom or independence is made synonymous with selfishness. We are left, simply, to condemn a solitary woman writer in the provinces, despising her for her coldness, and longing for the warmth, colour, passion, and energy, which have retreated with the man, Guy, into a distant metropolis.

Idealisation/idolisation of the male as the locus of energy is intensified in *Do Me a Favour* (1963). A successful writer, Monica Bristow, suspends her career for the sake of Dan Lindsay, a dashingly Byronic type, with dark features, high cheekbones, thick-set jaw, rakish alcoholic behaviour, aristocratic roots and all. Frequent lapses into Lawrentian prose indicate disturbingly masochistic features on the part of the woman writer. Monica wants to be brutalised, as if this will awaken her out of her work into real life. 'She wanted him to make love to her as harshly as he could, without compassion or being gentle—there was merely what she supposed was an animal yearning for him'. The further their romantic affair proceeds, the further she sinks into this mine, 'The deeper she penetrated, she began to see into the darkness and to know'. A classic romance plot nicely contains this knowledge in a cosy marriage, an unexpected pregnancy, and a 'placid contentment'. Monica accommodates herself completely to Dan's larger-than-life, egotistical existence. She experiences a 'complete loss of purpose for anything but this', and 'She wanted to build round her a big, noisy, stable family, with Dan in the centre . . . It was essentially a feminine dream . . . she loved him—she would have done anything he wanted'. 'Dan's company was all she wanted.' For all their generational differences, the women in the novel uphold identical values. Monica goes a little further than her elders along a path towards a career, but happily recedes into a marital enclosure. She vindicates the words of the old Mrs Christoff, who tells her: 'Your career is important. You write well. But marriage and children is a greater career in the end—for a woman . . . children are a greater gift than knowledge.' Monica—and Susan Hill—defend a similarly Victorian notion of women's role. Whereas *The Enclosure* had given Virginia an ending of despair for her devotion to work, *Do Me a Favour* gives Monica the joys of self-sacrifice, in her choice of heart, instead of art.

In *Gentleman and Ladies* (1968) and *A Change for the Better* (1969) humane values are sustained with difficulty against a dark awareness that everything returns to ashes and dust.
—*Rosemary Jackson*

By retreating into domestic security, Monica blinds herself to the unpalatable 'terrible truths' which hang outside. These truths are perceived only too clearly by Peter Goosens, a tragic, doomed figure who is the first in a long series of similarly depressed protagonists in Hill's work. Peter is constricted by the 'hell' of London and the horrors of his marriage. Everything exists, for him, over an edge of violence. He is drawn towards death. 'He pulled the blade over his skin slowly, with a tense, terrifying desire to use it on himself or her [his wife] with violence.' 'In the end, there was no cure for what he had to live with.' Just as in Virginia Woolf's *Mrs Dalloway* (1925), where death instincts are channelled into the suicidal figure of Septimus Smith, who impales himself by falling onto sharp railings, so, in ***Do Me a Favour,*** destructive instincts are concentrated into Peter, who throws himself into the Thames from Waterloo Bridge. 'The river below was running high, but not rough, and it looked filthy—it just went on and on . . . [he swung] up on to the railing.' It is the first of many deaths by drowning in Hill's fiction. When Monica watches an insect crawling over a picture of a sea storm, she reintroduces this motif of drowning, but refuses to accept that sense of futility which it evokes.

> She sat still, and suddenly noticed a small insect—an ant or tiny winter fly—on the opposite wall. It was crawling, very slowly, hardly moving . . . [it] made its way across the glazed canvas. She saw it go up the side of a grey rock, over the edge and down again, getting caught in a rush of foam that broke over it, and going down again, into the sea, across the sea to the other edge of the picture, a tiny black speck, moving, it seemed, without any legs, just moving aimlessly across the picture. Perhaps it did have an aim.

The conjecture in this 'perhaps' is translated into a certainty, in Monica's world, by confining herself to recognised aims for a woman, of producing children and protecting her husband. This plot sets the pattern for Hill's subsequent fiction. Images of futility and death are produced by a finite number of natural objects—moths, crows, peacocks, flies, insects, corpses, bones, birds of prey, 'owls, ravens, hedgehogs, snakes—augurs of death and mischance', and they darken Hill's world, drawing her most vulnerable subjects towards suicide. Opposed to them, and set comparatively lightly in the balance, are less convincing pictures of community, of family life and love, and a promise of summer.

In *Gentleman and Ladies* (1968) and *A Change for the Better* (1969) humane values are sustained with difficulty against a dark awareness that everything returns to ashes and dust. The title of the first indicates an imbalance in Hill's writing between the importance attached to male and female characters. Apart from a local vicar and two bird-like doctors, the only man in the novel is Hubert Gaily, a ponderous

middle-aged figure, slow but innocent in his child-like existence with his mother. He is the centre of a female universe. He hangs on to domestic routine in a defence against a grotesque reality, living in fear of change. 'Maybe it was only to be expected, a sudden change that tilted your world sideways, slipped the ground from under you a shade.' Outside little enclaves of love and caring established by Hubert, his friend Florence Ames (whose name recalls Dickens's innocent Florence in *Dombey and Son* and Amy in *Little Dorrit*), and Dorothy Shottery, lies a bleak world of the dead, dying and indifferent. There is very little plot. The novel opens with the funeral of Faith Lavender, an old spinster, and closes with that of her sister, Isabel. The third, Kathleen, suffers a stroke and paralysis, which make her infantile. The three Lavender sisters are a Chekhovian trio, slowly dying in an English countryside, surrounded by similarly empty female lives. Pictures of these female friends accumulate into a stark tableau of suffering, which is something of a *danse macabre*. Every woman is locked in her sense of isolation, resenting her lack of freedom, but too trapped by hostile circumstance to act. Isabel merely laments her wasted years. At twenty-eight, 'She had looked out of her bedroom window upon an unjust world, upon undeserved sadness, upon concatenation of ill-luck, upon at least equal odds of sickness, spinsterhood and narrow horizons'. Alida Thorne, a sixty-one-year-old acquaintance, has her mother put away into a nursing home in a final bid for self-fulfilment, but is portrayed as a bitter, selfish woman. Her mother, Eleanor, is 'carted away like a splitting and discarded mattress beside someone's dustbin' into a world where the only possible movement is into death or dementia, where 'Each day passed, that was all'. None of them is 'free from the threat' of immanent decay. They all live in fear. 'The thoughts of madness and senility frightened her', 'there are no words to convey the fear, the blank fear'. Even Hubert ponders 'death and dying. You had to think of it, now and then.' Rather like Elizabeth Gaskell's *Cranford* a century earlier, *Gentleman and Ladies* accumulates portraits of female gentility which barely cover an apprehension of futility. Grotesque similes are all to do with the traps of women's lives. 'The sunlight showed up a dead fly on its back beneath the window. Isabel started. She did not like to be reminded of dead things, even flies, by the stiff, still bits of leg.' Gaily remembers reading about 'a woman, crushed to death by a car that had pinned her against a wall. She had been walking to the shops, doing nothing, carefree, and it had killed her.' They are images simply presenting what is—their static form makes it impossible to imagine difference.

A Change for the Better gives no sense of change at all. Various lonely old people sit, waiting for the end, in an English seaside resort, out of season. Major Carpenter, looking out to sea, thinks of the deaths approaching his friend Isepp and himself, and complains that 'We are caught like rats in a trap'. Deirdre Fount, an ageing divorcee, longs for the death of the mother who has trapped her in restrictive habits, but when her desire is realised, she sinks back into her mother's character. Her name recalls Synge's *Deirdre of the Sorrows.* Only old Mrs Carpenter determines not to be imprisoned by such defeatism.

> She is very young, she thought, not yet forty, and already she has given in, she is afraid of life, she will have nothing to look forward to in the future. Well, that shall be a warning to me . . . [I must make] some effort to live my life independently . . . My future is entirely up to me.

Placing the one note of self-determination in the voice of an old widow, without a trace of irony or ambiguity, severely qualifies any sense of women's growth in *A Change for the Better.* Things are irredeemably stuck and static. None of the women escapes. Movement is confined to the ebb and flow of the sea, which erases all their lives, and to Deirdre's son, James, who rejects her and leaves to make a life of his own. It is clear, in these early novels, that Susan Hill has little faith in women's strength. She effects a virtual polarisation of 'female' and 'male' qualities: characters in whom the first predominate cannot compete on equal terms and they sink back, defeated, into actual death or into analogous states of death-in-life. *I'm the King of the Castle* (1970) is a carefully structured narrative along these lines of conflict between 'female' and 'male', resulting in the acquiescence of the 'female' part, which is reluctant to assert itself on 'male' terms.

Central to *I'm the King of the Castle* is a classic drama of rivalry for a family/kinship structure. Eleven-year-old Charles Kingshaw comes with his widowed mother, Helena, to stay at the Warings, a Gothic mansion owned by Joseph Hooper, whose wife, Ellen, has been dead for six years. Helena gradually replaces Ellen in the father's affections. But in the traditional family structure of father-mother-child which results, there is no room for both Charles and Edmund, Hooper's eleven-year-old son. One of the boys has to be excluded. The narrative built around this drama is a well-sustained, tense account of Charles Kingshaw's increasing sense of persecution and alienation. Unable to fight, and unwilling to abuse his integrity by happily giving in to the Hoopers as his mother does, Kingshaw moves away from the Warings to the woods outside, eventually drowning himself in an enclosed pool. Here, he is safe. 'He liked the smell, and the sense of being completely hidden. Everything around him seemed innocent.' But its innocence, its immunity to adult corruption, is at the cost of ceasing to be alive. Kingshaw's suicide indicates a despairing conviction on Hill's part, that moral innocence is incompatible with survival in an adult world whose rules are patriarchal. Kingshaw refuses to accept Hooper's masculine values. He does not enjoy hunting and killing, he hates war games, he plays with dolls as opposed to toy armies, he chooses not to employ his power to hurt others. He says, 'I can *do* anything. He knew that he would not.' It is this choice which determines his necessary death in a world dominated by the Hoopers and what they represent. 'He was only good at plodding along by himself, not at competing', and 'he knew that he was the loser.' 'He might as well give up, as he always gave up in the end . . . he knew that there was no more hope for him . . . It was pointless.' 'He was not cowardly. Just realistic, hopeless. He did not give in to people, he only went, from the beginning, with the assurance that he would be beaten. It meant that there was no surprise, and no disappointment about anything . . . He knew that there was no hope, really.' This defeatism is of the same kind which kills Peter Goosens in *Do Me a Favour* and darkens the scenes of *Gentleman and Ladies* and *A Change for the Better.* Innocence, childhood, truth, beauty, goodness, are assumed to be incompatible with entrance into adulthood. But behind Hill's humanistic vision there lie some telling sexual differences which reveal this negativity to be a rejection, and fear, of patriarchy.

Kingshaw and Hooper do not compete on equal terms. Kingshaw represents the 'feminine' and Hooper the 'masculine'. Kingshaw owns nothing and is therefore seen as being nothing, as a mere cipher. Hooper (his name suggests, hoop, ring, trap) is his father's son, a little man of property, with a tradition of economic strength and material security behind him. He taunts Kingshaw, that 'Anybody who hasn't got a father is useless'. This judgement is quickly internalised. Kingshaw thinks, 'It was his father's fault really, because his dying had been the start of it all, the not having enough money, and living in other people's houses . . . He wished she [his mother] was dead, instead of his father'. Both boys perceive that their drama is a reflection of what is happening between Mr Hooper and Mrs Kingshaw.

Hooper sees it as reinforcing his power, and he says condescendingly, 'Look, it's all right, Kingshaw, it's only what ladies do. If she hasn't got a husband, she's got to find one', but Kingshaw is nauseated by his mother's surrender, 'He wanted to shake her . . . He was sick with shame at her'. The two levels of plot, adult and child couples, parallel one another, and make it possible to read Kingshaw's drowning as a violent image of his mother's emotional suicide in the marriage in which she loses her identity. Unable to be a 'man', yet unwilling to play the losing role of 'woman', Kingshaw is left with no alternative but death. His isolation cannot be preserved indefinitely in the real world. 'He liked being alone, because he was used to it, he was safe with himself. Other people were unpredictable.' It is guaranteed only in a fatal, watery enclosure. 'This was his place. It was where he wanted to be . . . when the water had reached up to his thighs, he lay down slowly and put his face full into it and breathed in a long, careful breath.' He can accept neither his own nor his mother's sexuality. After seeing a calf born, he wants to erase the 'terrible truths' of birth, and of sexuality, but he realises that innocence has been lost. 'You could never return to the time of not-knowing.' In retreat from such knowledge and from the difficult sexual politics of an adult world, Kingshaw (just before adolescence) sinks into an almost intra-uterine state, in a pool of death in which impossible growth is no longer demanded.

Such withdrawal into perfect states of death, or of death-in-life, is thematically central to the tales collected in *The Albatross and Other Stories* (1971). They are similarly hopeless about the possibilities of sustaining innocence, or joy, or security, in an adult world. The title story concentrates goodness in characters who are killed or estranged from ordinary life. Ted Flint, the sole figure of strength, is killed in a violent seastorm. Dafty Duncan, the retarded consciousness at the centre of the tale, is cut off from normality. He experiences the world as a relentlessly cold place, and external scenes are literally and metaphorically ice-bound, in landscapes which come to predominate in Susan Hill's imaginative world. 'The air shone with frost . . . It was cold enough, now, to freeze the sea.' 'The gutters were all frozen over, icicles hanging in a clear smooth stream down from the backyard tap . . . Outside, nothing moved, it was as though the world had been bound by ice and frost and only he was free and alive . . . Out on the path, beside the sea wall, the cold was like a solid block through which he had to pass. He thought the skin of his face would peel off.' This ice landscape is an objectification of Duncan's estrangement from life: his mind is 'numbed', 'blocked off', he is not engaged with things. He tries to 'clear out the frozen feeling, understand what he must do'. A slow thaw sets in only when Duncan has killed his mother: violence against her life-denying restraints and indifference erupts in Duncan's manic action of tipping her in her wheelchair, into the sea, then setting fire to their home. But he is not released by this violence. He immediately hides in a barn where 'He felt safe, dark. So this was where he had wanted to be, then. This place', and later he is removed to an actual prison. No one with any vitality is left to enjoy the thaw which moves through the natural world in the tale's ending. Other stories in *The Albatross* are equally hopeless. Solitary figures make pathetic attempts to release themselves from years of frustrating isolation, but they all end in ludicrous failure. Miss Parson, the sixty-nine-year-old spinster in **'Cockles and Mussels'**, dies from food poisoning after a timid excursion into the night life of a seedy seaside resort. 'I have lived too sheltered a life, she thought, I have never known enough about the truth of things, about what really goes on' but her lonely Saturday night out is 'a little too aimless, too trivial to count as life.' Like the heroines of Jean Rhys, these isolated females are trapped in their own futility. A solitary woman in **'Friends of Miss Reece'** (whose name is homonymous with that of Rhys) can do or say nothing, as she

lies dying of cancer. Isolation is presented as a tragic, but apparently inevitable, condition of female maturity.

Even in **'Somerville'**, where the isolate is a selfish old man, a sense of inevitability militates against a critical perspective which would read withdrawal as cowardly or wrong. Somerville sees no-one, exists from day to day, caring only for himself and one hedgehog, a version of himself. He is unable to respond with compassion when a young local girl visits him, and is repulsed by her talk of birth—she is unmarried, pregnant—and death—her grandmother is dying of cancer. He cannot face these physical truths. 'He felt tainted by the mess of other people's lives.' He seeks to distance illness, pain, sexuality, emotional demands, into a vague realm of unpleasantness which need not infect him.

> Somerville thought, do not tell me this, it has nothing to do with me, I want to hear nothing of your grandmother. I have thought of all that, gone through all those questions and solved them, years ago, the problems of living and dying. It is sealed and packed away, that knowledge. I will not listen to you. It is nothing to me.

His enclosure is an aesthetic one. Like Virginia, in *The Enclosure,* Somerville has withdrawn into a perfect isolation as a way of anaesthetising himself against painful experience. He is a portrait of the artist, 'a spare, rational, ascetic man, a believer in the symmetry and clarity of life, obsessed by the beauty of the knowledge that the world contained five regular solids, no more and no less, a romantic'. He cannot face change. He does not open his mail. He lives in a romantic universe, in nostalgic love for Barton, a dead friend from his youth, reading and re-reading Barton's last letter, which had described the land of ice and snow in which they were stuck. '"You don't care about anything here", Barton had written, "except the bloody cold, and keeping yourself moving, on your feet, keeping on . . . I can tell you, I know what hell is and it isn't hot, it's cold, it's this frozen, bloody country"'. Somerville chooses to stay in this infernal landscape, rather than move into somewhere less known or less fixed.

David Barton is the most romantic of Hill's male idols. He is everything she most values in terms of humanist ideals. He has all that lesser mortals lack, 'some quality—gaiety, composure, and sensitivity' which make of him 'a good man'.
—*Rosemary Jackson*

John Hilliard in *Strange Meeting* (1971) is a younger version of Somerville. He, too, is a lonely figure. 'He had . . .

the odd sense of completeness, of holding everything within himself, of detachment.' He is cut off from ordinary existence. 'It was like being under water or some mild anaesthetic, everything around Hilliard and within him was remote, people parted and moved and reformed in bright, regular patterns, like fragments in a kaleidoscope.' Like Somerville, he idealises a young male friend, Barton.

David Barton is the most romantic of Hill's male idols. He is everything she most values in terms of humanist ideals. He has all that lesser mortals lack, 'some quality—gaiety, composure, and sensitivity' which make of him 'a good man'. Subjected to horrific scenes in the French trenches during the First World War, Barton hangs on to his humanism by reading Henry James and Sir Thomas Browne, and by playing Schubert, Mozart, Brahms on a portable gramophone, whilst shells explode around him. His idealism is ravaged by his meeting with death, as he comes to 'know' truths which had previously been distant and had left his innocence intact. He sees corpses piled together, 'bloated and black, unburied for weeks' and perceives a new emptiness, a nausea, in things. There is 'Something old and bad and dead, a smell, a feeling you get as you walk across the street. It is not simply the bodies lying all about us, and the fact that the guns are firing, it is something else, something . . . ', something which makes him feel old, as if 'he had seen and heard all that he ever needed to see, all the fear that there could be'. His face is transformed from being childish into one which 'knows'. Literature and music cease to signify in the face of this knowledge of inhumanity and death. Barton tears to shreds his volumes of Thomas Browne, ashamed of their pretence of order or beauty. Life, he thinks, is 'wicked and pitiless, it's all one Godawful mess, and how can I let that man, that great man, lull me into a kind of acquiescence? Be romantic about it? Is that right?'

This questioning of art and its humanistic values is gradually silenced in *Strange Meeting.* Barton's lost illusions are rediscovered by Hilliard, who takes upon himself Barton's life after the latter's disappearance in battle. Hilliard finds in Barton's perfect family the security he had always desired, 'to have a family, to whom you were so close, about whom you could talk so lovingly, people you missed every day, and admitted to missing'. 'It was as though he had been standing in a dark street looking into a lighted room and been invited in'. Hilliard purchases from Harrods the collected works of Sir Thomas Browne, and some Henry James and E. M. Forster, as he assumes Barton's role as a guardian of moral value. The horrors of war seem to be redeemed by this inheritance. Hilliard re-surfaces from a shell hole, with 'death, all around him', in which he has dreamt of swimming with his sister, Beth. In the dream, she transforms into Barton who tells him that everything is all right. Against the nightmare offensives of *Strange Meeting,* this imagery of

sea, water, and redemptive drowning, suggests another safe, romanticised and childish condition, which is far removed from the military, 'masculine' world at the novel's centre, and cannot be reconciled with it. Hilliard's own emotional detachment, expressed in that crucial opening dream of ice and snow, which I quoted at the beginning, is resolved, as he moves toward Barton's human warmth and love. But Barton is significantly absent by the end. That intangible 'something' which he represented survives only in nostalgic recollection, at one remove. Through this nostalgia, a romantic idealism is preserved intact, despite the novel's constant betrayal of the vulnerability, and inviability, of such ideals.

> ***The Bird of Night*** **continues that tragic polarity which is found throughout Hill's fiction, in positing an either/or choice between art/life, romanticism/actuality. The first is beautiful, but cold, inhuman, whilst the second is messy and limited, but alive.**
>
> **—*Rosemary Jackson***

This kind of ambivalence towards romantic difference, at its most extreme in Susan Hill's loving portraits of artist figures who are doomed to non-existence, is dramatically presented in the divided narrative of *The Bird of Night* (1972). In many ways, this novel echoes Thomas Mann's *Dr Faustus* (1947), in which a pedantic scholar, Serenus Zeitblom, recounts the tragic death-in-life of a great composer, Adrian Leverkühn. Susan Hill's much simpler version of romantic possession is occasionally embarrassing at the side of Mann's original, but it relies upon a similar structure. An English Egyptologist, Harvey Lawson, mediates the doomed life of a great poet, Francis Croft. Like Leverkühn, Francis is seen as mad, but a genius. He suffers all the pains of romantic agony, his suffering being the price of his art. He is unable to participate in ordinary living. He calls himself 'the bird of night', the owl who 'does not praise the light'. 'He believed in good, and, most especially, in evil, in God, but more personally, in the Devil.' When the text shifts into the artist's deranged consciousness, it tries to give an experience of madness from within, in an elliptical idiom taken from the Bible, Blake, and English literature.

> 'He casts forth his ice like morsels; who can stand before his cold?'

I shall soon go away to live in a wood for the wood likes to have night-owls, that it may have matter for wonder, and if it is winter with you in your North country, look carefully at the six-cornered snowflake, and give thanks for that. I send you greetings and goodwill, for I cannot love you.

Art and ordinary life, or simple caring, are assumed to be incompatible. Francis, like his predecessors Kingshaw in *King of the Castle* and Dafty Duncan in *The Albatross,* is a childish, immature figure. He is surrounded by Harvey's mystification of the artist, as if he were of a superior sensibility, and by definition outside normal categorisation. 'No tight, careful little structure will contain the man', Harvey claims, 'His work overflows . . . He was a man of violent feelings, a man of beliefs and passions, he was a poet with a vision, he had everything, everything to say.' Like his hero in Coleridge's *Ancient Mariner,* Francis inhabits a metaphorical landscape of ice and snow, which images his closure within a romantic egotism. His dark vision imposes periodic bouts of madness which are intolerable, and drives him to repeated suicide attempts, culminating in a successful one as he sacrifices himself by letting his blood in the local church. Harvey's awe-full devotion to Francis permits no ironical perspective on a dedication to romanticism, even though its ending is death. *The Bird of Night* continues that tragic polarity which is found throughout Hill's fiction, in positing an either/or choice between art/life, romanticism/ actuality. The first is beautiful, but cold, inhuman, whilst the second is messy and limited, but alive. Yeats posed the problems of romantic withdrawal in similarly absolute terms in his poem 'The Choice':

> The intellect of man is forced to choose
> Perfection of the life, or of the work,
> And if it take the second must refuse
> A heavenly mansion, raging in the dark.

By articulating difficulties in these extreme terms, Hill makes it impossible to envisage art as a force for life. Her artists are all estranged, damned figures, 'raging in the dark', and denying all that is human and warm.

Nearly all of Susan Hill's writing presents problems in such a manner that no positive resolution seems possible: a passive acknowledgement of tragic inevitability is the dominant mood. The stories in *A Bit of Singing and Dancing* (1973) are in this vein: they are bleak pictures of ordinary people confronting lost illusions, with nothing to put in the place of their romantic expectations. In the title story, Esme Fanshaw, in her fifties, is liberated by her mother's death and a small inheritance. She feels anything is possible. 'She thought, this is how life should be, I should be daring, I should allow myself to be constantly surprised. Each day I should be ready for some new encounter.' But her mother is replaced by a man, Amos Curry, a door-to-door salesman and street entertainer. He enters her house as a paying guest, and a dull awareness at lost opportunities seeps into the story, despite its surface perkiness. 'Now, all the plans she had made . . . were necessarily curtailed, and for the moment she felt depressed, as though the old life were going to continue.' Esme, like Deirdre Fount in *A Change for the Better,* and

Hill's other aging female victims, is seen with a shrug of the shoulders which arouses pathos rather than anger. The reader is numbed into a similar disbelief in the possibility of change. The same collection contains many hopeless cases, trapped in hotels, boarding houses, empty mansions, old people's homes, geriatric wards, sterile marriages. **'How soon can I leave?'** is a sad tale of two lonely women, Miss Bartlett and Miss Roscommon, the first always rebelling against the other's claustrophobic affection, and longing for autonomy. Miss Bartlett keeps resolving to start a new life, aware that her role has been unremittingly passive: 'she had never chosen, only drifted through her life from this to that, waking every morning to the expectation of some monstrous good fortune dropped in her lap'. She dares to make a stand, and leaves Miss Roscommon's house for her own, only to find it physically crumbling around her. Aware that she is too weak to realise her desire for freedom, Miss Bartlett returns to her friend's enclosure, to find her a corpse on the living room floor. For Hill's unfulfilled ladies, there is neither leaving nor returning, only a constant, static, dissatisfaction.

> **Humour . . . is always a long way away from Hill's fiction, nowhere more so than in her solemn tale of grieving, *In the Springtime of the Year* (1974).**
> —*Rosemary Jackson*

This misery is explicitly related to women's oppression within patriarchal society in some scenes of *A Bit of Singing and Dancing*. In **'The Peacock'**, fifty-four-year-old Daisy Buckingham looks back on her empty married life. She remembers how she had learnt to silence her own anger at being restrained, and had been taught shame at her sporadic outbreaks of violence when she desired freedom.

> She had felt frustration and anger and misery welling up within her like a boil, she had thought, I am only thirty four years old, I am still young. I have surely hope and fulfilment before me, why should I be in this place, why should I be still tied to my father, how can I bear it?

Marriage had appeared to be her only means of survival within a social structure which castigates unmarried women as failures. Within a month of her father's death, Daisy meets and weds Humphrey, 'a man she had married for fear that there might prove to be no alternative'. Daisy does not comprehend the nature of her discontent, but there are strong intimations of its origins in a male-dominated family structure. She protests too much that Humphrey is not the cause of her misery:

> She tried to pin down what she wanted, what was

really wrong. It was not Humphrey, it could not be Humphrey, for he had come as the answer to her prayer, he was a good man and he had taken her out of the old life . . . it had not, in the end, been excitement that she had longed for, she had been very content to settle for something else, for the status of a wife, for security from the shame of spinster-hood. . . .

Daisy's unhappy life is symbolically portrayed in a telling episode when she is accidentally trapped in a summerhouse, and finds herself locked in with a male peacock. She hates the bird as a creature of bad fortune, and wants to escape. 'She wanted to scream, to claw and hammer at the closed door. Oh help me.' She is impotent. She is a mere absence. 'I have never known myself, never tested myself, I have never truly lived.' She is unable to release herself from the locked house, anymore than she can escape from her marriage. Her promises of self-fulfilment sink into mere daydreams. Unlike many contemporary depictions of elderly women daring to assert themselves, such as Angus Wilson's *Late Call* (1963), Susan Hill's tales of eleventh-hour bids for female freedom are always pathetic failures. Another story in this volume, **'Missy'**, narrates the frustrated attempt of old Mrs Ebbs to escape from a geriatric ward. 'She had a right to choose. . . All her life, she had let others decide, father and husband, she had been as helpless as she was now, in this bed.' She walks out into the night, convinced 'she was entirely free', but is incarcerated again. In **'The Custodian'**, an old man who assumes a female role towards a young boy, mothering him, caring for him, is rejected by the boy's father. He is abandoned, as a weak, house-bound figure, no longer necessary. The hopelessness here, despite its male protagonist, is related to the inertia and impotence which are generated by a passive female condition. The mother figure is left, isolated, to wait for death. Having survived ice and snow, in the hope that 'ahead . . . lay only light and warmth and greenness', s/he meets with no reward for playing a woman's role. 'Happiness did not go on.' These tales are so relentless in depicting the futility of women's aspirations towards fulfilment, that they might appear parodic, were it not for the tragic, pathetic manner in which they are told.

Humour, in fact, apart from occasional streaks of black comedy, is always a long way away from Hill's fiction, nowhere more so than in her solemn tale of grieving, *In the Springtime of the Year* (1974). Structurally and thematically, this is much simpler than her previous novels. Its biblically-named characters, Ruth, Ben, and Jo, point to the novel's religious quality: it is a parable of finding meaning in life. Ben is killed whilst felling an elm tree, trapped underneath it in a crucifixion posture. Ruth, his young widow, and other local characters, seek to come to terms with this apparently meaningless death. Time after time, Ruth experiences mere

futility. 'There was no point . . . For there is only this world and the misery of it . . . the whole world should never have been.' Ratheman, a curate whose young daughter dies, loses his Christian faith in a similar sense of nihilism. '"There was no meaning to it . . . there is only cruelty, there is no purpose in any of it. It means *nothing*."' It is only through a religious conviction of the soul's immortality that Ruth learns to accept Ben's death. His end comes to seem right and necessary in a natural cycle. 'Birth and death and resurrection, and one tunnel led into the next.' An old labourer, Potter, who was with Ben's corpse, has a parallel experience of transfiguration. Ben's death, like Christ's, redeems them. Potter says 'I couldn't doubt the truth after that . . . It was death and—and life. I'd never doubt that now.' Through these spiritual awakenings, Ruth ceases to be a stranger in the world. She moves from winter—again ice landscapes dominate much of the novel—to spring, with a symbolic scene of resurrection on Easter Day. She is able to stand, simply, on the earth, and to accept a cyclical changing of seasons, since death and birth merge into one.

> The first ice and a hard frost came . . . Her breath smoked on the steel-cold night air, and the grass and the vegetable tops were coated with a thin frost, like powdered sugar . . . There was winter. There would be spring.

Lying behind the Christian, and at times Lawrentian, metaphysics of *In the Springtime of the Year,* there are some hints of Ruth's growth towards independence as a woman. Ben's death releases her to be herself. 'She . . . did not know how she might live for the rest of her life. But Ben was dead, and laid in his grave, and she would move on, from one day to the next.' She is not a radical female figure. But she does come to realise that her passivity had been related to her conditioned dependence upon a father or male protector. 'Until now she had brought about no real developments in her life by any exercise of her own will; things had happened to her, and she had accepted that . . . She was afraid of taking any initiative with time and circumstance, people and places. She had never done so, because her father had been there, and Ben.' Ben, like Prince Charming, had seemed to awaken her, 'She had been a chrysalis muffled in an opaque, papery shroud and it was Ben who had awakened her', but her subsequent awakening to herself is much more difficult. Ruth learns that it is not enough to 'simply wait' for outside influences. She moves out of her lonely cottage to assist Ratheman's family and to help Ben's unmarried pregnant sister, Alice. In social terms, women's position does not seem to have advanced far beyond Elizabeth Gaskell's *Ruth* (1853), which recounts the desertion of an unsupported pregnant woman. But in terms of the development of Hill's fiction, Ruth is a step forwards. Like Sylvia Plath's Esther, in *The Bell Jar,* who listens to her body pulsing life, 'that old heartbeat, I am, I am', Ruth gradually discovers her own life, independently of male protection. 'She took a deep breath, held it within herself, let it go softly, she thought, I am myself.'

Throughout Susan Hill's novels and stories, the same themes and motifs have recurred and have led gradually towards a resolution of the problem of withdrawal from adult experience—a problem she presents as related to detachment as an artist and retreat as a woman. *In the Springtime of the Year,* with its ending of minor triumph, lets the woman move towards self-discovery and re-entry into community life. But feminist issues are conflated with metaphysical ones, as Ruth learns the value of her own life through an apprehension of grace and love. This is typical of a confusion in Hill's presentation of women. On the one hand she presents their problems as actual and socially determined. Her victims are trapped in oppressive social structures, and their frustration stems from unhappy marriages, loneliness, alienation as spinsters, and ostracisation as artists. On the other hand, their 'real' selves are presented in relation to eternal rather than historical time, and they are seen to be suffering from the fact of being mortal. They are caught, with her male victims, 'like rats in a trap', their immanent deaths threatening them with a sense of futility, of never having actually 'lived'. Her women, and her 'female' men, are locked in hopeless situations, ignorant of their desire for freedom until they have lost the youth/energy/courage/power necessary to realise that desire. They end in fantasies of what-might-have-been, or in actual defeat by death. Susan Hill's posing of metaphysical questions, the priority she gives to ageing characters facing their own extinction, means that basic feminist issues are elided. Because of this, any optimism is the result of 'grace', of religious faith, and *not* the result of a conviction that human beings have the power to control their own destinies. One form of passivity has been exchanged for another. Her women, and men, are no more 'free' at the end of her work than they were in *The Enclosure.*

In the radio plays collected in *The Cold Country,* Susan Hill's central preoccupations are dramatised in a clear, distilled form: they reveal the illusory nature of any resolution to the problem of enclosure, at least in the terms she has stated it. *The End of Summer* (1971) introduces her familiar notion of the impossibility of sustaining happiness and childlike innocence. Tom and Sally, young lovers, are isolated on an island, surrounded by a flooding river. Water, rain, owls, cats, cocks, ravens, foxes, bats, monsters are constant motifs, reminders of distress. They haunt Sally with their implications of death. Tom tells her she has an 'overdeveloped sense of fate, of doom, of disaster . . . it's very neurotic', but Sally cannot resist it. She is terrified of approaching winter, of ice, and rather than witness its slow petrifaction, she drowns herself in the flood. There is no final resurrection: the play ends with the sound of endless rain. *Lizard in the Grass* (1971) revolves round Jane, an orphan

in a convent boarding school, isolated in her visions of death by drowning. She has a long imaginary dialogue with John, a spirit who keeps her company like a medieval *memento mori* figure, whispering 'It is generall / To be mortall . . . No man may him hide / From Death, hollow-eyed', until all we hear is the sea and the tolling of a single funeral bell. *The Cold Country* (1972) is, perhaps, Susan Hill's bleakest piece, uncompromising in its icebound landscape. It is set in a region of ice and snow, with four men stranded in a tent in uncharted territory, in the middle of a blizzard. One of them, Jo, ventures outside and is frozen to death. Of the others, Barney is killed with an ice-axe, his murderer, Chip, leaves the tent to go to his own death, and only Ossie remains, to await his inevitable end as 'wind and blizzard take over'. In their extreme situation, the four men keep asking what life means. 'Why don't we all go outside and lie down face first in the snow and die? Why are we bothering at all? Have you asked yourselves that?' They discover only that 'there is no answer. Not now. Not for us.' 'The world is a bleak place. You look for a bolt hole, that's all.' Their long day's journey into night promises no escape, except into the ultimate enclosure of death.

> **Hill's images of the female role within patriarchal culture are unequivocally bleak ones of wasted lives. She silences women's utterance of quiet anguish in a familiar and traditional manner.**
> **—*Rosemary Jackson***

Literary allusions echo throughout *The Cold Country,* as they do in all of Hill's writing. The folk refrain, used as an epigraph to this essay, is central in setting the mood, as is the traditional mourning lyric, the Lyke-Wake Dirge. Another central literary motif is Hans Andersen's fairy tale, *The Snow Queen.* Barney remembers his mother reading it to him. The Snow Queen had no heart, she was pure, cold reason, made entirely of ice, 'her eyes gleamed like two bright stars but there was no rest or repose in them'. She inhabited a palace whose halls were 'all alike, vast, empty, icily cold and dazzlingly white. No sounds of mirth ever resounded through these dreary spaces. No cheerful scene refreshed the sight.' The Snow Queen stands as an allegorical figure behind all the many sequences of ice, snow, frost, and winter in Hill's fiction, embodying in her cold body all those aspects of death-in-life which had militated against 'ordinary' engagement with the world from *The Enclosure* onwards: aesthetic detachment, narrow rationality, asceticism, inhumanity, indifference, egotism, idealism, quests for perfection. It is no accident that this figure is a female spectre, presented as abusing her power. A movement away from her cold, palatial enclosure, her Tennysonian Palace of Art, is made to coincide, in Hill's fiction, with a renunciation, not only of art, but also of female autonomy.

Strip Jack Naked (1974) finally moves away from the sterility of that cold country, at least in its desire. Its heartless centre, James, is a consummation of Hill's idealistic characters. Like Hamm in Beckett's *Endgame*, James sits in his wheelchair, withdrawn from life. His first words are, 'Grey, grey and grey. Why does the sun never shine now?' He has left behind a world of colour and change. His enclosure is 'bleak', 'austere', permitting 'nothing superfluous', allowing nothing to get out of control. It permits neither dancing, nor laughter, nor music, nor alteration. Randal, his brother-in-law, calls it 'a burial place', as if it were a removal to 'the womb, or the cradle'. James claims to have seen everything, to have reached the truth in his ascetic purity. But Randal reminds him that his perfect life is sustained at the cost of not really living.

> What has it done for you, this precious three years locked away in this house? This . . . 'purging', this inner voyage of discovery, this sack-cloth and ashes game? It's driven you mad.

In fact, James has withdrawn into his monastic existence in order to avoid the pain of his child's death and his wife's subsequent suffering. Jane, his wife, endured a mental breakdown after the child's death (by drowning), and through her suffering has moved on, into life. 'I feel different', she tells him, 'Clean. As if I'd been put into cold storage and then brought out again and . . . very slowly thawed. Restored. Ice-maiden . . . I used to be that. Heartless. But now it *beats*.' She insists that his negativity, his defeatism, is wrong. The enclosure is of his own choosing.

> Diana: I don't understand why you are here. Why you like it.
> James: Does it seem to you that I like it?
> Diana: Then go. You are perfectly free.
> James: Not so.
> Diana: There are no locks.

Gradually, James moves away from his self-imposed condition of death-in-life. Shadows shift from black into violet, his grey surroundings begin to be coloured. He realises that it is stasis which is cowardly. 'Death is easy, Randal. Dying is easy. Sitting still among the shadows is easy . . . But . . . to live . . . That is the hardest thing of all. And I must do it. I must.' It recalls a central quotation from *Strange Meeting,* where Barton had marked out Thomas Browne's words, 'It is a brave act of valour to condemn death but where life is more terrible, it is then the truest valour to live'. James's resolution to 'get up and walk', to find colour and change, puts an end to those various retreats into aestheticism, de-

spair, suicide, death, or mere vacuous endurance, which had, until then, and *In The Springtime of the Year,* characterised Hill's timorous protagonists.

Not surprisingly, in terms of the opposition that Hill constructed between 'art' and 'life', the resolution of that feeling of being enclosed in an inhuman aestheticism involves her in a complete repudiation of fiction. Randal reminds James in *Strip Jack Naked* that outside his perfect grey world, everything is chaotic. 'Life is disorganised and messy . . . Outside the door of this room. There are loose ends, questions, various answers and sometimes . . . no answers. A series of choices, awkward events . . . accidents. Distress.' In the name of engagement with these external contingencies, a cold country of art is renounced altogether. Susan Hill abandoned fiction in the late 1960s in a gesture towards a less etiolated, less enclosed, activity—and a more respectable female role—maternity. In doing so, she made explicit certain assumptions which had been present throughout her writing. Instead of clarifying or confronting difficult ideological issues, about the role of the artist within contemporary culture, and the problem of women's oppression within patriarchy, Susan Hill's work evades them. Her art is trapped within a tradition of humanism—and its essentially realistic mode (made slightly expressionistic by grotesque images and a filtering of experience through non-adult minds). Her women are trapped in their ignorance of the political roots of their misery. Attempts to resolve these questions on an apolitical, metaphysical level prove both unsatisfactory and, as Hill's fiction illustrates, impossible. It is no accident that Susan Hill's work has been so well received by a liberal literary tradition, for it ends by silencing its own timorous interrogation of some of the fatal and crippling effects of a patriarchal, 'male' culture and retreats into a familiar 'female' enclosure of defeatism.

Hill's images of the female role within patriarchal culture are unequivocally bleak ones of wasted lives. She silences women's utterance of quiet anguish in a familiar and traditional manner. Woman's 'voice [is] stilled', her 'body [made] mute, always foreign to the social order'—for in Kristeva's words, 'in the entire history of patrilineal or class-stratified societies, it is the lot of the feminine to assume the role of waste. . .'.

Kenneth Muir (essay date 1982)

SOURCE: "Susan Hill's Fiction," in *The Uses of Fiction: Essays on the Modern Novel in Honour of Arnold Kettle,* edited by Douglas Jefferson and Graham Martin, The Open University Press, 1982, pp. 273-85.

[*Below, Muir assesses the achievement of Hill's fiction up to her hiatus from writing, discussing her narrative method, characterization, and themes.*]

When Susan Hill, to the dismay of her admirers, announced that she had decided to write no more novels, her reasons were complex. It was partly her feeling that the novel on which she was working, and which she destroyed, was inferior to her best, partly her newly found happiness in marriage and motherhood, and partly, one suspects, her realization that she ought to let her talent lie fallow. She had been writing since her schooldays and her mature work, written between the ages of twenty-six and thirty-two, included two volumes of short stories, a collection of radio plays, and six novels. She had won several prizes and was increasing her reputation with each successive volume, varied as they were. This seems, therefore, to be a convenient moment to consider her present achievement. It will be necessary in this brief essay to confine our attention to the six novels and the volumes of short stories. These are: *Gentleman and Ladies* (1968); *A Change for the Better* (1969); *I'm the King of the Castle* (1970); *Strange Meeting* (1971); *The Albatross* (1971); *The Bird of Night* (1972); *A Bit of Singing and Dancing* (1973); *In the Springtime of the Year* (1974).

Elspeth Thackeray, a character in 'The Peacock' (in *A Bit of Singing and Dancing*) who is taking a correspondence course on Creative Writing, is gently satirized for following the instructions on how to create character:

> After observing people carefully you could then take a step farther on, you might invent a background for them, imagine them in their home environment, or at their place of work.

So she observes Daisy Buckingham, another guest at the hotel, and the central character of the story; but her observation tells her nothing of the inner thoughts and feelings—that she hated living in Africa, although she looked back on her stay with nostalgia, that she hated the hotel when she had stayed at it with her father years before, although it had been transformed by memory into a charming place, that she hoped her husband, although she recognized that he was a good man and a good husband, would die of a heart attack.

Obviously Susan Hill's method differs from Elspeth Thackeray's. She possesses to an extraordinary degree the quality which has been called the essential *dramatic* gift, the power of identifying herself with a wide variety of characters, all very different from the young graduate who wrote the novels and stories. Only one of them is told in the first person, but we look at events through the eyes of an eleven-year-old schoolboy, a mentally defective boy, a soldier in the trenches, a middle-aged railway clerk, a mad poet and his Egyptologist friend, the old man in 'The Custodian', the dying old woman in 'Missy'. It was presumably this qual-ity that led one critic to compare Susan Hill to Tolstoy, though she is more akin to Turgenev or Chekhov.

> **Susan Hill often uses old and middle-aged women as her personae; but the only one of her tales where a young woman is so used is *In the Springtime of the Year*, where the bereaved Ruth Boyce, widowed at twenty-one, is the character through whose eyes and memories we watch the action and her gradual recovery.**
> —*Kenneth Muir*

When we are reading (as to Susan Hill when she was writing) *I'm the King of the Castle*, we see nearly everything through the eyes of Charles Kingshaw—his genteel, husband-seeking mother, his enemy, Edmund Hooper, his friend, Fielding, and his terrors, his hopes and his ultimate despair. He is given no idea of feeling that such a boy might not have, and the style never calls attention to itself, but only to the object, the feeling, the idea, or the landscape. Although an extraordinary tension is built up in the course of the book by the ordeals that Charles undergoes and by the temporary turning of the tables on his persecutor in Hang Wood, the story unfolds so naturally that we become conscious of the art only when we close the book and come to analyse it.

Susan Hill often uses old and middle-aged women as her personae; but the only one of her tales where a young woman is so used is *In the Springtime of the Year*, where the bereaved Ruth Boyce, widowed at twenty-one, is the character through whose eyes and memories we watch the action and her gradual recovery. This is accomplished through the affection and care of her fourteen-year-old brother-in-law, through the healing power of the countryside and of the village rituals (such as the decorating of graves for Easter Day), and through her ministering to the griefs and troubles of others. But although the dedication of the book may suggest that Susan Hill had herself suffered a bereavement, the heroine is differentiated from the novelist in almost every other way.

The second quality displayed by Susan Hill is what may be called the innocent eye. This is apparent not merely in the vividness of her landscapes, so that we seem to be seeing them for the first time, but also in the apparent avoidance of sophistication in the way in which she presents people's behaviour, however eccentric or cruel. This is what they did; this is how it happened. Another kind of novelist, for example, would have made explicit the sexual element in the friendships described in *Strange Meeting* and *The Bird of Night*. Here, and elsewhere, Susan Hill gains considerably from her reticence about sex and from her avoidance of psychological analysis. Her husbands and wives are mostly divorced or widowed or aged, and although the middle-aged booking-clerk in *Gentleman and Ladies* does marry for love at the end of the book, Mr Hooper has sexual fantasies about his life with Mrs Kingshaw, and the motor salesman in *A Change for the Better* picks up any available woman, Susan Hill is as reticent as the hero of *Gentleman and Ladies* when he proposes to Florence Ames at the seaside:

> They began to climb one of the long, steep wooded paths up from the shore.
>
> "You will marry me?" Gaily said suddenly, "won't you? When things are—are clear? That will be all right?"
>
> They paused for a moment to recover breath.
>
> "I would like that," she said. "Yes. I would like that very much."

They pause because they are middle-aged people going up a steep hill, not for a kiss.

Susan Hill, for all her objectivity, uses the novel, in Auden's famous phrase about the greatest art, to teach men to unlearn hatred and to learn love. The characters are divided into sheep and goats: those who are loving, life-enhancing, and filled with a purpose beyond themselves, and those who are possessive, unloving, and dying inwardly.
—*Kenneth Muir*

To speak of the innocent eye does not imply that Susan Hill is unaware of the 'dark' side of life; many of her readers, indeed, feel that the atmosphere of her world is sombre and depressing. Her favourite English novelist is not George Eliot, but Dickens; and though she lacks his melodramatic intensity, his grotesque humour, and his flamboyance, she shares his appreciation of the odd and eccentric, a compassion for the aged, the lonely and the persecuted, and his obsession with violence. A summary of her plots would read like headlines from one of the more lurid Sunday newspapers. A half-witted boy murders his mother (and burns the house down), a teenager commits infanticide; two old men engage in a suicide pact; an eleven-year-old boy drives another to suicide; an old man is saved from death by cancer by dying of a heart-attack; a young agricultural labourer is killed by a falling tree; a nurse murders a geriatric patient because she fouls her bed; an old woman dies of food poisoning; a boy watches his father drown; a mad poet kills him-

self; and, sadder than all this violence, are the aimless and meaningless lives of many of her characters.

In *Gentleman and Ladies* the self-deceived Alida Thorne intrigues to have her invalid mother placed in a home, feeling guilty about it, although the mother is happier for the change. In the same book neurotic Isabel bullies her meek sister Kathleen, is furious that her other sister has left money to a hospital and jewelry to a friend, instead of to her, and buries the jewelry in the garden when the legatee refuses to accept it. The significance of the title *A Change for the Better* is that it is ironical. Mrs Fount, who runs a draper's shop with her mother, dreams vaguely, like the three sisters of Chekhov's play, of starting a new life; but when her mother dies she is unable to make a new start. Another character comments:

> She is very young . . . not yet forty, and already she has given in, she is afraid of life, she will have nothing to look forward to in the future.

Susan Hill extracts some bitter comedy from the continual bickering between Mrs Fount and her dreadful mother. She is always defeated and by the end of the book she has become very like her mother. Such characters are defeated by life, defeated ultimately by their own personal inadequacies. The author treats them compassionately, but ruthlessly and realistically. The painful effect of the stories would be alleviated only by our recognition of their truth, if it were not for characters in all the novels, and in some of the stories, who stand out against the prevailing hopelessness.

Susan Hill, for all her objectivity, uses the novel, in Auden's famous phrase about the greatest art, to teach men to unlearn hatred and to learn love. The characters are divided into sheep and goats: those who are loving, life-enhancing, and filled with a purpose beyond themselves, and those who are possessive, unloving, and dying inwardly. In *Gentleman and Ladies,* the genteel rentiers of Haverstock are either snobs, who regard Hubert Gaily as common, or sympathetic, like Dorothea Shottery, who appreciates his goodness. The snobs are also the selfish ones, Alida Thorne and Isabel Lavender. It is characteristic of the good people that they admit to mixed motives and evil thoughts. Dorothea, for example,

> had expected to get satisfaction from refusing Faith's jewellery, because it seemed an action on principle, and because there was always a surreptitious pleasure to be gained from snubbing Isabel.

Later in the book, when she is praised for her generosity, Dorothea thinks:

> I am not generous. If the truth were known, it is only because I have for so long been lonely that I

welcome demands for help. It is only that I feel that I may make a new friend and be rewarded with company.

Kathleen, on hearing of Isabel's death, thinks

I am not a vindictive woman . . . but I am glad that my sister is dead, for all my life I have suffered under her.

Even Hubert, whose affectionate and grumbling relationship with his mother is beautifully presented and who had dutifully stayed with her all his life, had wished at one moment that she were dead, since he could not apply for promotion elsewhere so long as she was alive.

Hubert's 'goodness' is illustrated through the book by his thoughtfulness for others—his joining in the funeral service in the first chapter, his helping an old woman to her seat in the bus, his mending of Mrs Shottery's gate, his organizing the village fair (not without satisfaction to himself). The goodness of Gaily is made explicit when Florence arranges for him to meet Mrs Shottery:

"I'd like to meet anyone—if you say so."

"Then you shall. She is a good person."

"Good?"

Nobody ever said a person was good, like that. They were nice, or all right, kind or likeable or easy to get on with. Not good, right out like that.

"I can't say I know any of what you'd call *good* people."

She turned to him in surprise.

"Not," Gaily said, worried, "not that I meet bad people. No, it's just-well, it's not a word you tend to apply, is it? You know . . ." He began to confuse himself. "I'm not sure what it means," he finished up, "a good person."

"Why," she said, "*you* are a good person! It is quite easy. That is what it means."

There is the same contrast in *A Change for the Better* between the life-enhancers and their opposites. The Founts, as we have seen, are spiritually dead or dying; but James, although born into a strange household from which adult males have been extruded, is saved, partly by his talents as a musician, partly by his determination to stand up against his mother and grandmother, and partly by the encouragement

of his music teacher, Ralph Porlock. There is one very funny episode when James's grandmother goes off to interview Porlock because she suspects him of homosexual tendencies. He confronts her on the doorstep holding a meat-cleaver and causes her considerable alarm. She does not know that he was about to cut up a hare. He reluctantly invites her inside but does not ask her to sit down; so she perches on the back of a chair. She funks a direct accusation and her hints are too vague and confused to be understood. Porlock finally says:

"Madam, I do not yet know why you have come to see me. I am, as you have said, a busy man. I would be grateful if you would now speak out plainly."

Mrs Oddicut flushed. She could not now say anything about the time he and the boy spent here together, she could not ask what they talked about, and say that she did not think it altogether suitable.

So she pretends that she had come because James was in danger when he came down the cliff path at night:

"Things have happened there, girls have been— have been set upon. Accosted."

"Once, yes. In the middle of a summer afternoon."

"Nobody knows what may be the danger, then, on a dark winter's evening."

"Tush, madam. No more than the danger outside your own house."

Mrs Oddicut goes away 'red about the neck with anger'. Porlock smiled to himself 'because as he got older, he found the quest for the risible more and more fully rewarded.'

The foul-tempered Major Carpenter behaves intolerably to his sweet-tempered wife; but there is some comedy in his irrational behaviour, in his snobbery, and in his Blimpish prejudices:

The people of whom Major Carpenter disapproved were—almost all summer visitors, all conference members, the Jewish businessmen from Hampstead and engineering executives from the Midlands, solicitors and retired Diocesan Bishops.

Mrs Carpenter spends her time in making up for her husband's rudeness, and when he dies she is able to make a new, and happier, life for herself. Yet the reader can feel some pity even for the Major, who is upset by the death of an old friend, and himself afraid of dying.

We are given a glimpse of one happy household in the town, to which James Fount is invited by a school friend, Schwartz. He persuades his mother to let him go on holiday with the Schwartzes, although she had arranged for him to stay in an hotel with her. But at the end of the book she finds herself behaving just like her mother:

> James Fount got off the cane chair and picked up his satchel.
>
> "I'm going to tea with Schwartz," he said.
>
> "I *beg* your pardon? How dare you tell me what you are or are not going to do, without so much as asking my permission."
>
> "I'm sorry. *May* I go to tea with Schwartz?"
>
> "Oh go on, go on, do what you like, I do not care for you. You have more feeling for your friend Schwartz and his family than you have for me."
>
> James Fount left the shop.
>
> I am saying all the things to him that I vowed I would never say, thought Mrs Fount. I am becoming more and more like my own mother was with me and I cannot help myself, for now I understand. I see it all and I am miserable and afraid.

We know that James will get his way and go to a boarding school on a music scholarship.

There had been many unpleasant and selfish and foolish characters in [Hill's] previous books, but Edmund is evil. When all excuses have been made—family pride, snobbery, his motherless state, his father, the barbarous ideology of his school— Edmund is cruel and evil.
                                        —*Kenneth Muir*

In *I'm the King of the Castle,* the victim, Charles Kingshaw lives in an unsympathetic or hostile environment. His mother, because she is so anxious to marry Mr Hooper, cannot be his confidante; Mr Hooper, though generous according to his lights, is unable to understand either his own son or Charles; and Edmund resents the invasion of his territory by Charles, and therefore persecutes him. The persecution takes understandable forms: locking his victim in a room containing a frightening collection of moths, putting a stuffed crow on his bed in the middle of the night, locking him in a shed, and so on. Near the end of the book, when Edmund is away,

Charles meets Fielding, the son of a neighbour, normal, good-natured and friendly; but this friendship is ruined by the return of Edmund. This and his mother's imminent marriage to Mr Hooper increase Charles's unhappiness; and when Mr Hooper arranges to pay his fees so that he can join Edmund at his school, he despairs and commits suicide. When Edmund finds the body, he

> thought suddenly, it was because of me, I did that, *it was because of me,* and a spurt of triumph went through him.

There had been many unpleasant and selfish and foolish characters in the previous books, but Edmund is evil. When all excuses have been made—family pride, snobbery, his motherless state, his father, the barbarous ideology of his school—Edmund is cruel and evil. This is made apparent not merely by his bullying, but by his refusal to respond to Charles's acts of kindness. In Hang Wood, when he is terrified of a thunderstorm, when he is afraid that they will starve to death, and when he is nearly drowned, he is cared for by Charles; yet when they are found Edmund accuses Charles of trying to drown him. Later in the book, when he breaks his leg in a climbing accident, he accuses Charles of having pushed him, although Charles had tried to help him to safety. The Fieldings merely provide a glimpse of a world outside the nightmare of schoolboy cruelty; to have given them a larger share in the book would have lessened the tension.

Characters in the earlier books had been cruel and selfish— Isabel Lavender, for example, or Mrs Oddicut—but here Susan Hill faces directly the mystery of iniquity: Edmund, although his cruelty is adolescent and merely verbal, is as evil as the demi-devil, Iago.

Strange Meeting was suggested by the first performance of Britten's *War Requiem* in Coventry Cathedral (1962), although some nine years elapsed before the novel was written. During the interval Susan Hill read a large number of books about the First World War, including those by Graves, Blunden, and Chapman. The Owen poem which provided the title is about the meeting after death of a German and an English soldier: in the novel the strange meeting is the close friendship between two English officers on the Western Front, and the death of one of them. The authenticity of the setting is the result of an amalgam of multitudinous sources, so that no direct borrowing can be detected. This is a remarkable imaginative feat. But the real subject is friendship rather than war: war provides a threat, a background, a quickener to the friendship. John Hilliard, the older of the two men, comes from a cold, respectable and conventional family, and he is himself reserved and emotionally inexperienced. David Barton comes from a warm, out-going, affectionate family, and he himself is loving and beloved. The contrast between the two families continues what we have seen in the previous novels; but Hilliard undergoes a conversion by love, so that when David is killed he is absorbed into the Barton family.

When he is home on leave at the beginning of the book, John is revolted by the uncomprehending attitude of his family to the realities of the war and by the sentimental attitude of a retired cavalry major. He hopes to be able to talk openly with his sister Beth, to whom he used to be close, and hears that she is to marry a middle-aged solicitor for security. When he gets to know David, he is astonished at his openness and the difference between their two families.

> "No. I didn't want to come out here at all, I was in a blue funk. I'd have done more or less anything . . . but I'm fit and of age, I couldn't slip through the net. So I suppose I'd better make the most of it."
>
> "Do you always tell people everything you're feeling?"
>
> Barton looked round at him in surprise. "Generally. If I want to. If they want to hear." He paused and then laughed. "Good Lord, we're not at school now, are we?"
>
> Hilliard did not reply.
>
> "Besides, it's the way we were brought up. To say things, tell people what you feel. I don't mean to force it on anyone. But not to bottle things up."

The letters from the Barton family begin to include messages to John, and then letters to him:

> He said again and again. "They don't know me. They don't know me," holding the envelopes, looking at the writing upon them, feeling the smoothness of the letter paper between his fingers.
>
> As always, Barton laughed. "Of course they do!"
>
> "They haven't seen me, we have never met."
>
> "Oh, that's practically superfluous by now."

These friendly letters contrast painfully with those he receives from his own family; and, when he is badly wounded and in hospital, the affectionate letters he gets from Mrs Barton contrast with the visit of his mother:

> "You look very beautiful, mother. You always look very beautiful."
>
> She inclined her head, smiled at him, as Royalty

would smile. She wore a dark fuchsia dress, full-skirted, and with a coat of deeper, more purplish red, a hat with purple feathers. When she walked away, the other men in the room looked up from their books and letters, and watched her go.

The theme of friendship is continued in the next novel, *The Bird of Night,* in more difficult circumstances. For Francis Croft is a great poet, who suffers from recurrent periods of madness, and the narrator, Harvey, looks after him with selfless devotion for many years. The title is taken from a Hölderlin poem, and the novel was written at Aldeburgh, where Britten composed his Hölderlin settings. Of the mad poets to whom Susan Hill refers,—Clare, Smart, and Blake—none was given to violence, whereas Hölderlin and Croft were. But we are meant to understand, perhaps, that when poets are mad, it is because the society in which they live is at fault. Harvey says:

> And if he is mad, it is because one man's brain cannot contain all the emotions and ideas and visions that are filling his without sometimes weakening and breaking down.

Harvey tells the story thirty years after Croft's death and his narrative is interspersed with prose quotations from the poet's notebooks. Susan Hill does not, however, risk quoting any of Croft's poems (as Pasternak quoted Zhivago's), for Croft is supposed to be the greatest poet of his age, one who had written during the First World War, and afterwards developed, as Owen might have done if he had survived. Harvey is himself a writer so that by using him as the narrator Susan Hill can allow herself a more 'literary' style than in her previous books, with a good deal of imagery and some splendid Suffolk and Dorset landscapes.

It will be remembered that the start of Hölderlin's madness coincided with the death of the lady he called Diotima: Croft seems to have no interest in women—his madness begins when his brother shoots a bird. Harvey is jealous; and his resentment of the academics who pester him for information about the dead poet, although suggested by the theses and articles about Sylvia Plath after her suicide, may have been due to his possessive love.

Towards the end of the book Croft's father comes to visit him in the Battersea asylum, and there is a meeting between him and Harvey, which brings out the difference between the two men, and between Croft and his father. The father disapproves of Harvey for not having the poet sent to an asylum years before, 'in the privacy of some clinic —Austria—Switzerland . . . There is no history of insanity in my family.' His reputation as a poet adds to his father's fear that his madness will become public knowledge; and when Harvey remarks that 'very many men of seventy had lost their sons in the war', he replies:

> I had rather he were dead than this, there would have at least been no shame in it. I should not have had to wake every morning of my life and fear for his future. At least I should have known.

Harvey realizes that 'there was no hope at all of sympathy left between us'.

The last of the novels, *In the Springtime of the Year,* has a less ambitious theme but a tauter construction. In the place of the first person narrative, the action is viewed through the eyes of Ruth. We learn nothing except what she sees and hears; our knowledge of the other characters in the book is her knowledge or her opinion, which we are willing to accept as true because she emerges as a kind and loving person. She is proud and independent and determines to come to terms with her bereavement on her own. She stays on in the cottage, refusing to see the clergyman who comes to bring spiritual comfort, and visited only by Jo, the one member of the family who is like her dead husband in temperament. He is one of the Hill characters who is sensitive, caring, and open-hearted, whereas his mother, Mrs Boyce, had resented Ruth's marriage with Ben, is conventional in her ideas, and regards Ruth's behaviour after the death of her husband as unfeeling because she does not weep in public and refuses to take a last look at the corpse.

> She saw the expression on Alice's face, remembered what she had said that night. "You've not even feeling enough to cry." But she could not go upstairs, the sight of his body, lying in a coffin, which would soon be sealed up forever, would be more than she could bear. And it would mean nothing, now. She looked around the room. So they had all been up? Yes. She imagined the file of dark mourners mounting the stairs and peering down into the coffin. At Ben. Ben. How could they? How could so many people have touched him and looked at him, unasked, since the moment of his death, when she herself had not?

Mrs Boyce is a self-deceiver, hoping to live a vicarious life through her daughter, Alice, who would marry a gentleman and become the lady she might have been herself:

> "I could have been Someone, Miss, had a real life, I could . . ."

> "We all know what you fancy you could have been. A lady! we've heard it all our lives and do you suppose we believe it? Why should we? And does it matter? Because whatever you might have been is a day-dream, isn't it, an escape from the truth? You live in a day-dream. But *this* is real, this is what you are, here, a woman of fifty, married to a farm hand. Well why can't you be satisfied, why not make do?"

Alice, tired of her mother's fantasies, has an affair with a man she doesn't love. Ruth, although she cannot understand how any woman could behave in this way, nevertheless shelters her when she is repudiated by her mother, and goes vainly to intercede on her behalf. Just before this she has tried to comfort the clergyman whose beloved child has died, and who has lost his faith as a result and proposes to resign from Holy Orders:

> Because she has died and now I know that everything I believed in and lived for has died with her. Because my life is a lie. I am a lie. How can I visit them, people sick, people dying and in distress, needing truth, what have I to say to them? How can I take services in the church and preach and pray and know that it is all a lie? I used to know what words to say, but there are no words, and there is no help for anyone. I think of how I went to people and talked to them, about death and goodness and consolation, and I feel ashamed, I knew nothing, I had never felt what they felt.

The naked grief of a professed and professional Christian prevents the reader from feeling that Ruth's grief for her husband had been alleviated too easily in the course of the book; and the clergyman's bereavement has been placed near the end both to show Ruth's concern for others and to remind us of what she herself had suffered. There is also a contrast between the possessive love of the clergyman and Ruth's selfless but reciprocal love for her husband which enables her to endure.

It is too early to assess Susan Hill's achievement, as her future work may well surpass what she has already done. She is younger now than George Eliot was when she published *Scenes from Clerical Life*; and the qualities we have outlined—the purity of her style, her ability to identify with a wide range of characters quite unlike herself, and her sensitive moral discrimination—are the best guarantee of her future development. She is one of the finest writers of the seventies: we may hope that she will emerge as the outstanding novelist of the last quarter of the century.

Mary Jane Reed (essay date April 1983)

SOURCE: "Recommended: Susan Hill," in *English Journal*, Vol. 72, No. 4, April, 1983, pp. 75-6.

[*In the essay below, Reed compares* The Bird of Night, In the Springtime of the Year, *and* Strange Meeting, *emphasizing the humanity of the main character of each novel.*]

Susan Hill's novels were not best-sellers when they were published in the early 1970s, nor would they be today, for they are short, have no complex plots, and do not exploit the sensual or bizarre. But each novel is a masterful probe into human emotions and needs. Her characters come alive not because of what they do but how they feel and react to others and to their environment. Hill's style is clear and the structure of her work is simple. Her novels are a paradox, easy to read yet profound in exploring our complex behavior and the universal problems we encounter—death, war, seclusion, even madness. Hill never exploits human tragedy. Suffering and grief illustrate the importance of human relationships and reaching out.

> **Susan Hill's novels were not best-sellers when they were published in the early 1970s, nor would they be today, for they are short, have no complex plots, and do not exploit the sensual or bizarre. But each novel is a masterful probe into human emotions and needs. Her characters come alive not because of what they do but how they feel and react to others and to their environment.**
> **—*Mary Jane Reed***

Unfortunately, of her ten novels, only five have been published in the United States—***In the Springtime of the Year*** (London: 1974; New York: Saturday Review Press, 1974), ***Strange Meeting*** (London: 1971; New York: Saturday Review Press, 1972), ***The Bird of Night*** (London: 1972; Baltimore: Penguin, 1973), ***I'm the King of the Castle*** (London: 1973; New York: Viking, 1970), ***Gentleman and Ladies*** (London: 1968; New York; Walker, 1969; now out of print in America), and a short story collection ***The Albatross and Other Stories*** (London: 1970; New York: Saturday Review Press, 1975).

The ultimate test for many of Hill's characters is a confrontation with death. Defining death and accepting its aftermath when it steals a loved one is the basis of ***In the Springtime of the Year.*** Ruth was devastated when her husband was crushed under a fallen tree, and the novel begins and ends with the twenty-one-year-old widow closing the door behind her. Yet each closing is different, symbolic of the metamorphosis in her mourning from the self-inflicted isolation of her grief to her coming out of herself to help others, the curate mourning his young daughter, and Alice bemoaning her unwanted pregnancy.

But the road to altruism is paved with agony. Hill describes Ruth's desperation at the onset of the novel as worse than being lonely. Her hell was "being absolutely alone." She felt wronged by a hostile "inevitable" force and violently rejected everyone except her young brother-in-law Jo. Not until she reached out did she alter hostility into acceptance.

Her acceptance was bittersweet, for she had to be purged of his haunting presence before conceding that no one was to blame for his death, that it was simply "one stage in completing the pattern." Selling Ben's possessions gave her strength to meet Potter, the only witness of the accident, to learn every detail of her husband's death. Through Potter, Hill focuses on that single moment when death occurs. He had felt "entirely alone with death and known that it was good. If he had ever doubted immortality, he could not doubt it now. Awe had come over him, and a kind of reverence, he had knelt and been, for a while, paralysed, for the whole wood was filled with this momentous thing, this parting of body and soul."

Through confrontation and not isolation, Ruth finds strength to accept the inevitable, to move out of herself, to realize that "man must make the journey of grief himself" but others strengthen our re-entry into reality.

Hill's precise imagery portrays nature as a backdrop to human suffering. The donkey's bray and the "smell of sweet stocks" pierce Ruth's empty dead world. In her acute, lethargic isolation she would "sit and sit as though the blood was dammed up within her." She had to run from the "ashen, sepulchral faces" to the hillside amid the "thin dart of sunlight . . . caught on a cobweb laid out on the hawthorn," for Ben had been her savior from the "chrysalis muffled in an opaque, papery shroud."

Unlike ***In the Springtime of the Year*** where a single death resounds throughout an entire town, death is rampant in ***Strange Meeting.*** Through junior officer Barton, the atrocities the British encounter during World War I dramatically unfold. But the power of the novel lies not in facing death but in our need for human compassion and communication that is Hill's trademark.

Barton expresses his feelings in letters to his family. His charm endears him to his comrades, and a certain mystique makes him enigmatically refreshing to fellow officer Hilliard who feels stifled by the dull reserve of his upper-class British family. Hilliard's ironic revelation is that he would rather fight alongside Barton than endure his sterile home where truths and emotions are camouflaged in silence.

Barton's letters explicitly expose his attitudes in a vivid commentary of the war from the cafes with "bad beer and comfortable chairs" to the bloody chaos of combat. He describes the "litters of armies" and "the sweet rotten trench smell of soil and chlorine and blood and the mustard gas like garlic." More important, he describes his feelings about death and his personal responsibility about the war. The accidental death of a young private provoked this reaction: "I thought of it all, how he'd been born and had a family. I thought of everything that had gone into making him and it wasn't that I was afraid . . . I just wanted him alive again."

How does Barton resolve death? To be unfeeling. Yet this is not his character. Barton's real conflict is not in coming to terms with death. He is plagued with altruistic guilt, for he is helpless to stop the fighting. He feels guilt for ravishing the earth, uprooting and disturbing all nature. He briefly risks his life to rescue a hedgehog.

> Unlike *In the Springtime of the Year* where a single death resounds throughout an entire town, death is rampant in *Strange Meeting*. Through junior officer Barton, the atrocities the British encounter during World War I dramatically unfold. But the power of the novel lies not in facing death but in our need for human compassion and communication that is Hill's trademark.
> —*Mary Jane Reed*

When his death occurs, it does not trigger torment within Hilliard as Ruth endured in *In the Springtime of the Year.* Because of their "strange meeting," Hilliard's emotional renaissance had such a profound, everlasting effect that even the death of his dear friend could not shatter his newfound freedom. Ironically, Hill demonstrates that amid death people can be resurrected to learn to love.

Our need to reach out is never so present as in *The Bird of Night.* In this virtually plotless novel, Harvey exemplifies a total giving of self as he resigns from the British Museum to devote the next twenty years caring for a poetic genius who simultaneously endures fame and madness. *The Bird of Night* is Hill's most difficult novel because of Francis' progressive madness and the incessant shifting in time from Harvey's narration to the interjection of Francis' journal, his documented stream of consciousness.

Why does a man relinquish his life to assume caring for another? Harvey answers, "Because I had glimpsed into the heart of his despair, because I had shared it a little . . . that I understood why I must stay with him."

Because of his progressive madness, Francis is erratic in his allegiance to man and nature. He tries to kill his brother for having shot a bird, yet he had no affinity for nature. He fears

animals and confesses that "all stars have sharpened points." Hill's imagery reflects his inner torment in his "blood-filled" nightmares where he sees his flesh "putrefy and rot" and fall away from his bones. He is not at rest with himself and certainly not in harmony with nature. Unlike Ruth in *In the Springtime of the Year,* Francis can derive no strength from nature. Unlike Barton in *Strange Meeting,* he has no compassion for the wild, natural world people destroy. And it is this inherent alienation, this total "inwardness" that justifies his madness and explicates Hill's recurrent theme—everyone's need for human compassion. He is as Hill writes in *In the Springtime of the Year,* "absolutely alone." He has fallen beyond the depths of loneliness to madness.

In Harvey in *The Bird of Night,* Ruth in *In the Springtime of the Year,* and Barton in *Strange Meeting,* we witness the positive effects of reaching out to others and experience a compassion and understanding for those hurting. Hill never needs to define or eulogize this awareness, for she examines and understands the human spirit. There is no place for morbid absurdity in these stories.

K. R. Ireland (essay date Fall 1983)

SOURCE: "Rite at the Center: Narrative Duplication in Susan Hill's *In the Springtime of the Year,*" in *The Journal of Narrative Technique,* Vol. 13, No. 3, Fall, 1983, pp. 172-80.

[*Below, Ireland identifies the scene at Helm Bottom as the mise en abyme of* In the Springtime of the Year, *emphasizing its primary relation to the themes and structure of the novel.*]

It is almost a decade since Susan Hill's last novel appeared. Similar to E. M. Forster in one respect at least, that of having written a handful of mature novels before giving up the form, she paradoxically invites, by her novelistic silence, a retrospective consideration of her work. Much-read but little analyzed, her work has a fluency and economy soon taken for granted, a simplicity of surface that is deceptive. *In the Springtime of the Year* (1974), her sixth and arguably most accomplished novel, received critical acclaim when it was published, but in the absence of any academic attention, certain features of the book's narrative structure have gone unnoticed. One feature especially, that of interior duplication or *mise en abyme,* makes an unobtrusive but carefully judged appearance, testifying to her subtle overall control and effective presentation of material.

Auden's description of Rilke as the "Santa Claus of loneliness" is one that might be adopted, with some modification, for Susan Hill. All her novels, it has been observed, focus on "the same kind of lonely, dislocated experience. The characters are always somehow unaccommodated, outside ordinary intercourse; there is always the pathos of an excited, complex sensibility that has to stay closed-off and inarticulate. . . ." Each novel explores a particular set of relationships, ranging from possessiveness and jealousy (*Gentleman and Ladies,* 1968, *A Change for the Better,* 1969), cruelty (*I'm the King of the Castle,* 1970), fear and intimacy (*Strange Meeting,* 1971), to madness (*The Bird of Night,* 1972) and grief (*In the Springtime of the Year,* 1974). Living "at the edge" in terms of mental stability, the central characters of these novels vary in age and sex from elderly spinsters and retired people to schoolboys, from a soldier and a poet to a young widow. They share a sense of guilt and responsibility exploited by family and kin, and a spiritual or geographical isolation making them vulnerable to events, so that, not surprisingly, death frequently intrudes. Two novels actually culminate in suicide, and the sixth and final novel only narrowly escapes, to close on a note of qualified hope.

In the Springtime of the Year is a study of the effects on a 19-year-old woman of the sudden death of her husband, a forester, killed while felling timber. Although Ben Bryce's family lives nearby, it has long shown resentment and lack of sympathy towards Ruth, and she now suffers in virtual solitude, tended only by her 14-year-old brother-in-law Jo. The novel traces the course of Ruth's emotional responses to Ben's death, from an initial terror and numbness, through despair interrupted by brief moments of vision, to an ultimately precarious sense of consolation based upon altruism. By dividing the narrative into three unequal parts, such that the first and third are temporally sequential and spatially subordinate to the central "embedded" section, Susan Hill skirts the danger of monotony inherent in a straightforward linear presentation of the material. Thus, the first part is set six months after Ben's death, while the second part opens on the day before that event in February and closes with the Easter weekend, leaving the third part to continue from August into December. For Ruth, sunk in depression, the approach of Easter represents "suffering and death and resurrection . . . despair and hope and certainty," but a scene which occurs before its arrival and is located at the very center of the novel seems in many ways more decisive. It is also a scene best conceived of in terms of the *mise en abyme.*

The procedure which this phrase connotes dates back as far as the Renaissance at least, but was outlined by André Gide in the 1890s and developed further by critics of the French New Novel in the 1960s and 1970s. Referring to his partiality for thematic duplication within a work of art, Gide contends that such duplication can illuminate a work and confirm its overall proportions. As pictorial models, he cites paintings by Memling, Quentin Metzys and Velasquez in which mirrors afford a second, if distorting view of a de-

picted scene; as literary models, Gide alludes to the play-within-a-play of *Hamlet,* to marionette scenes in Goethe's novel *Wilhelm Meister,* and to the story read to Roderick in Poe's *The Fall of the House of Usher.* For Gide, however, such models do not correspond as closely to the effects intended in his own works as does an analogy from heraldry, whereby one escutcheon encloses a second, positioned at the heart-point (*en abyme*). It has since been shown that this inner coat-of-arms never exactly reproduces the outer by which it is subsumed, though Gide's formula retains its value nonetheless. His brief discussion concludes with the claim that this effect of "inescutcheon" or *mise en abyme* is characteristic of the psychological novel.

> While, in practice, it might be difficult to demonstrate in a given text that a *mise en abyme* actually preceded and generated the whole of the narrative, or that, alternatively, it developed later to fulfill a need to provide an internal mirror of events, at least its functions in different contexts can be examined.
> —*K. R. Ireland*

More recent commentators, especially those involved with the *nouveau roman,* have chosen to ignore this latter feature in favor of approaches derived from structural semantics. The critic and novelist Jean Ricardou, for instance, sees the functions of the *mise en abyme* as those of narrative summary and enrichment. Its roles may be antithetical or revelatory: challenging the narrative by acting as counterpoint (Poe's *The Fall of the House of Usher*) or revealing the narrative's own self-awareness (Robbe-Grillet's *Le Voyeur*). These roles may, in turn, be further divided into semantic operations of repetition, condensation and anticipation. Ricardou's concern, and that of many practitioners of the French New Novel, is with the *mise en abyme* not simply as a fragment foreshadowing the whole of the narrative, but as the matrix of that whole. Thus, it comes to function as a model issuing directives for the production of the larger narrative, which then becomes the *mise en périphérie* of the micro-narrative. In the extreme case of *La prise de Constantinople* (1965), Ricardou uses the letters of his own name as the generative basis of his novel.

While, in practice, it might be difficult to demonstrate in a given text that a *mise en abyme* actually preceded and generated the whole of the narrative, or that, alternatively, it developed later to fulfill a need to provide an internal mirror of events, at least its functions in different contexts can be examined. Of the two anglophone examples cited by Gide, that of Shakespeare's tragedy has become a *locus classicus* of interior duplication. The play-within-a-play is located at the very center (III, ii.) of *Hamlet,* and in strict terms offers two mirrors rather than one mirror of the larger events, since a dumb-show precedes and enacts the argument of "The Mouse-trap" itself. It is Hamlet who chooses the play and who inserts lines of his own into the given text, while the avowed intention, to "catch the conscience of the king," proves successful. In its narrative relation to the main play, "The Mouse-trap" is retrospective, an "external analepsis," and in its performance it is only half-completed, King Claudius leaving when the Player King is poisoned. The *mise en abyme* in *Hamlet* thus has the status of a stage-work acted out in public, using a model familiar to initiator and performers, and carrying personal meaning for its chief spectator.

In Poe's *The Fall of the House of Usher,* second of Gide's anglophone examples, the book read to Roderick by the narrator most clearly represents the *mise en abyme,* though an allegorical poem titled "The Haunted Palace" placed at the very center of the larger narrative offers, as in *Hamlet,* a further internal mirror. It is the unnamed narrator who, within a prose narrative, vainly chooses a prose romance, the *Mad Trist* of Sir Launcelot Canning, in order to divert the doomed recluse. Usher's own recognition of the close correspondence between events offstage during the reading and those in the romance stresses the narrowness of the "internal prolepsis," so that the *mise en abyme,* here generating suspense but represented by a partial and incompleted performance, barely foreshadows the catastrophe. As Roderick's friend, the first-person narrator is an observer and a participant in a private performance, the literary model for which is familiar to speaker and listener alike, the outcome of which destroys both master and mansion. The functions of the *mise en abyme* in the context of Susan Hill's novel are different once again.

In the relevant scene, forming the second half of Chapter Six of *The Springtime of the Year,* Ruth visits Helm Bottom, site of Ben's death a month previously. Earlier chapters have detailed his funeral and other people's reactions to his death, and have focused especially on his widow's distracted grief, epitomized by her nocturnal vigils at the graveyard. Only her excursion to the sea with Jo, which earns his mother's re-proof in the first half of Chapter Six, has brought the slightest relief from despair. At Helm Bottom, however, Ruth now becomes soothed and quietened by happy memories of the past, in contrast with the storm of emotions aroused at the graveyard. The choice of name itself also carries the notion of reversal or contrast, since "helm," according to the OED, still signifies in dialect the crown, top or summit of anything, and in Old English referred to the leafy top of a tree. Ben's death beneath an elm tree, whose bark appeared fresh but whose center was rotten, may be pertinently recalled. Another sense of "helm" is that of a handle, tiller or wheel by which a ship's rudder or steering gear is managed, and in a more figurative sense, that by which affairs are managed.

Ben's relationship to Ruth is here exactly defined, and his loss causes her quite literally to drift:

> She had brought about no real developments in her life by any exercise of her own will; things had happened to her, and she had accepted that, and could not tell if it had been right or wrong, good or bad. She was afraid of taking any initiative with time and circumstance, people and places. She had never done so, because her father had been there, and Ben.

In a third, more circumscribed sense, "helm" is a North-Country name for a cloud which forms over a mountain-top before or during a storm, and a "helm-wind" refers to a violent wind met in the Pennines. Thus, in a novel with indeterminate geography, even this localized meaning conveys the force of Ben's death and its aftereffects.

It is significant that this scene at Helm Bottom, at the symmetrical center of the novel, should be graced by weather which suggests for the first time, "a sense of the approaching spring" (86). By this allusion to the book's title, the thematic as well as structural centrality of the scene is emphasized, and the new season is contrasted with the physical detail of the dead leaves remaining from the old year. Arrived at the bottom of the slope, in what proves a symbolic as well as physical sense, Ruth pauses at the sound of chanting from high, childish voices. She retreats behind an oak to watch a small, slow procession which emerges from the woods. The group comprises five children from the village, all girls and all dressed in white, the first of whom carries a small, white box. As they approach, they sing disjointedly the nursery rhyme of "Cock Robin," and halt near the fallen elm tree. Their leader, Jenny Colt, sets down the box, a hole is dug, the box is buried and the chanting recommences. After sticking a cross made of twigs into the ground, the group's leader bows in respect and rejoins the others who retire through the trees, leaving behind the grave of a bird or small animal.

To designate this scene as a *mise en abyme* clearly implies thematic duplication within a micro-narrative, but it also introduces here a significant reduction in the scale of performers themselves. Thus, the mourners are children, five in number, echoing the survivors of the Bryce family (Ruth; Jo and Alice; Arthur and Dora), but far fewer than the "column of mourners like black ants" at Ben's funeral. The coffin has become a small, white box, sufficiently light to be carried in the girl's hand, rather than requiring shoulders for support. Their clothes are adapted from adults', and their whiteness, like that of the box, contrasts with the conventional black of the adult ceremony. They sing a nursery rhyme in place of a hymn, use a rusty garden trowel instead of a spade, and endlessly incant the only fragment of the funeral service they know. Lacking any more substantial material, they make a cross from twigs, while the object of mourning in the grave is no human body, but that of a small creature whose scale matches that of the young mourners.

It is made quite apparent that the children act out their ritual with a specific ceremony in mind. Not only do they dig a grave close to the fallen elm where Ben lost his life, but their leader, Jenny Colt, is the sister of the young forester David Colt, who brought the first news of the accident to Ruth. The nursery rhyme embedded in this brief scene offers, like the dumb-show in *Hamlet* and the allegorical poem in *Usher,* a second internal mirror, or rather echo, of the larger events, and is especially appropriate in this context. While the story of the mating of Robin with Wren is centuries-old, it is his death and burial rather than their marriage that has endured in rhyme, and it is this same kind of emphasis which dominates Susan Hill's larger narrative too. By using the classic nursery rhyme liturgy of "Cock Robin" with its doleful sequence of question and response, and allowing the phonetic similarity of "Ben"/"Robin" to resonate throughout, the narrative establishes suggestive links which are further reinforced by giving Jenny Colt, the children's pallbearer, the same first name as the Wren who "bears the pall" in the nursery rhyme. Being herself childless and, at nineteen, young enough to be related in spirit to the child-mourners she is watching, Ruth must regard Jenny Colt as her surrogate, the Wren lamenting her Robin.

The choice of Helm Bottom for the *mise en abyme* of the children's ceremony also involves semantic condensation, in so far as the site of death now merges with the site of burial. It becomes, too, the site of rejuvenation, in terms of Ruth's identification with the youthful actors. By their white robes, the children mark themselves off from the world of adult convention and proclaim their innocence, while Ruth's past abhorrence of the "ashen" faces of mourners "black as crows" at Ben's funeral now merges with other images, of people in the early church "who wore white at a funeral for rejoicing." This association of whiteness, together with the link between the earlier ceremony and the reduced model, conveyed by the typical epithet of "old-young" which Susan Hill applies to the children's faces, prepares the reader for a brief account of Ruth's reactions to the scene. Leaving the solid oak, she goes to sit on the fallen elm, at the same moment as the sun breaks through, and she feels a moment of happiness. This "assurance that she would survive" recalls an earlier epiphany at the church service for Ben, when a reading from the Book of Revelation accompanies Ruth's perception of an inner unifying light: "She felt faint, not with grief but with joy, because love was stronger than death." Now, at Helm Bottom, she senses that she will one day emerge from the dark tunnel, remade and whole; were she to die soon, she tells herself, at least she would no longer feel alone, unloved and unprotected.

This gradual reawakening of concern for other proves later to be the vital support by which she clings to life and ultimately justifies her existence, so that on the last page of the novel, hearing about an old man's fate, she "felt appalled, at the isolated death, that the man had no friends, no care. She must not let anyone in her own life come to that." At the end of the scene at Helm Bottom, therefore, the first stage in that process has begun, as Ruth experiences a sense of relief on behalf of the youthful mourners. Her own thoughts provide the framework for that reaction: "The children were safe, because they had been able to act out the ritual of death and funeral, they would not come to harm." For days afterwards, she is gladdened by memories of the scene and at night the white figures inhabit her dreams. Ruth's attraction to the graveyard is now replaced by that of Helm Bottom, where she comes to the elm tree to remember her past life. For, "only by remembering might she piece the pattern together and understand it. Until now, she had only seen it in flashes, as though a light had been turned on to a picture, but turned off again, at once, before she had had a clear view of it." The scattered epiphanies of the past, now reinforced by her experience at Helm Bottom, prepare the way for her spiritual illumination on Easter Sunday, when she feels for the first time ever that she is part of the life around her, part of some "great, living and growing tapestry, every thread of which joined with and crossed and belonged to every other, though each one was also entirely and distinctly itself."

By contrast with *Hamlet* and *Usher,* the chief character of **Springtime** has little to say in the choice of the *mise en abyme,* beyond making the voluntary decision to watch the ritual funeral. The intention behind its staging by the children would appear to be their imitation of a traditional event in the adult world. Its success, however, unrealized by and incidental to the performers, must be measured by its effect upon the unseen observer. Ruth's momentous decision, on Good Friday, in the chapter next-but-one, to dispose of Ben's possessions, carries the sanction of the scene at Helm Bottom: "She remembered the children in the wood. Well, she would copy them; somehow, she would drag the sacks down to the meadow, or into the copse, and either bury them or make a pyre and burn them in the garden." Thus, the children's burial of the white box becomes the trigger for Ruth's burial of the past, which must precede a fresh start. In narrative terms, the purpose of the ritual is to objectify Ruth's experience for the first time, to prepare her to view her situation as if she were outside it, to exorcise the barren claims of the graveyard. By adopting elements from the pastoral elegy and using children as actors, a new ambience is created in which complex issues appear simplified, the outlines of emotion are softened, distanced and depersonalized, grief is granted dignity, and the possibility of consolation and reassurance in some permanent principle is finally held out. Later, when she comes to the aid of the curate Ratheman, whose young daughter has just died, she recognized a parallel case, a further objectification of her own earlier self: "Ruth realized at last how she herself had been, and how it had seemed to others, when she had shut herself away, or spent hours in the woods, or beside Ben's grave at night, all sense of time lost." It can hardly be accidental that Ruth encounters the hysterical curate, who prompts her first show of initiative, activity and altruism, in the woods at Helm Bottom.

Set alongside the ritual of Easter, presented at some length in the novel, the children's enactment of the burial service appears transient and private, though, as indicated, it is a necessary prerequisite to the public celebration of Easter by which it is followed. While *Springtime* shows the spatial reduction common to all examples of *mise en abyme,* it differs from *Hamlet* and *Usher* in adding a reduction in the physical scale of its performers, and introducing a different mode (dramatic) from its overall norm (narrative), whereas the *mise en abyme* in *Hamlet* is dramatic within a dramatic framework, and that in *Usher* is narrative within a [narrative] framework. Unlike Poe's and Shakespeare's, Susan Hill's example is non-literary and non-secular, emphasizing by its dramatic mode the notion of objectification, and by its status as religious ritual the importance of the spiritual in the novel as a whole. The proximity of interests between Ruth and the children is unequalled by that between the factions in the other works, the narrator and Roderick, Hamlet and Claudius.

This relationship of affinity, rather than sympathy or outright antagonism, is supplemented, further, by the fact that the *mise en abyme* in Susan Hill's novel is the only one of the three examples which offers a completed rather than a partial performance, since "The Mouse-trap" and the *Mad Trist* are not acted out or read out to their conclusions. In this connection, it would be apposite to refer to Ricardou's conception of the *mise en abyme* as a model issuing directives for the production of the larger narrative. Thus, the effect of reassurance which the (completed) performance has on Ruth is projected into the note of qualified hope at the end of the larger narrative, while the corresponding (incomplete) *mise en abyme* in *Hamlet* and *Usher* anticipate the physical downfall of their chief characters. In its relation to the larger narrative, finally, the *mise en abyme* of *Springtime,* by contrast with the other two works, appears as an "internal analepsis," referring back to an event which has occurred since the novel's starting-point. Its role proves revelatory, in Ricardou's terms, and its psychological aspect, proposed by Gide, is here borne out. All three anglophone examples treat the theme of death: in *Hamlet* the *mise en abyme* re-enacts the manner of death, in *Usher* it narrowly foreshadows its approach, in *Springtime* it relives the funeral rites. While the first two are concerned with process, the third is concerned with product, and while in *Hamlet* the micro-narrative contains no hint of the eventual outcome, and in *Usher*

it patently overdetermines it, in *Springtime* the ritual ceremony achieves a sense of tenuous balance: it serves both an analeptic and proleptic function, by its imitation of a past event and its anticipation of a future direction.

By consideration of one narrative feature, it is not meant to suggest that others may not be relevant in discussion of the novel. It would be possible, for instance, to use the analogy of a pictorial triptych as an approach to *Springtime.* With a central panel twice the width of its wings, this would roughly correspond to the dimensions of the novel's three parts, the first and third of which are temporally successive and in advance of the central section containing the *mise en abyme* and the Easter sequence. In novel and triptych alike, the outer sections fold over or embed the vital second section; where the pictorial model composes a church altarpiece often depicting the Madonna, the literary model offers a "meditation on love and death," a verbal Pietà not of Virgin Mother grieving for Son, but of widow for husband; the Easter narrative and shared spiritual experience would anchor both pictorial and literary models.

Whatever the value of using the triptych as an approach, the analogy underscores the value of considering structural as well as thematic features, and of relating each to other. Serious shortcomings in any area obviously can not be redeemed by mere felicities of structure, but the latter, on the other hand, can reinforce already existing strengths. Critics of *Springtime* have usually pointed to a certain simple-mindedness or indulgence, a lack of vulgarity, a trend towards quietism or melodrama, and an overliterate inner consciousness. Others, more favorably disposed, have commented on a lack of sentimentality, a delicate rendition of the countryside which blends inner and outer weather, a fastening on moments of genuine feeling and vision, an unfashionable concentration on the fundamentals of life. This intensity of concentration, Susan Hill's particular strength, whereby the private concerns of characters viewed in their isolation reach an obsessional level, results too from a classical purity of narrative marked by an absence of subplots, ideologies or panoramic ambitions, which could distract from or counter-balance the prime thrust. In *Gentleman and Ladies* (1968) and *Springtime* (1974), Susan Hill employs the identical trigger of a family death, but in the intervening years and novels moves gradually from multiple relationships to a single character spiritually and geographically isolated from any community ("it was a mile to the next house and three to the village"). It is in her last novel that this bracketing out of extraneous elements is most rigorously applied, the focus most narrow and sharp. The relative brevity, or short-windedness, of her novels is perhaps the inevitable outcome of such intensity, which over any longer stretch could prove intolerable for the reader. At the very extreme of self-preoccupation by the main character, then, there emerges in *Springtime* the possibility of piecing together some pattern, of grasping hold of some reassurance, or belonging to some community. By emphasizing the structural as well as thematic centrality of the rite which constitutes the *mise en abyme* in Susan Hill's last novel, it is hoped to direct critical attention not only to the value of narrative duplication as a general procedure, but also, and perhaps more pertinently, to a more careful analysis of her other works than it has hitherto received.

Maria Schubert (essay date 1990)

SOURCE: "Susan Hill Focusing on Outsiders and Losers," in *English Language and Literature: Positions & Dispositions,* edited by James Hogg, Karl Hubmayer, and Dorothea Steiner, Institut für Anglistik und Amerikanistik der Universität Salzburg, 1990, pp. 91-101.

[*In the following essay, Schubert discusses the ways Hill's marginalized, often female characters illuminate the main themes of her fiction, especially in* Gentleman and Ladies, A Change for the Better, *and* I'm the King of the Castle.]

The problems of women as an underprivileged even an oppressed section of society are almost inevitably a subject for female novelists today. In her novels and short stories Susan Hill too comes up against questions of female independence and individuality and makes them part of her preoccupation, but the circle of her sympathy is wider, more inclusive. The focus of her attention is on the weak links in the social chain generally, on the outsiders and losers, the old and the sick, children dominated or neglected by their parents, middle-aged women who want to begin a new life, on the mentally ill and eccentrics who all have difficulty holding their own. An unsigned review in the TLS made the point that "Miss Hill seems most at home when she writes about old people and children". What fascinates her so much about old people and children is that "the gulf between what they can feel and what they can do or say is deepest, and she identifies with them because of that". Certainly old people and children offer an extreme case of the outsider in his limited capacity to act which makes it a particularly profitable undertaking for a critic to concentrate on this aspect of her novels. The novels in which children and old people offer a specially interesting object of study are *Gentleman and Ladies* (1968), *A Change for the Better* (1969), and *I'm the King of the Castle* (1970), and to these I shall confine my investigation. Reality is too demanding, too harsh and too uncompromising for these sensitive and vulnerable people; they are only too well aware of their position as outsiders and of the few possibilities left them to change their lives for the better. Many of them remain outsiders all their lives, they are always the losers in a hostile world which has no time for fringe groups. Suicide is often the only escape

for Susan Hill's protagonists, the end of social humiliation and misunderstanding from one point of view, the end of human failure from another.

"Hill seems to pose their problems in metaphysical terms—as to whether life is worth living at all—, but behind these there are considerable economic and emotional factors which have determined their senses of 'failure'". The answer to the question whether life is worth living at all is implicit in Susan Hill's work: life is worth living, it is even worth living for the old and sick, the handicapped, the idiots, and even for the young widow for whom life seems to have become meaningless without her husband. In spite of this affirmation it is made clear in Susan Hill's novels and short stories that "death is not always the worst thing that can happen to people". From her first novel *The Enclosure* (1961) to *Lanterns across the Snow* (1987) death is a central theme; indeed "plots, themes, and motifs", as Rosemary Jackson notes, "recur with a striking similarity in different texts, as they move toward a resolution of a basic desire to enter life". This recurrence of themes does not, however, make for monotony; on the contrary, it presses on the reader the urgency and importance of the issues Susan Hill has to convey as she moves from novel to novel and from story to story.

> Although each of her books has had its own distinctive atmosphere, almost its own colour . . . — they all focus on the same kind of lonely, dislocated experience. The characters are always somehow unaccommodated, outside ordinary intercourse, there is always the pathos of an excited, complex sensibility that has to stay closed-off and inarticulate.

Her works also "characteristically explore states of isolation, loss, and detachment", but in spite of these negative aspects of life with which Susan Hill is primarily concerned, she cannot be said to have a negative view of humanity in general or of the human condition in particular. Like Thomas Hardy, whose short stories she selected and published with an introduction and notes, she seems to believe that the struggle of life is always worthwhile, that there is always hope. Without ever being sentimental, she manages to express deep-felt compassion for all who suffer, for man, who is an alien in an impersonal and inhuman world.

***Gentleman and Ladies* offers a portrait of village life, of ageing women constantly reminded of illness and death—the novel significantly opens with a funeral.**
—Maria Schubert

Susan Hill's early novels *The Enclosure* (1961) and *Do Me a Favour* (1963) are occupied in the main with male-female relationships. Her characteristic focus and style first made themselves apparent in *Gentleman and Ladies* and *A Change for the Better.* Here she turns to the problems of old and middle-aged people for whom life seems to have nothing to offer, of whom, however, a few finally succeed in changing their lives for the better by 'personal effort', not because fate is being kind to them. The author presents short episodes from the lives of these people in simple, lucid and rather formal prose. The stiffness and inflexibility of the characters, manifested in their daily routines, in their never-changing habits, which often border on the absurd and gro-tesque, their rigid viewpoints are perfectly reflected by the constant formal use of the characters' full names. The de-vice recurs in many subsequent novels and short stories, but Catherine Wells Cole's criticism that this "practice can, in Hill's later novels, degenerate into a mannerism" does not seem to be justified; it is a technique which always serves a distinct purpose: that of revealing a formal emptiness so characteristic of the lives of, say, a Mrs Deirdre Fount, a Mrs Winifred Oddicott (*A Change for the Better*) or a Mrs Hel-ena Kingshaw (*I'm the King of the Castle*). In this connec-tion it is interesting to note that while Susan Hill rarely refers to characters by their first names, in some short stories the reader never gets to know their Christian names and some characters, like 'the boy' in **"Friends of Miss Reece"** (*The Albatross and Other Stories,* 1971) and 'the boy' in **"The Custodian"** (*A Bit of Singing and Dancing,* 1973) remain anonymous. The names themselves are not less significant: in particular the women who people Susan Hill's novels and short stories have all rather peculiar names, e.g., Dorothy Shottery, Alida Thorne, the three Lavender sisters Faith, Isabel, and Kathleen, Florence Ames, Ada Gaily, Deirdre Fount, Winifred Oddicott, Hilda Pike, Avis Parson, Ruby Rourke, and many others. The names isolate their bearers, emphasize the fact of their being outsiders and contribute to the atmosphere of detachment, impersonality, and alien-ation.

Gentleman and Ladies offers a portrait of village life, of ageing women constantly reminded of illness and death—the novel significantly opens with a funeral. The gentleman of the title, Hubert Gaily, who is regarded as the outsider in the village community (the fact that he is wearing boots at the funeral is mentioned several times), becomes by the end of the novel a real 'insider' because of his solid and reli-able character and his readiness to help. He and his mother Ada, both of them strikingly anachronistic figures, contrib-ute a lot to relieve the gloomy atmosphere of the novel. Ada Gaily's insistence upon the daily routines, the keeping of old habits and familiar domestic practices and her son's not wanting to stick to all these rules, of taking the laundry out on Wednesdays and going out for a drink only on Saturdays reveal the author's comic vein at its best. "Routine was the stuff of life to Ada Gaily, had always been so" and now she

is "too old for all this shifting and altering". Also her son Hubert likes a certain routine in his life, he "was even pre-pared to go so far as to admit that monotony was the most comfortable way". This changes when he gets to know Flo-rence Ames, a widow whom he wants to marry. Middle-aged Hubert Gaily, a "ponderous" man, is one of many figures in Susan Hill's work who have considerable problems with communication in general and even greater difficulties in conveying their feelings. His clumsy efforts to propose to Florence Ames and to make his intentions clear to his mother, with whom he has been living up to now (for 54 years!), are grotesque in the extreme and brilliantly described by the author. Nevertheless, Hubert Gaily is a convincing character who is not only appreciated, but also accepted by people once they know him better, just as his grim old mother is a good-natured woman at heart, so that in spite of being townsfolk they are made part of the village commu-nity of Haverstock and find their way to a fuller life.

Other characters in the novel are less fortunate, however, Alida Thorne, a lonely woman of sixty-one, who "has her mother put away into a nursing home in a final bid for self fulfilment . . . is portrayed as a bitter, selfish woman", who does not find contentment and a real meaning to her life. In spite of her newly gained freedom, the fashionable new dresses, hats and coats bought in London and the prospect of a holiday she is not happy, whereas her mother, Eleanor Thorne, does splendidly at 'The Gantry', a beautiful old manor house, now transformed into a nursing home for old people, of which she has happy youthful memories. Unlike Ada Gaily or Deirdre Fount and Winifred Oddicott (*A Change for the Better*) Eleanor Thorne, though almost ninety, is only too well aware "that things change" and she is not too old "to accept the difference in life." She is very lively and alert for her age and has "a most agile mind" and her views on marriage are, in a way, remarkable:

> "But I do not believe, you know, that an unhappy marriage is preferable to a contended single life. There are a great many people, I think, men and women, who are perfectly satisfied living indepen-dently. Of course, that has not always been the gen-eral view. *We* were all encouraged to marry, we were branded as failures in our day, if we did not. There was the terrible burden of being the daughter left at home, the maiden aunt. But things are different now. Oh, indeed!"

Eleanor Thorne definitely has an experience of life which gives her a deep insight into the complexities of human na-ture and the human condition. Though the reader does not know which time is referred to when she is speaking of "our days" and "now", because "like much of Hill's work", the novel "is not precisely located in time" and at the same time "faintly anachronistic", Eleanor Thorne's pronouncements on marriage and the single life sound very modern. She is an amiable old lady with an admirable personality, having led a happy life as a young girl, as a mature woman, and also in old age. She has always regarded life from a very positive viewpoint; she has learned to accept fate—her husband died when her daughter Alida was only three years old—and she has thoroughly enjoyed what life has had to offer her. She pities the younger generation, not only because they "do not dance", but also because they "lead such serious, earnest lives", and she feels sorry for her daughter Alida who has not been able to derive the same pleasure as she from the experience of life. "'My daughter does not have patience with memories. I wonder if it is because she has so few of her own. I am guilty in that respect. Perhaps I sheltered her from experience. But she did not seem to want to see it'", she says to Miss Cress, the matron. Though Eleanor Thorne never complains about her selfish and heartless daughter, she is very upset when Alida, to soothe her own bad conscience, decides to take her home for a week's holiday. She has no desire to leave 'The Gantry', where she has been treated with kindness, respect, and understanding by the matron and the other patients; but fate is merciful again, and she dies before Alida can take her home.

Mrs Clemency, her friend and fellow-patient at 'The Gantry' "wondered constantly about the background that had caused such a terrible situation ... to have a daughter, an only child, of whom one was afraid and with whom one hated to stay, was beyond her comprehension". Here Susan Hill touches a most interesting and relevant subject, namely the hereditary and environmental influences on the development of a human being. The reader is not given much information about Alida's childhood, but from what he knows of her mother Eleanor, he wonders why she has not developed into a more pleasant person than she seems to be. One is reminded of a passage in Aldous Huxley's *The Genius and the Goddess* (1955), in which John Rivers reflects about his daughter Molly, whom he does not understand at all:

> "... Look at Molly, for example. She had a mother who knew how to love without wanting to possess. She had a father who at least had sense enough to try to follow his wife's example ... There were no quarrels in the household, no tragedies or explosions. By all the rules of psychology-fiction, Molly ought to be thoroughly sane and contented. Instead of which" ... He left the sentence unfinished.

Life does not always take the course expected by people or assumed by psychologists on the basis of certain premises which have proved correct in thousands of cases. There are other forces at work which cannot be foreseen or reckoned with. Just as John Rivers does not understand his daughter, Eleanor Thorne does not understand hers. Perhaps the answer to the puzzle lies in the theory of Alfred Adler:

> Alle Vorstellungen von Kräften, die auf das Kind einwirken und seine Entwicklung bestimmen, übersehen den wichtigsten Faktor, die Entscheidungsfähigkeit des Kindes. Es ist nicht das Opfer verschiedener Einflüsse, denen es ausgesetzt war, im Gegenteil, das Kind bestimmt ihre Bedeutung.

Alida, one might say, has become the victim of her own inability to lead these influences into positive channels; she herself is responsible for the dullness and dissatisfaction of her life. She has always been an outsider, as it were by her own design, and there is little hope for a fuller life in the years left to her.

In *A Change for the Better* the problems are basically the same. The characters are again middle-aged or old and there is very little plot. This time the setting is Westbourne, a faded seaside resort and the atmosphere of decay hovers over people's lives which are again characterized by isolation, detachment, alienation, and death. As in the previous novel there are many outsiders and losers who are defeated by fate or their own inability to make the best of things. The problems of the generation gap, here between Deirdre Fount and her mother, are also portrayed with ironic brilliance. The language, again formal and precise and lacking any tone of sentimentality, has been highly praised by critics. What is new in the novel is the first of many portraits of children. Susan Hill draws them with the professional skill of a writer and an insight which might be called feminine, even maternal. Interestingly, all the children in her work, only a few excepted, are boys. Whether this is purely accidental or an imbalance, or whether personal reasons might have influenced her choice in this respect cannot be precisely said.

Her child-characters are all highly convincing portraits of human beings, very often the victims of incompetent parents and nurses. They are suppressed, held in subjection and hardly ever treated as equals by adults who completely lack understanding and believe merely in authority and the keeping up of appearances. They are often cruelly treated by fate and trapped by restrictive social conventions and rules. Together with the old and sick people of the novels, they are always the weaker ones, the losers—only James Fount, Deirdre's son, is different. Though he appears a very shy and reserved boy and though he has certainly a difficult life with two women, his mother and his grandmother, and no man in the house, he is not defeated by them and he is finally one of the few winners of the story. In spite of his tender years he knows exactly what he wants and sticks firmly to his plans, whether they concern the railway holiday on which he wants to go with his friend, the school he will attend, or his future in general. He always succeeds in persuading his mother to acquiesce against her previous intentions. He manages and organizes everything alone, the only support coming from Mr Porlock, his music teacher, who is well aware of the boy's talent—he plays the flute excellently—and who advises him to be trained at a boarding school specialising in music.

His relationship to his mother, like many of the mother-son relationships in Susan Hill's work, is characterized by detachment, alienation, and a lack of closeness and understanding. Like Ada Gaily, Helena Kingshaw (*I'm the King of the Castle*), Hilda Pike ("The Albatross", *The Albatross and Other Stories*) or Constance Hilliard (*Strange Meeting*, 1971) Deirdre Fount does not really know her son; he is a stranger to her just as she is a stranger to her own mother, so that there seems to be a vicious circle which seems always to exclude the possibility of close parental relationships. Somehow the bonds of blood seem to be detrimental to happy unions and the children, as a sort of substitute for parental warmth and understanding, turn to people outside their families for support and affection (e.g., Martha in "Somerville", *The Albatross,* 'the boy' in "Friends of Miss Reece", *The Albatross,* Duncan Pike in "The Albatross", *The Albatross,* Marcel Piquet in "Red and Green Beads", *A Bit of Singing and Dancing,* and John Hilliard in *Strange Meeting*).

Unlike her son James, Deirdre Fount does not succeed in realising her plans for the future, of selling the draper's shop which she runs with her mother, of moving to another town, and above all, of living independently. When her mother dies quite unexpectedly in an accident, she fails to accomplish the long-desired change. Her former enthusiasm, her optimism and her hope for a better future suddenly give way to resignation and apathy. As long as her exasperating mother was alive, Deirdre Fount was rebellious; once she is dead, she sinks into lethargy and indifference. The reader is disappointed at this sudden change in her, this loss of initiative, which is not so much the result of her bad conscience about her mother's death, for which she feels partly guilty, as due to 'feminine failure'. As Rosemary Jackson puts it:

> It is clear, in these early novels, that Susan Hill has little faith in women's strength. She effects a virtual polarisation of 'female' and 'male' qualities: characters in whom the first predominate cannot compete on equal terms and they sink back, defeated, into actual death or into analogous states of death-in-life.

Flora Carpenter is not so easily defeated, although she is seventy and has just lost her husband; she does not despair or give up. She has made plans for the future; she means to leave the Prince of Wales Hotel, take a flat, enrol in a modern embroidery class, and do charity work of some kind. Like Eleanor Thorne she is a very gentle woman with an experience of life that has made her tolerant and open-minded. She

feels that it is time to lead her own life and in spite of her mourning for her husband, whom she had loved and whose life she had shared for fifty years, she is looking forward to a new freedom:

> . . . I have spent so long, ever since I was only a girl following in the wake of my husband, trying to think of him and make him happy, for that was my duty, and I was happy to do it. I have just now begun to realize that I do not know what it means to stand up alone and be independent, and that is an experience everyone should have before they die.

Flora Carpenter has always had the talent to do the right thing at the right moment. When Doctor Rogers tells her that her husband is seriously ill—probably cancer—she decides not to tell him the truth because she knows him too well, knows his aversion to doctors and his hatred of hospitals. She also knows her son's wife too well to accept her invitation to stay three weeks with them after her husband's death" . . . 'I know that she does not enjoy having guests in the house. Perhaps they have only invited me because they feel it is their duty, they have made the gesture' . . . 'perhaps I am judging harshly, . . . But, in any case, I shall not go, . . .'". This making of gestures, the keeping up of appearances is a recurrent theme in Susan Hill's fiction, revealing an aspect of social hypocrisy. Just as Auriole Carpenter, Flora's daughter-in-law, offers to take her for three weeks because "'. . . that seems fair. It will be long enough to make the journey worthwhile, and not long enough for us to get on top of one another . . .'", Alida Thorne wants to take her mother home for a week's holiday, neither longer nor shorter.

An excellent example of Susan Hill's ironic manner is the scene in which Miss Violet Prug, an acquaintance of Flora Carpenter, invites her after her husband's death and remarks in an apologetic manner "'. . . I did not think it at all necessary to hold back until anything like a "decent interval" might be supposed to have passed. Because it is now that you will be in need of your friends . . .'". The novel ends with Mrs Carpenter pitying Deirdre Fount who is "not yet forty" but has already "given in", a woman with no future. She has not only lost her mother, her son, who wants to go away, and her husband, whom she divorced shortly after marrying him, but also the belief in herself.

In *I'm the King of the Castle* Susan Hill is concerned with the relationship between two boys, Charles Kingshaw and Edmund Hooper, which ends with Charles's suicide. When Charles cannot bear Edmund's cruelties any longer, he drowns himself in a little pond in the nearby wood, the only place where he feels safe. He is one of Susan Hill's great losers; he cannot fight and he cannot act against his convictions; thus death is the only possibility open to him to escape from a life of terror. His persecutor Edmund Hooper is the same age as he, ten years old. Edmund regards him as an intruder at 'Warings', an old Victorian house, the family property of the Hoopers. The fact that Edmund seems to be more attached to the house than to his father—his mother has been dead six years—sets the events in motion that lead to the final catastrophe. Charles Kingshaw does not behave in the least like an intruder; he does not want or claim anything; on the contrary, he hates the sinister house with its secret corners and the Red Room, full of terrifying things. Edmund cruelly and unscrupulously takes advantage of Charles's fears and anxieties till he cannot bear the persecution any longer. Tragically, there is no one to help him in this terrible situation; Mr Hooper has no idea of what is going on in his house and Charles's mother is so busy with her own problems that she does not realize the seriousness of the boy's difficulties. Widowed herself, she has been forced to take various jobs as a housekeeper, always living in other people's houses or flats with her son. Charles wished "she was dead, instead of his father", and this cruel and inhuman wish points to the whole drama of the boy's life at Warings, the misery and despair of a child growing up in circumstances that cannot influence his development in a positive way. Had his father not died and had they been well provided for, his mother need not have accepted the job as Mr Hooper's housekeeper and the fatal involvement with Edmund would not have come about. Although Charles is only ten, he poignantly feels the important role money plays in life and that lack of money causes great problems. He hates his mother also for trying to attract Mr Hooper's attention and wanting to marry him, because sexuality is for him a factor of human life he either does not understand or denies completely. For Helena Kingshaw a new marriage would not only mean a desirable financial security, but also protection and the satisfaction of her physical desires, which are never mentioned explicitly, however. The absence of explicit sexual reference, characteristic of Susan Hill's fiction, does not imply a downgrading of the importance of this vital aspect of experience; it expresses a preference for an oblique mode of communication, almost innovative after years of the demonstrative breaking of sexual taboos, once doubtless a great merit in literature. The importance of sexuality is most convincingly conveyed in her novel *In the Springtime of the Year* (1974) in the suffering inflicted upon Ruth, the protagonist, by her young husband's death. Here Susan Hill describes Ruth's inexpressible grief and loneliness with the insight of someone who has experienced the pain of loss herself.

Charles Kingshaw, though he first deceives himself by not admitting his mother's aspirations to himself and Edmund, is fully aware that "in the traditional family structure of father-mother-child . . . , there is no room for both Charles and Edmund" and that one of them "has to be excluded". Charles knows only too well that he must be the one excluded, because he is the weaker of the two boys, though their roles are reversed twice when they run away into the woods and when they climb the ruins of Leydell Castle. Charles, however, has a last refuge he can flee to when the worst comes to the worst, when his mother marries Mr Hooper and when they are supposed to be a family and live at Warings. It is his boarding school where everything is familiar to him, where he knows his place and need not fight for his position among the others and, above all, where Edmund cannot persecute him any longer. When he learns that Mr Hooper wants him to attend Edmund's school, which is so much better than his own, and is even prepared to pay for him, he is terrified because then there would be no end to Edmund's humiliations and cruelties. And when Edmund claims Charles's only friend Anthony Fielding, whom he had met when Hooper was in hospital, as his friend and excludes Charles from their company, he gives up, he has "finished" with his enemy, he will no longer be tortured by him.

Helena Kingshaw [in *I'm the King of the Castle*] is perhaps the most incompetent of all incompetent mothers in Susan Hill's fiction. She fails completely to realize the difficulties in the relationship between the two boys, fails to see the cruelties and humiliations her son is exposed to.
—*Maria Schubert*

Edmund's successful attempts to uncover all of Charles's weaknesses and to hit him where he is most vulnerable, lead to a state of nervous tension in Charles that results finally and inevitably in suicide. The psychologist Erwin Ringel suggests that the capacity of a mentally healthy person to tolerate psychic disturbance is boundless. "Seelische Störungen— . . . —setzen aber diese Toleranzfähigkeit in geringerem oder größerem Maße herab, sodaß traumatisierende Außenfaktoren zum Motiv der Selbstmordhandlung werden können". In Charles's case the ability to tolerate Edmund's humiliations has been considerably reduced, partly by reason of his vulnerability and his sensitiveness in general, so that he cannot bear these traumatic experiences any longer. The inclination to suicide is greater, Ringel says, "je stärker die psychologische Fehlentwicklung eines Menschen ist". Charles has actually worked himself into such a state of neurotic tension that he sees everything worse than it really is. This does not mean, however, that Edmund's humiliations are nothing, a trifle; on the contrary, they are mean and intended to destroy. Had Charles been different, had he been more self-assured, invulnerable like Anthony Fielding who "would not bring out the worst in Hooper, as Kingshaw himself did", the situation would never have escalated so. Erwin Ringel expresses the opinion that a tremendous "Antriebskraft" is needed, "um den Selbsterhaltungstrieb auszuschalten. Nur eine hochgradige dynamische Einengung, niemals aber bloß rationale 'Überlegung' vermag dieselbe freizusetzen". Obviously, for Charles the wish to die has become stronger than the wish to live, but only in the end, not before all his attempts to cope with his problems have failed. Charles has operated several defence mechanisms and strategies to make life possible for him in Mr Hooper's house, and he has tried hard to make his unbearable situation clear to his mother.

Helena Kingshaw is perhaps the most incompetent of all incompetent mothers in Susan Hill's fiction. She fails completely to realize the difficulties in the relationship between the two boys, fails to see the cruelties and humiliations her son is exposed to. In her simple mind the problems between the two boys are mainly caused by jealousy; she believes it is only a question of time till the two boys grow to be happy to enjoy each other's company, glad not to be alone any longer. Like so many parents in Susan Hill's work, Helena Kingshaw and Mr Hooper do not know their sons; they have absolutely no idea of what is going on between the children. Helena cannot escape the reproach of being egoistic, calculating and, at the same time, obtuse,—qualities of character which make it impossible for her to judge the situation. Whenever Charles complains to her about Edmund's behaviour or simply tries to make clear his necessities to her, she refuses to take him seriously; she wears her mask of hypocrisy and pretends to be upset, shocked, or hurt by his rude criticism, by his outspoken wishes, by his open and frank judgments. The characterization of Helena finds its ironic climax at the end of the novel when she consoles Edmund, who feels the triumph of Charles's suicide, his victory over the enemy, the hated intruder:

> "Now, it's all right, Edmund dear, everything is all right", Mrs Helena Kingshaw put an arm out towards him, held him to her. "I don't want you to look, dear, you mustn't look and be upset, everything is all right".

This reaction of a mother at the sight of her drowned son does not need any comment. Susan Hill could not have chosen a better tone and language to reveal Helena Kingshaw's character, the emptiness and superficiality of a human life that leads to the destruction of lives. The vicious circle is finally closed, leaving no hope. Susan Hill's view of education in this novel invites comparison with Alice Miller's view in her book *Am Anfang war Erziehung* that education is actually harmful to children;

> Sämtliche Ratschläge zur Erziehung der Kinder verraten mehr oder weniger deutlich zahlreiche, sehr verschieden geartete *Bedürfnisse des Erwachsenen,* deren Befriedigung dem lebendigen Wachstum des Kindes nicht nur nicht förderlich ist, sondern es geradezu verhindert. Das gilt auch für die Fälle, in

> denen der Erwachsene ehrlich davon überzeugt ist, im Interesse des Kindes zu handeln.

This is exactly the case in *I'm the King of the Castle,* where Helena Kingshaw's principles of education are more or less based on her own needs in her doubtless difficult situation, though she believes she only wants the best for her son, and Alice Miller's fear that the child must inevitably suffer from such education is clearly justified. Charles's relationship to his mother has never been a good one,—before they came to 'Warings', she had clung too much to him, because he was all she had after his father's death.

Erwin Ringel warns against the danger of regarding children as partner substitutes, because "ein Kind ist ein Partner schlechthin, ist ein eigenständiger, selbständiger Mensch, dem wir von Anfang an immer größere Räume der Freiheit zugestehen müssen". Helena Kingshaw has failed to give her son the freedom necessary for a child's positive development, and she has failed to treat him as a genuine partner, to show respect for him, so that he is neither able to achieve self-confidence nor to realize his own mode of life. His suicide can be regarded as the only possible way of articulating his true self at the cost of his life.

The psychological background of Edmund Hooper's childhood is not less interesting or problematic. After his wife's death Mr Hooper tries to be a good father to his son, but he does not know how to treat him. Doubtless Edmund is a difficult child, so that the father's task is not an easy one. But unlike Charles's mother Mr Hooper is fully aware of his shortcomings in general and his incompetence as a father in particular. "It was his wife who had known the way, and she had died without leaving a set of rules for him to follow. He blamed her for it". As he lacks any intuition or natural talent in this respect, he badly needs such a set of rules to show him how to deal with children, but whether this would have helped him to establish a satisfactory relationship with his son is a different question. Though we do not know anything about Edmund's childhood while his mother Ellen was still alive, the reasons of his wickedness and his cruelty may be located, though not necessarily, in these earlier years.

Having examined the complex psychological background of the lives of criminals, Alice Miller believes that it is very difficult for many people to understand the simple fact that every persecutor has been a victim himself. "Dabei ist es doch sehr naheliegend, daß ein Mensch, der sich von Kind auf frei und stark fühlen durfte, kein Bedürfnis hat, einen anderen zu erniedrigen". Perhaps Edmund has never been able to feel free and strong; perhaps Ellen Hooper was not such a competent mother as her husband believes her to have been. Mr Hooper's memories of his marriage with Ellen are less than happy. "There had been the politeness of his marriage, the elaborate courtesy of the double bed, he had suffered from the cold gap between his permitted behaviour, and his desires". The words convey a deep sadness, a deep frustration to the reader. This short reference to the sexual aspect of this marriage possibly also reveals, to some extent, the atmosphere of the family in which Edmund grew up. The dispassionate style here is characteristic of the whole novel and represents a perfect vehicle for conveying the bitterness of life, the complete lack of love.

Anita Brookner (review date 24 October 1992)

SOURCE: "The Curious Incident of the Dog," in *Spectator,* Vol. 270, No. 8572, October 24, 1992, p. 34.

[*In the following review, Brookner concentrates on gothic aspects of* The Mist in the Mirror, *admiring the novel's "certain pluckiness of tone."*]

Yet another Victorian pastiche, this time by Susan Hill in her Gothic or ghost story mode. I say Victorian, though the period is uncertain. The stately clubman's tone is reminiscent of Henry James, while the multitudinous weather systems hint at Dickens: there is a transparent borrowing of the famous description of fog in the first chapter of *Bleak House,* although in this instance the identical syntax is applied to rain. As the unnamed narrator strides through a murky London he seems to be in Conan Doyle country; later on, the hero is conveyed by steam trains, although a telephone number is given. All in all, a rather too insistent nudging of one's instant response reflexes. One can see this successfully transferred to television, with manservants, dilapidated manor houses, pitiless moorland, and substantially clothed figures looming through the mist. There are no dogs, however, and no policemen. But there is, significantly, a reproduction on the jacket or a painting by the marvellous Atkinson Grimshaw, and unfortunately this picture says more than a thousand words.

[*The Mist in the Mirror*] is a story of a haunting, and of the difficulty of escaping a family curse. The story is told by James Monmouth, an elderly man encountered by the narrator at his club. In due course, and in true Henry James tradition, the narrator receives from Monmouth three large notebooks containing a memoir of his life and of the peculiar destiny that met him when he returned to England after 20 years spent travelling abroad. On arriving at the docks in London Monmouth is full of optimism: he has a plan for his future, which is to investigate the life of Conrad Vane, a world famous traveller in whose footsteps he has been diligently following these past 20 years.

All augurs well, until he becomes aware of a boy of 12 or 13 who appears to be shadowing him. This boy wears an

expression of infinite distress, and crops up at various intervals in Monmouth's not very intelligent progress. His announced intention of writing a biography of Conrad Vane elicits head-shakings and mutterings from acquaintances met along the way, including the psychic Lady Qincebridge, who turns pale in a railway carriage, begs Monmouth to cease his enquiries, and invites him to her stately pile for Christmas. Before this we have been introduced to Theodore Beamish, Holborn bookseller, who offers Monmouth 'dinner' and whose advice is 'Leave be'. 'Dinner' consists of mutton pies and treacle pudding. Scholars may deduce further chronological pointers from this detail.

> I was not convinced by *The Mist in the Mirror,* although I was oppressed by it, which may have been the author's intention. Where she succeeds is in capturing a certain pluckiness of tone, highly necessary for those venturing down peculiarly tricky paths.
> —*Anita Brookner*

Obviously the full story and the point of the mystery cannot be recounted here. Suffice it to say that Susan Hill leads us expertly from one ancient foundation to another, that Monmouth, who will not leave be, encounters even greater hardship as he progresses both physically and spiritually, and that the dénouement is oddly unsatisfactory, since it is clear that Susan Hill has been stalking two horses all the time and that one of her narratives fails to integrate successfully with the other. If one is pursued one is entitled to envisage a pursuer, and this character, almost entirely absent, is only reintroduced at the end. Which is to say that a whole area of menace has been left out of the story, and that the unfortunate Monmouth, last seen locked into an abandoned church, is the victim of imperfect understanding rather than of a deadly opponent.

We notice here the same story-telling device last noted in P. D. James's new novel, that of the unsuspecting hero voluntarily undertaking a deadly pilgrimage, whereas a little common sense would have told him to do nothing of the kind. This usually works to the hero's detriment, since the reader tends to think him a bit of a fool. I was not convinced by *The Mist in the Mirror,* although I was oppressed by it, which may have been the author's intention. Where she succeeds is in capturing a certain pluckiness of tone, highly necessary for those venturing down peculiarly tricky paths.

Toby Fitton (review date 30 October 1992)

SOURCE: "Directions from Afar," in *Times Literary Supplement,* No. 4674, October 30, 1992, p. 21.

[*In the review below, Fitton puzzles out the mystery of* The Mist in the Mirror, *noting that some questions remain "satisfyingly unanswered."*]

The mood of [*The Mist in the Mirror*] is autumnal, very suitable for a ghost story set in a moist and misty past. Its general context is conventional, that of an M. R. James story. An aged habitué of a Pall Mall club urgently presses on a fellow-member, whose light conversation about ghosts he has overheard, the manuscript reminiscence of a personal experience which had distressed him as a young man. The more specific context is less easy to place, especially in time. There are indications that the main narrative is of the early 1920s, but the plot seems to belong more to late-Victorian England, with the cab-ranks, pea-soupers and ill-lit quaysides of Sherlock Holmes's London as one of its main locations.

As a young orphan, the elderly clubman James Monmouth was sent out to Africa to be brought up on a remote farm with a British pioneer settler as his guardian. Attracted by the writings of an English traveller named Conrad Vane, he sets out after his guardian's death on a voyage of discovery—following Vane's earlier routes. Vane himself proves to be elusive, and research into his life leads Monmouth into some inexplicable situations.

Newly arrived in London to continue his work on Vane, Monmouth—though well off—takes seedy lodgings in a dockland tavern. His main informants urge him to desist. "Leave be, don't tempt fate", urges the seedy antiquarian bookseller who knows more than he is prepared to admit; "Be wary", says the headmaster of Vane's school. An amateur medium who offers Monmouth a refuge warns him to keep back. More admonitory than any of these is the chilling, recurrent appearance of a ragged boy, distant, anxious and pleading, who becomes Monmouth's familiar.

In the earlier chapters, it is puzzling that Monmouth shows a distinct lack of curiosity about his own background while becoming increasingly zealous and fascinated by the pursuit of Vane's life, especially when unsavoury details start to emerge. Surely the two must be related? So it turns out. The names of Vane and Monmouth were indeed once before conjoined in an episode that seems to forbid biographical research. Monmouth presses on warily, finding that documents and furnishings, sounds and places, begin to produce resonances of his own lost childhood—a tantalizing response deep within him whose significance he cannot quite grasp.

He soon finds his way to a remote ancestral property in Yorkshire, where the echoes of his childhood continue but are crowded out by evil immanences that eventually involve him

in an ordeal of the soul. He manages to extricate himself and to allay the evil haunting him.

The narrative proceeds, throughout, by an accumulation of hint and rumour and warning. This is traditional and effective, particularly as it becomes uncreasingly apparent that Monmouth's pursuit of Vane and of his own missing inheritance have no earthly origin but are directed from afar. Questions of mere chronology seem to lose their importance, and Susan Hill's traditional formula succeeds less in resolving the plot than in leaving plenty unexplained. Who was the miserable urchin? Who the guardian? Has the ghost been fully exorcised by being written into a story, or is it merely dormant? Such questions are left satisfyingly unanswered.

Peter Kemp (review date 15 October 1993)

SOURCE: "Imitation Gothic," in *Times Literary Supplement,* No. 4724, October 15, 1993, p. 19.

[*In the review of* Mrs. de Winter *below, Kemp complains that Hill's imitation of Daphne du Maurier's narrative style "is unstirred by any imaginative power."*]

In recent years, Susan Hill has taken to the literary equivalent of manufacturing reproduction furniture. With *The Woman in Black* and *The Mist in the Mirror,* she turned out a pair of antique-look ghost tales, modelled on M. R. James prototypes but also incorporating chunks of replica Dickens and Wilkie Collins. Now she is engaged in marketing another line of imitation: *Mrs de Winter,* her latest fictional commodity, is a simulated sequel to Daphne du Maurier's *Rebecca.*

Other than commercially, emulating that 1938 bestseller would be a profitless task, you'd think, and so it very soon proves. When the story starts—twelve years on from the fateful night Manderley went up in flames—Mrs de Winter, who has spent the intervening period living overseas with Maxim, has just returned to England with him for his sister's funeral. As she narrates what ensues, it rapidly becomes apparent that her prose style, never very distinguished, has sadly deteriorated during her long sojourn abroad. Not the most concise of communicators in *Rebecca,* she is now punishingly prolix. Parts of her story are, in fact, related in duplicate: weary of "running away, running away", she hopes Rebecca is "long, long dead" and "quite, quite forgotten", but "deep, deep fears" make her feel such optimism is "stupid, stupid".

When not caught up in this stylistic stutter, Mrs de Winter, as given voice by Hill, shows an extensive penchant for trios of adjectives. Dozens of instances of this strew her story.

Though happy with "loving, solicitous, tender" Maxim, she is still tormented by thoughts of "tall, slender, black-haired" Rebecca and her "bold, amused, triumphant" gaze. With the reappearance of "motionless, black, gaunt" Mrs Danvers, a "deranged, deluded, vengeful" figure with a "terrible, relentless, insane" voice, "hard, bitter, dreadful" laugh and "bright, mad, staring" eyes, Mrs de Winter suffers "dreadful, restless, haunted" nights, seems to hear a voice saying "Go, go, go", and asks herself "What shall I do? What shall I do? What shall I do?"

In recent years, Susan Hill has taken to the literary equivalent of manufacturing reproduction furniture.
                                        —*Peter Kemp*

One thing she does is to express with some profuseness her soulful sentiments about the English countryside ("a magic place, a scene from some fairy-tale and I sitting at the casement"). Among paragraphs heavily freighted with her sightings of flora and fauna, ornithological observations are particularly copious (suggesting that Hill may have simultaneously considered writing a sequel to du Maurier's story, "The Birds", the book abundantly comments on crows, seagulls, owls, an eagle, a robin, blackbirds, sparrows, larks, pigeons, ducks and geese). These not very vital nature notes are supplemented by long interludes of fervid, if somewhat vague, travelogue. Journeying round Europe, Mrs de Winter informs you that she has seen "beautiful things, breathtaking, unforgettable; houses and mountains and gardens and palaces, seas and skies and churches and lakes". She has marvelled over "the colours of individual pieces of food" on plates, and known cities such as "ancient, hidden, secret" Venice and "old, mysterious" Istanbul.

Though twelve years older, Mrs de Winter doesn't seem discernibly more mature than she was in *Rebecca*. Blushes and juvenile gaucheness still afflict her. But what appeared girlishness in the earlier book now seems retardation. Unaccountably, though a formidably wealthy middle-aged matron, she quivers timorously when Mrs Danvers, now reduced to companioning an elderly lady in Oxfordshire, visits her.

Just as the novel's lavish expenditure of banality in its descriptive passages seems designed to camouflage the fact that it hasn't got much of a plot, so Mrs de Winter's bewildering trepidation seems there to cover up the dearth of any real menace or suspense. The *frissons* in *Rebecca*—which gave it its famed appeal to adolescent girls—partly came from the young heroine's struggle to be accepted by adults who cow and snub her. Further Gothic thrills are transmitted by Maxim's saturnine sexuality and the mysteries of Manderley.

In *Mrs de Winter,* though, Maxim has softened into a husbandly nonentity and Manderley is replaced by a cosy, rosy property in the Cotswolds. Bathos accompanies the reappearance of characters from *Rebecca* and the reworking of dramatic highlights from it: as when, peering from a lofty window in Italy, Mrs de Winter fancies she again hears Mrs Danvers urging her to jump and kill herself. There's a neatish twist by which *Rebecca*'s concluding scene—the ashes of Manderley blown on "the salt wind from the sea"—is redone with a different set of ashes. But where the earlier book, fuelled by du Maurier's emotional turmoil, had a lurid energy that galvanized its story despite the inert prose, *Mrs de Winter,* written from no personal compulsion, is unstirred by any imaginative power.

Rachel Billington (review date 7 November 1993)

SOURCE: "Still Dead after All These Years," in *New York Times Book Review,* November 7, 1993, p. 23.

[*Below, Billington compares* Mrs. de Winter *to Daphne du Maurier's* Rebecca, *finding the former derivative.*]

That fascinating author Ivy Compton-Burnett, when asked whether she had ever thought of writing a sequel to any of her novels, answered: "No. But then my novels end with a full stop, as it were." Part of the magic of Daphne du Maurier's *Rebecca* (1938) is that it starts in the middle and finishes without a full stop, as it were. The temptation to continue such a publishing gold mine was obviously great.

Reading *Mrs. de Winter* feels rather like watching a magician trying to perform a trick while holding a top hat in one hand and the conjuring circle's instruction manual in the other.
                                    —*Rachel Billington*

"Last night I dreamt I went to Manderley again." The famous first line to *Rebecca* sets the tone for what has the air of an elegiac dream itself, a long backward look. The story is told by the second Mrs. de Winter, recalling her arrival as a humble new bride in the deep Cornish countryside. But all its passion and emotion and much of its narrative drive come from the story of the first Mrs. de Winter, the incomparably brilliant and beautiful Rebecca.

In effect, du Maurier is already writing a kind of sequel, cleverly combining an exciting past with a dullish present. Eventually, of course, Rebecca is revealed to have been as cruel as she was beautiful and Maxim de Winter turns out to be not just a gloomy Victorian-style hero but also a murderer.

Du Maurier's structure in what was her sixth novel sets up a particular challenge for Susan Hill, who faces the task with *Mrs. de Winter* of inventing a sequel to a sequel. It is surprising that instead of taking a deep breath and giving herself the freedom to build a forward-moving plot with her two central characters, she has decided to move in exactly the opposite direction. Ms. Hill's 13th book opens with a return to Cornwall, and the new Mrs. de Winter looks back much as she did in the first book, except that now the magnificent ghost of Rebecca has to reach us from even farther away in the mists of time. Furthermore, Ms. Hill has created no new characters, with the single exception of a dull country neighbor, almost indistinguishable from Maxim's sister, whose funeral opens her book.

There are some new events. The de Winters find a Manderley replacement home in the West Country. There are unpleasant confrontations with Rebecca's two disreputable supporters: the housekeeper, Mrs. Danvers; and Rebecca's lover, Jack Favell. There is a doomed party for the neighborhood that spawns despair and eventual tragedy. But such scenes are virtual replays of scenes we have already lived through in *Rebecca*. Lacking the breath of new invention, *Mrs. de Winter* has only the quiet impact of an echo.

Possibly Susan Hill embarked on this project in a spirit of homage to its famous predecessor. Certainly her pages-long descriptive passages seem to be an attempt to capture the atmospheric air of foreboding that is so important in explaining the success of *Rebecca*. Unfortunately, Ms. Hill's trees and shrubs and pinking blackbirds express heavy nostalgia but no sense of threat.

That erstwhile figure of terror Mrs. Danvers has become a pathetic old woman and Jack Favell a tattered drunk. An early attempt to inject mystery is half-hearted, and the failing relationship between Maxim and Mrs. de Winter hardly helps to raise the level of tension. He is too clearly a self-pitying bore, she a self-pitying doormat.

In all fairness, Ms. Hill has found a psychologically appropriate and dramatic end to her sequel, but that is not enough for a book of nearly 400 pages. Perhaps a good literary novelist like Susan Hill, whose work includes *I'm the King of the Castle, Air and Angels* and *The Mist in the Mirror,* should not have taken up the reins from an inspired second-rate novelist like Daphne du Maurier. *Pace* Margaret Forster, whose biography suggests that du Maurier's work contained but concealed such interesting themes in her life. *Rebecca* is a bravura performance arising out of passionate conviction. Reading *Mrs. de Winter* feels rather like watching a magician trying to perform a trick while holding a top hat in one hand and the conjuring circle's instruction manual in the other.

Kathryn Hughes (review date 26 November 1993)

SOURCE: "Play It Again," in *New Statesman and Society,* Vol. 6, No. 280, November 26, 1993, pp. 44-5.

[*In the following review, Hughes laments the specter of "literary ventriloquism" that hangs over* Mrs. de Winter, *likening its demerits to Emma Tennant's* Pemberley, *a sequel to Jane Austen's* Pride and Prejudice.]

Pemberley [by Emma Tennant] and *Mrs de Winter* comprise codas to two of English literature's most loved and enduring texts. Thus *Pemberley* tells the story of what-happened-next to Elizabeth Bennett, Mr Darcy and the rest of the cast of Jane Austen's *Pride and Prejudice*. Mrs de Winter, meanwhile, fast-forwards to a point ten years beyond the end of Daphne de Maurier's *Rebecca* to discover the fate of Mrs Danvers, Maxim de Winter and, of course, the nameless narrator.

Both texts, significantly, concern the non-appearance of heirs. Elizabeth Bennett has been married a full year, and while her sisters Jane and Lydia have produced the required sons. Eliza herself remains embarrassingly unencumbered. Likewise, the second Mrs de Winter, at 34, has begun to give up hope of materialising the tribe of robust, playful boys who already live inside her head.

In their concentration on the non-appearance of the next generation, both texts draw attention to the lack of closure in the original novels. While *Pride and Prejudice* appeared to offer the classic marriage plot of high-realist fiction, it also offered a teasing commentary upon it, refusing to tie up the ends as neatly as Mrs Bennett—and the reader—desired. In *Pemberley,* Emma Tennant reminds us that the finicky courtship rituals, the dancing and the walks in the park have a deadly serious end: the safe handing over of property from one generation to the next through a male heir. Only with Elizabeth pregnant can the story be said to be over.

In the same way, Susan Hill returns to de Maurier's *Rebecca* [in *Mrs de Winter*] and worries away at the little tags and tears in the concluding chapter. Far from wrapping things up nicely, de Maurier's resolution is morally—and novelistically—untenable. Hill's task is to work out the moral plot of *Rebecca* to its final conclusion. Not until Maxim de Winter has paid for the murder of his first wife with his own life can the ghost of Rebecca be laid to rest.

Both Tennant's and Hill's novels are tacked seamlessly on

to their predecessors. The reproduction of tone and character is faultless. True, Tennant allows herself to peer into Elizabeth and Darcy's bedroom in a manner which would have been impossible for Jane Austen, but she does it with such grace that her gentle voyeurism seems to extend rather than intrude upon our understanding of the original.

Hill's achievement, by contrast, is more laboured. While Tennant can simply bring all her characters to Pemberley (Darcy's country seat) for an extended Christmas holiday, Hill has to work hard to get Mrs Danvers from Cornwall to Gloucestershire and to produce a chance meeting in Venice between the de Winters and a still grizzling Mrs Van Hopper. Resorting to contrivance and coincidence as de Maurier never had to, Hill's narrative fails to find the urgent drive of its predecessor.

Logical and accomplished though *Pemberley* and **Mrs de Winter** may both be, the question remains as to why two such prominent talents as Hill and Tennant should be engaged on what, when it comes down to it, is nothing more than literary ventriloquism. For despite all the fancy arguments about intertextuality and knowing pastiche, the fact is that writing sequels to fabulous best-sellers represents a commercial and artistic safe bet.

Just as Hollywood now ransacks 1960s television series to turn tested formulas into big box office, so novelists seem to look to yesterday's smash hits to guarantee at least a modest success. In *Pemberley,* for instance, Tennant has no need to worry about those slow and difficult opening chapters where characters have to be introduced and relationships explained. She can plunge straight into the thick of the action, sure that she is neither boring nor confusing her readers.

In this world of endless literary recycling there is no reason why the characters from *Pride and Prejudice* and *Rebecca* could not be given their own fanzine and sent on a series of endless adventures. The corollary of low-risk writing is, after all, low-risk reading. Where once upon a time the postmodernist reader was an alert creature, ever on the look out for subtle nods at other texts, these days he or she is more likely to be a lazy sentimentalist, happy to reread old favourites.

Yet there is always the possibility that out of such deadness might come renewal. In this case, the ceremonial sealing-off of two such open texts as *Pride and Prejudice* and *Rebecca* could just represent the point at which the contemporary novel's obsession with the burden of its own past is laid to rest, leaving the way for something new to happen.

Ernest H. Hofer (essay date 1993)

SOURCE: "Enclosed Structures, Disclosed Lives: The Fictions of Susan Hill," in *Contemporary British Women Writers, Narrative Strategies,* edited by Robert E. Hosmer Jr., St. Martin's Press, 1993, pp. 128-50.

[*Below, Hofer provides an overview of Hill's fiction, tracing the movement away from an "enclosed" narrative structure to a more "open" one.*]

Susan Hill, now concentrating on writing plays and fiction for children, as well as idylls of country life, is chiefly known for a series of intensely realized narratives composed over a brief six-year period:

> Quite suddenly, a door opened, something fell into place—it's hard to know exactly how to put it—and I began to write as I had known somehow that I could. Between 1968 and 1974—when I look back, I am astonished at how short a time it actually was—I wrote six novels, two collections of short stories, and half a dozen full-length radio plays.

During this extraordinary creative period she gained sympathetic critical attention and indeed three major literary awards before passing her thirtieth year. Good reviews, a willing publisher—such encouragement would project the average writer into permanent composition, the next novel always assumed to be on the drawing boards. Unlike her friend Iris Murdoch, however, who manages to publish a new novel as regularly as Christmas, Hill decided to alter course. The so-admired narrative structure of her novels, the distance, 'the simple intensity', disappeared. 'How could a woman so brilliantly imagine a soldier in the trenches of the Great War?' Such questions, asked by astonished critics, became obsolete.

> This is where we get to this question that fascinates me, what was I compensating for, writing fiction that somehow when I was married and had children, didn't need to be compensated for any more and therefore the ability to write fiction, or need to write fiction, whichever, went from me and was replaced by the ability to go on writing in an off-the-top-need to express myself in this serious fictional form had gone. Why, how, I don't know.

One wonders about that term, 'serious fictional form'. By comparison one can sense what she means. Her kind of imagination, her discipline, which turned out structures of cool, often somberly understated portraits—as a clinical psychologist might—simply faded as a light fades. From revealing so little, except by controlled indirection and understatement to the perceptive reader, she began to reveal so much in her non-fiction. From the chaste style of her novels, powerful in their suggestiveness, Hill turned into a writer intent on self-revelation: a psychologist this time of self, willing to talk about life in the country and bringing up baby. The contrast—and this is the unique part—could not be more dramatic. For unlike any other current British novelist, this writer deliberately withdrew from the stage where she had been applauded. Withdrew without apology, determined to open a new chapter in her emotional life. Where before that energy went into an intense creative process; now it went into the creation of a family and a pastoral life.

> **Susan Hill is at pains to remind us that she was an only child, and that her relatively unhappy youth reflected her solitary predicament as well as a crucial move from her beloved Scarborough to 'a Midland City'. Her days were not spent with playmates, in short. Instead she devoured Hardy, Dickens, the Brontës. These three, particularly Dickens, provided her with early inspiration.**
> **—Ernest H. Hofer**

Our task therefore is a peculiar one: to show Susan Hill growing in strength and confidence, producing a prose accepted as individual and unique, and to trace her reasons for abdication as well as, possibly, contradiction.

Susan Hill is at pains to remind us that she was an only child, and that her relatively unhappy youth reflected her solitary predicament as well as a crucial move from her beloved Scarborough to 'a Midland City'. Her days were not spent with playmates, in short. Instead she devoured Hardy, Dickens, the Brontës. These three, particularly Dickens, provided her with early inspiration. Her reclusive youth, especially latterly in Coventry, found her writing vignettes, indeed peopling her world with the playmates she lacked in daily life. In consequence, writing became an outlet for an enclosed, though preternaturally active imagination. No wonder, then, that she wrote and published a novel while still in the sixth form of her grammar school, another before graduating from London University.

The Enclosure, she called that first 'novel of apprenticeship', and the term may be applied to the whole panorama of her work. Though unobtainable today and repudiated by Hill herself, it concerns Virginia (a young writer), so devoted to her craft that she disappoints a young husband. He eventually leaves her to her writing and her pregnancy: 'She seemed to be living in an enclosure which she hated with an agonizing intensity, but out of which she would not let herself escape'. Her wish to be a writer, obsessive to a de-

gree, prevented her fulfillment as a person. She became enclosed in a dilemma of her own making. Rosemary Jackson remarked, 'Female freedom or independence is made synonymous with selfishness'. True perhaps in a political sense, but the emphasis here seems to be the lure of two modes of behaviour, each in conflict with the other, forming a psychological impasse: to write or to love, both in high gear. To be enclosed in such a dilemma, of course, became the personal problem of Susan Hill herself. Indeed the novel, such as it is, previews the future concerns of its author.

Do Me a Favour (1963) is the second novel of apprenticeship, following two years after *The Enclosure.* A similar expression of frustration encloses the protagonist, another woman writer, who this time buckles under the admonition proclaimed by an 'experienced' lady of ideas, Mrs Christoff: 'Your career is important. You write well. But marriage and children is a greater career in the end—for a woman . . . children are a greater gift than knowledge'. If Susan Hill could create such a fictional scene at nineteen, it becomes easier for us to understand why it became an *idée fixe* later on.

But the 'serious fictional form' began in earnest in 1968 with *Gentleman and Ladies* and *A Change for the Better,* a year later, both designed to focus on a highly emotionally enclosed relationship—of a mother and son, in *Gentleman,* and a mother and daughter, in *A Change.*

But Gaily, the middle-aged son in *Gentleman,* bonded, actually *enslaved* to his mother since boyhood (we never hear of daddy) manages by a superhuman act of will to break out of the enclosure. He meets Florence Ames in the launderette. She is equally mummified, but equally receptive, her middle-aged loneliness under control, of course. In the second meeting, again doing their laundry, we catch these two forlorn beings trying to emerge from their programmed enclosure into recognition of one another. Hill's method of detached, incisive observation takes the form of dialogue and unemphatic action:

> 'Oh, I didn't think you would come,' she said, and laughed, not at all a confused laugh, but quiet, and at herself rather than at him, looking down at her cupped hands as she did so.
>
> 'I'd have to keep a promise.' He stood awkwardly by her table.
>
> 'A man of your word,' she said.
>
> 'That's it. I hope so.'
>
> 'Aren't you going to sit down?' She said that as though she wondered whether it was the correct thing to say.

'I'll get myself a coffee. Will you have another?
You'd no need to have bought your own.'

'Oh, I had to, in case you didn't come. You can't
just sit here.'

'No,' he said. 'No.'

In the cool world of Susan Hill, in the world of enclosure,
this is in a sense a breaking-out of the womb, a first signal
that these two are to be in love, dependent. Florence Ames
will be the instrument of rescue from the mother/son enclosure.

In **Change** Mrs Deidre Fount is an embittered daughter of
Mrs Winifred Oddicott. (We remember the full names: Hill
distances herself from the characters by the constant, formal use of the first and last names, even 'Mrs'.) James is
the son of Mrs Fount. The three live uneasily together by
necessity: Mrs Fount is divorced and needs to work at the
notions' shop run by her mother. The scene is the seaside
resort, reminiscent of Scarborough, so familiar to Hill and
used so often to give accurately her remarkable sense of
place.

Further, in **Change,** Hill is concerned to show the effect of
the yoking of three generations, and the voice in the middle,
Mrs Fount, tied to her mother, tied to her son, is a logical
choice to carry the burden of the enclosure. In her consciousness, writ large, we as readers can observe the building tension, the crisis caused when the son tries to break out of the
enclosure. Poignant perhaps best describes the mounting
confrontations which beset Mrs Fount because she watches
with terrible inevitability the very process of her failure to
communicate with James. It duplicates inexorably the sad
relationship she suffers with her mother. The enclosure that
has encircled her is as tight as a boa constrictor.

Hill uses this time the device of a limited stream of consciousness to advance our understanding of the deteriorat-
ing circumstances:

> I have done wrong, thought Deidre Fount, when she
> woke in the middle of the night, I have done wrong
> and it is a judgment upon me. I have quarrelled with
> my mother and spoken harsh words to her, I have
> wished her dead, I have made her unhappy and can-
> not help it. But now my own son will not look me
> in the eyes, and he will think about me in the same
> way, and talk about me with his friends. As soon
> as he is able he will go away.

Finally, in the climax, the enclosure she was born into alienates Mrs Fount completely from the very son she hopes to
keep close, within the enclosure. She makes reservations to

take him away from his school chum, on holiday alone with
herself. But friend Schwartz has already issued a counter invitation. The scene is in the shop; Mrs Fount has reached
the point of no return:

> 'Oh go on, go on, do what you like, I do not care
> for you. You have more feeling for your friend
> Schwartz than you have for me.'
>
> James Fount left the shop.
>
> I am saying all the things to him that I vowed I
> would never say, thought Mrs Deidre Fount. I am
> becoming more and more like my own mother was
> with me and I cannot help myself, for now I under-
> stand. I see it all and I am miserable and I am afraid.

As readers we watch her during this view of her consciousness: at last she understands the full consequences of an inherited enclosure.

The question of when the factual experience, the visual
record, becomes transmuted into fiction gets explored by
Susan Hill in the Introduction to the Longman's edition of
her next novel **I'm the King of the Castle** (1970), repub-
lished ten years after the Hamish Hamilton first edition.

The setting for **King** is the West Country, near the borders
of Dorset and Wiltshire, an area new to Susan Hill. Setting,
'place', always figures importantly in all her works. But after writing four novels and still being in her mid-twenties,
she felt need of a change of scene and took a cottage in this
'new' area:

> I had never been to the West Country, and at once
> loved that very typical, rural corner of it, explored
> the fields and woods around the cottage, sat and
> watched deer feed in the evenings, stayed up all
> night watching for badgers, had a terrifying expe-
> rience with a crow, one hot afternoon, read and fret-
> ted, and wandered about in that restless way a writer
> does when things are just starting to simmer deep
> inside him but aren't yet ready to boil over onto the
> page.

'Hang Wood' bordered the cottage in actuality and turns up
later in the novel, as do two boys she casually met: they became prototypes for Kingshaw and Hooper, though metamorphosed into boys totally different from the simple lads who
walked down her path. Hardy might have been an influence
here (she edited him later), for like his Wessex, the country
setting and its inhabitants (Fielding, in **King** especially) can
be identified, though re-focused.

In the Hill novel the two young boys become yoked, enclosed in an enforced relationship that leads finally to the suicide of Kingshaw. The intensity of the incidents leading to the tragedy are dispassionately related, factually noted, and seem to take on a logic all of their own. The public questioned the credibility of a schoolboy suicide, however. Hill defended the conclusion as recently as 1988 in a televised explanation of her narrative strategy. Released by the BBC with Bruce Jamson as producer, this curious televised documentary allows Susan Hill opportunity to recreate the highlights of her story. She talks about the sadistic evil she built up in the words and deeds of Hooper, Kingshaw's ever-present persecutor. She goes on to discuss the claustrophobia of the enclosure:

> 'It's a book about being trapped,' Hill says on screen. 'No one believed Kingshaw. Probably they *did* believe him, but there was too much at stake.'

What was at stake: the uninspired union, marriage finally, of the Hooper father to the Kingshaw mother. In consequence they fail to listen to Kingshaw's pleas, giving Hooper top billing by virtue of territorial rights, all the privileges of his longevity. 'Go out and play together,' says Mummy in a flash of exasperated unawareness. Conventional, unimaginative, middle-class: all these words spring to mind. Hill never condescends to pen such generalizations. Her narrative subtly loads our consciousness with these terms, however, by highlighting the relationship between the boys, placing the elders in an unfocused authoritarian role.

Kingshaw therefore has no recourse except to try to escape. He runs straight for the dreaded woods. As he starts through the cornfield, the symbolic malevolence of nature then becomes manifest:

> He could only hear the soft thudding of his own footsteps, and the silky sound of the corn, brushing against him, then there was a rush of air, as the great crow came beating down and wheeled about his head . . . The beak opened and the hoarse caaw came out again and again from inside the scarlet mouth . . . Then there was a single screech, and the terrible beating of wings, and the crow swooped down and landed in the middle of his back.

The bird recalls the incident Hill experienced the first day she had walked in Hang Wood herself. She transmutes it here into a symbolic incarnation of evil. Indeed the black bird turns up in every subsequent book, even the non-fiction, perhaps most dramatically in *The Bird of Night.*

Later that night, back at Warings, the forbidding house where the boys are 'enclosed', Hooper, who had watched the black bird attack Kingshaw, sneaks into Kingshaw's room with a stuffed crow from the collection displayed downstairs in the 'museum' of his father. He drops it on Kingshaw's bed, its black coat glistening. By such methodical, tension-laden incidents, Hill prepares the reader for the tragic finale. Structure thus supplies data, suggests meaning.

Actually Susan Hill goes a step further in this grisly tale by allowing the reader insight into Kingshaw's mind. We watch the boy's gradual acceptance of the inevitability of his predicament, its no-way-out enclosure. This is perhaps the most poignant aspect of this method of slow revelation, incident piled upon incident. For Kingshaw knows and we know he knows, when he is at last shut out of any parental protection, that he is doomed to the Hooper terror-enclosure. There is no escape now. And so the rush into the woods, to the stream where the boys had been swimming and Kingshaw had previously saved Hooper's life, ends with two sentences which reveal the terrible agony of Kingshaw, and his relief at escape. We understand that the act is deliberate; his dignity remains intact as he seeks peace:

> He began to splash and stumble forwards, into the middle of the stream, where the water was deepest. When it had reached up to his thighs, he lay down slowly and put his face into it and breathed a long, careful breath.

The year 1971 saw the publication of *Strange Meeting,* perhaps the most adventuresome imaginative excursion Susan Hill has attempted, both in subject matter and in time warp. To understand what she accomplished, it is imperative to examine the conditioning which prepared a woman of twenty-nine to write a novel primarily about men, set in the trenches of the Great War.

The donnee goes back a decade, when the younger Susan visited her eight maternal aunts who could never recover from the loss of their one idealized brother, killed in the 1914-18 conflict. Uncle Sidney Owen became a person eminently worthy of study for Susan. Indeed, she decided to read about everything that happened, politically and personally, to ordinary human victims of that conflagration. A year after her research began—in 1962—she attended a performance of Benjamin Britten's *War Requiem.*

> It was Britten, the man whose work has had more influence upon mine than anyone else's (including other writers), who first brought me back to my memories of Great Uncle Sidney Owen. In 1962 I went to a performance of Britten's *War Requiem.* I didn't know in advance much about what it was going to be like, or about, I only knew that what music of his I had already heard I had responded to at once, and that it had remained with me, in my mind and my heart, had fired my imagination. But I was not at all prepared for the effect that performance

of the *War Requiem* was to have on me. I came out of it feeling dazed, as though something very important had happened—to me, I mean, as well as in musical terms—I can't easily explain it or even describe it. But one result was that I became filled with the desire to write something myself about the First World War.

This time Susan Hill rented a cottage in Aldeburgh, home of Benjamin Britten and the Aldeburgh Festivals—a seacoast town again reminiscent of her own coastal childhood and indeed of the setting for *Peter Grimes.* 'I know Aldeburgh through my own emotions and my creative imagination and each book that I [later] wrote there and which has left its mark upon me . . . it is a landscape of the spirit'.

After her research in London and elsewhere, the actual writing of the novel took only three months. Sensitive to place, Susan Hill found the Aldeburgh setting ideal for this particular composition. The terrain had echoes of the same war terrain she was trying to re-create:

> When it was gray and cold, those marshes took on something of the aspect of the fields of Flanders. Here and there, people had dumped old bicycle wheels and tin oil drums, and they had half sunk in the mud, and rusty metal loomed up out of the pools of water, like the debris of a battlefield. When I took a break from writing, I walked on those marshes, early and late. In the end, I began to hear the boom of guns in the boom of the sea, and the cries of wounded men in the cries of the seagulls, to see blood, not the red of the early sunset, staining the water of the pools and ditches.

So the narrative strategy Hill employs in *Strange Meeting* is complex, unlike most modern novels: scholarship, Britten's music, the coastal furniture, plus the 'workings and productions of my subconscious and of my imagination'. It met with a mixed response. One critic found the tour-de-force unrewarding, the structural devices we have noted as disclosing so much about character, less than adequate in *Strange Meeting.* Claire Tomalin felt the 'very restraint and precision of the detail manage to undermine the reality of the central relationship, which fades into a fantasy woven round a discoloured sepia photo of two handsome young Englishmen'.

Perhaps we can argue that this same matter-of-fact style manages to keep what might turn into mawkish sentimentality, credible and moving. Without the restraint so typical of Hill, the story (as Kenneth Muir points out) in other hands might turn gruesome or become burdened with sexual innuendoes.

There is considerable space devoted to a realistic depiction of trench warfare in *Strange Meeting,* but that is backdrop for a more intimate drama, stage front, of two young men forced into one another's company by virtue of their army assignment. Hilliard could not be a more cramped, stereotypical English upper middle-class product: he is the senior lieutenant, son of non-communicating parents. He cannot meet people, or indeed even talk to his parents, except in the most level, conventional way. Then Barton arrives in his billet, a newly assigned junior lieutenant, a doctor's son, with none of the built-in hang-ups of class that strangle Hilliard.

But we must build up these impressions from artfully placed details. Back in England these two would never have met, but if they had, would not have been be able to talk, as Hilliard would have been consumed by shyness and inbred prejudice. Here in the novel, at a French farmhouse before going up to the front, the two confront one another. Barton, still idealistic, new to the war, transparently nice, unaffected, has brought a volume each of Henry James and Sir Thomas Browne with him. So opposite in temperament is Barton to Hilliard, that rather in spite of himself, Hilliard opens up to Barton: Hilliard who cannot talk to his own mother (who persists in sending packages from Fortnum's 'to the boys').

Suddenly, in this classless limbo, Hilliard makes a human contact which his family and home (at the top of the village where control was of the highest priority) has never provided. For instance, a day or two into their friendship, Hilliard asks Barton if he always tells people 'everything you're feeling'.

> Barton looked around at him in surprise.

> 'Generally. If I want to. If they want to hear.' He paused and then laughed. 'Good Lord, we're not at school now, are we?'

> Hilliard did not reply.

> 'Besides, it's the way we were brought up. To say things, tell people what you feel. I don't mean to force it on anyone. But not to bottle things up.'

> 'I see.'

Barton's family, equally 'open', become introduced to Hilliard through correspondence. 'It was as though he had been standing in a dark street looking into a lighted room and been invited in.' Hilliard's life, in fact, is being altered for the better by the war. But Susan Hill's plan is far more complex; she creates a Barton almost prelapsarian in his goodness (but credible nevertheless) in order to make more dramatic the later impact of the stench of death, the discomfort of the trenches, the meaninglessness of individual lives pitched into battle. Then—at the front—the disclosure emerges for us: the roles of the two men become reversed. The more pragmatic, hardened Hilliard must now help the more naive Barton. This spiritual interdependency becomes vivid and indeed possible only because of the sordid conditions.

The first confrontation Barton has with death is so horrifying that it alters his personality overnight. His withdrawal and his silence disturb Hilliard, who has learned to depend on Barton's ebullience and affection. Finally, one wet night before Barton's fatal run into no-man's land on a ridiculous mission to identify dead bodies as German or English, Hilliard manages—with difficulty—to break through to Barton, to talk about death . . .

> But the worst of it [Barton says] has been that I haven't known how to face myself. That Private who was snipered . . . looking at him I could have wept and wept, he seemed to be all the men who had ever been killed, John. I remember everything about him, his face, his hair, his hands, I can remember how pale his eyelashes were and I thought of how alive he's been, how much there had been going on inside him—blood pumping round, muscle working, brain saying do this, do that, his eyes looking at me. I thought of it all, how he's been born and had a family, I thought of everything that had gone into making him—and it wasn't that I was afraid and putting myself in his place down there on the ground. I just wanted him alive again.

It is at this point, the personal drama played out against the boom of cannon and the unexpressed recognition that one or both friends may not survive the next twenty-four hours, that Hilliard and Barton communicate best. Must we wait for an emergency to be our best, Susan Hill seems to suggest . . .

The roles of the two men are reversed again: Hilliard now quotes Sir Thomas Brown to Barton, his former teacher, and eventually gets Barton to smile as he looks at the tattered binding of the beloved book which he had hurled into the mud. Hilliard starts to speak—

> 'Are you afraid of what else is to come?'

> 'I'm afraid of myself. Of what I am becoming, of what it will do to me.'

> 'Are you afraid of your own dying?'

> Barton's face lighted up at once. 'Oh, no. I've thought about that too. No. I have never really been afraid of that.'

> 'It is a brave act of valour to condemn death, but when life is more terrible, it is the truest valour to live.'

> Barton smiled. 'I've just torn all that up.'

> 'But I have just learned it by heart.'

> 'And is it true?'

Susan Hill's use of dialogue here subtly places Hilliard into the role of leader. It is his point of view, now; he controls the action. We as readers must interpret, to assess this passage as crucial in the relationship between the two men. Further, the passage is selective, extremely economical, for the implications are up to us to make: Hill has given us the data, though removed herself. (As Kenneth Muir says, 'Susan Hill gains considerably from her reticence about sex and from her avoidance of psychological analysis'.

> [*Strange Meeting*] can be dismissed by some for going over material familiar from *All Quiet on the Western Front* onwards; the battle scenes are extremely realistic; the letters home possibly excessive. But *Strange Meeting* covers a far wider canvas.
> —*Ernest H. Hofer*

Then, at the end, when Barton dies and Hilliard, wounded, returns to England, it's first to the home of the Barton family, not to his own. He is met at the station by a friend of the family, and as they drive away, Hilliard names the streets and lanes, much to the surprise of the driver. No, he had not been here before, he answered. 'But then he thought that that was not true, he had been here, he had spent hours here with Barton, as they had talked in the apple loft and the tents and dugouts and billets . . .'. Susan Hill, by these quiet structural devices—getting into a car at the station, looking out at the town—conveys to us the depth of feeling, unexpressed, which Hilliard learned about person and place from his friendship with Barton.

The novel, finally, can be dismissed by some for going over material familiar from *All Quiet on the Western Front* onwards; the battle scenes are extremely realistic; the letters home possibly excessive. But *Strange Meeting* covers a far wider canvas. The two main characters, but also the Commanding Officer, and the Adjutant, are drawn with feeling and perspicacity. Factual though the novel essentially is, precise in its details, it likewise possesses an emotional quality not found before in Susan Hill. If it sounds 'like a true story', as the *Observer* critic complained, these 'facts' at the same time disclose latent political and psychological problems, even deep-felt emotion. By talking about the lanes and streets of Barton's Warwickshire, Hilliard discloses his affection and admiration for Barton and all he represents. The enclosure of Barton/Hilliard, indeed, discloses a microcosm of England and war.

Between 1971 and 1975 Susan Hill also wrote a number of memorable short stories, varying in length, and finally collected in two volumes: *The Albatross and Other Stories* (1971), and *A Bit of Dancing and Singing* (1975). Ruth Fainwright declared in the *Times Literary Supplement* that shorter length gave admirable 'restraint' to Hill's talent, particularly in the long story, or novella, *The Albatross,* which she found 'dark and simple as Tolstoy, yet avoiding both the suggestion of brutality and the sentimental moral pleading often found in such tales of elemental relationships'.

As in *King,* Hill concentrates on the enclosure of an intensely felt mother-son relationship in *The Albatross,* perhaps the most concentrated and effective of all the tales in these two volumes. She traces, inexorably, the day-to-day deterioration of the enclosed relationship, thus disclosing the real nature of Hilda Pike and son Dafty Duncan, whose proper name is Duncan Pike. Hill implements her strategy shrewdly, this time encouraging us to make a very difficult judgment. 'Dafty' of course refers to the boy's mental problem; he is 'slow' rather than schizoid, for example, but vulnerable and shy nevertheless. Susan Hill follows the young boy's grotesquely difficult youth in a series of telling incidents which enlist our support for him even to the point of justifiable homicide. We give him a verdict of 'innocent', rather to our surprise.

Again we are on the coast, this time in a sea-swept fishing village. The sea and the often inclement weather combine to become as important as any character in the piece. For weather penetrates the lives of all the inhabitants: boats become endangered by gales; awful winter freezes reduce the townspeople to a sullen acceptance of their lot. The sea pounds the shore, pounds too at them individually, especially if one of the fishing boats has failed to return.

Just so Hilda Pike's words pound at the consciousness of her son Duncan, whom she obviously cannot forgive for being 'slow', but whom she can the more easily dominate. Like the storm, her barrage sets up a rhythm, a bitter obbligato spoken from a wheelchair: she is handicapped. Both as servant and son, Duncan's enclosure with his mother has become suffocating, airtight, constant. That is until Ted Flint, a swashbuckling, easy-going fisherman, offers him a job and unwittingly threatens Hilda's position.

Using the logic of 'what he is', Hilda proceeds to pour scorn on the offer Flint has made to Duncan. What she really fears is long separations, their tight enclosure in the stuffy cot-

tage blasted apart. Her words to Duncan, gathering new storm as the weather also rages, construct a modulated, terrifying coherence. Every word she now utters discloses her true nature. We recall that Hooper gradually beat Kingshaw into submission in *King.* Here too Hilda will accept nothing but total compliance from Duncan.

So this enforced isolation, this unnatural enclosure, becomes intolerable, as it did for Kingshaw. In *King* the result was suicide to escape from enclosure. Here the burden of the albatross (his mother), which he must carry around with him, becomes unendurable. Calmly, deliberately, he overdoses his mother during 'pill time' and then pushes her, 'asleep', off the end of the breakwater wall. A message again seems to rise from these awful incidents—lack of freedom, enforced enclosure, leads eventually to a breaking-point, to death—that final enclosure.

The same formula works for the other stories in *The Albatross.* 'The Friends of Miss Reece', for example, concerns the story of an old woman, Miss Reece, who has one good friend in her nursing home, one fellow conspirator, a small boy. This 'odd couple' became attached through their fear and opposition to a sadistic head nurse, Wetherby. They learn quietly to circumvent her orders, slyly to defy her, but also to reduce her tyranny by being kind to each other. The enclosure this time also results in death, but Miss Reece wants to die. As part of their pact, Miss Reece asks the young boy to open her window against Wetherby's strict orders, and catches a fatal pneumonia. The agent, this small boy, has the same function in the structure of the narrative as did Ted Flint in *The Albatross* or Schwartz, the young friend in *Change.*

Less tragic, more poignant, perhaps, are the stories in *A Bit of Singing and Dancing,* a collection first published in 1973. The title story is particularly affecting, and seems a more benign version of *A Change for the Better.* The enclosure again involves a dominating mother and a subservient daughter bound for economic reasons to live together longer than they should.

Finally in *A Bit* Esme's mother dies, though her spirit lives on like a ghostly albatross. Nevertheless, Esme decides to break the spell and take in a lodger, a male one at that. Mother's ghost rattles almost audibly for even considering such a step. Esme, however, persists, as Mr Curry appears very correct in dress and manner, an acceptable gent for her part of town, a solidly middle-class area. They set up the arrangement; the rent comes in promptly. One day weeks later Esme stumbles on Mr Curry re-living his earlier music hall professional days at a busy intersection at the seafront. There he is, tap dancing and singing, a cap for coins at his feet. Coins that eventually pay for the rent.

> **[*In the Springtime of the Year*] is dedicated to 'the happy memory of David', a man she had loved deeply, and who had died very suddenly. 'Everything I felt and experienced about David's dying went into the novel,' she told Dr Anthony Clare in a radio interview in 1989. 'And I still dream about him once a month, sixteen years after he died,' she continued.**
> **—*Ernest H. Hofer***

At first she is shocked, realizing that mother was right after all. Why had she strayed outside the enclosure in the first place? As she is about to ask Mr Curry to pack his bags, she reviews her options, her life options, and mother does not prevail.

> She went down into the kitchen and made coffee and set it, with a plate of sandwiches and a plate of biscuits, on a tray, and presently Mr Curry comes in, and she called out to him, she said, 'Do come and have a little snack with me, I am quite sure you can do with it, I'm sure you are tired.' And she saw from his face that he knew that she knew.

And so Esme breaks out of the confinement of her enclosure by realizing that the structure of her life—rigid, uncompromising—had little to offer a lonely spinster. She experiences an epiphany in the last scene: her life, its parameters, its shortcomings, are disclosed in a flash of recognition. Just in time she changes course.

But the most extended treatment of breaking down inherited or acquired enclosure occurs in what Susan Hill calls her one frankly autobiographic novel, *In the Springtime of the Year,* a novel which bridges her 'serious' work prior to her marriage in 1975 and her subsequent non-fiction.

It is dedicated to 'the happy memory of David', a man she had loved deeply, and who had died very suddenly. 'Everything I felt and experienced about David's dying went into the novel,' she told Dr Anthony Clare in a radio interview in 1989. 'And I still dream about him once a month, sixteen years after he died,' she continued.

First published in 1974, *Springtime* tells the story of a young forester-husband—Ben—who is fatally felled by a tree, and his young wife Ruth, who is emotionally felled by the incident. This is the final exorcism, Susan Hill tells us further, of the pain David's death had caused, transmuted to the stage of *Springtime.* If, as she has stated in her essays, Susan Hill wrote fiction to make sense of experience, then here, certainly, she is doing so in relation to herself. The voice of her sorrow is Ben's sympathetic, sensitive younger brother; Christianity provides spiritual solace. Slowly, like water heating imperceptibly slowly, Ruth warms to the reality of her loss and gains strength from it.

Spring parallels Ruth's awakening: days are longer; flowers, berries, jams, herbs, windfalls, even cooking in her kitchen again, become objective correlatives symbolic of her groping toward recovery. The awakening from her sad torpor takes specific spiritual form in an epiphany she experiences when she comes upon children in the forest, dressed in white, acting out in nursery rhyme, the ritual of burial. They dig a grave near the fallen elm which crushed Ben and killed him. The leader of the children is Jenny Colt, sister of the young forester David Colt, who first brought the news of Ben's tragic death to Ruth, indeed, had witnessed the death. So the youngsters manage in this symbolic tableaux (in Chapter 6) to direct Ruth's path to spiritual illumination on Easter Sunday, when love overcomes death in the Christian sense and also in her personal return to physical and spiritual fitness.

What triggered this major step in Ruth's return to equilibrium was 'the play within the play' (so to speak) of the children in white at Helm Bottom. Now at long last Ruth can return and look at the tree which had felled Ben, and also talk to David Colt. By extension, by starting to bury the past in this objectification of her grief, Ruth can consider helping others, like the curate and his wife. The beautiful enclosure represented by the marriage of Ben and Ruth had been destroyed by death. By methodically measuring the extent of the enclosure, the extent of the grief, Susan Hill at the same time discloses the secret of a life in process of recovery. The special marital enclosure, at first destroyed by Ben's death, is at the end of the novel rediscovered on a spiritual, Christian level.

Springtime, therefore, acts as a transition between the Susan Hill of serious fiction and *The Magic Apple Tree,* a review of country life, with many references to those same windfalls, recipes, and jams that Ruth used as therapy in *Springtime.* Seven years went by, and in 1981, in her regular column called *World of Books in the Daily Telegraph,* the following statement appeared in a piece called **'Writing a Book':**

> I have done with novels, I gave them up seven years ago and have absolutely no intention of returning to them, and no more desire to do so than I have of smoking a cigarette again. Prose fiction of any kind is a chapter of my life closed, as it were, for all manner of reasons I won't go into here.

Two years later in 1983 *The Woman in Black* appeared in the bookstores. Was it a return to 'serious writing', or an experiment in a new genre? A ghost story, a gothic tale, a story within a story, a Jamesian revival: all these critical terms may be applied to this new work. But a word about the circumstances of its composition seems to be in order.

Susan Hill had married in 1975 and soon had one daughter, though like her own mother, she was getting to a period in life, the late thirties, when child-bearing could be risky. But she wanted another child, soon. She tells us frankly in *Family* that a miserable miscarriage then left her bereft, desperate to 'try again'. As she put it, she fretted, examined herself minutely for early signs of pregnancy, eager to conceive so as to eliminate the memory of the miscarriage, and indeed not get beyond the safe age of easy delivery. It is during this period of heightened stress that she wrote *The Woman in Black*. 'Month after month, I burst into tears of anguish, frustration, misery. I counted ahead—nine months from July—August—September—October, and saw my baby recede into the far future.'

Susan Hill wrote *The Woman* in seven weeks, enclosed, in a manner of speaking, by a burning psycho-physical need. She had to have an outlet. Writing this uncharacteristic piece was the answer. It is (with its archaic language of about 1910) mannered, suggestive, chilling, similar in setting to *The Turn of the Screw*, even to the story within a story and the scene round the fire at Christmas, at the start. Like James again, there is a first-person narrator telling the story within a story, married now a second time and reflecting on horrors which occurred during a previous marriage.

Woman received notices calling attention to its atmosphere and that Susan Hill wrote 'like one possessed'. A more extensive review by Stephen Bann appeared in the *London Review of Books,* mentioning its characteristics as a gothic novel, and differentiating it from the contemporary 'horror tale'. But one feels critics simply did not know what to do with this surprising novel which does not in any way resemble the more serious and important achievements of previous novels.

But if *Springtime* by vote of author and critics exorcised the memory of David, then perhaps *Woman* reverberates with a similar personal echo. Critics have avoided the implications of the story itself as related to its author directly. Could it be another exorcism?

The woman in the novel, the lady in black, who hovers frequently around the narrator, appears in the haunted house on the end of the causeway and is obviously overwhelmed with the death of a child, her child. The ghosts of mother and child return regularly to the house, indeed they possess the nursery where the crib is being rocked—empty of child. The lawyer closing 'the estate', sleeping at Eel Marsh House, actually hears the shrieks and yells and strained gratings of the mother, child, horse and trap as they all disappear into quicksand, the driver having lost his way along the causeway, owing to the sudden blanketing of mist. The enclosure of mother-child-house will haunt the area forever, as we are told by all the local inhabitants.

The drama intensifies in London when the lawyer is confronted by the carry-over of the ghostly events into his own personal life: he watches as his own wife and child in pony and trap pass before him, and die as the horse becomes maddened and gallops away dragging wife and child to their deaths. Fantasy thus turns into reality; the phantoms of the misty causeway turn tragically into the confrontation of death in reality. This re-enactment of the same haunting enclosure first displayed to the lawyer in Crythin, the tiny village on the north coast, provides the chief chill of the novel. The narrator can never be free of this two-tiered memory. He is enclosed permanently in its prison. And perhaps the enclosed structure, the ghostly and the actual represented here, discloses the subconscious torment of Hill herself: 'writing like one possessed', or as she says, with 'a need to go on at all costs'. Is the book therefore a reprieve from anxiety for Susan Hill herself?

Finally, to summarize. What must a reader deduce from the strange paradox of Susan Hill's two distinct writing objectives? The one structurally so clinical and objective, the other so intimate and open, both so deliberate and confident?

Simply, at first, in her novels and short stories, Susan Hill kept the reader remarkably distanced. She devised a credible enclosure for her characters, from First World War lieutenants to seaside landladies, where by virtue of the almost relentless objectification of characteristics, the plight of the Important Person was gradually revealed. By so structuring that tight enclosure, its parameters coolly and effectively measured and planned, Susan Hill's persona come to life. Faithful adherence to structure, it can thus be said, becomes a dynamic of exposure. We *SEE.*

What has happened after *Springtime* and the maverick *Woman in Black* might be dubbed psychological turnabout. A change in personal goals demolished the writing of 'the serious novel' only to replace it with an entirely different ambition, just as prolific: the anti-novel. She no longer needed to project feeling and opinion from the medium of the imagination. When she married Stanley Wells on Shakespeare's birthday, 1975, this author of revealed structures and disclosed lives had undergone a personal revolution:

> [She is speaking of her marriage ceremony] The headline read: 'Novelist weds in Stratford.'

> Novelist? For a moment, I wondered who they meant. I knew I had told my publisher I would be

starting a new book soon, but in truth I wasn't feeling like a writer, a novelist, at all. I wasn't sure I ever wanted to write another word, my mind was on quite other things.

So far only two novels have appeared since the 'ban'. One asks: Is it possible to let an imagination so fertile and inventive as Susan Hill's lie passive, yea dormant, indefinitely? Only the future will tell.

Merle Rubin (review date 12 January 1994)

SOURCE: A review of *Mrs. de Winter,* in *Christian Science Monitor,* January 12, 1994, p. 17.

[*In the excerpt below, Rubin finds that Hill's sequel is "a little duller and more predictable" than Daphne du Maurier's novel.*]

For much of her professional life, British writer Daphne du Maurier was dogged by feelings of disappointment at not being considered a serious artist.

Rebecca, du Maurier's most celebrated novel, published in 1938 and shortly thereafter made into a classic Hitchcock film, is still widely read today. But its fame overshadowed her subsequent work, including such novels as *My Cousin Rachel* (1951), *The Scapegoat* (1957), and *The House on the Strand* (1969), and her short stories, the best-known of which furnished further material for Hitchcock: "The Birds."

Ironically, some of the very qualities that once relegated du Maurier to second-class literary citizenship now excite the interest of feminist scholars engaged in reexamining women's lives and writings. Romantic myths of brooding, strong-willed aristocratic men, lovelorn Cinderellas, mysterious mansions, and cruel, beauteous rivals reveal something about the ways in which women have seen themselves....

> In her novel *Mrs. de Winter,* Hill deftly captures the keynotes of du Maurier's style and the intense self-conscious, impressionable sensibility of the original narrator-heroine, wisely following du Maurier's lead in never mentioning this self-effacing lady's first name.
>
> —*Merle Rubin*

Du Maurier was constantly bombarded by requests from people wanting to write sequels to *Rebecca.* One wonders if she might have looked more favorably on such an attempt

if it were by a novelist already established in her own right, like Susan Hill. In her novel *Mrs. de Winter,* Hill deftly captures the keynotes of du Maurier's style and the intense self-conscious, impressionable sensibility of the original narrator-heroine, wisely following du Maurier's lead in never mentioning this self-effacing lady's first name.

Ten years into the future, Hill's *Mrs. de Winter* is convincingly the same person, but a little older and wiser. "I had gone from being a gauche, badly dressed girl to being an uninterestingly, dully dressed married woman . . . ," she wryly remarks. She is still vulnerable to her own active imagination. This time, however, it is guilt rather than jealousy that threatens the de Winters' marital happiness.

Hill reintroduces characters, themes, and situations from du Maurier's original novel rather as a composer might rework motifs from a symphony's earlier movements in its final one. But in another way, she undercuts the thrust of du Maurier's original work by changing from a story about jealousy to a story about guilt. Hill's most original contribution, thus, is also the most contrary to the spirit of du Maurier's book, where it is made abundantly clear that the evil Rebecca not only deserved to die, but connived at her own shooting because she knew she had a fatal disease. Hill has replaced du Maurier's fierce, slightly over-the-top romanticism with a severe, if rather heavy-handed, moralism, which ultimately makes this accomplished and skillfully written sequel a little duller and more predictable than the remarkable novel that inspired it.

Gale Harris (review date Spring 1994)

SOURCE: "Dreaming of Manderley," in *Belles Lettres,* Vol. 9, No. 3, Spring, 1994, pp. 23-4.

[*In the following review, Harris looks into the reasons why* Mrs. de Winter *fails "to replicate the success of [Daphne] du Maurier's* Rebecca."]

What happens to a writer who has mined her craft to create a fantasy existence for herself and then finds that her inner conflicts no longer inspire the fiction for which she has become famous? Margaret Forster's new biography of Daphne du Maurier explores the development and decline of a woman who truly "lived to write." In a genre that receives little respect from critics, du Maurier's suspense novels introduced a unique psychological complexity that accomplished more than sensationalizing her plots. Few readers perceived the subtle themes that reflected du Maurier's inner turmoil.

Drawing on previously unavailable documents, Forster sympathetically reveals the forces that drove du Maurier's fiction and caused her collapse when they could no longer be released through that medium.

Du Maurier recognized that she had a rare and privileged childhood. She was the granddaughter of author George du Maurier, and her father, Gerald, was one of the most popular actors of his generation. But the du Maurier household had hidden troubles. Gerald's backstage affairs and his wife's tolerance of them taught Daphne that nothing was what it seemed and that a complicated double standard governed sexual relations.

Du Maurier also was tormented by a desire to be a boy, not only to have greater freedom but also to satisfy her father's craving for a son. In fact, du Maurier was convinced that she *was* a boy and her outward form was a mistake. At 22, after exploring physical attractions to men and women, du Maurier concluded that the boy within her had no chance for survival and must be locked in a box inside of her. She resolved to live as a woman, to "run the race with the rest of the pack instead of being a damned solitary hound missing the game." Yet never did she consider her behavior a suppression of "Venetian" (her code word for lesbian) tendencies, which she claimed to abhor. To sustain this charade, du Maurier retreated further into solitude and her own fantasy world, "the one place she was truly happy."

Writing became an antidote for her aimlessness, and she believed it was the only talent she possessed. Writing also provided the financial means for escaping the control of her parents and husband. Du Maurier's fiction reflected her fascination with place and her cynicism concerning relationships between men and women. Her initial writings portrayed boys searching for happiness or women longing for "something greater" and rebelling against being female. Later, she wrote in the first person as a man, a perspective that freed her to write more honestly about her own experiences and allowed the "boy-in-the-box" to come out in her imagination.

Forster wrote this illuminating biography with the full cooperation of du Maurier's children, who warned her that du Maurier was a "chameleon." Letters discovered after Forster's original biography was completed shed further light on the gap between reality and fantasy in du Maurier's life. Forster uses these letters and du Maurier's diaries to deftly reconstruct the development of the writer's confused sexual identity and her career as a novelist. Forster convincingly demonstrates the links between the two and hypothesizes that du Maurier's

> whole life's work was an attempt to defy reality and create for herself a world far more exciting and true than the one in which she lived. . . . When her abil-

ity to do this left her, and reality at last confronted her, her life was not worth living; the death of the writer was indeed the death of the self.

Forster builds her case and du Maurier's story without sensationalizing details about the writer's affairs with men and women, her stifling relationship with her father, and her troubled marriage. She relates du Maurier's need for solitude with neither apology for what might be considered neglect of her personal relationships nor rhetoric about the autonomy of women. She sympathetically but astutely discusses how du Maurier used Jungian theory to relabel and further deny her attraction to women. Forster's objectivity is admirable, but it also produces a curiously dispassionate book. One imagines, however, that it might please du Maurier, who probed her own feelings reluctantly but with courage and honesty.

Mrs. de Winter, Susan Hill's recently published sequel to Rebecca, includes all of du Maurier's standard elements but lacks the "real power and strange passion" that helped make du Maurier's most famous novel unforgettable.
—Gale Harris

Forster's biography helps to explain why it is impossible to replicate the success of du Maurier's best novels. The intricate twists of her plots, her strong sense of atmosphere and place, and the interior monologues exploring the psychology of her characters have become standard ingredients of suspense novels. But few other writers have drawn on such an extensive and vital fantasy life, or have been so haunted by the subterfuges and pretenses of personal relationships.

Mrs. de Winter, Susan Hill's recently published sequel to *Rebecca,* includes all of du Maurier's standard elements but lacks the "real power and strange passion" that helped make du Maurier's most famous novel unforgettable. Although Hill attempts to recreate the dreamlike settings and mysterious events of *Rebecca,* her lush language cannot hide the fact that nothing remarkable ever happens.

Mildly sinister events are soon clumsily explained. During the sequel's climax, obviously intended to parallel the ball at Manderley, the shoddy, dissolute villains of *Rebecca* reappear and hurl impotent threats that unbelievably precipitate a new disaster.

Like du Maurier, Hill is interested in the balance of power between the sexes. In ***Mrs. de Winter,*** Hill examines with her characteristic sensitivity the minor movements of relationships that underlie ultimately decisive events. She chronicles the ebb and flow of mastery within the de Winter's marriage and the wife's slow recognition of a need for things that a life of exile cannot give her. Hill's delicate insights and prose add a fine luster to many episodes, but they alone cannot fashion a deserving sequel to *Rebecca.* This enduring favorite, like du Maurier's life, remains a fascinating and incomparable study of the human psyche.

Charlotte Moore (review date 26 October 1996)

SOURCE: "Breaking Out in Spots," in *Spectator,* Vol. 277, No. 880, October 26, 1996, p. 46.

[*In the following review, Moore profiles the characters in* Listening to the Orchestra, *questioning whether they know they are alive.*]

'She had always kept her own company and her thoughts and feelings turned inwards. To tell things would be to her like undressing.' 'She' is the nameless young woman in the title story of *Listening to the Orchestra*; with the utmost delicacy and care her creator, Susan Hill, undertakes the task of 'undressing' her characters. Each of these four short stories exposes someone who is 'turned inwards', 'holding onto' themselves, but the exposure is never brutal. The inside is turned out through glimpses, oblique angles, and precise juxtapositions.

Like a still-life painter, Hill rearranges familiar elements in each story. Some of these elements are physical details—seagulls, pots of tea, boils, harsh haircuts, thin mattresses, abandoned books, even marble horse troughs, are reworked and repositioned—but words and emotions are also treated as physical facts. Sour, thick, bare, pinched, greasy, inward, silent, loneliness, anxiety, deadness, waste—such words are placed throughout the stories as a kind of gloomy punctuation. But these arrangements are neither repetitive nor uninventive. The pared-down prose leaves no room for mistakes; like a tightrope walker without a safety net, Hill has to maintain a perfect balance. She succeeds in doing so with scarcely a wobble.

The first two stories, **'Listening to the Orchestra'** and **'The Brooch',** are set in English seaside towns, **'Elizabeth'** is about rural Ireland, and **'Antonyin's',** the last, centres round a bar in Vldansk, a desolate city somewhere beyond what used to be the Iron Curtain. In the first, a friendless young woman disappointed in love is lured by a clairvoyant. In the second, a child witnesses the humiliation of her uncle, a blind commercial traveller. The eponymous Elizabeth is an 11-year-old who watches her mother die in 'a caravan that smelled of rustiness and mice'. In the last, an English businessman flees the clutches of a deformed seamstress who

wants to marry him, only to find that he has not escaped at all—'She would not leave his head'.

In each case, the inward-looking, orderly protagonist is challenged by a character who seems to know more about them than they know about themselves. The atmosphere is one of melancholy shot through with menace; safe in the warmth of the seaside hotel, the orchestra playing *The Merry Widow,* Myrna the clairvoyant offers the lonely girl the comfort of a jolly shopping trip. But 'late wasps sailed past the curved windows', and that is all we need to know about Myrna and her motivations.

Myrna is paralleled in the other stories by a Jew who sells fake jewellery to the blind uncle, a ferrety Irish poacher called Minchy Fagin, and the misshapen would-be-bride, half child, half toad, who has warts on her face that are 'pink and crinkled like the underside of small mushrooms'. These are bad fairies: they mesmerise, they expose, they threaten, they turn illusions to dust. But they also point the way to the only exit from the barren landscape of the interior self. 'There's a world beyond yourself you must break through to,' Elizabeth's doomed mother tells her. Each story presents us with the precise moment when such a breakthrough could be, must be, achieved.

'Her loneliness had been buried in mess and clutter, muffled in cloth. His was laid bare as a bone in this space.' In her self-created space Susan Hill lays bare the loneliness of these abbreviated lives. The blind man's niece asks herself, 'When I am dead, will I know it?' The four stories in this little volume ask their characters if they know that they are alive.

Robert McCrum (review date 8 December 1996)

SOURCE: "McCrum on Susan Hill," in *Observer Review,* December 8, 1996, p. 15.

[*In the review below, McCrum offers praise for* Listening to the Orchestra, *which he observes "is a reminder of the virtues of the traditional English story."*]

Susan Hill is, of course, an established English writer who first caught the attention of the reading public in the early Seventies, with her stories and novels *I'm the King of the Castle* (1970), *Strange Meeting* (1971), *Bird of Night* (1972), and *A Bit of Singing and Dancing* (1973). In recent years she has written for children. She is, in the bald, blunt language of the book trade, a 'name' author; a name, moreover, that is an almost cast-iron guarantee of a certain kind of English fiction. And now here in Long Barn Books, the publishing imprint she has created for herself this season, we have a re-patenting of her trademark Englishness.

There is nothing wrong with publishing your own book, and in the age of desktop publishing (DTP), quite a lot to be said for it. (In recent times, a number of established writers, notably Jill Paton Walsh and Timothy Mo, have, from a variety of motives, chosen this road, with mixed results.) But the problem that no amount of self-publishing can surmount is always going to be one of distribution: it's with the tedious business of actually getting the books into the shops that publishers score—'excel' is too strong a word.

There's also a problem with perception, or at least with PR. Inevitably, a number of unworthy thoughts occur to the reviewer facing a book that an established author has published herself. Why has she abandoned her publisher? Did she jump, or was she pushed? What hidden saga of disappointment and rage lurks behind the simple paperback format of this edition? Is the book a bizarre assertion of authorial vanity? An episode of literary autism that will eventually become forgotten? Is it, in fact, any good?

I am happy to report that, short as it is, *Listening to the Orchestra* strikes me as quite as good as Susan Hill's earlier work. The title story, set in a *fin-de-saison* seaside hotel, is as chilly and wistful as anything she has ever done: a solitary, lost girl arrives at a resort hotel 'dragging her suitcase on its little wheels across the town from the station'. At first she finds loneliness 'like a crater in the ground'. But then she meets Myrna, the seaside mystic who holds out the prospect of an intimacy so disturbing ('her fat little hands had rings like brilliant, raised warts') that the little refugee can think only of moving to Australia and recovering the security of her solitude. 'There was nothing more she wanted, nothing else she would know.'

> **Some critics will sneer that [the stories in *Listening to the Orchestra*] are old-fashioned (they are), unambitious (perhaps) and emotionally repressed (probably), but behind the stifled sympathies of these pages is an understanding of the human heart unknown to many, more acclaimed, contemporary English writers.**
> **—Robert McCrum**

The three other stories in this collection are united by a typically strong evocation of place—an Irish village in '**Elizabeth**', a faded East European city in '**Antonyin's**', the remorseless English seaside again in '**The Brooch**'—and by Hill's eye for detail:

'At Pitt's café, they always had the same order, and that was another ritual—a slice of apple pie and a slice of treacle tart, a pot of tea, a milky cocoa, and a bowl of water for the dog. She slipped the pie crust to it under the table feeling the slippery nose and mouth cold against her fingers.'

The passage of time has done little to soften or moderate Hill's hallmark bleakness. Her smile is, so to speak, like the silver plate on a coffin. If you like the short story to give you some kind of joy or uplift, then these tales are not for you. But to the lover of plain English prose, as clear and uncomplicated as a pane of glass, this nicely produced little volume, with its unfussy typography, is a reminder of the virtues of the traditional English story. It is only too easy to imagine these read aloud on Radio Four.

Some critics will sneer that these stories are old-fashioned (they are), unambitious (perhaps) and emotionally repressed (probably), but behind the stifled sympathies of these pages is an understanding of the human heart unknown to many, more acclaimed, contemporary English writers. Admirers of Susan Hill will hope that these stories eventually reach a wider audience in a more conventional format.

FURTHER READING

Criticism

Beauman, Sally. "Rereading Rebecca." *New Yorker* 69, No. 37 (8 November 1993): 127-38.
    Condemns *Mrs. de Winter* as "a vapid, incoherent ghost of a book, stained by infirmity of purpose on every page" in a reevaluation of the literary merits of *Rebecca.*

Sellers, Frances Stead. "Spirits of the Season." *Washington Post* (4 December 1994): 17, 20.
    Admires the "right touch of magic" in *The Christmas Collection.*

Wright, Jane Barker. Review of *Reflections from a Garden* by Susan Hill and Rory Stuart. *Horticulture* LXXIV, No. 9 (November 1996): 57-8.
    Admires "this challenging, endearing, maddening collection," noting that "the always good and occasionally fine writing, the attractive production, and the flashes of insight will please."

Additional coverage of Hill's life and career is contained in the following sources published by Gale: *Contemporary Authors,* Vols. 33-36R; *Contemporary Authors New Revision Series,* Vol. 29; *Dictionary of Literary Biography,* Vols. 14 and 139; *DISCovering Authors Modules: Most-studied* and *Novelists;* and *Major Twentieth-Century Writers.*

Stephen King
1947-

(Full name Stephen Edwin King; has also written under the pseudonyms Richard Bachman and John Swithen) American novelist, short story writer, scriptwriter, nonfiction writer, autobiographer, and children's author.

The following entry presents an overview of King's career through 1996. For further information on his life and works, see *CLC,* Volumes 12, 26, 37, and 61.

INTRODUCTION

King is a prolific and immensely popular author of horror fiction. In his works, King blends elements of the traditional gothic tale with those of the modern psychological thriller, detective, and science fiction genres. His fiction features colloquial language, clinical attention to physical detail and emotional states, realistic settings, and an emphasis on contemporary problems. His use of such issues as marital infidelity and peer group acceptance lend credibility to the supernatural elements in his fiction. King's wide popularity attests to his ability to tap into his reader's fear of and inability to come to terms with evil confronted in the everyday world.

Biographical Information

King was born in Portland, Maine, on September 21, 1947, to Donald Edwin King, a U.S. merchant marine, and Nellie Ruth Pillsbury King. His father abandoned the family when King was only two years old. King, his brother, and his mother went to live with relatives in Durham, Maine, then various other cities. They returned to Durham permanently in 1958. King was very close to his mother, who supported the family with a series of low-paying jobs and read to him often as a child. She later encouraged King to send his work to publishers. She died of cancer in 1973 without seeing the enormous success her son achieved as a writer. King published his first short story, "I Was a Teenage Grave Robber," in *Comics Review* in 1965. He also wrote his first full-length manuscript while still in high school. King received a scholarship to the University of Maine at Orono, where he majored in English and minored in speech. He has a deep political awareness, and was active in student politics and the anti-war movement. With the exception of his short story "The Children of the Corn," he has avoided setting his stories in the 1960s and '70s because of the painful and difficult issues associated with the time period. After his graduation in 1970, King was unable to get a teaching job; instead he got jobs pumping gas and then working in a laun-

dry. On January 2, 1971, King married Tabitha Jane Spruce, also a novelist; they have three children. King spent a short time teaching at the Hampden Academy in Hampden, Maine, until the success of his first novel *Carrie* (1974) enabled him to focus on writing full time. In 1978 he was writer-in-residence and an instructor at the University of Maine at Orono, which resulted in his writing *Stephen King's Danse Macabre* (1981), a series of essays about the horror genre.

Major Works

King's fiction has extended into a variety of categories within the horror genre, including vampires (*'Salem's Lot* [1975]), zombies (*Pet Sematary* [1983]), possession (*Christine* [1983]), and supernatural powers (*Carrie*). He has also successfully branched out into science fiction, fantasy, and westerns. Most of his adult protagonists are ordinary, middle-class people who find themselves in some supernatural nightmare from which they cannot escape. Many of his stories have elements of gothic fiction. Although several of the novels set up a clash between good and evil, the moral order in King's world is often ambiguous, with no clear victor. *The*

Stand (1978) presents a conflict between good and evil, in which survivors of a world-decimating virus must battle against enormous odds to survive and defeat the demonic Randall Flagg and his followers. In several of King's works a religious undertone is evident, but he avoids overtly religious references. King plays on people's deepest fears in order to draw the reader into his narratives. Often the horror results from social reality instead of a supernatural influence. The breakdown of the social structures of love and understanding leads to a struggle between the individual and society and results in disaster. In *Carrie*, the title character is an adolescent who feels like an outsider in her high school. She suffers several humiliations until she finally loses control and gains revenge against her tormentors by destroying guilty and innocent alike with her telekinetic abilities. Even children are not immune from terror in King's writing. Children have acted as both threatened protagonists, such as Tad Trenton in *Cujo* (1981), and threatening antagonists, such as Gage Creed in *Pet Sematary*. Often children are sacrificed as a result of their parents' actions, including Creed in *Pet Sematary*, Danny Torrance in *The Shining* (1977), and Charlie McGee in *Firestarter* (1980). The perversion and corruption of the innocent is a recurring theme in King's fiction. Louis Creed in *Pet Sematary* cannot resist the lure of the Micmac burial ground, and his surrender to its evil lure is his and his family's undoing. Jack Torrance cannot resist exploring the dark secrets of the Overlook Hotel in *The Shining*, and his curiosity leads him to insanity and eventually destruction. Arnie Cunningham succumbs to the lure of his possessed automobile in *Christine*. King is not afraid to take risks or use shocking gore in his fiction. In the novella *Different Seasons* (1982), a pregnant woman is beheaded in a car accident on the way to give birth, but her body survives. A doctor then helps the beheaded corpse give birth. King has also written several novels under the pseudonym Richard Bachman which rarely contain elements of the supernatural or occult, focusing instead on such themes as human cruelty, alienation, and morality.

Critical Reception

Much of the critical discussion concerning King's work revolves around the value and importance of his novels as literature. Many reviewers dismiss King's fiction as lacking in literary merit because it is popular and because he produces so much of it. Others insist upon a critical commentary on specific aspects of King's fiction before dismissing the author as a panderer of popular trash. Reviewers who have analyzed King's novels often praise him for the rhythm and pacing of his narratives. Others praise the author for his ability to make the unreal seem so plausible. Tony Magistrale said, "one of the major reasons for King's commercial and critical success as a horror writer is his uncanny ability to blend and convolute the artifacts of everyday reality, replete with brand names and actual geographical locations, with the incongruous and startling details of an imagined realm." Critics who dismiss King's work usually accuse him of being a formula writer, but his supporters assert that this is part of King's talent. James Egan stated, "King employs the Gothic and the melodramatic in accordance with the demands of popular formula literature, for he intends to offer his readers a combination of stock thrills and intriguing innovations, the security of the familiar and the unsettling delights of the unknown." Several reviewers criticize King for relying on coincidental plots and sketchy characterizations. Andy Solomon asserted, "By now, everyone knows Stephen King's flaws: tone-deaf narration, papier-mâché characters, clichés, gratuitous vulgarity, self-indulgent digressions." In recent reviews, however, critics praised King attempting to improve his characterization, especially his depictions of women, most notably with his characters Jessie Burlingame in *Gerald's Game* (1992) and Dolores in *Dolores Claiborne* (1992). Even those critics who question the value of King's writing as literature acknowledge his commercial success and enormous popularity.

PRINCIPAL WORKS

The Star Invaders [as Steve King] (short story collection) 1964

Carrie: A Novel of a Girl with a Frightening Power (novel) 1974; movie edition published as *Carrie*, 1975

'Salem's Lot (novel) 1975

Rage [as Richard Bachman] (novel) 1977

The Shining (novel) 1977

The Stand (novel) 1978; revised edition, 1990

Night Shift (short story collection) 1978; also published as *Night Shift: Excursions into Horror*, 1979

Another Quarter Mile: Poetry (poetry) 1979

The Dead Zone (novel) 1979; movie edition published as *The Dead Zone: Movie Tie-In*, 1980

The Long Walk [as Richard Bachman] (novel) 1979

Firestarter (novel) 1980

Cujo (novel) 1981

Roadwork: A Novel of the First Energy Crisis [as Richard Bachman] (novel) 1981

Stephen King's Danse Macabre (nonfiction) 1981

Creepshow (short story collection) 1982

The Dark Tower: The Gunslinger (novel) 1982

Different Seasons (short story collection) 1982

The Running Man [as Richard Bachman] (novel) 1982

Stephen King's Creepshow: A George A. Romero Film (screenplay) 1982

Christine (novel) 1983

Cycle of the Werewolf (short story collection) 1983; also published as *The Silver Bullet*, 1985

Pet Sematary (novel) 1983; (screenplay) 1989

Cat's Eye (screenplay) 1984

The Eyes of the Dragon (juvenile novel) 1984

The Talisman [with Peter Straub] (novel) 1984

Thinner [as Richard Bachman] (novel) 1984

Silver Bullet (screenplay) 1985

Stephen King's Skeleton Crew (short story collection) 1985

It (novel) 1986; first published in limited edition in Germany as *Es,* 1986

Maximum Overdrive [writer and director] (screenplay) 1986

Misery (novel) 1987

The Tommyknockers (novel) 1987

The Dark Half (novel) 1989

The Dark Tower: The Drawing of Three (novel) 1989

My Pretty Pony (children's novel) 1989

Four Past Midnight (novellas) 1990

Needful Things (novel) 1991

Dolores Claiborne (novel) 1992

Gerald's Game (novel) 1992

Rose Madder (novel) 1995

Desperation (novel) 1996

The Regulators [as Richard Bachman] (novel) 1996

Bag of Bones (novel) 1997

CRITICISM

Tony Magistrale (essay date Spring 1985)

SOURCE: "Inherited Haunts: Stephen King's Terrible Children," in *Extrapolation,* Vol. 26, No. 1, Spring, 1985, pp. 43-9.

[*In the following essay, Magistrale explores the role of children in King's work.*]

On March 25, 1984, in Boca Raton, Florida, Stephen King delivered the closing address at the International Conference on the Fantastic in the Arts. Following a discussion about King's childhood readings in the horror genre, someone in the audience asked the author the question, "What terrifies you the most?" King's reply was emphatic and immediate: "Opening the door of my children's bedroom and finding one of them dead."

King's dread that his offspring could be harmed has not inhibited his use of infantile and adolescent characters throughout his writing, which has achieved wide notoriety and brought a degree of untoward fame on its author. It is a fiction centering on excursions into terror, surreal fantasies which spring suddenly to life, the dark spirits that inhabit a deserted town or hotel. His stories are populated with demons and ghosts, monsters and phantoms. And his youthful protagonists are besieged by a variety of these creatures. This siege is in keeping with the foreword to his collection of short tales in *Night Shift,* where King insists that a requisite for a successful horror story is its ability to "hold the reader or listener spellbound for a little while, lost in a world that never was, never could be." Yet one of the major reasons for King's commercial and critical success as a horror writer is his uncanny ability to blend and convolute the artifacts of everyday reality, replete with brand names and actual geographical locations, with the incongruous and startling details of an imagined realm. In creating this blend, King displays no neglect for the humans who inhabit his works, be they children, many of whom appear to be endowed with either supernatural powers or an uncommon trait, or adult protagonists, the majority of whom are, by and large, middle-class men and women eking out a living in contemporary America. For varied reasons (sometimes accidental, usually deliberate) these characters find themselves suddenly and helplessly enmeshed in the Gothic machinery of a nightmare from which they will not awaken. King's people are not superhuman, but ordinary, flawed, and vulnerable. In his tales, good must struggle against evil, and from the encounter become less good. Behind this moral backdrop, he invests the majority of his protagonists with a persuasive sympathy: we care about these people, hope they will somehow discover a way to survive, and continue reading about the unfolding of their fates with a curious mixture of fascination and apprehension, because in many ways his literary characters represent our own fears and values.

> **One of the major reasons for King's commercial and critical success as a horror writer is his uncanny ability to blend and convolute the artifacts of everyday reality, replete with brand names and actual geographical locations, with the incongruous and startling details of an imagined realm.**
>
> —*Tony Magistrale*

King's most memorable and important characters, and the ones to whom we as readers grow increasingly attached, are his children. Frequently they form the moral centers of his books, and from them all other actions seem to radiate. In King's fiction, children embody the full spectrum of human experience; they are identified with the universal principles of ethical extremes. Some represent the nucleus for familial love. They are often healing forces, as in *Cujo* and the first halves of *The Shining* and *Pet Sematary,* enabling parents in unstable marriages to forgive one another's human failings. On this level of being, many of King's children represent the principle of good in a corrupt world; they seem both divinely inspired and painfully cursed with prophetic knowledge. Danny Torrance in *The Shining,* Carrie White in *Carrie,* and Charlie McGee in *Firestarter* possess superhuman abilities that trigger death and destruction, and yet these children elicit our sympathy because they appear more often in the role of victim than victimizer. It is not really the children who are responsible for their various acts of destruction, but the adults who mislead and torment them.

At the other moral pole are the adolescent hunters—the denim fascists in **"Sometimes They Come Back,"** *Christine,* and *Carrie*—who portray ambassadors from an immoral world, their sole purpose being to wreak destruction on anyone or anything weaker than or different from themselves. These "children" have completely severed their bonds with innocence; in their vicious lust to exploit sex, alcohol, and violence, they model their behavior on an extreme conception of adulthood. They want all the pleasures of worldly experience, with none of the responsibilities. Thus, they are simply young versions of the corruption which animates King's adult society. If they manage to live long enough, they will become the Jack Torrances (*The Shining*), John Rainbirds (*Firestarter*), and Greg Stillsons (*Dead Zone*) of the next generation.

> **The theme of innocence betrayed is at the heart of *Carrie*. Indeed, this concept unifies the major work of King's canon: throughout his fiction, the power of evil to malign and pervert innocence is omnipresent.**
> —*Tony Magistrale*

The adults in King's world act frequently as children; they explore places where they have no business going, their behavior is often immature and without conscience, and their institutions—the church, the state's massive bureaucratic system of control, the nuclear family itself—barely mask an undercurrent of violence that is capable of manifesting itself at any given moment. The daily interactions in their marriages and neighborhoods bring out the worst in King's adult characters; they revert to the meanness of adolescence, acknowledging their selfish urges only after they have set in motion a series of events which lead to catastrophe. Throughout the novel *Carrie,* for example, Carrie White is forced into the role of persecuted outsider. Her first and greatest impediment to a normal life is her mother, a woman indoctrinated with a fierce religious fanaticism who refuses to teach Carrie the adjustment skills necessary for survival in the real world. Consequently, Carrie's discovery of her menstrual period—the initial event associated with the emergence into womanhood—brings her only fear and loathing. Her mother translates the biological function into a symbol of corruption sent by God to punish women. As a direct result of her mother's negative sermonizing, and motivated by the final humiliation of having a bucket of pig's blood

dropped on her head at the senior prom, Carrie uses her telekinetic powers to destroy everything in sight. Since no one is either willing to, or capable of, guiding Carrie through the difficult transition from adolescence to adulthood, distinctions between good and evil lose their significance for her, and Carrie's night of carnage includes those who are innocent along with those who are culpable. Her only introductions to adulthood are presented through images of violence and pain, and all of Carrie's subsequent reactions become a grotesque reflection of what she has experienced personally. As King himself explains the novel in *Danse Macabre,* "Carrie can only wait to be saved or damned by the actions of others. Her only power is her telekinetic ability, and both book and movie eventually arrive at the same point: Carrie uses her 'wild talent' to pull down the whole rotten society."

The theme of innocence betrayed is at the heart of *Carrie.* Indeed, this concept unifies the major work of King's canon: throughout his fiction, the power of evil to malign and pervert innocence is omnipresent. Louis Creed (*Pet Sematary*), Jack Torrance (*The Shining*), and Arnie Cunningham (*Christine*), sacrifice their families and sanities when they succumb to the lure of evil. Evil becomes a pervasive force that these characters cannot resist. Creed is attracted to the power of the Micmac burial ground despite its obvious dangers; Torrance probes the history of decadence and violence in the Overlook hotel and yearns to become part of it; and in his automobile from hell, Arnie Cunningham surrenders both his personality and his soul to avenge a lifetime of frustration. In King's novels and stories, there are few heroes; at best his major characters endure, but they seldom prevail. Like the young protagonist in the tale **"Graveyard Shift,"** his men and women are usually (and often literally) overwhelmed by the legions of the underworld.

The most effective dramatization of King's dark vision occurs through the interaction of adults and children. His children, in spite of their goodwill and special gifts, are shaped and motivated by adults who are enmeshed in a personal struggle with evil. Most often, his young protagonists—Gage Creed, Danny Torrance, Charlie McGee—are forced to pay for their fathers' sins of curiosity; their innocence is the price for an intimate examination of evil.

The short story **"Children of the Corn"** is one of the more sophisticated illustrations of this formula. A young couple, their marriage in disarray, stumble upon Gatlin, Nebraska, a town where time has apparently stopped. Instead of August 1976, Burt and Vicki discover calendars and municipal records that go no further than 1964: "Something had happened in 1964. Something to do with religion, and corn . . . and children." Moreover, there are no adults in this town, only children under the age of nineteen.

The time period is certainly of crucial importance to the

story's meaning. But King never completely explains its mystery. Nor is it clear immediately why all the adults have been killed and why no child is permitted to survive past the age of nineteen. Like Vicki and Burt, the reader is supplied only with information about an Old Testament Jehovah whom the children worship in the corn fields. In return for their human sacrifices, he invests the crop with a special purity: "In the last of the daylight [Burt] swept his eyes closely over the row of corn to his left. And he saw that every leaf and stalk was perfect, which was just not possible. No yellow blight. No tattered leaves, no caterpillar eggs, no burrows."

Reading King's best fiction is like visiting a city with innumerable corners of intriguing complexity and atmospheres that reward lingering absorption. **"Children of the Corn"** encourages the reader to linger over multiple interpretations. On the most obvious level, it is a story of religious fanaticism dedicated to a malevolent deity. But such a reading does not, however, explain the significance of the 1964 time setting—the initial period of active involvement by American forces in Vietnam—and its relationship to the fertility of the Nebraska corn. Both appear irrevocably linked. Listening to the radio outside the town, Vicki and Burt hear a child's voice: "There's some that think it's okay to get out in the world, as if you could work and walk in the world without being smirched by the world." And later in the story, after he has learned the awful secret of the town, Burt wonders if human sacrifices were ordained because the corn was dying as a result of too much sinning.

Although King is cautious to avoid so overt a nexus, the reader with any sense of history will recall the violation of the land in Vietnam by such toxic chemicals as Agent Orange. Man's technology carried the poisoning of the soil, not to mention the levels of death and carnage, to the point at which the land itself (the allegorical corn god) demanded repentance. If we place the events of this story in such a context, it becomes possible to understand why all the adults past the (draft?) age of nineteen are sacrificed. These are the individuals who were most responsible for the war, for the "adult sins" that defiled and destroyed acres of Vietnamese landscape, thousands of American and Vietnamese lives, and, finally, what was left of America's innocence. For Vietnam was, among other things, America's collective cultural emergence into the "adult world" of sin and error. Our loss of innocence and our recognition of self-corruption is what gave impetus to the antiwar movement. In trying to decide whose side God favored in this war we were shown with painful certitude that life is a more complicated mixture of good and evil than we earlier had assumed. King's own view on the immorality of the Vietnam experience, as expressed in *Danse Macabre,* corresponds precisely with such an interpretation: "By 1968 my mind had been changed forever about a number of fundamental questions. . . . I did and do

believe that companies like Sikorsky and Douglas Aircraft and Dow Chemical and even the Bank of America subscribed more or less to the idea that war is good business."

Burt and Vicki are therefore sacrificed because they are adult representatives of fallen, post-Vietnam America. Both have strayed from any sense of a belief in God, their marriage is in disharmony; both appear as selfish, stubborn, and unforgiving individuals, they are anxious to pass through Nebraska and travel on to "sunny, sinful California"; and Burt is a Vietnam veteran. References to this last point are made on three separate occasions, but the most significant reference occurs immediately after Burt discovers the 1964 time setting. While standing on a sidewalk in the town, he smells fertilizer. The odor had always reminded him of his childhood in rural upstate New York, "but somehow this smell was different from the one he had grown up with. . . . There was a sickish sweet undertone. Almost a death smell. As a medical orderly in Vietnam, he had become well versed in that smell." The association between Vietnam and Nebraska and its corn fields, and the disenchantment inherent in adult experience, is maintained on similar symbolic levels throughout the story. Nebraska and its corn are in the "heartland" of America, its moral center, and out of an effort to reestablish the purity and innocence of an earlier era, both the corn and the land itself seem to be demanding adult penance for a sin that originated in 1964.

King's corn god is furious with the adult world, demanding blood in exchange for reclaiming the land from its state of spiritual and physical barrenness. Burt discovers the god's maxim written on the cover of the town's registry: "Thus let the iniquitous be cut down so that the ground may be fertile again saith the Lord God of Hosts." The very fact that the ground needs to be made "fertile again" suggests that it has suffered from some kind of pestilence. And the "disease of the corn" in this tale, while ambiguous throughout, can be interpreted in terms of American defoliation of the Vietnamese landscape, as well as the more symbolic cultural "illness" of moral guilt and spiritual taint that accompanied American war involvement.

The human sacrifices in **"Children of the Corn"** have been successful; vitality has been restored to the American soil. The corn itself grows in flawless rows. Moreover, as Burt discovers while running wounded through the open fields, the soil even contains a mysterious recuperative power: "The ache in his arm had settled into a dull throb that was nearly pleasant, and the good feeling was still with him." The corn deity has made the land, and all that comes in contact with it, into an agrarian Arcadia, a neo-Eden of pristine perfection and harmony. But to maintain this environment, the corn deity exacts from this symbolic American community in Nebraska a never-ending cycle of adult penance and revenge. In fact, at the conclusion of the story the corn god lowers the age of sacrifice from nineteen to eighteen, suggesting that the inherited guilt and shame of Vietnam will never be completely exorcised.

In *Danse Macabre,* on the other hand, King states that he has "purposely avoided writing a novel with a 1960's time setting. . . . But those things did happen; the hate, paranoia, and fear on both sides were all too real." King may not have directed his energies into a full-length novel, but in **"Children of the Corn"** he has provided us with a frightening little allegory of the decade's major historical event. It is also interesting, given the time setting for **"Children of the Corn,"** that the "adult world" is interpreted as sinful and in need of punishment. In the sixties, American youth were in the streets directing a cultural critique of the mores and values of their parents. The adults were the enemy; they had perpetuated the war in Vietnam and had sent America's children to perform the killing and the dying.

In Stephen King's Gothic landscape, horror often springs from social reality: the failure of love and understanding triggers disaster. King's world is a fallen one, and evil is perpetuated through legacies of sin, based in social, cultural, mythical, and historical contexts, and handed down from one generation to the next. Adulthood, because of its litany of selfish mistakes, broken marriages, cruel machinations, and drunken excesses, fully embodies this legacy of human corruption; adults show themselves capable of betrayal at any point. The inevitable violence and cruelty which are the usual end results of adult values and behavior force King's adolescent protagonists to relinquish their tentative hold on innocence and sensitivity. Gage Creed, the young boy in *Pet Sematary,* becomes a grotesque extension of The Wendigo, a creature from the pre-Christian world, because the human adults, Louis Creed and Jud Crandall, avail themselves of the unholy power within the Micmac burial ground. Charlie McGee's childhood in *Firestarter* is abruptly and hideously fragmented by the government's manipulation of her parents' chromosomes and the Shop's desire to extend the experiment. The child is caught in a conflict over the morality of using her superhuman powers. Knowing her confusion, the Shop engages in psychic blackmail, forcing her to refine her abilities and use them for destructive purposes. Although she cooperates with their devious methods, Charlie loses both parents, is betrayed by a surrogate father, and faces an uncertain future of fear and flight. In the short story **"Last Rung on the Ladder,"** an attorney becomes so involved with his career and his reputation in the world that he fails to heed the plea for help issued from his misdirected younger sister. As a child, he was always there to protect her and lend his support, but as an adult he is too preoccupied. When she finally commits suicide, in large measure because of his failure to become involved, he is left with the enormous burden of responsibility.

Finally, King's novella, *Apt Pupil,* from the collection *Different Seasons,* works from a similar set of suppositions. Todd Bowden, a precocious adolescent fascinated with the grisly details of Nazi Germany, discovers an aging war criminal, Dussander, sharing his suburban American neighborhood. Over a period of years the child's fascination deepens into obsession, as he practices more devious and intricate methods of extracting a personal history from the Nazi officer. Through the course of their long relationship, the boy is slowly transformed into a version of the Nazi adult: his interest in schoolwork and sports is abandoned in favor of stalking and butchering helpless drunks and indigent street people. It is a complex, albeit overwritten, study of negative adult influence and the corrupting fusion of evil: the Nazi's oral history of death camp atrocities exacts an intimate, active response from the high school student. Todd may never have been a paragon of moral purity or innocence (in fact his psychological torment of the officer suggests quite the opposite), but steady contact with Dussander pushes him into a deeper, more serious, and personal participation in evil. By the conclusion of the novella, the child relinquishes all control over his own life; he is forged from the same furnace of hate that created the Nazi.

King's children, like those found in Dickens' novels, illustrate the failings of adult society. The destruction of their innocence accomplishes more than a simple restating of the universal theme of the Fall from Grace; it enlarges to include a specific critique of respective societies and cultures as well. Like Todd Bowden in *Apt Pupil,* the children in **"Children of the Corn"** are neither symbols of purity nor sensitivity. Yet, similar to many of King's other, more sympathetic adolescents—Carrie, Charlie McGee, Danny Torrance, Gage Creed—they are victimized by the inherited sins of an older world. In each of these examples, the children are constrained to pay for the mistakes of their elders; they do so, significantly, at the expense of their own transition into adulthood.

Clive Barker (essay date January 1986)

SOURCE: "Stephen King: Surviving the Ride," in *Fantasy Review,* January, 1986, pp. 6-8.

[*In the following essay, Barker discusses King's success with, and commitment to, the horror genre.*]

First, a confession: I have no thesis. I come to these pages without an overview to propound; only with a substantial enthusiasm for the work of Stephen King and a potpourri of thoughts on fear, fiction, dreams and geographies which may bear some tenuous relation to each other and to King's fiction.

Theoretical thinking was never a great passion of mine, but ghost-trains are. And it's with a ghost-train I begin.

It's called—ambitiously enough—L'Apocalypse. To judge from the size of the exterior, the ride it houses is an epic; the vast, three-tiered facade dwarfs the punks who mill around outside, staring up with a mixture of trepidation and appetite at the hoardings, and wondering if they have the nerve to step out of the heat of the sun and into the stale darkness that awaits them through the swinging doors.

Surely, they reassure themselves, no fun-fair ride can be as bad as the paintings that cover every inch of the building suggest: for the pictures record atrocities that would have turned de Sade's stomach.

They're not particularly good paintings; they're rather too crudely rendered, and the gaudy primaries the artists have chosen seem ill-suited to the subject matter. But the eye flits back and forth over the horrors described here, unable to disengage itself. In one corner, a shackled man is having his head sliced off; it seems to leap out at us, propelled by a geyser of scarlet blood. A few yards from this, above a row of arches that are edged with canary-yellow lights, a man watches his bowels being drawn from his abdomen by a Cardinal in an advanced state of decomposition. Beside the entrance booth, a crucified woman is being burned alive in a chamber lined with white-hot swords. We might be tempted to laugh at such grand guignol excesses, but we cannot. They are, for all the roughness of their presentation, deeply disturbing.

I've never ridden L'Apocalypse. I know it only as a photograph, culled from a magazine some dozen years ago, and treasured since. The photograph still speaks loudly to me. Of the indisputable glamour of the horrible; of its power to enthrall and repulse simultaneously. And it also reminds me—with its sweaty-palmed punks queuing beneath a crystal blue sky for a chance at the dark—that nobody ever lost money offering a good ride to Hell.

Which brings us, inevitably, to the architect of the most popular ghost-train rides in the world: Mr. Stephen King.

It's perhaps redundant, in a book celebrating Stephen King's skills, for me to list his merits at too great a length. We his readers and admirers, know them well. But it may be worth our considering exactly what he's selling us through the charm and accessibility of his prose, the persuasiveness of his characters, the ruthless drive of his narratives.

He's selling death. He's selling tales of blood-drinkers, flesh-eaters, and the decay of the soul; of the destruction of sanity, community and faith. In his fiction, even love's power to outwit the darkness is uncertain; the monsters will devour that too, given half a chance. Nor is innocence much of a defense. Children go to the grave as readily as the adult of the species, and those few Resurrections that circumstance grants are not likely to be the glory promised from the pulpit.

> **Many reasons have been put forth for King's popularity. A common element in most of the theories is his plausibility as a writer. In the novels—though rather less in the short stories—he describes the confrontation between the real and the fantastic elements in his fiction so believably that the reader's rational sensibilities are seldom, if ever, outraged.**
> —*Clive Barker*

Not, one would have thought, a particularly commercial range of subjects. But in King's hands their saleability can scarcely be in question. He has turned the horror genre—so long an underdog on the publishing scene—into a force to be reckoned with.

Many reasons have been put forth for King's popularity. A common element in most of the theories is his plausibility as a writer. In the novels—though rather less in the short stories—he describes the confrontation between the real and the fantastic elements in his fiction so believably that the reader's rational sensibilities are seldom, if ever, outraged. The images of power, of loss, of transformation, of wild children and terrible hotels, of beasts mythological and beasts rabid and beasts human—all are dropped so cunningly into the texture of the world he conjures—morsel upon morsel—that by the time our mouths are full, we're perfectly willing to swallow.

The net effect is akin to taking that ride on L'Apocalypse, only finding that the dummies on either side of the track, enacting over and over their appalling death scenes, closely resemble people we know. The horror is intensified immeasurably. We are no longer simply voyeurs, watching some artificial atrocity unfold in front of our eyes. We are intimately involved with the sufferers. We share their traumas and their terrors. We share too their hatred of their tormentors.

This is by no means the only approach to writing dark fantasy of course. Many authors choose to plunge their readers into the world of the subconscious (which is, surely, the territory of such fiction charts) with scarcely a glance over their shoulders at the "reality" the reader occupies. In the geography of the fantastique, for instance, Prince Prospero's castle—sealed so inadequately against the Red Death—

stands far deeper in the world of pure dream than does the Overlook Hotel, whose rooms, though no less haunted by violent death, are far more realistically evoked than Poe's baroque conceits.

There are, inevitably, losses and gains on both sides. Poe sacrifices a certain accessibility by his method; one has to embrace the fictional conventions he has employed before the story can be fully savored. He gains, however, a mythic resonance which is out of all proportion to the meagre pages *The Masque of the Red Death* occupies. He has, apparently effortlessly written himself into the landscape of our dreams.

King's method—which requires the establishing of a far more elaborate fictional "reality"—wins out through or commitment to that reality, and to the characters who inhabit it. It also earns the power to subvert our sense of the real, by showing us a world we think we know, then revealing another view of it entirely. What I believe he loses in the tradeoff is a certain ambiguity. This I'll return to later.

First, a couple of thoughts on subversion. It has been argued, and forcibly, that for all the paraphernalia of revolution contained in King's fiction—the weak discovering unlooked-for strength and the strong faltering; the constant threat (or promise) of transformation; a sense barely hidden beneath the chatty surface of the prose, that mythic elements are being juggled here—that, despite all this apocalyptic stuff, the author's worldview is at heart a conservative one. Is he perhaps a sheep in wolf's clothing, distressing us with these scenes of chaos in order to persuade us to cling closer to the values that his monsters jeopardize?

I admit to having some sympathy with this argument, and I admire most those of his tales which seem to show the world irredeemably changed, with no hope of return to the comfortable, joyless, death-in-life that seems to be the late twentieth century ideal. But if there is evidence that gives weight to such argument, there is also much in King's work which is genuinely subversive: imagery which evokes states of mind and conditions of flesh which, besides exciting our anxieties, excites also our desires and our perversities.

Why, you may ask, do I put such a high value upon subversion?

There are many reasons. The most pertinent here is my belief that fantastic fiction offers the writer exceptional possibilities in that direction, and I strongly believe a piece of work (be it play, book, poem) should be judged by how enthusiastically it seizes the opportunity to do what it can do uniquely. The literature of the fantastic—and the movies, and the paintings—can reproduce, at its best, the texture of experience more closely than any "naturalistic" work, because it can embrace the complexity of the world we live in.

Which is to say: our minds. That's where we live, after all. And our minds are extraordinary melting pots, in which sensory information, and the memory of same, and intellectual ruminations, and nightmares, and dreams, simmer in an ever-richer stew. Where else but in works called (often pejoratively) fantasies can such a mixture of elements be placed side by side?

> **From the beginning, [King has] never apologized, never been ashamed to be a horror author. He values the genre, and if horror fiction is in turn more valued now than it was ten or twenty years ago it is surely in no small degree his doing.**
> **—*Clive Barker***

And if we once embrace the vision offered in such works, if we once allow the metaphors a home in our psyches, the subversion is under way. We may for the first time see ourselves as a totality—valuing our appetite for the forbidden rather than suppressing it, comprehending that our taste for the strange, or the morbid, or the paradoxical is contrary to what we're brought up to believe, a sign of our good health. So I say—subvert. And never apologize.

That's one of King's crowning achievements. From the beginning, he's never apologized, never been ashamed to be a horror author. He values the genre, and if horror fiction is in turn more valued now than it was ten or twenty years ago it is surely in no small degree his doing. After all, the most obsessive of rationalists must find it difficult to ignore the man's existence: he's read on buses and trains; in Universities and Hospitals; by the good, the bad, and the morally indifferent.

At this juncture it may be worth remembering that the dreams he is usually concerned to evoke are normally known not as dreams but as nightmares. This is in itself worthy of note. We have other classes of dreams which are as common as nightmares. Erotic Dreams, for instance; dreams of humiliation. But it's only the dream of terror which has been graced with a special name, as though we recognize that this experience, of all those that come to us in sleep, carries some essential significance. It is perhaps that in our waking lives we feel (rightly or wrongly) that we have control over all other responses but that of fear? Certainly we may use the word nightmare freely to describe waking experience ("the traffic was a nightmare," we casually remark), but seldom do our lives reach that pitch of terror—accompanied by the blood-chilling sense of inevitability—that informs the dream of dread.

In reading a good piece of horror fiction, we may dip into

the dreaming state at will; we may even hope to interpret some of the signs and signals that nightmares deliver to us. If not that, at least there is some comfort in knowing that these images are shared.

(An aside. One of the pleasures of any fiction is comparing the intricacies of response with other readers, but this process takes on a wonderfully paradoxical quality when two horror enthusiasts are exchanging views on a favorite book or film. The gleeful detailing of the carnage, the shared delight, as the key moments of revulsion and anxiety are remembered: we smile, talking of how we sweated.)

There are many kinds of nightmare. Some have familiar, even domestic settings, in which commonplace particulars are charged up with uncanny and inexplicable power to intimidate. It is this kind of nightmare that King is most adept at evoking, and the kind with which he is probably most readily identified. It is in a way a natural progression from rooting outlandish horrors—*Carrie; 'Salem's Lot*—in settings so familiar we might occupy them, to making objects from those settings—a dog, a car—themselves the objects of anxiety. I must say I prefer the earlier books by quite a measure, but that's in part because the Apocalypses conjured seem so much more comprehensive, and I have a practically limitless appetite for tales of the world turned inside out.

The other kind of nightmare is a different experience entirely and it is not—at least in the conventional sense—about threat. I mean the kind of dream voyage that takes you out of any recognizable context, and into some other state entirely. The kind that lifts you up (perhaps literally; for me such nightmares often begin with falling that turns into flight) and whips you away to a place both familiar and utterly new, utterly strange. You have never been to this place in your waking life, of that your dreaming self is certain; but there are presences here familiar to you, and sights around every corner that you will recognize even as they astonish you.

What actually happens on these voyages will run from the banal to the Wagnerian, depending on the dreamer's sense of irony, but the way this second sort of nightmare operates upon your psyche is totally different from the first. For one thing, the fears dealt with in the first sort are likely to be susceptible to analysis. They are fears of authority figures, or terminal disease, or making love to Mother. But the second kind is, I believe, rooted not in the specifies of the personality, but is something more primitive; something that belongs to our response as thought-haunted matter to the world we're born into. The images that come to overwhelm us in this region are not, therefore, projections of neurosis; they are things vast; contradictory; mythological.

King can conjure such stuff with the best of them; I only regret that his brilliance as a creator of domestic demons has

claimed him from writing more of that other region. When he turns his hand to it, the effect is stunning. *The Mist,* for example, is a story that begins in familiar King territory, and moves through a variety of modes—including scenes which, in their mingling of the monstrous and the commonplace work as high, grim comedy—towards a world lost to humanity, a world that echoes in the imagination long after the book has been closed. In the final section of the story the survivors encounter a creature so vast it doesn't even notice the protagonists:

> . . . Its skin was deeply wrinkled and grooved, and clinging to it were scores, hundreds, of those pinkish 'bugs' with the stalk-eyes. I don't know how big it actually was, but it passed directly over us. . . . Mrs. Reppler said later she could not see the underside of its body, although she craned her neck up to look. She saw only two Cyclopean legs going up and up into the mist like living towers until they were lost to sight.

There is much more of breathtaking imaginative scope in *The Stand,* and in a more intimate, though no less persuasive fashion, in *The Shining* and *'Salem's Lot.* Moments when the terror becomes something more than a fight for life with an unwelcome intruder; when the horror reveals itself, even in the moment of causing us to recoil, as a source of fascination and awe and self-comprehension.

This is the root of the ambiguity I spoke of before, and to which I said I would return. Wanting an encounter with forces that will challenge our lives—that will deliver us once and for all into the regions of the gods ("I had a dream that I saw God walking across Harrison on the far side of the lake, a God so gigantic that above the waist He was lost in a clear blue sky."—*The Mist*)—yet fearful that we are negligible things and so far beneath the concern of such powers that any confrontation will simply kill us.

Charting that ambiguity is, I would suggest, a function that fantasy genre uniquely fulfill. It is perhaps the liability of King's virtues that such ambiguity is often forfeited in exchange for straightforward identification with the forces of light. King's monsters (human, sub-human and Cyclopean) may on occasion be comprehensible to us, but they seldom exercise any serious claim on our sympathies. They are moral degenerates, whose colors are plain from the outset. We watch them kick dogs to death, and devour children, and we are reinforced in the questionable certainty that we are not like them; that we are on the side of the angels.

Now that's fiction. We are not. Darkness has a place in all of us; a substantial place that must, for our health's sake, be respected and investigated.

After all, one of the reasons we read tales of terror is surely that we have an appetite for viewing anguish, and death, and all the paraphernalia of the monstrous. That's not the condition of the angels.

It seems to me vital that in this age of the New Righteousness—when moral rectitude is again a rallying-cry, and the old hypocrisies are gaining acolytes by the hour—that we should strive to avoid feeding delusions of perfectibility and instead celebrate the complexities and contradictions that, as I've said, fantastic fiction is uniquely qualified to address. If we can, we may yet keep from drowning in a wave of simplifications that include such great, fake dichotomies as good versus evil, dark versus light, reality versus fiction. But we must be prepared to wear our paradoxes on our sleeve.

In King's work, it is so often the child who carries that wisdom; the child who synthesizes "real" and "imagined" experience without question, who knows instinctively that imagination can tell the truth the way the senses never can. That lesson can never be taught too often. It stands in direct contradiction to the basic principles which we are suckled upon and are taught make us strong in the world. Principles of verifiable evidence; and of the logic that will lead, given its head, to terrible but faultlessly logical, insanities.

I return again to the list of goods that King is selling in his fiction, and find my summary deficient. Yes, there is death on the list; and much about the soul's decay. But there's also vision.

Not the kind laid claim to by politicians or manufacturers or men of the cloth. Not the vision of the better economy, the better combustion engine, the better Eden. Those visions are devised to bind and blind us. If we look too long at them we no longer understand what our dreams are telling us; and without that knowledge we are weak.

No, King offers us another kind of vision; he shows us adults what the children in his fiction so often take for granted: that on the journey which he has so eloquently charted, where no terror shows its face but on a street that we have ourselves trodden, it is not, finally, the stale formulae and the trite metaphysics we're taught from birth that will get us to the end of the ride alive; it is our intimacy with our dark and dreaming selves.

James Egan (essay date Spring 1986)

SOURCE: "'A Single Powerful Spectacle': Stephen King's Gothic Melodrama," in *Extrapolation,* Vol. 27, No. 1, Spring, 1986, pp. 62-75.

[*In the following essay, Egan analyzes King's use of elements of the gothic and the melodramatic in his work.*]

The Gothic tradition which has survived into the twentieth century, after passing through the hands of the Gothic dramatists, Mary Shelley, Bram Stoker, Henry James, and Shirley Jackson, has evolved into a complex mixture of the sensational, the sentimental, the melodramatic, and the formulaic. True, a Gothic work such as Jackson's *The Haunting of Hill House* occasionally achieves belletristic status, but most examples of the genre can be appropriately categorized as "popular" fiction. Stephen King's numerous references and allusions make plain his familiarity with the Gothic tradition, particularly that part which begins with the publication of *Frankenstein.* One finds in King many Gothic conventions of setting, plot, characterization, and theme, along with an assortment of melodramatic techniques which accentuate his Gothic motifs and help to shape the world view which permeates his fiction. It must be emphasized, however, that the Gothic and the melodramatic in King are virtually inseparable, just as they are in the Gothic tradition itself. Equally important, one must recognize that King employs the Gothic and the melodramatic in accordance with the demands of popular formula literature, for he intends to offer his readers a combination of stock thrills and intriguing innovations, the security of the familiar and the unsettling delights of the unknown.

As Elizabeth MacAndrew has argued, Gothic literature highlights vice. King treats vice consistently, luridly, graphically. One of the main plots of ***The Dead Zone*** details the exploits of Frank Dodd, a rapist-murderer who stalks a succession of young women and ends his spree with the killing of a nine-year-old. Dodd's behavior follows the strangely consistent pattern of the deranged mind, a pattern which King describes in detail. After slapping a victim around and then raping her, Dodd savors the joy of murder: "He began to throttle [Alma Frechette], yanking her head up from the bandstand's board flooring and then slamming it back down. Her eyes bulged. Her face went pink, then red, then congested purple. Her struggles began to weaken." Eventually, the novel's psychic detective, John Smith, identifies Dodd; but Dodd declines to surrender quietly. Instead, he cuts his throat with a razor blade, spraying a bathroom with blood, and hangs around his neck "a sign crayoned in lipstick. It read: I CONFESS." Several humans confront a huge, rabid St. Bernard in ***Cujo.*** Cujo mauls Joe Camber and his friend, Gary Pervier, and traps Donna Trenton and her son, Tad, in Donna's car. King devotes a substantial section of the novel to the brutal, life-or-death struggle between Donna and Cujo. The dog bites her, and she in turn slams the car door repeatedly on the dog's head. For melodramatic effect, this war of attrition goes on in nearly unbearable heat and humidity, conditions which cause Tad to go into convulsions and finally contribute to his death. More than a rabid animal, Cujo is evil, a demonic reincarnation of Dodd returned to prey on the innocent once again. Sex competes with violence in *Cujo* as Steve Kemp, Donna's rejected lover, vandalizes her home while she battles the dog. Kemp's orgiastic violence does additional duty as a symbolic rape: sexually aroused, he nearly demolishes the Trenton home and then masturbates on Donna's bed.

Sex and violence also combine sensationally in *Firestarter*. John Rainbird, a bizarre, deformed hit-man for The Shop, a shadowy government espionage agency, strangles his victims slowly, hoping to witness death as they draw their last breaths. After learning of Charlie McGee, the adolescent girl with pyrokinetic abilities, he becomes fascinated with the child's power and personality. Rainbird wants to become "intimate" with Charlie—he seems to have fallen in love with her. His grotesque appearance and peculiar intentions evoke the stereotype of the child molester. Gruesome destruction is panoramic in *Carrie*. Following repeated harassment by her mother and her peers, Carrie White turns her telekinetic powers on the town of Chamberlain: water mains explode, gasoline stations erupt into flames, and the population stumbles about in a state of chaos—all of this because Carrie has become a vindictive, seemingly demonic character who seeks revenge on each and every one of her tormentors and even upon those who did not harm her. Once a victim, Carrie evolves into a methodical executioner whose vendetta take up the final third of the novel. Doubt and guilt do not impede Carrie, who simply kills whomever she chooses. The novel shifts, with melodramatic rapidity, from Carrie the victim to Carrie the avenger.

> **King's drastic, violent subject matter fits in with his essentially Gothic themes. He stresses the primordial power and pervasiveness of the unknown, the irrationality and unpredictability of the human psyche, and the moral reality of good and evil.**
>
> —*James Egan*

King's emphasis on blood and gore does not always depend upon vice, however. *The Breathing Method,* one of four novellas included in *Different Seasons,* qualifies as a "tale of the uncanny" told at a mysterious gentlemen's club in New York. Miss Standfield, an unwed pregnant woman who has diligently practiced controlled breathing in order to make delivery easier, is beheaded in a traffic accident while on the way to the hospital to give birth. Her body, though, remains alive, and the narrator, Dr. McCarron, helps the "corpse" deliver its child. But McCarron's excursion into the supernatural has not yet ended, for as he prepares to leave, Miss Standfield's head "mouthed four words: *Thank you, Dr.*

McCarron." McCarron informs the head that Miss Standfield has delivered a boy, and the head obligingly dies. The determined innocent-in-distress, Miss Standfield, has heroically, melodramatically, cheated fate and triumphed against all odds. Though diversified, the incidents cited above all emphasize "violence, physical disaster, and emotional agony" which is both Gothic and melodramatic. King starkly polarizes and exaggerates innocence and malignancy for intensified emotional effect.

King's drastic, violent subject matter fits in with his essentially Gothic themes. He stresses the primordial power and pervasiveness of the unknown, the irrationality and unpredictability of the human psyche, and the moral reality of good and evil. King's metaphysics of the Dark Fantastic provides a contemporary rendering of concepts that have permeated Gothicism for more than two centuries. King treats the Dark Fantastic as an environment where the primitive, superstition, and rudimentary incarnations of good and evil hold sway. In such an environment, those who refuse to take the fantastic seriously or who continue to explain it in terms of the realistic are usually its victims. How valid, King asks, are the empirical and psychological paradigms upon which contemporary society relies to explain reality? And what of the nature of reality itself? Should one conclude that reality is chaotic and menacing? Can subjective phenomena such as the Dark Fantastic be understood objectively? King makes, moreover, a highly plausible assertion about the relationship of the known to the unknown: the territory of the unknown is immense and probably expanding, not diminishing, despite the increasing sophistication of modern investigative methods. Since King deals with the volatile, explosive behavioral eruptions are to be expected. The plot, characterization, rhetoric, and world view of his fiction support these thematic premises and may be viewed, in melodramatic terms, as vehement arguments for them.

Critical consensus holds that melodrama stresses plot over character, plot which relies considerably upon coincidence and accident. Melodramatic plots feature rapid movements from one crisis to another and frequently terminate in death crises, or they accentuate "crucial times in life that seem to determine one's fate once and for all." King's characteristically fast-moving and episodic plots often depend upon coincidence to link together a series of crises which hinge on or end in death. He builds *The Stand* around several subplots which trace the lives of half a dozen people who try to survive a plague that destroys virtually the entire population of the earth. In order to survive, the main characters must surmount disaster after disaster. Above all, they must avoid the Dark Man, Randall Flagg, and finally confront him—in each case they are at risk. Everyone encounters hazards in the form of emotional agony, encounters with death or near misses, and the need to kill. Nick Andros loses his lover, Rita, to a drug overdose, Mother Abagail must stare down Flagg's menacing animal familiars on a lonely Nebraska road, and Harold Lauder must deal with maddening jealously after the woman he loves rejects him for another. *The Stand* ends in a holocaust when an atomic bomb destroys Flagg's assembled forces. *The Dead Zone* opens with the protagonist's dangerous fall while ice skating as a youth, proceeds to an auto accident which leaves him in a coma for five years, and then traces his encounters with a rapist-murderer. Before the novel closes, he tries to assassinate a diabolical politician, only to be shot in the attempt. One seldom finds a dull—or normal—moment. Clearly, much of what happens to Smith seems accidental or coincidental, particularly his astounding awakening and apparently full recovery from a lengthy coma.

King uses a variety of specific plot devices, moreover, to keep the level of suspense high in his crisis fiction. Short, fast-paced, rapidly changing scenes are commonplace, notably in *'Salem's Lot, The Stand,* and *The Shining.* Though his novels tend to be long, he breaks narrative detail down into many miniature, self-contained episodes, a favorite tactic of melodramatists. Multiple narrative viewpoints are another suspense tactic. In *The Stand* and *'Salem's Lot* he tells the story from the vantage points of many characters, often switching points of view as he changes chapters. The effect is both panoramic and provocative because important details are provided in small increments.

King likewise creates suspense with the thriller tactic of ending chapters on a climactic high note which whets the reader's curiosity, or by providing clues and hints which create a state of nervous anticipation. As it draws to a close, *The Shining* evolves into a continuous chase scene, a suspense device in itself. Danny Torrance has, in fact, been the object of a chase since the novel opened. An early chapter ends with Danny being stung by wasps while he sleeps, another when the ghost of Room 217 tries to strangle him, and a third when the hedge animals pursue him through the snow to the front porch of the Overlook Hotel. The suspense generated at the end of each chapter holds the reader's attention: one grows more curious about who or what will be Danny's final pursuer. King fancies murder-mystery plots and effectively utilizes the suspense inherent in such plots. In *Cujo,* Donna Trenton and her son turn up missing and the planting of clues begins. The police discover Donna's car has vanished, Vic Trenton tells them about the taunting note he received from Donna's ex-lover, Steve Kemp, and the police soon apprehend Kemp. Once the clues rest in the hands of the authorities, the reader waits eagerly for them to deduce that Donna took the car to Joe Camber's garage for repairs and wonders how long it will take for her to be rescued from Cujo.

An equally important way of creating thrills is intrinsic to the Gothic genre itself. The deliberate, necessary blurring of appearance and reality in most of King's fiction keeps the reader uncertain and therefore attentive to plot developments. In *The Mist* a group of people huddles inside a supermarket while an impenetrable, acrid mist blankets the world outside and carnivorous creatures prowl around. What the creatures may be, where they came from, how they might behave, and the extent to which insanity has infected those inside the market are all uncertain matters. The ambiguity of the situation makes distinctions between truth and falsehood problematical at best. A similar motif appears in *'Salem's Lot*—the Lot has been invaded by a vampire and his familiar. Is an "invasion" by a vampire possible, or no more than a mass hallucination? If vampires are real, might they be killed by the methods folklore prescribes? Who faces the greatest danger from the undead? Few of these questions allow for definite answers and suspense grows out of the uncertainty.

A final suspense gambit, clearly a stock melodramatic one, consists of delaying the "inevitable and wholly foreseen" denouement. Perhaps King's clearest and most emphatic use of this tactic occurs in *Christine,* the story of a 1958 Plymouth inhabited by the demonic spirit of its former owner, Roland LeBay. Arnie Cunningham, a lonely, socially isolated teenager, becomes frenzied as soon as he passes LeBay's house and notices the car for sale. It becomes apparent from the outset that Christine has a relentless supernatural grip on Arnie and that he will readily do her bidding. The plot makes it equally clear that Arnie's closest friend, Dennis Guilder, suspects and fears Christine's malign influence. A romantic and a revenge plot intervene, but the denouement methodically arrives: Christine turns Arnie into a human lackey and Dennis finally succeeds in destroying the evil machine.

King's emphasis on fast-moving, thrilling plots moves his work in the direction of another melodramatic convention, allegorically simple good and evil characters whose appearances correspond with their inner natures. He typically delineates such characters, moreover, as extremes of vice or virtue, freely adopting the Gothic convention that neurotic and obsessional emotional dynamics are the aspects of a character's psyche to be stressed, in addition to the Gothic preoccupation with guilt, fear, and madness. His characters act more out of compulsion than out of free choice. Like many other melodramatists, King plays up the consistent dual result of compulsion: victimization by a variety of aggressors, including nature, society and evil individuals, and subsequent aggression. Finally, characterization in King fits in with the traditional melodramatic striving after pathetic effects. Jack Torrance, protagonist-turned-antagonist of *The Shining,* suffers from a variety of unresolved psychological problems, including memories of a family-abusing father, alcoholism, and an explosive temper. When he arrives at the Overlook, Jack is driven to discover its dark secrets by his inner demons of guilt, paranoia, and self-destructiveness.

These inner demons join forces with the demons who inhabit the Overlook to transform Jack into a victim and then into an aggressor. The amount of free will he possesses remains open to serious question from the story's outset.

King portrays Carrie White as a victim from early childhood until death. Denied a normal maturation and social life by her mother's religious fanaticism, she becomes the perpetual butt of jokes and harbors fantasies of vengeance against her many tormentors. After Carrie's humiliation at the prom, fantasies evolve into aggressive obsessions, and then into overt madness during her telekinetic vendetta against Chamberlain. Surely madness compromises the matter of free will, yet Carrie's dilemma loses none of its pathos. The reader can easily sympathize with her because of her frustrated, empty life and because she possesses powers which mystify and perhaps control her. Carrie's vendetta, of course, also creates sympathy for the innocent victims who must pay for her lifetime of deprivation. Driven by a messianic desire to save civilization, John Smith in *The Dead Zone* has the ability to "see" the future. But his second sight reveals to him only the dark side of awareness—he can predict what will be, but can rarely convince others. A melodramatic simplicity stands out in Smith's character when King plays him off against his two primary antagonists, a rapist-murderer and a ruthless politician—obviously society can only profit from his exposure of these evildoers. Still, society refuses to listen, preferring to suspect Smith and his "gift." This pariah-like treatment intensifies Smith's obsession to carry out his quest, and pathos mixes with irony as he pushes onward to save his uncaring fellow man. Predictably, Smith dies as he lived, only vaguely aware of the mysterious forces which drive his personality. He does not pause for detailed reflection. He acts.

The single-natured yet relatively complex villain acts as the moving force in melodrama generally, and in Gothic melodrama demonic-seeming villains predominate. King's villains blend into the tradition of Gothic melodrama: monopathic, relentless, obsessed, they are his most fully realized and intriguing characters. Randall Flagg is literally a demon, a shape-shifter who can become a man, an animal, or a disembodied force. Evil displays itself in Flagg's very appearance, for those who dream of him see only a faceless man. Though Flagg may be surrounded by a supporting cast of criminals and semi-demons, he has no rival as *The Stand's* most interesting villain. Harold Lauder and Nadine Cross rediscover a truism, that all who serve Flagg eventually become his pawns. The Dark Man's cruelty knows no limits: he crucifies his victims, turns them into slobbering imbeciles, or hurls them from the upper floors of buildings. He broods endlessly over his relentless ambition to destroy his enemies in Boulder, led by the saintly Mother Abagail, and works tirelessly to build an arsenal. Both demon and workaholic, Flagg eventually falls victim to another melodramatic con-

vention, namely that "Evil can only destroy itself, no matter how hard it tries." John Rainbird, the huge, grotesquely scarred Indian of *Firestarter,* looms as the most physically conspicuous Gothic villain in King's fiction. His sinister freakishness evokes pathos when he encounters Charlie McGee, the innocent adolescent heroine. Here, beyond doubt, appearances alone are reliable measures of good and evil. Rainbird lives for a single purpose, to kill, doing so with ingenuity and pleasure. A creature of almost pure malignancy, monopathic, devoid of qualities higher than a powerful survival instinct. Rainbird dominates the novel. Before Andy and Charlie McGee can escape from The Shop, they must confront him, must either destroy him or be destroyed.

In constant danger themselves, women in Gothic melodrama often become a source of danger to others as well. "King follows this convention of characterization closely, establishing his female characters, for the most part, as vulnerable stereotypes in order to make the convention operate more effectively. Soon after the Torrance family's arrival at the Overlook, Wendy turns into a target of Jack's mania. In order to fight back, she jeopardizes Danny by using him as a psychological weapon or a bargaining chip. Susan Norton, a heroine-turned-predator in *'Salem's Lot* is coveted by the vampire Barlow. Susan signals danger for the novel's two main protagonists, Ben and Mark, because of her close relationship with both before she became a vampire. Fran Goldsmith of *The Stand* suffers as the object of Harold Lauder's unrequited love. Even though she finds Lauder's diary and realizes that he plans revenge by killing Stu Redman, her new lover, she cannot determine where and when Lauder will strike, or whether he intends to kill her also. In the end, Fran becomes both victim and threat when Lauder decides to retaliate by detonating a hidden bomb at a meeting of the Boulder citizens' council where Stu will be present; not surprisingly, several innocent people perish. Women, then, generally serve as targets of villainy and objects of pathos so that King's male villains can remain the most powerful figures and the initiators of his fiction's primary action.

Small children and elderly people, Michael Booth argues, serve to "reinforce pathetic effects" in melodrama, and this is their primary purpose in King's fiction. The theme of virtue in distress, a convention of the sentimental novel, King applies primarily to children. Tad Trenton in *Cujo* surely merits pity because he is at the mercy of a panoply of forces he cannot understand: hunger, thirst, a distressed mother, a rabid dog, and supernatural powers. Billy Drayton's position in *The Mist* offers little improvement. The boy has lost his mother, gotten trapped in a crowd of increasingly demented strangers, and been singled out as a sacrificial offering to propitiate carnivorous beasts. Charlie McGee's dilemma may be the most pitiable of all, for she is "gifted" with pyrokinesis, a talent which causes her endless anxiety.

If pyrokinesis itself were not problem enough, The Shop captures and uses her as a psychological guinea pig, John Rainbird lusts after her, and she must use her "gift" to kill nearly the entire staff at The Shop's compound. King's child characters are purposely one-dimensional, stereotypical innocents-in-distress whose misfortunes invariably invoke pity. He treats the elderly in similar fashion—for example, Jud Crandall in *Pet Sematary,* Matt Burke in *'Salem's Lot,* and Mother Abagail in *The Stand* each of whom faces a hazardous situation, a superior human opponent, or the supernatural. Like the children, these three must cope with complex problems alone, and their physical infirmities parallel the physical immaturity of the children. Pathos arises from the reader's fear that the older people, despite their heroic efforts, cannot finally escape the status of dependents. When the elderly die at the villain's hands or in the battle against him, however, they at least assure themselves of the mildly heroic stature reserved for virtuous characters in the sentimental tradition.

King relies upon bombastic rhetoric, a fundamental part of Gothic melodrama, to underscore the effects of his plotting and characterization. In the following passage from *'Salem's Lot,* Straker, the human familiar of the vampire Barlow, has just strung young Mark Petrie from a ceiling beam to wait for Barlow's return. Straker cannot resist teasing his victim: "You're trembling young master . . . your flesh is white—but it will be whiter! Yet you need not be so afraid. My Master has the capacity for kindness. . . . There is only a little sting, like the doctor's needle, and then sweetness. . . . You will go see your father and mother, yes? You will see them after they sleep." This sarcastic gloating naturally encourages the reader's sympathy for the helpless boy, and emotions polarize, the normal effect of bombast. Straker's bombast echoes the good-evil dichotomies found elsewhere in the novel, the juxtaposition of totally negative and purely positive. Carrie White's mother indulges in an equally blatant outburst when she tries to discourage Carrie from making a dress for the prom: "'Take it off, Carrie. We'll go down and burn it in the incinerator together, and then pray for forgiveness. We'll do penance.' Her eyes began to sparkle with the strange, disconnected zeal that came over her at events which she considered to be tests of faith. 'I'll stay home from work and you'll stay home from school. We'll pray. We'll ask for a Sign. We'll get us down on our knees and ask for the Pentecostal fire.'" Anything but subtle, Mrs. White's diatribe provokes confrontation, as melodramatic bombast usually does. Rhetoric magnifies the emotional conflicts that divide Carrie and her mother, branding Mrs. White as the aggressor and Carrie as the victim. Predictably, her mother's bluntly emotional appeal prompts Carrie to make an emphatically emotional response—a direct, uncompromising denial.

King's handling of subject matter, plot, characterization, and rhetoric implies a world view consistent with the world view of melodrama. Melodrama emphasizes the equitable rewarding of virtue and punishment of vice, and perpetuates the "fantasy of a world that operates according to our heart's desires." Since melodrama sets before us a world of clarity, simplicity, either-or dichotomies, and absolutes, appearance and reality conveniently correspond. Melodrama stresses as well fate and fate's victims. Whether or not fate figures as a cosmic culprit, melodrama encourages pity for victims and outrage at evildoers. Several of King's theories about horror fiction align themselves with the melodramatic world view. A major purpose of such fiction, he asserts, is to "confirm our own good feelings about the status quo by showing us extravagant visions of what the alternative might be." The writer of horror fiction functions, therefore, as "an agent of the status quo," the norm, operating according to what could be construed as a fantasy of a universe governed according to certain fixed principles. Horror stories, he argues, are "conservative," essentially the same as the morality plays of earlier centuries. In effect, horror stories, like other species of melodrama, support a conventional morality. The horror story's "strict moralities," in fact, make it a "reaffirmation of life and good will and simple imagination." King defines the horror story, finally, as an "invitation to lapse into simplicity," a definition which supports the melodramatic preoccupation with absolutes, extremes, dichotomies.

> **An accomplished melodramatic strategist, King understands horror fiction's formulaic nature and that a formula writer must blend conventions with inventions. His Gothic melodrama provides the "emotional security" inherent in anticipated, standardized subject matter, settings, character and plot types, and themes, while the exciting effects he seeks often derive from his innovative experiments with the familiar.**
>
> **—James Egan**

King's fictive practices confirm his belief in the world view of melodrama. Sensationalistic vice tends to be punished grimly: John Rainbird is incinerated, Randall Flagg flees to the nether world, and Jack Torrance forfeits his soul to the transcendent evil of the Overlook. Although not all of King's villains are punished so drastically, their ends are invariably frustrated. As demonstrated earlier, the innocent suffer abundantly, but suffering frequently vindicates their purity or rightness. This premise seems particularly true of child characters. Mark Petrie of *'Salem's Lot* believes in the supernatural and in vampire lore, a belief shared by few of the adults he deals with. Mark loses his parents, his friends and nearly his life; however, his suspicions finally prove correct.

John Smith of *The Dead Zone,* a childlike adult, undergoes a similar experience: the well-meaning Smith meets with recurring skepticism and frustration. Yet, in the book's climactic confrontation scene his suspicions about Gregg Stillson are justified—Stillson reveals his villainy when he holds a child in front of him to ward off Smith's bullets. King's dependence upon stereotypical figures, moreover, reinforces a world view that accentuates absolutes, clarity, and simplicity. Since characters are usually delineated as extremes of good or bad, reader recognition of a particular character's nature, motivations, and values rarely proves difficult. Again, in view of the one-dimensional nature of characters, the changes they undergo are easily anticipated and not unduly complex. Nothing will cause a Stillson or a Barlow, for example, to relent in his pursuit of a singular, clearly announced goal. King also provides clarity by means of his characters' preferences for immediate, direct action over lengthy, involved introspection. The major decisions they make often take on an either-or simplicity. All characters in *The Stand,* major or minor, must choose between the goodness of Mother Abagail and the evil of the Dark Man—the moral middle ground quickly vanishes for both character and reader. The bombastic rhetoric to which King's villains, particularly, seem addicted further illustrates the world of moral and psychological extremes in which they function. Bombast reduces potentially complex issues to simple, emotionally charged ones, establishing morally convenient polarizations. Plot, finally, moves so rapidly from crisis to crisis that it traps characters in the identities they assume early in a story. This crisis plotting necessitates limited, often fated characters who change little, irrespective of the dilemmas that assail them. Though it often appears to generate ambiguity, plotting probably resolves at least as much ambiguity as it creates.

An accomplished melodramatic strategist, King understands horror fiction's formulaic nature and that a formula writer must blend conventions with inventions. His Gothic melodrama provides the "emotional security" inherent in anticipated, standardized subject matter, settings, character and plot types, and themes, while the exciting effects he seeks often derive from his innovative experiments with the familiar. As suggested earlier, King evokes horror and fear by treating a variety of sensational subject matter: gruesome deaths, torture, sexual aberrations, grave-robbing, a worldwide plague, and the like. He offers a haunted house in *'Salem's Lot,* a haunted hotel in *The Shining,* and a wide range of demons, vampires, monstrous, quasi-human villains, and occult powers. Ventures into the unknown, his plots dramatize confrontations with immanent evil, the dark side of the human psyche, and with transcendent evil, the unfathomable mysterium.

King's variations in the formulas of Gothic melodrama are generally noteworthy and often striking. *Christine* features a haunted automobile, *Cujo* a dog inhabited by the malingering spirit of a psychotic murderer, and *The Shining* a menagerie of hedge animals seeking human prey. Technically, King has not created a new species of Gothic being in each instance, but he surely has made substantial changes in the conventional werewolf or ghost figure. Even his relatively traditional villains evoke contemporary versions of the freakish: Randall Flagg recalls Charles Manson and Frank Dodd the sexual deviate whose bizarre exploits are chronicled in tabloids. King's "wild-talent" novels (*Carrie, The Shining, The Dead Zone, Firestarter*) represent a dramatic innovation in the Gothic convention of the character who possesses extreme "sensibility." He substitutes telekinesis, pyrokinesis, and other forms of parapsychological sensitivity for the heightened emotions of a figure such as Poe's Roderick Usher. The protagonists of the "wild-talent" stories each manifest an advanced awareness or power that sets them apart from the rest of humanity. King's settings fulfill a dual purpose, providing novelty of a sort while simultaneously encouraging a strong sense of reader identification. Even though twentieth-century Gothic settings have grown increasingly localized and familiar, traces of remoteness and the unfamiliar still remain. King has all but obliterated those traces. References to rock music, media celebrities, politicians, and miscellaneous easily recognized items of popular culture stand out in his work. Paul McCartney, Elvis Presley, and Walter Cronkite are each referred to in *The Dead Zone,* along with Arthur Bremmer and a woman named Moore, two would-be political assassins who aimed at George Wallace and Gerald Ford, respectively. In *Firestarter,* Mr. Coffee and Cremora are essential parts of Cap Hollister's office equipment, and in *Carrie,* King cites *The Reader's Digest* as the source of a story about the White case. King's "brand-names" approach to setting emphatically asserts that Gothic horror cannot be dismissed as obscure and remote; on the contrary, it has an immediate, domestic, and specifically American quality. In short, King has democratized and universalized the Dark Fantastic without depending solely on myth.

A final innovation involves plot and works similarly. Often a large plot segment consists of either a realistic feature of another genre or an entire realistic sub-genre itself. *The Dead Zone* follows the conventions of the political novel closely, so that Gregg Stillson's rise to power identifies the work as both a political novel and a Gothic tale. Early on, Stillson becomes a successful candidate for office and steadily acquires power, approximating in several ways the stereotype of the fascist manipulator found in modern American political fiction. The reader can witness in Stillson's career the machinations of actual demagogues such as Hitler and Huey Long, both of whom are mentioned in the story, along with Sinclair Lewis' treatment of demagoguery, *It Can't Happen Here.* The political plot of *The Dead Zone* suggests that King intends for the Gothic and the realistic to overlap until they are virtually indistinguishable. His plotting may be considered both an argument for the pervasiveness of the Dark Fantastic and a response to the formulaic demand for novelty.

The popular success of King's fiction grows out of his skillful blending of the Gothic, the melodramatic, and the formulaic. King's own observations on the horror genre suggest several reasons why his work has enjoyed such popularity. These comments deserve attention because they indicate the extent to which he understands and controls his medium and his craft. Horror, he points out, stimulates the reader's curiosity; we are simply fascinated by the dark side, for example, by freaks, who are morbidly "attractive" yet "forbidden" and therefore appealing. Horror satiates our curiosity about such "forbidden" delights since "horror is, by its very nature, intriguingly alien and aberrant." The "purpose" of horror fiction, as he sees it, is to "explore taboo lands," to probe the anxieties of its readers; at the least, tales of terror stimulate "simple aggression and . . . morbidity." Horror has proven itself capable of localizing and making concrete our "free-floating anxieties" of all sorts, political, economic, and psychological. Fears, of course, are universal, and if they can be intensified and made immediate, they will appeal. Clearly, horror caters to the reader's rebelliousness as well; we read to dare the nightmare, to show "that we can ride this roller coaster." Society, in fact, sanctions horror, recognizing in the idiom an invitation "to indulge in deviant, antisocial behavior by proxy." The reader can rebel because he has the equivalent of mob approval, having joined a conspiracy to "destroy the outsider."

Perhaps the most pervasive appeal of horror derives from its indulgence of the reader's innate fascination with death; horror invites us by providing a "rehearsal for our own deaths," by treating death as though it were a "single powerful spectacle" seen through the eyes of a child. Catharsis, escape, and the return to normality, however, must also be part of horror's aesthetic in order for that aesthetic to appeal to readers so powerfully. The "melodies of the horror tale," according to King, "are simple and repetitive . . . but the ritual outletting of these emotions seems to bring things back to a more stable and constructive state again." One partakes of horror, in part, to reestablish his "feelings of essential normality." Readers long for escape from the abundance of horrors real life surrounds them with, and fictive horror obliges by helping us to "rediscover the smaller . . . joys of our own lives . . . by showing us the miseries of the damned."

King's analysis of the aesthetics of horror establishes numerous credible reasons for the appeal of his own fiction. The melodramatic and formulaic qualities of his work imply several additional reasons, for melodramatic and formulaic literature have traditionally enjoyed considerable popularity. Generally, his aesthetic of horror can be explained in terms of the melodramatic and the formulaic. King notes that horror fiction endures because it meets universal needs, essentially the same claim that Daniel Gerould makes for melodrama: "Melodrama is material available to everyone, its devices, characters and situations instantly known, implanted by the culture in the psyche of each of its members. This material may easily be aroused, activated, used." Robert Heilman concurs when he argues that audiences cannot do without melodrama, not only because it is exciting and invigorating in itself, but because it takes us away from complex and "dull or unproductive" contemplations of the "tragic consciousness." Melodrama, then, seems pervasive and permanent. King stresses that horror literature elicits fear and terror, both of which are highly appealing, and melodrama itself evokes analogous emotional reactions. Gerould claims that, owing to its "primal theatrical energy of aggression, anxiety, and eroticism," melodrama caters to the "eternal human longing to be terrified." John Cawelti has demonstrated that the idea of melodrama cannot be dissociated from violence, sensationalism, and terror. The success of any melodramatist, in short, may well depend upon his ability "to feel and project fear."

King considers horror fiction to be simple, explicit, repetitive, and direct rather than complex. Melodrama and formula literature could be characterized similarly, and like horror fiction they make ample allowances for escapism. Simplicity itself often proves exhilarating, a welcome relief which most readers can, at least occasionally, tolerate large amounts of. King magnifies and intensifies emotion, emotion which "takes us out of ourselves" and entices us to escape. He centers much of his fiction around violence, tacitly recognizing that "because it rouses extreme feelings, the representation of violence is an effective means of generating the experience of escape" from boredom and routine. King argues as well that horror fiction regularly attempts to probe taboos, a concern it shares with formula literature in general; the investigation of taboos "permits the audience to explore in fantasy the boundary between the permitted and the forbidden." Like horror fiction, melodrama and the formulaic are emotionally charged, aimed at producing thrills and allowing the reader to violate taboos vicariously and harmlessly.

> **The reasons why Stephen King has become virtually a brand name during the past decade become apparent when one examines his work objectively.**
> —*James Egan*

Several additional features of King's work, all of them intrinsic to melodrama, further account for its popularity. Monopathy or oneness in characters produces a corresponding reaction in readers: as a result of his contact with melodramatic virtue and vice, one experiences a unity of feeling. Since he does not need to deal with a full range of emotions, the reader's reactions will be incomplete but they will also be intense and carefully channeled. Melodrama presents, moreover, a "clear menace," something we search for subconsciously, a menace which demands an emphatic denial. King calls up an abundance of such menaces: perversely evil characters, demons, a nuclear accident, and a plague, to name a few. Thus, the reader can easily determine that "guilt belongs to monstrous individuals," such as Flagg or Rainbird, with whom he is "not identified." Melodrama likewise employs the "disaster principle," stimulating us to feel the uncomplicated responses of pity for victims and indignation at evildoers. The "disaster principle" provides the additional benefit of self-pity when the reader identifies with an innocent character, for example, John Smith or Tad Trenton. King entices his readers with a number of psychological rallying points in addition to a variety of escape routes, both overt and subtle, and they respond to these appeals overwhelmingly, with a narrowly focused, intense enthusiasm.

The reasons why Stephen King has become virtually a brand name during the past decade become apparent when one examines his work objectively. He has given careful consideration to the aesthetics of horror fiction and has attained a sophisticated awareness of his strengths and weaknesses as a practitioner of a popular genre. King's treatments of the Gothic and macabre are the opposite of impulsive meanderings—he consistently seeks to create a "single powerful spectacle." That goal dictates a strategy which can best be described as melodramatic and formulaic, and one which places him in a loosely defined but densely populated tradition that has existed from the beginning of literary history. Irrespective of one's attitude toward violence or sensationalism, King deserves credit for understanding his subject matter, craft, and audience well. King proposed in *'Salem's Lot* to celebrate "superstition and ignorance," his synonyms for the mysterious, the supra-rational, and the anti-scientific. His wildfire popularity suggests that he has found a large audience willing to share in that celebration.

Michael McDowell (essay date 1986)

SOURCE: "The Unexpected and the Inevitable," in *Kingdom of Fear: The World of Stephen King,* edited by Tim Underwood and Chuck Miller, New American Library, 1986, pp. 83-95.

[*In the following essay, McDowell asserts that King's novels are effective because of their rhythm.*]

It was with some hesitation that I agreed to write about Stephen King's work. I was trained as an academic, with an eye towards analysis and criticism, but now I have only contempt for the sapping methods of literary "appreciation" taught in colleges and graduate schools. The idea of analyzing a volume of writing that I think very good seems unappealing and pointless. Increasingly, I find myself in the critical vein that either gushes, "Oh God it's great you've got to read it!" or moans, "Can you believe that anybody would publish this," or is silent from indifference. So that I think the best—and probably most helpful—reaction to King's work is a simple, "Oh God I've read everything, and I haunt the bookstores waiting for the next one."

Certainly, that is the common reaction.

Another hesitation is that my view of King and his work is probably skewed. In the first place, I know the man, and like him very much. For another thing, I am a writer of occult fiction myself, and therefore read King with a more specialized eye than his usual admirer. Usually, in fact, to be read by another writer is like having a carpenter over. He's not going to admire your taste in decoration, he's going to be looking at how you *built* the house. You try to show him the new living room furniture, and he wants to know what kind of cement you put in the foundations. When I read Stephen King, I'm looking to see how he puts the damn books and stories together, and what makes them stand so straight and solid.

This innate, technical evaluation is in operation every time I read a book of fiction. (For pleasure, I have to make do with books on astronomy and particle physics.) I pick up a book with a promisingly lurid cover. On page twelve I've guessed not only the premise, but five important plot points, and the ending. I always know what's coming next. Discordances of tone grate. Misshapen or improbable dialogue sounds in my mind like Hanna-Barbera voices. It's a great tribute to King that by some point in the story, I no longer think about the cement in the cellar foundations and don't care how tight the sashes are in the window frames. I'm simply propelled room to room through the narrative, as by an energetic host, gaping and wary and fearing. It can take me a great while to finish one of King's books, simply because he transforms me into a timid reader. "Oh God," I think, "he's not going to do *that,* is he?" I put the book down for a space, till I have courage to pick it up again and make sure that, indeed, he is going to do it.

He always does, of course. No wet fuses. And the climaxes are exactly right. The dynamite is laid, stick by stick, and every one of them goes off, in a precise, rhythmic pattern.

Which brings me to the point of this little essay.

Stephen King's rhythm.

It is what stands out most for me in the books, it is what makes me sweat with jealousy when I read him, it is what—I suspect—makes the narratives so enormously effective.

It has become increasingly apparent to me that books rise or fall by the rhythm of the narrative. A story can carry you along—despite lapses in grammar, probability, or tone—if the rhythm is right. This rhythm is manifest in many ways, and in different measurements—that is to say that there are rhythms that are apparent on a scale of kilometers (an entire book), and rhythms that are manifest on a scale of centimeters (a sentence or two), and everything in between. In fact, a novel may be looked at as a series of interlocking rhythms. Five sentences that are rhythmically just right form a good paragraph; five good paragraphs, set up just so, make a good section to be separated by asterisks; six good sections make a very good chapter; and then all you have to do is write thirty of those, arrange them in the right order, smooth down the lumps, and now you have a good, rhythmic book—one that propels the reader forward. Prologue to *fin.*

People out there who don't write books, or who write books thoughtlessly, are saying, "That can't possibly be how it's done." But it is. It's how Stephen King writes, and I know because, one, it's how I write and I recognize the phenomenon when I see it; and two, he's told me so.

Of course you can't freehand a chart of arcs and say, "Well, here's the shape and rhythm of my new novel." But you can have a story in mind, and start writing it. The rhythm begins to develop on its own accord. It's astonishing how quickly it's established—usually for me by the end of the second chapter. And every book's rhythm is different, just as the tone of every book is different. Then, as you proceed further and further into the story, the rhythm becomes more complex, and more demanding. You can't always feel when it's right, but by God, you surely do know when it's *wrong.* When it's wrong—and you're conscientious—you stop and fix it, and then you go on. At the end, you sit down, read the book through—not for spelling errors, not for the rightness of the dialogue or the plausibility of motivation—but to make sure that it reads well. Which is to say, to make certain that the rhythm is right.

Some scenes, you'll invariably find, are overlong considering their importance. This would mean that a reader would spend longer with them than he should. It's a fault most obvious in transitions between disjointed sections. So you trim them back so that the amount of space they take up on the printed page is commensurate with their relative importance to the narrative.

On the other hand, some important scene may not be given its proper weight in the story simply because you wrote it too briefly. Then, even if you got everything in the first time, you have to write a few more pages, simply so that the reader will be slowed down a bit during the important bits.

Of course, there are no hard and fast rules about length *versus* importance. You know when it's wrong, and you can have a pretty good idea when it's right. If you write as much as King does (or as I do), the process of meting out space in a narrative becomes second nature. You don't often get it wrong. There's a little mental tape measure that reads off in pretty exact measurements. "This scene ought to get twelve pages. This transition ought to be three paragraphs and a snatch of dialogue. This can't be more than a page and a half."

To illustrate:

A few months ago, Stephen King asked me to read through the manuscript of his new novel, *Misery,* and tell him what I thought. I gladly acceded to the request, and devoured the book. I liked it very much, and saw many things to praise, and very few to object to. I made one small suggestion for a refinement of cruelty, and King said, "Very nice. I'll add it. Anything else?"

"The climax needs one more beat," I said. "I have no idea what it should be, but you need about six more pages of *something.* To slow it down. Because now it's over too quickly. Just a beat, that's all."

"I felt that," King replied. "But I was hoping I was wrong. I wasn't. I'll fix it."

And I know that he will have fixed it by the time the book is published. Because I've never come across even so small a lapse as that in one of his published books. I was gratified to find that error in rhythm, in fact, because it showed me that he had to work (even if only a little) to establish his perfectly rhythmic narratives. It wasn't *all* sheer and casual talent.

What this also shows, I think, is that the process of creating a rhythm actually exists. When I said that *Misery*'s climax needed an extra beat, King knew exactly what I was talking about. A build-up needs a pay-off, and the pay-off has to be in proper proportion to the build-up. Otherwise, the story is unbalanced, and in some way the reader will be dissatisfied. All through King's books, there are smaller build-ups and pay-offs, culminating in a final pay-off that balances everything that came before. One great arc encompasses all the smaller ones. The pattern may be worked out subconsciously, or by instinct, but it's still no accident.

I remember when a consciousness of this kind of narrative rhythm first came into focus for me. It wasn't after studying literature through four years of college and three of graduate school. It was reading **The Shining.** And it was the scariest moment in the book, the point at which the boy Danny, having willed away the vision of the dead, drowned woman in Room 217, finds her bloated hands round his neck.

> Time passed. And he was just beginning to relax, just beginning to realize that the door must be unlocked and he could go, when the years-damp, bloated, fish-smelling hands closed softly around his throat and he was turned implacably around to stare into the dead and purple face.

What happens next?

What happens next is that we get a new chapter. And it's not a chapter telling us what happens to Danny, and whether he's killed, whether he's only injured, whether he's able to will the ghastly residue away. It's a chapter dealing with Jack's parents.

I never read ten pages so quickly in my life, desperate to know what had become of the boy.

And when I found him again, at the beginning of the *next* chapter, Danny had bruises on his neck and was half-catatonic—but he wasn't dead.

At that point, I put the book down, and I said, aloud, "What a cheap device!"

Then I immediately incorporated the technique into the book that I was writing at the time.

Now, of course, the trick seems obvious. Bring the narrative to a fever of suspense—and then maintain that suspense by switching focus to an unrelated incident. While some poor victim hangs over the edge of the cliff by a fraying rope, pebbles spilling into his face, we switch to his distressed girlfriend begging a skeptical park ranger for assistance in finding him. The boyfriend can hang there for quite a while, in fact, till we get back to him. It's a cheap use of rhythm, but done correctly, it works. And it may be done *so* well, in fact, that the manipulated reader feels nothing but a straightforward anxiety for the poor victim at the end of the rope.

For me, the great lesson of that narrative sequence from **The Shining** was the importance of rhythm. I'm faintly embarrassed that it took this sledgehammer example of the thing to show me that. Now, I'm happy to say, I can be appreciative of much subtler sequence rhythms in King's work.

I much admire **Rita Hayworth and Shawshank Redemption,** the first of the four novellas that comprise **Different Seasons,** and as I read it, I was astonished by the delicacy of the construction. To nearly any reader, it is apparent that the climax of the story will be the attempt of Andy Dufresne to escape from Shawshank prison. The middle part of the story consists of various legal attempts that Dufresne makes to avoid or to shorten his term in prison. His trial. His model prisoner attitude. His discovery of the real murderer. Each of these fails, as we know it will. Then, at last, he's left with only one solution—an escape from the prison. What we've been waiting for. Something clever, something harrowing.

And of course, I assumed, a great deal of suspense would be tied up in whether he makes it or not.

Here again, King astonished me.

Only three-quarters of the way into the narrative, I came across this paragraph:

> In 1975, Andy Dufresne escaped from Shawshank. He hasn't been recaptured, and I don't think he ever will be. In fact, I don't think Andy Dufresne even exists anymore. But I think there's a man down in Zihuatanego, Mexico named Peter Stevens. Probably running a very new small hotel in this year of our Lord 1977.

When I read that paragraph, I looked up from the book puzzled and shocked. I flipped to the end of the story, and saw that there was a good quarter of the narrative to go. Why give away the fact that Dufresne makes his escape, and survives? How would the rest of the story maintain a balance of suspense against what had come before?

The answer should have been obvious—the narrative maintained suspense through rhythm.

What I thought would come next was a detailing of the escape. But I was wrong.

What came next was the *discovery* of the escape by the consternated officials of the prison, told in completely satisfying detail. But still we didn't know *how* the escape was accomplished. And it is this that comes next, the narrator's methodical analysis of what *must* have happened, because it couldn't have happened any other way. Then at the last, a coda—the narrator's release from prison, and his resolve to join up with Dufresne in Mexico.

Thus, three very satisfying sections of narrative follow the "give-away" of Dufresne's successful escape, and each of them is a payoff for something set up earlier in the book. The corrupt prison officials' comeuppance. The method of Dufresne's harrowing escape. And—what came as a pleasant surprise—the resolution of the narrator's future.

None of these passages would have been half so effective if we'd been troubled with wondering whether Dufresne would succeed with his escape. That question put to rest in a brief paragraph, we're able to relish the solution of three more questions.

Rita Hayworth and Shawshank Redemption has a lovely, audacious shape, and I can't believe that it requires another writer to appreciate it fully.

There is another example of bold rhythm in *Apt Pupil,* the second and longest novella in *Different Seasons.* The very title of the piece leads us to believe that Todd will be instructed in Nazi Dussander's evil, and (because King never pulls his punches), we realize well before the end that Todd will take his rifle to the edge of the freeway and begin picking off motorists—in a feeble imitation of the concentration camps' commanders' power to decide, casually and arbitrarily, who is to live and who to die. That snipering will be the Apt Pupil's graduation exercise, and it will end the story. That's the Inevitable Conclusion to the story.

But I know that while King delivers the inevitable, he never delivers it in quite the way I expected it. If I'm waiting at the front door, waiting for the bell, he goes around to the back, and knocks.

So what, I wondered, would be the Surprise to temper the Inevitability?

Here's how *Apt Pupil* ends:

> *"I'm king of the world!"* he shouted mightily at the high blue sky, and raised the rifle two-handed over his head for a moment. Then, switching it to his right hand, he started towards that place above the freeway where the land fell away and where the dead tree would give him shelter.
>
> It was five hours later and almost dark before they took him down.

In other words, the snipering happens, but we don't see it. But all our worst imaginings—of what misery a young man with a rifle above a freeway can cause in the space of five hours—are excited by that simple, final sentence. This long story ends with a jolt precisely commensurate with what has gone before.

I remember when I first read that, I was shocked by its cold brevity. Then disturbed—because I sat back and thought to myself, "All right, just how many people did he kill, and who were they, and if I had been driving along that freeway, would he have picked *me* out for death?"

And then I nodded a little nod of professional acknowledgment to King, who had done it again. Provided me with the unexpected and the inevitable.

King likes horror movies. King has written them, and for every script he's written, he's probably seen three hundred. In a film, it is an easy matter to give the viewer a jolt. The hapless victim—let's make her a girl this time—climbs naked out of bed and peers through a darkened window, checking out that strange noise outside. She sees nothing. She turns back to her boyfriend, and says, "I didn't see any—" At that moment of course, a great hairy arm crashes through the window, grabs her around the throat, and a moment later, she spills backward through the sash in a shower of glass, never to be seen again. Later the boyfriend dies as well. (This is another in the "Fuck and Die" school of film production.)

Ominous music leads up to the jolt, the jolt comes in a *sforzando* of strings, and the audience gasps and represses (or does not repress) its screams.

There are times when [the rhythm of King's writing] is so important that the words themselves almost don't matter— when the sound of the words in the brain and their length and their alternation is to be considered much more than any specific meaning they convey.
—*Michael McDowell*

But how do you do the equivalent in a book?

To *see* a hand crash through the window when you're not expecting it is not the same thing as to read, "She turned away from the window and reassured her boyfriend that there was nothing outside. Then a great hairy arm crashed through the window and caught her around the neck."

Not the same thing at all.

The difficulty is this. In a film, you can have five minutes of real (or is it "reel"?) time leading up to the climactic moment, and then the climactic moment takes less than a second. You have no control over the speed or the sequence of the action.

You can't do that in a book, because you can't control a reader's pace. You can't say, "All right, Gentle Reader, here's a slow part where I'm building suspense. Wait a minute, I'm still building—feel that terror mount?—a couple of paragraphs more, just to make sure you're good and primed, and now—and now—*voy-la!*—here's the surprise! Here's the great hairy arm through the window, and my God, weren't you scared?"

I've read books like that. I've even said hypocritically nice things to authors who write after that fashion, and if I'm not damned for *that*, I won't be damned for anything.

You just can't do it the way the movies can.

Or can you?

King obviously can, because his books are genuinely frightening. They deliver honest jolts. And they do it—have you guessed?—through rhythm.

There are ways of slowing a reader down and speeding him up. They are, in their way, quite technical, and have to do with the length of sentences, the length of words within those sentences, with the length and the alternation of the paragraphs the sentences make up.

A succession of long paragraphs, each composed of long sentences with great big words in them, is a lulling read. A good writer can make such a passage almost hypnotic. Then a one-line paragraph can jolt you right out of that trance. From the same sequence in *The Shining,* dealing with Danny's exploration of Room 217:

> A long room, old fashioned, like a Pullman car. Tiny white hexagonal tiles on the floor. At the far end, a toilet with the lid up. At the right, a washbasin and another mirror above it, the kind that hides a medicine cabinet. To the left, a huge white tub on claw feet, the shower curtain pulled closed. Danny stepped into the bathroom and walked toward the tub dreamily, as if propelled from outside himself, as if this whole thing were one of the dreams Tony had brought him, that he would perhaps see something nice when he pulled the shower curtain back, something Daddy had forgotten or Mommy had lost, something that would make them both happy—
>
> So he pulled the shower curtain back.
>
> The woman in the tub had been dead for a long time . . .

Notice particularly how the last sentence of the paragraph describing the bathroom runs on, repetitious and soothing and dreaming. Then that's cut off by a single line of simple action—"So he pulled the shower curtain back"—which is given a paragraph of its own. Then the next paragraph begins in a terrible, matter-of-fact way—and that's the jolt.

When I say that the method for achieving this jolt is techni-

cal, I'm not suggesting that King did anything other than sit down at his keyboard and type out those very words, first draft, as they appear there. The technique is in his brain, and probably he doesn't know any way to write except in this casually efficient and effective manner. But to have constructed that passage in any other way would not have been either as efficient or effective. King's technique placed the words, the sentences, the paragraph breaks, the very punctuation in the manner that would precisely maximize the current of the jolt.

There are times when this rhythm is so important that the words themselves almost don't matter—when the sound of the words in the brain and their length and their alternation is to be considered much more than any specific meaning they convey. In the above passage, I would put the sequence, "as if this whole thing were one of the dreams Tony had brought him, that he would perhaps see something nice when he pulled the shower curtain back, something Daddy had forgotten or Mommy had lost, something that would make them both happy," into that category. The repetitious, stringalong nature of the passage is the giveaway—at least to me, who use it frequently—that it's the lulling rhythm at work on the reader here, and not the actual content of Danny's groping mind.

By the same token, there are ways of speeding a reader up.

One-sentence paragraphs is one. Short sentences within those short paragraphs.

Even sentence fragments to serve as paragraphs.

Rapid alteration of dialogue, with no adverbs (". . . , he admonished balefully") and as few identifying tags as possible (". . . , said the dead saleslady").

> **A bad writer may tell a story, and the story he tells may be a good one. But if he can't control the reader, the good story he tells won't be told well, and the reader won't be satisfied. I really do believe it is as simple as that.**
> **—*Michael McDowell***

Put so badly, these sound—once again—like the cheapest of the cheap devices. But they work, and good writers use them. From the first page to the last.

And, contrariwise, bad writers don't use them. A bad writer may tell a story, and the story he tells may be a good one. But if he can't control the reader, the good story he tells won't be told well, and the reader won't be satisfied. I really do believe it is as simple as that.

Someone once asked me what I thought horror fiction did. What its purpose was. (King is asked this question frequently as well. It is only a very little less annoying that "Where do you get your ideas?") I don't know what he stipulated as the purpose of horror fiction, but I replied that when I wrote horror fiction, I tried to take the improbable, the unimaginable, and the impossible, and make it seem not only possible—but inevitable.

That is to say, the writer of horror fiction propels—or tries to propel—the reader up in a spiraling succession of improbabilities, and convince him that there is no other way that the story could unfold. That he presents the reader, at every turn, with a surprise—that after a moment's consideration becomes an inevitability.

You want the reader to say to himself, "Oh God that was a surprise, and a scary one, and I should have seen it coming, but I didn't, and yes—the author is right—it couldn't have been any other way." (This is, of course, only a little better than reciting the splendid review that the *New York Times* is going to accord your next work.)

This combination of the Unexpected and the Inevitable is, I think, what King probably does best. The foundation for the success of our belief in his narrative is laid, as has been often said, in the crushing normality of his settings and characters. I would add also that his characters' thoughts are crushing normal as well. That's why we believe in them. The action unfolds with a semblance of worldly verisimilitude, and then the unexpected intrudes. The descriptions of the horrors tend to be flattened rather than heightened: "The woman in the bathtub had been dead for a long time . . ." (This is surely better, one can see, than "The terrified boy stared at the naked, corrupting, purulent, *grinning* corpse of what had once probably been a cheerful middle-aged woman . . ." Which is how some writers of horror fiction write, I'm sorry to say.) King's flatness in these descriptions accords the horrors the same legitimacy as his characters' lawn-mowers, and their thirst for a cold Pabst, and their tedious marital squabbles.

It is this rhythm of the mundane and the unnatural—the *crushingly* mundane and the *stupefyingly* unnatural, I think I can say—that provides the power of King's horror. That the same language is used for both gives a terrible credence to the reality of the unnatural. I admire Lovecraft—and considering King's tributary story *Jerusalem's Lot,* it appears that he did too. It may be that he still does, but there seems to me to be little left of that progenitor in King. No obscure eldritch adjectives, no *unthinkable* monstrosities, no *unnameable* deities, no *indescribable* horrors, and no straggling dead man's ravings to end a story as the flapping obscenity sweeps down out of the sky and bursts through the shutters. King's characters may go mad, King's narration does not. It remains clear-eyed, matter-of-factual, observing entirely too much for the reader's comfort.

(What King still has in common with Lovecraft is the overwhelming sense of place. Castle Rock is not as overtly sinister as the valley of the Miskatonic, but nasty things happen there. And if there's not an actual map of Castle Rock on King's bulletin board, I've a pretty good idea that if he were set down in that mythical municipality, he'd been able to get from the TasTee Freeze to the Dew Drop Inn without asking directions from a homicidal cop.)

In this regard, the alternation of the mundane with the unnatural, King employs a kind of flatness—an absence of rhythmic alternation. When the corpse trundles on in a King novel, there are no Bernard Herrmann strings in the background, but the same Muzak that was playing before plays on, to disconcerting effect. In this case, it is the *absence* of a perceptible rhythm that lends its heightening effect.

I don't really think it would matter if not a single reader of King's work understood, in a technical way, how his books are built on interconnecting and intersecting rhythms. For despite his narrative expertise, King's books work for most in a way that they perceive as visceral. And, as I say, I no longer belong to the camp that analyzes, draws apart, deduces formulae and sketches diagrams. I'm happy to say I'm on that side that passes around a book (not a reviewer's copy, but one paid for with American currency at a book store or a supermarket or a shop that sells cigars and lottery tickets) and says, "Hey listen, you got to read this, and I promise you, it'll give you fucking nightmares."

Carol A. Senf (essay date 1987)

SOURCE: "Donna Trenton, Stephen King's Modern American Heroine," in *Heroines of Popular Culture,* edited by Pat Browne, Bowling Green State University Popular Press, 1987, pp. 91-100.

[*In the following essay, Senf discusses the female protagonists of King's* Cujo *and asserts that "Donna especially in her display of courage becomes a new American heroine, a strong woman with whom women in the twentieth century can be proud to identify."*]

For the past ten years Stephen King has been an enormously popular writer, and part of the reason for that popularity is the fact that his books feature ordinary human characters with whom the reader can readily identify. Moreover these ordinary people become heroes and heroines because they confront unspeakable horrors with courage and conviction.

By far the strongest of King's heroines is Donna Trenton in *Cujo.* To establish her as a modern American heroine, King does two things: First he places her in a realistic environment and shows her confronting the same problems that face ordinary human beings today; second he deliberately contrasts her with the dependent women of earlier Gothic literature and horror films, the women her son Tad thinks of when he dreams of warning her about the monster in his closet: *"Be careful, Mommy, they* [monsters] *eat the ladies! In all the movies they catch the ladies and carry them off and eat them!"* (King's italics). Though Tad never confesses his fears to his mother, Donna is aware of the tradition of female weakness and passivity. A former librarian, she repeatedly compares herself—sometimes facetiously but more often seriously—to a damsel in distress and her husband to the knight who will rescue her. In fact, King reveals that Donna must abandon the notion that the heroine is someone to be rescued. Only then can she attempt to save both her son and herself from the rabid Cujo, a monster that King emphasizes is a symbol for all the evil forces against which human beings must struggle, only then can she become a suitable representative of the modern, more assertive woman.

In a similar fashion, Charity Camber, a working class version of the trapped American woman, accepts responsibility for herself and her son and escapes from a brutal and abusive husband. A lesser version of the heroine, Charity is also a strong and courageous woman with whom twentieth-century readers can be proud to identify.

By far the strongest of King's heroines is Donna Trenton in *Cujo.*
—*Carol A. Senf*

Although King is often identified as a writer of supernatural horror because of his early novels, *Salem's Lot* and *The Shining,* his emphasis on ordinary human life is clear from the very beginning of *Cujo,* which he prefaces with the following quotation from W. H. Auden's "Musee des Beaux Arts":

> About suffering they were never wrong,
> The Old Masters: how well they understood
> Its human position; how it takes place
> While someone else is eating or opening a window
> or just walking dully along . . .

By choosing this quotation, King emphasizes the human rather than the superhuman; and he distances himself still further from his early novels in the rest of *Cujo.* Reinforcing the ordinary quality of human suffering is the first page of the novel, which identifies the monster in Castle Rock, Maine, as a sick human being:

> He was not werewolf, vampire, ghoul, or unnameable creature from the enchanted forest or from the snowy wastes; he was only a cop named Frank Dodd with mental and sexual problems.

King is obviously playing with the readers' expectations. However, the figure of Frank Dodd, a sick and destructive human being rather than a vampire or a haunted house, will appear again and again in the novel, sometimes linked with Cujo, another example of an evil that occurs within the natural world:

> Screaming, he got both hands under the dog's muzzle again and yanked it up. For a moment, staring into those dark, crazed eyes . . . he thought: *Hello, Frank. It's you, isn't it? Was hell too hot for you?* (King's italics)

Despite Sheriff Bannerman's reference to Dodd's return from the grave, however, King expects the reader to recognize that Cujo and Dodd are both examples of evil within the natural world, not supernatural Evil.

In addition to being about natural evil, *Cujo* is about women. Although Bannerman, Joe Camber, and Gary Pervier are men victims of Cujo and Vic Trenton is practically destroyed by the death of his son, *Cujo*—more than King's other novels (with the possible exception of *Carrie*) focuses on women's experiences. From the first paragraph, which catalogues Frank Dodd's six victims—all women or young girls—to the last, the novel scrutinizes the lives of women in twentieth-century America.

Aware of male fears of women, King is able to use this understanding in his books. *Carrie's* extraordinary power is unleashed in one terrifying night that destroys an entire town, but *Cujo* reveals that women terrify men even with less extraordinary strength.
—*Carol A. Senf*

Danse Macabre, a work in which King combines autobiography with his analysis of the horror tradition, reveals that King understands the complexities of women's lives, especially the ways their lives are influenced by their relationships with men. For example, comments on the movie *Alien* illustrate his awareness of men's condescending attitudes to women:

> The Sigourney Weaver character, who is presented as tough minded and heroic up to this point, causes the destruction of the mothership *Nostromo . . .* by

going after the ship's cat. Enabling the males in the audience, of course, to relax, roll their eyes at each other, and say either aloud or telepathically, "Isn't that just like a woman?"

Furthermore King is aware that men's attitudes to women range far beyond gentle condescension to fear and outright hostility; and his discussion of the movie *The Stepford Wives* comments on men's hostility to liberated women. In fact, King is aware that he shares some of these fears:

> If *The Stepford Wives* concerns itself with what men want from women, then **Carrie** is largely about how women find their own channels of power, and what men fear about women and women's sexuality . . . which is only to say that, writing the book in 1973 . . . I was fully aware of what Women's Liberation implied for me and others of my sex. The book is . . . an uneasy masculine shrinking from a future of female equality. . . . Carrie White is a sadly misused teenager. . . . But she's also Woman, feeling her powers for the first time. . . .

Aware of male fears of women, King is able to use this understanding in his books. Carrie's extraordinary power is unleashed in one terrifying night that destroys an entire town, but **Cujo** reveals that women terrify men even with less extraordinary strength. Arriving on the scene after his wife has finally overcome Cujo, Vic Trenton wants to escape rather than offer her comfort for her ordeal:

> He didn't know what he had expected, but it hadn't been this. He had been afraid, but the sight of his wife . . . standing over the twisted and smashed thing in the driveway, striking it again and again with something that looked like a caveman's club . . . that turned his fear to a bright, silvery panic. . . . For one infinite moment, which he would never admit to himself later, he felt an impulse to throw the Jag in reverse and drive away . . . to drive forever. What was going on in this still and sunny door yard was monstrous.

Especially perceptive here are King's recognition that men rarely admit their fear of women openly and his use of the word "monstrous" to describe one man's response to a woman's exhibition of power. He knows that such exhibits are so rare that they inspire awe and terror.

Although **Cujo** culminates with Donna's horrifying ordeal and her need for exceptional courage, most of the novel takes place within the minds of Donna and Charity as they face more ordinary problems. Douglas Winter observes of the novel that its "storyline evolves about two marriages," and that both of these "marriages are in jeopardy."

Of the two Charity is less interesting, and King spends less time on her because her problems are less psychologically complex. This is not to say that her problems are not serious—in some ways more serious than Donna's—for Charity is married to a physically abusive man:

> Joe had used his hands on her a few times in the course of their marriage, and she had learned. . . . Now she did what Joe told her and rarely argued. She guessed Brett was that way too. But she feared for the boy sometimes.

Most of the sections that involve Charity focus on her attempts to show her son a better way of life, one that is physically very different from their life with Joe. Escaping even briefly from Joe requires both luck and skill—the good luck of winning the lottery and skill in the courage to approach her husband. In fact, King reveals that she could "sometimes gain the upper hand just by seeming brave. Not always, but sometimes." King also lets the reader know that these moments of bravery are risky, however, for the Camber marriage, like so many other marriages, is essentially unequal: "Joe could go places alone or with his friends, but she couldn't, not even with Brett in tow. That was one of their marriage's ground rules."

Joe's power over Charity stems both from his greater physical strength and from the economic advantage of having money to spend as he chooses. Probing Charity's mind after she wins the lottery, King reveals to the reader how economic dependence on their husbands affects women:

> Lady Luck had singled her out. For the first time in her life, maybe for the only time, that heavy muslin drape of the everyday had been twitched a little, showing her a bright and shining world beyond. She was a practical woman, and in her heart she knew that she hated her husband more than a little, but that they would grow old together, and he would die, leaving her with his debts and . . . perhaps with his spoilt son.

In short, five thousand dollars isn't enough to provide her and Brett with more than a brief escape.

If King had stopped his portrait here, the reader would be left with a kind of caricature of an unliberated woman who is trapped by economic dependence and fear of physical power. However, King recognizes that many women are not able to take charge of their lives because they are also trapped by powerful internal compulsions, in Charity's case by love for the man who continues to victimize her:

> Was she going to kid herself and say that she did not, even now, in some way love the man she had

married? That she stayed with him only out of duty, or for the sake of the child (*that* was a bitter laugh; if she ever left him it would be for the sake of the child)? . . . That he could not, sometimes at the most unexpected moments . . . be tender. (King's italics)

Passages like this one focus on the kinds of complex emotional issues that King's ordinary characters face every day and negate a criticism so often leveled against popular writers like King—that they create nothing but caricatures. Moreover, it negates Chelsea Quinn Yarbro's specific criticism that King cannot "develop a believable woman character between the ages of seventeen and sixty." Both Donna and Charity are believable human beings because they confront the ordinary problems faced by the readers. The character of Charity, however, is more clearly modeled on an older notion of the heroine as a person to be rescued by someone else, by circumstance, or by luck. Less heroic than Donna, Charity escapes from her husband largely because of luck rather than because of skill and self knowledge. Nonetheless, at the end of the novel, she is a confident and independent woman who is working to achieve her own goals. Such independence and preparation for her son's college education could not have happened while she was married to Joe Camber.

If Charity is believable, strong, and almost heroic, Donna is an ordinary woman who becomes the modern American heroine. Middle class and college educated—a librarian married to an advertising executive—Donna is also much more articulate about her condition as a woman and about everything that being a woman means.

Despite these differences, King very carefully highlights significant similarities in the two women. The first of these similarities is the fact that Donna, like Charity, is aware of her physical limitations. Although Donna is a large woman—five-eleven and "an inch taller than Vic when she wore heels"—and an athlete, she is easily physically intimidated by both Steve Kemp and Joe Camber; and King's careful relating of Donna's thoughts also reminds us of how women are—more often than men—influenced by their physical condition:

> Falling off the back porch when she was five and breaking her wrist.

> Looking down at herself . . . when she was a high school freshman and seeing to her utter shame and horror that there were spots of blood on her light blue linen skirt. . . . Holding Tad in her arms, newborn, then the nurse taking him away; she wanted to tell the nurse not to do that . . . but she was too weak to talk. . . .

Furthermore, though her husband is not the kind of man to employ physical force, King makes it clear that Vic is in control, for Donna "hadn't wanted to come to Maine and had been appalled when Vic had sprung the idea on her." Such details suggest that the Trenton marriage is unequal and that Vic makes the important decisions.

King, who is exceptionally sensitive to material culture in the twentieth century, further reveals the inequality in their marriage by focusing on the cars they drive, an emphasis that clearly reveals Donna's economic dependence. Vic drives an expensive imported sports car, a Jaguar, while Donna drives one of the least expensive automobiles ever produced in Detroit, the Ford Pinto. In this way King reveals that Vic is a man who likes to pamper himself; and, when he shows that Vic is totally aware of the media attention to the dangers associated with driving the Pinto, he also reveals that such pampering may be at the expense of his family. Ironically, however, Donna and Tad don't die inside a burning Pinto. Donna survives, and Tad dies of dehydration when Cujo traps them inside the Pinto during three of the hottest days of the year.

> **Recognizing his readers' needs, Stephen King makes Donna Trenton a new kind of heroine. First, he presents her as an ordinary human being, one troubled by the same kinds of problems that confront ordinary human beings, and he shows that such an ordinary human being can live with dignity and courage. Finally he has this ordinary person confront an exceptional—almost superhuman—adversary.**
>
> —*Carol A. Senf*

Furthermore, like Charity Camber, Donna feels trapped though her feelings of entrapment are only partially due to lack of money. A former professional, Donna contemplates going back to work. However, she ultimately labels it a "ridiculous notion, and she shelved it after running some figures on her pocket calculator." Here—as elsewhere—King uses financial worries to emphasize ordinary problems, the kind of problems a reader might face. However, despite the reference to money here and elsewhere in the novel—Vic's new advertising agency is having financial difficulty, for example—Donna's problems are not lack of money, but the fact that she has too much time on her hands—time to worry about her loss of identity. Donna recognizes the problem:

> She started to sharpshoot at Vic about little things, sublimating the big things because they were hard to define and even harder to articulate. Things like

loss and fear and getting older. Things like being lonely and then getting terrified of being lonely. . . . Feeling jealous because his life was a daily struggle to build something . . . and her life was back here, getting Tad through the day.

Donna's later heroism is foreshadowed when King shows that she can't escape the loneliness in the ways that are acceptable for women: volunteer work, "hen parties," and soap operas. A doer and a confronter rather than an escapist, Donna tries to fill her life in traditionally acceptable ways—through housework and through caring for her son. She realizes, however, that this work won't last because "every year the world gets another little slice of him." Ultimately her loneliness and sense of frustration lead her to a disastrous affair with Steve Kemp, a man as physically brutal as Joe Camber and certainly more psychologically abusive.

The affair with Kemp is an illustration of Donna's weakness—of her tendency to drift until someone else provides her with a solution. On the other hand, the scene in which she ends the affair even though he threatens to rape her in her own kitchen foreshadows the final climactic scene when she decides that she cannot depend on someone else:

> She had been afraid to use her loudest voice, and had done so only when it became absolutely necessary. Because that was where civilization came to an abrupt, screeching halt. That was the place where the tar turned to dirt. If they wouldn't listen when you used your very loudest voice, a scream became your only recourse.

Ironically, although Donna fears the absence of civilization, she will discover herself only when she has rid herself of civilization and its expectations for women. Screaming at Kemp, she discovers her power over him: "And if I get a chance to tear your balls off or put one of your eyes out, I won't hesitate." It is a power that women rarely achieve.

Trapped by Cujo in the Pinto, which becomes a symbol of her entire life as a dependent, Donna slowly begins to take control of her life. At first, clearly expecting to be rescued—by Vic, by the mailman when he comes to the Cambers, by anyone—she remains like the old style passive heroine:

> She didn't know why no one had answered the SOS she had been beeping out. In a book, someone would have come. It was the heroine's reward for having thought up such a clever idea. But no one had come.

Alone in the Pinto, with only her four-year-old son for company, Donna becomes a new kind of heroine, a woman who takes control of her life rather than waiting for someone—

the proverbial knight—to save her. In fact, Donna begins to realize during the ordeal that she is a new kind of woman:

> That had been the first time she had really believed—believed in her gut—that she was going to grow up and become a woman, a woman with at least a fighting chance to be a *better* woman than her own mother, who could get into such a frightening state over what was really such a little thing. . . .

Finally, forced again by external circumstances to take matters into her own hands, Donna contrasts herself to the heroines of earlier literature, the traditional damsels in distress:

> The time had come, and Donna knew it. . . . No one was going to come. There was going to be no knight on a silver steed riding up Town Road No. 3—Travis McGee was apparently otherwise engaged.
>
> Tad was dying.

Reminding the reader again that *Cujo* takes place in the real world, King has Donna's victory over Cujo come too late to save Tad. The little boy dies while his mother is battling the monster; and Donna, who had earlier saved his life when his tongue blocks his windpipe and who finally overcomes the monstrous dog, cannot bring him back to life. It is thus a hollow victory. Her marriage in jeopardy and her son dead, Donna has lost all the things that supposedly provided meaning for traditional heroines. Realizing, however, that the modern heroine must not be afraid to confront life, readers should feel purged by their vicarious participation in her victory. As Donna herself recognizes before she leaves to do battle, this ability to confront one's problems is all that matters:

> Had this terrible vigil been only a matter of hours, or had it been her whole life? Surely everything that had gone before had been a dream, little more than a short wait in the wings? The mother who had seemed to be disgusted and repulsed by all those around her, the well-meaning but ineffectual father, the schools, the friends, the dates and dances—they were all a dream to her now. . . . Nothing mattered, nothing *was* but this silent and sunstruck dooryard where death had been dealt and yet more death waited in the cards. . . . The old monster kept his watch still. . . .

King seems to realize here that his readers—especially his women readers—are ready for a new kind of heroine, a woman who is prepared to leave behind triviality—the constant dusting of pottery knickknacks that Donna equates with women's lives—and confront the unspeakable with courage and conviction.

Recognizing his readers' needs, Stephen King makes Donna Trenton a new kind of heroine. First, he presents her as an ordinary human being, one troubled by the same kinds of problems that confront ordinary human beings, and he shows that such an ordinary human being can live with dignity and courage. Finally he has this ordinary person confront an exceptional—almost superhuman—adversary.

Stephen King has become an immensely popular writer, and part of that popularity is undoubtedly his ability to write a suspenseful story. However, another—and probably more important—reason for his popularity stems from his ability to create characters with whom the readers can readily identify. Although most of his novels focus on men characters, *Cujo* scrutinizes the problems that confront twentieth-century American women. Donna and Charity are ordinary women, one middle class, well educated and articulate; the other, working class, uneducated, and less introspective. Despite seemingly overwhelming odds, each woman manages to take control of her life. Donna especially in her display of courage becomes a new American heroine, a strong woman with whom women in the twentieth century can be proud to identify.

James Egan (essay date Winter 1989)

SOURCE: "Sacral Parody in the Fiction of Stephen King," in *Journal of Popular Culture,* Vol. 23, No. 3, Winter, 1989, pp. 125-41.

[*In the following essay, Egan discusses how the sacral parody common to gothic literature is at work in King's fiction.*]

Leslie Fiedler's observation in *Love and Death in the American Novel* that the Gothic is a parodic medium, "a way of assailing clichés by exaggerating them to the limit of their grotesqueness," has generally been supported by subsequent analyses of Gothic literature. Rosemary Jackson points to Gothic's tendency to "invert romance structures," for example, the quest, by twisting the quest into a "circular journey to nowhere." Coral Ann Howells makes explicit what Fiedler had implied, namely that in Gothic novels the structure of the external world breaks down, that the Gothic idiom destabilizes. William Patrick Day's recent study offers the most sophisticated reading of the parodic tendencies of Gothic and the implications of those tendencies. If, as Day contends, the Gothic parodies both romance and realistic fiction, and if the "Gothic world is one of unresolved chaos, of continuous transformation . . . of the monstrous that is the

shadow of the human," resolution in such a world would be grotesque or absurd, the articulation of the basic intent of the parodic. If the "wasteland of the Gothic is a world in which cruelty, violence and conflict are the only principles upon which the characters can act, only to destroy themselves," an atmosphere of radical distortion and mutation becomes normative, akin to the aesthetic direction of the parodic.

> **King's Gothic world not only identifies itself but, in the most extreme instances, mimics its own identity by bonding itself to religious concepts, so that the "monstrosity" of his Gothic often relates directly to his "inversion of the numinous."**
> *—James Egan*

Not only can Gothic fantasy exhibit the "disintegration of the spiritual," but the Gothic has long contained "a religious undercurrent of meaning." Nineteenth-century Gothic writers occasionally employ religious images to define man as "eternal victim" or place guilty wanderers at the center of essentially Calvinistic parables of sin and retribution. To cite several familiar examples of Gothic's incorporation of the sacral, Shelley's *Frankenstein* works ironic variations on creation, Resurrection and Adamic motifs, Stoker's *Dracula* invokes a largely Christian ritual to defeat the vampire, and Lovecraft's universe features a pantheon of dark gods. Stephen King's habits as a Gothicist have been much discussed, but his consistent development of Gothicism's parodic tendencies and the direction of his parody deserve more attention. Douglas Winter notes that in *The Mist* King accentuates the powerful shaping influences of science, materialism and religion and questions the worth of such influences. Tony Magistrale has argued, more specifically, that "one of the major elements linking Stephen King's fiction to the inclusive gothic tradition is its attack on the very foundations and values upon which society is built." Some of those values are societal bonds, science and religion. King depicts both government and organized religion as "spiritually bankrupt" and religious extremists are conspicuous in his fiction.

His attack upon Christian religious traditions, impulses and assumptions is, I would suggest, more comprehensive and sophisticated than either Winter or Magistrale indicates. King's Gothic world not only identifies itself but, in the most extreme instances, mimics its own identity by bonding itself to religious concepts, so that the "monstrosity" of his Gothic often relates directly to his "inversion of the numinous." King mocks religious targets, both literally and allegorically, by means of fairly conventional satiric stratagems, primarily caricature, ironic inversion, the grotesque and the burlesque and satiric juxtaposition. Rarely does he use humor as a form of catharsis, but rather as a device of intensification. King's sacral parody serves two primary purposes, to define the Gothic nightland more fully and to test the conventional religious beliefs of the normative world. Though his Gothic universe characteristically inverts and mimics the routinely sacral, King's stance toward the sacral does not appear uniformly negative. In some cases, an encounter with the Gothic underworld affirms the power of the sacral and sets the boundaries of the underworld. In others, escape from the darkness becomes possible when a secular credo replaces the sacral. King's parodic targets fall into several categories, categories which invariably overlap. My discussion presupposes a close relationship among these religious targets and the categories I employ have been selected because in each of them a particular target receives prominent emphasis. King occasionally mimics rather specific doctrinal issues, but for the most part his parodic emphasis falls on Christianity in the broadest sense.

Religious derives gone awry, particularly fundamentalist obsessions and the ludicrous, grotesque and violent consequences of such obsessions surely qualify as one of the primary targets of King's sacral parody. Several of his characters are obsessed in this fashion, for example, Vera Smith, mother of protagonist John Smith in *The Dead Zone.* Though the issue seems far from clear to anyone else, Vera considers her son's return to life after a long coma as the Lord's work, part of the providential plan, believing that "all actions of the creature happen under the lordship of the creator" and that the "Lord is always present, active, responsible and Omnipotent." She refuses to consider another Christian idea of providence, namely that "God's sovereignty is hidden to mankind, discernible only by faith, and then not as a clearly perceptible pattern." After the accident which nearly killed Johnny, Vera turns ever more zealously to her pronounced fundamentalist beliefs in an attempt to explain and justify his misfortune. A reliance on the "inerrancy of the Bible" typifies fundamentalism, yet that reliance has often proved troublesome for fundamentalists because of the ambiguity of highly personal interpretations of the Bible; and so it goes with Vera Smith. Her obsession grows into a fanatical zeal, culminating in her belief that Christ plans to come to earth in a flying saucer to commune with His faithful and to reward believers such as herself. Here King takes aim at the ludicrous consequences of fanatical "zeal," long a fundamentalist characteristic, as well as at the eschatalogical bent of fundamentalism, its belief in a vivid, apocalyptic "end to the existing order of things." Vera's zealous response to Johnny's trip into the unknown actually distances her from her son, who becomes a living icon, a way to verify her perception of the ways of the divine and her own manic zeal. Vera has begun to run in circles, so that the more she practices her beliefs, the more ineffectual and preposterous they seem. Vera's obsessions have distorted her

into a comic character; she has become a caricature, a woman whose religious predilections have become the dominant features of her personality. While these predilections may well be a response to divine love and to a providential plan, they also alienate her from the husband and son she claims to love. The strong evangelical zeal historically associated with fundamentalism likewise manifests itself in Vera, who tries, aggressively and repeatedly, to convince Johnny that a divinely ordained mission awaits him. Yet King darkens her evangelistic quest before it can really begin, implying that evangelism alienates, spreading confusion and dissension. Directly after Johnny's accident, as she leaves the hospital with Sarah, Vera, "looking dreamily up at the moon," announces: "It isn't in God's plan for Johnny to die." Then she smiles: "In that smile Sarah suddenly saw Johnny's own easy, devil-may-care grin, but at the same time she thought it was the most ghastly smile she had ever seen in her life." Imagistically and thematically, King treats Vera's compulsive evangelism as a mixture of the ludicrous and the "ghastly."

> The cataclysmic ending of *Carrie* . . . may be read allegorically as the mutation of evangelism into a parodic form. Carrie mimics her mother's excesses, taking them to massively destructive ends; she finally becomes the "Angel's Fiery Sword" her mother wanted her to be, a demonic evangelist who presides over a hellish, fiery holocaust.
>
> —*James Egan*

Vera Smith, however, merely echoes perhaps the most dangerous fundamentalist fanatic in all of King's fiction, the mother of Carrie White in *Carrie.* A militant, literal biblicist, a church unto herself, a tyrannical twentieth-century Puritan who insists that private reading and meditation on God's word must be enforced at all costs, Mrs. White embodies many fundamentalist clichés and their destructive consequences. She stands committed to the fundamentalist assumptions that neither an ordained ministry, nor a formal theological education, nor group reinforcement should be required for the true believer. The Gothic world tests, by means of Carrie's parapsychological powers, the efficacy of Margaret White's assumptions. Unfortunately for her, the Word has no explanation for the telekinetic prowess Carrie displays at an early age, except to suggest that Carrie should be labeled the "Devil's child, Satan spawn." Her pathological horror and "ever-present" fear of sin, an evangelical trait, along with a fundamentalist zeal for proselytizing, lead her into a crusade to convert Carrie into a replica of herself, so much so that she tries to conceal from her daughter the more "awkward" aspects of sexuality, such as breasts and menstruation. She strives as well to convert non-believers outside of her home, but with little success; unfortunately for Carrie, these failures probably redouble her mother's attempts to keep her "pure." Mrs. White's horror of sin and desire to spread God's Word turn the White home into a grotesque, darkly comic environment. She regularly punishes Carrie by locking her in a closet for hours to beg forgiveness before a glowing crucifix, on the assumption that torture will lead naturally to moral improvement. In a particularly ludicrous scene, after Carrie has endured the humiliation of experiencing in a school shower her first menstrual period, she returns home to confront a mother who decides that prayer is the answer to menstruation:

> [Carrie's] sobs were too strong to allow more [than the word 'Momma']. The latent hysterics had come out grinning and gibbering. She could not stand up. She could only crawl into the living room with her hair hanging in her face, braying huge, hoarse sobs. Every now and again Momma would swing her foot. So they progressed across the living room toward the place of the altar, which had once been a small bedroom.

As Carrie and her mother lurch toward the place of atonement, we are reminded of a serio-comic religious procession punctuated by screaming, kicking and "grinning." Margaret White, however, proves very capable of directing the same sort of violence toward herself, and she does so when Carrie refuses to abstain from going to the prom:

> Momma screamed. She made her right hand a fist and struck herself in the mouth, bringing blood. She dabbled her fingers in it, looked at it dreamily, and daubed a spot on the cover of the Bible.

Self-mutilation here translates as a distorted form of punishment, a propitiation to a presumably angry God, yet the ritual of atonement borders on the absurdly comic. Irrespective of her intentions, Mrs. White plays the fool, the slapstick, dreamy-eyed buffoon who has managed to punch herself in the mouth.

The cataclysmic ending of *Carrie,* moreover, may be read allegorically as the mutation of evangelism into a parodic form. Carrie mimics her mother's excesses, taking them to massively destructive ends; she finally becomes the "Angel's Fiery Sword" her mother wanted her to be, a demonic evangelist who presides over a hellish, fiery holocaust. Unlike her mother, Carrie makes converts—converts who come to believe in the power of the unknown. Fundamentalist religious postures have been mocked by the fierce "zeal" of telekinesis. By trying so hard to preserve Carrie's purity and to create a saint, Margaret White has helped to fashion a demon who rejoices in the chaos she creates.

In both novels King presents the reader with what Elizabeth MacAndrew calls a statement of the grotesque "which contains a pervasive comic element arising from and producing that uncomfortable sense of the incongruously horrible that makes the viewer laugh as he inwardly groans." Ironically, Mrs. White's "psychological monstrosity" may be seen as a tangible example of the shadowy moral evils she so thoroughly fears. Again ironically, the religious excesses of Margaret White and Vera Smith distort both women to the point that they come to resemble zealous automatons, character types occasionally found in the Gothic universe. King's dark humor offers no catharsis here.

Ministers, priests, sacraments and formal rites and rituals are likewise parodied in King's fiction. The Reverend Lowe in *Cycle of the Werewolf* qualifies as a case in point. A werewolf responsible for monthly killings, Lowe experiences little introspection, yet King's mocking touches can easily be seen when such introspection occurs. Near the end of the Novel, Lowe examines his situation, realizing that he is a werewolf, the scriptural Beast reincarnated, but still he declares, *"I am a man of God."* Lowe has undergone a parodic version of an examination of conscience. Despite his earnest declaration, the reader recalls that Lowe has a Gothic double, that he is very much a bestial creature from the Gothic universe, who hardly seems intent on spreading the gospel. If Lowe's examination of conscience contains elements of prayer, those elements are somewhat suspect because they do not provide a "means of grace" for him. Earlier, when the minister imagines his congregation metamorphosing into an assembly of werewolves, a grotesquely comic element surfaces. Indeed, as Randall Larson argues, pentecostalism may be one of King's targets here, yet other evidence of mimicry appears as well. Lowe's parishioners perform a parodic "low-church" ritual, a sharing of fellowship, but their evangelistic zeal has become bloodlust. For Lowe as well as his parishioners metamorphosing into a werewolf means experiencing a grotesquely rapturous ecstasy. By means of satiric juxtaposition King links ecstasy with bestial regression, riddling the notion of rapture with dark elements of self-delusion and degradation. Lowe's vision of his congregation suggests that an ominous metamorphosis awaits those who reach for the "high." A final religious irony underlies the story's parody. At no point can Lowe discover why or how he has become a werewolf. He seems to have been fated, in a mockery of traditional low-church notions of "election," to carry the mark of the Beast and to descend periodically into a hellish underworld, for no apparent reason. Lowe's status as unenlightened victim calls into question the providential scheme of things, the supposed divine benevolence, and adds an ironic twist to the identities and purposes of those called to do the Lord's work. So also does Lowe's belief that *"if it's the Lord's will,"* he will find Marty Coslaw, who has discovered his duplicity, *"And silence him. Forever."* Christian providence appears to have a demonic equivalent. Lowe dies without ever recognizing an overriding purpose or sense of individual wrong doing which would account for this dark "election" as a werewolf. In the absence of that purpose, a Gothic foreboding figures importantly in the story.

Father Donald Callahan in *'Salem's Lot* meets a fate similar to Lowe's when he challenges the Gothic universe manifesting itself as Barlow, the king vampire. We learn that Callahan, suffering from a crisis of faith and identity, very much needs the support and consolation his venerable traditions and rituals would presumably give him. Early encounters with Barlow show Callahan the victor who manages to exorcise the vampire from his sanctuary, the Marsten House. Yet Barlow boasts that he will eventually win, and makes good on his boast. In the crucial confrontation scene between the two, the sacred flame of Callahan's cross feebly flickers out, and the vampire contemptuously tosses the cross away. Then he initiates the failed priest into the Gothic universe by forcing Callahan to drink his blood, an appropriately Gothic "exorcism," a reversal of the sacraments of Baptism and the Eucharist. Callahan becomes a Cain-figure, an outcast with the devil's mark upon him, who can no longer enter the church he once served. True, Callahan can easily be faulted as an individual whose weak faith caused him to be drawn into the Gothic underworld. Yet does his failure not reflect the failure of his rituals, his sacraments, his church itself as well? King leaves the matter open to question, yet one may safely conclude that a priest with a crisis of faith and a drinking problem, on a mission of good, discovers no convincing proof in the rituals he practices that such rituals can keep back the darkness or refute the vampire's mocking laugh. If the sacramental system was designed to "secure God's aid in correct living" and to "protect against the crises of life," Callahan has not been its beneficiary. The priest's formal system of religious practice works no more effectively for him than Mrs. White's fundamentalist improvisations did for her.

The ways and workings of mysticism, affective and suprarational approaches to the *Visio Dei,* are still another form of the sacral which King consistently undercuts, though his parody of the *Visio* seems more indirect and allegorical than do most of his other sacral inversions. Christian mysticism "stresses that God can be known in immediate fashion, not merely by inference." In order to possess the *Visio Dei,* an intense and fulfilling experience of transcendent truth which unites the mystic with God and allows him to see God in the whole world, the mystic must pass through several stages of purification. Having awakened supra-rationally to a "consciousness of Divine Reality," the mystic must undergo various purgations to heighten his illumination of the divine, notably a mystic death, the "Dark Night of the Soul." To lift the "veil of imperfection" and to achieve a heightened consciousness of God, a mystic needs to experience psychic fatigue and emptiness. Despite the Dark Night of the Soul, the transcendent union with God ultimately achieved promises to be positive and uplifting—a transfigured vision of the universe allows the mystic to see beauty in all things and to achieve peace, rest and often bliss. The extrasensory powers possessed by several of King's characters serve as a metaphor of mystical perception and its varied results, some of which are plainly affirmative. Mother Abagail in *The Stand,* for example, remains steadfast during the epidemic of plague because of her visionary apprehension of an important role she has been given to play in heading a mission against the demonic adversary, Randall Flagg. After leading her pilgrims to Boulder, she vanished without explanation into the wilderness, explaining on her deathbed that her mystical vision had become blurred, requiring that she submit herself to purgation and endure the Dark Night of the Soul, thereby to offer proper guidance to her followers. After her sojourn in the wilderness, Abagail regains enough of her mystical insight to define the proper way to defeat Flagg. Her purification and repentance allow for the birth of a new self and she dies in union with the divine.

For the most part, though, King treats the *Visio* and the mystical way less reverently. If mystics typically attain a transfigured vision of the universe, the experience of several of King's characters suggests that they encounter the parodic opposite, that King deflates mysticism by means of burlesque, allowing the mystical to intrigue and compel characters, only to leave them disenchanted or traumatized. Rather than experiencing the *Visio,* these characters gain insights into its inversion, the Gothic underworld; their dark trips into the unknown call mystical ecstasy into question. If a "mystical adventure" may be defined as a "going forth" from the normal self, what happens to Carrie White might qualify as "mystical," but hardly as an "adventure." Carrie's telekinesis gives her, in addition to the ability to move objects, an immediate and intense awareness of the feelings and perceptions of those around her. As her telekinesis develops, so does her heightened insight. Carrie comes to perceive, in her "mystical" fashion, not the "beauty in all things," but the malignity in the hearts of her peers and her mother. For Carrie, the mystical Dark Night of the Soul becomes a venture into the Gothic darkness. She experiences pain and death rather than the *Visio Dei,* the emptiness of the void rather than fulfillment through unity with the One.

Similar problems afflict Danny Torrance in *The Shining.* Throughout the novel, King portrays Danny as a "sincere acolyte," an innocent whose "shine" allows him to make first contact with the Gothic world of the Overlook Hotel, to sense the darkness waiting to envelop him and his family. Though King does not add an explicitly religious dimension to Danny's life, as he did with Mother Abagail and Carrie, the notion of acolyte works metaphorically to suggest that Danny leads a procession or pilgrimage of sorts; technically, the term "acolyte" refers to a "cleric in the highest of the four minor orders of the Western church." Figuratively, then, Danny's heightened powers read as another version of the mystical. Before he arrived at the Overlook, moreover, Danny's shine had acquainted him with other forms of darkness: quarreling, alcoholism, child abuse. When Tony, Danny's contact in the world beyond the here and now, warns him about "redrum," the reader recognizes the continuation rather than the onset of a pattern, even though Danny himself realizes that his shine sometimes alerts him to dark possibilities that do not develop into facts. What happens at the Overlook, however, accentuates the problematic nature of mystical insight. Danny was born with a sophisticated power from whose potentially dangerous effects he has virtually no protection. His shine makes him highly attractive to the dark forces that inhabit the hotel, and Danny is vulnerable because, although he senses danger, he usually cannot locate it precisely. He confronts in innocence many of the hotel's traps, a number of which are religious inversions. When the ghost of Room 217 tries to strangle him, Danny encounters a parodic "welcome" into the afterlife, a grotesquely distorted *Visio* which traumatizes him. Nor does his mystical sensitivity alert him to his father's demonic ecstasy. After Jack strikes his bargain with the hotel, he erupts into a murderous "rapture," a frantic desire to destroy Danny and Wendy, so as to enjoy a "higher truth" by meeting the hotel's demonic manager. The Gothic world of the Overlook seems to strip Danny's *Visio* of its affirmative qualities. He has not been uplifted by his mystical abilities, has not found ecstatic happiness or even harmony with the world around him, has not been able to understand more than a little of the actual workings of his shine. Rather, his raptures, premonitions and trips out of his body have typically been horrific, a burlesque deflation of the alleged effects of mysticism and of mystical religion's contention that good should be sought in "that which is above and beyond this life." The Overlook's voracious attempts to assimilate Danny mock mysticism's exaltation of a "union with God in which the self disappears."

John Smith's mystical-seeming powers are equally unsettling in *The Dead Zone.* Smith recognizes his talents early on and feels "uncomfortable" about them even after he wins big at the wheel of fortune. After his lengthy coma, Smith's abilities intensify greatly, but with equivocal results. Dark visions haunt him: he senses the catastrophic fire at Cathy's, the horror of Frank Dodd and his mother and the menace of Gregg Stillson. Yet Smith's knowledge seems overwhelming, inundating, and his warnings are feared as often as they are heeded. He evolves into a Cassandra-figure, a pariah besieged by fanatics of all sorts and the cynicism of a culture dubious of mystical awareness. Eventually, despite Smith's concession that he has become a Jeremiah-like prophet on a mission to stop Stillson, a mission his insight has led him to, he can appreciate the moral ambiguity of his planned assassination and must wrestle with the thought that "This was

no holy business he was on." King creates the appearance of mystical awareness in Smith's case, seemingly to illustrate the frustrations, the unsettling moral paradoxes and the lack of reassurance connected with such awareness. Johnny's acceptance of his "mission," one presented in implicitly religious terms, further dramatizes that transcendence and illumination are not necessarily the rewards of those who possess mystical sensitivity. In the three novels discussed, King undercuts the *Visio* by suggesting that psychic fragmentation and radical, mutated psychic development accompany it; by rendering ambivalent and ironic the higher levels of consciousness available to those who experience it; and by upsetting the normal balance between pain and pleasure which characterizes the mystical state by accentuating pain, darkness and calamity.

With its series of ironic resurrections which unify the varied forms of sacral parody in the novel, **Pet Sematary** represents perhaps the most thoroughgoing inversion of Christian motifs in all of King's fiction. He evokes the Christian concept of Resurrection through Scriptural quotes and paraphrases at the opening of each division of the book, only to deny it with his plot, characterization and thematic emphases. The Pet Sematary is the nexus of the Gothic universe, an ageless and forbidding place seemingly far older than Christianity. King defines the Gothic universe, in part, by means of allusions to Lovecraft's Cthulhu mythos. On one of his last trips to the Micmac burying ground, Louis Creed hopes that the strange shapes he sees around him are not "the creatures which leap and crawl and slither and shamble in the world between . . . [the] dark and draggling horrors on the nightside of the universe." Yet his experiences rebuke his hopes. The platform on which the burying ground stands resonates with age and alienness, as do many ceremonial locations in Lovecraft's mythos tales. When Creed ascends the forty-five steps to the platform for the first time, he wonders whether the Micmacs who allegedly carved them were *"Tool bearing Indians."* On a later trip, he "cocked his head back once and saw the mad sprawl of the stars. There were no constellations he recognized and he looked away again, disturbed." Again King recalls a Lovecraftian sense of the void. Eventually Louis Creed concludes that the "grave markers in the Pet Sematary, those rude circles" recall a *"much older God than the Christian one."* Carrying Gage through Little God swamp, Creed encounters various personifications of his deepest fears, a "grisly, floating head," "its mouth drawn down in a rictus" and "a diffuse, ill-defined watermark . . . better than sixty feet high. It was no shade, no insubstantial ghost; he could feel the displaced air of its passage, could hear the mammoth thud of its feet coming down, the suck of mud as it moved on." Creed has seen the Wendigo, the God-figure of the burying ground, whose monstrous material presence recalls Lovecraft's mythos creatures at the same time that it mocks the presumed anthropomorphism and aetherial nature of the Christian God. The succession of dark priest-figures in the novel, moreover, echoes Lovecraft's mythos priests. Judd Crandall tells Creed of Stanny B, a Canuck "medicine man" of sorts, who "was a proper Christian and would preach on the Resurrection when he was drunk enough," a shape-shifter who, Crandall thinks, metamorphoses into an Indian as he leads Crandall to the burying ground. Crandall himself undergoes a similar metamorphosis, speaking of the Micmac past as though he had actually experienced it, becoming a shadowy "hood" which seems to "surround a blankness" as he leads Creed to the burying ground for the first time, and finally a priest who helps Louis bury the family cat and construct a cairn over Church's grave. Throughout the novel, King blurs Crandall's identity, and his knowledge and purposes are never clear. As did Stanny B, however, Crandall understands the dark rituals of the burying ground and the ceremonial formulas necessary to petition eldritch forces. Like Lovecraft's mythos priests, Crandall serves as the often terrified but still willing agent of the elder gods.

That the burial ground offers passage into an alien and terrifying universe the animals and people who return to life well demonstrate. As the book unfolds, a progression of demonic resurrections occurs, each in some way more complex and ominous than the last. A sustained mockery of Christian notions of the afterlife unites these resurrections. After Creed brings Church back to life, the cat lurches, sways and behaves like a snake, its animal vitality replaced by the confused energies of a creature scrambling for a foothold in the now unfamiliar world of the living. Church comes to resemble a demon in animal form, full of bizarre menace and peculiar power. Crandall finally tells Louis the story of Timmy Baterman, a World War Two casualty brought back to life by his father. To Crandall, Timmy seems *"damned,"* possessed of a preternatural knowledge of dark secrets in the lives of those who confront him. The return of the damned to an earthly existence plainly satirizes the Christian notion of a benign providential control of the afterlife.

If *Pet Sematary* illustrates the malevolent energies of the Gothic and implies at least the partial triumph of those energies, *The Stand* indicates the limited and qualified nature of any such triumph. Because of the inherent instability of the Gothic world, it will inevitably fragment and mock its own devices.

—*James Egan*

Pet Sematary's most acute horrors, however, involve the rebirth of Gage and Rachel Creed. Louis buries Gage with a guarded optimism, but the resurrection of his son animates a demonic being more vindictive and aggressive than Timmy Baterman, one who kills and cannibalizes out of pure malignity. If Gage has become a reanimated body from which the original soul has fled, his presence inverts the Christian belief that the unique personality survives after death. In desperation, Louis buries Rachel, who returns as the "best" and therefore the most terrible of the novel's parodic resurrections, the soul mate of the dark magician, the bride of the Frankenstein Doctor Louis Creed has become. Creed has finally succeeded in keeping open the passage to the Gothic world itself. The horror of *Pet Sematary* derives from our comprehension of how ominous that world can be. Timmy, Gage and Rachel, then, call into question the Christian perception of Resurrection in the spirit by reducing resurrection to a material level and equating it with the evocation of Gothic doubles who embody the monstrous, torture, madness and death. These bodies brought back from the dead resemble in no way Christ's glorified body, nor do they suggest a Christian Resurrection of the Just. King links a demonic creation motif to his resurrection parody in *Pet Sematary,* finally, to expand the range of the parody. Louis Creed devolves into an anti-creator whose "works" ridicule the Christian assumption that man was made in God's image. Gage and Rachel embody the darkness of his own heart; he has remade them into images of himself which allow the Gothic world an opportunity to exert its mocking, nihilistic force and to deny the sacral, the vivifying message of Christian Resurrection. To compound the irony of Creed's final predicament, he seems as much the mad victim of the burying ground's narcotic power as the powerful "creator" of diabolic life forms.

If *Pet Sematary* illustrates the malevolent energies of the Gothic and implies at least the partial triumph of those energies, *The Stand* indicates the limited and qualified nature of any such triumph. Because of the inherent instability of the Gothic world, it will inevitably fragment and mock its own devices. One of King's most fully realized Gothic worlds rises out of the post-apocalyptic ashes of *The Stand,* and again sacral parody figures prominently in his definition and development of that world. In the other novels discussed, a normative and empirical world exists in contradistinction to the Gothic shadowland, but in *The Stand* the epidemic of superflu decimates virtually the entire human population and much of the normative along with it. The reasons why the survivors have endured are not yet clear, and many of them possess uncommonly keen psychic perception. As Douglas Winter points out, however, Gothic fiction has traditionally played a major part in the apocalyptic; in a variety of ways the "new world" of *The Stand* is "haunted," so that in the rival empires of Boulder and Las Vegas the Gothic, not unexpectedly, manifests itself in uncommonly diverse and complex fashion. The novel's plot details an epic conflict between a foreboding Gothic world and a flawed but essentially righteous one. From the story's beginning, Randall Flagg, Gothic shape-shifter and apocalyptic Antichrist, establishes himself and his objectives with the help of sacral parody. Flagg sets the tenor of his demonic rule by recruiting Lloyd Henreid as his right-hand man, his "St. Peter," offering to "slip the keys to the kingdom right in [Lloyd's] hand," and then quoting Scripture to suggest to Lloyd that in the new realm of Antichrist, "the meek . . . shall inherit the earth." Flagg attempts to convert Nick Andros with another familiar ploy, this time echoing Satan's temptation of Christ on the pinnacle of the temple by whispering to Andros, "Everything you see will be yours if you will fall down on your knees and worship me" (Luke 4:1-13). As Flagg gains control of Las Vegas and the regions west of it, he takes up residence in a mammoth temple, the MGM Grand Hotel, where his growing legions of followers can worship him. Flagg underscores his reign of terror by crucifying those who oppose him and by impregnating the "virgin" Nadine Cross in an appropriately Gothic mimicry of the Incarnation.

The unstable, self-parodic nature of Flagg's empire soon becomes apparent, however; almost as soon as it reaches an apex, Flagg's power wanes. He loses control of the catatonic Nadine and tosses her out of a window, destroying his own offspring in the process. Proving that the "effective half-life of evil is always relatively short," Flagg's psychic perception falters and he loses sight of Tom Cullen, who escapes from Las Vegas with abundant information about Flagg's activities. His allies and followers, lieutenants as well as rank and file, begin to desert him, reflecting in their behavior the "dreadful insecurity" characteristic of Gothic fiction, their fear of a "contingent world which is altogether unpredictable and menacing." The instability of Flagg's empire has evoked a Gothic sort of paranoia in his followers. He succumbs, finally, not to desertion by his faithful, but to confrontation by his double and rival, the fire demon, Trashcan Man. Trash, Flagg comes to understand, may be stronger than himself. Trash begins his rebellion by burning and bombing the air force Flagg has assembled to attack Boulder. After this episode Trash feels repentant and dreams of atonement: "if he found something . . . something *big* . . . and brought it to the dark man in Las Vegas, might it not be possible. And even if REDEMPTION was impossible, perhaps ATONEMENT was not." Trash selects a nuclear bomb as a token of propitiation and presents it to Flagg, but the bomb detonates, destroying the Dark Empire of the west. Flagg cannot control the course of events or this climactic confrontation with his double. Instability has degenerated into chaos in a Gothic environment whose parodic impulse ultimately turns on itself. Trash's sacral gesture of atonement implies that even at its apex the intrinsically destabilized Gothic universe cannot achieve coherence through religious inversion.

The destruction of Las Vegas, finally, points to the limits King chooses to place on the Gothic world of *The Stand.* A fire demon has served as a providential agent by turning the apocalyptic fires of purgation on Flagg's empire: the ball of electricity generated by Flagg to torture his Boulder captives grows to a "tremendous size" and a mysterious hand appears in the sky, *"The Hand of God!"* which seemingly directs Flagg's electricity toward the cart holding Trash's bomb. The apocalyptic plague which aided Flagg's rise to power has given way to an apocalyptic judgement which will, at least temporarily, free the world of his influence. King has opted to curtail the chaos and terror of the Gothic underworld by denying the "possibility that the Gothic atmosphere will take over completely and that the conventional, stable division between self and Other will disappear completely."

King's sacral parody uses the Gothic universe to mock Christian conventions, but the novels in question are not devoid of affirmation or lacking in constructive redefinition of the sacral. The examples of Father Callahan, Carrie and Margaret White and Louis Creed illustrate the formidable power of the Gothic underworld, a world fully capable of destroying those who enter it. Not all who enter the vicinity of the underworld, however, meet the same fate. The Boulder colony escapes by providential fiat and Ellie Creed because of her physical distance from her father's transactions with the burial ground.

Another group does battle with the darkness and emerges with at least a qualified victory. In *Cycle of the Werewolf* Marty Coslaw can destroy the werewolf in part because he believes in the power and extent of the underworld. While Constable Neary denies all evidence pointing to Reverend Lowe as the werewolf, Marty accepts what his eyes and instincts tell him. He has not been corrupted by a false mythology which would maintain that a minister could not become a Gothic beast because of the protection his sacral role allegedly provides. Marty engages the darkness, in detective-like fashion, and investigates its mysteries without allowing himself to become enthralled by them. Another child survivor is Danny Torrance, who undergoes some daunting tests: the child-ghoul in the Overlook's playground, the hedge animals, the ghost of Room 217 and, worst of all, his own father. Danny also believes in the Gothic but resists enthrallment. In the climactic scene when he must confront the Jack-thing that stalks him through the halls of the Overlook, Danny faces down the darkness by empirically and matter-of-factly denying the inversions and distortions that support the Jack-thing. His denial does not refute the underworld itself, but rather defines correctly the Gothic qualities that adults typically fail to see. Mark Petrie and Ben Mears succeed in *'Salem's Lot,* where Father Callahan had failed, destroying Barlow and most of the vampire colony. Mark leads the way by accepting the power of the underworld and doubting the intrinsic supremacy of the sacral to the Gothic. He confronts the Gothic world as an ingenious detective might, fully appreciating its menacing riddles, but denying that the power of the Gothic can benefit him. In part because he imitates Mark, Ben Mears manages to stake Barlow and to profit from the saving power of the sacred cross. Though Ben uses sacral devices, his own energy and ingenuity are his deepest resources of strength.

The survivors of the battles enumerated above embody a code or strategy which helps them to escape the terminal effects of the darkness. Their basically secular value systems allow them to maintain a careful distance from unqualified reliance upon conventional icons of and assumptions about the sacral and about institutionalized forms of it. They accept the fact that the Gothic can overwhelm the sacral and that coming to terms with the underworld means respecting its fierce powers. In effect, these characters "Gothicize" themselves; they defeat the monstrous with implicitly mocking gestures of defiance toward conventional and easy religious assumptions, rebellious gestures which reflect basic impulses of the Gothic itself. By so doing they can confront the Gothic without becoming enthralled by its most attractive qualities, and investigate it with enough detachment to make them effective detectives. Gothic postures of defiance, then, allow them to be in the Gothic world but not of it. King also relocates the intrinsic strength of the sacral by linking that strength with the innocence and purity of childhood. Childhood often possesses in his fiction an immense natural ability to negate the distortions of the underworld, to protect children from enthrallment, largely because King's child protagonists trust their own instincts, their native cunning, intuition, resourcefulness and purity. Recognizing that the systems and icons of adults regularly fail, these children turn to their own "simplicity" and frequently find their salvation in it. For King's adult characters, the taking on of childlike attitudes often becomes a metaphoric denial of Gothic enthrallment and a commitment to survival.

King's sacral parody consistently illustrates that in the Gothic universe a variety of Christian religious beliefs or procedures are inverted and turned awry, from fundamentalism to mysticism, rapture and communion with the Godhead, to sacraments and rituals, to Resurrection and the notion of divine providence. Dark, grotesque humor, often connected with the Gothic motifs of decay and breakdown, arises from that parody. Sacral parody not only reinforces Magistrale's argument that King implies the dissolution of "traditional concepts of social solidarity," but suggests that the weaknesses of the conventionally sacral may invoke Gothic horror. The Gothic archetypes examined by William Day, finally, help to clarify the nature and direction of King's parody. Somewhat predictably, King creates a Gothic underworld where conventional values are suspended or irrelevant. Again typically, he describes many sacral versions of the radical mutation and distortion characteristic of Gothic. King does present his Gothic environments as destabilizing and occasionally as self-parodic, but he stops short of nihilism, of insisting that there can be "no ascent from the underworld."

Though he evidently questions the efficacy of the sacral, King's invocation of providence in *The Stand* and the escape routes scattered through his fiction mitigate somewhat the radical Gothic belief in the total "disintegration of the spiritual." For King, enough human qualities remain uncorrupted to allow for some measure of protection against the terrors of the nightland.

Andy Solomon (review date 2 September 1990)

SOURCE: "Scared but Safe," in *New York Times Book Review*, September 2, 1990, p. 21.

[*In the following review, Solomon argues that although there is nothing new in King's* Four Past Midnight, *it is a difficult book to put down.*]

A decade ago, in *Danse Macabre,* Stephen King made his literary esthetic clear: "I try to terrorize the reader. But if . . . I cannot terrify . . . I will try to horrify; and if I find I cannot horrify, I'll go for the gross-out. I'm not proud." The figures on his royalty checks suggest this strategy works, and he sticks to it closely in *Four Past Midnight.* Unlike Mr. King's adventurous novel *The Eyes of the Dragon,* this quartet of short novels risks few departures from earlier form.

By now, everyone knows Stephen King's flaws: tone-deaf narration, papier-mâché characters, clichés, gratuitous vulgarity, self-indulgent digressions. Each is amply present in these pages ringing with echoes of earlier King. Most tales revisit the old Maine setting. The characters are types rather than individuals. Even the taste for the crude looks familiar—five pages rendered with more detail than we care for to describe a man's getting interrupted in the bathroom by a phone call.

Not proud at all, Mr. King rehashes plot devices as well. Like an earlier work, *The Stand,* one of these novellas, *The Langoliers,* eliminates all humanity but for a few survivors, this time on a plane that has passed through a "time rip." This ploy of minimizing his cast serves Mr. King's purpose; he constantly relies on there being no one around with the common sense his characters invariably lack—until the last moment when, miraculously, they realize exactly how to avert catastrophe.

However, we don't read Stephen King for common sense, originality or insight into the adult world. Many who wouldn't want the fact broadcast read this master of suspense to escape their helpless fear of the headlines and to re-experience the more innocent terrors of childhood, to be once again a preschooler whose heart pounds from a nightmare.

> **As the poet laureate of pop, Mr. King is read by many who might otherwise never read fiction at all. He creates an immediate and familiar landscape and could form the ideal bridge from the Road Runner to Dostoyevsky's Raskolnikov.**
> —*Andy Solomon*

In this collection, only *Secret Window, Secret Garden,* because it is about an adult's psychological disintegration, fails to achieve that effect. *The Langoliers* exploits the primal infant's fear of abandonment, even of ceasing to exist. *The Library Policeman* reawakens the most haunting dimensions of childhood admonitions. In *The Sun Dog,* the terrifying agent is a boy's Polaroid camera. Mr. King's recurring tactic of making the ordinary function in a bizarre way always hooks the child in us. Significantly, this "simplified" Polaroid is too complex inside to fix. We had hoped, growing up, for comforting knowledge of how the world works, but the technology opening onto the 21st century has outraced us.

Also abundant here is another source of Mr. King's mass appeal, springing ironically from his clichéd diction, what Paul Gray in *Time* magazine once called "postliterate prose." Admittedly lazy,—he says "I'm a lazy researcher"—Mr. King often avoids laboring at description by summoning pre-existing images from cartoons, old movies, television shows and commercials. Here, sinister men wear "white *Andromeda Strain* suits." People wind up in a "dreary version of Fantasyland." A ruffled adulterer, when caught, looks "like Alfalfa in the old Little Rascals." Men wish for guns "like the one Dirty Harry wore." Slacks are "the color of Bazooka bubble gum."

As the poet laureate of pop, Mr. King is read by many who might otherwise never read fiction at all. He creates an immediate and familiar landscape and could form the ideal bridge from the Road Runner to Dostoyevsky's Raskolnikov.

There is little here Mr. King has not done before, but once again he proves difficult to lay aside.

Gail E. Burns and Melinda Kanner (essay date 1990)

SOURCE: "Women, Danger, and Death: The Perversion of the Female Principle in Stephen King's Fiction," in *Sexual Politics and Popular Culture,* edited by Diane Raymond, Bowling Green State University Popular Press, 1990, pp. 158-72.

[*In the following essay, Burns and Kanner discuss the relationship between women and evil in King's work and assert, "On a complex and subtextual level, women are represented in ways that reveal male fear and envy of female sexuality and reproductive biology."*]

I hope that this study may lessen the male-centering propensity and shed new light on the psychosexual role of woman; that it may indicate how much more that is feminine exists in men than is generally believed, and how greatly woman's influence and strivings have affected social institutions which we still explain on a purely masculine basis.

With these words, the psychologist Bruno Bettelheim expresses the mission of his cross-cultural inquiry into *rites de passage.* With these words, one might well begin an inquiry into the construction and situation of women in the world of Stephen King's fiction.

In all societies, relations between men and women are expressed, in part, through the symbolic acquisition of the powers and capabilities not normally under the control of one sex or the other. Women seek to capture the social, economic, and political control typically enjoyed and exercised by men; men, on the other hand, symbolically mimic female biological capabilities, most notably menstruation and childbirth, revealing envy of that which they lack.

In a complex, large-scale society such as ours, we turn our attention to the artifacts of popular culture to gain insight into our myths, our irreconcilable conflicts, our symbolic envies. To this end, Stephen King's work provides fertile ground for the anthropologist.

> **King himself and critics alike have commented that he cannot write convincing female characters. Our investigation reveals that the construction of female characters in *Pet Sematary,* as in his other fiction, draws upon and reinforces widely, if unconsciously, shared cultural myths about the female principle.**
> —*Gail E. Burns and Melinda Kanner*

Eric Norden's 1983 *Playboy* interview with Stephen King reveals something of King's attitudes about sex, sexual relations, and women. Asked if he has any "sexual hang-ups," King replies that his only sexual problem is that he is a sufferer of "periodic impotence." Asked why explicit sex is largely absent from his novels and stories, he replies that, first he is uncomfortable with sex, second, he has trouble creating believable romantic relationships which would be necessary to avoid arbitrary or perfunctory sex, and finally, that he has, in fact, included an S & M fantasy in one of his novellas. Norden continues in this line of questioning:

> Norden: Along with your difficulty in describing sexual scenes you apparently also have a problem with women in your books . . .
>
> King: Yes, unfortunately, I think it is probably the most justifiable of all those [criticisms] leveled at me . . . I recognize the problems but can't yet rectify them.

The women in King's fiction, then, are not carefully crafted, three-dimensional characters. The problem King has with women has nothing to do with writing women convincingly. Rather the deeply unconscious, culturally shared understandings of what constitutes Woman that emerge from the pages of these novels provide the basis for this analysis.

King himself and critics alike have commented that he cannot write convincing female characters. Our investigation reveals that the construction of female characters in *Pet Sematary,* as in his other fiction, draws upon and reinforces widely, if unconsciously, shared cultural myths about the female principle. This paper explores the construction of women in Stephen King and draws upon his controversial novel, *Pet Sematary,* as exemplary of the representation of women in King's fiction.

Precisely because of his immense popularity, Stephen King provides fertile ground for scholarly analysis. Although critical and academic audiences for the most part ignore, denigrate, or otherwise declare King's fiction as unworthy of serious consideration, the vast popularity of this body of popular culture suggests an area for investigation by the social scientists as well as the literary critic.

Since the 1974 publication of his best-selling novel, *Carrie,* Stephen King has received vast popular attention. His novels and collections of stories, in press continuously from their first publication and frequently converted into theatrical and made-for-television movies, have generated unprecedented levels of readership and media attention. Infrequently has this positive and sustained popular reception been matched with critical enthusiasm. The schism which traditionally has inhibited serious investigation of popular culture is dramatically reflected in the lack of academic reactions to Stephen King. Certain notable exceptions do exist. Two general categories of critical treatment address the various dimensions on which King exists as a phenomenon.

First, the predominant approach to King's fiction, written by fans-cum-critics, glorifies King's literary product as unrec-

ognized genius. These authors have contributed significantly to deepening King's appeal through their attention to his biography and its connections to his writing, their plot expositions, and their detailed cataloguing of the corpus of King's work. However valuable their contributions, this treatment has done little to advance our understanding of the underlying culturally shared symbols which account in large measure for King's popularity.

A second treatment of King has begun to explore the possibilities of scholarly interpretations by locating King's fiction in the context of theme and genre, of metaphor and archetype.

The recent publication of Hoppenstand and Browne's *The Gothic World of Stephen King* provides a collection of essays which understands King's fiction and films in the light of the contemporary re-telling of traditional horror myths, the struggle of adolescents in an adult world, the adult reliving of childhood horrors and interpretations of morality.

The high-culture low-culture dichotomy which has all but precluded serious literary analysis of King's fiction places the burden of untangling King's signification system on the shoulders of popular culture studies. The literary quality of King's work is not at issue, nor are the myriad explanations for his popular success. The aim here is to understand the women in King's fiction in the larger cultural context, to come to terms with those unconsciously shared and understood ideals, values, and understandings which give his plots and characters meaning, which give his images sustained potency.

In a recent made-for-cable-TV program, *Stephen King's Women of Horror,* horror writers and filmmakers, including Clive Barker, John Carpenter, and Anthony Hickox, comment on the role of women in horror fiction. John Carpenter, a director of horror films, observes:

> In society we have a lot of mixed feelings about women, what they should do and what they shouldn't do, and I think you see it reflected in horror movies all the time. It's a kind of anxiety level on the bottom. Women's traditional roles . . . there's a lot of confusion. The confusion comes from men a lot of the time.

Female reproductive potential, sexuality, and death are forged by King in a manner that invariably locks his female characters into particular, sexually defined roles. Although this analysis focuses on *Pet Sematary,* a cursory examination of the larger context of Stephen King's work reveals that the powerful reproduction/sexuality/death dialectic is present in all his work and provides the symbolic matrix in which all girls and women are embedded. Menstruation, mothering, and female sexual desire function as bad omens, prescient clues that something will soon be badly awry.

Women as mothers are incapable of caring for or protecting their children. In King's world, mothers are pathetically unable to save their offspring: witness Donna and Tad Trenton (*Cujo*), Wendy and Danny Torrance (*The Shining*), Vicky and Charlie McGee (*Firestarter*). Indeed, mothers and maternal figures alike are very often the agents of destruction, as in the cases of Margaret White (*Carrie*), Heidi Halleck (*Thinner*), and Annie Wilkes (*Misery*). King consistently portrays women at the mercy of their hormones, a force of nature that he links with the supernatural and which results in death rather than life.

Women in traditional horror fiction are portrayed as victims, targets of evil, easily terrorized, susceptible to the seductive forces of vampires and murderers. Where women are represented as the agents of horror themselves, they traditionally have appeared as "devourers, vampires, seductresses who can make you crash because you're listening to their song." Women in King's fiction are neither vacant, screaming victims nor are they evil incarnate. The ways in which women embody evil and act as conduits for the supernatural are ambiguous and drawn from culturally and socially shared understandings. The evil that women are and the evil women do in King is ambiguous, derived from precisely the forces of life and attraction.

Carrie White (*Carrie*) and Roberta Anderson (*Tommyknockers*) experience some sort of dysmenorrhea which functions as a portent of their personal destruction and, through them, the destruction of their communities. In each case King defines menstruation as the trigger for the paranormal/supernatural events of these novels. Carrie's and Bobbie's reproductive potential cannot result in life; instead it is perverted and becomes the transmitter of mutation and death. This biological conundrum is a hallmark of King's fictional females.

Bobbie Anderson, as she discovers and progressively uncovers the mysterious evil buried beneath the earth, lays open a trench.

> She began to unbutton her jeans so she could tuck
> in her blouse, then paused. The crotch of the faded
> Levi's was soaked with blood. Jesus. Jesus Christ.
> This isn't a period. This is Niagara Falls.

Days later, as she resumes her exploratory digging:

> Her period had started again, but that was all right;
> she had put a pad in the crotch of her panties even
> before she went out to weed the garden. A Maxi.

Women who do manage to give birth generally fail their children in the most fundamental ways. This failure is linked consistently in King's novels to their sexuality, manifest as excessive or inadequate. Donna Trenton, for example, watches her son die of dehydration and is helpless to act until it is too late. Cujo, the rabid St. Bernard, keeps the mother-child dyad trapped in a disabled Pinto for three days, but it is the mother, Donna, not Cujo, who sets the tragic circumstances in motion and is therefore ultimately responsible for her son's death. The car has not been repaired because her sexual relationship with the local tennis pro, Steve Kemp, estranges her from Vic, her husband, creates havoc in the household, and results in the fatal car break-down.

> He [Steve Kemp] had known Donna was cooling
> it, but she had struck him as a woman who could
> be manipulated with no great difficulty, at least for
> a while, by a combination of psychological and
> sexual factors. By fear, if you wanted to be crude.

Wendy Torrance's lack of decision nearly results is her son Danny's death. She knows of her husband's recurrent violence; his past alcoholic rages have resulted in child abuse including the broken arm of the infant Danny. Wendy, however, ignores Jack's erratic behavior, his inability to write, and even her growing suspicions that he is drinking again. She takes no measure to end the abuse, to save herself or her son. It is, in fact, Danny's telepathic distress signal to Halloran that results in their rescue from the Overlook.

Why is Billy Halleck (*Thinner*) afflicted with a gypsy curse? Because he killed the old man's daughter. But what caused the fatal automobile accident? Heidi Halleck, who is masturbating her husband Billy as they cruise along a busy city street. The facts that it is female desire, female sexual initiation, and, most importantly perhaps, sexual expression which cannot result in conception all function significantly in the sex/death dialectic.

As Heidi Halleck's desire realizes its expression, this temptation-turned-tragedy results in the death of seven people, including the entire Halleck family.

> But he couldn't speak. The pleasure woke again
> at the touch of her fingers, playful at first then
> more serious . . . The pleasure mixed uneasily
> with a feeling of terrible inevitability . . . Then:
> *Thud/thud.*

And, when blame is clearly assigned to the granddaughter of the deceased, the underlying cause of the tragedy is made public.

> He was getting a jerk-off job from his woman and
> he ran her down in the street.

Heidi unwittingly passes on the gypsy curse to their daughter, through her roles as biological creator and maternal nurturer. They share a strawberry pie, laden with placental, vaginal, and menstrual imagery. The pie, presented to Billy by the old gypsy man, will undo the curse when Billy feeds it to another woman. The imagery of the pie is explicit.

> This thing—*purpurfargade ansiket*—you bring into the world like a baby. Only it grows faster than a baby, and you can't kill it because you can't see it— only you can see what it *does*.

The pie, with a "darkish slit" under which a blood-like ooze pulsed, would extract the curse from Billy, contain it, and, finally implant it in the eater. As Billy followed the old man's instructions, allowing the blood from his knife wound to spill into the pie, his wound healed, the pie sealed itself, and

> He collapsed back against the park bench, feeling wretchedly nauseated, wretchedly *empty*—the way a woman who has just given birth must feel, he imagined.

The conjunction of the expression "the curse" with the bloody mass seeping from a dark slit, the perverse restorative, life-giving powers of the pie, the urgency of oral incorporation of the pie by another, and the ultimate responsibility for the series of devastations aimed at Heidi present an ambiguous exposition of the female to the reader.

In *Firestarter,* another case of an inadequate mother precipitates tragic events. The Shop, a nefarious secret agency, comes after Charlie because of her telepyrotechnic powers. That ability is the result of some genetic mutation caused by drugs used in an experiment for which her parents volunteered. Yet the most rudimentary knowledge of biology assigns the blame to Vicky for that mutant gamete. The evil which pursues them can only be construed as punishment for her flagrant disregard of her future reproductive role.

> "I'm Vicky Tomlinson. And a little nervous about this, Andy McGee. What if I go on a bad trip or something?"

He ended up buying her two Cokes, and they spend the afternoon together. That evening they had a few beers at the local hangout. It turned out that she and the boyfriend had come to a parting of ways, and she wasn't sure exactly how to handle it. He was beginning to think they were married, she told Andy; had absolutely forbidden her to take part in the Wanless experiment. For that precise reason she had gone ahead and signed the release form and was now determined to go through with it even though she was a little scared. . . .

How do you explain to a seven-year-old girl that Daddy and Mommy had once needed two hundred dollars and the people they had talked to said it was all right, but they had lied?

Her subsequent inability to defend herself and Charlie results in her own grisly death and Charlie's abduction by the evil secret agents.

Carrie's mother, Margaret White, is not, in any conventional sense maternal, but rather a hyperbole of perverted female sexuality and maternity. Her extreme puritanical view of sex—in the best Freudian tradition—produced a very strange girl.

After Carrie's humiliating public first menstruation, she returns home, hoping to find explanation from her mother.

"Why didn't you *tell* me? . . . Oh, Momma, I was so *scared!*"

Her mother articulates the connection of female sexuality, menstruation, motherhood, and evil:

> And Eve was weak and loosed the raven on the world . . . and the raven was called Sin, and the first Sin was Intercourse. And the Lord visited Eve with a Curse, and the Curse was the Curse of blood. And Adam and Eve were driven out of the Garden and into the World and Eve found that her belly had grown big with child.

Carrie's menarche somehow endows her with incredible telekinetic powers through which she punishes her classmates, her mother, and the entire town. Specifically, it is her rage at the ignominious outcome of her first date that prompts her to unleash her talents. This date with Tommy, particularly when they are chosen King and Queen of the Prom, is heavy with sexual implication and death imagery. In the recollection of a classmate, Norma Watson, the moment is described.

> All at once there was a huge red splash in the air. Some of it hit the mural and ran in long drips. I knew right away, even before it hit them, that it was blood. Stella Horan thought it was paint, but I had a premonition just like the time my brother got hit by a hay truck. Carrie got it the worst.

Annie Wilkes (*Misery*), although not biologically a mother, assumes a demented maternal role in Paul Sheldon's life. The fact that she is a killer nurse—notably in a hospital nursery— again punctuates King's death/reproduction theme. She disables and infantilizes Paul with drugs, rendering him dependent on her for all his needs.

Castration imagery figures prominently in Annie's terrorist maternity. First, a hobbling episode, representing both dependence and castration:

> Just a little pain. Then this nasty business will be behind us for good, Paul . . . She gripped the handle farther up in her left hand and spread her legs like a logger . . . The axe came whistling down and buried itself in Paul Sheldon's left leg just above the ankle.

Then later, the surgical removal of another of Paul's appendages in the thumbectomy.

> Then he had been still and let her give him the injection and this time the Betadine had gone over his left thumb as well as the blade of the knife . . . As the humming, vibrating blade sank into the soft web of flesh between the soon-to-be-defunct thumb and his first finger, she assured him again in her this-hurts-Mother-more-than-it-hurts-Paulie voice that she loved him.

The contrast between Annie and Misery Chastain, the voluptuous heroine of Paul's best-selling books, might be amusing were it not for Annie's crazed torture of the bedridden novelist. It is Misery's death in childbirth which catalyzes Annie's perverted mothering and underscores both the dangers of women who fail to fulfill their proper roles and the power of the male author over the death and resurrection of his female characters.

Women occupy particularly horrible roles in King's fiction. They are not, typically, wide-eyed, screaming, terror-stricken virgins, nor are they recognizable villains who suck the blood of those who would fall prey to their seductive powers. Rather they are the evil which results from the perversion of convention, the misuse of female sexual desire, the dangers of the empty, or emptying womb, the destruction which is unleashed by a failed mother.

> **Rachel Creed, the mother in *Pet Sematary,* is a good, if ineffective mother who provides the link between the dangers of life and mysteries of death. Failed by her own possessive, fearful parents and witness to her sister Zelda's agonizing, slow death, Rachel produces Ellen and Gage—children who themselves are doomed.**
> **—*Gail E. Burns and Melinda Kanner***

In *Stephen King's Women of Horror,* narrator Strozier notes

It is precisely their essence of femininity, the seductiveness in women that provides a perfect launching point for exploring the taboos of our society, the physical attractions, the compulsions, and attractions . . . The corruption of one's nature is a prime target for horror writers.

The emotions which surround sex and motherhood are compelling. The manipulation of these feelings serves to disorient, confuse, upset, and attract the reader. King has particular interest in "scaring women to death."

> It would be sexist to say that only ladies care about their children—in fact, it would be a downright lie—but there does seem to be such a thing as a "maternal instinct," and I go for it instinctively.

Indeed. Quite apart from King's ability to scare women, or men for that matter, his effectiveness depends upon hitting responsive chords, seeking out and bruising cultural sore spots, reflecting and creating images at reflexive and unconscious levels.

> The soil of a man's heart is stonier, Louis—like the soil up there in the old Micmac burying ground. Bedrock's close. A man grows what he can . . . and he tends it.

Pet Sematary elaborates the dysfunctionally dangerous, and destructive female principle in the world of Stephen King. The reproductive power of women, distorted in King's novels, becomes the object of envy and perversion. Sex expressed outside the context of procreative intercourse, sex initiated by a female, becomes linked with death rather than life. In this perversion, the power of procreation—of resurrection—becomes the property of men rather than women.

Rachel Creed, the mother in *Pet Sematary,* is a good, if ineffective mother who provides the link between the dangers of life and mysteries of death. Failed by her own possessive, fearful parents and witness to her sister Zelda's agonizing, slow death, Rachel produces Ellen and Gage—children who themselves are doomed. Deserted by his father and protected by his mother, Louis Creed fathers Ellen and Gage in the only distorted ways he can piece together from his skill as a physician and his role as a watchful and complaint "son" to the older neighbor Jud Crandall.

Prompted by Rachel's pathological inability and unwillingness to educate their daughter, Ellie, in matters of death, Louis Creed submits to the tutelage of Jud Crandall, his surrogate father, to learn the secrets of resurrection buried in the man's arcane knowledge.

Rachel's abdication of responsibility is revealed after a visit to the local pet cemetery, a burial ground established by children to honor their dead pets. Ellie's matter-of-fact approach to death is matched by her father's pragmatic, honest responses and contrasted with her mother's paranoid and terrified refusal to expose the child to death in any manifestation. Ellie's next exposure to the possibilities of death held by life comes with the neutering of her male cat, Church. Finally, the accidental death of Church while Rachel, Ellie, and Gage are visiting Rachel's parents set in motion the text of life restored and subtext of sex and death.

This perversion of reproduction is played out in several dimensions. Through two themes King juxtaposes the central elements and resolves the conflicts which inhere: Opposing forces are inverted, transformed and reversed.

At the center of the mother/father opposition are the dismal, dysfunctional childhoods of Rachel and Louis. Rachel, the daughter of upper middle class, urban parents, is dominated and controlled by her father, Irwin Goldman. Disapproving of Rachel's relationship with Louis from the start, Goldman offers Louis a "scholarship" for his medical school education in exchange for Louis' termination of his relationship with Rachel. The offer rejected, Louis severs himself from the Goldmans in every way possible. Rachel remains, at least partly, under the domination of her parents, succumbing to their pressure and accepting their gifts.

The parent/child mania in this relationship comes from Rachel's childhood. Her older sister, Zelda, had died of spinal meningitis when Rachel had been left by her parents, alone, at age eight, to watch her disabled and dying sister. Rachel was never *told* about death, but rather initiated into its mysteries. Rachel, the product of a politely dysfunctional home, transmits the destruction of ignorance to her own daughter, Ellie. By failing to tell Ellie about death, she leaves her maternal responsibility to Louis.

Louis, a child raised by his mother alone, suffers a different dysfunction. His mother, too, protected him. Where Rachel, as her mother before her, failed to instruct the daughter in the mysteries of death, Louis' mother misled him in matters of birth, about women finding babies in dewy grass when they really wanted one. "Louis had never forgiven his mother for telling it—or himself for believing it." Early in his life, Louis is educated about the natural place of death from his undertaker uncle, and by the same mother who had lied to him about sex. In his mind, Jud Crandall's voice and his mother are merged for him as he recalls the death of his first love at age twelve. The mysteries of death, unknown to Rachel, remain mysterious. The secrets of burial are as much a part of Louis' knowledge as his skill as a physician.

Rachel Creed, like the Biblical Rachel, will weep for her children and not be comforted, because they are not.

The pet cemetery is the site of death and burial and it is the perversely fertile soil, the soil of a man, for rebirth. This is signalled early by Rachel in an argument with Louis about confronting Ellie with the facts of death. Louis argues that Ellie knows the "facts of life," or the mechanics of human reproduction. "Where babies come from has nothing to do with a goddam pet cemetery," Rachel screams at Louis. Indeed, for the men in *Pet Sematary,* the pet cemetery has everything to do with where "babies" come from. The conversion of death into life, the reversal of natural processes, depends upon a complexly woven code of sex and death, in which all ordering, all processes, all functions become perverted.

Four major manifestations of the conjunction of sex and death form the center of the text: First, the juxtaposition of sexual encounters between Louis and Rachel with a death related episode; second, the metaphorical description of the pet cemetery's attraction and the pull of death is like the power and irresistibility of sexual attraction; third, the coincidence of castration actuality, anxiety, and threats with death imagery and death episodes; finally, the specifically sexual nature of the "knowledge" that those who return from the Micmac burial ground articulate in their resurrected state.

Sexual encounters between Louis and Rachel becomes linked with death when they are non-procreative—oral sex, masturbation—or when they occur at Rachel's instigation. On his first day as head of University Medical Services, the same day that Rachel was to schedule the castration of Ellie's cat, Louis Creed presides over the death of a young man fatally injured by an automobile. This man, Victor Pascow, in his dying words, warns Louis about the pet cemetery, speaks the words that Jud would speak ("a man's heart is stonier"). When Louis returns home that evening, Rachel greets him with seduction: a hot bath and a masturbatory sexual encounter. The occurrence of death followed by sex is repeated when Church, the now un-dead cat, brings home a Christmas Eve present of a dead crow, which he deposits at the Creed doorstep. Again, as Louis disposes of the crow, Pascow, Jud, Church, and Louis are conjoined in a prelude to sex. When Louis joins Rachel in bed, she greets him again with female-initiated sex, this time fellatio. Sex, when expressed in any way other than one which will result in conception, becomes the link with death. Initiated by Rachel, following Louis' encounters with death, these sexual liaisons confer upon Louis not the powers of female reproductive capabilities, but an inversion of these powers: their accumulation endows him with power of resurrection. The reversal of the sex-conception sequence into the death-sex sequence provides the transforming joint.

A second death/sex conjunction appears in the frequent comparisons between the pull of death and the attraction of the pet cemetery with sex. The necessity of man submitting to the demands of the burial ground is described as something

> you do because it gets hold of you. You do it because that burial place is a secret place, and you want to share the secret . . . you make up reasons . . . they seem like good reasons . . . but mostly you do it because you want to. Or because you have to.

After Jud calls Louis to deliver the sad news that Church's dead body lies on the road, another victim of the truck route, Louis contemplates how wrong this all seems, how he believed his family would be exempt from such tragedy in another death/sex connection.

> He remembered one of the guys he played poker with, Wikes Sullivan, asking him once how he could get horny for his wife and not get horny for the naked women he saw day in and day out. Louis tried to explain to him that it wasn't the way people imagined in their fantasies—a woman coming in to get a Pap smear or to learn how to give herself a breast self-examination didn't suddenly drop a sheet and stand there like Venus on the half-shell. You saw a breast, a vulva, a thigh. The rest was draped in sheet, and there was a nurse in attendance, more to protect the doctor's reputation than anything else. Wicky wasn't buying it. A tit is a tit, was Wicky's thesis, and a twat is a twat. You should either be horny all the time or none of it. All Louis could respond was that your wife's tit was different. *Just like your family's supposed to be different,* he thought now. Church wasn't supposed to get killed . . .

Other imagery links male sexuality and the male power of resurrection through the burial ground. Jud describes to Louis some of the secrets he has kept from his wife, Norma.

> I used to go up to the whorehouse in Bangor betimes. Nothing many a man hasn't done, although I s'pose there are plenty that walk the straight and narrow. I just would get the urge—the compulsion, maybe—to sink it into strange flesh now and then . . . Men keep their gardens too, Louis.

Castration, first of Church the cat, then Louis's own castration fears are tied to death and the recreation of life. Before their moving to Maine, Louis intervened on behalf of Church and obstructed a scheduled neutering by canceling the vet appointment. There is the strong suggestion that the cat's virility and Louis' own masculinity are somehow pieces of one puzzle.

> In fact there had been some trouble over that back

in Chicago. Rachel had wanted to get Church spayed, had even made the appointment with the vet. Louis canceled it. Even now he wasn't really sure why. It wasn't anything simple or as stupid as equating his masculinity with that of his daughter's tom . . . but most of it had been a vague but strong feeling that it would destroy something in Church that he himself valued . . .

The anticipation of Church's neutering precipitates Ellie's questions about death. The second and successful scheduling of the vet appointment comes immediately before Louis's encounter with the dying Pascow. In a dream, as Louis imagines life had Gage lived, had he not been killed in the same road where Church died, he re-writes the scenario by saving Gage from certain death. In his scenario, his closest contact with himself is genital, as though saving Gage was somehow an act of procreation.

> He yanked Gage backward and landed on the ground at the same instant, crashing his face into the rough gravel of the shoulder, giving himself a bloody nose. His balls signaled a much more serious flash of pain—Ohh, if I'd'a known I was gonna be playing football, I woulda worn my jock—but both the pain in his nose and the driving agony in his testes were lost in the swelling relief of hearing Gage's wail of pain and outrage . . .

As Louis embarks on his grave-robbing to recover the body of his son, he encounters the physical obstacles that might block his entrance into the cemetery. As he begins his ascent of the cemetery wall, he comes upon decorative arrow tips at the top of the fence. He realizes that his testicles, not to mention his internal organs, are in peril. As if by protecting his testicles, becoming aware of them, saving Church's sexual potency, unconsciously hurting himself in his fantasy rescue of Gage, Louis invests his testes with the power of resurrection.

Equally important is the nature of the knowledge of sexual intimacies announced by those who return from the dead. Timmy Baterman, a figure from Jud's past, was the only other human re-buried and, importantly, resurrected by his father in the Micmac cemetery. When Timmy returned from the dead, he reveals his secret knowledge.

> 'Your wife is fucking that man she works with down at the drugstore, Purinton. What do you think of that? She screams when she comes. What do you think of that?'

When Gage returns and confronts Jud in prelude to his death at the hands of the un-dead toddler, he reveals the secrets of Norma's sex life, again underscoring the connection of non-procreative sex and the world of death.

> Norma's dead and there'll never be no one to mourn you . . . What a cheap slut she was. She fucked every one of your friends, Jud. She let them put it up her ass . . .

Then, just before the fatal blow is delivered, Gage speaks to Jud in Norma's voice, telling him how she and her lovers laughed at him, how they made love in their bed, how she knew of his whorehouse visits. As Jud lunges to silence Gage, Gage strikes him with a scalpel from his father's medical bag. The father's instrument of life becomes the son's instrument of death.

Pet Sematary reveals a slight departure from King's typical treatment of women. Rather than the direct conduit of danger, destruction, and evil, Rachel Creed provides two rather more insidious and vital connections for the horrors of rebirth.
—Gail E. Burns and Melinda Kanner

Sex provides several vital connections through which Louis acquires the powers to produce a version of life. First as the aftermath of Louis's encounters with death, sex with Rachel allows Louis to gain access to female reproductive powers through this post-mortem contact. Next, the desire to visit the Micmac burial ground to bury first Church then Gage, is presented as like sexual desire. Third, the power to resurrect life is initiated through and invested in male sex organs and male sexuality. Finally, sex becomes the secrets held by the dead who return and share them with the living.

Pet Sematary reveals a slight departure from King's typical treatment of women. Rather than the direct conduit of danger, destruction, and evil, Rachel Creed provides two rather more insidious and vital connections for the horrors of rebirth.

The inadequacies of her own childhood disable her as a mother. Her fatal failure lies in her inability to teach her daughter that which a mother must teach: the mysteries of death. Her pathological inability to deal with death, and thereby save her family, results from the failures of her own parents.

Through her sexual behavior—desire, initiation, preferred forms of expression—she enables Louis to capture that which he lacks as a man, as a father, and as a physician: the ability to give, not simply save, life. Louis's role as a physician-turned-father-grave-robber-turned-life-giver is central to the conversion. Louis, who has presided over dozens of deaths, whose life was built upon saving life and relieving suffering, sought not the ultimate goal of his profession but the ultimate, collective male fantasy. A man's heart is stonier, Louis is told by Jud Crandall, and man tends his garden, grows what he can. What is grown in this stonier ground is a rockier life, born of the captured and distorted power of female reproduction.

Rather than victims or diabolical villains, women in Stephen King's fiction are the triggers of evil, the literal embodiment of danger. On a complex and subtextual level, women are represented in ways that reveal male fear and envy of female sexuality and reproductive biology. Not unlike the myth and ritual that symbolically play out and, to an extent, resolve male ambivalence toward women, King's women are dangerous figures indeed, to be feared as lovers, wives, and mothers.

Scores of societies known to anthropology play out similar dramas in symbolic and expressive forms. The *couvade,* for example, is a conspicuously ceremonial event in which men symbolically mimic post-partum recovery after their wives give birth. Institutionalized transvestism and clothing exchange, dramatic male rites of passage which entail genital blood-letting, and masquerade cults in which males exaggerate female fertility are, like the underlying drama in *Pet Sematary,* the symbolic working out of male envy and ambivalence. This resolution is derived from and responsible for shaping essential and unconsciously shared images.

Those women who are neither sexually linked to men nor maternally linked to children are not immune from male antagonism. Their failure to fulfill their expected, validated sociobiological functions renders them no less dangerous to their communities. Their sexuality is their vulnerability; the realization of their sexual desire results in destruction and death. Mothers fail their children, witness their abuse, and stand helpless to prevent their deaths. Finally, and most vividly illustrated in *Pet Sematary,* the ultimate perversion of the female principle is illustrated in the male appropriation of the powers of reproduction.

Chris Pourteau (essay date Summer 1993)

SOURCE: "The Individual and Society: Narrative Structure and Thematic Unity in Stephen King's *Rage,*" in *Journal of Popular Culture,* Vol. 27, No. 1, Summer, 1993, pp. 171-78.

[*In the following essay, Pourteau discusses the struggle of the individual against society in King's* Rage.]

The seemingly popular conception among literary critics that Stephen King's writing ability is somehow "less" than those writers usually considered "great writers," or "literary writers," stems from the "considerable comment and controversy" about his "prodigious popularity and productivity." A primary thesis of Mark Schorer's essay, "Technique as Discovery," establishes that writers who may be properly termed "artists" are those writers who consciously craft their works. Schorer says that, unlike H. G. Wells (whose overconfidence and disregard for the artistry of his profession necessitated his present-day obscurity), these artists will endure. The crafting of the work, according to Schorer, is what gives the work meaning; thus, through analyzing an artist's technique, we may discover the meaning of the work. In recent years, Stephen King has been granted Schorer's title of "artist" by such critics as Anthony Magistrale, Joseph Reino, and Douglas E. Winter. Despite his "prodigious popularity and productivity," King's reputation as a "literary" writer grows daily.

Anthony Magistrale argues that "The theme of innocence betrayed . . . unifies the major work of King's canon." Children, particularly, become victims as their characterization naturally implies a more innocent, corruptible state. As Magistrale suggests, "In King's novels and stories, there are few heroes; at best his major characters endure, but they seldom prevail . . . King's people are not superhuman, but ordinary, flawed, and vulnerable." Thus, King's works are often morality plays between good and evil, though his characters are not easy to pigeon-hole into moral categories.

Bernard J. Gallagher calls King's novels "psychological allegories," arguing that "external social pressures from the public world have led to a debilitating psychic fragmentation" of some of King's characters. As Gallagher suggests, the primary tension in King's work stems from the battle between the individual and society to control the individual's freedom:

> King believe[s] that the individual's relationship to his environment and to other individuals is based upon a complex interchange in which external events affect the unconscious which in turn disturbs the balance of the id, ego, and superego, which in turn disturbs the individual.

Gallagher, states that "he [King] may be nothing less than a closet Freudian who has chosen to abandon the Freudian emphases on infantile regression and the Oedipal conflict." Though Gallagher may go too far when positing King's abandonment of the Oedipal conflict, particularly when we see that conflict expressed so dramatically in *Rage,* he nevertheless recognizes the important psychological tension between the individual and society in King's works.

Looking at King's adolescent character types more specifically, Tom Newhouse says,

> King's novels and stories that depict teenage life are profoundly critical of the parental expectations, conservative values, and peer pressures which teenagers must face. In addition, King's teen protagonists come into awareness engaging the contradictions between the logical realm of routine activity and the darker regions of violent, destructive impulses. They are often outsiders who turn to violence as a response to exclusionary social environments which deny them acceptance, or who resort to destructive attitudes that they believe will advance them upward.

As Newhouse defines it, King's "brand of fiction" combines "social realism and archetypal horror, exposing deficient institutional and social values and the flimsy rational biases on which they are founded." In his analysis of *Rage,* Newhouse describes the novel as a treatise against authority, and, "though Charlie's revolt has a basis in genuine madness," the real motivation behind Charlie's civil disobedience is the "all too familiar" repression of the individual by society. Accepting Newhouse's assertion that this theme of the individual vs. society is the primary tension running through *Rage,* an examination of the structure of the novel should show, as Mark Schorer suggests, that this theme is evident in the technique of the novel.

In his essay, "The Concept of Point of View," Mitchell A. Leaska offers three classifications for narrative point of view: 1) omniscient narration, in which the writer controls and has access to all points of view in the narrative, 2) limited narration, in which the perspective of the storyteller is limited either to first or third person and sometimes colored by the interpreter's own psychological condition, and 3) non-narrated presentation, in which the character presents, in present tense, the reality of the text directly to the reader. King, to some extent, employs all three narrative techniques in *Rage.*

In Chapters 10 and 35, we have direct, present-tense addresses by Charlie to the reader. Chapter 10 is a discussion of "sanity," with Charlie standing "(metaphorically speaking . . .)" before the reader and telling us that he is "perfectly sane." Chapter 35 is Charlie's sign-off chapter, i.e. his last address to the reader, and his final announcement: "That's the end. I have to turn off the light now. Good night. . . ." The two chapters engender in the reader a sense of proximity to Charlie. Both chapters indicate examples in *Rage* of an obliterated narrative; Charlie has obliterated his *own* narration, for no longer are the readers separated from him by the narrative construction of the very past events he has described.

The classification of limited narration will only be mentioned briefly here, as it is obvious and occupies 32 of the novel's 35 chapters. At least two levels of this narration occur in *Rage:* the first is Charlie's relation of the events on that May morning to the reader; the second is when Charlie tells us of relating his autobiography to his classmates while he holds them hostage. While, in one sense, he is Leaska's first-person observer (for example, during the camping trip with his father when he hears the older men denigrating his mother and all women in general), he is also the narrator-participant during the primary narrative. His present state of mind, filled with the tension of his struggle with society, is reflected in his presentation of authority figures:

> School administrators and teachers are seen as hollow bullies, deluded by an authority that belies a weakness which is ultimately revealed during the tense confrontation, and parents are portrayed either as insensitive brutes or dark sexual monsters, like Charlie's Navy recruiter father.

The presence of the omniscient narrator is a debatable one, but, perhaps, an inescapable conclusion when examining Chapter 33 of the novel. Chapter 33 is an interoffice memo describing the catatonic mental state of Ted Jones, the classroom representative of the social norm, who, as a result of his "humbling" by Charlie's teachings and the class's physical assault, has retreated into that state. Yet, since it is learned (in Chapter 34) that Charlie's mail is censored by his own psychiatrists (he was committed to Augusta State Hospital on August 27, 1976), and the memo (dated November 3, 1976) is presented alone, without comment by Charlie, the reader may assume Charlie's ignorance of both the memo and Ted Jones's fate. Such an assumption, however, implies the presence of an outside controller of the narrative. The only solution to the problem of control in Chapter 33 (other than an outside fictional compiler, of which the reader is given no evidence since Charlie's narrative is, apparently, a direct, spoken address to the reader), is an omniscient narrator. Though we never hear the "voice" of that narrator, its presence is the only way to explain the inclusion of the memo in the novel. This shifting point of view reflects the individual/social tension thematically developed by King and structurally developed in the narrative; Charlie's struggle with society is mirrored by a struggle for control of the novel itself.

Rage is divided into 35 chapters (forming 170 pages), varying from half a page to 12 pages in length. The events of 29 of those chapters occur two years before Charlie's "present" (when he is telling the story), and entail the events taking place between the hours of 9:05 am and 1:00 pm on the day Charlie takes over his class. With the exception of Chapter 33, as noted above, the reader can assume that Charlie has a varying measure of control of the narrative throughout the novel.

His intrusions in various chapters of the narrative serve a specific purpose. Chapter 5, in which he transcends the primary time of action to a prior time of action, the camping trip with his father, sets up the Oedipal tension played out within the theme of individual vs. society in all Charlie's rebellions against authority. Chapter 10, as described earlier, allows Charlie a non-narrated, dramatic presentation of his theories on sanity. Chapter 15 represents a dramatic pause between Charlie and the reader as he briefly describes the class's silent reaction to his tale of Oedipal tension described in Chapter 14. Chapter 35 is Charlie's revelation that his rebellion, perhaps, was not as successful as he had at first hoped; it shows his own vulnerability and the final clamping down of society on Charlie, the individual.

A dual purpose of these chapters remains consistent throughout all four of them. They share a common characteristic: they break-up the flow of the narrative, allowing Charlie to control the presentation of the events to the reader. In Chapter 5, Charlie decides to obliterate the narrative restraints he had set for himself by telling of the camping trip with his father which occurred when Charlie was a boy. In Chapter 10, Charlie steps completely outside the narrative structure to theorize on the concept of sanity. In Chapter 15, Charlie's dramatic pause allows the reader to assess the effect of his Oedipal conflict on his secondary audience, his classmates. In Chapter 35, the reader learns from Charlie that society, for the moment at least, has beaten him, and it is ironic that he briefly retakes control of the narrative to prove that point. Except for this last chapter (the control of which is debatable since the reader learns of the ultimate failure of Charlie's struggle and that he must end the narrative because he must "turn off the light now," a restraint placed upon him by the society which has conquered him), these explicit examples of Charlie's narrative control occur in the first half of the novel.

The narrative of Chapters 16-31 is told in past tense but is set entirely within the classroom. Though some characteristics of the narrative are similar to the first half of the novel, the authorial control Charlie established by sectioning off the narrative before Chapter 16 is nonexistent thereafter. One characteristic shared between the two halves of the novel is Charlie's account of his relationship with his father. These descriptions which occur in the second half of the novel, in Chapters 16, 29, and briefly at the end of Chapter 22, however, do not break the primary time of action as it is broken in the first half of the novel. These stories are again told to the reader during that time, for they are stories which Charlie tells to the class while he holds it hostage. By getting rid of the quotation marks which ordinarily characterizes his dialogue with his classmates in these chapters, Charlie places the reader in the classroom with the rest of his hostage audience. Thus, Charlie is not narrating a story second-hand to the reader *about* his revelations to his classmates (and their subsequent revelations to him); the reader is, instead, placed within the classroom and experiencing those revelations first-hand, as they happen.

Though Charlie maintains some control over the narrative in the second half of the novel, he cannot step outside its boundaries and becomes obligated to his peer audience. He must shape his narrative based on their reactions and despite the fact that his peers, with the exception of Ted Jones of course, support him after their initial shock of Charlie's murder of Mrs. Underwood and Mr. Vance, Charlie must gauge their responses and mediate his actions accordingly. While giving a treatise on individual rebellion against an oppressive system, Charlie, ironically, finds himself reliant on his new society's (his peers') acceptance of him in order to "teach" them.

The last four chapters of the novel, Chapters 32-35, reaffirm society's control over the narrator, each in its own unique manner. Chapter 32 is a transcript of the court writ establishing Charlie's conviction of two murders, its judgment of his insanity, and its sentencing of him to Augusta State Hospital. Though Charlie's awareness of the writ gives him control over its presentation (his comment after the transcript confirms his awareness of it), the court's decision is the first step in society's final subjugation of the individual. Chapter 33, the interoffice memo, as already noted, is outside Charlie's narrative and, thus, not controlled by him.

The subjugation of the individual by society is presented here [in *Rage*] in at least three important ways.
—Chris Pourteau

Chapter 34, however, is a bit more ambiguous. This chapter is a transcript of a letter, evidently from Charlie's best friend, Joe McKennedy. After a first reading of the letter, the reader might think it would please Charlie, for in it we learn that Joe has become a successful undergraduate at Boston University, that Charlie's friends are still "pulling for [him]," and that those of his classmates whom he has influenced toward self-reliance have become productive, though independent, members of society. Thus, on the surface, all has turned out for the best—for everyone but Charlie.

The subjugation of the individual by society is presented here in at least three important ways. First, McKennedy's text has been replaced in several instances by "[Following has been censored as possibly upsetting to patient]"; thus, the hospital controls what Charlie may read, what *version of reality*

he may receive from the outside world. Second, the letter has no signature, simply ending with a "With love, your friend," and a blank page. The reader has to guess that McKennedy wrote the letter based on his self-reference as an "old buddy" of Charlie's, and the only character who qualifies for that position, based on Charlie's narrative, is Joe McKennedy. Whether McKennedy chose not to sign the letter (which seems unlikely) or the hospital censored his name, the obliteration of the signature takes away the *personal* identity of the letter's writer. Third, the letter writer warns Charlie that, "It would sure be a loss to the world if you clammed up and just scrunched in a corner all day." Taken in the context that Charlie's confession to both the reader and his classmates had provided him with some measure of freedom, this warning is especially significant. Indeed, it foreshadows the next chapter, where the reader learns that Charlie is happy to be able to keep a secret again from the hospital staff. Thus, Charlie has lost the liberating capacity he had found, the ability to confront and defeat his personal weaknesses through confession.

Chapter 35, as noted before, is Charlie's final, questionable attempt to control the narrative. Ultimately, however, the power to continue speaking is not his. His need to keep a secret again, to internalize his struggle for individuality, is particularly dramatic when the reader realizes that Charlie is in the ultimate situation of social control, psychiatric observation. It seems that Charlie himself knew this might happen, for, in Chapter 31, the last free act of his narrative is making a false grab for his gun, hoping that Philbrick, the police officer who has come down alone to the classroom (at Charlie's request) to personally escort Charlie out, will shoot him dead. Though Philbrick shoots him three times, Charlie survives and is tried for his crimes.

Thus, *Rage* exhibits a common theme of King's fiction, the struggle of the individual against society. As Mark Schorer suggests in his definition of the artist, thematic unity should extend itself to King's technique, and, indeed, the narrative structure parallels that struggle. In the first 15 chapters of *Rage,* Charlie Decker maintains some measure of authorial control by moving away from his primary narrative three separate times. Between Chapters 16 and 31, however, he is locked within the framework of his own narrative and must tailor his actions within the narrative, and portions of the narrative itself, to his audience. The final four chapters, each representative of the social repression of the individual, lock Charlie's cell and throw away the key. Though Charlie regains control of the narrative in the final chapter, it is only to tell the reader that he has lost his struggle for individualism.

Karen A. Hohne (essay date Fall 1994)

SOURCE: "The Power of the Spoken Word in the Works of Stephen King," in *Journal of Popular Culture,* Vol. 28, No. 2, Fall, 1994, pp. 93-103.

[*In the following essay, Hohne analyzes the use of official and unofficial language in King's fiction.*]

Orality seems straightforward and decorative, occurring in texts as either the voice of the poet or the people and apparently functioning very much on the text's surface. In fact, as a way of embodying and/or discussing power, it can be a central organizing factor in a text. Orality indicates power relations both in terms of who values the spoken word and how that word behaves towards other languages. Precisely because orality is a large and flexible category, containing many oralities, it is useful for authors and complex for scholars. It may, for instance, be dialogizing and internally persuasive or monologic and authoritative. It may function as a container of knowledge, preserving a history unvalued by those in power and only occasionally sanctified by being written down, or it may work as a mobile dispenser of silence and death, obliterating all voices not its own. Because it is polymorphous, it is a good vehicle for double-voicedness in texts, gesturing simultaneously towards both ends of the power spectrum.

> **Orality's double-sidedness is often disregarded whenever the term is applied to texts, but a fine example of its slippery dual nature is Stephen King's writing, where there is a great tension between the heteroglossic orality that is slang speech, which codifies a knowledge rejected by those in power, and monologic orality, which embodies that power.**
> **—*Karen A. Hohne***

When it is recorded, orality may preserve a poetic tendency to involve word play and consciousness of words' sounds as well as their meaning, as, for instance, dialect stories do or, for a perhaps more familiar example, rap does (where the supposed spontaneity of the moment is even usually carefully duplicated on the record—party sounds, inappropriate snorts of laughter, etc.). But generally when it is captured and preserved in a more or less static text (in such forms as the fairy tale or epic poem), orality's playfulness is frozen; it stops being an open, welcoming, hands-on endeavor, a work of the world and of empowerment, and becomes closed, forbidding, esoteric, and disempowering (the distance between epic poetry and rap, for instance, is above all the distance between the power that rules and the power of the people). Although epic poetry comes from folk epic and these two are connected in the mobius strip of literature, re-

corded oral narratives tend to be as flat and monologic as the spoken-aloud forms are orchestral and dialogizing.

Orality's double-sidedness is often disregarded whenever the term is applied to texts, but a fine example of its slippery dual nature is Stephen King's writing, where there is a great tension between the heteroglossic orality that is slang speech, which codifies a knowledge rejected by those in power, and monologic orality, which embodies that power.

Bakhtin designated the two language sets functioning in the dialect story as literary (written) and extraliterary (oral), but in actually working with double-accented texts, I found the terms official and unofficial more helpful, since they preserve the languages' very important relationship to both power and to authority, and since clearly orality may be either official or unofficial, as is the case with King.

Official language is a set of verbal and non-verbal authoritative languages which attain value in society based on their association with entrenched power. Thus included in this category as verbal languages we find not simply the language of high literature, but the political rhetoric of the State, the languages of legal documents, of "distinguished" journalism, academia (including the language of this paper), and so on. Official language usually literally embodies its association with the ruling forces by an adherence to the rules for speech; it is grammatically correct according to the grammars penned by those who (consciously or not) serve entrenched power.

In contrast, unofficial language as a category is composed of languages not valued (or perhaps even illegal or forced underground) by a particular society and which usually are furthermore rule-breaking in their form as well as their spirit, being ungrammatical, slangful, bastardized, and illogical. Unofficiality embraces otherness, borrowing from various aspects of unofficial culture—slang, obscenities, advertising, popular music, yellow journalism, B movies, comic books, etc. It is the speech of the marginalized majority—of rural folk or uneducated workers, of children, criminals, or minorities (to refer back to *The Shining,* for instance, the speech of the child Danny or the black cook, Mr. Halloran). However, unofficial ideology is distinguished by how it behaves as well as by its vocabulary and syntax. It is internally persuasive, constantly trying to enter into dialogue, and generally does not attempt to exile others to absence or strip them of their rightful voices. The only otherness unofficiality opposes is the otherness that wants to obliterate otherness—authoritativeness.

As aggressive as unofficiality is in its demystification of officiality, it does not usually attempt to gain the position of power, to officialize itself by obliterating officiality and clambering onto the vacated throne. It seeks only to unseat, not to be coronated. When unofficiality copies officiality's distinguishing feature, hatred of the other, it rejects all language borrowings and becomes monologic. Such an unofficiality occurs in the **"The Mist"** in the person of the fearsome Mrs. Carmody, whose own personal religious language, churchless and therefore powerless, becomes a vehicle for death (which perhaps simply indicates the real power unofficiality *does* have). Languages not in power that nevertheless reject internal persuasiveness for authoritativeness are simply officiality's poorest cousins, the lumpen proletariat of language. They are always lurking on the very fringes of society but never discover the positive aspects of life on the fag end. Instead, they dream of the day when they may be allowed to enter the society's center and thence exercise their authoritativeness to the fullest extent—i.e. through the tender attentions of fascist persuasion—death, torture, and silence. And we must assume that they will be made use of, just as the lumpen proletariat has been made use of, by an authoritativeness in fear of losing the power backing its words.

In works like **The Shining** and **The Stand,** however, we see the grubby-faced mongrel of internally persuasive unofficiality meeting prim officiality with the general result that unofficial language/ideology sticks out its tongue and reveals official language/ideology as a lie.

The kind of narrative which showcases this sort of double-accentuation takes monologism as its topic, revealing its negative effects. But these texts are no one-sided depictions of the horrors of some version of dictatorship, real as those horrors are. They speak not only monologism's deadly fallout, but its slithery attractions and stinky comforts. If official language is usually the language of the author/reader, then taking monologism as a subject to be deconstructed means deconstructing monologism not just out there somewhere in the world, but in the internal world; in other words, writing (and reading, if one reads dialogically) this kind of story means attempting to demystify oneself.

King is perhaps best known precisely for those narrators whose language is torn between the unofficiality of everyday spoken speech and the officiality of literary narration. Rather than make use of the officialized orality of the epic or fairy-tale, they string sentences together with "and" and repeat phrases in the redundant stutter of conversational, and their speech is full of highly unofficial slang and obscenities. But even in terms of their unofficiality one is not allowed to forget that they are individuals negotiating a heteroglossic world. Various unofficialities interact in these characters; in their speech we encounter bits of rock songs, advertising jingles, set phrases born on TV, and idiolects. King's readers *live* in this unofficiality, which is, outside of the book, constantly under attack by officiality; here that same unofficiality is celebrated and accepted as a vital aspect of the narrative of readers' lives, and when officiality

attacks, precisely in order to silence all this difference and to force the acceptance of its version of our lives, unofficiality strikes back and wins. This accounts for a great deal of King's popularity; he is the native son who wants to liberate the liberating mother tongues.

In most of King's novels the sensitivity to unofficiality is so great that there are attempts made to counteract the possible negative effects of literary narration on unofficial language. Some of the most dialogic moments occur when more-or-less unmediated thought penetrates the narrator's speech. It is indeed difficult to speak aloud without excessively monologizing, for these intrusive thoughts, rather than seconding or ratifying the oral narrative speech, contradict it and thereby take on the role of the unofficial, revealing the narrator's speech as inadequate to the world. It is as if orality, when given the job of narrative work normally performed by literary language, becomes officialized enough to require another sort of "spoken" speech, thought, to derail any monologic tendencies. Thought is then to spoken as spoken is to written. Thought may appear as a commentary on the speech of oneself or others, or as part of internal dialogue. It generally utilizes typeface to signify (a wonderfully curious situation given the orality we are dealing with) and often lacks punctuation (just as orality does).

It is fairly common in literature for thought to comment on the speech of others; however, in this example from **The Shining** we hear the internal unofficial other speaking in its own voice—not linearly, not in rule-bound sentences, but in fragments, circles:

> Jack's hands were clenched tightly in his lap, working against each other, sweating. *Officious little prick, officious*
>
> "I don't believe you care much for me, Mr. Torrance. I
>
> *little prick, officious—*
>
> don't care. Certainly your feelings toward me play no part in my own belief that you are not right for the job."

For a somewhat more subtle usage, where one insists on one's own internal, unofficial word over the official word imposed from without, there is the story of a boy who finds a tiger in

> The bathroom
>
> (!*basement*!)

Of course, the internal, unofficial other who cleaves to "basement" is proven correct—there really IS a tiger in the boys' room—just as the cage of dead, hypercorrect speech of the hotel manager in the previous excerpt is broken open both by Jack's unofficial language and by what actually happens at the Overlook Hotel.

Heteroglossia is manifested in internal dialogue as well. Notice the difference between the language inside and outside of parentheses in the following example. Both the form and the content are different. Unofficial speech, fenced in by parentheses and thus nearly literally marginalized, not only uses obscenities but rejects punctuation. Rule-abiding officiality, in contrast, is as always attempting to cover over lived life with its own lying version of things (here, the good father/murderous abuser), but its linear authority can be made to disintegrate under the stress unofficiality knows how to apply. Recalling the time he physically abused his son, Jack tells himself

It was an accident He fell down the stairs.

(o you dirty liar)

It was an accident I lost my temper.

(you fucking drunken waste god wiped snot out of his nose and that was you)

Listen, hey, come on, please, just an accident—

What appears on the microlevel organizes the macrolevel of these works as well. In speech so correct it sounds affected, the hotel manager tells us the official version of the Overlook Hotel's brilliant history as the grand stopping place of presidents (center of society). But Jack, a mere caretaker (margin of society), finds a scrapbook full of newspaper articles (certainly an unofficial version of a "real" book) in the basement; the unofficial story he puts together from the scrapbook gives the lie to the official version—the fine old hotel is actually a charnel house produced by corruption in high places. Unofficiality appears likewise as the Shining itself (the clairvoyant abilities of Mr. Hallorann and Danny). A non-linear means of cognition, the Shining is considered the knowing of the mentally ill and the simple, yet has the power to unmask officiality.

Official language, the peddler of a dangerously false knowledge which pretends to know everything, to encompass the universe within itself, may appear in various guises. All of its versions buy into the system of power and thus in the final instance serve the same master; they scramble over each other's backs in an attempt to be first and best at giving voice to those who rule. Officiality knows that other official languages all recognize authority, even if that authority is other than itself; should those other official languages attempt to

garner for themselves monologic power, officiality understands and can even forgive, since monologism and the urge to it is the only value in its world. Officialities thus have few difficulties in appearing side by side. A version of official language I have elsewhere called Scientific because of its use of science-peculiar buzzwords and syntax occurs in King and normally leads to lethal consequences, but official language is not limited to this incarnation. Religious language proves to be a particularly virulent strain of officiality for King, occurring again and again. A good example is **"Children of the Corn,"** where children in the grip of religiospeak sacrifice passers-by and their own comrades to a blood-spattered god. But scientific and religious officialities may easily coexist in the same text, as in **"The Mist,"** where blundering, know-it-all science, our present religious authority, overwhelms and destroys most of the world, and a recrudescence of old-time religion does its best to kill off the remainder. Science and religion, which appear to be completely opposed (when viewed from the rational/irrational axis), are thus revealed as identical in terms of their negative relationship to otherness: if it is other, eradicate it.

Literary language, perhaps the most invisible of all authoritative words for academics, appears in each of King's works, and as we know, there is an official space for orality within literary language as poetry and fairy tale—thus its double-voicedness as a category.
—*Karen A. Hohne*

In works where the unofficial word emerges triumphant, the velvet glove that covers officiality's iron fist is, all unknown to it, slid off, and officiality's literal or figurative monstrosity is revealed; this is quite different from the situation normal to society at large. There, unofficiality is allowed a precarious validity only at the margins, yet since our lives are awash in unofficiality, its absence from the privileged sorts of communication we employ emphasizes the unofficiality of our lives. It is then with great relief we take up a horror novel of King's type. In these the monstrosity is officiality itself.

Literary language, perhaps the most invisible of all authoritative words for academics, appears in each of King's works, and as we know, there is an official space for orality within literary language as poetry and fairy tale—thus its double-voicedness as a category. Even in his use of slang King draws attention to language, and this language self-consciousness fits the classic Formalist definition of poetry. It would seem strange for an author who produces works so crammed with validated unofficiality to create anything which touts officiality, but there are works in King's corpus where unofficiality not only does not triumph but appears to be smashed. The problem is that orality's connection to poetry and the fairy tale pulls the text away from heteroglossia and possible dialogism. We find these monologic capabilities demonstrated in novels like *The Eyes of the Dragon* and *The Dark Tower.*

These official languages are necessary to (or necessarily) reproduce the monologic relations of the society depicted— generally some version of feudalism, which is wonderfully fitting. When authoritative language is used to limn a monologic world, no space is left for us to work out a compromise with that world; we must accept or reject it in its entirety. Not only are the world's imperfections carefully smoothed over by their convenient absence, but the authoritative force of that world does not allow us to look at the white space, the margin, that signifies imperfection's existence. Only Evil, which is presented as individual deformation of universally accepted morality, a big or small glitch in an otherwise smooth-running machine, may counter officiality's bland narrative. But we are not permitted to wonder if there is anything wrong with the machine itself. On the contrary, bare-faced inequity is presented as normal and good, and if we would be normal and good, we must accept it as such. These works are in fact reader-hostile—there is nowhere for us to enter into the work; what's more, the lack of dialogized heteroglossia is antagonistic to our life experience.

A novel which speaks monologue is not going to be powered by a plot that deliberately works to subvert its world. On the contrary, the plot in these novels, like their language, lauds officiality. Instead of depicting positive transformation, which can only come about in the field of dialogism (as at the end of *The Shining,* for instance, where a new and completely different sort of "family" is formed), the plot born of a monologized world moves towards an entrenchment of the status quo. In *Eyes* the rightful king (certainly a fine representation of officiality), imprisoned by a usurping magician (unofficiality in its "evil" guise), destroys the magician and re-takes his throne to the usual rejoicing of the peasants, who, as always, are there to assure us that the lives of the people are just grand under authoritarianism. This sort of story has appeared over and over both in older horror novels and other writing. Here officiality smears unofficiality by attributing to it its own crimes—murder, torture, intrigue, etc. (that is, the activities practiced openly by kings rather than magicians)—and denies unofficiality its voice by killing off its speakers. Unofficiality is presented as an ugly deviation from the beautiful order of officialized society. It is an *evil* way of knowing precisely because it is an *other* way of knowing.

Unofficiality is here not permitted to speak its own language; instead, it is ventriloquized by officiality. Often these villains are gleefully self-condemning, tooting the horn of their own evil as no real villain would. Curiously, however, many readers identify with the villains rather than the heroes of this sort of work. This is not a function of the alleged difficulty of presenting good people as interesting but of readers' deep realizations that the story being told concerns them directly; the villain is their own life experience, which speaks a language different from the official version and which therefore is called evil. Contrast this to works where what horror has historically considered evil is openly depicted as attractive and even gets away in the end, thereby subverting the entire world of officiality. This latter is a progressive trend, for it means accepting one's own unofficiality and perhaps even taking pride in it. But since novels like *The Eyes of the Dragon* are told from the point of view of officiality, unofficiality is represented as an evil to be snuffed out. Then officiality can resume its rule, painting itself as universal, seamless, and ahistorical.

We see the same sort of reversal of the roles normally played by officiality and unofficiality in *The Dark Tower,* a work both poetic and poetry-inspired. The gunslinger, a sort of traveling officiality minus the bad makeup of civilization, pursues an alternative Satan of the trickster variety who carnivalizes wherever he goes. Rather than using a mixture of spoken slang and literary language, as appears in texts like *The Shining,* the narrator speaks in the officialized speech of the fairy tale or epic: "He was still unbedded, but two of the younger slatterns of a West-Town merchant had cast eyes on him." Although out of context the lifelessness of this particular officiality is so apparent that it is almost humorous, it is difficult while reading to resist the power of the narrator's authoritative word—one must either accept it or pull out of the book. Thus it becomes easy for us to see the Man in Black, who kills one person and reanimates two, as demonic, whereas the gunslinger, who kills at least 38 people, including a young boy devoted to him, seems heroic. If one recalls that in *The Shining* as well as other of King's works a child represents unofficiality's power, the significance of the boy's sacrifice to officiality's quest in this novel is clear.

In these works heteroglossia cannot and does not give birth to dialogism. It is merely decorative (in fact, "poetic"), lending a pleasant local color rather than representing alternative worldviews. The well-crafted characterization through language that is one means of introducing heteroglossia into novels like *The Shining* does not occur here. Instead, these characters are, like their worlds, flat. In *Eyes,* for instance, individuals' speech may be class-distinct, but this language differentiation is reminiscent of a snobby British novel where flower girls drop their h's and cloddish workmen stretch out their diphthongs like taffy—in other words, otherness may aspire only to (powerless) quaintness. It is noticeable that whenever otherness appears as unofficiality in these novels it is either incomprehensible and (therefore) ridiculous or it is simply an estrangement of our own world, which makes it even more ridiculous—the Amoco pump worshipped as a thunder-god, for instance. We laugh at our own estranged unofficiality, forgetting that officiality's most damaging effect on those who must have truck with it is the loathing and fear towards the unofficial other it produces, be that other another living being or an individual within the speaker's own psyche.

> **King's works provide a paradigm illustrating the tension between official and unofficial languages/ideologies that exists not only in literature but throughout our society.**
> —*Karen A. Hohne*

Since what heteroglossia there is has no dialogic life, the rich internal dialogue that weaves together books like *The Shining* is missing. Thought simply does not generally disrupt the flow of speech, and when it does, no illuminating spark of difference is struck. Instead, it is much more in line with what one would expect from a traditional novel:

> They [Brown and the gunslinger] looked at each other across the shadows, the moment taking on overtones of finality.
>
> —*Now* the questions will come.
>
> But Brown had nothing to say.

These heroes may even, like the gunslinger, as many an outlaw before and since, be inarticulate in their native language, which is quite appropriate, for the heroes of these works are deaf to heteroglossia. It is significant that in *The Drawing of the Three* the gunslinger has great difficulty not only with the "foreign" words of our world but with the codes of his own; likewise, in *The Dark Tower,* when he tries to read the clues left behind by the Man in Black, he thinks

> —Perhaps the campfires are a message, spelled out letter by letter. *Take a powder.* Or, *the end draweth nigh.* Or maybe even, *Eat at Joe's.* It didn't matter.

Indeed, it does not matter to one who does not prize heteroglossia; to him, all difference must be equal to inferiority. Officiality has no need to be wor(l)dly-wise; its tongue is a gun, its word a bullet. It would be difficult to find a better metaphor for officiality's attitude towards otherness.

King's works provide a paradigm illustrating the tension between official and unofficial languages/ideologies that ex-

ists not only in literature but throughout our society. In one of the sorts of novels he produces, orality appears in its official guise, as epic language, to tell the only story it is capable of telling—that of a world monologized. In such a world, heteroglossia cannot be dialogized; rather, other languages are mere surface decoration, and difference is an occasion for the expression of moral superiority and humor that excludes and objectifies otherness. Such novels are manifestations and exercises of the existing power relations. The plot of this sort of novel must be the story of officiality's triumph (there can be no other story). They are perhaps precisely those which will meet with greater acceptance from individuals taken up with officiality's literary business, for despite the fact that the far more vital works are those which turn away from literariness to make use of our own very living languages, these officialized works buy wholeheartedly into the literary system, which act therefore justifies them. In these tales, unofficiality is nowhere permitted to speak; instead, crimes, particularly those which officiality has itself committed, are attributed to unofficiality in absentia. This story and the way it works occur not only within the confines of a book but frequently out in the world.

The authoritativeness of such narratives draws us in, making us into exactly the sort of reader they demand—one who may easily stomach oppression because she laughs at her own (unofficial) self with a laugh emanating from self-hatred rather than demystification. But smothering difference means ultimately becoming inarticulate oneself, as the gunslinger illustrates, and likewise is apparent in society as a whole, where officiality, able to use only itself as reference, has less and less to say about the world we live in. This lack of substance is perceived by many and accounts for the popularity of texts which speak another language, another world, as some works of King do.

These texts are precisely the other side of orality, the other story, which likewise takes monologue as its subject, but this time depicts it from without rather than within, thus exposing the cracks in the deadly mechanism. The power of "simple," "ordinary," "everyday" speech is revealed as a force non-linear, fragmentary, and circular and thus peculiarly fitted to debunking rigid, straight-line officiality. Again the plot is related to what is going on in the work's language, but here heteroglossia leads to a real interaction of languages that produces something other than the same old story from which we must be excluded unless we mutilate ourselves and others. Unofficialized texts, in contrast, point to the power of our own unofficial languages in a society overdetermined by officiality, a power simply waiting to be wielded. These stories tell us to speak in our own true voices, all of them, to exploit multiplicity and fragmentation, to realize the lesson incorporated in the Babel myth. The tower to heaven is always being built again by officiality, but the real might of Babel was not the tower. It was the languages which are, since officiality tells the tale, presented as a curse. We see that other versions of Babel, such as those told by King, reveal this curse to be in fact the possibility of liberation.

Michael Wood (review date 19 October 1995)

SOURCE: "Horror of Horrors," in *New York Review of Books,* Vol. 42, No. 16, October 19, 1995, p. 54.

[*In the following review, Wood discusses the mythological allusions of King's* Rose Madder *and asserts, "The magical picture of* Rose Madder . . . *reminds us through fantasy how fantastic the unimagined everyday world can be."*]

Stephen King has become a household name in at least three senses. He is a writer pretty much everyone in the English-speaking world has heard of, if they have heard of writers at all. He is regularly read by many people who don't read many other writers. And, along with Danielle Steel and a few others, he is taken to represent everything that is wrong with contemporary publishing, that engine of junk pushing serious literature out of our minds and our bookstores. The English writer Clive Barker has said, "There are apparently two books in every American household—one of them is the Bible and the other one is probably by Stephen King." I don't know what Barker's source is for this claim, but I wonder about the Bible.

Do we know what popular literature is? When is it not junk? Is it ever (just) junk? Who is to say? What is the alternative to popular literature? Serious, highbrow, literary, or merely . . . unpopular literature? Stephen King responded with eloquent anger in an argument over these issues conducted in the PEN newsletter in 1991. He thought best-selling authors came in all kinds. He said he found James Michener, Robert Ludlum, John le Carré, and Frederick Forsyth "unreadable," but enjoyed (among others) Elmore Leonard, Sara Paretsky, Jonathan Kellerman, and Joyce Carol Oates. This seems sound enough to me, although I have to confess to liking Ludlum and le Carré as well. "Some of these," King continued, "are writers whose work I think of as sometimes or often literary, and all are writers who can be counted on to tell a good story, one that takes me away from the humdrum passages of life . . . and enriches my leisure time as well. Such work has always seemed honorable to me, even noble."

What had made King angry was the term "better" fiction, which Ursula Perrin had used in an open letter to PEN ("I am a writer of 'better' fiction, by which I mean that I don't write romance or horror or mystery") complaining about the profusion of worse fiction in the bookstores—"this rising sea of trash" were her words. "Ursula Perrin's prissy use of the word 'better,'" King says, "which she keeps putting in quotation marks, makes me feel like baying at the moon." Perrin's examples of writers of "better" fiction were John Updike, Kurt Vonnegut, Jr., and Alice Hoffman.

> **The English writer Clive Barker has said, "There are apparently two books in every American household—one of them is the Bible and the other one is probably by Stephen King." I don't know what Barker's source is for this claim, but I wonder about the Bible.**
>   —*Michael Wood*

But King was wrong, I think, to assume that Perrin's argument could rest only on snobbery, and he himself owes his success not to some all-purpose skill in entertainment but to his skill in a particular genre, and to his reader's expectations of that genre. There is a real difficulty with the rigidity and exclusivity of our literary categories; but it is no solution to say that exclusivity is the problem. What happens perhaps is that the tricky task of deciding whether a piece of writing (of any kind) is any good is repeatedly replaced by the easier habit of deciding which slabs or modes of writing we can ignore. Even King, who not only should but does know better, confuses fiction that is popular with popular fiction, best sellers with genres, and his line about the humdrum passages of life and the enrichment of leisure time is as condescending in its mock-demotic way as the idea of "better" fiction. No one would read Stephen King if that was all he managed to do.

Genres do exist, however we name them, and the work they do is honorable, even noble. When we say writers have transcended their genre, we often mean they have abandoned or betrayed it. Genres have long and complicated histories, richer and poorer, better and worse. They may be in touch with ancient and unresolved imaginative energies, or whatever haunts the back of a culture's mind; and they permit and occasionally insist on allusions the writer may have no thought of making. Stephen King, however, *has* thought of making allusions, and thought of it more and more, as the excursions into classical mythology of *Rose Madder* make very clear.

What's interesting about *Carrie,* King's first novel, published in 1974, is the way it sustains and complicates its problems, gives us grounds for judgment and then takes them away. The genre here (within the horror genre) is the mutant-disaster story, which in more recent years has become the virus novel or movie. Sixteen-year-old Carietta White has inherited awe-inspiring telekinetic powers, and in a fit of fury wipes out whole portions of the Maine town where she lives, causing a death toll of well over four hundred. Carrie has always been awkward and strange, cruelly mocked by her companions at school, and liked by no one. Her mother is a morbid fundamentalist Christian who thinks that sex even within marriage is evil. The town itself is full of rancor and hypocrisy and pretension—the sort of place where the prettiest girl is also the meanest, the local hoodlums have everyone terrorized, and the assistant principal of the school has a ceramic ashtray in the form of Rodin's *Thinker* on his desk—so that without any supernatural intervention at all there's plenty to go wrong, and plenty of people to blame. Carrie's terrible gift for willing physical destruction is an accident, the result of a recessive gene that could come up in anyone, and the novel makes much play with the idea of little Carries quietly multiplying all over the United States like bombs rather than children. The last image in the novel is of a two-year-old in Tennessee who is able to move marbles around without touching them, and this is the portentous question the novel pretends to address: "What happens if there are others like her? What happens to the world?"

This is a big question, but it's not as important as it looks, because apart from being unanswerable in the absence of any knowledge of the characters and lives of the "others like her," it mainly serves to mask another question, which is the most urgent question of the horror genre as Stephen King practices it: What difference does the supernatural or fanciful element make, whether it's telekinesis or death-in-life? What if it's only a lurid metaphor for what's already there? Carrie White is not a monster, even if her mother is. Carrie has been baited endlessly, and when someone is finally nice to her and takes her to the high-school prom, the evening ends in nightmare: pig's blood is poured all over her and her partner, a sickening echo and travesty of the opening scene in the novel, where Carrie discovers in the shower room that she is menstruating and doesn't know what's happening to her. Human folly and nastiness take care of this entire region of the plot, and Carrie's distress and rage are what anyone but a saint would feel. But then she has her powers. The difference is not in the rage but in what she can do about it, and this is where contemporary horror stories, like old tales of magic, speak most clearly to our fears and desires.

Edward Ingebretsen, S.J., in an interestingly argued book whose subtitle confirms King's status even in the academic household, speaks of religion where I am speaking of magic. "Once-religious imperatives," he says, "can be traced across a variety of American genres, modes, and texts." "The deflective energies of a largely forgotten metaphysical history live on, not only in churches, but in a myriad other centers of displaced worship." Ingebretsen has a nice sense of irony—I hope it's irony—dark and oblique like his subject: "A major comfort of the Christian tradition is the terror it generates and presupposes . . ." He certainly understands how King, while seeming to offer escape from the humdrum passages of life, shows us the weird bestiary lurking in those apparently anodyne places. "Change the focus slightly and King's horror novel [in this case *Salem's Lot*] reintroduces the horrific, although the horrific as it routinely exists in the real and the probable." "Routinely" is excellent.

It's true that religious hauntings are everywhere in American life, but because they are everywhere, they don't really help us to see the edge in modern horror stories, the way these stories suggest that we have returned, on some not entirely serious, not entirely playful level, to the notion that superstitions are right after all, that they offer us a more plausible picture of the world than any organized religion or any of our secular promises. It's not only that the old religion is still with us, but that even older ideas have returned to currency. This is a very complicated question, but the notion of magic will allow us to make a start on it.

Magic is the power to convert wishes into deeds without passing through the cumbersome procedures of material reality: taking planes, hiring assassins, waiting for the news, going to jail. It bypasses physics, connects the mind directly to the world. All of Stephen King's novels that I have read involve magic in this sense, even where nothing supernatural occurs, where the only magic is the freedom of fiction to move when it wants to from thought to act. Would you, if you could, immediately and violently get rid of anyone and anything you dislike? If you were provoked enough? And could be sure of getting away with it? The quick response, of course, is that you know you shouldn't, and probably wouldn't. The slow response is the same, but meanwhile, if you're not really thinking about it, you probably let it all happen in your head, which is a way of saying yes to the fantasy of immense violence while feeling scared about it.

This must be a large part of the delight of this kind of horror fiction. Is this really all right, even in a novel? There's a relish in the thought of Carrie's destroying her miserable town; we can't wait for another gas station to blow up. But there's also an ugly comfort in feeling Carrie's an alien and a freak, not one of us, and above all in knowing, at the end, that she's dead. At the heart of *Carrie* is a conversation between Susan, the one girl in town who worries about Carrie, and Susan's amiable boyfriend, who dies for his attempt at niceness. They have no idea of what's going to happen; they know only that everyone's always been mean to Carrie.

> "You were kids," he said. "Kids don't know what they're doing. Kids don't even know their reactions really, actually, hurt other people. . . ."

> She found herself struggling to express the thought

this called up in her, for it suddenly seemed basic, bulking over the shower-room incident the way sky bulks over mountains.

"But hardly *anybody* ever finds out that their actions really, actually, hurt other people! People don't get better, they just get smarter. When you get smarter you don't stop pulling the wings off flies, you just think of better reasons for doing it."

And what if, the question about magic continues, you grant to these people, without improving their moral awareness in any significant degree, inconceivable powers to hurt? To wipe out cities or abuse their wives? It wouldn't matter whether you called these powers telekinesis or Mephistopheles. Carrie's relative innocence—she's not smart and she doesn't pull the wings off flies—helps to focus the question but makes the powers all the scarier. Fortunately it's only a fantasy.

If we want to see what a genre novel looks like when it's barely in touch with any imaginative energies, either ancient or modern, we can look at King's ***The Langoliers,*** a short work published in ***Four Past Midnight,*** and recently adapted as a lumbering mini-series for ABC. The genre here is the end-of-the-world-as-we-know-it story, combined with a disaster in technology (airplane, ocean liner, skyscraper). A plane leaves Los Angeles and flies through a fold in time into the past—or rather into an alternative world which the present has abandoned, into the past as it would be if it vanished the moment we turned our backs on it. The plane lands at Bangor, Maine, which turns out to be deserted, nothing but stale air and tasteless food. The plane manages miraculously to refuel and to fly back through the time fold. There is a nasty moment when it arrives in Los Angeles too early—this is the future, and just as deserted as the past, but not as dead and tasteless. The good news is that you only have to wait a while for the present to get here.

> The novel and the movie called *Dolores Claiborne* are good illustrations of the way in which the same story can be told twice and mean different things each time. The novel is all about what people do when there's nowhere to go. The movie is about doing what you can but still having nowhere to go, and every image in it—the sea and the sky, the bare landscape, the half-abandoned houses—reinforces this feeling.
> —*Michael Wood*

There are possibilities here, and the hint of a genuine anxi-

ety about the fading past, a sort of mixture of disbeliefs about it: that it's still there, that it's actually gone. King writes engagingly in his introduction of "the essential conundrum of time"—"so perfect that even such jejune observations as the one I have just made retain an odd, plangent resonance"—but he hasn't worked all that hard at this version of it, and obviously felt his novel needed something more, which he provided in the shape of huge bouncing balls which are eating away at the earth—well, not just the earth, but reality itself. The balls are black and red, they have faces and mouths and teeth; they are "sort of like beachballs, but balls which rippled and contracted and then expanded again. . . ." "Reality peeled away in narrow strips beneath them, peeled away wherever and whatever they touched. . . ." Apart from telekinesis, King has written about vampires, rabid dogs, cats back from the dead, zombies, a demon automobile, and a whole barrage of ghosties and ghoulies. But sort of like beachballs?

The novel and the movie called ***Dolores Claiborne*** are good illustrations of the way in which the same story can be told twice and mean different things each time. The novel is all about what people do when there's nowhere to go. The movie is about doing what you can but still having nowhere to go, and every image in it—the sea and the sky, the bare landscape, the half-abandoned houses—reinforces this feeling. I don't think the movie intends to be depressing. It intends to be beautiful and uplifting, all about courage and coming through, and Kathy Bates, as Dolores Claiborne, is full of fight and dignity. But she can't compete with all those images, which in another context might well suggest freedom or an unspoiled world.

Still, it is the same story, in spite of the different tilts of meaning and of obvious and extensive changes in the development of characters and their part in the plot. Dolores Claiborne, accused of two murders, has committed one but not the other. In the second case, where she is innocent, the evidence is damning. She was seen with a rolling pin raised above the head of the aged and now dead woman whose housekeeper she was, and she has inherited a fortune through the woman's death.

In the first case, when she killed her husband nearly thirty years ago, the evidence was sparse because she took care to get rid of most of it—of all of it that she could find. She killed him, not just because he was a drunk and because he beat her, and not just to be free of him, but because he was molesting their daughter, and she could see no future for any of them in the world as long as he was alive. Obliquely but unmistakably instructed by her employer ("'An accident,' she says in a clear voice almost like a schoolteacher's, 'is sometimes an unhappy woman's best friend.'"), Dolores arranges for her drunken husband to fall down an old well he can't get out of. Like all bad characters in good horror stories, he takes a long time dying, indeed seems virtually unkillable. The same trope animates the battered and dying bad guy in *The Langoliers;* "There was something monstrous and unkillable and insectile about his horrible vitality."

This may remind us that murder in fiction is always too easy or too hard—that it is a fiction, a picture not of killing but of the way we feel about killing. Will Dolores, guilty the first time, get convicted the second time? Will her daughter, who suspects her of murder, ever trust her again? Would her daughter understand if she heard the whole story? Both the novel and the movie answer these questions, and both use the total eclipse of the sun in 1963 as their dominant visual image. This is the day of the murder of the husband, ostensibly a good time to get away with it, but really (that is, figuratively) a time of strange darkness when all bets are off and all rules suspended: this is the magic of the story, the moral telekinesis. Dolores doesn't need supernatural aid to kill her husband, she just needs, magically, for a few hours, to be someone else.

We are back in the world of *Carrie,* where rage is both understandable and terrifying. Carrie can read minds as well as move objects, and a phrase used about her helps us to see something else these novels are about: "the awful totality of perfect knowledge." The novels don't have perfect knowledge, or imagine anyone has it, except by magic. But then the magic, as well as giving anger a field day, would also give us a glimpse of the inside of anger, as if we could read it, as if it could be perfectly known. We might then want to say, not that to understand everything is to forgive everything, but that to understand everything is unbearable.

Stephen King is still asking his question about magic in *Rose Madder,* his most recent novel. It takes two forms here, or finds two instances. One involves a psychopathic cop, Norman Daniels, addicted to torturing his wife but shrewd enough to stop before she dies or before the evidence points only to him. He is also a killer, but even his wife doesn't know how crazy he is until she leaves him. Yet he's thought to be a good guy down at the station, recently promoted for his role in a big drug bust. His wife thinks every policeman is probably on his side, if not actually like him. Until King introduces a good cop around page 300, it looks as if the police force itself is the psychopath's version of telekinesis, what moves the world for him. There is a disturbing moment at the beginning of the novel, borrowed from Hitchcock but subtly and swiftly used, when Norman, having beaten his wife badly enough to cause a miscarriage, decides to call the hospital. "Her first thought is that he's calling the police. Ridiculous, of course—he *is* the police."

The other, more elaborate form of the question concerns Norman's wife, Rose. She finally finds the nerve to run away, after fourteen years of what King describes as sleep:

The concept of dreaming is known to the waking mind but to the dreamer there is no waking, no real world, no sanity; there is only the screaming bedlam of sleep. Rose McClendon Daniels slept within her husband's madness for nine more years.

Rose starts a new life in a distant city; makes new friends, gets a job reading thrillers for a radio station. You will have guessed that Norman goes after her and catches up with her at the climax of the novel, and that there is much maiming and murder and fright along the way, and you will have guessed right. The violence is inventive and nasty, and Norman is as truly scary a fictional character as you could wish to keep you awake at nights. He owes a certain amount to the Robert De Niro character in *Taxi Driver,* but when King himself refers to the actor and the movie—he pays his dues—the gesture isn't merely cute, it's amusing and polite, a casual tip of the hat. Norman is madder than the De Niro figure, his murder score is much higher, and—this is really distressing—he is often funny. Norman glances at a picture of Lincoln, for example, and thinks he looks "quite a bit like a man he had once arrested for strangling his wife and all four of his children."

What you won't have guessed is that the novel has a classical streak, and that King is quite consciously connecting his own modern mythology to a well-known ancient one. Rose buys a painting—it's called *Rose Madder,* after the color of the dress of the woman who is the chief figure in it, but the title, for us, also plays on the double meaning of "mad," on Rose's need to get angry and the craziness that may result—and discovers that she can step into it, become part of its world and have adventures there. The picture appears to be a rather banal classical landscape, with a ruined temple, and vines, and thunderheads in the sky. What's going on there, as Rose learns when she visits, is a mixture of the myths of the Minotaur in the maze and of Demeter looking for Persephone, her daughter by Zeus, after Persephone as been abducted into the underworld.

The creature in the maze isn't exactly the Minotaur, since it's all bull, and it's called Erinyes, a name which means fury, and is one of Demeter's epithets. Later the bull becomes Norman, or Norman becomes the bull: the monster is a metaphor for the less-than-human male. It's an engaging feature of King's play with these images that he doesn't forget the risks he's taking, and when Rose sees a pile of creaturely crap in the mythological maze she knows what it is: "After fourteen years of listening to Norman and Harley and all their friends, you'd have to be pretty stupid not to know bullshit when you see it."

The mother seeking her child is not exactly Demeter either, since Rose is told the mother is "not quite a goddess," and Demeter was undoubtedly the real thing. The mother is also decaying, having "drunk of the waters of youth" without getting immortality to go with it; and she is not exactly, or not always, a woman. She is a feminine principle, Carrie's rage in a calm disguise, telekinesis in a classical garb, and sometimes she looks like a spider or a fox. A literal vixen and cubs introduced in another part of the novel—in the world which is not that of the painting—set up the idea of rabies, whose name means rage, and whose name is rage in several European languages. "It's a kind of rabies," Rose thinks, picturing some mythological equivalent of the disease, a consuming anger which could destroy a near goddess. "She's being eaten up with it, all her shapes and magics and glamours trembling at the outer edge of her control now, soon it's all going to crumble. . . ."

This woman is a figure for the anger Rose may not be able to control or return from. The last pages of the novel are like an afterward to *Carrie.* Rose knows the power of her anger, but her anger also knows her, and won't let her go. In a trivial quarrel in her happy new life, after the gruesome and entirely satisfactory mangling of Norman in the spooky world of the painting—not only in that world, though, Norman's not coming back—Rose has to make "an almost frantic effort" not to throw a pot of boiling water at her harmless second husband's head. She finds peace in an encounter, not with the near goddess of the picture, but with the vixen of the American countryside, with the puzzle of rabies in that clever female face. "Rosie looks for madness or sanity in those eyes . . . and sees both." But only sanity is actually there—a matter of luck, no doubt, of the way the disease ran among the local wildlife—and when she sees the vixen much later, Rose has become confident of her own resistance to the power to hurt, knows the madness (or the magic) has faded. These are the last words of the book: "Her black eyes as she stands there communicate no clear thought to Rosie, but it is impossible to mistake the essential sanity of the old and clever brain behind them."

King writes very well at times: "Her shadow stretched across the stoop and the pale new grass like something cut from black construction paper with a sharp pair of scissors," "Huge sunflowers with yellowy, fibrous stalks, brown centers, and curling, faded petals towered over everything else, like diseased turnkeys in a prison where all the inmates have died." The second example is a bit ripe maybe, but it's effective. But then we also get "riding through a dream lined with cotton"; "shards of glass twinkling beside a country road"; "the unforgiving light of an alien sun"; "she . . . was fearfully enchanted"; and "what she felt like was tiny speck of flotsam in the middle of a trackless ocean." This is not popular writing, it's yesterday's posh writing, and it's consistent with Rosie's thinking of *Madame Bovary* and Norman's muttering a line from *Hamlet.* Perhaps this is "better" fiction after all.

But of course what we are looking for in this novel is not felicity of phrase but invention and dispatch, and racking fictional anxiety, and King supplies them in good measure. He also gives us a pretty generous clue to what he is up to with his mythology. Within the world of the painting the bull gets out of the maze, and Rose worries that this may mean not only that the bull is loose but that the world has become his maze. The world of the painting, at least. A voice in her head, eager to help King out, takes her thought further. "This world, all worlds. And many bulls in each one. These myths hum with truth, Rosie. That's their power. That's why they survive." This is heavy-handed as explanation, but doesn't really hamper the functioning of the myth. The magical picture of *Rose Madder* does what the beachballs of *The Langoliers* just won't do: reminds us through fantasy how fantastic the unimagined everyday world can be. The trouble, in such a scenario, is not that dreams don't come true but that we could scarcely live with them if they did. Or that we are already living with them.

Edwin F. Casebeer (essay date 1996)

SOURCE: "Stephen King's Canon: The Art of Balance," in *A Dark Night's Dreaming: Contemporary American Horror Fiction,* edited by Tony Magistrale and Michael A. Morrison, University of South Carolina Press, 1996, pp. 42-54.

[In the following essay, Casebeer traces influences from King's life that have affected his writing and delineates different stages and common elements in his fiction.]

Stephen King is the most popular horror novelist today (and also the most popular novelist). He is the only writer ever to have made the Forbes 500; his annual income exceeds that of some third-world countries. His works are a significant percentage of the book industry's annual inventory. The average American recognizes his name and face. Yet, paradoxically, his novels also top the lists of censored authors. Perhaps that is because he creates fiction and cinema about that which we would rather avoid: modern meaninglessness, physical corruptibility, and death. Do the fictional situations he presents argue for a decline in our culture's energy for life, a descending depression and despair that lends enchantment to the graveyard, the kind of apocalyptic view that often ends centuries and heralds new human hells? Or is his appeal understandable in a way that affirms our culture and its willingness to deal with its dilemmas?

If we begin with Stephen King's status among his immediate peers—the horror novelists—the reasons for his broad appeal are clear. He has taken command of the field by writing representative masterworks: the vampire novel (*'Salem's*

Lot), the monster novel (*The Dark Half*), wild talent fiction (*Carrie*), zombie fiction (*Pet Sematary*), diabolic possession fiction (*Christine*), and realistic horror fiction (*Misery*). His presence in the field extends to its very boundaries.

But King is actually a genre novelist; that is, he writes in all of the major popular genres now marketed to the country's largest reading population: horror, fantasy, science fiction, the western, the mystery, and the romance. While he works in pure forms (*'Salem's Lot* as a vampire novel, *Cycle of the Werewolf* as a werewolf novel, *The Talisman* as a quest fantasy, and *The Running Man* as science fiction), he often mixes genres. An early example is *The Stand,* particularly its first published edition, which begins as one form of the science fiction novel (the apocalyptic), evolves into a second form (the utopian), and concludes as a fantasy which blends elements of the quest like Tolkien's *Lord of the Rings* trilogy with Christian apocalyptic fantasy like *The Omen* trilogy. Similarly, his *Dark Tower* trilogy combines apocalyptic science fiction with Arthurian quest fantasy, itself subordinated to the western, and then introduces science fiction's alternate worlds concept. The standard detective mystery does much to shape *The Dark Half, Needful Things,* and *Dolores Claiborne,* while the Gothic romance and the feminist novel are essential features of *Misery, Gerald's Game,* and *Dolores Claiborne.* The resulting breadth gives his fiction a much wider appeal than might come to a "pure" horror writer.

Stephen King is the most popular horror novelist today (and also the most popular novelist). . . . Yet, paradoxically, his novels also top the lists of censored authors. Perhaps that is because he creates fiction and cinema about that which we would rather avoid: modern meaninglessness, physical corruptibility, and death.
—*Edwin F. Casebeer*

But King's appeal is even broader than that of a genre writer. From the beginning of his career, he was responsive to those horror writers of his decade, like Ira Levin, who moved from the traditional confines of the *fantastique* to establish analogies between the world that we all occupy and the horror novel's traditional settings, situations, plots, and characters. King, too, grounds fantasy in realism. In fact, his earliest published work, *Rage* (published under the Richard Bachman pseudonym), is a capable realistic novel. Motivated by his own boyhood and his involvement with his children, King's early novels demonstrate strong characterizations of preadolescent boys and small children.

In the ensuing years, he has added to his palette, and now is taking up the challenge of realistic female protagonists.

King's appeal thus broadens even further: this realism opens up a subtext that addresses urgent contemporary concerns. From his youth, he has been a man of his generation; a man with deep political awareness and involvement. As has been elaborated critically by such works as Tony Magistrale's *Landscape of Fear* and Douglas Winter's *The Art of Darkness,* King has created many novels which allegorically address current social dilemmas: the corruption of school and church (*Rage, Carrie, Christine*), the government (*The Long Walk, Firestarter, The Running Man, The Stand, The Dead Zone*), the small town (*'Salem's Lot, It, Needful Things, Tommyknockers*), the family (*The Shining, Cujo, It, Christine*), and heterosexual relationships (*Gerald's Game, Dolores Claiborne*). Thus, King's work offers more than mere escape fiction or "adrenaline" fiction; it urges readers to confront squarely and disturbingly the horror in their own lives. The resulting depth connects him to an audience drawn to literature more "serious" than horror or genre fiction. His model has inspired enough followers to cause horror fiction to move to the front of bookstores and the top of the *New York Times'* bestseller list. It is not so much that the reading public has developed a perverse taste for horror as it is that, emulating King, horror writers have broadened and deepened their art enough to address us all on issues of consequence.

Although King's thematic reach is wide and deep, ascertaining his position on any given issue is not simple. This ambiguity also underlies his broad appeal, for vastly different readers may arrive at vastly different conclusions about his agenda.
—*Edwin F. Casebeer*

Paramount among these issues is death. As James Hillman pointed out in *Revisioning Psychology,* contemporary Western culture is the first extensive culture which has had to consider death as an ending, rather than as a transformation. Instead of believing in a transformation into an angel or devil, animal, or star, today's rationalists regard being as matter and unanimated being as refuse. Founded upon such materialism, the contemporary state and school have reinterpreted reality so as to provide for the here and now, and have maintained a polite skepticism about other realities. King repeatedly dramatizes, from an evolving perspective, the dilemma in which we find ourselves: we are without resources before the imminence of our own deaths and the catastrophe of the deaths of those we love. Adopting (such as in *Carrie*) a contemporary existentialist attitude (where the only constants are isolation, decay, and death), King explores such values (acts, creations, children) as may survive death or those entertained by other cultures (as in *The Stand*). In other novels (such as *The Talisman* and *The Dark Tower* series) King will entertain the possibilities suggested by post-Einsteinian physicists (the multiverse, the reality of process and the nonexistence of time, space, and matter). As in *It*, King looks at possibilities suggested by the psychoanalytic architects of reality, particularly the Jungian theory of an archetypal dimension underlying matter—a dimension that can be apprehended and molded by the artistic imagination. Although King sometimes ends his novels in nausea (*Pet Sematary*) or nothingness (*Carrie*), normally he views the human condition in terms of possibilities and affirmations. Again representative of his generation—and his American community (small-town New England)—those affirmations are based upon what is possible for the individual, particularly the individual not blinded by rationalism. He displays deep distrust for any human configuration larger than the family.

Although King's thematic reach is wide and deep, ascertaining his position on any given issue is not simple. This ambiguity also underlies his broad appeal, for vastly different readers may arrive at vastly different conclusions about his agenda. King seems, in a novel like *The Stand*, to be able to appreciate the validity of the opposed positions of a small-town Christian, Republican American with a high school education and a sophisticated, liberal, and urban existentialist. In a way, like Shakespeare, he does not conclusively resolve a plot or commit irrevocably to the agenda of a specific character or group of characters involved in the conflict. But his noncommitment is so submerged that readers normally assume (as they have with Shakespeare for centuries) that he agrees with them; he economically gestures toward the possibility of gestalt, not a specific gestalt. On the contrary, his chief artistic talent—the talent that has kept all of his work in print throughout his career and is likely to keep it in print—is his ability to balance opposing realities. The reader must resolve the issues. If we supinely regard King as simply a popular artist and expect a canned resolution, we often will find his resolutions unsatisfying. If we invest the energy in tipping his balance toward ourselves, we will behold in the artistic experience an affirming and illuminating mirror of our problems and our solutions.

Such a mirror develops not only from King's choice of situations of great concern to us, but by his technique of characterization. Here again, he achieves balance, gains breadth and depth of appeal. In one sense, King is a highly accomplished realist with a keen eye for the nuances of image and voice; but, in another, his characters are archetypal with origins in myth and folktale. Characters fall into two large groups—the sketch and the multidimensional. One of his true talents is the sketch: he is able to populate novels like *'Salem's Lot, The Stand*, and *The Tommyknockers* with hundreds of briefly executed, vivid characters—each effi-

ciently caught in a telling and representative moment that is often grotesque and generally memorable. King can make credible, as in *The Stand*, a plot that quite literally involves a whole country. He sketches characters from the South, New York, New England, the West, from the rural and urban blue-collar class, the middle class, the criminal and indigent, the police, the army, the entertainment world, and the clerks and functionaries of cities and small towns from all over America. These characters, placed in highly detailed topographies, create for us the realistic element of his fantasies so central in enabling us to accept their supernatural premises. As King said in an interview with Magistrale: "The work underlines again and again that I am not merely dealing with the surreal and the fantastic but, more important, using the surreal and the fantastic to examine the motivations of people and the society and the institutions they create."

King's realistic techniques for creating the primary multidimensional characters significantly differs from those producing the sketch. Generally speaking, he avoids the customary expository visual portrait of a primary character; he prefers to develop the character internally. Thus, by beginning in the character's sensorium, we can project more quickly and directly into it than we might if the objectification of a physical description was between us and it: existing as the bound Jessie Burlingame in *Gerald's Game*, we see, hear, touch, taste, and smell her experience of her world; and from these physical experiences we enter into and share her psychological presence. Generally, we find that psychological presence to be archetypal—the anima. Like any popular artist working with the stereotypical, King is always on the border of creating Jungian personae and plots emanating from the cultural unconscious. Therefore, however individually a multidimensional character may be textured, it feels very familiar as we settle into it.

But King goes a step further, particularly in his more epic novels, by exemplifying the theories of such neo-Jungian thinkers as Hillman: (1) the human psyche is basically a location for a cast of personae in dynamic relationship with one another; (2) the one-persona psyche—humanity's current and dominant commitment to unity, integration, and control—is pathological (the excesses of the rationalistic materialist); and (3) the universe and its inhabitants can only be seen clearly through multiple and dynamic perspectives. Thus, except in novellas and short stories, King generally prefers multiple points of view. Here he is influenced by modernists (such as Faulkner) and by cinema: perspective follows setting—and if the setting contains different characters, he still develops multiple points of view. In the larger novels, typically King pits a group of comrades against a common threat, a dynamic for which he found precedent in both Tolkien's *The Ring* trilogy and Stoker's *Dracula*. Though the details produced by setting and sensorium conceal the fact, each comrade is a persona—a specialized and archetypal figure such as the child, the old man, the lover, the teacher, the healer, etc. As the plot progresses and each persona contributes its vision, the remaining personae subsume these perspectives and evolve into a single (hero or heroine) or dyadic (lovers or parent/child) protagonist with the capacity to defeat or stalemate the antagonist, which itself is often a persona embodying death, decay, or meaninglessness.

Just as often, however, the antagonist is the monstrous. King has a particularly complex attitude toward such a persona. Like Clive Barker, King is able to see the positive side of the monstrous—its incredible energy and commitment, its individuality, and its ability to function in the unknown. Unlike Barker, he is not ready to embrace the monstrous and let it transform him. Again, balance prevails. In *Danse Macabre,* King analyzes the function of author and antagonist in novels. For him, the authorial is not the autobiographical; the "King" is another persona—the folksy, small-town Maine citizen of the commercials, of the prefaces, and of the authorial asides. The persona of the author agrees with the norms of the community. But the antagonist (as monster) is that shadow aspect of us which finds its reality in the individual, the bizarre, and the grotesque. This antagonist seeks to tyrannically control or to destroy rather than to belong, which is dynamic rather than centered and driven rather than ordered. We contain both and we come to the novel to experience both. Their conflict will never be settled, for it is the essence of what they are: opposites that define one another. Although Thad Beaumont, the protagonist of *The Dark Half,* wins his conflict with George Stark (the monster within him) we learn in *Needful Things* that he has lost his love, his art, and his family—he has settled back into alcoholism. In summary, the traditional horror novel, such as Bram Stoker's *Dracula,* excises or conquers the antagonist; the postmodernist horror novel, such as Clive Barker's works, transforms the protagonist into the antagonist, or vice versa; and King's novels balance these processes.

The end result of such a dynamic perception of character and structure is that the novel becomes psyche: that is, it is the location of archetypal personae and their dynamics. It is the interface between the psyches of writer and reader, a template of the soul, a mirror in which we see ourselves most clearly in terrain we least care to explore, the nightworld of death and monstrosity. Seen from the above perspectives, King becomes a modern shaman employing magic (the fantasy image, childhood imagination) to lead his culture into self-discovery where it most needs to look while maintaining commitment to love, family, and community—for King is also a husband, father, and highly visible "social" presence. Again he balances: he is of the tribe and he directs the tribe. No wonder we read him; no wonder we approach him with caution.

Because of his inclination to balance consecutive novels by opposing them to one another, these propositions apply more to the broad characteristics and processes of the canon rather than to individual novels. But his novels also fall into categories in which the same striving toward the balancing of opposing forces is evident: the community, the child, the writer, the woman, and the quest. These categories not only provide a more useful way of approaching King's fiction specifically than would a chronological or genre discussion, but they also focus the preceding theoretical discussion. Each category is a broad, shared foundation with the reader upon which and through which King can consistently design and redesign his social allegories and the psyche's archetypal templates that so consistently and profoundly link him with his audience.

King's writings about the community establish him as one of the country's major regionalist writers whose influences can be traced to the New England Gothic writers, Thornton Wilder's *Our Town,* and the novels of William Faulkner. The community which King most often chooses to present is one inspired by the town of his childhood—Durham, Maine. Sometimes the town is Jerusalem's Lot of the *'Salem's Lot* stories, Haven of *The Tommyknockers,* or Castle Rock—the setting of such works as *The Body, Cujo, The Dead Zone, The Dark Half,* and *Needful Things.* A citizen of his region, King believes that the most politically viable unit is one small enough to hear and respond to individual opinion; as in *The Stand,* cities like New York regularly appear in an advanced state of disruption and the federal government responds only to the reality of its paper and its power.

Although community is more feasible in a small town than in a large city, in King's small towns it is rare. More frequently, their citizens (as in *'Salem's Lot, The Tommyknockers,* and *Needful Things*) are caught up in materialistic pursuits that lead them into conflict with their neighbors. This conflict results in a community held together by conformity rather than cooperation, with narcissism and the closed door, fealty to no code but self-gratification, and apocalypse simmering beneath the surface. Yet—to stress King's seeking of balance in this category—there appears the option of a better way of life. The Boulder Free Zone of *The Stand* comes closest to such a utopia: it is small, it accords a place to each according to need and talent, and it attends to the individual. But King is ambivalent about such a grassroots democracy; the true reason for the survival of the Free Zone is the emergence of an elite presiding coterie composed of exceptional individuals with exceptional social conscience. When events demand the sacrifice of most of these people and the Free Zone becomes too large for rule by their dialogue, Stu Redman and Fran Goldsmith (the surviving hero and heroine) conclude that their community now is simply recycling the former decadent and materialist world. They opt for a more viable social unit: the family.

And they leave the Free Zone for the locale of King's own family, Maine.

To understand King's strong focus on the family and the child requires recognition that during his career he has been a husband and father of two boys and a girl. During their childhood, he generally worked at home, but brought his family with him on the rare occasions when he left Maine. Thus, his family is often major material; he need only look up from the word processor to find grist. And as his own children have aged, so has the presence of the child diminished in his novels. The category of the child arises for a second reason: in his own development, King has had to reencounter himself as child and boy in order to remove the blocks to his becoming a man: "The idea is to go back and confront your childhood, in a sense relive it if you can, so that you can be whole." Also in this category are early novels such as *Rage* (begun while he was in high school), *The Long Walk,* and *Carrie* (written by a young man dealing with problems posed by family and organized adult society).

Among King's most endearing characters are small children such as Danny Torrance of *The Shining* and Charlie McGee of *Firestarter.* In their characterization, he avoids the potential sentimentality that often sinks such efforts by manipulating sentences that seamlessly weave together the diction and phrasing of both child and adult, thus conveying the being of the one and the perspective of the other. The second paragraph introducing Danny provides an example: "Now it was five o'clock, and although he didn't have a watch and couldn't tell time too well yet anyway, he was aware of passing time by the lengthening of the shadows, and by the golden cast that now tinged the afternoon light." The first subordinate clause is childishly run-on in structure and uses Danny's diction, while the second main clause is complex-compound within itself—its subordinate elements are parallel and its diction is the polysyllabic format typical of the narrator in King's lyric mode. Such a combination of styles and perspectives works so well because King adheres to the romantic belief that the child is the father of the man. It may be that children are superior in wisdom and psychological talents to adults simply because the latter are corrupted by psyches shrunken by materialism and rationalism—but they are superior. Thus, Danny is one with time and space, almost godlike in his perception of those dimensions in the haunted Hotel Overlook, while Charlie's power over the material world establishes her as an angel of apocalypse when she incinerates the Shop (King's version of the CIA).

King's adolescents can also be superior to his adults. In fact, the major reason for grouping the adolescent with the child is that, normally, King's adolescents are prepubescent: they have no explicit sexual identity and are still more child than adult. It is in such adolescents that we see his attempt to achieve yet another kind of balance—between the two stages

of life. While the child has intimations of immortality, the adult has knowledge of death. Thus, the Castle Rock novella *The Body* (made into the excellent film by Rob Reiner entitled *Stand By Me*) initiates its four boys by leading them not into a sexual encounter, but into another rite of passage: their first encounter with death as the corpse of a fifth boy. Similarly, in *It,* a group of boys encounters and prevails over the protean incarnation of every human's deepest fear; and in *The Talisman,* co-written with Peter Straub, a trio of boys (an archetypal id, ego, and superego) transcend the force of this reality to enter a reality in which death is unempowered. Sometimes, as in *Carrie, The Stand,* and *Christine,* death and sexuality are negatively related: as Carrie becomes sexual, she becomes monstrous and an angel of the apocalypse. The sexual foreplay of Nadine and Harold in *The Stand* is a clear symptom of their degenerate state. As Arnie becomes sexual, Christine corrupts him—even Arnie's benevolent alter ego, Dennis, discovers that his first love turns to ashes. In his most recent novels, King demonstrates a mature and central sexuality; but in the novels of this earlier period, in which he is reencountering his boyhood, sexuality leads to adulthood which leads to diminished psychological resources and death.

Coincidental with King's emphasis on the child and the boy is his emphasis on the family (often in a pathological phase). One of the earliest and most powerful of these novels is *The Shining,* which, long before systems theory, dramatized the point that the pathological individual is a symptom of the pathological family and that both must undergo treatment. Jack Torrance's obsessions and his wife's posture as victim are inheritances from their parents which bind them together and threaten Danny. In *Christine,* Arnie's pathological family environment leads to his destruction and theirs, while Dennis's family supports and creates him in its image. *It* provides the reader with a wide range of family dynamics, both successful and unsuccessful, and relates such to the girl and boys who are the protagonists. The most powerful of the numerous family novels is the tragic *Pet Sematary,* which develops for the reader a realistically ideal family which is demolished by its own estimable values when its child is senselessly killed. The question posed by the novel is whether the family can survive the death of a child. The answer is no. In this system, the death of a child kills the family.

A subject as close to King as the child and the family is that of the writer—a character who dominates as either protagonist or antagonist in a wide range of short stories, novellas, and novels (most significantly *'Salem's Lot, The Shining, It, Misery, The Tommyknockers,* and *The Dark Half*). The novelist-protagonist who dominates *'Salem's Lot* is more a product of King's youthful ideals than his experience. Like King, Ben Mears (a "mirror") undertakes a novel which will allow him to productively relive his childhood. But Ben's conflict with the vampire Barlow enlarges him to mythic proportions: as the personae about him converge and provide him understanding, faith, wisdom, and imagination, he develops a godlike perception and power. Metaphorically, when he encounters and conquers the vampire that is feeding on the town, he becomes the archetype of an elemental "good . . . whatever moved the greatest wheels of the universe." The following novel, *The Shining,* establishes balance by becoming an exact opposite to its predecessor: the alcoholic Torrance (a playwright this time) is the monster. King sees this particular writer as a failure because he stops writing—Torrance's writing block leads to psychosis. Among the complex communities of *The Stand,* a similar opposition is in the contrast between Larry (the successful musician) with Harold (the unsuccessful writer): although his success nearly destroys him, Larry literally enacts a second crucifixion that saves the world; abnegating art for dark vision, Harold still manages some dignity before succumbing to demonic forces. Both figures physically resemble King: Larry has King's height and current physique and Harold has the height and King's adolescent physique. Although the hero is blond and the villain dark-haired, both have hair the quality of King's. In *It,* where the child's imagination is the only weapon of the adult against the death and meaninglessness of the eponymous evil, the novelist Bill Denbrough (who this time resembles Peter Straub) regains this state most easily and thus is a vital element of the protagonistic band.

Balancing again, King writes two novels—*Misery* and *The Tommyknockers*—which countervail such optimistic authorial characterizations. In *Misery* the primary subject is the negative relationship of the reader and the writer: the reader is the writer's enemy. Readers regularly read the genre writer rather than the literary artist—in *Misery,* this is the Gothic novelist. Since the readers' choice enforces conventions and confines the writer's creative talent, in a sense the audience "writes" the genre novel. Apparently tiring of these limitations, King personifies his tyrannical audience in the archetypal figure of Annie, who literally limits the aspiring literary artist, Paul Sheldon, to genre fiction by drugs, bondage, and torture. Despite such a negative response to whether readers are the motivation for writing, King gives the issue a serious and detailed treatment: his writing of a Gothic romance novel within a realistic novel and his exploration of the psychological processes of writers and their relationship with those of readers is a fascinating and original effort. And, again, he negates his own negation by undercutting Paul's distaste for genre fiction by his admiration for this bloodily extracted romance, even though its creation mutilated him.

While *Misery* suggests that the literary artist's social influence is more negligible than that of a genre novelist by creating a character with a conflicting literary agenda, *The Tommyknockers* approaches the same issue by creating two authors: (1) the genre novelist, Bobbi Anderson, whose dark

vision unleashes an alien presence which enslaves her community; and (2) the literary artist, poet Jim Gardener, whose self-sacrifice saves that community. Both are competent and dedicated writers who hold one another's work in esteem. But both are fatally flawed. Bobbi's kind of writing leaves her psychologically open to outside control (from audience and alien): she becomes the conduit which unearths and directs a cosmic darkness to the human community. Jim is armed against such possession, but isolated from the community by an art aspiring to the ideal. He has the vision to see through the darkness—he can and does die for the community, but it will never buy his books. As in *Misery,* King's final position on the writer's value is extremely pessimistic.

After writing *Misery* and *The Tommyknockers,* King entered a hiatus. For him, writing had become an existential act. He had the money but he felt controlled and depleted by the audience that he did have and despaired of the existence of any other kind of audience. Why continue to write? Developmental theory, such as Gail Sheehy's *Passages,* suggests that other processes were affecting King. He was passing through a chronological period from the age of 38 to 42 in which a man or woman working in the public area generally experiences extreme conflict as life takes a new direction: he or she reaches the end of a horizontal direction in which new territory and material are claimed through a process of conflict (a masculine direction), and a vertical direction where depth rather than width is sought through the development of nurturance and personal relationships (a feminine direction).

> In *Gerald's Game* and *Dolores Claiborne,* King picks up a gauntlet. Long criticized for unidimensional female characters in such articles as Mary Pharr's "Partners in the *Danse:* Women in Stephen King's Fiction," he apparently decided that a new direction for growth both as human and as artist would be appropriate in accepting the challenge to create convincing women.
> —*Edwin F. Casebeer*

King emerged from his hiatus with an ambitious contract for four books—he wrote five (the last two of which were novels solely about women). But before he undertook this feminine direction, he closed the canon to children, Castle Rock, and writers. Children had by this time become lesser characters. The people of Castle Rock, given a slight nudge by a minor demon, destroyed themselves in the apocalyptic cataclysm ending *Needful Things.* The resolution of the issue of the writer in *The Dark Half* was more complex. The opposition of popular writer and artist in *Misery* and *The Tommyknockers* is here internalized in *The Dark Half:* warring for the soul of a writer are his personae as literary artist (Thad Beaumont) and as genre novelist (George Stark). The artist wins, but the victory is pyrrhic. Closer examination reveals that Beaumont's friends, wife, and children are psychologically akin to his nemesis. We find out in the sequel, *Needful Things,* that not only has the artist lost friends and family, but also the will to write. He is an alcoholic and the circle is closed. King leaves the issue behind him unresolved: it is what it is.

In *Gerald's Game* and *Dolores Claiborne,* King picks up a gauntlet. Long criticized for unidimensional female characters in such articles as Mary Pharr's "Partners in the *Danse:* Women in Stephen King's Fiction," he apparently decided that a new direction for growth both as human and as artist would be appropriate in accepting the challenge to create convincing women. Written simultaneously, the novels are most productively regarded as two poles in a meta-narrative process. At the one pole is the heroine of *Gerald,* Jessie Burlingame—economically and socially privileged, childless, and in her own eyes significant only as her husband's sexual object. At the other pole is Dolores, a figure apparently based on King's mother (to whom he dedicates the novel)—economically and socially underprivileged, a mother, and in her own eyes significant in herself. Through their telepathic awareness of one another and through their experience of the same eclipse as a central incident in their lives, King establishes the commonality of these two very different women: it lies in the fact that they are whole only in those years before and after men entered their lives—the period of the eclipse. In *Gerald,* King dramatizes the entry of Jessie into an eclipse through the seduction and domination by her father; she exits the eclipse by killing her dominating husband, Gerald. The subsequent fragmenting of her victim persona into a community of sustaining female personae provides her with the resources to free herself from a literal bondage. In *Dolores,* the titular figure is a mother and wife who exits the eclipse by murdering a husband who also seeks to sexually exploit his daughter. In either case, the women experience one horror in common: the entry of men and sexuality into their lives. By erecting such contrasting poles as Jessie and Dolores, and yet maintaining both as sympathetic characters with a shared dilemma, King writes paired novels sympathetic to a wide spectrum of women and evades an easy condemnation of his women characters as unidimensional.

Overall, King's canon is a quest. But his battle cry is not "excelsior!" The direction is downwards and the path is a spiral. Many of King's characters experience life as a quest: Ben Mears of *'Salem's Lot* questing for self and conquering the vampire; *The Tommyknockers'* Gardener questing for death and finding self; the comrades of *The Stand* marching against the Dark One and founding the New Jerusalem; the boys of *It* killing fear; and the boys of *The Talisman* killing death. The gunslinger of *The Dark Tower* series is, however, probably most typical of King: he seeks to understand what the quest itself is. His enemies become his friends, his guides his traitors, his victims those he has saved, and his now a then. Paradox; transformation; balancing the dualities, an emergent, tenuous, ever-fading, and ever-appearing balance—these are the duplicitous landmarks in the terrain of King's work and his life. Both are open enough and fluent enough to mirror us and ours as we seek to make our own accommodations with modern monsters, personal meaninglessness, social chaos, physical decay, and death.

FURTHER READING

Criticism

Keesey, Douglas. "'The Face of Mr. Flip': Homophobia in the Horror of Stephen King." In *The Dark Descent,* edited by Tony Magistrale. New York: Greenwood Press, 1992, pp. 187-201.

> Asserts that "one of the socially specific fears most often represented in King's horror is homophobia."

Quinn, Judy. "King of the Season." *Publishers Weekly* 243, No. 32 (5 August 1996): 293-94.

> Discusses the simultaneous publication of King's *Desperation* and *The Regulators* under his pseudonym, Richard Bachman.

Additional coverage of King's life and career is contained in the following sources published by Gale: *Authors and Artists for Young Adults,* **Vols. 1 and 17;** *Bestsellers,* **Vol. 90:1;** *Contemporary Authors,* **Vols. 61-64;** *Contemporary Authors New Revision Series,* **Vols. 1, 30, and 52;** *Dictionary of Literary Biography,* **Vol. 143;** *Dictionary of Literary Biography Yearbook,* **Vol. 80;** *DISCovering Authors Modules: Novelists* **and** *Popular Fiction and Genre Authors; Junior DISCovering Authors; Major Twentieth-Century Writers; Something about the Author,* **Vols. 9 and 55; and** *Short Story Criticism,* **Vol. 17.**

Carol Shields

1935-

American-born Canadian novelist, short story writer, poet, dramatist, and critic.

The following entry presents an overview of Shields's career through 1997. For further information on her life and works, see *CLC,* Volume 91.

INTRODUCTION

A Canadian-American born and raised in Chicago, Shields achieved a historic literary feat when her novel *The Stone Diaries* (1993) earned Canada's Governor General's Award and the American Pulitzer Prize and National Book Critics Circle Award, and was short-listed for Britain's Booker Award.

Biographical Information

Shields was born June 2, 1935, to Robert and Inez Warner in Oak Park, Illinois, a prosperous suburb of Chicago. She has described her years growing up as safe and happy, but also insular. Shields earned a bachelor's degree from Hanover College in Indiana; while studying for a year in England, she met Donald Shields, a Canadian engineering graduate student. The two married in 1957 and Shields moved to Canada. For the next few years, Shields focused on family, giving birth to five children and following her husband across Canada as his career progressed. Shields took a magazine writing course at the University of Toronto and sold stories to the Canadian Broadcasting Co. and British Broadcasting Co. In her late twenties, she revived an earlier interest in poetry writing. When the family moved to Ottawa, Shields enrolled in the graduate department in English at the University of Ottawa, writing a masters thesis on Susanna Moodie. It was at this time that Shields began writing fiction; in 1976 she published *Small Ceremonies*. The book received critical acclaim in Canada and Shields was encouraged to continue writing. While she attracted a modest Canadian following with her subsequent works, she did not gain attention outside of Canada until publishing *Swann* (1987), which was short-listed for the prestigious Governor General's Award. Following the success of *Swann,* many of Shields' earlier works were released in the United States and Britain. Shields has resided in Winnipeg, Manitoba for a number of years, teaching English and creative writing at the University of Manitoba, where she is now chancellor.

Major Works

Shields's fiction has focused on the common, almost banal, events of middle-class, middle-age characters. However, far from being uneventful, these characters' lives are marked by identity crises, self doubts, and anxieties. Her first published novel, *Small Ceremonies,* set in early 1970s Canada, focuses on Judith and Martin Gill, an academic couple, and their children. Through Judith's efforts to write a biography and the family's interaction with one another and others, Shields poses questions about public and private knowledge and how people construct identity. *Happenstance* (1980) and *A Fairly Conventional Woman* (1982) continue Shields's exploration of how people come to know themselves and others. Later published in a single volume, the two works follow a married couple during one weekend; *Happenstance* is written from the husband's perspective and *A Fairly Conventional Woman* from the wife's. Together the works illustrate the isolation that occurs within the marriage and the degree to which the characters misunderstand one another and themselves. In *Various Miracles* (1985) and to a greater extent in *Swann: A Mystery,* Shields began to experiment with form while remaining constant in theme. *Swann* consists of five chapters, with each of the first four written from the perspective of one of the characters and the final chapter written as a screenplay which reveals crucial information about the cast. The novel focuses on the illusive identity of Mary Swann, a poor farmer's wife from rural Ontario, whose single volume of poetry was published after she was killed by her husband. To each character Swann and her poetry represent something different, and each character struggles to create an identity for her, even as the artifacts of her life begin to mysteriously disappear. *The Stone Diaries* is written in the form of a journal recording the life of Daisy Goodwill Fletts. In it Fletts discusses the events of her life as she attempts to define its meaning. *Larry's Party* (1997) focuses on similar concerns of self-identity, but is written from the perspective of an average middle-aged man. In addition to her novels, Shields has written two critically acclaimed short story collections and three poetry collections.

Critical Reception

Critics are consistent in their praise of Shields's work. From the beginning of her career, critics have commended Shields's descriptive powers and ability to capture the nature of everyday life, comparing her with A. S. Byatt, Margaret Atwood, and Alice Munro. In reviewing her first three books, Julie Beddoes wrote, "Shields can create vivid and often picturesque characters with such sympathy that one is convinced their eccentricities are the stuff of everyday life." Elizabeth Benedict remarked, "Shields is wickedly accurate about the intricacies of marriage, parenthood and the battle of the sexes, and an astute observer and satirist of social trends." However, most critics agree that Shields began a transformation of her literary career with *Various Miracles* and has built upon this with each subsequent work. In her review of *Swann*, Diane Turbide concluded that the novel's plot was better developed and less banal than her earlier works. Other reviewers have noted that nothing truly frightening threatens Shields's characters, although she has captured a more urgent tone in her later books. In addition, some critics have questioned the accuracy of classifying her as a feminist.

PRINCIPAL WORKS

Others (poetry) 1972
Intersect (poetry) 1974
Small Ceremonies (novel) 1976
Susanna Moodie: Voice and Vision (criticism) 1976
The Box Garden (novel) 1977
Happenstance (novel) 1980
A Fairly Conventional Woman (novel) 1982
Various Miracles (short stories) 1985

Swann: A Mystery (novel) 1987
The Orange Fish (short stories) 1989
A Celibate Season [with Blanche Howard] (novel) 1991
The Stone Diaries (novel) 1993
Thirteen Hands (play) 1993
Coming to Canada (poetry) 1995
Larry's Party (novel) 1997

CRITICISM

Bruce MacDonald (review date July 1976)

SOURCE: "Quiet Manifesto: Carol Shields's *Small Ceremonies*," in *International Fiction Review*, Vol. 3, No. 2, July, 1976, pp. 147-50.

[*In the review below, MacDonald praises* Small Ceremonies *and places Shields within the Canadian literary tradition.*]

At a time when some Canadian writers are getting on cultural bandwagons, or are partially blinded by the myths which they have created for themselves, it is refreshing to come across a novel like ***Small Ceremonies*** by Carol Shields. Her novel, as the title suggests, concerns itself with the small acts of a quiet family in a relatively peaceful Canadian academic community. Very little happens in the novel, yet subtly and with considerable skill Mrs. Shields unfolds the character of the narrator, Judith Gill, her English professor husband, Martin, and their two children, Meredith and Richard.

The problems for the family arise after their return from a sabbatical year in England. The Canadian experience of the characters is portrayed against a wider, multi-cultural background which highlights both the more general humanity and the peculiarly Canadian quality of their responses. The "small ceremonies," like the English high tea on Sunday evenings, which define their English experience help them to identify the subtle differences and nuances of their Canadianness.

The setting is Canada in the early 1970's and the characters beyond the Gill family circle help not only to add complication to the life of the family, but also to give a sense of the times in which they live, when large, archetypal action is obsolete and a more intimate understanding is required. Roger Ramsey, Can. Lit. professor at the university, and Ruthie St. Pierre, librarian and translator, live commonlaw in defiance of social morality when society has ceased to care about that sort of protest; Nancy Krantz, Judith's best friend, is an activist in all the "anti-" organizations, but is ultimately unattached to anyone or anything; and most prominent, Furlong Eberhardt, famous Canadian novelist, who teaches in the East and writes in mythopoeic patterns about his "roots" in the West, is blissfully unaware of the reality around him. Unlike the protest and obtuseness of her friends Judith Gill roots her observations firmly in her immediate world, more Canadian even than Eberhardt's, arriving at her larger discoveries through a fidelity to the minuteness of her experience.

There are interesting relationships between *Small Ceremonies* and Frederick Philip Grove's work which are important on the levels of both art and tradition.
—*Bruce MacDonald*

Beyond the delicate Jane Austenish portrait of family and friends which is the main substance of the novel (*Emma* comes to mind), the work poses two major literary questions—one about the relationship between art and life and the second about the relationship between Shields's novel and the Canadian literary tradition. As Jane Austen in *Northanger Abbey* demonstrates what her art is not and what it hopes to be, so *Small Ceremonies* is a literary statement with the intentions but not the trumpeting connotations of "manifesto."

There are interesting relationships between *Small Ceremonies* and Frederick Philip Grove's work which are important on the levels of both art and tradition. Most obviously Furlong Eberhardt, Canadian novelist, has mysterious origins and a Germanic name like Grove. Furlong's real name is Rudyard, which suggests Kipling but also Rudyard Clark of Grove's *The Master of the Mill*. John Spalding of Shields's novel immediately suggests Abe Spalding of Grove's *Fruits of the Earth*. Furlong's novels, all of them set in the prairies, also suggest a modern equivalent of Grove. These "clues" are more significant when we discover that Shields and Grove are both involved in a similar aesthetic exploration of whether it is possible to determine the social and individual realities of the human experience through the dialectic of fiction. A passage from *The Master of the Mill* about this problem can almost be seen as a summary of Shields's concerns: "What is the reality in us? That which we feel ourselves to be? Or that which others conceive us to be?" It is through the tension between public knowledge and private awareness that Shields explores the reality of her narrator and other characters. The consequent ironies pervade the novel and reach beyond the art to include the writer herself.

Carol Shields is a biographer, poet, novelist; Judith Gill, her narrator, is a biographer and, by virtue of her position as narrator, a novelist (she has a sister who is a poet): Carol has recently published a critical study of Susanna Moodie's works [*Susanna Moodie: Voice and Vision*]; Judith is busy throughout the novel writing a biography of Susanna Moodie: Carol is married to a professor of civil engineering and has five children; Judith is married to an Associate Professor of English and has two children: Carol has studied and lived in England; the Gills go to England on sabbatical. Although drawn from Shields's own experience this novel is more than loosely disguised autobiography, however. The whole question posed by Grove, of how we know ourselves and others, is involved here. At the end of Shields's novel we find that neither public nor private knowledge of the self, neither biography nor autobiography is final or definitive. Fiction, as the dialectical recreation in precise terms of the individual in a specific social context, is the only public reality.

Judith, the biographer, cannot comprehend what Susanna Moodie was like as a human being even with all the evidence she has at her disposal; she cannot comprehend her husband and children even though they live in the same house; and it is only with great difficulty that she comes to terms with herself, not as an abstract personality but as a member of a family and society where individuality cannot be separated from the paraphernalia of living. When reality is transmuted into fiction Judith, Furlong, and John Spalding, all of them writers, find that it is impossible to "plagiarize from real life" in their art. Biography, fiction, even autobiography is only one limited view of the whole complex of life which defines the individual. Even of Susanna Moodie's own autobiographical novel Judith is forced to say, "But, of course, it isn't really Susanna; it's only a projection, a view of herself." And perhaps Judith Gill is a view of Carol Shields who finds something about herself in Susanna and can only account for the ambiguity of existence in the multiple levels of irony in the interplay between reality, autobiography, biography, and fiction in the novel.

The question of Canadianness is important to the conception of this novel as well, overtly in the person of Furlong Eberhardt, who, like Grove, was not originally Canadian, and more subtly in the relationship the novel establishes with the Canadian literary tradition. Furlong is conveyed to us through ironies as Judith herself is. He is first the great Canadian novelist who sells to an American company the movie rights of his "Canadian" masterpiece which he has indirectly plagiarized from an Englishman. Further irony lies in Furlong's origins which are not Canadian, although he is able to appear Canadian by adopting all the standard Canadian literary myths. However, the ironies do not stop there. The description of Furlong on pages 28-29 of the novel is based on the dust jacket of Kent Thompson's first novel—he has similar American/Canadian origins, though not hidden. But the even larger irony lies in the fact that Carol Shields is, like Kent Thompson, originally from the mid-Western United States, although in this novel peculiarly sensitive to the Canadian scene. Grove, Eberhardt, Thompson, Shields, are all "foreigners" in a nationalistic sense, yet all "Canadian" writers, and here the established nature of Grove's reputation is a necessary anchor to make the other ironies legitimate and real. Shields cannot be easily dismissed as un-Canadian (I do not wish to suggest she is) since her ironies have a genuine Canadian flavor. As with the autobiographical concerns the mode here is irony which encompasses Shields herself, and which suggests some of the ambiguities which arise in attempting to define the Canadianness of the Canadian tradition.

> ***Small Ceremonies* promises much, not of the same, but of a clarity of social vision akin to Jane Austen's, which can lead to further insights into the society Carol Shields has adopted and come to understand. One hopes that she will be able to maintain in future the "balancing act between humour and desperation" which makes the ironies and tensions of this novel enlightening and very human.**
> **—*Bruce MacDonald***

Small Ceremonies consciously and subtly recognizes a Canadian literary tradition and stakes its claim within it, proclaiming gently what it is and what it is not going to emulate. It is not Furlong Eberhardt's type of Can. Lit., "Saskatchewan in powder form. Mix with honest rain water for native genre." Shields avoids many of the standard Canadian formulas which often obscure rather than clarify the ideas implied by them—man vs. nature, urban vs. wilderness, moral vs. natural, materialistic vs. idealistic. Margaret Atwood is the most distinguished of the formularizers and Shields is staying carefully away from that camp. She also consciously sidesteps the tendency which developed in the 1960's to equate "creativity" with the scribbling of the gut reaction in immature prose. With the growing desire of Canadians and Canadian institutions for a Canadian literature this type of insensitive, gut-analysis has spilled over even into published works and is characterized by Ludwig in a "creative writing" class in *Small Ceremonies:* "Ludwig poked with a blunt and dirty finger into the sores of his consciousness, not stopping at his subtle and individual response to orgasm and the nuances of his erect penis. On and on." Again, on a more eminent level one is reminded here of *Beautiful Losers,* and Shields's conscious avoidance of that particular type of superficiality, without castrating her own prose, is welcome.

Small Ceremonies reminds one often of Margaret Laurence's *Fire-Dwellers,* with its emphasis on the housewife coming to terms with herself and her family. There is even an overt echo of Laurence's novel when Judith wants to assure Roger and Ruthie that in spite of their loss of romance "everything will be just fine," a phrase reminiscent of the oft repeated "Everything's all right" of *The Fire-Dwellers.* Shields's novel, however, avoids the blatant, often vulgar and loud declarations of Laurence's. Because much is similar in obvious things, the difference of tone is most striking. Shields's is a more quiet, more subtle, more delicately ironic portrayal of suburban existence and of what it means to Judith to come to terms with herself and her family.

Small Ceremonies then proclaims itself as existing beyond many of the conventional formulas and myths of the contemporary Canadian scene. It does not indulge in the kind of "mandatory sex scenes" which are often taken as proof of the "honesty" of "self-expression," and so it moves beyond the superficies of that sort of conformity. Above all it conveys in a quiet, precise style the glance, the subtle change of tone, the shortsighted immediacy of interiors and people, and the small ceremonies which are an index of the cohesiveness of any society or family. The novel is an affirmation in its own unobtrusive way of the unity of a Canadian society where not all behavior is loud and archetypal but some is delicate and on the verge of unself-conscious authenticity.

The novel works on all these levels simultaneously with very little loss of control. For a first novel, and given the complexity of the ironies and literary purposes of the work, it is a feat worthy of a much more experienced writer. *Small Ceremonies* promises much, not of the same, but of a clarity of social vision akin to Jane Austen's, which can lead to further insights into the society Carol Shields has adopted and come to understand. One hopes that she will be able to maintain in future the "balancing act between humour and desperation" which makes the ironies and tensions of this novel enlightening and very human.

Malcolm Page (essay date 1980)

SOURCE: "*Small Ceremonies* and the Art of the Novel," in *Journal of Canadian Fiction,* Vol. 28, No. 29, 1980, pp. 172-78.

[*In the essay below, Page discusses Shields's observations about fiction, biography, and sources in* Small Ceremonies.]

Carol Shields' first novel, *Small Ceremonies* (1976), is short, light and readable, a first-person study of nine months in the life of a woman of forty, scrutinizing herself and her circle. Thus reviewer John Parr appropriately describes it as "a familiar enough life story of quiet desperation except that

Judith Gill, who tells her own tale of woe, enlivens it with many satiric flourishes." Another reviewer, Robert A. Lecker, says the book is "a reasonably entertaining story about the significant trivialities of everyday suburban existence," in which "nothing particularly exciting happens," and DuBarry Campau terms it "a pleasant, unpretentious book" with "wit, delicacy, and deft, realistic perceptions."

However, one should not think that the subject is merely suburbia and the everyday—though illnesses, parties, and so on do occupy considerable space. Judith, the central character, is a writer of biographies who has made one unsuccessful attempt at a novel, and Martin, her husband, is a Milton expert seeking more creative ways of expressing his scholarly insights. The other characters include Furlong Eberhardt, an admired Canadian author of ten novels, and the Englishman, John Spalding, who has produced seven unpublished novels before his eighth is accepted. These people discuss and write about many of the problems of being authors—or would-be authors.

Shields, in fact, poses and examines a range of issues about the nature of fiction and of biography. Where do novelists find their ideas? How important is plot? What is originality, and does it matter? What are novelists like? Do they differ from biographers in their perceptions of life? What is the place of fact in fiction? When does biographical speculation become biographical fiction?

Judith has published two biographies: of the first barrister in Upper Canada and of a prairie suffragette of the nineties—both modest and manageable subjects. She turns next to Susanna Moodie, writing the book during the nine months covered in *Small Ceremonies.* She struggles to understand Moodie—can she really never have told her husband that she was responsible for the Lieutenant-Governor offering him a job? What can a relationship in which she always called her husband by his surname have been like? How did she come to change "from a rather priggish faintly bluestockinged but ardent young girl into a heavy, conventional, distressed, perpetually disapproving and sorrowing woman?" Moodie leaves a few clues of "unconscious self-betrayal," mainly in her novels, particularly in *Flora Lindsay,* where "by watching Flora, I am able to see Susanna as a young woman. But, of course, it isn't really Susanna; it's only a projection, a view of herself." After the book is completed, Judith tells Furlong she still does not know whether she succeeded in finding and expressing the truth about Moodie:

> "And did you do it this time, Judith? Did you really wrap it up?"
>
> I sense his genuine interest. And am oddly grateful for it. "No, not really," I admit. "I have a few

hunches. About the real Susanna. But I can't quite pin it all down."

> "You mean she never came right out and admitted much that was personal?"
>
> "Hardly ever. I had to look at her through layers and layers of affection."

Shields' novel contains a selection of the kind of documents with which the biographer has to work, and which could—just possibly—provide inspiration to the novelist. Scattered through *Small Ceremonies* are the letter left by a 9-year-old girl in her room when her apartment is rented out; samples of the lists left by her father; excerpts from Spalding's journal; Judith's sketchy "Notes for Novel"; a snatch of Martin's lecture-notes; itemized biographical sketches of Martin and Furlong; four letters exchanged between Judith and Spalding when he plans a visit to Canada; a newspaper clipping; and even a party invitation. These are really all observed and interpreted for the reader by Judith. She comments on the difficulty of giving life—and true life—to such papers: "There is never never enough material. . . . Characters from the past, heroic as they may have been, lie coldly on the page. They are inert, having no details of person to make them fidget or scratch; they are toneless, simplified, stylized, myths distilled from letters; they are bloodless. There is nothing to do but rely on available data, on diaries, bills, clippings, always something on paper."

Judith is the perennial observer, slightly aside from life, which she regrets but cannot change: "I became a full-time voyeur. On trains I watched people, lusting to know their destinations, their middle names, their marital status and always and especially whether or not they were happy. I stared to see the titles of the books they were reading or the brand of cigarette they smoked. I strained to hear snatches of conversations." On the last page, she accepts this destiny: "I am a watcher, an outsider whether I like it or not, and I'm stuck with the dangers that go along with it. And the rewards." Perhaps "watchers" make better biographers than do novelists.

Judith's curiosity extends to Furlong when she discovers that his real first-name is Rudyard, and she secretly researches his past. Eventually she finds that he is American-born, though purporting to express a uniquely Canadian consciousness—then she playfully threatens to write *his* biography. She also enjoys speculating about the unseen Spalding in England, placing him as a "silly, silly, silly little man. Paranoiac, inept, ridiculous." At the end of the book, Spalding turns up, and Martin and Judith discuss their impressions:

"He seems okay," Martin says. "Not quite the nut I expected."

"Me either. Where did I get the idea he was going to be short?"

"And fat! Christ, he's actually obese. Cheerful guy though. . . ."

"He certainly is different than what I expected. It's a good thing we had him paged at the airport or we'd never have found him."

"Funny, but he said the same thing about us."

"What?"

"That he wouldn't have recognized us in a thousand years. He had us pictured differently."

Judith may be as wrong about Susanna Moodie as she was about Spalding. The difference is the product of Judith's imagination. She resists speculation in her biographies: "If one does enlarge on data, there is the danger of trespassing into that whorish field of biographical fiction." Fiction she finds fascinating but difficult: "Unlike biography, where a profusion of material makes it possible and even necessary to be selective, novel writing requires a complex mesh of details which has to be spun out of simple air. . . . The most obvious fact about fiction struck me afresh: it all had to be made up." Furlong tells her that basically she mistrusts fiction: "It's your old Scarborough puritanism, as I've frequently told you. Judith Gill, my girl, basically you believe fiction is wicked and timewasting. The devil's work. A web of lies."

Judith likes true stories about people; "my children," she observes, "are like me in their lust after other people's stories." This reflection leads her to look back to her childhood and to realise, "unlike Martin, whose family tree came well stocked with family tales, I am from a bleak non-storytelling family" with just three anecdotes: "That was all we had: my father's adventures in the stairwell, which never developed beyond the scientific rationale for fainting, my mother's teapot and rash and her near-brush with fame." These three are true stories: Shields enjoys the ambiguity in the word "story."

Judith's three family anecdotes were fact, though handed down in polished, practised form. She had facts on Moodie and Furlong, clues and speculations eventually checked against fact for Spalding. What, Shields wonders, are the true, actual, real sources of what is described as fiction? Is fiction "made up," as Judith thinks, or are its origins more truly in life?

Four novels are described within the novel ***Small Ceremonies***. Poor Spalding has written no less than seven novels, all rejected, which Judith finds and reads when she comes to occupy their flat. While she finds them all "totally and climactically boring," she judges the one most likely written first to have "a plot of fairly breathless originality." Judith does not outline the plot, and she can only guess whether it originated in Spalding's experience or imagination: "Had he lived this plot himself or simply dreamed it up? The rest of the books were so helplessly conventional that it was difficult for me to credit him with creativity at any level. Still, it seemed reasonable, since the least of us are visited occasionally by genius, that this book might have been his one good idea." Or, as Judith wonders later, might Spalding have taken the idea from someone else? Or may the plot blend living and dreaming?

Judith reads Spalding's manuscript at a moment when she is dissatisfied with the limitations of biography and is toying with writing a novel. She tells Martin, "I'm tired of being boxed in by facts all the time. Fiction might be an out for me. And it might be entertaining too." But he replies: "You're too organized for full-time fantasy." All she has are nine short notes, one or two of which might be the germ of short stories, the rest at best paragraphs. And at once she faces writer's block.

A year later, back in Canada, she is still considering writing a novel and audits the Creative Writing seminar taught by Furlong, where in ten weeks she is expected to produce a novel. Having drafted a good first chapter, she is stuck for some weeks, then, desperate, suddenly remembers Spalding's good plot and uses it. At the time she has no difficulty in rationalizing "borrowing" another's plot: "A good idea should never be orphaned. . . . I thought of the Renaissance painters, and happily, gleefully, drew parallels; the master painter often doing nothing but tracing in the lines, while his worthy but less gifted artisans filled in the colours. It had been a less arrogant age in which creativity had been shared; surely that was an ennobling precedent. For I didn't intend anything as crude as stealing John Spalding's plot outright . . . All I needed to borrow was the underlying plot structure." The moral point raised is a difficult one: to what extent can the use of the plot of an unpublished book, for another book not intended for publication, be considered stolen? No sooner has Judith finished the book and given it to Furlong than she regrets it, because "the bones of my stolen plot stuck out everywhere like great evil-gleaming knobs, accusing me, charging me." So she directs Furlong to destroy it.

Furlong, however, takes over the plot and uses it in his next novel, the third novel we read of, the highly praised *Graven Images*. Judith is furious when she discovers this: "I had been used. Used by a friend. Taken advantage of. Furlong who had been trusted (although not always loved) had stolen something from me and that act made him both thief and enemy." A month later she manages to confront Furlong who, in his usual bland way, denies her charge: "Writers don't steal ideas. They abstract them from wherever they can. I never stole your idea. . . . Writers can't stake out territories. It's open season. A free range. One uses what one can find. One takes an idea and brings to it his own individual touch." And so on, ending by invoking Shakespeare as a borrower of plots. Sceptical though the reader is about anything Furlong says, perhaps what distinguishes this third treatment of the plot is precisely Furlong's "individual touch." Earlier, in a television interview, Furlong has given a public answer to the question of where he found the plot: "A writer's sources are never simple. Always composite. The idea for *Graven Images* came to me in pieces. True, I may have had one generous burst of inspiration, for which I can only thank whichever deity it is who presides over creative imagination." In fact, if there ever were a "burst of inspiration," it was Spalding's. In a neat tailpiece, however, Spalding reads the novel and does not recognize his own plot, though he found it "a ripping good yarn." Have Judith and Furlong actually changed it so much as to make it unrecognizable? Judith's 16-year-old daughter greatly admires *Graven Images* and makes her own distinction between fact and fiction when she defends the novel to her mother: "It's not supposed to be real life. It's not biography. It's sort of a symbol of the country. You have to look at it as a kind of extended image."

When Spalding finally writes a novel which a publisher accepts, his source is Judith and her family, their names thinly disguised, staying their year in England. Spalding has few facts, though he says that "one can tell something about people simply by the fact that they have occupied the same quarters." He has also drawn on the weekly letters from Judith's son to his daughter. Asked about the precise use he has made of them, he is evasive: "I didn't exactly *base* the novel on it. Just got a general idea of the sort of people you were, how you responded to things. That sort of thing." He explains this to them, guiltily, "so that when you read it, if you read it, you won't think I've—well—plagiarized from real life. If such a thing is possible." Spalding is clear about his source for this, his first accepted novel, yet he was obviously short of information. Judith, with her experience of the problems of using facts, guesses they may all be unrecognizable: "I have seen how facts are transmuted as they travel through a series of hands; our family situation seen through the eyes of pre-adolescent Richard and translated into his awkward letter-writing prose, then crossing cultures and read by a child we have never seen, to a family we have never met, then mixed with the neurotic creative juices of John Spalding and filtered through a publisher—surely by the time it reaches print, the least dram of truth will be drained away."

Finally, there is the novel we actually have, *Small Ceremonies.* This takes the form of a journal, divided into nine sections for the months September to May (in 1973-74, from the reference to Princess Anne's wedding), each made up of five or six separate entries. We are asked to infer that this is Judith's diary (presumably extracts from it)—at a time when most of her energies are going into the Moodie biography. She does, however, at times explain things to the reader (notably at the start of the November section, introducing her friends) in a manner not quite within the journal convention. The novel purports to be more nonfiction, Judith still unable to write a novel—even the kind of shapeless snatches from life that someone lacking creative gifts might come up with. One could even see this as Spalding's novel, guessing about the unseen Canadians, and a few passages (such as the description of their house) can easily be seen as drawing heavily on the son's letters to the girl. This view must fail, though, if the description of Spalding's novel as about the Gills' year in England is taken as the truth.

Judith judges *Graven Images* Furlong's best novel because "it was the first book he had ever written which contained anything like a structure." As biographer and novelist, she knows the central importance of form: "It's the arrangement of events which makes the stories. It's throwing away, compressing, underlining. Hindsight can give structure to anything, but you have to be able to see it." Her husband Martin strengthens this thread in the novel's pattern. He breaks from the grind of writing scholarly articles to weave a tapestry to illustrate the themes of *Paradise Lost,* how they enter and disappear, blend then separate. Judith is angry when she is told of this, ostensibly because Martin will look ridiculous, more importantly because he has not told her and because he has surprised her when she had placed him as incapable of surprising her. Martin succeeds not only in producing a teaching aid and impressing a conference but also in creating a work of art, which art galleries bid for and which he sells profitably to a collector. Martin has understood and expressed Milton's "arrangement," and has accomplished the leap from words to another medium.

Small Ceremonies does not, of course, solve the mysteries of the art of the novelist, of form, plot, the use of fact, and the workings of the creative imagination. Shields has shown how various and obscure the sources may be, the complexities of the inevitable association between fact and fiction. And, in so doing, she has left us the conundrum of the association between her own life and work—for, in real life, her next book touches on biography; its subject, a critical study of the work of Susanna Moodie [*Susanna Moodie: Voice and Vision*].

Maria Horvath (review date November 1982)

SOURCE: "Ordinary People," in *Books in Canada,* Vol. 11, No. 9, November, 1982, pp. 18-19.

[In the following review, Horvath argues that A Fairly Conventional Woman *fails to live up to the high standards Shields established in her earlier novels.]*

Carol Shields began her writing career as a poet, and her first three novels reflect a poetic view, a lyrical perspective. Two of them, *Small Ceremonies* and *Happenstance,* were especially notable for their imagery and for Shields's skillful handling of the musings of the main characters. In them Shields portrayed suburban life in great detail, but her descriptions, even of the prosaic, were almost always fresh and insightful. And because of their curiosity and imagination, her characters were appealing. Most important, she wrote with a delicate touch, so lightly that the reader discovered much more about the characters than the narrators apparently intended to reveal. Unfortunately *A Fairly Conventional Woman* is a weak successor to her previous accomplishments.

Readers of Shields's novels have already met the heroine, Brenda Bowman, wife of the historian Jack Bowman in *Happenstance.* We saw her only briefly before, because she was at a national crafts convention in Philadelphia. In her present novel Shields seems to have lost command of her character. In *Happenstance,* as seen through her husband's eyes, Brenda was a fascinating creature, a prize-winning quilter, gifted, artistic, still exciting to her husband after 20 years of faithful marriage. But in *A Fairly Conventional Woman,* which tells her side of the story of that week-long visit to Philadelphia, Brenda is quite an ordinary person. The title is not ironic.

Brenda's tale begins the day before the trip. She goes through all the motions of everyday life, preparing breakfast and laying out the table, planning the drive to the airport, worrying about her daughter, who's becoming overweight.

> But there is so much still to do, and she hasn't started packing. Two of her blouses need pressing: the green one, the one that goes with her suit and with the pants outfit as well, and the printed one, which she plans to wear to the final banquet. At 3:15 she is having her hair cut, tinted, and blown dry at a new place over on Lake Street which has wicker baskets and geraniums in the window and scarlet and silver wallpaper inside. And if there's time, she wants to make a casserole or two to leave for Jack and the children—lasagna maybe, they love lasagna. Not that they aren't capable of looking after themselves; even Rob can cook easy things— scrambled eggs, hamburgers—and Laurie's learned to make a fairly good Caesar salad. They're not ba-

bies any more, Brenda says to herself, neither of them.

This unnecessary attention to minutiae is a problem throughout the book. Shields records in meticulous detail, for example, the chit-chat with the man in the seat next to Brenda on the plane:

> "Of course, I'm young." He shot her a glance which seemed to Brenda to be partly apologetic, partly sly. "I've got lots of time to develop my, you know, my potential."
>
> "Oh yes," Brenda said. "That's true."
>
> "Hey, look out there."
>
> "Clouds."
>
> "Pretty, huh?"
>
> "Yes."

She transcribes in the same manner the interminably long interview with the woman at the desk of the hotel, the proceedings of the convention's meetings, and the small talk at the reception. What one asks, is the point of all this tedious detail? Is the author trying to show the contrast between the banality of real life and the creative energy of an artist's life? Is she telling us that a gifted artist can also be boring? Shields never makes this clear.

In her other books, Shields used dramatic irony to create friction between the main characters' knowledge of themselves and what her readers learned about them. In *Small Ceremonies,* for example, the heroine, a writer of biographies, slowly and carefully researched the lives of her subjects. She studied both the dramatic events and the commonplace happenings in their lives. In the end she pieced together a fascinating picture; there was a sense of discovery and surprise. In a similar way, and with equal excitement at the discovery, the reader got to know the heroine.

Carol Shields is a good writer and should not be judged by [*A Fairly Conventional Woman*] alone.
—*Maria Horvath*

There are no such surprises about Brenda Bowman in *A Fairly Conventional Woman.* She is just what she herself says she is—orderly, good-hearted, a realist, neither introspective nor original. The few hints of a more complex character are not followed up: "What did this mean, this new impatience, this seething reaction to petty irritations. . . . Part of it, she sensed, was regret, for lately she had been assailed by a sense of opportunities missed." We are not told what these opportunities were, nor the difference that seizing them might have meant.

Because Brenda is quite predictable, the tension of the novel's one significant encounter quickly dissipates. Will she or won't she succumb to the temptation of a brief extra-marital affair at the convention? The reader knows long before Brenda decides.

In a few places Shields writes with the imagination of her previous books, as in her description of how Brenda is inspired to design her beautiful quilts:

> . . . the patterns themselves seemed to come from some more simplified root of memory; sometimes they arrived as a pulsating rush when she was pulling weeds in the yard or shovelling snow off the front walk, but more often they appeared to her early in the morning before she opened her eyes, an entire design projected on the interior screen of her eyelid. She could see the smallest details, the individual stitches. All the pieces were there, the colours and shapes and proportions selected and arranged. When she opened her eyes to the light, she always expected the image to dissolve, but it remained intact, printed on an imaginary wall or beating slowly at the back of her head.

And Shields has developed a sharp, witty voice. Anyone who has attended a conference of any kind will laugh aloud at the pronouncements and jargon of the amateur politicos, the turgid analysis by the keynote speaker ("'The history of craft is a history of renunciation,' he croons into the microphone."), and the pretentiousness of the guest lecturer, with her talk on "Quilting Through the Freudian Looking-Glass: A New Interpretation."

Carol Shields is a good writer and should not be judged by this book alone. I look forward to her next novel and hope it will combine the imagery of her previous books with the satirical tone heard briefly in this one.

Carol Shields with Harvey De Roo (interview date Winter 1988)

SOURCE: "A Little Like Flying: An Interview with Carol Shields," in *West Coast Review,* Vol. 23, No. 3, Winter, 1988, pp. 38-56.

[*In the following interview, Shields discusses genre, form, and her writing process as they relate to several of her works.*]

[*Roo:*] *You display a good deal of formal versatility in your writing. You have published poems, short stories, novels (and a film script within one of them), and are working on a play. What dictates your choice of form?*

[Shields:] This question of form! I am, to tell you the truth, more indifferent to the boundaries between literary forms than your question indicates. Recently I went to Ottawa to sit on a Canada Council Jury and discovered, when we sifted through applications, that those writers who want to apply in a new genre (switching from poetry to fiction, play writing to poetry and so on) must apply in a completely separate, vaguely second-rate competition called 'Explorations'. I was surprised, since writing of all kinds interests me—the formulations of language. Who, after all, can distinguish between a novel and a series of connected stories? It is stunning, and distressing, to think of all the critical energy that has been wasted on genre classification. Is Susanna Moodie's *Roughing It in the Bush* a novel or a series of essays or autobiography or what? Does Daphne Marlatt write poetry or fiction? Where are we to 'place' the prose poems that are enjoying such a vogue right now, and doesn't that very term—prose poems—wink at our confusion? There is a very real sense in which each literary text makes its own form—certainly this is the case with Mrs. Moodie. Authoritative cultural compartments are puzzling, and I can't help wondering if people don't resent getting stuck in one form, and if the plays they eventually write will be analyzed for 'poetic' structures, or their poems for 'dramatic' voice.

Then you would argue there are no significant formal differences among genres, that you achieve the same thing(s) no matter what form you choose? That each presents no challenges or rewards peculiar to itself?

Well, literature has always been defined by separation, beginning with the division between the written and the spoken, and the genres of our literature—I'm talking about officially sanctioned Western literature—evolved separately, became hardened and set, and were accorded differing degrees of respectability and assigned specific spheres of substance. Conventional theory would have us believe that poetry is a more concentrated, more musical version of prose, that poetry pops off in our heads like a flash bulb, and prose like a steadily radiating incandescence, yet we can all point to prose that is dense and elliptical, and poetry that is sprawling, extravagant, deliberately diluted, serpentine. The matter of form is not really a writer's problem, but it may put a strain on readers' expectations; we talk about a poetry audience, for instance, and believe, without much evidence, that these rarified readers will bring to the text a degree of care unknown to the more forgiving fiction audience.

I like to think that these categories of reader response are breaking down as rapidly as the boundaries between genres, and that this process has been accelerated by feminist writing.

Well, this is the point of thinking you're at now. But, since you have chosen to write in different forms, I'll ask if there has been a chronology to your choice of form which is significant to your development as a writer. And, more specifically, why you have published no books of poems since your two back in the early seventies.

My early writing—that done in my twenties—consists of about a dozen highly conventional stories, all of them forgettable. Oh, very forgettable! The short story wasn't a form that interested me much, but I didn't think I could write a novel until I had served some sort of apprenticeship in shorter forms. I know now how foolish this was, and when I began, very late in my twenties, to write poetry, it was because that was exactly what I wanted to do, what really interested me. I was, for about five years, enchanted with the making of these little 'things'. (I remember once reading an essay by Gary Geddes in which he called poems 'little toys' one carries around in the head—that was exactly what I felt.) It was exhilarating. I don't think I ever wrote with such giddy elation or revised with so much ardour. I was strict with myself too. As I finished each poem, I asked myself: is this what I really mean? (Oddly, this was a question I hadn't thought to put to myself before.) There was a second question too: does this poem contain an idea? I knew I didn't want to write poems made out of the lint of unfocused feeling; my reading of such poems had made me distrustful of the form. I wanted to make hard, thoughtful, honest poems like those I had discovered by Philip Larkin.

> **I had in mind about twenty short stories which would come from all sorts of imaginative angles, or slants. What a wonder it was to me to step out on to the page, uncommitted to a voice and unfettered by a design—and what an awful terror.**
> —*Carol Shields*

Years later I turned to short fiction again. I was stuck in the middle of a novel (*Swann*); I knew what I wanted to do with the book, but didn't know how to make it fly. I wanted to talk about art and culture, who gets to make it and name it, and how it becomes established. But who in my novel was to pose these questions? Surely one voice would not be enough. I also wanted the novel to be a kind of pocket that contained itself, a demonstration, if you like, of what it was all about. Well, it was going badly, and a friend of mine, an-

other writer, Sandy Duncan, gave me some good advice. 'Why don't you just quit', she said. I did—it seemed I needed someone's permission—and the very next day began a novel that became *A Fairly Conventional Woman.* I went back to *Swann* after that, feeling I had found a way to solve the problem of voice, that I would need not one voice but a kind of chorus, and then, once again, I ran into difficulties. The novel had become a cluster of mysteries, and the trick was to get them all working together like a set of gears. How could I set this in motion? I decided to rescue myself by spending a year experimenting with different narrative approaches.

I had in mind about twenty short stories which would come from all sorts of imaginative angles, or slants. What a wonder it was to me to step out on to the page, uncommitted to a voice and unfettered by a design—and what an awful terror. But as I wrote one story, the idea for the next was already forming in my head. It was a little like flying, or at least like being a few inches off the ground. I tried hard to keep a loose hold on these stories and allow them to take their own shape. The resulting book, *Various Miracles,* did not, in fact, make use of all the narrative balls I wanted to juggle, but did open up my writing to the extent that I felt I could go back to the novel, that at least some of its problems could be solved. I suppose that writing year was like a mini-sabbatical. I felt bolder for it, healthier. The range of possibility appeared dazzling—anything was allowed, *everything* was allowed. And I was so late in finding this out.

I met a friend one afternoon in a book store. We were both going through a bin of books, looking for something wonderful to read. 'But why are you here?' he said. 'You can just go home and write the book you want to read.'

It made me laugh, but he was partly right, I think. I *am* always trying to write the novel I want to read, the play I want to see, making the very thing that seems to be missing from my experience. It's not just a case of 'wanting to do it better'; it's wanting to know whether it's possible. When I started writing novels in the seventies, I wanted to write the kind of novel I couldn't find on the library shelf. Where were the novels about the kind of women I knew, women who had a reflective life, a moral system, women who had a recognizable domestic context, a loyalty to their families, a love for their children? (Most of the novels written during this period were about women who left their families, who struck off in search of 'freedom', whatever that is.) The closest I could come to a world I recognized was in women's magazines, but the language was so eroded and the sentiment so false that these stories were unreadable. I knew it must be possible to look at the real lives of women. To be contemporary without being—God forbid—hip. And to be serious without being ponderous. I hoped, anyway, that it was possible.

I love theatre, but am often frustrated by the plays I see. There is in many plays a kind of dramatic exaggeration that I find uncomfortable (and, well, I just don't believe it, all that hurling of crockery). There is also a lack of intellectual rigour, and an easy dependence on mental aberration. Now why should this be? And, more serious still, there are surprisingly few plays about the so-called middle class, despite the fact that audiences for drama are overwhelmingly middle class. I suppose the plays I've written—including the one I've just finished—are attempts to find out if this kind of play is possible. Is it possible to make a play about reasonable, sane, articulate people talking about how they survive the life they're born into?

There doesn't seem to be much tidy chronology to my choice of form; I've drifted from one to the other, completing one thing at a time and moving on, finding perhaps a shifting of emphasis with certain tensions relaxed and others brought forward. Like most writers I am always thinking: what next? And then, more worrying: will there be a next? I do want to finish a half-completed book of poems. For a long time I believed I had forgotten how to enter a poem. It may be that I have.

You imply that experimentation began during the writing of **Swann**. *But you had played radically with perspective before:* **Swann** *wasn't the first novel to see you write from a male point of view. In* **Happenstance** *you sustain Jack Bowman as the centre of consciousness for the whole book. Was that strategy adopted out of the sense that men and women are significantly different, that therefore writing from a man's perspective would constitute a writer's challenge for you, a woman?*

I think I started with the opposite view—that men and women are more alike than we think, responding similarly to experience, but perhaps expressing those responses differently. The language of men and women has been differently conditioned, as we all know—by turns covert, self-protective, flamboyant, abstract, cryptic. These differences are fascinating, and a little frightening. But, of course, I knew I had only to write about one man, not 'man', and that lightened the burden of authenticity.

In **Happenstance** and *A Fairly Conventional Woman*, Brenda and Jack, whether talking about history or friendship, are remarkably alike, but their ideas are embedded in different language patterns, so that they only seem to be irreconcilable. I wanted these two novels to be about people who loved each other, but who remained, ultimately, strangers, one to the other. The gulf between them is language, not belief, and since most resolutions are made in silence—I do believe this—they are able to find their measure of understanding.

What kind of perceptual and technical problems did crossing that distance between female and male languages present? Why did you want to cross it? What did you think you would gain? What did you gain?

Well, one of the rewards, compensations, perhaps, of being a writer is the freedom to leave one's own skin and see with another's eyes. Old eyes, young eyes, male eyes, blind eyes. Surely there is always some refreshment in taking a different perspective. The world is made new. I think about these things all the time. And, of course, I love to set up a narrative problem and work my way though it. The solutions—or partial solutions anyway—have a way of opening up fresh questions. There is real joy in this.

Why did you make Jack an historian?

History was what I found myself thinking about at that time—what is it? What is it for? How much can it hold? But in a sense all my books have been about retrieval from the past. (I owe this insight to an astute reviewer; I wish I could remember who).

Let's go to your first novel. **Small Ceremonies** *takes the mystery of human personality and human exchange as its subject. Would that be a fair characterization of your work generally?*

Yes. The mystery of personality and the unknowability of others. Otherness. Even if we were allowed to go up to strangers and ask the most intimate of questions—and how I would love to do this—we would still remain in a state of ignorance about their lives. And yet moments do occur, as we all know, when we seem almost to enter into another body and sense something of its essence. These random glimpses appear to have little to do with how long we've known someone or the nature of what we might reveal. In *The Orange Fish* there is a story called '**Collision**' that deals (more overtly than elsewhere, I think) with one of those moments when the barriers between two people suddenly and briefly and mysteriously dissolve.

The usual subjects in your earlier novels are women whose primary reality is domestic, but who stretch outwards from their domestic centre, and claim an activity beyond that of wife and mother. How does that extension relate to their domestic lives?

I suppose I start with the assumption that everyone in the world has a domestic life. A bed to sleep in. A bowl to eat from. Walls and windows. Something to provide light. These things, which have to be secured and maintained, are comforting but they're much more than that. More than anything else they locate us in time and space. Perhaps domesticity's ubiquitous and essential nature is the reason it is missing from so much of our literature. In writing about women who had a domestic context—Charleen, Brenda, Judith, even Rose Hindmarch and Sarah Maloney—I had no intention of creating super-women who skillfully combined domesticity with a career. Domesticity is like breathing. It goes on and on. Most people do something else besides breathe—write, teach, quilt, something. I'm writing a book now about a woman who is a folklorist in love with a man who's a disk-jockey.

I hear a lot of talk these days about the new 'language-centred texts' and wonder what on earth is meant by this. Surely the best writing has always been language-centred.
—Carol Shields

In those novels, husbands and wives have 'projects' which take them beyond their identities as couples and families. Judith's work as biographer, Martin's tapestry, Jack's book, and Brenda's quilts—how did you conceive of these different projects as they reflect these characters?

Judith is writing a biography, trying to see through some of that opaqueness of personality, and Martin, less tormented than Judith by human mystery, is dallying with forms. Jack's book is a joyless task, part of the career package taken on early in his life. His real calling is speculation, not writing; he is a man who is always thinking—this enriches his life but is not directly negotiable in terms of his profession. Brenda is luckier. She loves what she's doing. Her 'career' has evolved almost whimsically, though she is already feeling by the end of the novel some of the ways in which she will be rewarded or judged. I like to write about work, by the way, and wonder why we don't see more of it in our fictions. Anita Brookner is one of those writers who is careful to include the working life of her characters. And John Updike.

You are fascinated by language in much of your work. **Small Ceremonies** *strikes the note, exploring many aspects—biography, novels (Furlong's, Spalding's, Judith's), anecdotal 'stories' (Judith's, Nancy Krantz's, Martin's, Judith's mother's & father's), letters, even Roger's thesis. What does this emphasis on language tell us about you as a writer?*

I was surprised myself at how the people in this book kept trying to define themselves through different forms of language. The various texts and tales they bore seemed to say: 'This is how I see it.' I think about language all the time. Words. Their specific weight and connotative clouds. Language has always seemed to me to be a kind of proof of our spiritual nature. Some of the stories in *Various Miracles,* and

also in my most recent book, *The Orange Fish,* are about the failure of language, the abuse of language, the gaps in language, and others are about the sudden ways in which language releases our best instincts by connecting us one to the other. For example, Kay, in the story **'Times of Sickness and Health'** belongs to a Talk Circle. Barbara and Peter in **'Milk Bread Beer Ice'** are brought together through the repetition of the title phrase. I hear a lot of talk these days about the new 'language-centred texts' and wonder what on earth is meant by this. Surely the best writing has always been language-centred.

Your first four novels make sets of twins: **Small Ceremonies** *is Judith Gill's book, as* **The Box Garden** *is Charlene Forrest's; but they are sisters, and both books share their attempts to deal with a loveless childhood.* **A Fairly Conventional Woman** *is an exploration of Brenda Bowman and her view of herself and her marriage, as* **Happenstance** *is such an exploration of her husband Jack. In what ways did the second novels grow out of the first ones? How do they act as companion pieces to their respective predecessors?*

The first two novels touch only tangentially, meeting perhaps only in the sisters' different ways of looking at their childhood and their mother. I see *Happenstance* and *A Fairly Conventional Woman* (Lord, I hate that title!) as fitting together like a puzzle. Both Jack and Brenda possess a partial sense of the history of their marriage, and the irony of it is that neither realizes, and never will, how close they are in their formulation. Marking off their comprehended territory, teasing it through their separate voices, was the happiest writing I've ever done. (*A Fairly Conventional Woman* is my favourite book—perhaps I'm not allowed to say this.)

Of course you are! But you say you hate its title. Let me name one I love: **Various Miracles.** *What relation does that title bear to the stories in the book?*

In a curious way, we carry certain important ideas the whole distance with us. No wonder writers are accused of writing the same book over and over. We are—might as well admit it—preoccupied by particular ways of looking at the world. I have always been compelled, and comforted, too, by the idea of the transcendental moment, that each of us is allotted a few random instances in which we are able to glimpse a kind of pattern in the universe. All my books, I think, even the early books of poetry, try to isolate and examine those odd, inexplicable moments. The accidental particles of our lives, for instance, suddenly align themselves, bringing about illumination, clarity, revelation or extraordinary coincidence—which are in themselves reaffirming. I suppose each of the stories in *Various Miracles* hangs on this fragile faith. What is one to do with such moments? We seldom speak of them for fear of being misunderstood, and I am told that our language is poor in the kind of vocabulary these events demand. Nevertheless, they must be paid attention to. They are, as my title suggests, miracles.

These transcendental moments. In your earlier books, you present a fairly realistic picture of domestic life; but in the midst of it you sometimes give your characters such moments, which refresh them and bolster them for more normal times. There is the wonderful ending of **Small Ceremonies,** *for example, or Charleen Forrest's rush of happiness in the subway in* **The Box Garden.** *Would it be fair to say that the most important move with* **Various Miracles** *was a decision to focus on such moments in life, rather than on the everyday which embeds them? And concomitant with that an escape from the constraints of plot?*

I am endlessly interested in this idea of everydayness, what exactly we mean when we speak of ordinary life. In my story **'Soup du Jour'** I've tried to come at it directly (more or less directly anyway). Ordinary life, depending on how we define it, constrains or frees us. I am not, to go back to your question, anxious to abandon the material we're embedded in, but rather to reveal it for what it is—necessary oxygen. But plot—now there's something I've never been good at and haven't much interest in but which I felt in my early books I had to provide. I suppose a narrative has to have a degree of tension, but I'm finding interesting ways of providing that tension that avoid the old, artificial rhythms of convergence, catastrophe and reconciliation. It seems to me we can only accept this cycle ironically these days, if at all.

> **The praise for my recent books has indeed been offset by a certain amount of casual disparagement of my earlier novels. What can I say? One, after all, has a certain affection for previous work; it seems natural to want to protect that work and to point out ways in which it has been undervalued.**
> **—Carol Shields**

Most readers would argue that with the publication of **Various Miracles,** *a new author emerged, radically different from that other author called Carol Shields, who had written novels to that point. Would you agree?*

The praise for my recent books has indeed been offset by a certain amount of casual disparagement of my earlier novels. What can I say? One, after all, has a certain affection for previous work; it seems natural to want to protect that work and to point out ways in which it has been undervalued. There are problems in my early books, but they did deal with serious subjects; I have never for one minute regarded the lives of women as trivial, and I've always known that

men and women alike possess a domestic life that very seldom finds its way into our fiction. All four of my early novels have a countertext, too, which is only occasionally alluded to in reviews, a kind of mirror commentary, though it seems awfully pompous to speak in such terms.

Beneath the apparent story is an echo of art: biography and fiction in **Small Ceremonies,** poetry in **The Box Garden.** **Happenstance** and **A Fairly Conventional Woman** have what I like to think is a fairly innovative form—broken time sequences, correspondences of voice and incident and interpretation. **The Box Garden** has a structural secret too—perhaps too well hidden, since no one's ever noticed it.

Language has been important to me from the beginning; every phrase has mattered, its shape and balance and resonance. What I have learned, though, in my later books is that I can trust the reader, that I can step off in mid-air, so to speak, and take the reader along. That I don't need to tie up all the ends quite so neatly. That it's okay not to be charming all the time. That I don't need to explain everything. Maybe it comes down to being older and braver. And having a few solid books on the shelf.

I suppose it sounds unacceptably naive to say I didn't know rules could be so easily broken. Part of this has to do with being a woman, especially a woman of my generation. Also, I was somewhat poisoned by literature courses in which we were required to dismember our texts—plot, setting, characters and themes—and I suppose I really believed that writers sat down with this kind of checklist. There was so much prohibition in my schooling. Fragments, for instance. No sin was greater than to leave a sentence fragment on the page. What a surprise it was to find that many of the writers I admired, Updike for instance, used them all the time and to great effect. I was scornful, too, of so-called 'experimental' writing. Bored to death by it. (Most of it really was boring, though I think we need a certain amount of avant-garde writing to keep us alert). But after **The Box Garden** I decided that I was going to abandon formal plot, and the next two novels were a lot more elastic.

And what else? Reading Russell Hoban. Reading Grace Paley and Angela Carter. Films made a difference, the way they can cut and jump. And reading a certain amount of postmodern fiction—much of it deadly and pretentious, but there were glimpses (William Gass) of new places one could dive from. And I had come to a place where I felt I could risk failing, knowing that I was not going to have an enormous audience anyway. I felt I would always be able to find a publisher—because this is important, after all. And I kept reminding myself that if I wrote the books I wanted to read, surely I would find a dozen or so readers of similar temperament. I wanted to try out a few things—write a one-sentence story, for instance (I never did, but did produce a one-sentence chapter in *Swann*). I wanted to try writing from a void, completely masking the narrator, but haven't managed it yet. Now I am trying to make a sort of hyper-reality jump and 'bending' tone by writing about love in a serious way. It's hard. When people ask me what I'm writing I find it hard to say I'm in the middle of a love story. I keep wanting to apologize or explain. It's ridiculous.

The epigraph from Emily Dickinson that you use in **Various Miracles**—*'Tell all the truth but tell it slant': why did you use it? What does that mean to you?*

In general, I distrust epigraphs, the pretentiousness they hint at, the free ride and borrowed grandeur. Nevertheless, I was unable to resist that line from Emily Dickinson as an epigraph for *Various Miracles.* Of course I have misappropriated her meaning. She was talking about going at the truth sideways in order to protect herself from truth's blinding brilliance. I am talking about approaching stories from subversive directions; my 'slant' involves angles of perspective, voice, and layered perception and structure. I'm interested in abandoning the old problem-solution story—what a set-up it comes to be!—and the punishment of those smug advances in self awareness—'and then John realized. . .'. I like endings that veer off in strange directions, rising rather than falling, or endings that make sudden leaps into the future or the past, bringing about a different quality of oxygen altogether. And I like to approach stories from multiple perspectives, hidden perspectives, from the eyes of children, through objects even or a stumbled-upon phrase: 'Wendy is back.' What I like best is to set up a story traditionally (the title story in *The Orange Fish,* for example) then turn it upside down or take it into another reality.

Let's move back to titles—and their role in a book. You have said that the second part of the title of **Swann**—A Mystery—*was your publisher's addition to the finished work, that it was not part of your own conception. Do you find the term useful? Does it give us any insight into the novel?*

Titles are a problem for me. Strange; you would think that if you could write a book you could write a title, but with two exceptions—*Others* and *Happenstance*—the titles of my books have been the result of editorial decisions. My original title for *Small Ceremonies* was—but I can't even remember, it was so uninspired. The original title for *Swann* was *The Swann Symposium.* It was decided that this was too academic and would appeal to too narrow an audience. My publisher, Stoddart, added *A Mystery* to the title, and I have not been able to decide whether or not this was a good idea. (The American edition, published in July by Viking, has dropped *A Mystery* from its title.) I don't read traditional mysteries. I don't know the expectations mystery readers bring to their reading. *Swann* does have what I think of as a tinker-toy mystery, the disappearing manuscripts of Mary

Swann, but the real mystery, the one that interests me, is the mystery of human personality and the creation of art, a question that pops up in all my books, even the two early books of poetry—the fact that art is bigger than those who make it, that it comes from unexpectedly common clay, and that its actual creation resists the analytical tools we apply to it. I've known writers to blink when reading their own books and to ask themselves: 'Did I really write this?' It's as though a writer enters a sort of trance while working, or, by working on a book over a long period of time, is able to draw into that work a multitude of selves.

Are you saying that some of your fiction is 'given' as well as 'made'? That it sometimes just comes from somewhere and you take it down?

I've never really had the sensation that my books were 'writing themselves', although ideas do seem to come my way quite freely. I have drawers full of notes and notions, and people are always passing on interesting observations to me. But I am very conscious of making my books, wrenching them into life. They are not, in other words, 'given' to me. I've never really known what I hear some writers describe—an effortless outpouring, as though a hand were guiding the pen.

Besides the chorus you needed to articulate the problem of art and culture you alluded to earlier, were you after anything else in dividing **Swann** *into various voices? Did it give you anything you weren't expecting?*

Swann was a difficult book for me to write. Twice I stopped and worked on other books, only to return to it later. I mentioned earlier the problems I was trying to solve, the kind of integration of parts I was hoping for. How was I to do this? I had tried various narrative techniques in my early novels, first person in the first two, third person in the third and fourth. Writing *Happenstance* gave me some experience in writing from a male perspective. Parts of *Various Miracles* made use of an omniscient story teller's voice. It occurred to me that the solution to my difficulty with *Swann* might be a highly schematic approach using a number of different narrative stances. The most interesting for me to write was the Frederic Cruzzi section which employs a sort of splintered omniscience—my own invention, I like to think: his life as seen through artefacts, friends, dreams, reports, letters, rhetorical exercises, a tour of his house, and so on. The different styles, the different perspectives carry the four main characters through a parallel time frame, and deliver them at the same moment in time and space. Why would I create such an elaborate scheme?—because I hoped it would give the book texture and insight and, ultimately, because it gave me pleasure to write it this way.

Why did you choose to end **Swann** *with a film script?*

At last the four characters in *Swann* came together. I felt at this point that I was watching them, that they had gone out of my consciousness, released as it were from my controlling hand. I was left with what felt like theatre, and so I decided to end the book with a play. It didn't work. It was too confining, though I tried all sorts of ways of shifting the scenery. The idea of a film script seemed to offer a good deal more flexibility, and gave me a chance, too, to nod in the direction of crime films. I worried that readers would have trouble reading a film script—I had never read one myself—but reasoned that they would find themselves at home in the text after the first few pages. I thought that perhaps a parallel situation might be my own reaction to watching films with subtitles; for the first ten minutes I can't stand it, and then, abruptly, I forget they're there. In some ways I think of the novel as two books, the film script being the second—an extra romp and an additional point of view, and demonstration, on the making of art.

Several reviewers have been unhappy with the ending of **Swann***; how would you answer their dissatisfaction?*

A number of readers and reviewers had difficulty not so much with the screenplay as with my abrupt declaration that all the characters, including Mary Swann, were fictional. That surprised me since I had thought that the idea of fiction as seamless illusion had long since been put behind us. I suppose, though, I knew that some readers would be puzzled, and put out, by the screenplay. I thought it was worth the risk. *Swann,* after all, is about appearance and reality, about the whole nature of what is fictional, what is invented. I wanted to turn the whole novel upside down, inside out. I'm not sorry.

The question of person you mentioned a moment ago: when I read **Small Ceremonies** *and* **The Box Garden***, I felt that the first person was perfect for stories that had so close a narrative focus in the main character. But the next two novels operate just as much 'inside' main character, yet are in the* third *person. What is the difference to you between first and third person narration? What strategies do they help to further?*

I switched to third person in *Happenstance* because it felt too risky using the first person 'I' with a male character. And I found the switch oddly rewarding; I felt less trapped by voice; I could stay close inside Jack's consciousness, as close as I liked, but could also move him around more easily and bring to surfaces a measure of disinterestedness. On the other hand, there's something spacey and springy about using the first person, and I've found it's useful occasionally to start things off that way and then transpose to a third person.

Let's look at your most recent book. Do you see **The Orange Fish** *as carrying on the experiments you began with*

Various Miracles*? Are you working out the same sorts of narrative problems as in the previous volume?*

Yes and no. The book doesn't fully reflect the range of my most recent work. I had originally planned to include seven less traditional stories, my 'little weirdies' as my friend Kent Thompson calls them. (Among them was **'Dressing Up for the Carnival'**, **'Soup du Jour'**, **'Dying for Love'**, and **'Reportage'**.) I was going to make **'Dressing Up for the Carnival'** the title story, in fact, then scuttled it when my editor, Ed Carson, didn't want that story in. For some reason Ed wanted this book to be more accessible. It wasn't so much that he didn't like these stories—he simply felt they didn't work thematically with the others.

I originally intended the stories in this book to revolve loosely around the idea of ageing—something I was thinking a good deal about at the time. **'The Orange Fish'** was an attempt to enter a realm of reality in which age was not linear but rather the result of multiplication. (It surprised me that the story was read by many reviewers not as a fabulation, but as a sermon about materialism and that the couple were thought to be 'real' people.)

When I read the proofs for the book I realized that the theme of ageing had been rather lost, and that what the stories shared was a view of language, how it serves and also fails us. As in *Various Miracles,* there were certain 'experiments': in **'Hazel'**, for instance, I wanted to reproduce the chorus of voices in her head—her daughters, her mother-in-law, her best friend, her dead husband—that directed her life, but that gradually faded. (I think we all carry around with us a similar tape-recorded set of directives.) **'Fuel for the Fire'** was an attempt to write a non-ironic story.

This change of plan and of title. We'll assume a title provides a way in to a book, and that a title derived from one of the stories is asking us to view the whole from the perspective of that story. So, why **The Orange Fish***?*

Does the title serve the book? In a sense, yes. The eye of the orange fish is ultimately mysterious. Each of the stories, I think, draws mystery from some unlikely object or observation or phrase. The sign Milk Bread Beer Ice, the conch shell in **'Hazel'**, the blisterlilies in **'Today Is the Day'**.) My favourite story in the book is **'Collision'** because I think it relocates the whole idea of traditional plot.

When you write, do you simply have a story to tell, or do you have a technical problem you are setting out to solve?

There's always a technical problem, and, oddly enough, the problem, like a coat hook, gives me something to hang the fiction on. For example, I had originally hoped that each section of *Swann* would stand alone as a novella, and that the film script too would have an independent existence. This doesn't quite happen—everything leans just a few degrees on everything else—but it is the kind of problem that I like to play with. I have a hard time knowing what sets a piece of writing on its course. Sometimes it's just a word or a phrase, sometimes a problem or a puzzle. Often a piece starts with an observation, something odd, something surreal, the one thing that doesn't fit in. I remember once writing a poem about a man I saw who was sitting on his front lawn in front of an ironing board, typing. Another time I wrote a story about an elderly woman I happened to see, who was mowing her lawn, wearing a pair of terrible shorts and a man's hat. Another story came into being when I saw a sign in a hairdressers saying 'Karen is back.' Who is Karen, I wondered, and why is her return being announced to the public? I try to enter the story at the point that interests me most, and after that it's a question of 'piecing' it together.

> **I'm an economical writer, doing a great many drafts, but with no large abandoned projects. I suppose this reflects the time and society in which I grew up. We were taught as children to be task-oriented, to finish what we started.**
> **—Carol Shields**

How does this 'piecing it together' work? Do you have any principles of development that you follow?

I write it over and over, and each time it gets longer, thicker. I think about it while I do other things, walking, driving, shopping, cooking. Sometimes I wake up in the morning with a new paragraph in my head. I have the very real sense when I'm working that I'm making something, and it is this 'making' that gives me such intense pleasure. I especially love rewriting. I love, in my mother's words, 'taking pains.' It's the first hacking out of the first draft that I find so painful, and the fear, always there, that this time it won't work.

You have said that the constraints of your domestic life led you to the habit of writing only a few hours a day. Has that regimen affected the nature of what you have written?

I'm an economical writer, doing a great many drafts, but with no large abandoned projects. I suppose this reflects the time and society in which I grew up. We were taught as children to be task-oriented, to finish what we started. When I started writing seriously in the early seventies I had very little time I could call my own. If I managed to catch one hour a day I felt fortunate, and I usually tried for an hour late in the morning before my children came home for lunch. I might also, on a good day, find an additional half an hour in the late afternoon to go over what I had written, perhaps even add-

ing a line or two. The next day I started again. This was the way my first two novels were written, and they do feel to me today a little thin. Gradually my free time expanded, but I must confess that I'm not much more productive. I can do about two new pages a day and not more. I need to think about what I am writing, let it stir. I remember that one of my children once said to me, 'Mummy, why are you moving your lips?' I was of course planning my next scene. Writing.

Certain things in writing fiction are more problematical than others. But, as you develop your craft, you get the 'hang' of them; some of them become easier. Some, however, become more difficult. What changes have occurred in this regard since you first began writing fiction? What things are most challenging for you at the moment?

I'm trying right now to write a serious novel about love, love between a man and a woman, and have discovered that the language of love has been trivialized in our society and that the literature of love is more than a little fluffy. Lovers are silly people, childish, envied but barely tolerated. How am I going to make this love credible, intelligent?—that's the question I ask myself these days. I worry, too, about age, that certain forms of creativity are taken from us, and also the bravado to bluster our way into a new piece of writing. I worry sometimes that my love of style overcomes the substance of my writing. Sometimes I see clearly enough that a piece of writing is overworked and lacking in freshness, that it is in fact less than honest, and that I've sacrificed something important merely to make the words dance. I once wrote eight pages describing a hotel lobby, right down to the ash trays on the coffee tables—the most terrible kind of indulgence, like painting a fingernail over and over. I know I'm being dishonest when I start throwing in the names of wild flowers or the brand names of cigarettes. That's when I have to sit back and remind myself of what I learned when I was twenty-nine years old and beginning to write poetry. (It's not enough, it seems, to learn these things once—we keep having to repeat the lesson, absorbing it again and again and again) I have to stop and take a deep breath. And speak directly, sternly, to the words on the paper, and ask: 'Is this really what I mean?'

Eleanor Wachtel (essay date May 1989)

SOURCE: "Telling It Slant," in *Books in Canada*, Vol. 18, No. 4, May, 1988, pp. 9-14.

[*In the following essay, Wachtel provides an overview of Shields's life and career.*]

Four years ago, when Carol Shields turned 50, her writing

turned a corner. The titles tell all. Before: *Small Ceremonies, The Box Garden, Happenstance,* and *A Fairly Conventional Woman.* After: *Various Miracles, Swann: A Mystery,* and now, *The Orange Fish.* "You get older and braver," she says, "braver about what you can say and what can be understood."

Her first four novels presented reliable pictures of middle-class, domestic life. Shields is expert at evoking the feelings and concerns of ordinary people—their ambivalence about their families, their jobs, and their mates. Her characters think. They try to be nice. And they often get stuck in boring situations—with spouses, parents, or colleagues. It's not the mad trapped housewife that Shields finds in suburbia, but relatively happy families coping with change, recognizing some uneasiness around the edges, but committed to the safety of the familiar. It's that world of dirty dishes, tired casseroles, and the acute desperation of school projects. The virtues, joys, and griefs of everyday life are cherished. Shields doesn't satirize; she reassures, but not in a smug or cloying way. Her style is often ironic, affectionately mocking—especially of academic life—lightly humorous, with a delicacy and subtlety of language that elicit (not entirely appropriate) comparisons with Jane Austen. These early books not only deal with prosaic subjects—which are, of course, the stuff of life—but they are "fairly conventionally" written. There's more attention to language and craft than is commonly recognized, but they're essentially naturalistic.

In *Various Miracles,* Shields's 1985 collection of short fiction, the lid came off. Shields began to experiment with different ways (and voices) to tell stories. She flouted conventions against literary coincidence, building the title story ["**Various Miracles**"] on a series of "miraculous" circumstances, creating an imaginative interweaving of events that lead to a playful "trick" ending. A character in the story is also a character in a manuscript in the story—a Russian doll-like construction. Shields takes a leaf from the postmodernist's book and writes, "Sometimes it's better to let things be strange and to represent nothing but themselves." The stories lift off the ground, take some sharp corners and find their own way, often at curious angles.

The book's epigraph is Emily Dickinson's "Tell the truth but tell it slant." Shields bends its meaning a little. In Dickinson's poem, the truth is so brilliant that if we look at it directly, we'll be blinded. Shields interprets this obliqueness as an invitation to experiment with a range of narrative approaches—omniscient, direct, fractured. "Telling the story from the slant," she says, "can sometimes lead you into the presence of an unreliable narrator, the narrator who understands everything, except what is central." This is what Shields developed in her next novel, *Swann: A Mystery*—a wonderful book, more adventurous than anything she'd ever done. Told from the point of view of four solitaries, each in

search of a kind of family or connection, the book is a double mystery, about the missing manuscripts of a dead poet, and the profound mystery of human personality.

> **It's not the mad trapped housewife that Shields finds in suburbia, but relatively happy families coping with change, recognizing some uneasiness around the edges, but committed to the safety of the familiar. It's that world of dirty dishes, tired casseroles, and the acute desperation of school projects. The virtues, joys, and griefs of everyday life are cherished.**
> *—Eleanor Wachtel*

Carol Shields is sitting at a restaurant, looking like a character from one of her early novels. What used to be called sensibly dressed: a soft cream-coloured sweater fastened at the neck with a gold bow pin. Matching skirt, pumps. Simple stud earrings; pearl ring and gold bracelet on one hand; gold wedding band and diamond engagement ring on the other. Shields is thin, with short blond hair and clear blue eyes behind thick-lensed glasses, which she removes and folds on the table. She has a small, soft, sometimes hesitant voice. She admits to a certain passivity, a reticence. And then disarms by saying, "Okay, ask me something personal." But when you do, she becomes abstract or ducks behind a book she's read. "Print is her way of entering and escaping the world." (*Various Miracles*)

"It concerns me," she confesses, "that the books I've read have been a big part of the way I experience the world—maybe more than for other people. And I do wonder if there is maybe something substandard about that." Surprising from a woman who's raised five children, published ten books, and who's lived in the U.S., England, France, Toronto, Ottawa, Vancouver, and Winnipeg. But learning to read at four, she claims, "realizing that those symbols meant something that I could be part of," was the central mystical experience of her life. She speculates that her early fascination with language may have been related to her short-sightedness, that instead of engaging with visual images, she got hooked on language and the magic it contained.

Carol Shields grew up in Dick-and-Jane-land. Oak Park is an older, stable suburb of Chicago, famous for its early 20th-century Frank Lloyd Wright houses. It was homogeneously white and middle class. Shields and her slightly older twin siblings lived with their parents in a large white stucco house. Her father managed a candy factory. Her mother, of Swedish stock and also a twin, taught fourth grade until she had children of her own, and then resumed after the war when there was a teacher shortage. While still a young woman, her mother boarded with Ernest Hemingway's parents, who lived in Oak Park. Shields captured this incident in an early poem, and in greater detail in a new story called **"Family Secrets"** in *The Orange Fish.* What amazed Shields was how her mother was never curious to read Hemingway despite living under his roof. In the story, the daughter speculates on her mother's life and its hidden corners, and ultimately treasures her own bundle of secrets.

The only books around Carol's house were her parents' childhood reading—Horatio Alger and *Anne of Green Gables* and Louisa May Alcott. Her mother read to her a lot—even pedestrian series like *The Bobbsey Twins*—and until eighth grade, Carol attended the local library's story hour. "That combination of drama and narrative was something I loved," she says. Central to her recollection of this time is her fondness for Dick and Jane—those school readers. "I *understood* Jane," she says almost ingenuously. "I suppose I imagined a life for her that wasn't really there in the reader, but she was someone I found interesting and related to. Jane was very sturdy and knew her own mind, I always thought. And I loved the way that Dick was so good to her, so protective of her, so unlike most brothers. Everyone was terribly good to everyone else; there were no bad intentions. They seemed like real people to me and their world seemed wonderfully safe and ordered. Probably even safer and more ordered than my own safe and ordered world. This sort of extraordinary goodness is very appealing to children."

She pauses. "What a place to grow up! Like growing up in a plastic bag is how I think of it—a very safe place to grow up." But surely a plastic bag is more suffocating than safe? "It's funny," she says. "I always knew that something was wrong with it, but I never knew what it was until I went away. What was wrong was that there wasn't enough: it was all very good, it just wasn't enough. Everyone went to church. I can't believe this, everyone went to church."

Shields recently went home for her high school's 35th reunion. She stood on a familiar corner and experienced "the opposite of nostalgia"—relief that she'd escaped. Her parents were timid people, so any intellectual expectations she sensed came from an affluent, kindly school system. "All my teachers at that time were unmarried, middle-aged and bosomy," she says, aware of the fulfilled stereotype. "They were wonderful women and very caring." But it was limited—or insulated. "Imagine growing up a few blocks from where James T. Farrell lived and not knowing it." Farrell, an early communist, is famous for the *Studs Lonigan* trilogy, a powerful indictment of the American dream.

But Shields was locked into her own dreamy childhood. She was the class poet, turning out sonnets that she knew even then were infused with false rhetoric. She was encouraged

by her parents and teachers, published in the school paper, and liked to write. Shields didn't actually think she could be a writer until much later—in her late 20s. The high school yearbook said she was the one who'd write the novel. "But I never believed that for a minute. I'd never met a writer. It was like wanting to be a movie star." Her parents wanted her to have a career "to fall back on." This was the '50s and "we all knew we would get married and have children."

Shields went to Hanover College, a small conservative school in Indiana. "I did what most people did: I just sent off for all kinds of university catalogues and chose one that looked like a 'Father Knows Best' college." Shields is mildly self-deprecating, not ironic. She regrets not being "braver" and going to a bigger urban school. She even found herself sucked into a sorority, unable to buck convention. "Education was wasted on me," she says. "I was much more interested in falling in love and going to dances." But she read. And one "lucky" thing was a junior year exchange program with Exeter University in England. It was a great revelation to encounter a truly academic atmosphere where people took their subjects seriously. Carol thrived. She also met Donald Shields, a Canadian engineering grad student, whom she married when she graduated. By this time, she'd forgotten about being a writer. "I was just interested in being in love and having a house—the whole *Ladies' Home Journal* thing." In fact, when her mother first met Don, she told him she hoped he'd encourage Carol to keep on writing, and Don looked blank. They were engaged to be married and Carol had never mentioned to him that she wrote. It wasn't until they were settled in Toronto, with the first of their five children, that Don suggested she take a University of Toronto course in magazine writing.

"I can't remember much about it except that a woman lectured to us once a week. She wore a big hat and she never took it off. There were about 40 of us and she said, 'When you send in a manuscript, you should use a paper-clip and not a staple.'" At the end of the term, students were expected to write something, so Carol wrote a short story. A few months later, the teacher called. She'd sold her story to CBC Radio—the old John Drainie program, 15 minutes narrated by Drainie. But even this success didn't galvanize Shields. She figured she'd write stories when she had the chance. And about once a year she'd "stir her stumps" and write a story and sell it to the CBC or BBC. She was busy, full of energy. She still read a lot and there was never a year when she wasn't taking "some course or other" in law or English. By the time she was 25, she had three children and was living in Manchester, where Don got his Ph.D. Yet Shields feels that she had a prolonged childhood, that she stayed in a sort of infancy, and didn't really wake up until her late 20s. There's a line in her fourth novel, *A Fairly Conventional Woman,* about a housewife on the verge of artistic recognition: "What a dumb sap she was, detained too long in girlhood, an abstainer from adult life." And although Shields clearly has done a lot in her life, it fits her self-perception as a passive observer, able to mediate with life primarily through books—her own and others'. Intrigued by history and biography, she lives these interests vicariously, through her characters: the biographer Judith Gill of her first novel, **Small Ceremonies,** and the historian Jack Bowman of her third, **Happenstance.** Of all her characters, it is with Jack the observer that Shields says she most identifies.

Suddenly, as if to underline her position as bystander, she leans across the table and says, *sotto voce,* "I've just been to New York and it's a great place to eavesdrop because they talk so loud and about such interesting things. Can you hear what they're saying at the next table? I think she's a writer because she was talking about writing books, but now she's talking about cooking so maybe she writes cookbooks." Shields smiles, resumes eating and demurely waits for another question.

On the boat home from England, Shields read Betty Friedan's *The Feminist Mystique.* She thought about going to law school. She joined a "Great Books" discussion group and she had another baby. She also started reading the English poet, Philip Larkin. Excited by the honesty of his writing, she started writing poetry again. At that time, CBC Radio had a Young Writers' Competition. The cut-off was 30; Shields was 29. She wrote seven poems. It was the first time in her life that she took her writing seriously. She won.

> I spoke to [P. K. Page] about her work and asked what one of her poems meant. She said, "I haven't the faintest idea." At this time I was rather severe about these things, and I thought, "If she doesn't know what it means, why am I going to try and figure it out?" Since then, I've met all sorts of poets who don't understand their writing and I've even written things I don't quite understand.
>
> —*Carol Shields*

"That led me into a period, of about five years, writing poetry," she explains. "It was an enormously happy writing time. I was very strict with myself. I followed Larkin's set of rules: no pretty language. If anything was pretty, out it went. Unfortunately, I also borrowed some of his despair, I think, in my first few poems. I can remember my friends being a little worried about me."

She published in *The Canadian Forum* and a few other

magazines. Then the family moved to Ottawa, where her husband was associated with the University of Ottawa. This meant free tuition for Carol. "Being very thrifty about these things, I decided I'd better take advantage of it." She enrolled in a master's program in English and discovered Susanna Moodie. "First I was going to do a thesis on P. K. Page because I liked her poetry. I even interviewed her when she was in Ottawa. I spoke to her about her work and asked what one of her poems meant. She said, 'I haven't the faintest idea.' At this time I was rather severe about these things, and I thought, 'If she doesn't know what it means, why am I going to try and figure it out?' Since then, I've met all sorts of poets who don't understand their writing and I've even written things I don't quite understand."

Shields was drawn to Moodie's trashy English novels and what they revealed about her Canadian work, *Roughing It in the Bush* and *Life in the Clearings.* She was surprised by the sibling rivalry that surfaced between Moodie and her sister, Catharine Parr Trail, who was a little older and more beautiful. She was also struck by the male-female relations in those books. Moodie paid lip service to the supremacy of men and then depicted weak men and strong women. There was a recurring tableau of the recumbent male being nursed back to health by the upright female. Shields wrote her thesis in the early '70s when feminism was in the air, but "being out of things is sort of my hobby," she jokes. Like her socialism—she describes herself as "an instinctive pink"—Shields's feminism is latent. She values the lives of women, especially the women friends she's kept all her life. But, she says, "I never went through those consciousness-raising sessions. A lot of my experience of what a woman's life could be—seeing other patterns of being—came from reading American and British fiction, not from reality." At the same time, Shields was annoyed that most women were portrayed as bitches or bubble-heads in fiction, a lot less kind and dumber than the women she knew. She started to think about writing a novel.

While still in graduate school, however, she published two small books of poetry, **Others** and **Intersect.** "Portraits" is how she thinks about those poems. They're about friends, parents, children; a married couple's bedtime rituals, a family dinner, anniversaries, a child learning to talk—the furniture of her novels.

During work on her thesis, she also got her first job—editorial assistant for a scholarly quarterly, *Canadian Slavonic Papers.* A "jobette" she calls it, conscious of its relative insignificance. But it was important, not only because she passed it on to Charleen, heroine of her second novel, **The Box Garden,** but because "all those years I was at home with children, I never thought I would have a job." Now she teaches part-time at the University of Manitoba.

The only story with a nice firm shape to it is the story of a human life, but so much of it is unknowable.
—Carol Shields

Shields dropped out of university for one term to try to write a novel, a literary whodunit, perhaps foreshadowing *Swann: A Mystery.* It was rejected by three publishers. "But they wrote very nice letters so I thought I would try again." This time she had more confidence, having written one book and a thesis. She wrote two pages a day, every day, and at the end of nine months, she had a novel, *Small Ceremonies.* Although the book isn't programmatic, there were several things she wanted it to feature: a heroine with a reflective side to her life; a woman who had friends; a context in which there were children; and some of the "leftover" Susanna Moodie material that was too conjectural for her thesis. The result was an intelligent, quiet book about Judith Gill, a biographer of Susanna Moodie, who also tries to write a novel while on sabbatical in England with her husband. The book signposted some recurring themes: an academic environment with a satirical edge; a middle-class woman who's not entirely content; and a fascination with biography coexistent with an awareness of its limitations. Drawn by her feeling of connection with the past, Shields wanted to fill in the spaces, the silences of Susanna Moodie's life. The things Moodie left out of her own writing were the authentic parts; what's there is less so. It's like reading a negative. "How do you retrieve someone who is dead and try to build up with the nib of your pen that personality who was, in a sense, voiceless about things that mattered?" This is a question she poses again in *Swann: A Mystery,* in which a quartet of characters try to resurrect the silent, dead poet, Mary Swann, who was brutally murdered by her husband 15 years before the novel begins. Shields's answer is to turn to fiction rather than biography because it can delve into the place where "ninetenths" of our lives occurs: in our heads. "The only story with a nice firm shape to it is the story of a human life," she says, "but so much of it is unknowable." Invention can fill in those gaps. And it can record those small rituals that give ordinary life its continuity. Although the title was serendipitous (chosen by her publisher), a sense of the ceremonial—*small* ceremonies—is very important to Shields. It's how we keep ourselves glued together and hold emptiness at bay. "Habit is the flywheel of society, conserving and preserving and dishing up tidy, edible slices of the cosmos." (*Swann: A Mystery*)

It's a philosophy present in all of Shields's writing. "Dailiness to be sure has its hard deposits of ennui, but it is also, as Mary Swann suggests, redemptive."

Carol Shields's 40th birthday was another turning point in her life. After three rejections, a publisher accepted *Small Ceremonies,* her thesis on Susanna Moodie [*Susanna Moodie: Voice and Vision*] was also to be published (as *Voice and Vision*), and she was off for a year in France during her husband's sabbatical. The day after she arrived in Brittany, she started her next novel, *The Box Garden,* which takes up the story of Judith Gill's sister, Charleen. "I wanted to get back into a novel quickly," she says. "There is a kind of post-partum feeling after a book." She missed her characters and decided to pick up another thread in the same family. The writing went easily and it too was finished in nine months. In some ways less successful than *Small Ceremonies,* it suffered from her susceptibility to her editor's advice. *Small Ceremonies,* she was told, didn't have a lot happening. So Shields added plot, a pseudo-kidnapping and police, to *The Box Garden.* "You can imagine how I much I know about these things," she says. "I should have listened to my doubts."

Shields looks back on those novels, (soon to be reissued in paperback), and is surprised by how stingy she was with detail. "I think I wrote very thinly. Part of it had to do with only writing for an hour a day and not having time to think over what I was doing. I seemed to write in spare little scenes where you're supposed to pick up the interior sense from exterior details. Now I'm interested in interior details—going really where film and television can't go. I like a dense texture, even in short stories."

In **"Collision,"** an odd story in the new collection, *The Orange Fish,* Shields describes the accidental collision of two people in a tiny eastern European country. An indigenous film-maker and an American tourist development consultant face a downpour outside a restaurant, where each has been dining with others. Neither can speak the other's language. They share an umbrella for a kilometre to the town square. This linking in time is an example of a recurrent motif in Shields's work—what might be called numinous moments. Fifteen minutes and it's over. But "sacredness attaches itself invisibly to certain rare moments." (*The Orange Fish*)

Naturally, this is based on Shields's own experience. She was in Tokyo, not Europe, but she walked under a stranger's umbrella, rhythmically in step, and felt that she could have gone on like that forever. "I believe in these moments," she says, "when we do feel or sense the order of the universe beneath the daily chaos. They're like a great gift of happiness that comes unexpectedly."

Shields also recognizes their obverse. Days when she senses the fragility of all our arrangements and how vulnerable we are to loss and tragic reversal. "It doesn't matter how insulated you are," she says, "you have these frightening glimpses of the utter meaninglessness of your life. It's a kind of angst when you suddenly feel that you're alone and powerless and nothing makes any sense. It's the opposite of those transcendental moments when you perceive the pattern of the universe." Shields is interested in capturing both those extremes and finding a language to express them. In *Swann: A Mystery,* these flashes occur back to back when the 80-year-old retired editor, Frederick Cruzzi, is first blissfully happy with his wife and their simple meal together, and then horror-stricken when he thinks she has inadvertently destroyed Mary Swann's poems. It's not simply alternate joy and despair—each comes with the certainty of revelation.

Swann explores that gap between appearance and reality. What is really at the core of a person? How much do we actually see? The poet Mary Swann herself is a complete unknown, a woman who lived virtually without record. Shields creates four sympathetic characters who appropriate her life, and reconstruct it to fit their needs—and as Shields sees it, their desire to connect with someone. It's Shields's first novel without children, something she only realized after it was finished. Her own children have grown, left home. It's given her greater freedom, but even after four years, she misses them. "It's very hard to sit down at the dinner table with just two people," she says.

Why isn't Shields better known? Is it because quiet books are tagged for quiet promotion? That women's lives and a "domestic" circumference are of only marginal interest? Or that her changing publishers over the years has meant a limited commitment to her as an author?
—*Eleanor Wachtel*

There are no conspicuous children in *The Orange Fish*—except for the occasional childhood flashback of the narrator. Shields likes to play with time. History orders the past, arranging events on a time line. She also projects forward into a future from which to look back on this moment in the present. Sometimes, as in the end of the story, **"Hinterland,"** it's a flattened future, like the images in a pop-up book, recognizable and folded inside each other.

The experimentation that was unleashed in *Various Miracles* is only partly present in *The Orange Fish.* There is even a story totally without irony—"not a scrap," she says. "I felt I was so ironic I was getting lockjaw." Shields isn't interested in postmodernism *per se,* but in the kinds of freedom she can get working out a narrative idea. She figures these kinds of styles are in the air and acquired by osmosis. One friend suggested it came from living in Manitoba, Bob Kroetschland, but Shields says no, like most things, it's from reading. Her work has struck responsive chords in other writers—from Kent Thompson's "postcard fiction" to Aritha van Herk, who recently wrote: "I have an image of Carol Shields. . . . I do not know the real woman, at least not well enough to count, but I do know this floating and powerful florentine engraving on air who nets fictions as turned and strange as brass rubbings, the articulate spines of fish, slender piles of knuckle bones."

Donna Smyth, a Halifax writer, was dazzled by the virtuosity of *Swann.* "The writing is superb," she says. "And as always with a Carol Shields book, you come away with this reverence for the way we are able to celebrate together what we are and what we don't know about each other. It's a real mystery, that."

Why isn't Shields better known? Is it because quiet books are tagged for quiet promotion? That women's lives and a "domestic" circumference are of only marginal interest? Or that her changing publishers over the years has meant a limited commitment to her as an author? *Swann* is only now coming out in paperback, a year and a half after publication, (and its nomination for a Governor General's Award). But surely the cumulative impact of *The Orange Fish* and *Swann* and *Various Miracles* within four years, plus the American release of *Swann* and *Various Miracles* this spring (by Viking/Penguin) will change that. Or is it the old regional conundrum? Shields hasn't lived in Toronto since she started publishing. She's moved a lot so she hasn't even been identified with a particular "region" and her books are set in France or Chicago or Scarborough—not Winnipeg.

In that last-named city, her spacious apartment overlooks the curve of the Assiniboine River. It's the first time she's ever *not* lived in a large Victorian house, and she wasn't sure about it at first. The place is on the seventh floor and there are trees that come as high as the windows, lots of light and no curtains. The living room has a fireplace and a wall of books. Shields boasts of only two things—"excellent reading lamps everywhere" and art that she and her husband have been collecting since they first lived in England. Her favorite is a Joe Fafard litho called "Bird's Eye" with an egg-shaped world floating in space and his trademark cows. In her kitchen is a print called "The Orange Fish." Now you feel as if you're inside one of her clever stories; the title story of the new book is about a couple who hang a litho called "The Orange Fish" in their kitchen.

Shields is fascinated by the way we share memories: how even people who are very close will remember things differently. And also, the silences between people, the acceptable silences. Of her early *A Fairly Conventional Woman* (her favourite of all her novels), she says "I wanted to write about two people who were more or less happily married, but who were, in fact, strangers to each other and always would be, and the value of that strangeness."

Shields's next novel, *Bodies of Water*, is about love and the search for the other, "or maybe not." Shields feels the need for an other. "Our own lives really aren't quite enough for us, we have to live some of our lives vicariously or it's just too narrow. Who we bump up against, what they mean to us, is what's interesting."

She recalls an image by the 8th-century historian, the Venerable Bede. How our actual life is such a little thing that it's like a bird in the darkness suddenly finding a way into the banquet hall and flying through, looking down at all the banqueters, and then flying out the other side. Shields says what a wonderful image that is, then adds, "I always thought how much better it would be if there were two birds flying together."

Donna E. Smyth (essay date July 1989)

SOURCE: "Shields' Swann," in *Room of One's Own*, Vol. 13, Nos. 1 & 2, July, 1989, pp. 136-46.

[*In the essay below, Smyth explores the meaning of identity for the protagonist in* Swann.]

> We believe we are at home in the immediate circle of beings. Beings are familiar, reliable, ordinary. Nevertheless, the lighting is pervaded by a constant concealment in the double form of refusal and dissembling. At bottom, the ordinary is not ordinary; it is extra-ordinary.
>
> (Martin Heidegger, *Origins of the Work of Art*)

Who is Swann? This question haunts the text, teasing readers and characters into laughter, frustration, recognition. Bittersweet mysteries of life. Shields insists on them, on us as mysterious creatures, riddled with doubt and anxiety, shot through with a capacity for concealment, for relief in the warmth of the body next to us in the bed, in the small pleasures and ceremonies of everyday life, in the song the poet sings.

Mary Swann, farmer's wife, poet. Lived in obscurity outside the small town of Nadeau, Ontario. Died violently at the hands of her husband who then shot himself. No note, no explanation. Only Mary's poems left behind and a few artifacts from the hard-scrabble farm where she lived most of her adult life. One child, a daughter, who lives in California, a world away, selves away from the farm.

Mary Swann, discovered long after her death and brought to the light of literary day by Sarah Maloney, feminist academic in this fictional weave. Sarah writes the "seminal" article on Swann which sets the academic bloodhounds in full pursuit.

Mary Swann, the Canadian Emily Dickinson, murdered? Why? What was inside the head of this ordinary woman who wrote such extraordinary poetry? Morton Jimroy, academic biographer, pursues these mysteries for the biography he is writing in the fiction in which he is a character.

Mary Swann, the poor farm woman who sometimes sent her poems to the local paper, and had several conversations with Rose Hindmarch, lonely librarian and town clerk of Nadeau. Rose creates the Mary Swann Memorial Room in the local museum of which she is curator in the fiction in which she is a character.

Mary Swann, who, on that fatal snowy afternoon, came to the door of Frederic Cruzzi, international intellectual, editor of the local paper, and co-publisher with his wife, Hildë, of obscure but deserving regional Canadian poets. Came to the door with her poems and her frozen feet. Was murdered later that evening by her brute of a husband. Cruzzi, who later with Hildë edits and publishes the poems which appear in the fiction in which he and Hildë are characters.

Fictions within fiction. This existential mystery plays with us like any good mystery, weaving a complicated plot, scattering clues. Not only has Mary Swann been murdered but then, at a crucial academic conference, copies of her notebook, her only poems, articles about her life and work start to disappear. At first the other characters think these artifacts are merely mislaid or lost. Then it becomes clear that somebody is deliberately stealing them. Why? For what purpose?

Multi-tiered, intricately structured, the novel leads us to questions which demand factual answers but the facts are few and hard to come by and seem elusive as fiction. And, out of these facts, the human imagination shapes new realities which some might call fiction. The Swann poems, for example, as Exhibit One. The text reveals them to us as powerful in their own right/write:

> Blood pronounces my name
> Blisters the day with shame
> Spends what little I own,
> Robbing the hour, rubbing the bone.

But are these really Swann's poems? Consider, for example, that Hildë wraps the fish bones in the original manuscript—a bag of scraps of song—and then she and Frederic have to painstakingly reconstruct them. Hildë, who is herself a poet but cannot focus her energies in poems, completes many lines which are blurred, wavery, disappeared with fish juice and slime and scales. Consider, too, the final scene where, the poems, having disappeared again, are once more being reconstructed lovingly, with care, in a collective effort by a group of scholars who ordinarily would be fiercely competitive with each other, but, in this miraculous moment of re-creation, are absorbed in a divine task. Shields' final "Director's Note" states:

> The faces of the actors have been subtly transformed. They are seen joined in a ceremonial act of reconstruction, perhaps even an act of creation. There need be no suggestion that any one of them will become less selfish in the future, less cranky, less consumed with thoughts of tenure and academic glory, but each of them has, for the moment at least, transcended personal concerns. (*Swann*)

Consider, too, the name: Swann. Enough to conjure up the past, Marcel Proust's past where memory/imagination/desire are the creation of Time, in Time. In Heidegger's terms, Time as the horizon of Being. Being, which we can only know as being-in-the-world, reveals her to us. Two things then: first, memory slippage into imaginative reconstruction—Sarah's articles, Jimroy's biography, Rose's memorial room, all focused around the elusive figure of Mary Swann (and, as we have seen, the poems themselves). Memory, which "plays tricks on us," as Shields hints when the narrator comments on the bedroom of Frederic and Hildë Cruzzi:

> The scenes that have taken place in this room are unguessable. Memory, that folded book, alters and distorts our most intimate settings so that passion, forgiveness, and the currency of small daily bargains are largely stolen from us—which may be just as well. (*Swann*)

Second, the everyday thingness of the world—these "small daily bargains" signalled by Mary Swann's stubborn "ordinariness." Sarah, thinking about one of Mary's poems, says:

> She spelled it out. The mythic heavings of the universe, so baffling, so incomprehensible, but when squeezed into digestible day-shaped bytes, made swimmingly transparent. Dailiness.... Whenever I meet anyone new, I don't say, "Tell me about your belief system." I say, "Tell me about your average day." (*Swann*)

What is attractive to Sarah is sheer frustration to Jimroy:

> And he will have to deal also with the peculiar ordinariness of Mary Swann's letters and even the subjects of those letters. Pleading letters to Eaton's returning mailorder underwear. Letters to her daughter, Frances, in California, letters full of bitter com-

plaint about the everlasting Ontario winter.... (*Swann*)

Jimroy, the biographer, creates life out of these sordid (to him) details, a life shaped like art, truthful as he can be to the original, honest as he can be in his male abstractness. Wonderful scene where Jimroy takes Rose Hindmarch to dinner in the local hotel to pump her for more details about Mary Swann and they discuss the "blood poem." Jimroy interprets the poem as sacramental symbolism whereas Rose, in trouble with her own menopausal body, sees the poem quite clearly as a woman's statement of biological necessity. Jimroy interprets one of the "water poems" as having similar religious significance, not hearing when Rose tells him that water might be important to a woman who lives on a farm without running water and without a washing machine.

Meeting of Jimroy and Rose is very funny—and meant to be—and yet—neither of them is right and neither of them is wrong. Or, rather, both are. The poems can read either way, both ways; it is the beings who are stuck in their temporal/biological zones just as Mary Swann was stuck in hers but escaped through her poems. Temporary transcendence is what the poems offer readers too. And even Jimroy has his authenticity: his "honouring" of questions; his genuine love of poetry:

> When he thought of the revolution of planets, the emergence of species, the balance of mathematics, he could not see that any of these was more amazing than the impertinent human wish to reach into the sea of common language and extract from it the rich dark beautiful words that could be arranged in such a way that the unsayable might be said. (*Swann*)

Jimroy, the negative, "sour" pole in this fiction. Sarah, his sweet complement and never-to-be sweetness of his own. By the time Jimroy gets to meet Sarah, she has married her juggler and is pregnant. Rose Hindmarch, contrast to Sarah in her unattractiveness, her "spinsterhood," her fate, but Rose with a sweetness of her own, a spirit not daunted. Frederic Cruzzi, contrast to Rose in his sophistication, contrast to Jimroy in his "sweetness," his love of life and people, at eighty more complex than Sarah at twenty-eight. It is Cruzzi who figures, embodies what Heidegger calls "aletheia": unconcealment, truth at the heart of Being and thinking, truth which is both an opening and a concealing. This is the riddle at the heart, of the heart. Cruzzi, word-man and intellectual, for instance, also knows the opposite pole:

> Once in a while, walking like this in shadowed woodland at three o'clock on a winter afternoon, or hearing perhaps a particular phrase of music, or approaching a wave of sexual ecstasy, Cruzzi has felt

a force so resistant to the power of syntax, description or definition, so savage and primitive in its form, that he has been tempted to shed his long years of language and howl monosyllables of delight and outrage. (*Swann*)

It is Cruzzi who experiences most directly the existential negative of Being which would/could cancel us out. It begins with revelation, a feeling, a mood. Cruzzi, having been slightly ill, thinks of Hildë out ice-fishing:

> just as everyday articles—preserving jars, teaspoons, loaves of bread—take on the look of sacred objects when seen in exceptional light, so he sometimes looked at his wife and saw her freshly and with the full force of vision. (*Swann*)

These "seizures of the heart," as the narrator calls them, give a meaning to Being—it is the loving gaze which fuses subject and object. But when Hildë reveals that she has inadvertently sullied the Swann poems, the energy pole is suddenly negative. Cruzzi cries out, "No!", throws up his arm, later he hits Hildë, knocks her down as perhaps Mary Swann's husband knocked her down before shooting her. The narrator comments:

> For Cruzzi, though he never came close to admitting it, not even to himself, it was a wail of denial. Because the darkness, or whatever it was that engulfed him, had dissolved for the briefest of moments, and what he glimpsed was the whole of his happiness revealed in a grotesque negative image. He was a man weakened by age and standing in a remote corner of the world, a man with a sore throat, a little drunk, and before him, facing him, was a thickish person without beauty. (*Swann*)

The negative pole of Being nauseates, frightens, cancels the loving gaze, makes a mockery of the meanings we carefully construct for our lives. It is a moment of total loss. This is the existentialist hell which gapes before us and Cruzzi like the medieval mouth of hell and then, mercifully, closes again, withdraws. Cruzzi has not killed Hildë but he might have and they both know it. Later, talking to Sarah about the murder of Mary Swann, Cruzzi uses the phrase "something snapped," thinking of Swann's husband, thinking of himself.

So much for motivation, explanation. Another cliché comes to mind: these things happen. They happen and we construct meanings for them after the event, the crime. We collect evidence, documents, testimony, and elaborate a rationale to make bearable the irrational nature of Being. Sometimes this rationale is called law, sometimes religion or psychology or art. Morton Jimroy, articulate in irritation, thinks:

Didn't these monied Stanford sharpies realize that literature was only a way for the helpless to cope? Get back to your tennis courts, he wanted to shout. Out into the sunshine! Live! Universities are nothing but humming myth factories. Dear God. How we love to systemize and classify what is rich and random in life. (*Swann*)

This is the same man who cannot bear the thought that Mary Swann read Edna Ferber instead of Jane Austen. We laugh at Jimroy's contradictions but also recognize them as our own. And Jimroy has his own moments of loss, as when he completes the biography of the American poet, John Starman (Shields' names are sometimes deliciously shameless), and finds him a hollow man: "the hollowness rang loud. And it rang with a double echo for Jimroy, announcing not only deadness at the centre of life, but a disenchantment with surfaces. The discovery of emptiness affected him like the beginning of a long illness" (*Swann*). Around this time, Jimroy also loses Audrey, his awkward but loving wife, because he did not recognize the grace she could grant him.

When Sarah Maloney faces the moment of loss, she decides to marry and have a baby, putting human flesh and love between her and emptiness. Rose Hindmarch chooses busyness but lives more clearly than the other characters in her essential aloneness. Cruzzi lives through the existential awareness of loss before he actually loses Hildë, who dies suddenly.

The loss of the Mary Swann artifacts, memorabilia, and poems, is, then, emblematic of other losses. Maybe this is why the novel ends with Mary's lost but reconstructed poem, "Lost Things," where the thingness of being-in-the-world withdraws itself, hides itself, sheds its human-shaped thingness to become:

> part of a larger loss
> Without a name
> Or definition or form
> Not unlike what touches us
> In moments of shame. (*Swann*)

We do know, at last, who the Mary Swann thief is but we don't know what will happen to him. And it doesn't matter. This is where Shields really subverts the conventional mystery ending with its punishments about to happen, its loose ends tied up. What really matters in **Swann** is the group of academics who have become, for the moment, a loving community as they piece together *Swann's Songs.* In the end, this mystery novel reveals itself as a kind of existentialist divine comedy.

But such a "critical" label does not do justice to the writing, the elegance and energy, the exuberant detail enjoyed for its own sake. Take the matter of meals, for instance. We know exactly what Sarah Maloney has for supper, for breakfast, for lunch (cheese on pita) and what Rose Hindmarch ate with Morton Jimroy at that hotel dinner—double pork chop platter with mashed potatoes, turnip, and mound of apple sauce, choice of rice pudding or rhubarb pie for desert. We hear about Hildë Cruzzi's walnut cake (although we don't get the recipe) and her skill with lake trout, filleted and grilled in butter. Partly, these fleshly delights are parodic of the kind of detail that make up much of the substance of ordinary mystery novels. But they are also part of the sensuous style, the "zest" of *Swann.*

As always in a Shields' novel, the major characters take on a life of their own. What is interesting here is how cleverly those lives intersect with the plot—it bears a second and third reading to realize how Brownie (Sarah's boyfriend), for instance, decidedly a minor character, is kept in focus until the surprise ending. Other minor characters too are oddly appealing—Audrey, Jimroy's wife, and how she meets up with Daisy Hart in Florida and we just know those two will have a great time on their auto trip.

> *Swann* seems to have released Shields from some of the constraints of her previous work. This "fairly conventional" writer has a depth of talent, a wild side on the far side of the "ordinary" that can, at times, "light up the workshop"—Heidegger's description of illumination of Being.
> —*Donna E. Smyth*

And then, there is the major character who is missing: Mary Swann. Like the other characters, we readers catch glimpses of her, know fragments of her, develop our own theories about her. For someone not there, she seems very real. Yet her reality is fictitious. More fictitious than Jimroy, Sarah, Rose, Frederic? Than the reader's realities? This absurdity leaves us laughing but also thinking.

Swann has to be a "turning platform"—in Nicole Brossard's words—for Shields as a writer. Here she is more playful, more daring than her earlier conventional novels at the same time as she is parodying a popular conventional form. The text is rich and varied: it includes letters, poems, narration, a cinematic ending. The pace is fast, the cuts and shifts often breathtaking—wait a minute, did the narrator say Sarah got married to that juggler on Christmas Eve?

There are, of course, continuities with the other works: Shields' celebration of life's small ceremonies, of human love, of the "ordinary" in which the miraculous may at any moment be revealed. Her women characters are wonderfully

shaped out of the stuff of female experience. Rose Hindmarch rises above cliché to touch us and make us laugh. She is so embedded in small-town Canadian life that we know Nadeau almost as well as Rose because, in some ways, Rose is Nadeau. And yet she is also capable of the transcendent moment: her night with Jean, the Mary Swann Memorial Room, her trip to the Symposium. Sarah Maloney is a rather different character register for Shields—a feminist academic who has a career before she chooses marriage. Through Sarah, Shields gently satirizes both feminism and academia but she also valorizes mother-daughter relationships in the loving portrait of Sarah with her mother.

Swann seems to have released Shields from some of the constraints of her previous work. This "fairly conventional" writer has a depth of talent, a wild side on the far side of the "ordinary" that can, at times, "light up the workshop"—Heidegger's description of illumination of Being. Which makes us think this "swann song" is no closing but an opening for Shields and her readers.

Clara Thomas (essay date July 1989)

SOURCE: "A Slight Parodic Edge: *Swann:* A Mystery," in *Multiple Voices: Recent Canadian Fiction,* edited by Jeanne Delbaere, Dangaroo Press, 1990, pp. 104-15.

[*In the following essay, originally published in 1989, Thomas discusses* Swann*'s illusive and complex nature.*]

No writer has shown us more clearly than has Carol Shields in *Swann* the paradoxical and illusory nature of *things* we covet, collect, think we possess and, in the end, lose. In *Swann* exactly 125 of the poems of the murdered Mary Swann were printed in a collection called *Swann's Songs* by the eccentric, crotchety journalist, publisher, humanist and editor, Frederic Cruzzi. Of the 250 copies originally printed, only 20 are known to have survived at the outset of the story; we learn later of the narrow escape all of the poems had in a crazy domestic disaster in the Cruzzis' home even before publication; in the end, all the eager owners of the poems have lost their copies, and even the love poems, discovered by Willard Lang under the linoleum in the deserted Swann kitchen, are gone—stuffed into a pillow-case and dropped out of a hotel window by Brownie, the book-dealer who has a passion for cornering markets: comic books, Mary Swann's poems, they're all the same to him. He hasn't read a book in years, but as artifacts their sheer physical presence, together with his urge to possess, lures him into the most bizarre labyrinths of stealth, theft and betrayal of trust.

Nor has any author shown us more clearly the flip side of the coin, the celebration of the 'redemptively ordinary' and the comfort that our *things* bring us. Sarah Maloney, feminist writer, teacher and *Swann's* central character, self-aware and good-naturedly self-mocking, muses over the shibboleths of her time:

> God is dead . . . the sixties are dead, John Lennon and Simone de Beauvoir are dead, the women's movement is dying—checking its inventory, let's say—so what's left?

The quotidian is what's left. Mary Swann understood that, if nothing else.

> A morning and an afternoon and
> Night's queer knuckled hand
> Hold me separate and whole
> Stitching light my daily soul.

Dailiness to be sure has its deposits of ennui, but it is also, as Mary Swann suggests, redemptive.

Sarah, at twenty-eight the author of the best-selling *The Female Prism,* was able to buy the 'Hansel and Gretel house' which she loves, with her royalties: 'No posters or prayer rugs or art deco here and no humanoid shapes draped in Indonesian cotton. I've got tables; I've got a more than decent Oriental rug; I've got lamps (Lord, make me a Spartan, but not yet.).' She finds her beautiful shoes, dresses and blouses 'richly satisfying': 'I've read my Thoreau, I know real wealth lies in the realm of the spirit, but I'm still a person who can, in the midst of depression, be roused by the rub of a cashmere scarf in my fingers.'

There are two further characteristic Shields signatures in *Swann:* The characters' and plot's involvement in the random chances that govern so much of our lives, and the aphorisms studding the text. As do many of the stories in *Various Miracles,* the entire saga of Mary Swann begins with an illustration of the strange synchronicity, or sometimes, serendipity, of events and our tenuous hold on what Sarah Maloney calls 'that lucent dotted line' we would like to believe leads to the future. Exhausted by Olaf Thorkelson, who hounds her to marry him, Sarah goes away to rest in a cottage he knows on a lake in Wisconsin. There, playing house in a ramshackle cabin, reading flyspecked novels and piles of old magazines, she comes upon a little book of poems called *Swann's Songs.* From this, the first of the novel's many chance happenings, all else follows.

Carol Shields is good at aphorisms and she has fun spotting them around the text: 'Clever men create themselves, but clever women, it seems to me are created by their mothers'; 'the longest hour of the week is the one wrenched from the machinery of habit'; 'The charm of falsehood is not that it distorts reality, but that it creates reality afresh.' All of the

quoted poetry of Mary Swann is aphoristic, gnomic, Dickinsonian of course—a congruence comically exploited in the text and, on Shields' part, a remarkable authorial invention and device as well as a solid story foundation: 'She has lately been recognized as a distinguished, though minor, contributor to the body of Canadian literature, and there are those who have gone so far as to call her the Emily Dickinson of Upper Canada.'

Shields wrote the fourth and final part of *Swann: A Mystery* as a film script, complete with camera and sound directions assembled around and within the dialogue. In it she provided the dénouement of her story, but more than that, much more, she invited her reader to enjoy the dénouement of her *writing* of the story, not with the smug 'the joke's on you' tone so familiar to mystery-story addicts, but with a happy, edge-of-farcical 'We've all been in this together. Now let's see the final nonsense. And by the way, don't think I'm going to wrap up all the answers for you'. We have certainly all been implicated: the writer in creating her 'mystery', the readers in a willed suspension of disbelief in the interests of their own continued pleasure in the tale being told. One of her 'Director's Notes' blandly gives her game away: 'This scene, in which the four main characters assemble their separate clues, may be played with a very slight parodic edge.' Truth to tell, we've been reading a novel whose edge is more than slightly parodic from the start.

Swann is a work whose plot is engrossing and self-sufficient: it also offers us, if we want it, a very large bonus of fun in the post-modern, critical-theory style. Shields plays the delightful game of deconstructing her own work, inviting us to share, if we wish, her bubbling awareness of all the self-reflexive, intertextual goodies she sets in front of us. The plot-line of *Swann* is only one of its mysteries; its text is a banquet of them, if we wish to recognize and enjoy them. Parody is not, however, the end and final purpose of this novel: rather, Shields has chosen it as a vehicle on which to build. When she sets up a 'parodic edge' it is, finally, to overplay and dignify it by a humanizing process that makes her characters linger on after the last page is turned, not as familiar caricatures to be laughed at, but as real people to be marvelled at—and remembered.

There is no mystery about *who* killed Mary Swann, though between page 17, when she enters the text, and page 43, we are treated to a nice build-up. The woman who wrote the 125 poems of *Swann's Songs* was a farm wife who lived outside the little town of Nadeau, Ontario, and 'that man [her husband] put a bullet right through her head and chopped her up into little pieces.' There is no answer, ever, to the mystery of *why* he killed her. 'Something just snapped' is the best guess. Other mysteries there are aplenty. Within the entire conglomerate of conventions that make up the mystery story, the 'discourse', if you prefer, of the Whodunit, the prime consideration (and quarry) of the hunt is, of course, the villain. Conventionally, he commits the murder; in *Swann,* the deed disposed of 'pre-text', the distinctly unconventional villain is out to corner the market on the Swann papers—the existent copies of *Swann's Songs,* Mary Swann's notebook, the two remaining photographs, the additional love-poems found under the linoleum of the Swanns' empty kitchen.

He is not the only villain though. A whole group of people are out to make or enhance their reputations out of exploiting Mary Swann: Sarah Maloney ('in a sense I invented Mary Swann and am responsible for her'); Frederic Cruzzi, retired newspaperman who published *Swann's Songs,* her book of poems; 'the' Morton Jimroy, biographer of Ezra Pound, John Starman and now Mary Swann; Willard Lang, the professor who is organizing the Swann Symposium in Toronto, a gathering that provides the setting for the climax and dénouement of the plot; Syd Buswell, the scholar in Ottawa who found the four additional poems underneath the linoleum in the kitchen of the deserted Swann farmhouse. Even Rose Hindmarch, town clerk, librarian and curator of the Swann memorial room in Nadeau's Local History Museum, owes a good part of her meagre self-esteem to her reputation among scholars as the one person in Nadeau who had known Mary Swann. The ones we come to know the best, Sarah, Jimroy, Rose and Cruzzi, are all guilty of violating the tenuous reality of the woman behind the poems: Sarah, by bringing Mary Swann into the light in the first place and by keeping Mary's notebook, given to her by Rose, but discarding her rhyming dictionary as if that somehow demeaned the poetry; Jimroy, by wanting *things* and stealing them and by undertaking to claim her life, death and poetry by translating it all into his biographic version; Rose, by embroidering her few exchanges of words with Mary Swann almost into the intimacy of friendship in order to ingratiate herself with her interviewers as well as to satisfy their insatiable curiosity. And Frederic Cruzzi began the whole process of her second, metaphorical murder by publishing her poems in the first place. A plethora of villains indeed!

The real hero of any mystery story, as we all know, is the Great Detective. Who is the Poirot-Wimsey-Campion-Marlowe-Fletch-Dalziel of *Swann*? Frederick Cruzzi is his token representative, the one who begins to suspect what is going on before any of the rest of them, but his detective role is displaced in the text, minor compared to the weight and substance of the character Shields makes of him.

'Sarah Maloney' is the title of the first of the five parts of *Swann*. Sarah tells her story in the present, up until the morning after her marriage to Stephen Stanhope and her leaving for Toronto and the Symposium. In 65 pages we get to know her quite well, well enough certainly to know that she is, as

she says of Rose Hindmarch, 'a good woman'. On the superficial level she is a wish-fulfilment figure for the young feminist, a successful academic who achieved that one-in-a-million miracle, a best-seller, out of her Ph.D. thesis. She is given to us, however, as a character-in-depth. Sarah is intensely and ironically self-aware, in love with Brownie who is not the marrying kind, uncertain about Stephen but warmly committed to his baby whom she is carrying, attentive to her mother ('you might say I'm a professional daughter, or at least a serious hobbyist'), and beginning to be uneasy: 'Once I knew exactly what freedom meant and now I have no idea. Naturally I resent the loss of knowledge.' She both cherishes and laughs at the idiosyncrasies that make her a fully believable, complex individual—her love of *things,* her passion for writing and receiving letters:

> Among my friends I'm known as the Queen of Correspondence. . . . It's a guilty secret of mine that I write two kinds of letters, one-drafters and two-drafters. For old friends I bang out exuberant single-spaced typewritten letters. . . . But in my two-draft letters I mind my manners, sometimes even forsaking my word processor for the pen.

The love and care she feels for her mother, her friends and her baby make her warmly human, as does the combination of relief and wonder she feels at the strange but harmless outcome of her mother's operation. Sarah Maloney marks an advance, I believe, in our gallery of young feminists: the bewilderment, victim-syndrome, and defensive hard edges of early Engel or Atwood heroines are absent. Sarah's complexity, lightly worn, makes Joan of *Lady Oracle,* Renee of *Bodily Harm* and even Rita of *The Glassy Sea* a little old-fashioned and anachronistic, believable enough in the time of their writing, necessary even, but out-dated today.

'What I need is an image to organize my life. A flower would be nice', she says. Two pages later she gives us the dual image that does organize her life and that resonates with meaning for countless women. She sits down in her kitchen to write her paper for the Swann Symposium on her second-hand word-processor. Sarah not only loves real things, she is grounded in them, in dailiness. She lives with her worlds by bringing them together, enjoying the gleam of her yellow kettle in the one, recognizing the efficiency of her machine in the other: 'Oh that miraculous little green clearing key!'

Part II, Morton Jimroy's story, is told in the third person, a wise choice on Shields' part. She lets us hear enough of his voice to know that a steady diet of it would be too thick with self-delusion and self-pity to bear. By moving away both to show and tell us about Morton she can and does signal sympathy, in spite of the inept pettiness of a fearful, insecure man whose academic reputation as a biographer of the great is all he has. Her portrait could easily have been a carica- ture, the holding up to ridicule of every bumbling academic from Lucky Jim onward, but she circles around him, balanc- ing parodic highlights with all too human shadows until we understand and even cheer for his hard bought modicum of gallantry. In California, far from his Winnipeg home, work- ing alone on Christmas Day, Jimroy has a moment of trans- figuration. He is happy, happy devising his own Mary Swann, happy with the inimitably pompous and totally mis- taken phrase he has just penned: 'It is highly probable that Swann read Jane Austen during this period. . . .':

> He lifts an arm in salutation, shouting, in his cheery broken tenor, 'Merry Christmas,' and smiling broadly at the same time to show them that his life may be foolish, it may be misguided and strange and bent in its yearnings, but it's all he has and all he's likely to get.

And cold indeed is the reader who doesn't cheer him on.

With Part III, 'Rose Hindmarch', Shields moves more deeply, obviously and daringly into what contemporary criti- cal theorists call intertextuality—for Rose is straight out of Mariposa. She is, at first, like an omitted character in Leacock's gallery, companion to Josh Smith, Dean Drone, Peter Pupkin and the rest: 'Rose Helen Hindmarch wears a number of hats. "I wear too many hats for my own good", she has been heard to say'. Then we hear about her mul- tiple jobs in Nadeau—town clerk, librarian, curator, church elder, town councillor. In the section 'Some Words of Ori- entation', Shields is speaking in a voice and tone inescap- ably Leacockian. She leads the reader geographically through the town as does Leacock at the beginning of *Sun- shine Sketches,* pointing out the landmarks with a humour that closely echoes his:

> *Leacock:* Up and down the Main street are tele- graph poles of cedar of colossal thickness, stand- ing at a variety of angles and carrying rather more wires than are commonly at a transatlantic cable station.

> *Shields:* The museum, taking up all of the second floor of the old school is small by anyone's stan- dards, though it manages to attract more than 500 visitors annually. . . . Be sure to see the interesting old washing machine, *circa* 1913, and to take in the various articles of clothing that include a 'christen- ing gown from the nineties' and a woman's grey wool walking costume, piped in red (1902).

Likewise, in the section 'Here Comes Rose Now', Shields puts her narrator and reader in exactly the same relative po- sitions as does Leacock:

> *Leacock:* Walk on this June afternoon halfway down the Main Street—or, if you like, halfway up from the wharf—to where Mr. Smith is standing at the door of his hostelry. You will feel as you draw near that it is no ordinary man you approach. It is not alone the huge bulk of Mr. Smith (two hundred and eighty pounds as tested on Netley's scales). It is not merely his costume, though the chequered waistcoat of dark blue with a flowered pattern. . . .

> *Shields:* Here comes Rose now, a shortish woman with round shoulders and the small swelling round- ness of a potbelly, which she is planning to work on this fall.

> Never mind the leather coat and boots and gloves, there's something vellum and summery in Rose's appearance, and she almost sings out the words, 'Good evening'.

So much for the manner and context of Rose's setting and a nice acknowledgement that any Ontario literary small town does well to pay tribute to Mariposa, the first great one. From the start Shields' narrative voice enters the text to di- rect our sympathy and compassion for Rose as Leacock would never have done: 'There are moments when she ex- periences an appalling sensation of loss, the nagging suspi- cion that beneath the hats is nothing but chilly space or the small scratching sounds of someone who wants only to please others.' Once Rose is established in her place, the whole movement of her section is not toward further cari- cature, as in Leacock, but away from it.

The section could be called 'The Humanizing of Rose Hindmarch', and, finally, it is as complete and satisfying a story and as replete with invitations to understanding and empathy as is the remarkable 'Mrs. Turner Cutting the Grass' from *Various Miracles.* Like Jimroy's section, but more compellingly, I believe, Rose's section ends with a small but very important moment of transcendence. Tired but happy in the midst of her party, Rose forgets the nagging anxieties of her self-doubts and her frightening bleeding:

> Happiness seizes her, exhausted though she is by the loss of blood and the preparations for the party. In recent weeks she has had the feeling that some poisonous sorrow has seeped into her life, and now, this afternoon, from nowhere comes a sudden shine of joy. . . .

> . . . and then, out of the blue, she remembers a line from one of Mary Swann's poems. It just swims into her head like a little fish.

> A pound weighs more

When grief had gone before

With Part IV, 'Frederic Cruzzi', we are satisfyingly, unmistakably in the world of Robertson Davies. How could one avoid connecting 'retired newspaper editor Frederic Cruzzi of Grenoble, Casablanca, Manchester, and Kingston, Ontario, aged eighty', who suffers no fool gladly, writes snappy letters to obtuse correspondents and castigates the yahoos with glee, to Samuel Marchbanks? Or, for that matter, in his wide travels, European sensibility and considerable wisdom, to Dunstan Ramsay? Or, for that matter, with Davies himself—as his persona says in *The Papers of Samuel Marchbanks,* 'let us call ourselves two sides of a coin'.

In this, the penultimate section of *Swann,* Shields has a more complicated, demanding task than in any of her first three sections. Not only does she embark on the humanizing of a character with the caricature outline of Marchbanks; she has also to provide all the background to the publication of *Swann's Songs.* Until now we have been in the dark about this, for the story started *in media res* as we've had no hint of the adventures of publication. Shields weaves the two processes beautifully together, rounding out Cruzzi in his mellowing present, setting Hilde, the wife he loved, now dead, beside him and climaxing with the stunning—and harrowing—story of the first making of the text of *Swann's Songs,* whose Proustian title he and Hilde gave the poems and later regretted: 'An inexplicable lapse of sensibility. A miscalculation, an embarrassment.'

The night Mary Swann visited Cruzzi and left him her poems, her husband murdered her: 'something snapped'. The same night, when Frederic Cruzzi found that Hilde had dumped the heads and entrails of the fish she'd caught and cleaned into the bag of poems, he struck out in rage, knocking her down: '*something snapped.* . . . He had never completely understood what constituted a crime of passion'. Later, reconciled, past the shock of his betrayal of himself and Hilde, they spent the whole night salvaging poems, making Mary Swann's manuscript:

> By midnight . . . they were referring to Hilde's transcribed notes, and not the drying, curling, fish-stinking poems on the table, as 'the manuscript'. . . .

> By now—it was morning—a curious conspiracy had overtaken them. Guilt, or perhaps a wish to make amends, convinced them that they owed Mrs. Swann an interpretation that would reinforce her strengths as a poet. They wanted to offer her help and protection, what she seemed never to have had.

This is the central surprise and revelation of *Swann: A Mystery.* There never was a text of Mary Swann's poems authentic to her own words. Cruzzi had agreed to speak at the Swann Symposium, but he was not now, or ever, about to tell the bizarre story of *Swann's Songs.* We, the readers, are reasonably sure of the identity of the 'villain' who is bent on cornering the Swann market. We are not surprised, then, with the Christmas Eve robbery of Cruzzi's four copies of the poems as well as his file on Mary Swann. But we do understand and share in the confusion and guilt of the old man, and in his limited reassurance:

> Gazing at the shelf, Cruzzi felt pierced with the fact of his old age, his helplessness, and the knowledge that a long-delayed act of reprisal had taken place. . . . As he sorted through twenty years of manuscripts and correspondence, he listened to Handel's *Messiah* on the radio and felt a feeble tide of balance reassert itself. . . . By late afternoon he was finished. Everything was in place. Everything was in place, with only the file on Mary Swann missing. He supposed he should be grateful, but instead found his face confused by tears.

For four-fifths of *Swann: A Mystery* we have been moved from caricature and stereotype to the powerful illusion of 'real people'. Now, the initial Director's Note of Part V, 'The Swann Symposium', instructs us to swing back to artifice and artificiality: this is a 'film', we are told; all the elements are 'fictional creations'; it may be described '(for distribution purposes) as a thriller.' For her final dénouement Shields has moved us into the conventions, the discourse, of yet another genre. She has assembled all the pieces of her puzzle, and now she breaks it all up under our eyes, forcing us to remember that our suspension of disbelief has been just that and only that. Shields is the maker of the text and she can choose the games to play. Her Symposium scenes have wonderful elements of parody of every academic conference in the world. They also have major infusions of farce, with much hide-and-seek among the characters, in and out of bedrooms, washrooms, conference rooms, with sudden dowsing of lights, concealing, locked doors and, finally a pillow-case stuffed with Mary Swann's poems pitched out of a 24th-floor hotel window into the snow.

In the final scene, participants in the Symposium are seated in a circle, 'laboriously reassembling' a new text of the poems:

> Director's Final Note: the faces of the actors have been subtly transformed. They are in a ceremonial act of reconstruction, perhaps even in an act of creation. There need be no suggestion that anyone of them will become less selfish in the future, less cranky, less consumed with thoughts of tenure and academic glory, but each of them has, for the moment at least, transcended personal concerns.

All along Carol Shields has made this text: under her aegis Mary Swann wrote her poems; Frederic and Hilde Cruzzi made their text; now the Swann scholars are making yet another final text. 'Lost Things' is the poem they are reassembling in the final scene, and that poem (or their version of it) ends the text of *Swann: A Mystery.* This is a wonderful ending, on the one hand a fitting closure to such a romp through techniques and genres, on the other a final Shields signature, a humanizing of the whole group. *Things* vanish, become disconnected from us, separate us; shared and caring feeling and enterprise join us into community.

To try to analyse *Swann: A Mystery* is rather like dissecting a butterfly with a hoe. *Swann* is a 'murder' answering De Quincey's requirements: more than that, much more, it is a novel whose hallmarks are wit, wisdom, play, skill and great good nature, one to be enjoyed—and remembered.

Ursula Hegi (review date 20 August 1989)

SOURCE: "Carrion Conspiracy," in *Los Angeles Times Book Review,* August 20, 1989, p. 2.

[In the following review, Hegi discusses the issue of stolen identity in Swann.*]*

What happens when literary criticism takes a writer's work so far from her intent that, finally, it loses its essence? Carol Shields asks disturbing questions about the nature of theft in her novel, *Swann.* Who is the real thief—the person who steals the last rare copies of a murdered poet's book, the scholars who use her poems to seek recognition for themselves, or her husband who brutally murders her?

Fifteen years after Canadian poet, Mary Swann, is killed without an apparent motive, a symposium is held in Toronto, drawing Swann experts from all over the United States and Canada. Shields focuses on four of the participants—a critic, a biographer, a publisher, and a town clerk.

The feminist critic, Sarah Maloney, considers herself Swann's discoverer. Exulting in the "womanly brilliance" she bestows on her postgraduate students, she indulges in a running, internal commentary on her thoughts, feelings, and actions. This tireless reflection is amusing at first but soon becomes repetitive and transforms a potentially complex character into a caricature.

Her correspondence with Swann's biographer, Morton Jimroy, evolves from their mutual interest in the work of the murdered poet. Sarah likes to believe that Mary Swann "invented modern poetry." She keeps it a secret that Swann worked with a rhyming dictionary which resulted in unfortunate choices such as nerves/preserves, shelf/myself, light/bite. Certain that her connection to Swann will bring her recognition at the symposium, she distorts Swann's poems and life to fit her interpretation.

Jimroy is flattered by Sarah's letters and indulges in sexual fantasies in which she seduces him. A lonely, silly, and pompous man, he still carries the presence of his ex-wife, Audrey, with him, romanticizing even those habits that used to annoy him, making anonymous phone calls to her late at night and, eventually, to Sarah.

As a biographer, he is drawn to his own flaws in people he writes about—Pound's "elephantiasis of the ego" and Starman's emptiness. He ignores the "peculiar ordinariness of Mary Swann's letters" in his attempt to link "Mary Swann's biographical greyness with the achieved splendour of Swann's songs." He starts off as an interesting character but, as with Sarah, Shields overworks his peculiarities until he becomes a caricature of himself.

Rose Hindmarch, the town clerk in Nadeau where Swann lived, has been invited to the symposium because she has convincingly exaggerated her relationship with the reticent poet.

The fourth major participant in the symposium is 80-year-old Frederic Cruzzi, Swann's publisher, the last person to see her alive. The winter day Swann arrived at his house unannounced with her manuscript, "her face was small, purplish . . . eyes squeezed shut . . . hunched sweatered shoulders and the whiteness of scalp under scanty hair. . . ." He never saw her again because that night, when she got home, her husband killed her.

Cruzzi and his wife, Hilde, founded Peregrine, a small press, and published regional authors they both believed in. Their relationship is alive and convincing. "The two of them occasionally made gifts to each other of their dreams." Cruzzi is by far the strongest character in *Swann,* revealing a uniqueness and depth that make it puzzling why Shields didn't develop her other characters with the same skill.

As the date for the Swann Symposium draws closer, the last known copies of Swann's book, her hand-written journal, and a few unpublished poems disappear mysteriously. The suspense, however, is transparent since Shields, in the early pages of the novel, introduces the person who has the incentive and proximity to steal Swann's material.

Yet, this deliberate theft illuminates the real theft which is far more subtle and damaging, a theft that has been happening from the moment Swann brought a bag filled with loose papers to Cruzzi, and the publisher and his wife spent all night reconstructing the poems that were nearly destroyed by accident. "A curious conspiracy had overtaken them. Guilt, or perhaps a wish to make amends, convinced them that they owed Mrs. Swann an interpretation that would reinforce her strengths as a poet."

The real theft continues with Maloney's discovery of the poet. "In a sense I invented Mary Swann and I am responsible for her," with Jimroy's leading questions which provide him with material that will bring him fame, with the corruption of Rose Hindmarch as she embroiders stories about her friendship with Swann. It's a theft that implicates the scholars at the symposium who spout their competing theories without regard to the integrity of Mary Swann's poetry.

Anita Clair Fellman (review date December 1989)

SOURCE: "A World Made of Words," in *Women's Review of Books,* Vol. VII, No. 3, December, 1989, p. 16.

[*In the following review, Fellman discusses Shields's interest in form and personality in* Swann *and her investigations into order and chaos in the stories in* Various Miracles.]

Now that the US and Canada have signed a free trade treaty, perhaps it will be possible for more than one or two Canadian women writers to slip past the US cultural border. High on my list of imports is Carol Shields, whose fifth novel, *Swann,* and collection of short stories, *Various Miracles,* have just been published in the US. Shields, who was nominated for a Governor General's Award for *Swann,* and is the subject of a recent special issue of the Canadian feminist literary quarterly, *Room of One's Own,* has enriched Canadian fiction writing and poetry, and deserves to be better known in the US. Ironically, although she lives in Winnipeg, she was born and raised in the Chicago area, and takes her settings and her characters from both countries.

The fascination of other people's lives and the essential unknowability of even those closest to us are threads that run through all of Shields' work. She is preoccupied with individuals who work with words and those who perceive the world largely through books. The middle-class protagonists in her first three novels, *Small Ceremonies, The Box Garden* and *Happenstance,* are respectively a biographer, a poet and a historian. Although the main characters in each of these novels are psychologically connected, at levels they are not always aware of, they are also profoundly mysterious to each other.

Swann is a bigger, funnier, more dazzling and expansive undertaking than Shields' earlier, somewhat constrained work, concerned not only with the difficulty of knowing

other people, but also with the questions posed by the unknown origins of creativity. When it was published in Canada two years ago, the novel was entitled *Swann: A Mystery.* The mystery is a double one. First and foremost is that of Mary Swann herself. Her drab Ontario farm life offered nothing to explain her "preternatural ability to place two ordinary words side by side and extract a kilowatt, and sometimes more, much more, from them," as one character describes her poetry. Her biographer can find no literary influences on her; not having read any poetry (except nursery rhymes to her daughter), Swann apparently reinvented modern poetry on her own. The second mystery has to do with the gradual disappearance of every artifact pertaining to the poet and of every known copy of her poems. In the course of the novel only one of these two mysteries really gets solved, and that is one that astute readers will readily solve themselves.

The main characters of the book are four very diverse people who have come, in one way or another, to have a stake in Mary Swann's growing literary reputation. Sarah Maloney is a successful young Chicago feminist literary scholar who "discovered" a small volume of Swann's poems by accident more than fifteen years after the poet's inexplicable, violent death at the hands of her husband. Morton Jimroy is a famous Winnipeg biographer of poets. Rose Hindmarch is a part-time librarian and museum curator in the small town near which Swann had lived. And Frederic Cruzzi is a small-town Ontario retired newspaper editor and poetry publisher who had published Swann's poems posthumously.

The motives behind their interest in Swann, revealed in the first four sections of the book, are a combination of the personal and professional. Sarah Maloney is drawn to Mary Swann's poetry because of its affirmation of the redemptive power of dailiness. The ballast of the quotidian is needed in the difficult days of the 1980s, Sarah thinks, and as a feminist she relishes the fact that Mary Swann drew her inspiration from the most mundane of tasks and scenes, creating wonderful poetry premised on the saving grace of routine. Sarah herself needs the reliability of routine; not only does she give her days a firm pattern, but she marries a juggler, someone who can always make order out of flying objects. Having brought Swann to the attention of the world, Sarah now thinks of herself as her maternal caretaker, her protector against the greedy literary men who, she is sure, would eat Swann up "inch by inch."

Morton Jimroy has chosen Swann because after two biographies of poets whom he came to despise as individuals, he wants to write about someone he can admire and champion. Jimroy, however, comes to have as complicated a relationship with Swann as he had with his previous subjects. And in his desire to portray her as an important poet, he begins to reinterpret Swann's poems to minimize the female metaphors, to look for signs that she had transcended her womanhood. "She wasn't writing poems about housewife blues," he tells Rose Hindmarch. "She was speaking about the universal sense of loss and alienation, not about washing machines breaking down."

So eager is the well-meaning Rose to be consulted as the supposed expert on Swann's life that she fabricates whole conversations beyond the minimal greetings she and the poet had exchanged at the library charge desk. For Frederic Cruzzi, the poems are forever associated with his beloved, now-dead wife, who had been co-publisher of their little poetry press, and with his residual guilt for the tinkering they had done, unasked, with Swann's work. All these largely sympathetic characters commit various acts of dishonesty to protect their investment in Swann; Shields gives a wonderfully ironic and funny portrayal of the process of mythologizing a previously unknown literary figure.

For the last several years, Shields has been experimenting with form, and *Swann* shows the fruits of this experimentation. The four protagonists are each accorded a section of the novel, and in each the style, tone, even voice differ. Sarah Maloney's section reveals her to be an engaging, somewhat self-conscious young woman. Recalling her first meeting with Rose, she confesses, "I often frighten people. I frighten myself, as a matter of fact, my undeflectable energy probably. I did what I could to put Rose at her ease. . . . In an hour she was won over, so quickly won over that I winced with shame."

> When all four characters are brought together in the last section for the Swann Symposium [in *Swann: A Mystery*], which is to be the culmination of their efforts to anoint Swann as a major poet, Shields uses a screenplay form. While inventive, this is not quite as successful as the preceding sections, partly because the satire becomes too broad, but also because the task here is intrinsically more difficult.
> —*Anita Clair Fellman*

Shields' playfulness reaches a peak with Frederic Cruzzi's section, which is something of a parody of Robertson Davies' work. Here there is a selection from Cruzzi's correspondence, a record of his dreams, a description of one of the most important days of his life. There is also a one-sentence autobiography more than a page long, which contains, among other things, a description of Cruzzi's wife-to-be:

a rather large-boned girl with straight yellow hair

parted in the middle, who had grown up in the hamlet of La Motte-en-Champsaur (where her father kept goats) and who was possessed of a shining face in which Cruzzi glimpsed the promise of his future happiness, though it took him a week before he found the courage to declare his love—in the museum at Gap, as it happened, standing before a hideous oil painting, even then peeling away from its frame, depicting Prometheus being fawned on by a dozen lardy maidens—

When all four characters are brought together in the last section for the Swann Symposium, which is to be the culmination of their efforts to anoint Swann as a major poet, Shields uses a screenplay form. While inventive, this is not quite as successful as the preceding sections, partly because the satire becomes too broad, but also because the task here is intrinsically more difficult. The convergence of four characters who scarcely know each other, but whom we know quite well, is a little too neat.

Mary Swann was as close to "Anonyma" as it is possible to be in the Western industrialized world. Shields' story suggests that the process of creation, while mysterious, is democratic, and can be communal and open-ended as well.

In *Various Miracles,* a collection of short stories first published in Canada two years before *Swann,* Shields explores the parallel to her interest in the mysteriousness of the personality. Here it is our fleeting glimpses of both the order and chaos of the universe that fascinate her. "Several of the miracles that occurred this year have gone unrecorded," begins the title story. A wonderful series of homely coincidences and parallel events is then detailed, including a dream divided between a husband and wife. As the husband awakes from his part of the dream and watches his rapturously dreaming wife, "he felt how utterly ignorant he was of the spring that nourished her life."

For Shields the moments of revelation are more often of unexpected symmetries and "the million invisible filaments of connection" than they are of utter randomness and emptiness. In **"Home,"** each passenger and the pilot on a transatlantic flight experiences, for different reasons, an extraordinary sense of well-being. Their collective happiness causes the walls of their aircraft to become momentarily translucent. In **"The Journal,"** an unknown combination of reasons permits Sally and Harold a night in which "they are minutely and ecstatically joined and where they exchange, as seldom before in their forty-year lives, those perfect notices of affection and trust and rhapsody." These visions of harmony coexist with Shields' depictions of the obverse, the moments of revelation in which people realize the patternlessness of the universe. In **"Invitations,"** a woman seated alone, absorbed in a book, awakens in the stream of people passing by her window on their way to a series of parties a sense of the futility of their destinations, the emptiness and disappointment of their lives. In **"Purple Blooms,"** the narrator gives three dissatisfied people in her life a copy of a book written by a local poet. She sees them all in the park that afternoon, seeking the author's autograph and claiming that the book has helped them make healing connections. The narrator waiting her turn to have her copy signed pulls out another book of poetry to read, this one a celebration of the randomness and disorder of the world. As she reads, with the other people reading over her shoulder, the world around her fades, leaving only "a page of print, a line of type, a word, a dot of ink, a shadow on the retina that is no bigger than the smallest violet in the woods."

The power of the printed word to overcome reality, or, more accurately, to define reality, is the theme of several stories in the collection. In **"Pardon,"** people's deep grievances against each other are miraculously expunged by an unexplained flurry of verbal and written apologies and pardons. In **"Words,"** an ill-considered ban on speech renders people incapable of human intercourse and action.

The 21 stories are economically short. Shields offers intense, layered scenes, rather than elaborated narratives. Each story is a glimpse of a captured moment in a mysterious world. These moments may or may not have deeper meaning. "Only rarely," one of her characters says, "do they point to anything but themselves . . . . They're useless, attached to nothing, can't be traded in or shaped into instruments to prise open the meaning of the universe . . . they are what life is made of."

Herb Weil (essay date 1990)

SOURCE: "From 'Dying for Love' to 'Mrs. Turner': Narrative Control in Stories by Carol Shields," in *Contemporary Manitoba Writers: New Critical Studies,* edited by Kenneth James Hughes, Turnstone Press, 1990, pp. 163-76.

[*In the essay below, Weil considers structure and narration in Shields's short stories.*]

i

My first thought this morning is for Beth, how on earth she'll cope now that Ted's left her for the dancer Charlotte Brown. I ask myself, what resources does a woman like Beth have, emotional resources? (**"Dying,"** *Made*)

These two sentences begin Carol Shields' **"Dying for Love,"** a story that has been reprinted twice within a year

of its original publication (1989). After the first paragraph, the story-teller (perhaps better conceived as what we used to call "the implied author") unobtrusively vanishes—or at least does not explicitly refer to herself until the final paragraphs of the first segment:

> Despite my uneasiness about Beth's ability to cope emotionally, and despite her insomnia, she somehow manages to get up most mornings. . . .

> Beth . . . wonders what would happen if she took all twelve pills plus the gin. She doesn't know. I don't know either.

This section is the first of three segments in the story. Each is devoted to one woman who may be in danger of dying (because of love or the absence of love). After we learn that Beth empties the gin down the sink and grinds the pills down the garburator, the first segment concludes, "Life is a thing to be cherished, she thinks, and this thought, slender as a handrail, gets her through one more night." Does this last line involve the narrator more intimately than does traditional omniscience? Unnamed, she presents explicitly only feelings, attitudes, and especially worries that are directly relevant to her characters and their situations. (Different readers will quite appropriately weigh differently phrases, rhythms, tones that suggest the technique of leaving insecure any distinctions between teller and creator.) How important is it that Beth and Ted have no last names while Charlotte does? Do all readers sense that the speaker in the second paragraph, partly by revealing intimate details, is *constructing* the characters?

> Habits accrue in that time, especially habits of the night when bodies and their routines get driven into hard rituals of washed skin. . . . Beth curls, but sinuously; her backbone makes a long smiling capital C on the bedsheet, or used to, before Ted told her he was leaving her for Charlotte.

Within this brief story, and in most of her work, Shields creates a wide variety of relations between narrator and characters, situations, actions; between narrator and "implied author"; between each of these and her readers. Often we feel less encouraged to treat the events as if they had happened to the author than we do in other overtly "confessional" fiction, as, for example, by Alice Munro. Nor do we find here the "conspicuously" artificial sub-genre of alleged autobiography—at least in the literal sense best typified by Machado de Assis in which the speaker (after his own death) tells his story, or more typically, when the narrator is of a gender or an age, or lives in a time, that we know cannot be that of the author. In **"Dying for Love"** most readers will recognize a very self-conscious narrator, playing with some of the tones implied by her title. How strongly does "dying for" resonate of trite clichés, of transitory pleasures? Do these overtones make it far-fetched to take the phrase literally? Why then does "dying for" rather than "love" dominate in creating the tone?

As we read the story, how convincing are the threats that the cliché-sense will turn into actual death because of what the character, at least, continues to feel is love? But does the narrator feel it as love? Does the author? The second segment begins, "But then there's Lizzie in Somerset; my fears for Lizzie grow day by day. Her predicament is clear and so is her fate, although I would do anything, or almost anything, to assist her in the avoidance of that fate." Then the narrator again disappears. Four pages later, in the closing lines of this segment, she returns.

> Who can tell.
>
> One of the advantages in my relationship with Lizzie is my freedom to discard those possibilities she can't yet imagine. All she understands is that both love and the lack of love can be supported.

From the vagueness or false precision of "almost anything" the narrator advances with her character to the finely tuned tone of this final sentence that blends calculation and self-reassurance.

The final, shortest segment begins, "Elsewhere, nearer home, a woman named Elizabeth is lying on her bed in the middle of the afternoon with a plastic dry-cleaner's bag drawn up over her face. . . ." How important for the reader is the change to the overt absence of the "I" from this sequence until the very last sentence of the story? Surely the first three words of this segment remind any alert reader of her presence. But how firm is the pressure? Need the good reader make much of this? Or of the apparently gratuitous "named"?

The segment and the story end in two long sentences. The first presents the apparently factual—if emotionally loaded—statement, "She is a woman whose life is crowded with not-unpleasant errands. . . ." How decisive should we consider the change of tone with the return of the author in the final sentence?

> Not that this is much of a handrail to hang on to—she knows that, and so do I—but it is at least continuous, solid, reliable in its turnings and better than no hand-rail at all.

Shields encourages many different responses: of hope, of worry, of emphasis upon strengths or upon fragility. In this final sentence, for the first time, the "I" knows precisely what the character knows. The story has moved from an extremely

nervous series of questions about another person, allegedly external, with whom the "I" feels strong empathy: "The nights will be terrible for her, I'm sure of that. . . ." Does the possible sense that the narrator (as well as the actual author) may have created the characters make her detachment much less? And consequently her handrail much more fragile? We sense here an implied author in a well-controlled but insecure relation to the narrator she has created.

ii

In vivid contrast to Beth, Lizzie, and Elizabeth is the focal character in **"Mrs. Turner Cutting the Grass."** Few would be less likely to die for love. Unlike the three distinct "heroines" who share variants of the same first name but receive no other, Mrs. Turner seems at first to be captured in that title of address. Not until the third page, after our sense of her has been well established, do we learn that the high school girls on their way home

> are ignorant of that fact . . . that she, Mrs. Turner, possesses a first name—which is Geraldine.
>
> Not that she's ever been called Geraldine. Where she grew up in Boissevain, Manitoba, she was known always—the Lord knows why—as Girlie Fergus. . . .

This story, a frequently anthologized prize-winner and favourite of many of Shields' readers, begins:

> Oh, Mrs. Turner is a sight cutting the grass on a hot afternoon in June! She climbs into an ancient pair of shorts and ties on her halter top and wedges her feet into crepe-soled sandals and covers her red-gray frizz with Gord's old golf cap—Gord is dead now, ten years ago, a seizure on a Saturday night while winding the mantel clock.

At first, this story seems more conventional and familiar than much of the author's recent work. The tone of these first statements seems detached, the unnamed and undescribed narrator hardly sympathetic to her[?] subject. We assume that we are in the world of satire, perhaps of broad comedy (with the temporal jump between sentences), as the story races along with the unencumbered mower:

> The grass flies up around Mrs. Turner's knees. Why doesn't she use a catcher . . . [?] Everyone knows that leaving the clippings like that is bad for the lawn. . . .
>
> . . . [And worse] Roy is far more concerned about the Killex that Mrs. Turner dumps on her dandelions. . . .

. . . But he and Sally so far have said nothing to Mrs. Turner about her abuse of the planet because they're hoping she'll go into an old-folks home soon or maybe die, and then all will proceed as it should.

High-school girls on their way home . . . are mildly, momentarily repelled by the lapped, striated flesh on her upper thighs. . . .

The things Mrs. Turner doesn't know would fill the Saschers' new compost pit, would sink a ship, would set off a tidal wave. . . . Back and forth, back and forth she goes with the electric lawn mower, the grass flying out sideways like whiskers. Oh, the things she doesn't know!

Smoothly, almost glibly, convincingly, the things Mrs. Turner does not know—not just about grass clippings but about Neil Young, cellulite, "the vocabulary of skin care," the concerns of the chorus of neighbours, and apparently of the narrator—give way to facts that the passing girls and the young parents do not know. Sharply in mid-sentence, the story turns. Until its final paragraph, roughly four-fifths of the story tells us about matters that the girls and the young married couple next door would want to know, but do not even suspect. And finally we learn, too, about the fame of Girlie Fergus, a public persona that she herself does not imagine.

Let us return to look more closely at the major shift in mid-sentence from the "present tense" of an old lady cutting the grass, an old lady so ignorant of facts about contemporary life that she does not even seem to inhabit the same psychological world as any of the unsympathizing characters mentioned. When the narrator moves from the chatty, relaxed, somewhat superior present tense that confidently invites readers to share the story-teller's views, we find the author there waiting to be noticed. There is nothing insistent. Shields gives us a life story that few could have predicted, but which includes only what could well have happened. With the greatest tact, the author creates a past that seems far-fetched but possible. She encourages a range of interpretation: many readers will skim happily along assuming a simple mimetic narrative. Others will feel more aware of an author neatly constructing people and events. The story will work well for both sorts of audience.

In the next paragraph, we quickly learn that Girlie was "the one who got herself in hot water. . . . Girlie got caught one night—she was nineteen—in a Boissevain hotel room with a local farmer, married, named Gus MacGregor." By the next paragraph Girlie has escaped, sneaking out to catch a bus to Winnipeg, another to Minneapolis, to Chicago, to New York City. However wretched the journey, New York is "immense and wonderful." She loves her job as usherette at the Movie Palace in Brooklyn, quickly moves in with "a man

named Kiki. . . . His skin was as black as ebony. . . . [She has a baby] boy, rather sweetly formed, with wonderful smooth feet and hands." Deserted by Kiki, she leaves her baby in a beautiful carriage on the porch of a house that "she particularly liked. . . . She has no idea what happened to Kiki . . . [or] to her son," but she doesn't worry much. She returns home a year later. Frighteningly embraced and accepted by her family, she quickly leaves to marry "a tonguetied man . . . who loved every inch of his house. . . . And he loved every inch of his wife, Girlie, too, saying to her once and only once that he knew about her past . . . and that as far as he was concerned the slate had been wiped clean." In the single brilliant fast-paced paragraph devoted to this marriage, we learn too of the one time on a passionate picnic when he worshipped Girlie, or at least her body. We barely have time to wonder whether it matters that his sense of knowing all about the past stops at Boissevain. What would he think about New York? What should we?

After Gordon Turner dies, Girlie and her two sisters travel. To Disneyland, to seven countries of Europe, to New Orleans, to Mexico; finally, "three years ago they did what they swore they'd never have the nerve to do: they got on an airplane and went to Japan." This trip and one of its "results," a book of poems, receive the most extensive treatment in the story. Another tourist in the group, the "Professor," a bald, "trim," unsuccessful poet, almost continuously jotting, after his return publishes "a solid little book" which becomes very popular. The favourite poem, always demanded in readings, is his "A Day at the Golden Pavilion":

> [It] was not really about the Golden Pavilion [in Kyoto] at all, but about three midwestern lady tourists who . . . had talked incessantly and in loud, flatbottomed voices about . . . indigestion, sore feet, breast lumps . . . who back home in Manitoba should receive a postcard. . . . They were the three furies . . . who for vulgarity and tastelessness formed a shattering counterpoint to the Professor's own state of transcendence. . . .

> One of the sisters . . . particularly stirred his contempt, she of the pink pantsuit, the red toenails, the grapefruity buttocks. . . .

Always this reading evokes laughter and self-satisfied applause from the students who know "the irreconcilable distance between taste and banality."

Again in mid-paragraph the narrator steps in and corrects her last statement. A new distance combines with a new strong commitment: "Or perhaps that's too harsh; perhaps it's only the difference between those who know about the world and those who don't." Here the distance, strongly reinforced by the assertion that begins the next paragraph—

"It's true Mrs. Turner remembers little about her travels. . . . What does it matter? She's having a grand time"—suggests a range of legitimate responses for the readers in deciding the stance and tones of the implied author. The irony toward the youths who already know so much about taste and banality at first offers a range of tones for the implied voice. The revision, "that's too harsh," even modulated by "perhaps," forecloses possibilities, ensuring that with more acute precision we see through the smug students and even more through the self-satisfied poet. (Even Gus MacGregor had received a name—if no physical, social, or other description.)

The three concluding paragraphs return us to the present, primarily in Winnipeg, with an explicit yoking of celebration and irony: "Her sisters have long forgotten about her wild days." To the Local History Museum, Em has donated her father's pipe, her mother's wedding veil, and "a white cotton garment labeled 'Girlie Fergus' Underdrawers. . . .' If Mrs. Turner knew the word *irony* she would relish this. Even without knowing the word irony, she relishes it." This past and her "fame" contrast vividly with the way in which the poem brought her, however nameless, into the consciousness of so many audiences. With careful vagueness, the narrator leaves the patronizing professor who has won "an important international award" and who has sold rights to "a number of foreign publishers." Circling to the first six paragraphs, the final one returns to Mrs. Turner. But now, we see things only through her vision—and that created by the narrator—never through that of the high school girls or the neighbours, or, in another world, of the college students. Mrs. Turner waves to the girls (who have become timid), "she hollers hello to Sally and Roy. . . ." And finally, the narrator makes overt the vision she shares with her heroine, a vision that Mrs. Turner could never come close to formulating: "She cannot imagine that anyone would wish her harm. All she's done is live her life." Mrs. Turner would never make such claims, but she would no doubt feel pleased, if embarrassed, should she read this description (so unlike the crude ungenerous satiric poem). Only now does the author dare to conclude, with symbolic images and finally with her first explicit celebration: "The green grass flies up in the air, a buoyant cloud swirling about her head. Oh, what a sight is Mrs. Turner cutting her grass and how, like an ornament, she shines."

The author has chosen a subject and created for her a biography that very few of her readers are likely at first to find appealing. She leaves open crucial questions. How can the deserted child, the devoted husband be so quickly dropped? But her movement from satire and irony to the final praise permits her to lead her reader (as Jane Austen did with Emma and Mrs. Bates) away from participating in the narrow-minded alleged superiority of characters early in the story. That we accept as well the contrasting didactic style

which the ending incorporates and transforms suggests how skillfully the narrator has earned our trust.

iii

"Mrs. Turner Cutting the Grass" and **"Dying for Love"** succeed, I think, for most readers, both those who focus upon the strategies of the implied author and those more casual (say, for example, readers sympathetic and alert, but not studying the stories or, at least, not these aspects of the stories). If one attends to the careful timing and tones of authorial control one should have a richer, more complex appreciation, but those only intermittently aware of this craft need never feel excluded from the audience addressed. Two other stories in *Various Miracles,* however, make, in their very distinct ways, much more explicit demands upon their readers. The brief title story [**"Various Miracles"**] (placed first, just before **"Mrs. Turner"**) immediately confronts the reader with the presence of a strongly manipulating author. Even the title, like that of the earlier novel, *Small Ceremonies,* links a vague or weak initial adjective that normally would not arouse any special interest with a stronger noun which has overtones (or at least distant memories) of religion. The nouns have a formality usually denied by the adjectives, and this makes us aware of a creator intentionally starting with the weaker word.

The initial terse paragraph, both casual and authoritative, establishes the tone: "Several of the miracles that occurred this year have gone unrecorded." Each of the six "miracles" begins with a date and an almost identical form of presentation, although after two very brief miracles, each new one receives a longer description. The first sets the pattern: "Example: On the morning of January 3, seven women stood in line at a lingerie sale in Palo Alto, California, and by chance each of these women bore the Christian name Emily." While some readers will think more of coincidence than of miracles, others will stress the way, perhaps arbitrarily, that the "author" (for the narrator never receives distinguishing traits or past experiences and never explicitly refers to her[?]self) creates and arranges the examples. But the third miracle (dropping "Example") adds a different order of reality.

> On March 30 a lathe operator in a Moroccan mountain village dreamed that a lemon fell from a tree into his open mouth, causing him to choke and die. He opened his eyes, overjoyed at being still alive, and embraced his wife . . . she was dreaming . . that a lemon tree had taken root in her stomach . . . she began to tremble . . . with happiness and intoxication . . her face radiant. What he saw was a mask of happiness so intense it made him fear for his life.

By now, the earlier convincing mimetic realism may seem

to have become completely irrelevant. The "miracles" lie in the power of the creator's imagination and skill. To refuse (or fail) to delight in this exultant artifice would leave the reader incapable of enjoying this story.

Particularly deft in expressing another completely different relation of story-teller to material is the much more extended **"Dolls, Dolls, Dolls, Dolls."** Starting with a long unquoted letter she has received from a friend who was visiting a doll factory in Japan, the narrator then recalls how she herself was given one doll every year until she was ten. She goes on to describe a visit in the suburbs of Paris to "one of the finest archeological museums in Europe" where her daughter insists that the pre-Christian icons might be dolls. The story-teller feels "sick with sudden inexplicable anger" when her husband tries to correct the child, but then immensely relieved when he shrugs, smiles, and says, "'You might be right. Who knows'." The fourth section, corresponding to the final repetition in the title, presents a story in itself as the speaker and her sister share both recollections and a strange forgetfulness about their childhood. These lead the speaker to remember the terrible murder of a little girl, "ten years old, my age" and especially her own horrible fears and attempts to cope with them for the rest of that summer. A battered old doll, Nancy Lynn, "protects" her, although "I knew she was lifeless. . . . Human love, I saw, could not always be relied upon. There would be times when I would have to settle for a kind of parallel love."

To discuss the *oeuvre* of Carol Shields in mid-career would require consideration not only of her 11 books, including novels, stories, poems, and a play, but also of her uncollected reviews. Instead, by focusing upon four stories—especially through extensive quotations—we can see how central to her work is the range of tones rather than of subject matter or of location.
—*Anita Clair Fellman*

In this vivid story, close to a meditation, Shields presents us with nothing that could not be factually or autobiographically true. In this example of an increasingly widespread sub-genre, she achieves a brilliant success, comparable to the best stories of the unheralded master, James McConkey. The work can be considered as memoir, as autobiography, or as fiction. But unlike the stories of McConkey or the gripping monologue *No Place Like Home* by Shane McCabe (the outstanding critical and popular favourite at the 1990 Winnipeg Fringe Festival), **"Dolls"** would be in no way diminished if its facts were no more literally true than those of **"Mrs. Turner"** or of **"Dying for Love."** Shields achieves here a

convincing effect of autobiographic truth in which we never go outside the thoughts and the memories set off in the extremely credible narrator, who might well be the author. We read the story *as if* its events and feelings were true.

To discuss the *oeuvre* of Carol Shields in mid-career would require consideration not only of her 11 books, including novels, stories, poems, and a play, but also of her uncollected reviews. Instead, by focusing upon four stories—especially through extensive quotations—we can see how central to her work is the range of tones rather than of subject matter or of location. We can often hear an effective speaking voice, especially in its needling humour. We always find carefully crafted comments upon characters and their situations, but how often do we consider these apart from our awareness of their construction? When her command of various tones results in our immediate assent, we will often subsequently find how our noticing the artifice increases the vividness and the resonance of the scene. Readers may well differ in deciding whether the word "miracle" should apply to extreme coincidence or to the comeback of a losing player or to the creation suddenly bursting out from unpromising material. But we should all share the delight, as we read, when, contrasting the initial description of Mrs. Turner's attire, we discover the exquisite tact of the final sentence in the story: "Oh, what a sight is Mrs. Turner cutting her grass, and how, like an ornament, she shines."

Running as sub-texts through this essay have been the varying relations of reader-response theory to the narrator and to the author. More overt have been the relations of the implied author (sometimes the "I") to the characters, the ideas they embody or express, and the events of the stories. Some of Shields' more intriguing resonances come if we now attend consciously to a sequence of relations leading from those internal ones we have discussed to those of the work to the reader. In **"Mrs. Turner,"** for example, as we have seen, the reader is engaged from the first lines in a wide variety of ways. But the reader's retrospective engagement will prove quite unlike his/her initial response. At first, most of us may well share the views of the teen-age girls, the selfish ecologically minded neighbours, or the poem about Mrs. Turner—however little we may identify with those characters in other respects. By the end of the story, most of us will agree that Mrs. Turner is an ornament, for Shields has transformed this initially unattractive character through a final vision without mockery or condescension.

Some will not want to stop at this closure. Isn't the poet, especially, treated with mockery and condescension? However important or unimportant one feels one's answer is to this last question, readers of Carol Shields may suspect that she is—or was—prepared to write other stories about these other characters she has created—so that in the vision of the whole, mockery and condescension give way to compassion and celebration.

Isobel Armstrong (review date 3 January 1991)

SOURCE: "Designs for Living," in *Times Literary Supplement,* No. 4587, January 3, 1991, p. 21.

[*In the following review of the expanded edition of* Happenstance, *Armstrong discusses the significance of daily events in the lives of the two characters.*]

The two novellas between the covers of ***Happenstance*** are arranged so that which story you read first is a matter of chance. Whichever end of the book you start with will actually be a beginning. The stories are not arranged as a sequence, but read from front to back and from back to front of the book, so that their endings converge in the middle, printed upside down to one another. Likewise, the histories of Jack Bowman and his wife, Brenda, *nouveau* middle-class Americans from middle America, both in their forties, converge at O'Hare Airport, Chicago, after they have been away from one another for a week.

Domestic rules, like the form of the stories, have been inverted; Brenda has been at a craft conference in Philadelphia, winning recognition ("*Second Coming* receives Honourable Mention", a local newspaper announces of her apocalyptically named quilt) and surviving, among other experiences, a naked couple *in flagrante delicto,* who have usurped her hotel room. Her husband, a historian with an ebbing belief in his work, is involved in a more sombre black comedy of bewildered domesticity. He is left with two awkward adolescent children, a friend's broken marriage and a neighbour's suicide.

There is no suggestion that one novella, husband's or wife's, takes precedence over the other. Indeed, this is a way of rewriting hierarchical narrative, just as the form itself points to a renegotiation of the marriage relationship. But the novel is not a post-modern experiment in open-endedness. Rather the reverse. Like an orderly quilt pattern, the narrative time of the two stories comes together neatly, edge to edge. With brilliant formal skill, each story is made to act as figure and ground to the other. As all good patterns do, the design of the narrative produces a number of relationships simultaneously. The stories cleave together, expanding in one tale what is barely mentioned in the other—Brenda's earlier estrangement from Jack, Jack's loving exasperation with his father—turning the same event inside out and back to front.

The same control, working with energetic brio, organizes dazzling contrasts of hilariousness and subtlety, high com-

edy and sombre complexity. Jack endures the blow-drying of his snow-soaked boxer shorts by a lascivious secretary—who really loves him. A potentially light-hearted affair modulates into seriousness when Brenda learns that her friend's daughter, at eighteen, simply disappeared.

By the end of their stories Jack and Brenda have changed places. Jack exchanges the grand narrative of "History" and truth for smaller dreams and fictions and the unrecorded details which slip out of the reach of documentation. Brenda's world grows larger as she discovers, in parallel with her growing power as a designer, the richness and design of her own life. She begins to acknowledge "the shiver of history" as Jack begins to doubt it. Each constructs a new pattern.

But it is a pattern which is also a patchwork: part of the exuberance of the book comes from the way trivial scraps of experience are used to make and change the pattern of lives, particularly the detritus of the fast-food culture of Reaganite America—lifestyle columns, cooking articles, gossip features, women's magazines, reviews, beauty tips, fake events, reportage. The characters are comically exposed to its coercive banality. Brenda, still escaping from pink bathrooms and matching towels, reads with wonder about a strawberry rinse to nourish pubic hair, and catches herself regretting that she missed out on a televised love-in in the 1960s. Jack is haunted by a magazine article about men's inability to make close friendships and exasperated by his father's library of popular psychology—*Take Charge of Your Life, Living Adventurously*—which, movingly, does actually allow his father to change a little. And a mean newspaper review causes a suicide. Trivia *counts.*

Both husband and wife say "I love you" to someone else, meaning it, and yet both confirm the marriage. They choose, and the novel is about choice. That is why it does not point towards post-modern lack of closure despite the innovative symmetry of its form. But is does explore the complexity of choice. Jack, giving up his book on Native American society and the theories which almost historicize him out of existence, still wonders, from his post-Watergate, post-Vietnam context, how far his life was made by "those curious mid-fifties, the sunny optionless Eisenhower days". Brenda, seeing that our stories can have more than one ending, sees also that she has chosen *not* to do things.

The double structure of the narrative actually achieves a genuinely intra-subjective novel, where two mutually independent subjects exist, not the solipsist modern subject and its distant objects. But choice does not guarantee control: happenstance asserts itself; a lost eighteen-year-old and the presence of a neighbour's brain-damaged child make that clear.

Happenstance has been at work in the back-to-front publication of Carol Shields's work in England. Her most recent work, another innovative novel, **Mary Swann** (1987, reviewed in the *TLS* of November 16, 1990), was published here last year. The two novellas under review were first published in Canada in 1980 and 1982. Happenstance is also likely to identify her as a novelist of the school of Margaret Atwood. But, like her characters, she has constructed her work with the authentic independence of an important writer.

D. O. Spettigue (review date Autumn 1991)

SOURCE: "Impressions," in *Canadian Literature,* No. 130, Autumn, 1991, pp. 149-50.

[*In the following review of* The Orange Fish, *Spettigue compares Shields' writing with the work of Alice Munro.*]

Twelve stories in the post-post fashion. They begin casually, they wander about, sometimes they have little story line, perhaps no closure. They have theme, though; they have, usually, a consistent point of view. Carol Shields is a critic, is a novelist, is an excellent writer of short stories; she knows how these things work. She must remind her readers of Alice Munro.

Not that you would confuse Shields and Munro, though the worlds they draw many of their subjects from are often the same: the professional maze, with its own rules for survival; the domestic scene, banal but viewed in an odd light; the perpetual, depressing puzzle of the generations—**"Family Secrets"** is a title for either author. But though they both deliver the knockout blow concealed in casualness, Shields is clearer, crisper—devastating but perhaps not quite so devastating as the more diffuse Munro.

The title story, initially one that seems an unlikely choice, insinuates its significance, but you know it's there: that momentary flash of numinousness in the dull disorder of existence. The inadequacy of the response. Bulwarking a collapsing marriage, the couple in **"The Orange Fish"** buy a print of a fish, which briefly gives their lives a focus and a lift. Almost immediately a fish cult develops; they attend meetings and find themselves extolling the fish. The fish appears on pins and t-shirts, it is everywhere, it begins to die.

Parodic. You think, this writer's cleverness cannot merely mimic, it must parody the forms it exploits. So in **"Today Is the Day"** the annual ritual of planting brings the village women briefly back to an earlier language, an earlier community where both the few words and the silence are fertile, "weaving a stratagem of potent suggestion overlain by a wily, votive grammar of sign and silence."

There is always something wistful in those luminous moments. No transcendence is claimed, but only a brief and unexpected excitement, a glimpse of possibilities, of colour. In **"Collision"** the East-Bloc documentary-film maker, Martä, shares for a few heightened moments the umbrella of the American Brownstone, consultant on tourist entertainments. Nothing more. The bright moment will not change their lives, nor do they even speak—they have no common language. Two ships that pass in the rushhour, to speak in metaphor as, we are told, "more and more we *must* do." More and more too, the narrator tells us, we acknowledge the world's activity as the accumulating of biographical minutiae. Life is not action, not conflict, but the endless recording of trivia. Is Shields saying, We write therefore we are? Perhaps not even write, but file. In the age of archives, of self-awareness, self-analysis, what else is there?

Martä's encounter with Brownstone is one of the non-events that overflow the silent record, a significance only within the life because that is all there is, brightness that does nothing, goes nowhere. The gap it fills is not so much a need as an inevitability. In the beginning was the biographer.

These are, as the narrator indicates, stories of metaphor; they are impressionistic, catching spots of time as the painter might catch spots of light. In **"Fuel for the Fire"** the widowed father brings loads of scrap lumber, anything that will burn, including, finally, bowling pins; and the daughter-narrator draws her metaphorical conclusions:

> the sight of burning fires, like right now, this minute, how economical it is, how it eats up everything we give it, everything we have to offer.

As the father's other interest is food, both metaphors inform the conclusion.

There are conclusions, tentative ones of course. Again as in Munro, there is much comment, and more than in Munro much impressionistic speculation on the wry vagaries of life. Increasingly in these post-moderns the impossibility of communication, the betrayals of personal relations, the unforgivingness of time, add up to the futility of life, the uncertainty of everything but death. These "real" worlds conceal the others where the bright moments flash and fade. Where communication fails in silence, so silence can be momentary communication, as the narrator finds after she and her husband have been unscrambling road signs, "the real death of words."

As in Munro's "underground caves paved with kitchen linoleum," these are the "true" world—the world of feeling and fiction—underlying all the realities, and the pretences that have to pass for realities just to keep us going. Like

Munro, Shields gets it brightly, deceptively, disturbingly right.

Rita Donovan (review date April 1992)

SOURCE: "A Fine Romance," in *Books in Canada,* Vol. XXI, No. 3, April, 1992, p. 40.

[*In the following review of* The Republic of Love, *Donovan argues that Shields has taken the typical romance and infused it with depth and realism.*]

Carol Shields a romance writer? In her latest novel, **The Republic of Love,** Shields takes the reader on a foray into the cold landscape of the late 20th century. Her two protagonists, Fay McLeod and Tom Avery, personably document their respective states: Fay, a recently involved, now single folklorist who is studying the mermaid myth, and Tom, a lonely late-night talk-show host with three failed marriages under his belt. That they will meet and fall in love is inevitable; it is the stuff of romance novels. And, indeed, it is one of the devices Shields purposely adopts from the genre.

Technically, the book is crisply divided into parallel chapters alternating the narratives of Fay and Tom. Their stories progress separately, although minor characters familiar to them both pass from narrative to narrative. Roughly halfway through the book, Fay and Tom meet and fall immediately in love. Interestingly, although their lives now interweave, the narrative threads of their stories are kept separate, presumably to allow the reader to assess Fay through Tom's eyes and Tom through Fay's. This very successfully gives Shields ample room for irony.

Because of these structural decisions, the essential isolation of each character is underlined. Indeed, loneliness is one of the predominant themes in the novel. It contrasts with the longing for independence that several characters exhibit (Fay's father among them), and Shields also explores this duality—the consolatory woman figure and the impenetrable female, the essentially contradictory nature of the psyche—in describing Fay's mermaid research.

We see the loneliness. Tom is afraid of Friday nights. Fay is afraid to go home to an empty apartment. As Tom notes: "Misery does not love company. The lonely can do very little for each other. Emptiness does not serve emptiness."

Is romance possible under these circumstances? And what is romance, anyway? And what is love? These questions plague the citizens of **The Republic of Love,** and they are the basis for what surrounds the bare-boned story of Tom and Fay. No one seems to have definitive answers to these simple questions (simple if you live in a romance novel). Fay asks, "What does it mean to be a romantic in the last decade of the twentieth century?" Her brother Clyde answers "To believe anything can happen to us." Later Fay's father says almost the same thing: "You never know what's going to happen. What's just around the corner." This nicely complements a thought Tom has as he ponders that, despite his problems, "he wakes up most mornings believing that he is about to enter a period of good fortune."

Is this *naïveté*? As if Fay's and Tom's own existences aren't enough to convince them, all around they witness the wreckage of love, the compromises that have been made. Fay looks to her parents' settled life and finds it suffocating (yet, ironically, will later be distraught when her father leaves her mother). Fay says, "No one should settle for being half-happy." And her friend answers, "Really?" As Fay later observes: "The lives of others baffle her, especially the lives of couples." Yet despite the evidence of disastrous manifestations of love, Fay and Tom *believe.* This is underlined in Fay's folklore studies, for example, when she describes folk credulity: "Believers . . . develop an aptitude for belief, a willed innocence."

This optimism is certainly part of most "romances," and Fay and Tom fall as completely in love as any couple in a romance novel. The *naïveté* seems somehow necessary in order for the couple to begin to love at all. Both characters talk about being "alive" when love comes to them. Fay speaks of "the ballooning sensation of being intensely alive," and Tom notes: "So this is what it feels like. To be coming awake."

They try their best to live up to the old-fashioned versions of love. But Fay and Tom don't live on the pages of a Harlequin romance, and Fay observes that while everyone seems to be searching for love, love itself is not taken seriously: "It's not respected." And the world intrudes, as it always will.

Theirs, then, must be an "open-eyed" romanticism; they must choose to love, just as they must choose to believe. Contrary to the cynical world around them, and contrary also to the naïve vision in old movies and romance novels, they must create a life that does not deny dead marriages and dying friends, while also not denying the liberating "coming to life" that their love inspires.

Without these qualifications, Shields would have given us a charming tale with little direct bearing on the times. But Fay and Tom earn their right to love. They know the stakes, and they know the odds. So when Shields allows them to honeymoon in Tom's apartment and the storm outside "maroons" them there, the reader feels that they are entitled to their brief stay on their "island," before the world lays claim to them.

Carol Shields has created a sophisticated story in the romance of Fay and Tom. And the "happy ending," so traditional to the romance novel, is here refurbished, updated, and—most happily—earned.

Susan Elizabeth Sweeney (essay date 1993)

SOURCE: "Formal Strategies in a Female Narrative Tradition: The Case of *Swann: A Mystery*," in *Anxious Power: Reading, Writing, and Ambivalence in Narrative by Women*, State University of New York Press, 1993, pp. 19-32.

[*In the following essay, Sweeney argues that in* Swann, *Shields focuses on the meaning and ambiguity of feminist literature.*]

My department, like many others, is debating how best to incorporate minority authors, marginalized texts, and unconventional genres into the canon—into the canon, that is, which we teach our sophomore majors in a two-semester course entitled "Traditions of English Literature." At a departmental discussion on whether to include Adrienne Rich in this syllabus, one of my colleagues, a narrative theorist and stalwart formalist, said he would gladly teach Rich's poetry in the context of her feminism—but only if he was persuaded that her feminism was expressed in the *form* as well as the *content* of her poetry.

I, too, am a formalist. I am also a feminist. I believe that women *do* write differently than men—because, as women, they respond differently to a literary tradition which is primarily composed by men, for men, and of men, and in which women appear often as muses and mistresses but seldom as readers or writers. Such a masculine tradition, Sandra Gilbert and Susan Gubar explain, prompts intensely divided emotions in a female writer: "feelings of alienation from male predecessors coupled with her need for sisterly precursors and successors . . . her need for a female audience together with her fear of the antagonism of male readers, her culturally conditioned timidity about self-dramatization, her dread of the patriarchal authority of art, her anxiety about the impropriety of female invention."·More important, a female writer may feel ambivalent toward language itself, toward the very acts of reading and writing—since they are both the measure of her powerlessness and the means for her to articulate it. And this ambivalence is expressed in the form and content of the narratives she writes.

Because, as Lawrence Lipking says, "a woman's poetics must begin . . . with a fact that few male theorists have ever had to confront: the possibility of never having been empowered to speak," feminist theorists must first give a name to the silence surrounding female art. In "Toward a Feminist

Poetics," Elaine Showalter coins the term "gynocritics" for such a poetics of women's writing. Josephine Donovan warns that "a women's poetics" should reflect "a woman-centered epistemology" and an awareness of the diversity of women's experiences; Jane Marcus describes a "feminist aesthetic" as the "obstinacy and slyness" with which women write for their silenced sisters, and overcome their own anxious authorship, "by keeping a hand in both worlds"—one of masculine discourse, the other of everyday feminine tasks. Rachel Blau DuPlessis defines a "female aesthetic" more precisely as "the production of formal, epistemological, and thematic strategies by members of the group Woman, strategies born in struggle with much of already existing culture." In women's writing, DuPlessis explains, these strategies include speaking in multiple voices, inviting the reader's participation, "not seeking the authority of the writer," and articulating a "both/and vision born of shifts, contraries, negations, contradictions". Susan Lanser calls for a feminist narratology which would address the surface and the subtext of such feminine texts, as well as the narrative frame that binds them. Reading an anonymous feminine text, Lanser points out that "beneath the 'feminine' voice of self-effacement and emotionality . . . lies the 'masculine' voice of authority that the writer cannot inscribe openly."

Many feminist theorists, then, have helped to articulate a female aesthetic. I hope to extend their work by describing a female narrative poetics: specific narrative strategies with which women represent their ambivalence toward reading and writing. Many feminist critics have helped to reconstruct a female literary history which demonstrates a female aesthetic; I hope to extend their work by showing how these narrative strategies define a distinctly female narrative tradition.

Any female narrative poetics must take into account Virginia Woolf's artful essay *A Room of One's Own,* which began as a lecture on "women and fiction." Woolf explains that the female writer usually produces novels, not poems or plays—because for centuries she could observe and record human nature only in the sitting-room, and because "the novel alone was young enough to be soft in her hands." In her novels, moreover, she developed a "natural, shapely sentence proper for her own use," which Woolf elsewhere calls the "psychological sentence of the feminine gender": "capable of stretching to the extreme, of suspending the frailest particles, of enveloping the vaguest shapes." Men sometimes use such sentences, of course; but women design them specifically to "descend to the depths and investigate the crannies" of female consciousness. The feminine sentence—which expresses the most tenuous and shadowy extremes—shows how women manipulate narrative form in order to represent anxious power.

A Room of One's Own also imagines a female literary history, which ranges from "a lost novelist, a suppressed poet . . . some mute and inglorious Jane Austen" to a series of women named "Mary": Mary Beton, Mary Seton, and finally Mary Carmichael, an experimental novelist like Woolf herself. In order to delineate the formal characteristics of a female narrative tradition, I would like to cite another Mary: Mary Swann, the shadowy heroine of *Swann: A Mystery,* Carol Shields' satirical novel about the posthumous discovery of a female writer. If the name "Mary" evokes women's common experiences, then "Swann"—with its Proustian allusion—suggests that which is lost or forgotten. Indeed, Shields uses her fictitious "suppressed poet" to reconstruct yet another female literary history—one that includes Emily Dickinson, to whom Swann is compared; Pearl Buck and Edna Ferber, her favorite writers; and a contemporary feminist critic, who discovers her. Like Woolf in *A Room of One's Own,* then, Shields describes women's ambivalence toward language in a fictive history of female reading and writing.

The content of *Swann* (what narrative theorists would call its *story*) concerns the problems of becoming a female writer and of being included in the literary canon. Mary Swann—already dead before her story begins, like many female writers in women's narratives—was a poor and abused farmer's wife, geographically and culturally isolated in rural Ontario, unschooled, and apparently unversed in any literary tradition except for the two popular romances she borrowed each week from her town library. The two most significant facts of Swann's life are that it ended when her husband shot her, dismembered her body, and then shot himself; and that she left behind 125 haunting poems whose compression, resonance, and use of common meter recall Emily Dickinson. Fifteen years after her death, when a young feminist scholar discovers her only book (a cheap pamphlet entitled *Swann's Songs*), Swann suddenly becomes a literary phenomenon—the inspiration for MLA sessions, *PMLA* essays, a Mary Swann Memorial Room in her hometown, even a Swann Symposium. Yet she remains elusive. Her biographer can find no useful information on her life; no two readers can agree on a poem's meaning; and even the few proofs of her existence (her photograph, her pen, her notebook, her unpublished love poems, the remaining copies of *Swann's Songs*) mysteriously disappear. The content of Shields' novel, then, expresses her anxiety about the production and interpretation of women's writing by recounting the life and posthumous reception of a female writer.

More important, the narrative form of *Swann* (what narrative theorists would call its *discourse*) reflects this same anxiety. In *Swann,* Shields uses formal strategies that reveal her ambivalence toward reading and writing: interrupted, indirect, or dialogic narration; mixed genres and embedded texts (in particular, feminine texts which are absent or illegible); depictions of a feminine text's composition, publication, and interpretation; and an ambiguous ending.

The experimental narration of the novel's five sections reveals its ambivalence toward narrative authority. Each of the first four sections focuses on a different character (Sarah Maloney the feminist scholar, Morton Jimroy the biographer, Rose Hindmarch the town librarian, and Frederic Cruzzi the publisher of *Swann's Songs*); and each is narrated from a different point of view, organized in a different format, and written in a different prose style. The narration of the fifth section is even more playfully self-reflexive: it takes the form of an imaginary screenplay, "The Swann Symposium," in which characters' voices become audible and inaudible in a cacophony of "random phrases", "fragments of conversation," "overlapping voices", and interrupted or misunderstood speech:

> GINGER PONYTAIL: . . . splitting headache—
> CRINKLED FOREHEAD: . . . was a trifle
> disturbed by his remarks regarding—
> BIRDLADY: . . . blatantly sexist—
> GREEN TWEED SUIT: Slash, slash—
> GINGER PONYTAIL: Jesus, the smoke in here's
> thick enough to—
> WOMAN IN PALE SUEDE BOOTS: . . . and the
> noise—
> SILVER CUFFLINKS: . . . sorry, I didn't catch—

The extravagant multiplicity of narrative voices in the five sections of *Swann*—whether it takes the form of interrupted discourse, free indirect discourse, or dialogic narration—reflects, I think, a peculiarly feminine ambivalence toward narrative authority. It is as if Shields divides responsibility for telling her story among as many narrators as possible. And yet such attempts to disguise or diffuse narrative authority actually draw attention to her own authorial power. This ambivalence is clearly articulated in the "Director's Note" that introduces the screenplay:

> *The Swann Symposium* is a film lasting approximately 120 minutes. The main characters . . . are fictional creations, as is the tragic Mary Swann, *poète naïve,* of rural Ontario. The film may be described (for distribution purposes) as a thriller. A subtext focuses on the more subtle thefts and acts of cannibalism that tempt and mystify the main characters. The director hopes to remain unobtrusive throughout, allowing dialogue and visual effects (and not private passions) to carry the weight of the narrative.

This self-reflexive passage reveals Shields' conflicting desires: "to remain unobtrusive throughout" the novel, on the one hand; and obtrusively to assert her authority as its "director," on the other.

Swann reveals Shields' ambivalence not only about narrative authority, but about narrative itself. It combines various forms of narrative (autobiography, biography, epistolary novel, romance, ghost story, detective story, university novel) as well as other genres (poetry and drama). And it not only alludes to other texts that remain unwritten, such as Rose's letter to Morton Jimroy; it even embeds some of them, such as Frederic Cruzzi's "(Unwritten) One-Sentence Autobiography," "Short Untranscribed History of the Peregrine Press," and "Unwritten Account of the Fifteenth of December, 1965." *Swann* presents itself, then, as many different narrative and non-narrative texts—but also as a text that cannot be written or, according to Kristeva's definition of the feminine, as "that which is not represented, that which is unspoken, that which is left out."

In addition to mixing narrators, genres, and embedded texts, then, Shields reflects her ambivalence toward reading and writing by representing texts—in particular, feminine texts like Swann's poems—as "left out," illegible, blank, or altogether absent. Swann's body of work is dismembered, like her physical body, during the course of the narrative. Her love poems, for example, are hidden beneath her kitchen linoleum, only to be appropriated by one scholar, stolen by another, and never published at all. Her other poems, published posthumously in *Swann's Songs,* are written in an ink called "washable blue"—which, when the poems are accidentally soaked, results in "a pale swimmy smudge, subtly shaded, like a miniature pond floating on a white field. Two or three such smudges and a written page became opaque and indecipherable, like a Japanese water-colour." The novel thus represents the feminine text—Swann's manuscript—as an indecipherable image, a blank page, a missing sign.

Not surprisingly, Swann's inscrutable poems resist interpretation and confound her readers. Consider one poem whose meaning becomes less clear each time it is quoted:

> Blood pronounces my name,
> Blisters the day with shame,
> Spends what little I own,
> Robbing the hour, rubbing the bone.

In a series of self-reflexive passages (what Gerald Prince would call "reading interludes"), several characters (whom Naomi Schor would call "interpretants") try to make sense of this embedded feminine text. Sarah Maloney, the feminist scholar, reads it as a poem about "the inescapable perseverance of blood ties, particularly those between mothers and daughters." Morton Jimroy, the biographer, thinks it describes "the eating of the Godhead," "a metaphysical covenant with an inexplicable universe." Rose Hindmarch, the town librarian, thinks it concerns menstruation. And Frederic Cruzzi, the publisher, remembers deciphering the poem's almost illegible manuscript with his wife on the day of Swann's death:

The last poem, and the most severely damaged, began: "Blood pronounces my name." Or was it "Blood renounces my name"? The second line could be read in either of two ways: "Brightens the day with shame," or "Blisters the day with shame." They decided on *blisters.* The third line, "Spends what little I own," might just as easily be transcribed, "Bends what little I own," but they wrote *Spends* because—though they didn't say so—they liked it better.

What Mary Swann wrote on the page—let alone what she meant to say—remains obscure. *Swann* also represents ambivalence toward reading and writing, then, in the fate of this embedded feminine text, whose transcription, editing, and publication is so unreliable, and whose readers' interpretations are so hopelessly contradictory.

When Swann's poems literally disappear at the end of the novel, it becomes clear that such feminine texts must be read differently than masculine texts. The last scene of "The Swann Symposium" shows a meeting room in a hotel, "but there is no one at the lectern and no one, seemingly, in charge. People are seated in a sort of circle, speaking out, offering up remembered lines of poetry, laboriously reassembling one of Mary Swann's poems." The novel's ending describes the effects of reading the feminine text in this new way:

The faces of the actors have been subtly transformed. They are seen joined in a ceremonial act of reconstruction, perhaps even an act of creation. There need be no suggestion that any one of them will become less selfish in the future, less cranky, less consumed with thoughts of tenure and academic glory, but each of them has, for the moment at least, transcended personal concerns.

The ending suggests, then, that reading a feminine text appropriately—unlike the earlier solipsistic interpretations of "Blood Pronounces My Name"—empowers readers by allowing them to transcend "personal concerns" and unite with others. Indeed, this collaborative reconstruction resembles the "intersubjective encounter" that Patrocinio Schweickart describes in her feminist theory of reading.

Yet the novel also seems ambivalent about the validity of such feminist reading. Shields embeds this scene of collaboration within a series of unreliable narrative frames: Swann's absent text is reconstructed by a group of academics, who are played by hypothetical actors in a screenplay, which is produced only in the reader's imagination. More important, the text that results from this reading remains ambiguous. The poem that these readers reconstruct, line by line, is reprinted on the novel's last page under the heading: "LOST

THINGS By Mary Swann." It comments ironically on Swann's life, her art, and the elusive feminine text:

> . . . As though the lost things have withdrawn
> Into themselves, books returned
> To paper or wood or thought,
> Coins and spoons to simple ores,
> Lustreless and without history,
> Waiting out of sight
>
> And becoming part of a larger loss
> Without a name
> Or definition or form
> Not unlike what touches us
> In moments of shame.

This meditation on "lost things" reflects the novel's sense of women's writing and provides a satisfying closure. Yet it is also an appropriately ambiguous ending: because the poem appears only as it was reconstructed, it may not be the poem Swann wrote. The ending of *Swann,* then, leaves us with another embedded feminine text that remains both absent and present—thus raising additional questions about its interpretation and authorship, and about the nature of female reading and writing.

Carol Shields' self-reflexive narrative strategies suggest her ambivalence toward appropriating the power of language. Those same strategies recur throughout the history of women's narrative: disguised or deferred narrative authority (what in this volume Christine Moneera Laennec, after Christine de Pizan, calls "writing-without-having-written"); dialogic or interrupted narration (what in this volume Patricia Hannon calls "writing by addition" in seventeenth-century French fairy tales); mixed genres, modes of discourse, and *mises en abyme*; narrative codes, secrets, and subtexts (what Bonnie TuSmith describes, in this volume, as Maxine Hong Kingston's "strategy of ambiguity"); self-reflexive accounts of the composition, publication, or interpretation of a feminine text (such as the mother's story in Caroline Lee Hentz' *Ernest Linwood* or the handmaid's tale in Margaret Atwood's eponymous novel); descriptions of the dismemberment of female writing; embedded feminine texts that are both legible and illegible (such as the bewildering pattern in Gilman's "The Yellow Wallpaper," the white bedsheet in Dinesen's "The Blank Page," or the ghostly letters in Wharton's "Pomegranate Seed"); and unresolved or ambiguous endings. The formal strategies that Christine de Pizan, Marie-Catherine d'Aulnoy, Jane Barker, and other early female writers used to express their anxious power thus anticipated the characteristics of contemporary experimental fiction by Toni Morrison, Sandra Cisneros, Angela Carter, Kathy Acker, and others: dialogic narration, cross-genre writing, metafiction, and "writing beyond the ending" (as DuPlessis calls it). Indeed, the recurrence of these formal strategies—

from de Pizan's fifteenth-century prose to Shields' 1987 novel—defines a distinctly female narrative tradition.

This reading of *Swann: A Mystery* not only confirms the existence of a female poetics, but outlines a narrative tradition in which women represent their ambivalence toward reading and writing. It also suggests that a combination of critical approaches (narrative theory, reader-response criticism, and feminist theory) can serve critics as the "asbestos gloves," in Adrienne Rich's phrase, with which to handle the question of woman's language about which feminist theory itself is so ambivalent. Finally, in emphasizing the hidden authority of women's narrative, this reading of *Swann* indicates, as Lanser says, "that the powerless form called 'women's language' is . . . a potentially subversive—hence powerful—tool."

And to return to my colleague's implicit question: yes, the female writer's struggle with the social construction of femininity does shape the *form* as well as the *content* of her writing. In narrative, it has even produced a female tradition of experimental, ambiguous, and self-reflexive narrative strategies—a tradition which is legible to anyone who can be persuaded to read "otherwise" (in Molly Hite's phrase), to heed voices that "never [have] been empowered to speak". That such persuasion remains necessary explains why women are still so anxious about the power of their words.

Gail Pool (review date May 1994)

SOURCE: "Imagination's Invisible Ink," in *Women's Review of Books,* Vol. XI, No. 8, May, 1994, p. 20.

[*In the following review of* Happenstance *and* The Stone Diaries, *Pool argues that while similar in nature and focus, the latter is more complex.*]

You would expect that good books from a country as close to us (in every sense) as Canada would quickly find American covers. Apparently not. It has taken more than a decade for the first US edition of Carol Shields' *Happenstance* to appear, and I suspect we might not have it even now if her latest work, *The Stone Diaries,* had not been short-listed for last year's Booker Prize. Whatever their literary merit, awards are good promotion even for finalists, encouraging publishers to furnish early and out-of-print work. In Shields' case this is all to the good, and I hope we will soon see her earlier novels, *Small Ceremonies* and *The Box Garden.* Her work should be read in its entirety, that entirety hangs together so well.

Shields staked out her fictional territory early in her novel-writing life, and has explored it inventively ever since. Her realm of interest is the chronicling of lives, our efforts to find stories that give them shape and meaning. Underlying her own chronicling of people chronicling lives is the point that no one ever really knows enough. Shields' characters may be professional biographers or ordinary folk trying to make sense of their lives; all confront a picture that is inevitably incomplete. Beyond the mysteries of life (the role of fate or choice), we each have a particular perspective that determines what we see and miss, an individual framework that leads to readings that are sometimes comically, sometimes poignantly wrong. Nor do we readily enter other perspectives: in Shields' world, people misconstrue each other regularly, even if—perhaps especially if—they sleep together nightly.

With her eye on perspective, Shields plays nicely with viewpoints, shifting not only within books but even between them. In *Small Ceremonies,* the central character is biographer Judith Gill; in *The Box Garden,* the protagonist is Judith's sister. The setup offers great potential to enrich both books, but Shields uses it only modestly here, as if trying it out.

In her next two novels, though, she works this construction ingeniously. *Happenstance,* which first appeared in 1980, follows historian Jack Bowman's life over five days when his wife Brenda, a quiltmaker, is away at a handicrafts exhibit; *A Fairly Conventional Woman,* published in 1982, examines the same five days, focusing on Brenda. Together the novels create a vital portrait of a marriage. As the subtitle of this new edition suggests, it is a marriage "in transition." Fittingly, in this volume, the two stories are bound together but open from opposite sides of the book, each upside down to the other.

Jack's story takes place in Chicago, where Shields, now a Winnipeg resident, was born and raised. The Bowmans' suburb is comfortable, a word that applies equally well to Jack. At 43, he has a secure, unpressured research position. Married twenty years, he has two healthy if adolescent children. He meets his good friend Bernie Koltz weekly to discuss such topics as entropy or the death of God. As he sees it, he owes his good fortune to "happenstance," which has "made him into a man without serious impairment or unspeakable losses."

But during Brenda's absence, comfort disappears amidst a slew of comically depicted disasters: Bernie turns up, announcing his wife has left him; a neighbor, an amateur actor, is trashed in a review and attempts suicide; Jack's son has stopped eating; in the background, housekeeping degenerates, the kitchen overflows with gnawed bones, dirty glasses, wadded-up napkins.

Worst of all, Jack confronts a crisis. He learns that a book on the same subject as the one he is writing will soon appear; he may have to drop his project. If truth be told, it would be a relief. Only on chapter six after three years, he can barely face the boring text. "I'm a man who has lost his faith," he says dramatically, posing a bit for this crisis much as he has posed at writing his book.

A philosophizing fellow, Jack has trouble grounding himself in everyday reality. By contrast, there is nowhere else that Brenda lives. So we realize as, during her five days at the conference, she remembers her unmarried mother and unmissed father, and reflects on her years as a housewife and her recent quilting success.

For Brenda, these are heady days. A woman who hasn't traveled alone, she calls room service for the first time in her life. She wins honorable mention for her quilt, is interviewed by a reporter, meets feminists at the conference, is shaken to find her hotel room-mate having sex, gets horribly drunk and sick, meets a man for whom she feels an affinity. Not everything is wonderful, but everything is new.

Shrewdly depicting the same moments as seen by each spouse, Shields reveals different visions of the past as well as different views of the present. In Jack's story, the comedy depends partly on Brenda's forthcoming, continuing presence, which he never doubts. In Brenda's, though her love for Jack is clear, we find her reflecting on her anger, wondering if it means her life has been a mistake. Ruminating guiltily about taking over the guest room for her work, she realizes she deserves it: she is more serious about her work than Jack is about his. This, in view of their history, seems to me the most startling realization of all, one that Jack has yet to come to, though it lies just ahead.

Shields is expert at combining satire and sympathy. Alongside the gaps in Jack and Brenda's comprehension of each other lies the substance of all they share. Canny and unsentimental, this double chronicle captures not just this couple but men's and women's lives and marriages in our time.

If *Happenstance* is ingeniously constructed, it is nonetheless straightforward compared to *The Stone Diaries,* an intricate novel and complex commentary on living and telling lives. Simply described, it is the autobiography of Daisy Goodwill Flett, from her birth in Tyndall, Manitoba, in 1905, to her death in Florida in the nineties. It is very much a woman's story.

Starting with her birth and advancing approximately by decades, Daisy describes how her mother Mercy Stone died when she herself was born; how a neighbor, Clarentine Flett, cared for her and, in the midst of change of life, changed her life, abandoning her husband, Magnus, and taking Daisy to her son Barker in Winnipeg; how at Clarentine's death, Daisy's father, a stone worker, took her to Bloomington, Indiana, where he flourished in business; how she married a handsome alcoholic who fell out a window on their honeymoon; how, feeling swamped by her "tragic" story as orphan and widow, she went to Canada at 31, to visit—and marry—Barker Flett; how she lived as housewife and mother for twenty years, thrived in widowhood writing a gardening column, fell into depression when she was fired; how she moved to Florida and made a comfortable life. The final chapters, unsparing and grimly funny, chronicle her decline and death.

Throughout, Daisy generally refers to herself in the third person, perhaps because she has stationed herself as an observer, perhaps because she feels an absence in herself, an absence of self. Her detailed chronicle includes stories and descriptions alongside commentary about life, men and women, autobiography in general and the one she is writing.

Shields plays intriguingly here with invention and truth. The novel has not only a family tree, easily conceived of as pure invention, but also family photographs, which are sure to give a reader pause: pictures of whom? Daisy's narrative constantly raises the question of veracity. She cannot know what happened at her birth or past her death, though she relates both. And all her wonderful stories—including the ones about events she could never have witnessed.

Consider one of my favorite tales (unfortunately, condensed here): the laconic Magnus Flett, abandoned by Clarentine, misses her intensely. He doesn't understand why she left. Discovering her stash of novels, he reads them; he especially likes *Jane Eyre*.

> It astonished him, how these books were stuffed full of people. Each one was like a little world, populated and furnished. And the way those book people talked! ... Some of the phrases were like poetry, nothing like the way folks really spoke, but nevertheless he pronounced them aloud to himself and committed them to memory, so that if by chance his wife should decide to come home and take up her place once more, he would be ready.

Magnus practices: "O beautiful eyes, O treasured countenance, O fairest of skin."

But Clarentine never comes home. Magnus returns to his homeland, the Orkneys. Years later, Daisy, who never met her father-in-law, visits the Orkneys and discovers he is still alive. At 115, he is famous as the oldest man in the British Isles. But he is still more famous as the man who could recite *Jane Eyre* by heart.

Now I find this story both moving and hilarious. But what is true here? The "facts" are few. Magnus did, for example,

return to the Orkneys. It is interesting to imagine the various routes by which Daisy might have arrived at her tale.

Daisy doesn't hide the fact that her autobiography abounds in distortions and inventions. She warns us often. "The recounting of a life is a cheat," she observes. Daisy, she says,

> is not always reliable when it comes to the details of her life; much of what she has to say is speculative, exaggerated, wildly unlikely. ... Daisy Goodwill's perspective is off. Furthermore, she imposes the voice of the future on the events of the past, causing all manner of wavy distortion. She takes great jumps in time, leaving out important matters. ... Still, hers is the only account there is, written on air, written with imagination's invisible ink.

Daisy knows the power of storytelling: it was by this "primary act of imagination" that she determined to hold onto her life. She is also aware of different perspectives: she records with humor varied explanations of her breakdown, from her new-generation daughter's theory that it was the loss of her job to her friend's assertion that it was sex. And she is aware of her own perspective: her abiding sense of motherlessness and abandonment, the feeling of being "erased from the record of her own existence" (no picture of Daisy appears among her photographs) have influenced the story she tells. So we construct our life stories, the book suggests, seeing or inventing what we need, filling in the picture we cannot truthfully complete.

True or invented, a distinct person emerges from these pages. Her story is a quietly riveting chronicle of an ordinary life, valiant and tedious. If we finish *Happenstance* feeling "Yes, this is a marriage," we finish *The Stone Diaries* feeling "Yes, this is a life."

Mel Gussow (review date 10 May 1995)

SOURCE: "A Celebrator of the Little Things," in *New York Times,* Vol. CXLIV, No. 50057, May 10, 1995, p. B2.

[*In the following review of* The Stone Diaries, *Gussow provides background on the Shields's life and career.*]

The Stone Diaries, which won this year's Pulitzer Prize for fiction, is a rich, panoramic novel in the guise of a biography. As Carol Shields traces the life of Daisy Goodwill, from birth to death, through the 20th century, she creates a family tree and inserts an album of family photographs in the center of the book to underscore the tangibility of her characters.

"When I read biography," she said during an interview, "I always turn to the section of photographs and check the text against the image, again and again, so that when I'm finished reading the book, it opens all by itself to that place."

With the help of her editor, she said, she looked for photos that would reflect her feeling about her invented characters, eclectically gathering them from museums, antique stores and a Parisian postcard market. The last two pages of the photo insert are actually childhood pictures of Ms. Shields's son and four daughters.

At 59, the novelist has five grandchildren; she published her first novel when she was 40. Until then, in very traditional fashion, she brought up her children and managed the household as her husband pursued his career in civil engineering. When she took her first steps as a writer, she said, she felt a certain embarrassment and even guilt: "Sitting in an upstairs bedroom making up stories was not a fit occupation for a grown-up woman." As her confidence grew, so did her sense of storytelling.

Now she writes her novels in her office at the University of Manitoba, in Winnipeg, where she is a professor of English and her husband is dean of the engineering department. Her daughters are the first to read the books when they are finished. Looking back, she said she had no regrets about the long delay in her career. From her perspective, she began writing when she was ready to write.

She was born in Oak Park, Ill., and is a naturalized Canadian with dual citizenship and "a foot on either side of the border." As "a hyphenate," she is in the rare position of being eligible for awards in England, Canada and the United States. In this halcyon year, she has been gathering honors. *The Stone Diaries* was shortlisted for the Booker Prize in Britain, received the Canadian Governor General's Literary Award and won the National Book Critics Circle Award as well as the Pulitzer Prize.

For many people, she may seem like a new writer, but behind *The Stone Diaries* is a body of work including six novels and two collections of short stories and a loyal readership, especially in Canada, where she is accepted as one of its leading authors.

Ms. Shields has also written three plays and was in Toronto for the opening of *Thirteen Hands,* a wistful collage about three generations of bridge players. At the Alumnae Theater, she was greeted as a celebrity, a role she responds to with customary modesty: she is petite, genteel and soft-spoken. After the show, in keeping with the hominess of the work, date squares and Rice Krispie bars were served at a reception.

Although she wrote poems and stories in high school and college, she never really thought she could be a professional writer. For a young woman growing up in the 1950's, she said, such an aspiration was as distant as "wanting to be a movie star." She explained that her parents had encouraged her to study for her teaching license "so I would have something to fall back on, if I were widowed or divorced, or failed to find a husband."

Soon after graduating from college, she married Donald Shields, who is Canadian, and they moved to Toronto. In her spare time, she wrote poetry and published two slim volumes. Years later, with seeming casualness, her husband suggested that she take a night school course in writing, and with equal casualness she enrolled. To fulfill an assignment, she wrote a short story, and the teacher sold it to the Canadian Broadcasting Company, which broadcast it on a short-story series. Ms. Shields, who was packing to go to England with her family for three years, said she was "flabbergasted" at the sudden success.

Later, while studying for a master's degree at the University of Ottawa, she wrote a literary whodunit, which three publishers rejected with encouraging letters. Readers' reports agreed that she was manipulating her characters from a great distance. Because she had been preparing her thesis on Susanna Moodie, a 19th century Canadian writer, she decided to write a novel closer to her life, about a woman who is writing about Susanna Moodie.

Producing two pages a day, it took her nine months: her sixth child. On the day she turned 40, she and her husband were packing again, this time for a year's sabbatical in France, when she learned that the book (*Small Ceremonies*) had been accepted. It was, as she sees it, another case of serendipity. When the novel was published, one of the first letters of congratulation came from Alice Munro, the writer she most admired. Now the two are friends and have equal stature.

Ms. Shields's novels, which take place in the United States as well as Canada, deal with people quietly facing emotional crises. The writing is marked by sophistication and insight into familial and marital relationships. The novels are filled with chance meetings and seemingly random events, coincidences of life that she regards as synchronicity. As with those in Anne Tyler's novels, her characters are people who might otherwise be overlooked.

The protagonist of *Small Ceremonies* says: "I am a watcher. My own life will never be enough for me. It's a congenital condition, my only, only disease in an otherwise lucky life." When the passage was quoted to her, Ms. Shields readily accepted it as the author's voice. It is her role as closely watchful observer that has given her books their intimacy.

While others may think of *The Stone Diaries* as a break-through, for her, the most intricate work was her fifth novel, *Swann,* which deals with academic rivals vying for the life and art of what she calls a "poète naïve of rural Ontario." After that came *The Republic of Love,* a deeply romantic novel in which a Winnipeg man and woman undergo a series of unsatisfying relationships until they finally meet and instantly fall in love. Ms. Shields recently finished writing the screenplay for the film version, which might do for Winnipeg what "Sleepless in Seattle" did for Seattle.

Writing *The Stone Diaries,* she worried that the story was thin on plot. Then she came across a statement from the novelist Patrick White, who said that he never worried about plot, he just wrote about "life going on toward death." "I relaxed into that quotation," said Ms. Shields. "It's always seemed to me that this was the great primordial plot: birth, love, death."

In her novel *Happenstance,* one of the two leading characters is a quilt maker, "a 40-year-old woman who discovers she is an artist, and nothing in her life has prepared her for that knowledge." For Ms. Shields, writing is like quilt making, and the important thing is the creating. "I always feel I'm making something when I write a book, an artifact," she said, "and that's where the pleasure is."

Christine Hamelin (review date January-February 1996)

SOURCE: "Sadness and Light," in *Canadian Forum,* Vol. LXXIV, No. 846, January-February, 1996, pp. 46-7.

[*In the following review of* Coming to Canada, *Hamelin praises Shields's poetry, stating that in it readers hear the same poignant voice of her novels.*]

It is difficult to read Carol Shields' collection of poetry, *Coming to Canada,* without preconceptions; by now, we know her voice well and find ourselves looking for glimmers of Daisy Goodwill and shades of Mary Swann. And in fact the poems in this retrospective—which includes selections from *Others* (1972), *Intersect* (1974) and an earlier volume also entitled *Coming to Canada* (1992), as well as 33 new ones—have the same honest, unpretentious intensity as Shields' best fiction. Shields excels at character and description, and many of the poems are like little novels, tiny scenes held up to the light.

In his introduction, Christopher Levenson expresses surprise that the poems are not "as full of sweetness and light" as he had expected. But since most of them are tinged with an awareness of mortality, of missed opportunities, or a certain anxiety, this comment leaves one wondering if Shields is still a victim of what could be called the L.M. Montgomery Syndrome, where women who write about the domestic realm are often underrated. In fact, the reflective and philosophical bent of a number of the poems dispels the myth that Shields is a "women's writer", fixated on the family, and many of her images reveal a crueler or more bizarre underside of reality than is evident in her novels.

> **The reflective and philosophical bent of a number of the poems [in *Coming to Canada*] dispels the myth that Shields is a "women's writer", fixated on the family, and many of her images reveal a crueler or more bizarre underside of reality than is evident in her novels.**
> —*Christine Hamelin*

Levenson argues that in *Others,* Shields' preoccupation with the family leads to "a sense of stifling coziness", and adds that but for her wit and technical skill, the poems would be "debilitatingly trivial". And yet most of the poems deal with complex and often negative aspects of life. **"The New Mothers"** dispassionately describes a hospital where "egg-bald babies lie" like "insects in cases", crying "tiny metal tunes, / hairpins scratching / sky". Nor does **"Anne at the Symphony"** evoke coziness. Anne, "stilled in ether", permits "an alien clarinet / to scoop out an injury / we can't even imagine." The theory of life transmitted by "vinegar pure" flutes "bleeds like sand / through her faintly / clapping hands". Rather than celebrating "happiness, harmony and order", as Levenson suggests, these poems suggest a sadness and even emptiness behind the reassuring rituals of everyday life.

True, Shields grounds her work in the domestic, but she connects its specific details to larger concerns and sometimes terrifying realities, as in **"A Friend of Ours who Knits"**.

> The mittens that leap
> from her anxious wool annul
> old injuries and rehearse
> *her future tense.*
>
> *Her husband's career is secured*
> in cablestitch, and her children,
> double-ribbed, are
> *safe from disease.*
>
> knit, purl,
> she goes faster and faster,
> increase, decrease,
> now she prevents

storms, earthquakes, world wars.

In the "Coming to Canada" section of the volume, the speaker's voice is relaxed, personal and outward-reaching. The title generates certain expectations: that we will learn about Shields' feelings about immigrating to Canada, and perhaps that we will see ourselves reflected. But these poems deal mostly with Shields' youth in the U.S. They re-create early sensations such as blowing through a blade of grass, or learning to speak ("when language blew up a new balloon / almost every day"), as well as some more frightening aspects of childhood. In one poem, a child touches her dead grandmother's mouth, seeing this act as the first of many terrifying tests in the adult world. In another, a child thinking about religion concludes that "It was better not / To think about / The Holy Ghost".

Shields is at her best when she places personal details in a broader historical or political context, as in her subtle merging of the public and private effects of war in **"The Four Seasons"**. Less strong are the poems where she confronts philosophical issues directly, as in **"I/Myself,"** where she attempts to describe the nature of consciousness by comparing the complicated back of a radio to the inside of her head.

The title poem, **"Coming to Canada"**, juxtaposes a 1932 postcard, sent on the occasion of an aunt's Canadian honeymoon, with the poet's perception of Canada:

> It was cool and quiet there
> with a king and queen
> and people drinking tea
> and being polite and clean
> snow coming down
> *everywhere*

Years later, this clichéd view is displaced when the speaker settles in Canada, which becomes "here and now and home / the place I came to / the place I was from."

When Shields strikes the right balance between the personal and the political, the mundane and the philosophical, her writing is powerful indeed.
—Christine Hamelin

Like many other writers of her generation (one thinks of Margaret Atwood's moving poem about her father in *Morning in the Burned House*), Shields is preoccupied with the themes of the aging and death of parents or relatives. In **"Our Old Aunt Who Is Now in a Retirement Home"**, Auntie, "stewed / in authentic age" and caught "in her closet of brown breath," "lives from tray to tray, / briefly finger-

ing / squares of cake." "The final outrage", the poet discovers, is "not death, / but lingering". There is an unexpected gravity and sadness in many of her later poems, which confront the inevitability of time's passing and the heartbreak of old age through such situations as the selling of the family house, the painful recognition of aging felt at a class reunion or the choked anger of golden-agers on a tour of autumn leaves.

But not all of the new poems are overtly about time. In **"Work"**, which seems haunted by Susanna Moodie on whom Shields wrote her M.A. thesis [*Susanna Moodie: Voice and Vision*], the poet describes a couple stacking wood:

> Afterwards we drank tea
> and noticed how our hands shook
> clumsy as paws
> with the tiny cups,
> as though the shock
> of moving from brutal bark
> to flowered china
> *had been too great.*

Such elegance and control are more the rule than the exception in this deeply human collection of poems. When Shields strikes the right balance between the personal and the political, the mundane and the philosophical, her writing is powerful indeed. Many poems in *Coming to Canada* achieve that balance, and in them one recognizes the voice we have grown accustomed to through reading Shields' novels: a quiet, unpretentious voice speaking important truths.

Eunice Lipton (review date April 1996)

SOURCE: "Smaller than Life," in *Women's Review of Books*, Vol. XIII, No. 7, April, 1996, pp. 17-18.

[*In the following review of* Small Ceremonies *and* The Box Garden, *Lipton compares the protagonists from each novel.*]

Small Ceremonies and *The Box Garden,* Carol Shields' earliest published novels, unfold in Canadian suburbs and cars; they portray the lives of decent people who slowly pull meaning, sometimes wisdom, out of mundane pain and familiar satisfactions. Indeed, the books are like laboratories where Shields peruses the commonplace and discovers her metier. There is nothing in them that is larger than life. There is something, however, that makes *Small Ceremonies* and *The Box Garden* remarkable, particularly for women readers: the protagonist of each book is a woman who writes.

Small Ceremonies was published in Canada in 1976, *The*

Box Garden in 1977. I suspect they were originally intended as one book which didn't coalesce and so was divided into two. The main characters are two sisters who make appearances in both books. *Small Ceremonies* is told in Judith (McNinn) Gill's voice. She is a successful biographer of the unfamous and a wife and mother in her early forties, contentedly married to Martin, a Milton specialist who teaches at a nearby university. Their two children are Richard, nine, and Meredith, sixteen.

Judith is an efficient, decent person who has a professional interest in gossip and is somewhat given to envy. She is principled and correct and her decency elicits our respect. The family leads a steady, predictable life in a house near Toronto. Their friends include academics, one famous writer, graduate students, wives and mothers. There is no plot to speak of. Events unfold in chapters named for the months September through April; Judith's inner self, her musing writer's self, negotiates the days and seasons, assimilating details, references, memories.

The Box Garden is more structured, but so awkwardly that I was continually brushing aside narrative filaments in my attempt to keep Charleen (McNinn) Forrest, the other sister, in focus. She is a poet in her mid-thirties who lives with her fifteen-year-old son Seth in Vancouver. She earns a living at a boring, unremunerative job, editing an academic journal on botany. Charleen is a stubbornly passive, quite nervous person, always fretting and worrying. She lives mostly in her head and maintains a compulsive conversation with her superego. Unlike Judith, she is not a soothing presence. Her boyfriend, Eugene, is an orthodontist—and here Shields surely pushes the commonplace into your face: Can you take it? You can almost see her smiling, daring you. Charleen's friends can't, and it's an indication of an entirely different Charleen that she doesn't give a damn.

The narrative in *The Box Garden* takes Charleen and Eugene to Toronto to attend her mother's marriage. While there she meets her stepfather-to-be, spends time with her sister—they are forced to share their childhood bedroom while their male companions are put to sleep elsewhere—observes, if doesn't quite visit with, her mother. As might be expected, the sisters are different types of writers. Judith is matter-of-fact: "I am putting the finishing touches on Susanna Moodie." No Problem. Charleen is ironic: "'[My poetry is] about the minutiae of existence,' I said with mock solemnity." So self-effacing is Charleen that the reader is caught off guard when she refers to her last three volumes of published poetry.

Each sister describes a desolate childhood. Judith says to a friend, "'Do you know what it was that frightened me most about childhood? . . . That it would never end. . . . It was the terrible, terrible suffocating sameness of it all . . . the awful and relentless monotony.'" Charleen is more specific. When Eugene asks about her mother, "But she must have loved you. You and your sister?" Charleen responds:

> It's hard to explain . . . because she had loved us but with an angry, depriving love which, even after all these years, I don't understand. The lye-bite of her private rancour, her bitter shrivelling scoldings. When she scrubbed our faces it was with a single, hurting swipe. When we fell down and scraped our knees and elbows she said, "that will teach you to watch where you're going."

Judith voices an explanation for their vocations: "My sister Charleen, who is a poet, believes that we two sisters turned to literature out of simple malnutrition. Our own lives just weren't enough. . . . We were underfed, undernourished; we were desperate. So we dug in. And here we are, all these years later, still digging." As Charleen puts it, "My survival was hooked into my quirky, accidental ability to put words into agreeable arrangements. I could even remake my childhood, that great void in which nothing had happened but years and years of shrivelling dependence. I wrote constantly. . . ."

Neither book focuses on the psychological. Self-containment and domesticity set emotional contours. That's life, these books take for granted, all we've got: mothers, fathers, sisters, children, husbands, and lovers-soon-to-become husbands. Neither friends nor professional life figure. This is a world without allure, as if one doesn't even have to make a case for domesticity. Houses are banal, neighborhoods plain, husbands decent, children more or less manageable. There's no noise in these books, no unexpected movements, no smells. Nor is it so chilling that you run to bundle up in wools and flannels, sip hot tea in warm mugs, fall into a trance in front of the fireplace. It's not the acrid sadness of Raymond Carver's stories that makes you want to slit your throat or cry your heart out. No, in *Small Ceremonies* and *The Box Garden,* one accepts what one is given—genteel ordinariness with an occasional quiver of love, accomplishment, solace. Banality is the drear backdrop, the white noise against which Judith and Charleen make biographies and poems. And each in her different way wonders: what is a worthwhile life, why write, how do love and writing go together?

Judith manages better than Charleen. She's more stable and organized, her life more routinized. Charleen is a bit out of it, obsessively fretting as she does, self-described as the "pathetic younger-sister-from-the-west." The eponymous box garden is her metaphor. She plants a box of grass in her house and says, "Anyway grass can put up with almost anything." It's a secret garden that only she knows about. One pictures her lost in thought before the box, the static turned off. She can pretend to dullness, write the poems behind her back even as she publishes one book of poetry after the other to critical acclaim. There's nothing there, she can insist, only grass.

Both sisters sense something is wrong with them. Each uses the words "bravery" and "cowardice" too often. Judith comments about her daughter, "If she were braver she would be beautiful." She tells a friend that as a child, "I was a real coward." Charleen says, "I will never be brave. Never. I don't know what it was—something in my childhood probably—but I was robbed of my courage." And a few pages on: "And I, suffering from a lack of bravery, must expend all my energies preparing for the next test. And the next. And the next." Finally, "My hereditary disease, the McNinn syndrome, has riddled me with cowardice. . . ." What are these women missing in themselves? What would it mean to them to be brave?

Would Judith leave her husband and children, become a writer on her own, take back her family name, have intimate friends and lovers, move out of the suburbs? Would Charleen get rid of her busybody friends, get a better-paying job, tell her mother off? Certainly anger is not in their vocabulary. Judith, upon finding out that a prominent friend has plagiarized her own work, says: "My heart was beating wildly; I could feel it through the heavy quilting of my dressing gown. Anger almost choked me, but in spite of it (or maybe even because of it), I fell instantly asleep. . . ."

I have a feeling that these women's self-containment helps them write. The world hurls by on either side of them. They pull in the bits and pieces that they need. The churning is inside. They are masters at creating distance in their lives. One could say that these two books are about writing and distance, and more particularly about the distance these two different women must establish, insist on establishing, in order to write.

Judith says of her close friend, "Nancy who is my good, my best friend, has never been an intimate." Once, when she is quite ill with flu, her husband Martin out of sympathy—and loneliness—lies down next to her, and she says to herself, "I am obscurely angered that he has violated my bed with his presence." Judith likes distance. She gets at people's secrets in her books, she can invade her subjects' privacy. And they can't touch her. Charleen is unable to make the same separations. She says of herself: "I can never quite believe in the otherness of people's lives. That is, I cannot conceive of their functioning out of my sight." Charleen creates distance through obsessing.

One doesn't end up loving these women—Judith in particular—but the trajectory of their lives is intriguing. They are good people who work hard, who try to figure out the de-

cent way to be, not to hurt people, not to disturb themselves too much, to love quietly, soberly. And to keep on writing.

Diane Turbide (review date 29 September 1997)

SOURCE: "The Masculine Maze," in *Maclean's,* Vol. 110, No. 39, September 29, 1997, pp. 82, 85.

[*In the following review of* Larry's Party, *Turbide writes that once again Shields focuses on characters' self-evaluations although this time from the perspective of an average man.*]

By the end of a sunny Monday earlier this month, Winnipeg novelist Carol Shields had been put through the wringer. She had gingerly made her way through a scraggly hedge and leant against a tree to accommodate a magazine photographer. ("Make sure you show the manicure," she teased him, flashing russet-colored nails. "It's a rare thing.") She had been interviewed twice, once for print and once for TV, fielding questions about her new novel, *Larry's Party.* From her office at the University of Winnipeg, where she is chancellor, she had called ahead to a local Italian restaurant to pre-order a 6 p.m. meal for herself, husband Don and a guest. The dinner would be quick because she had to get to a 7:30 launch at the city's handsome superstore, McNally Robinson. And, oh yes, she had picked up a new green dress before heading home for a late afternoon photo shoot, this one for *People* magazine. Although Shields sailed through it all with a mixture of military precision and good humor, she says it takes its toll. "Just listening to yourself blathering on induces a certain amount of self-loathing," admits the Pulitzer Prize-winning author, 62, who is limiting promotion of her new book to two months. "I simply can't do that for a prolonged period. I have to get home between stops."

Home for the soft-spoken author is a highrise apartment that overlooks the winding Assiniboine River. The spacious, light-filled living room is filled with reminders of some of the 10 works of fiction she has created since her first novel, *Small Ceremonies,* was published in 1976. Over the mantlepiece is a print called "The Orange Fish," which figures in the title story of her 1989 short-story collection. Below the print is a snapshot showing three of her five children (who range in age from 29 to 39) and her six grandchildren; her best-selling 1993 novel, *The Stone Diaries,* contained real-life photos of some of those same family members in Shields's fictional biography of her heroine, Daisy Goodwill.

The Stone Diaries was the book that propelled Shields into the book-selling stratosphere. It appeared on all the major best-seller lists, and won her a sheaf of awards, including the Governor General's Literary Award and the Pulitzer Prize, as well as a Booker nomination. The book sold more than a million English-language copies worldwide, paving the way for reprinting new editions of her previous works. It also made film-makers sit up and take notice: Shields's 1987 book, *Swann: A Mystery,* became a feature film in 1996, and two other adaptations—one of *The Republic of Love* (1992) and another of *The Stone Diaries*—are currently in the works. Winnipeg film-maker Bruce Duggan, one of the producers of *The Republic of Love,* says that Shields's recent fame helped open doors when he went looking for financing for the movie. "When we started we didn't exactly get a thrilled reaction when we'd say it's a love story set in Winnipeg by a Canadian writer," he recalls. "But now, when we say it's a love story by Carol Shields, people are interested."

As Shields unveils *Larry's Party,* readers are more than just interested—they are plunking down $31 to buy the book in huge numbers. In Winnipeg, more than 900 people turned up at the home-town launch for *Larry's Party* on Sept 8, snapping up 350 copies, a record one-day sale for a single title at McNally Robinson. Within four days of the book's official Canadian release on Sept. 13, Random House went back to its printers to supplement its initial run of 50,000 hardcover copies. And all this before Shields had done any interviews with national media outlets. Meanwhile, the book has been selling briskly in Britain since its August launch (although it did not make this year's Booker Prize short-list). And Shields has already concluded the first leg of a 10-city American promotional tour.

It's an axiom of the book industry that women read more fiction than men. But *Larry's Party* may attract more male readers than usual, because Shields has set out to explore "what it's like to be an ordinary, middle-aged guy at the end of the century," as she puts it. The idea germinated with a lunch discussion among Shields's women friends about how the very definition of masculinity has changed dramatically as women's expectations of men have changed. And the story evolved as she canvassed male friends and family about their experience. "Of course," she recalls, "nearly every one of them said, 'But I'm not a typical guy.'" Don Shields, the author's husband of 40 years and the dean of engineering at the University of Manitoba, comments drolly on the curiosity he's encountered about his wife's book: "Every man born between 1948 and 1952 has spoken to me lately."

The novel covers a 20-year span in Larry Weller's life, between ages 26 and 46—"when the bedrock of a life is laid down," says Shields. The author tracks her character through two marriages and divorces, fatherhood, career changes, sexual ecstasy and impotence, illness and fleeting periods of contentment. The book is set during a social era, 1977 to the present, when gender roles have never been more confused. "I wanted to be very careful about not presenting Larry as a buffoon," Shields recalls. "Something has hap-

pened to the male image. You can't turn on the TV without seeing men mocked or portrayed as idiots—the way women were in the 1950s, with all those jokes about the mother-in-law or the lady driver or the dumb secretary."

Larry is not a buffoon, though he may seem inordinately good-natured and almost passive to some readers. Born into a loving but emotionally repressed working-class family, Larry grows up to be a mediocre student; he is also painfully inarticulate and beset by the usual sexual anxieties. He more or less drifts into a job as a floral designer. But a honeymoon visit to England and the famous Hampton Court maze leaves him with a passion for the green-leafed labyrinths, "their teasing treachery and promise of reward." His obsession plays a part in breaking up his first marriage and indirectly leads him to a second wife.

Shields also has a fondness for mazes, and says it was "pure pleasure" to research the arcane details of their history and designs. In a stroke of literary artfulness, Shields uses the maze—how its blind pathways and dead ends force people to retrace their steps, how it offers the hope of finding the one true path—as an extended metaphor for Larry's journey through life. But the cleverness of the device does not reduce the vitality of the characters within it. Larry remains endearing, not because of his eccentric occupation, but because he is so intent on understanding himself. Unsettled at 40, he cannot even take his own suffering too seriously. He cringes at the words "'midlife crisis' or 'male menopause,' those trumped-up diseases of trite and trivial contemporary man."

Larry may seem just another of "those barbecuers, those volunteer firemen, those wearers of muscle shirts" who are boringly predictable. But his life is touched by randomness and luck. Shields insists that her own career is very much the product of chance. "I drifted into writing fiction," she says. "I certainly never set out with a plan for a career path. With five children, I was just too busy." Born and raised in Oak Park, a suburb of Chicago, Shields was an exchange student in England when she met her husband, a Manitoban there on a scholarship. In 1957 they married and moved to Canada, living in several cities before settling in Winnipeg in 1980.

Shields wrote sporadically during most of the 1960s and '70s while she raised one son and four daughters. "I used to have about one hour a day, and my first novels were very short," she recalls. Daughter Catherine, a librarian who collaborated with her mother on a 1995 play, *Fashion Power Guilt and the Charity of Families,* recalls that her mother always wrote. "On long family car trips, she would always be-scribbling in a little notebook, with this abstracted look on her face," she says. "We just thought all Moms did that." Shields's early novels—*Small Ceremonies, The Box Garden, Happen-*

stance and *A Fairly Conventional Woman,* published between 1976 and '82—are gently satirical chronicles of the tensions in middle-class families. While the author continues to mine the same territory, she has become far more stylistically experimental in her recent books.

Shields still works at her writing almost every day, amid her duties as chancellor and her family obligations. She thinks that most novels and movies ignore the pre-eminence of work in peoples' lives. "When I came out of that movie *Four Weddings and a Funeral,* I was in a rage, just furious," she recalls. "Absolutely no one in that film had a job. People's work lives are written out of most novels, too, and considering how much time they spend working, it's curious."

Shields has served on the board of the Canada Council and for many years taught English and creative writing. She professes optimism about the future of fiction in Canada, pointing to the phenomenal amount of attention domestic novels are getting abroad. "Every time I'm in Europe," she says, "interviewers ask me to explain my theory on the explosion of writing in Canada." According to fellow Winnipeg writer Jake MacDonald, Shields takes a personal interest in nurturing younger talent. "Carol and her husband are like the royalty of Winnipeg book circles," he says. "They always make sure that you get invited to dinner, and they're unfailingly genial and gracious."

That generosity of spirit seems to infuse her fictional worlds, too. On balance, the universe of *Larry's Party* is benevolent: terrible things may happen, but there is also the redemption of love and friendship, the consolation of words and memory. People can be blindsided by happiness: Larry recalls standing on a Winnipeg street corner 20 years earlier, possessed by a sudden feeling of well-being. "Love was waiting for him. Transformation. Goodness. Work. Understanding. The enchantment and liberation of words. . . . All he had to do was stand still and allow it to happen."

In fact, while acknowledging that much fiction chronicles the prevalence of evil, Shields believes it is just as interesting to explore why its opposite endures. "I believe in goodness," she says. "I'm amazed by the amount of goodness in the world. And I think that makes me a very unfashionable writer." She notes with humor that even the English language seems to conspire against her. "I had my students get out their dictionaries and thesauruses and look up all the names for happiness and sadness," she recounts. "And do you know, the English language is much richer in the language of despair than joy. There's only a handful of words for happiness, and they tend to sound glib or even silly."

With *Larry's Party,* Carol Shields proves that there is a language for happiness that is original and engaging. And like all her fictional works—replete with the significance of small lives and small ceremonies—it is a resounding confirmation of the mystery of the ordinary.

FURTHER READING

Criticism

Addison, Catherine. "Lost Things." *Canadian Literature,* No. 121 (Summer 1989): 158-60.
    Argues that *Swann* is reflective of Shields herself.

Beaton, Virginia. A review of *A Celibate Season,* by Carol Shields and Blanche Howard. *Books in Canada* XX, No. 8 (November 1991): 51.
    Argues that *A Celibate Season* is well-written and believable.

Beddoes, Julie. "Sweet Nothings." *Books in Canada* 10, No. 5 (May 1981): 31-2.
    Argues that although Shields is successful in developing characters, *Happenstance* lacks a sufficient plot.

Benedict, Elizabeth. "Below the Surface." *Los Angeles Times Book Review* (17 April 1994): 3, 7.
    Favorably reviews *Happenstance, A Fairly Conventional Woman,* and *The Stone Diaries.*

Bessai, Diane. "Poetry from Ottawa." *The Canadian Forum* LV, No. 652 (July 1975): 36-8.
    Reviews *Intersect* and argues that Shields needs more editing of her poetry.

Campbell, Grant. A review of *Swann: A Mystery,* by Carol Shields. *Queen's Quarterly* 96, No. 1 (Spring 1989): 153-55.
    Praises the first half of *Swann* but finds the conclusion disappointing.

Collins, Anne. "Can This Marriage Be Saved—Again?" *Maclean's* 95, No. 42 (18 October 1982): 78.
    Argues that *A Fairly Conventional Woman* adds little to its sequel, *Happenstance.*

Fernández, Sandy M. A review of *Small Ceremonies* and *The Box Garden,* by Carol Shields. *Ms.* VI, No. 4 (January-February 1996): 90-1.
    States that neither *Small Ceremonies* nor *The Box Garden* is as good as *The Stone Diaries.*

Giltrow, Janet. "Strange Attractors." *West Coast Review* 23, No. 3 (Winter 1988): 57-66.
    Examines the creation and transmission of art in *The Orange Fish.*

Gould, Jean. "Our Chaotic World." *Belles Lettres* 7, No. 4 (Summer 1992): 20.

> Compares Shields's *The Republic of Love* to Alice Hoffman's *Turtle Moon.*

Groening, Laura. "Still in the Kitchen: The Art of Carol Shields." *Canadian Forum* LXIX, No. 796 (January-February 1991): 14-17.

> Argues that Shields is not a true feminist.

Helwig, Maggie. "Constructing Ourselves for Others." *The Canadian Forum* LXVII, Nos. 776-777 (February-March 1988): 48-9.

> Praises *Swann* as a daring and exciting novel.

Hill, Douglas. "Intimate Pleasures." *Books in Canada* 14, No. 7 (October 1985): 16-7.

> Argues that in *Various Miracles,* Shields transforms ordinary events into extraordinary stories.

Karlin, Danny. "Mary Swann's Way." *London Review of Books* 12, No. 18 (27 September 1990): 20-1.

> Praises Shields's confident tone and skillful character depictions in *Swann.*

Kemp, Peter. "Conjugal Arrangements." *Times Literary Supplement,* No. 4642 (20 March 1992): 21.

> Argues that Shields's combination of mythical, modern, exhilarating, and melancholy elements in *The Republic of Love* enlivens the love story.

Kietner, Wendy. "No Second Stage." *Canadian Literature,* No. 99 (Winter 1983): 116-19.

> Compares *A Fairly Conventional Woman* to Joan Barfoot's *Dancing in the Dark.*

Klinkenborg, Verlyn. "A Maze Makes Sense from Above." *New York Times Book Review* (7 September 1997): 7.

> Praises *Larry's Party* as an unusual account of a man's life.

Ledger, Brent. "Wild, Wild World." *Maclean's* 102, No. 23 (5 June 1989): 61.

> Argues that in *The Orange Fish,* Shields crafts profound stories out of the banal events of daily life.

Lipman, Elinor. "Making Winnipeg Safe for Mermaids." *New York Times Book Review* (14 March 1992): 14, 16.

> Favorably reviews *The Republic of Love.*

Messud, Claire. "Why So Gloomy?" *New York Times Book Review* (7 January 1996): 12.

> Compares *Small Ceremonies* and *The Box Garden.*

Prosser, David. "Unpunctually Yours." *Books in Canada* XXII, No. 6 (September 1993): 34-5.

> Reviews Shields's play *Thirteen Hands.*

Rubins, Josh. "They All Want a Piece of the Legend." *New York Times Book Review* (6 August 1989): 11.

> Favorably reviews *Various Miracles* but finds fault with *Swann.*

Sigurdson, Norman. "Carol Shields: Raising Everyday Lives to the Level of Art." *Quill & Quire* 53, No 11 (November 1987): 21.

> Argues that *Swann* is successful because it builds on Shields's earlier novels but adds more focus and drama.

Skuce, Joel. "Natural, Physical Simplicity." *Canadian Forum* LXXII, No. 824 (November 1993): 44-5.

> Argues that in *Coming to Canada,* Shields creates fine poetry from common incidences.

Thomas, Clara. "Reassembling Fragments: Susanna Moodie, Carol Shields, and Mary Swann." In *Inside the Poem: Essays and Poems in Honour of Donald Stephens,* edited by W. H.. New, pp. 196-204. Toronto: Oxford University Press, 1992.

> Examines the poetry Shields wrote in *Swann* to serve as the voice for Mary Swann.

Wallace, Bronwen. "Going Swimmingly." *Books in Canada* 18, No. 4 (May 1989): 32.

> States that *The Orange Fish* builds on Shields's earlier collection *Various Miracles.*

Werlock, Abby H. P. "Canadian Identity and Women's Voices: The Fiction of Sandra Birdsell and Carol Shields." In *Canadian Women Writing Fiction,* edited by Mickey Pearlman, pp. 126-41. Jackson: University Press of Mississippi, 1993.

> Compares the presentation of Canadian identity in the work of Sandra Birdsell and Carol Shields.

Whitlock, Gillian. "Fabulous Keys." *Canadian Literature,* No. 110 (Fall 1986): 157-60.

> Reviews *Various Miracles* and compares it to Marian Engel's *The Tattooed Woman.*

Wigston, Nancy. A review of *A Celibate Season,* by Carol Shields and Blanche Howard. *Quill and Quire* 57, No. 11 (November 1991): 18.

> Favorably reviews *A Celibate Season.*

Wilson, Dean. "Problematic Reaches." *Times Literary Supplement,* No. 4572 (16-22 November 1990): 1232.

> Favorably reviews *Swann* but finds the final chapter problematic.

Woodcock, George. "Testing the Boundaries." *Quill & Quire* 59, No. 8 (August 1993): 31.

    Reviews *The Stone Diaries* and praises Shields for her dexterity in handling an extensive plot.

Interview

Welsh-Vickar, Gillian. "A Fairly Unconventional Writer." *Canadian Author and Bookman* 63, No. 2 (Winter 1988): 7.

    Interview in which Shields discusses the themes that interest her as a writer.

Additional coverage of Shields's life and career is contained in the following sources published by Gale: *Contemporary Authors,* Vols. 81-84; *Contemporary Authors New Revision Series,* Vol. 51; and *DISCovering Authors: Canadian Edition.*

☐ Contemporary Literary Criticism

Indexes

Literary Criticism Series
Cumulative Author Index
Cumulative Topic Index
Cumulative Nationality Index
Title Index, Volume 113

How to Use This Index

The main references

Camus, Albert
1913-1960 ...... **CLC 1, 2, 4, 9, 11, 14,**
32, 69; DA; DAB; DAC; DAM DRAM,
MST, NOV; DC2; SSC 9; WLC

list all author entries in the following Gale Literary Criticism series:

BLC = *Black Literature Criticism*
BLCS = *Black Literature Criticism Supplement*
CLC = *Contemporary Literary Criticism*
CLR = *Children's Literature Review*
CMLC = *Classical and Medieval Literature Criticism*
DA = *DISCovering Authors*
DAB = *DISCovering Authors: British*
DAC = *DISCovering Authors: Canadian*
DAM = *DISCovering Authors Modules*
   DRAM = *dramatists;* **MST** = *most-studied*
   authors; **MULT** = *multicultural authors;* **NOV** =
   novelists; **POET** = *poets;* **POP** = *popular/genre*
   writers; **DC** = *Drama Criticism*
HLC = *Hispanic Literature Criticism*
LC = *Literature Criticism from 1400 to 1800*
NCLC = *Nineteenth-Century Literature Criticism*
PC = *Poetry Criticism*
SSC = *Short Story Criticism*
TCLC = *Twentieth-Century Literary Criticism*
WLC = *World Literature Criticism, 1500 to the Present*
WLCS = *World Literature Criticism Supplement*

The cross-references

See also CA 89-92; DLB 72; MTCW

list all author entries in the following Gale biographical and literary sources:

AAYA = *Authors & Artists for Young Adults*
AITN = *Authors in the News*
BEST = *Bestsellers*
BW = *Black Writers*
CA = *Contemporary Authors*
CAAS = *Contemporary Authors Autobiography Series*
CABS = *Contemporary Authors Bibliographical Series*
CANR = *Contemporary Authors New Revision Series*
CAP = *Contemporary Authors Permanent Series*
CDALB = *Concise Dictionary of American Literary Biography*
CDBLB = *Concise Dictionary of British Literary Biography*

DLB = *Dictionary of Literary Biography*
DLBD = *Dictionary of Literary Biography Documentary Series*
DLBY = *Dictionary of Literary Biography Yearbook*
HW = *Hispanic Writers*
JRDA = *Junior DISCovering Authors*
MAICYA = *Major Authors and Illustrators for Children and Young Adults*
MTCW = *Major 20th-Century Writers*
NNAL = *Native North American Literature*
SAAS = *Something about the Author Autobiography Series*
SATA = *Something about the Author*
YABC = *Yesterday's Authors of Books for Children*

Literary Criticism Series
Cumulative Author Index

Annensky, Innokenty (Fyodorovich) 1856-1909
TCLC 14
See also CA 110; 155

Annunzio, Gabriele d'
See D'Annunzio, Gabriele

Anodos
See Coleridge, Mary E(lizabeth)

Anon, Charles Robert
See Pessoa, Fernando (Antonio Nogueira)

Anouilh, Jean (Marie Lucien Pierre) 1910-1987
CLC 1, 3, 8, 13, 40, 50; DAM DRAM; DC 8
See also CA 17-20R; 123; CANR 32; MTCW

Anthony, Florence
See Ai

Anthony, John
See Ciardi, John (Anthony)

Anthony, Peter
See Shaffer, Anthony (Joshua); Shaffer, Peter (Levin)

Anthony, Piers 1934- .... **CLC 35; DAM POP**
See also AAYA 11; CA 21-24R; CANR 28, 56;
DLB 8; MTCW; SAAS 22; SATA 84

Antoine, Marc
See Proust, (Valentin-Louis-George-Eugene-) Marcel

Antoninus, Brother
See Everson, William (Oliver)

Antonioni, Michelangelo 1912- .... **CLC 20**
See also CA 73-76; CANR 45

Antschel, Paul 1920-1970
See Celan, Paul
See also CA 85-88; CANR 33, 61; MTCW

Anwar, Chairil 1922-1949 .... **TCLC 22**
See also CA 121

Apollinaire, Guillaume 1880-1918 **TCLC 3, 8, 51; DAM POET; PC 7**
See also Kostrowitzki, Wilhelm Apollinaris de
See also CA 152

Appelfeld, Aharon 1932- .... **CLC 23, 47**
See also CA 112; 133

Apple, Max (Isaac) 1941- .... **CLC 9, 33**
See also CA 81-84; CANR 19, 54; DLB 130

Appleman, Philip (Dean) 1926- .... **CLC 51**
See also CA 13-16R; CAAS 18; CANR 6, 29, 56

Appleton, Lawrence
See Lovecraft, H(oward) P(hillips)

Apteryx
See Eliot, T(homas) S(tearns)

Apuleius, (Lucius Madaurensis) 125(?)-175(?)
CMLC 1

Aquin, Hubert 1929-1977 .... **CLC 15**
See also CA 105; DLB 53

Aragon, Louis 1897-1982 .. **CLC 3, 22; DAM NOV, POET**
See also CA 69-72; 108; CANR 28; DLB 72;
MTCW

Arany, Janos 1817-1882 .... **NCLC 34**

Arbuthnot, John 1667-1735 .... **LC 1**
See also DLB 101

Archer, Herbert Winslow
See Mencken, H(enry) L(ouis)

Archer, Jeffrey (Howard) 1940- ..... **CLC 28; DAM POP**
See also AAYA 16; BEST 89:3; CA 77-80;
CANR 22, 52; INT CANR-22

Archer, Jules 1915- .... **CLC 12**
See also CA 9-12R; CANR 6, 69; SAAS 5;
SATA 4, 85

Archer, Lee
See Ellison, Harlan (Jay)

Arden, John 1930- **CLC 6, 13, 15; DAM DRAM**

See also CA 13-16R; CAAS 4; CANR 31, 65, 67; DLB 13; MTCW

Arenas, Reinaldo 1943-1990 . **CLC 41; DAM MULT; HLC**
See also CA 124; 128; 133; DLB 145; HW

Arendt, Hannah 1906-1975 .... **CLC 66, 98**
See also CA 17-20R; 61-64; CANR 26, 60;
MTCW

Aretino, Pietro 1492-1556 .... **LC 12**

Arghezi, Tudor .... **CLC 80**
See also Theodorescu, Ion N.

Arguedas, Jose Maria 1911-1969 **CLC 10, 18**
See also CA 89-92; DLB 113; HW

Argueta, Manlio 1936- ....**CLC 31**
See also CA 131; DLB 145; HW

Ariosto, Ludovico 1474-1533 .... **LC 6**

Aristides
See Epstein, Joseph

Aristophanes 450B.C.-385B.C. **CMLC 4; DA; DAB; DAC; DAM DRAM, MST; DC 2; WLCS**
See also DLB 176

Arlt, Roberto (Godofredo Christophersen) 1900-1942 **TCLC 29; DAM MULT; HLC**
See also CA 123; 131; CANR 67; HW

Armah, Ayi Kwei 1939- .. **CLC 5, 33; BLC 1; DAM MULT, POET**
See also BW 1; CA 61-64; CANR 21, 64; DLB 117; MTCW

Armatrading, Joan 1950- .... **CLC 17**
See also CA 114

Arnette, Robert
See Silverberg, Robert

Arnim, Achim von (Ludwig Joachim von Arnim) 1781-1831 ...... **NCLC 5; SSC 29**
See also DLB 90

Arnim, Bettina von 1785-1859 .... **NCLC 38**
See also DLB 90

Arnold, Matthew 1822-1888 **NCLC 6, 29; DA; DAB; DAC; DAM MST, POET; PC 5; WLC**
See also CDBLB 1832-1890; DLB 32, 57

Arnold, Thomas 1795-1842 .... **NCLC 18**
See also DLB 55

Arnow, Harriette (Louisa) Simpson 1908-1986 **CLC 2, 7, 18**
See also CA 9-12R; 118; CANR 14; DLB 6;
MTCW; SATA 42; SATA-Obit 47

Arp, Hans
See Arp, Jean

Arp, Jean 1887-1966 .... **CLC 5**
See also CA 81-84; 25-28R; CANR 42

Arrabal
See Arrabal, Fernando

Arrabal, Fernando 1932- .... **CLC 2, 9, 18, 58**
See also CA 9-12R; CANR 15

Arrick, Fran .... **CLC 30**
See also Gaberman, Judie Angell

Artaud, Antonin (Marie Joseph) 1896-1948
TCLC 3, 36; DAM DRAM
See also CA 104; 149

Arthur, Ruth M(abel) 1905-1979 ...... **CLC 12**
See also CA 9-12R; 85-88; CANR 4; SATA 7, 26

Artsybashev, Mikhail (Petrovich) 1878-1927
TCLC 31

Arundel, Honor (Morfydd) 1919-1973 **CLC 17**
See also CA 21-22; 41-44R; CAP 2; CLR 35;
SATA 4; SATA-Obit 24

Arzner, Dorothy 1897-1979 .... **CLC 98**

Asch, Sholem 1880-1957 .... **TCLC 3**
See also CA 105

Ash, Shalom

See Asch, Sholem

Ashbery, John (Lawrence) 1927- **CLC 2, 3, 4, 6, 9, 13, 15, 25, 41, 77; DAM POET**
See also CA 5-8R; CANR 9, 37, 66; DLB 5, 165; DLBY 81; INT CANR-9; MTCW

Ashdown, Clifford
See Freeman, R(ichard) Austin

Ashe, Gordon
See Creasey, John

Ashton-Warner, Sylvia (Constance) 1908-1984
CLC 19
See also CA 69-72; 112; CANR 29; MTCW

Asimov, Isaac 1920-1992 **CLC 1, 3, 9, 19, 26, 76, 92; DAM POP**
See also AAYA 13; BEST 90:2; CA 1-4R; 137;
CANR 2, 19, 36, 60; CLR 12; DLB 8; DLBY 92; INT CANR-19; JRDA; MAICYA;
MTCW; SATA 1, 26, 74

Assis, Joaquim Maria Machado de
See Machado de Assis, Joaquim Maria

Astley, Thea (Beatrice May) 1925- ... **CLC 41**
See also CA 65-68; CANR 11, 43

Aston, James
See White, T(erence) H(anbury)

Asturias, Miguel Angel 1899-1974 **CLC 3, 8, 13; DAM MULT, NOV; HLC**
See also CA 25-28; 49-52; CANR 32; CAP 2;
DLB 113; HW; MTCW

Atares, Carlos Saura
See Saura (Atares), Carlos

Atheling, William
See Pound, Ezra (Weston Loomis)

Atheling, William, Jr.
See Blish, James (Benjamin)

Atherton, Gertrude (Franklin Horn) 1857-1948
TCLC 2
See also CA 104; 155; DLB 9, 78, 186

Atherton, Lucius
See Masters, Edgar Lee

Atkins, Jack
See Harris, Mark

Atkinson, Kate .... **CLC 99**
See also CA 166

Attaway, William (Alexander) 1911-1986
CLC 92; BLC 1; DAM MULT
See also BW 2; CA 143; DLB 76

Atticus
See Fleming, Ian (Lancaster); Wilson, (Thomas) Woodrow

Atwood, Margaret (Eleanor) 1939- **CLC 2, 3, 4, 8, 13, 15, 25, 44, 84; DA; DAB; DAC; DAM MST, NOV, POET; PC 8; SSC 2; WLC**
See also AAYA 12; BEST 89:2; CA 49-52;
CANR 3, 24, 33, 59; DLB 53; INT CANR-24; MTCW; SATA 50

Aubigny, Pierre d'
See Mencken, H(enry) L(ouis)

Aubin, Penelope 1685-1731(?) .... **LC 9**
See also DLB 39

Auchincloss, Louis (Stanton) 1917- **CLC 4, 6, 9, 18, 45; DAM NOV; SSC 22**
See also CA 1-4R; CANR 6, 29, 55; DLB 2;
DLBY 80; INT CANR-29; MTCW

Auden, W(ystan) H(ugh) 1907-1973 **CLC 1, 2, 3, 4, 6, 9, 11, 14, 43; DA; DAB; DAC; DAM DRAM, MST, POET; PC 1; WLC**
See also AAYA 18; CA 9-12R; 45-48; CANR 5, 61; CDBLB 1914-1945; DLB 10, 20;
MTCW

Audiberti, Jacques 1900-1965 **CLC 38; DAM DRAM**
See also CA 25-28R

Audubon, John James 1785-1851 .. **NCLC 47**

Auel, Jean M(arie) 1936-**CLC 31, 107; DAM POP**
See also AAYA 7; BEST 90:4; CA 103; CANR 21, 64; INT CANR-21; SATA 91

Auerbach, Erich 1892-1957 .... **TCLC 43**
See also CA 118; 155

Augier, Emile 1820-1889 .... **NCLC 31**
See also DLB 192

August, John
See De Voto, Bernard (Augustine)

Augustine, St. 354-430 .... **CMLC 6; DAB**

Aurelius
See Bourne, Randolph S(illiman)

Aurobindo, Sri
See Ghose, Aurabinda

Austen, Jane 1775-1817 **NCLC 1, 13, 19, 33, 51; DA; DAB; DAC; DAM MST, NOV; WLC**
See also AAYA 19; CDBLB 1789-1832; DLB 116

Auster, Paul 1947- .... **CLC 47**
See also CA 69-72; CANR 23, 52

Austin, Frank
See Faust, Frederick (Schiller)

Austin, Mary (Hunter) 1868-1934 . **TCLC 25**
See also CA 109; DLB 9, 78

Autran Dourado, Waldomiro
See Dourado, (Waldomiro Freitas) Autran

Averroes 1126-1198 .... **CMLC 7**
See also DLB 115

Avicenna 980-1037 .... **CMLC 16**
See also DLB 115

Avison, Margaret 1918- **CLC 2, 4, 97; DAC; DAM POET**
See also CA 17-20R; DLB 53; MTCW

Axton, David
See Koontz, Dean R(ay)

Ayckbourn, Alan 1939- **CLC 5, 8, 18, 33, 74; DAB; DAM DRAM**
See also CA 21-24R; CANR 31, 59; DLB 13; MTCW

Aydy, Catherine
See Tennant, Emma (Christina)

Ayme, Marcel (Andre) 1902-1967 .... **CLC 11**
See also CA 89-92; CANR 67; CLR 25; DLB 72; SATA 91

Ayrton, Michael 1921-1975 .... **CLC 7**
See also CA 5-8R; 61-64; CANR 9, 21

Azorin .... **CLC 11**
See also Martinez Ruiz, Jose

Azuela, Mariano 1873-1952 . **TCLC 3; DAM MULT; HLC**
See also CA 104; 131; HW; MTCW

Baastad, Babbis Friis
See Friis-Baastad, Babbis Ellinor

Bab
See Gilbert, W(illiam) S(chwenck)

Babbis, Eleanor
See Friis-Baastad, Babbis Ellinor

Babel, Isaac
See Babel, Isaak (Emmanuilovich)

Babel, Isaak (Emmanuilovich) 1894-1941(?) **TCLC 2, 13; SSC 16**
See also CA 104; 155

Babits, Mihaly 1883-1941 .... **TCLC 14**
See also CA 114

Babur 1483-1530 .... **LC 18**

Bacchelli, Riccardo 1891-1985 .... **CLC 19**
See also CA 29-32R; 117

Bach, Richard (David) 1936- **CLC 14; DAM NOV, POP**
See also AITN 1; BEST 89:2; CA 9-12R; CANR

18; MTCW; SATA 13

Bachman, Richard
See King, Stephen (Edwin)

Bachmann, Ingeborg 1926-1973 .... **CLC 69**
See also CA 93-96; 45-48; CANR 69; DLB 85

Bacon, Francis 1561-1626 .... **LC 18, 32**
See also CDBLB Before 1660; DLB 151

Bacon, Roger 1214(?)-1292 .... **CMLC 14**
See also DLB 115

Bacovia, George .... **TCLC 24**
See also Vasiliu, Gheorghe

Badanes, Jerome 1937- .... **CLC 59**

Bagehot, Walter 1826-1877 .... **NCLC 10**
See also DLB 55

Bagnold, Enid 1889-1981 .... **CLC 25; DAM DRAM**
See also CA 5-8R; 103; CANR 5, 40; DLB 13, 160, 191; MAICYA; SATA 1, 25

Bagritsky, Eduard 1895-1934 .... **TCLC 60**

Bagrjana, Elisaveta
See Belcheva, Elisaveta

Bagryana, Elisaveta .... **CLC 10**
See also Belcheva, Elisaveta
See also DLB 147

Bailey, Paul 1937- .... **CLC 45**
See also CA 21-24R; CANR 16, 62; DLB 14

Baillie, Joanna 1762-1851 .... **NCLC 71**
See also DLB 93

Bainbridge, Beryl (Margaret) 1933-**CLC 4, 5, 8, 10, 14, 18, 22, 62; DAM NOV**
See also CA 21-24R; CANR 24, 55; DLB 14; MTCW

Baker, Elliott 1922- .... **CLC 8**
See also CA 45-48; CANR 2, 63

Baker, Jean H. .... **TCLC 3, 10**
See also Russell, George William

Baker, Nicholson 1957- **CLC 61; DAM POP**
See also CA 135; CANR 63

Baker, Ray Stannard 1870-1946 .... **TCLC 47**
See also CA 118

Baker, Russell (Wayne) 1925- .... **CLC 31**
See also BEST 89:4; CA 57-60; CANR 11, 41, 59; MTCW

Bakhtin, M.
See Bakhtin, Mikhail Mikhailovich

Bakhtin, M. M.
See Bakhtin, Mikhail Mikhailovich

Bakhtin, Mikhail
See Bakhtin, Mikhail Mikhailovich

Bakhtin, Mikhail Mikhailovich 1895-1975 **CLC 83**
See also CA 128; 113

Bakshi, Ralph 1938(?)- .... **CLC 26**
See also CA 112; 138

Bakunin, Mikhail (Alexandrovich) 1814-1876 **NCLC 25, 58**

Baldwin, James (Arthur) 1924-1987**CLC 1, 2, 3, 4, 5, 8, 13, 15, 17, 42, 50, 67, 90; BLC 1; DA; DAB; DAC; DAM MST, MULT, NOV, POP; DC 1; SSC 10; WLC**
See also AAYA 4; BW 1; CA 1-4R; 124; CABS 1; CANR 3, 24; CDALB 1941-1968; DLB 2, 7, 33; DLBY 87; MTCW; SATA 9; SATA-Obit 54

Ballard, J(ames) G(raham) 1930-**CLC 3, 6, 14, 36; DAM NOV, POP; SSC 1**
See also AAYA 3; CA 5-8R; CANR 15, 39, 65; DLB 14; MTCW; SATA 93

Balmont, Konstantin (Dmitriyevich) 1867-1943 **TCLC 11**
See also CA 109; 155

Balzac, Honore de 1799-1850**NCLC 5, 35, 53; DA; DAB; DAC; DAM MST, NOV; SSC**

5; **WLC**
See also DLB 119

Bambara, Toni Cade 1939-1995 **CLC 19, 88; BLC 1; DA; DAC; DAM MST, MULT; WLCS**
See also AAYA 5; BW 2; CA 29-32R; 150; CANR 24, 49; DLB 38; MTCW

Bamdad, A.
See Shamlu, Ahmad

Banat, D. R.
See Bradbury, Ray (Douglas)

Bancroft, Laura
See Baum, L(yman) Frank

Banim, John 1798-1842 .... **NCLC 13**
See also DLB 116, 158, 159

Banim, Michael 1796-1874 .... **NCLC 13**
See also DLB 158, 159

Banjo, The
See Paterson, A(ndrew) B(arton)

Banks, Iain
See Banks, Iain M(enzies)

Banks, Iain M(enzies) 1954- .... **CLC 34**
See also CA 123; 128; CANR 61; DLB 194; INT 128

Banks, Lynne Reid .... **CLC 23**
See also Reid Banks, Lynne
See also AAYA 6

Banks, Russell 1940- .... **CLC 37, 72**
See also CA 65-68; CAAS 15; CANR 19, 52; DLB 130

Banville, John 1945- .... **CLC 46**
See also CA 117; 128; DLB 14; INT 128

Banville, Theodore (Faullain) de 1832-1891 **NCLC 9**

Baraka, Amiri 1934-**CLC 1, 2, 3, 5, 10, 14, 33; BLC 1; DA; DAC; DAM MST, MULT, POET, POP; DC 6; PC 4; WLCS**
See also Jones, LeRoi
See also BW 2; CA 21-24R; CABS 3; CANR 27, 38, 61; CDALB 1941-1968; DLB 5, 7, 16, 38; DLBD 8; MTCW

Barbauld, Anna Laetitia 1743-1825**NCLC 50**
See also DLB 107, 109, 142, 158

Barbellion, W. N. P. .... **TCLC 24**
See also Cummings, Bruce F(rederick)

Barbera, Jack (Vincent) 1945- .... **CLC 44**
See also CA 110; CANR 45

Barbey d'Aurevilly, Jules Amedee 1808-1889 **NCLC 1; SSC 17**
See also DLB 119

Barbusse, Henri 1873-1935 .... **TCLC 5**
See also CA 105; 154; DLB 65

Barclay, Bill
See Moorcock, Michael (John)

Barclay, William Ewert
See Moorcock, Michael (John)

Barea, Arturo 1897-1957 .... **TCLC 14**
See also CA 111

Barfoot, Joan 1946- .... **CLC 18**
See also CA 105

Baring, Maurice 1874-1945 .... **TCLC 8**
See also CA 105; DLB 34

Barker, Clive 1952- .... **CLC 52; DAM POP**
See also AAYA 10; BEST 90:3; CA 121; 129; INT 129; MTCW

Barker, George Granville 1913-1991 **CLC 8, 48; DAM POET**
See also CA 9-12R; 135; CANR 7, 38; DLB 20; MTCW

Barker, Harley Granville
See Granville-Barker, Harley
See also DLB 10

Barker, Howard 1946- .... **CLC 37**

Author Index

See also DLB 90

Bond, Edward 1934- **CLC 4, 6, 13, 23; DAM DRAM**
See also CA 25-28R; CANR 38, 67; DLB 13; MTCW

Bonham, Frank 1914-1989 .... **CLC 12**
See also AAYA 1; CA 9-12R; CANR 4, 36; JRDA; MAICYA; SAAS 3; SATA 1, 49; SATA-Obit 62

Bonnefoy, Yves 1923- ... **CLC 9, 15, 58; DAM MST, POET**
See also CA 85-88; CANR 33; MTCW

Bontemps, Arna(ud Wendell) 1902-1973 **C L C 1, 18; BLC 1; DAM MULT, NOV, POET**
See also BW 1; CA 1-4R; 41-44R; CANR 4, 35; CLR 6; DLB 48, 51; JRDA; MAICYA; MTCW; SATA 2, 44; SATA-Obit 24

Booth, Martin 1944- .... **CLC 13**
See also CA 93-96; CAAS 2

Booth, Philip 1925- .... **CLC 23**
See also CA 5-8R; CANR 5; DLBY 82

Booth, Wayne C(layson) 1921- .... **CLC 24**
See also CA 1-4R; CAAS 5; CANR 3, 43; DLB 67

Borchert, Wolfgang 1921-1947 .... **TCLC 5**
See also CA 104; DLB 69, 124

Borel, Petrus 1809-1859 .... **NCLC 41**

Borges, Jorge Luis 1899-1986 **CLC 1, 2, 3, 4, 6, 8, 9, 10, 13, 19, 44, 48, 83; DA; DAB; DAC; DAM MST, MULT; HLC; PC 22; SSC 4; WLC**
See also AAYA 19; CA 21-24R; CANR 19, 33; DLB 113; DLBY 86; HW; MTCW

Borowski, Tadeusz 1922-1951 .... **TCLC 9**
See also CA 106; 154

Borrow, George (Henry) 1803-1881 **NCLC 9**
See also DLB 21, 55, 166

Bosman, Herman Charles 1905-1951 **T C L C 49**
See also Malan, Herman
See also CA 160

Bosschere, Jean de 1878(?)-1953 ... **TCLC 19**
See also CA 115

Boswell, James 1740-1795 . **LC 4; DA; DAB; DAC; DAM MST; WLC**
See also CDBLB 1660-1789; DLB 104, 142

Bottoms, David 1949- .... **CLC 53**
See also CA 105; CANR 22; DLB 120; DLBY 83

Boucicault, Dion 1820-1890 .... **NCLC 41**

Boucolon, Maryse 1937(?)-
See Conde, Maryse
See also CA 110; CANR 30, 53

Bourget, Paul (Charles Joseph) 1852-1935 **TCLC 12**
See also CA 107; DLB 123

Bourjaily, Vance (Nye) 1922- ....**CLC 8, 62**
See also CA 1-4R; CAAS 1; CANR 2; DLB 2, 143

Bourne, Randolph S(illiman) 1886-1918 **TCLC 16**
See also CA 117; 155; DLB 63

Bova, Ben(jamin William) 1932- ...... **CLC 45**
See also AAYA 16; CA 5-8R; CAAS 18; CANR 11, 56; CLR 3; DLBY 81; INT CANR-11; MAICYA; MTCW; SATA 6, 68

Bowen, Elizabeth (Dorothea Cole) 1899-1973 **CLC 1, 3, 6, 11, 15, 22; DAM NOV; SSC 3, 28**
See also CA 17-18; 41-44R; CANR 35; CAP 2; CDBLB 1945-1960; DLB 15, 162; MTCW

Bowering, George 1935- .... **CLC 15, 47**
See also CA 21-24R; CAAS 16; CANR 10; DLB

53

Bowering, Marilyn R(uthe) 1949- .... **CLC 32**
See also CA 101; CANR 49

Bowers, Edgar 1924- .... **CLC 9**
See also CA 5-8R; CANR 24; DLB 5

Bowie, David .... **CLC 17**
See also Jones, David Robert

Bowles, Jane (Sydney) 1917-1973 **CLC 3, 68**
See also CA 19-20; 41-44R; CAP 2

Bowles, Paul (Frederick) 1910-1986 **CLC 1, 2, 19, 53; SSC 3**
See also CA 1-4R; CAAS 1; CANR 1, 19, 50; DLB 5, 6; MTCW

Box, Edgar
See Vidal, Gore

Boyd, Nancy
See Millay, Edna St. Vincent

Boyd, William 1952- .... **CLC 28, 53, 70**
See also CA 114; 120; CANR 51

Boyle, Kay 1902-1992 **CLC 1, 5, 19, 58; SSC 5**
See also CA 13-16R; 140; CAAS 1; CANR 29, 61; DLB 4, 9, 48, 86; DLBY 93; MTCW

Boyle, Mark
See Kienzle, William X(avier)

Boyle, Patrick 1905-1982 .... **CLC 19**
See also CA 127

Boyle, T. C. 1948-
See Boyle, T(homas) Coraghessan

Boyle, T(homas) Coraghessan 1948- **CLC 36, 55, 90; DAM POP; SSC 16**
See also BEST 90:4; CA 120; CANR 44; DLBY 86

Boz
See Dickens, Charles (John Huffam)

Brackenridge, Hugh Henry 1748-1816 **N C L C 7**
See also DLB 11, 37

Bradbury, Edward P.
See Moorcock, Michael (John)

Bradbury, Malcolm (Stanley) 1932- **CLC 32, 61; DAM NOV**
See also CA 1-4R; CANR 1, 33; DLB 14; MTCW

Bradbury, Ray (Douglas) 1920- **CLC 1, 3, 10, 15, 42, 98; DA; DAB; DAC; DAM MST, NOV, POP; SSC 29; WLC**
See also AAYA 15; AITN 1, 2; CA 1-4R; CANR 2, 30; CDALB 1968-1988; DLB 2, 8; MTCW; SATA 11, 64

Bradford, Gamaliel 1863-1932 ...... **TCLC 36**
See also CA 160; DLB 17

Bradley, David (Henry, Jr.) 1950- .. **CLC 23; BLC 1; DAM MULT**
See also BW 1; CA 104; CANR 26; DLB 33

Bradley, John Ed(mund, Jr.) 1958- .. **CLC 55**
See also CA 139

Bradley, Marion Zimmer 1930- **CLC 30; DAM POP**
See also AAYA 9; CA 57-60; CAAS 10; CANR 7, 31, 51; DLB 8; MTCW; SATA 90

Bradstreet, Anne 1612(?)-1672 **LC 4, 30; DA; DAC; DAM MST, POET; PC 10**
See also CDALB 1640-1865; DLB 24

Brady, Joan 1939- .... **CLC 86**
See also CA 141

Bragg, Melvyn 1939- .... **CLC 10**
See also BEST 89:3; CA 57-60; CANR 10, 48; DLB 14

Brahe, Tycho 1546-1601 .... **LC 45**

Braine, John (Gerard) 1922-1986 **CLC 1, 3, 41**
See also CA 1-4R; 120; CANR 1, 33; CDBLB 1945-1960; DLB 15; DLBY 86; MTCW

Bramah, Ernest 1868-1942 .... **TCLC 72**

See also CA 156; DLB 70

Brammer, William 1930(?)-1978 .... **CLC 31**
See also CA 77-80

Brancati, Vitaliano 1907-1954 .... **TCLC 12**
See also CA 109

Brancato, Robin F(idler) 1936- .... **CLC 35**
See also AAYA 9; CA 69-72; CANR 11, 45; CLR 32; JRDA; SAAS 9; SATA 97

Brand, Max
See Faust, Frederick (Schiller)

Brand, Millen 1906-1980 .... **CLC 7**
See also CA 21-24R; 97-100

Branden, Barbara .... **CLC 44**
See also CA 148

Brandes, Georg (Morris Cohen) 1842-1927 **TCLC 10**
See also CA 105

Brandys, Kazimierz 1916- .... **CLC 62**

Branley, Franklyn M(ansfield) 1915- **CLC 21**
See also CA 33-36R; CANR 14, 39; CLR 13; MAICYA; SAAS 16; SATA 4, 68

Brathwaite, Edward Kamau 1930- . **CLC 11; BLCS; DAM POET**
See also BW 2; CA 25-28R; CANR 11, 26, 47; DLB 125

Brautigan, Richard (Gary) 1935-1984 **CLC 1, 3, 5, 9, 12, 34, 42; DAM NOV**
See also CA 53-56; 113; CANR 34; DLB 2, 5; DLBY 80, 84; MTCW; SATA 56

Brave Bird, Mary 1953-
See Crow Dog, Mary (Ellen)
See also NNAL

Braverman, Kate 1950- .... **CLC 67**
See also CA 89-92

Brecht, (Eugen) Bertolt (Friedrich) 1898-1956 **TCLC 1, 6, 13, 35; DA; DAB; DAC; DAM DRAM, MST; DC 3; WLC**
See also CA 104; 133; CANR 62; DLB 56, 124; MTCW

Brecht, Eugen Berthold Friedrich
See Brecht, (Eugen) Bertolt (Friedrich)

Bremer, Fredrika 1801-1865 .... **NCLC 11**

Brennan, Christopher John 1870-1932 **T C L C 17**
See also CA 117

Brennan, Maeve 1917- .... **CLC 5**
See also CA 81-84

Brent, Linda
See Jacobs, Harriet A(nn)

Brentano, Clemens (Maria) 1778-1842 **N C L C 1**
See also DLB 90

Brent of Bin Bin
See Franklin, (Stella Maria Sarah) Miles (Lampe)

Brenton, Howard 1942- .... **CLC 31**
See also CA 69-72; CANR 33, 67; DLB 13; MTCW

Breslin, James 1930-1996
See Breslin, Jimmy
See also CA 73-76; CANR 31; DAM NOV; MTCW

Breslin, Jimmy .... **CLC 4, 43**
See also Breslin, James
See also AITN 1; DLB 185

Bresson, Robert 1901- .... **CLC 16**
See also CA 110; CANR 49

Breton, Andre 1896-1966 **CLC 2, 9, 15, 54; PC 15**
See also CA 19-20; 25-28R; CANR 40, 60; CAP 2; DLB 65; MTCW

Breytenbach, Breyten 1939(?)- . **CLC 23, 37; DAM POET**

See also CA 113; 129; CANR 61

Bridgers, Sue Ellen 1942- .... **CLC 26**
See also AAYA 8; CA 65-68; CANR 11, 36;
CLR 18; DLB 52; JRDA; MAICYA; SAAS
1; SATA 22, 90

Bridges, Robert (Seymour) 1844-1930 **T C L C
1; DAM POET**
See also CA 104; 152; CDBLB 1890-1914;
DLB 19, 98

Bridie, James .... **TCLC 3**
See also Mavor, Osborne Henry
See also DLB 10

Brin, David 1950- .... **CLC 34**
See also AAYA 21; CA 102; CANR 24; INT
CANR-24; SATA 65

Brink, Andre (Philippus) 1935- **CLC 18, 36,
106**
See also CA 104; CANR 39, 62; INT 103;
MTCW

Brinsmead, H(esba) F(ay) 1922- .... **CLC 21**
See also CA 21-24R; CANR 10; CLR 47;
MAICYA; SAAS 5; SATA 18, 78

Brittain, Vera (Mary) 1893(?)-1970 . **CLC 23**
See also CA 13-16; 25-28R; CANR 58; CAP 1;
DLB 191; MTCW

Broch, Hermann 1886-1951 .... **TCLC 20**
See also CA 117; DLB 85, 124

Brock, Rose
See Hansen, Joseph

Brodkey, Harold (Roy) 1930-1996 .... **CLC 56**
See also CA 111; 151; DLB 130

Brodsky, Iosif Alexandrovich 1940-1996
See Brodsky, Joseph
See also AITN 1; CA 41-44R; 151; CANR 37;
DAM POET; MTCW

Brodsky, Joseph 1940-1996 **CLC 4, 6, 13, 36,
100; PC 9**
See also Brodsky, Iosif Alexandrovich

Brodsky, Michael (Mark) 1948- .... **CLC 19**
See also CA 102; CANR 18, 41, 58

Bromell, Henry 1947- .... **CLC 5**
See also CA 53-56; CANR 9

Bromfield, Louis (Brucker) 1896-1956 **T C L C
11**
See also CA 107; 155; DLB 4, 9, 86

Broner, E(sther) M(asserman) 1930- **CLC 19**
See also CA 17-20R; CANR 8, 25; DLB 28

Bronk, William 1918- .... **CLC 10**
See also CA 89-92; CANR 23; DLB 165

Bronstein, Lev Davidovich
See Trotsky, Leon

Bronte, Anne 1820-1849 .... **NCLC 71**
See also DLB 21, 199

Bronte, Charlotte 1816-1855 **NCLC 3, 8, 33,
58; DA; DAB; DAC; DAM MST, NOV;
WLC**
See also AAYA 17; CDBLB 1832-1890; DLB
21, 159, 199

Bronte, Emily (Jane) 1818-1848 **NCLC 16, 35;
DA; DAB; DAC; DAM MST, NOV, POET;
PC 8; WLC**
See also AAYA 17; CDBLB 1832-1890; DLB
21, 32, 199

Brooke, Frances 1724-1789 .... **LC 6**
See also DLB 39, 99

Brooke, Henry 1703(?)-1783 .... **LC 1**
See also DLB 39

Brooke, Rupert (Chawner) 1887-1915 **T C L C
2, 7; DA; DAB; DAC; DAM MST, POET;
WLC**
See also CA 104; 132; CANR 61; CDBLB
1914-1945; DLB 19; MTCW

Brooke-Haven, P.

See Wodehouse, P(elham) G(renville)

Brooke-Rose, Christine 1926(?)- .... **CLC 40**
See also CA 13-16R; CANR 58; DLB 14

Brookner, Anita 1928- **CLC 32, 34, 51; DAB;
DAM POP**
See also CA 114; 120; CANR 37, 56; DLB 194;
DLBY 87; MTCW

Brooks, Cleanth 1906-1994 **CLC 24, 86, 110**
See also CA 17-20R; 145; CANR 33, 35; DLB
63; DLBY 94; INT CANR-35; MTCW

Brooks, George
See Baum, L(yman) Frank

Brooks, Gwendolyn 1917- **CLC 1, 2, 4, 5, 15,
49; BLC 1; DA; DAC; DAM MST, MULT,
POET; PC 7; WLC**
See also AAYA 20; AITN 1; BW 2; CA 1-4R;
CANR 1, 27, 52; CDALB 1941-1968; CLR
27; DLB 5, 76, 165; MTCW; SATA 6

Brooks, Mel .... **CLC 12**
See also Kaminsky, Melvin
See also AAYA 13; DLB 26

Brooks, Peter 1938- .... **CLC 34**
See also CA 45-48; CANR 1

Brooks, Van Wyck 1886-1963 .... **CLC 29**
See also CA 1-4R; CANR 6; DLB 45, 63, 103

Brophy, Brigid (Antonia) 1929-1995 **CLC 6,
11, 29, 105**
See also CA 5-8R; 149; CAAS 4; CANR 25,
53; DLB 14; MTCW

Brosman, Catharine Savage 1934- ..... **CLC 9**
See also CA 61-64; CANR 21, 46

Brother Antoninus
See Everson, William (Oliver)

The Brothers Quay
See Quay, Stephen; Quay, Timothy

Broughton, T(homas) Alan 1936- ..... **CLC 19**
See also CA 45-48; CANR 2, 23, 48

Broumas, Olga 1949- .... **CLC 10, 73**
See also CA 85-88; CANR 20, 69

Brown, Alan 1950- .... **CLC 99**
See also CA 156

Brown, Charles Brockden 1771-1810 **N C L C
22**
See also CDALB 1640-1865; DLB 37, 59, 73

Brown, Christy 1932-1981 .... **CLC 63**
See also CA 105; 104; DLB 14

Brown, Claude 1937- **CLC 30; BLC 1; DAM
MULT**
See also AAYA 7; BW 1; CA 73-76

Brown, Dee (Alexander) 1908- .. **CLC 18, 47;
DAM POP**
See also CA 13-16R; CAAS 6; CANR 11, 45,
60; DLBY 80; MTCW; SATA 5

Brown, George
See Wertmueller, Lina

Brown, George Douglas 1869-1902 **TCLC 28**
See also CA 162

Brown, George Mackay 1921-1996 **CLC 5, 48,
100**
See also CA 21-24R; 151; CAAS 6; CANR 12,
37, 67; DLB 14, 27, 139; MTCW; SATA 35

Brown, (William) Larry 1951- .... **CLC 73**
See also CA 130; 134; INT 133

Brown, Moses
See Barrett, William (Christopher)

Brown, Rita Mae 1944- **CLC 18, 43, 79; DAM
NOV, POP**
See also CA 45-48; CANR 2, 11, 35, 62; INT
CANR-11; MTCW

Brown, Roderick (Langmere) Haig-
See Haig-Brown, Roderick (Langmere)

Brown, Rosellen 1939- .... **CLC 32**
See also CA 77-80; CAAS 10; CANR 14, 44

Brown, Sterling Allen 1901-1989 **CLC 1, 23,
59; BLC 1; DAM MULT, POET**
See also BW 1; CA 85-88; 127; CANR 26; DLB
48, 51, 63; MTCW

Brown, Will
See Ainsworth, William Harrison

Brown, William Wells 1813-1884 ... **NCLC 2;
BLC 1; DAM MULT; DC 1**
See also DLB 3, 50

Browne, (Clyde) Jackson 1948(?)- .... **CLC 21**
See also CA 120

Browning, Elizabeth Barrett 1806-1861
**NCLC 1, 16, 61, 66; DA; DAB; DAC; DAM
MST, POET; PC 6; WLC**
See also CDBLB 1832-1890; DLB 32, 199

Browning, Robert 1812-1889 **NCLC 19; DA;
DAB; DAC; DAM MST, POET; PC 2;
WLCS**
See also CDBLB 1832-1890; DLB 32, 163;
YABC 1

Browning, Tod 1882-1962 .... **CLC 16**
See also CA 141; 117

Brownson, Orestes (Augustus) 1803-1876
NCLC 50

Brownson, Orestes Augustus 1803-1876
NCLC 50
See also DLB 1, 59, 73

Bruccoli, Matthew J(oseph) 1931- ... **CLC 34**
See also CA 9-12R; CANR 7; DLB 103

Bruce, Lenny .... **CLC 21**
See also Schneider, Leonard Alfred

Bruin, John
See Brutus, Dennis

Brulard, Henri
See Stendhal

Brulls, Christian
See Simenon, Georges (Jacques Christian)

Brunner, John (Kilian Houston) 1934-1995
CLC 8, 10; DAM POP
See also CA 1-4R; 149; CAAS 8; CANR 2, 37;
MTCW

Bruno, Giordano 1548-1600 .... **LC 27**

Brutus, Dennis 1924- **CLC 43; BLC 1; DAM
MULT, POET**
See also BW 2; CA 49-52; CAAS 14; CANR 2,
27, 42; DLB 117

Bryan, C(ourtlandt) D(ixon) B(arnes) 1936-
CLC 29
See also CA 73-76; CANR 13, 68; DLB 185;
INT CANR-13

Bryan, Michael
See Moore, Brian

Bryant, William Cullen 1794-1878 . **NCLC 6,
46; DA; DAB; DAC; DAM MST, POET;
PC 20**
See also CDALB 1640-1865; DLB 3, 43, 59,
189

Bryusov, Valery Yakovlevich 1873-1924
TCLC 10
See also CA 107; 155

Buchan, John 1875-1940 ..... **TCLC 41; DAB;
DAM POP**
See also CA 108; 145; DLB 34, 70, 156; YABC
2

Buchanan, George 1506-1582 .... **LC 4**
See also DLB 152

Buchheim, Lothar-Guenther 1918- .... **CLC 6**
See also CA 85-88

Buchner, (Karl) Georg 1813-1837 . **NCLC 26**

Buchwald, Art(hur) 1925- .... **CLC 33**
See also AITN 1; CA 5-8R; CANR 21, 67;
MTCW; SATA 10

Buck, Pearl S(ydenstricker) 1892-1973 **CLC 7,**

39, 73; DAM NOV; SSC 3
See also CA 85-88; 116; CANR 23, 61; DLB
196; MTCW

Cameron, Carey 1952- .... **CLC 59**
See also CA 135

Cameron, Peter 1959- .... **CLC 44**
See also CA 125; CANR 50

Campana, Dino 1885-1932 .... **TCLC 20**
See also CA 117; DLB 114

Campanella, Tommaso 1568-1639 .... **LC 32**

Campbell, John W(ood, Jr.) 1910-1971 **C L C
32**
See also CA 21-22; 29-32R; CANR 34; CAP 2;
DLB 8; MTCW

Campbell, Joseph 1904-1987 .... **CLC 69**
See also AAYA 3; BEST 89:2; CA 1-4R; 124;
CANR 3, 28, 61; MTCW

Campbell, Maria 1940- .... **CLC 85; DAC**
See also CA 102; CANR 54; NNAL

Campbell, (John) Ramsey 1946-**CLC 42; SSC
19**
See also CA 57-60; CANR 7; INT CANR-7

Campbell, (Ignatius) Roy (Dunnachie) 1901-
1957 .... **TCLC 5**
See also CA 104; 155; DLB 20

Campbell, Thomas 1777-1844 .... **NCLC 19**
See also DLB 93; 144

Campbell, Wilfred .... **TCLC 9**
See also Campbell, William

Campbell, William 1858(?)-1918
See Campbell, Wilfred
See also CA 106; DLB 92

Campion, Jane .... **CLC 95**
See also CA 138

Campos, Alvaro de
See Pessoa, Fernando (Antonio Nogueira)

Camus, Albert 1913-1960**CLC 1, 2, 4, 9, 11, 14,
32, 63, 69; DA; DAB; DAC; DAM DRAM,
MST, NOV; DC 2; SSC 9; WLC**
See also CA 89-92; DLB 72; MTCW

Canby, Vincent 1924- .... **CLC 13**
See also CA 81-84

Cancale
See Desnos, Robert

Canetti, Elias 1905-1994**CLC 3, 14, 25, 75, 86**
See also CA 21-24R; 146; CANR 23, 61; DLB
85, 124; MTCW

Canin, Ethan 1960- .... **CLC 55**
See also CA 131; 135

Cannon, Curt
See Hunter, Evan

Cao, Lan 1961- .... **CLC 109**
See also CA 165

Cape, Judith
See Page, P(atricia) K(athleen)

Capek, Karel 1890-1938 ... **TCLC 6, 37; DA;
DAB; DAC; DAM DRAM, MST, NOV; DC
1; WLC**
See also CA 104; 140

Capote, Truman 1924-1984**CLC 1, 3, 8, 13, 19,
34, 38, 58; DA; DAB; DAC; DAM MST,
NOV; POP; SSC 2; WLC**
See also CA 5-8R; 113; CANR 18, 62; CDALB
1941-1968; DLB 2, 185; DLBY 80, 84;
MTCW; SATA 91

Capra, Frank 1897-1991 .... **CLC 16**
See also CA 61-64; 135

Caputo, Philip 1941- .... **CLC 32**
See also CA 73-76; CANR 40

Caragiale, Ion Luca 1852-1912 ..... **TCLC 76**
See also CA 157

Card, Orson Scott 1951-**CLC 44, 47, 50; DAM
POP**

See also AAYA 11; CA 102; CANR 27, 47; INT
CANR-27; MTCW; SATA 83

Cardenal, Ernesto 1925- .... **CLC 31; DAM
MULT, POET; HLC; PC 22**
See also CA 49-52; CANR 2, 32, 66; HW;
MTCW

Cardozo, Benjamin N(athan) 1870-1938
TCLC 65
See also CA 117; 164

Carducci, Giosue (Alessandro Giuseppe) 1835-
1907 .... **TCLC 32**
See also CA 163

Carew, Thomas 1595(?)-1640 .... **LC 13**
See also DLB 126

Carey, Ernestine Gilbreth 1908- .... **CLC 17**
See also CA 5-8R; SATA 2

Carey, Peter 1943- .... **CLC 40, 55, 96**
See also CA 123; 127; CANR 53; INT 127;
MTCW; SATA 94

Carleton, William 1794-1869 .... **NCLC 3**
See also DLB 159

Carlisle, Henry (Coffin) 1926- .... **CLC 33**
See also CA 13-16R; CANR 15

Carlsen, Chris
See Holdstock, Robert P.

Carlson, Ron(ald F.) 1947- .... **CLC 54**
See also CA 105; CANR 27

Carlyle, Thomas 1795-1881 . **NCLC 70; DA;
DAB; DAC; DAM MST**
See also CDBLB 1789-1832; DLB 55; 144

Carman, (William) Bliss 1861-1929**TCLC 7;
DAC**
See also CA 104; 152; DLB 92

Carnegie, Dale 1888-1955 .... **TCLC 53**

Carossa, Hans 1878-1956 .... **TCLC 48**
See also DLB 66

Carpenter, Don(ald Richard) 1931-1995**C L C
41**
See also CA 45-48; 149; CANR 1

Carpentier (y Valmont), Alejo 1904-1980**CLC
8, 11, 38, 110; DAM MULT; HLC**
See also CA 65-68; 97-100; CANR 11; DLB
113; HW

Carr, Caleb 1955(?)- .... **CLC 86**
See also CA 147

Carr, Emily 1871-1945 .... **TCLC 32**
See also CA 159; DLB 68

Carr, John Dickson 1906-1977 .... **CLC 3**
See also Fairbairn, Roger
See also CA 49-52; 69-72; CANR 3, 33, 60;
MTCW

Carr, Philippa
See Hibbert, Eleanor Alice Burford

Carr, Virginia Spencer 1929- .... **CLC 34**
See also CA 61-64; DLB 111

Carrere, Emmanuel 1957- .... **CLC 89**

Carrier, Roch 1937-**CLC 13, 78; DAC; DAM
MST**
See also CA 130; CANR 61; DLB 53

Carroll, James P. 1943(?)- .... **CLC 38**
See also CA 81-84

Carroll, Jim 1951- .... **CLC 35**
See also AAYA 17; CA 45-48; CANR 42

Carroll, Lewis ..... **NCLC 2, 53; PC 18; WLC**
See also Dodgson, Charles Lutwidge
See also CDBLB 1832-1890; CLR 2, 18; DLB
18, 163, 178; JRDA

Carroll, Paul Vincent 1900-1968 ...... **CLC 10**
See also CA 9-12R; 25-28R; DLB 10

Carruth, Hayden 1921- **CLC 4, 7, 10, 18, 84;
PC 10**
See also CA 9-12R; CANR 4, 38, 59; DLB 5,
165; INT CANR-4; MTCW; SATA 47

Carson, Rachel Louise 1907-1964 .. **CLC 71;
DAM POP**
See also CA 77-80; CANR 35; MTCW; SATA
23

Carter, Angela (Olive) 1940-1992 **CLC 5, 41,
76; SSC 13**
See also CA 53-56; 136; CANR 12, 36, 61; DLB
14; MTCW; SATA 66; SATA-Obit 70

Carter, Nick
See Smith, Martin Cruz

Carver, Raymond 1938-1988**CLC 22, 36, 53,
55; DAM NOV; SSC 8**
See also CA 33-36R; 126; CANR 17, 34, 61;
DLB 130; DLBY 84, 88; MTCW

Cary, Elizabeth, Lady Falkland 1585-1639
LC 30

Cary, (Arthur) Joyce (Lunel) 1888-1957
TCLC 1, 29
See also CA 104; 164; CDBLB 1914-1945;
DLB 15, 100

Casanova de Seingalt, Giovanni Jacopo 1725-
1798 ....**LC 13**

Casares, Adolfo Bioy
See Bioy Casares, Adolfo

Casely-Hayford, J(oseph) E(phraim) 1866-1930
TCLC 24; BLC 1; DAM MULT
See also BW 2; CA 123; 152

Casey, John (Dudley) 1939- .... **CLC 59**
See also BEST 90:2; CA 69-72; CANR 23

Casey, Michael 1947- .... **CLC 2**
See also CA 65-68; DLB 5

Casey, Patrick
See Thurman, Wallace (Henry)

Casey, Warren (Peter) 1935-1988 ..... **CLC 12**
See also CA 101; 127; INT 101

Casona, Alejandro .... **CLC 49**
See also Alvarez, Alejandro Rodriguez

Cassavetes, John 1929-1989 .... **CLC 20**
See also CA 85-88; 127

Cassian, Nina 1924- .... **PC 17**

Cassill, R(onald) V(erlin) 1919- .... **CLC 4, 23**
See also CA 9-12R; CAAS 1; CANR 7, 45; DLB
6

Cassirer, Ernst 1874-1945 .... **TCLC 61**
See also CA 157

Cassity, (Allen) Turner 1929- .... **CLC 6, 42**
See also CA 17-20R; CAAS 8; CANR 11; DLB
105

Castaneda, Carlos 1931(?)- .... **CLC 12**
See also CA 25-28R; CANR 32, 66; HW;
MTCW

Castedo, Elena 1937- .... **CLC 65**
See also CA 132

Castedo-Ellerman, Elena
See Castedo, Elena

Castellanos, Rosario 1925-1974**CLC 66; DAM
MULT; HLC**
See also CA 131; 53-56; CANR 58; DLB 113;
HW

Castelvetro, Lodovico 1505-1571 .... **LC 12**

Castiglione, Baldassare 1478-1529 ...... **LC 12**

Castle, Robert
See Hamilton, Edmond

Castro, Guillen de 1569-1631 .... **LC 19**

Castro, Rosalia de 1837-1885**NCLC 3; DAM
MULT**

Cather, Willa
See Cather, Willa Sibert

Cather, Willa Sibert 1873-1947 **TCLC 1, 11,
31; DA; DAB; DAC; DAM MST, NOV;
SSC 2; WLC**
See also AAYA 24; CA 104; 128; CDALB 1865-
1917; DLB 9, 54, 78; DLBD 1; MTCW;

13
See also CA 17-20R; CAAS 2; CANR 29, 55; DLB 6

del Castillo, Michel 1933- .... **CLC 38**
See also CA 109

Deledda, Grazia (Cosima) 1875(?)-1936 **TCLC 23**
See also CA 123

Delibes, Miguel .... **CLC 8, 18**
See also Delibes Setien, Miguel

Delibes Setien, Miguel 1920-
See Delibes, Miguel
See also CA 45-48; CANR 1, 32; HW; MTCW

DeLillo, Don 1936- **CLC 8, 10, 13, 27, 39, 54, 76; DAM NOV, POP**
See also BEST 89:1; CA 81-84; CANR 21; DLB 6, 173; MTCW

de Lisser, H. G.
See De Lisser, H(erbert) G(eorge)
See also DLB 117

De Lisser, H(erbert) G(eorge) 1878-1944 **TCLC 12**
See also de Lisser, H. G.
See also BW 2; CA 109; 152

Deloney, Thomas (?)-1600 .... **LC 41**
See also DLB 167

Deloria, Vine (Victor), Jr. 1933- ..... **CLC 21; DAM MULT**
See also CA 53-56; CANR 5, 20, 48; DLB 175; MTCW; NNAL; SATA 21

Del Vecchio, John M(ichael) 1947- ... **CLC 29**
See also CA 110; DLBD 9

de Man, Paul (Adolph Michel) 1919-1983 **CLC 55**
See also CA 128; 111; CANR 61; DLB 67; MTCW

De Marinis, Rick 1934- .... **CLC 54**
See also CA 57-60; CAAS 24; CANR 9, 25, 50

Dembry, R. Emmet
See Murfree, Mary Noailles

Demby, William 1922- **CLC 53; BLC 1; DAM MULT**
See also BW 1; CA 81-84; DLB 33

de Menton, Francisco
See Chin, Frank (Chew, Jr.)

Demijohn, Thom
See Disch, Thomas M(ichael)

de Montherlant, Henry (Milon)
See Montherlant, Henry (Milon) de

Demosthenes 384B.C.-322B.C. ...... **CMLC 13**
See also DLB 176

de Natale, Francine
See Malzberg, Barry N(athaniel)

Denby, Edwin (Orr) 1903-1983 .... **CLC 48**
See also CA 138; 110

Denis, Julio
See Cortazar, Julio

Denmark, Harrison
See Zelazny, Roger (Joseph)

Dennis, John 1658-1734 .... **LC 11**
See also DLB 101

Dennis, Nigel (Forbes) 1912-1989 .... **CLC 8**
See also CA 25-28R; 129; DLB 13, 15; MTCW

Dent, Lester 1904(?)-1959 .... **TCLC 72**
See also CA 112; 161

De Palma, Brian (Russell) 1940- .... **CLC 20**
See also CA 109

De Quincey, Thomas 1785-1859 ...... **NCLC 4**
See also CDBLB 1789-1832; DLB 110; 144

Deren, Eleanora 1908(?)-1961
See Deren, Maya
See also CA 111

Deren, Maya 1917-1961 .... **CLC 16, 102**

See also Deren, Eleanora

Derleth, August (William) 1909-1971 **CLC 31**
See also CA 1-4R; 29-32R; CANR 4; DLB 9; SATA 5

Der Nister 1884-1950 .... **TCLC 56**

de Routisie, Albert
See Aragon, Louis

Derrida, Jacques 1930- .... **CLC 24, 87**
See also CA 124; 127

Derry Down Derry
See Lear, Edward

Dersonnes, Jacques
See Simenon, Georges (Jacques Christian)

Desai, Anita 1937- **CLC 19, 37, 97; DAB; DAM NOV**
See also CA 81-84; CANR 33, 53; MTCW; SATA 63

de Saint-Luc, Jean
See Glassco, John

de Saint Roman, Arnaud
See Aragon, Louis

Descartes, Rene 1596-1650 .... **LC 20, 35**

De Sica, Vittorio 1901(?)-1974 .... **CLC 20**
See also CA 117

Desnos, Robert 1900-1945 .... **TCLC 22**
See also CA 121; 151

Destouches, Louis-Ferdinand 1894-1961 **CLC 9, 15**
See also Celine, Louis-Ferdinand
See also CA 85-88; CANR 28; MTCW

de Tolignac, Gaston
See Griffith, D(avid Lewelyn) W(ark)

Deutsch, Babette 1895-1982 .... **CLC 18**
See also CA 1-4R; 108; CANR 4; DLB 45; SATA 1; SATA-Obit 33

Devenant, William 1606-1649 .... **LC 13**

Devkota, Laxmiprasad 1909-1959 . **TCLC 23**
See also CA 123

De Voto, Bernard (Augustine) 1897-1955 **TCLC 29**
See also CA 113; 160; DLB 9

De Vries, Peter 1910-1993 **CLC 1, 2, 3, 7, 10, 28, 46; DAM NOV**
See also CA 17-20R; 142; CANR 41; DLB 6; DLBY 82; MTCW

Dexter, John
See Bradley, Marion Zimmer

Dexter, Martin
See Faust, Frederick (Schiller)

Dexter, Pete 1943- ... **CLC 34, 55; DAM POP**
See also BEST 89:2; CA 127; 131; INT 131; MTCW

Diamano, Silmang
See Senghor, Leopold Sedar

Diamond, Neil 1941- .... **CLC 30**
See also CA 108

Diaz del Castillo, Bernal 1496-1584 .... **LC 31**

di Bassetto, Corno
See Shaw, George Bernard

Dick, Philip K(indred) 1928-1982 **CLC 10, 30, 72; DAM NOV, POP**
See also AAYA 24; CA 49-52; 106; CANR 2, 16; DLB 8; MTCW

Dickens, Charles (John Huffam) 1812-1870 **NCLC 3, 8, 18, 26, 37, 50; DA; DAB; DAC; DAM MST, NOV; SSC 17; WLC**
See also AAYA 23; CDBLB 1832-1890; DLB 21, 55, 70, 159, 166; JRDA; MAICYA; SATA 15

Dickey, James (Lafayette) 1923-1997 **CLC 1, 2, 4, 7, 10, 15, 47, 109; DAM NOV, POET, POP**
See also AITN 1, 2; CA 9-12R; 156; CABS 2;

CANR 10, 48, 61; CDALB 1968-1988; DLB 5, 193; DLBD 7; DLBY 82, 93, 96, 97; INT CANR-10; MTCW

Dickey, William 1928-1994 .... **CLC 3, 28**
See also CA 9-12R; 145; CANR 24; DLB 5

Dickinson, Charles 1951- .... **CLC 49**
See also CA 128

Dickinson, Emily (Elizabeth) 1830-1886 **NCLC 21; DA; DAB; DAC; DAM MST, POET; PC 1; WLC**
See also AAYA 22; CDALB 1865-1917; DLB 1; SATA 29

Dickinson, Peter (Malcolm) 1927- **CLC 12, 35**
See also AAYA 9; CA 41-44R; CANR 31, 58; CLR 29; DLB 87, 161; JRDA; MAICYA; SATA 5, 62, 95

Dickson, Carr
See Carr, John Dickson

Dickson, Carter
See Carr, John Dickson

Diderot, Denis 1713-1784 .... **LC 26**

Didion, Joan 1934- **CLC 1, 3, 8, 14, 32; DAM NOV**
See also AITN 1; CA 5-8R; CANR 14, 52; CDALB 1968-1988; DLB 2, 173, 185; DLBY 81, 86; MTCW

Dietrich, Robert
See Hunt, E(verette) Howard, (Jr.)

Dillard, Annie 1945- **CLC 9, 60; DAM NOV**
See also AAYA 6; CA 49-52; CANR 3, 43, 62; DLBY 80; MTCW; SATA 10

Dillard, R(ichard) H(enry) W(ilde) 1937- **CLC 5**
See also CA 21-24R; CAAS 7; CANR 10; DLB 5

Dillon, Eilis 1920-1994 .... **CLC 17**
See also CA 9-12R; 147; CAAS 3; CANR 4, 38; CLR 26; MAICYA; SATA 2, 74; SATA-Obit 83

Dimont, Penelope
See Mortimer, Penelope (Ruth)

Dinesen, Isak .... **CLC 10, 29, 95; SSC 7**
See also Blixen, Karen (Christentze Dinesen)

Ding Ling .... **CLC 68**
See also Chiang, Pin-chin

Disch, Thomas M(ichael) 1940- .... **CLC 7, 36**
See also AAYA 17; CA 21-24R; CAAS 4; CANR 17, 36, 54; CLR 18; DLB 8; MAICYA; MTCW; SAAS 15; SATA 92

Disch, Tom
See Disch, Thomas M(ichael)

d'Isly, Georges
See Simenon, Georges (Jacques Christian)

Disraeli, Benjamin 1804-1881 .... **NCLC 2, 39**
See also DLB 21, 55

Ditcum, Steve
See Crumb, R(obert)

Dixon, Paige
See Corcoran, Barbara

Dixon, Stephen 1936- .... **CLC 52; SSC 16**
See also CA 89-92; CANR 17, 40, 54; DLB 130

Doak, Annie
See Dillard, Annie

Dobell, Sydney Thompson 1824-1874 **NCLC 43**
See also DLB 32

Doblin, Alfred .... **TCLC 13**
See also Doeblin, Alfred

Dobrolyubov, Nikolai Alexandrovich 1836-1861 **NCLC 5**

Dobson, Austin 1840-1921 .... **TCLC 79**
See also DLB 35; 144

Dobyns, Stephen 1941- .... **CLC 37**

See also CA 45-48; CANR 2, 18

Doctorow, E(dgar) L(aurence) 1931- **CLC 6, 11, 15, 18, 37, 44, 65, 113; DAM NOV, POP**
See also AAYA 22; AITN 2; BEST 89:3; CA 45-48; CANR 2, 33, 51; CDALB 1968-1988; DLB 2, 28, 173; DLBY 80; MTCW

Dodgson, Charles Lutwidge 1832-1898
See Carroll, Lewis
See also CLR 2; DA; DAB; DAC; DAM MST, NOV, POET; MAICYA; YABC 2

Dodson, Owen (Vincent) 1914-1983 **CLC 79; BLC 1; DAM MULT**
See also BW 1; CA 65-68; 110; CANR 24; DLB 76

Doeblin, Alfred 1878-1957 .... **TCLC 13**
See also Doblin, Alfred
See also CA 110; 141; DLB 66

Doerr, Harriet 1910- .... **CLC 34**
See also CA 117; 122; CANR 47; INT 122

Domecq, H(onorio) Bustos
See Bioy Casares, Adolfo; Borges, Jorge Luis

Domini, Rey
See Lorde, Audre (Geraldine)

Dominique
See Proust, (Valentin-Louis-George-Eugene-) Marcel

Don, A
See Stephen, SirLeslie

Donaldson, Stephen R. 1947- **CLC 46; DAM POP**
See also CA 89-92; CANR 13, 55; INT CANR-13

Donleavy, J(ames) P(atrick) 1926-**CLC 1, 4, 6, 10, 45**
See also AITN 2; CA 9-12R; CANR 24, 49, 62; DLB 6, 173; INT CANR-24; MTCW

Donne, John 1572-1631**LC 10, 24; DA; DAB; DAC; DAM MST, POET; PC 1**
See also CDBLB Before 1660; DLB 121, 151

Donnell, David 1939(?)- .... **CLC 34**

Donoghue, P. S.
See Hunt, E(verette) Howard, (Jr.)

Donoso (Yanez), Jose 1924-1996**CLC 4, 8, 11, 32, 99; DAM MULT; HLC**
See also CA 81-84; 155; CANR 32; DLB 113; HW; MTCW

Donovan, John 1928-1992 .... **CLC 35**
See also AAYA 20; CA 97-100; 137; CLR 3; MAICYA; SATA 72; SATA-Brief 29

Don Roberto
See Cunninghame Graham, R(obert) B(ontine)

Doolittle, Hilda 1886-1961**CLC 3, 8, 14, 31, 34, 73; DA; DAC; DAM MST, POET; PC 5; WLC**
See also H. D.
See also CA 97-100; CANR 35; DLB 4, 45; MTCW

Dorfman, Ariel 1942- ...... **CLC 48, 77; DAM MULT; HLC**
See also CA 124; 130; CANR 67; HW; INT 130

Dorn, Edward (Merton) 1929- ... **CLC 10, 18**
See also CA 93-96; CANR 42; DLB 5; INT 93-96

Dorris, Michael (Anthony) 1945-1997 .. **C L C 109; DAM MULT, NOV**
See also AAYA 20; BEST 90:1; CA 102; 157; CANR 19, 46; DLB 175; NNAL; SATA 75; SATA-Obit 94

Dorris, Michael A.
See Dorris, Michael (Anthony)

Dorsan, Luc
See Simenon, Georges (Jacques Christian)

Dorsange, Jean

See Simenon, Georges (Jacques Christian)

Dos Passos, John (Roderigo) 1896-1970 **C L C 1, 4, 8, 11, 15, 25, 34, 82; DA; DAB; DAC; DAM MST, NOV; WLC**
See also CA 1-4R; 29-32R; CANR 3; CDALB 1929-1941; DLB 4, 9; DLBD 1, 15; DLBY 96; MTCW

Dossage, Jean
See Simenon, Georges (Jacques Christian)

Dostoevsky, Fedor Mikhailovich 1821-1881 **NCLC 2, 7, 21, 33, 43; DA; DAB; DAC; DAM MST, NOV; SSC 2; WLC**

Doughty, Charles M(ontagu) 1843-1926 **TCLC 27**
See also CA 115; DLB 19, 57, 174

Douglas, Ellen .... **CLC 73**
See also Haxton, Josephine Ayres; Williamson, Ellen Douglas

Douglas, Gavin 1475(?)-1522 .... **LC 20**
See also DLB 132

Douglas, George
See Brown, George Douglas

Douglas, Keith (Castellain) 1920-1944**T C L C 40**
See also CA 160; DLB 27

Douglas, Leonard
See Bradbury, Ray (Douglas)

Douglas, Michael
See Crichton, (John) Michael

Douglas, (George) Norman 1868-1952**T C L C 68**
See also CA 119; 157; DLB 34, 195

Douglas, William
See Brown, George Douglas

Douglass, Frederick 1817(?)-1895**NCLC 7, 55; BLC 1; DA; DAC; DAM MST, MULT; WLC**
See also CDALB 1640-1865; DLB 1, 43, 50, 79; SATA 29

Dourado, (Waldomiro Freitas) Autran 1926- **CLC 23, 60**
See also CA 25-28R; CANR 34

Dourado, Waldomiro Autran
See Dourado, (Waldomiro Freitas) Autran

Dove, Rita (Frances) 1952-**CLC 50, 81; BLCS; DAM MULT, POET; PC 6**
See also BW 2; CA 109; CAAS 19; CANR 27, 42, 68; DLB 120

Doveglion
See Villa, Jose Garcia

Dowell, Coleman 1925-1985 .... **CLC 60**
See also CA 25-28R; 117; CANR 10; DLB 130

Dowson, Ernest (Christopher) 1867-1900 **TCLC 4**
See also CA 105; 150; DLB 19, 135

Doyle, A. Conan
See Doyle, Arthur Conan

Doyle, Arthur Conan 1859-1930**TCLC 7; DA; DAB; DAC; DAM MST, NOV; SSC 12; WLC**
See also AAYA 14; CA 104; 122; CDBLB 1890-1914; DLB 18, 70, 156, 178; MTCW; SATA 24

Doyle, Conan
See Doyle, Arthur Conan

Doyle, John
See Graves, Robert (von Ranke)

Doyle, Roddy 1958(?)- .... **CLC 81**
See also AAYA 14; CA 143; DLB 194

Doyle, Sir A. Conan
See Doyle, Arthur Conan

Doyle, Sir Arthur Conan
See Doyle, Arthur Conan

Dr. A
See Asimov, Isaac; Silverstein, Alvin

Drabble, Margaret 1939-**CLC 2, 3, 5, 8, 10, 22, 53; DAB; DAC; DAM MST, NOV, POP**
See also CA 13-16R; CANR 18, 35, 63; CDBLB 1960 to Present; DLB 14, 155; MTCW; SATA 48

Drapier, M. B.
See Swift, Jonathan

Drayham, James
See Mencken, H(enry) L(ouis)

Drayton, Michael 1563-1631 ...... **LC 8; DAM POET**
See also DLB 121

Dreadstone, Carl
See Campbell, (John) Ramsey

Dreiser, Theodore (Herman Albert) 1871-1945 **TCLC 10, 18, 35, 83; DA; DAC; DAM MST, NOV; SSC 30; WLC**
See also CA 106; 132; CDALB 1865-1917; DLB 9, 12, 102, 137; DLBD 1; MTCW

Drexler, Rosalyn 1926- .... **CLC 2, 6**
See also CA 81-84; CANR 68

Dreyer, Carl Theodor 1889-1968 ...... **CLC 16**
See also CA 116

Drieu la Rochelle, Pierre(-Eugene) 1893-1945 **TCLC 21**
See also CA 117; DLB 72

Drinkwater, John 1882-1937 .... **TCLC 57**
See also CA 109; 149; DLB 10, 19, 149

Drop Shot
See Cable, George Washington

Droste-Hulshoff, Annette Freiin von 1797-1848 **NCLC 3**
See also DLB 133

Drummond, Walter
See Silverberg, Robert

Drummond, William Henry 1854-1907**T C L C 25**
See also CA 160; DLB 92

Drummond de Andrade, Carlos 1902-1987 **CLC 18**
See also Andrade, Carlos Drummond de
See also CA 132; 123

Drury, Allen (Stuart) 1918- .... **CLC 37**
See also CA 57-60; CANR 18, 52; INT CANR-18

Dryden, John 1631-1700**LC 3, 21; DA; DAB; DAC; DAM DRAM, MST, POET; DC 3; WLC**
See also CDBLB 1660-1789; DLB 80, 101, 131

Duberman, Martin (Bauml) 1930- ..... **CLC 8**
See also CA 1-4R; CANR 2, 63

Dubie, Norman (Evans) 1945- .... **CLC 36**
See also CA 69-72; CANR 12; DLB 120

Du Bois, W(illiam) E(dward) B(urghardt) 1868-1963 .. **CLC 1, 2, 13, 64, 96; BLC 1; DA; DAC; DAM MST, MULT, NOV; WLC**
See also BW 1; CA 85-88; CANR 34; CDALB 1865-1917; DLB 47, 50, 91; MTCW; SATA 42

Dubus, Andre 1936- **CLC 13, 36, 97; SSC 15**
See also CA 21-24R; CANR 17; DLB 130; INT CANR-17

Duca Minimo
See D'Annunzio, Gabriele

Ducharme, Rejean 1941- .... **CLC 74**
See also CA 165; DLB 60

Duclos, Charles Pinot 1704-1772 .... **LC 1**

Dudek, Louis 1918- .... **CLC 11, 19**
See also CA 45-48; CAAS 14; CANR 1; DLB 88

Duerrenmatt, Friedrich 1921-1990 **CLC 1, 4,**

8, 11, 15, 43, 102; DAM DRAM
See also CA 17-20R; CANR 33; DLB 69, 124; MTCW

Duffy, Bruce (?)- .... **CLC 50**

Duffy, Maureen 1933- .... **CLC 37**
See also CA 25-28R; CANR 33, 68; DLB 14; MTCW

Dugan, Alan 1923- .... **CLC 2, 6**
See also CA 81-84; DLB 5

du Gard, Roger Martin
See Martin du Gard, Roger

Duhamel, Georges 1884-1966 .... **CLC 8**
See also CA 81-84; 25-28R; CANR 35; DLB 65; MTCW

Dujardin, Edouard (Emile Louis) 1861-1949
TCLC 13
See also CA 109; DLB 123

Dulles, John Foster 1888-1959 .... **TCLC 72**
See also CA 115; 149

Dumas, Alexandre (Davy de la Pailleterie)
1802-1870 .. **NCLC 11; DA; DAB; DAC; DAM MST, NOV; WLC**
See also DLB 119, 192; SATA 18

Dumas (fils), Alexandre 1824-1895 **NCLC 71; DC 1**
See also AAYA 22; DLB 192

Dumas, Claudine
See Malzberg, Barry N(athaniel)

Dumas, Henry L. 1934-1968 .... **CLC 6, 62**
See also BW 1; CA 85-88; DLB 41

du Maurier, Daphne 1907-1989 **CLC 6, 11, 59; DAB; DAC; DAM MST, POP; SSC 18**
See also CA 5-8R; 128; CANR 6, 55; DLB 191; MTCW; SATA 27; SATA-Obit 60

Dunbar, Paul Laurence 1872-1906 . **TCLC 2, 12; BLC 1; DA; DAC; DAM MST, MULT, POET; PC 5; SSC 8; WLC**
See also BW 1; CA 104; 124; CDALB 1865-1917; DLB 50, 54, 78; SATA 34

Dunbar, William 1460(?)-1530(?) .... **LC 20**
See also DLB 132, 146

Duncan, Dora Angela
See Duncan, Isadora

Duncan, Isadora 1877(?)-1927 .... **TCLC 68**
See also CA 118; 149

Duncan, Lois 1934- .... **CLC 26**
See also AAYA 4; CA 1-4R; CANR 2, 23, 36; CLR 29; JRDA; MAICYA; SAAS 2; SATA 1, 36, 75

Duncan, Robert (Edward) 1919-1988 **CLC 1, 2, 4, 7, 15, 41, 55; DAM POET; PC 2**
See also CA 9-12R; 124; CANR 28, 62; DLB 5, 16, 193; MTCW

Duncan, Sara Jeannette 1861-1922 **TCLC 60**
See also CA 157; DLB 92

Dunlap, William 1766-1839 .... **NCLC 2**
See also DLB 30, 37, 59

Dunn, Douglas (Eaglesham) 1942- **CLC 6, 40**
See also CA 45-48; CANR 2, 33; DLB 40; MTCW

Dunn, Katherine (Karen) 1945- .... **CLC 71**
See also CA 33-36R

Dunn, Stephen 1939- .... **CLC 36**
See also CA 33-36R; CANR 12, 48, 53; DLB 105

Dunne, Finley Peter 1867-1936 ...... **TCLC 28**
See also CA 108; DLB 11, 23

Dunne, John Gregory 1932- .... **CLC 28**
See also CA 25-28R; CANR 14, 50; DLBY 80

Dunsany, Edward John Moreton Drax Plunkett
1878-1957
See Dunsany, Lord
See also CA 104; 148; DLB 10

Dunsany, Lord .... **TCLC 2, 59**
See also Dunsany, Edward John Moreton Drax Plunkett
See also DLB 77, 153, 156

du Perry, Jean
See Simenon, Georges (Jacques Christian)

Durang, Christopher (Ferdinand) 1949-**C L C 27, 38**
See also CA 105; CANR 50

Duras, Marguerite 1914-1996 **CLC 3, 6, 11, 20, 34, 40, 68, 100**
See also CA 25-28R; 151; CANR 50; DLB 83; MTCW

Durban, (Rosa) Pam 1947- .... **CLC 39**
See also CA 123

Durcan, Paul 1944-**CLC 43, 70; DAM POET**
See also CA 134

Durkheim, Emile 1858-1917 .... **TCLC 55**

Durrell, Lawrence (George) 1912-1990 **C L C 1, 4, 6, 8, 13, 27, 41; DAM NOV**
See also CA 9-12R; 132; CANR 40; CDBLB 1945-1960; DLB 15, 27; DLBY 90; MTCW

Durrenmatt, Friedrich
See Duerrenmatt, Friedrich

Dutt, Toru 1856-1877 .... **NCLC 29**

Dwight, Timothy 1752-1817 .... **NCLC 13**
See also DLB 37

Dworkin, Andrea 1946- .... **CLC 43**
See also CA 77-80; CAAS 21; CANR 16, 39; INT CANR-16; MTCW

Dwyer, Deanna
See Koontz, Dean R(ay)

Dwyer, K. R.
See Koontz, Dean R(ay)

Dye, Richard
See De Voto, Bernard (Augustine)

Dylan, Bob 1941- .... **CLC 3, 4, 6, 12, 77**
See also CA 41-44R; DLB 16

Eagleton, Terence (Francis) 1943-
See Eagleton, Terry
See also CA 57-60; CANR 7, 23, 68; MTCW

Eagleton, Terry .... **CLC 63**
See also Eagleton, Terence (Francis)

Early, Jack
See Scoppettone, Sandra

East, Michael
See West, Morris L(anglo)

Eastaway, Edward
See Thomas, (Philip) Edward

Eastlake, William (Derry) 1917-1997 **CLC 8**
See also CA 5-8R; 158; CAAS 1; CANR 5, 63; DLB 6; INT CANR-5

Eastman, Charles A(lexander) 1858-1939
TCLC 55; DAM MULT
See also DLB 175; NNAL; YABC 1

Eberhart, Richard (Ghormley) 1904-**CLC 3, 11, 19, 56; DAM POET**
See also CA 1-4R; CANR 2; CDALB 1941-1968; DLB 48; MTCW

Eberstadt, Fernanda 1960- .... **CLC 39**
See also CA 136; CANR 69

Echegaray (y Eizaguirre), Jose (Maria Waldo)
1832-1916 .... **TCLC 4**
See also CA 104; CANR 32; HW; MTCW

Echeverria, (Jose) Esteban (Antonino) 1805-1851 .... **NCLC 18**

Echo
See Proust, (Valentin-Louis-George-Eugene-) Marcel

Eckert, Allan W. 1931- .... **CLC 17**
See also AAYA 18; CA 13-16R; CANR 14, 45; INT CANR-14; SAAS 21; SATA 29, 91; SATA-Brief 27

Eckhart, Meister 1260(?)-1328(?) ... **CMLC 9**
See also DLB 115

Eckmar, F. R.
See de Hartog, Jan

Eco, Umberto 1932- **CLC 28, 60; DAM NOV, POP**
See also BEST 90:1; CA 77-80; CANR 12, 33, 55; DLB 196; MTCW

Eddison, E(ric) R(ucker) 1882-1945 **TCLC 15**
See also CA 109; 156

Eddy, Mary (Morse) Baker 1821-1910 **T C L C 71**
See also CA 113

Edel, (Joseph) Leon 1907-1997 .. **CLC 29, 34**
See also CA 1-4R; 161; CANR 1, 22; DLB 103; INT CANR-22

Eden, Emily 1797-1869 .... **NCLC 10**

Edgar, David 1948- ... **CLC 42; DAM DRAM**
See also CA 57-60; CANR 12, 61; DLB 13; MTCW

Edgerton, Clyde (Carlyle) 1944- ...... **CLC 39**
See also AAYA 17; CA 118; 134; CANR 64; INT 134

Edgeworth, Maria 1768-1849 .... **NCLC 1, 51**
See also DLB 116, 159, 163; SATA 21

Edmonds, Paul
See Kuttner, Henry

Edmonds, Walter D(umaux) 1903- ... **CLC 35**
See also CA 5-8R; CANR 2; DLB 9; MAICYA; SAAS 4; SATA 1, 27

Edmondson, Wallace
See Ellison, Harlan (Jay)

Edson, Russell .... **CLC 13**
See also CA 33-36R

Edwards, Bronwen Elizabeth
See Rose, Wendy

Edwards, G(erald) B(asil) 1899-1976 **CLC 25**
See also CA 110

Edwards, Gus 1939- .... **CLC 43**
See also CA 108; INT 108

Edwards, Jonathan 1703-1758 .... **LC 7; DA; DAC; DAM MST**
See also DLB 24

Efron, Marina Ivanovna Tsvetaeva
See Tsvetaeva (Efron), Marina (Ivanovna)

Ehle, John (Marsden, Jr.) 1925- .... **CLC 27**
See also CA 9-12R

Ehrenbourg, Ilya (Grigoryevich)
See Ehrenburg, Ilya (Grigoryevich)

Ehrenburg, Ilya (Grigoryevich) 1891-1967
CLC 18, 34, 62
See also CA 102; 25-28R

Ehrenburg, Ilyo (Grigoryevich)
See Ehrenburg, Ilya (Grigoryevich)

Ehrenreich, Barbara 1941- .... **CLC 110**
See also BEST 90:4; CA 73-76; CANR 16, 37, 62; MTCW

Eich, Guenter 1907-1972 .... **CLC 15**
See also CA 111; 93-96; DLB 69, 124

Eichendorff, Joseph Freiherr von 1788-1857
NCLC 8
See also DLB 90

Eigner, Larry .... **CLC 9**
See also Eigner, Laurence (Joel)
See also CAAS 23; DLB 5

Eigner, Laurence (Joel) 1927-1996
See Eigner, Larry
See also CA 9-12R; 151; CANR 6; DLB 193

Einstein, Albert 1879-1955 .... **TCLC 65**
See also CA 121; 133; MTCW

Eiseley, Loren Corey 1907-1977 .... **CLC 7**
See also AAYA 5; CA 1-4R; 73-76; CANR 6

Eisenstadt, Jill 1963- .... **CLC 50**

Evarts, Esther
See Benson, Sally
Everett, Percival L. 1956- .... **CLC 57**
See also BW 2; CA 129
Everson, R(onald) G(ilmour) 1903- . **CLC 27**
See also CA 17-20R; DLB 88
Everson, William (Oliver) 1912-1994 **CLC 1, 5, 14**
See also CA 9-12R; 145; CANR 20; DLB 5, 16; MTCW
Evtushenko, Evgenii Aleksandrovich
See Yevtushenko, Yevgeny (Alexandrovich)
Ewart, Gavin (Buchanan) 1916-1995 **CLC 13, 46**
See also CA 89-92; 150; CANR 17, 46; DLB 40; MTCW
Ewers, Hanns Heinz 1871-1943 ..... **TCLC 12**
See also CA 109; 149
Ewing, Frederick R.
See Sturgeon, Theodore (Hamilton)
Exley, Frederick (Earl) 1929-1992 **CLC 6, 11**
See also AITN 2; CA 81-84; 138; DLB 143; DLBY 81
Eynhardt, Guillermo
See Quiroga, Horacio (Sylvestre)
Ezekiel, Nissim 1924- .... **CLC 61**
See also CA 61-64
Ezekiel, Tish O'Dowd 1943- .... **CLC 34**
See also CA 129
Fadeyev, A.
See Bulgya, Alexander Alexandrovich
Fadeyev, Alexander .... **TCLC 53**
See also Bulgya, Alexander Alexandrovich
Fagen, Donald 1948- .... **CLC 26**
Fainzilberg, Ilya Arnoldovich 1897-1937
See Ilf, Ilya
See also CA 120; 165
Fair, Ronald L. 1932- .... **CLC 18**
See also BW 1; CA 69-72; CANR 25; DLB 33
Fairbairn, Roger
See Carr, John Dickson
Fairbairns, Zoe (Ann) 1948- .... **CLC 32**
See also CA 103; CANR 21
Falco, Gian
See Papini, Giovanni
Falconer, James
See Kirkup, James
Falconer, Kenneth
See Kornbluth, C(yril) M.
Falkland, Samuel
See Heijermans, Herman
Fallaci, Oriana 1930- .... **CLC 11, 110**
See also CA 77-80; CANR 15, 58; MTCW
Faludy, George 1913- .... **CLC 42**
See also CA 21-24R
Faludy, Gyoergy
See Faludy, George
Fanon, Frantz 1925-1961 ... **CLC 74; BLC 2; DAM MULT**
See also BW 1; CA 116; 89-92
Fanshawe, Ann 1625-1680 .... **LC 11**
Fante, John (Thomas) 1911-1983 ..... **CLC 60**
See also CA 69-72; 109; CANR 23; DLB 130; DLBY 83
Farah, Nuruddin 1945- **CLC 53; BLC 2; DAM MULT**
See also BW 2; CA 106; DLB 125
Fargue, Leon-Paul 1876(?)-1947 ... **TCLC 11**
See also CA 109
Farigoule, Louis
See Romains, Jules
Farina, Richard 1936(?)-1966 .... **CLC 9**
See also CA 81-84; 25-28R

Farley, Walter (Lorimer) 1915-1989 **CLC 17**
See also CA 17-20R; CANR 8, 29; DLB 22; JRDA; MAICYA; SATA 2, 43
Farmer, Philip Jose 1918- .... **CLC 1, 19**
See also CA 1-4R; CANR 4, 35; DLB 8; MTCW; SATA 93
Farquhar, George 1677-1707 ... **LC 21; DAM DRAM**
See also DLB 84
Farrell, J(ames) G(ordon) 1935-1979 **CLC 6**
See also CA 73-76; 89-92; CANR 36; DLB 14; MTCW
Farrell, James T(homas) 1904-1979 **CLC 1, 4, 8, 11, 66; SSC 28**
See also CA 5-8R; 89-92; CANR 9, 61; DLB 4, 9, 86; DLBD 2; MTCW
Farren, Richard J.
See Betjeman, John
Farren, Richard M.
See Betjeman, John
Fassbinder, Rainer Werner 1946-1982 **CLC 20**
See also CA 93-96; 106; CANR 31
Fast, Howard (Melvin) 1914- **CLC 23; DAM NOV**
See also AAYA 16; CA 1-4R; CAAS 18; CANR 1, 33, 54; DLB 9; INT CANR-33; SATA 7
Faulcon, Robert
See Holdstock, Robert P.
Faulkner, William (Cuthbert) 1897-1962 **CLC 1, 3, 6, 8, 9, 11, 14, 18, 28, 52, 68; DA; DAB; DAC; DAM MST, NOV; SSC 1; WLC**
See also AAYA 7; CA 81-84; CANR 33; CDALB 1929-1941; DLB 9, 11, 44, 102; DLBD 2; DLBY 86, 97; MTCW
Fauset, Jessie Redmon 1884(?)-1961 **CLC 19, 54; BLC 2; DAM MULT**
See also BW 1; CA 109; DLB 51
Faust, Frederick (Schiller) 1892-1944(?) **TCLC 49; DAM POP**
See also CA 108; 152
Faust, Irvin 1924- .... **CLC 8**
See also CA 33-36R; CANR 28, 67; DLB 2, 28; DLBY 80
Fawkes, Guy
See Benchley, Robert (Charles)
Fearing, Kenneth (Flexner) 1902-1961 . **CLC 51**
See also CA 93-96; CANR 59; DLB 9
Fecamps, Elise
See Creasey, John
Federman, Raymond 1928- .... **CLC 6, 47**
See also CA 17-20R; CAAS 8; CANR 10, 43; DLBY 80
Federspiel, J(uerg) F. 1931- .... **CLC 42**
See also CA 146
Feiffer, Jules (Ralph) 1929- ..... **CLC 2, 8, 64; DAM DRAM**
See also AAYA 3; CA 17-20R; CANR 30, 59; DLB 7, 44; INT CANR-30; MTCW; SATA 8, 61
Feige, Hermann Albert Otto Maximilian
See Traven, B.
Feinberg, David B. 1956-1994 .... **CLC 59**
See also CA 135; 147
Feinstein, Elaine 1930- .... **CLC 36**
See also CA 69-72; CAAS 1; CANR 31, 68; DLB 14, 40; MTCW
Feldman, Irving (Mordecai) 1928- ..... **CLC 7**
See also CA 1-4R; CANR 1; DLB 169
Felix-Tchicaya, Gerald
See Tchicaya, Gerald Felix
Fellini, Federico 1920-1993 .... **CLC 16, 85**
See also CA 65-68; 143; CANR 33

Felsen, Henry Gregor 1916- .... **CLC 17**
See also CA 1-4R; CANR 1; SAAS 2; SATA 1
Fenno, Jack
See Calisher, Hortense
Fenton, James Martin 1949- .... **CLC 32**
See also CA 102; DLB 40
Ferber, Edna 1887-1968 .... **CLC 18, 93**
See also AITN 1; CA 5-8R; 25-28R; CANR 68; DLB 9, 28, 86; MTCW; SATA 7
Ferguson, Helen
See Kavan, Anna
Ferguson, Samuel 1810-1886 .... **NCLC 33**
See also DLB 32
Fergusson, Robert 1750-1774 .... **LC 29**
See also DLB 109
Ferling, Lawrence
See Ferlinghetti, Lawrence (Monsanto)
Ferlinghetti, Lawrence (Monsanto) 1919(?)- **CLC 2, 6, 10, 27, 111; DAM POET; PC 1**
See also CA 5-8R; CANR 3, 41; CDALB 1941-1968; DLB 5, 16; MTCW
Fernandez, Vicente Garcia Huidobro
See Huidobro Fernandez, Vicente Garcia
Ferrer, Gabriel (Francisco Victor) Miro
See Miro (Ferrer), Gabriel (Francisco Victor)
Ferrier, Susan (Edmonstone) 1782-1854 **NCLC 8**
See also DLB 116
Ferrigno, Robert 1948(?)- .... **CLC 65**
See also CA 140
Ferron, Jacques 1921-1985 .... **CLC 94; DAC**
See also CA 117; 129; DLB 60
Feuchtwanger, Lion 1884-1958 .... **TCLC 3**
See also CA 104; DLB 66
Feuillet, Octave 1821-1890 .... **NCLC 45**
See also DLB 192
Feydeau, Georges (Leon Jules Marie) 1862-1921 .... **TCLC 22; DAM DRAM**
See also CA 113; 152; DLB 192
Fichte, Johann Gottlieb 1762-1814 **NCLC 62**
See also DLB 90
Ficino, Marsilio 1433-1499 .... **LC 12**
Fiedeler, Hans
See Doeblin, Alfred
Fiedler, Leslie A(aron) 1917- . **CLC 4, 13, 24**
See also CA 9-12R; CANR 7, 63; DLB 28, 67; MTCW
Field, Andrew 1938- .... **CLC 44**
See also CA 97-100; CANR 25
Field, Eugene 1850-1895 .... **NCLC 3**
See also DLB 23, 42, 140; DLBD 13; MAICYA; SATA 16
Field, Gans T.
See Wellman, Manly Wade
Field, Michael 1915-1971 .... **TCLC 43**
See also CA 29-32R
Field, Peter
See Hobson, Laura Z(ametkin)
Fielding, Henry 1707-1754 **LC 1; DA; DAB; DAC; DAM DRAM, MST, NOV; WLC**
See also CDBLB 1660-1789; DLB 39, 84, 101
Fielding, Sarah 1710-1768 .... **LC 1, 44**
See also DLB 39
Fields, W. C. 1880-1946 .... **TCLC 80**
See also DLB 44
Fierstein, Harvey (Forbes) 1954- ... **CLC 33; DAM DRAM, POP**
See also CA 123; 129
Figes, Eva 1932- .... **CLC 31**
See also CA 53-56; CANR 4, 44; DLB 14
Finch, Anne 1661-1720 .... **LC 3; PC 21**
See also DLB 95
Finch, Robert (Duer Claydon) 1900- **CLC 18**

See also CA 57-60; CANR 9, 24, 49; DLB 88
Findley, Timothy 1930- . **CLC 27, 102; DAC; DAM MST**
See also CA 25-28R; CANR 12, 42, 69; DLB 53
Fink, William
See Mencken, H(enry) L(ouis)
Firbank, Louis 1942-
See Reed, Lou
See also CA 117
Firbank, (Arthur Annesley) Ronald 1886-1926
TCLC 1
See also CA 104; DLB 36
Fisher, M(ary) F(rances) K(ennedy) 1908-1992
CLC 76, 87
See also CA 77-80; 138; CANR 44
Fisher, Roy 1930- .... **CLC 25**
See also CA 81-84; CAAS 10; CANR 16; DLB 40
Fisher, Rudolph 1897-1934 **TCLC 11; BLC 2; DAM MULT; SSC 25**
See also BW 1; CA 107; 124; DLB 51, 102
Fisher, Vardis (Alvero) 1895-1968 ...... **CLC 7**
See also CA 5-8R; 25-28R; CANR 68; DLB 9
Fiske, Tarleton
See Bloch, Robert (Albert)
Fitch, Clarke
See Sinclair, Upton (Beall)
Fitch, John IV
See Cormier, Robert (Edmund)
Fitzgerald, Captain Hugh
See Baum, L(yman) Frank
FitzGerald, Edward 1809-1883 .... **NCLC 9**
See also DLB 32
Fitzgerald, F(rancis) Scott (Key) 1896-1940
TCLC 1, 6, 14, 28, 55; DA; DAB; DAC; DAM MST, NOV; SSC 6, 31; WLC
See also AAYA 24; AITN 1; CA 110; 123; CDALB 1917-1929; DLB 4, 9, 86; DLBD 1, 15, 16; DLBY 81, 96; MTCW
Fitzgerald, Penelope 1916- ... **CLC 19, 51, 61**
See also CA 85-88; CAAS 10; CANR 56; DLB 14, 194
Fitzgerald, Robert (Stuart) 1910-1985 **CLC 39**
See also CA 1-4R; 114; CANR 1; DLBY 80
FitzGerald, Robert D(avid) 1902-1987 **CLC 19**
See also CA 17-20R
Fitzgerald, Zelda (Sayre) 1900-1948 **TCLC 52**
See also CA 117; 126; DLBY 84
Flanagan, Thomas (James Bonner) 1923-
CLC 25, 52
See also CA 108; CANR 55; DLBY 80; INT 108; MTCW
Flaubert, Gustave 1821-1880 **NCLC 2, 10, 19, 62, 66; DA; DAB; DAC; DAM MST, NOV; SSC 11; WLC**
See also DLB 119
Flecker, Herman Elroy
See Flecker, (Herman) James Elroy
Flecker, (Herman) James Elroy 1884-1915
TCLC 43
See also CA 109; 150; DLB 10, 19
Fleming, Ian (Lancaster) 1908-1964 . **CLC 3, 30; DAM POP**
See also CA 5-8R; CANR 59; CDBLB 1945-1960; DLB 87; MTCW; SATA 9
Fleming, Thomas (James) 1927- .... **CLC 37**
See also CA 5-8R; CANR 10; INT CANR-10; SATA 8
Fletcher, John 1579-1625 .... **LC 33; DC 6**
See also CDBLB Before 1660; DLB 58
Fletcher, John Gould 1886-1950 .... **TCLC 35**
See also CA 107; DLB 4, 45

Fleur, Paul
See Pohl, Frederik
Flooglebuckle, Al
See Spiegelman, Art
Flying Officer X
See Bates, H(erbert) E(rnest)
Fo, Dario 1926- . **CLC 32, 109; DAM DRAM**
See also CA 116; 128; CANR 68; DLBY 97; MTCW
Fogarty, Jonathan Titulescu Esq.
See Farrell, James T(homas)
Folke, Will
See Bloch, Robert (Albert)
Follett, Ken(neth Martin) 1949- ..... **CLC 18; DAM NOV, POP**
See also AAYA 6; BEST 89:4; CA 81-84; CANR 13, 33, 54; DLB 87; DLBY 81; INT CANR-33; MTCW
Fontane, Theodor 1819-1898 .... **NCLC 26**
See also DLB 129
Foote, Horton 1916- **CLC 51, 91; DAM DRAM**
See also CA 73-76; CANR 34, 51; DLB 26; INT CANR-34
Foote, Shelby 1916- **CLC 75; DAM NOV, POP**
See also CA 5-8R; CANR 3, 45; DLB 2, 17
Forbes, Esther 1891-1967 .... **CLC 12**
See also AAYA 17; CA 13-14; 25-28R; CAP 1; CLR 27; DLB 22; JRDA; MAICYA; SATA 2
Forche, Carolyn (Louise) 1950- **CLC 25, 83, 86; DAM POET; PC 10**
See also CA 109; 117; CANR 50; DLB 5, 193; INT 117
Ford, Elbur
See Hibbert, Eleanor Alice Burford
Ford, Ford Madox 1873-1939 **TCLC 1, 15, 39, 57; DAM NOV**
See also CA 104; 132; CDBLB 1914-1945; DLB 162; MTCW
Ford, Henry 1863-1947 .... **TCLC 73**
See also CA 115; 148
Ford, John 1586-(?) .... **DC 8**
See also CDBLB Before 1660; DAM DRAM; DLB 58
Ford, John 1895-1973 .... **CLC 16**
See also CA 45-48
Ford, Richard 1944- .... **CLC 46, 99**
See also CA 69-72; CANR 11, 47
Ford, Webster
See Masters, Edgar Lee
Foreman, Richard 1937- .... **CLC 50**
See also CA 65-68; CANR 32, 63
Forester, C(ecil) S(cott) 1899-1966 ... **CLC 35**
See also CA 73-76; 25-28R; DLB 191; SATA 13
Forez
See Mauriac, Francois (Charles)
Forman, James Douglas 1932- .... **CLC 21**
See also AAYA 17; CA 9-12R; CANR 4, 19, 42; JRDA; MAICYA; SATA 8, 70
Fornes, Maria Irene 1930- .... **CLC 39, 61**
See also CA 25-28R; CANR 28; DLB 7; HW; INT CANR-28; MTCW
Forrest, Leon (Richard) 1937-1997 .. **CLC 4; BLCS**
See also BW 2; CA 89-92; 162; CAAS 7; CANR 25, 52; DLB 33
Forster, E(dward) M(organ) 1879-1970 **CLC 1, 2, 3, 4, 9, 10, 13, 15, 22, 45, 77; DA; DAB; DAC; DAM MST, NOV; SSC 27; WLC**
See also AAYA 2; CA 13-14; 25-28R; CANR 45; CAP 1; CDBLB 1914-1945; DLB 34, 98, 162, 178, 195; DLBD 10; MTCW; SATA 57
Forster, John 1812-1876 .... **NCLC 11**

See also DLB 144, 184
Forsyth, Frederick 1938- **CLC 2, 5, 36; DAM NOV, POP**
See also BEST 89:4; CA 85-88; CANR 38, 62; DLB 87; MTCW
Forten, Charlotte L. .... **TCLC 16; BLC 2**
See also Grimke, Charlotte L(ottie) Forten
See also DLB 50
Foscolo, Ugo 1778-1827 .... **NCLC 8**
Fosse, Bob .... **CLC 20**
See also Fosse, Robert Louis
Fosse, Robert Louis 1927-1987
See Fosse, Bob
See also CA 110; 123
Foster, Stephen Collins 1826-1864 **NCLC 26**
Foucault, Michel 1926-1984 . **CLC 31, 34, 69**
See also CA 105; 113; CANR 34; MTCW
Fouque, Friedrich (Heinrich Karl) de la Motte 1777-1843 .... **NCLC 2**
See also DLB 90
Fourier, Charles 1772-1837 .... **NCLC 51**
Fournier, Henri Alban 1886-1914
See Alain-Fournier
See also CA 104
Fournier, Pierre 1916- .... **CLC 11**
See Gascar, Pierre
See also CA 89-92; CANR 16, 40
Fowles, John 1926- **CLC 1, 2, 3, 4, 6, 9, 10, 15, 33, 87; DAB; DAC; DAM MST**
See also CA 5-8R; CANR 25; CDBLB 1960 to Present; DLB 14, 139; MTCW; SATA 22
Fox, Paula 1923- .... **CLC 2, 8**
See also AAYA 3; CA 73-76; CANR 20, 36, 62; CLR 1, 44; DLB 52; JRDA; MAICYA; MTCW; SATA 17, 60
Fox, William Price (Jr.) 1926- .... **CLC 22**
See also CA 17-20R; CAAS 19; CANR 11; DLB 2; DLBY 81
Foxe, John 1516(?)-1587 .... **LC 14**
See also DLB 132
Frame, Janet 1924- **CLC 2, 3, 6, 22, 66, 96; SSC 29**
See also Clutha, Janet Paterson Frame
France, Anatole .... **TCLC 9**
See also Thibault, Jacques Anatole Francois
See also DLB 123
Francis, Claude 19(?)- .... **CLC 50**
Francis, Dick 1920- **CLC 2, 22, 42, 102; DAM POP**
See also AAYA 5, 21; BEST 89:3; CA 5-8R; CANR 9, 42, 68; CDBLB 1960 to Present; DLB 87; INT CANR-9; MTCW
Francis, Robert (Churchill) 1901-1987 **C L C 15**
See also CA 1-4R; 123; CANR 1
Frank, Anne(lies Marie) 1929-1945 **TCLC 17; DA; DAB; DAC; DAM MST; WLC**
See also AAYA 12; CA 113; 133; CANR 68; MTCW; SATA 87; SATA-Brief 42
Frank, Bruno 1887-1945 .... **TCLC 81**
See also DLB 118
Frank, Elizabeth 1945- .... **CLC 39**
See also CA 121; 126; INT 126
Frankl, Viktor E(mil) 1905-1997 ...... **CLC 93**
See also CA 65-68; 161
Franklin, Benjamin
See Hasek, Jaroslav (Matej Frantisek)
Franklin, Benjamin 1706-1790 .. **LC 25; DA; DAB; DAC; DAM MST; WLCS**
See also CDALB 1640-1865; DLB 24, 43, 73
Franklin, (Stella Maria Sarah) Miles (Lampe) 1879-1954 .... **TCLC 7**
See also CA 104; 164

Fraser, (Lady) Antonia (Pakenham) 1932-
CLC 32, 107
See also CA 85-88; CANR 44, 65; MTCW;
SATA-Brief 32

Fraser, George MacDonald 1925- ...... CLC 7
See also CA 45-48; CANR 2, 48

Fraser, Sylvia 1935- .... CLC 64
See also CA 45-48; CANR 1, 16, 60

Frayn, Michael 1933-CLC 3, 7, 31, 47; DAM
DRAM, NOV
See also CA 5-8R; CANR 30, 69; DLB 13, 14,
194; MTCW

Fraze, Candida (Merrill) 1945- .... CLC 50
See also CA 126

Frazer, J(ames) G(eorge) 1854-1941TCLC 32
See also CA 118

Frazer, Robert Caine
See Creasey, John

Frazer, Sir James George
See Frazer, J(ames) G(eorge)

Frazier, Charles 1950- .... CLC 109
See also CA 161

Frazier, Ian 1951- .... CLC 46
See also CA 130; CANR 54

Frederic, Harold 1856-1898 .... NCLC 10
See also DLB 12, 23; DLBD 13

Frederick, John
See Faust, Frederick (Schiller)

Frederick the Great 1712-1786 .... LC 14

Fredro, Aleksander 1793-1876 .... NCLC 8

Freeling, Nicolas 1927- .... CLC 38
See also CA 49-52; CAAS 12; CANR 1, 17,
50; DLB 87

Freeman, Douglas Southall 1886-1953T C L C
11
See also CA 109; DLB 17

Freeman, Judith 1946- .... CLC 55
See also CA 148

Freeman, Mary Eleanor Wilkins 1852-1930
TCLC 9; SSC 1
See also CA 106; DLB 12, 78

Freeman, R(ichard) Austin 1862-1943 T C L C
21
See also CA 113; DLB 70

French, Albert 1943- .... CLC 86

French, Marilyn 1929-CLC 10, 18, 60; DAM
DRAM, NOV, POP
See also CA 69-72; CANR 3, 31; INT CANR-
31; MTCW

French, Paul
See Asimov, Isaac

Freneau, Philip Morin 1752-1832 ... NCLC 1
See also DLB 37, 43

Freud, Sigmund 1856-1939 .... TCLC 52
See also CA 115; 133; CANR 69; MTCW

Friedan, Betty (Naomi) 1921- .... CLC 74
See also CA 65-68; CANR 18, 45; MTCW

Friedlander, Saul 1932- .... CLC 90
See also CA 117; 130

Friedman, B(ernard) H(arper) 1926- CLC 7
See also CA 1-4R; CANR 3, 48

Friedman, Bruce Jay 1930- ...... CLC 3, 5, 56
See also CA 9-12R; CANR 25, 52; DLB 2, 28;
INT CANR-25

Friel, Brian 1929- .... CLC 5, 42, 59; DC 8
See also CA 21-24R; CANR 33, 69; DLB 13;
MTCW

Friis-Baastad, Babbis Ellinor 1921-1970C L C
12
See also CA 17-20R; 134; SATA 7

Frisch, Max (Rudolf) 1911-1991CLC 3, 9, 14,
18, 32, 44; DAM DRAM, NOV
See also CA 85-88; 134; CANR 32; DLB 69,

124; MTCW

Fromentin, Eugene (Samuel Auguste) 1820-
1876 .... NCLC 10
See also DLB 123

Frost, Frederick
See Faust, Frederick (Schiller)

Frost, Robert (Lee) 1874-1963CLC 1, 3, 4, 9,
10, 13, 15, 26, 34, 44; DA; DAB; DAC;
DAM MST, POET; PC 1; WLC
See also AAYA 21; CA 89-92; CANR 33;
CDALB 1917-1929; DLB 54; DLBD 7;
MTCW; SATA 14

Froude, James Anthony 1818-1894NCLC 43
See also DLB 18, 57, 144

Froy, Herald
See Waterhouse, Keith (Spencer)

Fry, Christopher 1907- CLC 2, 10, 14; DAM
DRAM
See also CA 17-20R; CAAS 23; CANR 9, 30;
DLB 13; MTCW; SATA 66

Frye, (Herman) Northrop 1912-1991CLC 24,
70
See also CA 5-8R; 133; CANR 8, 37; DLB 67,
68; MTCW

Fuchs, Daniel 1909-1993 .... CLC 8, 22
See also CA 81-84; 142; CAAS 5; CANR 40;
DLB 9, 26, 28; DLBY 93

Fuchs, Daniel 1934- .... CLC 34
See also CA 37-40R; CANR 14, 48

Fuentes, Carlos 1928-CLC 3, 8, 10, 13, 22, 41,
60, 113; DA; DAB; DAC; DAM MST,
MULT, NOV; HLC; SSC 24; WLC
See also AAYA 4; AITN 2; CA 69-72; CANR
10, 32, 68; DLB 113; HW; MTCW

Fuentes, Gregorio Lopez y
See Lopez y Fuentes, Gregorio

Fugard, (Harold) Athol 1932-CLC 5, 9, 14, 25,
40, 80; DAM DRAM; DC 3
See also AAYA 17; CA 85-88; CANR 32, 54;
MTCW

Fugard, Sheila 1932- .... CLC 48
See also CA 125

Fuller, Charles (H., Jr.) 1939-CLC 25; BLC 2;
DAM DRAM, MULT; DC 1
See also BW 2; CA 108; 112; DLB 38; INT 112;
MTCW

Fuller, John (Leopold) 1937- .... CLC 62
See also CA 21-24R; CANR 9, 44; DLB 40

Fuller, Margaret .... NCLC 5, 50
See also Ossoli, Sarah Margaret (Fuller
marchesa d')

Fuller, Roy (Broadbent) 1912-1991CLC 4, 28
See also CA 5-8R; 135; CAAS 10; CANR 53;
DLB 15, 20; SATA 87

Fulton, Alice 1952- .... CLC 52
See also CA 116; CANR 57; DLB 193

Furphy, Joseph 1843-1912 .... TCLC 25
See also CA 163

Fussell, Paul 1924- .... CLC 74
See also BEST 90:1; CA 17-20R; CANR 8, 21,
35, 69; INT CANR-21; MTCW

Futabatei, Shimei 1864-1909 .... TCLC 44
See also CA 162; DLB 180

Futrelle, Jacques 1875-1912 .... TCLC 19
See also CA 113; 155

Gaboriau, Emile 1835-1873 .... NCLC 14

Gadda, Carlo Emilio 1893-1973 .... CLC 11
See also CA 89-92; DLB 177

Gaddis, William 1922- CLC 1, 3, 6, 8, 10, 19,
43, 86
See also CA 17-20R; CANR 21, 48; DLB 2;
MTCW

Gage, Walter
See Inge, William (Motter)

Gaines, Ernest J(ames) 1933- CLC 3, 11, 18,
86; BLC 2; DAM MULT
See also AAYA 18; AITN 1; BW 2; CA 9-12R;
CANR 6, 24, 42; CDALB 1968-1988; DLB
2, 33, 152; DLBY 80; MTCW; SATA 86

Gaitskill, Mary 1954- .... CLC 69
See also CA 128; CANR 61

Galdos, Benito Perez
See Perez Galdos, Benito

Gale, Zona 1874-1938TCLC 7; DAM DRAM
See also CA 105; 153; DLB 9, 78

Galeano, Eduardo (Hughes) 1940- ... CLC 72
See also CA 29-32R; CANR 13, 32; HW

Galiano, Juan Valera y Alcala
See Valera y Alcala-Galiano, Juan

Galilei, Galileo 1546-1642 .... LC 45

Gallagher, Tess 1943- ...... CLC 18, 63; DAM
POET; PC 9
See also CA 106; DLB 120

Gallant, Mavis 1922- ...CLC 7, 18, 38; DAC;
DAM MST; SSC 5
See also CA 69-72; CANR 29, 69; DLB 53;
MTCW

Gallant, Roy A(rthur) 1924- .... CLC 17
See also CA 5-8R; CANR 4, 29, 54; CLR 30;
MAICYA; SATA 4, 68

Gallico, Paul (William) 1897-1976 ..... CLC 2
See also AITN 1; CA 5-8R; 69-72; CANR 23;
DLB 9, 171; MAICYA; SATA 13

Gallo, Max Louis 1932- .... CLC 95
See also CA 85-88

Gallois, Lucien
See Desnos, Robert

Gallup, Ralph
See Whitemore, Hugh (John)

Galsworthy, John 1867-1933TCLC 1, 45; DA;
DAB; DAC; DAM DRAM, MST, NOV;
SSC 22; WLC 2
See also CA 104; 141; CDBLB 1890-1914;
DLB 10, 34, 98, 162; DLBD 16

Galt, John 1779-1839 .... NCLC 1
See also DLB 99, 116, 159

Galvin, James 1951- .... CLC 38
See also CA 108; CANR 26

Gamboa, Federico 1864-1939 .... TCLC 36

Gandhi, M. K.
See Gandhi, Mohandas Karamchand

Gandhi, Mahatma
See Gandhi, Mohandas Karamchand

Gandhi, Mohandas Karamchand 1869-1948
TCLC 59; DAM MULT
See also CA 121; 132

Gann, Ernest Kellogg 1910-1991 ...... CLC 23
See also AITN 1; CA 1-4R; 136; CANR 1

Garcia, Cristina 1958- .... CLC 76
See also CA 141

Garcia Lorca, Federico 1898-1936TCLC 1, 7,
49; DA; DAB; DAC; DAM DRAM, MST,
MULT, POET; DC 2; HLC; PC 3; WLC
See also CA 104; 131; DLB 108; HW; MTCW

Garcia Marquez, Gabriel (Jose) 1928-CLC 2,
3, 8, 10, 15, 27, 47, 55, 68; DA; DAB; DAC;
DAM MST, MULT, NOV, POP; HLC; SSC
8; WLC
See also AAYA 3; BEST 89:1, 90:4; CA 33-
36R; CANR 10, 28, 50; DLB 113; HW;
MTCW

Gard, Janice
See Latham, Jean Lee

Gard, Roger Martin du
See Martin du Gard, Roger

Gardam, Jane 1928- .... CLC 43

See also CA 25-28R; CANR 11, 44; DLB 5, 193

Guest, Judith (Ann) 1936- **CLC 8, 30; DAM NOV, POP**
See also AAYA 7; CA 77-80; CANR 15; INT CANR-15; MTCW

Guevara, Che .... **CLC 87; HLC**
See also Guevara (Serna), Ernesto

Guevara (Serna), Ernesto 1928-1967
See Guevara, Che
See also CA 127; 111; CANR 56; DAM MULT; HW

Guild, Nicholas M. 1944- .... **CLC 33**
See also CA 93-96

Guillemin, Jacques
See Sartre, Jean-Paul

Guillen, Jorge 1893-1984 .... **CLC 11; DAM MULT, POET**
See also CA 89-92; 112; DLB 108; HW

Guillen, Nicolas (Cristobal) 1902-1989 **C L C 48, 79; BLC 2; DAM MST, MULT, POET; HLC; PC 23**
See also BW 2; CA 116; 125; 129; HW

Guillevic, (Eugene) 1907- .... **CLC 33**
See also CA 93-96

Guillois
See Desnos, Robert

Guillois, Valentin
See Desnos, Robert

Guiney, Louise Imogen 1861-1920 **TCLC 41**
See also CA 160; DLB 54

Guiraldes, Ricardo (Guillermo) 1886-1927 **TCLC 39**
See also CA 131; HW; MTCW

Gumilev, Nikolai (Stepanovich) 1886-1921 **TCLC 60**
See also CA 165

Gunesekera, Romesh 1954- .... **CLC 91**
See also CA 159

Gunn, Bill .... **CLC 5**
See also Gunn, William Harrison
See also DLB 38

Gunn, Thom(son William) 1929-**CLC 3, 6, 18, 32, 81; DAM POET**
See also CA 17-20R; CANR 9, 33; CDBLB 1960 to Present; DLB 27; INT CANR-33; MTCW

Gunn, William Harrison 1934(?)-1989
See Gunn, Bill
See also AITN 1; BW 1; CA 13-16R; 128; CANR 12, 25

Gunnars, Kristjana 1948- .... **CLC 69**
See also CA 113; DLB 60

Gurdjieff, G(eorgei) I(vanovich) 1877(?)-1949 **TCLC 71**
See also CA 157

Gurganus, Allan 1947- . **CLC 70; DAM POP**
See also BEST 90:1; CA 135

Gurney, A(lbert) R(amsdell), Jr. 1930- . **C L C 32, 50, 54; DAM DRAM**
See also CA 77-80; CANR 32, 64

Gurney, Ivor (Bertie) 1890-1937 ... **TCLC 33**

Gurney, Peter
See Gurney, A(lbert) R(amsdell), Jr.

Guro, Elena 1877-1913 .... **TCLC 56**

Gustafson, James M(oody) 1925- ... **CLC 100**
See also CA 25-28R; CANR 37

Gustafson, Ralph (Barker) 1909- ..... **CLC 36**
See also CA 21-24R; CANR 8, 45; DLB 88

Gut, Gom
See Simenon, Georges (Jacques Christian)

Guterson, David 1956- .... **CLC 91**
See also CA 132

Guthrie, A(lfred) B(ertram), Jr. 1901-1991 **CLC 23**
See also CA 57-60; 134; CANR 24; DLB 6; SATA 62; SATA-Obit 67

Guthrie, Isobel
See Grieve, C(hristopher) M(urray)

Guthrie, Woodrow Wilson 1912-1967
See Guthrie, Woody
See also CA 113; 93-96

Guthrie, Woody .... **CLC 35**
See also Guthrie, Woodrow Wilson

Guy, Rosa (Cuthbert) 1928- .... **CLC 26**
See also AAYA 4; BW 2; CA 17-20R; CANR 14, 34; CLR 13; DLB 33; JRDA; MAICYA; SATA 14, 62

Gwendolyn
See Bennett, (Enoch) Arnold

H. D. .... **CLC 3, 8, 14, 31, 34, 73; PC 5**
See also Doolittle, Hilda

H. de V.
See Buchan, John

Haavikko, Paavo Juhani 1931- .. **CLC 18, 34**
See also CA 106

Habbema, Koos
See Heijermans, Herman

Habermas, Juergen 1929- .... **CLC 104**
See also CA 109

Habermas, Jurgen
See Habermas, Juergen

Hacker, Marilyn 1942- **CLC 5, 9, 23, 72, 91; DAM POET**
See also CA 77-80; CANR 68; DLB 120

Haeckel, Ernst Heinrich (Philipp August) 1834-1919 .... **TCLC 83**
See also CA 157

Haggard, H(enry) Rider 1856-1925**TCLC 11**
See also CA 108; 148; DLB 70, 156, 174, 178; SATA 16

Hagiosy, L.
See Larbaud, Valery (Nicolas)

Hagiwara Sakutaro 1886-1942**TCLC 60; PC 18**

Haig, Fenil
See Ford, Ford Madox

Haig-Brown, Roderick (Langmere) 1908-1976 **CLC 21**
See also CA 5-8R; 69-72; CANR 4, 38; CLR 31; DLB 88; MAICYA; SATA 12

Hailey, Arthur 1920-**CLC 5; DAM NOV, POP**
See also AITN 2; BEST 90:3; CA 1-4R; CANR 2, 36; DLB 88; DLBY 82; MTCW

Hailey, Elizabeth Forsythe 1938- ..... **CLC 40**
See also CA 93-96; CAAS 1; CANR 15, 48; INT CANR-15

Haines, John (Meade) 1924- .... **CLC 58**
See also CA 17-20R; CANR 13, 34; DLB 5

Hakluyt, Richard 1552-1616 .... **LC 31**

Haldeman, Joe (William) 1943- .... **CLC 61**
See also CA 53-56; CAAS 25; CANR 6; DLB 8; INT CANR-6

Haley, Alex(ander Murray Palmer) 1921-1992 **CLC 8, 12, 76; BLC 2; DA; DAB; DAC; DAM MST, MULT, POP**
See also BW 2; CA 77-80; 136; CANR 61; DLB 38; MTCW

Haliburton, Thomas Chandler 1796-1865 **NCLC 15**
See also DLB 11, 99

Hall, Donald (Andrew, Jr.) 1928- **CLC 1, 13, 37, 59; DAM POET**
See also CA 5-8R; CAAS 7; CANR 2, 44, 64; DLB 5; SATA 23, 97

Hall, Frederic Sauser
See Sauser-Hall, Frederic

Hall, James
See Kuttner, Henry

Hall, James Norman 1887-1951 ..... **TCLC 23**
See also CA 123; SATA 21

Hall, (Marguerite) Radclyffe 1886-1943 **TCLC 12**
See also CA 110; 150

Hall, Rodney 1935- .... **CLC 51**
See also CA 109; CANR 69

Halleck, Fitz-Greene 1790-1867 .... **NCLC 47**
See also DLB 3

Halliday, Michael
See Creasey, John

Halpern, Daniel 1945- .... **CLC 14**
See also CA 33-36R

Hamburger, Michael (Peter Leopold) 1924- **CLC 5, 14**
See also CA 5-8R; CAAS 4; CANR 2, 47; DLB 27

Hamill, Pete 1935- .... **CLC 10**
See also CA 25-28R; CANR 18

Hamilton, Alexander 1755(?)-1804 **NCLC 49**
See also DLB 37

Hamilton, Clive
See Lewis, C(live) S(taples)

Hamilton, Edmond 1904-1977 .... **CLC 1**
See also CA 1-4R; CANR 3; DLB 8

Hamilton, Eugene (Jacob) Lee
See Lee-Hamilton, Eugene (Jacob)

Hamilton, Franklin
See Silverberg, Robert

Hamilton, Gail
See Corcoran, Barbara

Hamilton, Mollie
See Kaye, M(ary) M(argaret)

Hamilton, (Anthony Walter) Patrick 1904-1962 **CLC 51**
See also CA 113; DLB 10

Hamilton, Virginia 1936- .... **CLC 26; DAM MULT**
See also AAYA 2, 21; BW 2; CA 25-28R; CANR 20, 37; CLR 1, 11, 40; DLB 33, 52; INT CANR-20; JRDA; MAICYA; MTCW; SATA 4, 56, 79

Hammett, (Samuel) Dashiell 1894-1961 **C L C 3, 5, 10, 19, 47; SSC 17**
See also AITN 1; CA 81-84; CANR 42; CDALB 1929-1941; DLBD 6; DLBY 96; MTCW

Hammon, Jupiter 1711(?)-1800(?) ..**NCLC 5; BLC 2; DAM MULT, POET; PC 16**
See also DLB 31, 50

Hammond, Keith
See Kuttner, Henry

Hamner, Earl (Henry), Jr. 1923- ...... **CLC 12**
See also AITN 2; CA 73-76; DLB 6

Hampton, Christopher (James) 1946- **CLC 4**
See also CA 25-28R; DLB 13; MTCW

Hamsun, Knut .... **TCLC 2, 14, 49**
See also Pedersen, Knut

Handke, Peter 1942-**CLC 5, 8, 10, 15, 38; DAM DRAM, NOV**
See also CA 77-80; CANR 33; DLB 85, 124; MTCW

Hanley, James 1901-1985 ..... **CLC 3, 5, 8, 13**
See also CA 73-76; 117; CANR 36; DLB 191; MTCW

Hannah, Barry 1942- .... **CLC 23, 38, 90**
See also CA 108; 110; CANR 43, 68; DLB 6; INT 110; MTCW

Hannon, Ezra
See Hunter, Evan

Hansberry, Lorraine (Vivian) 1930-1965**CLC**

See also AAYA 9

Hebbel, Friedrich 1813-1863NCLC 43; DAM DRAM
See also DLB 129

Hebert, Anne 1916-CLC 4, 13, 29; DAC; DAM MST, POET
See also CA 85-88; CANR 69; DLB 68; MTCW

Hecht, Anthony (Evan) 1923- CLC 8, 13, 19; DAM POET
See also CA 9-12R; CANR 6; DLB 5, 169

Hecht, Ben 1894-1964 .... CLC 8
See also CA 85-88; DLB 7, 9, 25, 26, 28, 86

Hedayat, Sadeq 1903-1951 .... TCLC 21
See also CA 120

Hegel, Georg Wilhelm Friedrich 1770-1831
NCLC 46
See also DLB 90

Heidegger, Martin 1889-1976 .... CLC 24
See also CA 81-84; 65-68; CANR 34; MTCW

Heidenstam, (Carl Gustaf) Verner von 1859-1940 .... TCLC 5
See also CA 104

Heifner, Jack 1946- .... CLC 11
See also CA 105; CANR 47

Heijermans, Herman 1864-1924 .... TCLC 24
See also CA 123

Heilbrun, Carolyn G(old) 1926- .... CLC 25
See also CA 45-48; CANR 1, 28, 58

Heine, Heinrich 1797-1856 .... NCLC 4, 54
See also DLB 90

Heinemann, Larry (Curtiss) 1944- ... CLC 50
See also CA 110; CAAS 21; CANR 31; DLBD 9; INT CANR-31

Heiney, Donald (William) 1921-1993
See Harris, MacDonald
See also CA 1-4R; 142; CANR 3, 58

Heinlein, Robert A(nson) 1907-1988CLC 1, 3, 8, 14, 26, 55; DAM POP
See also AAYA 17; CA 1-4R; 125; CANR 1, 20, 53; DLB 8; JRDA; MAICYA; MTCW; SATA 9, 69; SATA-Obit 56

Helforth, John
See Doolittle, Hilda

Hellenhofferu, Vojtech Kapristian z
See Hasek, Jaroslav (Matej Frantisek)

Heller, Joseph 1923-CLC 1, 3, 5, 8, 11, 36, 63; DA; DAB; DAC; DAM MST, NOV, POP; WLC
See also AAYA 24; AITN 1; CA 5-8R; CABS 1; CANR 8, 42, 66; DLB 2, 28; DLBY 80; INT CANR-8; MTCW

Hellman, Lillian (Florence) 1906-1984CLC 2, 4, 8, 14, 18, 34, 44, 52; DAM DRAM; DC 1
See also AITN 1, 2; CA 13-16R; 112; CANR 33; DLB 7; DLBY 84; MTCW

Helprin, Mark 1947-CLC 7, 10, 22, 32; DAM NOV, POP
See also CA 81-84; CANR 47, 64; DLBY 85; MTCW

Helvetius, Claude-Adrien 1715-1771 .. LC 26

Helyar, Jane Penelope Josephine 1933-
See Poole, Josephine
See also CA 21-24R; CANR 10, 26; SATA 82

Hemans, Felicia 1793-1835 .... NCLC 71
See also DLB 96

Hemingway, Ernest (Miller) 1899-1961 C L C 1, 3, 6, 8, 10, 13, 19, 30, 34, 39, 41, 44, 50, 61, 80; DA; DAB; DAC; DAM MST, NOV; SSC 25; WLC
See also AAYA 19; CA 77-80; CANR 34; CDALB 1917-1929; DLB 4, 9, 102; DLBD 1, 15, 16; DLBY 81, 87, 96; MTCW

Hempel, Amy 1951- .... CLC 39

See also CA 118; 137

Henderson, F. C.
See Mencken, H(enry) L(ouis)

Henderson, Sylvia
See Ashton-Warner, Sylvia (Constance)

Henderson, Zenna (Chlarson) 1917-1983S S C 29
See also CA 1-4R; 133; CANR 1; DLB 8; SATA 5

Henley, Beth .... CLC 23; DC 6
See also Henley, Elizabeth Becker
See also CABS 3; DLBY 86

Henley, Elizabeth Becker 1952-
See Henley, Beth
See also CA 107; CANR 32; DAM DRAM, MST; MTCW

Henley, William Ernest 1849-1903 .. TCLC 8
See also CA 105; DLB 19

Hennissart, Martha
See Lathen, Emma
See also CA 85-88; CANR 64

Henry, O. .... TCLC 1, 19; SSC 5; WLC
See also Porter, William Sydney

Henry, Patrick 1736-1799 .... LC 25

Henryson, Robert 1430(?)-1506(?) ...... LC 20
See also DLB 146

Henry VIII 1491-1547 .... LC 10

Henschke, Alfred
See Klabund

Hentoff, Nat(han Irving) 1925-̄ .... CLC 26
See also AAYA 4; CA 1-4R; CAAS 6; CANR 5, 25; CLR 1, 52; INT CANR-25; JRDA; MAICYA; SATA 42, 69; SATA-Brief 27

Heppenstall, (John) Rayner 1911-1981 C L C 10
See also CA 1-4R; 103; CANR 29

Heraclitus c. 540B.C.-c. 450B.C. .. CMLC 22
See also DLB 176

Herbert, Frank (Patrick) 1920-1986CLC 12, 23, 35, 44, 85; DAM POP
See also AAYA 21; CA 53-56; 118; CANR 5, 43; DLB 8; INT CANR-5; MTCW; SATA 9, 37; SATA-Obit 47

Herbert, George 1593-1633 ..... LC 24; DAB; DAM POET; PC 4
See also CDBLB Before 1660; DLB 126

Herbert, Zbigniew 1924- .. CLC 9, 43; DAM POET
See also CA 89-92; CANR 36; MTCW

Herbst, Josephine (Frey) 1897-1969 CLC 34
See also CA 5-8R; 25-28R; DLB 9

Hergesheimer, Joseph 1880-1954 .. TCLC 11
See also CA 109; DLB 102, 9

Herlihy, James Leo 1927-1993 .... CLC 6
See also CA 1-4R; 143; CANR 2

Hermogenes fl. c. 175- .... CMLC 6

Hernandez, Jose 1834-1886 .... NCLC 17

Herodotus c. 484B.C.-429B.C. ...... CMLC 17
See also DLB 176

Herrick, Robert 1591-1674LC 13; DA; DAB; DAC; DAM MST, POP; PC 9
See also DLB 126

Herring, Guilles
See Somerville, Edith

Herriot, James 1916-1995CLC 12; DAM POP
See also Wight, James Alfred
See also AAYA 1; CA 148; CANR 40; SATA 86

Herrmann, Dorothy 1941- .... CLC 44
See also CA 107

Herrmann, Taffy
See Herrmann, Dorothy

Hersey, John (Richard) 1914-1993CLC 1, 2, 7,

9, 40, 81, 97; DAM POP
See also CA 17-20R; 140; CANR 33; DLB 6, 185; MTCW; SATA 25; SATA-Obit 76

Herzen, Aleksandr Ivanovich 1812-1870
NCLC 10, 61

Herzl, Theodor 1860-1904 .... TCLC 36

Herzog, Werner 1942- .... CLC 16
See also CA 89-92

Hesiod c. 8th cent. B.C.- .... CMLC 5
See also DLB 176

Hesse, Hermann 1877-1962CLC 1, 2, 3, 6, 11, 17, 25, 69; DA; DAB; DAC; DAM MST, NOV; SSC 9; WLC
See also CA 17-18; CAP 2; DLB 66; MTCW; SATA 50

Hewes, Cady
See De Voto, Bernard (Augustine)

Heyen, William 1940- .... CLC 13, 18
See also CA 33-36R; CAAS 9; DLB 5

Heyerdahl, Thor 1914- .... CLC 26
See also CA 5-8R; CANR 5, 22, 66; MTCW; SATA 2, 52

Heym, Georg (Theodor Franz Arthur) 1887-1912 .... TCLC 9
See also CA 106

Heym, Stefan 1913- .... CLC 41
See also CA 9-12R; CANR 4; DLB 69

Heyse, Paul (Johann Ludwig von) 1830-1914
TCLC 8
See also CA 104; DLB 129

Heyward, (Edwin) DuBose 1885-1940 T C L C 59
See also CA 108; 157; DLB 7, 9, 45; SATA 21

Hibbert, Eleanor Alice Burford 1906-1993
CLC 7; DAM POP
See also BEST 90:4; CA 17-20R; 140; CANR 9, 28, 59; SATA 2; SATA-Obit 74

Hichens, Robert (Smythe) 1864-1950 T C L C 64
See also CA 162; DLB 153

Higgins, George V(incent) 1939-CLC 4, 7, 10, 18
See also CA 77-80; CAAS 5; CANR 17, 51; DLB 2; DLBY 81; INT CANR-17; MTCW

Higginson, Thomas Wentworth 1823-1911
TCLC 36
See also CA 162; DLB 1, 64

Highet, Helen
See MacInnes, Helen (Clark)

Highsmith, (Mary) Patricia 1921-1995CLC 2, 4, 14, 42, 102; DAM NOV, POP
See also CA 1-4R; 147; CANR 1, 20, 48, 62; MTCW

Highwater, Jamake (Mamake) 1942(?)- C L C 12
See also AAYA 7; CA 65-68; CAAS 7; CANR 10, 34; CLR 17; DLB 52; DLBY 85; JRDA; MAICYA; SATA 32, 69; SATA-Brief 30

Highway, Tomson 1951-CLC 92; DAC; DAM MULT
See also CA 151; NNAL

Higuchi, Ichiyo 1872-1896 .... NCLC 49

Hijuelos, Oscar 1951- CLC 65; DAM MULT, POP; HLC
See also AAYA 25; BEST 90:1; CA 123; CANR 50; DLB 145; HW

Hikmet, Nazim 1902(?)-1963 .... CLC 40
See also CA 141; 93-96

Hildegard von Bingen 1098-1179 . CMLC 20
See also DLB 148

Hildesheimer, Wolfgang 1916-1991 .. CLC 49
See also CA 101; 135; DLB 69, 124

Hill, Geoffrey (William) 1932- CLC 5, 8, 18,

45; DAM POET
See also CA 81-84; CANR 21; CDBLB 1960
to Present; DLB 40; MTCW
Hill, George Roy 1921- .... **CLC 26**
See also CA 110; 122
Hill, John
See Koontz, Dean R(ay)
Hill, Susan (Elizabeth) 1942- .... **CLC 4, 113;**
DAB; DAM MST, NOV
See also CA 33-36R; CANR 29, 69; DLB 14,
139; MTCW
Hillerman, Tony 1925- . **CLC 62; DAM POP**
See also AAYA 6; BEST 89:1; CA 29-32R;
CANR 21, 42, 65; SATA 6
Hillesum, Etty 1914-1943 .... **TCLC 49**
See also CA 137
Hilliard, Noel (Harvey) 1929- .... **CLC 15**
See also CA 9-12R; CANR 7, 69
Hillis, Rick 1956- .... **CLC 66**
See also CA 134
Hilton, James 1900-1954 .... **TCLC 21**
See also CA 108; DLB 34, 77; SATA 34
Himes, Chester (Bomar) 1909-1984 **CLC 2, 4,**
7, 18, 58, 108; BLC 2; DAM MULT
See also BW 2; CA 25-28R; 114; CANR 22;
DLB 2, 76, 143; MTCW
Hinde, Thomas .... **CLC 6, 11**
See also Chitty, Thomas Willes
Hindin, Nathan
See Bloch, Robert (Albert)
Hine, (William) Daryl 1936- .... **CLC 15**
See also CA 1-4R; CAAS 15; CANR 1, 20; DLB
60
Hinkson, Katharine Tynan
See Tynan, Katharine
Hinton, S(usan) E(loise) 1950- **CLC 30, 111;**
DA; DAB; DAC; DAM MST, NOV
See also AAYA 2; CA 81-84; CANR 32, 62;
CLR 3, 23; JRDA; MAICYA; MTCW; SATA
19, 58
Hippius, Zinaida .... **TCLC 9**
See also Gippius, Zinaida (Nikolayevna)
Hiraoka, Kimitake 1925-1970
See Mishima, Yukio
See also CA 97-100; 29-32R; DAM DRAM;
MTCW
Hirsch, E(ric) D(onald), Jr. 1928- .... **CLC 79**
See also CA 25-28R; CANR 27, 51; DLB 67;
INT CANR-27; MTCW
Hirsch, Edward 1950- .... **CLC 31, 50**
See also CA 104; CANR 20, 42; DLB 120
Hitchcock, Alfred (Joseph) 1899-1980 **CLC 16**
See also AAYA 22; CA 159; 97-100; SATA 27;
SATA-Obit 24
Hitler, Adolf 1889-1945 .... **TCLC 53**
See also CA 117; 147
Hoagland, Edward 1932- .... **CLC 28**
See also CA 1-4R; CANR 2, 31, 57; DLB 6;
SATA 51
Hoban, Russell (Conwell) 1925- . **CLC 7, 25;**
DAM NOV
See also CA 5-8R; CANR 23, 37, 66; CLR 3;
DLB 52; MAICYA; MTCW; SATA 1, 40, 78
Hobbes, Thomas 1588-1679 .... **LC 36**
See also DLB 151
Hobbs, Perry
See Blackmur, R(ichard) P(almer)
Hobson, Laura Z(ametkin) 1900-1986 **CLC 7,**
25
See also CA 17-20R; 118; CANR 55; DLB 28;
SATA 52
Hochhuth, Rolf 1931- .. **CLC 4, 11, 18; DAM**
DRAM

See also CA 5-8R; CANR 33; DLB 124; MTCW
Hochman, Sandra 1936- .... **CLC 3, 8**
See also CA 5-8R; DLB 5
Hochwaelder, Fritz 1911-1986 **CLC 36; DAM**
DRAM
See also CA 29-32R; 120; CANR 42; MTCW
Hochwalder, Fritz
See Hochwaelder, Fritz
Hocking, Mary (Eunice) 1921- .... **CLC 13**
See also CA 101; CANR 18, 40
Hodgins, Jack 1938- .... **CLC 23**
See also CA 93-96; DLB 60
Hodgson, William Hope 1877(?)-1918 **T C L C**
13
See also CA 111; 164; DLB 70, 153, 156, 178
Hoeg, Peter 1957- .... **CLC 95**
See also CA 151
Hoffman, Alice 1952- ... **CLC 51; DAM NOV**
See also CA 77-80; CANR 34, 66; MTCW
Hoffman, Daniel (Gerard) 1923- **CLC 6, 13, 23**
See also CA 1-4R; CANR 4; DLB 5
Hoffman, Stanley 1944- .... **CLC 5**
See also CA 77-80
Hoffman, William M(oses) 1939- ...... **CLC 40**
See also CA 57-60; CANR 11
Hoffmann, E(rnst) T(heodor) A(madeus) 1776-
1822 .... **NCLC 2; SSC 13**
See also DLB 90; SATA 27
Hofmann, Gert 1931- .... **CLC 54**
See also CA 128
Hofmannsthal, Hugo von 1874-1929 **TCLC 11;**
DAM DRAM; DC 4
See also CA 106; 153; DLB 81, 118
Hogan, Linda 1947- ... **CLC 73; DAM MULT**
See also CA 120; CANR 45, 69; DLB 175;
NNAL
Hogarth, Charles
See Creasey, John
Hogarth, Emmett
See Polonsky, Abraham (Lincoln)
Hogg, James 1770-1835 .... **NCLC 4**
See also DLB 93, 116, 159
Holbach, Paul Henri Thiry Baron 1723-1789
LC 14
Holberg, Ludvig 1684-1754 .... **LC 6**
Holden, Ursula 1921- .... **CLC 18**
See also CA 101; CAAS 8; CANR 22
Holderlin, (Johann Christian) Friedrich 1770-
1843 .... **NCLC 16; PC 4**
Holdstock, Robert
See Holdstock, Robert P.
Holdstock, Robert P. 1948- .... **CLC 39**
See also CA 131
Holland, Isabelle 1920- .... **CLC 21**
See also AAYA 11; CA 21-24R; CANR 10, 25,
47; JRDA; MAICYA; SATA 8, 70
Holland, Marcus
See Caldwell, (Janet Miriam) Taylor (Holland)
Hollander, John 1929- .... **CLC 2, 5, 8, 14**
See also CA 1-4R; CANR 1, 52; DLB 5; SATA
13
Hollander, Paul
See Silverberg, Robert
Holleran, Andrew 1943(?)- .... **CLC 38**
See also CA 144
Hollinghurst, Alan 1954- .... **CLC 55, 91**
See also CA 114
Hollis, Jim
See Summers, Hollis (Spurgeon, Jr.)
Holly, Buddy 1936-1959 .... **TCLC 65**
Holmes, Gordon
See Shiel, M(atthew) P(hipps)
Holmes, John

See Souster, (Holmes) Raymond
Holmes, John Clellon 1926-1988 ...... **CLC 56**
See also CA 9-12R; 125; CANR 4; DLB 16
Holmes, Oliver Wendell, Jr. 1841-1935 **T C L C**
77
See also CA 114
Holmes, Oliver Wendell 1809-1894 **NCLC 14**
See also CDALB 1640-1865; DLB 1, 189;
SATA 34
Holmes, Raymond
See Souster, (Holmes) Raymond
Holt, Victoria
See Hibbert, Eleanor Alice Burford
Holub, Miroslav 1923- .... **CLC 4**
See also CA 21-24R; CANR 10
Homer c. 8th cent. B.C.- ... **CMLC 1, 16; DA;**
DAB; DAC; DAM MST, POET; PC 23;
WLCS
See also DLB 176
Hongo, Garrett Kaoru 1951- .... **PC 23**
See also CA 133; CAAS 22; DLB 120
Honig, Edwin 1919- .... **CLC 33**
See also CA 5-8R; CAAS 8; CANR 4, 45; DLB
5
Hood, Hugh (John Blagdon) 1928- **CLC 15, 28**
See also CA 49-52; CAAS 17; CANR 1, 33;
DLB 53
Hood, Thomas 1799-1845 .... **NCLC 16**
See also DLB 96
Hooker, (Peter) Jeremy 1941- .... **CLC 43**
See also CA 77-80; CANR 22; DLB 40
hooks, bell .... **CLC 94; BLCS**
See also Watkins, Gloria
Hope, A(lec) D(erwent) 1907- .... **CLC 3, 51**
See also CA 21-24R; CANR 33; MTCW
Hope, Anthony 1863-1933 .... **TCLC 83**
See also CA 157; DLB 153, 156
Hope, Brian
See Creasey, John
Hope, Christopher (David Tully) 1944- **C L C**
52
See also CA 106; CANR 47; SATA 62
Hopkins, Gerard Manley 1844-1889 .. **N C L C**
17; DA; DAB; DAC; DAM MST, POET;
PC 15; WLC
See also CDBLB 1890-1914; DLB 35, 57
Hopkins, John (Richard) 1931- .... **CLC 4**
See also CA 85-88
Hopkins, Pauline Elizabeth 1859-1930 **T C L C**
28; BLC 2; DAM MULT
See also BW 2; CA 141; DLB 50
Hopkinson, Francis 1737-1791 .... **LC 25**
See also DLB 31
Hopley-Woolrich, Cornell George 1903-1968
See Woolrich, Cornell
See also CA 13-14; CANR 58; CAP 1
Horatio
See Proust, (Valentin-Louis-George-Eugene-)
Marcel
Horgan, Paul (George Vincent O'Shaughnessy)
1903-1995 .... **CLC 9, 53; DAM NOV**
See also CA 13-16R; 147; CANR 9, 35; DLB
102; DLBY 85; INT CANR-9; MTCW;
SATA 13; SATA-Obit 84
Horn, Peter
See Kuttner, Henry
Hornem, Horace Esq.
See Byron, George Gordon (Noel)
Horney, Karen (Clementine Theodore
Danielsen) 1885-1952 .... **TCLC 71**
See also CA 114; 165
Hornung, E(rnest) W(illiam) 1866-1921
TCLC 59

See also CA 108; 160; DLB 70

Horovitz, Israel (Arthur) 1939-**CLC 56; DAM DRAM**
See also CA 33-36R; CANR 46, 59; DLB 7

Horvath, Odon von
See Horvath, Oedoen von
See also DLB 85, 124

Horvath, Oedoen von 1901-1938 ... **TCLC 45**
See also Horvath, Odon von
See also CA 118

Horwitz, Julius 1920-1986 .... **CLC 14**
See also CA 9-12R; 119; CANR 12

Hospital, Janette Turner 1942- .... **CLC 42**
See also CA 108; CANR 48

Hostos, E. M. de
See Hostos (y Bonilla), Eugenio Maria de

Hostos, Eugenio M. de
See Hostos (y Bonilla), Eugenio Maria de

Hostos, Eugenio Maria
See Hostos (y Bonilla), Eugenio Maria de

Hostos (y Bonilla), Eugenio Maria de 1839-1903 .... **TCLC 24**
See also CA 123; 131; HW

Houdini
See Lovecraft, H(oward) P(hillips)

Hougan, Carolyn 1943- .... **CLC 34**
See also CA 139

Household, Geoffrey (Edward West) 1900-1988 **CLC 11**
See also CA 77-80; 126; CANR 58; DLB 87; SATA 14; SATA-Obit 59

Housman, A(lfred) E(dward) 1859-1936 **TCLC 1, 10; DA; DAB; DAC; DAM MST, POET; PC 2; WLCS**
See also CA 104; 125; DLB 19; MTCW

Housman, Laurence 1865-1959 .... **TCLC 7**
See also CA 106; 155; DLB 10; SATA 25

Howard, Elizabeth Jane 1923- ..... **CLC 7, 29**
See also CA 5-8R; CANR 8, 62

Howard, Maureen 1930- .... **CLC 5, 14, 46**
See also CA 53-56; CANR 31; DLBY 83; INT CANR-31; MTCW

Howard, Richard 1929- .... **CLC 7, 10, 47**
See also AITN 1; CA 85-88; CANR 25; DLB 5; INT CANR-25

Howard, Robert E(rvin) 1906-1936 **TCLC 8**
See also CA 105; 157

Howard, Warren F.
See Pohl, Frederik

Howe, Fanny 1940- .... **CLC 47**
See also CA 117; CAAS 27; SATA-Brief 52

Howe, Irving 1920-1993 .... **CLC 85**
See also CA 9-12R; 141; CANR 21, 50; DLB 67; MTCW

Howe, Julia Ward 1819-1910 .... **TCLC 21**
See also CA 117; DLB 1, 189

Howe, Susan 1937- .... **CLC 72**
See also CA 160; DLB 120

Howe, Tina 1937- .... **CLC 48**
See also CA 109

Howell, James 1594(?)-1666 .... **LC 13**
See also DLB 151

Howells, W. D.
See Howells, William Dean

Howells, William D.
See Howells, William Dean

Howells, William Dean 1837-1920**TCLC 7, 17, 41**
See also CA 104; 134; CDALB 1865-1917; DLB 12, 64, 74, 79, 189

Howes, Barbara 1914-1996 .... **CLC 15**
See also CA 9-12R; 151; CAAS 3; CANR 53; SATA 5

Hrabal, Bohumil 1914-1997 .... **CLC 13, 67**
See also CA 106; 156; CAAS 12; CANR 57

Hroswitha of Gandersheim c. 935-c. 1002 **CMLC 29**
See also DLB 148

Hsun, Lu
See Lu Hsun

Hubbard, L(afayette) Ron(ald) 1911-1986 **CLC 43; DAM POP**
See also CA 77-80; 118; CANR 52

Huch, Ricarda (Octavia) 1864-1947**TCLC 13**
See also CA 111; DLB 66

Huddle, David 1942- .... **CLC 49**
See also CA 57-60; CAAS 20; DLB 130

Hudson, Jeffrey
See Crichton, (John) Michael

Hudson, W(illiam) H(enry) 1841-1922**TCLC 29**
See also CA 115; DLB 98, 153, 174; SATA 35

Hueffer, Ford Madox
See Ford, Ford Madox

Hughart, Barry 1934- .... **CLC 39**
See also CA 137

Hughes, Colin
See Creasey, John

Hughes, David (John) 1930- .... **CLC 48**
See also CA 116; 129; DLB 14

Hughes, Edward James
See Hughes, Ted
See also DAM MST, POET

Hughes, (James) Langston 1902-1967**CLC 1, 5, 10, 15, 35, 44, 108; BLC 2; DA; DAB; DAC; DAM DRAM, MST, MULT, POET; DC 3; PC 1; SSC 6; WLC**
See also AAYA 12; BW 1; CA 1-4R; 25-28R; CANR 1, 34; CDALB 1929-1941; CLR 17; DLB 4, 7, 48, 51, 86; JRDA; MAICYA; MTCW; SATA 4, 33

Hughes, Richard (Arthur Warren) 1900-1976 **CLC 1, 11; DAM NOV**
See also CA 5-8R; 65-68; CANR 4; DLB 15, 161; MTCW; SATA 8; SATA-Obit 25

Hughes, Ted 1930- **CLC 2, 4, 9, 14, 37; DAB; DAC; PC 7**
See also Hughes, Edward James
See also CA 1-4R; CANR 1, 33, 66; CLR 3; DLB 40, 161; MAICYA; MTCW; SATA 49; SATA-Brief 27

Hugo, Richard F(ranklin) 1923-1982 **CLC 6, 18, 32; DAM POET**
See also CA 49-52; 108; CANR 3; DLB 5

Hugo, Victor (Marie) 1802-1885**NCLC 3, 10, 21; DA; DAB; DAC; DAM DRAM, MST, NOV, POET; PC 17; WLC**
See also DLB 119, 192; SATA 47

Huidobro, Vicente
See Huidobro Fernandez, Vicente Garcia

Huidobro Fernandez, Vicente Garcia 1893-1948 .... **TCLC 31**
See also CA 131; HW

Hulme, Keri 1947- .... **CLC 39**
See also CA 125; CANR 69; INT 125

Hulme, T(homas) E(rnest) 1883-1917 **TCLC 21**
See also CA 117; DLB 19

Hume, David 1711-1776 .... **LC 7**
See also DLB 104

Humphrey, William 1924-1997 .... **CLC 45**
See also CA 77-80; 160; CANR 68; DLB 6

Humphreys, Emyr Owen 1919- .... **CLC 47**
See also CA 5-8R; CANR 3, 24; DLB 15

Humphreys, Josephine 1945- ..... **CLC 34, 57**
See also CA 121; 127; INT 127

Huneker, James Gibbons 1857-1921**TCLC 65**
See also DLB 71

Hungerford, Pixie
See Brinsmead, H(esba) F(ay)

Hunt, E(verette) Howard, (Jr.) 1918-. **CLC 3**
See also AITN 1; CA 45-48; CANR 2, 47

Hunt, Kyle
See Creasey, John

Hunt, (James Henry) Leigh 1784-1859**NCLC 70; DAM POET**
See also DLB 96, 110, 144

Hunt, (James Henry) Leigh 1784-1859**NCLC 1; DAM POET**

Hunt, Marsha 1946- .... **CLC 70**
See also BW 2; CA 143

Hunt, Violet 1866(?)-1942 .... **TCLC 53**
See also DLB 162, 197

Hunter, E. Waldo
See Sturgeon, Theodore (Hamilton)

Hunter, Evan 1926-. **CLC 11, 31; DAM POP**
See also CA 5-8R; CANR 5, 38, 62; DLBY 82; INT CANR-5; MTCW; SATA 25

Hunter, Kristin (Eggleston) 1931- .... **CLC 35**
See also AITN 1; BW 1; CA 13-16R; CANR 13; CLR 3; DLB 33; INT CANR-13; MAICYA; SAAS 10; SATA 12

Hunter, Mollie 1922- .... **CLC 21**
See also McIlwraith, Maureen Mollie Hunter
See also AAYA 13; CANR 37; CLR 25; DLB 161; JRDA; MAICYA; SAAS 7; SATA 54

Hunter, Robert (?)-1734 .... **LC 7**

Hurston, Zora Neale 1903-1960**CLC 7, 30, 61; BLC 2; DA; DAC; DAM MST, MULT, NOV; SSC 4; WLCS**
See also AAYA 15; BW 1; CA 85-88; CANR 61; DLB 51, 86; MTCW

Huston, John (Marcellus) 1906-1987 **CLC 20**
See also CA 73-76; 123; CANR 34; DLB 26

Hustvedt, Siri 1955- .... **CLC 76**
See also CA 137

Hutten, Ulrich von 1488-1523 .... **LC 16**
See also DLB 179

Huxley, Aldous (Leonard) 1894-1963 **CLC 1, 3, 4, 5, 8, 11, 18, 35, 79; DA; DAB; DAC; DAM MST, NOV; WLC**
See also AAYA 11; CA 85-88; CANR 44; CDBLB 1914-1945; DLB 36, 100, 162, 195; MTCW; SATA 63

Huxley, T(homas) H(enry) 1825-1895 **NCLC 67**
See also DLB 57

Huysmans, Joris-Karl 1848-1907**TCLC 7, 69**
See also CA 104; 165; DLB 123

Hwang, David Henry 1957- ... **CLC 55; DAM DRAM; DC 4**
See also CA 127; 132; INT 132

Hyde, Anthony 1946- .... **CLC 42**
See also CA 136

Hyde, Margaret O(ldroyd) 1917- ..... **CLC 21**
See also CA 1-4R; CANR 1, 36; CLR 23; JRDA; MAICYA; SAAS 8; SATA 1, 42, 76

Hynes, James 1956(?)- .... **CLC 65**
See also CA 164

Ian, Janis 1951- .... **CLC 21**
See also CA 105

Ibanez, Vicente Blasco
See Blasco Ibanez, Vicente

Ibarguengoitia, Jorge 1928-1983 ..... **CLC 37**
See also CA 124; 113; HW

Ibsen, Henrik (Johan) 1828-1906 **TCLC 2, 8, 16, 37, 52; DA; DAB; DAC; DAM DRAM, MST; DC 2; WLC**
See also CA 104; 141

See also CA 61-64; CAAS 5; CANR 8, 39, 66; DLB 27; MTCW; SATA 66

Jennings, Waylon 1937- .... **CLC 21**

Jensen, Johannes V. 1873-1950 ..... **TCLC 41**

Jensen, Laura (Linnea) 1948- .... **CLC 37**
See also CA 103

Jerome, Jerome K(lapka) 1859-1927**TCLC 23**
See also CA 119; DLB 10, 34, 135

Jerrold, Douglas William 1803-1857**NCLC 2**
See also DLB 158, 159

Jewett, (Theodora) Sarah Orne 1849-1909
TCLC 1, 22; SSC 6
See also CA 108; 127; DLB 12, 74; SATA 15

Jewsbury, Geraldine (Endsor) 1812-1880
NCLC 22
See also DLB 21

Jhabvala, Ruth Prawer 1927-**CLC 4, 8, 29, 94;**
DAB; DAM NOV
See also CA 1-4R; CANR 2, 29, 51; DLB 139, 194; INT CANR-29; MTCW

Jibran, Kahlil
See Gibran, Kahlil

Jibran, Khalil
See Gibran, Kahlil

Jiles, Paulette 1943- .... **CLC 13, 58**
See also CA 101

Jimenez (Mantecon), Juan Ramon 1881-1958
TCLC 4; DAM MULT, POET; HLC; PC 7
See also CA 104; 131; DLB 134; HW; MTCW

Jimenez, Ramon
See Jimenez (Mantecon), Juan Ramon

Jimenez Mantecon, Juan
See Jimenez (Mantecon), Juan Ramon

Jin, Ha 1956- .... **CLC 109**
See also CA 152

Joel, Billy .... **CLC 26**
See also Joel, William Martin

Joel, William Martin 1949-
See Joel, Billy
See also CA 108

John, Saint 7th cent. - .... **CMLC 27**

John of the Cross, St. 1542-1591 .... **LC 18**

Johnson, B(ryan) S(tanley William) 1933-1973
CLC 6, 9
See also CA 9-12R; 53-56; CANR 9; DLB 14, 40

Johnson, Benj. F. of Boo
See Riley, James Whitcomb

Johnson, Benjamin F. of Boo
See Riley, James Whitcomb

Johnson, Charles (Richard) 1948-**CLC 7, 51, 65; BLC 2; DAM MULT**
See also BW 2; CA 116; CAAS 18; CANR 42, 66; DLB 33

Johnson, Denis 1949- .... **CLC 52**
See also CA 117; 121; DLB 120

Johnson, Diane 1934- .... **CLC 5, 13, 48**
See also CA 41-44R; CANR 17, 40, 62; DLBY 80; INT CANR-17; MTCW

Johnson, Eyvind (Olof Verner) 1900-1976
CLC 14
See also CA 73-76; 69-72; CANR 34

Johnson, J. R.
See James, C(yril) L(ionel) R(obert)

Johnson, James Weldon 1871-1938 **TCLC 3, 19; BLC 2; DAM MULT, POET**
See also BW 1; CA 104; 125; CDALB 1917-1929; CLR 32; DLB 51; MTCW; SATA 31

Johnson, Joyce 1935- .... **CLC 58**
See also CA 125; 129

Johnson, Lionel (Pigot) 1867-1902 **TCLC 19**
See also CA 117; DLB 19

Johnson, Mel
See Malzberg, Barry N(athaniel)

Johnson, Pamela Hansford 1912-1981**CLC 1, 7, 27**
See also CA 1-4R; 104; CANR 2, 28; DLB 15; MTCW

Johnson, Robert 1911(?)-1938 .... **TCLC 69**

Johnson, Samuel 1709-1784**LC 15; DA; DAB; DAC; DAM MST; WLC**
See also CDBLB 1660-1789; DLB 39, 95, 104, 142

Johnson, Uwe 1934-1984 .. **CLC 5, 10, 15, 40**
See also CA 1-4R; 112; CANR 1, 39; DLB 75; MTCW

Johnston, George (Benson) 1913- ..... **CLC 51**
See also CA 1-4R; CANR 5, 20; DLB 88

Johnston, Jennifer 1930- .... **CLC 7**
See also CA 85-88; DLB 14

Jolley, (Monica) Elizabeth 1923-**CLC 46; SSC 19**
See also CA 127; CAAS 13; CANR 59

Jones, Arthur Llewellyn 1863-1947
See Machen, Arthur
See also CA 104

Jones, D(ouglas) G(ordon) 1929- ...... **CLC 10**
See also CA 29-32R; CANR 13; DLB 53

Jones, David (Michael) 1895-1974**CLC 2, 4, 7, 13, 42**
See also CA 9-12R; 53-56; CANR 28; CDBLB 1945-1960; DLB 20, 100; MTCW

Jones, David Robert 1947-
See Bowie, David
See also CA 103

Jones, Diana Wynne 1934- .... **CLC 26**
See also AAYA 12; CA 49-52; CANR 4, 26, 56; CLR 23; DLB 161; JRDA; MAICYA; SAAS 7; SATA 9, 70

Jones, Edward P. 1950- .... **CLC 76**
See also BW 2; CA 142

Jones, Gayl 1949- .... **CLC 6, 9; BLC 2; DAM MULT**
See also BW 2; CA 77-80; CANR 27, 66; DLB 33; MTCW

Jones, James 1921-1977 ...... **CLC 1, 3, 10, 39**
See also AITN 1, 2; CA 1-4R; 69-72; CANR 6; DLB 2, 143; MTCW

Jones, John J.
See Lovecraft, H(oward) P(hillips)

Jones, LeRoi .... **CLC 1, 2, 3, 5, 10, 14**
See also Baraka, Amiri

Jones, Louis B. .... **CLC 65**
See also CA 141

Jones, Madison (Percy, Jr.) 1925- .... **CLC 4**
See also CA 13-16R; CAAS 11; CANR 7, 54; DLB 152

Jones, Mervyn 1922- .... **CLC 10, 52**
See also CA 45-48; CAAS 5; CANR 1; MTCW

Jones, Mick 1956(?)- .... **CLC 30**

Jones, Nettie (Pearl) 1941- .... **CLC 34**
See also BW 2; CA 137; CAAS 20

Jones, Preston 1936-1979 .... **CLC 10**
See also CA 73-76; 89-92; DLB 7

Jones, Robert F(rancis) 1934- .... **CLC 7**
See also CA 49-52; CANR 2, 61

Jones, Rod 1953- .... **CLC 50**
See also CA 128

Jones, Terence Graham Parry 1942- **CLC 21**
See also Jones, Terry; Monty Python
See also CA 112; 116; CANR 35; INT 116

Jones, Terry
See Jones, Terence Graham Parry
See also SATA 67; SATA-Brief 51

Jones, Thom 1945(?)- .... **CLC 81**

See also CA 157

Jong, Erica 1942- . **CLC 4, 6, 8, 18, 83; DAM NOV, POP**
See also AITN 1; BEST 90:2; CA 73-76; CANR 26, 52; DLB 2, 5, 28, 152; INT CANR-26; MTCW

Jonson, Ben(jamin) 1572(?)-1637 .. **LC 6, 33; DA; DAB; DAC; DAM DRAM, MST, POET; DC 4; PC 17; WLC**
See also CDBLB Before 1660; DLB 62, 121

Jordan, June 1936- .... **CLC 5, 11, 23; BLCS; DAM MULT, POET**
See also AAYA 2; BW 2; CA 33-36R; CANR 25; CLR 10; DLB 38; MAICYA; MTCW; SATA 4

Jordan, Neil (Patrick) 1950- .... **CLC 110**
See also CA 124; 130; CANR 54; INT 130

Jordan, Pat(rick M.) 1941- .... **CLC 37**
See also CA 33-36R

Jorgensen, Ivar
See Ellison, Harlan (Jay)

Jorgenson, Ivar
See Silverberg, Robert

Josephus, Flavius c. 37-100 .... **CMLC 13**

Josipovici, Gabriel 1940- ....**CLC 6, 43**
See also CA 37-40R; CAAS 8; CANR 47; DLB 14

Joubert, Joseph 1754-1824 .... **NCLC 9**

Jouve, Pierre Jean 1887-1976 .... **CLC 47**
See also CA 65-68

Jovine, Francesco 1902-1950 .... **TCLC 79**

Joyce, James (Augustine Aloysius) 1882-1941
TCLC 3, 8, 16, 35, 52; DA; DAB; DAC; DAM MST, NOV, POET; PC 22; SSC 3, 26; WLC
See also CA 104; 126; CDBLB 1914-1945; DLB 10, 19, 36, 162; MTCW

Jozsef, Attila 1905-1937 .... **TCLC 22**
See also CA 116

Juana Ines de la Cruz 1651(?)-1695 ...... **LC 5**

Judd, Cyril
See Kornbluth, C(yril) M.; Pohl, Frederik

Julian of Norwich 1342(?)-1416(?) .... **LC 6**
See also DLB 146

Junger, Sebastian 1962- .... **CLC 109**
See also CA 165

Juniper, Alex
See Hospital, Janette Turner

Junius
See Luxemburg, Rosa

Just, Ward (Swift) 1935- .... **CLC 4, 27**
See also CA 25-28R; CANR 32; INT CANR-32

Justice, Donald (Rodney) 1925- .. **CLC 6, 19, 102; DAM POET**
See also CA 5-8R; CANR 26, 54; DLBY 83; INT CANR-26

Juvenal c. 55-c. 127 .... **CMLC 8**

Juvenis
See Bourne, Randolph S(illiman)

Kacew, Romain 1914-1980
See Gary, Romain
See also CA 108; 102

Kadare, Ismail 1936- .... **CLC 52**
See also CA 161

Kadohata, Cynthia .... **CLC 59**
See also CA 140

Kafka, Franz 1883-1924**TCLC 2, 6, 13, 29, 47, 53; DA; DAB; DAC; DAM MST, NOV; SSC 5, 29; WLC**
See also CA 105; 126; DLB 81; MTCW

Kahanovitsch, Pinkhes
See Der Nister

36R; CANR 25, 41, 68; DLBY 82; MTCW

Ludwig, Ken .... **CLC 60**

Ludwig, Otto 1813-1865 .... **NCLC 4**
See also DLB 129

Lugones, Leopoldo 1874-1938 .... **TCLC 15**
See also CA 116; 131; HW

Lu Hsun 1881-1936 .... **TCLC 3; SSC 20**
See also Shu-Jen, Chou

Lukacs, George .... **CLC 24**
See also Lukacs, Gyorgy (Szegeny von)

Lukacs, Gyorgy (Szegeny von) 1885-1971
See Lukacs, George
See also CA 101; 29-32R; CANR 62

Luke, Peter (Ambrose Cyprian) 1919-1995
CLC 38
See also CA 81-84; 147; DLB 13

Lunar, Dennis
See Mungo, Raymond

Lurie, Alison 1926- .... **CLC 4, 5, 18, 39**
See also CA 1-4R; CANR 2, 17, 50; DLB 2;
MTCW; SATA 46

Lustig, Arnost 1926- .... **CLC 56**
See also AAYA 3; CA 69-72; CANR 47; SATA
56

Luther, Martin 1483-1546 .... **LC 9, 37**
See also DLB 179

Luxemburg, Rosa 1870(?)-1919 ..... **TCLC 63**
See also CA 118

Luzi, Mario 1914- .... **CLC 13**
See also CA 61-64; CANR 9; DLB 128

Lyly, John 1554(?)-1606 **LC 41; DAM DRAM;**
DC 7
See also DLB 62, 167

L'Ymagier
See Gourmont, Remy (-Marie-Charles) de

Lynch, B. Suarez
See Bioy Casares, Adolfo; Borges, Jorge Luis

Lynch, David (K.) 1946- .... **CLC 66**
See also CA 124; 129

Lynch, James
See Andreyev, Leonid (Nikolaevich)

Lynch Davis, B.
See Bioy Casares, Adolfo; Borges, Jorge Luis

Lyndsay, Sir David 1490-1555 .... **LC 20**

Lynn, Kenneth S(chuyler) 1923- .... **CLC 50**
See also CA 1-4R; CANR 3, 27, 65

Lynx
See West, Rebecca

Lyons, Marcus
See Blish, James (Benjamin)

Lyre, Pinchbeck
See Sassoon, Siegfried (Lorraine)

Lytle, Andrew (Nelson) 1902-1995 ... **CLC 22**
See also CA 9-12R; 150; DLB 6; DLBY 95

Lyttelton, George 1709-1773 .... **LC 10**

Maas, Peter 1929- .... **CLC 29**
See also CA 93-96; INT 93-96

Macaulay, Rose 1881-1958 .... **TCLC 7, 44**
See also CA 104; DLB 36

Macaulay, Thomas Babington 1800-1859
NCLC 42
See also CDBLB 1832-1890; DLB 32, 55

MacBeth, George (Mann) 1932-1992 **CLC 2, 5,**
9
See also CA 25-28R; 136; CANR 61, 66; DLB
40; MTCW; SATA 4; SATA-Obit 70

MacCaig, Norman (Alexander) 1910- **CLC 36;**
DAB; DAM POET
See also CA 9-12R; CANR 3, 34; DLB 27

MacCarthy, (Sir Charles Otto) Desmond 1877-
1952 .... **TCLC 36**

MacDiarmid, Hugh **CLC 2, 4, 11, 19, 63; PC 9**
See also Grieve, C(hristopher) M(urray)

See also CDBLB 1945-1960; DLB 20

MacDonald, Anson
See Heinlein, Robert A(nson)

Macdonald, Cynthia 1928- .... **CLC 13, 19**
See also CA 49-52; CANR 4, 44; DLB 105

MacDonald, George 1824-1905 .... **TCLC 9**
See also CA 106; 137; DLB 18, 163, 178;
MAICYA; SATA 33

Macdonald, John
See Millar, Kenneth

MacDonald, John D(ann) 1916-1986 **CLC 3,**
27, 44; DAM NOV, POP
See also CA 1-4R; 121; CANR 1, 19, 60; DLB
8; DLBY 86; MTCW

Macdonald, John Ross
See Millar, Kenneth

Macdonald, Ross .... **CLC 1, 2, 3, 14, 34, 41**
See also Millar, Kenneth
See also DLBD 6

MacDougal, John
See Blish, James (Benjamin)

MacEwen, Gwendolyn (Margaret) 1941-1987
CLC 13, 55
See also CA 9-12R; 124; CANR 7, 22; DLB
53; SATA 50; SATA-Obit 55

Macha, Karel Hynek 1810-1846 .... **NCLC 46**

Machado (y Ruiz), Antonio 1875-1939 **TCLC**
3
See also CA 104; DLB 108

Machado de Assis, Joaquim Maria 1839-1908
TCLC 10; BLC 2; SSC 24
See also CA 107; 153

Machen, Arthur .... **TCLC 4; SSC 20**
See also Jones, Arthur Llewellyn
See also DLB 36, 156, 178

Machiavelli, Niccolo 1469-1527 **LC 8, 36; DA;**
DAB; DAC; DAM MST; WLCS

MacInnes, Colin 1914-1976 .... **CLC 4, 23**
See also CA 69-72; 65-68; CANR 21; DLB 14;
MTCW

MacInnes, Helen (Clark) 1907-1985 **CLC 27,**
39; DAM POP
See also CA 1-4R; 117; CANR 1, 28, 58; DLB
87; MTCW; SATA 22; SATA-Obit 44

Mackay, Mary 1855-1924
See Corelli, Marie
See also CA 118

Mackenzie, Compton (Edward Montague)
1883-1972 .... **CLC 18**
See also CA 21-22; 37-40R; CAP 2; DLB 34,
100

Mackenzie, Henry 1745-1831 .... **NCLC 41**
See also DLB 39

Mackintosh, Elizabeth 1896(?)-1952
See Tey, Josephine
See also CA 110

MacLaren, James
See Grieve, C(hristopher) M(urray)

Mac Laverty, Bernard 1942- .... **CLC 31**
See also CA 116; 118; CANR 43; INT 118

MacLean, Alistair (Stuart) 1922(?)-1987 **CLC**
3, 13, 50, 63; DAM POP
See also CA 57-60; 121; CANR 28, 61; MTCW;
SATA 23; SATA-Obit 50

Maclean, Norman (Fitzroy) 1902-1990 **CLC**
78; DAM POP; SSC 13
See also CA 102; 132; CANR 49

MacLeish, Archibald 1892-1982 **CLC 3, 8, 14,**
68; DAM POET
See also CA 9-12R; 106; CANR 33, 63; DLB
4, 7, 45; DLBY 82; MTCW

MacLennan, (John) Hugh 1907-1990 **CLC 2,**
14, 92; DAC; DAM MST

See also CA 5-8R; 142; CANR 33; DLB 68;
MTCW

MacLeod, Alistair 1936- **CLC 56; DAC; DAM**
MST
See also CA 123; DLB 60

Macleod, Fiona
See Sharp, William

MacNeice, (Frederick) Louis 1907-1963 **CLC**
1, 4, 10, 53; DAB; DAM POET
See also CA 85-88; CANR 61; DLB 10, 20;
MTCW

MacNeill, Dand
See Fraser, George MacDonald

Macpherson, James 1736-1796 .... **LC 29**
See also Ossian
See also DLB 109

Macpherson, (Jean) Jay 1931- .... **CLC 14**
See also CA 5-8R; DLB 53

MacShane, Frank 1927- .... **CLC 39**
See also CA 9-12R; CANR 3, 33; DLB 111

Macumber, Mari
See Sandoz, Mari(e Susette)

Madach, Imre 1823-1864 .... **NCLC 19**

Madden, (Jerry) David 1933- .... **CLC 5, 15**
See also CA 1-4R; CAAS 3; CANR 4, 45; DLB
6; MTCW

Maddern, Al(an)
See Ellison, Harlan (Jay)

Madhubuti, Haki R. 1942- **CLC 6, 73; BLC 2;**
DAM MULT, POET; PC 5
See also Lee, Don L.
See also BW 2; CA 73-76; CANR 24, 51; DLB
5, 41; DLBD 8

Maepenn, Hugh
See Kuttner, Henry

Maepenn, K. H.
See Kuttner, Henry

Maeterlinck, Maurice 1862-1949 ... **TCLC 3;**
DAM DRAM
See also CA 104; 136; DLB 192; SATA 66

Maginn, William 1794-1842 .... **NCLC 8**
See also DLB 110, 159

Mahapatra, Jayanta 1928- .... **CLC 33; DAM**
MULT
See also CA 73-76; CAAS 9; CANR 15, 33, 66

Mahfouz, Naguib (Abdel Aziz Al-Sabilgi)
1911(?)-
See Mahfuz, Najib
See also BEST 89:2; CA 128; CANR 55; DAM
NOV; MTCW

Mahfuz, Najib .... **CLC 52, 55**
See also Mahfouz, Naguib (Abdel Aziz Al-
Sabilgi)
See also DLBY 88

Mahon, Derek 1941- .... **CLC 27**
See also CA 113; 128; DLB 40

Mailer, Norman 1923- **CLC 1, 2, 3, 4, 5, 8, 11,**
14, 28, 39, 74, 111; DA; DAB; DAC; DAM
MST, NOV, POP
See also AITN 2; CA 9-12R; CABS 1; CANR
28; CDALB 1968-1988; DLB 2, 16, 28, 185;
DLBD 3; DLBY 80, 83; MTCW

Maillet, Antonine 1929- .... **CLC 54; DAC**
See also CA 115; 120; CANR 46; DLB 60; INT
120

Mais, Roger 1905-1955 .... **TCLC 8**
See also BW 1; CA 105; 124; DLB 125; MTCW

Maistre, Joseph de 1753-1821 .... **NCLC 37**

Maitland, Frederic 1850-1906 .... **TCLC 65**

Maitland, Sara (Louise) 1950- .... **CLC 49**
See also CA 69-72; CANR 13, 59

Major, Clarence 1936- **CLC 3, 19, 48; BLC 2;**
DAM MULT

See also BW 2; CA 21-24R; CAAS 6; CANR 13, 25, 53; DLB 33

Major, Kevin (Gerald) 1949- .. **CLC 26; DAC**
See also AAYA 16; CA 97-100; CANR 21, 38; CLR 11; DLB 60; INT CANR-21; JRDA; MAICYA; SATA 32, 82

Maki, James
See Ozu, Yasujiro

Malabaila, Damiano
See Levi, Primo

Malamud, Bernard 1914-1986**CLC 1, 2, 3, 5, 8, 9, 11, 18, 27, 44, 78, 85; DA; DAB; DAC; DAM MST, NOV, POP; SSC 15; WLC**
See also AAYA 16; CA 5-8R; 118; CABS 1; CANR 28, 62; CDALB 1941-1968; DLB 2, 28, 152; DLBY 80, 86; MTCW

Malan, Herman
See Bosman, Herman Charles; Bosman, Herman Charles

Malaparte, Curzio 1898-1957 .... **TCLC 52**

Malcolm, Dan
See Silverberg, Robert

Malcolm X .... **CLC 82; BLC 2; WLCS**
See also Little, Malcolm

Malherbe, Francois de 1555-1628 .... **LC 5**

Mallarme, Stephane 1842-1898 **NCLC 4, 41; DAM POET; PC 4**

Mallet-Joris, Francoise 1930- .... **CLC 11**
See also CA 65-68; CANR 17; DLB 83

Malley, Ern
See McAuley, James Phillip

Mallowan, Agatha Christie
See Christie, Agatha (Mary Clarissa)

Maloff, Saul 1922- .... **CLC 5**
See also CA 33-36R

Malone, Louis
See MacNeice, (Frederick) Louis

Malone, Michael (Christopher) 1942-**CLC 43**
See also CA 77-80; CANR 14, 32, 57

Malory, (Sir) Thomas 1410(?)-1471(?)**LC 11; DA; DAB; DAC; DAM MST; WLCS**
See also CDBLB Before 1660; DLB 146; SATA 59; SATA-Brief 33

Malouf, (George Joseph) David 1934-**CLC 28, 86**
See also CA 124; CANR 50

Malraux, (Georges-)Andre 1901-1976**CLC 1, 4, 9, 13, 15, 57; DAM NOV**
See also CA 21-22; 69-72; CANR 34, 58; CAP 2; DLB 72; MTCW

Malzberg, Barry N(athaniel) 1939- ... **CLC 7**
See also CA 61-64; CAAS 4; CANR 16; DLB 8

Mamet, David (Alan) 1947-**CLC 9, 15, 34, 46, 91; DAM DRAM; DC 4**
See also AAYA 3; CA 81-84; CABS 3; CANR 15, 41, 67; DLB 7; MTCW

Mamoulian, Rouben (Zachary) 1897-1987 **CLC 16**
See also CA 25-28R; 124

Mandelstam, Osip (Emilievich) 1891(?)-1938(?) **TCLC 2, 6; PC 14**
See also CA 104; 150

Mander, (Mary) Jane 1877-1949 ... **TCLC 31**
See also CA 162

Mandeville, John fl. 1350- .... **CMLC 19**
See also DLB 146

Mandiargues, Andre Pieyre de .... **CLC 41**
See also Pieyre de Mandiargues, Andre
See also DLB 83

Mandrake, Ethel Belle
See Thurman, Wallace (Henry)

Mangan, James Clarence 1803-1849**NCLC 27**

Maniere, J.-E.
See Giraudoux, (Hippolyte) Jean

Manley, (Mary) Delariviere 1672(?)-1724 **L C 1**
See also DLB 39, 80

Mann, Abel
See Creasey, John

Mann, Emily 1952- .... **DC 7**
See also CA 130; CANR 55

Mann, (Luiz) Heinrich 1871-1950 ... **TCLC 9**
See also CA 106; 164; DLB 66

Mann, (Paul) Thomas 1875-1955 **TCLC 2, 8, 14, 21, 35, 44, 60; DA; DAB; DAC; DAM MST, NOV; SSC 5; WLC**
See also CA 104; 128; DLB 66; MTCW

Mannheim, Karl 1893-1947 .... **TCLC 65**

Manning, David
See Faust, Frederick (Schiller)

Manning, Frederic 1887(?)-1935 ... **TCLC 25**
See also CA 124

Manning, Olivia 1915-1980 .... **CLC 5, 19**
See also CA 5-8R; 101; CANR 29; MTCW

Mano, D. Keith 1942- .... **CLC 2, 10**
See also CA 25-28R; CAAS 6; CANR 26, 57; DLB 6

Mansfield, KatherineTCLC 2, 8, 39; DAB; SSC 9, 23; WLC**
See also Beauchamp, Kathleen Mansfield
See also DLB 162

Manso, Peter 1940- .... **CLC 39**
See also CA 29-32R; CANR 44

Mantecon, Juan Jimenez
See Jimenez (Mantecon), Juan Ramon

Manton, Peter
See Creasey, John

Man Without a Spleen, A
See Chekhov, Anton (Pavlovich)

Manzoni, Alessandro 1785-1873 .... **NCLC 29**

Mapu, Abraham (ben Jekutiel) 1808-1867 **NCLC 18**

Mara, Sally
See Queneau, Raymond

Marat, Jean Paul 1743-1793 .... **LC 10**

Marcel, Gabriel Honore 1889-1973 . **CLC 15**
See also CA 102; 45-48; MTCW

Marchbanks, Samuel
See Davies, (William) Robertson

Marchi, Giacomo
See Bassani, Giorgio

Margulies, Donald .... **CLC 76**

Marie de France c. 12th cent. - **CMLC 8; PC 22**

Marie de l'Incarnation 1599-1672 ...... **LC 10**

Marier, Captain Victor
See Griffith, D(avid Lewelyn) W(ark)

Mariner, Scott
See Pohl, Frederik

Marinetti, Filippo Tommaso 1876-1944**TCLC 10**
See also CA 107; DLB 114

Marivaux, Pierre Carlet de Chamblain de 1688-1763 .... **LC 4; DC 7**

Markandaya, Kamala .... **CLC 8, 38**
See also Taylor, Kamala (Purnaiya)

Markfield, Wallace 1926- .... **CLC 8**
See also CA 69-72; CAAS 3; DLB 2, 28

Markham, Edwin 1852-1940 .... **TCLC 47**
See also CA 160; DLB 54, 186

Markham, Robert
See Amis, Kingsley (William)

Marks, J
See Highwater, Jamake (Mamake)

Marks-Highwater, J

See Highwater, Jamake (Mamake)

Markson, David M(errill) 1927- .... **CLC 67**
See also CA 49-52; CANR 1

Marley, Bob .... **CLC 17**
See also Marley, Robert Nesta

Marley, Robert Nesta 1945-1981
See Marley, Bob
See also CA 107; 103

Marlowe, Christopher 1564-1593**LC 22; DA; DAB; DAC; DAM DRAM, MST; DC 1; WLC**
See also CDBLB Before 1660; DLB 62

Marlowe, Stephen 1928-
See Queen, Ellery
See also CA 13-16R; CANR 6, 55

Marmontel, Jean-Francois 1723-1799 .. **LC 2**

Marquand, John P(hillips) 1893-1960**CLC 2, 10**
See also CA 85-88; DLB 9, 102

Marques, Rene 1919-1979 ..... **CLC 96; DAM MULT; HLC**
See also CA 97-100; 85-88; DLB 113; HW

Marquez, Gabriel (Jose) Garcia
See Garcia Marquez, Gabriel (Jose)

Marquis, Don(ald Robert Perry) 1878-1937 **TCLC 7**
See also CA 104; 166; DLB 11, 25

Marric, J. J.
See Creasey, John

Marryat, Frederick 1792-1848 .... **NCLC 3**
See also DLB 21, 163

Marsden, James
See Creasey, John

Marsh, (Edith) Ngaio 1899-1982 **CLC 7, 53; DAM POP**
See also CA 9-12R; CANR 6, 58; DLB 77; MTCW

Marshall, Garry 1934- .... **CLC 17**
See also AAYA 3; CA 111; SATA 60

Marshall, Paule 1929- .. **CLC 27, 72; BLC 3; DAM MULT; SSC 3**
See also BW 2; CA 77-80; CANR 25; DLB 157; MTCW

Marsten, Richard
See Hunter, Evan

Marston, John 1576-1634**LC 33; DAM DRAM**
See also DLB 58, 172

Martha, Henry
See Harris, Mark

Marti, Jose 1853-1895**NCLC 63; DAM MULT; HLC**

Martial c. 40-c. 104 .... **PC 10**

Martin, Ken
See Hubbard, L(afayette) Ron(ald)

Martin, Richard
See Creasey, John

Martin, Steve 1945- .... **CLC 30**
See also CA 97-100; CANR 30; MTCW

Martin, Valerie 1948- .... **CLC 89**
See also BEST 90:2; CA 85-88; CANR 49

Martin, Violet Florence 1862-1915 **TCLC 51**

Martin, Webber
See Silverberg, Robert

Martindale, Patrick Victor
See White, Patrick (Victor Martindale)

Martin du Gard, Roger 1881-1958 **TCLC 24**
See also CA 118; DLB 65

Martineau, Harriet 1802-1876 .... **NCLC 26**
See also DLB 21, 55, 159, 163, 166, 190; YABC 2

Martines, Julia
See O'Faolain, Julia

Martinez, Enrique Gonzalez

See also CA 118; DLB 149

Musgrave, Susan 1951- .... **CLC 13, 54**
See also CA 69-72; CANR 45

Musil, Robert (Edler von) 1880-1942 **T C L C 12, 68; SSC 18**
See also CA 109; CANR 55; DLB 81, 124

Muske, Carol 1945- .... **CLC 90**
See also Muske-Dukes, Carol (Anne)

Muske-Dukes, Carol (Anne) 1945-
See Muske, Carol
See also CA 65-68; CANR 32

Musset, (Louis Charles) Alfred de 1810-1857 **NCLC 7**
See also DLB 192

My Brother's Brother
See Chekhov, Anton (Pavlovich)

Myers, L(eopold) H(amilton) 1881-1944 **TCLC 59**
See also CA 157; DLB 15

Myers, Walter Dean 1937- . **CLC 35; BLC 3; DAM MULT, NOV**
See also AAYA 4, 23; BW 2; CA 33-36R; CANR 20, 42, 67; CLR 4, 16, 35; DLB 33; INT CANR-20; JRDA; MAICYA; SAAS 2; SATA 41, 71; SATA-Brief 27

Myers, Walter M.
See Myers, Walter Dean

Myles, Symon
See Follett, Ken(neth Martin)

Nabokov, Vladimir (Vladimirovich) 1899-1977 **CLC 1, 2, 3, 6, 8, 11, 15, 23, 44, 46, 64; DA; DAB; DAC; DAM MST, NOV; SSC 11; WLC**
See also CA 5-8R; 69-72; CANR 20; CDALB 1941-1968; DLB 2; DLBD 3; DLBY 80, 91; MTCW

Nagai Kafu 1879-1959 .... **TCLC 51**
See also Nagai Sokichi
See also DLB 180

Nagai Sokichi 1879-1959
See Nagai Kafu
See also CA 117

Nagy, Laszlo 1925-1978 .... **CLC 7**
See also CA 129; 112

Naidu, Sarojini 1879-1943 .... **TCLC 80**

Naipaul, Shiva(dhar Srinivasa) 1945-1985 **CLC 32, 39; DAM NOV**
See also CA 110; 112; 116; CANR 33; DLB 157; DLBY 85; MTCW

Naipaul, V(idiadhar) S(urajprasad) 1932- **CLC 4, 7, 9, 13, 18, 37, 105; DAB; DAC; DAM MST, NOV**
See also CA 1-4R; CANR 1, 33, 51; CDBLB 1960 to Present; DLB 125; DLBY 85; MTCW

Nakos, Lilika 1899(?)- .... **CLC 29**

Narayan, R(asipuram) K(rishnaswami) 1906- **CLC 7, 28, 47; DAM NOV; SSC 25**
See also CA 81-84; CANR 33, 61; MTCW; SATA 62

Nash, (Fredric) Ogden 1902-1971 . **CLC 23; DAM POET; PC 21**
See also CA 13-14; 29-32R; CANR 34, 61; CAP 1; DLB 11; MAICYA; MTCW; SATA 2, 46

Nashe, Thomas 1567-1601(?) .... **LC 41**
See also DLB 167

Nashe, Thomas 1567-1601 .... **LC 41**

Nathan, Daniel
See Dannay, Frederic

Nathan, George Jean 1882-1958 .... **TCLC 18**
See also Hatteras, Owen
See also CA 114; DLB 137

Natsume, Kinnosuke 1867-1916

See Natsume, Soseki
See also CA 104

Natsume, Soseki 1867-1916 .....:.. **TCLC 2, 10**
See also Natsume, Kinnosuke
See also DLB 180

Natti, (Mary) Lee 1919-
See Kingman, Lee
See also CA 5-8R; CANR 2

Naylor, Gloria 1950- **CLC 28, 52; BLC 3; DA; DAC; DAM MST, MULT, NOV, POP; WLCS**
See also AAYA 6; BW 2; CA 107; CANR 27, 51; DLB 173; MTCW

Neihardt, John Gneisenau 1881-1973 **CLC 32**
See also CA 13-14; CANR 65; CAP 1; DLB 9, 54

Nekrasov, Nikolai Alekseevich 1821-1878 **NCLC 11**

Nelligan, Emile 1879-1941 .... **TCLC 14**
See also CA 114; DLB 92

Nelson, Willie 1933- .... **CLC 17**
See also CA 107

Nemerov, Howard (Stanley) 1920-1991 **CLC 2, 6, 9, 36; DAM POET**
See also CA 1-4R; 134; CABS 2; CANR 1, 27, 53; DLB 5, 6; DLBY 83; INT CANR-27; MTCW

Neruda, Pablo 1904-1973 **CLC 1, 2, 5, 7, 9, 28, 62; DA; DAB; DAC; DAM MST, MULT, POET; HLC; PC 4; WLC**
See also CA 19-20; 45-48; CAP 2; HW; MTCW

Nerval, Gerard de 1808-1855 **NCLC 1, 67; PC 13; SSC 18**

Nervo, (Jose) Amado (Ruiz de) 1870-1919 **TCLC 11**
See also CA 109; 131; HW

Nessi, Pio Baroja y
See Baroja (y Nessi), Pio

Nestroy, Johann 1801-1862 .... **NCLC 42**
See also DLB 133

Netterville, Luke
See O'Grady, Standish (James)

Neufeld, John (Arthur) 1938- .... **CLC 17**
See also AAYA 11; CA 25-28R; CANR 11, 37, 56; CLR 52; MAICYA; SAAS 3; SATA 6, 81

Neville, Emily Cheney 1919- .... **CLC 12**
See also CA 5-8R; CANR 3, 37; JRDA; MAICYA; SAAS 2; SATA 1

Newbound, Bernard Slade 1930-
See Slade, Bernard
See also CA 81-84; CANR 49; DAM DRAM

Newby, P(ercy) H(oward) 1918-1997 **CLC 2, 13; DAM NOV**
See also CA 5-8R; 161; CANR 32, 67; DLB 15; MTCW

Newlove, Donald 1928- .... **CLC 6**
See also CA 29-32R; CANR 25

Newlove, John (Herbert) 1938- .... **CLC 14**
See also CA 21-24R; CANR 9, 25

Newman, Charles 1938- .... **CLC 2, 8**
See also CA 21-24R

Newman, Edwin (Harold) 1919- .... **CLC 14**
See also AITN 1; CA 69-72; CANR 5

Newman, John Henry 1801-1890 .. **NCLC 38**
See also DLB 18, 32, 55

Newton, Suzanne 1936- .... **CLC 35**
See also CA 41-44R; CANR 14; JRDA; SATA 5, 77

Nexo, Martin Andersen 1869-1954 **TCLC 43**

Nezval, Vitezslav 1900-1958 .... **TCLC 44**
See also CA 123

Ng, Fae Myenne 1957(?)- .... **CLC 81**

See also CA 146

Ngema, Mbongeni 1955- .... **CLC 57**
See also BW 2; CA 143

Ngugi, James T(hiong'o) .... **CLC 3, 7, 13**
See also Ngugi wa Thiong'o

Ngugi wa Thiong'o 1938- .. **CLC 36; BLC 3; DAM MULT, NOV**
See also Ngugi, James T(hiong'o)
See also BW 2; CA 81-84; CANR 27, 58; DLB 125; MTCW

Nichol, B(arrie) P(hillip) 1944-1988 **CLC 18**
See also CA 53-56; DLB 53; SATA 66

Nichols, John (Treadwell) 1940- .... **CLC 38**
See also CA 9-12R; CAAS 2; CANR 6; DLBY 82

Nichols, Leigh
See Koontz, Dean R(ay)

Nichols, Peter (Richard) 1927- **CLC 5, 36, 65**
See also CA 104; CANR 33; DLB 13; MTCW

Nicolas, F. R. E.
See Freeling, Nicolas

Niedecker, Lorine 1903-1970 .... **CLC 10, 42; DAM POET**
See also CA 25-28; CAP 2; DLB 48

Nietzsche, Friedrich (Wilhelm) 1844-1900 **TCLC 10, 18, 55**
See also CA 107; 121; DLB 129

Nievo, Ippolito 1831-1861 .... **NCLC 22**

Nightingale, Anne Redmon 1943-
See Redmon, Anne
See also CA 103

Nik. T. O.
See Annensky, Innokenty (Fyodorovich)

Nin, Anais 1903-1977 **CLC 1, 4, 8, 11, 14, 60; DAM NOV, POP; SSC 10**
See also AITN 2; CA 13-16R; 69-72; CANR 22, 53; DLB 2, 4, 152; MTCW

Nishida, Kitaro 1870-1945 .... **TCLC 83**

Nishiwaki, Junzaburo 1894-1982 .... **PC 15**
See also CA 107

Nissenson, Hugh 1933- .... **CLC 4, 9**
See also CA 17-20R; CANR 27; DLB 28

Niven, Larry .... **CLC 8**
See also Niven, Laurence Van Cott
See also DLB 8

Niven, Laurence Van Cott 1938-
See Niven, Larry
See also CA 21-24R; CAAS 12; CANR 14, 44, 66; DAM POP; MTCW; SATA 95

Nixon, Agnes Eckhardt 1927- .... **CLC 21**
See also CA 110

Nizan, Paul 1905-1940 .... **TCLC 40**
See also CA 161; DLB 72

Nkosi, Lewis 1936- .... **CLC 45; BLC 3; DAM MULT**
See also BW 1; CA 65-68; CANR 27; DLB 157

Nodier, (Jean) Charles (Emmanuel) 1780-1844 **NCLC 19**
See also DLB 119

Noguchi, Yone 1875-1947 .... **TCLC 80**

Nolan, Christopher 1965- .... **CLC 58**
See also CA 111

Noon, Jeff 1957- .... **CLC 91**
See also CA 148

Norden, Charles
See Durrell, Lawrence (George)

Nordhoff, Charles (Bernard) 1887-1947 **TCLC 23**
See also CA 108; DLB 9; SATA 23

Norfolk, Lawrence 1963- .... **CLC 76**
See also CA 144

Norman, Marsha 1947- **CLC 28; DAM DRAM; DC 8**

Richardson, Ethel Florence (Lindesay) 1870-
1946
See Richardson, Henry Handel
See also CA 105

Richardson, Henry Handel .... TCLC 4
See also Richardson, Ethel Florence (Lindesay)
See also DLB 197

Richardson, John 1796-1852NCLC 55; DAC
See also DLB 99

Richardson, Samuel 1689-1761LC 1, 44; DA;
DAB; DAC; DAM MST, NOV; WLC
See also CDBLB 1660-1789; DLB 39

Richler, Mordecai 1931-CLC 3, 5, 9, 13, 18, 46,
70; DAC; DAM MST, NOV
See also AITN 1; CA 65-68; CANR 31, 62; CLR
17; DLB 53; MAICYA; MTCW; SATA 44,
98; SATA-Brief 27

Richter, Conrad (Michael) 1890-1968CLC 30
See also AAYA 21; CA 5-8R; 25-28R; CANR
23; DLB 9; MTCW; SATA 3

Ricostranza, Tom
See Ellis, Trey

Riddell, Charlotte 1832-1906 .... TCLC 40
See also CA 165; DLB 156

Riding, Laura .... CLC 3, 7
See also Jackson, Laura (Riding)

Riefenstahl, Berta Helene Amalia 1902-
See Riefenstahl, Leni
See also CA 108

Riefenstahl, Leni .... CLC 16
See also Riefenstahl, Berta Helene Amalia

Riffe, Ernest
See Bergman, (Ernst) Ingmar

Riggs, (Rolla) Lynn 1899-1954 ..... TCLC 56;
DAM MULT
See also CA 144; DLB 175; NNAL

Riis, Jacob A(ugust) 1849-1914 ..... TCLC 80
See also CA 113; DLB 23

Riley, James Whitcomb 1849-1916TCLC 51;
DAM POET
See also CA 118; 137; MAICYA; SATA 17

Riley, Tex
See Creasey, John

Rilke, Rainer Maria 1875-1926TCLC 1, 6, 19;
DAM POET; PC 2
See also CA 104; 132; CANR 62; DLB 81;
MTCW

Rimbaud, (Jean Nicolas) Arthur 1854-1891
NCLC 4, 35; DA; DAB; DAC; DAM MST,
POET; PC 3; WLC

Rinehart, Mary Roberts 1876-1958TCLC 52
See also CA 108; 166

Ringmaster, The
See Mencken, H(enry) L(ouis)

Ringwood, Gwen(dolyn Margaret) Pharis
1910-1984 .... CLC 48
See also CA 148; 112; DLB 88

Rio, Michel 19(?)- .... CLC 43

Ritsos, Giannes
See Ritsos, Yannis

Ritsos, Yannis 1909-1990 .... CLC 6, 13, 31
See also CA 77-80; 133; CANR 39, 61; MTCW

Ritter, Erika 1948(?)- .... CLC 52

Rivera, Jose Eustasio 1889-1928 ... TCLC 35
See also CA 162; HW

Rivers, Conrad Kent 1933-1968 .... CLC 1
See also BW 1; CA 85-88; DLB 41

Rivers, Elfrida
See Bradley, Marion Zimmer

Riverside, John
See Heinlein, Robert A(nson)

Rizal, Jose 1861-1896 .... NCLC 27

Roa Bastos, Augusto (Antonio) 1917-CLC 45;

DAM MULT; HLC
See also CA 131; DLB 113; HW

Robbe-Grillet, Alain 1922-CLC 1, 2, 4, 6, 8, 10,
14, 43
See also CA 9-12R; CANR 33, 65; DLB 83;
MTCW

Robbins, Harold 1916-1997 ..... CLC 5; DAM
NOV
See also CA 73-76; 162; CANR 26, 54; MTCW

Robbins, Thomas Eugene 1936-
See Robbins, Tom
See also CA 81-84; CANR 29, 59; DAM NOV,
POP; MTCW

Robbins, Tom .... CLC 9, 32, 64
See also Robbins, Thomas Eugene
See also BEST 90:3; DLBY 80

Robbins, Trina 1938- .... CLC 21
See also CA 128

Roberts, Charles G(eorge) D(ouglas) 1860-1943
TCLC 8
See also CA 105; CLR 33; DLB 92; SATA 88;
SATA-Brief 29

Roberts, Elizabeth Madox 1886-1941 T C L C
68
See also CA 111; 166; DLB 9, 54, 102; SATA
33; SATA-Brief 27

Roberts, Kate 1891-1985 .... CLC 15
See also CA 107; 116

Roberts, Keith (John Kingston) 1935-CLC 14
See also CA 25-28R; CANR 46

Roberts, Kenneth (Lewis) 1885-1957TCLC 23
See also CA 109; DLB 9

Roberts, Michele (B.) 1949- .... CLC 48
See also CA 115; CANR 58

Robertson, Ellis
See Ellison, Harlan (Jay); Silverberg, Robert

Robertson, Thomas William 1829-1871NCLC
35; DAM DRAM

Robeson, Kenneth
See Dent, Lester

Robinson, Edwin Arlington 1869-1935T C L C
5; DA; DAC; DAM MST, POET; PC 1
See also CA 104; 133; CDALB 1865-1917;
DLB 54; MTCW

Robinson, Henry Crabb 1775-1867NCLC 15
See also DLB 107

Robinson, Jill 1936- .... CLC 10
See also CA 102; INT 102

Robinson, Kim Stanley 1952- .... CLC 34
See also CA 126

Robinson, Lloyd
See Silverberg, Robert

Robinson, Marilynne 1944- .... CLC 25
See also CA 116

Robinson, Smokey .... CLC 21
See also Robinson, William, Jr.

Robinson, William, Jr. 1940-
See Robinson, Smokey
See also CA 116

Robison, Mary 1949- .... CLC 42, 98
See also CA 113; 116; DLB 130; INT 116

Rod, Edouard 1857-1910 .... TCLC 52

Roddenberry, Eugene Wesley 1921-1991
See Roddenberry, Gene
See also CA 110; 135; CANR 37; SATA 45;
SATA-Obit 69

Roddenberry, Gene .... CLC 17
See also Roddenberry, Eugene Wesley
See also AAYA 5; SATA-Obit 69

Rodgers, Mary 1931- .... CLC 12
See also CA 49-52; CANR 8, 55; CLR 20; INT
CANR-8; JRDA; MAICYA; SATA 8

Rodgers, W(illiam) R(obert) 1909-1969CLC 7

See also CA 85-88; DLB 20

Rodman, Eric
See Silverberg, Robert

Rodman, Howard 1920(?)-1985 .... CLC 65
See also CA 118

Rodman, Maia
See Wojciechowska, Maia (Teresa)

Rodriguez, Claudio 1934- .... CLC 10
See also DLB 134

Roelvaag, O(le) E(dvart) 1876-1931TCLC 17
See also CA 117; DLB 9

Roethke, Theodore (Huebner) 1908-1963CLC
1, 3, 8, 11, 19, 46, 101; DAM POET; PC 15
See also CA 81-84; CABS 2; CDALB 1941-
1968; DLB 5; MTCW

Rogers, Samuel 1763-1855 .... NCLC 69
See also DLB 93

Rogers, Thomas Hunton 1927- .... CLC 57
See also CA 89-92; INT 89-92

Rogers, Will(iam Penn Adair) 1879-1935
TCLC 8, 71; DAM MULT
See also CA 105; 144; DLB 11; NNAL

Rogin, Gilbert 1929- .... CLC 18
See also CA 65-68; CANR 15

Rohan, Koda .... TCLC 22
See also Koda Shigeyuki

Rohlfs, Anna Katharine Green
See Green, Anna Katharine

Rohmer, Eric .... CLC 16
See also Scherer, Jean-Marie Maurice

Rohmer, Sax .... TCLC 28
See also Ward, Arthur Henry Sarsfield
See also DLB 70

Roiphe, Anne (Richardson) 1935- .. CLC 3, 9
See also CA 89-92; CANR 45; DLBY 80; INT
89-92

Rojas, Fernando de 1465-1541 .... LC 23

**Rolfe, Frederick (William Serafino Austin
Lewis Mary)** 1860-1913 .... TCLC 12
See also CA 107; DLB 34, 156

Rolland, Romain 1866-1944 .... TCLC 23
See also CA 118; DLB 65

Rolle, Richard c. 1300-c. 1349 ...... CMLC 21
See also DLB 146

Rolvaag, O(le) E(dvart)
See Roelvaag, O(le) E(dvart)

Romain Arnaud, Saint
See Aragon, Louis

Romains, Jules 1885-1972 .... CLC 7
See also CA 85-88; CANR 34; DLB 65; MTCW

Romero, Jose Ruben 1890-1952 .... TCLC 14
See also CA 114; 131; HW

Ronsard, Pierre de 1524-1585 ... LC 6; PC 11

Rooke, Leon 1934- .. CLC 25, 34; DAM POP
See also CA 25-28R; CANR 23, 53

Roosevelt, Theodore 1858-1919 ..... TCLC 69
See also CA 115; DLB 47, 186

Roper, William 1498-1578 .... LC 10

Roquelaure, A. N.
See Rice, Anne

Rosa, Joao Guimaraes 1908-1967 .... CLC 23
See also CA 89-92; DLB 113

Rose, Wendy 1948-CLC 85; DAM MULT; PC
13
See also CA 53-56; CANR 5, 51; DLB 175;
NNAL; SATA 12

Rosen, R. D.
See Rosen, Richard (Dean)

Rosen, Richard (Dean) 1949- .... CLC 39
See also CA 77-80; CANR 62; INT CANR-30

Rosenberg, Isaac 1890-1918 .... TCLC 12
See also CA 107; DLB 20

Rosenblatt, Joe .... CLC 15

See also Rosenblatt, Joseph
Rosenblatt, Joseph 1933-
See Rosenblatt, Joe
See also CA 89-92; INT 89-92
Rosenfeld, Samuel
See Tzara, Tristan
Rosenstock, Sami
See Tzara, Tristan
Rosenstock, Samuel
See Tzara, Tristan
Rosenthal, M(acha) L(ouis) 1917-1996 . C L C **28**
See also CA 1-4R; 152; CAAS 6; CANR 4, 51; DLB 5; SATA 59
Ross, Barnaby
See Dannay, Frederic
Ross, Bernard L.
See Follett, Ken(neth Martin)
Ross, J. H.
See Lawrence, T(homas) E(dward)
Ross, Martin
See Martin, Violet Florence
See also DLB 135
Ross, (James) Sinclair 1908- **CLC 13; DAC; DAM MST; SSC 24**
See also CA 73-76; DLB 88
Rossetti, Christina (Georgina) 1830-1894 **NCLC 2, 50, 66; DA; DAB; DAC; DAM MST, POET; PC 7; WLC**
See also DLB 35, 163; MAICYA; SATA 20
Rossetti, Dante Gabriel 1828-1882 . **NCLC 4; DA; DAB; DAC; DAM MST, POET; WLC**
See also CDBLB 1832-1890; DLB 35
Rossner, Judith (Perelman) 1935- **CLC 6, 9, 29**
See also AITN 2; BEST 90:3; CA 17-20R; CANR 18, 51; DLB 6; INT CANR-18; MTCW
Rostand, Edmond (Eugene Alexis) 1868-1918 **TCLC 6, 37; DA; DAB; DAC; DAM DRAM, MST**
See also CA 104; 126; DLB 192; MTCW
Roth, Henry 1906-1995 ..... **CLC 2, 6, 11, 104**
See also CA 11-12; 149; CANR 38, 63; CAP 1; DLB 28; MTCW
Roth, Philip (Milton) 1933- **CLC 1, 2, 3, 4, 6, 9, 15, 22, 31, 47, 66, 86; DA; DAB; DAC; DAM MST, NOV, POP; SSC 26; WLC**
See also BEST 90:3; CA 1-4R; CANR 1, 22, 36, 55; CDALB 1968-1988; DLB 2, 28, 173; DLBY 82; MTCW
Rothenberg, Jerome 1931- .... **CLC 6, 57**
See also CA 45-48; CANR 1; DLB 5, 193
Roumain, Jacques (Jean Baptiste) 1907-1944 **TCLC 19; BLC 3; DAM MULT**
See also BW 1; CA 117; 125
Rourke, Constance (Mayfield) 1885-1941 **TCLC 12**
See also CA 107; YABC 1
Rousseau, Jean-Baptiste 1671-1741 ...... **LC 9**
Rousseau, Jean-Jacques 1712-1778 **LC 14, 36; DA; DAB; DAC; DAM MST; WLC**
Roussel, Raymond 1877-1933 .... **TCLC 20**
See also CA 117
Rovit, Earl (Herbert) 1927- .... **CLC 7**
See also CA 5-8R; CANR 12
Rowe, Elizabeth Singer 1674-1737 ...... **LC 44**
See also DLB 39, 95
Rowe, Nicholas 1674-1718 .... **LC 8**
See also DLB 84
Rowley, Ames Dorrance
See Lovecraft, H(oward) P(hillips)
Rowson, Susanna Haswell 1762(?)-1824 **NCLC 5, 69**

See also DLB 37, 200
Roy, Arundhati 1960(?)- .... **CLC 109**
See also CA 163; DLBY 97
Roy, Gabrielle 1909-1983 **CLC 10, 14; DAB; DAC; DAM MST**
See also CA 53-56; 110; CANR 5, 61; DLB 68; MTCW
Royko, Mike 1932-1997 .... **CLC 109**
See also CA 89-92; 157; CANR 26
Rozewicz, Tadeusz 1921- .. **CLC 9, 23; DAM POET**
See also CA 108; CANR 36, 66; MTCW
Ruark, Gibbons 1941- .... **CLC 3**
See also CA 33-36R; CAAS 23; CANR 14, 31, 57; DLB 120
Rubens, Bernice (Ruth) 1923- .... **CLC 19, 31**
See also CA 25-28R; CANR 33, 65; DLB 14; MTCW
Rubin, Harold
See Robbins, Harold
Rudkin, (James) David 1936- .... **CLC 14**
See also CA 89-92; DLB 13
Rudnik, Raphael 1933- .... **CLC 7**
See also CA 29-32R
Ruffian, M.
See Hasek, Jaroslav (Matej Frantisek)
Ruiz, Jose Martinez .... **CLC 11**
See also Martinez Ruiz, Jose
Rukeyser, Muriel 1913-1980 **CLC 6, 10, 15, 27; DAM POET; PC 12**
See also CA 5-8R; 93-96; CANR 26, 60; DLB 48; MTCW; SATA-Obit 22
Rule, Jane (Vance) 1931- .... **CLC 27**
See also CA 25-28R; CAAS 18; CANR 12; DLB 60
Rulfo, Juan 1918-1986 ...... **CLC 8, 80; DAM MULT; HLC; SSC 25**
See also CA 85-88; 118; CANR 26; DLB 113; HW; MTCW
Rumi, Jalal al-Din 1297-1373 .... **CMLC 20**
Runeberg, Johan 1804-1877 .... **NCLC 41**
Runyon, (Alfred) Damon 1884(?)-1946 **T C L C 10**
See also CA 107; 165; DLB 11, 86, 171
Rush, Norman 1933- .... **CLC 44**
See also CA 121; 126; INT 126
Rushdie, (Ahmed) Salman 1947- **CLC 23, 31, 55, 100; DAB; DAC; DAM MST, NOV, POP; WLCS**
See also BEST 89:3; CA 108; 111; CANR 33, 56; DLB 194; INT 111; MTCW
Rushforth, Peter (Scott) 1945- .... **CLC 19**
See also CA 101
Ruskin, John 1819-1900 .... **TCLC 63**
See also CA 114; 129; CDBLB 1832-1890; DLB 55, 163, 190; SATA 24
Russ, Joanna 1937- .... **CLC 15**
See also CANR 11, 31, 65; DLB 8; MTCW
Russell, George William 1867-1935
See Baker, Jean H.
See also CA 104; 153; CDBLB 1890-1914; DAM POET
Russell, (Henry) Ken(neth Alfred) 1927- **C L C 16**
See also CA 105
Russell, William Martin 1947- .... **CLC 60**
See also CA 164
Rutherford, Mark .... **TCLC 25**
See also White, William Hale
See also DLB 18
Ruyslinck, Ward 1929- .... **CLC 14**
See also Belser, Reimond Karel Maria de
Ryan, Cornelius (John) 1920-1974 ..... **CLC 7**

See also CA 69-72; 53-56; CANR 38
Ryan, Michael 1946- .... **CLC 65**
See also CA 49-52; DLBY 82
Ryan, Tim
See Dent, Lester
Rybakov, Anatoli (Naumovich) 1911- **CLC 23, 53**
See also CA 126; 135; SATA 79
Ryder, Jonathan
See Ludlum, Robert
Ryga, George 1932-1987 **CLC 14; DAC; DAM MST**
See also CA 101; 124; CANR 43; DLB 60
S. H.
See Hartmann, Sadakichi
S. S.
See Sassoon, Siegfried (Lorraine)
Saba, Umberto 1883-1957 .... **TCLC 33**
See also CA 144; DLB 114
Sabatini, Rafael 1875-1950 .... **TCLC 47**
See also CA 162
Sabato, Ernesto (R.) 1911- **CLC 10, 23; DAM MULT; HLC**
See also CA 97-100; CANR 32, 65; DLB 145; HW; MTCW
Sa-Carniero, Mario de 1890-1916 . **TCLC 83**
Sacastru, Martin
See Bioy Casares, Adolfo
Sacher-Masoch, Leopold von 1836(?)-1895 **NCLC 31**
Sachs, Marilyn (Stickle) 1927- .... **CLC 35**
See also AAYA 2; CA 17-20R; CANR 13, 47; CLR 2; JRDA; MAICYA; SAAS 2; SATA 3, 68
Sachs, Nelly 1891-1970 .... **CLC 14, 98**
See also CA 17-18; 25-28R; CAP 2
Sackler, Howard (Oliver) 1929-1982 **CLC 14**
See also CA 61-64; 108; CANR 30; DLB 7
Sacks, Oliver (Wolf) 1933- .... **CLC 67**
See also CA 53-56; CANR 28, 50; INT CANR-28; MTCW
Sadakichi
See Hartmann, Sadakichi
Sade, Donatien Alphonse Francois, Comte de 1740-1814 .... **NCLC 47**
Sadoff, Ira 1945- .... **CLC 9**
See also CA 53-56; CANR 5, 21; DLB 120
Saetone
See Camus, Albert
Safire, William 1929- .... **CLC 10**
See also CA 17-20R; CANR 31, 54
Sagan, Carl (Edward) 1934-1996 **CLC 30, 112**
See also AAYA 2; CA 25-28R; 155; CANR 11, 36; MTCW; SATA 58; SATA-Obit 94
Sagan, Francoise .... **CLC 3, 6, 9, 17, 36**
See also Quoirez, Francoise
See also DLB 83
Sahgal, Nayantara (Pandit) 1927- .... **CLC 41**
See also CA 9-12R; CANR 11
Saint, H(arry) F. 1941- .... **CLC 50**
See also CA 127
St. Aubin de Teran, Lisa 1953-
See Teran, Lisa St. Aubin de
See also CA 118; 126; INT 126
Saint Birgitta of Sweden c. 1303-1373 **C M L C 24**
Sainte-Beuve, Charles Augustin 1804-1869 **NCLC 5**
Saint-Exupery, Antoine (Jean Baptiste Marie Roger) de 1900-1944 **TCLC 2, 56; DAM NOV; WLC**
See also CA 108; 132; CLR 10; DLB 72; MAICYA; MTCW; SATA 20

Schopenhauer, Arthur 1788-1860 . **NCLC 51**
See also DLB 90

Schor, Sandra (M.) 1932(?)-1990 ...... **CLC 65**
See also CA 132

Schorer, Mark 1908-1977 .... **CLC 9**
See also CA 5-8R; 73-76; CANR 7; DLB 103

Schrader, Paul (Joseph) 1946- .... **CLC 26**
See also CA 37-40R; CANR 41; DLB 44

Schreiner, Olive (Emilie Albertina) 1855-1920
TCLC 9
See also CA 105; 154; DLB 18, 156, 190

Schulberg, Budd (Wilson) 1914-... **CLC 7, 48**
See also CA 25-28R; CANR 19; DLB 6, 26, 28; DLBY 81

Schulz, Bruno 1892-1942**TCLC 5, 51; SSC 13**
See also CA 115; 123

Schulz, Charles M(onroe) 1922- .... **CLC 12**
See also CA 9-12R; CANR 6; INT CANR-6; SATA 10

Schumacher, E(rnst) F(riedrich) 1911-1977
CLC 80
See also CA 81-84; 73-76; CANR 34

Schuyler, James Marcus 1923-1991**CLC 5, 23; DAM POET**
See also CA 101; 134; DLB 5, 169; INT 101

Schwartz, Delmore (David) 1913-1966**CLC 2, 4, 10, 45, 87; PC 8**
See also CA 17-18; 25-28R; CANR 35; CAP 2; DLB 28, 48; MTCW·

Schwartz, Ernst
See Ozu, Yasujiro

Schwartz, John Burnham 1965- .... **CLC 59**
See also CA 132

Schwartz, Lynne Sharon 1939- .... **CLC 31**
See also CA 103; CANR 44

Schwartz, Muriel A.
See Eliot, T(homas) S(tearns)

Schwarz-Bart, Andre 1928- .... **CLC 2, 4**
See also CA 89-92

Schwarz-Bart, Simone 1938-.. **CLC 7; BLCS**
See also BW 2; CA 97-100

Schwob, (Mayer Andre) Marcel 1867-1905
TCLC 20
See also CA 117; DLB 123

Sciascia, Leonardo 1921-1989 . **CLC 8, 9, 41**
See also CA 85-88; 130; CANR 35; DLB 177; MTCW

Scoppettone, Sandra 1936- .... **CLC 26**
See also AAYA 11; CA 5-8R; CANR 41; SATA 9, 92

Scorsese, Martin 1942- .... **CLC 20, 89**
See also CA 110; 114; CANR 46

Scotland, Jay
See Jakes, John (William)

Scott, Duncan Campbell 1862-1947 **TCLC 6; DAC**
See also CA 104; 153; DLB 92

Scott, Evelyn 1893-1963 .... **CLC 43**
See also CA 104; 112; CANR 64; DLB 9, 48

Scott, F(rancis) R(eginald) 1899-1985**CLC 22**
See also CA 101; 114; DLB 88; INT 101

Scott, Frank
See Scott, F(rancis) R(eginald)

Scott, Joanna 1960- .... **CLC 50**
See also CA 126; CANR 53

Scott, Paul (Mark) 1920-1978 .... **CLC 9, 60**
See also CA 81-84; 77-80; CANR 33; DLB 14; MTCW

Scott, Sarah 1723-1795 .... **LC 44**
See also DLB 39

Scott, Walter 1771-1832 .. **NCLC 15, 69; DA; DAB; DAC; DAM MST, NOV, POET; PC 13; WLC**

See also AAYA 22; CDBLB 1789-1832; DLB 93, 107, 116, 144, 159; YABC 2

Scribe, (Augustin) Eugene 1791-1861 **N C L C 16; DAM DRAM; DC 5**
See also DLB 192

Scrum, R.
See Crumb, R(obert)

Scudery, Madeleine de 1607-1701 .... **LC 2**

Scum
See Crumb, R(obert)

Scumbag, Little Bobby
See Crumb, R(obert)

Seabrook, John
See Hubbard, L(afayette) Ron(ald)

Sealy, I. Allan 1951- .... **CLC 55**

Search, Alexander
See Pessoa, Fernando (Antonio Nogueira)

Sebastian, Lee
See Silverberg, Robert

Sebastian Owl
See Thompson, Hunter S(tockton)

Sebestyen, Ouida 1924- .... **CLC 30**
See also AAYA 8; CA 107; CANR 40; CLR 17; JRDA; MAICYA; SAAS 10; SATA 39

Secundus, H. Scriblerus
See Fielding, Henry

Sedges, John
See Buck, Pearl S(ydenstricker)

Sedgwick, Catharine Maria 1789-1867**NCLC 19**
See also DLB 1, 74

Seelye, John 1931- .... **CLC 7**

Seferiades, Giorgos Stylianou 1900-1971
See Seferis, George
See also CA 5-8R; 33-36R; CANR 5, 36; MTCW

Seferis, George .... **CLC 5, 11**
See also Seferiades, Giorgos Stylianou

Segal, Erich (Wolf) 1937- . **CLC 3, 10; DAM POP**
See also BEST 89:1; CA 25-28R; CANR 20, 36, 65; DLBY 86; INT CANR-20; MTCW

Seger, Bob 1945- .... **CLC 35**

Seghers, Anna .... **CLC 7**
See also Radvanyi, Netty
See also DLB 69

Seidel, Frederick (Lewis) 1936- .... **CLC 18**
See also CA 13-16R; CANR 8; DLBY 84

Seifert, Jaroslav 1901-1986 .. **CLC 34, 44, 93**
See also CA 127; MTCW

Sei Shonagon c. 966-1017(?) .... **CMLC 6**

Selby, Hubert, Jr. 1928-**CLC 1, 2, 4, 8; SSC 20**
See also CA 13-16R; CANR 33; DLB 2

Selzer, Richard 1928- .... **CLC 74**
See also CA 65-68; CANR 14

Sembene, Ousmane
See Ousmane, Sembene

Senancour, Etienne Pivert de 1770-1846
NCLC 16
See also DLB 119

Sender, Ramon (Jose) 1902-1982**CLC 8; DAM MULT; HLC**
See also CA 5-8R; 105; CANR 8; HW; MTCW

Seneca, Lucius Annaeus 4B.C.-65 . **CMLC 6; DAM DRAM; DC 5**

Senghor, Leopold Sedar 1906- **CLC 54; BLC 3; DAM MULT, POET**
See also BW 2; CA 116; 125; CANR 47; MTCW

Serling, (Edward) Rod(man) 1924-1975**C L C 30**
See also AAYA 14; AITN 1; CA 162; 57-60; DLB 26

Serna, Ramon Gomez de la

See Gomez de la Serna, Ramon

Serpieres
See Guillevic, (Eugene)

Service, Robert
See Service, Robert W(illiam)
See also DAB; DLB 92

Service, Robert W(illiam) 1874(?)-1958**TCLC 15; DA; DAC; DAM MST, POET; WLC**
See also Service, Robert
See also CA 115; 140; SATA 20

Seth, Vikram 1952-**CLC 43, 90; DAM MULT**
See also CA 121; 127; CANR 50; DLB 120; INT 127

Seton, Cynthia Propper 1926-1982 .. **CLC 27**
See also CA 5-8R; 108; CANR 7

Seton, Ernest (Evan) Thompson 1860-1946
TCLC 31
See also CA 109; DLB 92; DLBD 13; JRDA; SATA 18

Seton-Thompson, Ernest
See Seton, Ernest (Evan) Thompson

Settle, Mary Lee 1918- .... **CLC 19, 61**
See also CA 89-92; CAAS 1; CANR 44; DLB 6; INT 89-92

Seuphor, Michel
See Arp, Jean

Sevigne, Marie (de Rabutin-Chantal) Marquise de 1626-1696 .... **LC 11**

Sewall, Samuel 1652-1730 .... **LC 38**
See also DLB 24

Sexton, Anne (Harvey) 1928-1974**CLC 2, 4, 6, 8, 10, 15, 53; DA; DAB; DAC; DAM MST, POET; PC 2; WLC**
See also CA 1-4R; 53-56; CABS 2; CANR 3, 36; CDALB 1941-1968; DLB 5, 169; MTCW; SATA 10

Shaara, Michael (Joseph, Jr.) 1929-1988**CLC 15; DAM POP**
See also AITN 1; CA 102; 125; CANR 52; DLBY 83

Shackleton, C. C.
See Aldiss, Brian W(ilson)

Shacochis, Bob .... **CLC 39**
See also Shacochis, Robert G.

Shacochis, Robert G. 1951-
See Shacochis, Bob
See also CA 119; 124; INT 124

Shaffer, Anthony (Joshua) 1926- .... **CLC 19; DAM DRAM**
See also CA 110; 116; DLB 13

Shaffer, Peter (Levin) 1926-**CLC 5, 14, 18, 37, 60; DAB; DAM DRAM, MST; DC 7**
See also CA 25-28R; CANR 25, 47; CDBLB 1960 to Present; DLB 13; MTCW

Shakey, Bernard
See Young, Neil

Shalamov, Varlam (Tikhonovich) 1907(?)-1982
CLC 18
See also CA 129; 105

Shamlu, Ahmad 1925- .... **CLC 10**

Shammas, Anton 1951- .... **CLC 55**

Shange, Ntozake 1948-**CLC 8, 25, 38, 74; BLC 3; DAM DRAM, MULT; DC 3**
See also AAYA 9; BW 2; CA 85-88; CABS 3; CANR 27, 48; DLB 38; MTCW

Shanley, John Patrick 1950- .... **CLC 75**
See also CA 128; 133

Shapcott, Thomas W(illiam) 1935-... **CLC 38**
See also CA 69-72; CANR 49

Shapiro, Jane .... **CLC 76**

Shapiro, Karl (Jay) 1913-... **CLC 4, 8, 15, 53**
See also CA 1-4R; CAAS 6; CANR 1, 36, 66; DLB 48; MTCW

Sutro, Alfred 1863-1933 .... **TCLC 6**
See also CA 105; DLB 10
Sutton, Henry
See Slavitt, David R(ytman)
Svevo, Italo 1861-1928 . **TCLC 2, 35; SSC 25**
See also Schmitz, Aron Hector
Swados, Elizabeth (A.) 1951- .... **CLC 12**
See also CA 97-100; CANR 49; INT 97-100
Swados, Harvey 1920-1972 .... **CLC 5**
See also CA 5-8R; 37-40R; CANR 6; DLB 2
Swan, Gladys 1934- .... **CLC 69**
See also CA 101; CANR 17, 39
Swarthout, Glendon (Fred) 1918-1992**CLC 35**
See also CA 1-4R; 139; CANR 1, 47; SATA 26
Sweet, Sarah C.
See Jewett, (Theodora) Sarah Orne
Swenson, May 1919-1989**CLC 4, 14, 61, 106;
DA; DAB; DAC; DAM MST, POET; PC
14**
See also CA 5-8R; 130; CANR 36, 61; DLB 5;
MTCW; SATA 15
Swift, Augustus
See Lovecraft, H(oward) P(hillips)
Swift, Graham (Colin) 1949- ...... **CLC 41, 88**
See also CA 117; 122; CANR 46; DLB 194
Swift, Jonathan 1667-1745 **LC 1; DA; DAB;
DAC; DAM MST, NOV, POET; PC 9;
WLC**
See also CDBLB 1660-1789; DLB 39, 95, 101;
SATA 19
Swinburne, Algernon Charles 1837-1909
**TCLC 8, 36; DA; DAB; DAC; DAM MST,
POET; WLC**
See also CA 105; 140; CDBLB 1832-1890;
DLB 35, 57
Swinfen, Ann .... **CLC 34**
Swinnerton, Frank Arthur 1884-1982**CLC 31**
See also CA 108; DLB 34
Swithen, John
See King, Stephen (Edwin)
Sylvia
See Ashton-Warner, Sylvia (Constance)
Symmes, Robert Edward
See Duncan, Robert (Edward)
Symonds, John Addington 1840-1893 **N C L C
34**
See also DLB 57, 144
Symons, Arthur 1865-1945 .... **TCLC 11**
See also CA 107; DLB 19, 57, 149
Symons, Julian (Gustave) 1912-1994 **CLC 2,
14, 32**
See also CA 49-52; 147; CAAS 3; CANR 3,
33, 59; DLB 87, 155; DLBY 92; MTCW
Synge, (Edmund) J(ohn) M(illington) 1871-
1909 ... **TCLC 6, 37; DAM DRAM; DC 2**
See also CA 104; 141; CDBLB 1890-1914;
DLB 10, 19
Syruc, J.
See Milosz, Czeslaw
Szirtes, George 1948- .... **CLC 46**
See also CA 109; CANR 27, 61
Szymborska, Wislawa 1923-.............. **CLC 99**
See also CA 154; DLBY 96
T. O., Nik
See Annensky, Innokenty (Fyodorovich)
Tabori, George 1914- .... **CLC 19**
See also CA 49-52; CANR 4, 69
Tagore, Rabindranath 1861-1941**TCLC 3, 53;
DAM DRAM, POET; PC 8**
See also CA 104; 120; MTCW
Taine, Hippolyte Adolphe 1828-1893 . **N C L C
15**
Talese, Gay 1932-................................ **CLC 37**

See also AITN 1; CA 1-4R; CANR 9, 58; DLB
185; INT CANR-9; MTCW
Tallent, Elizabeth (Ann) 1954- .... **CLC 45**
See also CA 117; DLB 130
Tally, Ted 1952-................................... **CLC 42**
See also CA 120; 124; INT 124
Tamayo y Baus, Manuel 1829-1898 **NCLC 1**
Tammsaare, A(nton) H(ansen) 1878-1940
TCLC 27
See also CA 164
Tam'si, Tchicaya U
See Tchicaya, Gerald Felix
Tan, Amy (Ruth) 1952-**CLC 59; DAM MULT,
NOV, POP**
See also AAYA 9; BEST 89:3; CA 136; CANR
54; DLB 173; SATA 75
Tandem, Felix
See Spitteler, Carl (Friedrich Georg)
Tanizaki, Jun'ichiro 1886-1965**CLC 8, 14, 28;
SSC 21**
See also CA 93-96; 25-28R; DLB 180
Tanner, William
See Amis, Kingsley (William)
Tao Lao
See Storni, Alfonsina
Tarassoff, Lev
See Troyat, Henri
Tarbell, Ida M(inerva) 1857-1944 . **TCLC 40**
See also CA 122; DLB 47
Tarkington, (Newton) Booth 1869-1946**TCLC
9**
See also CA 110; 143; DLB 9, 102; SATA 17
Tarkovsky, Andrei (Arsenyevich) 1932-1986
CLC 75
See also CA 127
Tartt, Donna 1964(?)- .... **CLC 76**
See also CA 142
Tasso, Torquato 1544-1595 .... **LC 5**
Tate, (John Orley) Allen 1899-1979**CLC 2, 4,
6, 9, 11, 14, 24**
See also CA 5-8R; 85-88; CANR 32; DLB 4,
45, 63; MTCW
Tate, Ellalice
See Hibbert, Eleanor Alice Burford
Tate, James (Vincent) 1943- ..... **CLC 2, 6, 25**
See also CA 21-24R; CANR 29, 57; DLB 5,
169
Tavel, Ronald 1940- .... **CLC 6**
See also CA 21-24R; CANR 33
Taylor, C(ecil) P(hilip) 1929-1981 .... **CLC 27**
See also CA 25-28R; 105; CANR 47
Taylor, Edward 1642(?)-1729 ..... **LC 11; DA;
DAB; DAC; DAM MST, POET**
See also DLB 24
Taylor, Eleanor Ross 1920- .... **CLC 5**
See also CA 81-84
Taylor, Elizabeth 1912-1975 ..... **CLC 2, 4, 29**
See also CA 13-16R; CANR 9; DLB 139;
MTCW; SATA 13
Taylor, Frederick Winslow 1856-1915 **T C L C
76**
Taylor, Henry (Splawn) 1942- .... **CLC 44**
See also CA 33-36R; CAAS 7; CANR 31; DLB
5
Taylor, Kamala (Purnaiya) 1924-
See Markandaya, Kamala
See also CA 77-80
Taylor, Mildred D. .... **CLC 21**
See also AAYA 10; BW 1; CA 85-88; CANR
25; CLR 9; DLB 52; JRDA; MAICYA; SAAS
5; SATA 15, 70
Taylor, Peter (Hillsman) 1917-1994**CLC 1, 4,
18, 37, 44, 50, 71; SSC 10**

See also CA 13-16R; 147; CANR 9, 50; DLBY
81, 94; INT CANR-9; MTCW
Taylor, Robert Lewis 1912- .... **CLC 14**
See also CA 1-4R; CANR 3, 64; SATA 10
Tchekhov, Anton
See Chekhov, Anton (Pavlovich)
Tchicaya, Gerald Felix 1931-1988 .. **CLC 101**
See also CA 129; 125
Tchicaya U Tam'si
See Tchicaya, Gerald Felix
Teasdale, Sara 1884-1933 .... **TCLC 4**
See also CA 104; 163; DLB 45; SATA 32
Tegner, Esaias 1782-1846................. **NCLC 2**
Teilhard de Chardin, (Marie Joseph) Pierre
1881-1955 .... **TCLC 9**
See also CA 105
Temple, Ann
See Mortimer, Penelope (Ruth)
Tennant, Emma (Christina) 1937-**CLC 13, 52**
See also CA 65-68; CAAS 9; CANR 10, 38,
59; DLB 14
Tenneshaw, S. M.
See Silverberg, Robert
Tennyson, Alfred 1809-1892... **NCLC 30, 65;
DA; DAB; DAC; DAM MST, POET; PC
6; WLC**
See also CDBLB 1832-1890; DLB 32
Teran, Lisa St. Aubin de .... **CLC 36**
See also St. Aubin de Teran, Lisa
Terence 195(?)B.C.-159B.C. **CMLC 14; DC 7**
Teresa de Jesus, St. 1515-1582 .... **LC 18**
Terkel, Louis 1912-
See Terkel, Studs
See also CA 57-60; CANR 18, 45, 67; MTCW
Terkel, Studs .... **CLC 38**
See also Terkel, Louis
See also AITN 1
Terry, C. V.
See Slaughter, Frank G(ill)
Terry, Megan 1932- .... **CLC 19**
See also CA 77-80; CABS 3; CANR 43; DLB 7
Tertullian c. 155-c. 245 .... **CMLC 29**
Tertz, Abram
See Sinyavsky, Andrei (Donatevich)
Tesich, Steve 1943(?)-1996 .... **CLC 40, 69**
See also CA 105; 152; DLBY 83
Teternikov, Fyodor Kuzmich 1863-1927
See Sologub, Fyodor
See also CA 104
Tevis, Walter 1928-1984 .... **CLC 42**
See also CA 113
Tey, Josephine .... **TCLC 14**
See also Mackintosh, Elizabeth
See also DLB 77
Thackeray, William Makepeace 1811-1863
**NCLC 5, 14, 22, 43; DA; DAB; DAC; DAM
MST, NOV; WLC**
See also CDBLB 1832-1890; DLB 21, 55, 159,
163; SATA 23
Thakura, Ravindranatha
See Tagore, Rabindranath
Tharoor, Shashi 1956- .... **CLC 70**
See also CA 141
Thelwell, Michael Miles 1939- .... **CLC 22**
See also BW 2; CA 101
Theobald, Lewis, Jr.
See Lovecraft, H(oward) P(hillips)
Theodorescu, Ion N. 1880-1967
See Arghezi, Tudor
See also CA 116
Theriault, Yves 1915-1983 .... **CLC 79; DAC;
DAM MST**
See also CA 102; DLB 88

54; CDBLB 1960 to Present; DLB 15, 27,
139, 155; MTCW

Wajda, Andrzej 1926- .... **CLC 16**
See also CA 102

Wakefield, Dan 1932- .... **CLC 7**
See also CA 21-24R; CAAS 7

Wakoski, Diane 1937- **CLC 2, 4, 7, 9, 11, 40;**
DAM POET; PC 15
See also CA 13-16R; CAAS 1; CANR 9, 60;
DLB 5; INT CANR-9

Wakoski-Sherbell, Diane
See Wakoski, Diane

Walcott, Derek (Alton) 1930-**CLC 2, 4, 9, 14,**
25, 42, 67, 76; BLC 3; DAB; DAC; DAM
MST, MULT, POET; DC 7
See also BW 2; CA 89-92; CANR 26, 47; DLB
117; DLBY 81; MTCW

Waldman, Anne (Lesley) 1945- .... **CLC 7**
See also CA 37-40R; CAAS 17; CANR 34, 69;
DLB 16

Waldo, E. Hunter
See Sturgeon, Theodore (Hamilton)

Waldo, Edward Hamilton
See Sturgeon, Theodore (Hamilton)

Walker, Alice (Malsenior) 1944- **CLC 5, 6, 9,**
19, 27, 46, 58, 103; BLC 3; DA; DAB;
DAC; DAM MST, MULT, NOV, POET,
POP; SSC 5; WLCS
See also AAYA 3; BEST 89:4; BW 2; CA 37-
40R; CANR 9, 27, 49, 66; CDALB 1968-
1988; DLB 6, 33, 143; INT CANR-27;
MTCW; SATA 31

Walker, David Harry 1911-1992 .... **CLC 14**
See also CA 1-4R; 137; CANR 1; SATA 8;
SATA-Obit 71

Walker, Edward Joseph 1934-
See Walker, Ted
See also CA 21-24R; CANR 12, 28, 53

Walker, George F. 1947- . **CLC 44, 61; DAB;**
DAC; DAM MST
See also CA 103; CANR 21, 43, 59; DLB 60

Walker, Joseph A. 1935- .... **CLC 19; DAM**
DRAM, MST
See also BW 1; CA 89-92; CANR 26; DLB 38

Walker, Margaret (Abigail) 1915- **CLC 1, 6;**
BLC; DAM MULT; PC 20
See also BW 2; CA 73-76; CANR 26, 54; DLB
76, 152; MTCW

Walker, Ted .... **CLC 13**
See also Walker, Edward Joseph
See also DLB 40

Wallace, David Foster 1962- .... **CLC 50**
See also CA 132; CANR 59

Wallace, Dexter
See Masters, Edgar Lee

Wallace, (Richard Horatio) Edgar 1875-1932
TCLC 57
See also CA 115; DLB 70

Wallace, Irving 1916-1990 **CLC 7, 13; DAM**
NOV, POP
See also AITN 1; CA 1-4R; 132; CAAS 1;
CANR 1, 27; INT CANR-27; MTCW

Wallant, Edward Lewis 1926-1962**CLC 5, 10**
See also CA 1-4R; CANR 22; DLB 2, 28, 143;
MTCW

Walley, Byron
See Card, Orson Scott

Walpole, Horace 1717-1797 .... **LC 2**
See also DLB 39, 104

Walpole, Hugh (Seymour) 1884-1941**TCLC 5**
See also CA 104; 165; DLB 34

Walser, Martin 1927-.......................... **CLC 27**
See also CA 57-60; CANR 8, 46; DLB 75, 124

Walser, Robert 1878-1956 **TCLC 18; SSC 20**
See also CA 118; 165; DLB 66

Walsh, Jill Paton .... **CLC 35**
See also Paton Walsh, Gillian
See also AAYA 11; CLR 2; DLB 161; SAAS 3

Walter, Villiam Christian
See Andersen, Hans Christian

Wambaugh, Joseph (Aloysius, Jr.) 1937-**CLC**
3, 18; DAM NOV, POP
See also AITN 1; BEST 89:3; CA 33-36R;
CANR 42, 65; DLB 6; DLBY 83; MTCW

Wang Wei 699(?)-761(?) .... **PC 18**

Ward, Arthur Henry Sarsfield 1883-1959
See Rohmer, Sax
See also CA 108

Ward, Douglas Turner 1930- .... **CLC 19**
See also BW 1; CA 81-84; CANR 27; DLB 7,
38

Ward, Mary Augusta
See Ward, Mrs. Humphry

Ward, Mrs. Humphry 1851-1920 .. **TCLC 55**
See also DLB 18

Ward, Peter
See Faust, Frederick (Schiller)

Warhol, Andy 1928(?)-1987 .... **CLC 20**
See also AAYA 12; BEST 89:4; CA 89-92; 121;
CANR 34

Warner, Francis (Robert le Plastrier) 1937-
CLC 14
See also CA 53-56; CANR 11

Warner, Marina 1946-........................ **CLC 59**
See also CA 65-68; CANR 21, 55; DLB 194

Warner, Rex (Ernest) 1905-1986 ...... **CLC 45**
See also CA 89-92; 119; DLB 15

Warner, Susan (Bogert) 1819-1885 **NCLC 31**
See also DLB 3, 42

Warner, Sylvia (Constance) Ashton
See Ashton-Warner, Sylvia (Constance)

Warner, Sylvia Townsend 1893-1978 **CLC 7,**
19; SSC 23
See also CA 61-64; 77-80; CANR 16, 60; DLB
34, 139; MTCW

Warren, Mercy Otis 1728-1814 ..... **NCLC 13**
See also DLB 31, 200

Warren, Robert Penn 1905-1989**CLC 1, 4, 6,**
8, 10, 13, 18, 39, 53, 59; DA; DAB; DAC;
DAM MST, NOV, POET; SSC 4; WLC
See also AITN 1; CA 13-16R; 129; CANR 10,
47; CDALB 1968-1988; DLB 2, 48, 152;
DLBY 80, 89; INT CANR-10; MTCW; SATA
46; SATA-Obit 63

Warshofsky, Isaac
See Singer, Isaac Bashevis

Warton, Thomas 1728-1790 .....**LC 15; DAM**
POET
See also DLB 104, 109

Waruk, Kona
See Harris, (Theodore) Wilson

Warung, Price 1855-1911 .... **TCLC 45**

Warwick, Jarvis
See Garner, Hugh

Washington, Alex
See Harris, Mark

Washington, Booker T(aliaferro) 1856-1915
TCLC 10; BLC 3; DAM MULT
See also BW 1; CA 114; 125; SATA 28

Washington, George 1732-1799 .... **LC 25**
See also DLB 31

Wassermann, (Karl) Jakob 1873-1934**TCLC**
6
See also CA 104; DLB 66

Wasserstein, Wendy 1950-... **CLC 32, 59, 90;**
DAM DRAM; DC 4

See also CA 121; 129; CABS 3; CANR 53; INT
129; SATA 94

Waterhouse, Keith (Spencer) 1929- . **CLC 47**
See also CA 5-8R; CANR 38, 67; DLB 13, 15;
MTCW

Waters, Frank (Joseph) 1902-1995 .. **CLC 88**
See also CA 5-8R; 149; CAAS 13; CANR 3,
18, 63; DLBY 86

Waters, Roger 1944- .... **CLC 35**

Watkins, Frances Ellen
See Harper, Frances Ellen Watkins

Watkins, Gerrold
See Malzberg, Barry N(athaniel)

Watkins, Gloria 1955(?)-
See hooks, bell
See also BW 2; CA 143

Watkins, Paul 1964-........................... **CLC 55**
See also CA 132; CANR 62

Watkins, Vernon Phillips 1906-1967 **CLC 43**
See also CA 9-10; 25-28R; CAP 1; DLB 20

Watson, Irving S.
See Mencken, H(enry) L(ouis)

Watson, John H.
See Farmer, Philip Jose

Watson, Richard F.
See Silverberg, Robert

Waugh, Auberon (Alexander) 1939- .. **CLC 7**
See also CA 45-48; CANR 6, 22; DLB 14, 194

Waugh, Evelyn (Arthur St. John) 1903-1966
CLC 1, 3, 8, 13, 19, 27, 44, 107; DA; DAB;
DAC; DAM MST, NOV, POP; WLC
See also CA 85-88; 25-28R; CANR 22; CDBLB
1914-1945; DLB 15, 162, 195; MTCW

Waugh, Harriet 1944- .... **CLC 6**
See also CA 85-88; CANR 22

Ways, C. R.
See Blount, Roy (Alton), Jr.

Waystaff, Simon
See Swift, Jonathan

Webb, (Martha) Beatrice (Potter) 1858-1943
TCLC 22
See also Potter, (Helen) Beatrix
See also CA 117

Webb, Charles (Richard) 1939- .... **CLC 7**
See also CA 25-28R

Webb, James H(enry), Jr. 1946- .... **CLC 22**
See also CA 81-84

Webb, Mary (Gladys Meredith) 1881-1927
TCLC 24
See also CA 123; DLB 34

Webb, Mrs. Sidney
See Webb, (Martha) Beatrice (Potter)

Webb, Phyllis 1927-........................... **CLC 18**
See also CA 104; CANR 23; DLB 53

Webb, Sidney (James) 1859-1947 .. **TCLC 22**
See also CA 117; 163; DLB 190

Webber, Andrew Lloyd .... **CLC 21**
See also Lloyd Webber, Andrew

Weber, Lenora Mattingly 1895-1971 **CLC 12**
See also CA 19-20; 29-32R; CAP 1; SATA 2;
SATA-Obit 26

Weber, Max 1864-1920 .... **TCLC 69**
See also CA 109

Webster, John 1579(?)-1634(?) ... **LC 33; DA;**
DAB; DAC; DAM DRAM, MST; DC 2;
WLC
See also CDBLB Before 1660; DLB 58

Webster, Noah 1758-1843 .... **NCLC 30**

Wedekind, (Benjamin) Frank(lin) 1864-1918
TCLC 7; DAM DRAM
See also CA 104; 153; DLB 118

Weidman, Jerome 1913- .... **CLC 7**
See also AITN 2; CA 1-4R; CANR 1; DLB 28

CANR-8; MTCW; SATA 56
Wiggins, Marianne 1947- .... **CLC 57**
See also BEST 89:3; CA 130; CANR 60
Wight, James Alfred 1916-1995
See Herriot, James
See also CA 77-80; SATA 55; SATA-Brief 44
Wilbur, Richard (Purdy) 1921-**CLC 3, 6, 9, 14, 53, 110; DA; DAB; DAC; DAM MST, POET**
See also CA 1-4R; CABS 2; CANR 2, 29; DLB 5, 169; INT CANR-29; MTCW; SATA 9
Wild, Peter 1940- .... **CLC 14**
See also CA 37-40R; DLB 5
Wilde, Oscar (Fingal O'Flahertie Wills) 1854(?)-1900**TCLC 1, 8, 23, 41; DA; DAB; DAC; DAM DRAM, MST, NOV; SSC 11; WLC**
See also CA 104; 119; CDBLB 1890-1914; DLB 10, 19, 34, 57, 141, 156, 190; SATA 24
Wilder, Billy .... **CLC 20**
See also Wilder, Samuel
See also DLB 26
Wilder, Samuel 1906-
See Wilder, Billy
See also CA 89-92
Wilder, Thornton (Niven) 1897-1975**CLC 1, 5, 6, 10, 15, 35, 82; DA; DAB; DAC; DAM DRAM, MST, NOV; DC 1; WLC**
See also AITN 2; CA 13-16R; 61-64; CANR 40; DLB 4, 7, 9; DLBY 97; MTCW
Wilding, Michael 1942- .... **CLC 73**
See also CA 104; CANR 24, 49
Wiley, Richard 1944- .... **CLC 44**
See also CA 121; 129
Wilhelm, Kate .... **CLC 7**
See also Wilhelm, Katie Gertrude
See also AAYA 20; CAAS 5; DLB 8; INT CANR-17
Wilhelm, Katie Gertrude 1928-
See Wilhelm, Kate
See also CA 37-40R; CANR 17, 36, 60; MTCW
Wilkins, Mary
See Freeman, Mary Eleanor Wilkins
Willard, Nancy 1936- .... **CLC 7, 37**
See also CA 89-92; CANR 10, 39, 68; CLR 5; DLB 5, 52; MAICYA; MTCW; SATA 37, 71; SATA-Brief 30
Williams, C(harles) K(enneth) 1936-**CLC 33, 56; DAM POET**
See also CA 37-40R; CAAS 26; CANR 57; DLB 5
Williams, Charles
See Collier, James L(incoln)
Williams, Charles (Walter Stansby) 1886-1945 **TCLC 1, 11**
See also CA 104; 163; DLB 100, 153
Williams, (George) Emlyn 1905-1987**CLC 15; DAM DRAM**
See also CA 104; 123; CANR 36; DLB 10, 77; MTCW
Williams, Hank 1923-1953 .... **TCLC 81**
Williams, Hugo 1942- .... **CLC 42**
See also CA 17-20R; CANR 45; DLB 40
Williams, J. Walker
See Wodehouse, P(elham) G(renville)
Williams, John A(lfred) 1925-**CLC 5, 13; BLC 3; DAM MULT**
See also BW 2; CA 53-56; CAAS 3; CANR 6, 26, 51; DLB 2, 33; INT CANR-6
Williams, Jonathan (Chamberlain) 1929- **CLC 13**
See also CA 9-12R; CAAS 12; CANR 8; DLB 5

Williams, Joy 1944- .... **CLC 31**
See also CA 41-44R; CANR 22, 48
Williams, Norman 1952- .... **CLC 39**
See also CA 118
Williams, Sherley Anne 1944-**CLC 89; BLC 3; DAM MULT, POET**
See also BW 2; CA 73-76; CANR 25; DLB 41; INT CANR-25; SATA 78
Williams, Shirley
See Williams, Sherley Anne
Williams, Tennessee 1911-1983**CLC 1, 2, 5, 7, 8, 11, 15, 19, 30, 39, 45, 71, 111; DA; DAB; DAC; DAM DRAM, MST; DC 4; WLC**
See also CA 5-8R; 108; CABS 3; CANR 31; CDALB 1941-1968; DLB 7; DLBD 4; DLBY 83; MTCW
Williams, Thomas (Alonzo) 1926-1990**CLC 14**
See also CA 1-4R; 132; CANR 2
Williams, William C.
See Williams, William Carlos
Williams, William Carlos 1883-1963**CLC 1, 2, 5, 9, 13, 22, 42, 67; DA; DAB; DAC; DAM MST, POET; PC 7; SSC 31**
See also CA 89-92; CANR 34; CDALB 1917-1929; DLB 4, 16, 54, 86; MTCW
Williamson, David (Keith) 1942- ...... **CLC 56**
See also CA 103; CANR 41
Williamson, Ellen Douglas 1905-1984
See Douglas, Ellen
See also CA 17-20R; 114; CANR 39
Williamson, Jack .... **CLC 29**
See also Williamson, John Stewart
See also CAAS 8; DLB 8
Williamson, John Stewart 1908-
See Williamson, Jack
See also CA 17-20R; CANR 23
Willie, Frederick
See Lovecraft, H(oward) P(hillips)
Willingham, Calder (Baynard, Jr.) 1922-1995 **CLC 5, 51**
See also CA 5-8R; 147; CANR 3; DLB 2, 44; MTCW
Willis, Charles
See Clarke, Arthur C(harles)
Willy
See Colette, (Sidonie-Gabrielle)
Willy, Colette
See Colette, (Sidonie-Gabrielle)
Wilson, A(ndrew) N(orman) 1950- ... **CLC 33**
See also CA 112; 122; DLB 14, 155, 194
Wilson, Angus (Frank Johnstone) 1913-1991 **CLC 2, 3, 5, 25, 34; SSC 21**
See also CA 5-8R; 134; CANR 21; DLB 15, 139, 155; MTCW
Wilson, August 1945-**CLC 39, 50, 63; BLC 3; DA; DAB; DAC; DAM DRAM, MST, MULT; DC 2; WLCS**
See also AAYA 16; BW 2; CA 115; 122; CANR 42, 54; MTCW
Wilson, Brian 1942- .... **CLC 12**
Wilson, Colin 1931- .... **CLC 3, 14**
See also CA 1-4R; CAAS 5; CANR 1, 22, 33; DLB 14, 194; MTCW
Wilson, Dirk
See Pohl, Frederik
Wilson, Edmund 1895-1972**CLC 1, 2, 3, 8, 24**
See also CA 1-4R; 37-40R; CANR 1, 46; DLB 63; MTCW
Wilson, Ethel Davis (Bryant) 1888(?)-1980 **CLC 13; DAC; DAM POET**
See also CA 102; DLB 68; MTCW
Wilson, John 1785-1854 .... **NCLC 5**
Wilson, John (Anthony) Burgess 1917-1993

See Burgess, Anthony
See also CA 1-4R; 143; CANR 2, 46; DAC; DAM NOV; MTCW
Wilson, Lanford 1937- **CLC 7, 14, 36; DAM DRAM**
See also CA 17-20R; CABS 3; CANR 45; DLB 7
Wilson, Robert M. 1944- .... **CLC 7, 9**
See also CA 49-52; CANR 2, 41; MTCW
Wilson, Robert McLiam 1964- .... **CLC 59**
See also CA 132
Wilson, Sloan 1920- .... **CLC 32**
See also CA 1-4R; CANR 1, 44
Wilson, Snoo 1948- .... **CLC 33**
See also CA 69-72
Wilson, William S(mith) 1932-......... **CLC 49**
See also CA 81-84
Wilson, (Thomas) Woodrow 1856-1924**TCLC 79**
See also CA 166; DLB 47
Winchilsea, Anne (Kingsmill) Finch Counte 1661-1720
See Finch, Anne
Windham, Basil
See Wodehouse, P(elham) G(renville)
Wingrove, David (John) 1954- .... **CLC 68**
See also CA 133
Wintergreen, Jane
See Duncan, Sara Jeannette
Winters, Janet Lewis .... **CLC 41**
See also Lewis, Janet
See also DLBY 87
Winters, (Arthur) Yvor 1900-1968 **CLC 4, 8, 32**
See also CA 11-12; 25-28R; CAP 1; DLB 48; MTCW
Winterson, Jeanette 1959-**CLC 64; DAM POP**
See also CA 136; CANR 58
Winthrop, John 1588-1649 .... **LC 31**
See also DLB 24, 30
Wiseman, Frederick 1930- .... **CLC 20**
See also CA 159
Wister, Owen 1860-1938 .... **TCLC 21**
See also CA 108; 162; DLB 9, 78, 186; SATA 62
Witkacy
See Witkiewicz, Stanislaw Ignacy
Witkiewicz, Stanislaw Ignacy 1885-1939 **TCLC 8**
See also CA 105; 162
Wittgenstein, Ludwig (Josef Johann) 1889-1951 **TCLC 59**
See also CA 113; 164
Wittig, Monique 1935(?)- .... **CLC 22**
See also CA 116; 135; DLB 83
Wittlin, Jozef 1896-1976 .... **CLC 25**
See also CA 49-52; 65-68; CANR 3
Wodehouse, P(elham) G(renville) 1881-1975 **CLC 1, 2, 5, 10, 22; DAB; DAC; DAM NOV; SSC 2**
See also AITN 2; CA 45-48; 57-60; CANR 3, 33; CDBLB 1914-1945; DLB 34, 162; MTCW; SATA 22
Woiwode, L.
See Woiwode, Larry (Alfred)
Woiwode, Larry (Alfred) 1941- ....**CLC 6, 10**
See also CA 73-76; CANR 16; DLB 6; INT CANR-16
Wojciechowska, Maia (Teresa) 1927-**CLC 26**
See also AAYA 8; CA 9-12R; CANR 4, 41; CLR 1; JRDA; MAICYA; SAAS 1; SATA 1, 28, 83
Wolf, Christa 1929- .... **CLC 14, 29, 58**

Author Index

Literary Criticism Series
Cumulative Topic Index

This index lists all topic entries in Gale's *Classical and Medieval Literature Criticism, Contemporary Literary Criticism, Literature Criticism from 1400 to 1800, Nineteenth-Century Literature Criticism,* and *Twentieth-Century Literary Criticism.*

Topic Index

Contemporary Literary Criticism
Cumulative Nationality Index

Nationality Index

Nationality Index

Nationality Index

Nationality Index

Title Index

00006

ISBN 0-7876-5515-5